Y0-BVP-533

IF FOUND, please notify and arrange return to owner. This text is important for the owner's preparation for the Uniform Certified Public Accountant Examination.

Name of CPA Candidate _____

Address _____

City, State, Zip _____

Telephone ( ) _____

Additional texts are available at your local bookstore

or directly from John Wiley and Sons, Inc.

Order information and order forms can be found at the back of the book

———————————††———————————

CPA

EXAMINATION REVIEW

VOLUME I
OUTLINES and STUDY GUIDES

11th EDITION

Irvin N. Gleim, Ph.D., CPA
University of Florida
Gainesville, Florida

&

Patrick R. Delaney, Ph.D., CPA
Northern Illinois University
DeKalb, Illinois

JOHN WILEY & SONS

New York   Chichester   Brisbane   Toronto   Singapore

Permissions

The following items copyright © by the American Institute of Certified Public Accountants, Inc., are reprinted with permission:

1. *Uniform CPA Examination Questions and Answers*, 1973, 1974, 1975, 1976, 1977, 1978, 1979, 1980, 1981, 1982, 1983 and 1984. Those which have been adapted are so identified.

2. *Information for CPA Candidates* and *Content Specification Outlines for the Uniform Certified Public Accountant Examination*, Board of Examiners.

3. Definitions, example schedules, etc., from *Accounting Research Bulletins, APB Opinions, APB Statements,* and *The Code of Professional Ethics.*

4. Example audit reports from *Statements on Auditing Standards* and *Statements on Standards for Accounting and Review Services.*

5. Example financial statements from Industry Audit Guides: *Audits of Colleges and Universities, Audits of Voluntary Health and Welfare Organizations*, and *Hospital Audit Guide.*

6. Example Statement of Activity from SOP 78–10.

Reproduction and adaption of pronouncements, copyright © Financial Accounting Standards Board, High Ridge Park, Stamford, Connecticut 06905, with permission.

Reproduction of diagram titled "Sale and Leaseback Transaction" from Welsch, Zlatkovich, and Harrison, *Intermediate Accounting, Sixth Edition*, Richard D. Irwin, Inc., 1982, with permission.

Reproduction of "Combined Statement of Revenues, Expenditures, and Changes in Fund Balances—All Governmental Fund Types and Expendable Trust Funds," copyright © Municipal Finance Officers Association, Chicago, Illinois 60601, with permission.

Several examples in Chapter 13, "Taxes," are taken from Internal Revenue Service Publication 17.

Statement of changes in Fund Balances for an educational institution from *College and University Business Administration* with permission of the National Association of College and University Business Officers.

Table summarizing The Independent Auditor's Civil Liability, *The Accounting Review*, (April 1980, p. 320), with permission of American Accounting Association.

The following material in this manual was taken, with permission, from *Intermediate Accounting*, Fourth Edition, by Donald E. Kieso and Jerry J. Weygandt, John Wiley & Sons, Inc., 1983: Table entitled "Summary of APB Opinions and FASB Standards Pertaining to the Income Statement."

This publication is designed to provide accurate and authoritative information in regard to the subject matter covered. It is sold with the understanding that the publisher is not engaged in rendering legal, accounting, or other professional service.

If legal advice or other expert assistance is required, the services of a competent professional person should be sought.

From a declaration of principles jointly adopted by a Committee of the American Bar Association and a Committee of Publishers.

Copyright © 1984, by John Wiley and Sons, Inc. All rights reserved. Published simultaneously in Canada.

Reproduction or translation of any part of this work beyond that permitted by Sections 107 and 108 of the 1976 United States Copyright Act without the permission of the copyright owner is unlawful. Request for permission or further information should be addressed to the Permissions Department, John Wiley and Sons, Inc.

ISBN 0-471-80083-X

10 9 8 7 6 5 4 3 2 1

PREFACE

The objective of this volume is to provide, in an easily readable format, study outlines of all areas tested on the Uniform CPA Examination. The clear, concise phraseology supplemented by brief examples and illustrations is designed to help candidates quickly understand and retain the material. To make the task of preparing for the examination more manageable, we have structured both review volumes into 44 modules (manageable study units). The modular organization commences in Chapter 5 of this volume and in Chapter 2 of Volume II. Also, the multiple choice questions In Volume II have been grouped into topical categories within each module. These categories correspond to the sequencing of material as it appears within each of the corresponding modules in this volume. A significant feature of this volume concerns the tables summarizing the frequency and extent to which topical areas have been tested on each of the last nine exams. Our classification of the coverage of these exams is based on the AICPA's Content Specification Outlines for the Uniform Certified Public Accountant Examination which were effective beginning with the November 1983 exam.

The Eleventh Edition has been updated and revised to include changes in applicable law and new authoritative pronouncements through May 15, 1984. Additionally, other areas have been revised to improve the pedagogical treatment of the materials. Finally, coverage of some areas has either been reduced or expanded to reflect changes in exam coverage.

The authors are indebted to the American Institute of Certified Public Accountants and the Financial Accounting Standards Board for permission to reproduce and adapt their publications.

The authors deeply appreciate the enthusiastic and dedicated attitude of the many CPA candidates with whom the authors have had the pleasure to work. As always, the authors welcome any comments concerning materials contained in or omitted from this text. Please send these to Partick R. Delaney, c/o CPA Examination Review, P.O. Box 886, DeKalb, Illinois 60115.

Please read Chapter 1 carefully, especially "Attributes of Examination Success" and "Purpose and Organization of These Review Textbooks."

Good Luck on the Exam,

Irvin N. Gleim
Patrick R. Delaney
May 15, 1984

ABOUT THE AUTHORS

Patrick R. Delaney is Chair and Professor of Accountancy at Northern Illinois University. He received his PhD in Accountancy from the University of Illinois. He is past president of the Rockford Chapter, National Association of Accountants; is a member of the Illinois CPA Society's Accounting Principles Committee; and has served on numerous other professional committees. He is a member of the American Accounting Association, American Institute of Certified Public Accountants, and National Association of Accountants. Professor Delaney has published in *The Accounting Review* and is a recipient of NIU's Excellence in Teaching Award. He has been involved in NIU's CPA Review Course as director and instructor and has served as an instructor of NASBA's Critique Program.

Irvin N. Gleim is Professor of Accounting at the University of Florida and is a CPA, CIA and CMA. He received his PhD in Accountancy from the University of Illinois. He is a member of the American Institute of Certified Public Accountants, Florida Institute of Certified Public Accountants, American Accounting Association, American Business Law Association, Institute of Internal Auditors, Institute of Management Accounting, and National Association of Accountants. He has published professional articles in the *Journal of Accountancy, The Accounting Review,* and *The American Business Law Journal.* He has developed and taught both proprietary and university CPA review courses. He is author of *CIA Examination Review* and *CMA Examination Review*, both published by Accounting Publications, Inc.

ABOUT THE CONTRIBUTORS

Richard E. Baker, PhD, CPA, is Associate Professor of Accountancy at Northern Illinois University and teaches in the NIU CPA Review Course. Professor Baker prepared the Investments and Consolidation module.

John C. Borke, MAS, CPA, is an Assistant Professor of Accounting at the University of Wisconsin-Platteville. He has worked as a staff auditor with Peat, Marwick, Mitchell & Co. Professor Borke assisted in the revision of the Inflation Accounting module; prepared several other sections in Financial Accounting, including the section in Chapter 8 on the Conceptual Framework; and prepared the revision of Chapter 10, Cost Accounting.

Martin A. Bubley, MBA, CPA, prepared the revisions of Suretyship and Employer—Employee Relationships modules, in Chapter 6, Business Law.

John H. Engstrom, DBA, CPA, is an Associate Professor of Accountancy at Northern Illinois University. He revised Chapter 12, Governmental and Nonprofit Accounting.

Frank S. Forbes, JD, is Professor and Chairman, Department of Law and Society, College of Business Administration at the University of Nebraska-Omaha. Dr. Forbes made revisions in several business law modules.

Edward C. Foth, PhD, CPA, is an Associate Professor and Administrator of the Master of Science in Taxation Program at DePaul University. He has public accounting experience with Arthur Andersen & Co. and teaches in their Basic and Intermediate U.S. Tax Schools. Professor Foth is the author of Commerce Clearing House's *Study Guide For Federal Tax Course* and coauthor of their S Corporation Guide. He prepared Chapter 13.

William T. Geary, PhD, CPA, is an Associate Professor at The College of William and Mary. He has taught in several major CPA Review Programs and the NASBA Critique Program. Professor Geary prepared the revision of Leases and Pensions in Chapters 8 and 9.

Kurt Pany, PhD, CPA, is an Associate Professor of Accounting at Arizona State University. He is a member of the American Institute of Certified Public Accountants, and the American Accounting Association. Prior to entering academe, he worked as a staff auditor for Touche Ross & Co. Professor Pany prepared the Professional Responsibilities, Internal Control, Evidence, and Report modules in Chapter 5 and the Accountant's Legal Liability module in Chapter 6.

James H. Perkins, MS, MIS, CIA, CISA, CPA, EDP Audit Manager, Federal Reserve Bank of Cleveland. He previously worked as a Principal Research Manager—Audit Programs for the Bank Administration Institute in Rolling Meadows, Illinois and as a staff auditor for Deloitte Haskins & Sells. Mr. Perkins prepared the EDP Auditing module in Chapter 5.

John R. Simon, PhD, CPA, is Associate Professor of Accountancy at Northern Illinois University. He has taught in NIU's CPA Review Course for the past eight years and is presently the director of the course. He is a recipient of NIU's Excellence in Teaching Award. Professor Simon prepared the Earnings Per Share section of the Stockholders' Equity module and the Foreign Currency Translation portion of the Inflation module in Chapter 9.

Bart H. Ward, PhD, CPA, is a Professor of Accounting at the University of Oklahoma. He has previously contributed questions which have been used on the CPA exam and is now a member of the AICPA's Statistical Sampling Committee. He served as a Research Associate with the national office of Touche Ross & Co., and has taught sampling courses for Ernst & Whinney and conducted CPA review courses. He has published articles in the *Journal of Accounting Research, The Accounting Review, Financial Executive* and elsewhere. He has served as Chairman of the Audit Section of the American Accounting Association. He prepared the Statistical Sampling module in Chapter 5.

Harold Wright, JD, is Coordinator and Assistant Professor of Business Law at Northern Illinois University. He has taught in NIU's CPA Review Course for the past eleven years, has served as an instructor of NASBA's Critique Program, and is a recipient of NIU's Excellence in Teaching Award. Professor Wright prepared revisions, including the new section on Federal Consumer Protection Legislation, in Chapter 6, Business Law.

TABLE OF CONTENTS

As explained in Chapter 1, this volume is organized into 44 modules (manageable study units). Volume II is organized in a parallel fashion. For easy reference, both Volumes I and II have numbered index tabs indicating the first page of each module.

x

Acknowledgements

Writing an annualized text is always a publishing event and a rejuvenating human experience. The authors are most grateful to the many users of previous editions, both instructors and students who have so generously shared with us their satisfaction with our work and their suggestions for changes and improvements. We hope that this will continue for we have benefited from those communications.

This work continues to be a "community effort." In addition to those colleagues cited as contributors above, we would like to acknowledge and thank those many friends who gave us so many devoted hours to bring this 11th annualized edition to you so quickly after the May 1984 Examination: Diane Babich, Mary Ann Babich, Bruce Barron, David Charbonneau, Sandy Donnelly, Lee Gampfer, Ona Golden, Rudy Knappmeyer, Paula Krueger, Pam Miller, Nancy Thompson, Eileen Thorsen, Lester Welles, and Ray Wisbrock.

The authors are indebted to the following individuals who read parts of the manuscript and made helpful suggestions: Katherine B. Frazier, University of Colorado, Karola Jungbacker, University of Wisconsin-Oshkosh, James Marshall, Michigan State University, J. Hal Reneau, Arizona State University, S. Jay Sklar, Temple University, and G. William Glezen, University of Arkansas.

Several of our colleagues allowed us to use their charts or summaries in the text; these credits are noted with their contributions.

OTHER CONTRIBUTORS AND REVIEWERS

Michael Baker, BA, is a candidate for the MBA degree. Mr. Baker has worked as a staff auditor and senior tax specialist for Peat, Marwick, Mitchell & Co. He reviewed new material in Chapter 5, Auditing; revised Module 18 regarding tax preparer's liability and several sections in Module 27 on Deferred Taxes; reviewed Chapter 13, Taxes; and assisted in the preparation of the index.

Stephen J. Gilmour, MAS, CPA, is an Instructor of Accountancy at Northern Illinois University. He has public accounting experience with Peat, Marwick, Mitchell & Co. Mr. Gilmour revised Chapter 1–4 of this volume.

Bill Griesenauer, MAS, CPA, has accepted employment with Ernst & Whinney. Mr. Griesenauer reviewed new material; assisted in the revision of Chapter 8; prepared new material for several modules in Chapter 9, Financial Accounting; and assisted in the preparation of the index.

Darrel S. Grove, BS, is employed with Touche Ross & Co. Mr. Grove assisted in the revision of several modules in Chapter 9, Financial Accounting.

William Hartig, MBA, CPA. Mr. Hartig drafted outlines of financial accounting pronouncements in Chapter 8; assisted in the revision of several modules in Chapter 9, Financial Accounting; reviewed new material; and assisted in the preparation of the index.

Cindy Johnson, MAS, CPA, is an Instructor of Accountancy at Northern Illinois University. Ms. Johnson reviewed new material.

Carol Krenek, MAS, CPA, is an Instructor of Accountancy at Northern Illinois University. Ms. Krenek prepared and edited new material for the Inventory and Working Capital modules.

CHAPTER ONE

BEGINNING YOUR CPA REVIEW PROGRAM

To maximize the efficiency of your review program, begin by studying (not merely reading) this chapter and the next three chapters of this volume. They have been carefully organized and written to provide you with important information to assist you in successfully completing the CPA exam. Beyond providing a comprehensive outline of the material tested on the exam, Chapter 1 will assist you in organizing a study program to prepare for the exam (self-discipline is essential).

GENERAL COMMENTS ON THE EXAMINATION

Successful completion of the Uniform CPA Examination is an attainable goal. Keep this point foremost in your mind as you study the first four chapters in this volume and develop your study plan.

Purpose of the Examination[1]

The CPA examination is designed to measure basic technical competence, including

1. Technical knowledge and application of such knowledge
2. Exercise of good judgment
3. Understanding of professional responsibilities

The CPA examination is one of many screening devices to assure the competence of those licensed to perform the attest function and to render professional accounting services. Other screening devices are educational requirements, ethics examinations, etc.

The examination appears to test the material covered in accounting programs of the better business schools. It also appears to be based upon the body of knowledge essential for the practice of public accounting and, perhaps specifically, the audit of a medium-sized client. Since the examination is primarily a textbook or academic examination, you should plan on taking it as soon as possible after completing your undergraduate accounting education. Take the examination with the idea of passing all parts of the exam, since studying for the whole exam is synergistic; e.g., while you study for accounting theory, you often study material tested on the accounting practice section, and vice versa.

The difficulty of the examination is undoubtedly increasing. This phenomenon is directly related to the rapid expansion of accounting as a body of knowledge. The Institute has suggested that the level of the examination will proceed to the body of knowledge attainable from a five-year college accounting program.

---

[1] The following general comments are largely adapted from Information for CPA Candidates published by the American Institute of Certified Public Accountants. Information for CPA Candidates is usually sent to CPA candidates by their State Board of Accountancy as they apply to sit for the CPA examination. If you will not be immediately applying to your State Board of Accountancy to sit for the exam, you may wish to request a complimentary copy from your board or the AICPA. (Write to AICPA, Examination Division, 1211 Avenue of the Americas, New York, New York 10036.)

Examination Content

Guidance concerning topical content of the CPA exam can be found in a document prepared by the Board of Examiners of the AICPA entitled <u>Content Specification Outlines for the Uniform Certified Public Accountant Examination</u>.

The Board's objective in preparing this detailed listing of topics tested on the exam is to help "in assuring the continuing validity and reliability of the Uniform CPA Examination." These outlines are an excellent source of guidance concerning the areas and the emphasis to be given each area on future exams.

We have included the content outlines in this volume by placing each outline (Accounting Practice, Accounting Theory, Auditing, and Business Law) or portion thereof in the chapter containing related topical areas. Additionally, we have used the outlines as the basis for our frequency analysis of the last nine exams (May 1980 - May 1984). These outlines/frequency analyses should be used as an indication of the topics' relative importance on past exams.

The AICPA does not test new accounting and auditing pronouncements until approximately 12 months after they are issued. It is quite likely, however, that recent pronouncements (within 12 months) will be germane to some questions, because the AICPA frequently develops questions dealing with current issues and controversies in the accounting profession (the areas in which new pronouncements are likely). When a question appears on a topic on which a pronouncement has been issued in the previous 12 months, the graders give credit for the old rule as well as the new rule. CPA exam coverage of business law and tax law changes appears in Chapter 6 and Chapter 13, respectively.

Schedule of Examinations

The Uniform Certified Public Accountant Examination is given twice a year, usually the first consecutive Wednesday-Thursday-Friday in May and November.

Recent exams have followed the format presented in the schedule on the next page. Currently, the exam consists of 60% multiple choice (M/C) questions in all parts, but the time allocations within each part are different. For example, the 3 multiple choice questions on the Practice I exam were given 45-55 minutes each, for an average of about 2 1/2 minutes per individual multiple choice item. The 60 multiple choice items in Theory were assigned a time range of 90-110 minutes, or about 1 2/3 minutes per question. You should note the suggested time limits for each question as you begin working the exam. The subject and time schedules are at the top of the next page.

CPA EXAM SCHEDULE AND EXPECTED FORMAT

	Wednesday	Thursday	Friday

A.M.		Auditing
		8:30 a.m. – 12 noon
		5 Questions:
		    1 Question of 60 M/C
		    4 Essays
			Business Law
			8:30 a.m. – 12 noon
			5 Questions:
			    1 Question of 60 M/C
			    4 Essays

P.M.	Practice I
	1:30 – 6:00 p.m.
	5 Questions:
	    3 Questions of 20 M/C each
	    2 Problems
		Practice II
		1:30 – 6:00 p.m.
		5 Questions:
		    3 Questions of 20 M/C each
		    2 Problems
			Theory
			1:30 – 5:00 p.m.
			5 Questions:
			    1 Question of 60 M/C
			    4 Essays

You receive four scores; accounting practice is considered one section. Seventy-five is considered passing. Rules for partial credit on the examination vary from state to state (see "State Boards of Accountancy" below).

The dates for future CPA examinations are:

1984	November 7, 8, 9	1985	May 8, 9, 10 November 6, 7, 8
		1986	May 7, 8, 9 November 5, 6, 7

State Boards of Accountancy

The right to practice public accounting as a CPA is governed by individual state statutes. While some rules regarding the practice of public accounting vary from state to state, all State Boards of Accountancy use the Uniform CPA Examination and AICPA advisory grading service as one of the requirements to practice public accounting. Every candidate should inquire of his/her State Board of Accountancy to determine the requirements to sit for the exam, e.g., education, filing dates, references, and fees. A frequent problem candidates encounter is failure to apply by the deadline. APPLY TO SIT FOR THE EXAMINATION EARLY. ALSO, YOU SHOULD USE EXTREME CARE IN FILLING OUT THE APPLICATION AND MAILING THE REQUIRED MATERIALS TO YOUR STATE BOARD OF ACCOUNTANCY. If possible, have some friend review your completed application before mailing with check, photos, etc. Too many candidates are turned down for sitting for a particular CPA examination simply because of minor technical details overlooked (photos not signed on back, check not enclosed, question not answered on application, etc.). BECAUSE OF THE VERY HIGH VOLUME OF APPLICATIONS RECEIVED IN THE MORE POPULOUS STATES, THE ADMINISTRATIVE STAFF DOES NOT HAVE TIME TO

CALL OR WRITE TO CORRECT MINOR DETAILS AND WILL SIMPLY REJECT YOUR APPLICATION.
This can be extremely disappointing particularly after spending many hours in preparing to sit for a particular exam.

The various state requirements to take the CPA exam are listed on the following
page. The data are based on the CCH Accountancy Law Reporter, AICPA Legislative
Reference Service, and a survey of state boards. Note that the presentation is condensed and generalized; there are numerous "alternatives," etc. Be sure to inquire
of your state board for specific and current requirements.

It is possible for candidates to sit for the examination in another state as an
out-of-state candidate. Candidates desiring to do so should contact the State Board
of Accountancy in their home state. Addresses of all 54 Boards of Accountancy
appear on the next page.

ATTRIBUTES OF EXAMINATION SUCCESS

Your objective in preparing for the CPA exam is to pass. Other objectives such
as learning new and reviewing old material should be secondary. The following five
attributes of examination success discussed below are essential. You should study
the attributes and work toward achieving/developing each of them before the next
examination.

1. Knowledge of Material

Two points are relevant to "knowledge of material" as an attribute of examination success. First, there is a distinct difference between being familiar with
material and knowing the material. Frequently we (you) confuse familiarity with
knowledge. Can you remember when you just could not answer an examination question
or did poorly on an examination, but maintained to yourself or your instructor that
you knew the material? You probably were only familiar with the material. On the
CPA examination, familiarity is insufficient; you must know the material. For
example, you may be familiar with the concepts in accounting for leases (SFAS 13),
but can you compute the present value of an annuity due under a lease agreement and
record entries for the lessee and lessor? You also may be familiar with the general
rules distinguishing purchase and pooling (APB 16), but do you know how to treat
intercompany treasury stock holdings? Once again, a very major concern must be to
know the material rather than just being familiar with it. Discussion of the
material (knowledge) is required on the CPA examination, not familiarity. Second,

INDIVIDUAL STATE CPA REQUIREMENTS
Compiled May 1, 1984

	State Board address	Educ.[1]	Application deadline First time	Application deadline Re-exam	Exam[2] fee	Cond. re-[3] quirements	Life of[4] condition	Yrs. exp.	Cont. ed. requirements hrs./yrs.	
AL	1103 S. Perry St., Montgomery 36104	4	2-28,8-31	3-31,9-30	$125	2 or P	4NE	2-3	40	1
AK	Pouch D, Juneau 99811	2-4	60 days	same	$ 50	2 or P	5Y	2-4	60	2
AZ	1645 W. Jefferson St., Phoenix 85007	4	2-28,8-31	same	$100	2 or P	3Y	2	80	2
AR	1515 W. Seventh St., Ste. 320, Little Rock 72202	4	60 days	30 days	$100	2 or P	5NE	1-2	40	1
CA	2135 Butano Dr., Ste. 112, Sacramento 95825	0-4	3-1,9-1	same	$ 75	2 or P	3Y	2-4	80	2
CO	617 State Services Bldg., Denver 80203	4	3-1,9-1	same	varies	2 or P	5NE	0-1	80	2
CT	165 Capitol Ave., Hartford 06106	4	60 days	same	$100	2 or P,50	3Y	3	40	1
DE	P.O. Box 1401, Dover 19901	2	3-1,9-1	same	$100	2 or P,50	5NE	2-4	Yes[5]	
DC	614 H St., NW, Rm. 923, Washington 20001	4	90 days	60 days	$ 95	2 or P	5NE	2	Yes	
FL	4001 NW 43rd St., Ste. 16, Gainesville 32606	4[5]	2-1,8-1	3-1,9-1	$125	2 or P,50	5NE	0-1	16-64	2
GA	166 Pryor St., SW, Atlanta 30303	4	60 days	same	$125	2,40[5]	5NE	2-5	60	2
GU	P.O. Box P, Agana 96910	4	60 days	same	$ 60	2 or P,50	6NE	1-2		
HI	P.O. Box 3469, Honolulu 96801	5	3-1,9-1	same	$100	2 or P,50	6NE	2	80	2
ID	700 W. State St., 2nd Fl., Boise 83720	4	3-1,9-1	same	$ 75	2 or P,50	6NE	1-2	80	2
IL	10 Administration Bldg., 506 S. Wright, Urbana 61801	4	2-27,8-28	same	$100	2 or P,50	3 of N6E	0		
IN	1021 State Office Bldg., Indianapolis 46204	4	3-1,9-1	same	$100	2,50	6NE	2-6	80	2
IA	Executive Hills, West, 1209 Court Ave., Des Moines 50319	4	2-28,8-31	same	$ 90	2 or P,50	5NE	1-3	120	3
KS	503 Kansas, Rm. 236, Topeka 66603	4-5	3-15,9-15	same	$ 90	2,50	4 of N6E	5-2	40	1
KY	332 W. Broadway, Ste. 310, Louisville 40202	4	3-1,9-1	same	$ 75	2 or P,50	6NE	2-4	20	1[6]
LA	310 Masonic Temple Bldg., New Orleans 70130	4	3-1,9-1	same	$ 75	2,50	1 of N4E	2-6	90	3
ME	84 Harlow St., Bangor 04401	4	4-15,10-1	same	$ 80	2 or P	3Y	1-2	12	1
MD	501 St. Paul Place, Rm. 902, Baltimore 21202	4	60 days	same	$ 70	2 or P,50	5NE	0	40	1
MA	100 Cambridge St., Rm. 1524, Boston 02202	4	42 days	same	$115	2 or P,50	6NE	2-9	80	2
MI	P.O. Box 30018, Lansing 48909	4	60 days	same	$100	2 or P,50	6NE	2	40	1
MN	Metro Square Bldg., 5th Fl., St. Paul 55101	0-5	60 days	same	$100	2,50	5NE	1-6	120	3
MS	P.O. Box 55447, Jackson 39216	4	3-15,9-15	same	$ 90	2 or P,45	8NE	1-3	120	3
MO	P.O. Box 613, Jefferson City 65102	4[5]	3-1,9-1	same	$ 75	2 or P,50	Unlimited	0	—[5]	
MT	1424 9th Ave., Helena 59620-0407	4	3-15,9-15	same	$100	2 or P	5NE	1	120	3
NE	P.O. Box 94725, Lincoln 68509	0-4	3-31,9-30	same	$ 80	2 or P,50	5NE	2-4	120	3
NV	One East Liberty St., Suite 614, Reno 89501	4	3-1,9-1	same	$ 75	2 or P,35	6NE	2-4	80	2
NH	Two and One-Half Beacon St., Concord 03301-4447	4	4-1,10-1	same	$125	2,50	5Y	1-2	80	2[5]
NJ	1100 Raymond Blvd., Rm. 507-A, Newark 07102	4	2-1,8-1	same	$100	2 or P,50	6NE	2-4		
NM	P.O. Drawer 8770, Albuquerque 87198	4	3-1,9-1	same	$ 60	2,50	3Y	1	120	3
NY	Cultural Education Center, Albany 12230	4	90 days	60 days	$245	2 or P	6NE	1-2		
NC	P.O. Box 12827, Raleigh 27605	2	2-28,8-31	same	$125	2 or P	5NE	1-5	40	1
ND	Box 8104, Univ. Sta., Grand Forks 58202	0	3-15,9-15	same	$100	2 or P	5NE	0-4	120	3
OH	65 S. Front St., Ste. 222, Columbus 43215	4	3-1,9-1	4-1,10-1	$100	1	8Y	1-4	120	3
OK	265 West Ct., 4545 Lincoln Blvd., Oklahoma City 73105	0-4[5]	60 days	same	$100	2 or P	1 of 3 N6E	0-3	24	1
OR	403 Labor & Industries Bldg., Salem 97310	0-4	3-1,9-1	same	$ 75	2 or P,50	6NE	1-2	80	2
PA	P.O. Box 2649, Harrisburg 17105-2649	4	2-15,8-15	3-1,9-1	$ 80	1,20	Unlimited	1-2	80	2
PR	Box 3271, San Juan 00904	0-4[5]	60 days	same	$ 50	2	Unlimited	0-6		
RI	100 N. Main St., Providence 02903	4	45 days	same	$ 50	2 or P	Unlimited	1-2	120	3
SC	P.O. Box 11376, Columbia 29211	4	5 weeks or 35 days	same	$100	2 or P,40	3NE	2	60	2
SD	1509 S. Minnesota Ave., Ste. 1, Sioux Falls 57105	2	60 days	same	$120	2 or P	4Y	2	120	3
TN	408 Doctors Building, 706 Church St., Nashville 37219	4	3-1,9-1	same	$ 75	2 or P,50	6NE or 3Y	2-3	120	3
TX	1033 LaPosada, Ste. 340, Austin 78752-3892	2	2-28,8-31	same	$ 75	2	5Y	1-6		
UT	Heber M. Wells Bldg., 160 E. 300 S., Box 5802, Salt Lake City 84114	2	60 days	same	$ 75	2 or P,50	6NE	1-2	80	2
VT	109 State St., Montpelier 05602	0	4-1,10-1	same	$100	2 or P	6NE	2	80	2
VI	Royal Strand Bldg., Christiansted, St. Croix 00820	0	3-15,9-15	same	$100	2	Unlimited	2-6		
VA	3600 West Broad St., Richmond 23230	4	60 days	same	$ 85	2 or P,50	5NE	2,3&4		
WA	210 E. Union, Ste. H, EP-21, Olympia 98504	4	3-1,9-1	same	$ 75	2 or P,50	6NE	1	80	2
WV	825 Charleston National Plaza, Charleston 25301	4	3-1,9-1	same	$ 40[5]	1	3Y	0		
WI	P.O. Box 8936, Madison 53708	4	3-1,9-1	same	$ 50	2,50	2 of N4E	1½		
WY	2320 Capitol Ave., Cheyenne 82002	4	3-15,9-15	same	$125	2 or P	3Y	2	120	3

[1] Years of higher education

[2] First-time fee

[3] Number of parts, specific parts, and minimum scores on parts failed

[4] Y = years; NE = next exams

[5] Check with your local State Board for specific requirements

[6] Effective in 1985

The Uniform Certified Public Accountant Examination tests a literally overwhelming amount of material at a rigorous level. From an undergraduate point of view, the CPA examination includes material from the following courses:

Accounting
>   Intermediate Financial
>   Cost/Managerial
>   Tax
>   Auditing
>   Advanced Financial
>   Computer/Systems
>   Governmental

Business Law

Quantitative
>   (e.g., statistics, operations research,
>   production management, etc.)

Furthermore, as noted earlier, the CPA exam tests new material in all of these areas. In other words, you are not only responsible for material you should have learned in the above courses, but also for all new developments in each of these areas.

This text contains outlines of accounting topics from FASB pronouncements, financial accounting courses, cost accounting courses, etc. Return to the original material (e.g., FASBs, your accounting textbooks, etc.) when the outlines less than reinforce material you already know.

2. Solutions Approach

The solutions approach is a systematic approach to solve the complicated, sometimes ambiguous problems found on the CPA examination. Many candidates know the material fairly well when they sit for the CPA exam, but they do not know how to take the examination. Candidates generally neither work nor answer problems efficiently in terms of time or grades.

The solutions approach permits you to avoid drawing "blanks" on CPA exam problems; using the solutions approach coupled with grader orientation (see the next side heading) allows you to pick up a sizable number of points on questions testing material with which you are not familiar.

Chapter 3 outlines the solutions approach for practice problems, essay questions, and multiple choice questions. Example problems are worked as well as explained.

3. Grader Orientation

Your score on each section of the exam is determined by the sum of points assigned to individual questions. Thus, you must attempt to maximize your points on each individual question. The name of the game is to satisfy the grader, as s/he is the one who awards you points. Your answer and the grading guide (which conforms closely to the unofficial answer) are the basis for the assignment of points.

This text helps you develop grader orientation by analyzing AICPA grading procedures and grading guides (this is explained further in Chapter 2). The authors believe that the solutions approach and grader orientation, properly developed, are worth at least 10 to 15 points on each section to most candidates.

4. Examination Strategy

Prior to sitting for the examination, it is important to develop an examination strategy, i.e., a preliminary inventory of the questions, the order of working problems, etc.

Your ability to cope successfully with 19 1/2 hours of examination can be improved by

a. Recognizing the importance and usefulness of an examination strategy

b. Using Chapter 4 "Taking the Examination" and previous examination experience to develop a "personal strategy" for the exam

c. Testing your "personal strategy" on recent CPA questions under examination conditions (using no reference material and within a time limit)

5. Examination Confidence

You need confidence to endure the physical and mental demands of 19 1/2 hours of problem solving under tremendous pressure. Examination confidence develops from proper preparation for the exam including mastery of the first four attributes of examination success. Examination confidence is also necessary to enable you to overcome the initial frustration with problems for which you may not be specifically prepared.

This study manual (in conjunction with Volume II), properly used, should contribute to your examination confidence. The systematic outlines herein will provide you with a sense of organization such that as you sit for the examination, you will feel reasonably prepared (it is impossible to be completely prepared).

Reasons for Failure
The Uniform Certified Public Accountant Examination is a formidable hurdle in your accounting career. Candidates, generally with a college degree and an accounting major, face about a 30% pass rate nationally on each section of the exam. About 20% of all candidates (first-time and re-exam) sitting for each examination successfully complete that examination. The cumulative pass rate on the exam is about 70-75%; that is, the percentage of first-time candidates who eventually pass the exam. It is even higher for serious candidates (80%-90%) because a significant number of candidates "drop out" after failing the exam the first time.

Attempt to identify and correct your weaknesses before you sit for the examination based on your experience with undergraduate and previous CPA examinations. Also, analyze the contributing factors to incomplete or incorrect solutions to CPA problems prepared during your study program. The more common reasons for failure are

1. Failure to understand the requirements
2. Misunderstanding the text of the problem
3. Lack of knowledge of material tested
4. Inability to apply the solutions approach
5. Lack of an exam strategy, e.g., time budgeting
6. Sloppiness, computational errors, etc.
7. Failure to proofread and edit

These are not mutually exclusive categories. Some candidates get in such a hurry that they misread the requirements and the problem text, fail to use a solutions approach, make computational errors, and omit proofreading and editing.

PURPOSE AND ORGANIZATION OF THESE REVIEW TEXTBOOKS

Volume I and Volume II of CPA EXAMINATION REVIEW are designed to help you prepare adequately for the examination. Unfortunately (or fortunately, depending on your point of view), there is no easy approach (that is also effective) to prepare for successful completion of the exam.

The objective of Volume I is to provide study materials supportive to CPA candidates. While no guarantees are made concerning the success of those using this text, this volume promotes efficient preparation by

1. Explaining how to "satisfy the grader" through analysis of examination grading and illustration of the solutions approach

2. Defining areas tested previously through the use of the content specification outlines/frequency analyses described earlier. Note that predictions of future exams are not made. You should prepare yourself for all possible topics rather than gambling on the appearance of certain questions.

3. Organizing your study program by comprehensively outlining all of the subject matter tested on the examination in 44 easy-to-use study modules. Each study module is a manageable task which facilitates your exam preparation. Turn to the TABLE OF CONTENTS and peruse it to get a feel for the organization of this volume.

As you read the next few paragraphs which describe the contents of this book (Volume I), flip through the chapters to gain a general familiarity with the book's organization and contents.

Chapters 2, 3, and 4 of Volume I will help you "satisfy the grader."

    Chapter 2 Examination Grading and Grader Orientation
    Chapter 3 The Solutions Approach
    Chapter 4 Taking the Examination

Chapters 2, 3, and 4 contain material that should be kept in mind throughout your study program. Refer back to them frequently. Reread them for a final time just before you sit for the exam.

Chapter 5 (Auditing) and Chapter 6 (Business Law) each contain:

1. AICPA Content Specification Outlines combined with the authors' frequency analysis thereof
2. Outlines of material tested on that section of the examination

Chapters 7 through 13 outline the practice and theory sections of the CPA examination. Chapter 7, Accounting Practice and Accounting Theory, discusses the general coverage of the practice and theory sections of the examination. It also contains the AICPA Content Specification Outlines combined with the frequency analyses for all the financial accounting topics tested in the accounting practice and accounting theory parts of the exam. Chapter 8 contains outlines of the official pronouncements (ARB, APB, and FASB) which are tested in the accounting practice and accounting theory parts of the exam.

Outlines of the remaining topics tested in the practice and theory parts of the examination are contained in Chapters 9 (Financial Accounting), 10 (Cost Accounting), 11 (Quantitative Methods), and 12 (Governmental and Nonprofit Accounting).

The material in Chapter 13, Taxes, is currently tested only in the practice section. While the type of questions/problems differs between the practice and theory sections, the topics tested coincide very closely. The content specification outlines/ frequency analyses which relate to the topics covered in Chapters 10, 12, and 13 appear at the beginning of the appropriate chapters.

The first objective of Volume II is to provide CPA candidates with recent examination problems organized by topic, e.g., audit reports, consolidations, secured transactions, etc. In addition to the traditional approach of printing practice problems and essay questions, Volume II includes over 2,100 multiple choice questions (largely May 1979 to May 1984). Multiple choice questions are an effective means of studying the material tested on the exam (in contrast to studying the solutions approach). It is also necessary, however, to work with practice problems and essay questions to develop the solutions approach (the ability to solve CPA essay questions and practice problems efficiently).

The second objective of Volume II is to explain the AICPA unofficial answers to the examination questions/problems. The AICPA publishes unofficial answers to all past CPA examinations; however, no explanation is made of the approach that should have been applied to the examination questions/problems to obtain those unofficial answers. Relatedly, the AICPA unofficial answers to multiple choice questions provide no justification and/or explanation. Volume II provides: (1) AICPA unofficial answers for each question/problem, (2) an outline of the solution for each essay question, (3) an explanation of how to solve each practice problem, and (4) a one-paragraph explanation for each multiple choice question. The questions in Volume II are arranged in 44 modules which parallel the modules in Volume I.

A significant feature of these volumes is the grouping of multiple choice questions into topical categories. These categories correspond to the sequencing of material as it appears within the text of each corresponding module in Volume I. In the answer explanations for the multiple choice questions in Volume II, we have included headings which provide cross-references to the text material in Volume I. For example, in Module 26, Fixed Assets, a heading appears above the answers to those questions dealing with depreciation. This heading is identified by the letter "F." To find the topical coverage of depreciation in Volume I, the candidate would refer to the Table of Contents for Financial Accounting (Chapter 9) and look under the module title (Fixed Assets) for the letter "F." At the right on the line marked "F." would be the appropriate page number in Fixed Assets related to depreciation.

Other Textbooks

Since this text is a compilation of study guides and outlines, it may be necessary to supplement it with accounting textbooks and other materials. You probably
already have some of these texts or earlier editions of them. In such a case, you
must make the decision whether to replace them and trade familiarity (including
notes therein, etc.), with the cost and inconvenience of obtaining the newer texts
containing a more updated presentation.

Before spending time and money acquiring new texts, begin your study program
with CPA EXAMINATION REVIEW to determine your need for supplemental texts.

Ordering Other Textual Materials

You probably already have intermediate, advanced, and cost accounting texts for
theory and practice. Governmental accounting is generally covered sufficiently in
one or two chapters of an advanced accounting text. A law text and an auditing text
may also be needed to prepare for their respective sections. If you cannot order
desired texts through a local bookstore, write the publisher directly.

The pervasive need of candidates will be AICPA materials. Candidates should locate an AICPA member to order their materials, since members are entitled to a 20%
discount (educators obtain a 40% discount) and may place telephone orders. The
backlog at the order department is substantial; telephone orders decrease delivery
time from a month or more to about a week.

AICPA
   Telephone: (212) 575-6426   Address: 1211 Avenue of the Americas
                                                       New York, New York 10036

You may request shipment by first class, which is billed separately.

Working CPA Problems

The content outlines/frequency analyses, study outlines, etc., in Volume I will
be used to acquire and assimilate the knowledge tested on the examination. This,
however, should be only <u>one-half</u> of your preparation program. The other half should
be spent practicing how to work problems using Volume II, "Problems and Solutions."

Most candidates probably spend over 90% of their time reviewing material tested on the CPA exam. Much more time should be allocated to working old examination problems <u>under exam conditions</u>.

Working old examination problems (including essay questions) serves two functions. First, it helps you develop a solutions approach as well as solutions that will satisfy the grader. Second, it provides the best test of your knowledge of the material.

At a minimum, candidates should work one of the more complex and difficult problems (e.g., statement of changes in financial position, consolidated financial statement worksheet, process cost report) in each area or module.

After you have finished reviewing for each part of the exam, work the complete sample exam for that part of the exam. A complete sample exam is provided in the Appendix to Volume II.

SELF-STUDY PROGRAM

The following suggestions will assist you in developing a <u>systematic</u>, <u>comprehensive</u>, and <u>successful</u> self-study program to help you complete the exam.

CPA candidates generally find it difficult to organize and complete their own self-study program. A major problem is determining <u>what</u> and <u>how</u> to study. Another major problem is developing the self-discipline to stick to a study program. Relatedly, it is often difficult for CPA candidates to determine how much to study, i.e., determining when they are sufficiently prepared. The following self-study suggestions will address these and other problems that you face in preparing for the CPA exam. Remember that these are only suggestions. You should modify them to suit your personality, available study time, and other constraints. Some of the suggestions may appear trivial, but CPA candidates generally need all the assistance they can get to systemize their study program.

Study Facilities and Available Time

Locate study facilities that will be conducive to concentrated study. Factors that you should consider include

1. Noise distraction
2. Interruptions
3. Lighting
4. Availability, e.g., a local library is not available at 5:00 A.M.
5. Accessibility, e.g., your kitchen table vs. your local library
6. Desk or table space

You will probably find different study facilities optimal for different times, e.g., your kitchen table during early morning hours and local libraries during early evening hours.

Next review your personal and professional commitments from now until the exam to determine regularly available study time. Formalize a schedule to which you can reasonably commit yourself. In the appendix to this chapter, you will find a detailed approach to managing your time available for the exam preparation program.

Self-Evaluation

The CPA EXAMINATION REVIEW self-study program is partitioned into 44 topics or modules. Since each module is clearly defined and should be studied separately, you have the task of preparing for the CPA exam partitioned into 44 manageable tasks. Partitioning the overall project into 44 modules makes preparation psychologically easier, since you sense yourself completing one small step at a time rather than seemingly never completing one or a few large steps.

By completing the "Preliminary Estimate of Your Knowledge of Subject" inventory on the next page, organized by the 44 modules in this program, you will have a tabulation of your strong and weak areas at the beginning of your study program. This will help you budget your limited study time. Note that you should begin studying the material in each module by answering up to 1/4 of the total multiple choice questions in Volume II covering that module's topics (see instruction "5.A." in the next section). This "mini-exam" should constitute a diagnostic evaluation as to the amount of review and study you need.

Time Allocation

The study program below entails an average of 250 hours (Step "6." below) of study time. The breakdown of total hours is indicated in the left margin.

[3 hrs.] 1. Study Chapters 2-4 in this volume and Chapter 1 in Volume II. These chapters are essential to your efficient preparation program.

Time estimate includes candidate's review of the examples of the solutions approach in Chapters 2 and 3.

PRELIMINARY ESTIMATE OF YOUR PRESENT KNOWLEDGE OF SUBJECT:

No.	Module	Proficient	Fairly Proficient	Generally Familiar	Not Familiar
	AUDITING				
1	Professional Responsibilities				
2	Internal Control				
3	Audit Evidence				
4	Audit Reports				
5	Statistical Sampling				
6	Auditing EDP				
	BUSINESS LAW				
7	Contracts				
8	Sales				
9	Negotiable Instruments				
10	Secured Transactions				
11	Bankruptcy				
12	Suretyship				
13	Agency				
14	Partnership Law				
15	Corporations				
16	Antitrust & Government Regulation				
17	Federal Securities Law				
18	Accountant's Legal Liability				
19	Employer-Employee Relationships				
20	Property				
21	Insurance				
22	Trusts and Estates				
	PRACTICE AND THEORY				
23	Miscellaneous Financial				
24	Working Capital				
25	Inventory				
26	Fixed Assets				
27	Deferred Taxes				
28	Stockholders' Equity				
29	Present Value				
30	Inflation Accounting				
31	Ratio Analysis				
32	Partnerships				
33	Investments & Consolidations				
34	Costing Systems				
35	Planning, Control, and Analysis				
36	Standards and Variances				
37	Nonroutine Decisions				
38	Quantitative Methods				
39	Governmental and Nonprofit Acc.				
40	Individual Taxes				
41	Transactions in Property				
42	Partnership Taxes				
43	Corporate Taxes				
44	Gift and Estate Taxes				

2. Determine the order of studying for the four sections of the exam.

	Volume I	Volume II
Auditing	Chap 5	Chap 2
Business Law	Chap 6	Chap 3
Practice	Chap 7-13	Chap 4-8
Theory	Chap 7-12	Chap 4-7

If you have no preference, use the chronological order in the book. Note that you should study for practice and theory concurrently (recall that federal income taxes are not tested on theory).

$\boxed{\begin{matrix}1 \\ \text{hr.}\end{matrix}}$ 3. Begin Auditing and Business Law by studying the introductory material at the beginning of Chapters 5 and 6. Begin Practice/Theory by studying Chapter 7.

Time estimate: 15-30 minutes for each section.

4. For each section (Auditing, Law, and Practice/Theory) study one module at a time. The modules for each section of the exam are listed on the previous page in the self-evaluation section.

5. For each module:

$\boxed{\begin{matrix}38 \\ \text{hrs.}\end{matrix}}$ A. Work 1/4 of the multiple choice questions in Volume II (e.g., if there are 40 multiple choice questions in a module, you should work every 4th question). Score yourself.

This diagnostic routine will provide you with an index of your proficiency and familiarity with the type and difficulty of questions.

Time estimate: 3 minutes each, not to exceed 1 hour total.

$\boxed{\begin{matrix}72 \\ \text{hrs.}\end{matrix}}$ B. Study the outlines and illustrations in Volume I. Refer to outlines of authoritative pronouncements per instructions in Volume I. Also refer to your accounting textbooks and original authoritative pronouncements (this will occur more frequently for topics in which you have a weak background).

Time estimate: 1 hour minimum per module, with more time devoted to topics less familiar to you.

$\boxed{\begin{matrix}60 \\ \text{hrs.}\end{matrix}}$ C. Work the remaining multiple choice questions in Volume II. Study the explanations of the multiple choice questions you missed or had trouble answering.

Time estimate: 3 minutes to answer each question and 2 minutes to study the answer explanation of each question missed.

$\boxed{\begin{matrix}48 \\ \text{hrs.}\end{matrix}}$ D. Under exam conditions, work at least 2 essay questions and/or practice problems. Work additional essays/problems as time permits.

Time estimate: 20 minutes for each essay question, 45 minutes for each practice problem, and 10 minutes to review the unofficial answer and solution guide for each problem worked.

[28 hrs.] E. Work through the sample CPA examinations presented at the end of Volume II. Each exam should be taken in one sitting.

Take the examination under simulated exam conditions, i.e., in a strange place with other people present (e.g., your local municipal library). Apply your solutions approach to each problem and your exam strategy to the overall exam.

You should limit yourself to the allotted exam times, and spend time afterwards grading your work and reviewing your effort. It might be helpful to do this with other CPA candidates. Another person looking over your exam might be more objective and notice things such as clarity of essays, logic of problem presentations, etc.

Time estimate: To take the exam and review it later, approximately 5-6 hours for each part.

6. The total suggested time of 250 hours is only an average. Allocation of of time will vary candidate by candidate. Time requirements vary due to the diverse backgrounds and abilities of CPA candidates.

Allocate your time so you gain the most proficiency in the least time. Remember that while several hundred hours will be required, you should break the overall project down into 44 more manageable tasks. Do not study more than one module during each study session.

Using Notecards

Below are one candidate's notecards on exam topics which illustrate how key definitions, formulas, lists, etc. can be summarized on index cards for quick review. Since candidates can take these anywhere they go, they are a very efficient review tool.

Theory and Practice:

RETAIL INVENTORY	INCLUDE Bi	EXCLUDE Bi
MKUP + MKdwN	AVE COST	FIFO COST
MKUPS ONLY	CONVENTIONAL AVE L-C-M	FIFO L-C-M

CONSOLIDATIONS

Primary purpose of Consolidated F/S is to present for benefit of shareholders, CR of parent, the ni and B/S of a parent and its sub-"substance over form."

LIMITATIONS OF CONSOLIDATING -
• SUB INFO NOT DISCLOSED
• DIVERSIFICATION ELEMENTS HIDDEN
• LOSE INFO AS YOU AGGREGATE

Prepared by Cindy Johnson, former student, Northern Illinois University

Auditing:

<u>Tolerable error</u> - Max $ error for a bal.

<u>Ultimate Risk</u> - comb. of the risk that mat'l. error will occur & the risk that mat'l. error will not be detected by the auditor.

<u>Nonsampling Risk</u> -
- wrong audit proced.
- audit error,

con't.

<u>Sampling Risk</u> - may cause result diff. than pop. as a whole.

- Substantive Tests
1.) incorrect accep. β
2.) incorrect rejc. α

- Compliance
1.) Risk of overreliance
2.) Risk of underreliance

Prepared by Cindy Johnson, former student, Northern Illinois University

Business Law:

<u>NEGOTIABLE INSTRUMENT</u>

- in writing semi permeable movable form
- signed by appropriate person
- unconditional promise to pay sum certain in money

- words of negotiability
- No 2nd promise (collateral - OK)
- payable on demand or at definite date.

<u>ELEMENTS OF A BINDING AGREEMENT</u>

1) Manifestation of Mutual Assent
  a.) offer
  b.) acceptance
2) Reality of consent
3) Consideration
4) Capacity of Parties
5) Legality of object
6) Compliance w/ Statute of Frauds

Prepared by Cindy Johnson, former student, Northern Illinois University

Stop Using Calculators

As you know, calculators are not permitted on the CPA exam due to security problems (you can see the cathode ray answer displays at a considerable distance). Most CPA candidates are not used to working problems without calculators. Eliminate your dependence on a calculator throughout your CPA exam preparation program so you will

be able to make necessary computations quickly and accurately on the exam. To eliminate this dependence, practice computing the required answers utilizing mathematical shortcuts.

Levels of Proficiency Required

What level of proficiency do you have to develop with respect to each of the
topics to pass the exam? You should work toward a minimum correct rate on the Volume II multiple choice questions of 60 to 70% in accounting practice and 70 to 75%
in other areas.

In accounting practice, only 60 to 70% rather than 75% is recommended, because
this section of the CPA exam is "curved." We recommend 70 to 75% for the other
areas (accounting theory, auditing, and business law), because they are graded on
the basis of raw points. As explained in Chapter 2, recent exams in auditing,
business law, and accounting theory have been graded by adding "difficulty points"
to the candidates' raw scores.

Warning: Disproportional study time devoted to multiple choice questions (relative to essay questions/practice problems) can be disastrous on the exam. You
should work a substantial number of essay questions and practice problems under exam
conditions, even though multiple choice questions are easier to work and are used to
gauge your proficiency. The authors believe that a serious effort on essay questions and problems will also improve your proficiency on the multiple choice questions.

Conditional Candidates

Once you have a "leg up on the exam" (received partial credit for passing 2 or
more sections), you have to bear down on the remaining section(s). Unfortunately,
many candidates let up after conditioning the exam, relying on luck to get them
through the remaining section(s). As a result many candidates lose their
conditional status (as their time to complete the exam expires).

PLANNING FOR THE EXAMINATION

Overall Strategy

An overriding concern should be an orderly, systematic approach toward both your
preparation program and your examination strategy. A major objective should be to
avoid any surprises or anything else that would rattle you during the 2 1/2 days of

taking the examination. In other words, you want to be in complete control as much as possible. "Control" is of paramount importance from both positive and negative viewpoints. The presence of "control" on your part will add to your confidence and your ability to prepare for and take the exam. Moreover, the presence of "control" will make your preparation program more enjoyable (or at least less distasteful). On the other hand, a lack of organization will result in inefficiency in preparing and taking the examination, with a highly predictable outcome. Likewise, distractions during the examination (e.g., inadequate lodging, long drive) are generally disastrous.

In summary, your establishment of a systematic, orderly approach to the examination is of paramount importance.

1. Develop an overall strategy at the beginning of your preparation program (see below)
2. Supplement your overall strategy with outlines of material tested on each section of the CPA examination (see Chapters 5 through 13)
3. Supplement your overall strategy with an explicitly stated set of problem-solving procedures--the solutions approach
4. Supplement your overall strategy with an explicitly stated approach to each examination session (see Chapter 4)
5. Evaluate your preparation progress on a regular basis and prepare lists of things "to do" (see Weekly Review of Preparation Program Progress on following page)
6. RELAX: You can pass the exam. About 10,000 candidates successfully complete the exam each sitting. You will be one of them if you complete an efficient preparation program and execute well (i.e., use your solutions approach and exam strategy) while writing the exam.

The following outline is designed to provide you with a general framework of the tasks before you. You should tailor the outline to your needs by adding specific items and comments.

A. Preparation Program (refer to Self-Study Program discussed previously)
   1. Obtain and organize study materials
   2. Locate facilities conducive for studying and block out study time
   3. During your study program, if it becomes apparent that you will not be adequately prepared for all four parts of the upcoming exam, concentrate the majority of your study on your two strongest parts. For the two parts selected, devote much of your time to correcting weaknesses and the remainder for reviewing your strengths. CANDIDATES ADOPTING THIS STRATEGY MUST DO SO ONLY IN LIGHT OF THE PASS AND/OR CONDITION REQUIREMENTS APPLICABLE IN THE STATE IN WHICH THEY PLAN TO SIT.
   4. Develop your solutions approach (including solving essay questions and practice problems as well as multiple choice questions)
   5. Prepare an examination strategy

6. Study the material tested recently and prepare answers to actual exam questions on these topics under examination conditions
7. Periodically evaluate your progress

B. Physical Arrangements

1. Apply to and obtain acceptance from your State Board
2. Reserve lodging for examination nights

C. Taking the Examination (covered in detail in Chapter 4)

1. Become familiar with exam facilities and procedures
2. Implement examination strategies and the solutions approach

Weekly Review of Preparation Program Progress

Use the next two pages to reevaluate your preparation program progress. This procedure, taking only five minutes per week, will help you proceed through a more efficient, complete preparation program.

Make notes of materials and topics

1. That you have studied
2. That you have completed
3. That need additional study

Weeks to go   Comments on progress, "to do" items, etc.

    12

    11

    10

    9

8

7

6

5

4

3

2

1

0

APPENDIX

TIME MANAGEMENT FOR CPA CANDIDATES

Twice a year, candidates begin preparing for the CPA exam. They buy CPA review manuals, notebooks, dividers, pens, pencils, erasers, and even books that say to "keep a positive mental attitude toward this new and difficult assignment." All this is important to you as you begin studying for the exam. However, let us raise a note of caution--do not charge into your studies with such enthusiasm that you neglect to consider the magnitude of the task.

We know you have heard "war stories" from previous CPA candidates about the hundreds of hours that you will have to spend during the next three to four months working problems and reading official pronouncements. We know that all too often candidates do not realize the extent to which their time will be committed to studying for the exam. Common sense should tell you that finding those hundreds of hours for study will not be a simple task.

In this section of your CPA review program, we will help you to identify the hours you have available for studying for the CPA exam. We ask that you complete a short exercise using the "Time Analysis Matrix." After completing this exercise, you will have identified the "time blocks" that are currently available to you for study. This is an important exercise for you, whether you are a full-time student or a full-time practitioner.

Time Analysis Matrix. The "Time Analysis Matrix" (last page of this appendix) covers one complete week (i.e., seven days, twenty-four hours per day). The days of the week move across the matrix, while the hours of the day are listed down the left-hand side of the matrix. Each box represents a one-hour time block that is available to you. You have 168 (7 days x 24 hours) one-hour time blocks to work with every week.

Analyzing Your Fixed Time. Fixed time is the time you have allocated for SPECIFIC PURPOSES throughout your CURRENT WEEKLY SCHEDULE. For example, if you are a full-time student, your CURRENT CLASS SCHEDULE should represent fixed time. When you are in class, you cannot be in the library or the coffee shop. You are committed to using this time in a specific way. If you are working full-time, your normal working hours should be considered fixed time. Additionally, hours allotted to normal sleep time should be considered fixed time. IN SHORT, ANY HOURS YOU HAVE SPECIFICALLY COMMITTED TO USING REGULARLY DURING THE WEEK SHOULD BE CONSIDERED FIXED TIME.

Take a few moments and examine the TIME ANALYSIS MATRIX. Use a colored pencil or pen and shade in the time blocks that represent FIXED TIME in your CURRENT WEEKLY SCHEDULE. After you have finished shading in the time blocks, COUNT the shaded blocks and complete the following equations:

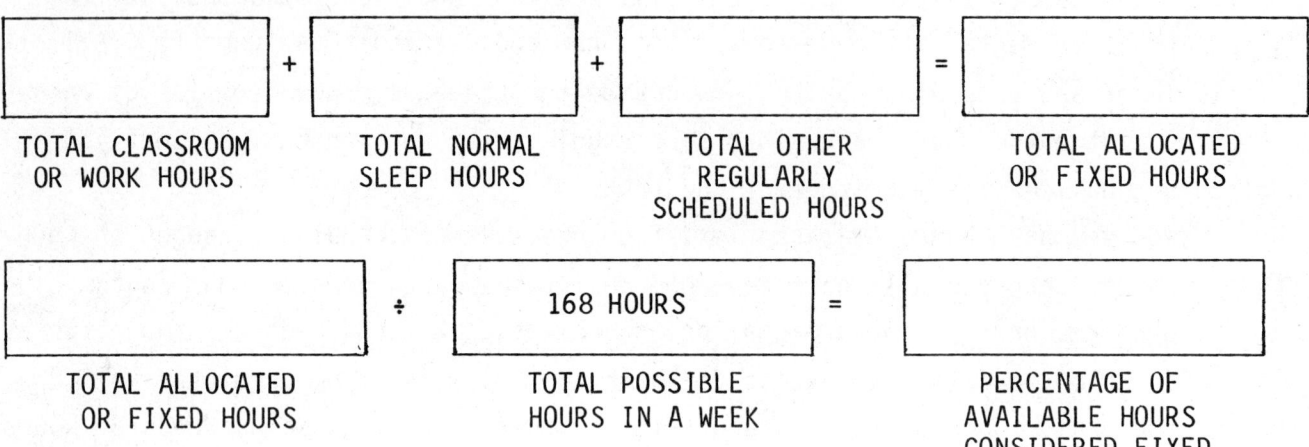

| TOTAL CLASSROOM OR WORK HOURS | + | TOTAL NORMAL SLEEP HOURS | + | TOTAL OTHER REGULARLY SCHEDULED HOURS | = | TOTAL ALLOCATED OR FIXED HOURS |

| TOTAL ALLOCATED OR FIXED HOURS | ÷ | 168 HOURS / TOTAL POSSIBLE HOURS IN A WEEK | = | PERCENTAGE OF AVAILABLE HOURS CONSIDERED FIXED |

Now for the Moment of Truth. If you are like most undergraduate students, your percentage of fixed hours should be around 46%. If this is true, you probably have approximately 54% or 91 hours per week that can be used in a DISCRETIONARY manner. It is with these DISCRETIONARY HOURS that PERSONAL TIME MANAGEMENT techniques can really be of help to you. If you can make the discretionary hours productive, you will find there is more than enough time to adequately prepare for the CPA exam.

If you are working full-time and studying for the exam through a review course or on your own, you will probably find that approximately 70% of your time will be fixed. Therefore, you have approximately 30% or 50 hours per week to use at your DISCRETION. You will have to work even harder at making the discretionary hours productive hours.

Approaching Your Discretionary Hours. CPA CANDIDATES DO NOT LIVE BY SOLVING PROB-LEMS ALONE! Believe it or not, even CPA candidates need time to relax and refresh their minds. However, you must carefully limit and properly sequence the discre-tionary time you spend relaxing and refreshing your mind.

Each hour on the TIME ANALYSIS MATRIX that is not shaded is considered discre-tionary. For each of these time blocks, you have to make an important decision. HOW DO YOU WANT TO USE EACH DISCRETIONARY HOUR? Take a few moments and shade in the discretionary time blocks. (Use a light-colored pencil which is a different color than the one used for FIXED TIME.) This will make them stand out so you can see the impact of this free time and where it is located on the matrix.

How do you make a discretionary hour become a PRODUCTIVE HOUR? As you look at
the discretionary hours on the time analysis matrix, where do you need both a PHYSI-
CAL and a MENTAL break? Think about your personal needs, since no two people work,
study, or rest in exactly the same way. Where you need BOTH the PHYSICAL and MENTAL
break period, WRITE THE LETTER "B" in the time block. Now the discretionary time
period has become a PRODUCTIVE-FIXED time period.

Review the time analysis matrix. At this point, you have allocated time blocks
to "fixed hours" and to "break hours." The REMAINING hours are what you have to
work with as you begin to set the remainder of your schedule.

Now--What Time Do You Have Left? At this point, any time blocks that are shaded as
DISCRETIONARY and do not contain the letter "B" are available for scheduling.
LOOK FOR TIME PERIODS THAT ARE AVAILABLE CONSISTENTLY FROM DAY TO DAY. For example,
you might find that 7-9 P.M. is open Monday through Friday. This would be a perfect
time slot for allocating to STUDY TIME. It is a reasonable length of study time,
and it is available every day. REASONABLENESS OF THE STUDY PERIOD AND CONSISTENCY
OF AVAILABILITY ARE "CRUCIAL" TO USING THE TIME BLOCKS AS PRODUCTIVE STUDY PERIODS.
Take a few moments and mark the time blocks you want to designate as STUDY PERIODS.
WRITE THE LETTER "S" in these time blocks.

The Final Analysis. Review the time analysis matrix and count the number of hours
you have designated as being FIXED. Next, count the number of hours you originally
designated as DISCRETIONARY, but which have now been marked as being DISCRETIONARY-
USED FOR BREAKS (i.e., the letter "B"). Finally, count the number of hours you have
marked as being DISCRETIONARY-USED FOR STUDY (i.e., the letter "S"). Complete the
following equation and see how you have allocated your time. ARE YOU GETTING THE
MOST OUT OF YOUR TIME? IF NOT, STEP BACK AND REWORK YOUR SCHEDULE.

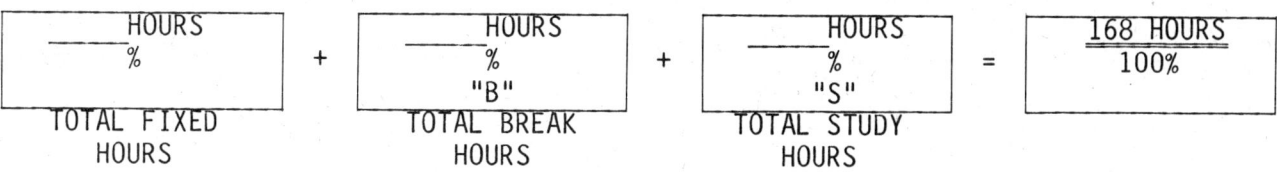

_____ HOURS %		_____ HOURS % "B"		_____ HOURS % "S"		168 HOURS 100%
TOTAL FIXED HOURS	+	TOTAL BREAK HOURS	+	TOTAL STUDY HOURS	=	

NOTE: For the FINAL ANALYSIS, consider time designated as neither FIXED nor
DISCRETIONARY-USED FOR STUDY to be DISCRETIONARY-USED FOR BREAKS. Therefore, "Break Time" will be used both for relaxation and for time not otherwise assigned for a specific purpose.

NOW IS THE TIME
TO MAKE A COMMITMENT

TIME ANALYSIS MATRIX

	MON	TUES	WED	THURS	FRI		SAT	SUN
1 am								
2 am								
3 am								
4 am								
5 am								
6 am								
7 am								
8 am								
9 am								
10 am								
11 am								
12 pm								
1 pm								
2 pm								
3 pm								
4 pm								
5 pm								
6 pm								
7 pm								
8 pm								
9 pm								
10 pm								
11 pm								
12 am								

CHAPTER TWO

EXAMINATION GRADING AND GRADER ORIENTATION

All State Boards of Accountancy use the AICPA advisory grading service. As your grade is to be determined by this process, it is very important that you understand the AICPA grading process and its implications for your preparation program and for the solution techniques you will use during the examination.

The AICPA has a full-time staff of CPA examination personnel whose responsibilities include

1. Preparing questions for the examination
2. Working with outside consultants who prepare questions
3. Preparation of grading guides and unofficial answers
4. Supervising and reviewing the work of examination graders

The AICPA examination staff is under the supervision of the AICPA Board of Examiners which has responsibility for the CPA examination.

This chapter contains a description of the AICPA grading process based on the description of AICPA grading in Information for CPA Candidates, AICPA grading guides, etc.

The AICPA Grading Process

The AICPA exercises very tight control over all the examination papers during the grading process and prior to their return to individual State Boards of Accountancy. Upon receipt from the exam sites, papers are assigned to control groups, reviewed for candidate numbers, and checked against state board records of examination papers submitted.

Multiple choice questions are graded electronically. Essay questions and practice problems are graded individually on the basis of grading guides. Grading guides consist of grading concepts, which are ideas, constructs, principles, etc., that can be clearly defined. Grading concepts for practice problems include amounts such as equivalent units of production and goodwill, as well as particular debits and credits in journal entries.

While tentative grading guides (answers) are prepared prior to the examination, the final grading guides are based upon two test gradings of samples of actual examinations. Once grading guides are developed, "production graders" perform the first grading of the examination. The "production graders" are practicing CPAs, university professors, attorneys, etc., retained by the AICPA on a per diem basis to grade the examination. These graders specialize in a single essay question or practice problem, and grade answers to that question for about six weeks. About 200 graders, some full-time, some part-time, are required for each examination.

After the multiple choice questions are machine-graded and returned to their respective examinations, the first grading of essay questions and practice problems begins. The control group of papers moves from grader to grader. Attached to each examination is a grading guide similar to the "Hypothetical Grading Guide" on page 32. The purpose of the first grading is to separate examinations as to pass, fail, and marginal.

The second grading is performed by reviewers who generally inspect the work of the "production graders" but emphasize review of the marginal examinations, i.e., papers with grades of 70 to 74. Papers with grades of 70 to 74 are regraded to grades of 69 or 75. One of the major reasons for this procedure is to relieve State Boards of Accountancy of requests for regrading failing papers "very near" 75. Most 72s, 73s, and 74s are regraded to 75. All of the questions on papers selected for regrading are reevaluated. Grade changes (when made) are made to the essay questions or practice problems. An analysis is undertaken of all essay questions and practice problems to differentiate sophisticated grading concepts (those included by most candidates passing the exam) from rudimentary grading concepts (those included by candidates both passing and failing the exam). Answers which include sophisticated grading concepts are generally graded up and papers with only rudimentary grading concepts are generally graded down. Note this procedure is only applied to papers in the 70 through 74 range. In all cases, as throughout the grading procedure, the candidate is given the benefit of the doubt.

The third grading is administered to papers that have several passing parts but have a failing score on a particular part. A fourth and final grading may be performed on papers that continue to have inconsistent grades after the third grading, e.g., 88, 84, 68, 89.

Note that the first grading is directed to individual questions while the second grading is directed to individual sections, e.g., Theory, Law, etc. The third grading is a review of failing parts written by candidates who have done well on other remaining parts (or for example, conditional candidates with one part to go). The fourth and final grading is directed to any remaining inconsistencies. It should be emphasized that answer format, presentation, logic, etc., are given more consideration on the regradings than on the first grading.

An adding machine tape totaling the grade on individual questions for each section is then prepared. The examination papers, grades, and grading tapes are returned to the individual state boards several weeks prior to the official grade release date. The grade release date is usually at the end of January for the November exam, and at the end of July for the May exam.

What Graders Are Looking For

Based on Information for CPA Candidates, the examination instructions, examination questions, unofficial answers, etc., the examiners appear to be looking for
1. Knowledge of the academic content of the typical undergraduate accounting major
2. Ability to apply this knowledge to specific situations with good judgment
3. Precise and concise use of the English language
4. Examination, evaluation, and classification of data in complex situations
5. Organization and presentation of accounting data
6. Application of accounting and auditing standards, procedures, etc., to specific situations
7. Reasonable facility with disciplines relatively close to accounting, e.g., quantitative methods, statistics, finance, economics, etc.

Multiple Choice Grading

In the past, conversion tables (or curves) have been developed for each overall question which consists of a number of individual multiple choice questions. However, there appears to be a move away from using grading curves to linear assignment of grades, i.e., one point was assigned for each correct response on the auditing, business law, and theory sections of the past several examinations. Grades on these parts have been modified by "difficulty points" whereby candidates are "spotted" points for attempting the multiple choice questions (note that this is a means of "curving" the grades on the entire section).

The November 1983 multiple choice point allocation and grading were typical of recent exams. Auditing, Business Law, and Theory presented all their multiple choice questions as Problem 1. For these sections, each correct response was worth 1 point. "Difficulty points" were awarded on the November 1983 exam as summarized in the following table.

	No. of MC	% of Section Grade	"Difficulty Points"	No. of Correct Responses for a 75	Correct Response Rate Req.
Auditing	60	60%	1	44	73%
Business Law	60	60%	9	36	60%
Theory	60	60%	6	39	65%
Practice	120	60%	N/A	N/A	N/A

Practice I and Practice II each had three problems consisting of 20 multiple choice items. Each problem made up 10% of the total grade of the practice portion of the exam. The conversion tables for the six multiple choice problems in Practice appear below.

Practice I						Practice II					
Problem 1		Problem 2		Problem 3		Problem 1		Problem 2		Problem 3	
No. correct	Grade	No. correct	Grade	No. correct	Grade	No. correct	Grade	No. correct	Grade	No. correct	Grade
20-16	10	20-17	10	20-17	10	20-18	10	20-16	10	20-18	10
15	9.5	16	9.5	16	9.5	17	9.5	15	9.5	17	9.5
14	9	15	9	15	9	16	9	14	9	16	9
13	8.5	14	8.5	14	8.5	15	8.5	13	8.5	15	8.5
12	8	13	8	13	8	14	8	12	8	14	8
11*	7.5	12*	7.5	12*	7.5	13*	7.5	11*	7.5	13*	7.5
10	7	11	7	11	7	12	7	10	7	12	7
9	6.5	10	6.5	10	6.5	11	6.5	9	6.5	11	6.5
8	6	9	6	9	6	10	6	8	6	10	6
7	5.5	8	5.5	8	5.5	9	5.5	7	5.5	9	5.5
6	5	7	5	7	5	8	5	6	5	8	5
5	4.5	6	4.5	6	4.5	7	4.5	5	4.5	7	4.5
4	4	5	4	5	4	6	4	4	4	6	4
3	3.5	4	3.5	4	3.5	5	3.5	3	3.5	5	3.5
2	3	3	3	3	3	4	3	2	3	4	3
1	2.5	2	2.5	2	2.5	3	2.5	1	2.5	3	2.5
0	0	1	2	1	2	2	2	0	0	2	2
		0	0	0	0	1	1.5			1	1.5
						0	0			0	0

Note that the ratio of correct responses over total questions required for a "75" on each question - 11/20, 12/20, 12/20, 13/20, 11/20, and 13/20, respectively - was cumulatively 72/120, for an overall 60% correct response rate.

Implications: Since grading is on a relative basis, do your best regardless of the difficulty of the questions. Perfect and use a "multiple choice question solutions approach" which is discussed in Chapter 3. If you are unsure about a particular question, you should guess, i.e., pick the "best" answer. This assumes that "your grade will be based on your total correct answers," i.e., no penalty for incorrect answers. The grading procedure for multiple choice questions is explained in the instructions at the beginning of each section of the exam. The importance of carefully reading and following these, and all other, instructions cannot be over-emphasized.

Essay Grading

To illustrate the grading of essay questions, we have included auditing question Number 3 from the November 1981 exam in this section. Following the question are the AICPA Unofficial Answer and a hypothetical grading guide.

Number 3

Dunbar Camera Manufacturing, Inc., is a manufacturer of high-priced precision motion picture cameras in which the specifications of component parts are vital to the manufacturing process. Dunbar buys valuable camera lenses and large quantities of sheetmetal and screws. Screws and lenses are ordered by Dunbar and are billed by the vendors on a <u>unit basis.</u> Sheetmetal is ordered by Dunbar and are billed by the vendors on the basis of <u>weight.</u> The receiving clerk is responsible for documenting the quality and quantity of merchandise received.

A preliminary review of the system of internal control indicates that the following procedures are being followed:

Receiving Report

1.   Properly approved purchase orders, which are prenumbered, are filed numerically. The copy sent to the receiving clerk is an exact duplicate of the copy sent to the vendor. Receipts of merchandise are recorded on the duplicate copy by the receiving clerk.

Sheetmetal

2.   The company receives sheetmetal by railroad. The railroad independently weighs the sheetmetal and reports the weight and date of receipt on a bill of lading (waybill), which accompanies all deliveries. The receiving clerk only checks the weight on the waybill to the purchase order.

Screws

3.   The receiving clerk opens cartons containing screws, then inspects and weighs the contents. The weight is converted to number of units by means of conversion charts. The receiving clerk then checks the computed quantity to the purchase order.

Camera lenses

4.   Each camera lens is delivered in a separate corrugated carton. Cartons are counted as they are received by the receiving clerk and the number of cartons are checked to purchase orders.

Required:

a.   Explain why the internal control procedures as they apply individually to receiving reports and the receipt of sheetmetal, screws, and camera lenses are adequate or inadequate. **Do not discuss recommendations for improvements.**

b.   What financial statement distortions may arise because of the inadequacies in Dunbar's system of internal control and how may they occur?

UNOFFICIAL ANSWER

a.   The adequacy of internal control is questionable whenever quantities are not blocked out on the copy of the purchase order that is sent to the receiving department, because this practice may cause the receiving clerk to bypass the counting and inspection procedures. The receiving clerk may only compare the purchase order and packing slip (or other document accompanying the shipment) and prepare a receiving report based on these documents. As a result of this weakness, incorrect quantities of merchandise or inferior quality merchandise may be received and accepted. However, in the case of Dunbar Manufacturing, Inc., in certain areas there are compensating controls.

Receipt of sheetmetal. Although the receiving clerk may only compare quantities on the purchase order and the bill of lading, there is a compensating control over quantities of sheetmetal received. This compensating control is the independent verification of weights received and date of receipt, which are provided in the bill of lading. However, sheetmetal with unacceptable quality specifications may still be received and accepted.

Receipt of screws. Since the receiving clerk weighs the screws upon receipt and the weight is converted to units, control over quantities received is adequate. Furthermore, screws of an unacceptable specification may be expected to be detected during the weighing and inspecting process.

Receipt of camera lenses. Because there are no controls that compensate for the weakness in checking actual receipt of camera lenses, there is inadequate control over the quantity and quality of lenses received.

b.   Inventory may be overstated and the cost of merchandise sold and income may be misstated because additions to inventory may be based on suppliers' invoices, which may include nonusable items or items that were not received. Further, because the company may have erroneously accrued the cost of nonusable items or items not received, accounts payable may be overstated.

Essay questions are generally graded based on the number of <u>grading</u> concepts in the candidate's solution. The grading guide is a list of the grading concepts and raw point(s) assigned to each concept. The total raw points listed are usually in excess of the maximum points which a candidate may earn on the question. A hypothetical grading guide for the preceding auditing essay question appears below.

<u>NOVEMBER 1981 AUDITING, NUMBER 3</u>
<u>HYPOTHETICAL GRADING GUIDE</u>*

	Grading points
a. Adequacy of internal control procedures	
<u>Receiving report</u> — <u>documentation</u> of the receipt of merchandise is <u>inadequate</u>	1
Because <u>quantities</u> are <u>not blocked out</u> on the purchase order copy sent to the receiving department	1
This may cause the receiving clerk to <u>by-pass</u> the established <u>counting procedures</u>	1
<u>Sheetmetal</u> — an adequate <u>compensating control</u> exists <u>over quantities</u> of sheetmetal <u>received</u>	1
Because the <u>bill of lading</u> provides <u>independent verification</u> of weights received	1
However, sheetmetal with <u>unacceptable</u> quality specifications may be <u>received and accepted</u> because <u>inspection</u> procedures are <u>by-passed</u>	1
<u>Screws</u> — <u>adequate control</u> exists <u>over quantity</u> of screws <u>received</u>	1
Because <u>weights</u> are <u>converted to units</u>	1
During the <u>weighing and inspecting</u> process screws of an <u>unacceptable quality</u> may be expected to be detected	1
<u>Camera lenses</u> — <u>no compensating controls</u> exist <u>over</u> the <u>receipt</u> of camera lenses	1
Therefore, <u>control</u> over the <u>quantity</u> and <u>quality</u> of lenses received is <u>inadequate</u>	1
b. Financial statement distortions which are possible include:	
<u>Inventory</u> may be <u>overstated</u>	1
<u>Cost</u> of sales may be <u>misstated</u>	1
<u>Accounts payable</u> may be <u>overstated</u>	1
The distortions are possible because supplier's invoice may be basis for additions to inventory allowing for inclusion of	
<u>Nonusuable items</u>	1
<u>Items</u> that were <u>not received</u>	1
Grading points possible	16

The conversion scale below converts the "raw" grading points shown above to the grade earned on the question.

CONVERSION SCALE

Grading Points Earned	16-14	13	12	11	10	9-8	7	6	5-4	3	2-1
Grade	10	9	8	7.5	7	6	5	4	3	2	1

TOTAL GRADE: NUMBER 3

Grade from Conversion Scale   _____

Demerit for form, etc.   _____

                                                                    ══════

Note: To obtain a passing grade (7.5 points) on this problem, a candidate would need to earn 11 of the possible 16 points (68%).

The AICPA Board of Examiners does not release the grading guides used for scoring essay questions and practice problems. The grading guide above was prepared by the authors to illustrate to candidates the manner in which points are allocated to grading concepts.

In the above grading guide, note that each grading concept is summarized by several keywords. Graders undoubtedly scan for these keywords during the first grading.

Another consideration is "cross-grading." Often candidates answer one requirement elsewhere than required; i.e., the answer to requirement "a" may be written as part of the answer to requirement "b." Frequently, the grading guides permit "cross-grading," i.e., giving credit in one part of the answer for a correct response in another part of the answer. To assure full credit, however, candidates should be very careful to organize their answers to meet the question requirements; i.e., you should answer requirement "a" in answer "a," answer requirement "b" in answer "b," etc. Additionally, the efficient use of time is of the utmost importance. If you have included grading concepts in one part of a question that are applicable to another part of the same question, do not repeat them. Simply refer the grader to your previous answer.

Two common misconceptions about the AICPA grading of essay questions have cost candidates points in recent years. First, answers should not consist of a listing (or outline) of keywords. Answers should be set forth in short, concise sentences, organized per the requirements of the question. Second, a candidate should not answer only one or two parts of a question very thoroughly and leave the remaining parts blank. Even though the grading guide may contain 3 times as many grading concepts as there are points available, each part of a question will usually have a limited number of attainable points.

Notice that the last grading concept in the example grading guide is "Demerit for form, etc." Grading guides may provide a penalty for sloppiness, inadequate form, etc. Alternatively, they may provide a bonus for good form and appearance. A closely related matter is the examiner's consideration of the candidates' ability to express themselves in acceptable written language. Recent examinations have contained the following paragraph in the instructions for each section of the exam:

> A CPA is continually confronted with the necessity of expressing opinions and conclusions in written reports in clear, unequivocal language. Although the primary purpose of the examination is to test the candidate's knowledge and application of the subject matter, the ability to organize and present such knowledge in acceptable written language will be considered by the examiners.

The grading guide might be thought of as a brief outline of the unofficial answer. Note the similarities between the grading guide and the unofficial answer.

Problem Grading

Problem grading guides are more structured than the grading guides for essay questions, because essay questions have an open-ended nature. Although some alternative calculations may be acceptable for practice problems, relatively little latitude is available in the problem solutions. Problem grading guides consist of check figures from throughout the unofficial answer. The grading of a practice problem is illustrated in the next chapter, The Solutions Approach.

Allocation of Points to Questions

Information for CPA Candidates states that the "maximum point values for each question are approximately proportional to the minutes allotted to the question in the suggested time budget printed in the examination booklet." Candidates should be concerned with point allocations for the purpose of allocating their time on the exam.

Grading Implications for CPA Candidates

Analysis of the grading process helps you understand what graders are looking for and how you can present solutions to "satisfy the grader." Before turning to Chapter 3 for a discussion of how to prepare solutions, consider the following conclusions derived from the foregoing grading analysis:

1. Your solutions should be neat and orderly to avoid demerits and to obtain bonuses

2. Allocate your time based on AICPA minimum suggested times
3. Do your best on every question, no matter how difficult

    a. Remember the exam is graded on a relative basis
    b. If a question is difficult for you, it probably is difficult for others also
    c. Develop a "solutions approach" to assist you

4. No supporting computations are required for the multiple choice questions; however, you will most likely use scratch paper to perform computations, etc. The multiple choice answers are machine-graded, and any related notes, computations, etc., are ignored.

    a. Conversely, supplementary computation sheets should be prepared for practice problems for submission to the grader

5. Essay solutions should be numbered and organized according to the problem requirements, e.g., a, b1, b2, c1, c2, c3, d1, d2

    a. Label your solutions parallel to the requirements
    b. Emphasize keywords
    c. Separate grading concepts into individual sentences or short paragraphs

        1) Do not bury grading concepts in lengthy paragraphs that might be missed by the grader. Include as many <u>sensible</u> grading concepts as possible.
        2) Use short, uncomplicated sentence structure
        3) DO NOT PRESENT YOUR ANSWER IN OUTLINE FORMAT

    d. Do not omit any requirements

6. Problem solutions should also be numbered and organized according to the requirements of the problem

    a. Solutions should be complete because of the finite number of grading concepts
    b. Label solutions neatly to help the grader find the required grading concepts (check figures)

        1) Reasonable abbreviations are fine, e.g., A/P for accounts payable
        2) Headings should be prepared for all schedules and statements
        3) Assumptions should be briefly stated indicating knowledge of alternative treatments

    c. All supporting calculations should be prepared answer sheet or computational sheets

        1) All such supporting calculations and schedules should be labeled
        2) In your answer, you should use references such as "See sched. A"

In summary, SATISFY THE GRADER. You need neat, readable solutions organized according to the requirements, which will also be the organization of the grading guides. Remember that a legible, well-organized solution gives a professional appearance. Additionally, recognize the plight of the grader having to decipher one mess after another, day after day. Give him/her a break with a neat, orderly solution. The "halo" effect will be rewarded by additional consideration (and hopefully points!).

**NOW IS THE TIME
TO MAKE A COMMITMENT**

CHAPTER THREE

THE SOLUTIONS APPROACH

The solutions approach is a systematic problem-solving methodology. The purpose is to assure efficient, complete solutions to CPA exam problems, some of which are complex and confusing relative to most undergraduate accounting problems.

Unfortunately, there appears to be a widespread lack of emphasis on problem-solving techniques in accounting courses. Most accounting books and courses merely provide solutions to specific types of problems. Memorization of these solutions for examinations and preparation of homework problems from examples is "cookbooking."

"Cookbooking" is perhaps a necessary step in the learning process, but it is certainly not sufficient training for the complexities of the business world. Professional accountants need to be adaptive to a rapidly changing complex environment. For example, CPAs have been called on to interpret and issue reports on new concepts such as price controls, energy allocations, and new taxes. These CPAs rely on their problem-solving expertise to understand these problems and to formulate solutions to them.

Practice Problem Solutions Approach Algorithm

The steps outlined below are only one of many possible series of solution steps. Admittedly, the procedures suggested are _very_ structured; thus, you should adapt the suggestions to your needs. You may find that some steps are occasionally unnecessary, or that certain additional procedures increase your own problem-solving efficiency. Whatever the case, substantial time should be allocated to developing an efficient solutions approach before taking the examination. You should develop your solutions approach by working old CPA problems.

Note that the steps below relate to any specific problem; overall examination or section strategies are discussed in Chapter 4.

1. Glance over the problem. Only scan the problem. Get a feel for the type or category of problem. Do not read it. Until you understand the requirements, you cannot discriminate important data from irrelevant data.

2. Study the requirements. "Study" as differentiated from "read." Candidates continually lose points due to misunderstanding the requirements. Underline key phrases and words.

2a. Visualize the solution format. Determine the expected format of the required solution. Develop an awareness of "schedule and statement format." Put headings on the required statements and schedules. Often a single requirement will require two or more statements, schedules, etc. A common example is a question followed by "why" or "explain." Explicitly recognize multiple requirements by numbering or lettering them on your examination booklet, expanding on the letters already assigned to problem parts.

3. Outline the required procedures mentally. Interrelate the data in the text of the problem to the expected solution format, mentally noting a "to do" list. Determine what it is you are going to do before you get started doing it.

3a. Review applicable principles, knowledge. Before immersing yourself in the details of the problem, quickly (30-60 seconds) review and organize the principles and your knowledge applicable to the problem. Jot down any acronyms, formulas, or other memory aids relevant to the topic of the question. Otherwise, the details of the problem may confuse and overshadow your previous knowledge of the applicable principles.

4. Study the text of the problem. Read the problem carefully. With the requirements in mind, you can now begin to sort out relevant from irrelevant data. Underline and circle important data. The data necessary for answering each requirement may be scattered throughout the problem. As you study the text, use arrows, etc. to connect data pertaining to a common requirement. List the requirements (a, b, etc.) in the margin alongside the data to which they pertain. Use a wild colored pen to mark up the problem. Heavy colored underlining and comments are attention getting and give you confidence.

4a. Prepare intermediary solutions as you study the problem. E.g., calculate goodwill, reconstruct accounts, prepare time diagrams, etc. You are able to perceive these required intermediary solutions because you already understand the problem requirements. These intermediary solutions, underlining, and notes in the text of the problem will drastically decrease re-reading time.

5. Prepare the solution. You now are in a position to write a neat, complete, organized, labeled solution. Label computations, intermediary solutions, assumptions made, etc., on your scratch sheets and turn them in with your solution (note: but not for multiple choice questions).

6. Proofread and edit. Do not underestimate the utility of this step. Just recall all of the "silly" mistakes you made on undergraduate examinations.

Corrections of errors and completion of oversights during this step can easily be the difference between passing and failing.

7. <u>Review the requirements</u>. Assure yourself that you have answered them all.

<u>Time Requirements for the Solutions Approach</u>. Many candidates bypass the solutions approach because they feel it is too time consuming. Actually, the solutions approach is a time saver, and, more importantly, it helps you prepare better solutions to all problems.

Without committing yourself to using the solutions approach, try it step-by-step on several essay questions and practice problems. After you conscientiously go through the step-by-step routine a few times, you will begin to adopt and modify aspects of the technique which will benefit you. Subsequent usage will become subconscious and painless. The important point is that you have to try the solutions approach several times to accrue any benefits.

<u>Schedule Layout</u>. Many candidates are concerned with how to "lay out" schedules and "set up" problems. As you visualize the solution formats, prepare the statement and schedule headings. This will help you understand the requirements and develop the necessary intermediary solutions, analyses, etc. Put the "headed" answer sheets aside until you have worked through the entire problem and are ready to "write up" your final solution.

In preparation for the examination, you should continually be concerned with schedule and statement formats. As you study topics, e.g., consolidations, statement of changes, etc., and work recent CPA problems, always note the schedule and statement formats. To assist you, numerous formats are illustrated throughout these texts. Recognize that there generally are several acceptable formats for most presentations. Become comfortable with the alternate presentations by comparing and contrasting unfamiliar formats to the format(s) with which you are familiar.

It is not necessary to "memorize" the format to be able to solve many financial accounting problems because the components (labels to be placed on the vertical axis and horizontal axis) are often listed in the requirements. For example, assume a problem has the following requirement:

a. Prepare a comparative schedule of <u>pretax accounting income</u> and <u>taxable income</u>, including supporting schedules of <u>sales</u>, <u>cost of goods sold</u>, <u>present-value computations</u>, and <u>investment income</u>

Analysis: The requirement calls for a schedule with two columns as follows:

Dom Corp.

COMPARATIVE SCHEDULE OF PRETAX ACCOUNTING
INCOME AND TAXABLE INCOME
For the Year Ended December 31, 1984

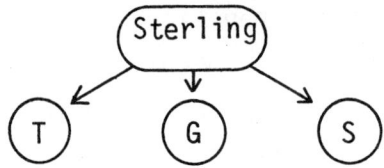

Note that the necessary supporting schedules are also listed in the requirement.

Diagrams are very important to help you understand interrelationships within a problem setting. You should practice using diagrams to analyze problems. For example, the Sterling Company may invest in Turner, Grotex, and Scott Companies, which may be diagrammed as:

A very important form of diagram is the time diagram. Time diagrams are frequently required to sort out a series of transactions. The following time diagram format facilitates analysis:

	19X1		19X2	

Diagrams are recommended for two reasons in addition to facilitating analysis of the problem. First, a diagram creates a firmer impression in your mind so as to prevent confusion while you are working the problem. A simple diagram, such as O ──────▶ S indicating that Operating Corp. invested in Service Corp., will often aid your solution. Second, time diagrams promote preparation of solutions in chronological order, which tends to make them more orderly and complete.

T-accounts (representing ledger accounts) are extremely useful to reconstruct account balances and flow of information from account to account. One example of information flows arises in cost accounting. Material, labor, and overhead costs flow into the work-in-process (manufacturing) account; then to finished goods inventory; then to cost of goods sold.

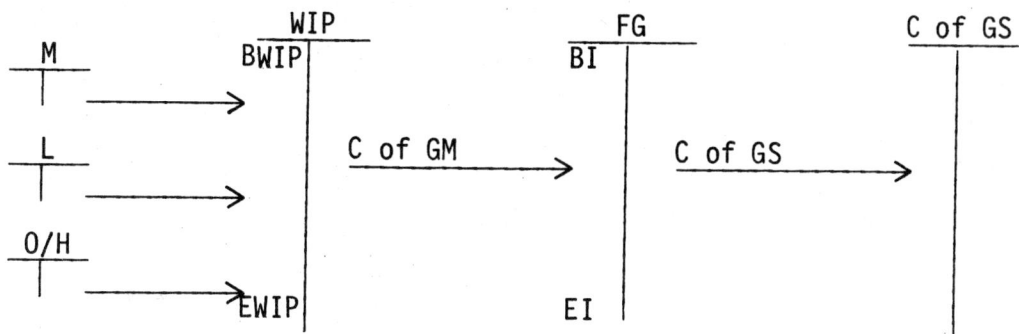

An example of T-account analysis to reconstruct ledger accounts is inherent in the solution to the problem below:

> With certain of its products, Hite Foods, Inc., includes coupons having no expiration date which are redeemable in merchandise. In the company's experience, 40% of such coupons are redeemed. The liability for unredeemed coupons at December 31, 1983, was $9,000. During 1984, coupons worth $18,000 were issued and merchandise worth $8,000 was distributed in exchange for coupons redeemed. The December 31, 1984, balance sheet should include a liability of
>
> a. $7,600.
> b. $8,200. (correct per the T-account below)
> c. $9,800.
> d. $13,000.

	Liability	
Beginning		9,000
40% of Issued		7,200
Redeemed	8,000	
Ending		8,200

Journal Entries. Many candidates have trouble with journal entries. When you come upon a seemingly difficult entry, diagram the economic event that occurred. Most economic events are transactions with third parties. What did we give up? What did we receive?

Also, always start with the easy elements of a journal entry. If we sold something for cash, debit cash and then worry about the credit. This is particularly important with compound/complex entries.

Journal entries are often a "solutions approach" in themselves. When you do not understand a transaction, e.g., amount of profit on a combined sale-financing lease, prepare the journal entries. Furthermore, journal entries can constitute a solutions approach even though they are not explicitly required in the solution, as in the preparation of consolidated worksheets.

Practice Problem Solutions Approach Example

The problem on the next two pages is Problem 4 from Part I of the May 1983 Examination in Accounting Practice. This problem will be worked using the solutions approach. Following this solution guide is the AICPA Unofficial Answer.

First, glance over the problem noting that it consists of two unrelated parts. Part "a" involves computations concerning the allowance for doubtful accounts. Part "b" involves certain dollar-value LIFO computations. The candidate should solve part "a" before beginning work on part "b." Therefore, steps 1-7 of the solutions approach will be applied first to part "a" and then to part "b."

Second, study the requirements. The first requirement in part "a" is to prepare an analysis of changes in the allowance for doubtful accounts. Visualize the solution format. The candidate should anticipate a schedule starting with the 1/1/82 balance in the allowance account and adjusting it for the effects of activity taking place during 1982 to determine the 12/31/82 balance. The second requirement in part "a" is the journal entry for the year-end adjustment to the allowance account.

Third, determine the steps to your solution. An organized approach to solving part "a" would involve evaluating each event detailed in the problem to determine its impact on the allowance account. Jot down journal entries, calculations, etc. as you proceed. Quickly review the accounting principles applicable to bad debt expense and the related allowance for doubtful accounts.

Fourth, study the text of the problem preparing intermediary solutions as you proceed.

a. Go through the problem using a felt tip pen to make marginal notes setting out key information (e.g., write-offs) and underlining key points (e.g., provision at 2% of credit sales). To the extent possible, use your felt tip pen to relate the tables of data given with the text of the problem.

b. Interim provisions during the year were 2% of credit sales ($9,000,000), or $180,000. These provisions increased the allowance account:

Bad debt expense	$180,000	
Allowance for doubtful accounts		$180,000

c. Accounts in the amount of $15,000 previously written off were recovered. This amount would increase the allowance account:

Accounts receivable	$15,000	
Allowance for doubtful accounts		$15,000
Cash	$15,000	
Accounts receivable		$15,000

Number 4 (Estimated time —— 45 to 55 minutes)

Number 4 consists of two unrelated parts.

Part a.   From inception of operations to December 31, 1981, Harris Corporation provided for uncollectible accounts receivable under the <u>allowance method: provisions were made monthly at 2% of credit sales</u>; bad debts written off were charged to the allowance account; recoveries of bad debts previously written off were credited to the allowance account; and, <u>no year-end adjustments to the allowance account were made.</u> Harris's usual credit terms are net 30 days.

The <u>balance in the allowance for doubtful accounts</u> was $130,000 at January 1, 1982. During 1982 credit sales totaled $9,000,000, interim provisions for doubtful accounts were made at 2% of credit sales, *(WRITE-OFFS)* $90,000 of bad debts were written off, and recoveries of accounts previously written off amounted to $15,000. Harris installed a computer facility in November 1982 and an aging of accounts receivable was prepared for the first time as of December 31, 1982. A summary of the aging is as follows:

(handwritten annotations: 1/1/82, 1982)

AGING AT 12/31/82

Classification by month of sale	Balance in each category	Estimated % uncollectible	
Nov-Dec 1982	$1,140,000	× 2% =	22,800
Jul-Oct	600,000	× 10 =	60,000
Jan-June	400,000	× 25 =	100,000
Prior to 1/1/82	70,000 ~~130,000~~	× 75 =	~~97,500~~ 52,500
	$2,270,000	REQUIRED 12/31/82 BAL?	~~280,300~~ 235,300

Based on the review of collectibility of the account balances in the "prior to 1/1/<u>82</u>" aging category, additional receivables totaling $60,000 were written off as of December 31, 1982. *(ADDL. WRITE OFFS)* Effective with the year ended December 31, 1982, Harris adopted a <u>new accounting method for estimating the allowance for doubtful accounts at the amount indicated by the year-end aging analysis</u> of accounts receivable.

TREATED as Change in estimate!

Required:

1.   Prepare a schedule analyzing the <u>changes in the allowance for doubtful accounts</u> for the year ended December 31, 1982. Show supporting computations in good form. *BAL + PROVISIONS + RECOVERIES - WRITE-OFFS + ADJUSTMENTS*

2.   Prepare the <u>journal entry for the year-end adjustment</u> to the allowance for doubtful accounts balance as of December 31, 1982.

Part b. On January 1, 1981, [NEW] Lucas Distributors, Inc., adopted the dollar value LIFO inventory method for income tax and external financial statements reporting purposes. However, Lucas continued to use the [OLD] FIFO inventory method for internal accounting and management purposes. In applying the LIFO method Lucas uses internal conversion price indexes and the multiple-pools approach under which substantially identical inventory items are grouped into LIFO inventory pools. The following data were available for Inventory Pool No. 1, which is comprised of products A and B, for the two years following the adoption of LIFO:

INV. POOL NO. 1 _FIFO basis per records_

	Units	Unit cost	Total cost	
Inventory, 1/1/81				
Product A	12,000	$30	$360,000	**BASE-YEAR PRICES**
Product B	8,000	25	200,000	
			$560,000	
	AT BASE PRICES			
Inventory, 12/31/81				
Product A	30 × 17,000	35	$595,000	
Product B	25 × 9,000	28	252,000	
	510,000	INDEX	$847,000	**Current Prices**
	225,000			
	735,000			
Inventory, 12/31/82				
Product A	30 × 13,000	40	$520,000	
Product B	25 × 10,000	32	320,000	
	390,000	INDEX	$840,000	**Current prices**
	250,000			
	640,000			

Required:

1. Prepare a schedule to compute the internal conversion price indexes for 1981 and 1982. Round indexes to two decimal places.

2. Prepare a schedule to compute the inventory amounts at December 31, 1981 and 1982, using the dollar value LIFO inventory method.

d. During 1982, $90,000 of bad debts were written off. At 12/31/82, additional receivables totaling $60,000 were written off. These amounts would decrease the allowance account:

    Allowance for doubtful accounts $150,000
        Accounts receivable $150,000

e. At year end, an aging analysis of accounts receivable was prepared. The required balance in the allowance account is computed to be $235,300 by taking the amount in each category and multiplying by the percentage estimated to be uncollectible, and adding the four products (see Schedule 1 in Unofficial Answer on following pages). In the "prior to 1/1/82" category, it is necessary to multiply the 75% expected uncollectible rate times $70,000 because $60,000 of the $130,000 was written off the same day. $70,000 is the correct amount because the wording of the problem implies that the $60,000 was written off subsequent to the preparation of the aging schedule but before the determination of the provision for doubtful accounts for 1982.

f. The allowance account is increased by $60,300 (from $175,000 to $235,300) as a result of the aging. The change in method of estimating uncollectible accounts is considered a change in estimate, handled currently and prospectively. Therefore, the entry is to debit bad debt expense and credit the allowance account.

    Bad debt expense $60,300
        Allowance for doubtful accounts $60,300

Fifth, prepare the solution (see following pages). All schedules should have a heading which includes the name of the company, schedule title, and period covered. Supporting schedules should be appropriately titled and referenced, e.g., "See Schedule 1." Journal entries should include an appropriate explanation.

Sixth, proofread and edit.

Seventh, review later, time permitting.

The candidate would now proceed to apply the same seven-step approach to part "b." We will start with step two.

Second, study the requirements. The first requirement in part "b" is a schedule to compute the internal conversion price indexes for a company using the dollar-value LIFO inventory method. The second requirement is the inventory amounts at the end of 1981 and 1982 using the dollar-value LIFO method.

Third, determine the steps to your solution. Review the accounting principles applicable to dollar-value LIFO inventory. Dollar-value LIFO bases inventory on "dollars" in inventory rather than "units." Remember that increases and decreases in inventory are measured in terms of base year dollars. Also, recall that individual layers in a dollar-value LIFO inventory are valued as follows:

$$\$ \text{ value LIFO} = \frac{\text{Inventory at}}{\text{base prices}} \times \frac{\text{Conversion}}{\text{price index}}$$

Fourth, study the text of the problem preparing intermediary solutions as you proceed.

a. Go through the problem using a felt tip pen to make marginal notes setting out key information (e.g., base-year prices) and underlining key points (e.g., dates). Use your felt tip pen to relate data presented within the text of the problem (e.g., amounts to compute conversion indexes).

b. The conversion price indexes required for 1981 and 1982 are computed by dividing ending inventory dollar amounts at year-end prices by ending inventory dollar amounts at base-year prices.

c. Ending inventory dollar amounts at year-end prices are given as $847,000 and $840,000 at December 31, 1981 and 1982, respectively.

d. Ending inventory dollar amounts at base-year prices are computed by multiplying the given quantities by the base-year prices of $30 for product A and $25 for product B, respectively.

	12/31/81	12/31/82
Product A:	17,000 x $30 = $510,000	13,000 x $30 = $390,000
Product B:	9,000 x $25 = 225,000	10,000 x $25 = 250,000
	$735,000	$640,000

e. The conversion price indexes are computed as:

$$\underset{1981}{\frac{\$847,000}{\$735,000} = 1.15} \qquad\qquad \underset{1982}{\frac{\$840,000}{\$640,000} = 1.31}$$

f. To satisfy requirement two, the inventory amounts at 12/31/81 and 12/31/82 must be computed using the dollar-value LIFO method.

g. At 12/31/81, the ending inventory in base-year prices (computed earlier) is $735,000. Since the beginning inventory (FIFO inventory on date of adoption of the dollar-value LIFO method) was $560,000, the ending inventory consists of a base layer of $560,000 and an incremental layer of $175,000 ($735,000 - 560,000). The incremental layer, added during 1981, is priced at the 1981 index by multiplying $175,000 by 1.15 (computed earlier).

	Inventory at base cost		Index	Inventory at LIFO cost
Base inventory	$560,000	x	1.00 =	$560,000
1981 layer	175,000	x	1.15 =	201,250
Total	$735,000			$761,250

h. At 12/31/82, the ending inventory in base-year prices (computed earlier) is $640,000. This is a decrease of $95,000 from 12/31/81, when inventory at base-year prices was $735,000. Therefore, some of the 1981 incremental layer of $175,000 has been depleted, and there is no incremental layer added in 1982. The 1982 ending inventory consists of the base layer of $560,000 and the remaining 1981 layer of $80,000 ($175,000 - $95,000). This $80,000 layer must again be priced at the 1981 index by multiplying $80,000 by 1.15.

	Inventory at base cost		Index	Inventory at LIFO cost
Base inventory	$560,000	x	1.00 =	$560,000
1981 layer (remaining)	80,000	x	1.15 =	92,000
Total	$640,000			$652,000

Fifth, prepare the solution (see following pages).

Sixth, proofread and edit.

Seventh, review later, time permitting.

UNOFFICIAL ANSWER
Number 4

Part a.

1.   Harris Corporation
              Analysis of Changes in the
            Allowance for Doubtful Accounts
          For the Year Ended December 31, 1982

Balance at January 1, 1982	$130,000
Provision for doubtful accounts ($9,000,000 x 2%)	180,000
Recovery in 1982 of bad debts written off previously	15,000
	325,000
Deduct write-offs for 1982 ($90,000 + $60,000)	150,000
Balance at December 31, 1982, before change in accounting estimate	175,000
Increase due to change in accounting estimate during 1982 ($235,300 − $175,000)	60,300
Balance at December 31, 1982, adjusted (Schedule 1)	$235,300

Schedule 1

Computation of Allowance for Doubtful Accounts
at December 31, 1982

Aging category	Balance	%	Doubtful accounts
Nov–Dec 1982	$1,140,000	2	$ 22,800
Jul–Oct	600,000	10	60,000
Jan–Jun	400,000	25	100,000
Prior to 1/1/82	70,000 [a]	75	52,500
			$235,300

[a] $130,000 − $60,000

2.   Harris Corporation
                      Journal Entry
                   December 31, 1982

Account	Dr.	Cr.
Provision for doubtful accounts	$60,300	
Allowance for doubtful accounts		$60,300

To increase the allowance for doubtful accounts at December 31, 1982, resulting from a change in accounting estimate.

Part b.

1.

Lucas Distributors, Inc.
Computation of Internal Conversion Price Index
for Inventory Pool No. 1
Double Extension Method

	December 31, 1981	*December 31, 1982*
Current inventory at current year cost		
Product A	17,000 × $35 = $595,000	13,000 × $40 = $520,000
Product B	9,000 × $28 = 252,000	10,000 × $32 = 320,000
	$847,000	$840,000
Current inventory at base cost		
Product A	17,000 × $30 = $510,000	13,000 × $30 = $390,000
Product B	9,000 × $25 = 225,000	10,000 × $25 = 250,000
	$735,000	$640,000
Conversion price index	$847,000 ÷ $735,000 = 1.15	$840,000 ÷ $640,000 = 1.31

2.

Lucas Distributors, Inc.
Computation of Inventory Amounts
under Dollar Value LIFO Method
for Inventory Pool No. 1
at December 31, 1981 and 1982

	Current inventory at base cost	*Conversion price index*	*Inventory at LIFO cost*
December 31, 1981			
Base inventory	$560,000	1.00	$560,000
1981 layer ($735,000 − $560,000)	175,000	1.15 (a)	201,250
Total	$735,000 (a)		$761,250
December 31, 1982			
Base inventory	$560,000	1.00	$560,000
1981 layer (remaining)	80,000 (b)	1.15 (a)	92,000
1982 layer	0	1.31 (a)	0
Total	$640,000 (a)		$652,000

[a] Per schedule for Required No. 1.
[b] After liquidation of $95,000 at base cost:

Product A (4,000 × $30)	$120,000
Product B (1,000 × $25)	(25,000)
Net	$95,000

The hypothetical grading guide below is a schedule of key solution figures showing the "raw" grading points assigned to these key figures.

MAY 1983 PRACTICE I, NUMBER 4
HYPOTHETICAL GRADING GUIDE*

Part a.

			Grading points
1.	Balance, 1/1/82	$130,000	1
	Provision for 1982	180,000	1
	Recoveries for 1982	15,000	1
	Deduct write-offs for 1982	90,000	1
		60,000	1
	Change in estimate	60,300	1
	Schedule 1		
	Multiply by correct percentages		1
	Balance, 12/31/82		1
2.	Debit to provision for and credit to allowance for doubtful accounts	60,300	1
	Explanation of entry		1

Part b.

1.	Conversion price index		
	12/31/81		
	Current inventory @ current cost	847,000	1
	Current inventory @ base cost	735,000	1
	12/31/82		
	Current inventory @ current cost	840,000	1
	Current inventory @ base cost	640,000	1
2.	12/31/81		
	Base inventory	560,000	1
	1981 layer current inventory @ base cost	175,000	1
	Inventory @ LIFO cost	201,250	1
	12/31/82		
	1981 layer (remaining) LIFO cost	92,000	1
	1982 layer	0	1
	Liquidation [Note (b)]	95,000	1
	Grading points possible		20

*The AICPA Board of Examiners does not release the grading guides used for scoring essay questions and practice problems. The grading guide below was prepared by the authors to illustrate to candidates the manner in which points are allocated to grading concepts.

The conversion scale below converts the "raw" grading points shown on the previous page to the grade earned on the problem.

Conversion Scale

Grading Points Earned	20-17	16	15	14	13	12	11	10	9	8	7	6	5	4	3	2	1	0
Grade	10	9.5	9	8.5	8	7.5	7	6.5	6	5.5	5	4.5	4	3.5	3	2.5	2	0

TOTAL GRADE: NUMBER 4

Grade from Conversion Scale _____

Demerit for form, etc. _____

_____

Note: To obtain a passing grade (7.5 points) on this problem, a candidate would need to earn 12 of the possible 20 points (60%).

Essay Question Solutions Approach Algorithm

The major difference between the solutions approach for problems and the one for essay questions is the use of a keyword outline. The keyword outline in the essay solutions approach takes the place of the intermediary solution in the problem solutions approach. Substitute the following two steps for step 4a, "Prepare intermediary solutions as you study the problem," from the practice problem "solutions approach."

4a. Write down keywords (concepts). Jot down a list of keywords (grading concepts) in the margin of the examination. The proximity of the keywords to the text of the question will be more efficient than making notes on a separate sheet of paper which may be misplaced.

4b. Organize the keywords into a solution outline. After you have noted all of the grading concepts that bear on the requirements, reorganize the outline for the entire answer. Make sure that you respond to each requirement and do not preempt answers to other requirements.

Essay Question Solutions Approach Example

To illustrate the use of the solutions approach in answering essay questions, we have included Question 3 from the November 1981 Examination in Auditing (same question that was used to illustrate grading in Chapter 2). The illustration appears on the next two pages.

Highlights of the Solutions Approach to Essay Questions

The outline should be made up of the keywords of all the grading concepts you can bring to bear on each of the requirements. The keywords should be listed in the margin of the examination.

After completion of the keyword outline, reorganize it for the entire answer. Make sure that you answer each requirement (and only that requirement) completely. Be careful not to preempt an answer to another requirement. The keyword outline for the example question should be similar to the grading guide in Chapter 2. Next, write up your solution and edit as needed. If you have time later, review your solution again.

Revisions may be made in the margin of your answer sheet. Alternatively, you might use only 3/4 of every page to write up your solution. The remaining 1/4 can then be used to add material and to make revisions which can be keyed to the text with asterisks. Alternatively, write on every other line. The solution will thus

Number 3

Dunbar Camera Manufacturing, Inc., is a manu-facturer of <u>high-priced</u> precision motion picture cam-eras in which the specifications of component parts are vital to the manufacturing process. Dunbar buys <u>valu-able</u> camera lenses and large quantities of sheetmetal and screws. Screws and lenses are ordered by Dunbar and are billed by the vendors on a unit basis. Sheet-metal is ordered by Dunbar and is billed by the vendors on the basis of weight. The <u>receiving clerk</u> is <u>responsible for documenting</u> the <u>quality and quantity</u> of merchandise received.

A <u>preliminary review</u> of the system of internal control indicates that the following procedures are being followed:

Receiving Report

1. Properly approved purchase orders, which are <u>prenumbered,</u> are filed numerically. The copy sent to the receiving clerk is an <u>exact duplicate</u> of the copy sent to the vendor. Receipts of merchandise are record-ed on the duplicate copy by the receiving clerk.

Sheetmetal

2. The company receives sheetmetal by rail-road. The railroad <u>independently weighs</u> the sheet-metal and reports the weight and date of receipt on a bill of lading (waybill), which accompanies all deliver-ies. The receiving clerk <u>only checks the weight</u> on the waybill to the purchase order.

Screws

3. The receiving clerk opens cartons contain-ing screws, then <u>inspects and weighs</u> the contents. The weight is converted to number of units by means of <u>conversion charts</u>. The receiving clerk then <u>checks the computed quantity</u> to the purchase order.

Camera lenses

4. Each camera lens is delivered in a separate corrugated carton. <u>Cartons are counted</u> as they are re-ceived by the receiving clerk and the <u>number of cartons is checked to purchase orders.</u>

Required:

a. Explain <u>why</u> the <u>internal control proce-dures</u> as they apply individually to receiving reports(1) and the receipt of sheetmetal(2), screws(3), and camera(4) lenses are adequate or inadequate. <u>Do not discuss recommendations for improvements.</u>

b. (1)What <u>financial statement distortions</u> may arise because of the inadequacies in Dunbar's system of internal control and how(2) may they occur?

<u>KEYWORD OUTLINE</u>

CONTROLS FOR QUANTITY AND QUALITY IMPORTANT FOR EXPENSIVE INVENTORY ITEMS

EXISTENCE OF RECEIVING CLERK IS GOOD

RECEIVING CLERK SHOULD NOT HAVE QUANTITIES ON PURCHASE ORDERS

INDEPENDENT WEIGHING IS A GOOD COMPENSATING CONTROL

NO QUALITY CHECK

GOOD CONTROL ON QUANTITY AND QUALITY

NO QUANTITY CHECK
NO QUALITY CHECK

#s REFER TO INDIVIDUAL PARTS OF THE REQUIREMENTS. THE SAME NUMBERING SCHEME IS USED IN THE KEYWORD OUTLINE (STEP 4A) AND SOLUTIONS OUTLINE (STEP 4B)

STEP 1:
Glance over quickly

STEP 2:
Study requirements

STEP 2A:
Visualize solution format
1. The solution will be in paragraph form
2. For Part a. one may expect the problem to have various weaknesses as well as strengths. The solution will have to discuss these strengths and weaknesses and how they relate to one another
3. For Part b. consider effects of weaknesses on inventory and cost of goods sold

STEP 3:
Outline required procedures mentally
1. Approach for Part a. will be to read the problem very carefully to first obtain an understanding of how the system works and then to evaluate its strengths and weaknesses
2. Approach for Part b. will be to consider whether misstatements of inventory item quantities and qualities may occur

STEP 3A:
Review applicable principles, knowledge
1. Recall AICPA's essential characteristics of internal accounting control (AU 320 30–48)
    a. Personnel (reliable, etc.)
    b. Segregation of functions (separate custody, record keeping, authorization)
    c. Execution of transactions
    d. Recording of transactions
    e. Access to assets (physically controlled)
    f. Comparison of accountability with assets

    Or, you may be familiar with other lists from other texts
2. Recall that when goods are received a firm needs to determine that
    a. Proper items received
    b. Proper quantity received
    c. Items in proper condition

STEP 4:
Study the text

STEP 4A:
Keyword outline

STEP 4B:
Organize key words into solutions outline
Part a.
Because this problem has introductory material followed by 4 distinct sections (receiving report, sheetmetal, screws, camera lenses) a possible approach is to consider strengths and weaknesses by such sections
1. Receiving report
    a. Quantity on copy of purchase order sent to receiving
    b. Limited tests of quality of materials when received
2. Sheetmetal
    a. Compensating—railroad weighs
    b. Receiving does not weigh
    c. Quality not tested
3. Screws
    a. Receiving clerk weighs— good control
    b. Weighing **may** serve as quality check
4. Camera lenses
    a. Is count actually made?
    b. No quality control check— lenses in cartons

Part b.
1. Potential F/S distortions:
    a. Overstate inventory
    b. Misstate cost of sales
    c. Overstate A/P
2. Using supplier's invoice as basis for additions could cause inventory to include
    a. Nonusable items
    b. Items not received

*STEP 5:
Prepare solution

*STEP 6:
Proofread and edit

*STEP 7:
Review

*See Unofficial Answers in Chapter 2

be easier for the grader to read. It will also be easier for you to proofread and edit. Remember, there is no limit on the number of answer sheets you may use.

NOTE: You <u>must write out</u> the answers to essay questions. <u>Keyword</u> outlines are not sufficient. The AICPA requires you to show an understanding of the grading concepts, not merely a listing of grading concepts.

Prepare brief paragraphs consisting of several concise sentences about each grading concept. The paragraphs may be numbered in an outline format similar to that of the unofficial answers.

<u>Multiple Choice Question Solutions Approach Algorithm</u>

1. Work individual questions in order

    a. If a question appears lengthy or difficult, skip it until you can determine that extra time is available. Put a big question mark in the margin to remind you to return to questions you have skipped or need to review.

2. Cover the choices before reading each question

    a. The answers are frequently ambiguous and may cause you to misread or misinterpret the question

3. Read each question carefully to determine the topical area

    a. Study the requirements first so you know which data are important
    b. Underline keywords and important data
    c. Identify pertinent information with notations in the margin of the exam
    d. Be especially careful to note when the requirement is an <u>exception,</u> e.g., "Which of the following is <u>not</u> an accounting change <u>handled</u> by the cumulative effect method?"
    e. If a set of data is the basis for two or more questions, read the requirements of each of the questions before beginning to work the first question (sometimes it is more efficient to work the questions out of order or simultaneously)

4. Anticipate the answer before looking at the alternative answers

    a. Recall the applicable principle (e.g., change in estimate); the applicable model (e.g., net present value); or the applicable code section (e.g., 1245)
    b. If accounting practice questions deal with a complex area like earnings per share, set them up like full-blown problems on scratch paper, if necessary, using abbreviations that enable you to follow your work (remember that these questions are machine-graded)

5. Read the answers and select the <u>best</u> alternative

    a. For accounting practice questions, if the answer you have computed is not among the choices, quickly check your math and the logic of your solution. If you don't arrive at one of the given answers in the allotted time, make an educated guess.

6. Mark the correct (or best guess) answer on the examination booklet itself

7. After completing all of the individual questions in an overall question, transfer the answers to the machine gradable answer sheet with extreme care

    a. Be very careful not to fall out of sequence with the answer sheet. A mistake would cause most of your answers to be wrong. SINCE THE AICPA USES ANSWER SHEETS WITH VARYING FORMATS, IT WOULD BE VERY EASY TO GO ACROSS THE SHEET INSTEAD OF DOWN OR VICE VERSA. Read the instructions carefully!
    b. Review to check that you have transferred the answers correctly
    c. Do not leave this step until the end of the exam as you may find yourself with too little time to transfer your answers to the answer sheet. The exam proctors are not permitted to give you extra time to transfer your answers.

Multiple Choice Question Solutions Approach Example

A good example of the multiple choice solutions approach is provided, using multiple choice question number 5 from the May 1983 Examination in Accounting Practice, Part I.

Step 3:

Topical area? Leases/Amortization of leasehold improvements

Step 4:

Principle? Leasehold improvements amortized over the __shorter__ of remaining life of lease or useful life of improvements

Step 4b:

Set up

$$\frac{\$64,000 \text{ of lease-}}{\text{hold improvements}}\Big/ 8 \text{ yrs.} = (\$8,000)$$

5. On __January 4, 1982__, Hadley Company signed a __10-year__ __nonrenewable lease__ for a building to be used in its manufacturing operations. __During January 1982__ Hadley __incurred the following costs:__

    8 yrs. < 10 yrs. ∴ use 8 yrs.

    • __$64,000 for general improvements to the__ leased premises with an estimated __useful life of (eight)__ years.

    • __$32,000__ for a (movable) assembly line equipment installation with an estimated __useful life of eight years.__ ∴ *Record as equipment.*

    __A full year's amortization__ is taken for the calendar year 1982. What amount should Hadley record as __amortization of leasehold improvements__ for 1982?

a.	$ 6,400	c.	$ 9,600
b.	$ 8,000	d.	$12,000

Currently, all multiple choice questions are scored based on the number correct; i.e., there is no penalty for guessing. The rationale is that a "good guess" indicates knowledge. Thus, you should answer all multiple choice questions.

Antithesis of a Solutions Approach

The mark of an inefficient solution is one wherein the candidate immediately begins to write an essay/problem solution. Remember, the final solution is one of the last steps in the solutions approach. You should have the solution under complete control (with the __keyword__ outline or intermediary solutions) before you begin your final solution.

Efficiency of the Solutions Approach

While the large amount of intermediary work in the solutions approach may appear burdensome and time-consuming, the technique results in more complete solutions in less time than with haphazard approaches. Moreover, the solutions approach really allows you to work out problems that you feel unfamiliar with at first reading. The solutions approach, however, must be mastered prior to sitting for the CPA examination. In other words, the candidate must be willing to invest a reasonable amount of time toward perfecting his/her own solutions approach.

In summary, the solutions approach may appear foreign and somewhat cumbersome. At the same time, if you have worked through the material in this chapter, you should have some appreciation for it. Develop the solutions approach by writing down the seven steps in the solutions approach algorithm at the beginning of this chapter, and keep them before you as you work recent CPA exam problems. Remember that even though the suggested procedures appear <u>very structured</u> and <u>time-consuming</u>, integration of these procedures into your own style of problem solving will help improve <u>your</u> solutions approach. The next chapter discusses strategies for the overall examination.

**NOW IS THE TIME
TO MAKE A COMMITMENT**

CHAPTER FOUR

TAKING THE EXAMINATION

This chapter is concerned with developing an examination strategy, e.g., how to cope with the environment at the examination site, what order to work problems, etc.

EXAMINATION STRATEGIES

Your performance during the 2 1/2 day examination is final and not subject to revision. While you may sit for the examination again if you are unsuccessful, the majority of your preparation will have to be repeated, requiring substantial additional amounts of time. Thus, examination strategies (discussed in this chapter) which maximize your exam-taking efficiency are very important.

Getting "Psyched Up"

The CPA exam is quite challenging and worthy of your best effort. Explicitly develop your own psychological strategy to get yourself "up" for the exam. Pace your study program such that you will be able to operate at peak performance when you are actually taking the exam. Many candidates "give up" because they have a bad day or encounter a rough problem. Do the best you can; the other candidates are probably no better prepared than you.

Examination Supplies

The AICPA recommends that candidates prepare their solutions in pencil. As you practice your solutions approach, experiment with pencils, lead types, erasers, etc., that are comfortable to use and also result in good copy for the grader. A hard lead pencil is recommended for better erasability and neatness.

In addition to an adequate supply of pencils and erasers, it is very important to take a watch to the examination. Also, take refreshments (as permitted), which are conducive to your exam efficiency. Finally, dress to assure your comfort during the exam. Layered clothing is recommended for possible variations in temperature at the examination site.

Do not take study materials into the examination room. You will not be able to use them. They will only muddle your mind and get you "up tight." Finally, DO NOT carry notes or crib sheets upon your person: This can only result in the gravest of problems.

Lodging, Meals, Exercise

Make advance reservations for comfortable lodging convenient to the examination facilities. Do not stay with friends, relatives, etc. Both uninterrupted sleep and total concentration on the exam are a must. Consider the following in making your lodging plans:

1. Proximity to exam facilities
2. Lodging and exam parking facilities
3. Availability of meals and snacks
4. Recreational facilities

Plan your meal schedule prior to and during the exam to provide maximum energy and alertness during the day and maximum rest at night.

Do not experiment with new foods, drinks, etc., during the examination time period. Within reasonable limits, observe your normal eating and drinking habits. Recognize that overconsumption of coffee during the exam could lead to a hyperactive state and disaster. Likewise, overindulgence in alcohol to overcome nervousness and to induce sleep the night before might contribute to other difficulties the following morning.

Tenseness should be expected before and during the examination. Rely on a regular exercise program to unwind yourself at the end of the day. As you select your lodging for the examination, try to accommodate your exercise pleasure, e.g., running, swimming, etc. Continue to indulge in your exercise program on the days of the examination.

To relieve tension or stress while studying, try breathing or stretching exercises. Use these exercises before and during the examination to start and to keep your adrenaline flowing. Do not hesitate to attract attention by doing pushups, jumping jacks, etc., in a lobby outside of the examination room if it will improve your exam efficiency. Remain determined not to go through another examination to obtain your certificate.

A problem you will probably experience during the exam related to general fatigue and tenseness is writer's cramp. Experiment with alternate methods of holding your pencil, rubbing your hand, etc., during your preparation program.

In summary, the examination is likely to be both rigorous and fatiguing. Expect it and prepare for it by getting in shape, planning methods of relaxation during the exam and exam evenings, and finally building the courage and competence to complete the exam (successfully).

Examination Facilities and Procedures

Visit the examination facilities at least the evening before the examination to assure knowledge of the location. Remember: no surprises. Having a general familiarity with the facilities will lessen anxiety prior to the examination.

Talking to a recent veteran of the examination will give you background for the general examination procedures, such as:

1. Procedure for distributing exam booklets, papers, etc.
2. Accessibility of restrooms
3. Availability of coffee and snacks at exam location
4. Admissibility of coffee and snacks in the exam room
5. Peculiar problems of exam facilities, e.g., noise, lighting, temperature, etc.
6. Permissibility of early departure from exam
7. A copy of his/her exam booklet
8. His/her experience in taking the exam
9. Any other suggestions s/he might make

As you can see, it is important to talk with someone who recently sat for the examination at the same location where you intend to sit. The objective is to reduce your anxiety just prior to the examination and to minimize any possible distractions. Finally, if you have any remaining questions regarding examination procedure, call or write your state board.

On a related point, do not be distracted by other candidates who show up at the examination completely relaxed and greet others with confidence. These are most likely candidates who have been there before. Probably the only thing they are confident of is a few days' vacation from work. Also, do not become distracted when they leave early: some candidates may leave after signing in for that session.

Arrive at the Examination Early

On the day of the exam, be sure to get to the examination site at least 30 minutes early to reduce tension and to get yourself situated. It is probably wise to sit away from the door and the administration table to avoid being distracted by candidates who arrive late, leave early, ask questions, etc., and proctors who occasionally converse. AVOID ALL POSSIBLE DISTRACTIONS. Stay away from friends. Find a seat that will be comfortable: consider sunlight, interior lighting, heating/air conditioning, pedestrian traffic, etc. Most states have assigned seating. If this is the case, you will be seated by your candidate ID number.

Usually the proctors open the sealed boxes of exams and distribute the booklets to candidates 10 minutes before the scheduled beginning of the examination. You are not permitted to open the booklet, but you should study the instructions printed on the front cover. The instructions generally explain:

1.   How to turn in examination papers
2.   Handling of:

   a. Multiple choice answer sheets
   b. Scratch sheets
   c. Columnar work sheets

3.   Examiners' consideration of the candidate's ability to express him/herself in acceptable written language

You will be given a supply of answer paper as you enter the exam room or as the test booklets are passed out. You will not be permitted to write anything except the headings on an adequate supply of columnar and lined answer paper. The heading is:

Candidate's No. _____

Date _____

State _____

Subject _____

Problem _____ Page _____

Do not use your name; write only your candidate number, which will be assigned to you at the beginning of the exam. If a problem requires a name signature, e.g., on an audit report, do not use your own name or initials.

You probably will not work the examination problems in order. There is a possibility of confusion since you cannot number your answer sheets consecutively until the end of the exam. To alleviate this problem, take 10 or 15 paper clips to the exam room to keep the answer sheets of each question separate and in order, while you answer other questions. At the end of the exam, put the packets of answer sheets in proper order and number them consecutively.

Inventory of the Examination Content

When you receive your examination booklet, carefully read the instructions. The objective is to review the standard instructions and to note any new or special instructions. After reviewing the instructions on the front of your examination booklet, make note of the number of questions/problems and the time allocated to each. Immediately after receiving permission to open the examination booklet, glance over each of the questions sufficiently and jot down the topics on the time schedule on the front of the exam booklet. This will give you an overview of the ensuing 3 1/2 or 4 1/2 hours of work.

Allocation of Time

Budget your time. Time should be carefully allocated in your attempt to maximize your points. Remember the maximum points available on each question are proportional to the suggested time allotments on the front of each exam booklet. Theoretically, time should be allocated so that you maximize points per minute.

While you have to develop your own strategy with respect to time allocation, some suggestions may be useful. First, consider the three sections that have essay questions (Auditing, Law, Theory) and are 210 minutes long. Allocate 5 minutes to read the instructions and to take an inventory, jotting the topics tested by question on the front cover. Write the topic next to the time allotment. Assuming 60 individual multiple choice and 4 essay questions, you should spend about 10 minutes keyword outlining each of the 4 essay questions. Then, plan on spending about 1 1/2 minutes working each of the individual multiple choice questions. (You will probably be adding grading concepts to your keyword outlines as you read the multiple choice questions.)

After completing these tasks, you now have spent 2 1/4 hours and have substantially completed both the multiple choice questions and essay questions. Revise the keyword outline and prepare the final solutions of the essay questions one at a time. Allocate about 15 minutes to each solution. Recognize that you can write all the grader will care to read in 15 minutes from a well-developed outline.

Finally, you have 10 minutes to proofread and edit. Remember that this is a hypothetical time allocation for illustrative purposes only.

Hypothetical Time Budget
210-Minute Essay Exam
(60 individual multiple choice, 4 essay questions)

	Minutes
Inventory of exam	5
<u>Keyword</u> outline of 4 essay questions	40
<u>Answer</u> 60 multiple choice questions	90
Completion of multiple choice question answer sheet	5
Final solution of 4 essay questions	60
Extra time	10
Total	210

Now consider the time allocation in the two practice parts which are 4 1/2 hours (270 minutes) in length. For a 4 1/2 hour practice section, consisting of three sets of multiple choice questions (each set containing 20 items), and 2 problems (that require schedules, entries, etc.), you should allocate 2 1/2 hours to the 60 multiple choice questions (2 1/2 minutes each) and about 1 1/2 hours (45 minutes each) to the 2 problems - which leaves about 1/2 hour of "extra time." The nature of practice problems does not lend itself to as precise a time allocation as the essay questions. It is important to keep track of the time spent on each problem during the examination. Write the time you start each problem near the top of the question to preclude your spending more than the suggested time on any one problem.

Order of Working Questions/Problems

Select the question/problem that you are going to work first from the notes you made on the front of your examination. Some candidates will select the question/ problem that appears easiest to get started and build confidence. Others will begin with the question/problem they feel is most difficult to get it out of the way. Multiple choice questions generally should not be worked first on the auditing, business law, and theory exams, since each question may contain 4 or 5 grading concepts (for possible inclusion in your essay solutions) as alternate answers. You should, therefore, work through the multiple choice questions only after you have keyword outlined all of the essay questions (but before you write up your final solutions).

Once you select a question/problem, you should apply the solutions approach. Practice problems should be worked through to the final stage, and all calculations and schedules should be labeled before leaving the problem. If you start another practice problem before completing one, you will have to rework (or at a minimum, waste time becoming familiar again with) the unfinished problem.

You should, however, leave a problem if you get stuck, rather than just sitting there "spinning your wheels." Later, when you come back and retool for the problem, you may be able to think of a new approach to "unlock" the solution. Likewise, proofreading and editing should be undertaken after working on one or more other problems, so you have a fresh perspective as you evaluate your own solution.

On the other hand, essay questions should be worked only through the keyword outline prior to moving on to the next question. Recall that essay questions are generally graded with an open-ended grading guide. Thus, you want to include as many grading concepts as possible in your solution. Waiting to write your essay solution until after all other questions have been dealt with will force you to take a fresh look at the question. As a result, additional grading concepts are often found. As you recognize grading concepts applicable to other questions, turn to the respective question and jot down the keywords (remember that the keyword outlines should be prepared in the margin of your exam booklet).

Note that the AICPA grading curves generally reflect decreasing returns to scale. That is to say, candidates get more credit for the first correct answer than for the last correct answer. This comes about through the use of base points; i.e., a relatively large amount of credit is given to the initial stages of the solution.

The existence of decreasing returns to scale in the AICPA grading curves implies that candidates should allocate more time to the questions/problems which are troublesome. The natural tendency is to write on and on for questions/problems with which you are conversant. Remember to do the opposite: spend more time where more points are available; i.e., you may already have earned the maximum allowable on the question/problem familiar to you.

Never, but never, leave a question blank, as this almost certainly precludes a passing grade on that section. Some candidates talk about "giving certain types of questions to the AICPA," i.e., no answer. The only thing being given to the AICPA is grading time since the grader will not have to read a solution. Expect a couple of "far out" or seemingly "insurmountable" questions/problems. Apply the solutions approach - imagine yourself having to make a similar decision, computation, explanation, etc., in an actual situation and come up with as much as possible.

Page Numbering

Carefully follow the instructions on the front of each exam booklet with regard to turning in papers. Remember that a lost answer is a zero. The typical instructions include:

1. Arrange your answers in numerical order and number them consecutively, e.g., if you have 15 sheets answering Practice I, number them 1 through 15
2. For practice problems, include scratch sheets (label all computations) as part of the answer
3. Write "continued" on the bottom of sheets when another answer sheet for the same problem follows
4. Printed answer sheets for multiple choice questions should be the first answers turned in, i.e., on top, and numbered 1

Postmortem of Your Performance

DON'T DO IT and especially don't do it until Friday evening. Do not speak to other candidates about the exam after completing sections on Wednesday evening, Thursday noon, Thursday evening, and Friday noon. Exam postmortem will only upset, confuse, and frustrate you. Besides, the other candidates probably will not be as well prepared as you, and they certainly cannot influence your grade. Often, those candidates who seem very confident have overlooked an important requirement(s) or fact(s). As you leave the exam room after each session, think only ahead to achieve the best possible performance on each of the remaining sections.

AICPA GENERAL RULES GOVERNING EXAMINATION

1. Read carefully the identification card assigned to you; sign it; make a note of your number for future reference; when it is requested, return the card to the examiner. Only the examination number on your card shall be used on your papers for the purpose of identification. The importance of remembering this number and recording it on your examination papers correctly cannot be overemphasized. If a question calls for an answer involving a signature, do not sign your own name or initials.

2. Seating during the exam is assigned according to your ID number in most states.

3. The only aids candidates are permitted to have in the examination room are pens, pencils, and erasers. Calculators, rulers, and slide rules are not permitted. Handbags and purses must be placed on the floor at candidates' locations during the entire time they are taking the exam. Briefcases, files, books, and other material brought to the examination site by candidates must be placed in a designated area before the start of the examination.

4. The fixed time for each session must be observed by all candidates. Each period will start and end promptly. It is the candidate's responsibility to be present and ready at the start of the period and to stop writing when told to do so.

5. Only two time warnings are given: (1) thirty minutes prior to the end of the session and (2) at the end of the session. (Additional warnings are not considered necessary.)

6. Candidates arriving late should not be permitted any extension of time, but may be allowed to take the examination with proctor approval.

7. Answers should be written in pencil and preferably using #2 lead. Use only one side of the paper. Use the plain sheets for calculations, working notes, etc. <u>Neatness and orderly presentation of work are important.</u> Credit cannot be given for answers that are illegible.

8. Use a soft pencil, preferably #2 lead, to blacken the spaces on the separate answer sheet for the multiple choice questions.

9. Heading up answer papers is allowed approximately ten minutes prior to the examination starting signal. Extra time is not allowed for this at the end of each session. Looking at questions before the starting signal is not allowed.

10. Answers must be submitted on paper furnished by the Board and must be completed in the total time allotted for each subject as stated on the printed examinations. Identify your answers by using the proper question number. Begin your answer to each question on a separate page and number pages <u>in accordance with the instructions on the printed examination booklets.</u> Arrange your answers in the order of the questions.

11. Attach all computations relating to the practice problems to the papers containing your answers. Identify them as to the problem to which they relate. The rough calculations and notes may assist the examiners in understanding your solution.

12. Stationery and supplies furnished by the Board shall remain its property and must be returned whether used or not. You may retain the printed examination booklets provided you do not leave the examination room before one-half hour prior to completion time. Leaving the examination room earlier than one hour after the examination begins is not permitted.

13. Any reference during the examination to books or other matters or the exchange of information with other persons shall be considered misconduct sufficient to bar you from further participation in the examination.

14. Smoking is allowed only in designated areas away from the general examination area.

15. No telephone calls are permitted during the examination session.

In addition to the above general rules, oral instructions will be given by the examination supervisor shortly before the start of each session. They should include the location and/or rules concerning

    a. Storage of briefcases, handbags, books, personal belongings, etc.
    b. Food and beverages
    c. Smoking
    d. Rest rooms
    e. Telephone calls and messages
    f. Requirements (if any) that candidates must take all parts not previously passed each time they sit for the examination. Minimum grades (if any) needed on parts failed to get credit on parts passed.
    g. Cheating
    h. Official clock, if any
    i. Additional supplies
    j. Assembly, turn-in, inspection, and stapling of solutions

The next section is a detailed listing (mind jogger) of things to do for your last-minute preparation. It also contains a list of strategies for the exam.

CPA EXAM CHECKLIST

One week before exam

1. Look over major topical areas, concentrating on schedule formats and the information flow of the formats.

   E.g.:

   FIFO or Wtd. Avg. Process Costing Flow
   Capital Budgeting Models
   Cost of Goods Manufactured Schedule
   Statement of Changes Format
   Long-Term Construction Accounting
   Inventory Methods
   Cost vs. Equity Method Investments
   Lessee-Lessor Accounting
   Minimum/Maximum Pension Limits
   EPS Calculations
   Governmental Fund Accounting
   Purchase, Pooling, Consolidation Methods
   Individual and Corporate Tax Formats
   Accounting Changes and Error Correction

2. Reread outlines (your own or those in *CPA Examination Review)* of most important SASs, underlining buzz words.

3. Review law notes, committing important terms and lists to notecards or abbreviated outlines.

4. If time permits, work through a few questions in your weakest areas so that techniques/concepts are fresh in your mind.

5. Assemble notecards and key outlines of major topical areas into a manageable "last review" notebook to be taken with you to exam.

What to bring

1. Registration material for the CPA exam.

2. Your hotel confirmation.

3. **Cash** — payment for anything by personal check is rarely accepted.

4. **Major credit card** — American Express, Master-Card, etc.

5. **Alarm clock** — this is too important an event to trust to a hotel wake-up call that might be overlooked.

6. **Food** — candidates may wish to pack a sack lunch for Thursday and Friday as time is often limited between the conclusion of the morning session and returning to the afternoon session in plenty of time to check in, since it is suggested that candidates arrive no later than 30 minutes prior to each session's starting time. Bring snack foods that will provide energy and sustenance, such as fruit and cheese.

7. **Clothing** that is comfortable and that can be layered to suit the temperature range over the three-day period and the examination room conditions.

8. **Watch** — it is imperative that you be aware of the time remaining for each session.

9. Your personal "last review" materials, pencils, erasers, leads, sharpeners, pens, etc.

While waiting for the exam to begin

1. Put ID card on table for ready reference to your number. Fill out attendance form that proctor will pick up prior to distributing exam booklet.

2. Fill out all page headings (except for question and page number) and divide papers on table into computational forms, essay sheets (use every other line when using this form), and columnar workpaper. Make sure your ID number is CORRECT on each answer sheet. Fill in ID number on M/C answer form, filling in circles that correspond to your ID number.

3. Realize that proctors will be constantly circulating throughout each exam session. You need only raise your hand to receive more paper at any time or paper will be available at nearby tables.

4. Take a few deep breaths and compose yourself. Resolve to do your very best and to go after every point you can get!

Before leaving for exam each day

1. Put ID card in wallet, purse, or on person for entry to take the exam. This is your official entrance permit that allows you to participate in all sections of the exam.

2. Remember your hotel room key.

3. Pack snack items and lunch (optional).

4. Limit consumption of liquids.

5. Realize that on Friday **a.m.** you must check out and arrange for storage of your luggage (most hotels have such a service) PRIOR TO departing for the Law and Theory sections in order to prevent late charges on your hotel bill.

Evenings before exams

1. Reviewing the evenings before the exams could earn you the extra points needed to pass a section. Just keep this last-minute effort in perspective and do NOT panic yourself into staying up all night trying to cover every possible point.

This could lead to disaster by sapping your body of the endurance needed to attack questions creatively during the next 7-8 hour day.

2. Before practice session, scan the general schedule formats to imprint the **flow** of information on your mind (e.g.: Stmt. of Changes and EPS formats, partnership "safe payment" schedule, lease formats, min./max. pension schedules, indiv. and corp. tax formats, etc.).

3. Scan tax notes, imprinting required percentages used for figuring investment tax credit, tax credit for the elderly, etc., on your mind.

4. Read over KEY notecards or most important outlines on topics in which you feel deficient.

5. Go over mnemonics you have developed as study aids (i.e., TIP, PIE, GODC for the ten GAAS in auditing). Test yourself by writing out the letters on paper while verbally giving a brief explanation of what the letters stand for.

6. Reread key outlines of important SASs on Wednesday evening so that buzz words will be fresh in your mind on Thursday a.m.

7. Reread key outlines or notecards for law on Thursday evening, reviewing important terms, key phrases, and lists (i.e., essential elements for a contract, requirements for a holder in due course, etc.) so that they will be fresh in your mind Friday a.m.

8. Scan an outline of APB 4, SFACs 1-4, and any other notes pertinent to answering theory questions, in order to imprint keywords.

9. Avoid postmortems during the examination period. Nothing you can do will affect your grade on sections of the exam you have already completed. Concentrate only on the work ahead in remaining sections.

10. GET A GOOD NIGHT'S REST! Being well rested will permit you to meet each day's challenge with a fresh burst of creative energy.

Practice

1. Open the exam booklet, noting the number of M/C questions (60 per section have been asked on recent exams) and the areas they cover (various financial, individual tax, managerial, etc.).

2. Scan the "required" sections of all non-M/C problems to get a feel for the nature of the topics covered, making a mental note of the time allotted to each section (exam point allotments parallel time allocation). Remember to divide allotted time per question proportionately over ALL

parts to a question (parts are often unrelated, so don't forget that if 40-50 minutes are allowed for Problem 5, that much time must be divided among all parts required). Knowing the nature of these problems that you will tackle later allows your subconscious to sort out needed facts for solving them as you work the M/C.

3. Reconcile the problem numbers with the questions listed on the front of the exam booklet and check consecutive page numbers in your booklet to reassure yourself that your booklet is complete, that no pages are stuck together, etc.

4. Begin working the M/C questions, noting the time begun at the start of each set. Realize that you have approximately 1½ to 2½ minutes per question. Use computational sheets rather than the exam booklet itself for computations so that you have ample room to develop mini-schedules, time lines, etc. Do not waste time labeling computations, because the grader will not use M/C computation sheets. It is wise to number your computations for your own use if you come back to a question, however.

5. Read each question **carefully!** Dates are extremely important! (E.g., a long-term contract problem using the percentage-of-completion method may give information for a contract begun in 1982 but ask for income recognized for year ended Dec. 31, 1984.)

6. If you are struggling with problems beyond your time limit, divide M/C into 2 categories and use this strategy
   a. Questions for which you **know** you lack knowledge to answer: Drawing from any resources you have, narrow answers down to as few as possible; then make your BEST GUESS.
   b. Questions for which you feel you should be getting correct answer: Put "?" by M/C number on exam booklet and label computational sheet so you can return later. Your mental block may clear, or you may spot a simple math error that now can be corrected, thus giving you extra points.

7. Remember: NEVER change a first impulse M/C answer later unless you are **absolutely certain** you are right. It is a proven fact that your subconscious often guides you to the correct answer.

8. Go on to problems while you are "hot!" You can transfer M/C answers to the computer form later when you are tired.

9. Work problems that you consider easiest first, noting time begun and time allotted. Your goal is to pick up extra time to allocate to problems you are weaker on.

10. Read "required" section, underlining and noting EVERY requirement that you are asked for.

11. Read factual information, underlining key facts, circling percentages and interest rates that you plan to use, crossing out extraneous information, etc.

12. Draw time lines, visualize schedule headings, schedule formats, etc., that will help you respond to requirements. Do not forget to put a heading on each schedule or statement.

13. Computations should be made on computation sheets which WILL be used by the grader as an "audit trail" to support your work. Label and cross-reference to schedules and work sheets as necessary. (E.g., when asked to show comparative balance sheets for 1983 and 1984, with the correct valuation of Investment in Subsidiary, show supporting computations by stating "See Schedule A on page . . .".)

14. Write legibly; be neat and organized. Leave space on schedules, etc., to add information that you might think of later.

15. For practice problems, format, organization, technique, disclosure, etc. are of critical importance.

16. Constantly compare your progress with the time remaining. NEVER spend more than the maximum time on any problem until ALL problems are answered and time remains. Fight the urge to **complete** one problem at the expense of another problem. Remember that there are more gradable points in the **beginning** stages of problems than toward the end (the law of diminishing returns applies!). Ten points is the maximum you can earn, so once you feel you have answered sufficiently, **move on!**

17. As each problem is completed, quickly reread the "required" section again to make sure you have responded to each requirement. Check off each completed problem on the form provided; this should prevent you from inadvertently leaving a problem unanswered. Paper clip together the pages used to answer each individual related part of a question and set them aside for later assembly before handing in.

18. Each test will include a problem or question for which you may feel unprepared. Accept the challenge and go after the points! Draw from all your resources. Ask yourself how GAAP would be applied to similar situations, scan the M/C for clues, look for relationships in **all** the available information given in the problem, try "backing into" the problem from another angle, etc. Every problem (no matter how impossible it may look at first glance) contains some points that are yours for the taking. Make your best effort. You may be on the right track and not even know it!

19. The cardinal rule is NEVER, but NEVER leave an answer blank!

20. When you see alternate routes to take in problem solving, explain to the grader any assumptions you are making and why. Should you run out of time on a problem that you know how to complete, write a note to the grader briefly describing what you would have done had time permitted.

21. If time permits, go back to any M/C questions that you "guessed" on.

22. Double check to make certain you have answered ALL parts of EVERY problem to the best of your ability.

23. Transfer M/C answers to the form provided. Be especially careful to follow the numbers exactly, because number patterns differ on each answer form! Don't wait until too late to make this transfer.

24. Assemble paper-clipped answer sheets in the correct order. Count total number of pages, counting M/C answer form as page 1. Consecutively number pages (i.e., Page 3 of 20).

25. Take assembled answers with "Degree of Completion" form to front of exam room where a proctor will staple them together.

Auditing

1. Check exam booklet for completeness as you note number of M/C questions (you can expect 60), and read "required" sections of essay questions, noting the time allotted to each question.

2. Reconcile the problem numbers with the questions listed on the front of the exam booklet and check consecutive page numbers in your booklet.

3. Use the solutions approach to briefly outline key concepts or mnemonics that apply to each requirement. These are fresh in your mind now and can be supplemented later after answering M/C questions. Your subconscious will also be working on added ideas.

4. The crucial technique to use for auditing M/C is to read each question CAREFULLY, underlining keywords such as "most, least, primary, special report, interim report," etc. Then READ EVERY CHOICE before you start eliminating inappropriate answers. In auditing, often the 1st or 2nd answer may **sound** correct but a later answer may be MORE CORRECT! Be discriminating! NEVER choose answer (a) or (b) BEFORE reading (c) and (d).

5. Begin the essay questions, carefully monitoring your time. Read all parts (a, b, c, etc.) of "required" section and organize your answer around the key concepts, mnemonics, buzz words that are responsive to part a, b, c, etc.

6. The most important technique to use for ALL essay questions is to constantly remind yourself that the grader assumes you know nothing (s/he cannot read your mind) and you, as a candidate for a professional designation, must convince him/her of your knowledge of the subject matter under question. NEVER OMIT THE OBVIOUS! Explain each answer as if you were explaining the concept to a beginning business student.

7. Recognize that some questions ask for general, rather than specific, responses allowing you to bring out **many** relevant points.

8. Using the key "buzz word" outline, develop well-organized, complete sentences that are responsive to each part of the question. Always answer essay questions using every other line of answer paper.

9. Points are allocated to quantity as well as quality of related ideas presented in an answer, so state in brief form as many relevant ideas as you can possibly think of in the time allowed. BE CREATIVE!

10. Auditing answers are often "list" oriented, so do not fall into the trap of developing only 2 or 3 ideas at the expense of running out of time to present more gradable concepts.

11. When an auditing question calls for audit procedures or programs to use in a certain business setting (such as a university book store buy-back revolving cash fund), you must BE SPECIFIC and tailor your procedures to the factual situation described. For example, it is not enough to tell the grader that proper segregation of duties is required; you must specify that where Jones has custody of cash, Smith should have recording responsibilities, etc.

12. Constantly compare your progress with the time. NEVER spend more than the maximum time on any question until ALL questions are answered and time remains.

13. As each question is completed, quickly reread the "required" section to make sure you have responded to each requirement.

14. Double check to make certain you have answered ALL parts of EVERY question to the best of your ability.

15. Transfer M/C answers to the form provided. Be especially careful to follow the numbers exactly, because number patterns differ on each answer form! Don't wait until too late. The proctors are not authorized to give you extra time for this.

16. Remember: A legible, well-organized, grammatically correct answer — using as many buzz words as appropriate — gives a professional appearance.

Business Law

1. Check exam booklet for completeness as you note number of M/C questions (you can expect 60), and read "required" sections of essay questions, noting the time allotted to each question.

2. Reconcile the problem numbers with the questions listed on the front of the exam booklet and check consecutive page numbers in your booklet.

3. Use the solutions approach to briefly outline key concepts that apply to each requirement. These are fresh in your mind now and can be supplemented later after answering M/C questions. Your subconscious will also be working on added ideas.

4. You will need the maximum time available for the law essay questions because they usually consist of 8 unrelated yet involved fact situations that you **must** address. Thus, you must use the minimum time allotted in answering the law M/C.

5. The crucial technique to use for business law M/C is to read through each fact situation CAREFULLY, underlining keywords such as "oral, without disclosing, subject to mortgage," etc. Then read EVERY CHOICE carefully before you start eliminating inappropriate answers. In business law, often the 1st or 2nd answer may sound correct, but a later answer may be MORE CORRECT. Be discriminating! Reread the question and choose the right response.

6. Law essay fact situations are often lengthy and involved. Read carefully and decide which areas of law apply.

7. The most important technique to use for ALL essay questions is to constantly remind yourself that the grader assumes you know nothing (s/he cannot read your mind) and you, as a candidate for a professional designation, must convince him/her of your knowledge of the subject matter under question. NEVER OMIT THE OBVIOUS! Explain each answer as if you were explaining the concept to a beginning business student.

8. Tell the grader that you are applying the UCC or Common Law, or the Act of 1933 or 1934, etc.

9. State the issue involved or the requirements that you are testing for (i.e., all 6 elements of a contract are present).

10. State the rule of law that applies to the issue.

11. Tell the grader how this affects the parties involved.

12. Limit discussion to relevant issues. Too often, candidates spend more time than allotted on a question they are sure of, only to sacrifice points on another question where those extra minutes are crucial.

13. Remember that on the law section you have a maximum of about 10 minutes per fact situation.

14. If you draw a blank as to a conclusion, telling the grader all the points of law that you know about the fact situation may salvage the question.

15. As each question is completed, quickly reread the "required" section to make sure you have responded to each requirement.

16. Double check to make certain you have answered ALL parts of EVERY question to the best of your ability.

17. Transfer M/C answers to the form provided. Be especially careful to follow the numbers exactly, because number patterns differ on each answer form! Don't leave this until too late.

18. Remember: A legible, well-organized, grammatically correct answer gives a professional appearance.

Theory

1. Use all of the techniques previously described.

2. Candidates often find time pressure the least intense on the theory section.

3. Recognize that you may be feeling a little "burned out" by Friday afternoon, so fight to stay sharp and go after the available points!

4. Use all the GAAP keywords applicable to the question asked, inasmuch as the grader will be looking for these as s/he seeks to award you points. (E.g.: "Depreciation is a **systematic** and **rational** allocation of asset cost over accounting periods according to the **pervasive expense recognition principle**.")

5. Remember, once again, DO NOT OMIT THE OBVIOUS! The grader cannot read your mind — you alone must explain all the pertinent points relevant to the question. Do so in clear, concise, well-organized sentences.

6. You've come too far to end the exam early, just because it's the last part and you feel you've written enough. Stick it out until they call for the exams.

CHAPTER FIVE

AUDITING MODULES

Number   Code

                        C. Accounting Cycles - 138
                            1. Sales, Receivables, Cash Receipts - 141
                            2. Purchases, Payables, and Cash Disbursements - 144
                            3. Inventories and Production - 148
                            4. Personnel and Payroll - 153
                            5. Property, Plant, and Equipment - 157
                            6. Overall Internal Control Checklists - 157
                        D. Other Considerations - 161
                            1. Required Communication of Material Weaknesses - 161
                            2. Reports on Internal Control - 161
                            3. Sampling - 163
                            4. Effects of EDP - 163
                            5. Flowcharting - 163
                            6. Effects of an Internal Audit Function - 163

    3   EVID   Audit Evidence - 164
                        Study Program for Audit Evidence Module - 165
                        A. Audit Evidence--General - 166
                            1. Competent and Sufficient Evidential Matter - 166
                            2. Types of Evidence - 168
                        B. Audit Evidence--Specific - 170
                            1. Types of Substantive Tests - 170
                                a. Analytical Review - 170
                                b. Tests of Details of Transactions and
                                    Balances - 171
                            2. Preparing Substantive Test Audit Programs - 172
                            3. Documentation - 177
                        C. Other Specific Evidence Topics - 178
                            1. Cash - 178
                            2. Receivables - 179
                            3. Inventory - 181
                            4. Marketable Securities - 181
                            5. Property, Plant, and Equipment - 182
                            6. Prepaids - 182
                            7. Payables (Current) - 183
                            8. Long-Term Debt - 184
                            9. Owners' Equity - 184
                           10. Engagement Letters - 185
                           11. Client Representation Letters - 186
                           12. Using the Work of a Specialist - 187
                           13. Inquiry of a Client's Lawyer - 188
                           14. Related Party Transactions - 189
                           15. Operational Auditing - 189

    4   REP   Audit Reports - 190
                        Study Program for the Reports Module - 191
                        A. Financial Statement Audit Reports--General - 192
                        B. Financial Statement Audit Reports--Detailed - 194
                            1. Circumstances Resulting in Departure from Auditor's
                                Standard Report - 194
                                a. Scope Limitations - 195

Module Module
Number Code

SUMMARY OF AUDITING TOPICS TESTED

The auditing section of the CPA exam tests the candidate's knowledge of generally accepted auditing standards (GAAS) and procedures as they relate to the CPA's functions in the examination of financial statements. It is essential that you have a recent copy of the codification of the Statements on Auditing Standards. The codified version, as opposed to the original Statements on Auditing Standards (the SASs) as issued, eliminates all superseded portions. Commerce Clearing House, Inc. (4025 W. Peterson Ave., Chicago, Illinois 60646) publishes the codification as the AICPA's Professional Standards. This codification also includes the Auditing Interpretations, Statements on Standards for Management Advisory Services, Statements on Management Advisory Services, Statements on Responsibilities in Tax Practice, and Statements on Standards for Accounting and Review Services. Many university bookstores carry this source as it is often required in the undergraduate auditing course.

You should also have an auditing textbook to assist you in your preparation. Be certain that your text includes the 1973 (as modified in 1978 and 1979) Code of Professional Ethics. Note that the Code is also now included in the Professional Standards.

This chapter reviews topics tested on the auditing section of the exam. Begin by studying the content of the recent auditing examinations as suggested in the "self-study program" which is in Chapter 1 of this volume. After studying each module in this volume, work all of the multiple choice and essay questions.

Recognize that most candidates have difficulty with statistical sampling and auditing EDP due to limited exposure in their undergraduate programs and in practice. Thus, you should work through the outlines presented in each study module and work the related questions. Unfortunately, this entire volume would be required to provide comprehensive textbook coverage of topics tested on the exam.

AICPA Content Specification Outline/Frequency Analysis

The AICPA Content Specification Outline of the coverage of auditing, including the authors' frequency analysis (last nine exams) thereof, appears on the following pages.

AICPA CONTENT SPECIFICATION OUTLINE/FREQUENCY ANALYSIS*
AUDITING

	May 1980	Nov. 1980	May 1981	Nov. 1981	May 1982	Nov. 1982	May 1983	Nov. 1983	May 1984
I. Professional Responsibilities									
A. General Standards and Rules of Conduct									
1. Proficiency	-	-	-	-	1	-	-	1	-
2. Independence	-	-	1	-	3	1	1	1	-
3. Due Care	-	1	2	-	-	-	-	-	-
4. Rules of Conduct	2	3	2	4	2	-	2	2	-
5. Miscellaneous**	-	1	1	1	-	2	1	-	2
B. Control of the Audit									
1. Planning and Supervision	-	1	3	1	4	-	1	-	-
2. Quality Control	1	1	1	-	2	1	3	1	2
C. Other Responsibilities									
1. Detection of Errors or Irregularities	-	-	2	1	1	1	-	1	-
2. Illegal Acts by Clients	-	-	2	1	1	-	2	2	-
3. Responsibilities in Management Advisory Services	1	1	-	-	1	1	1	1	1
4. Responsibilities in Tax Practice	-	3	1	1	1	2	-	2	1
5. Continuing Professional Education and Familiarity with Topics of Current Concern to the Profession	-	-	-	-	2	-	-	-	-
Total MC Questions	4	11	15	9	18	8	11	11	6
Total Essays	1	.5	-	-	-	-	-	-	-
Actual Percentage***(AICPA 15%)	14%	16%	15%	9%	18%	8%	11%	11%	6%
II. Internal Control									
A. Definitions and Basic Concepts									
1. Purpose of Auditor's Study and Evaluation	-	-	-	-	-	1	1	1	-
2. Definitions and Basic Concepts	2	-	-	1	1	3	4	2	2

*The classifications are the authors'.

**This classification has been added by the authors.

***The Actual Percentage was calculated by adding the Total MC Questions to
the 10 points for each essay (or portion of) relating to this area (i.e., I, II,
etc.), and dividing by 100 (total points for all auditing areas). The essays in
auditing are classified by area only.

AICPA CONTENT SPECIFICATION OUTLINE/FREQUENCY ANALYSIS (CONTINUED)
AUDITING

	May 1980	Nov. 1980	May 1981	Nov. 1981	May 1982	Nov. 1982	May 1983	Nov. 1983	May 1984
B. Study and Evaluation of the System									
1. Review of the System	1	2	1	2	2	1	-	1	2
2. Tests of Compliance	2	2	3	-	2	1	1	1	1
3. Evaluation of Weaknesses	1	1	-	1	-	-	-	-	-
C. Cycles									
1. Sales, Receivables, and Cash Receipts	-	-	1	2	-	4	3	1	-
2. Purchases, Payables, and Cash Disbursements	1	1	-	2	2	1	-	-	1
3. Inventories and Production	1	1	1	1	1	1	2	-	1
4. Personnel and Payroll	1	-	2	-	3	1	-	-	1
5. Property, Plant, and Equipment	1	1	1	1	-	-	-	-	-
D. Other Considerations									
1. Required Communication of Material Weaknesses	1	-	-	2	-	1	1	-	-
2. Reports on Internal Control	-	-	-	2	1	2	-	1	2
3. Sampling	1	2	2	4	3	1	3	1	2
4. Effects of EDP	4	4	5	2	1	2	2	4	6
5. Flowcharting	1	-	1	-	-	-	1	-	1
6. Effects of an Internal Audit Function	-	1	1	1	1	-	1	1	-
Total MC Questions	17	15	18	20	17	19	19	13	19
Total Essays	1.5	1	1	2	1	2	1	1	1
Actual Percentage (AICPA 30%)	32%	25%	28%	40%	27%	39%	29%	23%	29%
III. Audit Evidence and Procedures									
A. Audit Evidence									
1. Nature, Competence, and Sufficiency of Evidential Matter	6	4	2	2	3	2	1	2	2
2. Analytical Review Procedures	1	2	1	1	3	1	1	1	3
3. Evidential Matter for Receivables and Inventory	4	4	2	1	2	2	2	3	3
4. Evidential Matter for Long-Term Investments	-	1	-	1	-	-	-	-	1
5. Client Representations	1	-	-	1	1	2	1	1	2
6. Using the Work of a Specialist	-	-	1	-	-	-	1	1	2
7. Inquiry of a Client's Lawyer	1	1	-	1	-	2	2	1	2
8. Related Party Transactions	-	1	2	1	1	-	1	2	-

AICPA CONTENT SPECIFICATION OUTLINE/FREQUENCY ANALYSIS (CONTINUED)
AUDITING

	May 1980	Nov. 1980	May 1981	Nov. 1981	May 1982	Nov. 1982	May 1983	Nov. 1983	May 1984
B. Specific Audit Objectives and Procedures									
1. Tests of Details of Trans- actions and Balances	8	7	5	6	2	3	3	6	2
2. Documentation	-	1	-	2	-	2	-	-	-
C. Other Specific Topics									
1. Use of the Computer in Performing the Audit	2	-	3	1	1	2	1	2	-
2. Use of Statistical Sampling in Performing the Audit	3	2	-	1	1	-	2	5	2
3. Subsequent Events	-	-	-	1	1	-	-	-	1
4. Operational Auditing	1	-	-	-	-	1	1	-	-
Total MC Questions	27	23	16	19	15	17	16	24	20
Total Essays	1.5	1	2	1	2	1	2	2	2
Actual Percentage (AICPA 30%)	42%	33%	36%	29%	35%	27%	36%	44%	40%

IV. Reporting

	May 1980	Nov. 1980	May 1981	Nov. 1981	May 1982	Nov. 1982	May 1983	Nov. 1983	May 1984
A. Reporting Standards and Types of Reports									
1. Scope of Examination	-	-	-	-	-	3	1	1	-
2. Generally Accepted Accounting Principles	-	-	3	1	-	-	-	-	1
3. Consistency	4	1	1	1	2	1	3	3	1
4. Disclosure	-	-	-	1	-	-	-	-	-
5. Reporting Responsibilities	2	-	1	1	4	2	2	2	4
6. Unqualified	-	1	-	2	-	-	-	-	-
7. Qualified	-	1	-	-	1	1	1	-	-
8. Adverse	2	-	1	1	-	-	-	-	1
9. Comparative	-	1	1	-	-	2	3	1	2
10. Disclaimer	-	1	-	1	-	-	-	-	-
11. Compilation and Review	1	1	-	1	-	2	1	2	2
12. Review of Interim Financial Information	-	2	1	-	1	-	1	-	-
13. Special Reports	2	1	1	-	1	1	1	1	1
14. Negative Assurance	-	-	-	-	-	1	-	-	-
B. Other Reporting Considerations									
1. Subsequent Discovery of Facts Existing at the Date of the Auditor's Report	-	1	-	-	-	1	-	1	1
2. Dating of the Auditor's Report	-	-	1	2	-	-	-	-	-

AICPA CONTENT SPECIFICATION OUTLINE/FREQUENCY ANALYSIS (CONTINUED)
AUDITING

	May 1980	Nov. 1980	May 1981	Nov. 1981	May 1982	Nov. 1982	May 1983	Nov. 1983	May 1984
3. Part of Examination Made by Other Independent Auditors	1	-	1	1	-	1	1	1	-
4. Letters for Underwriters	-	-	-	-	-	-	-	-	-
5. Filing Under Federal Securities Statutes	-	1	-	-	-	-	-	-	-
6. Segment Information	-	-	-	-	-	1	-	-	1
7. Other Information in Documents Containing Audited Financial Statements	-	-	-	-	1	-	-	-	-
8. Supplementary Information Required by the FASB	-	-	-	-	-	-	-	-	-
9. Information Accompanying the Basic Financial Statements	-	-	-	-	-	-	-	-	1
Total MC Questions	12	11	11	12	10	16	14	12	15
Total Essays	-	1.5	1	1	1	1	1	1	1
Actual Percentage (AICPA 25%)	12%	26%	21%	22%	20%	26%	24%	22%	25%

OVERVIEW OF ·THE ATTEST FUNCTION

In this overview section the general nature of the attest function is first discussed. Second, is a discussion of the general nature of the attest function as it relates to financial statement information. Third, a diagram is provided for understanding the nature of audits of financial statements. A section on generally accepted auditing standards (GAAS) and Statements on Auditing Standards (SASs) follows.

Attest Function--General Nature

The purpose of the attest function is to provide third-party assurance or "attestation" as to whether appropriate criteria have been met. In the United States this attest function is most frequently performed by CPAs through financial statement audits, operational audits, and compliance audits.

Information on financial statement audits, the bulk of the auditing portion of the CPA exam, is presented in much greater detail throughout this module. Operational audits generally relate to evaluating whether the criteria of effectiveness and efficiency of various accounting processes have been met; operational auditing is considered in further detail in the audit evidence module. Compliance audits are directed at determining whether a client is in compliance with a law or an agreement (e.g., the criteria here may be to maintain certain ratio requirements as required by a debt agreement). Reports for compliance audits are discussed in the audit reports module. (See "Special Reports.")

The need for independent third-party attestation arises due to possible differences between management and others (stockholders, the government, etc.) as to

1. Beliefs as to activities in which the firm should engage
2. Beliefs as to the manner in which these activities should be performed
3. Reward structures (management's pay, at least in part, is a salary while investors receive interest, dividends, and/or capital gains)

Attest Function--Financial Statement Information

The purpose of third-party financial attestation is to provide assurance that financial statements, which have been prepared by management, follow appropriate criteria (e.g., generally accepted accounting principles). The preparation of financial information may be viewed as consisting of inputs (source documents) being processed (through use of journals, ledgers, etc.) to arrive at an output (the financial information itself). Or shown diagrammatically

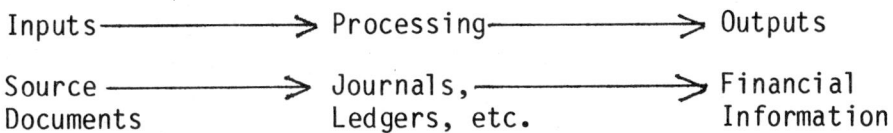

Inputs————————> Processing————————————> Outputs

Source ————————> Journals,————————————> Financial
Documents   Ledgers, etc.   Information

While CPAs often assist in the preparation of the financial statements, the attestation function conceptually begins with financial information.

Financial————————> CPA————————————————> Attested-to
Information   Attestation   Financial Information

A CPA collects various types of evidence relating to the propriety of the recording of economic events and transactions. In examining transactions CPAs must
satisfy themselves that

1. All significant transactions occurring during the period have been prop-
    erly recorded, classified and summarized in the statements, and
2. All significant transactions included in the financial statements did oc-
    cur during the period

In short, the attestation function helps assure that all transactions have been recorded at their proper amounts. A CPA serves a "control" function in the sense that
s/he helps to establish the likelihood that the entity's financial information follows the appropriate criteria to an acceptable degree.

Several forms of the attestation function are currently being performed by
CPAs. The primary form is the annual financial statement audit

Annual Financial ————> CPA ————————> Audited Annual
Statements   Audit   Financial Statements

In an <u>audit</u> the CPA renders an opinion on whether the financial statements of the
entity being audited have been prepared in conformity with generally accepted accounting principles (GAAP).

CPAs also become associated with financial information in performing engagements short of audits. For example, overall analytical and inquiry procedures may
be used when CPAs perform <u>reviews</u> of interim, annual, or forecast information. In
the case of interim financial information

Interim Financial ————> CPA ————————> Reviewed Interim
Information   Review   Financial Information

Because of the limited nature of the evidence gathering procedures in a review, the
CPA's report provides limited assurance with respect to whether the statements follow the appropriate criteria. In the case of reviewed interim financial information, for example, the report explicitly indicates the limited nature of the

review's procedures and states that no opinion regarding the statements as a whole
is expressed. The report's concluding paragraph indicates whether the CPA is aware
of any material modifications which need to be made to the statements for them to be
in conformity with generally accepted accounting principles.

     CPAs may also provide assistance to clients in the form of compilation and un-
audited statement services. Compilation services are performed for nonpublic companies which seek assistance in the preparation of financial statements. In the
case of public companies which are not required to have audits (primarily certain
utilities, banks, etc., which do not report to the Securities and Exchange Commission) similar assistance may be obtained through CPA preparation of unaudited statements. For both compilations and unaudited statements, note that the CPA's primary
role is to prepare the financial statements, an accounting as opposed to attestation
function (in fact, in the case of compilations, independence is not required). Accordingly, in both cases the CPA's report disclaims any opinion and gives no assurances with respect to whether the statements comply with the appropriate criteria.
(The Reports Module, Module 4, discusses these forms of association in further detail.)

     Finally, note that while attestation (i.e., reviewing and/or auditing) is often
considered an area within accounting, it is probably more accurate to consider it a
separate function which provides assurance ("attests") to the outputs generated by
the accounting process. One must be an accountant to be an auditor (or "reviewer"),
but one is not necessarily an auditor if one is an accountant. In other words,
auditors must be proficient as auditors as well as proficient as accountants.

Diagram of an Audit

     In the audit process an auditor gathers evidence to support a professional
opinion. This audit process is performed in compliance with GAAS--see page 86 for
these ten standards. The following diagram outlines the steps in the evidence collection and evaluation process in which an auditor forms an opinion.

DIAGRAM OF AN AUDIT

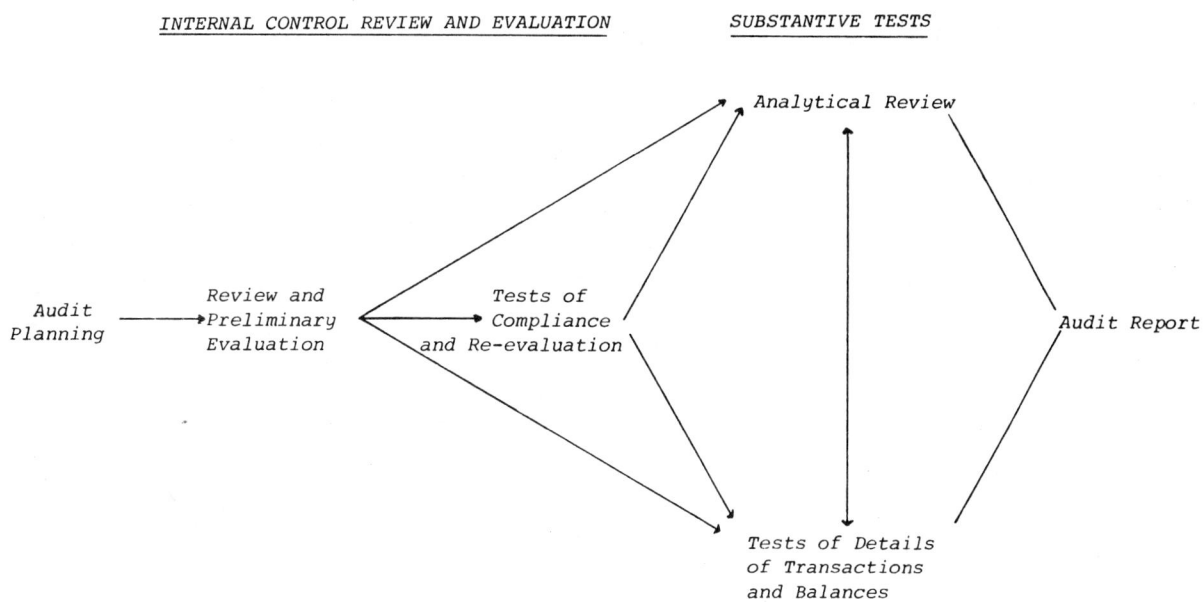

INTERNAL CONTROL REVIEW AND EVALUATION   *SUBSTANTIVE TESTS*

Kinney, William R., Jr., "Decision Theory Aspects of Internal Control System Design/Compliance, and Substantive Tests," Journal of Accounting Research (Supplement, 1975), p. 16 (adapted).

Audit Planning. The objective of this phase of an audit is to obtain an overall environmental understanding of the firm being audited. Evidence gathered includes information about the firm's characteristics and the characteristics of the firm's industry.

Internal Control Review and Evaluation--General. The second generally accepted auditing standard of field work requires a "proper study and evaluation" of internal control. Auditors first review the system and make a preliminary evaluation. The results of the preliminary evaluation are used to decide whether to perform tests of compliance and a reevaluation of internal control.

Internal Control--Review and Preliminary Evaluation. The auditor performs a conceptual review and preliminary evaluation of internal controls using questionnaires, checklists, flowcharts, and/or decision tables to gain and record an understanding of how the firm's controls are purported to work. At this point few actual transactions have been traced through the firm's accounting system, inasmuch as the auditor is simply gaining an understanding of how the accounting system is purported to function. Upon completion of the review, the auditor makes a preliminary evaluation based on the system as it has been described. After evaluating the firm's internal control in this manner, the auditor must decide whether the system seems strong enough to prevent, detect and correct material errors. If the auditor's preliminary evaluation determines that portions of the system are weak, a decision must be made to rely in large part on substantive tests--analytical review procedures, and/or tests of details of transactions and balances. On the other hand, if the system seems capable of preventing or detecting and correcting material errors, the auditor must decide whether it is more cost effective to perform compliance tests or to directly perform substantive tests.

Internal Control--Tests of Compliance and Reevaluation. In situations in which an auditor believes that an internal control system may be adequate to be relied upon, tests of compliance may be performed. In these tests auditors typically select various types of transactions which have been processed by the system and test whether the prescribed controls worked. Using the results of these tests of compliance, auditors reevaluate internal control. When auditors find an acceptable level of compliance with internal controls, less substantive testing is generally required than in cases in which there is a lower level of compliance.

Substantive Tests--General. Substantive tests are used to "substantiate" account balances. While compliance tests, as noted above, provide evidence as to whether prescribed procedures are being followed, substantive tests provide evidence as to whether actual account balances are proper. Two types of substantive tests are (1) Analytical Review and (2) Tests of Details of Transactions and Balances.

Substantive Tests--Analytical Review. In these tests auditors gather evidence with respect to relationships among various accounting and nonaccounting data such as industry and economy information. When unexpected changes occur (or expected changes do not occur) in these relationships, an auditor investigates further and obtains explanations. Ratio analysis is a frequently used analytical review procedure. The auditor would, for example, calculate a ratio and compare it to criteria such as budgets, prior year and industry data.

Substantive Tests--Tests of Details of Transactions and Balances. Auditors use these tests to detect dollar errors in the financial statements. The detail supporting individual financial statement accounts is tested to gain assurance that material errors do not exist in the accounts. Sending confirmations for year-end receivable accounts is an example.

Audit Report. There is a standard short-form audit report that is issued by CPAs when their examination and the results thereof were satisfactory. It is known as a "clean opinion" and is reproduced on the following page. This "clean opinion" is modified as the audit examination deviates from normal, or the financial statements do not comply with generally accepted accounting principles (GAAP).

Variations of the short-form report include

1. Unqualified (Clean opinion)
2. Qualified
3. Disclaimer
4. Adverse
5. Unaudited (including "compilation" and "review" reports)

The purposes and examples of each are outlined and illustrated in the audit report section of this chapter (also see the outline of SASs at the end of this chapter).

As a final step in this introduction, you will find it useful to read the standard short-form report carefully, and note the assertions made in it. Remember, the audit report is the objective and product of the audit.

To: Board of Directors and Stockholders   June 1, 19__
     ABC Company

     We have examined the balance sheets of ABC Company as of [at] December 31, 19X2 and 19X1, and the related statements of income, retained earnings, and changes in financial position for the years then ended. Our examinations were made in accordance with generally accepted auditing standards and, accordingly, included such tests of the accounting records and such other auditing procedures as we considered necessary in the circumstances.

     In our opinion, the financial statements referred to above present fairly the financial position of ABC Company as of [at] December 31, 19X2 and 19X1, and the results of its operations and the changes in its financial position for the years then ended, in conformity with generally accepted accounting principles applied on a consistent basis.

                                             /s/ Joe Smith, CPA

Some key assertions in the above report include

     Addressee
     Date

     Scope paragraph

        1. We have examined

        2. Client's financial statements
            Balance sheets
            Income statements
            Retained earnings statements
            Statements of changes in financial position

3.   Exam was according to GAAS including
     Tests of the accounting records
     Other auditing procedures
     As we considered necessary

Opinion paragraph

1.   In our opinion

2.   Statements fairly present
     Per GAAP (applied consistently)

Signature

Generally Accepted Auditing Standards

CPAs are to perform their examinations in compliance with generally accepted auditing standards. These auditing standards deal with measures of the quality of performance of the audit (as contrasted to auditing procedures which relate to acts to be performed by the auditor). The ten generally accepted standards may be categorized as general, field, and reporting standards.

General Standards

1.   The examination is to be performed by a person or persons having adequate technical training and proficiency as an auditor.

2.   In all matters relating to the assignment, an independence in mental attitude is to be maintained by the auditor or auditors.

3.   Due professional care is to be exercised in the performance of the examination and the preparation of the report.

Standards of Fieldwork

1.   The work is to be adequately planned and assistants, if any, are to be properly supervised.

2.   There is to be a proper study and evaluation of the existing internal control as a basis for reliance thereon and for the determination of the resultant extent of the tests to which auditing procedures are to be restricted.

3.   Sufficient competent evidential matter is to be obtained through inspection, observation, inquiries, and confirmations to afford a reasonable basis for an opinion regarding the financial statements under examination.

Standards of Reporting

1.   The report shall state whether the financial statements are presented in accordance with generally accepted accounting principles.

2.   The report shall state whether such principles have been consistently observed in the current period in relation to the preceding period.

3.   Informative disclosures in the financial statements are to be regarded as reasonably adequate unless otherwise stated in the report.

4. The report shall either contain an expression of opinion regarding the financial statements, taken as a whole, or an assertion to the effect that an opinion cannot be expressed. When an overall opinion cannot be expressed, the reasons therefore should be stated. In all cases where an auditor's name is associated with financial statements, the report should contain a clear-cut indication of the character of the auditor's examination, if any, and the degree of responsibility he is taking.

You should have these ten standards memorized (also by category) for the exam. The following mnemonics provide one way to remember these standards:

TIP (Training, Independence, Professional Care)
PIE (Planning, Internal Control, Evidence)
GODC (GAAP, Opinion, Disclosure, Consistency)

Note: That to form the third mnemonic (god with a soft c), one must reorder the reporting standards--1,4,3,2.

Statements on Auditing Standards

In 1939, the AICPA appointed the Committee on Auditing Procedure which issued 54 Statements on Auditing Procedure (SAP). In 1973 the Auditing Standards Executive Committee replaced the Committee on Auditing Procedure and issued Statement on Auditing Standards (SAS) No. 1 which was a codification of SAPs which had not then been superseded. The Auditing Standards Executive Committee issued 22 other SASs and was replaced in 1978 when the AICPA created the Auditing Standards Board which now has the responsibility for issuing pronouncements on auditing matters. The Auditing Standards Board has continued the series of SASs which are considered interpretations of GAAS per Ethics Rule 2.02 which requires compliance with GAAS. SAS 2 through 47 have been issued as of May 1, 1984.

All of the SASs (except superseded sections) are outlined at the end of this chapter in their codified order. You should study the SAS outlines as a separate topic and also refer to the appropriate SAS sections and paragraphs as you study the other sections of this chapter, e.g., audit reports, EDP, etc. At the beginning of each module in this chapter, a study program will refer you to appropriate SASs. A summary of this cross-reference is also set forth here to give you an additional overview of the topical coverage of the SASs.

Also included at the end of this chapter are outlines for the AICPA's Guide for a Review of Financial Forecasts and Statements on Standards for Accounting and Review Services (SSARS). These too should be studied as a separate topic, as well as with the topical material presented in this chapter.

Stan

SAS 1 Section		Module in This Book
100	Introduction	Overview
200	General GAAS	Overview
310	Adequate Planning and Supervision	EVID
320	Internal Control	IC
330*	Evidential Matter	EVID
400*	First 3 Reporting GAAS	REP
500*	Fourth Reporting GAAS	REP
901	Public Warehouses	EVID

		Module in This Book	New Codified SAS Section No.
SAS 2	Audit Reports	REP	509
SAS 3	EDP and Internal Control	EDP	321
SAS 4	Firm Quality Controls	RESP	Superseded by SAS 25
SAS 5	Meaning of Present Fairly	REP	411
SAS 6	Related Party Transactions	EVID	335
SAS 7	Predecessor-Successor Communications	EVID	315
SAS 8	Other Information	REP	550
SAS 9	Effect of an Internal Audit Function	IC	322
SAS 10	Limited Review	REP	Superseded by SAS 24
SAS 11	Using Specialists	EVID	336
SAS 12	Inquiry of Client's Lawyer	EVID	337
SAS 13	Limited Review Reports	REP	Superseded by SAS 24
SAS 14	Special Reports	REP	621
SAS 15	Comparative Financial Statements	REP	505
SAS 16	Detection of Errors and Irregularities	EVID	327
SAS 17	Illegal Acts	EVID	328
SAS 18	Replacement Costs	EVID	Deleted by Auditing Standards Board
SAS 19	Client Representations	EVID	333
SAS 20	Required Communications of Material Weaknesses in Internal Accounting Control	IC	323
SAS 21	Segment Reporting	REP	435
SAS 22	Planning and Supervision	EVID	311
SAS 23	Analytical Review Procedures	EVID	318
SAS 24	Review of Interim Financial Information	EVID	Superseded by SAS 36
SAS 25	The Relationship of Generally Accepted Auditing Standards to Quality Control Standards	RESP	161

*contains multiple subsections

		Module in This Book	New Codified SAS Section No.
SAS 26	Association with Financial Statements	REP	504
SAS 27	Supplementary Information Required by the Financial Accounting Standards Board	REP	553
SAS 28	Supplementary Information on the Effects of Changing Prices	REP	554
SAS 29	Reporting on Information Accompanying the Basic Financial Statements in Auditor-Submitted Documents	REP	551
SAS 30	Reporting on Internal Accounting Control	REP	642
SAS 31	Evidential Matter	EVID	326
SAS 32	Adequacy of Disclosure in Financial Statements	REP	431
SAS 33	Supplementary Oil and Gas Reserve Information	REP	555
SAS 34	The Auditor's Considerations When a Question Arises about an Entity's Continued Existence	REP	340
SAS 35	Special Reports--Applying Agreed-Upon Procedures to Specified Elements, Accounts, or Items of a Financial Statement	REP	622
SAS 36	Review of Interim Financial Information	EVID	722
SAS 37	Filings under Federal Securities Statutes	REP	711
SAS 38	Letters for Underwriters	REP	631
SAS 39	Audit Sampling	SS	350
SAS 40	Supplementary Mineral Reserve Information	EVID	556
SAS 41	Working Papers	EVID	339
SAS 42	Reporting on Condensed Financial Statements and Selected Financial Data	REP	552
SAS 43	Omnibus Statement on Auditing Standards	VARIOUS	1010*
SAS 44	Special-Purpose Reports on Internal Accounting Control at Service Organizations	IC	324
SAS 45	Omnibus Statement on Auditing Standards--1983	VARIOUS	1020*
SAS 46	Consideration of Omitted Procedures after the Report Date	EVID	390
SAS 47	Audit Risk and Materiality in Conducting an Audit	RESP VARIOUS	312
SAS 48	The Effects of Computer Processing on the Examination of Financial Statements	VARIOUS	(not avail. at press time)*

*Outlines of the paragraphs of this statement have been inserted in the outlines of the sections which it superseded.

PROFESSIONAL RESPONSIBILITIES

Professional ethics (responsibilities) have traditionally been focused at the individual practitioner level. The authoritative literature at that level includes the generally accepted auditing standards, the AICPA Code of Professional Ethics (hereafter the Code) and the Statements on Responsibilities in Tax Practice and Statements on Standards for MAS. During the past several years, however, a new series of Statements on Quality Control Standards (SQCS) has been started (to date only SQCS #1 on the system of quality control for a CPA firm has been issued) which addresses the issue of the qualitative standards which a CPA firm should follow.

Generally multiple choice questions are used to test the candidate's knowledge of the AICPA Code of Professional Ethics and, to a lesser extent, the Statements on Responsibility in Tax Practice, Statements on Standards for Management Advisory Services, and the Statement on Quality Control Standards. Occasionally essay questions have provided a description of a situation with ethical connotations and have required that the candidate list and describe any unethical behavior which has occurred.

Study Program for the Professional Responsibilities Module

This module is organized and should be studied in the following manner:

A. General Standards and Rules of Conduct

1. General Standards
2. Rules of Conduct

B. Control of the Audit

1. Planning and Supervision
2. Quality Control

C. Other Responsibilities

1. Detection of Errors or Irregularities
2. Illegal Acts by Clients
3. Responsibilities in Management Advisory Services
4. Responsibilities in Tax Practice
5. Continuing Professional Education and Current Topics

The above outline is based on the AICPA CPA Exam Content Specification Outline for Professional Responsibilities.

The following SAS sections pertain to Professional Responsibilities:

Section (AU)

110	Responsibilities and Functions of the Independent Auditor
150	Generally Accepted Auditing Standards
161	Relationship of Generally Accepted Auditing Standards to Quality Control Standards
201	Nature of the General Standards
210	Training and Proficiency of the Independent Auditor
220	Independence
230	Due Care in the Performance of Work
310	Adequacy of Planning and the Timing of Fieldwork
311	Planning and Supervision
312	Audit Risk and Materiality in Conducting an Audit
315	Communications Between Predecessor and Successor Auditors
327	Detection of Errors or Irregularities
328	Illegal Acts by Clients

Additionally, outlines of the Code of Professional Ethics, Statements on Quality Control, Management Advisory Services, and Tax Practice are presented in this module.

A. General Standards and Rules of Conduct

1. <u>General Standards (AU 210, 220, 230)</u>. The three general standards (recall TIP--Training, Independence, Professional Care) are personal in nature in the sense that they are concerned with the auditor's qualifications and the quality of his/her work. Note that training includes both the auditor's formal education and professional experience.

The second standard, which requires audit independence, requires both independence in fact and in appearance. The Code of Professional Ethics considers independence in detail. The third general standard states that, although infallibility is not assumed in an audit, due professional care must be exerted at all levels.

2. <u>Rules of Conduct (Code of Professional Ethics)</u>.
   a. <u>Overview</u>. The AICPA Code of Professional Ethics consists of four sections:
      1) Concepts
      2) Rules
      3) Interpretations
      4) Rulings

The concepts section is a positively phrased, philosophical essay on the ethical behavior of CPAs. There are five concepts with thirteen enforceable rules organized as follows:

1. Independence
   Rule 101--Independence
   Rule 102--Integrity and Objectivity

2. General and Technical Standards
   Rule 201--General Standards
   Rule 202--Auditing Standards
   Rule 203--Accounting Principles
   Rule 204--Other Technical Standards

3. Responsibilities to Clients
   Rule 301--Confidential Client Information
   Rule 302--Contingent Fees (Enforcement currently suspended)

4. Responsibilities to Colleagues
   (Enforcement of all Rules, Interpretations, and Rulings currently suspended)

5. Other Responsibilities and Practices
   Rule 501--Acts Discreditable
   Rule 502--Advertising and Other Forms of Solicitation
   Rule 503--Commissions
   Rule 504--Incompatible Occupations
   Rule 505--Form of Practice and Name

Additionally, interpretations of the rules of conduct have been made by the AICPA Division of Professional Ethics. The Division also issues rulings on specific factual situations. In the subsequent outline of the Code, the rules, interpretations, and rulings have been grouped by concept.

A one-sentence summary is presented for each of the ethics rulings issued by the AICPA. They are now published (starting in 1982) in Vol. 1 of the Professional Standards. While CPA candidates should read the rulings to better understand the ethics rules and interpretations, it is not necessary to memorize them--consider them to be illustrations.

The Code of Professional Ethics has been reproduced in most auditing texts. If you refer to the ethics code in your auditing text, make sure it is current.

A major recent change was the modification of rules 502 (to allow advertising) and 504 (to delete the prohibition against concurrent occupations which serve as a feeder to accounting practice, e.g., insurance sales). Also rules 401 (prohibiting encroachment on another CPA's practice) and 402 (requiring CPAs to notify other CPAs before offering employment to their employees) were eliminated. Thus, the "Responsibilities to Colleagues" section of the Code was at least temporarily eliminated.

   b. Overall review of the Code of Ethics. This section is meant to give you overall guidance on the information which you will need in order to be able to answer ethics questions. The information here is a combination of ideas to help you understand the framework of the Code as well as "must know" points which have ap- peared frequently on past exams. You must also be very familiar with the informa- tion presented in the Code of Ethics outline which appears in this module.

Know that the Code of Ethics sets forth minimum levels of acceptable conduct and that such a code is especially important in a discipline such as auditing in which it is difficult for outsiders to evaluate the quality of CPA services.

The Code derives its authority from the by-laws of the AICPA. Violation of the Code may result in admonishment, suspension, or expulsion from the AICPA. Court decisions have consistently held that even if an individual is not a member of the AICPA, that individual is still expected to follow the profession's Code of Ethics. Additionally, the individual state CPA boards and societies monitor ethical matters.

The Code applies to all services performed in public accounting, including tax and management advisory services, unless the wording indicates otherwise and in limited situations when a CPA is practicing outside the United States. A CPA is re- sponsible for compliance with the Code by all persons associated with him/her; this includes all other partners and those employees under his/her supervision.

CPAs not in public accounting are, nonetheless, subject to sections 102 (do not knowingly misrepresent facts or subordinate judgment) and section 501 (do not commit acts discreditable to the profession).

Independence Concept. Know that independence is defined as the ability to act with integrity and objectivity. The primary types of relationships which hinder independence are (1) financial and (2) those in which the CPA is virtually a part of management or an employee under management's control. Rule 101 is especially important. You must be able to distinguish between those situations in which the auditor must refrain during the period of the audit engagement (e.g., owning stock) vs. those in which the auditor must refrain during the period covered by the finan- cial statements (e.g., director or officer). Know that in tax matters a CPA may re- solve doubt in favor of a client if there is reasonable support for the position taken. In Management Advisory Services (MAS) engagements an auditor may not make actual decisions for an audit client. Also, be aware that members of the AICPA's SEC Practice Section (discussed below, under "B.2.a.") may not engage in executive recruitment, and that providing primary actuarial advice has been discouraged.

General and Technical Standards. Although a CPA should not render services without being aware of the applicable standards, the competence may be obtained after acceptance of an engagement. Concerning forecasts, a CPA is not to vouch for achievability (the Audit Reports module outlines review reports in which an auditor may vouch for the reasonableness of a forecast's assumptions). GAAP is to be followed unless it can be demonstrated that due to "unusual circumstances" (e.g., new legislation, new types of transactions), GAAP will make the financial statements misleading (the Audit Reports module discusses this in further detail under "Departures from Promulgated Principles"). A CPA must follow GAAS or be able to justify any departures therefrom in the audit working papers.

Responsibilities to Clients. Be aware that a CPA has a confidential relationship with his/her clients and may not disclose confidential client data without the consent of the client. However, as indicated in the outline (Section 301, point "b") there are exceptions to this rule. You must know them. Also, a CPA only has privileged communication with a client to the extent that state law allows it and then only in the state court system. Contingent fees are not acceptable; however, fees fixed by courts or, in tax matters, fees based on the results of judicial proceedings or the findings of governmental agencies are not regarded as contingent. A CPA may not accept a commission from a vendor for recommending his/her product to a client.

Responsibilities to Colleagues. A CPA testifying as an expert witness in court must testify with complete candor. Before accepting an engagement, it is desirable in all situations and required in some situations (see AU 315 outline concerning predecessor/successor auditors) to consult with the accountant already serving the client. Note that the objective here is to make it possible for the successor to consider the pertinent facts concerning the prospective client before accepting the engagement. Finally, all rules, interpretations, and rulings in this section of the Code are currently suspended.

Other Responsibilities. This section is composed of a miscellaneous group of responsibilities. Audit fees may be based on various factors in addition to actual hours worked. Advertising, while allowed, must not be false, misleading or deceptive. Any advertising comparisons with other firms and any indication of expertise in an area must be objectively verifiable. Retention of client records is discreditable (even if state law allows it). While a CPA may sell his/her practice, s/he must obtain client permission before turning over working papers (audit and other) to the purchaser. A CPA may not accept (or offer) a "forwarding fee" for referring a prospective client to another CPA.

c. Outline of the Code of Professional Ethics.

1) "Independence, integrity and objectivity. A certified public accountant should maintain his integrity and objectivity and, when engaged in
the practice of public accounting, be independent of those he serves."
POINTS: (1) Independence is defined as having the ability to act with
integrity and objectivity. Primary relationships which hinder objectivity are (a) financial and (b) those where the CPA is virtually a
part of management or an employee under management's control.
(2) While the appearance of independence is not required in MAS and
tax work, it is desirable.

101 Independence

a) A CPA or firm will not express opinion unless independent. A CPA is
not independent if there exist certain financial relationships with
client--during period of professional engagement or at time of
opinion.

1] Had or was committed to acquire financial interest in client

a] Any direct
b] Material indirect

2] Had any joint investment with any client, officer, stockholder,
etc. that was material

3] Had any loan to or from client, officer, stockholder, etc.
except

a] Borrowed by CPA or CPA firm not material to borrower's net
worth
b] Home mortgages
c] Other secured loans except loans guaranteed by CPA firm

b) A CPA is not independent if there exists a management or employee
relationship with client--during period covered by financial statements, period of professional engagement or at time of opinion as a

1] Promoter, underwriter, voting trustee, director, officer, employee, etc.
2] Trustee of any trust or executor of any estate having direct or
material indirect interest in the client

a] Or trustee of any pension or profit sharing trust of client

101 Interpretations

a) CPA who is a director of a nonprofit organization where the board is
large and representative of community leadership is not lacking independence if

1] Position is purely honorary
2] Position identified as honorary on externally circulated materials
3] Participation restricted to use of name
4] He does not vote or participate in management affairs

b) Retired CPA's association with clients does not impair firm independence if

1] Retired CPA is no longer active in firm

2] Client fees do not have a material effect on CPA's retirement payments

3] Retired CPA is not associated with firm

c) When a CPA performs writeup services, it <u>may</u> impair his independence. On the other hand, CPA's performance of manual or automated bookkeeping services may have no effect on independence.

    1] CPA must meet following requirements to retain appearance that CPA is not employee of client

        a] CPA cannot have any relationships with client that impair integrity and objectivity

        b] Client must accept statements as his own

            i] Client must have knowledge of business and financial operations to accept such responsibility

        c] CPA must not assume role of employee or management of the client

            i] CPA shall not consummate transactions or have custody of assets, etc.

           ii] Client must prepare source documents, etc.

        d] CPA must conform to GAAS and not eliminate tasks because he has done accounting work

    2] CPAs renting block computer time to clients are involved in a business and not a professional relationship

    3] When client qualifies for SEC regulation, client must assume all responsibility for the statements. (CPA would not be considered independent by SEC if he maintains the accounting records.)

d) Deleted, see "i)"

e) Meaning of "normal lending procedures"

    1] Rule 101 prohibits client-CPA loans except for certain types which are per normal lending procedures

    2] Normal lending procedures are the terms for "other borrowers", including

        a] Amount of loan and collateral

        b] Repayment terms

        c] Interest rate, points, closing costs, etc.

f) Effect of threatened litigation

    1] Client-CPA threatened or actual litigation impairs independence

        a] Adversary relationship exists possibly affecting

            i] Management's willingness to disclose data

           ii] Objectivity of auditor

    2] Generally litigation by client security holders or other third parties does not cause above problems or impair independence a] Unless material client-CPA cross-claims develop

     3] If independence is impaired, CPA should disassociate and/or disclaim an opinion for lack of independence

          a] CPA may re-sign report of prior year (when he was independent) if no material audit work is required (see section 505, Comparative Financial Statements)

g) Deleted, see "i)"

h) A CPA's (member's) financial interest in nonclients may have an effect on independence when those nonclients have financial interest (investee or investor) in the CPA's clients

     1] <u>Definitions</u>

        <u>Investor</u>--(1) a parent or (2) another investor that holds an interest in another company (investee) which gives it the ability to exercise significant influence over the investee

        <u>Material Investee</u>--investor's carrying amount of investment is 5% or more of investor's total assets or investor's equity in investee's income is 5% or more of the investor's income

        <u>Material Financial Interest</u>--5% or more of member's net worth

     2] Provisions

          a] Where a nonclient investee is material to a client investor, any direct or material indirect financial interest by a CPA in the nonclient investee impairs independence

          b] Where a client investee is material to a nonclient investor, any direct or material indirect financial interest of a CPA in the nonclient would impair independence

          c] Careful consideration should be given to situations involving brother-sister common control or client-nonclient joint ventures

          d] Where a nonclient investee is not material to a client investor, an immaterial financial interest of a CPA in the nonclient investee would not be considered to impair independence; a material one would

          e] Where a client investee is not material to a nonclient investor, an immaterial or material financial interest of a CPA in a nonclient investor will not generally impair independence with respect to the investee; the exception case is when the member owns so much of the nonclient so as to be able to significantly influence the nonclient's actions--not independent here

i) Meaning of independence terminology and the effect of family relationships on independence

     1] "He and his firm" in Rule 101 includes

          a] An individual member performing professional services requiring independence

          b] The proprietor of, or all partners or shareholders in, a firm

  c] All full and part time employees of a firm participating in the engagement

  d] All full and part time <u>managerial</u> employees of a firm in an office performing a significant portion of the engagement

   <u>Managerial</u> employees--distinguishing characteristics

    Position similar to partner, including authority to sign or give final approval for report issuance; examples include

    - Overall planning and supervision of engagements

    - Authority to determine when engagement is complete subject to final partner approval

    - Authority to negotiate and collect fees and to market services

    - Responsibility for job staffing, hiring, or training

    - Profit sharing is significant portion of compensation

  e] Any entity whose operating, financial, or accounting policies can be <u>significantly influenced</u> by one or more persons in a] through d] above

   Examples of individuals with <u>significant influence</u> over an entity

    - Promoter, underwriter, voting trustee, director, general partner

    - In a position making operating, financial or accounting policies (chief executive officer, chief financial officer, chief accounting officer, key assistants)

    - Meet APB 18, para 17 guidelines indicating influence

    - Holds 20 percent or more of limited partnership interest if the entity is a limited partnership

 2] Effect of family relationships on independence

  a] Spouse and dependent persons--same restrictions apply as to member, except that spouse may be employed by client if s/he does not exert <u>significant influence</u> over client's operating, financial or accounting policies. If spouse is in an <u>audit sensitive position</u> (subject to significant internal accounting controls--cashier, internal auditor, general accounting clerk, etc.) the member should not participate in the engagement.

  b] Nondependent close relatives (nondependent children, brothers, sisters, parents, grandparents, parents-in-law and respective spouses)--normally not considered, but member independence is impaired if

   1] A professional <u>participating on the job</u> has a close relative who has

    a] Significant influence (operating, financial or accounting)

b] An audit sensitive position
c] A material financial interest (to the relative) in client and the professional has knowledge of the financial interest

2] A <u>partner or managerial employee</u> in an office has a close relative who can exert significant influence (operating, financial, or accounting)

c] Other family considerations--consider whether a reasonable person aware of all facts and considering normal strength of character and normal behavior would question

<u>102 Integrity and Objectivity</u>[+] (See note below)

a) CPA shall not knowingly misrepresent facts
b) Shall not subordinate judgment to others including

1] Management services
2] Tax services

c) In tax, CPA may resolve doubt in favor of client if his position has reasonable support

Independence and Integrity Ethics Rulings

1. If a CPA accepts more than a token gift from a client, independence may be impaired.
2. A CPA may join a trade association, which is a client, without impairing independence, but not serve in a capacity of management.
3. If a CPA is cosignor of a client's checks, independence is impaired.
4. Independence is impaired if a CPA prepares a client's payroll.
5. If a client processes all original entry documents and transmits this data to a CPA for further processing, independence is not impaired if the conditions of Interpretation 101–3 are met.
6. If a CPA's spouse, as an employee, performs only bookkeeping services for a client, independence is not impaired.
7. Independence is impaired if a CPA supervises client office personnel on a monthly basis.
8. Extensive accounting and MAS services, including interpretation of statements, forecasts, etc., do not impair independence.
9. Independence is impaired if the CPA cosigns checks or purchase orders or exercises general supervision over budgetary controls.
10. The independence of an elected legislator (a CPA) in a local government is impaired with respect to that governmental unit.
11. Mere designation as executor or trustee, without actual services in either capacity, does not impair independence, but actual service does.

12. If a CPA is a trustee of a foundation, independence is impaired.
13. If a CPA's stock investment in a bank is not material, it does not impair independence with a client borrowing from that bank.
14. A CPA serving as director and treasurer of a local United Fund does not impair independence with respect to charities receiving money from the fund.
15. If a retired partner is still closely associated with the CPA firm, his serving on a client's board of directors impairs independence.
16. Independence is impaired if a member serves on the board of a nonprofit social club if the board has ultimate responsibility for the affairs of the club.
17. Membership in a country club does not impair independence.
18. Being chairman of a city council does not impair independence with respect to other governmental agencies not under the council's control.
19. Independence is impaired if a CPA serves on a committee administering a client's deferred compensation program.
20. Membership on governmental advisory committees does not impair independence with respect to that governmental unit.
21. A CPA serving as director of an enterprise would not be independent with respect to the enterprise's profit sharing and retirement trust.

[+]Some Rules do not have Interpretations. Those Rules are identified with a +.

22. Independence is impaired if the CPA's brother is a stockholder and vice-president of a closely held company.
23. Independence would not be impaired for a company owned by the uncle of a CPA's wife (infrequent personal contacts).
24. Independence would be impaired if a CPA's father serves on a school board.
25. Independence is impaired if a CPA's son is a director of a savings and loan association.
26. A CPA purchasing a public client's stock for his son's educational trust would impair independence.
27. A CPA's independence would be impaired if the CPA's spouse is trustee of a trust owning stock in the CPA's client.
29. A CPA's independence is impaired when owning bonds in a municipal authority.
31. A partner's ownership of an apartment in a co-op apartment building does not impair the firm's independence.
32. A CPA, who is president and a substantial stockholder in a company which is indebted on a mortgage loan to an S&L, does not impair the firm's independence with respect to the S&L.
33. A CPA impairs independence upon joining a client's employee benefit plan.
34. A partner's ownership of stock in a bank impairs firm independence with respect to the bank's trust fund.
35. A CPA's ownership of shares in a mutual investment fund which owns stock in the CPA's clients normally would not impair independence.
36. A CPA who is a member of an investment club, holding stock in a client, lacks independence.
38. A CPA serving with a client bank in a cofiduciary capacity, with respect to a trust, does not impair independence with respect to the bank or trust department (if the estate's or trust's assets were not material).
39. A CPA who acts as a transfer agent and/or registrar is not independent with respect to the company.
41. A CPA may audit a mutual insurance company that provides a retirement plan for the CPA's employees if the plan is not material to the insurance company.
42. A CPA firm's independence would not be impaired if the client, a stock life insurance company, underwrites a group term life insurance policy for the firm's partners if the amount at risk is not material to the insurance company's underwriting activities.

43. A CPA's independence would be impaired upon serving as treasurer of a charitable organization.
45. A CPA can be independent of a client in bankruptcy if the CPA's claim is fixed at the date of the bankruptcy filing.
47. A CPA who is a shareholder of a company serving as a mutual fund's investment advisor or manager is not independent to the mutual fund.
48. A university faculty member cannot be independent to a student senate fund because the student senate is a part of the university which is the CPA's employer.
51. A CPA who provides legal services to a client is not independent with respect to the client.
52. Independence is impaired if more than a year's fee remains unpaid for an extended period of time.
53. A CPA's independence, with respect to an employee benefit plan, is not impaired by being the auditor of the sponsoring company.
54. A CPA's independence is not impaired by rendering actuarial services to a client, if the client makes or approves all significant matters of judgment.
55. A CPA's independence is not impaired if the CPA is involved in hiring and instructing new personnel during a systems implementation. The client must make all significant management decisions and the CPA must restrict supervisory activities to initial instruction and training.
56. Independence is impaired by recruiting and hiring a controller and/or cost accountant for a client company. The CPA may, however, recommend position descriptions and candidate specifications as well as initially screen and recommend qualified candidates.
57. There is a possible violation of independence if a CPA firm recommends an outside service bureau in which partners have a financial interest.
58. Independence is impaired when a CPA owns a building and leases space to a client.
59. Independence is not impaired with respect to a brokerage client, if the investment accounts of partners and staff accountants at the brokerage firm are within the coverage provided by the Securities Investor Protection Corporation. Margin accounts, however, would create a loan relationship and impair independence.
60. Generally CPA's auditing employee benefit plans must be independent of the employer.
61. Participation by a CPA's spouse in an employee stock ownership plan of a client does not im-

pair independence until a right of possession of the stock exists.

62. A CPA may own a limited partnership interest (less than 20%) in a partnership in which a client owns less than 20% if neither is active in management in the partnership. If more than one client is involved, the aggregate investment (CPA plus clients) must be less than 50% of the interest of all limited partners.

2) "General and technical standards. A certified public accountant should observe the profession's general and technical standards and strive continually to improve his competence and the quality of his services."

201 General Standards

a) CPA must comply with the following general standards

1] Be able to complete all engagements with professional competence
2] Exercise due professional care
3] Shall adequately plan and supervise engagements
4] Obtain sufficient relevant data to afford a reasonable basis for all conclusions
5] Shall not allow his name to be associated with a forecast in such a manner that it appears the CPA is vouching for the achievability of the forecast

201 Interpretations

a) Competence to complete an engagement includes

1] Technical qualifications of CPA and staff
2] Ability to supervise and evaluate work
3] Knowledge of technical subject matter
4] Capability to exercise judgment in its application
5] Ability to research subject matter and consult with others

b) When a CPA is associated with forecasts he should determine that the following have been disclosed

1] Sources of the information used
2] Major assumptions
3] Work performed by CPA
4] Responsibility taken by CPA

c) If an audit client of another public accounting firm requests a CPA's advice on accounting or auditing matters, the CPA, before giving advice, should

1] Consult with the other accounting firm to determine that s/he has all of the available facts
2] Bear in mind that the client and its public accountant may have disagreed about the facts, accounting standards, or auditing standards

202 Auditing Standards

a) CPA must comply with GAAS (or be able to justify any departures before being associated with financial statements)

1] SASs are considered interpretations of GAAS

202 Interpretation

a) Unaudited statements

1] Rule 202 does not preclude a CPA from being associated with unaudited financial statements. However, any time a CPA is associated with any financial statements, the CPA must indicate the degree of responsibility taken.

203 Accounting Principles

a) CPA cannot state that financial statements are in conformity with GAAP if statements contain any departures from SFAS having a material effect on statements taken as a whole (except in "b", below)

b) Only exception is when CPA can show that statements would be misleading if SFAS were applied. CPA must then disclose

1] Departure
2] Approximate effects thereof
3] Reasons why compliance with SFAS would have been misleading

203 Interpretations

a) CPAs are to allow departure from SFAS only when results of SFAS will be misleading

1] Requires use of professional judgment
2] Examples of possible circumstances requiring departure are

a] New legislation
b] Evolution of a new form of business transaction

3] Examples not ordinarily requiring departure include

a] Unusual degree of materiality
b] Conflicting industry practices

b) FASB Interpretations are covered by Rule 203

1] Also unsuperseded ARBs and APBs

c) Statements of Financial Accounting Standards which stipulate that certain information should be disclosed outside the basic financial statements are not covered by Rule 203

204 Other Technical Standards[+]

a) CPA shall comply with all technical standards promulgated by bodies designated by AICPA council

1] The Accounting and Review Services Committee is designated to promulgate standards for unaudited financial statements of non-public companies

Competence and Technical Standards Ethics Ruling

1. A practicing CPA who prepares an unaudited financial statement for a company in which he is a stockholder, is deemed to be associated with unaudited financial statements, i.e., requires a disclaimer due to lack of independence.

2. A CPA employed by a corporation may perform examinations of corporate interests for internal purposes only. Reports to outsiders cannot indicate he is a CPA and must be on the corporate letterhead.

3. A CPA cannot accept the audit opinion issued by the controller of the client who is also a CPA.

4. A CPA may express an opinion on a prior fiscal year in which he prepared unaudited financial statements provided he can satisfy himself as to their fairness and comply with GAAS.

5. Unaudited interim reports issued by clients are considered associated with a CPA if the CPA's name is listed anywhere on or in the report.

6. A practicing CPA who prepares statements for a private club of which he is treasurer may issue the statements on CPA letterhead with proper disclaimer per Section 504.
7. A CPA who is in partnership with non-CPAs may sign the report with the firm name, his own name and indicate "certified public accountant."
8. A CPA selecting subcontractors for MAS engagements are obligated to select subcontractors on the basis of professional qualifications, technical skills, etc.
9. A CPA should be in a position to supervise and evaluate work of a specialist in his employ.

3)   "Responsibilities to clients. A certified public accountant should be fair and candid with his clients and serve them to the best of his ability, with professional concern for their best interests, consistent with his responsibilities to the public."
POINTS: (1) A CPA should hold in confidence information concerning the client's affairs; this, however, does not permit a CPA to acquiesce to client's unwillingness to make necessary disclosures in financial statements. (2) A CPA cannot accept a commission from a vendor for recommending his product or service to a client.

301 Confidential Client Information

a)   CPA shall not disclose confidential client data except with consent of client, except in "b" below

b)   Rule shall not preclude

    1]   Compliance with rules 202 and 203
    2]   Compliance with enforceable subpoena
    3]   Voluntary quality review under AICPA authorization
    4]   Responding to AICPA Trial Board or to an investigative body of a state CPA society

301 Interpretation

a)   Confidential relationship rule cannot prohibit CPA from carrying out his/her responsibility per GAAS

302 Contingent Fees[+]

a)   CPA shall not offer services on a basis contingent with findings, but

    1]   Fees may vary with the complexity of services rendered
    2]   Fees may be fixed by courts
    3]   In tax matters, findings of government agencies may determine fees
NOTE: Enforcement of Rule 302 is currently suspended, pending the results of a ballot of AICPA members.

Responsibilities to Clients Ethics Rulings

1. A member may utilize outside computer services to process tax returns as long as there is no release of confidential information.
2. With client permission, a CPA may provide P&L percentages to a trade association.
3. A CPA withdrawing from a tax engagement due to irregularities on the client's return should urge successor CPA to have client grant permission to reveal reasons for withdrawal.
4. A CPA who had audited an international union could not be retained by local unions bringing suit against the international union.
5. A CPA may use a records retention agency to store client records as long as confidentiality is maintained.
6. A CPA may be engaged by a municipality to verify taxpayer's books and records for the purpose of assessing property tax. The CPA must maintain confidentiality.

7. CPAs and their employees should not reveal the names of the CPA's non-public clients without client permission.

8. CPAs should not base their fee for work on a bond issue as a percentage of the total amount of the issue.

9. A CPA's fees for work on acquisitions of other companies should be based upon the services rendered and not the percentage of the acquisition price.

10. Expert witness fees may not be based upon the amount awarded.

11. Fees based upon the amount of mortgage commitments are contingent fees and a violation of Rule 302.

12. A fee based on taxes saved in preparing a return is a violation of Rule 302. There is a proper tax liability and no basis for tax savings.

13. Contingent fees for accounting services associated with a fire adjuster are not permitted.

14. A CPA has a responsibility to honor confidential relationships with non-clients. Accordingly, CPAs may have to withdraw from MAS engagements where the client will not permit the CPA to make recommendations without disclosing confidential information about other clients or non-clients.

15. If the CPA has conducted a similar MAS study with a negative outcome, the CPA should advise potential clients of the previous problems providing that earlier confidential relationships are not disclosed. If the earlier confidential relationship may be disclosed (through client knowledge of other clients), the CPA should seek approval from the first client.

4) "Responsibilities to colleagues. A certified public accountant should conduct himself in a manner which will promote cooperation and good relations among members of the profession."
POINTS: (1) Professional courtesy and friendship can never excuse lack of complete candor if CPA testifying as expert witness in court.
(2) It is desirable in all situations and required in some situations before accepting an engagement to consult with accountant already serving the client.

All rules, interpretations, and rulings are currently suspended.

5) "Other responsibilities and practices. A certified public accountant should conduct himself in a manner which will enhance the stature of the profession and its ability to serve the public."
POINTS: (1) Fees may be based on responsibility assumed, time, manpower and skills required, value of service to client, customary charges of colleagues, and other considerations. (2) While a CPA may refer a prospective client to another CPA, he may not receive a "forwarding fee" for the service.

501 Acts Discreditable

a) A CPA shall not commit a discreditable act

   1] E.g., violation of 102

501 Interpretations

a) Retention of client records after they are requested by client is a discreditable act

   1] E.g., cash disbursement spread sheets, adjusting journal entries, etc.
   2] CPA may keep a copy for files

b) Discrimination on basis of race, color, religion, sex, age, or national origin is discreditable to the profession

    c) In audits of governmental grants, governmental units, or other re-
cipients of governmental monies, failure to follow any required
governmental standards, procedures, etc. (in addition to generally
accepted auditing standards) is an act discreditable to the profession

502 Advertising and Solicitation

    a) CPA shall not seek clients by false, misleading, or deceptive ad-
vertising or solicitation

502 Interpretations

    a) Advertising should be in good taste and dignified

        1] No restrictions on type, media, frequency, art work, etc.
        2] May include names, addresses, telephone numbers, number of
partners, office hours, and date firm was established

            a] Services offered and fees (hourly and fixed)
            b] Educational and professional attainments
            c] Statements of position regarding the practice of accounting
or public interest topics

    b) False, misleading, and deceptive advertising is prohibited, includ-
ing those that

        1] Create false or unjustifiable expectations
        2] Imply the ability to influence the courts, regulatory agencies,
etc.
        3] Are self-laudatory, nonverifiable statements
        4] Nonverifiable comparisons with other CPAs
        5] Contain testimonials or endorsements
        6] Contain representation that professional services will be per-
formed for a stated fee, estimated fee, or fee range when it is
likely fees will be substantially increased
        7] Contain representations likely to be misunderstood by a reason-
able person

    c) Deleted due to revision of rule 502
    d) CPAs may render services to clients of third parties as long as all
promotion efforts were within the Code

503 Commissions

    a) CPA shall not pay or accept commissions to obtain or to refer
clients

        1] Rule does not apply to purchase and sale of practices

503 Interpretation

    a) Payment of commissions to obtain a client is prohibited to avoid a
client's paying fees without commensurate services

        1] Fees for professional services (not commissions) may be paid to
referring CPA

504 Incompatible Occupations[+]

    a) CPA shall not concurrently engage in occupations which create a con-
flict of interest

505 Form of Practice and Name

a) CPA may practice as

1] Proprietorship
2] Partnership
3] Professional corporation

b) CPA shall not practice under a firm name that

1] Includes a fictitious name
2] Includes specialization
3] Is misleading about form of organization

a] An individual may practice in the name of a former partner-ship for up to 2 years (applies when all other partners have died or withdrawn)

c) Firm may not designate itself as members of AICPA unless all part-ners or shareholders are members

505 Interpretations

a) CPA may have an interest in a commercial corporation performing services similar to public accounting if

1] Interest is not material to corporation's net worth
2] Relation to corporation is that of an investor

b) CPAs holding out to the public as being CPAs or public accountants and who participate in the operation of a separate business that offers services rendered by public accountants are required to ob-serve all of the Rules of Conduct in the operation of the business

Other Responsibilities Ethics Rulings

Due to rescinding the advertising and solicitation pro-hibition, the majority of the ethics rulings have been suspended.

2. A CPA may permit a bank to collect notes issued by a client in payment of fees.

3. A CPA employed by a firm with non-CPA prac-titioners must comply with the rules of conduct. If a partner of such a firm is a CPA, the CPA is responsible for all persons associated with the firm to comply with the rules of conduct.

33. A CPA who is a course instructor has the re-sponsibility to determine that the advertising materials promoting the course are within the bounds of rule 502.

38. A CPA who is controller of a bank may place his CPA title on bank stationery and in paid advertisements listing the officers and directors of the bank.

78. CPAs who are also attorneys may so indicate on their letterhead.

82. A CPA may write a financial management newsletter (being advertised for sale) with his name featured prominently.

86. A CPA may be engaged to verify financial or statistical facts used in a client's adver-tising and the CPA's name may be used in such advertising.

108. CPAs interviewed by the press should observe the code of professional conduct and not pro-vide the press with any information for publi-cation that the CPA could not publish himself.

109. A CPA who arranges for clients to purchase supplies at a discount may not accept a com-mission from a supplier but may only accept payment for common effort on behalf of the clients purchasing the supplies.

110. A CPA may represent a computer tax service providing services only to tax practitioners (not clients) and receive a fee for each tax return processed within his franchise area.

111. A CPA may buy a bookkeeping practice based on a percentage of fees received over a three-year period.

112. A CPA cannot pay a management specialist to refer potential clients to him.

113. A CPA may not refer potential life insurance customers to a spouse who is a life insurance agent.

114. A CPA may pay bonuses or otherwise share profits to employees from professional account-ing work where practice development is a fac-tor in determining bonus or profit sharing.

115. A CPA firm may conduct actuarial and administrative services for a client as a separate partnership.

117. A CPA may be a director of a consumer credit company if he is not the auditor.

127. A CPA may not both work for the state controller and practice public accounting as most businesses are subject to some form of state control.

132. A non-CPA partner to a CPA who specializes in taxes should not accept a position as a public member of a board of tax appeals for a recently established municipal income tax ordinance.

134. CPAs who share offices, employees, etc., may not indicate a partnership exists unless a partnership agreement *is* in effect.

135. CPA firms which are members of an association cannot use letterhead that indicates a partnership rather than an association.

136. Where a firm consisting of a CPA and a non-CPA is dissolved, and an audit is continued to be serviced by both, the audit opinion should be signed by both individuals, such that a partnership is not indicated.

137. The designation "non-proprietary partner" should not be used to describe personnel as it may be misleading.

138. A CPA may be a partner of a firm of public accountants when all other personnel are not certified, and at the same time practice separately as a CPA.

139. A CPA in practice with a public accountant would have to conform to the code of ethics, and would not be permitted to represent itself as a partnership of CPAs.

140. A partnership practicing under the name of the managing partner who is seeking election to high office may continue to use the managing partner's name plus "and Company" if the managing partner is elected and withdraws from the partnership.

141. A CPA in partnership with a non-CPA is ethically responsible for all acts of the partnership and those of the non-CPA partner.

144. A CPA firm may use an established firm name in a different state even though there is a difference in the roster of partners.

145. Newly merged CPA firms may practice under a title which includes the name of a previously retired partner from one of the firms.

146. CPA firms may not designate themselves as Members of the American Institute of Certified Public Accountants unless all their partners or shareholders are members of the AICPA.

147. A sole proprietor may not use in his firm title the designation "and Company" or "and Associates."

148. Two CPAs may use in their firm title the designations "and Company" or "and Associates."

155. A CPA firm in partnership with a computer corporation providing services only for the clients of the CPA firm (not directly to the public) would not be a violation of the Code.

156. A CPA may assist a corporation in developing a tabulating service to be offered to the public if he has no financial interest in the corporation and the CPA is not publicly connected with the tabulating service.

158. A CPA's association with a firm providing data processing services should be limited to that of a consultant. The CPA should not be an officer or shareholder.

159. A CPA firm may buy computer time at a discount from another CPA firm and bill it to his clients at regular rates.

167. A CPA should not recommend investments in tax-sheltered investments and receive a commission on the sale of such investments.

175. CPAs serving as bank directors should carefully consider the effect of their role as bank director with problems concerning:
1. Confidential client information
2. Conflict of interest (between bank and client)
3. Independence (after bank grants material loan to client)
4. Solicitation (using directorship to obtain clients)

176. A CPA firm's name, logo, etc., may be imprinted on newsletters and similar publications if the outside author or publisher is clearly indicated.

177. Performing centralized billing services for a doctor is a public accounting service and must be conducted in accordance with the code.

178. Unless a conflict of interest exists, simultaneous operation of an accounting practice and some other business or occupation does not violate the code.

179. Member firms of an association (or group) of separate CPA firms may not practice public accounting under the association's (group's) name.

180. A CPA in public practice must conduct a separate estate planning business in accordance with the Rules of Conduct.

Professional Corporation Characteristics (per AICPA council)

1. Name of firm shall contain only names of present and former shareholders
2. Purpose shall not be to provide services incompatible with CPA practice
3. Ownership shall be by persons eligible to practice public accounting
4. Transfer of shares must be made from shareholder who becomes ineligible to practice
5. To extent possible, all directors and officers shall be CPAs
6. Conduct of shareholders and employees shall be in accordance with AICPA standards
7. Liability of shareholders shall be jointly and severally except where adequate professional liability insurance is carried or capitalization is maintained

    a. $50,000 per shareholder and professional employee
    b. To a maximum of $2,000,000

B. Control of the Audit

1. Planning and Supervision (AU 310, 311, 312, and 315).

    a. Overall Planning Considerations. The first standard of fieldwork requires that work be adequately planned and supervised. The nature, extent, and timing of audit planning varies with the (1) size and complexity of the client, (2) the auditor's experience with the entity, and (3) the auditor's knowledge of the entity's business. Also, when a client has computer operations, the following need to be considered:

    1) Extent of usage
    2) Complexity of usage
    3) Organization structure of computer operations
    4) Availability of data
    5) Potential for using computer-assisted audit techniques

The auditor must be aware that specialized computer skills (either by staff or by outside consultants) may be needed to audit a firm with a computer system.

    Section 312 states that in planning an auditor must determine both a preliminary measure of materiality and an acceptable level of audit risk. The materiality measure is to be based on the definition in SFAC 2 which suggests that a material error is one which makes it probable that the judgment of a reasonable person relying on the information would have been changed or influenced.

    Audit risk is "the risk that the auditor may unknowingly fail to appropriately modify his opinion on financial statements that are materially misstated." At the overall financial statement level, audit risk is the chance that a material error exists and has been missed by the auditor. At the individual account-balance level,

audit risk is composed of three components--inherent risk, control risk, and detection risk.

Inherent risk refers to the likelihood of a material error occurring in an account, assuming no related internal accounting controls. This risk could be low,
for example, for petty cash when it is known that only a very limited amount was
spent during the year; it could be high for a general cash account with millions of
dollars of expenditures. To assess this risk the auditor will perform overall review techniques and will use his/her overall auditing knowledge.

Control risk is the risk that a material error will not be prevented or detected
on a timely basis by the system of internal accounting control. The auditor may
assess this risk through overall review techniques, internal control review techniques (e.g., questionnaires, flowcharts, etc.), and compliance tests.

Detection risk is the risk that an auditor's procedures will lead him/her to
conclude that a material error does not exist in an account balance when in fact
such an error does exist. The auditor's substantive tests are primarily relied upon
to control detection risk.

Note that detection risk is related to the effectiveness of the auditor's procedures, while inherent and control risk are elements of the client's accounting
system. When an auditor believes that an account has a high level of inherent
and/or control risk, detection risk should be set at a relatively low level. On the
other hand, a low level of inherent and control risk (as evidenced by the auditor's
evaluation and subsequent compliance testing) will justify allowing a higher
detection risk.

Several other considerations relating to materiality and audit risk at the
planning stage are important. First, the two concepts vary inversely--as the materiality level increases, the potential audit risk decreases. Second, both materiality and audit risk may be evaluated either quantitatively or nonquantitatively.
Third, if individual materiality levels are determined for each financial statement,
the smallest level so estimated should be used for audit planning purposes.

AU 311 presents additional planning assistance. We may divide the section's
overall planning considerations as follows:

Client considerations: 1. Type of business and industry
                          2. Accounting policies and procedures
                          3. Conditions requiring extension of audit procedures
                              (e.g., related party transactions)
                          4. Items likely to need adjustment

Audit considerations: 1. Anticipated internal accounting control reliance
                          2. Preliminary judgment about materiality levels
                          3. Reports to be issued

Additionally, various audit procedures are suggested at the audit planning stage.
We may categorize them as:

Review techniques:
1. Correspondence, prior workpaper, statement, etc.
2. Current interim statements
3. Authoritative (especially new) pronouncements
4. Effect of nonaudit services which have been performed

Detailed planning
techniques:
1. Need for consultants, specialists, internal auditors, etc.
2. Establish timing of audit work
3. Coordinate staff requirements

Client involvement:
1. Inquire about current developments
2. Discuss type, scope, timing, etc.
3. Coordinate client assistance in data collection

Note also that a written audit program is to be developed and used for the audit.

   b. Supervision Considerations (AU 311). Supervision includes instructing assistants, being informed on significant problems, reviewing audit work, and dealing
with differences of opinion among audit personnel. The complexity of the audit and
qualifications of audit assistants affect the degree of supervision needed. Procedures should be established for documenting any disagreements of opinions among
staff personnel; the basis for resolution of such disagreements should be documented.

   c. Communications Between Predecessor and Successor Auditors (AU 315). When a
potential new client has been served by another auditor in the past, the successor
auditor should, before accepting the engagement, obtain permission from the potential client to communicate with the predecessor auditor. The successor should question the predecessor on matters concerning the integrity of management, any disagreements, and the reasons for the change in auditors. The predecessor is normally
to respond promptly and fully (unusual circumstances such as impending litigation
may, however, cause a limited reply). If the engagement is accepted by the success-
or, other inquiries such as a review of the predecessor's work papers may be performed by the successor. Again, conditions such as litigation may preclude the predecessor from cooperating and may thus cause the successor to perform additional
audit procedures.

   d. Timing of Audit Procedures (AU 310). Many audit tests can be conducted at
almost any time during the year. For example, compliance testing may be performed
at an interim period with subsequent updating of tests through year end.

   A properly conducted audit will reflect the fact that the performance of certain
procedures needs to be synchronized. For example, the simultaneous examination of

cash, securities, and bank loans is desirable because these assets are readily negotiable.

2. Quality Control (QC 10-300).

    a. Overview. The nine quality control standards (outlined at the end of this
section) apply to the audit practice of all firms. As indicated earlier, while the
generally accepted auditing standards and the Code are primarily directed at the
individual practitioner level, the quality control standards apply to the CPA firm
itself.

    A major function of these quality control standards is to serve as the appro-
priate criteria for evaluation for independent peer reviews. In a peer review,
one's peers (other CPAs) evaluate the quality of the firm's audit work. A peer
review may be performed by:

        1) Another CPA firm
        2) An AICPA approved peer review commmittee
        3) A state society of CPA's approved peer review committee

    For quality control purposes the AICPA has also formed a "Division for CPA
Firms" which has two sections--the SEC Practice Section and the Private Companies
Practice Section. While membership in either of these sections is voluntary, member
firms of either section are required to submit to peer reviews (once every three
years) and may be penalized by the AICPA for work deemed to be substandard.

    The peer review process is new and is still being refined as more experience is
gained. The overall objective of the process is to help assure the performance of
the attestation function in a socially desirable manner. Possible benefits of peer
review include:

        1) Prevention of poor audit procedures due to the awareness of the firm's
            personnel regarding subsequent peer review

        2) Detection of poor audit procedures

        3) The reviewing firm may learn from the process

        4) Self-regulation by the profession may be more cost effective than the
            alternative of governmental regulation

Possible limitations of peer review are:

        1) It is costly to the reviewed firm and to the public to whom some portion
            of the cost is undoubtedly passed

        2) In cases where the roles of reviewer and reviewee switch, a lack of per-
            ceived and/or actual independence may result

        3) While it may be possible to determine whether a firm has followed its
            quality control standards, evaluating the actual adequacy of an audit
            (presumably the "bottom line" in peer reviewing) is difficult

4) The effectiveness of the sanctioning (penalization) process remains largely untested

To this point there have been few questions on quality control (the frequency analysis presented earlier in this chapter indicates only 1 or 2 multiple choice questions per exam). For multiple choice questions be familiar not only with the names of the nine standards but also with what they imply (e.g., Supervision policies provide assurance that work performed meets the firm's standards of quality). Essay questions on the nine quality control standards and/or on peer review seem likely in the future.

b. Outline of Quality Control Standards.

1) A system of quality control standards is required to assure the firm is providing professional services that comply with professional standards

a) Includes organization structure, policies and procedures
b) Should be appropriate in relation to the firm's

1] Size
2] Degree of operating autonomy within firm
3] Nature of practice
4] Organization structure
5] Other appropriate cost-benefit considerations

c) The system has inherent limitations

1] E.g., variance in individual performances, understanding of professional requirements, etc.

2) Quality control standards apply to auditing and accounting and review services

a) May be applied to other areas, e.g., MAS, tax, etc.
b) Should apply to work done by foreign offices and domestic affiliates

3) A firm shall consider each of the following interrelated elements of quality control in establishing quality control policies and procedures (quoted from SQCS #1)

a) Independence. "Policies and procedures should be established to provide the firm with reasonable assurance that persons at all organizational levels maintain independence to the extent required by the rules of conduct of the AICPA."

b) Assigning Personnel to Engagements. "Policies and procedures for assigning personnel to engagements should be established to provide the firm with reasonable assurance that work will be performed by persons having the degree of technical training and proficiency required in the circumstances."

c) Consultation. "Policies and procedures for consultation should be established to provide the firm with reasonable assurance that personnel will seek assistance, to the extent required, from persons having appropriate levels of knowledge, competence, judgment, and authority."

    d) <u>Supervision</u>. "Policies and procedures for the conduct and super-
vision of work at all organizational levels should be established
to provide the firm with reasonable assurance that the work performed meets the firm's standards of quality."

    e) <u>Hiring</u>. "Policies and procedures for hiring should be established
to provide the firm with reasonable assurance that those employed
possess the appropriate characteristics to enable them to perform
competently."

    f) <u>Professional Development</u>. "Policies and procedures for professional
development should be established to provide the firm with reasonable assurance that personnel will have the knowledge required to
enable them to fulfill responsibilities assigned."

    g) <u>Advancement</u>. "Policies and procedures for advancing personnel
should be established to provide the firm with reasonable assurance
that those selected for advancement will have the qualifications
necessary for fulfillment of the responsibilities they will be
called on to assume."

    h) <u>Acceptance and Continuance of Clients</u>. "Policies and procedures
should be established for deciding whether to accept or continue a
client in order to minimize the likelihood of association with a
client whose management lacks integrity."

    i) <u>Inspection</u>. "Policies and procedures for inspection should be
established to provide the firm with reasonable assurance that the
procedures relating to the other elements of quality control are
being effectively applied."

4) Responsibility for a quality control system shall be assigned to individuals to assure effective implementation based on

    a) Competence of individuals
    b) Authority delegated
    c) Extent of supervision over them

5) Quality control policies and procedures shall be communicated to the
firm's personnel

    a) Normally in writing
    b) Documentation expected to be more extensive in larger and multi-
office firms

6) The quality control system shall be monitored on a timely basis

    a) Monitoring includes the quality control element of inspection
    b) To assure effectiveness of the system
    c) Size, structure, and nature of practice determine monitoring func-
tion
    d) Includes timely modification of policies and procedures for

        1] New authoritative pronouncements
        2] Expansion of practice
        3] Opening of new offices, mergers, etc.

C. Other Responsibilities

1. Detection of Errors or Irregularities (AU 327). Review this section (and the outline) carefully as it is heavily examined. Distinguish between an error (an unintentional mistake such as a math error) and an irregularity (an intentional distortion such as fraud). Know that while an audit will not provide absolute assurance of detection of errors or irregularities, an auditor must plan his/her examination to search for such situations. When an auditor discovers such a situation, which leads him/her to believe that material errors or irregularities might exist, s/he should discuss further investigation with an appropriate level of management at least one level above those involved. Examination of such matters may, at management's discretion, be made either by the auditor or by management (with subsequent auditor review).

2. Illegal Acts by Clients (AU 328). This section is also heavily examined. Note that the further removed an item is from the recorded transactions (e.g., an unrecorded bank account in a foreign country in which the firm does no other business is far removed) the less likely it is that an auditor will discover the illegal act. In determining the materiality of an illegal act, consider the loss contingency aspect (SFAS 5) as well as the actual illegal payment (or other illegal occurrence). When a client refuses to give appropriate consideration to handling an illegal act (even an immaterial one), the auditor should consider withdrawing from the engagement. Notifying parties other than management and the board of directors of illegal acts is, however, the responsibility of management.

3. Responsibilities in Management Advisory Services.
    a. Overview. In 1982 a new series of pronouncements on management advisory services, Statements on Standards for Management Advisory Services (SSMAS), became effective. The old series, Statements on Management Advisory Services, while not enforceable, may in part be incorporated into future MAS standards.
    Know that SSMAS 1 distinguishes between a MAS consultation (usually oral and based on the CPA's existing personal knowledge--see "3.c." of the following outline) and a MAS engagement (a more thorough study--see "3.b." of outline). Also, for an audit client, a CPA shall not assume a role of management or any positions that might impair objectivity.

b. Outline of SSMAS 1 (MS 11) Definitions and Standards for MAS Practice.

   1) Management advisory services, in general

      a) Consist of advice and assistance on organization, personnel, planning, operations, controls, etc.

      b) Are often closely related to auditing, tax, and review services of CPAs

   2) Purpose of this series of statements is to

      a) Provide compliance guidance for Rule 201 of the AICPA Rules of Conduct

         1] Previous statements on MAS were not enforceable under Rule 201

         2] Previous statements may be consulted until new standards are issued

      b) Provide other appropriate standards under Rule 204 of the AICPA Rules of Conduct

   3) Definitions

      a) Management advisory services (MAS) - advice and technical assistance to help the client improve use of capabilities and resources

      b) MAS engagement - MAS form where an analytical approach is applied to a study or project

      c) MAS consultation - MAS form based on existing personal knowledge about the client, the circumstances, the technical matters involved, and the mutual intent of the parties

         1] Usually oral advice given in a short time frame

         2] Advice may be definitive (existing knowledge is adequate) or qualified (cost, time, scope or other limitations are present)

      d) MAS practitioner - any member of AICPA in public practice while performing a MAS service for a client

         1] Also any individual carrying out MAS for a client on behalf of an AICPA member

   4) Standards for MAS Practice

      a) General standards for both MAS engagements and MAS consultations per Rule 201

         1] Professional competence, due care, planning and supervision, sufficient relevant data and association with forecasts

      b) Technical standards applying to MAS engagements only, per Rule 204

         1] For an audit client, a practitioner shall not assume role of management or any positions that might impair objectivity

         2] An understanding (oral or written) with client should determine nature, scope, and limitations of services to be performed

         3] Potential benefits should not be explicitly or implicitly guaranteed and should be viewed objectively

            a] Identify estimates, disclose support for quantifications and describe limitations

   4] Significant information, limitations, qualifications, or reser-
      vations should be communicated to the client orally or in
      writing

c. Outline of SSMAS 2 (MS 12) MAS Engagements.

   1) Statement provides guidance on application of standards in SSMAS 1

      a) Management Advisory Services (MAS) are

         1] Engagements or
         2] Consultations
         3] Not recommendations and comments as direct result of observa-
            tions during audit compilations or review

   2) Nature of MAS engagements

      a) Involve gathering and analyzing appropriate information in order
         to develop conclusions and recommendations

         1] Information includes facts about client operating results,
            financial conditions, and systems and procedures

      b) Engagements vary in area of staffing requirements

         1] Variables include size, timing, complexity, and technical skills
         2] Some require joint participation including client personnel and
            practitioner

      c) Client may inquire concerning MAS matter unrelated to engagement

         1] Practitioner's response may fall within definition of MAS con-
            sultation depending on nature of inquiry and response
         2] If so MAS consultation standards apply

   3) Professional competence in MAS engagements

      a) Professional competence includes ability to

         1] Identify and define client needs
         2] Select and supervise staff
         3] Select and apply analytical process
         4] Apply relevant technical knowledge
         5] Effectively communicate and assist in implementation of recom-
            mendations

      b) Evaluating competence for engagement

         1] Assess combined abilities, education, and experience of staff
            (or other individuals retained for this engagement) and client
            personnel committed to this project
         2] Compare diverse skills needed with abilities available

   4) Planning and supervision of MAS engagements

      a) Practitioner should plan and supervise engagement in order to pro-
         vide reasonable assurance that work is in accordance with

         1] Understanding with client
         2] Professional standards (SSMASs and AICPA Rules of Conduct)

      b) If staff is needed, determine that sufficient number of skilled
         individuals are available

    c) Plan should be developed that

        1] Guides conduct, supervision, control, and completion of engagement
        2] Can be modified as necessary during engagement
        3] Includes consideration of approach and tasks required for completion

    d) Level of documentation and amount of supervision

        1] Is determined by professional judgment
        2] Criteria for judgment include skills of individuals involved and duration and complexity of engagement

    e) Direction of MAS engagement requires competence to

        1] Supervise personnel
        2] Evaluate quality and completeness of work performed
        3] Accept responsibility for successful completion of engagement

5) Sufficient relevant data

    a) Should be obtained in order to complete engagement in manner consistent with client understanding

        1] May be obtained by interview, observation, computation, research, analysis, and review of client documents

        2] Nature and quantity of information necessary will vary with scope and circumstances of engagement

            a] Normally will be information sufficient to analyze courses of action and support conclusions and recommendations

    b) Practitioner should exercise professional judgment in determining nature and quantity of information

        1] Practitioner should consider

            a] Objectives, nature, and scope of engagement
            b] Intended use of results

        2] In forming conclusions, source, reliability and completeness of data should be considered

6) Role of practitioner in MAS engagement

    a) Objective advisor

        1] Should not assume role of management
        2] Roles of all parties should be clearly defined in understanding with client

    b) Action on engagement results requires management approval

        1] Engagement should be structured to provide for review and approval of engagement findings, conclusions, recommendations, and other results

7) Client understanding in MAS engagements

    a) In reaching understanding with client, practitioner should consider

        1] Objectives and scope of engagement including nature of services to be performed

        2] Relationships, roles, and responsibilities of practitioner, client, and third parties
        3] Planned engagement approach, major activities and, where appropriate, methods to be used
        4] Means of communication for engagement status and results
        5] Work schedule and fee arrangements

    b) Nature and extent of documentation

        1] Determined by professional judgment
        2] Written documentation may be accepted proposal letter, confirmation letter, engagement arrangement letter, contract, or file memorandum
        3] Client confidentiality or other circumstances may make written documentation inappropriate

    c) Practitioner should modify client understanding, if circumstances change nature, scope or limitations of services to be performed

8) Client benefit in MAS engagements

    a) Practitioner should obtain understanding of possible benefit, tangible, and intangible, client wishes to achieve
    b) Results of engagement

        1] Should not be guaranteed either implicitly or explicitly
        2] Ultimately dependent on

            a] Effectiveness of client management in implementing recommendations
            b] Client management's ability to address changes and uncertainty

        3] Reservations concerning achievability of anticipated benefits should be expressed

    c) Potential benefits which are quantified

        1] Should be described as estimates with underlying support shown
        2] If estimated benefits or costs change significantly, client should be informed

9) Communication of results in MAS engagements

    a) Principal findings, results, conclusions, and findings should be reported

        1] Include underlying assumptions and major facts
        2] Communicate together with limitations, reservations, and other qualifications

    b) Interim client communications

        1] Desirable during lengthy complex engagements
        2] Encourage client involvement and decision making
        3] Keep client informed of results and progress

    c) Final reports may be oral or written depending on

        1] Understanding with client and degree with which results were provided in progress reports

           2] Intended use of results and sensitivity of material
           3] Need for a formal record

      d) When communicated orally, file memorandum concerning results and documentation provided should be considered

d. <u>Outline of SSMAS 3 (MS 13) MAS Consultations.</u>

  1) Statement provides guidance on

      a) Application of general standards of SSMAS 1 to MAS Consultations
      b) Establishment of technical standards for MAS consultations

  2) Nature of MAS consultations

      a) Situations in which MAS consultations occur

           1] Concurrent with other professional services or independently
           2] Topics may be one decision or continuing relation on wide variety of matters
           3] Interaction may be via telephone, nonbusiness setting, periodic meetings, or formal writings

      b) MAS consultations may be significant portion of services to clients

           1] Implicit and explicit understandings between client and practitioner form basis for client reliance on professional advice
           2] Consultation usually is based on practitioner's existing personal knowledge of technical matters and of client's financial, business, and personal affairs
           3] Response to inquiry may be immediate or after reference to client's file, technical information, and consideration of various alternatives

      c) MAS consultations may take form of

           1] Explicit recommendation
           2] Suggestion on a course of action or method of inquiry
           3] Limited analysis of options or pros and cons of alternative actions
           4] Technical research on a specific matter

  3) Due professional care in MAS consultations should provide for

      a) Clear communication of advice given
      b) Careful delineation of appropriate degree of reliance in light of qualifications that apply to advice

  4) Planning and supervision in MAS consultations

      a) Nature and extent of planning

           1] Will vary with complexity of entity and inquiry
           2] Will be mental process that consists of

               a] Understanding client inquiry and nature of service requested
               b] Considering subject of inquiry and knowledge of entity
               c] Determining steps necessary to respond

      b) Supervision of staff, if any, used will depend upon their qualifications and experience

5) Sufficient relevant data in MAS consultation

   a) Information provided by client to practitioner often is not veri-
      fied, corroborated or reviewed

      1] In these cases, inform client that advice given is dependent on
         accuracy and completeness of client information

   b) Relevance of information should be considered

      1] Is information sufficient to provide definite response
      2] If not, can a qualified response be given, or
      3] Is further study or analysis required to formulate response

6) Technical standards for MAS consultations (established under rule 204 of
   AICPA Rules of Conduct)

   a) Role of MAS practitioner--practitioner should not assume role of
      management or any positions that might impair objectivity

   b) Understanding with client--oral or written understanding should be
      reached with client outlining nature, scope, and limitations of con-
      sultation to be performed

   c) Client benefits--major consideration in consultations

      1] Benefits should be viewed objectively
      2] Client should be notified of any reservation concerning benefits
      3] No guarantees (explicit or implicit) should be given
      4] Estimates of quantifiable results should be identified as such,
         and support for them should be disclosed

   d) Communication of results--significant information and results should
      be disclosed with any limitations or reservations

      1] Written or oral communication may be used

7) Role of practitioner in MAS consultations

   a) General business adviser
   b) Practitioner must recognize and minimize possibility client might
      erroneously conclude practitioner has

      1] Assumed responsibility for decision
      2] Guaranteed benefits, either implicitly or explicitly
      3] Predicated advice on full consideration of all relevant informa-
         tion

8) Client understanding and communication of results in MAS consultations

   a) Inquiry, understanding, and response may take place in one conversa-
      tion
   b) Either party may presume that other has knowledge and understanding
      of pertinent matters not communicated

   c) Practitioner should recognize possibility of misunderstanding and
      take reasonable steps to prevent it by considering

      1] Specific or general nature of advice sought
      2] Financial and operational significance of advice given
      3] Limitations, lack of certainty, and incompleteness of informa-
         tion
      4] Complexity of inquiry, response, and qualifications

d) Nature and form of communication with client are matters of professional judgment

   1] May be oral or written as circumstances dictate is appropriate

4. Responsibilities in Tax Practice.

a. <u>Overview.</u> On most exams one or two multiple choice questions deal with issues raised in the Statements on Responsibilities in Tax Practice. Each of the Statements raises one major issue (e.g., how estimates are to be handled). Be aware that the standards related to the signature of a preparer and of a reviewer (TX 111 and TX 121) have been deleted. Read the following remaining outlines. You will be able to grasp the nature of the statements in a short period of time, and any questions on the exam will probably be quite easy to answer.

b. <u>Outline of Tax Statements.</u>

<u>Introduction (TX 101)</u>

1) Series of statements setting good standards of tax practice which outline CPA's responsibility to

   a) His client
   b) The government
   c) His profession

2) Objectives

   a) Identify and develop standards of responsibility in tax practices
   b) Encourage increased understanding of CPA's responsibilities by tax authorities
   c) To foster increased public compliance with and confidence in our tax system

3) Primary effect is educational

   a) Authority depends on general acceptability

<u>Signature of Preparer (TX 111)--Deleted</u>

<u>Signature of Reviewer: Assumption of Preparer's Responsibility (TX 121)--</u>
<u>Deleted</u>

<u>Answers to Questions on Returns (TX 131)</u>

1) CPA may sign return if he is satisfied that a reasonable effort has been made to provide appropriate answers

   a) Reason for unanswered question should be stated
   b) Possibility that an answer may be disadvantageous to client does not justify omission

2) CPA should be satisfied that a reasonable effort has been made to answer questions because

   a) The question may bear on the tax liability
   b) It is inconsistent with the CPA's professional stature to sign an incomplete return

3) Reasonable grounds may exist for omitting an answer, e.g.,

    a) Data is not readily available and is not significant to the tax liability

    b) May be significant but:

       1] Genuine uncertainty exists
       2] Not reliable enough to report

    c) Answer is voluminous but available at client offices

4) When reasonable grounds exist, they should be explained

Recognition of Prior Year Administrative Proceedings (TX 141)

1) Can a CPA sign a return in which an item is treated differently from a similar item in a prior administrative proceeding wherein the client executed a waiver?

    a) I.e., the taxpayer accepted the IRS finding and the effect thereof, e.g., assessment, etc.

    b) Administrative proceeding

       1] Exam by revenue agent
       2] District conference
       3] Appellate conference

2) CPA _may_ sign such a return if justified by the facts including

    a) Client's prior waiver may have been based on a lack of substantiation that exists now

    b) Client may have yielded even though reasonable support existed for his position

    c) Climate for client's position may have changed, e.g., new court decisions

3) The departure from the administrative proceeding waiver need not be disclosed

Use of Estimates (TX 151)

1) CPA may prepare tax returns using estimates if

    a) Use is generally accepted or
    b) It is impracticable to obtain exact data
    c) They are presented as estimates
    d) They are not unreasonable

2) Explanation

    a) Accounting judgments require the use of estimates, e.g., useful life and salvage value

    b) Accruals. Tax regulations require a reasonable estimate if exact amounts are not known

    c) Small expenditures are not practicable to record with accuracy, e.g., gas and sales taxes

    d) Unavailable data requires estimates

3) CPA should encourage use of appropriate records to support items on the tax return

Knowledge of Error: Return Preparation (TX 161)

   1) CPA's responsibility when he learns of error in prior period's return (or failure to file a return)

      a) CPA should advise client of error and recommend client action

         1] CPA so required by IRS regulations

      b) Continuation of method requiring commissioner permission is not an error

   2) CPA may advise client orally or in writing

      a) CPA may not inform IRS without client permission
      b) If client may be charged with fraud, send client to his attorney
      c) If CPA discovers error in audit but does not prepare the tax return, CPA should send the client to the preparer

   3) If the client does not correct the error, the CPA should consider withdrawing

      a) Depends on materiality
      b) Depends on whether CPA may prepare "true, correct, and complete" returns in subsequent years

         1] Each year's return is to stand by itself as to correctness

Knowledge of Error: Administrative Proceedings (TX 171)

   1) Errors which are subject of proceedings

      a) Errors include omissions
      b) Opinion concerned with errors that result in material understatement of tax liability
      c) Not errors when reasonable support exists for client position
      d) Not errors when client continues to use method requiring permission of Commmissioner
      e) Applies whether or not CPA prepared the return containing the error
      f) Opinion does not apply when CPA is retained by attorney to assist attorney relating to attorney's client

   2) CPA should request client agreement to disclose error to IRS

      a) If client refuses, CPA may be under duty to withdraw

         1] May affect any future relationship

      b) CPA may not make disclosures to IRS without client agreement due to confidential relationship

         1] CPA withdrawal, itself, during proceedings may also be construed as a violation of confidential relationship. Indicates existence of client problems to IRS.

Advice to Clients (TX 181)

   1) CPA should seek to assure that his advice appropriately serves needs of client. The CPA should consider

      a) Importance of transaction and amounts
      b) Specific or general nature of inquiry
      c) Time available to develop and submit advice
      d) Technical complications

e) Existence of authority and precedents
f) Tax sophistication of client

2) Written communications are recommended in important unusual transactions

a) Oral advice is acceptable in usual transactions

3) CPA may wish to advise client that

a) Advice reflects professional judgment
b) Subsequent developments may affect previous advice

Procedural Aspects of Preparing Returns (TX 191)

1) CPA may rely on data provided by client

a) CPA is not required to examine or review client data

1] CPA should ask questions when data appears incomplete or incorrect

b) CPA should encourage client to provide appropriate supporting data

2) CPA should make use of prior years' returns when feasible

a) Provides information to CPA about client
b) Avoids omissions and errors

3) CPA should not modify preparer's declaration

a) CPA may attach an explanatory rider in unusual circumstances

Positions Contrary to Treasury Department or Internal Revenue Service Interpretations of the Code (TX 201)

1) Issue: whether disclosure should be made in tax returns when positions are taken contrary to IRS Code and IRS Interpretations thereof

a) Assuming reasonable support exists for the contrary position

1] No disclosure is required for contrary positions to IRS interpretations
2] Disclosure should be made for contrary positions to the Code

b) No treatment can be made contrary to either IRS interpretation or the Code without reasonable support

1] Ethics Rule 102: "A member shall not knowingly misrepresent facts, and when engaged in the practice of public accounting, including the rendering of tax and management advisory services, shall not subordinate his judgment to others. In tax practice, a member may resolve doubt in favor of his client as long as there is reasonable support for his position."
2] Preparer's declaration: that the return "to the best of (his/ her) knowledge and belief . . . is true, correct and complete."

2) Reasonable support for a position contrary to the Code (return should state position taken)

a) Examples:

1] Legal opinions as to constitutionality of specific provisions
2] Published writings of tax specialists asserting the possibility of a lack of constitutionality
3] Possible conflicts between two sections of the Code

     b) It would be difficult to find reasonable support for positions contrary to Supreme Court decisions as it is the final authority

3) Reasonable support for a position contrary to an IRS interpretation or lower court ruling (disclosure is not required)

    a) Exists when CPA concludes the contrary position can be supported by competent authority, e.g.,

        1] IRS Code
        2] Legislative history
        3] Court decisions

4) CPA may wish to make disclosure even if not required due to

    a) Fraud and negligence penalties per section 6653
    b) Six-year statutory assessment period per section 6501(e)
    c) Various preparer penalties
    d) Treasury Department regulations are promulgated per IRS Code direction, i.e., quasi-legislative (see sections 1502 and 472)

5) Tax returns are client representations

    a) Client has final responsibility for positions taken
    b) Positions taken must be with full client acquiescence

5. Continuing Professional Education and Current Topics. Past questions in these areas have, for example, related to audit committees (see Internal Control Module) and the CPA's role in performing MAS. Future questions are difficult to predict. However, essay questions on quality control and peer review (both discussed earlier in this module) as well as on internal control reports (see Internal Control Module) and on forecasts (see Audit Reports Module) may be expected. To be prepared for current topics questions you should read articles in the Journal of Accountancy dealing with current developments in the profession.

INTERNAL CONTROL

Internal control describes an entity's organization and system of procedures which provide reasonable assurance that errors or irregularities will be prevented or detected on a timely basis. Internal control allows management, owners, auditors, etc., to rely on the results reported in financial statements without verifying the correctness of every financial transaction. On page 83 of the auditing overview section, the following "Diagram of an Audit" was presented and explained:

DIAGRAM OF AN AUDIT

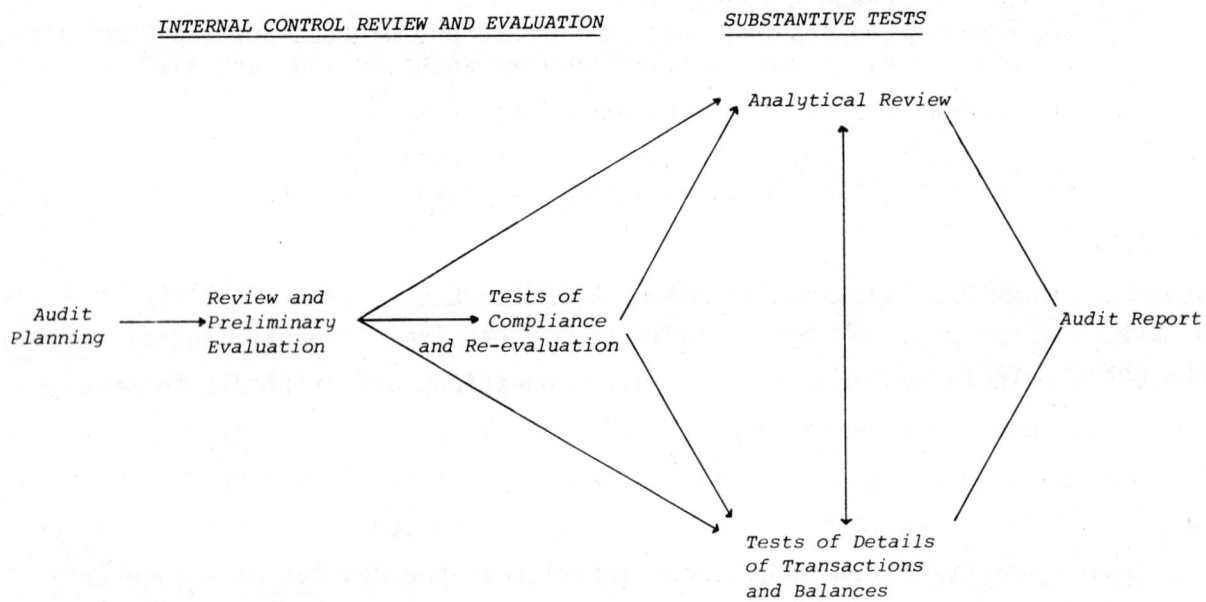

INTERNAL CONTROL REVIEW AND EVALUATION   *SUBSTANTIVE TESTS*

Kinney, William R., Jr., "Decision Theory Aspects of Internal Control System Design/Compliance, and Substantive Tests," Journal of Accounting Research (Supplement, 1975), p. 16 (adapted).

This module covers the review and evaluation of internal control and develops the relationships among internal control, compliance tests, and substantive tests.

Every CPA examination includes questions on internal control. Often an overall question presents a system or organization and requires the candidate to list weaknesses and make recommendations for improvements in internal control. Occasionally a question requires the preparation of an audit program to test compliance with prescribed internal controls. Multiple choice questions frequently require specification of a control which would, if present and operating properly, detect a stated

2

weakness or error. Objective questions also have appeared regarding organization responsibility, e.g., who should distribute payroll checks?

Study Program for the Internal Control Module

This module is organized and should be studied in the following manner:

A. Definitions and Basic Concepts

  1. Purpose of Auditor's Study and Evaluation
  2. Definitions and Basic Concepts
  3. Additional Considerations

B. Study and Evaluation of the System of Internal Control

  1. Review of Internal Control
  2. Preliminary Evaluation of Internal Control
  3. Tests of Compliance
  4. Reevaluation of Internal Control
  5. Summary

C. Accounting Cycles

  1. Sales, Receivables, and Cash Receipts
  2. Purchases, Payables, and Cash Disbursements
  3. Inventories and Production
  4. Personnel and Payroll
  5. Property, Plant, and Equipment
  6. Overall Internal Control Checklists

D. Other Considerations

  1. Required Communication of Material Weaknesses
  2. Reports on Internal Control
  3. Sampling
  4. Effects of EDP
  5. Flowcharting
  6. Effects of an Internal Audit Function

The above outline is based on the AICPA CPA Exam Content Specification Outline for Internal Control. However, since this volume has separate modules for sampling ("D.3." above) and for the effects of EDP, including flowcharting ("D.4." and "D.5." above), these topics are not covered in this module.

The following SAS sections pertain to internal control and are discussed in this module:

Section AU

320 The Auditor's Study and Evaluation of Internal Control

322 The Effect of an Internal Audit Function on the Scope of the Independent Auditor's Examination

323 Required Communication of Material Weaknesses in Internal Accounting Control

324 Special-Purpose Reports on Internal Accounting Control at Service Organizations

642 Reporting on Internal Accounting Control

A. Definitions and Basic Concepts

1. Purpose of Auditor's Study and Evaluation. The second standard of fieldwork reads:

> There is to be a proper study and evaluation of the existing internal control as a basis for reliance thereon and for the determination of the resultant extent of the tests to which auditing procedures are to be restricted.

Thus, the primary purpose of the auditor's study and evaluation of internal control is to determine whether the system may be relied upon to produce reliable financial information. If the auditor determines that internal control is strong, the scope of other audit procedures may be more restricted than in the case of weak internal control.

A secondary purpose of the study and evaluation is to provide a basis for constructive suggestions to clients concerning possible improvements in internal control.

2. Definitions and Basic Concepts. Section 320, with which you should be thoroughly familiar, contrasts accounting with administrative controls, and compliance with substantive tests. The section also outlines ten "basic concepts."

a. Accounting vs. administrative controls. Section 320 distinguishes between administrative and accounting controls and suggests that auditors should generally emphasize the latter. Administrative controls include the plan of organization, procedures, records, etc., over the process which leads to management's authorization of transactions. Accounting control is the plan of organization and the procedures and records to (a) safeguard assets and (b) safeguard the reliability of the financial records and is designed to provide reasonable assurance that:

1) Transactions are executed in accordance with management's authorization
2) Transactions are recorded to permit financial statements per GAAP and to maintain accountability over assets
3) Access to assets is controlled
4) Assets are periodically compared to recorded accountability

Section 642.04 states that safeguarding assets and providing reliable financial records ["(a)" and "(b)" above] are the "broad objectives" of internal accounting control while 1 through 4 above are the "operative objectives" of internal accounting control (note--AU 320 does not use this terminology).

The first operative objective suggests that transactions are to be executed in accordance with management's authorization. This authorization may be general (selling a product at the price indicated on a general price list) or specific (allowing special terms on a sale).

The second operative objective relates to proper recording of transactions. It is helpful here to disaggregate the proper recording of transactions as:

     a) All transactions should be recorded (completeness)
     b) Recorded transactions should

        1] have substance (existence)
        2] be properly valued (valuation)
        3] be properly classified (presentation)
        4] be recorded in proper period (completeness and existence)

     (The bracketed term refers to the evidential assertion most directly related. See Audit Evidence Module: Audit Evidence--General.)

The third operative objective relates to restricting access to assets. Here both direct and indirect access must be considered. Direct access control refers to limiting physical access to assets such as inventory. Indirect access refers to a situation, for example, in which an inadequate segregation of duties exists and an employee is able to fraudulently ship inventory to his/her home.

Finally, the fourth operative objective requires that the actual assets be periodically compared to the accounting records. An example here is the annual physical counting of inventory.

The Internal Accounting Control Hierarchy on the following page summarizes the above discussion. Know and understand the definition of internal accounting control, including the various objectives. The information will help you on a direct question asking for the definition as well as on questions which address the nature of compliance tests (which attempt to provide assurance that the internal control objectives are being met).

    b. Compliance vs. substantive tests. Compliance tests are undertaken to evaluate the existence and effectiveness of internal control procedures that have been prescribed by management. A compliance test may, for example, be used to test whether purchase orders were properly approved before an item was ordered.

A substantive test, on the other hand, directly tests a financial statement account balance. For example, confirmations are often used to substantiate the existence of accounts receivable. Tests which both test compliance and substantiate an account balance are known as "dual purpose" tests.

    c. Ten basic concepts. Section 320 presents ten basic concepts on internal control. Each concept is explained in the outline of Section 320. The first four basic concepts relate to the definition of accounting controls.

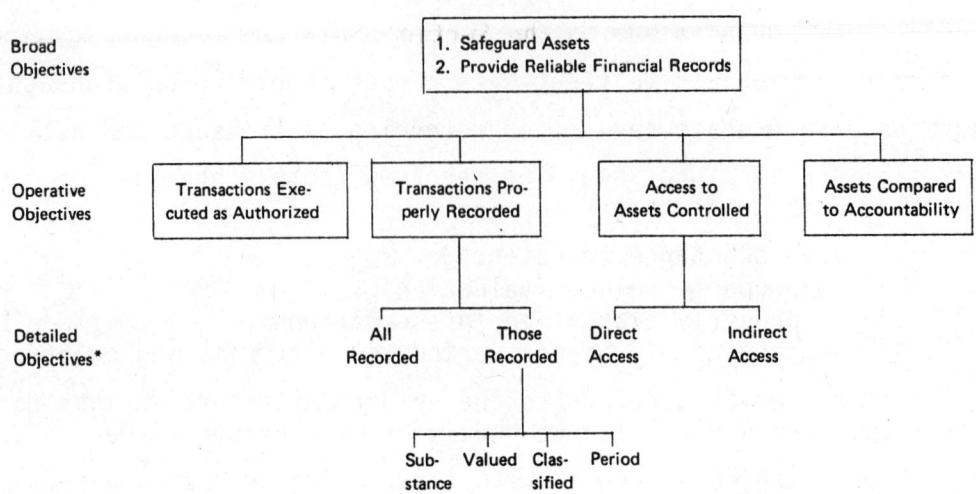

INTERNAL ACCOUNTING CONTROL HIERARCHY

*This term is not used in the Professional Standards

Management responsibility - to establish, maintain, supervise, and modify, as required, a system of internal control for the company

Reasonable assurance - the cost of controls should not exceed their expected benefit (multiple choice questions frequently test this definition)

Methods of data processing. While these concepts apply to both manual and computer systems, the following distinguish computer systems from manual:

1) Transaction trails may exist for a short period of time or only in computer readable form
2) Program errors that cause uniform mishandling of transactions may exist - clerical errors become less frequent
3) Computer controls may need to be relied upon instead of segregation of functions
4) Increased difficulty in detecting unauthorized access (to the computer)
5) Less documentation of initiation and execution of transactions
6) Effectiveness of manual control procedures using computer output is dependent on effectiveness of computer controls

Limitations. Auditors do not rely entirely on internal control, even if it seems excellent, since even the best system may break down due to:

1) Misunderstandings
2) Mistakes of judgment
3) Carelessness
4) Collusion
5) Management override (arises from the fact that management may not be subject to many of the internal control procedures)

The final six basic concepts from Section 320 are called the "essential characteristics of internal accounting control." These characteristics may be viewed as providing assurance to the auditor that our four operative objectives (part of the internal accounting control hierarchy) presented under "2.a." have been met. While there are numerous other lists of detailed internal accounting control character-

istics (see those provided at the end of this module), for purposes of the CPA exam
it is possible to consider them within the Section 320 essential characteristics
framework as follows:

> <u>Segregation</u> of Functions
>> separate--recordkeeping
>>> custodianship
>>> authorization
>>> operations
>
> <u>Personnel</u>
>> reliable
>> bonded
>> supervised
>> required vacations
>
> <u>Access</u> to Assets
>> physical control
>> control over computer data
>
> <u>Comparison</u> of Accountability with Assets
>> reconcile physical asset with detail accounting control
>
> <u>Execution</u> of Transactions
>> authorization
>> guidelines/policies
>
> <u>Recording</u> of Transactions
>> standardized procedures
>> more than 1 employee per transaction
>> exceptions investigated
>> proper records
>>> detail - control
>>> prenumbered (and accounted for)
>>> multiple copies

The above list of essential characteristics has been reordered so that the
mnemonic SPACER may be used to help remember them. These characteristics will be
used subsequently to find weaknesses in internal control systems.

3. <u>Additional Considerations</u>. In addition to the Section 320 definitions and basic
concepts, you should be familiar with the following areas that affect internal
control:

a. <u>Internal accounting control environment</u>. The AICPA's Special Advisory
Committee on Internal Accounting Control used this term to describe characteristics
of internal control. Examples include an active, effective internal audit department, and reliable, bonded employees.

b. <u>Audit committee</u>. A committee of outside (nonmanagement) directors whose
member's functions typically include:

1) Nominating the firm's public accounting firm
2) Discussing broad, general matters concerning the type, scope, and timing of the audit with the public accounting firm
3) Discussing internal control weaknesses with the public accounting firm
4) Reviewing the financial statements and the public accounting firm's audit report
5) Working with the firm's internal auditors

B. Study and Evaluation of the System of Internal Control

The approach which auditors use to review and evaluate internal control involves four steps:

1. Review of Internal Control
2. Preliminary Evaluation of Internal Control
3. Tests of Compliance
4. Reevaluation of Internal Control

The relationships among these four steps are presented in the flowchart on the next page. We now discuss in detail each of these four steps.

1. Review of Internal Control. Auditors review internal control through use of techniques such as discussions with key personnel and through examination of available system support. The objective is to determine how the internal control system is purported to work. Section 320 emphasizes an approach of considering particular classes of transactions when reviewing and evaluating internal control. Consistent with this "class of transactions" concept for analyzing an accounting system's strengths and weaknesses is an approach, now used by many of the largest firms of reviewing and evaluating internal control based on "transaction cycles" such as:

a. Sales, Receivables, and Cash Receipts
b. Purchases, Payables, and Cash Disbursements
c. Inventories and Production
d. Personnel and Payroll
e. Property, Plant, and Equipment

Understanding the nature of these cycles (discussed in detail later in this module) is important to you because the CPA exam frequently contains both essay and multiple choice questions which require a basic knowledge of them. Frequently, candidates are asked to prepare a compliance test audit program or to evaluate internal control weaknesses for a particular transaction cycle.

An effective approach for reviewing internal control is to obtain an understanding of how each of the above transaction cycles is purported to work. This knowledge of the system is usually obtained by using:

Detailed Flowchart of the Relationship
of Internal Control to the Audit

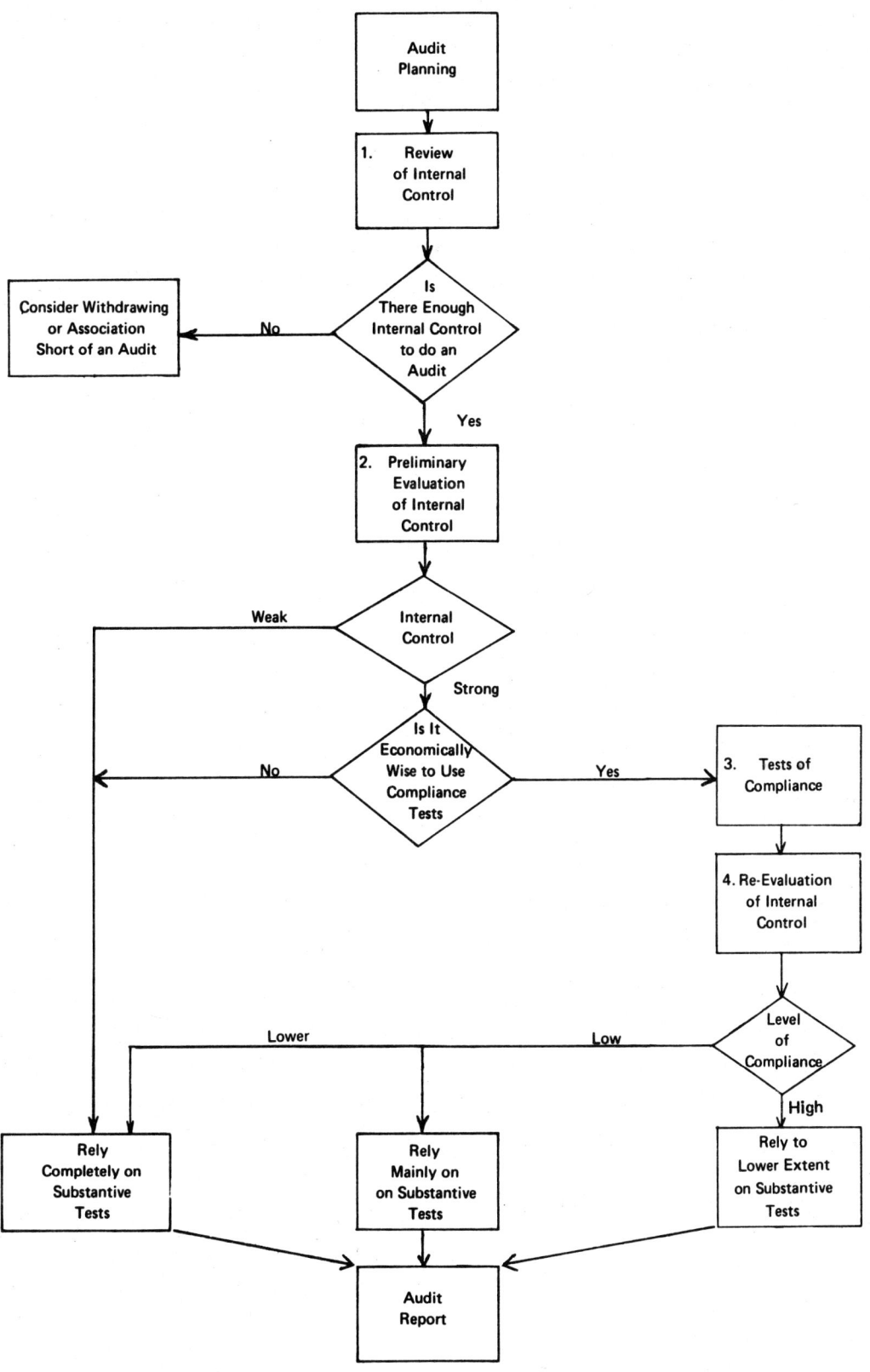

a) Questionnaires
b) Narrative memoranda
c) Flowcharts

The advantages and disadvantages of using questionnaires, memoranda, and/or flowchart methods are:

Method	Advantages	Disadvantages
Questionnaire	1. Easy to complete 2. Comprehensive list of questions make it unlikely that important portions of internal control will be overlooked 3. Weaknesses become obvious (generally those questions answered with a "no")	1. May be answered without adequate thought being given to questions 2. Questions may not "fit" client adequately
Memoranda	1. Tailor-made for engagement 2. Requires a detailed analysis and thus forces auditor to understand functioning of system	1. May become very long and time consuming 2. Weaknesses in system not always obvious 3. Auditor may overlook important portions of internal control system
Flowchart	1. Graphic representation of system 2. Usually makes it unlikely that important portions of internal control will be overlooked 3. Good for EDP systems 4. No long wording (as in case of memoranda)	1. Preparation is time consuming 2. Weaknesses in system not always obvious (especially to inexperienced auditors)

(Note: Flowcharts, including symbols, are discussed in the Auditing EDP module.)

In addition to questionnaires, memoranda, and flowcharts, auditors may prepare "decision tables" to evaluate internal control. Decision tables are a graphic method of describing the logic of decisions. Various combinations of conditions are matched to one of several actions. In an internal control setting, the various important controls are reviewed and, based on the combination of answers received, a preliminary internal control evaluation (step 2 page 135) is made. Subsequently, compliance testing (step 3 page 136) is used to determine whether the conditions are actually in existence. The following extremely simplified table will provide you with the information you need for the CPA exam (note, for example, in the case of segregation of functions, a series of detailed segregation conditions--not one summary--would be used).

Conditions   Rules

	1	2	3	4	5	6	7
1) Segregation of function adequate	y	y	y	y	n	n	n
2) Personnel competent	y	y	n	n	y	y	n
3) Proper execution of transactions	y	n	y	n	y	n	-

Actions

	1	2	3	4	5	6	7
1) Rely to low extent on substantive tests	x						
2) Rely mainly on substantive tests		x	x		x		
3) Rely completely on substantive tests				x		x	x

Note that for decision rule 7, after the first two conditions have received "no's" it doesn't matter what the third condition is--internal control will not be relied upon. Also, while a decision table is an efficient means of describing the logic of an internal control evaluation process, it does not provide an analysis of document flow as does a flowchart.

The auditor may, however, omit the above methods when s/he does not plan to rely on the internal control system to restrict substantive tests. In such cases, documentation may be limited to a record of reasons for deciding not to extend the review.

2. Preliminary Evaluation of Internal Control. After reviewing the system, the CPA forms an opinion on how the system is purported to work. Recall that a CPA is interested in determining whether:

a. Transactions executed as authorized

   1) General authorization
   2) Specific authorization

b. Transactions properly recorded

   1) All recorded
   2) Recorded transactions should

      a) have substance
      b) be properly valued
      c) be properly classified
      d) be recorded in proper period

c. Access to assets controlled

   1) Direct access
   2) Indirect access

d. Assets compared to accountability

(Recall that this is our "internal accounting control hierarchy")

For each transaction cycle, the auditor may form an opinion concerning the likelihood that the above objectives were met. Remember, at this point, the auditor is basing his/her decision entirely on how the system is _purported_ to work--s/he has not tested the system yet to determine whether it _actually_ works as _purported_.

A decision is, at this point, made on which controls should be tested with compliance tests. If controls seem weak in an area, there is no real need to test them and to find out that they are indeed bad--it is unlikely that a system has been described as being weaker than it actually is. In such a case, substantive tests will be relied upon entirely.

If controls seem strong, an auditor will decide whether it is cost-justified to perform compliance tests, thereby reducing the scope of substantive tests, or whether substantive tests should be relied on completely.

3. _Tests of Compliance_. Tests of compliance are used to determine whether the purported controls (as noted through flowcharts, etc.) are actually working. The CPA exam occasionally requires the candidate to prepare a compliance test audit program. A question on the exam could, for example, describe a purchase, payables, and cash disbursements cycle for a firm and ask the candidate to develop an audit program. An organized approach for solving this type of question is to consider for yourself what you believe to be the objectives of compliance tests. The internal control operative objectives presented above may be used and adapted for the various transaction cycles.

You would, for example, in the case of cash disbursements, consider audit procedures to determine whether transactions are executed as authorized. Procedures would include determining that proper evidence of authorization exists (e.g., initialed purchase orders). While the unofficial solutions prepared by the AICPA often do not directly deal with objectives, you may wish to answer the questions using this objectives framework and then check whether your answer includes the key concepts suggested by the AICPA. (Note: The Evidence module provides further information on preparing audit programs as well as detailed lists of possible audit procedures.)

4. _Reevaluation of Internal Control_. The auditor reevaluates internal control based on the results obtained during compliance testing. If the controls are working, and if the system is producing reliable information, the system may be relied upon to a greater extent than in the case in which controls are found to be ineffec-

tive. Thus, controls which are found to be ineffective will result in a greater dependence upon substantive testing.

The entire four-step approach for the study and evaluation of internal control
(review, preliminary evaluation, tests of compliance, reevaluation) may be illustrated through use of an example. Assume that you have been told by the controller
that two secretaries are present and open all mail together each morning. These
secretaries are supposed to prepare a list of all cash receipts, which is then to be
forwarded to the accounts receivable clerk. The cash, according to the controller,
is then given to the cashier who deposits it each day. To keep the example simple,
assume, based on this and other internal control information which you have gathered
during a preliminary review, that internal control over receivables seems to be
strong. Subsequently, you decide to perform compliance tests (with the objective of
determining whether the system described is the one actually in operation and one
which may be relied upon to process cash receipts properly). Also assume that you
have decided that, if the results of your compliance tests indicate that controls
are operating as described, one substantive test will be to confirm 30 of the firm's
250 accounts receivable. That is, despite strong internal controls, some substantive tests must be performed (see internal control concept of "limitations" page
130).

However, when you performed the compliance test of observing the opening of the
mail, you discovered that the secretaries had decided to minimize their work by each
individually performing the task every other week. Also, you discovered that the
secretaries decided to omit the step of preparing a list of cash receipts and have
started forwarding all receipts to the accounts receivable clerk who then forwards
them to the cashier who deposits them periodically.

You have discovered that the controls over cash receipts are <u>not</u> as strong as
you had been initially led to believe. In this situation, you might decide that a
higher than acceptable likelihood exists that an embezzlement of cash receipts could
occur. You might then decide to increase the scope of your substantive tests; you
could, for example, confirm more accounts than originally had been planned. You
might also decide to expand your investigation of bad debt write-offs to determine
that accounts have not been collected and subsequently been fraudulently written
off. Note that, if you had originally obtained a more accurate description of the
client's internal control (or lack thereof) over cash receipts, you might have decided to omit the compliance tests and might have initially planned more substantive
tests.

5. Summary. The approach presented above may be summarized as follows:

    a. Review of Internal Control

        1) Obtain and analyze available documentation such as procedure manuals, job descriptions, flowcharts, decision tables and organization charts

        2) Discuss function of system (by transaction type) with appropriate personnel

        3) Record understanding of system--use flowcharts, narrative memoranda, questionnaires, decision tables and other means

        4) Decide whether there appears to be adequate internal control to perform an audit

    b. Preliminary Evaluation of Internal Control

        1) Evaluate internal control system as it has been described by considering:

            a) What types of errors could occur

            b) What accounting control procedures should prevent or detect these errors

            c) Do these controls appear to exist in the system

        2) For areas which seem to have adequate control, determine whether it is cost justified to perform some compliance tests in addition to substantive tests

        3) For areas with inadequate control rely on substantive tests

    c. Tests of Compliance

        1) Test whether prescribed procedures are followed satisfactorily

        2) Summarize results of tests by transaction type

    d. Reevaluation of Internal Control

        1) Based on results of tests of compliance, determine how much reliance is to be placed on internal controls

        2) Modify substantive tests as necessary

C. Accounting Cycles

We now consider CPA exam questions which ask the candidate to identify internal control weaknesses in a particular cycle or to determine an audit test which will meet some specified objective. For many candidates, these questions are especially difficult. The difficulty is frequently the result of the fact that the candidate (1) does not have an understanding of the various source documents and accounting records and how they relate to one another in an accounting system, and (2) does not know what types of detailed internal accounting controls over the source documents and accounting records should exist. To help you prepare for these questions, we are presenting a brief summary.

In the overview section we suggested that an accounting system may be viewed as follows:

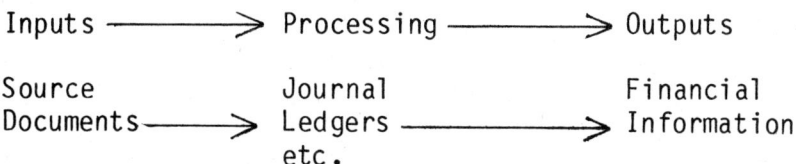

The diagram of "The Financial Accounting Reporting Cycle" on the next page presents an accounting system in further detail. At this point, simply look it over and note the difference between source documents (inputs), accounting records such as journals and ledgers which are used to process the inputs (processing), and financial statements (outputs). Recall that our objectives are to (1) learn an approach for addressing questions pertaining to internal control weaknesses, and (2) learn how to answer other questions pertaining to the effectiveness of audit tests.

One approach for questions pertaining to internal control weaknesses is to:

1) Read the problem to identify the type of transaction cycle

2) Obtain an understanding of how the accounting system works by rereading the problem in detail (and possibly informally flowcharting it if the description is very detailed)

3) Use the internal control characteristics (SPACER--segregation, personnel, access, comparison, execution, recording) to identify internal control weaknesses

4) Recall typical internal control weaknesses (presented subsequently) for the transaction cycle involved to find additional internal control weaknesses

Steps 1 and 2 are clearly necessary since you need to understand the problem and its requirements. While performing the second step, think about the controls the system appears to have. Bear in mind that one way of considering controls is to classify them by whether they are (1) preventive, (2) detective, and/or (3) corrective.

Preventive controls are typically most effective since they are designed to prevent an error or irregularity from occuring (e.g., two persons opening the mail which includes cash receipts may prevent embezzlements). Detective and corrective controls most frequently occur together. They detect and correct an error or irregularity which has already occurred (e.g., bank account reconciliation by an individual not otherwise involved with cash receipts or cash disbursements). While these controls are typically cheaper to institute than preventive controls, they may detect errors too late. They may detect that an employee embezzled $1,000,000, but may only be corrective in the sense that an embezzlement loss journal entry is made in cases where the employee has disappeared. For purposes of the CPA exam, ask

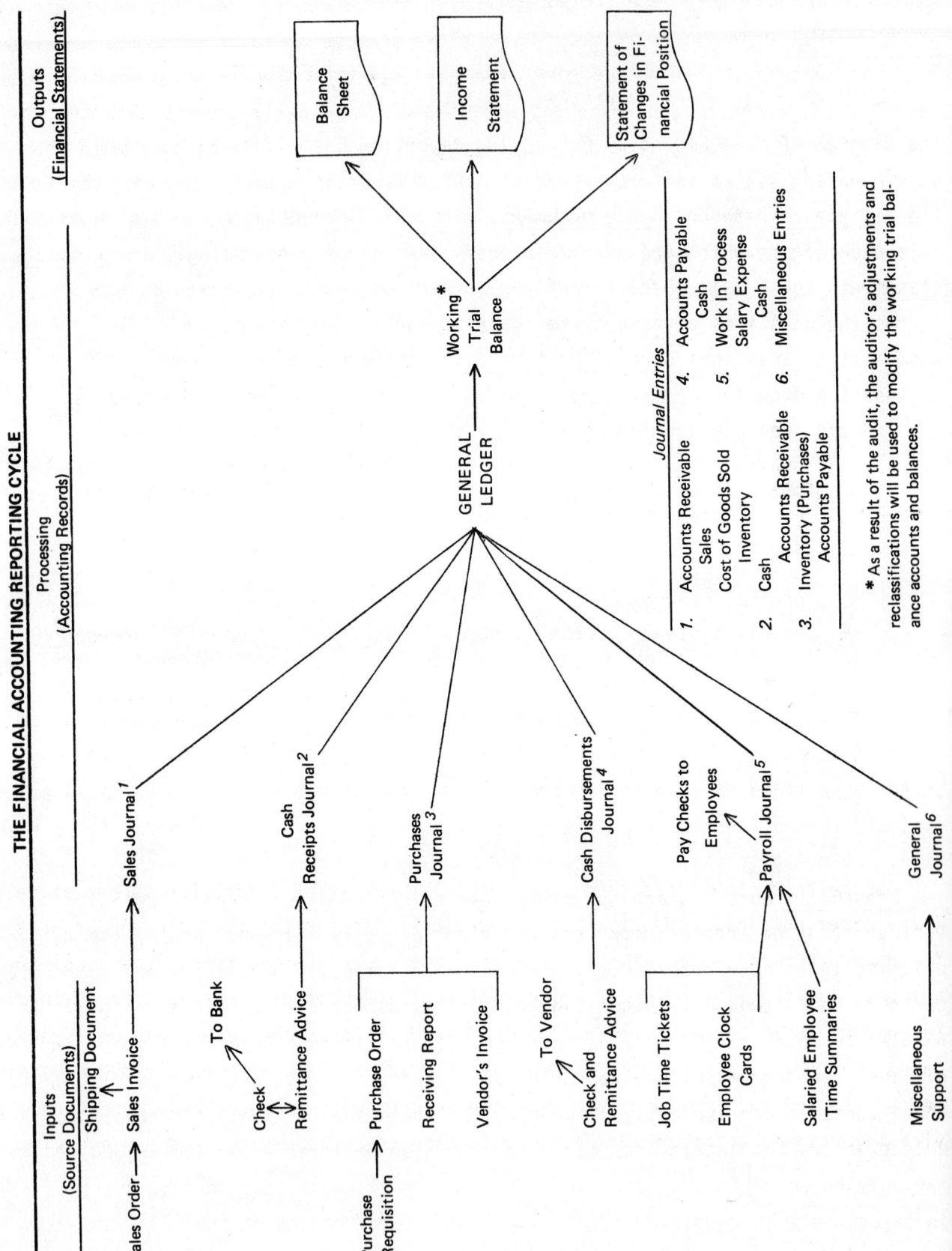

THE FINANCIAL ACCOUNTING REPORTING CYCLE

| Inputs (Source Documents) | Processing (Accounting Records) | Outputs (Financial Statements) |

Balance Sheet

Income Statement

Statement of Changes in Financial Position

Working Trial Balance*

GENERAL LEDGER

Journal Entries

1. Accounts Receivable
      Sales
   Cost of Goods Sold
      Inventory

2. Cash
      Accounts Receivable

3. Inventory (Purchases)
      Accounts Payable

4. Accounts Payable
      Cash

5. Work In Process
   Salary Expense
      Cash

6. Miscellaneous Entries

* As a result of the audit, the auditor's adjustments and reclassifications will be used to modify the working trial balance accounts and balances.

Sales Order → Sales Invoice → Sales Journal¹

Shipping Document

Cash Receipts Journal²

To Bank

Check
Remittance Advice

Purchase Requisition → Purchase Order → Purchases Journal³

Receiving Report

Vendor's Invoice

To Vendor

Cash Disbursements Journal⁴

Check and Remittance Advice

Job Time Tickets

Pay Checks to Employees

Employee Clock Cards

Payroll Journal⁵

Salaried Employee Time Summaries

Miscellaneous Support → General Journal⁶

yourself how effective each of the detective and corrective controls is--their effectiveness depends on the details of the system being examined.

When using the internal control characteristics to find internal control weaknesses, the segregation of functions (step 3) is especially important since many of the weaknesses relate to an inadequate segregation. Recall that an inadequate segregation exists whenever one individual is performing two or more of the following: recordkeeping, custodianship, authorization. For example, when a cashier (custodian) authorizes the write-off of bad debts (authorization), a weakness exists.

We may now analyze in detail each of the following accounting cycles:

1. Sales, Receivables, and Cash Receipts
2. Purchases, Payables, and Cash Disbursements
3. Inventories and Production
4. Personnel and Payroll
5. Property, Plant, and Equipment

1. <u>Sales, Receivables, and Cash Receipts.</u>   The following is a possible flow of documents:

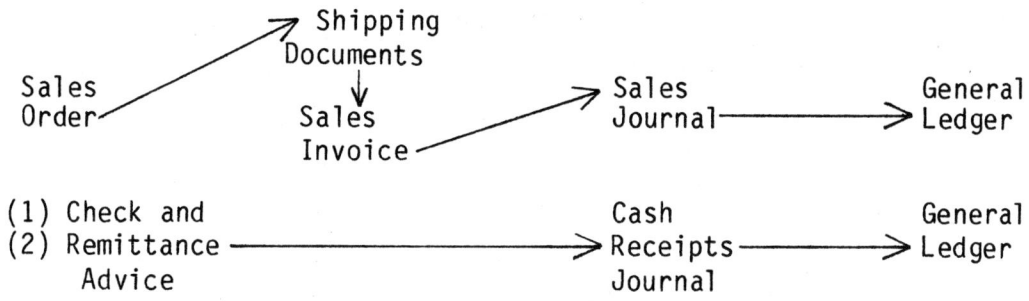

(1) Sent to banks
(2) List or remittance advice is used to make entries

Assume that the firm's sales personnel prepare sales orders for potential sales (many other possibilities, such as the customer filling out the sales order, are found in practice). The sale is approved by the credit department, the goods are shipped, and the billing department (a part of accounting) prepares a sales invoice (a copy of which becomes the customer's "bill"). After the sales invoice is prepared, the sales journal, the general ledger, and the accounts receivable subsidiary ledger are posted. The customer pays the account with a check, and a remittance advice is enclosed to describe which invoice the check is paying. As a preventive control, two individuals open the mail which includes these customer remittances. The checks are listed and sent to the cashier who daily deposits them in the bank (recall that the checks should not go to the accounting department, as that would give accounting custody of assets [checks in this case] as well as recordkeeping responsibility). Another copy of the list of checks and the remittance advices is sent to accounting to be used to post the cash receipts journal, which is subsequently posted to the general and accounts receivable subsidiary ledgers.

Major controls frequently missing in CPA questions

Sales

1) Credit granted by a credit department
2) Sales orders and invoices prenumbered and controlled
3) Sales return credit memoranda prenumbered and matched with receiving reports

Accounts Receivable

1) Subsidiary ledger reconciled to control ledger regularly
2) Individual independent of receivable posting reviews statements before sending to customers
3) Monthly statements sent to all customers
4) Write-offs approved by management official independent of recordkeeping responsibility

Cash Receipts

1) Cash receipts received in mail listed by individuals with no recordkeeping responsibility--
      cash goes to cashier
      remittance advices go to accounting
2) Over the counter cash receipts controlled (cash register tapes)
3) Cash deposited daily
4) Employees handling cash are bonded
5) Bank reconciliation prepared by individuals independent of cash receipts recordkeeping

Sales, Receivables and Cash Receipts Questions

Multiple Choice:

Question	Answer

1. (579,A1,15)   An auditor is testing sales transactions. One step is to trace a sample of debit entries from the accounts receivable subsidiary ledger back to the supporting sales invoices. What would the auditor intend to establish by this step?

   a.   Sales invoices represent bona fide sales.
   b.   All sales have been recorded.
   c.   All sales invoices have been properly posted to customer accounts.
   d.   Debit entries in the accounts receivable subsidiary ledger are properly supported by sales invoices.

(d)   The question is asking what an auditor would intend to establish by tracing a sample of debit entries from the accounts receivable subsidiary ledger back to supporting sales invoices. By undertaking this step, the auditor would determine that the entries in the accounts receivable subsidiary ledger are properly supported by sales invoices. Therefore, answer (d) is the correct answer. Answer (a) would answer the question: "What would the auditor accomplish by tracing sales invoices back to customers' purchase orders, sales invoices, shipping documents and sales agreements?" Answer (b) would answer: "What would the auditor accomplish when tracing approved customer purchase orders to credit entries in sales?" Answer (c) would answer: "What would the auditor accomplish by tracing sales invoices to the accounts receivable subsidiary ledger?"

2. (578,A1,3)   A client's physical count of inventories was lower than the inventory quantities shown in its perpetual records. This situation could be the result of the failure to record

   a.   Sales.
   b.   Sales returns.
   c.   Purchases.
   d.   Purchase discounts.

(a)   The question is asking what situation could cause the actual inventory to be lower than the amount recorded in the perpetual records. If sales had not been recorded, the perpetual inventory records would not reflect the shipment of inventory resulting in inventory overstatement. Therefore, answer (a) is the correct answer. Answers (b) and (c) would answer a question in which the physical count were higher than the perpetual records since physical goods would be in inventory with no recordkeeping having been performed. Purchase discounts, answer (d), relates to the cost of items involved as opposed to the quantity.

3. How would you test credit sales for understatements?

   ANSWER: Compare a sample of approved sales orders to the subsequent posting in the sales journal (and through to the general ledger). You are interested in finding out whether the approved sales order made it all the way to the general ledger. Note that you may find over-statements by this audit procedure (e.g., a $10 sale recorded for a higher amount) but that the primary emphasis is in finding understatements.

4. How would you test credit sales for overstatements?

   ANSWER: Opposite of 1 above.

5. Are you mainly testing for over or understatements of cash when you agree remittance advices to the cash receipts journal?

   ANSWER: Understatements. That is, did the cash which the firm received get recorded?

6. What could cause a remittance advice with no subsequent cash receipt entry?

    ANSWER: An embezzlement.

7. Should there be a sales invoice for each sales order?

    ANSWER: No. Sales in process and sales not approved will not be invoiced.

Problem

The following page presents a cash receipts problem (Internal Control module, Problem 8) with weaknesses highlighted. Note that a quick reading of the problem reveals that it relates to the sales, receivables and cash receipts cycle. A flow-chart is probably not necessary since few documents are involved. Next, using the internal control characteristics and the major controls, you may isolate weaknesses. Also, the "unofficial solution" contains 7 numbered points. They may be derived as:

Internal Control Characteristic	"Unofficial Solution" Point Number
Segregation of Functions	1,3
Personnel	--
Access to Assets	2,5,7
Comparison of Accountability with Asset	2,3,6
Execution of Transactions	2,3
Recording of Transactions	2,3,4

In most cases more than one of the internal control characteristics could help you to arrive at the points in the "unofficial solution." Also, you will probably (hope-fully) find that, even though you haven't memorized the major controls, they come to your attention when the problem provides information such as the fact that deposits are only made on Fridays.

2. **Purchases, Payables, and Cash Disbursements.** The following is a possible flow of documents:

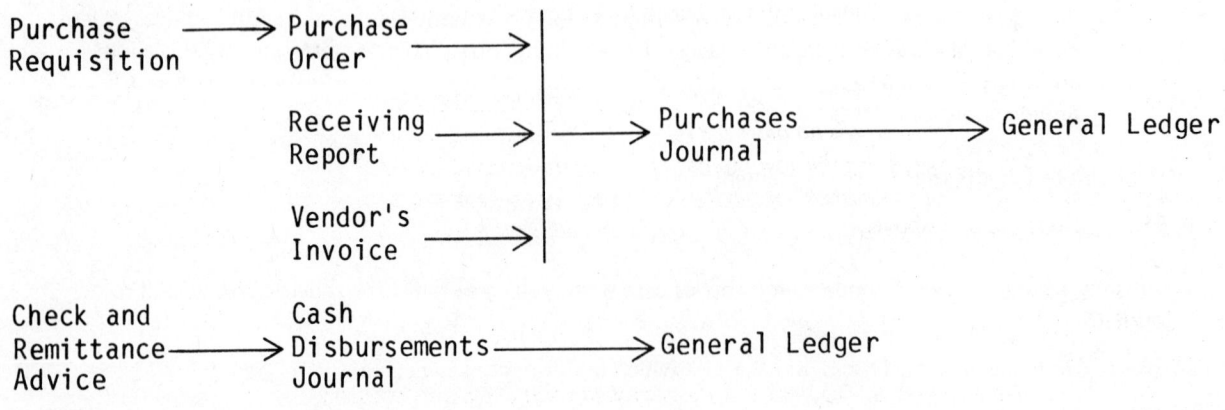

Problem

Cash Receipts IC Weaknesses (1180,A4)

(15 to 25 minutes)

MAJOR PROBLEM 2 CLERKS CONTROL AUTHORIZATION, CUSTODY AND RECORDKEEPING (NO ENTRY MADE IF CASH DISAPPEARS).

INADEQUATE SEGRE- GATION -- ONE SHOULD COLLECT CASH, OTHER SHOULD AUTHORIZE ADMISSION.

CASH NOT DEPOSITED DAILY (ACCESS TO ASSETS)

CASH REGISTER WITH TAPE NEEDED HERE.

NO INDEPENDENT COUNT OF PAYING PATRONS

ONLY ONE ENTRY PER WEEK (RECORDING)

OTHER

IS BONDING POSSIBLE OR REASONABLE?

WHO RECONCILES THE BANK ACCOUNT

The Art Appreciation Society operates a museum for the benefit and enjoyment of the community. During hours when the museum is open to the public, two clerks who are positioned at the entrance collect a five-dollar admission fee from each nonmember patron. Members of the Art Appreciation Society are permitted to enter free of charge upon presentation of their membership cards.

At the end of each day one of the clerks delivers the proceeds to the treasurer. The treasurer counts the cash in the presence of the clerk and places it in a safe. Each Friday afternoon the treasurer and one of the clerks deliver all cash held in the safe to the bank, and receive an authenticated deposit slip which provides the basis for the weekly entry in the cash receipts journal.

The board of directors of the Art Appreciation Society has identified a need to improve their system of internal control over cash admission fees. The board has determined that the cost of installing turnstiles, sales booths or otherwise altering the physical layout of the museum will greatly exceed any benefits which may be derived. However, the board has agreed that the sale of admission tickets must be an integral part of its improvement efforts.

Smith has been asked by the board of directors of the Art Appreciation Society to review the internal control over cash admission fees and provide suggestions for improvement.

Required:

Indicate weakness in the existing system of internal control over cash admission fees, which Smith should identify, and recommend one improvement for each of the weaknesses identified.

Organize the answer as indicated in the following illustrative example:

Weakness	Recommendation
1. There is no basis for establishing the documentation of the number of paying patrons.	*1. Prenumbered admission tickets should be issued upon payment of the admission fee.*

Note: Refer to Problem 8 for a complete solution to this problem.

Assume that the purchase requisition is an internal document sent by the department in need of the supplies to the purchasing department. The purchasing department determines the proper quantity and vendor for the purchase and prepares a purchase order. One copy of the purchase order is sent to the vendor. Another copy is sent to the receiving department to allow receiving personnel to know that items received have been ordered; however, the copy of the purchase order sent to receiving will not have a quantity of items on it so as to encourage personnel to count the goods when they are received. When the goods are received, a receiving report is prepared by the receiving department and forwarded to the accounting department. A vendor's invoice or "bill" is received by the accounting department from the vendor. When the accounting department has the purchase order, receiving report and vendor's invoice, the purchase is recorded in the purchases journal since evidence exists that the item was ordered, received, and billed. A check and remittance advice is subsequently sent to the vendor in accordance with the terms of the sale.

Major Controls Frequently Missing in CPA Exam Questions

Purchases

1) Prenumbered purchase orders used
2) Separate purchasing department makes purchases
3) Purchases personnel independent of receiving and recordkeeping
4) Suppliers' monthly statements compared with recorded payables

Accounts Payable

1) Accounts payable personnel independent of purchasing, receiving and disbursements
2) Clerical accuracy of vendors' invoices tested
3) Purchase order, receiving report and vendor's invoice matched

Cash Disbursements

1) Prenumbered checks with a mechanical check protector used
2) Two signatures on large checks
3) Checks not signed without appropriate support (purchase order, receiving report, vendor's invoice). Treasurer is a check signer.
4) Support for checks cancelled after payment
5) Voided checks mutilated, retained, and accounted for
6) Bank reconciliations prepared by individual independent of cash receipts recordkeeping
7) Physical control of unused checks

Purchases, Payables, and Cash Disbursement CPA Exam Questions

Short Answers

1. Which documents need to be present before payment is approved?

    ANSWER: Purchase order, receiving report, vendor's invoice (This shows that the firm ordered the goods, received the goods, and has been billed for the goods).

2. How can a firm control disbursements so that if a duplicate invoice is sent by the supplier the payment will not be made a second time?

    ANSWER: Cancel the required supporting documents in "1" after the invoice is paid the first time.

3. What audit test could be used to determine whether recorded purchases represent valid business expenses?

    ANSWER: Compare a sample of recorded disbursements with properly approved purchase orders, purchase requisitions, vendors invoices and receiving reports.

4. What audit procedure would test whether actual purchases are recorded?

    ANSWER: Select a sample of purchase requisitions and agree them to the purchase orders and to the purchases journal (as well as to subsequent general ledger posting).

5. Should there be a purchase order for each purchase requisition?

    ANSWER: No. Several requisitions may be summarized on one purchase order and some requisitions may not be approved.

The above are meant to assist you in obtaining an overall understanding of auditing procedures and accounting controls. Note that entire courses (and majors) in systems analysis address these issues. The purpose of the above is to give the individual who has a very limited systems background a starting point for analysis.

Problem

The following is a purchase/disbursements problem (Internal Control Module, Problem 2). This type of question does not require a knowledge of internal control weaknesses. What is necessary is an understanding of how accounting systems generally work. This question is typical of a number of questions which have presented a flowchart with certain information on operations omitted--the candidate is to determine what description belongs in the blocks, circles, etc. which simply contain a number or letter.

First, you must know the common flowchart symbols (presented in the auditing EDP module under "Flowcharting"). This information will be helpful to you because when you see, for example, a trapezoid, you will know that a manual operation has been performed. Additionally, for such problems, you should consider the department the missing information is in and that department's purpose (e.g., the purchasing department purchases appropriate goods from vendors at acceptable prices). Finally, consider both the step preceding and succeeding the missing information to provide you with a clue as to what is being represented.

Starting with A in the purchasing department, we note that an approved requisition has been received from stores. Step A represents some form of manual operation (due to the existence of a trapezoid) out of which a 5-copied purchase order as well as the requisition come. The only possible manual operation here is the preparation of a 5-part purchase order. At this point, the various copies are either filed or sent elsewhere (the circles represent connectors to other portions of the flowchart or possibly represent a document leaving the system). In this case, we see the various copies being filed and sent to receiving and vouchers payable. Step B represents a copy being sent elsewhere. When we consider the fact that the purpose of the purchasing department is to purchase the items, it becomes obvious that this copy must be sent to the vendor - otherwise no order would occur.

Because a receiving report appears for the first time under step C, it obviously represents the preparation of a receiving report. Next are connectors D and E. We know that the use of the circle indicates that something - probably a document or form of some sort - has been received. For D, a clue is given in that requisition 1 has also been received. We know that this is from purchasing by recalling that requisition 1 and purchase order 5 were sent to vouchers payable - this is shown on the flowchart under purchasing. Similarly, we know that receiving sent a copy of the receiving report to vouchers payable and that E and G relate to it. Thus, through understanding the nature of the various symbols and by considering preceding and succeeding information, we are able to determine the nature of the omitted information. Finally, when you have practiced on problems such as this one, you might wish to use the entire flowchart to assist you in obtaining an understanding of how a purchases and disbursement system can work. Note also that problem number 10 in Internal Control is similar to this one except that is relates to a sales system.

3. Inventories and Production. Inventories and production fit under the first two cycles. However, due to the unique nature of inventories, separate coverage is warranted. Two cases will be considered here: a nonmanufacturing firm and a manufacturing firm.

Assume you are auditing a retailer who purchases products from a wholesaler and then sells the goods to the public. As in the acquisitions and payments cycle, purchase requisitions and purchase orders are used and controlled to purchase the inventory items which are of a "finished goods" nature. Likewise, when ordered goods

Problem 2   Purchases and Disbursements Flowchart (583,A5)

(15 to 25 minutes)

The following illustrates a Manual System for Executing Purchases and Cash Disbursements Transactions.

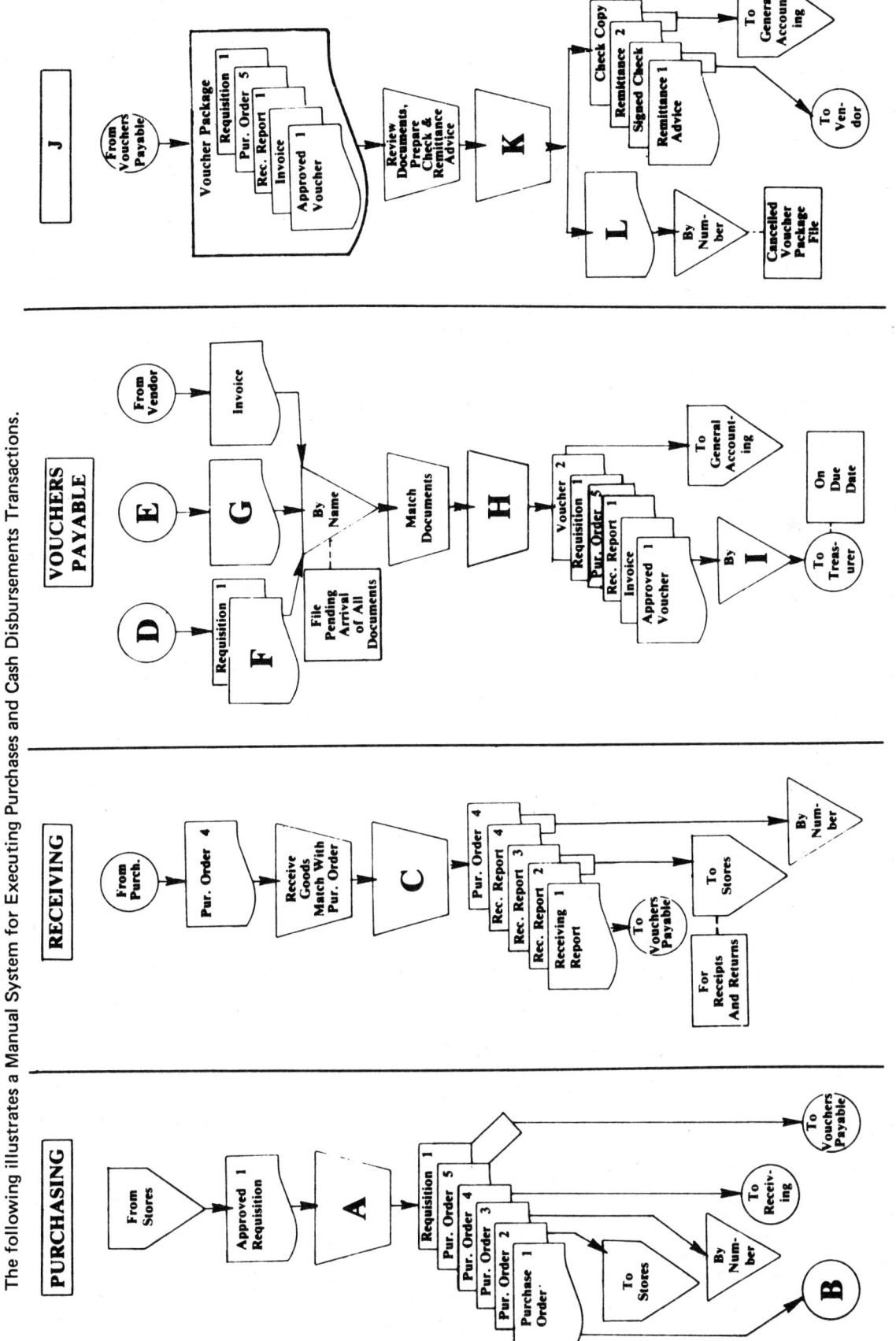

Required: Indicate what each of the letters (A) through (L) represent. Do not discuss adequacies or inadequacies in the system of internal control.

are received, a receiving report is filled out by personnel in the receiving department. Perpetual inventory records are maintained for large dollar items. The firm
has calculated economic reorder points and quantities. When quantities on hand
reach the reorder point, a purchase requisition is prepared and sent to the purchasing department which places the order.

At the end of the year, a physical inventory is taken in which items on hand are
counted. In the case of items for which perpetual records exist, the perpetuals are
corrected for any errors--large errors must be explained. For items without perpetual records, the total on hand is used to adjust the cost of goods sold at year end
(beginning inventory + purchases - ending inventory = cost of goods sold).

The case of the manufacturing firm is somewhat more involved. Recall that
basically three types of inventory accounts are involved. First, supplies and raw
materials are purchased from suppliers in much the same manner as described above
for the nonmanufacturing firm. Second, work in process is the combination of raw
materials, direct labor and factory overhead. Third, when the items in process have
been completed, they are transferred at their cost (typically standard cost) to
finished goods. Finally, when the goods are sold, the entry is to credit finished
goods and to debit cost of goods sold.

Work in process is controlled through use of a standard cost system as described
in elementary cost accounting courses. Recall that raw materials are those which
typically can be directly identified with the product (e.g., transistors in a
radio). Direct labor is also identified with the product (e.g., assembly line
labor). Overhead includes materials not specifically identified with the product
(amount of glue used) and supervisory, non-administrative labor. Variances may be
calculated for all three components--raw materials, direct labor, and overhead.
Variances will be allocated between cost of goods sold and ending inventory (finished goods and work in process) based on the proportion of items sold and those
remaining in inventory, although any "abnormal" waste will be directly expensed.
This allocation is necessary because generally accepted accounting principles require that the firm report inventory based on the lower of actual cost or market -
not standard cost.

Major Controls Frequently Missing in CPA Exam Questions

1) Perpetual inventory records for large dollar items
2) Prenumbered receiving reports prepared when inventory received;
   receiving reports accounted for

3) Adequate standard cost system to cost inventory items
4) Physical controls against theft
5) Written inventory requisitions used
6) Proper authorization of purchases and use of prenumbered purchase orders

Inventories and Production CPA Exam Questions

Multiple Choice

(578,A1,12)   When verifying debits to the perpetual inventory records of a non-manufacturing company, an auditor would be most interested in examining a sample of purchase

a.   Approvals.
b.   Requisitions.
c.   Invoices.
d.   Orders.

(c)   The question is asking what an auditor would be interested in for the verification of debits to the perpetual inventory records. The invoice from the vendor (purchase invoice) will show the number and cost of items sent to the client company. Therefore, answer (c) is the correct answer. Answer (a) would answer a question relating to internal controls over purchases. Answer (b) would answer: "When verifying that recorded purchases of inventory were asked for by stores an auditor would be most interested in examining a sample of purchase?" Answer (d) would answer "When verifying that recorded purchases in inventory have been properly ordered an auditor would be most interested in examining a sample of purchase?"

(578,A1,50)   To best ascertain that a company has properly included merchandise that it owns in its ending inventory, the auditor should review and test the

a.   Terms of the open purchase orders.
b.   Purchase cut-off procedures.
c.   Contractual commitments made by the purchasing department.
d.   Purchase invoices received on or around year end.

(b)   The question is asking how to best ascertain that a company has properly included merchandise that it owns in its ending inventory. Purchase cut-off procedures include the other choices and are thus more complete. Therefore, answer (b) is the correct answer. Answers (a) and (c) would be especially good answers for a question such as "To ascertain the amount of future purchase commitments a firm has an auditor should review and test the?" Answer (d) would answer "An effective procedure for determining that a proper year-end cut-off of purchases has occurred is to review and test the?"

The following is an inventory example problem (Internal Control Module, Problem 6) with weaknesses highlighted. Also, using the internal control characteristic weaknesses may be derived as:

Internal Control Characteristic	"Unofficial Solution" Point Number
Segregation of Functions	2,4,6,7
Personnel	--
Access to Assets	6
Comparison of Accountability with Asset	2
Execution of Transactions	1,3,5
Recording of Transactions	1,2,7,4,6

Internal Control Weaknesses
(1173,A6)

(25 to 30 minutes)

INTRODUCTORY
MATERIAL

You have been engaged by the management of Alden, Inc., to review its internal control over the purchase, receipt, storage, and issue of raw materials. You have prepared the following comments which describe Alden's procedures.

Raw materials, which consist mainly of high-cost electronic components, are kept in a locked storeroom. Storeroom personnel include a supervisor and four clerks. All are well trained, competent, and adequately bonded. Raw materials are removed from the storeroom only upon written or oral authorization of one of the production foremen.

GOOD PERSONNEL
POLICIES! (PERSONNEL)

ORAL AUTHORIZATION
MAKES REMOVAL
WITHOUT WRITTEN
ENTRY POSSIBLE
(RECORDING OF
TRANSACTIONS, ACCESS
TO ASSETS)

INADEQUATE RECORDING,
PERPETUAL RECORDS
NEEDED FOR VALUABLE
INVENTORY ITEMS
(HIGH COST ELECTRONIC
COMPONENTS) (RECORDING
OF TRANSACTIONS, COMPARI-
SON OF ACCOUNTABILITY
WITH ASSETS)

There are no perpetual-inventory records; hence, the storeroom clerks do not keep records of goods received or issued. To compensate for the lack of perpetual records, a physical-inventory count is taken monthly by the storeroom clerks who are well supervised. Appropriate procedures are followed in making the inventory count.

MAY NOT BE AN
ECONOMICAL QUANTITY
(AN ADMINISTRATIVE
CONTROL)

After the physical count, the storeroom supervisor matches quantities counted against predetermined reorder level. If the count for a given part is below the reorder level, the supervisor enters the part number on a materials-requisition list and sends this list to the accounts-payable clerk. The accounts-payable clerk prepares a purchase order for a predetermined reorder quantity for each part and mails the purchase order to the vendor from whom the part was last purchased.

INADEQUATE SEGREGATION,
ACCOUNTS PAYABLE PERFORM
PURCHASING FUNCTION
AND PAYABLE FUNCTION
(SEGREGATION OF FUNCTIONS)
MAY NOT BE BEST
VENDOR (EXECUTION
OF TRANSACTIONS)

INADEQUATE SEGREGATION,
STOREROOM SHOULD NOT
BE FIRST TO RECEIVE
GOODS. (SEGREGATION OF
FUNCTIONS)
HIGH COST ITEMS NEED
QUALITY INSPECTION

When ordered materials arrive at Alden, they are received by the storeroom clerks. The clerks count the merchandise and agree the counts to the shipper's bill of lading. All vendors' bills of lading are initialed, dated, and filed in the storeroom to serve as receiving reports.

NO PRENUMBERED
RECEIVING REPORTS
(RECORDING OF TRANS-
ACTIONS)

Note: Refer to Problem 6 for a complete solution to this problem.

4. Personnel and Payroll. The following is a possible flow of documents:

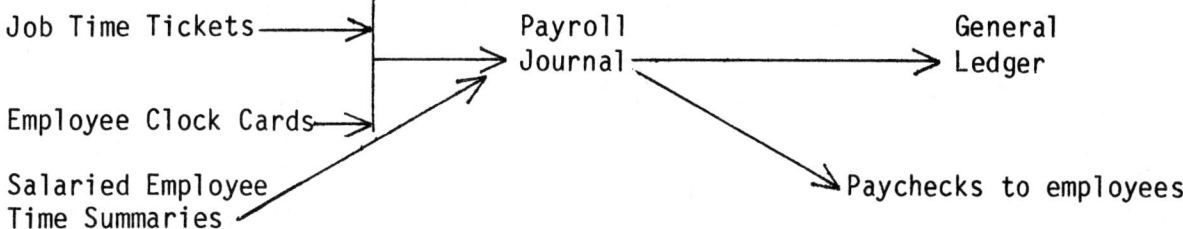

Job Time Tickets ───────⟶┐
                         ├⟶ Payroll   General
                         │⟶ Journal ───────────⟶ Ledger
Employee Clock Cards─────⟶┘
                                                  ↘ Paychecks to employees
Salaried Employee ╱
Time Summaries ╱

   Assume that a separate personnel department maintains complete, up-to-date
records for each employee. Included in such records is information on level of
education, basic payroll information, experience, and authorization for any changes
in pay rates. Assume that the firm's factory, direct labor personnel use a time
clock to punch in each morning and out each evening. Their employee clock card thus
shows the total hours worked each day. These direct labor personnel also fill out
job time tickets for each job they work on each day. At the end of each week their
supervisor compares job time tickets with employee clock cards which have already
been signed by the employees. Assume also that salaried and other employees fill
out weekly time summaries indicating hours worked. All of the above information is
sent to the payroll accounting department whose function it is to prepare the payroll journal and to prepare the unsigned payroll checks. The checks are then signed
by the treasurer and distributed by an independent paymaster who has no other payroll functions. The internal auditing department periodically compares the payroll
department's file on each employee with that in the personnel department's file to
determine that no unauthorized changes in payroll records have been made. Employees
with cash handling and recordkeeping responsibilities are covered by fidelity bonds,
a form of insurance which protects an employer against losses caused by dishonest
employees (fidelity bonds also serve as a control when new employees are hired since
the insurer will typically perform a background check on prospective employees).

Major Personnel and Payroll Controls Frequently Missing in CPA Exam Questions

   1) Segregate: Timekeeping
                   Payroll Preparation
                   Personnel
                   Paycheck Distribution
   2) Time clocks used where possible
   3) Job time tickets reconciled to time clock cards
   4) Time clock cards approved by supervisors (overtime and regular hours)
   5) Treasurer signs pay checks

6) Unclaimed pay checks controlled by someone otherwise independent of the payroll function (locked up and eventually destroyed if not claimed). In cases in which employees are paid cash (as opposed to checks) unclaimed pay should be deposited into a special bank account.

Personnel and Payroll CPA Exam Questions

Multiple Choice

17. (1179,A1,5) For internal control purposes, which of the following individuals should preferably be responsible for the distribution of payroll checks?

    a.   Bookkeeper.
    b.   Payroll clerk.
    c.   Cashier.
    d.   Receptionist.

17. (d) From an internal control viewpoint, the person to distribute payroll checks should follow the dictum of separation of functional responsibilities: record keeping, custodianship, authorization, and operations. The receptionist would be independent of those keeping payroll records [answer (a)], preparing the payroll [answer (b)], and those with custodianship over cash [answer (c)].

35. (579,A1,37)   Effective internal control over the payroll function would include which of the following?

    a.   Total time recorded on time-clock punch cards should be reconciled to job reports by employees responsible for those specific jobs.
    b.   Payroll department employees should be supervised by the management of the personnel department.
    c.   Payroll department employees should be responsible for maintaining employee personnel records.
    d.   Total time spent on jobs should be compared with total time indicated on time-clock punch cards.

35. (d) The requirement is an effective internal control technique over the payroll function. Note that you are looking for the best answer of the four alternatives. Total time spent on individual jobs should be compared with total time per the time clock. This will insure that all time is properly allocated to individual jobs, and excess time was not incurred that was not chargeable to specific jobs. Answer (a) is incorrect because employees should not be permitted to reconcile or check their own job reports, i.e., there should be a separate review. Answers (b) and (c) are incorrect because the payroll department and the personnel department should be separate, as they have separate functional responsibilities. The personnel department authorizes the hiring and pay levels of employees whereas the payroll department expends funds. These functional responsibilities should be separate, and neither department should supervise the other department.

The following page presents a payroll problem (Internal Control Module, Problem 7) in a flowchart format with weaknesses highlighted. Exam questions which provide such a detailed flowchart often cause candidates significant problems. While reading the problem to identify the type of transaction cycle is not difficult, obtaining an understanding of how the system works requires careful thought, especially for those with very limited audit experience. When presented with a detailed flowchart such as this one, it is helpful to determine the point at which the transactions originate and to "walk one through."

The narrative background for Problem 7 makes clear that this flowchart starts with payroll clerk Number 1 determining the employment status of factory employees and then preparing clock cards. Give thought to the actual operation being performed. Here, for example, the clerk has information (such as withholding data) obtained from personnel. After the clock cards have been prepared, they are distributed to the factory. Consider for yourself what happens in the factory - think about the daily punching in and out and submission of time cards to the factory foreman. It might help you to imagine that you are the foreman, for example, and that you are reviewing the clock cards and preparing the summary (which is filed and never used again - a sure sign that the report is either unnecessary, or, as in this case, not properly utilized). In like manner, work through the entire system.

The next step is to study the flowchart again, this time using your knowledge of internal control to find weaknesses. As indicated earlier, the characteristics of internal control (SPACER) and the above list of typical control weaknesses will help. Using SPACER, the solution's weaknesses may be derived as:

Internal Control Characteristic	"Unofficial Solution" Point Number
Segregation of Functions	a1,a2,a3,a6,a7,a8,a9,a10,b1
Personnel	b3,b4,b5
Access to Assets	a5
Comparison of Accountability with Asset	a4
Execution of Transactions	a1,a2,a3,a4,b2
Recording	a1

Again, recall that it is not important which characteristic jogs your memory as to a weakness.

Payroll IC Weaknesses
(580,A5)

(15 to 20 minutes)

A CPA's audit working papers contain a narrative description of a **segment** of the Croyden Factory, Inc., payroll system and an accompanying flowchart as follows:

The internal control system with respect to the personnel department is well-functioning and is **not** included in the accompanying flowchart.

At the beginning of each work week payroll clerk No. 1 reviews the payroll department files to determine the employment status of factory employees and then prepares time cards and distributes them as each individual arrives at work. This payroll clerk, who is also responsible for custody of the signature stamp machine, verifies the identity of each payee before delivering signed checks to the foreman.

At the end of each work week, the foreman distributes payroll checks for the preceding work week. Concurrent with this activity, the foreman reviews the current week's employee time cards, notes the regular and overtime hours worked on a summary form, and initials the aforementioned time cards. The foreman then delivers all time cards and unclaimed payroll checks to payroll clerk No. 2.

Required:

a. Based upon the narrative and accompanying flowchart, what are the weaknesses in the system of internal control?

b. Based upon the narrative and accompanying flowchart, what inquiries should be made with respect to clarifying the existence of **possible additional weaknesses** in the system of internal control?

Note: Do not discuss the internal control system of the personnel department.

CROYDEN INC., FACTORY PAYROLL SYSTEM

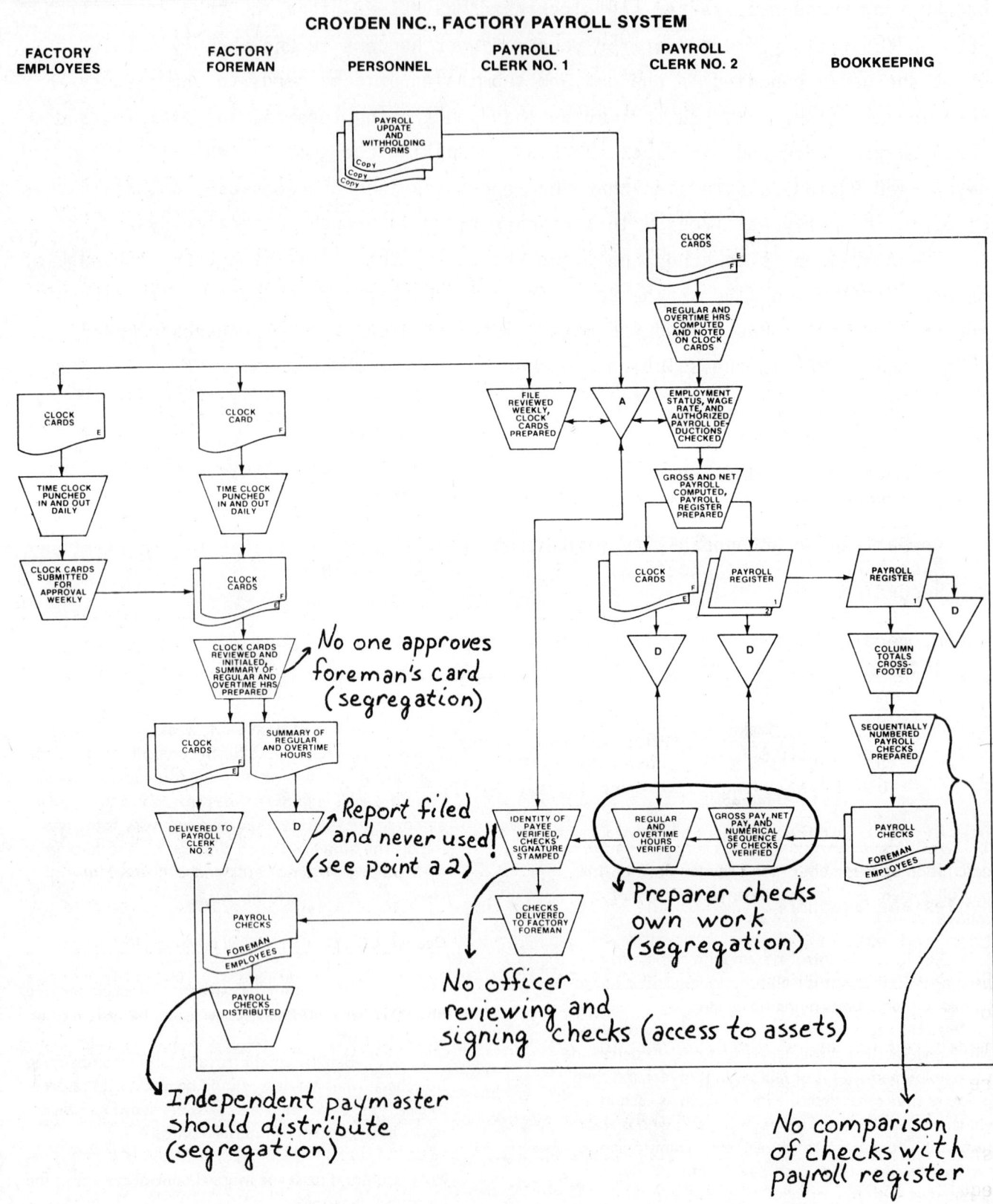

5. Property, Plant, and Equipment. This cycle is a subset of the acquisition and payment cycle. Assume that a firm must obtain board of director approval for purchases over a certain amount. Otherwise, the purchase is handled similarly to a merchandise purchase. As in the case of merchandise purchases, the item is recorded as an addition when some form of purchase authorization is present with a vendor's invoice and a receiving report. The firm then selects an appropriate life and depreciation method (e.g., straight-line, sum-of-the-years'-digits, double-declining balance) for depreciation purposes. Depreciation entries are made in the general journal with a debit to depreciation expense (manufacturing overhead for manufacturing equipment) and a credit to accumulated depreciation. The firm must also have controls to determine that repair and maintenance expenses have not been capitalized.

Asset retirements are recorded by removing the asset and accumulated depreciation from the general ledger -- a gain (loss) may occur on the transaction. In cases of exchanges of assets, the firm has policies to determine that GAAP is followed in recording the transaction.

Major Property, Plant and Equipment Controls Frequently Missing in CPA Exam Questions

1) Major asset acquisitions are properly approved by the firm's board of directors
2) Detailed records are available for property assets and accumulated depreciation
3) Written policies exist for capitalization vs. expensing decisions
4) Depreciation properly calculated
5) Retirements approved by an appropriate level of management
6) Physical control over assets to prevent theft

6. Overall Internal Control Checklists. The following internal control checklist outline gives the controls which are typically necessary in various transaction cycles and accounts. While the lists are clearly too lengthy to memorize, review them and obtain a general familiarity. Candidates with little actual business experience will probably find them especially helpful. Study in detail the checklists on cash receipts (checklist #3), cash disbursements (#4), and on payroll (#14) -- as indicated above, a large percentage of the internal control weakness type questions relate to these three areas.

The checklists are organized into subtopics -- generally by category of balance sheet account, e.g., cash, receivables, fixed assets, liabilities, shareholders' equity, etc. The related nominal accounts should be considered with the real accounts, e.g., depreciation and fixed assets, sales and accounts receivable.

1. General

>   Chart of accounts
>   Accounting procedures manual
>   Organizational chart to define responsibilities
>   Absence of entries direct to ledgers
>   Posting references in ledgers
>   Review of journal entries
>   Use of standard journal entries
>   Use of prenumbered forms
>   Support for all journal entries
>   Access to records limited to authorized persons
>   Rotation of accounting personnel
>   Required vacations
>   Review of system at every level
>   Appropriate revision of chart of accounts
>   Appropriate revision of procedures
>   Separation of recordkeeping from operations
>   Separation of recordkeeping from custodianship
>   Record retention policy
>   Bonding of employees
>   A conflict of interest policy

2. Cash funds

>   Imprest system
>   Reasonable amount
>   Completeness of vouchers
>   Custodian responsible for fund
>   Reimbursement checks to order of custodian
>   Surprise audits
>   No employee check cashing
>   Physically secure
>   Custodian has no access to cash receipts
>   Custodian has no access to accounting records

3. Cash receipts

>   Detail listing of mail receipts
>   Special handling of postdated checks
>   Daily deposit
>   Cash custodians bonded
>   Cash custodians apart from negotiable instruments
>   Bank accounts properly authorized
>   Handling of returned NSF items
>   Comparison of duplicate deposit slips with cash book
>   Comparison of duplicate deposit slips with detail A/R
>   Banks instructed not to cash checks to company
>   Control over cash from other sources

>   Separation of cashier personnel from accounting duties
>   Separation of cashier personnel from credit duties
>   Use of cash registers
>   Cash register tapes
>   Numbered cash receipt tickets
>   Outside salesmen cash control
>   Daily reconciliation of cash collections

4. Cash disbursements

>   Numbered checks
>   Support for check signature
>   Limited authorization to sign checks
>   Signing of blank checks
>   All checks accounted for
>   Detail listing of checks
>   Mutilation of voided checks
>   Proper authorization of persons signing checks
>   Control over signature machines
>   Check listing compared with cash book
>   Control over interbank transfers
>   Prompt accounting for interbank transfers
>   Checks not payable to cash
>   Physical control of unused checks
>   Cancellation of supporting documents
>   Control over long outstanding checks
>   Reconciliation of bank account
>   Independence of person reconciling bank statement
>   Bank statement direct to person reconciling
>   No access to cash records or receipts by check signers

5. Investments

>   Proper authorization of transactions
>   Under control of a custodian
>   Custodian bonded
>   Custodian separate from cash receipts
>   Custodian separate from investment records
>   Safety deposit box
>   Record of all safety deposit visits
>   Access limited
>   Presence of two required for access
>   Periodic reconciliation of detail with control
>   Record of all aspects of all securities
>   Availability of brokerage advices, etc.
>   Periodic internal audit
>   Securities in name of company
>   Proper segregation of collateral
>   Physical control of collateral
>   Periodic appraisal of collateral
>   Periodic appraisal of investments
>   Adequate records of investments for application of equity method

6. Accounts receivable and sales

Sales orders prenumbered
Credit approval
Credit and sales departments independent
Control of back orders
Sales order and sales invoice comparison
Shipping invoices prenumbered
Names and addresses on shipping invoice
Review of sales invoices
Control over returned merchandise
Credit memoranda prenumbered
Matching of credit memoranda and receiving
  reports
Control over credit memoranda
Control over scrap sales
Control over sales to employees
Control over C.O.D. sales
Sales reconciled with cash receipts and A/R
Sales reconciled with inventory change
A/R statement to all customers
Periodic preparation of aging schedule
Control over payments of written off
  receivables
Control over A/R write offs, e.g., proper
  authorization
Control over A/R written off, i.e., review for
  possible collection
Independence of sales, A/R, receipts, billing,
  and shipping personnel

7. Notes receivable

Proper authorization of notes
Detailed records of notes
Periodic detail to control comparison
Periodic confirmation with makers
Control over notes discounted
Control over delinquent notes
Physical safety of notes
Periodic count of notes
Control over collateral
Control over revenue from notes
Custodian of notes independent from cash
  and recordkeeping

8. Inventory and cost of sales

Periodic inventory
Written inventory instructions
Counts by noncustodians
Control over count tags
Control over inventory adjustments
Use of perpetual records
Periodic comparison of G/L and perpetual
  records

Investigation of discrepancies
Control over consignment inventory
Control over inventory stored at warehouses
Control over returnable containers with
  customers
Are receiving reports prepared
Receiving reports in numerical order
Independence of custodian from record-
  keeping
Adequacy of insurance
Physical safeguards against theft
Physical safeguards against fire
Adequacy of cost system
Cost system tied into general ledger
Periodic review of overhead rates
Use of standard costs
Use of inventory requisitions
Periodic summaries of inventory usage
Control over intracompany inventory
  transfers
Purchase orders prenumbered
Proper authorization for purchases
Review of open purchase orders

9. Prepaid expenses and deferred charges

Proper authorization to incur
Authorization and support of amortization
Detailed records
Periodic review of amortization policies
Control over insurance policies
Periodic review of insurance needs
Control over premium refunds
Beneficiaries of company policies
Physical control of policies

10. Intangibles

Authorization to incur
Detailed records
Authorization to amortize
Periodic review of amortization

11. Fixed assets

Detailed property records
Periodic comparison with control accounts
Proper authorization for acquisition
Written policies for acquisition
Control over expenditures for self construc-
  tion
Use of work orders
Individual asset identification plates
Written authorization for sale
Written authorization for retirement
Physical safeguard from theft

Control over fully depreciated assets
Written capitalization--expense policies
Responsibilities charged for asset and
   depreciation records
Written depreciation records
Responsibilities charged for asset and
   depreciation records
Written depreciation policies
Detail depreciation records
Depreciation adjustments for sales and
   retirements
Control over intracompany transfers
Adequacy of insurance
Control over returnable containers

12.   Accounts payable

Designation of responsibility
Independence of A/P personnel from
   purchasing, cashier, receiving functions
Periodic comparison of detail and control
Control over purchase returns
Clerical accuracy of vendors' invoices
Matching of purchase order, receiving report,
   and vendor invoice
Reconciliation of vendor statements with A/P
   detail
Control over debit memos
Control over advance payments
Review of unmatched receiving reports
Mutilation of supporting document at
   payment
Review of debit balances
Investigation of discounts not taken

13.   Accrued liabilities and other expenses

Proper authorization for expenditure and
   incurrence
Control over partial deliveries
Postage meter
Purchasing department
Bids from vendors
Verification of invoices
Imprest cash account
Detailed records
Responsibility charged
Independence from G/L and cashier functions
Periodic comparison with budget

14.   Payroll

Authorization to employ
Personnel data records
Tax records
Time clock
Review of payroll calculations
Imprest payroll account
Responsibility for payroll records
Compliance with labor statutes
Distribution of payroll checks
Control over unclaimed wages
Profit sharing authorization
Responsibility for profit sharing computations

15.   Long-term liabilities

Authorization to incur
Executed in company name
Detailed records of long-term debt
Reports of independent transfer agent
Reports of independent registrar
Otherwise adequate records of creditors
Control over unissued instruments
Signers independent of each other
Adequacy of records of collateral
Periodic review of debt agreement compliance
Recordkeeping of detachable warrants
Recordkeeping of conversion features

16.   Shareholders' equity

Use of registrar
Use of transfer agent
Adequacy of detailed records
Comparison of transfer agent's report with
   records
Physical control over blank certificates
Physical control over treasury certificates
Authorization for transactions
Tax stamp compliance for cancelled certi-
   ficates
Independent dividend agent
Imprest dividend account
Periodic reconciliation of dividend account
Adequacy of stockholders' ledger
Review of stock restrictions and provisions
Valuation procedures for stock issuances
Other paid-in capital entries
Other retained earnings entries

D. Other Considerations

1. <u>Required Communication of Material Weaknesses</u>. Section 323 requires auditors to communicate to senior management and to the board of directors or its audit committee material weaknesses in internal accounting control which were noted during the audit (Section 642 details the report to be issued). A material weakness in internal accounting control is a condition in which the specific control procedures or the degree of compliance therewith does not reduce to a <u>relatively low level</u> the risk that <u>errors</u> or <u>irregularities</u> in amounts that could be <u>material</u> in relation to the financial statements being audited <u>may occur and not be detected</u> within a timely period by employees in the normal course of performing their assigned functions. While the communication is preferably to be in writing, oral communications in some circumstances may be acceptable--in such cases the auditor should document the discussion in the working papers. If a weakness noted in a prior year remains uncorrected, the auditor should either repeat it in this year's communication, or should refer to his/her previous communication.

2. <u>Reports on Internal Control</u>. Section 642 outlines four general types of reports on internal accounting control:

    a. <u>Separate opinion on internal accounting control</u>. Section 642 allows accountants to issue an opinion on internal accounting control. The publicly available report addresses the issue of whether the firm's internal accounting control system can prevent or detect material errors or irregularities. Section "D" of the outline of Section 642 summarizes the report issued.

    b. <u>Report made as part of a financial statement audit</u>. As indicated earlier, Section 323 requires auditors to communicate to senior management and to the board of directors or its audit committee material weaknesses in internal control. Also, regardless of whether weaknesses are found, auditors may be asked to provide a report. Section "E" of the outline of Section 642 summarizes the report issued.

    c. <u>Report based on criteria established by regulatory agencies</u>. Section 642 allows reporting on internal accounting control when the criteria have been prescribed by a regulatory agency. While CPAs do not assume responsibility for the criteria, they should report any weakness discovered which is not covered by the prescribed criteria. Section "F" of the outline of Section 642 summarizes the report issued.

d. Other special purpose reports. These reports, described briefly in Section 642 and Section "G" of the outline, are for management, another independent accountant, or other specified third parties. While no specific report form is suggested, the accountant must disclaim an opinion on whether the system meets the overall objectives of internal accounting control. Section 324 provides more specific guidance on the preparation and use of these reports for service centers (e.g., EDP Service Centers and bank trust departments holding assets for employee benefit plans).

e. Summary of internal accounting control reports. For the first three types of reports outlined in Section 642, note that each report starts with a paragraph describing the scope of the auditor's work (no suggested report form is provided for the fourth type of report). Also, each report includes paragraphs similar to, or the same as, the following:

> The management of XYZ Company is responsible for establishing and maintaining a system of internal accounting control. In fulfilling this responsibility, estimates and judgments by management are required to assess the expected benefits and related costs of control procedures. The objectives of a system are to provide management with reasonable, but not absolute, assurance that assets are safeguarded against loss from unauthorized use or disposition, and that transactions are executed in accordance with management's authorization and recorded properly to permit the preparation of financial statements in accordance with generally accepted accounting principles.
>
> Because of inherent limitations in any system of internal accounting control, errors or irregularities may occur and not be detected. Also, projection of any evaluation of the system to future periods is subject to the risk that procedures may become inadequate because of changes in conditions, or that the degree of compliance with the procedures may deteriorate.

The above two paragraphs summarize (1) management's responsibilities, (2) the objectives of internal control, and (3) the limitations of a system of internal control.

Several of the most important differences in the four types of reports on internal control may be summarized as:

	Report 1 Separate Opinion on Internal Accounting Control	Report 2 Report Made as Part of a Financial Statement Audit	Report 3 Report Based on Criteria Established by Regulatory Agencies	Report 4 Other Special Purpose Reports
I. *Use of Report*	Unrestricted	Management, a specified regulatory agency, or other specified third party	Regulatory agency, management	Management, another accountant, other specified third party
II. *Source for Proper Review Procedures*	SAS No. 30, paragraphs 13 thru 35*	Normal audit procedures	SAS No. 30, paragraph 55 and regulatory agency's criteria	SAS No. 30, paragraph 60 plus agreed upon procedures.
III. *Important Differences in Opinion Paragraphs*	In our opinion, the system . . . taken as a whole was sufficient to meet the objectives stated above . . .	. . . we do not express an opinion on the system . . . taken as a whole . . . However, our study disclosed no condition we believe to be a material weakness . . .	. . . we believe . . . procedures were adequate for the agency's purposes . . . in relation to the grant . . .	Disclaim opinion (see paragraph 61)

*These procedures may also be applied to other types of engagements.

[1]Adapted from C. E. Arrington and K. Pany, "SAS No. 30: Clarifying and Extending the Accountant's Involvement with Reporting on Internal Accounting Control," Journal of Accounting Auditing and Finance (Summer, 1981) p.369, Warren, Gorham and Lamont, reprinted with permission.

3. Sampling -- See Statistical Sampling module

4. Effects of EDP -- See Auditing EDP module

5. Flowcharting -- See Auditing EDP module

6. Effects of an Internal Audit Function. Section 322 discusses the effect of an internal audit function on the CPA's audit. Note that the CPA may use the internal auditor's work--although the CPA remains responsible for such work. Before using such work, the CPA should review the competency and the objectivity of the internal auditors. Competency may be evaluated through inquiries about internal audit staff educational backgrounds, training, and supervision. Objectivity relates primarily to the organizational level to which the internal auditors report. Also, the CPA may wish to review the regular work of the internal auditors to evaluate competence and objectivity.

AUDIT EVIDENCE

The entire financial statement audit may be described as a process of evidence accumulation and evaluation. This process enables the auditor to formulate an informed opinion as to whether the financial statements are presented fairly in accordance with generally accepted accounting principles. The following "Diagram of an Audit" was first presented and explained in the auditing overview section:

DIAGRAM OF AN AUDIT

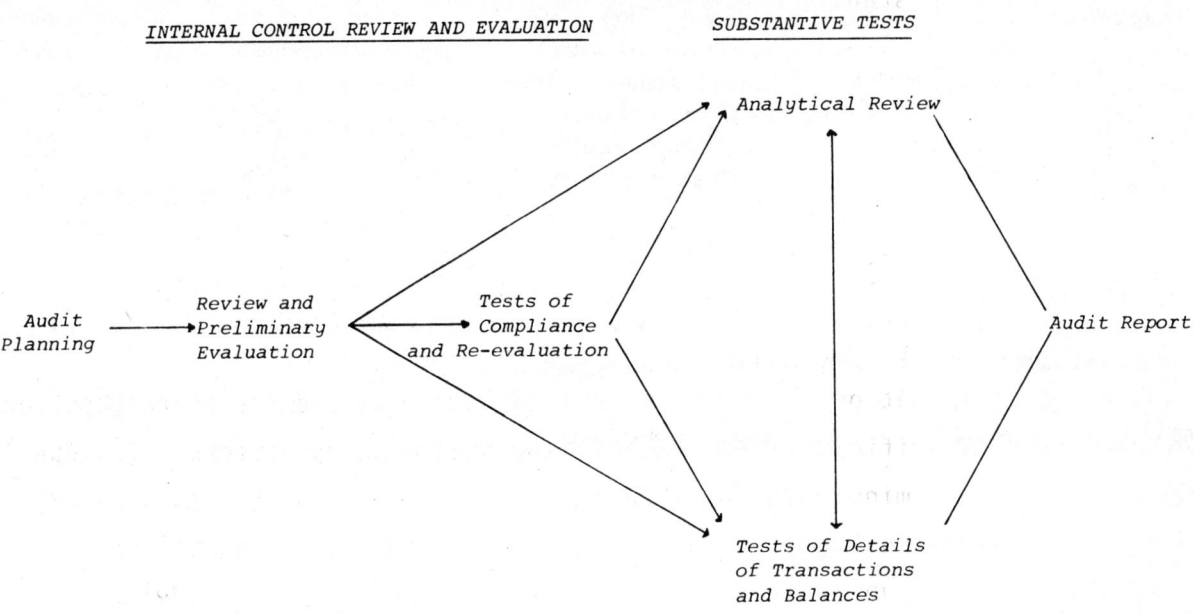

Kinney, William R., Jr., "Decision Theory Aspects of Internal Control System Design/Compliance, and Substantive Tests," Journal of Accounting Research (Supplement, 1975), p. 16 (adapted).

This module covers "evidential matter" as a concept and discusses types of evidential matter generated through performance of substantive tests--both analytical review techniques and tests of details of transactions and balances.

Numerous questions on evidence appear on each CPA Exam. Multiple choice questions frequently ask the candidate to select the audit procedure most likely to detect errors which have occurred in given accounting records. Essay as well as multiple choice questions are used to test whether the candidate can distinguish among various concepts such as:

1) Competent vs. sufficient evidence
2) Analytical review vs. tests of details of transactions and balances
3) Audit objectives vs. audit procedures

Additionally, candidates may be required to prepare an audit program.

Study Program for Audit Evidence Module

This module is organized and should be studied in the following manner:

A. Audit Evidence--General

   1. Competent and Sufficient Evidential Matter
   2. Types of Evidence

B. Audit Evidence--Specific (Substantive Tests)

   1. Types of Substantive Tests

     a. Analytical Review
     b. Tests of Details of Transactions and Balances

   2. Preparing Substantive Test Audit Programs
   3. Documentation

C. Other Specific Evidence Topics

   1. Cash
   2. Receivables
   3. Inventory
   4. Marketable Securities
   5. Property, Plant, and Equipment
   6. Prepaids
   7. Payables (Current)
   8. Long-Term Debt
   9. Owners' Equity
   10. Engagement Letters
   11. Client Representation Letters
   12. Using the Work of a Specialist
   13. Inquiry of a Client's Lawyer
   14. Related Party Transactions
   15. Operational Auditing

This module covers information included in the Audit Evidence and Procedures section of the AICPA Content Specification Outline with the following exceptions: (1) Use of the Computer in Performing the Audit is covered in the Auditing EDP module; (2) Use of Statistical Sampling in Performing the Audit is covered in the Statistical Sampling module; and (3) Subsequent Events are covered in the Reports module.

The following SAS sections pertain to audit evidence:

Section (AU)

318	Analytical Review Procedures
326	Evidential Matter
331	Receivables and Inventories
332	Long-Term Investments
333	Client Representations
335	Related Party Transactions
336	Using the Work of a Specialist
337	Inquiry of a Client's Lawyer Concerning Litigation, Claims, and Assessments

Section (AU)

339   Working Papers

340   The Auditor's Considerations When a Question Arises About an Entity's Continued Existence

390   Consideration of Omitted Procedures after the Reported Date

435   Segment Information

553   Supplementary Information Required by the Financial Accounting Standards Board

554   Supplementary Information on the Effects of Changing Prices

555   Supplementary Oil and Gas Reserve Information

556   Supplementary Mineral Reserve Information

722   Review of Interim Financial Information

Read the various sections and study the outlines for each of the above SASs separately. After studying each outline, attempt to summarize in your own words the "sum and substance" of the pronouncement. If you cannot explain the pronouncement in your own words, you do not understand it. Go back and study it again.

A. Audit Evidence--General

1. Competent and Sufficient Evidential Matter. The ultimate goal of an audit is to express an opinion as to whether the financial statements of the audited firm are presented fairly in conformity with generally accepted accounting principles. When management prepares financial statements which purport to be in conformity with generally accepted accounting principles, certain assertions (implicit or explicit) are made. Section 326.03 identifies and classifies these assertions as

   a. Presentation and disclosure--Components of financial statements are properly classified, described and disclosed (e.g., inventories are properly classified on the balance sheet)

   b. Existence or occurrence--Components of financial statements exist at a given date and transactions have occurred during a given period (e.g., inventories physically exist)

   c. Rights and obligations--Assets are rights of the entity and liabilities are obligations at a given date (e.g., firm has legal title to inventory)

   d. Completeness--All transactions and accounts presented (e.g., all inventory items included on balance sheet)

   e. Valuation or allocation--Components of financial statements included at appropriate amounts (e.g., inventories are properly stated at lower of cost or market)

(PERCV--as in, "I perceive the need to pass the CPA exam.") Note the relationship between existence and completeness. The existence assertion relates to whether the recorded amount is bona fide (e.g., recorded receivables are legitimate). Completeness, on the other hand, addresses the issue of whether all transactions have been recorded (e.g., are all receivables recorded?). An auditor must test for both existence and completeness. Auditing texts frequently refer to this as "2-directional testing."

Evidential matter is gathered in an audit to determine whether the above assertions have been met. To this end, the third standard of fieldwork requires that:

> Sufficient competent evidential matter is to be obtained through inspection, observation, inquiries, and confirmations to afford a reasonable basis for an opinion regarding the financial statements under examination.

Competent evidential matter may be thought of as being reliable. Section 326 states that, to be competent, evidential matter must be both valid and relevant (know these criteria). The validity of evidence is affected by the circumstances under which it is obtained. Section 326.18 states that the following presumptions (which have been asked directly and indirectly on several previous exams) relate to the validity of audit evidence:

a) Direct personal knowledge of the auditor obtained through physical examination, observation, computation, and inspection is more persuasive than information obtained indirectly.

b) Other things being equal, evidence from independent sources outside the enterprise provide greater assurance of reliability than that secured solely within the enterprise.

c) Accounting data developed under strong internal accounting control provides more assurance of reliability than data developed under weak internal accounting control.

Competent evidence must also be relevant to the financial statement assertion under consideration. Thus, a receivable confirmation may be more directly relevant to the existence assertion than to the valuation assertion. That is, a debtor might confirm the amount as being owed--whether it will ever be paid is another issue.

The concept of sufficient evidence refers to the quantity of evidence that an auditor must gather. Sufficient evidence has been gathered when audit risk (see discussion in Planning and Supervision--Professional Responsibilities Module) is considered to be at a low, acceptable level. Thus, if highly competent evidence is available, audit risk will be controlled with less evidence than in situations where the available evidence is of a lower competence.

Section 326.19 suggests that in the great majority of cases the auditor finds it necessary to rely on evidence that is persuasive rather than convincing: an acceptable level of audit risk does not indicate that <u>all</u> uncertainty be eliminated for sufficient evidence to have been gathered. The auditor must be able to form an opinion within a reasonable length of time, at a reasonable cost. However, the difficulty or expense involved in testing a particular item is not in itself a valid reason for omitting a test. Auditors use professional <u>judgment</u> to determine the extent of tests necessary to obtain <u>sufficient</u> evidence. In exercising this professional judgment, auditors consider both the materiality of the item in question (e.g., dollar size) as well as the <u>relative risk</u> of the item (e.g., cash, due to its liquidity, may have a higher relative risk than do certain property, plant, and equipment items).

The following example distinguishes between competent vs. sufficient evidence. Assume that an auditor has highly credible evidence on one account receivable for $400 out of a total receivable balance of $1,000,000. While this evidence is competent, most auditors would suggest that it is not sufficient evidence for the $1,000,000 balance; to be sufficient, more evidence verifying the account's <u>total</u> value must be collected.

2. <u>Types of Evidence</u>. Section 326.13 distinguishes between the underlying accounting data and all corroborating (supporting) information available to the auditor. <u>Underlying accounting data</u> includes books of original entry (journals), general and subsidiary ledgers, related accounting manuals, and informal and memorandum records such as worksheets supporting cost allocations, computations, and reconciliations.

<u>Corroborating evidence</u> is the supporting documentation that is the basis for a transaction being recorded in the journals and ledgers. While every text seems to have its own list of types of corroborating evidence, the following list seems quite adequate (memorize them by remembering the first letter of each category--AICPA IS).

> <u>A</u>uthoritative documents
> <u>I</u>nternal control
> <u>C</u>alculations
> <u>P</u>hysical existence
> <u>A</u>uthoritative statements--by client and by third parties
> <u>I</u>nterrelationships
> <u>S</u>ubsequent events

<u>Authoritative documents</u> such as truck titles, vendor's invoices, etc., support ownership and transactions.

<u>Internal control</u> is a form of audit evidence by itself. The adequacy thereof determines the extent and types of additional evidence required.

<u>Calculations</u> by auditor such as calculation of depreciation expense, tax liabilities, etc., support the application of GAAP.

<u>Physical existence</u> is determined by observation and count.

<u>Authoritative statements</u> by client provide support for the treatment of certain items in the recording and aggregation of transaction data. Authoritative statements by third parties such as confirmations provide evidence concerning the status of transactions with third parties.

<u>Interrelationships</u> within the data such as interest expense and accrued interest payable, unusual items, etc., provide assurance as to the reasonableness of items and the absence of material irregularities or errors.

<u>Subsequent events</u> confirm the status of estimates and assertions at the financial statement date. For example, subsequent collection of receivables gives evidence of their collectibility. Court award of a law suit pending at year end is evidence of the year-end payable or receivable.

Since the competency of evidence depends upon the financial statement assertion under consideration (recall PERCV), the auditor must use professional judgment when deciding which type of evidence is most appropriate in a specific situation. Conceptually, the auditor should attempt to gather a sufficient quantity of competent evidence at a minimum cost.

Audit procedures (acts to be performed) are undertaken by the auditor to obtain the corroborating evidence discussed above. Some of the terms (i.e., "buzz words") that you will find in written audit procedures are listed below. Review the terms and relate them to one or more of the categories of corroborative evidence. (Note: each "buzz word" indicates a specific action that the auditor would take while performing an audit procedure.)

> Analyze (account transactions)
> Compare (beginning balances with last year's audit figures)
> Confirm (payables and receivables)
> Count (cash, inventory, etc.)
> Examine (authoritative documents)
> Foot (totals)
> Inquire (for explanations of accounting treatments)
> Interrelate (interest expense with liabilities)
> Observe (inventories)
> Prove (totals)
> Read (minutes of directors' meetings)
> Recalculate (client's figures)
> Reconcile (beginning and ending balances)
> Trace or retrace (bookkeeping procedures)
> Review (legal documents)
> Scan (for unusual items)

B. Audit Evidence--Specific (Substantive Tests)

As noted earlier, the ultimate aim of an audit is to express an opinion on whether the firm's financial statements are fairly presented in conformity with generally accepted accounting principles. Substantive tests are designed to assist the auditor in reaching this goal by ascertaining whether the specific balances of financial statement accounts are in conformity with generally accepted accounting principles. Recall that while compliance tests are used to test the "means" of processing (the internal accounting control system), substantive tests are used to directly test the "ends" of processing--the financial statements.

When evaluating evidence, the objective is to obtain an estimate of the total error in the financial statements and to determine whether it exceeds a material amount. The auditor estimates the likely error in the financial statements and attempts to determine whether an unacceptably high audit risk exists. Note here that in the evaluation of audit evidence, because of information obtained during the audit, the auditor may revise his/her preliminary estimate of materiality (see discussion in Planning and Supervision--Professional Responsibilities Module).

1. Types of Substantive Tests. Substantive tests are of two types: (a) Analytical Review and (b) Tests of Details of Transactions and Balances.

a. Analytical Review. Analytical review procedures are substantive tests which can be used to study and compare relationships among data. They may be performed at the beginning of the audit or at any time thereafter. Perhaps the most familiar example of analytical review procedures used in auditing is the calculation of ratios. However, some firms also use such techniques as regression and time series analysis as a part of their analytical reviews.

In ratio analysis, the auditor calculates a ratio and compares it to some pertinent criterion such as:

    1) Itself in a prior period
    2) Its budgeted value
    3) Industry data
    4) Other financial information
    5) Other nonfinancial information

The auditor then further investigates the accounts relating to any ratios which seem to be inconsistent with the above criteria.

Ratios may be classified as:

1) Profitability (e.g., NI ÷ assets)
2) Short-term solvency (e.g., working capital ratio)
3) Long-term solvency (e.g., debt to equity)
4) Efficiency (e.g., turnover ratios such as average collection period for receivables)

Ratios have certain limitations:

1) The guidelines for evaluation may be inadequate (e.g., Why is an industry average good? Why should the ratio be the same as last year?)
2) It is difficult to determine whether a change in a ratio is significant or due to random error.
3) Cost-based accounting records hinder comparisons between firms of different ages and/or asset compositions.
4) Accounting differences hinder comparisons between firms (e.g., if one firm uses LIFO and another uses FIFO the information is not comparable).
5) Ratios present only "circumstantial" evidence in that a "significant" difference only leads to additional audit procedures as opposed to direct detection of an error.

b. <u>Tests of Details of Transactions and Balances</u>. These tests are used to examine the actual details making up the various account balances. For example, if receivables total $1,000,000 at year end, tests of details may be made of the individual components of the total account. Assume the $1,000,000 is the accumulation of 250 individual accounts. As a test of details, an auditor might decide to confirm a sample of these 250 accounts. Based on the results of the auditor's evaluation of internal accounting control and compliance tests, the auditor might determine that 60 accounts should be confirmed. Thus, when responses are received and when the balances have been reconciled, the auditor has actually tested the detail behind the account; the <u>existence</u> of the accounts has been confirmed. As an additional test (and also as an alternate procedure when confirmation replies have not been received from debtors), the auditor may examine cash receipts received after year end on individual accounts. This substantive test provides evidence pertaining to both the <u>existence</u> and the <u>valuation</u> of the account.

2. Preparing Substantive Test Audit Programs. The CPA exam frequently requires the candidate to prepare an audit program. This skill, obviously necessary in practice, is generally tested through essay questions. Three approaches have been used in these problems.

  a. The exam describes an internal control area of a company and requires the candidate to prepare a compliance test program
  b. The exam describes a financial statement account(s) of a company and requires the candidate to prepare a substantive test program
  c. The exam asks questions on an area in which a SAS prescribes specific audit procedures and requires the candidate to prepare an audit program

The compliance test program was discussed in the Internal Control module. We now discuss the second and third types of programs.

Approach for a Substantive Test Program. As noted earlier under "Audit Evidence--Specific (Substantive Tests)," statements which purport to be in conformity with generally accepted accounting principles contain certain assertions: presentation and disclosure, existence or occurrence, rights and obligations, completeness, valuation or allocation (PERCV). Auditors gather evidence to form an opinion with respect to these assertions. The experienced auditor should be able to prepare an audit program for an audit area (e.g., inventory) to test whether these assertions are supportable. The process is one in which specific audit objectives are developed (also either explicitly or implicitly) based on the assertions being made in the financial statements. Finally, audit procedures to meet these audit objectives are selected and listed in an audit program. These relationships may be illustrated as:

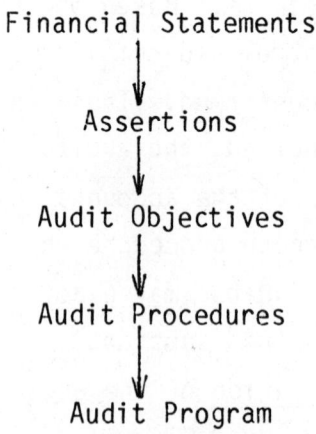

Financial Statements

Assertions

Audit Objectives

Audit Procedures

Audit Program

For purposes of the CPA exam, consider two possible approaches for auditing an account: (1) direct tests of ending balance ("tests of balances") and (2) tests of inputs and outputs during the year ("tests of details of transactions"). First, the auditor may directly test ending balances for high turnover accounts such as cash, accounts receivable, accounts payable, etc. (e.g., confirm year-end balances). The second approach, tests of inputs and outputs during the year, is used most extensively for low turnover accounts (e.g., fixed assets, long-term debt, etc.). For example, for fixed assets, a low turnover account, the emphasis will be on vouching additions or retirements--not on auditing the entire account for a continuing audit engagement. While the distinction between approaches will probably help you on audit program problems, bear in mind that in an audit it is not an either/or proposition--a combination of approaches with an emphasis of one approach over the other will generally be used.

To prepare a substantive test audit program use the following three step approach:

1) Determine whether the program should have an ending balance or input/output emphasis
2) Write as the first step of your audit program: "Test the adequacy of internal accounting control over the account"
3) Use the PERCV assertions to develop your audit program

The following tables present summarized substantive audit programs for the major balance sheet accounts. Although the tables are constructed to present the pertinent procedures under only one assertion, be aware that most audit procedures provide support for multiple assertions. For example, while receivable confirmations are listed under the "existence or occurrence" assertion, it may be argued that confirmations provide evidence with respect to all five assertions. The purpose is to use the PERCV assertions as an aid to organizing your thoughts; do not worry about which assertion an audit procedure "fits best under." Also, you should understand the listed procedures well enough to be able to explain them in detail on the CPA exam. Additionally, when writing audit programs for a balance sheet account, include procedures used to audit the related income statement accounts. For example, analytically reviewing bad debt expense may provide evidence as to the valuation of receivables; recalculating interest expense may provide evidence as to the existence of long-term debt; and recalculating depreciation and analytically reviewing repairs and maintenance expense may provide evidence as to the completeness and/or valuation of property, plant, and equipment. Finally, the CPA exam may ask for the auditor's "objectives" in the audit of an account. The approach suggested here may be easily adapted to answer this type of question. In the case of long-term debt, for example, the following could serve as objectives:

1) Determine whether internal control over long-term debt is adequate
2) Determine whether long-term debt disclosures comply with GAAP (presentation and disclosure)

3) Determine whether recorded long-term debt exists at year end (existence or occurrence)
4) Determine whether long-term debt represents an obligation to the firm at year end (rights and obligations)
5) Determine whether all long-term debt has been completely recorded at year end (completeness)
6) Determine whether all long-term debt has been properly valued at year end (valuation)

In addition to the summary audit procedures presented here, Section C of this module describes, in further detail, major audit procedures for the various accounts.

SUMMARY AUDIT PROCEDURES: CASH, RECEIVABLES, INVENTORY

	Cash	Receivables	Inventory
Presentation and Disclosure	1. Review disclosures for compliance with GAAP 2. Inquire about compensating balance requirements and restrictions	1. Review disclosures for compliance with GAAP 2. Inquire about pledging, discounting 3. Review loan agreements for pledging, factoring	1. Review disclosures for compliance with GAAP 2. Inquire about pledging 3. Review purchase commitments
Existence or Occurrence	1. Confirmation 2. Count cash on hand 3. Prepare bank transfer schedule	1. Confirmation 2. Inspect notes 3. Vouch (examine shipping documents, invoices, credit memos)	1. Confirmation of consigned inventory and inventory in warehouses 2. Observe inventory count
Rights and Obligations	1. Review cutoffs (receipts and disbursements) 2. Review passbooks, bank statements	1. Review cutoffs (sales, sales returns) 2. Inquire about factoring of receivables	1. Review cutoffs (sales, sales returns, purchases, purchase returns)
Completeness	1. Perform analytical review procedures 2. Review bank reconciliation (obtain cutoff statement for reconciling items).	1. Perform analytical review procedures	1. Perform test counts and compare with client's counts/summary 2. Inquire about consigned inventory 3. Perform analytical review procedures
Valuation	1. Foot summary schedules 2. Reconcile summary schedules to general ledger 3. Test translation of any foreign currencies	1. Foot subsidiary ledger 2. Reconcile subsidiary ledger to general ledger 3. Examine subsequent cash receipts 4. Age receivables to test adequacy of allowance for doubtful accounts 5. Discuss adequacy of allowance for doubtful accounts with management	1. Foot and extend summary schedules 2. Reconcile summary schedules to general ledger 3. Test inventory pricing 4. Examine inventory quality

SUMMARY AUDIT PROCEDURES: MARKETABLE SECURITIES, PROPERTY, PLANT AND EQUIPMENT, PREPAIDS

	Marketable Securities	**Property, Plant, Equipment**	**Prepaids**
Presentation and Disclosure	1. Review disclosures for compliance with GAAP 2. Inquire about pledging 3. Review loan agreements for pledging	1. Review disclosures for compliance with GAAP 2. Inquire about liens and restrictions 3. Review loan agreements for liens and restrictions	1. Review disclosures for compliance with GAAP 2. Review adequacy of insurance coverage
Existence or Occurrence	1. Confirmation of securities held by third parties 2. Inspect and count 3. Vouch (to available documentation)	1. Inspect additions 2. Vouch additions 3. Review any leases for proper accounting 4. Perform search for unrecorded retirements	1. Confirmation of deposits and insurance 2. Vouch (examine insurance policies miscellaneous support for deposit)
Rights and Obligations	1. Review cutoffs (examine transactions around year end)	1. Review minutes for proper approval of additions	(See existence or occurrence)
Completeness	1. Perform analytical review procedures	1. Perform analytical review procedures 2. Vouch major entries to repairs and maintenance expense	1. Perform analytical review procedures
Valuation	1. Foot summary schedules 2. Reconcile summary schedules to general ledger 3. Test amortization of premiums and discounts 4. Recompute long- vs. short-term portions 5. Perform lower of cost or market tests	1. Foot summary schedules 2. Reconcile summary schedules to general ledger 3. Recalculate depreciation	1. Foot summary schedules 2. Reconcile summary schedules to general ledger 3. Recalculate prepaid portions

SUMMARY AUDIT PROCEDURES: PAYABLES (CURRENT), LONG-TERM DEBT, OWNERS' EQUITY

	Payables (Current)	Long-Term Debt	Owners' Equity
Presentation and Disclosure	1. Review disclosures for compliance with GAAP 2. Review purchase commitments	1. Review disclosures for compliance with GAAP 2. Inquire about pledging of assets 3. Review debt agreements for pledging and events of default	1. Review disclosures for compliance with GAAP 2. Review information on stock options, dividend restrictions
Existence or Occurrence	1. Confirmation 2. Inspect copies of notes and note agreements 3. Vouch payables (examine purchase order, receiving reports, invoices)	1. Confirmation 2. Inspect copies of notes and note agreements 3. Trace receipt of funds (and payment) to bank account and cash receipts journal	1. Confirmation with registrar and transfer agent (if applicable) 2. Inspect stock certificate book (when no registrar or transfer agent) 3. Vouch capital stock entries
Rights and Obligations	1. Review cutoffs (purchases, purchase returns)	1. Review cutoffs (examine transactions around year end) 2. Review minutes for proper authorization (and completeness)	1. Review minutes for proper authorization 2. Inquire of legal counsel on legal issues 3. Review articles of incorporation and bylaws for propriety of equity securities
Completeness	1. Perform analytical review procedures 2. Perform search for unrecorded payables (examine unrecorded invoices, receiving reports, purchase orders) 3. For payroll, review year-end accrual 4. Inquire of management as to completeness	1. Perform analytical review procedures 2. Inquire of management as to completeness	1. Perform analytical review procedures 2. Inspect treasury stock certificates
Valuation	1. Foot subsidiary ledger 2. Reconcile subsidiary ledger to general ledger 3. Recalculate interest expense (if any)	1. Foot summary schedules 2. Reconcile summary schedules to general ledger 3. Vouch entries to account	1. Agree amounts to general ledger 2. Vouch dividend payments 3. Vouch all entries to retained earnings 4. Recalculate treasury stock transactions

Approach for a Program for Areas in Which SASs Prescribe Procedures.   The
following are areas in which the SASs list the specific procedures which the auditor
is to apply:

Specific Types of Transactions

Illegal Acts	328.04 - .09
Related Parties	335.09 - .15
Litigation (Loss Contingencies)	337.04 - .07

Information with which "limited" procedures are required

Information in Documents	
Containing Audited Statements	550.04
Interim Reviews	722.06
Compilations	AR100.10
Reviews	AR100.27

Supplemental Information Required by the FASB	
General Procedures	553.07
Effects of Changing Prices	555.05
Mineral Reserve Information	556.04

Areas in which "audit" procedures are required

Receivables and Inventories	331
Long-Term Investments	332.04 - .05
Segmental Information	435.04
Subsequent Events	560.10 - .12
Analytical Review	318.06

Other	
Other Auditors Involved	543.02 - .13
Public Warehouses	901.07,.32; 331.14 - .15

Memorizing the procedures in each of the areas would be a difficult task. A
more manageable approach is to first review them well before the exam and then,
again, shortly before the exam. Note the similarities within areas of the required
procedures. For example, procedures for illegal acts and related parties certainly
overlap. Be cautious not to cover this area too "lightly." This is the type of
problem on which, without adequate preparation, a candidate may "blank out" and
receive little or no credit for his/her solution.

3. Documentation (AU ¶339). Candidates should be familiar with the information in
the outline of Section 339 as to the function and types of workpapers, factors affecting the structure and content of workpapers, and the guidelines as to what

workpapers should include. You should know the AICPA's two suggested purposes for workpapers: (1) to aid in the conduct of the audit; (2) to provide support for the auditor's opinion.

Additionally, candidates should be aware of the following terms:

Working Trial Balance--A listing of ledger accounts with current year-end balances (as well as last year's ending balances), with columns for adjusting and reclassifying entries as well as for final balances for the current year. Typically both balance sheet and income statement accounts are included.

Lead Schedules--Schedules which summarize like accounts, the total of which is typically transferred to the working trial balance. For example, a client's various cash accounts may be summarized on a lead schedule with only the total cash being transferred to the working trial balance.

Index--The combination of numbers and/or letters given to a workpaper page for identification purposes. For example, cash workpaper may be indexed A-1.

Cross-Reference--When the same information is included on two workpapers, auditors indicate on each workpaper the index of the other workpaper containing the identical information. For example, if Schedule A-1 includes a bank reconciliation with total outstanding checks listed, while Schedule A-2 has a detailed list of these outstanding checks plus the total figure, the totals on the two workpapers will be cross-referenced to one another.

Current Workpaper Files--files which contain corroborating information pertaining to the current year's audit program (e.g., cash confirmation).

Permanent Workpaper Files--files which contain information that is expected to be used by the auditor on many future audits with the client (e.g., schedules of ratios by year).

C. Other Specific Evidence Topics

1. Cash. While no specific SAS sections pertain to cash, you should be familiar with several "tools" which the auditor uses in his/her audit of cash. Either a two or a four column bank reconciliation is prepared to reconcile the difference between the cash per bank and per books. The four column approach (also called a proof of cash) offers the advantage of allowing the auditor to test whether or not: (1) all cash receipts recorded on the books have been deposited in the bank, (2) all deposits in the bank are recorded on the books, (3) all book cash disbursements have been paid by the bank, and (4) all bank cash disbursements are recorded on the books. Note that a four column reconciliation will not detect (1) checks written for the wrong amounts and so recorded on both the books and the bank statement, and (2) unrecorded checks which have not cleared the bank.

A bank confirmation is sent on a standard form to the banks with which a firm deals to obtain the year-end balance in the account (per bank). Also, recall that

the form asks for replies from the bank as to loans outstanding, contingent liabilities, and various security agreements under the Uniform Commercial Code.

A bank transfer schedule shows the dates of all deposits and withdrawals between
the various bank accounts of the client. It is prepared using the bank statements
for the periods before and after year end as well as by using the firm's accounting
data. A bank transfer schedule is especially effective for detecting kiting--the
overstatement of cash by recording a deposit without a corresponding withdrawal at
year end. The following is an example of kiting for a client that has two bank accounts (one in Valley State Bank and one in First City Bank):

Date   Situation

12/1   *Bookkeeper writes himself a $10,000 check on the Valley account and cashes
        it--no journal entry is made.*

12/2   *Bookkeeper loses the money gambling in Bullhead City.*

12/31   *Bookkeeper, fearing the auditors will detect the irregularity, covers up the
        shortage by*

        1. *Writing a $10,000 check on First City account and depositing it in the
            Valley account (this will cover up the shortage).*

        2. *Not recording check in cash disbursements journal until after year end.*

        3. *Not listing check as outstanding on 12/31 bank reconciliation.*

*The following is an example of a bank transfer schedule which will detect the kit-
ing:*

| | | | Date | | | | Date | |
	Amount	Bank Drawn on	Books	Bank	Bank Deposited in		Books	Bank
Kiting	$10,000	First City	1/2	1/2	Valley		1/2	12/31

Additionally, note that while independent two column bank reconciliations of the
two accounts would not detect the kiting, a four column reconciliation of the Valley
account would.

A cutoff statement is a bank statement for the first 8-10 business days after
year end. It is sent by the bank directly to the auditor, who uses it primarily as
evidence in determining whether the reconciling items on the year-end bank reconciliation have been properly reflected (e.g., an outstanding check has been recorded
at the proper value).

2. Receivables (AU ¶331.03 - .08). Review the outline of this section. From the
earlier discussion of financial statement assertions (PERCV), recall that confirmations most directly address the existence assertion.

Note especially that two types of confirmations are defined. Debtors are asked to respond to <u>positive</u> confirmations regardless of whether they agree with the amount on the confirmation. Debtors are asked to respond to <u>negative</u> confirmations only if they disagree with the amount on the confirmation. Receivable confirmation is a generally accepted auditing procedure and a CPA must be able to justify not using it. This SAS Section suggests that the positive form is preferable for large accounts and when there is reason to believe that there may be a large number of accounts with errors. The negative form is useful when there is good internal control, small dollar balances, and when the auditor believes that those receiving the confirmation will give them consideration. Note that when no replies are received for negative confirmations the assumption (which may be questionable) is made that the debtor agrees that s/he owes the amount on the confirmation. In the case of nonreplies to positive confirmations, alternative procedures must generally be performed (e.g., examination of shipping documents, subsequent cash receipts, sales agreements).

An <u>aging schedule</u> is used by auditors to address the receivable <u>valuation</u> assertion. Such a schedule summarizes receivables by their "age" (e.g., 0-30 days since sale, 31-60 days since sale. . . .). Estimates of the likely amount of bad debts in each age group are then made (typically based on historical experience) to estimate whether the amount in the allowance for doubtful accounts is adequate at year end.

Accounts receivable may be used to assist in <u>lapping</u>, an embezzlement scheme in which cash collections from customers are stolen. To keep the embezzlement from being discovered, the embezzler corrects the customers' accounts within a few days by posting other cash receipts to the accounts for which the proceeds have been embezzled. A simplified lapping scheme is shown below:

Date	Situation	Bookkeeping Entry		
1/7	Jones pays $500 on account	No entry, bookkeeper cashes check and keeps proceeds		
1/8	Smith pays $200 on account	Cash	500	
		Accounts Receivable--Jones		500
	Adams pays $300 on account			
1/9	Brock pays $500 on account	Cash	500	
		Accounts Receivable--Smith		200
		Accounts Receivable--Adams		300
1/10	Bookkeeper determines Brock is unlikely to purchase from firm in future	Allowance for Doubtful Accounts	500	
		Accounts Receivable--Brock		500

Lapping most frequently occurs in situations in which one individual has both recordkeeping responsibility and custody of cash. Auditors frequently use techniques such as the following to detect lapping:

   a. Analytical review--Calculate average age of receivables and receivable turnover (lapping will increase average age and decrease turnover)

   b. Confirmations--Emphasize old accounts and written off accounts and investigate all exceptions noted (watch for posting of cash receipts after an unusually long time)

   c. Deposit slips--

     1) Obtain authenticated deposit slips from bank and compare names, dates and amounts on remittance advices to information on deposit slips (where possible)

     2) Perform surprise inspection of deposits, and compare deposit slip with remittances

   d. Bookkeeping system--

     1) Compare remittance advices with information recorded
     2) Verify propriety of noncash credits to accounts receivable
     3) Foot cash receipts journal, customers' ledger accounts, and accounts receivable control account
     4) Reconcile individual customer accounts to account receivable control account
     5) Compare copies of monthly statements with customer accounts

3. Inventory (AU ¶331.09-.13). Review the outline of this section. Note that the observation of the counting of inventory (which primarily addresses the existence assertion) is also a generally accepted auditing procedure from which departure must be justified. If the client uses statistical methods, the auditor must be satisfied that the sampling plan has statistical validity. Also, in cases of very good internal control, the client may count a portion of the inventory before year end with reliance on controls through year end.

4. Marketable Securities (AU ¶332). Review the outline. Recall the criteria for deciding whether the cost, equity, or consolidated basis should be used for the investments. Also, recall the distinction in accounting treatment for long-term vs. short-term investments in marketable equity securities as well as the necessity of amortizing discounts/premiums on bonds in the case of long-term debt securities (recall that discounts/premiums on short-term debt securities are not amortized).

An auditor typically inspects any securities which are held by a client (often in a safe deposit box) and confirms securities held by third parties (e.g., a bank). Because of the liquid nature of securities, the inspection is generally performed simultaneously with the audit of cash, bank loans (e.g., a revolving credit agreement), and other related items. A client employee should be present during the inspection to avoid confusion over any missing securities. In examining the security certificates, the auditor determines whether securities held are identical to the recorded securities (certificate numbers, number of shares, face value, etc.).

5. Property, Plant, and Equipment (PP&E). The audit of PP&E consists largely of an analysis of the year's acquisitions and disposals (an input and output approach) when the opening balance has already been audited. The entire account balance must be audited in detail for a first year audit.

Acquisitions are vouched to vendors' invoices, certificates of title, etc. For sales and trades of PP&E the auditor traces cash receipts to the cash receipts journal and recalculates any gains (losses). Disposals may occur due to retirements or thefts of PP&E items. Simple retirements of equipment are often difficult to detect since no journal entry may have been recorded to reflect the event. Unrecorded or improperly recorded retirements (and thefts) may be discovered through examination of changes in insurance policies, consideration of the purpose of acquisitions, examination of property tax files, discussions, observation, or through an examination of debits to accumulated depreciation.

CPA exam questions frequently address the relationship between repairs and maintenance expense and PP&E. Remember: an examination of the details of repairs and maintenance expense may reveal understated acquisitions, since an acquisition may have been improperly expensed. On the other hand, the examination of PP&E may reveal expenses which may have improperly been capitalized (understated repairs and maintenance).

An analysis of rent expense and the supporting leasing agreements should be made to detect unrecorded capital leases.

6. Prepaids. Prepaids typically consist of items such as insurance and deposits. Insurance policies may be examined and the prepaid portion of any expenditure may be recalculated. Additionally, policies may be confirmed with the firm's insurance agent and/or payments may be vouched. The lack of insurance on an asset ("self-insurance") will not typically result in a report modification, although such a situation may be discussed by the client in the footnotes to the financial statements. Also, an auditor may serve an advisory role by pointing out assets which, unknown to management, may have inadequate insurance.

Deposits and other prepaid amounts are typically immaterial. In those situations in which they are considered material, an auditor may confirm their existence, recalculate prepaid portions, and examine any available support.

7. <u>Payables (Current)</u>. Auditors typically review purchase orders, receiving reports, purchase agreements, and vendors' invoices to examine <u>recorded</u> payables. Because both purchase agreements and vendors' invoices are externally generated, they are generally considered reliable.

Confirmations may be sent. However, confirmation procedures are sometimes omitted due to the availability of externally generated evidence and due to inability of confirmations to adequately address the completeness assertion. (Auditors are primarily concerned about the possibility of understated payables--a major payable may not be confirmed if it is omitted from the trial balance of payables.) Accounts payable confirmations are most frequently used in circumstances involving bad internal control, bad financial position, and when vendors do not send month-end statements. However, when an auditor has chosen to confirm payables despite the existence of vendor statements, the confirmation will frequently request the vendor to send the month-end statement to the auditor. The balance per the client's books is not included on the confirmation. Confirmations are typically sent to major suppliers (not necessarily largest year-end balances), disputed accounts, and to a sample of other suppliers based on the premise that understated payables exist. The client will probably have established the largest credit lines with its major suppliers and thus the potential for the largest understatement exists in such accounts.

The auditor's "search for <u>unrecorded</u> liabilities" is an effort to discover any liabilities which may have been omitted from recorded year-end payables. Procedures such as the following are used:

1. Examination of vendors' invoices and statements
2. Examination, after year end, of the following to test whether proper cutoffs have occurred

    a. Cash disbursements   c. Unrecorded vouchers (receiving reports,
    b. Purchases   vendors' invoices, purchase orders)

Additionally, note that the internal control system is analyzed to determine how effective it is likely to be in preventing and detecting the occurrence of such errors.

Recall that payables are to be recorded when title to goods passes. For items shipped FOB shipping point, title generally passes when the item is shipped; for items shipped FOB destination, title generally passes when the goods are received. This part of the examination must be coordinated with inventory observation procedures.

Other current liabilities include accrued items (e.g., salaries payable). Such liabilities may be recalculated for reasonableness.

8. <u>Long-Term Debt</u>. Auditors test new borrowings, repayments, and ending debt balances. Minutes of director and/or stockholder meetings will be reviewed to determine whether new borrowings have been properly authorized. The proceeds of any new borrowings will be traced to the cash receipts journal, deposit slips, and bank statements.

Repayments will be traced to the cash disbursements journal, cancelled checks, and to cancelled notes. If a debt trustee is used, it will be possible to obtain information through a confirmation on whether the repayments have been made.

Considerable analysis is performed on ending debt balances. Confirmations are frequently used. For situations in which the debt is owed to banks, recall that the standard bank confirmation (see "1. <u>Cash</u>.") requests such debt information. Direct confirmation with other creditors is also typically performed.

The CPA also reviews all debt agreements to determine compliance with various restrictions and to test the propriety of the classification between long- and short-term liabilities. Also, the examination of debt agreements will often disclose pledged assets and/or any required compensating cash balances which need to be disclosed.

Interest expense and accrued year-end interest payable will also be recalculated. Analytical review techniques can be used to test the reasonableness of interest expense as compared to outstanding debt.

9. <u>Owners' Equity</u>. Clients use one of two approaches for capital stock transactions. First, a stock certificate book may be used which summarizes, through "stubs," the outstanding certificates (the stockholders hold the actual certificates); cancelled certificates (for repurchased stock or received when a change in stock ownership occurs) are held by the client. When a stock certificate book is used the auditor will reconcile outstanding shares, par values, etc. with the "stubs" in the book. Confirmations may be sent to stockholders.

The second approach, typically used by large firms, is to engage a transfer agent and registrar to manage the firm's stock transactions. In such cases the number of shares issued and outstanding will usually be confirmed directly by the transfer agent and registrar.

As in the case of long-term debt, changes in equity accounts will be traced to supporting evidence, such as director and stockholder meeting minutes, journals, deposit slips, and bank statements. Approval for dividends will be traced to director minutes. Analytical review techniques may be used to test the reasonableness of the total dividends (e.g., multiply shares outstanding times per share dividend). If the client uses a "dividend paying agent," such as a bank or the transfer agent, confirmation of total dividends paid may be possible.

Because the profession has adopted an "all inclusive" form of income statement, few entries will be made into <u>retained earnings.</u> Little effort need be exerted for a continuing client. The audit procedures for dividends outlined above will allow the auditor to determine the propriety of that debit to retained earnings. The entry to record for the year's net income (loss) is readily available. Finally, the nature of any prior period adjustments is examined to determine whether they meet the criteria for an adjustment to retained earnings. Recall that the type of adjustment typically encountered is a correction of prior years' income.

10. <u>Engagement letters.</u> Engagement letters document and confirm the auditor's acceptance of the appointment, outline the objectives and scope of the audit, outline the extent of auditor responsibility to the client, and indicate the form of any reports to be issued by the auditor. Engagement letters are recommended on both audits and reviews. While the Auditing Standards Board has not issued a sample engagement letter, the following sample was published by the International Auditing Practices Committee:

To the Board of Directors or the appropriate representative of senior management:

You have requested that we audit the balance sheet, statements of income and changes in financial position of .... as of and for the year ending .... We are pleased to confirm our acceptance and our understanding of this engagement by means of this letter. Our audit will be made in accordance with applicable authoritative pronouncements in ....(name of country) with the objective of our expressing an opinion on the financial statements.

In forming our opinion on the financial statements, we will perform sufficient tests to obtain reasonable assurance as to whether the information contained in the underlying accounting records and other source data is reliable and sufficient as the basis for the preparation of the financial statements. We will also decide whether the information is properly communicated in the financial statements.

Because of the test nature and other inherent limitations of an audit, together with the inherent limitations of any system of internal control, there is an unavoidable risk that even some material misstatement may remain undiscovered.

In addition to our report on the financial statements, we expect to provide you with a separate letter concerning any material weaknesses in internal control which come to our notice.

May we remind you that the responsibility for the preparation of financial statements including adequate disclosure is that of the management of the company. This includes the maintenance of adequate accounting records and internal controls, the selection and application of accounting policies, and the safeguarding of the assets of the company. As part of our audit process, we will request from management written confirmation concerning representations made to us in connection with the audit.

We look forward to full cooperation with your staff and we trust that they will make available to us whatever records, documentation and other information are requested in connection with our audit.

Our fees, which will be billed as work progresses, are based on the time required by the individuals assigned to the engagement plus direct out-of-pocket expenses. Individual hourly rates vary according to the degree of responsibility involved and the experience and skill required.

This letter will be effective for future years unless it is terminated, amended or superseded.

Please sign and return the attached copy of this letter to indicate that it is in accordance with your understanding of the arrangements for our audit of the financial statements.

X, Y, Z and Company

11. Client Representation Letters (AU ¶333). Review the outline and note that representation letters are required for audits. Representation letters, while not a substitute for other audit procedures, ordinarily confirm in writing oral representations which have been made by management to the auditor and thereby reduce the likelihood of misunderstandings. They are to be signed by the chief executive officer and the chief financial officer at the close of the audit (dated last day of significant fieldwork). Management refusal to provide such written representation is a limitation in the scope of the audit sufficient to preclude an unqualified opinion. The following is a sample representation letter:

(Date of Auditor's Report)

(To Independent Auditor)

In connection with your examination of the (identification of financial statements) of (name of client) as of (date) and for the (period of examination) for the purpose of expressing an opinion as to whether the (consolidated) financial statements present fairly the financial position, results of operations, and changes in financial position of (name of client) in conformity with generally accepted accounting principles (other comprehensive basis of accounting), we confirm, to the best of our knowledge and belief, the following representations made to you during your examination.

1. We are responsible for the fair presentation in the (consolidated) financial statements of financial position, results of operations, and changes in financial position in conformity with generally accepted accounting principles (other comprehensive basis of accounting).

2. We have made available to you all —
   a. Financial records and related data.
   b. Minutes of the meetings of stockholders, directors, and committees of directors, or summaries of actions of recent meetings for which minutes have not yet been prepared.

3. There have been no—
   a. Irregularities involving management or employees who have significant roles in the system of internal accounting control.
   b. Irregularities involving other employees that could have a material effect on the financial statements.
   c. Communications from regulatory agencies concerning noncompliance with, or deficiencies in, financial reporting practices that could have a material effect on the financial statements.

4. We have no plans or intentions that may materially affect the carrying value or classification of assets and liabilities.

5. The following have been properly recorded or disclosed in the financial statements:
    a. Related party transactions and related amounts receivable or payable, including sales, purchases, loans, transfers, leasing arrangements, and guarantees.
    b. Capital stock repurchase options or agreements or capital stock reserved for options, warrants, conversions, or other requirements.
    c. Arrangements with financial institutions involving compensating balances or other arrangements involving restrictions on cash balances and line-of-credit or similar arrangements.
    d. Agreements to repurchase assets previously sold.

6. There are no —
    a. Violations or possible violations of laws or regulations whose effects should be considered for disclosure in the financial statements or as a basis for recording a loss contingency.
    b. Other material liabilities or gain or loss contingencies that are required to be accrued or disclosed by Statement of Financial Accounting Standards No. 5.

7. There are no unasserted claims or assessments that our lawyer has advised us are probable of assertion and must be disclosed in accordance with Statement of Financial Accounting Standards No. 5.

8. There are no material transactions that have not been properly recorded in the accounting records underlying the financial statements.

9. Provision, when material, has been made to reduce excess or obsolete inventories to their estimated net realizable value.

10. The company has satisfactory title to all owned assets, and there are no liens or encumbrances on such assets nor has any asset been pledged.

11. Provision has been made for any material loss to be sustained in the fulfillment of, or from inability to fulfill, any sales commitments.

12. Provision has been made for any material loss to be sustained as a result of purchase commitments for inventory quantities in excess of normal requirements or at prices in excess of the prevailing market prices.

13. We have complied with all aspects of contractual agreements that would have a material effect on the financial statements in the event of noncompliance.

14. No events have occurred subsequent to the balance sheet date that would require adjustment to, or disclosure in, the financial statements.

_____	_____
(Name of Chief Executive Officer and Title)	(Name of Chief Financial Officer and Title)

(Section 333, Appendix)

12. Using the Work of a Specialist (AU ¶336). Read the outline and note especially that the auditor may use the work of a specialist (in cases such as the valuation of an inventory, for example). The specialist is not referred to in the audit report unless his/her report is the cause for other than an unqualified report.

13.   Inquiry of a Client's Lawyer (AU ¶337).   Read the key points in the outline. The client's lawyer is the primary source for information on loss contingencies. Refusal of the lawyer to reply is a scope limitation which may affect the audit report.   In the case of unasserted claims which the client has not disclosed, the lawyer is not required to note them in his/her reply to the auditor; however, the lawyer is generally required to inform the client of the omission and to consider withdrawing if the client fails to inform the auditor.   The following is a sample lawyer's letter:

> In connection with an examination of our financial statements at (balance sheet date) and for the (period) then ended, management of the Company has prepared, and furnished to our auditors (name and address of auditors), a description and evaluation of certain contingencies, including those set forth below involving matters with respect to which you have been engaged and to which you have devoted substantive attention on behalf of the Company in the form of legal consultation or representation. These contingencies are regarded by management of the Company as material for this purpose (management may indicate a materiality limit if an understanding has been reached with the auditor). Your response should include matters that existed at (balance sheet date) and during the period from that date to the date of your response.

Pending or Threatened Litigation (excluding unasserted claims)

> [Ordinarily the information would include the following: (1) the nature of the litigation, (2) the progress of the case to date, (3) how management is responding or intends to respond to the litigation (for example, to contest the case vigorously or to seek an out-of-court settlement), and (4) an evaluation of the likelihood of an unfavorable outcome and an estimate, if one can be made, of the amount or range of potential loss.] Please furnish to our auditors such explanation, if any, that you consider necessary to supplement the foregoing information, including an explanation of those matters as to which your views may differ from those stated and an identification of the omission of any pending or threatened litigation, claims, and assessments or a statement that the list of such matters is complete.

Unasserted Claims and Assessments (considered by management to be probable of assertion, and that, if asserted, would have at least a reasonable possibility of an unfavorable outcome)

> [Ordinarily management's information would include the following: (1) the nature of the matter, (2) how management intends to respond if the claim is asserted, and (3) an evaluation of the likelihood of an unfavorable outcome and an estimate, if one can be made, of the amount or range of potential loss.] Please furnish to our auditors such explanation, if any, that you consider necessary to supplement the foregoing information, including an explanation of those matters as to which your views may differ from those stated.
>
> We understand that whenever, in the course of performing legal services for us with respect to a matter recognized to involve an unasserted possible claim or assessment that may call for financial statement disclosure, if you have formed a professional conclusion that we should disclose or consider disclosure concerning such possible claim or assessment, as a matter of professional responsibility to us, you will so advise us and will consult with us concerning the question of such disclosure and the applicable requirements of Statement of Financial Accounting Standards No. 5. Please specifically confirm to our auditors that our understanding is correct.

Please specifically identify the nature of and reasons for any limitation on your response. [The auditor may request the client to inquire about additional matters, for example, unpaid or unbilled charges or specified information on certain contractually assumed obligations of the company, such as guarantees of indebtedness of others.]

(Section 337, Appendix)

14. <u>Related Party Transactions (AU ¶335)</u>. Review the outline. The primary problem with related party transactions is that the price at which a transaction occurs may not be the one which would have resulted from "arm's length bargaining." Note the procedures suggested in Section 337 for discovering related party transactions. Further note that it is generally not possible for the auditor to determine whether such a transaction would have occurred, if no related party had existed, and, if so, the price thereof.

15. <u>Operational Auditing</u>. Operational audits, generally performed by internal auditors, typically evaluate the <u>effectiveness</u> and <u>efficiency</u> of various accounting processes. For example, an operational audit of the sales, receivables, and cash receipts cycle would deal largely with administrative controls as well as accounting controls and would emphasize whether the process was efficient and effective. A financial statement audit on the other hand would deal more directly with accounting controls and the safeguarding of assets and the accuracy of the financial records.

AUDIT REPORTS

The report represents the primary product of auditor association with client financial statements. The following "Diagram of an Audit," originally presented in the auditing overview section, shows the relationship of the audit report to the entire financial statement audit:

DIAGRAM OF AN AUDIT

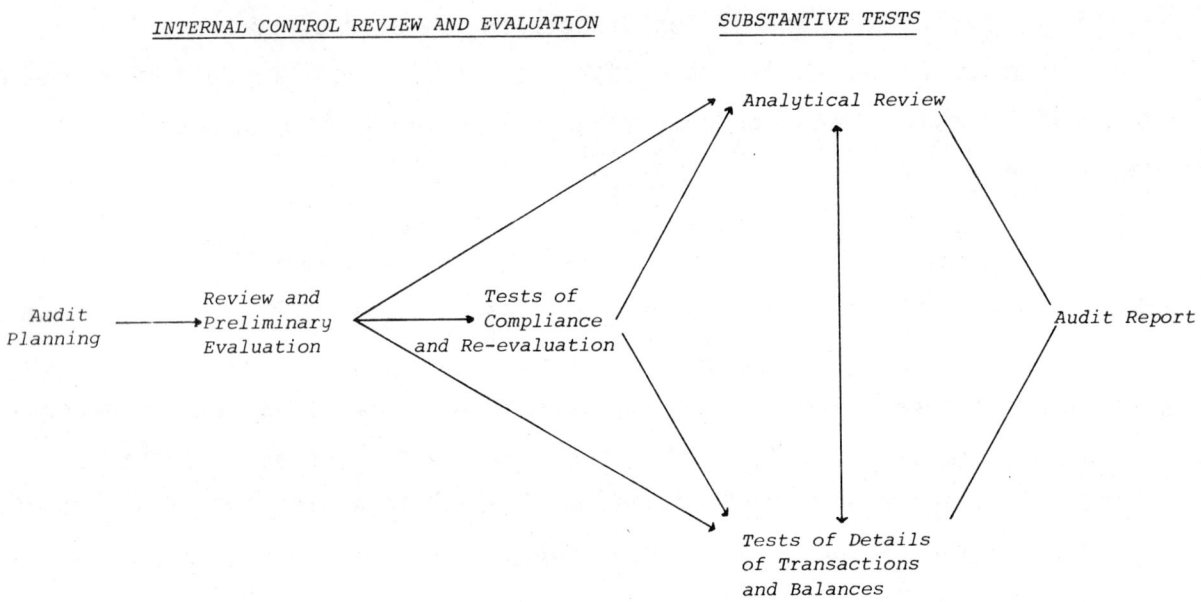

INTERNAL CONTROL REVIEW AND EVALUATION   *SUBSTANTIVE TESTS*

Kinney, William R., Jr., "Decision Theory Aspects of Internal Control System Design/Compliance, and Substantive Tests," Journal of Accounting Research (Supplement, 1975), p. 16 (adapted).

This module primarily covers audit reports, but also includes information on other reports (e.g., compilation reports, review reports, special reports). Candidate knowledge of reports is tested on every examination. While most of the report questions refer to audit reports, a significant number of questions refer to the other types of reports which auditors issue. Essay questions in this area often describe a situation and ask the candidate to prepare an appropriate audit report. Multiple choice questions present a circumstance which calls for a departure from the standard short-form report and ask specifically what type of report is to be issued.

Study Program for the Reports Module

This module is organized and should be studied in the following manner:

    A. Financial Statement Audit Reports--General
    B. Financial Statement Audit Reports--Specific
    C. Auditor Association Other Than Audits

All of the following sections of Statements on Auditing Standards apply to reports:

Section (AU)

410	Adherence to GAAP
411	The Meaning of "Present Fairly"
420	Consistency of Application of GAAP
431	Adequacy of Informative Disclosure
435	Segment Information
504	Association with Financial Statements
505	Reports on Comparative Financial Statements
509	Reports on Audited Financial Statements
530	Dating of Report
543	Part of Examination Made by Other Independent Auditors
545	Inadequate Disclosure
546	Reporting on Inconsistency
550	Other Information in Documents Containing Audited Financial Statement
552	Reporting on Condensed Financial Statements and Selected Financial Data
553	Supplementary Information Required by the Financial Accounting Standards Board
560	Subsequent Events
561	Subsequent Discovery of Facts Existing at the Date of the Auditor's Report
621	Special Reports
622	Special Reports--Applying Agreed-Upon Procedures to Specified Elements, Accounting or Items of a Financial Statement
631	Letters for Underwriters
722	Review of Interim Financial Information
730	Unaudited Replacement Cost Information

Additionally, you should read the outlines of Statements on Standards for Accounting and Review Services which follow the outlines of the Statements on Auditing Standards (page 362).

Statements on Standards for Accounting and Review Services (SSARS)

SSARS 1, Compilation and Review of Financial Statements
SSARS 2, Reporting on Comparative Financial Statements
SSARS 3, Compilation Reports on Financial Statements Included in Certain Prescribed Forms
SSARS 4, Communications Between Predecessor and Successor Accountants
SSARS 5, Reporting on Compiled Financial Statements (consists solely of changes to SSARS 1 which have been integrated into the outline of that statement)

The above SAS sections are very detailed. In this module we present an overview of the information in the various sections. In order to simplify the discussion, the topics are covered in a sequence which is somewhat different than the order in which they are presented in the codified professional standards. The best way to cover this material is to first read the background material on an SAS section presented in this module. Then, read the actual SAS section together with the SAS outline presented subsequently in this volume. The purpose of this module is to present you with overall information which will make it easier for you to follow the actual SASs.

This module covers the topics listed in the Reporting area of the AICPA Content Specification Outline plus subsequent events which the AICPA includes in the Audit Evidence and Procedures area of the Outline.

A. Financial Statement Audit Reports--General

The objective and primary product of the audit is the audit report. The following standard short-form report was originally presented in the overview section:

To: Board of Directors and Stockholders   June 1, 19X3
     ABC Company

>   We have examined the balance sheets of ABC Company as of [at] December 31, 19X2 and 19X1, and the related statements of income, retained earnings, and changes in financial position for the years then ended. Our examinations were made in accordance with generally accepted auditing standards and, accordingly, included such tests of the accounting records and such other auditing procedures as we considered necessary in the circumstances.

>   In our opinion, the financial statements referred to above present fairly the financial position of ABC Company as of [at] December 31, 19X2 and 19X1, and the results of its operations and the changes in its financial position for the years then ended, in conformity with generally accepted accounting principles applied on a consistent basis.

                                                        /s/ Joe Smith, CPA

Some key assertions in the above report include:

Addressee (company, board of directors and/or stockholders--not management)
Date (normally last day of field work)

Scope paragraph

    1. We have examined

    2. Client's financial statements
        Balance sheets
        Income statements
        Retained earnings statements
        Statements of changes in financial position

3. Exam was according to GAAS including
       Tests of the accounting records
       Other auditing procedures
       As we considered necessary

Opinion paragraph

1. In our opinion

2. Statements fairly present
       Per GAAP (applied consistently)
Signature (Firm name)

Remember that the generally accepted auditing standards (GAAS) include four reporting standards (GAAP, Opinion, Disclosure, Consistency--the GODC mnemonic presented in the Overview Section). Read Section 410, 411, and 431 (we will cover the numerous other sections on audit reports below). Note especially in Section 411 that the "present fairly" term in the opinion paragraph is generally to be interpreted within the framework of GAAP. That is, if financial statements are in conformity with GAAP, they generally do present fairly. Also, note in Section 411 that when alternate acceptable principles exist (e.g., LIFO and FIFO), the auditor may conclude that more than one accounting principle is acceptable--that is, the auditor does not in general have to decide whether the client is using the "best" one. However, there may be unusual circumstances in which accounting principles may make the financial statements misleading (e.g., new legislation); in such cases, not too surprisingly, the principle is not to be followed.

In 1982 an amendment to Section 411 clarified the authority of sources of GAAP. The following four level hierarchy was established:

	Category	Included items
a.	Authoritative body pronouncements	FASB Statements FASB Interpretations APB Opinions AICPA Accounting Research Bulletins
b.	Other expert pronouncements	AICPA Industry Audit Guides and Accounting Guides AICPA Statements of Position
c.	Widely recognized pronouncements and practices	FASB Technical Bulletins AICPA Accounting Interpretations Widely accepted industry practices
d.	Other accounting literature	APB Statements AICPA Issues Papers FASB Statements of Financial Accounting Concepts Other Professional Association and Regulatory pronouncements Accounting textbooks and articles

In cases of conflict between the accounting treatment suggested by the categories the higher category prevails (e.g., "a" would prevail over "b"); for conflicts within a category the one most closely approximating the transaction's economic substance prevails.

Also, Section 430 was revised in October of 1980 (now Section 431) to include a statement that when the auditor issues a qualified or an adverse opinion, the report should provide, if <u>practicable</u>, the information causing the departure from an unqualified report. Thus if the client omits information in the footnotes concerning a loan agreement's restriction of future dividends, the auditor would provide the additional information. But, if the client has omitted a statement of changes in financial position, an auditor would not be required to prepare it, since it is not practicable to directly obtain this information from the client's records.

B. Financial Statement Audit Reports--Detailed

1. <u>Circumstances resulting in departure from the auditor's standard report.</u>
The AICPA does not present a list of necessary conditions for an auditor to render a standard, unqualified report. Instead, Section 509 describes the following circumstances that "result in a departure from the auditor's standard report":

    a) Scope limitations
    b) Opinion based, in part, on report of another auditor
    c) Departure from a generally accepted accounting principle
    d) Departure from a promulgated accounting principle
    e) Accounting principles not consistently applied
    f) Uncertainties
    g) Emphasis of a matter

Also, scattered throughout the SASs are the following additional conditions which may cause the auditor to depart from the standard report:

    h) Lack of independence
    i) Segmental accounting information
    j) Additional information included with basic financial statements

The candidate should be familiar with the effect each of the above circumstances has on an auditor's report. In the following pages we summarize some of the most basic "must know" material. While the outlines on the various audit report sections present the information in more detail, we here provide the candidate with a more structured, organized approach to these topics than is possible with the outlines alone. Also, note that samples of the various types of audit reports are presented in Section 509.29-509.47.

a. Scope limitations (Au ¶509.10-.13). Scope limitations result in either a qualified (except for) opinion or a disclaimer. The type of report issued depends on the importance of the omitted procedures. This assessment is affected by the nature and magnitude of the potential effects of the matters in question and by their significance to the financial statements (e.g., number of accounts involved).

Two types of scope limitations need to be considered--client imposed and circumstance imposed. Client imposed result when a client will not allow an auditor to perform an audit procedure (e.g., confirm receivables). Circumstance imposed occur in situations other than the client saying, "No, I will not allow you to perform that procedure." For example, although a bad internal control system which makes it impossible for the auditor to perform the audit may be management's fault, it is considered circumstance imposed. The following summarizes the effect of scope limitations on the report.

SCOPE LIMITATION DECISIONS

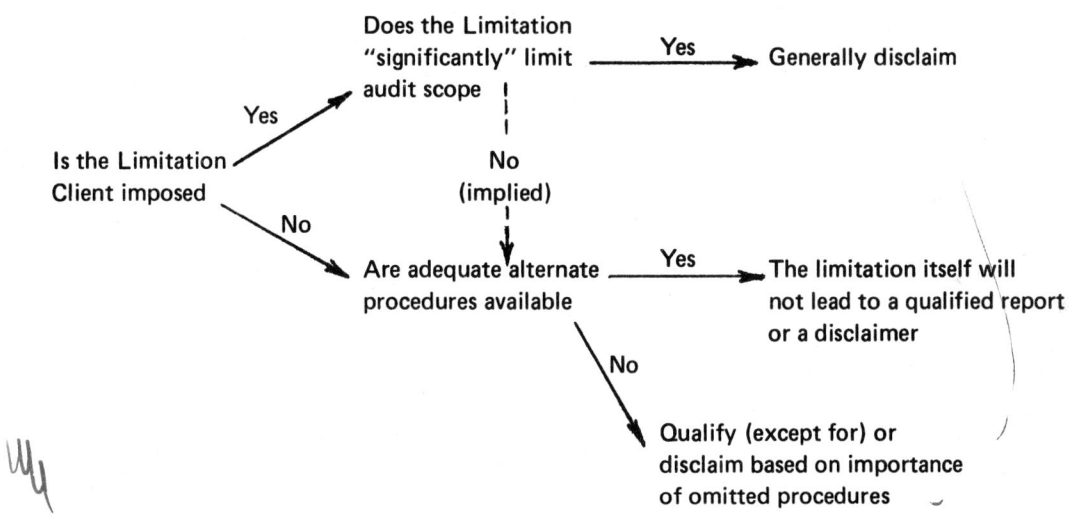

Finally, an auditor may be asked to report on only one statement (e.g., the balance sheet). If the auditor's access to information underlying the financial statements is not limited, such a situation does not involve a scope limitation. That is, scope limitations are related to audit procedures, not reporting objectives.

b. Opinion based, in part, on report of another auditor (Au ¶509.14, 543). Opinions based, in part, on the report of another auditor differ from the standard report, but are still unqualified. This situation arises when two or more auditors are involved in the audit of a single entity. An example of this is the case in which one audits the entire firm except for a subsidiary in a distant location.

While the auditor who audited the single subsidiary will generally give an audit report on it, and while the auditor who audited the remainder of the firm could give a report on that portion, there will generally be a preference (and indeed often a legal requirement) for an audit report on the overall firm.

The overall audit report must be signed by the <u>principal</u> auditor. The principal auditor is chosen based on the materiality of the portion of financial statements examined, knowledge of the overall financial statements, and the importance of the components audited. The principal auditor is required to:

1) Make inquiries into the other auditor's <u>reputation</u> (e.g., contact AICPA, state society of CPAs, other practitioners, bankers)

2) Obtain representation from other auditor of <u>independence</u>

3) Ascertain that other auditor <u>knows</u> U.S. auditing <u>standards</u>, SEC standards (if appropriate), and knows that statements are a component of the overall firm

If the results of any of the above inquiries are unsatisfactory, the principal auditor must either modify the overall audit report (qualify or disclaim), or audit the component. If the results of the inquiries are satisfactory, the following summarizes the principal auditor's required decisions and responsibilities:

PRINCIPAL — OTHER AUDITOR RELATIONSHIP

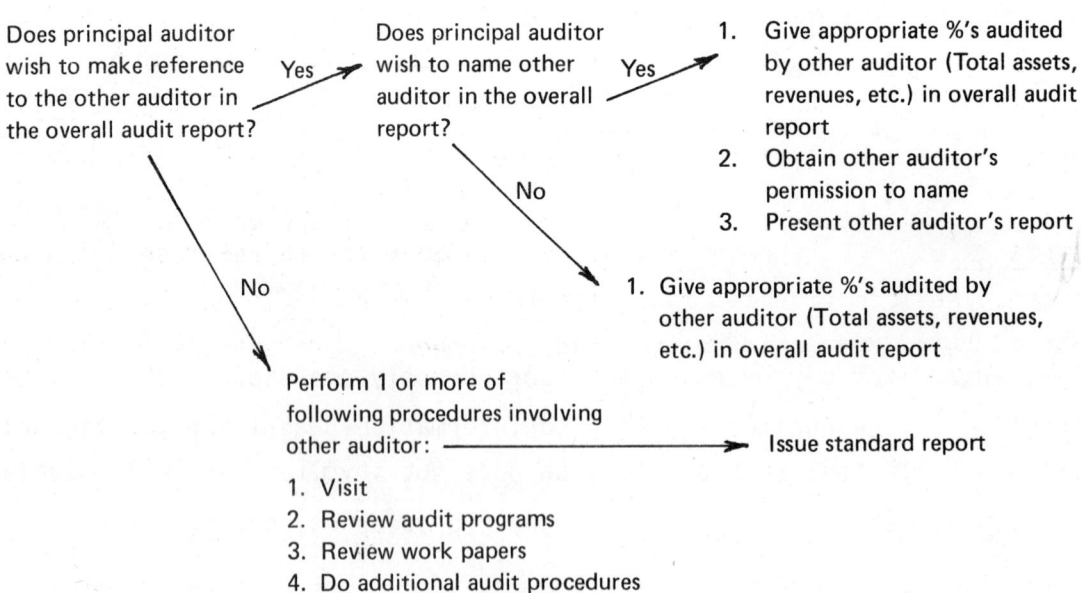

The decision to make reference to the other auditor indicates <u>divided responsibility</u> between the auditors and is <u>not</u> considered an audit report qualification. The decision <u>not</u> to make reference to the other report indicates that the principal

auditor assumes responsibility for the work of the other auditor. Reasons for assuming responsibility include:

    1) The other auditor is an affiliate of the principal auditor
    2) The principal auditor hired the other auditor
    3) The portion audited by the other auditor is not material
    4) Other miscellaneous reasons as the principal auditor (or client) desires

Finally, note that in situations in which the other auditor's report is other than
unqualified, the materiality of the matter causing the departure from a standard
report of the other auditor to the principal financial statements determines whether
the principal auditor's report must be modified.

    c. <u>Departures from a generally accepted accounting principle</u> (Au ¶509.15-.17,
545). Departures from GAAP result in either a qualified (except for) opinion or an
adverse opinion. Examples of departures from GAAP include the use of an unacceptable inventory valuation method (e.g., current sales value) and incorrectly treating a lease (e.g., treating a capital lease as an operating lease).

    The type of report depends on the materiality of the departure. <u>Know</u> that mate-
riality depends on:

    1) Dollar magnitude of effects
    2) Significance of item to enterprise
    3) Pervasiveness of misstatement
    4) Impact of misstatement on financial statements taken as a whole

Conceptually, as departures become more material the likelihood of an adverse opinion increases.

    The correct information, if available, is to be included in a middle explana-
tory paragraph to the qualified or adverse report. When the information is not
available, the middle paragraph of the report should state so. Also, the <u>Profes-
sional Standards</u> explicitly require (545.04-.05) that the unjustified omission of a
statement of changes in financial position results in a qualified (except for) opinion and <u>not</u> in an adverse opinion; the auditor need not present the missing statement in the middle paragraph of his/her report.

    d. <u>Departure from a promulgated accounting principle</u> (Au ¶509.18-.19). In this
case, which relates to Ethics Rule 203 (See Professional Responsibilities Module),
the auditor <u>agrees</u> with the client that a departure from GAAP is justified due to
<u>unusual</u> circumstances (e.g., new legislation or a new type of transaction). An un-
qualified report is issued which includes a separate paragraph describing the departure.

    e. <u>Consistency</u> (Au ¶509.20, 420, 546). A lack of consistency in following
accounting principles generally results in a qualified report (some call it a

modified report). Reread APB 20 on accounting changes when studying this section.
While the term "except for" arises in principle changes which are accounted for by
means other than retroactive restatement, consistency exceptions are often not considered to be either "subject to" or "except for" exceptions. Also, in this case
the auditor will not, in general, add a middle paragraph to the audit report to describe the inconsistency.

The general rule is that changes in accounting principles result in consistency
exceptions while changes in accounting estimates, corrections of clerical errors,
and minor reclassifications of accounts from one year to the next do not result in
consistency exceptions. For changes in business entities, changes among carrying
bases (cost, equity, consolidated) for continuing subsidiaries result in a consistency exception; poolings, and changes in subsidiaries (creation, cessation, purchase, or disposition) are not consistency exceptions. The most frequent cases may
be summarized as:

Type of change	Consistency exception	Restate prior year
I. Change in Accounting Principle		
1. GAAP to GAAP	Yes	No[1]
2. Non-GAAP to GAAP	Yes	Yes
3. GAAP to non-GAAP	Yes[2]	No
4. For newly acquired assets in an existing class of assets (whether 1, 2, or 3 above)	Yes	No[1]
5. For a new class of asset (whether 1, 2, or 3 above)	No	No[1]
II. Change in Accounting Estimate		
1. Judgmental adjustments	No	No
2. Inseparable estimate and principle change	Yes	No
III. Change in Entity		
1. Changes between carrying basis (cost, equity, consol.)	Yes	Yes
2. Pooling	No	Yes
3. Changes in subsidiaries (creation, cessation, purchase or disposition)	No	No
IV. Correction of Error		
1. Error in principle (I.2., above)	Yes	Yes
2. Error not involving application of a principle	No	Yes
V. Change in Statement Format		
1. Classifications and reclassifications	No	Yes
2. Revised basis for Statement of Changes in Financial Position	No	Yes

[1]The following "exceptions" call for restatement:
    a. LIFO to another method
    b. Method of accounting for long-term-construction-type contracts
    c. To or from "full cost" method in extractive industries

[2]Note that "I.3." will also result in a departure from GAAP exception

Several other items are frequently examined. The audit report for a firm in its first year of existence deletes the standard report's final phrase "applied on a basis consistent with the prior year." However, for a firm which has been in existence for more than one year which is having its first audit, the phrase is included in the report. A change which is immaterial this year, but is expected to become material in the future, does not result in a consistency exception if the client has properly disclosed it in the footnotes. Finally, if the auditor does not concur with the change in principle, or if the change has not been properly accounted for, the auditor must also include exceptions based on departures from GAAP ("c" above).

   f. Uncertainties (Au ¶509.21-.26, 509.39-.40, 340). In cases in which the outcome of significant matters is not susceptible to reasonable estimation, a qualified (subject to) opinion or a disclaimer may be appropriate. Examples here include uncertainty regarding the firm's continued existence (a "going concern" exception) due to factors such as the lack of adequate working capital. Also, other significant factors that do not endanger the existence of the firm may result in this type of qualification (e.g., lawsuits). A middle paragraph is added to the report discussing the uncertainty. In general, the "subject to" qualification will be adequate. (This is the only case in which a "subject to" qualified report is issued.)

   g. Emphasis of a matter (Au ¶509.27). The auditor may wish to emphasize a matter regarding the financial statements, but, nevertheless, intends to render an unqualified opinion. Examples include cases in which the entity is a component of a larger entity, or in which related party transactions exist, or in cases drawing attention to an important subsequent event. Such information is included in an explanatory middle paragraph.

   h. Lack of independence (Au ¶504.08-.10). When an auditor is not independent, a disclaimer must be issued. No mention of the reason for the lack of independence or of any audit procedures followed is to be given in the report. This type of situation might occur in the case in which a partner in the CPA firm has neglected to sell an equity (e.g., common stock) interest in the firm being audited. The Code of Professional Ethics explicitly defines this as a case in which the CPA firm is not independent.

   i. Segmental accounting information (Au ¶435). Inaccurate segmental information leads to a qualified (except for) opinion or an adverse opinion. The measure of materiality for segmental information is in relation to the financial statements taken as a whole; thus, the auditor is not required to apply auditing procedures that would be necessary to express a separate opinion on the segmental information. Note that errors in, or omissions of, segmental information are a special type of departure from a generally accepted accounting principle ("c" above).

j. Additional information included with basic financial statements (Au ¶550, 551, 553). Several types of information are included here. Section 550 deals with other information in documents containing audited statements. This relates to the case in which the audited financial statements are included in a published annual report which includes other information (e.g., president's letter, graphs, pictures). The auditor is to read the annual report and note any inconsistencies between the financial statements and the other information provided. If the audited statements are inconsistent with the other information, one or both of the following must be true:

1) Financial statements are incorrect--this will lead to a qualified (except for) opinion or an adverse opinion since it is a departure from GAAP (see "c" above)

2) Other information is incorrect--this will lead to an unqualified report with an explanatory paragraph, and/or withholding use of the audit report and/or withdrawal from the engagement

Finally, the auditor may note no inconsistency, but may believe that the other information *seems* incorrect. In such cases the auditor is to discuss the matter with the client, consult with other parties such as legal counsel, and use judgment as to other steps to follow.

Section 553 deals with supplementary information required by the FASB. Because this information is not audited, inaccuracies in it or omissions of it will lead to an explanatory paragraph in the audit report and not affect the audit opinion paragraph (which deals with audited financial information). Current cost information is an example of this supplementary information.

Section 551 deals with long-form reports. These reports primarily arise in the case of small clients whose annual report is composed of the audited financial statements plus several extra, more detailed, schedules and explanatory materials. The auditor is to either explicitly disclaim an opinion on this additional information or, if s/he has audited it in detail, expand the audit report to include reference to it. If the information is to be audited, the measure of materiality is in relation to the financial statements taken as a whole.

Section 552 (para .09-.11) addresses the situation in which selected financial data, derived from audited financial statements, are presented in a client prepared document (e.g., annual report) which also includes the audited financial statements. The auditor may report only on the financial data which may be derived from the audited financial statements. In this situation, a third paragraph is added to the normal short-form report in which the auditor states whether the selected financial data are fairly stated in all material respects in relation to the financial statements.

Summary. The table on the next page summarizes much of the "key" information from the above discussion. The last three columns of the table discuss required report format modifications. It is probably not necessary to memorize these three columns. When considering a circumstance resulting in departure from the standard report, simply ask yourself the following:

1) Did the circumstance change the scope of my audit?--if yes, the scope paragraph is modified
2) Did the circumstance change my overall opinion on the statements?--if yes, the opinion paragraph is modified

Finally, remember that, in general, when either the scope or opinion paragraph is being modified, an explanatory middle paragraph is required. The only exceptions are the case of involvement of other auditors and the case of a lack of consistency.

2. Other Audit Issues. Several additional audit report issues are of concern to the candidate.

a. Dating the report (Au ¶530). The date of completion of fieldwork should generally be used as the date for the audit report. In cases in which a subsequent event (see below) has occurred after this date, the auditor may either use dual dating of the report (for example, March 2, 19X8 except for footnote X as to which the date is March 6, 19X8), or may change the report date to the date of the subsequent event (March 6 in our example). However, when using the second alternative, the auditor increases his/her responsibility for all material events through the latter date and audit procedures must, therefore, be extended through that date.

b. Comparative statements (Au ¶505). When comparative statements are issued (that is, financial statements for two or more periods are presented) the auditor must report on the statements for these years. In certain instances the report of

SUMMARY OF STANDARD REPORT DEPARTURES

Circumstance	Type of Opinion	Report Format Modifications		
		Scope Paragraph Modified?	Middle Explanatory Paragraph Added?	Opinion Paragraph Modified?
a. Scope limitation				
1. Client imposed	"Generally Disclaim" but possibly Qualified (except for)	Yes	Yes	Yes
2. Circumstance imposed	Qualified (except for) or Disclaimer	Yes	Yes	Yes
b. Other auditor involved				
1. Make reference	Unqualified	Yes	No	Yes
2. Not make reference	Unqualified	No	No	No
c. Departure from GAAP	Qualified (except for) or adverse	No	Yes	Yes
d. Justified departure from promulgated principle	Unqualified	No	Yes	No
e. Inconsistency				
1. Restatement	Qualified ("after giving retroactive effect")	No	No	Yes
2. No restatement	Qualified (except for)	No	No	Yes
f. Uncertainty	Qualified (subject to) or disclaimer	No	Yes	Yes
g. Emphasis of a matter	Unqualified	No	Yes	No
h. Lack of independence	Disclaimer	*	*	*
i. Segmental information	Qualified (except for) or adverse	No	Yes	Yes
j. Additional information included				
1. Documents containing audited statements				
a. Financial statements incorrect	Qualified (except for) or adverse	No	Yes	Yes
b. Other information incorrect	Unqualified	No	Yes	No
2. Supplementary incorrect (unaudited footnotes)	Unqualified	No	Yes	No
3. "Long form" reports				
a. Separate Report on other information to be issued	Unqualified	No	No	No
b. No separate Report on other information to be issued	Unqualified	No	Yes	No

*In cases in which the auditor is not independent a one paragraph disclaimer is issued.

the prior year may differ from when it was originally presented (subsequent resolution of an uncertainty, discovery of an uncertainty in a subsequent period, subsequent restatement of prior period statements).

    c. <u>Piecemeal opinion not permitted (Au ¶509.48)</u>. Piecemeal opinions were positive expressions of opinion on certain identified items in the financial statements for a client for which the auditor was either disclaiming an opinion or expressing an adverse opinion on the financial statements taken as a whole. They are considered inappropriate because of the belief that the positive piecemeal opinion might overshadow or contradict the overall report.

3. <u>Subsequent Events and Subsequent Discovery of Facts Existing at the Date of the Audit Report (Au ¶560, 561)</u>. These two sections deal with accounting issues (e.g., how to measure and disclose certain events) as well as the audit reporting issue of the effects of subsequent events on an audit report. Section 560 breaks down subsequent events into two types:

    a. Those events that provide additional evidence with respect to conditions that existed at the date of the balance sheet (for which the financial statements are to be adjusted)

    b. Those events that provide evidence with respect to conditions that did not exist at the date of the balance sheet (for which there is to be footnote disclosure)

Section 560 also deals with the auditing issues involved when these types of events are noted prior to release of the audit report. Section 561 deals with the auditing disclosure issues involved when these events are not discovered until after the release of the financial statements. Read especially carefully the outline of the auditor's reponsibilities with respect to these events--numerous questions have been asked relating to subsequent events.

4. <u>Report Preparation</u>. Questions frequently require the candidate to prepare an audit report which reflects certain departures from the standard form, or to list deficiencies in a report which the question presents. See, for example, Problems 1, 2, and 4 in the Reports module.

    The best approach for preparing a report is to start with the standard short-form report and to make necessary adaptations. The standard short-form report is presented here for your convenience:

June 1, 19X3

To: Board of Directors and Stockholders
   ABC Company

   We have examined the balance sheets of ABC Company as of [at] December 31, 19X2 and 19X1, and the related statements of income, retained earnings, and changes in financial position for the years then ended. Our examinations were made in accordance with generally accepted auditing standards and, accordingly, included such tests of the accounting records and such other auditing procedures as we considered necessary in the circumstances.

   In our opinion, the financial statements referred to above present fairly the financial position of ABC Company as of [at] December 31, 19X2 and 19X1, and the results of its operations and the changes in its financial position for the years then ended, in conformity with generally accepted accounting principles applied on a consistent basis.

/s/ Joe Smith, CPA

You should have the standard short-form report memorized. The following key assertions in the above report may help in memorization as well as provide assistance in modifying reports:

   Addressee (company, board of directors and/or stockholders--_not_ management)
   Date (last day of field work)
   Scope paragraph

      1. We have examined
      2. Client's financial statements
         Balance sheets
         Income statements
         Retained earnings statements
         Statements of changes in financial position
      3. Exam was according to GAAS including:
         Tests of the accounting records
         Other auditing procedures
         As we considered necessary
   Opinion paragraph
      1. In our opinion
      2. Statements fairly present
         Per GAAP (applied consistently)
   Signature (Firm Name)

   While the various SASs present numerous types of reports which are other than the standard short-form, it is _not_ necessary to memorize them. Use the following 4-step approach to prepare (and evaluate) reports:

   Step 1. Determine the overall type of report to be issued
   Step 2. Determine whether the scope paragraph of the standard short-form report needs to be modified
   Step 3. Determine whether an explanatory middle paragraph needs to be added
   Step 4. Determine whether the opinion paragraph of the standard short-form report needs to be modified

   a. _Determine the overall type of report to be issued._ That is, use the information presented earlier in this module to determine whether an unqualified, qualified (subject to or except for), adverse, or disclaimer report is necessary. In this step you are setting your objective--to prepare the proper type of report.

   b. Determine whether the scope paragraph of the standard short-form report
needs to be modified. Ask yourself: did the matter of concern (or, if more than
one reason for departure from the standard short-form report exists, did any of the
matters of concern) significantly restrict the scope of the audit procedures which
the auditor performed? If the answer is yes, unless the auditor is satisfied with
the adequacy of alternate procedures, the scope paragraph is modified--see Scope
Limitations presented earlier in this module.

   As presented several pages earlier in the table entitled Summary of Standard
Report Departures, the circumstances in which the scope paragraph will be modified
are scope limitations (client and circumstance imposed) and when reference to other
auditors is made.

   When the scope paragraph is to be modified, the actual modification is not difficult. For scope restrictions, the underlined phrase is added to the scope paragraph:

We have examined the balance sheet of ABC Company as of [at] December 31, 19X2 and 19X1, and the related statements of income, retained earnings, and changes in financial position for the years then ended. Except as explained in the following paragraph, our examinations were made in accordance with generally accepted auditing standards and, accordingly, included such tests of the accounting records and such other auditing procedures as we considered necessary in the circumstances.

   In the case of other auditors, the standard short-form scope paragraph's first
two sentences remain the same, but the following sentences are added:

We did not examine the financial statement of B Company, a consolidated subsidiary, which statements reflect total assets and revenues constituting X percent and Y percent respectively, of the related consolidated totals. These statements were examined by other auditors whose report thereon has been furnished to us, and our opinion expressed herein, insofar as it relates to the amounts included for B Company, is based solely upon the report of the other auditors.

Don't memorize the above wording. Simply remember that in the first sentence you
mention the portion of the assets and revenues audited by the other auditor, and in
the second sentence you note that you are relying on the other auditor's report.

   c. Determine whether an explanatory middle paragraph needs to be added. The
general rule is that, if there is a departure from the standard short-form report,
an explanatory paragraph will be necessary. As indicated in the Summary of Standard
Report Departure, the exceptions to the rule are:

        1)   Other auditors involved
        2)   Inconsistency (consistency exceptions)
        3)   Lack of independence (when a brief one paragraph disclaimer is issued)
        4)   Long-form reports when a separate report on other information is to be
             issued

The middle paragraph simply explains the matter of concern. The following is an example for a scope limitation:

We did not observe the taking of the physical inventories as of December 31, 19XX (stated at $.....), and December 31, 19X1 (stated at $.....), since those dates were prior to the time we were initially engaged as auditors for the Company. Due to the nature of the Company's records we were unable to satisfy ourselves as to the inventory quantities by means of other auditing procedures.

The following is an example of an explanatory paragraph for a departure from GAAP:

The Company has excluded from property and debt in the accompanying balance sheet certain lease obligations, which in our opinion should be capitalized in order to conform with generally accepted accounting principles. If these lease obligations were capitalized, property would be increased by $....., long-term debt by $..... and retained earnings by $..... as of December 31, 19XX and net income and earnings per share would be increased (decreased) by $..... and $..... respectively, for the year then ended.

As a final example, the following explanatory paragraph relates to an uncertainty exception:

As discussed in Note X to the financial statements, the company is defendant in a lawsuit alleging infringement of certain patent rights and claiming royalties and punitive damages. The company has filed a counter action, and preliminary hearings and discovery proceedings on both actions are in progress. The ultimate outcome of the lawsuits cannot presently be determined, and no provision for any liability that may result has been made in the financial statements.

d. Determine whether the opinion paragraph of the standard short-form report needs to be modified. The general rule here is that, if a report other than unqualified is to be issued, this paragraph will be modified. In addition, if the principal auditor makes reference to other auditors, a modification is required. While there are numerous circumstances which affect the opinion paragraph (see Summary of Standard Report Departures), here are the primary ones:

Division of Responsibility. The only modification is the insertion of the underlined phrase:

In our opinion, based upon our examination and the report of other auditors, the financial statement . . . . . .

Qualified report--subject to. The modification is:

In our opinion, subject to the effects of such adjustments, if any, as might have been required had the outcome of the uncertainty referred to in the preceding paragraph been known, the financial statements. . . . .

Qualified report--except for. The report's opinion paragraph is modified to include:

In our opinion, except for the effects of not capitalizing lease obligations, as discussed in the preceding paragraph, the financial statements. . . . . . .

Adverse Opinion.   The following is the opinion paragraph from an adverse report:

> In our opinion, because of the effects of the matters discussed in the preceding paragraph, the financial state-
> ments referred to above do not present fairly, in conformity with generally accepted accounting principles, the financial
> position of X Company as of December 31, 19XX, or the results of its operations and changes in its financial position
> for the year then ended.

Note that, again, the primary change is the addition of a phrase after "In our
opinion." However, the final five words of the standard short-form opinion paragraph ("applied on a consistent basis") are also deleted.

Inconsistency.   When a consistency exception is to be issued, recall that the
scope paragraph is not modified and an explanatory middle paragraph is not required.
The opinion paragraph used includes the standard short-form opinion paragraph with
an additional description of the inconsistency. If the change is one which should
be reported by restating the financial statements of prior years (see the Inconsistency section of this module) the following phrase is added after the "applied on a
consistent basis" conclusion of the standard report:

> after restatement for the change, with which we concur, in the method of accounting for . . . (description of change). . .

If the change is one which should be reported by means other than by restating the
additional information the following is added:

> except for the change, with which we concur in the method of accounting for . . . (description of change). . .

C. Auditor Association Other Than Audits

As indicated in the overview section, auditors become involved with financial
information in performing engagements other than "full" audits. These forms may be
categorized as: 1) other forms of auditor association with historical financial
statements, and 2) other reports.

1. Other forms of auditor association with historical financial statements. Here
we discuss 4 primary "other" forms of auditor association. The candidate should be
very familiar with each of these forms of association.

a. Unaudited statements (Au ¶504). For those relatively few public firms which
are not required to have annual audits, the option of unaudited statements exists.
In this case, a simple disclaimer of opinion is generally issued; also each page of
the financial statements should be marked "unaudited." However, if the auditor is

aware of any significant departure from GAAP, s/he should suggest that the statements be revised and, failing that, should include such information in the disclaimer.

b. <u>Compiled or reviewed statements (AR 100-500)</u>. When a CPA has <u>compiled</u> financial statements for a nonpublic entity, a disclaimer of opinion is issued--it is dated as of the date of completion of the compilation. Each page of the financial statements is to be marked "See Accountant's Compilation Report." If management elects to exclude disclosures such as footnotes from the financial statements, a special form of the disclaimer is available (AR 100.21). Other disclosures from GAAP are to be described in an explanatory paragraph to the report.

Compilation report examples:

Accountant's Compilation Report

I (we) have compiled the accompanying balance sheet of XYZ Company as of December 31, 19XX, and the related statements of income, retained earnings, and changes in financial position for the year then ended, in accordance with standards established by the American Institute of Certified Public Accountants.

A compilation is limited to presenting in the form of financial statements information that is the representation of management (owners). I (we) have not audited or reviewed the accompanying financial statements and, accordingly, do not express an opinion or any other form of assurance on them.

Third Paragraph if Disclosures Are Omitted

Management has elected to omit substantially all of the disclosures (and the statement of changes in financial position) required by generally accepted accounting principles. If the omitted disclosures were included in the financial statements, they might influence the user's conclusions about the company's financial position, results of operations, and changes in financial position. Accordingly, these financial statements are not designed for those who are not informed about such matters.

The following paragraph is added to the compilation report if the financial statements have been prepared on a comprehensive basis other than GAAP:

These financial statements (including related disclosures) are presented in accordance with the requirements of (name of body), which differ from generally accepted accounting principles. Accordingly, these financial statements are not designed for those who are not informed about such differences.

The <u>review</u> form of association, which calls for audit procedures far short of an audit (see outline), may be performed for a public or for a nonpublic firm. The review report provides limited assurance to users, in the sense that a statement is made that the auditor is not aware of any material modifications which need to be made to the financial statements. Departures from GAAP are to be treated similarly as in the compilation case.

Review report examples:

Accountant's Review Report

I (we) have reviewed the accompanying balance sheet of XYZ Company as of December 31, 19XX, and the related statements of income, retained earnings, and changes in financial position for the year then ended, in accordance with standards established by the American Institute of Certified Public Accountants. All information included in these financial statements is the representation of the management (owners) of XYZ Company.

A review consists principally of inquiries of company personnel and analytical procedures applied to financial data. It is substantially less in scope than an examination in accordance with generally accepted auditing standards, the objective of which is the expression of an opinion regarding the financial statements taken as a whole. Accordingly, I (we) do not express such an opinion.

Based on my (our) review, I am (we are) not aware of any material modifications that should be made to the accompanying financial statements in order for them to be in conformity with generally accepted accounting principles.

Accountant's Review Report with Exception

I (we) have reviewed the accompanying balance sheet of XYZ Company as of December 31, 19XX, and the related statements of income, retained earnings, and changes in financial position for the year then ended, in accordance with standards established by the American Institute of Certified Public Accountants. All information included in these financial statements is the representation of the management (owners) of XYZ Company.

A review consists principally of inquiries of company personnel and analytical procedures applied to financial data. It is substantially less in scope than an examination in accordance with generally accepted auditing standards, the objective of which is the expression of an opinion regarding the financial statements taken as a whole. Accordingly, I (we) do not express such an opinion.

Based on my (our) review, with the exception of the matter(s) described in the following paragraph(s), I am (we are) not aware of any material modifications that should be made to the accompanying financial statements in order for them to be in conformity with generally accepted accounting principles.

As disclosed in note X to the financial statements, generally accepted accounting principles require that inventory cost consist of material, labor, and overhead. Management has informed me (us) that the inventory of finished goods and work in process is stated in the accompanying financial statements at material and labor cost only, and that the effects of this departure from generally accepted accounting principles on financial position, results of operations, and changes in financial position have not been determined.

or

As disclosed in note X to the financial statements, the company has adopted [description of newly adopted method], whereas it previously used [description of previous method]. Although the [description of newly adopted method] is in conformity with generally accepted accounting principles, the company does not appear to have reasonable justification for making a change as required by Opinion no. 20 of the Accounting Principles Board.

c. <u>Reviewed quarterly statements (AU ¶722)</u>. The review form of association discussed above is also appropriate for firms wishing to have quarterly financial statement reviews. The reports issued are essentially the same as those presented above, except that they are modified to relate to one quarter.

d. <u>Condensed financial statements (AU ¶552.01-.08)</u>. A firm which must file a set of audited financial statements at least annually with a regulatory agency may also choose to prepare condensed financial statements for other purposes. In such cases an auditor's report on such condensed statements should be issued which discloses:

1) That the auditor has expressed an opinion on the complete audited financial statements
2) The date of the audit report on the complete statements

3) The type of opinion expressed on the complete statements
4) Whether the condensed statements are fairly stated in relation to the complete financial statements

On the other hand, for a client which is <u>not</u> a public entity and, therefore, is not required to file complete annual audited financial statements, an adverse opinion is recommended for the condensed statements (see footnote 6 of AU ¶552).

2. <u>Other Reports</u>. Auditors also become involved with a variety of other types of information which result in the following reports:

a) Special reports
b) Letters for underwriters
c) Forecast review reports

In addition, recall that auditors issue reports on internal control which are summarized in the internal control module.

a. <u>Special reports (Au ¶621)</u>. Be aware that this section deals with four basic types of reports. First, comprehensive basis statements refer to financial statements prepared on some basis other than GAAP (e.g., cash or tax basis). Note here that, in general, a three paragraph report is issued with a scope paragraph, an explanatory paragraph which describes the comprehensive basis, and an opinion paragraph which states whether the financial statements follow the comprehensive basis. Also, terms such as "balance sheet" and "income statement" are not used for comprehensive statements--use, for example, "statement of assets and liabilities arising from cash transactions."

Comprehensive basis of accounting report examples:

Tax Basis Statements

We have examined the statement of assets, liabilities, and capital—income tax basis of ABC Partnership as of December 31, 19X1, and the related statements of revenue and expenses—income tax basis and of changes in partners' capital accounts—income tax basis for the year then ended. Our examination was made in accordance with generally accepted auditing standards and, accordingly, included such tests of the accounting records and such other auditing procedures as we considered necessary in the circumstances.

Cash Basis Statements

We have examined the statement of assets and liabilities arising from cash transactions of XYZ Company as of December 31, 19X1, and the related statement of revenue collected and expenses paid for the year then ended. Our examination was made in accordance with generally accepted auditing standards and, accordingly, included such tests of the accounting records and such other auditing procedures as we considered necessary in the circumstances.

Tax Basis Statements

As described in Note X, the Partnership's policy is to prepare its financial statements on the accounting basis used for income tax purposes; consequently, certain revenue and the related assets are recognized when received rather than when earned, and certain expenses are recognized when paid rather than when the obligation is incurred. Accordingly, the accompanying financial statements are not intended to present financial position and results of operations in conformity with generally accepted accounting principles.

In our opinion, the financial statements referred to above present fairly the assets, liabilities, and capital of ABC Partnership as of December 31, 19X1, and its revenue and expenses and changes in its partners' capital accounts for the year then ended, on the basis of accounting described in Note X, which basis has been applied in a manner consistent with that of the preceding year.

Cash Basis Statements

As described in Note X, the Company's policy is to prepare its financial statements on the basis of cash receipts and disbursements; consequently, certain revenue and the related assets are recognized when received rather than when earned, and certain expenses are recognized when paid rather than when the obligation is incurred. Accordingly, the accompanying financial statements are not intended to present financial position and results of operations in conformity with generally accepted accounting principles.

In our opinion, the financial statements referred to above present fairly the assets and liabilities arising from cash transactions of XYZ Company as of December 31, 19X1, and the revenue collected and expenses paid during the year then ended, on the basis of accounting described in Note X, which basis has been applied in a manner consistent with that of the preceding year.

The second type of special report is that on special elements or accounts. An auditor may, if allowed to perform whatever procedures s/he believes are necessary, render an opinion on one or more accounts (e.g., rentals). On the other hand, if an auditor is hired to perform only agreed upon procedures, negative assurance is given.

Special elements report examples:

Specified Element of Statements

We have examined the schedule of gross sales (as defined in the lease agreement dated March 4, 19X1, between ABC Company, as lessor, and XYZ Stores Corporation, as lessee) of XYZ Stores Corporation at its Main Street store, [City], [State], for the year ended December 31, 19X1. Our examination was made in accordance with generally accepted auditing standards and, accordingly, included such tests of the accounting records and such other auditing procedures as we considered necessary in the circumstances.

In our opinion, the schedule of gross sales referred to above presents fairly the gross sales of XYZ Stores Corporation at its Main Street store, [City], [State], for the year ended December 31, 19X1, on the basis specified in the lease agreement referred to above.

Agreed Upon Procedures

Trustee
XYZ Company

At your request, we have performed the procedures enumerated below with respect to the claims of creditors of XYZ Company as of May 31, 19XX, set forth in the accompanying schedules. Our review was made solely to assist you in evaluating the reasonableness of those claims, and our report is not to be used for any other purpose. The procedures we performed are summarized as follows:

a. We compared the total of the trial balance of accounts payable at May 31, 19XX, prepared by the company, to the balance in the company's related general ledger account.
b. We compared the claims received from creditors to the trial balance of accounts payable.
c. We examined documentation submitted by the creditors in support of their claims and compared it to documentation in the company's files, including invoices, receiving records, and other evidence of receipt of goods or services.

Our findings are presented in the accompanying schedules. Schedule A lists claims that are in agreement with the company's records. Schedule B lists claims that are not in agreement with the company's records and sets forth the differences in amounts.

Because the above procedures do not constitute an examination made in accordance with generally accepted auditing standards, we do not express an opinion on the accounts payable balance as of May 31, 19XX. In connection with the procedures referred to above, except as set forth in Schedule B, no matters came to our attention that caused us to believe that the accounts payable balance might require adjustment. Had we performed additional procedures or had we made an examination of the financial statements in accordance with generally accepted auditing standards, other matters might have come to our attention that would have been reported to you. This report relates only to the accounts and items specified above and does not extend to any financial statements of XYZ Company, taken as a whole.

The third type of special report is one which results from an engagement in which an auditor is hired to test whether a client is in compliance with some form of an agreement. For example, an auditor may give negative assurance to a banker on whether a client is in conformity with restrictions in a debt agreement.

Compliance report examples:

Contractual Compliance (in Short-Form)

We have examined the balance sheet of XYZ Company as of December 31, 19X1, and the related statements of income, retained earnings, and changes in financial position for the year then ended. Our examination was made in accordance with generally accepted auditing standards and, accordingly, included such tests of the accounting records and such other auditing procedures as we considered necessary in the circumstances.

In our opinion, the financial statements referred to above present fairly the financial position of XYZ Company as of December 31, 19X1, and the results of its operations and changes in its financial position for the year then ended, in conformity with generally accepted accounting principles applied on a basis consistent with that of the preceding year.

In connection with our examination, nothing came to our attention that caused us to believe that the Company was not in compliance with any of the terms, covenants, provisions, or conditions of sections XX to XX, inclusive, of the Indenture dated July 21, 19X0, with ABC Bank. However, it should be noted that our examination was not directed primarily toward obtaining knowledge of such noncompliance.

Contractual Compliance (Separate Report)

We have examined the balance sheet of XYZ Company as of December 31, 19X1, and the related statements of income, retained earnings, and changes in financial position for the year then ended, and have issued our report thereon dated February 16, 19X2. Our examination was made in accordance with generally accepted auditing standards and, accordingly, included such tests of the accounting records and such other auditing procedures as we considered necessary in the circumstances.

In connection with our examination, nothing came to our attention that caused us to believe that the Company was not in compliance with any of the terms, covenants, provisions, or conditions of sections XX to XX, inclusive, of the Indenture dated July 21, 19X0, with ABC Bank. However, it should be noted that our examination was not directed primarily toward obtaining knowledge of such noncompliance.

The fourth special report is that in which a client is required to present information on prescribed forms or schedules. For example, a state corporation commission may require all corporations within its jurisdiction to present assets, liabilities, and equities on a standard form. If that form calls upon the auditor to make an assertion which s/he believes to be unjustified, s/he is to either reword the form or attach a separate report to the form.

b. Letters for underwriters (Au ¶631). When a public firm wishes to issue new securities to the public, the underwriters of the securities will generally ask the firm's auditor to give "comfort" on the financial and accounting data in the prospectus which is not covered by the accountant's opinion. In these cases, auditors may generally give negative assurance (a statement that nothing came to the CPA's attention that caused him/her to believe that the information does not meet a specified standard) on accounting related matters. The letter to the underwriter will generally refer to one or more of the following: CPA independence, compliance of the CPA's audit with various requirements, unaudited interim financial information, changes subsequent to the balance sheet date, various tables.

    c. Reviewed forecasts. In October 1980 the AICPA released its Guide for a Review of a Financial Forecast. (See outline of this guide immediately following the outline of SAS 1, Section 901.) While retaining the AICPA's long held policy that a CPA should not vouch for the achievability of a forecast (see Responsibilities module), the guide outlines review procedures for circumstances in which a CPA wishes to report on a forecast's assumptions. The following standard report is issued when the auditor is satisfied with the reasonableness of the forecast's assumptions:

> The accompanying forecasted balance sheet, statements of income, retained earnings, and changes in financial position, and summary of significant forecast assumptions of XYZ Company as of December 31, 19XX, and for the year then ending, is management's estimate of the most probable financial position, results of operations, and changes in financial position for the forecast period. Accordingly, the forecast reflects management's judgment, based on present circumstances, of the most likely set of conditions and its most likely course of action.

> We have made a review of the financial forecast in accordance with applicable guidelines for a review of a financial forecast established by the American Institute of Certified Public Accountants. Our review included procedures to evaluate both the assumptions used by management and the preparation and presentation of the forecast. We have no responsibility to update this report for events and circumstances occurring after the date of this report.

> Based on our review, we believe that the accompanying financial forecast is presented in conformity with applicable guidelines for presentation of a financial forecast established by the American Institute of Certified Public Accountants. We believe that the underlying assumptions provide a reasonable basis for management's forecast. However, some assumptions inevitably will not materialize and unanticipated events and circumstances may occur; therefore, the actual results achieved during the forecast period will vary from the forecast, and the variations may be material.

As indicated in the outline of the forecast guide, the guide discusses circumstances which will cause the accountant to depart from the above report. Be generally familiar with them. Note that there is no qualified report on forecasts. If exceptions are noted, the report is adverse; if there are significant scope limitations, a disclaimer is issued.

Summary

    The CPA exam has recently asked questions which have required candidates to either prepare or be aware of information provided in reports other than those based on the standard unqualified report. For example, in May 1982, candidates were required to analyze a report based on agreed upon procedures; in November 1982, candidates were required to prepare a review report. Memorizing all of the miscellaneous reports is difficult, at best. The following table summarizes most of the key elements of the types of reports on which questions have been asked for the individual not interested in memorizing the details of each report. By including these key elements in an answer, the candidate will at least receive a significant portion of the available credit without memorizing the report itself.

SPECIAL REPORTS SUMMARY*

	Comprehensive basis	Special elements — a. Opinion	Special elements — b. Agreed upon procedures	Compliance reports — a. Within standard report	Compliance reports — b. Separate report	Nonpublic entity — Compilation	Nonpublic entity — Review	Forecast review
Scope Paragraph	1. Standard report except for, in first sentence (a) names of statements (b) name reporting basis used	1. Standard report except for, in first sentence (a) names of accounts (b) name reporting basis used	1. We have applied agreed upon procedures 2. Report solely for your information 3. Describe procedures applied	1. Standard report	1. Standard report except for, add "and have issued our report thereon dated ——" (to end of first sentence)	1. We have compiled (list statements) in accordance with standards established by AICPA.	1. We have reviewed (list statements) in accordance with AICPA standards 2. All information is representation of management	(Second para of report) 1. Forecast reviewed in accord with AICPA guidelines for a review 2. Review included evaluation of management's assumptions and of preparation and presentation 3. No responsibility to update
Explanatory Paragraph	1. Describe basis (or refer to footnote which describes) 2. Statements not intended to present in conformity with GAAP	1. Description of reporting basis if not given in scope paragraph	No explanatory paragraph	No explanatory paragraph	No explanatory paragraph	No explanatory paragraph	1. Review principally inquiry and analytical procedures 2. Less in scope than audit 3. Do not express an opinion	(First para of report) 1. Forecast is management's estimate of most probable results 2. Forecast reflects management's judgment of most likely conditions and actions
Opinion (Assurance) Paragraph	Opinion 1. Standard report except for (a) names of statements (b) refer to reporting basis used	Opinion 1. Standard report except for (a) names of accounts (b) name reporting basis used	Negative assurance 1. We do not express an opinion 2. No matters came to our attention which need adjustment 3. If additional procedures had been performed other matters might have come to our attention 4. Report relates only to above accounts and items	Opinion and negative assurance 2 paragraphs: A. Standard opinion para B. Negative assurance on compliance para 1. Nothing came to our attention to lead us to believe not in compliance 2. Exam was not directed primarily toward obtaining knowledge of such noncompliance	Negative assurance 1. Nothing came to our attention to lead us to believe not in compliance 2. Exam was not directed primarily toward obtaining knowledge of such noncompliance	Disclaimer 1. Compilation only presents financial statements which are management's representations 2. Have not audited or reviewed, express no opinion	Negative assurance 1. Not aware of material modifications to be in conformity with GAAP	Opinion We believe . . . . 1. (a) forecast in conformity with AICPA guidelines (b) forecast assumptions reasonable 2. Actual results will vary
How to Report Departures from Reporting Criteria	1. Same as standard report	1. Add comment to opinion para and add explanatory para describing 2. If significant client interpretations of criteria have been made add explanatory para describing	1. Prepare schedules summarizing accounts 2. Add comment to negative assurance para and add explanatory para describing	1. Add comment to negative assurance para and add explanatory para describing	1. Add comment to negative assurance para and add explanatory para describing	1. Add sentence to disclaimer para disclosing departure and add explanatory para (after disclaimer) describing 2. If footnotes omitted, add explanatory para (after disclaimer) so stating and state that they might influence a user's conclusions	1. Add comment to negative assurance para and add explanatory para (after negative assurance) describing	1. Unreasonable assumptions or improper presentation—adverse opinion and add para describing 2. Scope limitations—disclaimer and add para describing

*Note that no report form has been proposed for the Special Reports based on Prescribed Forms or Schedules.

STATISTICAL SAMPLING

Statistical sampling has been tested on most recent auditing examinations, usually in the form of multiple choice questions. Until November 1982, a statistical sampling essay question had not appeared since May 1977. The adoption of a new standard (SAS 39, Section 350) increases the probability of this subject being tested (as evidenced by the November 1982 essay question). The essentials of this new standard are outlined beginning on page 311, and should be reviewed in order to become familiar with the concepts and new terminology which it stresses. Coverage of statistical sampling appears in the Auditing Content Specification Outline/ Frequency Analysis under "II.D.3." and "III.C.2." A comparison of some of this terminology with older, traditional terminology appears on page 219.

The new standard provides guidance for planning, performing, and evaluating audit samples, and covers nonstatistical as well as statistical sampling. Therefore, questions dealing with the distinction between audit sampling and nonsampling procedures as well as the concepts of sampling risk, tolerable error and projection of results for nonstatistical as well as statistical audit samples, can be expected. Exam questions often deal with the relationships between such statistical concepts and other basic audit concepts such as audit objectives, reliance on internal controls, materiality, and audit decision making. Questions of a mathematically technical nature are less likely to appear. However, basic formulas such as those appearing on pages 237 and 238 should be memorized.

Study Program for Statistical Sampling Module

This module is organized and should be studied in the following manner:
A. Basic Statistical Auditing Concepts
B. Planning for Audit Sampling
C. Variables Based Sampling
D. Attribute Sampling
E. Probability Proportional to Size (PPS) (Dollar-Unit) Sampling
F. Statistical Sampling Formulas and Relationships
G. Overview of Audit Sampling

A.   Basic Statistical Auditing Concepts

1. Quick Reference Symbol Key (see next page)

Symbol	Term
UR	Ultimate Risk (also known as Audit Risk)
TD	Allowable Risk of Incorrect Acceptance for Substantive Test of Details.
α	Alpha Risk
IC	Risk of Internal Accounting Control Failure
AR	Risk of Analytical Review Failing
TE	Tolerable Error
a	Average Precision per Item (Substantive Testing)
pre	Precision Percentage (Attribute Sampling)
σ^2	Variance
σ	Standard Deviation
n	Sample Size
N	Population Size
$\sigma/\sqrt{n}$	Standard Error
z	Reliability Coefficient
x	Observed Value of Sample Item
$\bar{x}$	Sample Mean
$N\bar{x}$	Expected Value of Population Total
p	Expected Rate of Error
q	1-p
FPC	Finite Population Correction Factor

2. Definitions*

   a. Population, Universe, Field - Group of items to be examined, the total value of which is to be projected (e.g., trade accounts receivable) or the actual error rate of which is to be estimated (e.g., invoices for approval)

   b. Sample - A selected group of items from a population chosen with the expectation that they will be representative of the population. Every item in the population must have an opportunity to be chosen.

      1) Judgmental Sample - Sample selected without probability basis

*Initially, you may want to peruse these definitions and refer to them later as they appear in the discussion.

2) Probability Sample - Sample selected so that likelihood of any item being selected is known prior to selection

   a) Random Sample - Sample selected, with replacement, so that every item in the population has an equal opportunity to be chosen and selection is independent, i.e., the selection of any one item has no influence on the probability for selection of any other item

   b) Stratified Sample - Sample selected so that every item in a sub-group of the population (strata) has the same probability of selection, but the probability of selection varies for different subgroups, e.g., selection with higher probability assigned to all inventory items with values in excess of $100,000

   c) Systematic Sample - A sample selected on a probability basis but without independence of selection, e.g., selection of every 100th trade receivable ledger item

c. Tolerable Error - The maximum monetary error for a balance or class of transactions which may exist without causing the financial statements to be materially misstated. It is related to materiality in that tolerable error as planned for and combined for the entire audit plan must not exceed preliminary materiality level estimates.

d. Tolerable Rate - The maximum rate of deviations from a prescribed control procedure which the auditor can tolerate without altering his planned reliance on the control

e. Risk - Likelihood, chance, or probability of reaching an incorrect audit conclusion

   1) Ultimate Risk (UR) - The combined risk that material errors in the financial statements will (1) occur, and (2) go undetected by the application of auditing procedures. In SAS 45 it is suggested that in the future the term "audit risk" will be used to replace the term "ultimate risk."

   2) Nonsampling Risk - Risk of error due to selection of inappropriate audit procedure or misapplication of audit procedure, e.g., human errors

   3) Sampling Risk - Inherent risk of error due to random chance of observing a set of items which are not typically representative of the population

      a) Substantive Sampling Risks:

         1] Allowable Risk of Incorrect Acceptance for Substantive Test of Details (TD) - Risk that sampling evaluation will support acceptance of book value when book value is materially misstated. E.g., if TD = .20 there will be one chance in five (20/100) that the sampling evaluation will support acceptance when material misstatement is present. As UR (Ultimate Risk) is allowed to increase, TD will be allowed to increase.

         2] Allowable Risk of Incorrect Rejection - Risk that sampling evaluation will not support acceptance of book value in the absence of material error. E.g., if set at 10% there will be one chance in ten that the sampling evaluation will not support acceptance even though the book value is correct.

b) Risks related to the sufficiency of audit samples in substantive testing:

1] Risk of Internal Accounting Control Failure (IC) - Risk that internal accounting controls will fail to detect and correct errors equal to tolerable error given that such errors exist. E.g., if controls are reasonably strong the auditor might set IC = .4. If controls are exceptionally strong IC could be set lower, say IC = .2.

2] Risk of Analytical Review and Other Substantive Tests Failing (AR) - Risk that analytical review and other relevant substantive tests will fail to detect errors equal to tolerable error given that such error occurs and is not detected by internal accounting controls. If analytical review provides only weak evidence relative to the audit sampling objective, AR would be high, say AR = .9. If analytical review is stronger, then AR could be set at a lower level, say, AR = .6.

3] Illustration of relationships among risks. Increasing IC (risk of internal accounting control failure) will lead the auditor to a reduction in TD (allowable risk of incorrect acceptance for substantive tests of detail). Increasing AR (risk of analytical review and other nonsampling substantive testing failing) will lead the auditor to a reduction in TD.

4] Combined numeric example of relationships among substantive sampling risks:

If UR = .05, IC = .30, and AR = .50
Then TD = UR/(IC x AR)
       = .05/(.3 x .5)
       = .33

c) Compliance Testing Risks:

1] Allowable Risk of Overreliance - Maximum acceptable risk that sample results will support planned degree of reliance on internal accounting control when true compliance rate does not justify such reliance

2] Allowable Risk of Underreliance - Maximum acceptable risk that sample results will not support planned degree of reliance on internal accounting control when true compliance rate supports such reliance

f. Reliability - The complement of a risk (1.0-risk). Also called Confidence Level in statistical applications. Proportion of times, e.g., 95% or 90%, that use of planned sampling procedure will lead to avoidance of error associated with the risk being considered.

g. Comparison of Terminologies - Many auditing texts and other sources now available have not been converted to the new risk and uncertainty terminology of SAS 39. The following table may be useful in bridging from more traditional sources to the terms adopted in SAS 39.

Traditional Terminology	SAS 39 Terminology
Materiality of Test	Tolerable Error
Combined Risk Ultimate Risk	Ultimate Risk (UR)
Beta Risk (β) Risk of Type II Error	Allowable Risk of Incorrect Acceptance for Substantive Tests of Details (TD)
Alpha Risk (α) Risk of Type I Error	Allowable Risk of Incorrect Rejection
1 - Reliability Assigned to Internal Control*	Risk of Internal Accounting Control Failure (IC)
1 - Reliability of Supplemental Substantive Tests*	Risk of Analytical Review and Other Substantive Tests Failing (AR)
Critical Error Rate	Tolerable Rate
1 - Reliability of Compliance Test	Risk of Overreliance

*These two elements are sometimes combined and treated as a single factor, i.e., 1 - reliability of internal controls and other relevant factors.

h. Precision - A measured range of the accuracy of a statistical result. E.g., if sample results indicate that A/R are between $240,000 and $260,000, the overall precision is plus or minus $10,000 $\left(\frac{260,000 - 240,000}{2} \right)$.

In attribute sampling, precision is the difference between the error rate observed in the sample and the maximum rate of error which is likely to exist in the population given the observed error rate and a specified reliability level.

i. Probability Distribution - Relationship among all possible values of an unknown quantity and the relative chance that each such value is the true value of that quantity

3. Statistical Measurements

a. Mean - Expected value or average value of a population or sample

b. Measures of Dispersion

1) Range - Difference between highest and lowest value

2) <u>Variance</u> - Denoted σ^2; a measure of the degree of compactness in a population. Populations with smaller standard deviations are more tightly distributed (i.e., more nearly identical in value) than populations with larger standard deviations which range over broader sets of values. The variance is computed by finding the average squared value of the difference between each item in the population and the mean of the population.

3) <u>Standard Deviation</u> - σ; the square root of the variance

4) <u>Standard Error</u> - Standard deviation of the distribution of all possible mean values of a sample of given size. The larger the sample the smaller standard error becomes.

5) <u>Skewness</u> - A measure of the lack of symmetry in a distribution:

   a) Positive (right) skewness - Tail of distribution on right
   b) Negative (left) skewness - Tail of distribution on left
   c) EXAMPLE:

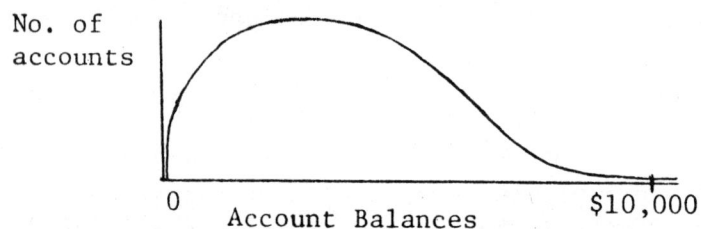

   d) Typically, accounting populations are positively skewed

6) <u>Finite Population Correction Factor (FPC)</u> - The basic sample size formula is based on an infinite population size where the sample constitutes 0% of the population. When the sample constitutes a larger proportion of the population, there is a better chance that any extreme values in the population will be sampled. Remember that the extreme values have the greatest effect on the sample figures; thus, it is important to examine them. As a practical matter, ignore the FPC if sample size (n) is less than 20% of the population size (N). An approximation of the formula for the finite population correction factor (FPC) is:

$$FPC = \sqrt{1 - \frac{n}{N}}$$

4. <u>Normal Distribution Properties</u>

   a. For <u>any</u> normal distribution, the following fixed relationships exist concerning the area under the curve <u>and</u> the distance from the mean in standard deviations. This table assumes a <u>two-tailed</u> approach. It places in each 'tail' an equal percentage of the area not included in the standard deviation distance.

Distance in Stan. Dev. (Reliability coefficient)	Area Under the Curve (Reliability level)	
+ 1.0	68%	
− 1.64	90%	*
1.96	95%	*
2.0	95.5%	
2.7	99%	

*Most frequently employed on exam

Example where $\sigma = 10$

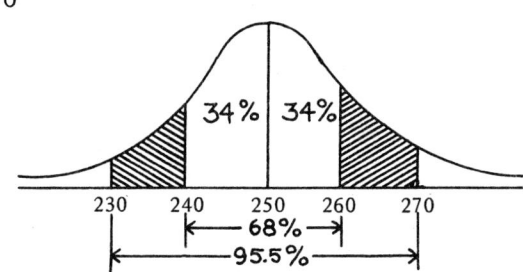

b. In words, plus or minus one standard deviation from the mean of a normal
    distribution contains 68% of the items in the population described by the
    distribution. Or, if you draw one item from the population described by the
    distribution, 68% of the time it will have a value X $\pm$ 1 σ (in the above
    example, 68% of the items described by the distribution are between 240 and
    260).
c. You should memorize the above relationships, e.g., $\pm$ 1.96 σ = 95% reli-
    ability (5% risk). Note that the 1.96 is known as a reliability coefficient
    (confidence coefficient) and the related percentage (e.g., 95%), a confi-
    dence level, or reliability level.
d. It is useful to note that values of either more than 270 or less than 230
    ($\pm 2\sigma$) only occur with frequency of 4.5%
e. If the auditor is concerned only about the relationship between the area
    of the normal curve and the distance from the mean in only a single direc-
    tion, then a one-tailed approach is appropriate

    1) In the example, values of more than 270 occur with a frequency of 2.25%
        (4.5 ÷ 2). Therefore, for one-tailed testing only 2.25% of the dis-
        tribution lies beyond +2.00 (rather than $\pm$ 2.00) standard deviations
        of the distribution.

B. Planning for Audit Sampling

1. Relate audit objectives to evidential test planning

    a. The audit objective should be chosen to provide competent evidence about
        one or more assertions related to management's financial statement repre-
        sentations (substantive objectives), or to provide evidence about the
        reliability of internal accounting control procedures related to such
        assertions (compliance objectives).

1) The auditor may decide, for example, that he wishes to determine whether goods shipped from inventory are billed. This audit objective may be related to the completeness of sales and to the existence of inventories as asserted by management.

    a) Substantive tests related to this objective could include tests of inventory on hand at year end

    b) Compliance tests related to this objective could include tests of control over back ordered shipments

b. Define the population of audit interest

1) The auditor must determine what class of transactions or balances are relevant to the objective

2) *EXAMPLES:*

    a) *All inventory item balances classified as currently available for resale could constitute the population of interest for tests of inventory on hand*

    b) *All credit sales transactions during one year which could not be filled at time of initial sales order might constitute the population of interest for testing controls over back orders*

c. Determine an appropriate source of evidence about the population

1) The auditor should relate the class of transactions or balances of interest to a specific physical source of evidence (often called a frame) which is available from existing client systems

2) If a statistical approach to audit sampling is being considered, it is important to establish a unique correspondence between the frame and the items in the population

3) *EXAMPLES:*

    a) *An inventory subsidiary ledger file and supporting client inventory counts could be used as a frame and source of evidence in doing substantive tests related to the existence of inventory*

    b) *A back order log and supporting documents could be used as a frame in testing control over back orders*

2. Determine whether audit sampling is appropriate

a. Audit sampling is usually considered when the auditor has no special knowledge allowing him to concentrate on the examination of particular items likely to contain error

b. When examination of key or risky transactions is sufficient to reduce the total of remaining items to an immaterial level, audit sampling from the remaining items need not be employed

c. When examination of key items and/or risky items alone will not sufficiently reduce audit risk, then audit sampling will usually be considered

    d. Audit sampling is not required for acquiring understanding of systems. A "walk through" of a few transactions will usually suffice. E.g., an auditor might follow a cash disbursement process by observing the preparation and flow of documents related to the disbursement process. This might involve observation of the requisition procedures by a user department, the preparation and forwarding of purchase orders in a purchasing department, the preparation of a receiving report at a warehouse location, and the receipt of an invoice for the goods by the accounting section. Observing these procedures once or twice in order to acquire understanding of the disbursement voucher system, while a legitimate audit activity, is not considered an audit sampling activity.

3. Determine whether a statistical or nonstatistical audit sample will be used

    a. Either approach is acceptable and either can provide sufficient evidence

    b. Statistical sampling helps design efficient samples and provides measured evaluation of risks and audit results

    c. Nonstatistical approaches can be less costly, especially with regard to evaluation, and do not require specially trained auditors

4. Determine whether to use an attribute or variable estimation type plan

    a. <u>Estimation of Variables</u> - Sampling for continuous variables (dollars, pounds, etc.). E.g., estimating the total dollar amount of accounts receivable by estimating the average receivable in the population based upon the average receivable in the sample and multiplying the sample average times the number of receivables in the population.

    b. <u>Estimation of Attributes</u> - Sampling for the existence or nonexistence of a particular condition. In auditing this typically involves sampling for an error rate, e.g., estimating the error rate in sales invoice pricing.

    c. Note that attribute sampling is applicable to compliance tests (of internal control) and variables sampling to substantive tests

[Note: Once a decision has been reached concerning the type of plan (attribute or variable) design, selection, performance, and evaluation should be completed accordingly.]

C. <u>Variables Based Sampling</u>

1. <u>Step One</u> - Determine the appropriate use of sample results. When planning for substantive tests of detail using variables sampling, the auditor must choose one of the following two objectives:

    a. If the auditor wishes to project a best estimate of an underlying true value for use in establishing a basis for valuing a population in the absence of sufficient supporting records, or in lieu of a client value, then estimation should be considered

1) Estimation objectives are appropriate when the amount in question is believed to be materially in error or unreliable

2) In such cases, there is no intention of accepting the client's reported book value. Therefore, the risk of overauditing (but not the risk of accepting a materially misstated balance) needs to be considered.

b. If the auditor wishes to determine, based on sampling, whether or not a book value is acceptable, then a hypothesis testing strategy should be employed. Both the risk of overauditing and the risk of accepting a materially misstated book value must be considered.

2. Step Two - Determine which selection technique to use

a. Different sample selection techniques can be employed to choose items for audit sampling tests

b. Judgmental Selection is generally not used as part of a statistical sampling plan. But an auditor may use an approach which includes comparison of his sample size with sample sizes based on statistical formulas. Generally, a judgmental sample should include the following types of items:

1) A large number of high-value items so as to cover a substantial proportion of the overall dollar value
2) At least one item from each type or subcategory
3) An emphasis on possible problem areas based on auditor's experience with the client
4) Items initiated by each person, department, etc., with responsibility for initiating that type of transaction
5) Any item which appears to be unusual, e.g., even dollar amounts, etc.
6) If nonstatistical audit sampling is used, random or systematic selection plans are preferred if representative results are required. The AICPA audit guide on sampling which is now in exposure draft stage also recommends the use of a judgmental stratification involving not less than two strata with a proportionately larger sample size for the larger dollar stratum.

c. Random Selection samples are those in which every item in the population has an equal chance of being drawn, and the chance of an item being selected is not influenced by whether any other item is selected. A probability sample is one in which certain classes of items have different probabilities of being selected, e.g., stratified sampling. Probability samples, however, are also based on random selection.

d. Systematic Sample Selection - Obtaining a random start and taking every nth item. For example, a sample of 40 from a population of 1,000 would require selecting every 25th item after selecting the starting point from items 1 to 25.

1) A variation of this is to use systematic sampling with multiple starts. Using the same sample above with 2 random starts would require taking every 50th item from two random starts between 1 and 50.

2) The problem with systematic sampling is that the population may be systematically ordered such as having the identification number of all large items ending in 9. In such a case one does not obtain the randomness desired because a 9 may never be selected.

e. Stratified Sample Selection - Breaking the population down into subpopula-
    tions (strata), and applying different selection probabilities among strata,
    but the same selection probability within each strata

f. Cluster (Block) Sample Selection - Sample groups of items rather than
    individual items. Dispersion within clusters should be greater than dis-
    persion between clusters. A common problem can be illustrated with an
    extreme example: suppose you pull a block of payroll records for the same
    class of employees with identical salaries, deductions, etc. You would
    really be testing one transaction instead of 50.

    Cluster sampling is frequently used when testing documents that are filed
    sequentially. Clients may request that auditors use a group of
    sequentially-numbered documents to save time in pulling and replacing
    documents.

g. Multiple Stage Sample Selection - Sampling of primary units first, e.g.,
    stores; then sampling secondary units within primary units, e.g., items in
    stores, and so on

3. Step Three - Determine which characteristic of the sample and population to
    observe/measure - variables sampling

    a. Audit estimates may be based on the audit value of items in a sample. E.g.,
        the total dollar value of accounts receivable could be estimated by deter-
        mining the average value of receivables sampled after audit, and multiplying
        this average by the number of receivables in the population. This procedure
        is called simple extension or mean per unit sampling.

    b. There are three alternatives to calculating the average value of the audited
        sample items to "infer" the population average value

        1) Difference Method - Sampling for the difference between audit and
            book figures. Difference sampling will usually reduce sample size
            as the distribution of differences will probably have less dispersion
            than distribution of basic variables (e.g., book values).

        2) Ratio Method - Sampling to estimate the ratio of audit to book value.
            Ratio sampling has a similar effect as difference sampling but is not
            subject to bias when large errors are associated with large items in
            the population (and small errors with small items) as in difference
            sampling.

        3) Regression Method - Sampling to estimate a book value through finding
            the best regression line fit for the relationship between audit and
            book values, and projecting the total value accordingly

    c. The best choice is the characteristic which will likely provide the most
        efficient result; that is, the characteristic that for any given sample
        size, n, will produce the most reliable result for a given precision (or
        the most precise result at a specified risk level)

    d. Difference-, ratio-, or regression-based estimation of variables are
        usually more efficient in typical audit circumstances involving relatively
        few errors of fairly small size

        1) Difference estimation is most efficient when errors between audit and
            book values are of approximately the same size regardless of the size
            of the items in question

      2) Ratio estimation is most efficient when errors between audit and book values are proportional to the size of the items, i.e., smaller items-smaller errors, larger items-larger errors

      3) Regression estimates are most effective when sampling error results in large differences between average book value of audited accounts and average book value of all items in the population

4. Step Four - Establish audit sampling risks. The auditor must relate the risk of incorrect acceptance based on a sample for a substantive test to other sources of audit evidence which might contribute to overall reliance. All sources of reliance should be related to the ultimate risk of incorrect acceptance of material monetary errors. If the auditor has chosen a hypothesis testing objective for audit sampling, consideration should also be given to controlling the risk of incorrect rejection of a client's book value. Five basic risks and the basic risk determination model from SAS 39 are discussed below.

   a. Basic risks to be assessed:
     1) TD = allowable risk of incorrect acceptance as indicated by results of audit sampling tests of detail
     2) UR = ultimate risk usually set at 5 to 10%
     3) IC = risk that internal control will fail to detect existing material errors
     4) AR = risk that analytical review and/or other substantive testing aside from the representative sample itself will fail to detect any existing material error
     5) Allowable risk of incorrect rejection is the planned risk that sample results will support the conclusion that material error is present when in fact the book value is not materially misstated. Necessary in planning hypothesis tests.

   b. Allowable risk of incorrect acceptance as a result of audit sampling tests of detail, TD, may be modeled or computed as follows according to SAS 39:

$$TD = UR/(IC \times AR)$$

EXAMPLE:

With, UR = 5%
*   IC = 20% (indicating moderately strong control)*
*   AR = 80% (indicating little reliance on nonsampling*
*   substantive tests)*

TD is determined as follows:

TD = .05/(.2 x .8) = .05/.16 = 31%

Learn this equation and its meaning for the exam!

5. Step Five - Determine appropriate sample size, based on risk assessments, tolerable error assessment, and the variation (dispersion) of the population from which the sample will be drawn or the auditor's expectation about errors in the population

a. Nonstatistical

  1) If a nonstatistical approach to audit sampling has been adopted, the auditor may consider the relationships implied by the risk model in arriving at an appropriate risk factor for TD. The AICPA exposure draft on sampling in auditing suggests the following approach:

| | Assurance Factor | |
Degree of Allowable Risk (TD)	Little Error Anticipated	Some Error Anticipated
Substantial	1.5	3
Moderate	2.3	4
Little	3	6

$$\text{Sample Size} = \frac{\text{Book Value of Population To Be Sampled}}{\text{Tolerable Error}} \times \text{Assurance Factor}$$

  2) This is a simplified Probability Proportional to Size (PPS) approach and should be used only in conjunction with a sample selection plan which calls for at least two strata with sample size in each stratum proportional to the book value of the stratum

b. Statistical

  1) Statistical sample sizes for variables hypothesis testing may be determined by application of the following formula:

  a)
  $$n = \frac{z_\alpha^2 \sigma^2}{a^2}$$

  Where, n = sample size
  α = planned level (%) of risk of rejecting a proper amount
  z_α = reliability coefficient (# of std. errors) associated with planned risk of rejecting a proper amount
  a = precision per item in the population (as determined below)
  σ = standard deviation (estimated) of the population to be sampled, and

  b) $$a = \frac{TE/N}{1 + z_{TD}/z_\alpha}$$

  Where, TE = tolerable error (material amount)
  N = number of items in population to be sampled
  z_{TD} = reliability coefficient (number of standard errors) associated with planned risk of accepting, based on sample results, an amount which is materially misstated

c) EXAMPLE:

   The auditor in preparing to conduct an audit hypothesis test of an account balance of $100,000 has determined that:

   TE = $10,000

   α = .10 (hence z_α = 1.64 because α is a two-tailed test)

   TD = .16 (hence z_{TD} = 1.0 because TD is related to a one-tail test)

   σ = $10 (based on a sample of book values) and computed as follows:

   $$\sigma = \sqrt{\frac{\Sigma(x_i - \bar{x})^2}{n-1}}$$

   Where, x_i = observed value of an item in the sample of book values

   $\bar{x}$ = avg. of all observed values in the sample of book values

   To determine n, the auditor first computes, a, average precision per item as follows:

   $$a = \frac{TE/N}{1 + z_{TD}/z_\alpha}$$

   $$= \frac{10,000/3,000}{1 + 1.0/1.64} = \frac{3.333}{1.61}$$

   = 2.07   So that,

   $$n = \frac{z_\alpha^2 \cdot \sigma^2}{a^2}$$

   $$n = \frac{1.64^2 \cdot 10^2}{2.07^2} = \frac{269}{4.28}$$

   n = 63

2) As a rule of thumb, population precision, N·a, can be arbitrarily set at 1/2 TE in order to conservatively establish an acceptably low allowable risk of accepting a material error in a book value

3) For estimation sampling, use equation from step "5.b.1)a)" with a "z" value determined by the number of standard errors associated with the planned risk of projecting an audit value which is materially in error

a)   The risk of projecting an audit value which is materially in error
     would normally be set at a low level (5% - 10%) because the auditor
     will have previously determined that the book value is materially in
     error (or absent) and hence that IC is near 100%

b)   Potter Company asks its CPA's assistance in estimating the average
     gross value of the 5,000 invoices processed during June 1971. The
     CPA estimates the population standard deviation to be $10. If he
     wishes to achieve (average) precision of $\pm$ $2 with a 95% level of
     confidence (reliability), he should draw an unrestricted random
     sample of

     a)   418 elements
     b)   186 elements
     c)   122 elements
     d)   96 elements

The following graph is useful in setting up an analysis of this
problem.

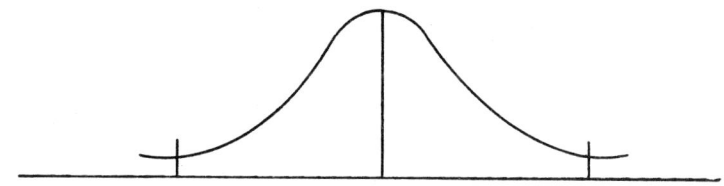

True Average Value
              True Average Value -$2   True Average Value +$2

The horizontal axis represents the distribution of invoice balances.

The CPA wants the hypothetical (you only take one sample) distribution to include 95% of its area within $2 of the true avg. value.

Plus or minus two dollars equals average precision. The same distance is equal to the reliability coefficient times the dollar value
of the standard error $\left(\dfrac{\sigma}{\sqrt{n}}\right)$.

Since the objective of the question is to determine "n" (sample
size), one can do so as follows:

$$\text{Average precision} = \text{Reliability coefficient} \times \text{Standard error}$$

Numeric Example	Notation
$\$2 = 1.96 \times \dfrac{\$10}{\sqrt{n}}$	$a = z\,\dfrac{\sigma}{\sqrt{n}}$
$\sqrt{n} = \dfrac{1.96 \times 10}{2}$	$\sqrt{n} = z\,\dfrac{\sigma}{a}$
$n = \dfrac{1.96^2 \times 10^2}{2^2}$	$n = \dfrac{z^2\,\sigma^2}{a^2}$
$n = 96$	

6. <u>Step Six</u> - Select Sample Items from the population and <u>perform audit procedures</u> on the sample

    a. Proper audit procedures must be applied to each item selected

        1) Any value other than "book" must be noted for the statistical evaluation

        2) Each error must be analyzed to determine whether it is an "exception" or one of many of a similar type. E.g., if an auditor finds that a discount was not granted, s/he must decide whether the deviation was a simple error or a symptom of failure to apply management's discount policy.

           a) Thus, the audit procedures are expanded to some degree for each error
           b) Any other unusual items, relationships, etc., that come to the attention of the auditor should be analyzed

    b. Avoid nonsampling error such as:

        1) Failure to use a random sample
        2) Failure to recognize an exception
        3) Failure to evaluate sample results properly
        4) Failure to use correct sampling method
        5) All other errors in carrying out the sampling plan

7. <u>Step Seven</u> - Project and Evaluate Results

    a. Nonstatistical approach

        1) SAS 39 requires <u>projection</u> of a sample result to the population as a whole

        2) It is therefore inappropriate to pass as immaterial errors in a sample simply because the total of those errors actually observed is immaterial

3) One method of projecting results is to project each stratum (or the population as a whole, if an unstratified sample was used) by dividing the amount of error in the sample by the fraction of total dollars from the population which have been included in the sample

4) *EXAMPLE: An auditor may have selected a sample to be representative of trade receivables. The sample includes 10 percent of the book values of the account balance. If the auditor has found $1,000 of error in the sample, his best estimate of error in the population would be calculated to be $10,000 ($1,000 ÷ 1/10).*

5) Total projected error should be compared with tolerable error to determine whether there is excess risk of material error in the population. If projected total error is greater than or close to tolerable error, the risk of material error may exceed acceptable levels. The account balance should be evaluated accordingly.

b. Statistical Approach

1) Evaluation of variables samples requires computation of a mean value, $\bar{x}$, for the sample of n items. If total rather than average value is being estimated, a projection of that total, X, equal to N multiplied by $\bar{x}$ $(X = N\bar{x})$.

2) Basic statistical evaluation of hypothesis test results requires construction of an interval of values which the auditor finds acceptable based on the sampling plan, and a comparison of the interval with the book value reported by the client

a) If the book value exists within the interval $X \pm (\text{pre} \cdot N)$, then the auditor may accept the book value knowing that the risk of having accepted a value which is materially incorrect is acceptably low

b) If the book value is not within the interval $X \pm (\text{pre} \cdot N)$, then the auditor may reject the book value with an acceptably low risk of having rejected an amount which is not materially in error. Follow-up may include:

1] Expansion of sample
2] Follow-up work on the balance by the client, or
3] The determination of an appropriate adjustment, or
4] Consideration of a qualification based on misstatement of the amount in question

3) Practical considerations requiring modification of basic evaluation method

a) The estimated standard deviation used in planning a sample application may be significantly different from the best available estimate derived after considering the audited values of the sample items

1] The achieved standard deviation estimate for the ratio, difference, or regression methods may be much smaller than the estimate used in planning, thus the achieved value of pre·N will be smaller than planned

a] If so, the auditor may still be able to accept a client balance even though the book value is <u>not</u> within the achieved interval Nx ± (pre·N)

b] One approach in such a circumstance is to compare the book value and the audit estimate after adjusting the estimate for possible sampling error. The amount of the adjustment is equal to the achieved precision of the estimate. If the difference between the book value and the far end of the achieved precision range surrounding the audit estimate is less than tolerable error, the book value can be accepted. In other words, if the two-sided confidence interval for the total audit value is completely within the book value plus and minus the amount considered material, the auditor may accept the hypothesis that the book value is not misstated by a material amount.

c] E.g., if book value is $200,000; N$\overline{x}$ is $185,000; achieved precision is $10,000; and tolerable error is $30,000; then:

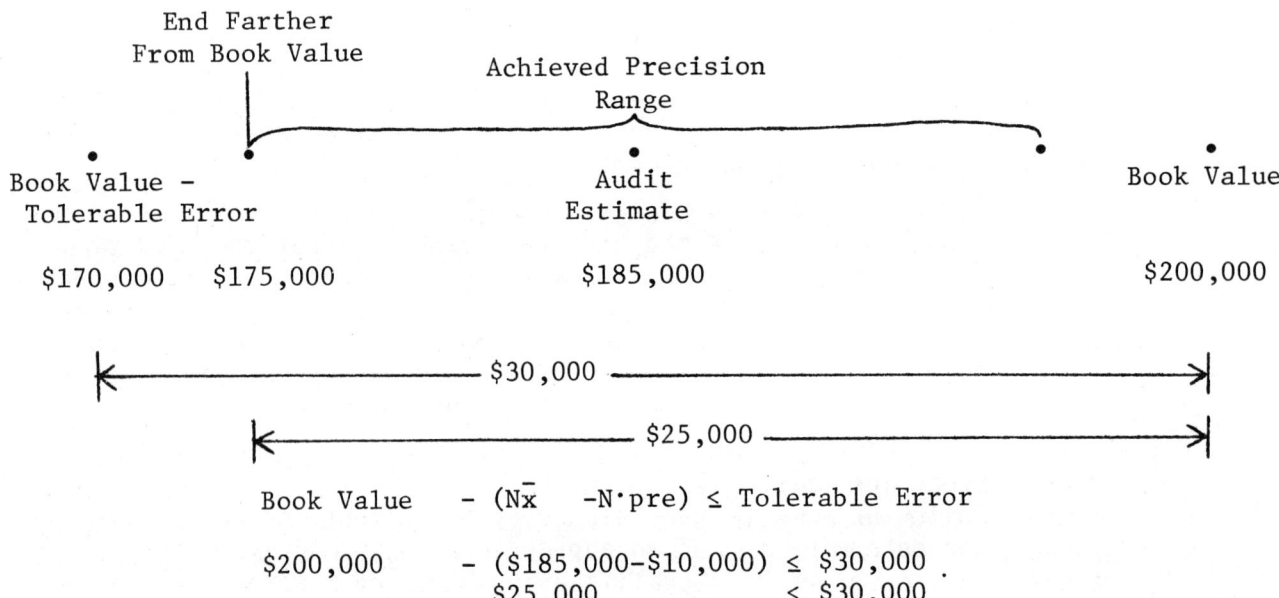

Book Value   − (N$\overline{x}$ −N·pre) ≤ Tolerable Error

$200,000   − ($185,000−$10,000) ≤ $30,000
             $25,000   ≤ $30,000

So the book value can be accepted.

d] This approach is valid (and conservative) in circumstances in which the acceptable level of risk of incorrect rejection is not larger than twice the risk of incorrect acceptance

        2] The achieved standard deviation estimate may, in unusual cases, be larger than the estimated standard deviation used in planning. If so, the auditor may wish to consider expanding the sample or performing other tests before accepting or rejecting the book value.

    b) Systematic errors discovered as a result of audit evaluation of sample items may require extended audit procedures regardless of the statistical conclusions reached

    c) When the book value cannot be accepted based on statistical evaluation, the auditor or client may need to do extended testing before reaching a conclusion about the size of any required adjustment

D. Attribute Sampling

1. Step One - Determine which form of attribute sampling to use. Acceptance and discovery sampling are special forms of attribute sampling. Either can be used for compliance tests of internal control.

    a. Acceptance Sampling - Sampling for an error rate to be able to say that the error rate is less than a specified level with a stated degree of confidence, e.g., taking a sample and based on the sample size and number of errors, one can state that the error rate is below an auditor's specified tolerable error limit with a given level of confidence

    b. Discovery Sampling - Sampling for critical errors, e.g., forgeries. Like acceptance sampling, the objective is to be able to state that the error rate is below a certain tolerable level with a stated degree of confidence (e.g., less than 1% error with 95% confidence); thus, the error rate will be less than 1% 95 times out of 100. If one finds one critical error, however, one stops using sampling and examines all transactions because the presumption (with critical errors) is that there are no errors.

    c. Both acceptance and discovery sampling result in assurance (confidence) that an error rate is less than a specified percentage, e.g., 95% confidence that the error rate is less than 5%. This assurance is achieved by observing a sufficiently small error rate in a sufficiently large sample to make such a statement.

2. Step Two - Determine method of selecting the sample

    a. Haphazard sample selection is acceptable for use with a judgmental audit sample test

    b. Block sample selection is generally not the most appropriate means of selecting compliance samples

    c. Random selection or systematic selection (as discussed above) should be used if a statistical compliance sampling approach has been selected

    d. Sequential sampling is a sampling plan in which the sample is taken in several steps with each step conditional on the results of the previous step

3. Step Three - Define the error (deviation condition) which will determine whether each item in the sample was properly or improperly handled

    EXAMPLE: If the prescribed procedure to be tested requires the cancellation of each paid disbursement voucher, the error (deviation condition) would be defined as a paid but uncancelled voucher.

4. Step Four - Establish acceptable audit sampling risk (risk of arriving at wrong conclusion based on sample results). Since the auditor usually relies on compliance sample results as the primary source of evidence about the reliance to be placed on controls, a low level of risk of overreliance is normally selected.

    a. Risk levels between 1% and 10% are considered low
    b. Many auditors establish a single risk level for all such tests

5. Step Five - Determine appropriate sample size

    a. Sample size for basic attribute testing for compliance purposes is frequently determined by reference to appropriate tables which relate sample sizes to:

        1) Expected occurrence rate, p, specified by the auditor, and
        2) Approximate size of the population: less than 1,000 items, 1,000 - 2,000, 2,000 - 5,000, etc., and
        3) Maximum tolerable rate of error as specified by the auditor

    b. Alternatively the sample size formula which follows can be used:

    $$n = \frac{z^2 \cdot p \cdot q}{pre^2}$$

    where   p = expected error rate
             q = 1-p, e.g., if the expected error rate is 4%, q = .96
           pre = maximum tolerable error rate less expected error rate
             z = reliability coefficient, i.e., the number of standard deviations of sampling distribution required to fit within the precision range in order to achieve specified risk level established in Step Four above

        1) For substantial reliance on a control, tolerable rates below 7% are usually selected
        2) Moderate reliance usually requires a tolerable rate of less than 12% to be considered

    c. Attribute sampling illustrations

        1) The CPA believes the client's vouchers contain a 3% error rate (expected error rate). The CPA wants to assure himself that the error rate is not above 5% (maximum tolerable error rate). The precision is ± 2% (maximum tolerable error rate minus the expected error rate). The CPA wants a 95% confidence level, i.e., not more than a 5% risk of overreliance.

$$n = \frac{z^2 \times p \times q}{pre^2}$$

$$n = \frac{1.96^2 \times .03 \times .97}{.02^2}$$

$$n = \frac{4 \times .0291}{.004}$$

$$n = 291$$

The difference in determining sample size between variables sampling and attribute sampling is caused by substituting:

$$\sqrt{\frac{pq}{n}} \quad \text{for} \quad \frac{\sigma}{\sqrt{n}}$$

2) In connection with his examination of the financial statements of Juicy Melons, Inc., a CPA is testing the effectiveness of the company's inspection system for purchases from melon growers. For one lot of 2,000, company inspectors found the bad melon rate to be 4%. If the CPA wishes to sample from this lot with a confidence level of 90% and a precision (confidence interval) of ± 2%*, the required sample size is 230. If the precision is changed to ± 1% and other specifications remain the same, the required sample size is

    1) 684
    2) 460
    3) 251
    4) 230

The answer is (1), 684, because of the finite population correction factor, even though sample size formula results in a sample of 1036.

$$n = \frac{1.64^2 \times .04 \times .96}{.01^{2*}}$$

$$n = \frac{2.7 \times .0384}{.0001} = 1036$$

$$1036 \sqrt{1 - \frac{n}{N}}$$

$$1036 \sqrt{1 - \frac{1036}{2000}}$$

---

*Precision is given here and need not be calculated as in "c.1)" on the previous page.

1036 $\sqrt{.5}$

1036 x .7 or 684 approximately

d. Suggested guidelines for nonstatistical compliance sampling which can be related to the statistical approach just described are as follows:

  1) If tolerable rate of error is 5% and no deviations are expected, a sample of size n = 60 might be sufficient to conclude that there is an acceptably low sampling risk, and that the deviation rate is less than the tolerable (5%) rate

  2) Without expanding the sample beyond 60, if two or more errors are subsequently discovered, results would not usually support reliance at the planned level

6. Step Six - Select Sample items from the population and perform audit procedures on those items

  a. Proper audit procedures should be applied to all items in the sample

   1) However, randomly selected items for which the control being tested is not applicable should be excluded from the sample for evaluation purposes

   2) *EXAMPLE: In a test of control procedures over purchase discounts taken, one or more randomly selected invoices may be for purchases for which no discount terms exist. If so, the auditor should note in audit workpapers that the item(s) is not subject to discount control procedures. It is important, then, to realize that sample size for the purpose of evaluating control of discounts is reduced accordingly. If planned sample size was the minimum required, then an additional randomly selected item(s) should be chosen accordingly.*

  b. Each exception should be analyzed to determine whether it is an isolated instance or a recurring type of error

7. Step Seven - Project and Evaluate Results

  a. Compute an error rate for the sample by dividing the number of deviations observed by the sample size

  b. Compare the sample rate with the expected rate. If the computed sample error rate exceeds the expected rate used in planning for sample size, risk of relying on internal control may be unacceptably high.

  c. Statistical attribute samples for compliance tests may be evaluated with tables used in selecting sample size

   1) Find the maximum upper limit on error rate actually achieved for the specified risk level and actual number of deviations observed. This maximum upper limit on error should be compared with tolerable error.

   2) If tolerable error exceeds the limit from the sampling table, reliance is appropriate

d. In evaluating attribute sample results, the auditor must decide the effect on the substantive tests

1) If internal control is very good, there is less need to rely on substantive tests, (e.g., IC, the risk of control failure, can be low), or vice versa
2) All errors should be analyzed to determine their nature, extent, and effect
3) The discovery of irregularities (fraud) ordinarily requires broader consideration of implications for subsequent audit action than does the discovery of an error or mistake

E. Probability Proportional to Size (PPS) (Dollar-Unit) Sampling

1. PPS sampling is an emerging type of sampling plan whose use in audit practice is increasing. This type of plan has not received attention on the exam to date, but may appear soon.

2. PPS Sampling - Individual dollars within an item or balance, rather than items or balances per se, are defined as the sampling units, e.g., a 1,000 dollar transaction item would contain 1,000 dollar sampling units. Items selected are selected with probability proportional to size, e.g., a 1,000 dollar item is 10 times as likely to be selected as a 100 dollar item.

3. PPS can be used for compliance or substantive purposes

4. If more than a few errors are expected in a sample, PPS type plans are inefficient. Therefore, this type of sampling plan should not be used unless very few errors can reasonably be expected.

F. Statistical Sampling Formulas and Relationships

1. Variables

a. $n = \dfrac{z_\alpha^2 \sigma^2}{a^2}$

b. $a = \dfrac{TE/N}{1+z_{TD}/z_\alpha}$

c. $TD = UR/(IC \times AR)$

2. Attributes

$$n = \frac{z^2 \cdot p \cdot q}{pre^2}$$

Note: Especially "F.1.c." and possibly "F.1.a." are more likely to be tested from memory than other formulas.

3. Relationships

   a. Table of Effects

Factor	Change in Factor	Impact on Sample Size
Population Dispersion i.e., σ^2, or σ	Increases (Decreases)	Increases (Decreases)
Ultimate Risk, UR	Increases (Decreases)	Decreases (Increases)
Risk of Internal Control Failure, IC	Increases (Decreases)	Increases (Decreases)
Risk of Analytical Review Failure, AR	Increases (Decreases)	Increases (Decreases)
Tolerable Error	Increases (Decreases)	Decreases (Increases)

   b. Explanations

   1) As population dispersion, e.g., standard deviation, increases, sample size increases
   2) As ultimate risk, UR, increases the allowable risk of accepting a materially misstated balance, TD, can increase thus decreasing sample size
   3) As the risk of control failure, IC, or the risk of analytical review, AR, failing increases the allowable risk of accepting a materially misstated balance, TD, should be decreased, thus increasing sample size
   4) As tolerable error, TE, increases, sample size may be decreased

G. <u>Overview of Audit Sampling</u>

1. Planning
    a. Carefully formulate audit objective
    b. Define the population (class of transactions or balances) germane to audit objective
    c. Determine appropriate source of evidence about the population
    d. Determine whether audit sampling is required

        1) Audit sampling is usually considered when the auditor has no special knowledge about which items or groups of items are most likely to be in error and,
        2) If examination of key or risky items alone is not sufficient to reduce audit risks to acceptable levels, audit sampling is advisable

    e. Determine whether a statistical or nonstatistical approach will be used for audit sampling

2. Steps in Sampling
    (Complete listing on following page.)

2. Steps in Sampling

Step	Variables	Attributes
1. Determine Audit Objective	Determine whether audit objective requires estimation sampling or hypothesis testing.	Determine whether to use acceptance or discovery sampling.
2. Determine Selection Technique	Determine selection technique (e.g., random, systematic, stratified random, etc.).	Determine sample selection method (e.g., haphazard, random, etc.).
3. Define (Select) the Characteristic to be Evaluated	Select the characteristic to be observed, (e.g., differences between audit and book values, ratio of audit to book, etc.).	Precisely define the error (deviation condition) to be tested.
4. Establish Sampling Risks	Establish sampling risks, i.e., TD, UR, AR, and risk of incorrect rejection. Remember: $TD = UR/(IC \times AR)$	Establish acceptable sampling risk, i.e., risk of overreliance.
5. Determine Sample Size	Determine sample size by relating risks to population dispersion and tolerable error.	Determine sample size by relating (usually through use of tables) expected error rate, tolerable error rate, and population size to risk of overreliance
6. Select and Perform Audit Tests	Select sample items and perform audit tests of substantive detail.	Select sample and perform audit tests of compliance.
7. Project and Evaluate Results	Project and evaluate results. Remember that projection of results to population is required for nonstatistical and statistical samples.	Project an error rate and compare with expected rate or evaluate projected upper limit on error in relation to planned tolerable error rate.

AUDITING EDP

There are very few financial information systems today that are not automated. Whether they exist on a micro or a mainframe, automation proliferates throughout the financial system. Therefore, the audit of an EDP system can no longer be considered a separate audit from the audit of the financial information system. However, there is a specialized degree of knowledge that is required to evaluate the system of controls in an automated environment.

Knowledge of EDP systems and audit procedures appropriate thereto are regularly tested on the auditing section of the exam. The questions more recently were scattered multiple choice questions testing candidates' knowledge of basic EDP concepts and terms, i.e., what is machine language or knowing the limitations of input-output testing. When EDP is tested as an essay question, you will be required to either explain the difference between general controls and application controls (including giving examples in a small computer system, distributed, data-base, or batch environment) or be able to flowchart an EDP environment. Other questions use EDP terminology but require no EDP knowledge for determining the right answer. Therefore, do not feel you cannot answer a question until you read it and determine what it is testing.

If you have limited time to study, you should concentrate on understanding flowcharting principles. This will have applicability on numerous non-EDP questions dealing with general internal control. If you want to be fully prepared, then a complete review of this section and reference to supplementary materials (i.e., beginning EDP texts) is necessary when the material in this section is new to you. This should prepare you to perform reasonably well on the exam. Keep in mind that review of these materials cannot make you an expert. However, the material in this section will enable you to understand the complexities of automated environments and at the same time understand that the basic principles of internal control still prevail.

Study Program for the Auditing EDP Module

The organization of the material in this module corresponds to four areas of knowledge.

I. Principles of Auditing EDP Systems

The AICPA is in the process of revising SAS 3. Under the revised SAS 3, the AICPA will consider auditing EDP systems to be a normal extension of the audit. This section will present the basic principles which you can use in answering questions on the exam that ask about auditing the entire system as well as multiple choice questions testing specific terms.

II. Unique Characteristics of Specific EDP Systems

In addition to the batch environment, there are other specific EDP environments that you should be familiar with. This section describes the unique control characteristics in each of those environments. An essay question on the exam may ask you to detail the control objectives or control weaknesses in one of these environments.

III. Flowcharting

Flowcharting is an important tool available to the auditor in an automated environment. This section describes the various flowcharting techniques that the auditor can use and that may be tested in an essay question on the exam.

IV. EDP Definitions

Buzz words proliferate in the EDP environment. This section describes some of the more common terms that you may find tested in various multiple choice questions. If this material is new to you, then begin by reading the section on EDP definitions. This will provide you with the basic vocabulary that is used throughout the entire section.

I. Principles of Auditing EDP Systems

If a client uses EDP, the auditor must be capable of understanding the entire system to evaluate the client's internal control (SAS 3, para 4). Note that EDP systems are integral parts of the accounting system. Thus, the auditor's primary concern is with the system's internal control, i.e., does the system provide reasonable assurance that errors and irregularities have been and will be prevented or detected on a timely basis by employees in the course of their normal activities.

The audit procedures applicable to evaluating the internal controls in EDP systems are (1) review of the system, (2) tests of compliance, and (3) evaluation to

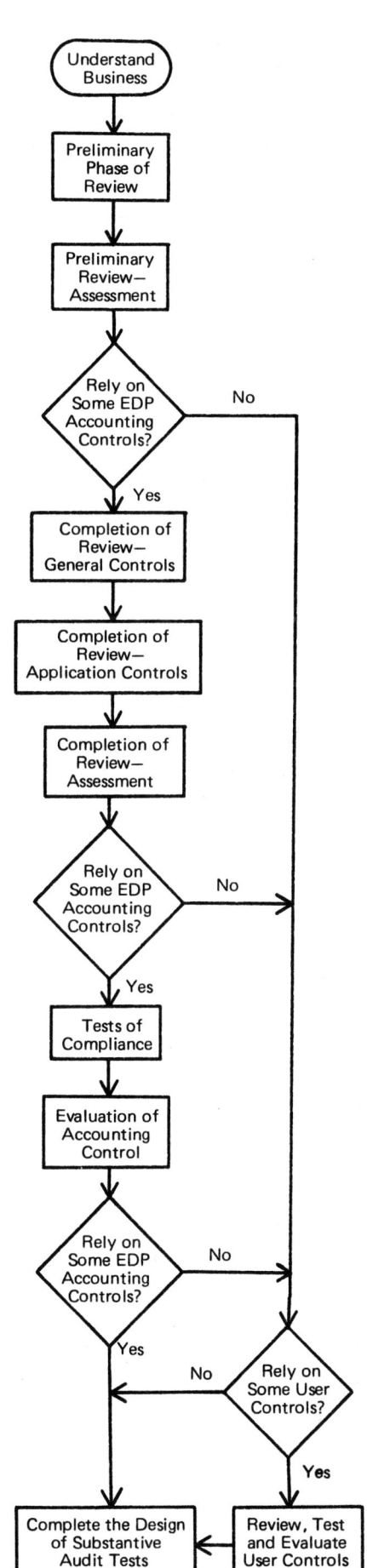

OBJECTIVES:

1. Flow of transactions and significance of output.
2. Extent to which EDP is used in significant accounting applications.
3. Basic structure of accounting control, including both EDP and user controls.

1. Assess significance of EDP and non-EDP accounting controls.
2. Determine extent of additional review within EDP.
3. Develop preliminary design of substantive tests.

1. Determine the effect of strengths and weakness on application controls.
2. Identify general controls on which reliance is planned and determine how they operate.
3. Design tests of compliance.

1. Identify applications and related controls on which reliance is planned, and determine how the controls operate.
2. Design tests of compliance.

1. Assess effectiveness of EDP and non-EDP accounting controls.
2. Review preliminary design of substantive procedures.

1. Provide reasonable assurance that controls are functioning properly.
2. Determine and document when, how, and by whom.

1. Consider the types of errors and irregularities that could occur.
2. Determine the accounting control procedures that prevent or detect such errors and irregularities.
3. Determine whether the necessary control procedures are prescribed and followed satisfactorily.
4. Evaluate weaknesses and assess their effect on the nature, timing, and extent of substantive procedures.

NOTE: User controls are those outside the EDP system, i.e., traditional controls such as total payroll, dollars of inventory, etc., kept by user departments.

determine the extent of the substantive tests (as described in SAS 1, Section 320). The process is flowcharted on page 243. The flowchart is taken from the AICPA Audit Guide: "The Auditor's Study and Evaluation of Internal Control in EDP Systems." The discussion is based on the classification of controls presented in the guide.

Following the evaluation of the internal controls, the auditor performs the various substantive tests necessary to evaluate the reasonableness of the records produced by the system. The purpose of this section is to assume that in your evaluation of internal control you do not have the option of auditing around the computer at the three decision points on the flowchart. Also assume that the scope of your evaluation dictates that you must recommend additional controls if none exist or the ones that exist are not effective. This section will explain what controls should exist and recommend common testing procedures for your evaluation of both the EDP environment (general controls) and each accounting process (application controls).

A. Evaluating the EDP Environment

The EDP environment requires specialized controls to compensate for the controls that were lost in the conversion from the traditional manual processing system. Those controls that affect multiple accounting applications are classified as general controls. The audit guide categorizes general controls into five areas.

1. Organization and Operation Controls

The EDP department is responsible for execution of transactions and maintaining the records of those transactions. Therefore, controls must be in place that ensure (1) no transaction can be initiated within EDP, (2) authorization for those transactions is separated from EDP, and (3) within EDP the execution and recording functions remain separate.

Segregation of duties provides the control mechanism for maintaining an independent processing environment and meeting the control objective. First, the EDP department should be segregated from the user departments organizationally. Secondly, key functions within EDP are defined to ensure maximum segregation of duties. The key functions are:

a. Systems Analyst - The systems analyst is responsible for designing the system to be developed within the specifications formulated jointly with the user department that has ultimate responsibility for the project. A system flowchart may be used as the tool to define the system requirements.

b. Applications Programmer - The applications programmer is responsible for designing detailed programs from the general specifications provided by the systems analyst. The programmer will write, test, and debug the detailed program specifications.

c. Systems Programmer - The systems programmer is responsible for implementing, modifying, and debugging the software necessary for making the hardware work (systems software).

d. Operator - The operator is responsible for ensuring the day to day execution of software operations. S/he mounts magnetic tapes on the tape drives, supervises operations on the operators console, accepts any required input, and distributes the output that is generated.

e. Librarian - The librarian is responsible for custody of both the records that are electronically maintained (primarily magnetic tapes but can be magnetic disks or paper generated files) and maintenance of the documentation library.

f. Quality Assurance - The quality assurance function is a relatively new function established primarily to ensure that new systems under development and old systems being changed are adequately controlled and that they meet the user's specifications.

The auditor's compliance tests should include inquiring, observing, discussing, and reviewing the existence of an appropriate organization chart, the responsibility for initiation and authorization of transactions, and the custody of the electronic records and documentation. Any discrepancies should be reported and the appropriate controls recommended.

2. Systems Development and Documentation Controls

Within EDP, new systems are constantly being developed that either replace old systems or introduce a new system that enhances an old system. This environment requires unique controls to be functioning to ensure that the integrity of the overall system is maintained.

The most common controls that should be present include the following.

a. Design Methodology - All new systems being developed should flow through a distinctive process that has specific control points at which the overall direction of the system can be evaluated. A common type of methodology is SDLC (systems development life cycle). SDLC presents distinctive processes through which the systems are developed. To compliance test the system the auditor can, first, determine if the systems development department is using a methodology and, second, review the process to determine if there are adequate control points. To perform substantive testing the auditor can evaluate the system to ensure that the applications controls are in place.

b. Change Control Process - To effect a change on a system that is presently operating (known as the live system), a formal change process must be in place which provides for formal approval of the change(s) to be implemented. Once the change is approved, developed, tested, and ready for implementation, the live system is replaced with the fully tested system that incorporates the change. It is the auditor's responsibility to ensure that a formal change control process is functioning (compliance tests). Secondly, the auditor ensures that each change made to the systems is properly authorized (tracking the change process and substantive testing changes made). In addition, the auditor will need to review any "quick fixes" that occurred to the live system while it was operating and inquire why these changes could not have gone through the formal change process. This includes program changes as well as direct fixes to existing electronic records (files).

3. Hardware and Systems Software Controls

The reliability of EDP hardware today has increased dramatically over the last decade. This is primarily due to the chip technology. However, it is additionally due to many of the controls built into the hardware and systems software. The primary controls that you should be aware of include the following.

a. Parity Check - A special bit is added to each character stored in memory that detects if the hardware loses a bit during the internal movement of the character.

b. Echo Check - Primarily in telecommunications transmissions. During the sending and receiving of characters, the receiving hardware repeats back to the sending hardware what it received and automatically resends any characters that it detects were received incorrectly.

c. Diagnostic Routines - The systems software maintains statistics on the operations of the computer, e.g., number of jobs run, percentage of utilization of the computer by time period, number of errors occurring, etc. These reports are reviewed by operations management to improve efficiency and highlight past problems for future planning.

d. Boundary Protection - Most CPUs have multiple jobs running simultaneously (multiprogramming environment). To ensure that these simultaneous jobs cannot destroy or change the allocated memory of another job, the systems software contains boundary protection controls.

The auditor should determine the controls that exist within the system during compliance testing and ensure that they are functioning. During substantive testing, the auditor should take advantage of the information compiled in the diagnostic routines and use that as part of the overall evaluation. The use of audit software or utility programs (discussed later) can reformat information that is stored electronically to aid in the evaluation of the system.

4. Access Controls

In order to function within the EDP environment individuals require access to resources. Access can be effected either physically or electronically. With the advent of today's computer hackers, who have illegally electronically accessed unauthorized information, the emphasis is currently on ensuring adequate controls over electronic access to data. A properly controlled environment should include controls over both physical access to EDP operation as well as data communications.

    a. Physical Access Controls

        1) Limited Access Room - The physical facility that houses EDP equipment must have controls to limit access to only authorized individuals. There are many alternatives to limit access including using a guard, automated key card access, and manual key locks.

        2) Visitor Entry Logs - Any individual who wants to enter a secure area must be authorized by an appropriate individual, recorded in a visitors' log, and escorted while in the secure area. The use of badges displayed by all employees quickly distinguishes visitors and draws attention to their activities.

    b. Data Communications Controls

        1) User Identification - Each potential user of the EDP system should be issued an individual user account number and a secret password that no individual can retrieve electronically or manually from the system. These passwords should be reissued periodically to ensure that multiple individuals are not aware of more than one password. Upon termination or transfer, an individual's account and password should be deleted. There are security packages available to add to the EDP system to implement the controls above, e.g., Top Secret, ACF2, and RACF.

        2) Call Back - On highly sensitive systems, a user dials up the system, identifies him/herself, and the system terminates the session. Then, either manually or electronically, the system looks up the authorized telephone number for that individual and calls him/her back and re-establishes communications. This is the primary preventive technique for stopping computer hackers from trying to masquerade as an authorized user from an unauthorized telephone number.

        3) Multiple Level Security - Once an individual is identified as an authorized user of the system, restrictions can be placed on the information the user can read and/or change. This will further control access to sensitive information and limit changes to stored data to only those users who have been properly authorized.

The auditor performing compliance tests of access controls should determine what controls are available and whether they are being implemented. Substantive tests can include reviewing the detailed implementation program of the security software package that is being used to determine which users have been given access to what information and whether they are authorized.

5. Data and Procedural Controls

The EDP environment must be clearly defined to the most finite detail and appropriately documented so that each individual responsible for processing knows what to do in each situation that could occur. To ensure that this happens, specific controls must be implemented to prevent an unnecessary stoppage or error in processing.

a. Operations Manual - The operations manual specifies the responsibilities of the EDP operators. Every detail should be explained, from how to bring the computer up from a cold start to how to restart the machine if an error occurs.

b. Backup and Recovery - To ensure the preservation of historical records and the ability to recover from an unexpected error, files created within EDP are backed up in a systematic manner. The most common method used is called the Grandfather-Father-Son method. In a batch processing environment, detail files are updated with each run. The detail file being updated is the father. The new file is the son. The file from which the father was developed is the grandfather. The father, grandfather, and great-grandfather are backup files that should be stored both on- and off-premises. If the son were destroyed, for example, it could be reconstructed by rerunning the father file and the related transactions file.

c. Contingency Processing - Detailed plans must be developed to prepare for: (1) an outage of the EDP processing center of less than 6 hours, (2) an outage of 6-12 hours, and (3) an outage over 12 hours. The contingency plan will detail responsibilities of individuals as well as alternate processing sites to be utilized. There is a new service being sold that allows EDP centers to pay a service fee to be able to use an unused facility for backup if they incur an emergency. These backup centers are called shells.

d. Processing Control - There should be adequate administrative controls to ensure that all of the jobs required to be processed are run in a timely manner (controlled through a production schedule by the EDP Operations Manager), that all hardware errors and malfunctions are corrected and have been corrected (controlled through an operator's log), and that distribution of output is controlled.

e. File Protection Ring - A file protection ring is a processing control to ensure that an operator does not use a magnetic tape as a tape to write on when it actually has critical information on it.

During compliance testing the auditor should determine, through audit techniques such as interviews and internal control questionnaires, which controls have been implemented. During substantive testing the auditor can test the detail, e.g., monitor a test of the contingency plan.

B. Evaluating the Accounting Process

Each accounting application that is processed in an EDP environment is controlled during the three steps through EDP: input, processing, and output. The input step converts human readable information into computer readable information. Ensuring the integrity of the records while in the computer is controlled in the processing step. Presentation of the results of processing to the user occurs at the output step. This section will present common controls that should be present

at each of those steps and will then conclude with the most common audit techniques
that can be used to test the process, during compliance testing and substantive
testing.

1. Input Controls

    To ensure the integrity of the human readable data into the computer readable
format, there are many common controls that can be used.

    a. Preprinted Form - Input operators process a large quantity of repetitive
        data. If the information is preassigned a place on the input form used, the
        operator could consistently look for the information in those locations.

    b. Check Digit - A check digit is a suffix digit related algorithmically to the
        preceding digits of the number. It is used to verify that the number was
        entered into the computer system correctly (within the applications program
        there is software code that recomputes the check digit).

    c. Control, Batch, or Proof Total - A total of one numerical field for all the
        records of a batch that normally would be added, e.g., total sales dollars.

    d. Hash Total - A total of one field for all the records of a batch where the
        total is a meaningless total for financial purposes, e.g., a sum of account
        numbers added together.

    e. Record Count - A control total used for accountability to ensure all the
        records received are processed.

    f. Reasonableness and Limit Tests - Contained in the initial software program
        that the data is run through are tests for each input field, as appropriate.
        These tests check for dollar amounts that are too high (e.g., sale of pen
        for $1,000), fields expected to be only numeric (e.g., sales field contain-
        ing 10A0), or a code field containing an invalid choice (e.g., a field that
        indicates the sex of an individual where 1 = man and 2 = woman and contains
        a 3 in the field).

    g. Menu Driven Input - If input is being entered into a CRT, then the operator
        should be greeted by a menu and prompted as to the proper response to
        make [e.g., What score did you get on the Auditing part of the CPA exam
        (75-100)?].

2. Processing Controls

    Once the input has been accepted by the computer, it usually is processed
through multiple steps. Therefore, the throughput controls are essential (those
controls that ensure the integrity of the data through all of the processing steps).
Those controls include record counts, hash totals, and control totals established
during the input step and revised during processing as needed. Additional controls
that need to be established include the following.

    a. Checkpoint/Restart Capability - If a particular process requires a signifi-
        cant amount of time to process, it is desirable to have software within the
        application that allows the operator the ability to restart the application

at the last checkpoint passed as opposed to restarting the entire application.

b. Error Resolution Procedure - Individual transactions may be rejected during
processing as a result of the error detection controls in place. There
should be complementary controls that ensure those records are corrected and
reentered into the system.

3. Output Controls

Prior to the release of output to the user, there should be appropriate controls
in place to ensure that processing was accomplished according to specifications.
The following controls are frequently used to maintain the integrity of processing.

a. Control Total - The user of the application will frequently give the operator the expected result of processing ahead of time to allow the operator
to verify that processing was completed properly.

b. Limiting the Quantity of Output and Total Processing Time - Time restraints
and output page generation constraints are often automated within the job
being run to ensure that, if processing is being done in error, the job will
not utilize the resources needlessly.

c. Error Message Resolution - Following each job the system provides technical
codes indicating the perceived success the computer felt it had with the
running of the job. The operator should be trained in recognizing these
codes and appropriate reactions that should be made to them. This can
include calling users in the middle of the night and telling them their
application does not run and asking for their response to correct the
problem.

4. Audit Techniques

There are many techniques which auditors can use to test EDP applications. The
following are some of the more common ones.

a. Audit Software - Using either a specific audit software computer program, a
system utility software package, or developing a program in a higher level
language (e.g., COBOL), the auditor must use the computer to aid in the
audit. The most common types of reports that software is used for include:

1) Test extensions, footings, etc.
2) Print items over a certain amount
3) Select and print confirmations
4) Perform other statistical tests
5) Compare items in different files
6) Summarize data, e.g., aged accounts receivable
7) Analyze data for inconsistencies

b. Test Data - A set of dummy transactions is developed to determine if the
controls that are purported to be in effect are functioning as intended.
This technique is used primarily for system debugging purposes as opposed to
auditing due to the complexity of developing an adequate deck.

c. Controlled Processing and Reprocessing - Once a program has been tested, the
auditor need not test it again unless there have been substantial changes.

However, this requires assurance be provided that the programs used in processing are the same programs tested. Subsequently the auditor parallel
tests the system and compares the results with processing done utilizing the
controlled file. This procedure is primarily used when auditing service
centers which use the same program for multiple clients.

II. Unique Characteristics of Specific EDP Systems

Section I described the definitional approach to general and application controls. The problem for you on the exam will be to apply those controls to the
processing environment that the question calls for. For example, it would not be
appropriate to talk about batch controls in a data-base environment. The purpose of
this section is to describe each system so that you will be able to apply the
appropriate general and application controls.

A. Batch Processing

If the question does not specify the operating environment, then you can assume
it is talking about a batch environment. In a batch environment, it should be
fairly simple for you to discuss control principles, since any business data
processing course you had, or any review of a beginning data processing book
that you made, centered primarily on a batch environment.

Therefore, there are two key principles you should keep in mind:

1. Transactions flow through the system in batches. In any particular batch,
transactions may be adding, changing, or deleting existing information in the
master file. When these changes occur, balancing controls are maintained
throughout the change process. Therefore, the audit trail is straightforward
and easy to follow.

2. If CRTs are used in this environment, it may appear to the user of the system as
though changes are occurring immediately to the master file. In actuality, a
dummy file is set up, and the transactions are batched to change the actual file
later in the day. One example of this, memo post system, is being used in the
banking industry. Therefore, the controls over the batched transactions should
leave a good audit trail.

B. Data-Base Processing Environment

The most difficult processing environment to understand is the data-base
environment. The easiest way to describe this environment is to look at a
typical university. Usually, each department keeps a set of records on each of
its students. In addition, the bursar, payroll (if you are working for the
university), and eventually the alumni office all maintain their individual
student files. If you have an address change, you must notify each of those
entities in order to ensure that your records are accurate.

In a data-base environment, it is recognized that there is duplicate (common)
information within each of those university entities. Therefore, why not strip
off the duplicate information, just maintain in that department the unique
information, and refer to the central file for common information?

In addition, that central file of information and all of the interconnected files can be accessed directly if it is an online real-time (OLRT) environment. Usually, any user can either read, modify, or delete information on the file from CRTs. Because of this, the emphasis on batch controls is useless. There could be some batch access to these files late at night during the production runs, but the vulnerability of this environment is direct access and immediate changes to files.

The emphasis on controls in this environment should be placed on the following:

1. Terminal Security - There are terminal security software packages as discussed before that not only identify the user of the system, but limit the user to see only predesignated sections of the information file. That software can also limit the user to only read the information and not change it.

2. Backup and Recovery - Keep in mind that the data base environment is using a daily dump of the entire file (see Section IV on EDP definitions for a discussion)

3. Audit Software - Audit software packages usually test historical records. Therefore, if they are used, they will access the backup files stored in sequential files.

4. Integrated Test Facility (ITF) - More internal audit organizations are exploring the possibility of setting up the audit department as a simulated wholly owned subsidiary of the company in an ITF environment

5. User Department - Controls in this environment must start at the user department, with strict controls over who is authorized to make changes to the data base

6. Computer Personnel - Firms are establishing a new position entitled database administrator (DBA). The DBA serves as the keeper of the data ensuring that its integrity is maintained. Associated duties may include coordinating access authority over the data files. This person should not have access to assets, since it can be assumed s/he has access to records.

Overall, remember that transactions are initiated primarily at user terminals, and the files are usually updated immediately.

C. Service Bureau/Center

Service bureaus are simply computer centers not usually directly owned by the company. The company is renting time at the center. Therefore, the following controls should be maintained.

1. Contract - In the contract with the service center it should be stated that the company explicitly owns the data files and records maintained at the center

2. Independence - Either batch controls or online controls (depending on the particular system being rented) should be maintained at the user's own location. This includes having batch controls over information transmitted to the center and independent verification of information on the data base.

3. Backup and Recovery - Backup files should be under the control of the user, not the service center

It is very easy to fall into the old buddy routine, but many a service bureau has abruptly folded when a major client decided to bring its processing in-

house, or some other calamity befell the center, leaving the remaining users to
fend for themselves.

4. Timesharing System Considerations - If the service center has online access,
    then there are increased concerns. Many clients use the central computer simul-
    taneously. In the same way that the controls applicable to in-house batch
    processing are also applicable to service bureaus, standard real-time controls
    also apply to timesharing operations. The major problem is protection of data
    (both stored and in process) from destruction and unauthorized access. Data-
    protection controls include:

    1) Boundary protection
    2) Passwords on header labels
    3) Interlock·
    4) Physical security of library storage

As systems like timesharing and online real-time systems advance, internal
auditors will be affected in many ways:

    1) Better internal control systems will be required
    2) Better data integrity controls will be needed
    3) Alternative approaches to the audit trail will have to be developed
    4) Procedures will be required to assure that the system being subjected
        to the audit tests is the same system that produced the data
    5) Better data security controls will be needed
    6) Internal auditors will have to keep abreast of new technology
    7) Procedures must be developed to perform audits at reasonable costs

D. Distributed Systems

Distributed systems represent a network of remote computer sites each having a
small computer that is connected to the main computer system, i.e., payroll,
accounts payable, and accounts receivable could all have a separate computer
which communicates to the main system.

These smaller computers have the capabilities of:

    1) Operating as stand-alone devices
    2) Communicating with other smaller computers
    3) Communicating with the main computer

The advantages of distributive systems include:

    1) Reduced load on the main computer system
    2) Faster turnaround for each of the remote locations

Audit considerations include:

    1) Each location must be audited as a separate unit to verify the integrity
        of the data processed
    2) The continuity of data communicated by the remote locations should be
        verified through additional audit procedures

E. Small Computer Environment

With the proliferation of micro and mini computers, controls over these environments need to be emphasized. However, even if the computer can now be carried
around in a briefcase or fit in the palm of your hand, the control objectives
have not changed. It is still necessary to have physical security over the

unit, backup capability for the diskettes, and trained personnel that are authorized to access the corporate information.

The emphasis in this environment should center around the following:

1. Security - In this small computer environment, security over hardware is not as critical as security over the software. Most companies can easily replace the hardware, but may suffer a severe setback if they lose the software. Security should include: diskettes being kept in locked cabinets overnight, backup copies of the diskettes kept in a different location, custodians appointed who have control over the diskettes, and independent verification of the applications being processed on the small computer system.

2. Corporate Policies - At most companies, no one person knows the extent of how these small computers are being utilized company-wide. Executive management must issue a directive that, at a minimum, states management must be kept abreast on a periodic basis as to how the computers are being utilized. Then management is in a position to assess the impact of the small computers on the corporation taken as a whole.

3. Personnel - Personnel that are given authorization to purchase hardware and software should be required to attend professional education programs that caution them on the pitfalls of purchasing fly by night equipment and "garage-developed" software. In addition, the personnel who maintain the files on these small computer systems should be properly trained to prevent unintentional errors.

    Overall, remember that the basic control concepts still apply, they simply have to be adapted to this environment where adequate segregation of duties and key-accessed computer rooms are nonexistent.

F. Electronic Funds Transfer (EFT) Systems

    There are two common types of EFT systems. The first is retail EFT and the second is wholesale EFT. Retail EFT systems interact directly with the consumer, e.g., ATM (automated teller machine) or POS (point of sale) terminal. All of these systems automate the data input process with the customer.

    Wholesale funds transfer systems are utilized to transfer funds between one bank and a second bank. The equivalent of the Gross National Product (GNP) is transferred every three days over wholesale funds transfer lines.

    The controls that should be present in wholesale funds transfer systems must be preventative (that is, prevent the transaction from being released) as opposed to detective (a control that tells you when an error has occurred). This is primarily due to the speed of the transaction and the exponential costs in recovering funds sent in error.

    In both the retail and wholesale environments, controls must be in place to ensure:

    a. Compliance with government regulations
    b. Maintenance of the sophisticated equipment
    c. Adequate training of personnel

    The auditor's responsibility is to ensure that the controls are in place. In wholesale funds transfer systems, extensive substantive tests must be performed due to the high risk inherent in the high dollar volumes transferred.

G. The Audit Workstation

More internal audit departments and a few external audit firms are ending their
dependence on audit software programs run on the mainframe and are using the
microcomputer workstation. Using a micro with 256K minimum, one floppy disk
drive, one hard disk drive, a communication modem, a printer, and the associated
software, today's auditor can examine the data much more closely than ever
before.

1. Determine Data Needed - At this step we analyze the information stored on the
    main frame and determine what information would be useful to the audit under
    review.

2. Write Extract Program - On a one-time basis, write a program that extracts the
    information required and places it in a format that can be transferred to the
    audit micro.

3. Run Extract Program - As often as required run the extract program to create the file that will be transferred to the micro.

4. Download Extracted File - This is the most technical step in the process. However, there are some new software packages available for the micro that make this process relatively simplistic.

5. Run Analysis - You are now free of the main frame to be able to perform the analysis you want. Using a spreadsheet package you can prepare financial statements, generate ratios, and prepare totals. Using a graphics package you can graph trend analysis. Using a data-base package you can run statistical analysis. If you want something more you can write your own software.

6. Prepare Report - You now have the necessary analysis to develop a much more substantial analytical report.

7. Workpapers - To document your analysis, you can write your report using a word processing package and can save the results electronically.

The audit workstation is the trend for the future and could replace many traditional auditing concepts.

III. Flowcharting

Flowcharting is a procedure used in systems development, documentation, and internal control evaluation to graphically show step-by-step progression of document (information) preparation, authorization, flow, storage, etc. It can also show the steps in decision making. The more common flowcharting symbols are illustrated on page 258.

A. Types and Definitions. Flowcharts may be one of several types.

1. System Flowchart - Graphic analysis of a data-processing application, usually prepared by a systems analyst. The system flowchart is general in nature and stresses flows of data rather than computer program logic.

2. Program Flowchart - A graphic representation of the detailed steps and logic of the computer program itself. On the top of page 257 is printed an excerpt from a program flowchart which appeared on the May 1970 CPA exam.

3. Document Flowchart - A graphic presentation of the flow of documents from one department to another, showing the source, flow, and final disposition of the various copies of all documents

4. Audit (Internal Control) Flowchart - Most easily defined as a combination of systems and document flowcharts, showing:

   a. The flow of documents through various departments, and
   b. The various major processing steps through which the documents go. Particular attention is given to highlighting internal control procedures.

B. Internal Control Flowcharts emphasize document flows and major processing steps. The horizontal axis generally describes departments and/or individuals. On page 259 is an example of an internal control flowchart that appeared on the May 1980 CPA exam.

Program Flowchart

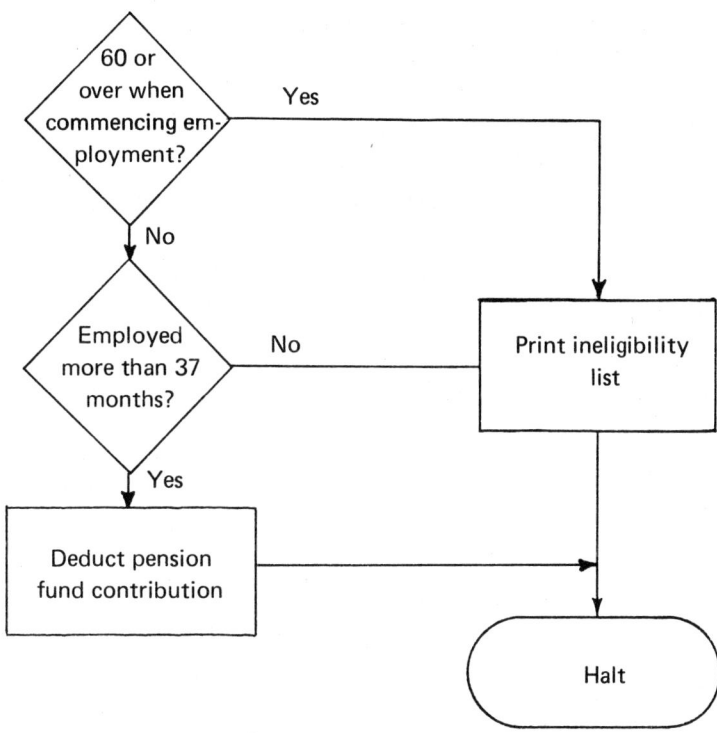

The flowchart depicts the following description of a payroll system.   The numbers in the text correspond to the numbers on the flowchart.

The internal control system with respect to the personnel department is well-functioning and is not included in the accompanying flowchart.

At the beginning of each work week payroll clerk No. 1 reviews the payroll department files to determine the employment status of factory employees and then prepares time cards and distributes them as each individual arrives at work. This payroll clerk, who is also responsible for custody of the signature stamp machine, verifies the identity of each payee before delivering signed checks to the foreman.

At the end of each work week the foreman distributes payroll checks for the preceding work week. Concurrent with this activity, the foreman reviews the current week's employee time cards, notes the regular and overtime hours worked on a summary form, and initials the aforementioned time cards. The foreman then delivers all time cards and unclaimed payroll checks to payroll clerk No. 2.*

---

*Taken from the May 1980 Uniform CPA Examination, Auditing, Number 5.

Common Flowchart Symbols

DOCUMENT.

OPERATION. Process resulting in change in the information or the flow direction.

MANUAL OPERATION. Offline process.

PUNCHED CARD. Input-output and storage function.

INPUT/OUTPUT. General input-output symbol.

MAGNETIC TAPE. Input-output and storage function.

DECISION. Determines which alternative path is followed.

OFFLINE STORAGE.

FLOWLINE. Indicates sequence of information and operations.

DIRECTION FLOW. Indicates direction of information flow.

CROYDEN INC., FACTORY PAYROLL SYSTEM

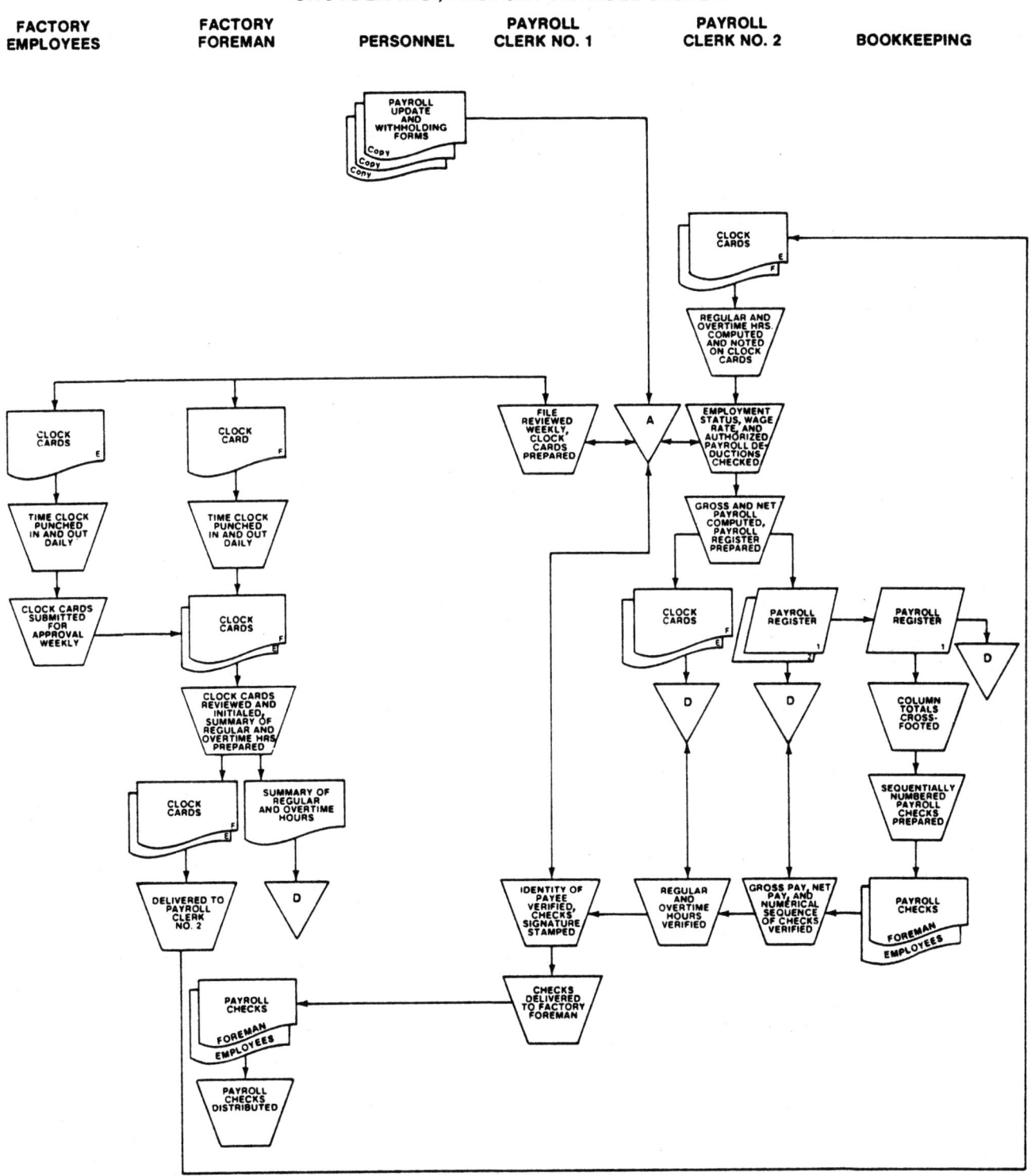

| FACTORY EMPLOYEES | FACTORY FOREMAN | PERSONNEL | PAYROLL CLERK NO. 1 | PAYROLL CLERK NO. 2 | BOOKKEEPING |

IV. EDP Definitions

This section reviews the basic terminology that is used in automated environments.

A. Hardware

1. Computer hardware consists of the configuration of physical EDP equipment. (Software consists of the computer programs that tell hardware what to do.)

   a. CPU (Central Processing Unit, Main Frame) - The central processing unit or principle hardware component of a computer contains an arithmetic/logic unit, primary storage, and a control unit. The major function of the CPU is to fetch stored instructions and data, decode the instructions, and carry out the instructions in the arithmetic/logic unit.

      1) The arithmetic/logic unit adds, subtracts, multiplies, compares, etc.
      2) The primary storage contains the data and program steps that are being processed by the CPU
      3) The control unit keeps track of addresses in the computer, status of programs, etc.

   b. Console - A computer component used for communication between the operator and the computer. The console may have indicators and switches, or be of a teletype nature. It may be part of the CPU or peripheral equipment.

   c. Peripheral Equipment - All non-CPU hardware that may be placed under the control of the central processor. Classified as online or offline (see below), this equipment consists of input, storage, output, and communication devices.

   d. Controllers - Hardware units designed to operate (control) specific input/output units, i.e., card reader controllers, magnetic tape controllers, etc. These devices eliminate the need for the central processing unit to operate the input/output devices.

   e. Channels - Hardware units designed to handle the transfer of data into or out of primary storage (memory). Thus, the central processing unit need not handle the transfer of data.

   f. Buffer Memory (or Buffer) - Temporary storage unit used to hold data during input/output operations. It compensates for the vast differences in speed between the CPU and the input/output units.

   g. Offline - Peripheral equipment not in direct communication with the CPU, e.g., punched cards to a card reader. The operator must intervene to connect offline equipment or data to the CPU.

   h. Online - Peripheral equipment in direct communication with, and under the control of, the CPU, e.g., disk drives controlled by the CPU

   i. Interpreter - A machine which makes punched cards easily readable to humans (it prints the contents of a card on the card itself)

   j. Verifier - A machine used to test whether keypunching errors exist on punched cards

2. <u>Input devices</u> provide a means of transferring data into CPU storage

    a. <u>Card Reader</u> - An input device, consisting of a mechanical or electrical punched card reader and related circuitry, that converts data from punched cards into binary-coded data which are transferable to the CPU or storage

    b. <u>Paper Tape Reader</u> - A device capable of sensing information from holes punched on a paper tape. May also be an output device.

    c. <u>Magnetic Tape Reader</u> - A device capable of sensing information recorded as magnetized spots on a magnetic tape. May also be an output device and storage medium.

    d. <u>Magnetic Ink Character Reader</u> - Device that reads characters by scanning characters which have been printed using a magnetic ink, e.g., bank check readers

    e. <u>Optical Scanner</u> - Reads characters based on their shapes

    f. <u>Console</u> - May be an input device

    g. <u>Key-to-Tape and Key-to-Disk</u> - Systems in which input data can be entered (keyed) directly onto magnetic tape or magnetic disk (as opposed to being initially recorded on cards and then copied to tape or disk through the use of a computer program)

3. <u>Storage Devices</u> - Devices which store data that can be subsequently used by the CPU. Classified as random or sequential access.

    a. <u>Random Access</u> - Data can be accessed directly regardless of how it is physically stored. Disks are random access devices.

    b. <u>Sequential Access</u> - Data must be processed in the order in which it is physically stored. Magnetic tape is a sequential storage device. Only magnetic tape (below) is limited to being only a sequential storage device.

    c. <u>Primary Memory</u> - Primary random storage directly accessed and utilized by CPU

    d. <u>Magnetic Drum (Drum)</u> - The fastest and most expensive secondary direct access device; it is becoming obsolete

    e. <u>Magnetic Tape</u> - (Can either be an input or an output device.) Retrieval of information on magnetic tape is limited to sequential access. However, tape allows access to, and transfer of, data at a faster rate than punched cards. Cheapest type of storage available. It is used extensively for backing up direct access disk files.

    f. <u>Magnetic Disk (Disk)</u> - Disks are secondary random access devices which allow data to be retrieved directly without searching through other stored data. In addition, magnetic disks also allow the transfer data to the CPU at a faster rate.

4. <u>Output</u> - Devices to produce readable data (or machine readable data, when further processing is required)

    a. <u>Cathode Ray Tube (CRT)</u> - Combination typewriter/television device for sending and receiving data

    b. <u>Card Punch</u> - Device similar to (may be part of) a card reader, which produces output in the form of punched cards

      c. Printer - Prints data on computer paper, or directly onto invoices, checks, etc.

      d. Paper Tape - Tape punched with machine readable holes. This is also an input device.

      e. Plotter - Device to graph output, e.g., mathematical functions, temperatures, etc.

      f. COM (Computer Output to Microfilm) - A device which records output directly on microfilm. This frequently takes the place of the printer or magnetic tape output.

5. Remote Systems - In some companies, in addition to hardware located at a centralized site or in the central EDP room, access and sometimes processing capabilities are provided in other rooms or even other buildings or cities

      a. Terminals - Teletype, typewriter or CRT devices used for input/output (communication) with CPU

      b. Point-of-Sale Devices - A terminal connected to a computer which takes the place of a cash register or similar device. It allows instant credit checks, etc.

      c. Modem - A hardware device used to convert digital signals from terminals and the CPU into analog signals for transmission across data lines and then to convert the signal back to digital for use by the receiving terminal or CPU

      d. Microcomputer - Desktop computer

      e. Distributed Systems - Processing is performed at the location closest to the user

B. Software

Software consists of the instructions which tell the computer hardware to perform the desired processing.

1. Types of Programs

      a. Operating System - The instructions which control the overall functioning of the CPU and its peripheral equipment. Several different operating systems permit a single configuration of hardware to function in several different modes.

          1) Multiprogramming - The operating system processes a program until an input/output operation is required. Since input or output can be handled by peripheral hardware (channels and controllers), the CPU can begin executing another program's instructions. Several programs appear to be concurrently processing.

          2) Multiprocessing - Multiple CPUs process data while sharing peripheral units

          3) Virtual Storage - The operating system separates user programs into segments automatically. To the user it appears as though there is unlimited memory available for programs, even though the program is still confined to a physical segment of memory.

    b. Utility Program (or Routine) - A standard program for performing a commonly required process, such as sorting, merging, etc.

    c. Application Programs - Used to perform the desired data processing tasks, e.g., preparation of payroll, updating of accounts receivable, etc.

    d. Source Program - Program written by a programmer in a source language (FORTRAN, COBOL, etc.) that will be converted into an object program

    e. Object Program - Program that has converted source program using a compiler to a set of machine readable instructions, i.e., instructions to be followed by the CPU

    f. Compiler Program - Produces a machine language object program from a source program language

    g. Data-Base Management System (D.B.M.S.) - A comprehensive software package for the purpose of creating, accessing, and maintaining a data base

    h. Converter - A program or device which changes data from one form to another

2. Programming Terminology

    a. Edit - To correct input data prior to processing

    b. Loop - A set of program instructions performed repetitively. Repetition continues a predetermined number of times, or until all data have been processed

    c. Desk Checking - Review of a program by the programmer for errors before the program is run and debugged on the computer

    d. Core or Storage Dump - A listing of the contents of storage in machine code

    e. Pass (Run) - A complete cycle of a program, including input, processing and output

    f. Debug - To find and eliminate errors in a computer program. Many compilers assist debugging by listing errors in the program such as invalid commands

    g. Patch - A section of coding inserted into a routine to correct a mistake or alter the routine

    h. Address - A location in storage

C. Data Organization for EDP Operations

1. Bit - A binary digit (0 or 1 represented by a positive or negative charge, hole or no hole, etc.)

2. Byte (Character) - A group of bits which represents a character, whether alphabetic, numeric, or alphanumeric

3. Alphabetic - Characters from the alphabet

4. Numeric - Digits

5. Alphanumeric - Alphabetic, numeric, and special characters. Special characters are pluses, minuses, dollar signs, etc.

6. Field, Item, Word - A group of related characters (e.g., a social security number) or a subdivision of record (e.g., a group of columns on a punched card earmarked for one item) is called a field

7. Record - A group of related items or field of data handled as a unit (e.g, an employee's pay record for one week)

8. Block - A group of records held or processed as a unit by the computer to improve input/output efficiency

9. File - An organized collection of related records (e.g., all the weekly pay records year-to-date), which is usually arranged in sequence

10. Master File - A file containing relatively permanent information used as a source of reference and periodically updated with a detail (transactions) file (e.g., permanent payroll records)

11. Detail File - A file containing current transaction information used to update the master file (e.g., hours worked by each employee during the current period, used to update the payroll master file)

12. Data Base - A series of related files combined to eliminate unnecessary redundancy of data items and to establish logical connections between data items, i.e., payroll and personnel files are combined eliminating redundant SSN, name, etc.

D. Documentation

Documentation is the written description of a system, application, or program designed to substantiate or to advise about some aspect of the system, application, or program.

1. Program Documentation - Describes a single program. It consists of the following sections:

    a. Problem Statement - Clear statement of the problem to be solved and the objectives of the program

    b. System Flowchart - Includes the source and nature of input, computer operations, and the disposition of output

    c. Operating Instructions - To be used by the operator when running the program

    d. Record Layouts - E.g., sample report formats

    e. Program Flowcharts - Including the logic

    f. Program Listing - In the source language

    g. Test Data - To test the controls and accuracy of the program

    h. Approval and Change Sheet - Includes initial authorization to use, record of periodic review, and proper authorization of any changes

2. System - Overall description of a related set of programs (an application, e.g., payroll, inventory, etc.)

3. Operations - The operating instructions taken from the run manual. Note that the operator is not given access to the other parts of the run manual, e.g., programs. This control precludes tampering with the program, the test data, etc.

4. User Instructions - To personnel preparing input or receiving output: how to prepare input and what to expect in output

5. Library or File Control Instructions - Relate to the structure, storage, and safeguarding of files

E. Modes of EDP Operation

EDP operations can be classified several ways.

1. Systems can be differentiated based on the timing of transaction processing. Two types of systems using this basis for differentiating are:

   a. Batch Processing - Records are collected into groups (batches) before processing

      1) *EXAMPLE. All payroll records are run at one time. The computer oper-ator for the payroll follows the instructions in the run manual pro-gram and begins the execution. The input is probably punched cards con-taining employees' identification numbers and hours worked. This in-put will be matched to the employee master file for pay rate and payroll deductions data. The program will then compute the weekly payroll, print the pay checks, update year-to-date payroll records, summarize the payroll data for management, report payroll exceptions and trends, and compute the liability for payroll deductions and taxes, etc.*

      The process would be under continual review by a control group. After completion of the run, the program, files, and blank checks (special printed computer cards) would be returned to the library.

   b. Online Real-Time Systems - Processing time is instantaneous in these sys-tems. This requires related records and programs to be online, not in an offline library.

      1) Definition of terms

         a) Online - A terminal or input device that is in direct communication with the central processing unit

         b) Real-Time - The CPU response is made in sufficient time to affect the decision making process or the process being monitored

         c) Integrated Systems - Multiple files or data base. Each transaction that affects multiple files updates all files in one processing run rather than separate runs for each file, i.e., duplicate operations are minimized.

         d) Data Base - A system of individual files which are integrated into a larger collection of related files. There may be either a single data base, which would contain all files, or a number of interre-lated data bases, which comprise the system.

         e) Paging - A technique used in virtual storage to segment programs and data files which are being used

2) Operation of online real-time systems

a) Communications Controller - An input device that scans incoming messages from terminals for correctness, assigns priorities, and puts them into an input queue for later processing by the CPU

b) Supervisory Program - The operating system in an online real-time system. It takes the messages produced by the communications controller, determines which files and which programs are needed for processing those transactions, and controls the actual processing of the transactions.

c) Input Terminals - Any device used as a source for the transactions. It could be a teletype or typewriter-type terminal.

d) Location of Files and Programs - In an online real-time system, all active files and programs are stored on magnetic disks as opposed to the usual library storage procedures of a batch processing system. The files and programs are fetched by the supervisory program after analysis of which files and programs are required by the individual transactions.

3) *EXAMPLE: A company has an online employee timekeeping system. Employees have plastic identification cards that are read by the timeclock. Employees, as they complete jobs, also input the number of the job completed. As the data are inputted, the computer checks to see if the employee has submitted a reasonable job number, e.g., is the employee scheduled to work on that job? If the job number does not appear correct, the computer rejects the input message on the data entry terminal. Names of absent or tardy employees are printed out periodically for supervisors or foremen on a printer located in the production department. Reports of employees with variations from standard times are also produced periodically.*

The timekeeping system may also store the employees' hours for periodic payroll processing. In fact, many online real-time systems also contain applications which are processed using batch processing.

2. Systems may also be differentiated based on the physical location of the equipment. Using this criterion, the following are the two major categories:

a. In-House Systems - Computer hardware and personnel are maintained by the company which utilizes them

b. Non-In-House Systems - Main processing hardware belongs to another organization. The most common off-premise systems are:

1) Block time - Rental of time by one firm of another organization's computer

2) Timesharing - Access to another organization's computer is provided through terminal devices. User has the impression of being the sole user of the system, when in reality the computer is sharing its time with a number of users.

3) Service Bureaus - Use of an outside organization to provide a wide range of data-processing services (from systems analysis and design through actual running of programs with data) for a fee. Also called Facilities Management if the company uses an outside management team to run its EDP operation under contract.

F. Systems Design

A general knowledge of systems design is tested on the auditing section of the exam. Note that systems design can apply to noncomputer areas as well. The following comprises the components of a typical design process.

1. Feasibility Study - Investigation of the present system, determination of information and processing requirements, evaluation of the possible application of computer data processing, selection of the best alternative, and an evaluation of the proposed alternative's cost effectiveness and impact on the organization. Top management should approve of the final decision before any further work is performed.

2. Preparation of Specifications - Definition of hardware and/or software requirements for submission to vendors to solicit proposals or for in-house decision purposes

3. Selection of Hardware/Software - The evaluation of vendor or in-house proposals and selection of the best alternatives

4. System Development - Analyze the impact of the new system, analyze the information requirements, develop any software, test the software, schedule delivery of the hardware, and conduct training sessions for the potential users

5. Implementation - Conversion to the new system, usually done while the old system is still in place to allow parallel operation until the new system is ascertained to be operating correctly

STATEMENTS ON AUDITING STANDARDS

The next 104 pages outline the nonsuperseded sections of SAS 1 through SAS 48 as of May 1, 1984. Note that the outlines are presented in codified sequence rather than chronological sequence (see listing of SAS Sections below). Study these SAS outlines in conjunction with the related topical material, e.g., ethics, reports, etc., in this chapter. Additionally, outlines are presented of

1. AICPA Guide for a Review of a Financial Forecast
2. SSARS 1-5 - Compilation and Review of Financial Statements

Statements on Standards for Accounting and Review Services (SSARS) are a series of AICPA pronouncements to set standards for engagements to prepare unaudited statements.

Status of SASs

The chronological listing of superseded and amended sections of SASs will facilitate your crossing out the superseded sections in your original pronouncements.

		Now SAS Section
SAS 1		
Para 110.05-110.08	Superseded by SAS 16	327
Para 150.06	Superseded by SAS 43	1010*
Para 310.05-315.09	Superseded by SAS 45	1020
Para 311.03, .09, .10	Superseded by SAS 48	—**
Para 318.07	Superseded by SAS 48	—**
Para 320.33-.34, .37, .57-.58, .65-.68	Superseded by SAS 48	—**
Para 320.70	Amended by SAS 23	318
Para 320.74	Superseded by SAS 9	322
Para 320A.01-320B.36	Superseded by SAS 39	350
Para 320.49-320.55	Superseded by SAS 43	1010
Para 326.12	Superseded by SAS 48	—**
Para 330.01-330.15	Superseded by SAS 31	326
Para 331.14-331.15	Superseded by SAS 43	1010
Para 410.03-410.04	Superseded by SAS 5	411
Para 420.15-420.16	Superseded by SAS 43	1010
Para 430.01-430.06	Superseded by SAS 32	431
Para 510.01-515.10	Superseded by SAS 2	509
Para 516.01-516.10	Superseded by SAS 26	504
Para 516.11-516.12	Superseded by SAS 15	505
Sec. 517-518	Superseded by SAS 26	504
Para 535.01-542.04	Superseded by SAS 2	509
Para 543.18	Superseded by SAS 7	315
Para 544.01	Superseded by SAS 2	509
Para 545.01, 545.05	Amended by SAS 21	435
Para 547.01-547.04	Superseded by SAS 2	509
Para 560.12d	Amended by SAS 12	337
Para 610.01-610.06	Superseded by SAS 29	551
Section 620	Superseded by SAS 14	621
Para 630.01-630.53	Superseded by SAS 38	631
Para 640.01-641.06	Superseded by SAS 30	642
Para 710.01-710.11	Superseded by SAS 37	711
Para 901.01-901.05, .28, .32	Superseded by SAS 43	1010
SAS 2 (now Section 509)		
Para 39	Amended by SAS 43	1010
Para 49	Superseded by SAS 15	505
SAS 4	Superseded by SAS 25	161

The changes resulting from SASs 43 and 45 (omnibus opinions) have been integrated into our SAS outlines. The AICPA will print SAS 43 in codified Section 1010 and SAS 45 in codified Section 1020, respectively.
**Codification number not available at time of publication.*

		Now SAS Section
SAS 5		
Para 5-6	Superseded by SAS 43	1010
SAS 6	Superseded by SAS 45	1020
SAS 7 (now Section 315)		
Para 11	Superseded by SAS 15	505
SAS 10	Superseded by SAS 36	722
SAS 13	Superseded by SAS 36	722
SAS 14 (621)		
Para 15-17	Superseded by SAS 35	622
SAS 15 (505)		
Para 13-15	Superseded by SAS 26	504
SAS 18	Deleted	
SAS 24	Superseded by SAS 36	722
SAS 30 (now Section 642)		
Para 2, 60	Amended by SAS 44	324
SAS 33	Superseded by SAS 45	1020
SAS 38		
Para 47, 51, 56	Amended by SAS 43	1010
SAS 39		
Para 46	Amended by SAS 43	1010

110 Responsibilities and Functions of the Independent Auditor

Para 110.05-.08 Superseded by SAS 16, now Section 327

A. The objective of an ordinary audit examination is expression of opinion on

   1. Conformity with GAAP

   2. Consistent application

B. Auditor and management responsibilities

   1. Statements are representations of management

      a. Adequate system of IC is management responsibility

   2. Professional qualifications

      a. Adequate education and experience

      b. Informed judgment of a qualified professional person

      c. CPA's responsibility to the profession is to adhere to professional standards

150 Generally Accepted Auditing Standards

Para 150.06 superseded by SAS 43

A. Standards deal with measures of quality of procedures undertaken and objectives of procedures

   1. Procedures are acts to be performed

B. AICPA general standards (para 150.02)

   1. The examination is to be performed by a person or persons having adequate technical training and proficiency as an auditor

   2. In all matters relating to the assignment, an independence in mental attitude is to be maintained by the auditor or auditors

   3. Due professional care is to be exercised in the performance of the examination and the preparation of the report

C. AICPA standards of fieldwork

   1. The work is to be adequately planned and assistants, if any, are to be properly supervised

2. There is to be a proper study and evaluation of the existing internal control as a basis for reliance thereon, and for the determination of the resultant extent of the tests to which auditing procedures are to be restricted

3. Sufficient competent evidential matter is to be obtained through inspection, observation, inquiries, and confirmations to afford a reasonable basis for an opinion regarding the financial statements under examination

D. AICPA standards of reporting

1. The report shall state whether the financial statements are presented in accordance with generally accepted accounting principles

2. The report shall state whether such principles have been consistently observed in the current period in relation to the preceding period

3. Informative disclosures in the financial statements are to be regarded as reasonably adequate unless otherwise stated in the report

4. The report shall either contain an expression of opinion regarding the financial statements, taken as a whole, or an assertion to the effect that an opinion cannot be expressed. When an overall opinion cannot be expressed, the reasons therefore should be stated. In all cases where an auditor's name is associated with financial statements, the report should contain a clear-cut indication of the character of the auditor's examination, if any, and the degree of responsibility he is taking.

E. Materiality

1. More evidence is required for more important items and those for which the possibility of material error is greater

F. Relative risk

1. More evidence is required for items more susceptible to irregularity
2. The stronger the system of IC, the lower the relative risk

G. GAAS are applicable to the extent they are relevant in the circumstances, to all other services governed by SASs, unless specified otherwise

161 The Relationship of Generally Accepted Auditing Standards to Quality Control Standards (SAS 25)

A. Individuals are responsible for complying with GAAS per Ethics Rule 202

1. Firms should also endeavor to comply with GAAS

   a. By establishing quality control policies and procedures
   b. Nature and extent depend on firm's

      1) Size
      2) Autonomy of personnel and practice offices
      3) Nature of practice
      4) Organizational structure
      5) Appropriate cost-benefit considerations

B. GAAS and quality control standards are related

1. GAAS relate to conduct of individual audits
2. Quality control standards relate to overall audit practice
3. Quality control standards may affect conduct of audits and overall practice

C. Effective 11/79

201 General Standards are Personal in Nature

A. Qualification of auditor

B. Quality of work

210 Training and Proficiency

A. Proper education and experience are necessary

1. Professional experience under proper supervision is necessary
2. Auditor with final responsibility must have seasoned judgment

B. Formal education and professional experience complement one another

C. CPA must consider objectively and exercise independent judgment when evaluating management's assertions

220 Independence

A. Independence is necessary for impartial findings

1. In state of mind
2. In fact
3. In appearance; guard against presumption of loss of independence
4. SEC stresses independence
5. Many companies stress independence by having a CPA appointed by

   a. Board of directors
   b. Election by stockholders

230 Due Care

A. CPA must observe GAAS

1. Critical review at every level of supervision
2. Concerns what CPA does and how well he does it

B. From Cooley on Torts

1. One who offers services must exercise possessed skill and exercise reasonable care
2. If a specialized skill is prerequisite, he should possess common level of such skill; otherwise fraud
3. No one guarantees faultless work

310 Adequacy of Planning and the Timing of Fieldwork

A. Early appointment of the CPA facilitates the audit and is generally efficient

1. Permits early consideration of accounting problems and possible modification of accounting procedures

B. Appointment near or after the close of the period

1. CPA should ascertain that an adequate examination is possible
2. Qualified or disclaimer may be necessary

C. Many audit tests may be performed any time during the year

1. When a significant part of the examination is carried out at midyear and IC found effective, year-end transactions may consist of

a. Ratio analysis
b. Investigation of unusual transactions

2. The CPA must satisfy himself that IC continues to be effective at year end

D. Tests of procedures are particularly appropriate for high volume accounts

E. Performing substantive tests at an interim date

1. Factors to be considered before performing tests at an interim date

a. Cost of subsequent tests necessary in remaining period (period after principal substantive tests through year end)

b. Effectiveness of remaining period substantive tests if internal accounting controls are not being relied upon

c. Existence of rapidly changing business conditions which might cause management to misstate financial statements

d. Predictability of year-end balances

2. Extending interim date audit conclusions to balance sheet date

a. Compare interim balances with year-end balances for unusual changes and perform other analytical review and/or substantive tests of details

b. Consider implications of interim period errors in determining scope of remaining period tests

3. Coordinate timing of audit procedures such as

a. Related party transactions
b. Interrelated accounts and accounting cutoffs
c. Negotiable assets (e.g., cash) and liabilities (e.g., loans)

311 Planning and Supervision (SAS 22)

Para 3, 9, and 10 superseded by SAS 48, section number not available

A. This section provides guidance concerning compliance with the first standard of fieldwork, including

1. Preparing audit programs
2. Obtaining knowledge of the entity's business
3. Dealing with differences of opinion among firm personnel

B. Audit planning: development of an overall strategy for conduct and scope of the audit

1. Nature, extent, and timing of planning vary with

a. Size and complexity of client
b. Auditor's experience with the client
c. Auditor's knowledge of the client's business

2. In planning, the auditor should consider

a. Client's type of business and industry
b. Client's accounting policies and procedures
c. Methods used to process accounting information, including the use of service centers

    d. Anticipated reliance on internal accounting control
    e. Preliminary estimates of materiality levels
    f. Items likely to require adjustments
    g. Conditions requiring extension or modification of audit procedures
    h. Nature of reports to be rendered by the auditor

3. Audit procedures applicable to planning the examination

    a. Review correspondence, prior year's workpapers, statements, etc.
    b. Determine the effect of nonaudit services to the client on the examination
    c. Inquire about current client developments
    d. Read current interim statements
    e. Discuss type, scope, timing, etc., of examination with client
    f. Consider effects of applicable authoritative pronouncements
    g. Coordinate client's preparation of data needed by auditor
    h. Determine need for consultants, specialists, and internal auditors
    i. Establish timing of audit work
    j. Coordinate staff requirements

4. A written audit program should be prepared

    a. Instructs assistants on the work to be done
    b. Details audit procedures which are necessary
    c. Which reflects the results of planning considerations and procedures
    d. Changing conditions may require modifications of the planned audit procedures

5. The auditor should obtain adequate knowledge of client's business to plan and perform the examination per GAAS

    a. Including events, transactions, and practices which may have a significant effect on the statements
    b. This knowledge should include

        1) Type of business
        2) Types of products and services
        3) Capital structure
        4) Related parties
        5) Locations of business
        6) Production and distribution methods
        7) Means of compensation
        8) Environmental conditions affecting business
        9) Industry accounting practices
       10) Financial trends and ratios

    c. This knowledge assists the auditor in

        1) Identifying problem areas
        2) Assessing overall conditions in which accounting data are developed
        3) Evaluating the reasonableness of estimates
        4) Evaluating reasonableness of management representations
        5) Evaluating appropriateness of GAAP and adequacy of disclosures

    d. Knowledge obtained through experience with entity or industry and inquiry of personnel

e.   When a client has computer operations, an auditor should consider the following when determining the nature, extent, and timing of audit procedures

1)   Extent computer used
2)   Complexity of computer use
3)   Organization structure of computer operations
4)   Availability of data (limited data retention policies may exist in computer operations)
5)   Computer-assisted audit techniques may be helpful and/or necessary

f.   If specialized computer skills are needed, the auditor should obtain either staff or outside professional assistance

1)   A staff specialist requires the same supervision and review as any assistant
2)   AU 336 (SAS 11) provides guidance when using outside professional assistance

C.   Supervision: directing efforts of assistants <u>and</u> determining attainment of the audit objectives

1.   Supervision includes

a.   Instructing assistants
b.   Being informed of significant problems
c.   Reviewing the audit work
d.   Dealing with differences of opinion among audit personnel

2.   The extent of supervision depends on the complexity of the audit and qualifications of audit assistants
3.   Audit assistants should be informed of

a.   Their responsibilities
b.   The objectives of the audit procedures
c.   Other matters affecting the nature, extent, and timing of audit procedures
d.   The need to point out any problems to the auditor with final responsibility

D.   Each assistant's audit work should be reviewed to determine adequacy and the effect on final audit conclusions

E.   All audit personnel should be aware of procedures to be followed concerning disagreements on accounting and auditing issues

1.   The procedures should allow assistants to document disagreement and disassociate with tentative conclusions by senior personnel

2.   The basis for resolution of these disagreements should be documented

312   Audit Risk and Materiality in Conducting an Audit (SAS 47)

A.   Statement gives guidance on (1) audit risk and (2) materiality when planning <u>and</u> performing an audit

1. <u>Audit risk</u>--risk that auditor unknowingly fails to modify opinion on financial statements which are materially misstated

   NOTE: Not included in this definition are risks relating to losses from litigation, adverse publicity, and the risk that an auditor erroneously concludes that financial statements are misstated (see AU 350).

2. <u>Materiality</u> (per SFAC 2)--magnitude of omission or misstatement of accounting information that, in light of surrounding circumstances, makes it probable that judgment of reasonable person relying on information would have been changed or influenced

   a. Financial statements are materially misstated when errors or irregularities (hereafter, simply "errors") individually or in aggregate cause departures from GAAP due to

      1) Misapplications of GAAP
      2) Departures from fact
      3) Omissions

   b. Individual and aggregate effect of errors should be considered by making judgments of their

      1) Nature and amount
      2) Qualitative and quantitative nature

         EXAMPLE: An otherwise immaterial illegal act may be considered material if a reasonable possibility of contingent liability exists.

3. Both audit risk and materiality should be considered in (1) <u>planning</u> the audit and in (2) <u>evaluation</u> of whether financial statements follow GAAP

B. In <u>planning</u> the audit, auditor should make a preliminary judgment of materiality and attempt to limit audit risk to low level

   1. Judgments of materiality and audit risk may be in quantitative or non-quantitative terms
   2. Nature, timing, and extent of planning will depend upon size and complexity of entity and on auditor's experience with and knowledge of firm to be audited
   3. While materiality levels include overall level for each financial statement, for planning purposes, lowest amount so obtained would ordinarily be considered material

      EXAMPLE: If $100,000 is material for income, but $200,000 for financial position, the lower amount would be used for planning.

   4. Changes in audited entity's circumstances (e.g., merger) may result in

      a. Modification of auditor's preliminary materiality judgment and/or
      b. Materiality judgment to be used in evaluating audit findings

         NOTE: The section is discussing two materiality judgments--(1) preliminary and (2) evaluation.

C. Audit risk and materiality vary inversely for an account or class of transactions (hereafter, simply "account")

   1. For example, risk that an account is misstated by a large amount may be low while risk of a small misstatement may be high

2. Holding other planning considerations equal, either a decrease in audit risk or a decrease in the amount considered material will cause

    a. Selection of a more effective auditing procedure
    b. Performance of auditing procedures closer to balance sheet date
    c. Increasing extent of a particular auditing procedure

3. Audit risk at the account level must be controlled to allow an overall financial statement low level of risk

4. Audit risk

    a. Components

        1) Inherent risk--risk that an account could be materially in error, when aggregated with other errors, assuming there were no related internal accounting controls. This risk varies by account (e.g., cash is more susceptible to theft than an inventory of coal).

        2) Control risk--risk that internal accounting control will not prevent or detect an error which could be material when aggregated with other errors

        3) Detection risk--risk that auditing procedures will not detect an error which could be material when aggregated with other errors

    b. Relationships among components

        1) Inherent and control risks exist independently of the audit while detection risk relates to auditor's procedures

        2) Acceptable detection risk should vary inversely with the inherent and control risks

    c. Professional judgment is used to assess inherent risk and control risk

        1) Separate or combined assessments are acceptable
        2) If either is assumed to be at less than maximum level of risk, basis for reliance should be disclosed (e.g., questionnaires, checklists)

5. It is not appropriate to rely completely on assessments of inherent risk and control risk.

    a. Substantive tests for material accounts are necessary

D. When evaluating audit findings, auditor should aggregate known, uncorrected errors and should also consider qualitative factors

1. The aggregation of errors should include auditor's best estimate of total error in the accounts

    a. This is known as "likely error"

2. Risk of material error is generally greater for accounts which include accounting estimates (e.g., inventory obsolescence, uncollectible receivables)

3. A difference between audited estimated amount which is supported by evidence and the financial statement amount would not be considered likely error unless auditor believes financial statement amount is unreasonable

4. Known prior period errors should be aggregated with current likely errors to determine total likely error

5. When total likely error is material, auditor must either qualify or issue adverse opinion if management does not eliminate the error

6. As aggregate likely error increases, risk of misstatement increases

   a. Auditor must recognize that undetected errors may still exist
   b. If audit risk is unacceptably high, auditor should perform additional auditing procedures

315 Communications Between Predecessor and Successor Auditors (SAS 7)

Para 11 superseded by SAS 15, now Section 505

A. Successor auditor is one who has accepted or is considering acceptance

   1. This section applies to all new audit engagements per GAAS
   2. Communication initiative is with successor auditor

B. Required communications (written or oral) before accepting engagement

   1. Successor should obtain prospective client permission for communication

      a. If client refuses, consider implications

   2. Successor inquiries should include

      a. Integrity of management
      b. Disagreement with client over accounting principles, auditing procedures, etc.
      c. Reasons for change in auditors

   3. Predecessor should respond candidly

      a. If response is limited, so indicate and consider implications

C. Other inquiries should be made which affect the successor's audit, e.g., beginning balances and GAAP consistency

   1. Successor may consult with and review predecessor's work papers to determine consistency of application of GAAP

      a. Successor should obtain client permission to review predecessor's work papers

         1) Certain conditions, e.g., litigation, may preclude predecessor from cooperating
         2) Successor should not refer to predecessor auditor in the audit report

   2. Alternative is to apply auditing procedures to prior years

D. If the successor auditor during the investigation of the client becomes aware of information relevant to the predecessor auditor, such should be disclosed at a meeting with the predecessor and client

318 Analytical Review Procedures (SAS 23)

Para 7 superseded by SAS 48, section number not available

A. Statement provides guidance on use of analytical procedures in audits per GAAS

    1. Does not specify extent of reliance on tests of transactions and/or analytical procedures

        a. That decision is based on

            1) Competence and sufficiency of evidential matter
            2) Cost benefit analysis

    2. Analytical review procedures evaluate financial data based on comparison of interrelationships

        a. Based on premise that known relationships exist

            1) Provide evidential matter contemplated by third standard of fieldwork

        b. Auditor should investigate significant fluctuations/unusual items

B. Analytical review procedures may be performed

    1. During initial audit planning to help determine nature, extent, and timing of other procedures

        a. May identify significant matters requiring special attention

    2. In conjunction with other procedures applied to individual elements of statements
    3. At or near the conclusion of examination, i.e., an overall review

C. Analytical review procedures include the following (analysis may be done in terms of dollars, percentages, ratios, etc.)

    1. Comparison of financial data with comparable data of previous periods
    2. Comparison of financial data with anticipated results, e.g., budgets
    3. Study of interrelationships that would be expected to conform to predictable patterns, e.g., gross profit rates
    4. Comparison of client data with industry data
    5. Comparison of financial data with relevant nonfinancial data

D. The following factors should be considered in performing analytical reviews

    1. The nature of the entity, e.g., consolidated vs. single company statement
    2. Scope of the engagement, e.g., overall statements vs. specified elements of the statements
    3. Availability of client financial data
    4. Availability of relevent nonfinancial data
    5. Computer system ability to store, retrieve, and analyze data
    6. Reliability of financial and nonfinancial data
    7. Comparability of available industry financial data

E. Auditor should investigate unusual items identified by analytical review procedures

    1. Begin by suitable inquiry of management

        a. Evaluate reasonableness of responses
        b. Consider need to corroborate replies
        c. Perform additional procedures if explanation is unsatisfactory

2. Items to consider when determining nature and extent of additional procedures

    a. Analytical review procedure objective, e.g., audit planning
    b. Nature of the item
    c. Auditor's knowledge of entity's business
    d. Results of other auditing procedures
    e. Auditor's study and evaluation of internal control

3. Auditor should be aware of effect of his/her findings on scope of his/her examination of related accounts

320 Study and Evaluation of Internal Control (IC)

Para 3, 33-34, 37, 57-58, 65-68 superseded by SAS 48, section number not available

Para .49-.55 superseded by SAS 43, now Section 1010

Para .74 superseded by SAS 9, now Section 322

A. Outline of Section 320

    1. Purpose
    2. Definition and basic concepts
    3. Study of the system
    4. Evaluation of system
    5. Correlation with other auditing procedures

B. Purpose

    1. Establish a basis of reliance thereon in determining

        a. Nature of audit tests
        b. Extent of audit tests
        c. Timing of audit tests

    2. Constructive suggestions to improve IC are only a by-product of IC evaluation

        a. A special engagement may be warranted for this purpose

    3. Three developments producing need for this revised statement on IC

        a. Increased trend in MAS services and special engagements regarding IC
        b. Increased use of computers
        c. Trend toward integrating accounting systems into management information systems

C. Definitions and basic concepts

    1. Old definition of IC stressed objectives

        a. "Plan of organization . . ."

            1) Safeguard assets
            2) Check accuracy of financial statements
            3) Promote operational efficiency
            4) Adherence to managerial policies

        b. CPAs stressed first two--accounting controls

2. Need for clarification

    a. Alternate meanings of safeguarding assets

        1) Protection against something undesirable
        2) Protection against both intentional and unintentional errors
        3) Protection against only intentional errors

    b. Alternate purposes of reliability of financial records

        1) External reporting
        2) Internal reporting

3. The new AICPA definition of IC emphasizes the flow of transactions

    a. Transactions are the basic components of business

        1) Authorization
        2) Execution
        3) Recording
        4) Accountability for resulting assets

    b. Ultimate authority is with stockholders and board, but much authority is delegated to management

        1) General--setting of sales prices and credit limits
        2) Specific--employment of a specific person

    c. Execution encompasses the exchange of assets between third parties or within the business
    d. Recording includes all recordkeeping of the transaction
    e. Accountability is comparing physical assets with records

4. Administrative control. "Plan of organization and the procedures and records that are concerned with the decision processes leading to management's authorization of transactions. Such authorization is a management function directly associated with the responsibility for achieving the objectives of the organization and is the starting point for establishing accounting control of transactions." (para 320.27)

5. Accounting control. "Plan of organization and the procedures and records that are concerned with the safeguarding of assets and the reliability of financial records and consequently are designed to provide assurance that

    a. Transactions are executed in accordance with management's general or specific authorization
    b. Transactions are recorded as necessary

        1) To permit preparation of financial statements in conformity with generally accepted accounting principles or any other criteria applicable to such statements and

        2) To maintain accountability for assets

    c. Access to assets is permitted only in accordance with management's authorization
    d. The recorded accountability for assets is compared with the existing assets at reasonable intervals and appropriate action is taken with respect to any differences" (para 320.28)

6. Administrative and accounting control are not always mutually exclusive, because accounting data is used for management decisions

7. Basic concepts (implicit in accounting control)

   a. <u>Management responsibility.</u> Management is responsible for establishment and maintenance of IC

   b. <u>Reasonable assurance.</u> The objectives of IC are reasonably assured, but not guaranteed

      1) Cost-benefit analysis must be applied to IC systems resulting in accounting control procedures being applied on test basis

   c. <u>Method of data processing</u>

      1) The following distinguish computer processing from manual processing

         a) Transaction trails may exist for a short period or only in computer readable form with computers

         b) While clerical errors disappear with computer processing, program errors may result in all like transactions being processed incorrectly

         c) Internal control objectives normally achieved through segregation of functions in manual systems may need to be controlled through computer controls such as password control

         d) Decreased human involvement in handling transactions in computer systems may make detection of errors caused by unauthorized access to computer difficult to detect on timely basis

         e) Ability of management to perform analytical tests of data with computer may improve system internal control

         f) Initiation and execution of transactions by computer may not be well documented

         g) While computer prepared reports may be used to help perform manual control procedures, their effectiveness is dependent on effectiveness of firm's computer controls

      2) Computer general controls (relate to all or many accounting activities) and application controls (relate to individual accounting activities), as in manual systems, have the objectives of (1) safeguarding assets and (2) providing reliable financial records

   d. <u>Limitations.</u> Possible errors arise from

      1) Mistakes in judgment
      2) Misunderstanding of instructions
      3) Personal carelessness
      4) Distraction or fatigue
      5) Collusion
      6) Perpetrations by management
      7) Changes in conditions
      8) Deteriorating degree of compliance

   e. <u>Personnel.</u> The objectives of accounting control depend on the competence and integrity of personnel

      1) In small business, control procedures may be performed by owner managers

  f. <u>Segregation of functions</u>. Avoid allowing any individual to be in position to perpetrate and conceal errors or irregularities

   1) Examples

    a) In manual system individual recording disbursements should not reconcile bank account

    b) In computer system individual entering information to execute disbursements should not receive reconciliation information from computer

  g. <u>Execution of transactions</u>.

   1) Requires independent evidence that authorizations are issued by persons within the scope of their authority

   2) Transactions should conform with their authorizations

  h. <u>Recording of transactions</u>.

   1) Proper amount
   2) Proper period
   3) Proper classification
   4) Depends on independent source of information that transactions have been executed
   5) Transactions should be recorded as promptly as possible

  i. <u>Access to assets</u>. Limited to authorized personnel

   1) Both physically and through preparation of documents

  j. <u>Comparison of recorded accountability with assets</u>.

   1) E.g., cash, inventory, securities, etc., counts and bank reconciliations
   2) Independent comparison should be made for items susceptible to loss
   3) The frequency of comparison to safeguard assets depends on the nature of the assets
   4) The frequency of comparisons to achieve reliable statements depends on the materiality
   5) Action on discrepancies depends on

    a) Nature of asset
    b) System in use
    c) Amount and cause of discrepancy

D. Study of the IC system

 1. <u>Scope of Study</u>

  a. Accounting control is within scope of study and evaluation of IC under GAAS, administrative control is not

  b. Study consists of two parts

   1) <u>Review of system</u>--knowledge and understanding of procedures and methods prescribed
   2) <u>Tests of compliance</u>--reasonable degree of assurance that they are <u>actually being applied</u>
   3) Some portions of "1)" and "2)" above may be performed concurrently

2. <u>Review of System</u>--purpose is to obtain sufficient knowledge and understanding about the accounting system <u>and</u> the internal accounting control system

   a. To determine whether IC procedures exist that

      1) Provide a basis for reliance in determining nature, extent, and timing of substantive tests, <u>or</u>
      2) Aid auditor in designing substantive tests in absence of such reliance

   b. Preliminary phase of review should provide

      1) Understanding of the control environment including

         a) Organizational structure
         b) Methods of communication responsibility and authority
         c) Methods used to supervise the system (including internal audit)

      2) Understanding of the flow of transactions including

         a) Various classes of transactions
         b) Methods used to authorize, execute, record, and subsequently process (including data processing) transactions

      3) Understanding obtained by combination of

         a) Previous experience with entity
         b) Inquiry
         c) Observation
         d) Reference to prior-year working papers
         e) Reference to client-prepared descriptions of system

   c. Conclusions that may be reached after preliminary phase

      1) Further study unlikely to lead to reduced substantive testing
      2) Cost of further study and evaluation of system design and doing the compliance tests exceeds benefit of expected reduction of audit effort (substantive testing)
      3) If one of two conclusions above is reached, audit documentation need only be a record of reasons for deciding not to extend review

         a) Documenting his/her understanding of the IC system is <u>not</u> required of the auditor (e.g., it is not necessary to complete an IC questionnaire)

      4) Continue testing of the system to determine effectiveness of specific control procedures, either individually or in combination, concerning their significance in detecting or preventing errors or irregularities

         a) Absence of a specific control procedure may not be a weakness if other procedures achieve same purpose

   d. Information required to review the design of the system is usually obtained from

      1) Inquiries of appropriate client personnel
      2) Review of written documentation
      3) Observation of transaction processing and handling of related assets

e. On completion of system design review, the auditor should make a pre-liminary evaluation that

1) Specific control procedures are suitably designed for him to rely on, or

   a) Compliance testing would be performed on these controls

2) Specific control procedures will not be relied on

   a) Compliance testing would <u>not</u> be performed on these controls
   b) Substantive testing would be expanded

f. Documenting the review of system

1) Extent of auditor's documentation depends on

   a) Anticipated reliance on internal accounting controls
   b) Nature of the entity's system
   c) Entity's documentation of that system

2) Auditor should document his/her

   a) Understanding of the system
   b) Bases of conclusions for reliance

3) Documentation used may be

   a) Answers to questionnaires
   b) Narrative memorandums
   c) Flowcharts
   d) Decision tables

g. Auditors should consider interdependence among controls--this concern may be greater in computer systems due to concentration of functions

h. Computer application controls are often dependent upon existence of general controls

1) For example, general controls relating to access to computer pro-grams affect application controls relating to a customer billing program
2) It may be more efficient to first review general control procedures

3. <u>Tests of compliance.</u> Provides reasonable assurance the prescribed IC is in use and operating

a. Necessary if IC is to be relied on to determine

1) Nature of substantive tests
2) Timing of substantive tests
3) Extent of substantive tests

b. CPA may decide not to rely on IC because

1) Prescribed IC is not satisfactory
2) Effort to test compliance is greater than resultant saving in sub-stantive tests

c. Tests of compliance are closely related to substantive tests

1) Audit procedures often provide evidence of compliance and also sub-stantive evidence

4. Nature of compliance tests

    a. Were necessary procedures performed?

    b. How were they performed?

    c. Who performed them?

        1) Some aspects of control leave an audit trail, e.g., vouchers, and can be verified through inspection of documents

        2) Other aspects of control have no audit trail, e.g., segregation of duties, are only subject to inquiry

5. Timing and extent of compliance tests

    a. Reasonable assurance depends on timing, nature, extent of tests, and results obtained

    b. Tests of control procedures leaving an audit trail should be applied to the whole year. When done during interim work, additional year-end work may not be necessary depending on

        1) Results of interim tests

        2) Inquiries of remaining period

        3) Length of remaining period

        4) Nature and amount of transactions or balances

        5) Evidence of compliance in substantive tests

    c. Subjective or statistical testing may be used

    d. Statistical sampling allows CPA to quantify reasonableness of sample size and sample evaluation

    e. While manual system may generally provide for documentation of performance of control procedures, computer system may provide no visible evidence of internal control procedures performed

        1) In such cases, auditor may use computer-assisted audit techniques such as (1) re-performing the processing and/or (2) a test data approach

    f. In both computerized and manual systems, procedures which leave no trail should be tested through inquiries and observation

    g. Functions considered incompatible in manual system may be controlled in computer system through

        1) Segregation within data processing department

        2) Segregation between data processing and user departments

        3) Control over access to data and computer operations

6. Evaluation of IC system

    a. Summary

        1) Consider possible errors and irregularities

        2) Determine control procedures to prevent or detect such errors and irregularities

        3) Determine whether such procedures are prescribed <u>and</u> in effect

        4) Evaluate effect of deficiencies in IC system on

            a) Substantive tests

            b) IC comment letter

    b. Emphasis on controls for particular classes of transactions

      1) Controls of different classes of transactions are not offsetting, e.g., strong inventory control does not counterbalance weak cash control

      2) Overall evaluations are not useful in determining extent of substantive tests

      3) In some cases, a more narrow evaluation may be appropriate, e.g., cash disbursements for advertising

    c. CPA's evaluation of IC for each class of transactions should be considered satisfactory if no material weakness exists

      1) A material weakness is one which would permit material errors in statements without detection within a timely period

      2) Auditor is required to report such weaknesses as described in Section 323

E. Correlation of IC study with other procedures

    1. Ultimate purpose of IC evaluation is to contribute to a reasonable basis for an opinion

    2. Two classes of substantive tests (required by third standard of fieldwork)

      a. Tests of transactions and balances

      b. Review of ratios, trends, unusual fluctuations

        1) Which are analytical review procedures -- see Section 318

    3. Purpose of substantive tests is to substantiate validity and propriety of accounting transactions or balances

    4. Cannot place reliance on IC to the exclusion of substantive tests

    5. Reliance on substantive tests may vary inversely with reliance on IC

      a. Relative reliance varies with circumstances

      b. Effectiveness is overall consideration

    6. Substantive tests may be applied subjectively or statistically

320 A Relationship of Statistical Sampling to GAAS

Superseded by SAS 39, now Section 350

320 B Precision and Reliability for Sampling

Superseded by SAS 39, now Section 350

321 The Effects of EDP on the Auditor's Study and Evaluation of Internal Control (SAS 3)

A. Introduction

    1. Internal control objectives are independent of the method of data processing

      a. EDP organization and procedures are influenced by the method of data processing

    2. Data processing systems may be wholly manual or combinations of manual, mechanical, and EDP systems

    3. If EDP is used, CPA needs to understand the entire system to identify and evaluate the accounting control features

B. EDP accounting control procedures

1. General controls

    a. Plan of organization of EDP activity
    b. Procedures to review, test, approve, and change programs
    c. Hardware controls
    d. Access controls
    e. Other data and procedural controls

2. Application controls provide reasonable assurance

    a. Input controls -- data received for processing are

        1) Properly authorized
        2) Converted into machine readable form
        3) Intact (not lost, modified, etc.)

    b. Processing controls -- data processing has been performed as intended

        1) All transactions processed as authorized
        2) No authorized transactions omitted
        3) No unauthorized transactions

    c. Output controls -- process is accurate and only authorized personnel receive the output

3. EDP controls may be performed within the

    a. EDP department
    b. User department
    c. A separate control group

C. EDP effects on accounting controls

1. Segregation of functions. Incompatible functions are those which allow a person both to perpetrate and conceal errors.

    a. Incompatible functions are more likely in EDP systems due to the concentration of clerical activities. For example

        1) Persons having opportunity to make unapproved changes in programs
        2) Persons in position to make unapproved changes in data files
        3) Persons who can make unapproved changes in supervisory programs

            a) Supervisory programs perform standardized data handling functions, e.g., "operating systems" and "data management systems"

    b. In lieu of controls in the EDP department, compensating controls may be installed in user departments and control groups

        1) Frequently supplemented by internal audit procedures

2. Execution of transactions. Procedures to assure that steps in the transaction cycle are executed in accordance with specific or general authorizations.

3. Recording of transactions. Procedures to assure recording transactions in the amounts, time periods, and accounts that the transactions were executed.

    a. Data conversion controls are required for the conversion to machine readable form
    b. The effectiveness of control over recording is dependent on

        1) Functioning of EDP procedures
        2) Follow up by users of the output

4. Access to assets. EDP personnel have access to assets if they can prepare documents, e.g., checks, shipping orders, etc., to release the assets.

   a. Use compensating (outside EDP department) controls

5. Comparisons of assets with recorded amounts. Personnel may insert incorrect physical inventory count data.

   a. Use recording controls

D. Review of the system

1. The preliminary phase is to understand the flow of transactions including

   a. Extent of EDP use
   b. Basic structure of accounting control
   c. Knowledge is acquired by

      1) Inquiring of client personnel
      2) Observation of employees
      3) Reviewing documentation

2. Based on the preliminary phase, the auditor will conclude

   a. Accounting controls in the EDP system appear to warrant reliance thereon

      1) Requires compliance tests

   b. Accounting controls are weak and do not warrant reliance

      1) Determine impact on examination. If examination is to continue to be feasible, extend substantive tests to compensate for lack of accounting controls.

   c. Not to rely on the EDP accounting controls (and not undertake compliance tests) because:

      1) Effort required would exceed benefits (reduction of substantive tests), or
      2) EDP accounting controls may be redundant

E. Tests of compliance

1. The purpose is to provide reasonable assurance that the accounting controls are being applied as prescribed and are effective

2. The concern is

   a. Were necessary procedures performed?
   b. How were they performed?
   c. By whom were they performed?

3. EDP accounting control procedures may

   a. Leave visible evidence of performance

      1) Error listings
      2) Approval and change sheets

   b. Leave no visible evidence of performance but may be tested in the EDP system

      1) Reasonableness tests
      2) Valid character tests

     c. Leave no visible evidence of performance <u>nor</u> are testable in the system but are observable

        1) Segregation of duties

F. Evaluation of the system

    1. Evaluation of the EDP system of internal control is not unlike the evaluation of any other system of internal control

       a. It should be undertaken as a part of the evaluation of the overall internal control evaluation

322 The Effect of an Internal Audit Function on the Scope of the Independent Auditor's Examination (SAS 9)

Supersedes Section 320.74 of SAS 1

A. The work of internal auditors cannot be substituted for the work of the CPA, but the auditor should consider the procedures performed by internal auditors in determining the nature, timing, and extent of audit procedures

B. If the work of the internal auditor may be a factor in determining the nature, timing, or extent of the audit work, the auditor should

    1. Review the competence and objectivity of the internal auditors

       a. Competence contemplates qualifications and may be indicated by hiring, training, and supervising practices
       b. Objectivity may be indicated by the organization status of the internal auditor and internal audit reports

    2. Evaluate the work of the internal auditor

       a. Examine documentary evidence on a test basis

          1) Scope appropriate?
          2) Auditor programs adequate?
          3) Working papers documented?
          4) Conclusions appropriate?
          5) Reports consistent with work?

       b. The auditor should also perform some tests of the work of the internal auditor, e.g., examine transactions or balances the internal auditor examined

C. When the work of the internal auditors on internal control is significant, the auditor should arrange to have access to internal auditor's workpapers and reports

    1. The internal auditor's work frequently is more useful when discussed with the auditor prior to performance

D. Internal auditors may also be used in performing substantive and compliance tests

    1. The competence and objectivity of internal auditors should be considered
    2. The work of internal auditors should be supervised and tested

E. The auditor must make all of the judgments concerning matters affecting the audit report

323 Required Communication of Material Weaknesses in Internal Accounting Control (SAS 20)

Amends para 320.68, 640.01, .12, .13 of SAS 1

A. Requires auditors to communicate to senior management and the board of directors or its audit committee material weaknesses (definition is in Au 320) in internal accounting control discovered in audits per GAAS

   1. The weaknesses affect the nature, extent, and timing of audit tests
   2. Reporting the weaknesses is not required to comply with GAAS

      a. The report is incidental to the audit examination (and study of internal control)

B. The auditor may become aware of weaknesses during the internal control review, tests of compliance, or substantive tests, but

   1. The auditor may skip tests of compliance and rely on substantive tests, and
   2. The auditor is not required to evaluate every control, and
   3. The audit examination is done on a sample basis
   4. Thus, all material internal control weaknesses may not be disclosed

C. Management is responsible for establishing and maintaining an internal accounting control system

   1. Management obtains knowledge of internal control weaknesses from

      a. Other levels of management
      b. Internal auditors
      c. Independent auditors

   2. Thus, the auditor should communicate any material weaknesses to management

      a. Preferably in writing to reduce misunderstandings

         1) If orally, document in workpapers

   3. Due to the possible effects of weaknesses, they should be communicated at the earliest practicable date

      a. Even during interim work

   4. The auditor is not required to communicate the absence of weaknesses or immaterial weaknesses
   5. Uncorrected weaknesses (per previous communications) should be recommunicated
   6. When corrective action is not practicable, a summary of the circumstances is sufficient
   7. Corrective action may be suggested

      a. Additional studies to this end are not part of an examination per GAAS

324 Special Purpose Reports on Internal Accounting Control at Service Organizations (SAS 44)

A. Statement provides guidance on independent auditor's use of special-purpose report on certain aspects of internal control of organization that provides following services to auditor's client

1. Executing transactions and maintaining related accountability
2. Recording transactions and processing related data
3. Various combinations of these services

B. Definitions

1. Client organization--entity for which financial statements are being examined
2. User auditor--auditor who reports on financial statements of client organization
3. Service organization--entity (or a segment thereof) that provides services to client organization
4. Service auditor--auditor who reports on certain aspects of service organization's system of internal accounting control

C. Examples of service organizations

1. Service centers that provide data processing functions for other organizations
2. Trust departments of banks that invest and hold assets for employee benefit plans

D. Factors affecting user auditor's decision to obtain a service auditor's report

1. Service organizations maintaining controls that interact with client organization's control

   a. E.g., EDP service center processes client's payroll, orders, billings, etc.
   b. User auditor should identify significant classes of transaction processed by service organization and obtain understanding of flow of transactions through entire accounting system

      1) Service auditor's report on design of system may be useful but does not provide user auditor with basis for reliance on controls because no assurance regarding compliance is provided

   c. If user auditor plans to rely on system of internal accounting control, and

      1) Control procedures necessary to achieve objectives of internal accounting control are located at client organization and are operating

         a) Place reliance on controls at client organization

      2) Control procedures necessary to achieve objectives of internal accounting control are located at service organization

         a) Apply appropriate procedure at service organization, or
         b) Obtain service auditor's report covering both design of service organization's system and compliance tests directed to specific objectives of internal accounting control; report should

            1] Provide user auditor with understanding of

               a] Flow of transactions through part of client organization's system maintained by service organization

               b] Extent to which control procedures have been designed to meet specific control objectives

    2] Include service auditor's opinion as to whether control procedures and compliance with them are sufficient

    3] If report does not cover procedures on which the user auditor intends to rely, s/he may

      a] Arrange to have service auditor perform agreed-upon procedures, or

      b] Perform his/her own compliance tests at service organization

   c) User auditor should consider whether combination of internal accounting control procedures at client organization and service organization provides basis for reliance

   d) Control weaknesses in service organization's system should be considered weaknesses in client organization's system

 2. Service organizations maintaining controls that do not interact with client organization controls

  a. E.g., Trustees of employee benefit plans that hold and invest assets for plans

  b. If service organization is authorized to execute transactions without specific authorization and client organization is not able to maintain adequate controls, user auditor should

   1) Rely on internal accounting controls at service organization, or

   2) Apply substantive tests at service organization

  c. If service organization executes transaction only with specific authorization of client organization, client organization can maintain independent record of transactions thereby maintaining adequate controls

   1) In these cases, it still may be more efficient to restrict substantive tests of client's records by relying on controls at service organization

  d. If user auditor intends to rely on controls at service organization s/he may

   1) Obtain appropriate service auditor's report, or

   2) Apply auditing procedures at service organization or request service auditor to make tests

E. Considerations in using service auditor's report

 1. Obtaining and evaluating service auditor's report

  a. Contact service organization through client

  b. If no report or if report is not appropriate, user auditor may

   1) Apply procedures at service organization, or

   2) Request service auditor to apply procedures

  c. Make inquiries concerning service auditor's professional reputation per SAS 1, Section 543.10a (AU 543.10a)

  d. If necessary, discuss with service auditor scope and results of his/her work

  e. If unable to achieve audit objectives, qualify or disclaim an opinion due to scope limitations

2. If timing of service auditor's report does not coincide with period covered by financial statements, auditor should consider guidance provided by SAS 1, Section 320.65 (AU320.65)

3. Reference to service auditor's report

   a. In opinion on financial statements, make no reference

   b. In opinion on internal control, refer to service auditor's report in accordance with SAS 30, para 45 (AU642.45)

F. Responsibilities of service auditors for special-purpose reports

  1. His/her service should be performed in accordance with GAAS and any other relevant standards

  2. Service auditor need not be independent with regard to each client organization

  3. Type of engagement and type of report should be established by service organization

     a. Reports on design of system

       1) Useful for

         a) Providing user auditor with understanding of system

         b) Designing compliance and substantive tests

         c) Do not provide basis for reliance on controls

       2) Required information is obtained through discussion with service organization personnel, reference to documentation and walk-throughs

         a) Tests of compliance are not required

       3) Opinion as of specified date should include description of

         a) Significant changes in system that auditor becomes aware of

         b) Circumstances in which control objectives are not achieved

       4) Elements of special-purpose reports in addition to those described in SAS 30, para 61 (AU642.61)

         a) Description of system

         b) Description of specific control objectives

         c) Purpose of procedures performed

         d) Inherent limitations of internal control

         e) Service auditor's opinion concerning control procedures described

     b. Reports on both design of system and certain compliance tests

       1) Useful for

         a) Providing user auditor with understanding of system including relationship of service organization's controls to those of client

         b) Providing basis for reliance on service organization's internal accounting controls

         c) Designing compliance and substantive tests at client organization

       2) Required information is obtained through discussion with service personnel, reference to documentation, tests of compliance and other procedures

         a) Circumstances found where control objectives are not achieved should be described

         b) Report will not necessarily include list of each compliance deviation

    3) Elements of special-purpose reports in addition to those described in SAS 30, para. 61 (AU642.61)

         a) Description of system

         b) Description of specific control objectives

         c) Inherent limitations of internal control

         d) Service auditor's opinion concerning control procedures described and degree of compliance therewith

c. Reports on system of segment of service organization

    1) May be useful when it is unlikely that client organizations will maintain controls that interact with those of service organization

         a) Do not ordinarily include description of design of system

         b) Includes service auditor's opinion on internal controls applied by segment of service organization [Guidance is per SAS 30, paras 3-46 (AU642.03-.46)]

         c) In report on system, basis for assessing materiality of potential errors or irregularities is financial statements of service organization rather than segment

         d) Report will not necessarily include list of each compliance deviation error found

         e) Service auditor must also consider materiality of errors or irregularities found in relation to assets held for affected client organization

             1] If material, service auditor should request service organization to report this, and

             2] If service organization does not report errors or irregularities, service auditor should describe them in report

326 Evidential Matter (SAS 31)

Para .12 superseded by SAS 48, section number not available

Supersedes Section 330 of SAS 1

A. This statement, which interprets the third standard of fieldwork, analyzes the decision process auditors follow in obtaining and evaluating evidence

    1. Auditor's judgment is the measure of validity of audit evidence, whereas legal evidence is circumscribed by strict rules

B. Assertions (explicit or implicit) are representations made by management and include several types

    1. <u>Existence or occurrence</u> assertions state whether

        a. Assets or liabilities existed at a specific date, e.g., inventories on the balance sheet are available for sale

        b. Recorded transactions occurred during the period, e.g., sales on the income statement are the results of exchanges of goods or services for a valid asset

2.   Completeness assertions state whether all transactions and accounts meeting tests for inclusion under GAAP are included in the financial statements, e.g., all purchases have been recorded and are included in financial statements

3.   Rights and obligations assertions state whether assets are rights of the entity and liabilities are obligations of the entity as of the balance sheet date, e.g., capital leases

4.   Valuation or allocation assertions state whether asset, liability, revenue and expense elements are shown in the financial statements at the proper amounts, e.g., accounts receivable at net realizable value and fixed assets at cost less accumulated depreciation

5.   Presentation and disclosure assertions state whether elements of financial statements are properly classified, described, and disclosed, e.g., extraordinary items meet the criteria of APB 30

C.   Assertions are used to develop audit objectives and design substantive tests

1.   Audit objectives are formulated with regard to the entity's specific circumstances including

   a.   Essence of its economic activity
   b.   Industry accounting practices

2.   Objective-procedure relationship is not always one-to-one

   a.   An audit objective may require application of more than one procedure
   b.   An audit procedure may relate to more than one objective

3.   Factors which auditors weigh in selecting specific substantive tests include

   a.   Extent of reliance on internal accounting control
   b.   Relative risk of material errors or irregularities
   c.   Anticipated effectiveness and efficiency of specific tests
   d.   Nature and materiality of items to be tested
   e.   Types and competence of evidential matter which can be obtained
   f.   Essence of the audit objective to be tested

      1)   E.g., in formulating tests to achieve an objective concerning the assertion of existence or occurrence, auditor takes items included in an amount and searches for evidence

      2)   E.g., in formulating tests to achieve an objective concerning completeness, auditor chooses evidence indicating an item should be included in financial statements and looks for the item in the statements

4.   While methods of applying audit procedures may be influenced by existence of computer, auditor's objectives do not change

   a.   Existence of computer may make inspection, inquiry, or confirmation impossible without computer assistance

5.   Professional judgment of the auditor considering specific circumstances determines the nature, timing, and extent of the procedures to be used on a given audit

a. Procedures used should be adequate to fulfill specific audit objectives

b. Evidential matter secured should be sufficient for auditor to assess validity of specific assertions contained in the elements of the financial statements

D. Evidential matter supporting the financial statement consists of

1. Underlying accounting data including books of original entry, general and subsidiary ledgers, accounting manuals, informal and memorandum records

a. Presence of the above alone is not sufficient support for the financial statements; however, in the absence of evidence regarding propriety and accuracy of this underlying data, an opinion is not justified

b. Auditor tests underlying accounting data using analysis and review by

1) Retracing procedural steps of accounting, process including worksheets, allocations, etc.
2) Recalculating allocations, etc.
3) Reconciling related types and applications of common information

c. If system is properly designed and maintained above tests will provide persuasive evidence regarding presentation of financial statements in conformity with GAAP

2. Corroborating evidence which provides additional support and includes

a. Documentary items (e.g., checks, invoices, contracts, minutes of meetings)
b. Confirmations and other written representations
c. Information gathered by the auditor through inquiry, observation, inspections, and physical examination
d. Other information available or developed by auditor which allows him/her to form conclusions using valid reasoning

E. Competence of evidential matter is a function of its validity and relevance; since validity is influenced so heavily by circumstances, the generalizations below are subject to exceptions

1. External evidential matter gathered from unbiased outsiders gives greater assurance than internally obtained evidence
2. Financial statements processed from accounting data under conditions of adequate internal control are more reliable than those processed in entities with weak internal control
3. Corroborating evidential matter obtained directly is more persuasive than that obtained indirectly

a. E.g., physical examination, observation, computation, and inspection

F. Sufficient competent evidential matter must be obtained to give the auditor a basis for forming an opinion

1. Auditors use professional judgment to assess whether the quantities and types of evidential matter are sufficient

a. Usually it is necessary to rely on persuasive rather than convincing evidence for both

1) Individual financial statement assertions, and
2) Assertion that the financial statements taken as a whole present financial position, results of operations, and changes in financial position in accordance with GAAP

   b. Time and cost constraints must be considered by auditor
   c. Usefulness of evidence including relative risk must bear a rational re-
       lationship to the cost of securing evidence

G. Evaluation of evidential matter must be made with reference to attainment of
   specific audit objectives

   1. If substantial doubt exists relative to any materially significant asser-
       tion, auditor must not form an opinion until sufficient competent evidential
       matter has been gathered to eliminate the substantial doubt

   2. If removal of substantial doubt is not possible, auditor must express a
       qualified opinion or disclaimer of opinion

327 The Independent Auditor's Responsibility for the Detection of Errors or
     Irregularities (SAS 16)

Supersedes para 110.05-.08 of SAS 1

A. Per GAAS, auditors should search for errors and irregularities having a material
   effect on the statements (per appropriate auditing procedures)

   1. Error - unintentional mistakes in statements

       a. Math or clerical mistakes
       b. Misapplication of GAAP
       c. Oversight, misinterpretation

   2. Irregularity - intentional distortion of statements

       a. Fraud - deliberate misstatement
       b. Defalcation - misappropriation of assets
       c. Causes of irregularities

           1) Misrepresentations and omissions of transactions
           2) Manipulation, falsification of records, documents
           3) Omission of data from records
           4) Recording fictitious transactions
           5) Intentional misapplication of GAAP
           6) Misappropriation of assets

B. Business controls and independent audits provide reasonable assurance that
   material errors or irregularities are prevented or detected

   1. Business controls include

       a. Legal requirements
       b. Board of Director's oversight
       c. Audit committee activities
       d. Internal audit function

           1) Internal control procedures

C. The auditor's examination is influenced by the possibility of errors or
   irregularities, i.e., attitude of professional skepticism

   1. Internal controls and substantive tests

       a. Management is responsible for establishing and maintaining internal
           control system
       b. Summary of evaluation of internal control (para 320.65, SAS 1)

      1) Consider possible errors and irregularities
      2) Determine control procedures to prevent or detect such errors and irregularities
      3) Determine whether such procedures are prescribed and in effect
      4) Evaluate effect of deficiencies in IC system on

         a) The nature, extent, and timing of audit tests
         b) Suggestions to management

  c. Auditors do not rely entirely on internal control to detect and prevent errors and irregularities

      1) Substantive tests can detect errors and irregularities in systems with satisfactory internal control

  d. Customary audit procedures produce evidence of errors or irregularities, e.g.,

      1) Discrepancies within the accounting records
      2) Discrepancies revealed by audit confirmations
      3) Low response rates to confirmations
      4) Undocumented transactions
      5) Improperly recorded transactions
      6) Large, unusual, year-end transactions

2. The integrity of management. Management can override controls to record or control transactions.

  a. Circumstances which may encourage misstatement of statements

      1) Client in industry experiencing failures
      2) Client lacks sufficient working capital or credit

  b. Factors to consider in evaluating the possibility of management misrepresentations or override of controls

      1) Nature of client entity
      2) Susceptibility to irregularities
      3) Degree of authority at various management levels
      4) Prior experience with client

  c. Circumstances causing auditor concern

      1) Client does not correct internal control weaknesses
      2) High turnover of financial executives
      3) Understaffed accounting and financial departments

  d. Unless there is evidence to the contrary, auditors can assume no overriding of controls or no material misrepresentations

3. Inherent limitations of an audit

  a. Audits provide reasonable (but not absolute) assurance that statements are not materially affected by errors or irregularities

      1) Cost-benefit analysis requires audit techniques to be applied on a sample basis

  b. Unfortunately, the auditor may be misled by falsified records, documents, in the absence of evidence indicating falsification

      1) Procedures cannot be undertaken to confirm the truthfulness of all representations received by the auditor

        2) Also the auditor cannot be expected to detect unrecorded transactions without evidence of omissions

    c. Auditor is not insurer or guarantor

        1) Must comply with GAAS

D. When the auditor believes material errors or irregularities may exist, s/he should discuss the need for further investigation with appropriate levels of management

    1. If top management may be involved, the auditor should consult the audit committee or board of directors

    2. The examination should be expanded to determine existence and effect of errors or irregularities

        a. Attorneys may be consulted on legal matters

    3. If the auditor is unable to obtain sufficient competent evidence, consider

        a. Qualification
        b. Withdrawal with written explanation

    4. For errors or irregularities not material to statements, e.g., a petty cash defalcation, refer matter to client

        a. Consider effect of immaterial irregularities to other aspects of the audit

328   Illegal Acts by Clients (SAS 17)

A. Audits cannot be relied on to detect illegal acts

    1. Audits concern financial, not legal matters

        a. Auditor may become aware of illegal acts
        b. As an illegal act is less related to the financial statements, the less likely the auditor will discover it

B. Audit procedures that may identify illegal acts

    1. Audit procedures may reveal illegal acts even though they are not designed specifically to detect illegal acts, e.g.,

        a. Evaluation of internal control
        b. Management inquiries

    2. The auditor should recognize the possibility that illegal acts may have a material effect on the statements
    3. If the auditor believes illegal acts may have occurred, procedures are needed to determine the nature and the effect of the statements

C. Internal control evaluation and related tests of transactions and balances may disclose illegal acts

    1. IC review and tests may detect transactions suggesting illegal acts

        a. Unauthorized transactions
        b. Improperly recorded transactions
        c. Incomplete or untimely recording of transactions

    2. Throughout the audit, transactions and balances are tested which may indicate the possibility of illegal acts

      a. Unusual or questionable purpose transactions

      b. Improper accounting for taxes, government contracts, etc.

D. Through inquiries of management and others, e.g., client's attorneys, illegal acts may come to the auditor's attention

  1. Auditor should inquire of

      a. Client's compliance with laws, etc.

      b. Client procedures for prevention and detection of illegal acts

  2. The auditor may learn of governmental investigation regarding violations of statutes and regulations

      a. Occupational, health and safety

      b. Food and drug

      c. Truth in lending

      d. Environmental protection

      e. Price fixing, antitrust, etc.

  3. Unless the auditor learns of the above from external sources, client, or client attorney, the auditor cannot be expected to detect the illegal acts

E. Materiality of illegal acts

  1. Monetary effects

      a. Fines

      b. Penalties

      c. Damages

      d. Expropriation of assets

      e. Discontinuance of foreign operations

  2. Loss contingencies should be evaluated in terms of SFAS 5

  3. Effect of illegal acts on the operation of the client

      a. E.g., possible loss of major customers, etc.

F. Auditor should bring illegal acts discovered to appropriate client personnel, e.g., members of the audit committee, so that

  1. Remedial action may be considered

  2. Statement disclosure or adjustments may be made

  3. Disclosures on other documents may be made

G. If illegal acts having a material effect are not properly disclosed and accounted for, the auditor may have to

  1. Qualify for lack of compliance with GAAP (e.g., disclosure)

  2. Qualify due to an uncertainty (effect not known)

  3. Disclaim for lack of audit evidence (limitation of scope makes it impossible for auditor to gather sufficient evidence on legality or amounts involved)

  4. Auditor should withdraw if client refuses to accept other than unqualified opinion

H. An auditor's decision to withdraw or dissociate from clients not taking corrective action upon detection of illegal act depends on

  1. Reliability of management representations

  2. Possible effects of continuing relationship

3. Legal counsel's advice

I. Normally a CPA has no legal obligation to notify third parties of the client's illegal acts

330 Evidential Matter
Superseded by Section 326 (SAS 31)

331 Evidence for Receivables and Inventories

A. Confirmation of receivables and observation of inventory are generally required

   1. Auditor who does not employ them has the burden of justifying the opinion expressed

B. Confirmation date, method, and number should be determined by

   a. Effectiveness of IC
   b. Possibility of disputes, inaccuracies, etc.
   c. Probability that debtor will confirm
   d. Materiality of the receivables

   1. Positive confirmation

      a. Requires either

         1) Receipt of response from debtor
         2) Use of alternative procedures for evidence of receivable validity

      b. Should be used with large receivables or when discrepancies are expected

   2. Negative confirmations are useful when

      a. IC is satisfactory
      b. Large number of small receivables
      c. Debtors are likely to respond

   3. Nonreplies of positive confirmations should always be followed up

      a. For significant nonreplies alternative procedures may include evidence of subsequent cash receipts, cash remittance advices, etc.

   4. A combination of positive and negative confirmations may be used
   5. Confirmation may be made of account balances or individual items in the account balance

      a. Latter useful when debtor records will not permit confirmation of account balances

C. Inventories

   1. CPA must be present when inventory quantities are determined by physical count

      a. Suitable observations, tests, inquiries, etc., to satisfy CPA as to inventory quantities and condition

   2. If client has well maintained perpetual records, CPA observation can be performed during or after year under audit

3. Statistical sampling count method must

    a. Be statistically valid
    b. Be properly applied
    c. Have reasonable precision and reliability

4. Tests of accounting records alone are <u>not</u> sufficient

5. A CPA may satisfy himself as to prior period's inventory with appropriate tests if satisfied with current inventory by

    a. Tests of prior transactions
    b. Review of prior count records
    c. Gross profit tests

D. Inventories held in public warehouses

1. Direct confirmation in writing from custodian is ordinarily obtained
2. If such inventories represent a significant portion of current or total assets, auditor should

    a. Review and test owner's control procedures in investigating and evaluating performance of the warehouseman
    b. Obtain report from independent accountant as to the reliability of the system of internal accounting control relevant to custody of goods and, if applicable, pledging of receipts

        1) Alternatively, test the system to gain assurance that information received is reliable

    c. Observe physical counts where reasonable and practical
    d. Confirm with lenders pertinent details of pledged receipts, if any

332 Evidence for Long-Term Investments

A. Examination objectives

1. Compliance with GAAP

    a. Carrying values of long-term investments
    b. Investor's shares of investee's earnings
    c. Related disclosures

B. Evidence for existence, ownership, and cost

1. Inspection and count of securities and records
2. Confirmation of independent custodian

C. Evidence for carrying value and earnings therefrom

1. Audited statements are sufficient
2. Unaudited statements are not, by themselves, sufficient

    a. Extent and nature of audit procedures determined by materiality of investment
    b. Investee's CPA may be used

3. Market quotations when based on reasonable broad and active market
4. Personal evaluations (by client personnel or others) of investment carrying value greater than book value are acceptable (occurs when book value does not reflect market value)

5. When collateral is important with regard to collectibility, ascertain

    a. Existence
    b. Market value
    c. Transferability

D. Equity Method

1. CPA must satisfy himself as to client's methods of accounting for investments in common stock

    a. Investor's ability to exercise significant influence
    b. Circumstances that are basis for conclusion
    c. When 20% to 50% presumption is not followed, obtain evidence to satisfy that presumption has been overcome, and disclose appropriately

2. Investor includes proportionate share of investee's earnings from investee's most recent reliable statements

    a. May use unaudited interim statements which may in turn require audit procedures
    b. Any time lag should be consistent from year to year

        1) If change in time lag has material effect express consistency exception in opinion

3. Events subsequent to investee's most recent reliable statements should be treated (in accounts or disclosed) in the same manner as subsequent events of investor

    a. Such events may be so significant as to cause loss in investment which should be recognized

4. Eliminate intercompany profit and loss

333 Client Representations (SAS 19)

A. Requires CPAs to obtain written representations from management, i.e., required for compliance with GAAS

1. Only part of evidential matter and not a substitute for other auditing procedures
2. Reduces possibility of auditor-client misunderstandings
3. Confirms and documents oral representations
4. Auditor's reliance on written client representations is reasonable unless there is contradictory evidence

B. Generally, written representations are obtained on

1. Management's acknowledgement of responsibility for financial statement presentation per GAAP
2. Availability of all financial and related data
3. Completeness and availability of all minutes of meetings
4. Absence of errors and unrecorded transactions
5. Related party transactions
6. Noncompliance with contractual agreements
7. Information concerning subsequent events
8. Management or employee irregularities
9. Noncompliance with regulatory requirements
10. Management's intentions affecting statement items, e.g., current assets

11. Disclosure of compensating balances
12. Obsolete inventories
13. Sales commitment losses
14. Satisfactory title, liens, etc., on assets
15. Repurchase agreements
16. Purchase commitment losses
17. Violations of laws, regulations, etc.
18. Other disclosures required per SFAS 5, "Accounting for Contingencies"
19. Unasserted claims probable of assertion
20. Capital stock options, repurchase agreements, etc.

C. Written representations may be limited to material matters

   1. On an individual or collective basis
   2. As determined by an auditor-client understanding
   3. Except items "1," "2," "3," and "8" above

D. Miscellaneous

   1. The auditor may require written representations on other items

     a. E.g., interim data in audited statements

   2. Written representations regarding consolidated statements should specify applicability to parent and/or subsidiaries

   3. Written representations should be addressed to auditors

     a. Dated as of date of auditor's report
     b. Signed by chief operating and chief financial officers
     c. Written representations may also be obtained from others

E. Scope limitations

   1. Management's refusal to furnish necessary written representations precludes an unqualified opinion

     a. May affect reliance on other representations

   2. If precluded from necessary auditing procedures but given written representations, auditor should qualify or disclaim

     a. I.e., written representations cannot take the place of other auditing procedures

335 Related Parties (SAS 45)

A. From an accounting viewpoint, related party transactions need to be adequately disclosed

   1. Also, transactions should reflect their substance (rather than their form)
   2. Examples possibly indicative of related party transactions

     a. Borrowing or lending at interest rates above or below the market rate
     b. Selling real estate at a price significantly different from its appraised value
     c. Exchanging property for similar property in a nonmonetary transaction
     d. Loans with no scheduled repayment terms

B. From an audit viewpoint, the objectives are first to determine existence of related parties and second to identify and examine related party transactions

1. Compliance with GAAS does not assure detection of all related party transactions

    a. CPA should evaluate management organization to determine potentiality of related party transactions
    b. Related party transactions may be motivated by

        1) Lack of sufficient working capital
        2) Urgent desire for favorable EPS trends
        3) Optimistic EPS forecast
        4) Dependence on a few transactions, customers, etc.
        5) Declining industry profitability
        6) Rapid expansion of business
        7) Excess capacity
        8) Significant litigation
        9) Significant obsolescence

2. Procedures to determine existence of related parties

    a. Does client have procedures for related party transactions?
    b. Ask client for names of all related parties
    c. Review SEC filings
    d. Determine names of officers of all employee trusts
    e. Review stockholder listings of closely held companies
    f. Review prior workpapers for the names of related parties
    g. Inquire of predecessor and/or principal auditors
    h. Review material investment transactions

3. Procedures to identify related party transactions

    a. Provide audit personnel with related party names
    b. Review B of D minutes (and other committees)
    c. Review SEC filings
    d. Review client "conflict of interest" reports
    e. Review nature of transactions with major customers, suppliers, etc.
    f. Consider whether unrecorded transactions exist
    g. Review records for large, nonrecurring transactions
    h. Review for compensating balances
    i. Review legal invoices
    j. Review confirmations of loans receivable and payable for guarantees

4. Procedures (beyond management inquiry) should be applied to determine the purpose, nature and extent of the transactions

    a. Understand the purpose of the transaction
    b. Examine supporting documents
    c. Verify existence of required approval
    d. Evaluate reasonableness of amounts to be disclosed
    e. Consider simultaneous or joint audit of intercompany balances
    f. Inspect/confirm transferability and value of collateral
    g. Extend auditing procedures further as necessary to understand transactions

        1) Confirm transaction details with other party
        2) Inspect evidence held by other party
        3) Confirm information with intermediaries, e.g., banks
        4) Refer to trade journals, credit agencies, etc.
        5) Seek assurance on material uncollected balances

C. Disclosure of related party transactions

1. Auditor must be satisfied that related party disclosures per SFAS 57 are presented and that sufficient competent evidence has been gathered

2. It will often not be possible to determine whether transaction would have taken place if firms had not been related

    a. Unsubstantiated management comments concerning transaction's terms approximating arm's-length transactions may lead to qualified or adverse opinion

336   Using the Work of a Specialist (SAS 11)

A. The auditor may use the work of a specialist to obtain competent evidential matter, e.g.

    a. Valuation of drugs, art, securities, etc.
    b. Physical quantities of mineral reserves, etc.
    c. Actuarial determinations
    d. Interpretation of regulations, agreements, etc.

1. A specialist is a person (firm) possessing special skills or knowledge other than auditing or accounting

    a. E.g., actuaries, appraisers, attorneys, engineers, etc.
    b. Thus, section does not apply to CPA staff members
    c. Nor does it apply to client staff with special skills regarding only the client, e.g., plant or credit manager

B. Selecting a specialist

1. Through inquiry, consider

    a. Professional certification, license, etc.
    b. Reputation and standing
    c. Relationship to client

2. Specialist related to client may be acceptable, but unrelated specialist is better

3. Documented understanding of the work should exist among auditor, client, and specialist

    a. Objectives and scope
    b. Specialist's relationship to client
    c. Methods or assumptions used
    d. Comparison of methods or assumptions with those used last year
    e. Specialist's understanding of auditor's use of specialist's findings
    f. Form and content of specialist's report

C. The auditor ordinarily uses the work of the specialist if methods or assumptions used by the specialist appear reasonable

1. The auditor needs a sufficient understanding (preferably documented) of the methods and assumptions used by the specialist to determine whether the findings are suitable evidence

2. The specialist's findings should support the related financial statement representations

3. The auditor should test accounting data used by the specialist

4. If the client and specialist are related, an outside specialist should corroborate the findings of the related specialist

      a. Or the auditor should perform additional work on the specialist's

         1) Assumptions
         2) Methods
         3) Findings

D. When the specialist's findings are unreasonable or there is a difference between the specialist's findings and the financial statement representations, the auditor should perform additional procedures

    1. When the auditor cannot resolve, qualify, or disclaim for lack of sufficient competent evidential matter
    2. If auditor concludes statements do not conform with GAAP, issue qualified or adverse opinion

E. No reference to specialist in the audit report unless the report was a qualification or disclaimer (or other modification)

    1. Reference could indicate qualification or division of responsibility which is not intended
    2. If report modified as a result of findings of specialist, reference to specialist may be made to facilitate understanding of modification

337 Inquiry of a Client's Lawyer Concerning Litigation, Claims, and Assessments (SAS 12)

Amends Section 560.12 of SAS 1

A. Management has the responsibility for policies and procedures to identify, evaluate, and account for contingencies per GAAP

    1. GAAP for litigations, claims, and assessments (hereafter contingencies) are in SFAS 5 "Accounting for Contingencies"

B. The auditor should obtain evidential matter regarding

    1. Condition or circumstances indicating a possible loss from litigation, claims, and assessments
    2. Period in which the cause for legal action occurred
    3. Degree of probability of an unfavorable outcome
    4. Range of potential loss

C. Audit procedures

    1. Management is the primary source of information about contingencies
    2. The auditor should

      a. Inquire as to the policies and procedures adopted for identifying, evaluating, and accounting for contingencies

      b. Obtain a description and evaluation of all pending contingencies at the balance sheet date and any contingencies arising after the balance sheet date

      c. Examine relevant documents including correspondence and invoices from lawyers

      d. Obtain management's written assurance that all unasserted claims required to be disclosed by SFAS 5 (per client's lawyer) are disclosed

         1) Obtain client's permission and inform lawyer

    3. The auditor should request the client to communicate with relevant attorneys concerning contingencies

    a. Evidential matter from inside counsel may be corroborative, but is not a
       substitute for information outside counsel refuses to provide

  4. Other audit procedures which may reveal pending or possible contingencies

    a. Reading Board of Directors' and other appropriate meeting minutes
    b. Reading contracts, leases, correspondence, and other similar documents
    c. Guarantees of indebtedness on bank confirmations
    d. Inspecting other documents for possible client-made guarantees

D. The auditor should request that management send a letter of audit inquiry to the
   client's attorneys concerning contingencies

  1. To be included in the letter of audit inquiries

    a. Identification of client, subsidiaries, and period of examination
    b. A list and evaluation prepared by management of pending or threatened
       contingencies for which lawyer has been engaged and devoted substantial
       attention

       1) Request that the lawyer indicate

          a) Nature of the matter
          b) Progress of case
          c) Action client intends
          d) Likelihood of unfavorable outcome
          e) Range of potential loss
          f) Management's list is complete

    c. A list and evaluation prepared by management of unasserted claims con-
       sidered probable of assertion with a reasonable possibility of unfavor-
       able outcome

       1) Request that the lawyer comment on items where disagreement exists

    d. Statement by the client that client understands lawyer will advise cli-
       ent when unasserted claims may have to be disclosed per SFAS 5

       1) Request that the lawyer confirm this understanding

    e. Request that the lawyer specifically identify nature of and reasons for
       any limitations

  2. No inquiry of immaterial items is necessary if client and auditor agree on
     materiality limits
  3. The auditor may have the client request the lawyer provide the above infor-
     mation in a conference

    a. The auditor should appropriately document the conference

  4. The auditor should inquire about the reasons for changes in or resignation
     of attorneys

    a. Attorneys sometimes have to resign their engagement if clients disregard
       their advice

E. Limitations on the scope of a lawyer's response

  1. Lawyers may limit their response to items to which substantial attention has
     been given

    a. The response may also be limited to material items

    b. Such limitations are not limitations on the scope of the auditor's examination

  2. Refusal to furnish information requested in inquiry letter is a limitation on the scope of the auditor's examination sufficient to preclude an unqualified report

  3. Due to inherent uncertainties, a lawyer may be unable to respond as to the

    a. Likelihood of an unfavorable outcome, or

    b. Range of potential loss

    c. If the effect of the matter could be material the auditor ordinarily could not issue an unqualified opinion

338 Working Papers

Superseded by SAS 41, now Section 339

339 Working Papers (SAS 41)

Supersedes Section 338 of SAS 1

A. Auditor should prepare and maintain working papers designed to meet circumstances of a particular engagement

  1. Information included represents principal record of work done and conclusions reached concerning significant matters

B. Functions and nature of working papers

  1. Main functions of working papers are to

    a. Support auditor's opinion

    b. Provide a representation regarding observance to standards of fieldwork

    c. Aid auditor in the conduct and supervision of the engagement

  2. Working papers are records kept during the engagement of

    a. Procedures applied

    b. Tests performed

    c. Information obtained

    d. Pertinent conclusions reached

  3. Examples of working papers

    a. Audit programs

    b. Memoranda

    c. Letters of confirmation and representation

    d. Schedules or commentaries prepared or obtained

    e. Data stored on tapes, films, or other media

  4. Factors affecting auditor's judgment of quantity, type, and content of working papers

    a. Nature of engagement

    b. Nature of auditor's report

    c. Nature of financial statements, schedules, or other information being reported on

    d. Nature and condition of client's records

    e. Degree of reliance on internal accounting control

    f. Needs in particular circumstances for supervision and review of work

C. Content of working papers ("a.," "b.," and "c." are fieldwork standards)

1. Working papers should be sufficient to show that financial statements were reconciled with the accounting records and that the standards of fieldwork had been observed

    a. Adequate planning and supervision
    b. Adequate review of internal control
    c. Sufficient competent evidential matter has been obtained

D. Ownership and custody of working papers

1. Property of auditor, subject to ethical limitations relating to confidential client relationship
2. Not a substitute for client records
3. To be reasonably safeguarded and retained for reasonable period of time

340 The Auditor's Considerations When a Question Arises About an Entity's Continued Existence (SAS 34)

A. This statement gives guidance regarding the auditor's considerations when information comes to his/her attention that raises a question about an entity's ability to continue in existence; auditor should consider

1. Firm's solvency
2. Firm's chance of losing key personnel, principal customers, key suppliers, or primary revenue producing assets

B. According to GAAP, the auditor is not required to search for evidence relating to an entity's continued existence since the going concern is an underlying assumption in financial accounting. However, the auditor is required to consider any contrary information obtained through the audit process.

1. Includes information relating to the going concern at the date of the financial statements that comes to the auditor's attention at any time up to the date of his report

    a. Solvency problems (negative trends, default on loans)
    b. Internal problems (loss of key management)
    c. External problems (loss of key suppliers)

C. Mitigating factors which should be considered by the auditor in evaluating the significance of the contrary information include

1. Alternative means of maintaining adequate cash flows

    a. Asset disposal
    b. Debt financing available
    c. Cost factors (reduce or delay expenditures)
    d. Equity factors

2. Other factors

    a. Qualified persons available to replace lost management
    b. Alternative suppliers to replace lost suppliers

D. The auditor should also consider management plans which are responsive to the observed conditions that resulted in the contrary information. These plans should be evaluated as to their underlying assumptions, using the auditor's knowledge of the entity and the company's past budget variances.

E. The auditor's function is not predicting future events; and an unqualified opinion does not guarantee that the entity will continue beyond the date of the opinion

    1. The auditor should consider the adequacy of the disclosure related to the entity's ability to continue in existence

    2. A qualified opinion should be issued, if necessary, for full disclosure

350 Audit Sampling (SAS 39)

Supersedes Sections 320A and 320B of SAS 1

A. This statement provides guidance on the use of sampling in an audit of financial statements

    1. Audit sampling is the application of an audit procedure to less than 100 percent of the items within an account balance or class of transactions

        a. The purpose of audit sampling is to evaluate some characteristic of an account or class of transactions

        b. Use of a few items to gain understanding of systems or operations is not covered by guidance in this SAS

    2. Both nonstatistical and statistical approaches to sampling are addressed in this statement

    3. Sampling is usually considered when the auditor has no special knowledge indicating that errors or irregularities are likely to occur

B. The use of audit sampling relates to the third standard of fieldwork which requires sufficient, competent evidential matter to be obtained to afford a reasonable basis for an opinion

    1. Sufficiency relates to the design and size of an audit sample

        a. The size of a sample depends on the objective and the efficiency of the sample

        b. Both statistical and nonstatistical sampling can provide sufficient evidential matter

        c. Both statistical and nonstatistical sampling require that the auditor use professional judgment

    2. The competence of evidential matter is a matter of auditing judgment. The auditor should ask whether the sample is representative of the population.

C. Uncertainty and audit sampling. The third standard of fieldwork implies some degree of uncertainty.

    1. The concept of sampling is well established in auditing practice

    2. There are some items that do not justify the acceptance of any uncertainty; therefore, they will be examined 100 percent

    3. The statement refers to uncertainty as <u>ultimate risk</u>, UR, which consists of the risk of errors in the accounting process and the risk that the auditor will not detect material errors

        a. The auditor relies on internal accounting controls to reduce the first risk

        b. The auditor relies on substantive tests to reduce the second risk. Substantive tests include

            1) Detail tests (tests of transactions)

2) Analytical reviews
3) Tests of ending balances

4. Ultimate risk includes uncertainties due to sampling, called sampling risk, and uncertainties due to factors other than sampling, called nonsampling risk

   a. Sampling risk arises from the possibility that the conclusions derived from the sample will differ from the conclusions that would be derived from the population (the sample is nonrepresentative of the population). Sampling risk varies inversely with sample size.

   b. Nonsampling risk arises from uncertainties due to factors other than sampling. For example

      1) Inappropriate audit procedures for a given objective, and
      2) The failure to recognize errors. This risk can be reduced through adequate planning and supervision (SAS 22) and adherence to quality control standards (SAS 25).

D. Auditor judgment is used in assessing sampling risk

   1. In performing substantive tests, the auditor is concerned with two aspects of sampling

      a. The risk of incorrect acceptance
      b. The risk of incorrect rejection

   2. In performing compliance tests, the auditor is concerned with two aspects of sampling

      a. The risk of overreliance on internal accounting control
      b. The risk of underreliance on internal accounting control

   3. Risks "1.a." and "2.a." relate to the ability to detect material misstatements, while risks "1.b." and "2.b." relate to the efficiency of the audit. (Note: "1.a." and "2.a." are usually of greater concern.)

E. Sampling in substantive tests of details

   1. In planning a sample the auditor should consider

      a. The relationship of the sample to the relevant audit objective
      b. Preliminary estimates of materiality levels (the maximum error is called tolerable error for the sample)
      c. The auditor's allowable risk of incorrect acceptance, TD
      d. Characteristics of items comprising the account balance or class of transactions to be sampled

   2. The auditor must select a population from which to sample and which is consistent with the specific audit objective of concern

      a. The population consists of items in the account balance or transaction class of interest
      b. E.g., understatement due to omission could not be detected by sampling recorded items. Sampling from subsequent activities records would be preferred.

   3. The extent of substantive tests required will vary inversely with the auditor's reliance on internal accounting controls, 1-IC

   4. The greater the reliance on analytical review and other substantive tests of a nonsampling nature, 1-AR, the greater the allowable risk of incorrect

acceptance and, thus, the smaller the required sample size for substantive tests

5. The auditor uses his/her judgment in determining which items should be individually tested and which items should be subject to sampling

   a. The efficiency of a sample may be improved by separating items subject to sampling into relatively homogeneous groups

F. In <u>selecting</u> sample items, the auditor should insure that

1. The sample is representative of the population
2. All the items have an equal chance of being chosen
3. Acceptable random-based selection techniques include

   a. Random sampling
   b. Stratified random sampling
   c. Probability proportional to size
   d. Systematic sampling

G. In <u>performing</u> audit procedures on items included in a sampling and in <u>evaluating</u> sample results, the auditor should

1. Apply auditing procedures to each sample item

   a. Unexamined items should be evaluated to determine their effect on the sample results
   b. In addition, the auditor should consider the reasons for his/her inability to examine the item (e.g., a lack of supporting documentation)

2. Compare error results of the sample (including errors from the 100 percent examined items) to the tolerable error

   a. This evaluation requires the use of judgment in both statistical and nonstatistical sampling
   b. The auditor should also consider the qualitative aspects of the errors

      1) The nature and cause of the misstatement
      2) The possible relationship of the misstatement to other phases of the audit

   c. An irregularity usually requires more consideration than an error
   d. The auditor should consider projected error results in the aggregate from statistical and nonstatistical sources when evaluating whether the financial statements as a whole may be misstated

H. Sampling in compliance tests of internal accounting controls

1. In planning a sample the auditor should consider

   a. The relationship of the sample to the objective of the compliance test
   b. The maximum rate of deviations from prescribed control procedures that would support his planned reliance
   c. The auditor's allowable risk of overreliance

      1) Low levels usually required because compliance tests are the primary source of evidence about whether a control procedure is being applied as prescribed
      2) Quantitatively the auditor might consider 5% to 10% risk of overreliance as acceptable

   d. The characteristics of the population of interest

          1) The auditor should consider the likely rate of deviation
          2) The auditor should consider whether to test controls singly or in combination

  2. The auditor should realize that deviations from important control procedures of a given rate ordinarily result in errors or irregularities at a lower rate

I. Sample selection should insure that

  1. The sample is representative of the population
  2. The probability of inclusion of every element in the population is <u>known</u>

J. Performance and Evaluation

  1. Follow the same techniques as noted in substantive sampling (letter "G")
  2. Whether statistical or nonstatistical sampling is used, if the auditor decides that he is not going to rely on internal controls, the planned substantive tests should be adjusted

K. Dual purpose samples have two purposes

  1. To test compliance with a control procedure (compliance tests)
  2. To test whether the recorded dollar amounts of a transaction are correct (substantive tests)

    a. The auditor usually assumes that there is an acceptably small risk of compliance deviations being greater than the tolerable level
    b. The size of the sample should be the larger of the samples otherwise designed for two separate purposes

L. Selecting a Sampling Approach

  1. Statistical or nonstatistical approaches can provide sufficient evidential matter
  2. Choice between statistical and nonstatistical approach depends on relative

    a. Cost
    b. Effectiveness

  3. Statistical sampling helps

    a. Design efficient sampling plans
    b. Measure sufficiency of evidential matter
    c. To quantitatively evaluate sample results

390   Consideration of Omitted Procedures After the Report Date

A. This section provides guidance on auditor's responsibility when s/he realizes, subsequent to date of audit report, that one or more necessary procedures may have been omitted

  1. This section only covers case in which there is <u>no</u> indication that financial statements depart from GAAP. (See AU 561 when errors exist.)

  2. Although auditor has no responsibility to retroactively review his/her work, such postissuance review may occur as part of internal inspection or peer review
  3. In all such circumstances, auditor may be well advised to consult attorney

B. When it is determined that procedure has been omitted, auditor must

1. Assess its importance. (Consider other procedures which may have compensated for its omission.)

    a. If omission is considered important and if auditor believes individuals are relying on financial statements, procedures (or alternate procedures) should be promptly applied
    b. If financial statement errors are detected, consult AU 561
    c. If unable to apply procedures, consult attorney

410   Adherence to GAAP

Para .03 & .04 superseded by SAS 5, now Section 411

GAAP are accounting principles, practices, and methods of applying them

411   The Meaning of "Present Fairly in Conformity with GAAP" in the Independent Auditor's Report (SAS 5)

Supersedes para 410.03-.04 of SAS 1

A. GAAP is a technical term encompassing the conventions, rules, procedures, etc., (includes detailed rules as well as broad guidelines) that define accepted practice

   1. Form a standard to measure financial presentation

B. CPA's opinion that statements present fairly in conformity with GAAP

   1. Sources of GAAP in order of their authority are

       a. Pronouncements of body designated by AICPA to establish accounting principles pursuant to rule 203 of Code of Ethics

           1) Includes SFASs, FASB Interpretations, APBs, and ARBs

       b. Pronouncements of bodies of expert accountants that follow a due process

           1) Includes AICPA Industry Audit Guides and Accounting Guides and SOPs

       c. Practices or pronouncements widely recognized as GAAP

           1) Includes FASB Technical Bulletins, AICPA Interpretations and industry practices

       d. Other accounting literature

           1) Includes APB Statements, AICPA Issues Papers, SFACS, pronouncements of other professional associations or regulatory agencies, and textbooks and articles

   2. Appropriateness of principle depends on circumstances

       a. Principle selection should be based on the substance of the transaction
       b. Principle application should be related to the effect on the overall statements
       c. Principle with limited usage may have general acceptance
       d. More than one principle may be appropriate where criteria for selection among alternatives have not been established

   3. The statements and footnotes are relevant to their use, understanding, and interpretation

4. The presentation is neither too detailed nor too condensed
5. The statements fairly reflect the underlying transactions

C. The auditor's judgment of fairness should be applied within the framework of GAAP

420 Consistency of Application of GAAP
Para .15 and .16 replaced with new paras from SAS 43

A. Objectives

   1. Assure that comparability has not been materially affected by changes in accounting principles or application thereof

      a. Lack of consistency may cause lack of comparability

         1) Other factors unrelated to consistency may cause lack of comparability, e.g., differing business events

      b. Comparability may be affected by

         1) Accounting changes

            a) Change in principle
            b) Change in estimate
            c) Change in entity

         2) Error in prior statements
         3) Classification changes
         4) Substantially different transactions

   2. Provide appropriate reporting if such a change takes place

B. Changes affecting consistency (affect report)

   1. Change in principle

      a. E.g., changing depreciation method for all assets

   2. Change in reporting entity

      a. Consolidated in place of individual statements
      b. Changing subsidiaries in consolidated group

         1) Not from purchase, sale, etc., of subsidiary

      c. Changing companies in combined statements

         1) Not from purchase, sale, etc., of a company

      d. Changing among accounting or consolidation methods for investments in common stock
      e. Application of pooling of interests

   3. Correction of an error in principle

      a. Change from unacceptable to acceptable principle

   4. Change in principle inseparable from a change in estimate

C. Changes not affecting consistency. (Does not require comment in report but may require footnote disclosure.)

   1. Change in estimate
   2. Error correction not involving principle
   3. Changes in classification

4.   Variations in format of funds statements
5.   Changes made in terms used to express "changes in financial position" (cash, net quick assets, or working capital)
6.   Substantially different transactions
7.   Changes not affecting current statements, but expected to affect future statements

   a.   Disclose in period of change

8.   Qualify report for changes not affecting consistency that are <u>not</u> properly disclosed in footnotes

D.   When CPA reports only on current period, report on consistency in relation to preceding period (even if preceding period statements are not presented). When reporting on more than one period, report on consistency between all periods (and that of preceding year, if presented).

E.   Consistency report phraseology

1.   "On a basis consistent with that of the preceding year" for reports on a single year
2.   "Applied on a consistent basis" for two or more years
3.   No mention if initial accounting period of a company

430   Adequacy of Informative Disclosure

Superseded by Section 431 of SAS 1

431   Adequacy of Disclosure in Financial Statements

Supersedes Section 430 of SAS 1

A.   This statement interprets the third standard of reporting

> "Informative disclosures in the financial statements are to be regarded as reasonably adequate unless otherwise stated in the report."

B.   Presentation in accordance with GAAP embraces adequate disclosure of all material matters of form, arrangement, and content of financial statements and their appended notes, e.g., classification of statement items and valuation bases

1.   If management omits the required information, the auditor

   a.   Should express qualified or adverse opinion, and
   b.   Should provide information in his/her report, if practicable; however, an auditor need not assume position of preparer, e.g., prepare an omitted basic financial statement

2.   In most cases, the auditor should not make available information obtained in confidence which is not required to be disclosed under GAAP per Ethics Rule 301, e.g., competitive information

435   Segment Information (SAS 21)

A.   Provides guidance on examining and reporting on statements required to include segment information

1.   Segment disclosures required by SFAS 14 include data on

   a.   Operations in different industries
   b.   Foreign operations and export sales
   c.   Major customers

    2.   Audit objective is to have basis for determining compliance with SFAS 14

B. Segment audit procedures

    1.   The nature, timing, and extent of audit procedures may be affected by the following:

        a.   Segment data materiality is determined by more than relative size

           1)   Qualitative as well as quantitative factors
           2)   Significance to a particular entity
           3)   Pervasiveness of the data or error

        b.   Internal control and degree of integration, centralization, uniformity, etc., of records
        c.   Nature, number, size, etc., of industry and geographic segments

           1)   Nature and number of subsidiaries, divisions, etc.

    2.   Tests of the underlying accounting records should consider classification of transactions and balances among industry and geographic segments

    3.   Auditors should apply the following procedures to segment data

        a.   By inquiry, determine methodology used to develop segment data and evaluate reasonableness
        b.   By inquiry, determine method of accounting for intersegment sales

           1)   Test intersegment sales as necessary

        c.   Analytically review segment information (apply SFAS 14 percentage tests)

           1)   Current year to previous year and budgeted data
           2)   Other interrelationships expected to have predictable patterns

        d.   Inquire as to methods of allocating common costs and assets

           1)   Test allocations as necessary

        e.   Determine whether segment information has been presented consistently

           1)   Including proper disclosures of changes per SFAS 14

C. Reporting on segment data

    1.   Auditor's standard report applies to segment data as it does to any other disclosures

        a.   Unless segment data are clearly marked "unaudited"
        b.   No referral in report to segment data if per GAAS and GAAP
        c.   Item material to segment data may be immaterial to overall statements

           1)   Qualitative as well as quantitative, i.e.,

               a)   Significance of matter to particular entity
               b)   Pervasiveness of the matter
               c)   Impact of the matter

    2.   If any material error or omission in segment data exists, modify report describing error or data omitted

        a. Omitted segment data do not have to be presented in audit report

    3.   If the nature and effect of changes in reporting segment data are not disclosed or restated (if required by SFAS 14), opinion should be modified

a. If appropriate disclosure, restatement, etc., per SFAS 14 is given, no mention in report is necessary

1) Unless a change in accounting principle

b. Segment inconsistencies occur because

1) Change in accounting for intersegment sales or allocation of joint expenses
2) Change in method of determining segment profitability
3) A change in accounting principle
4) A change in requiring retroactive restatement

a) Statements as a whole have been retroactively restated
b) Segments have been redefined

4. Auditors should qualify on statements as a whole if unable to conclude whether the entity is required to provide segment information

5. Auditor may also report separately on segment data

a. See Section 621 "Special Reports" for separate reports
b. Since segment data are per GAAP, all reporting GAAS apply
c. Materiality is related to segment disclosures, not overall statements

504 Association with Financial Statements (SAS 26)

A. This SAS defines "association" with financial statements as contemplated in the fourth standard of reporting

1. The objective of the fourth standard is to prevent misinterpretation of the degree of responsibility assumed by the accountant when his name is associated with statements in a manner implying compliance with GAAS

a. The fourth standard requires expression of an opinion or assertion that an opinion cannot be expressed

2. Applied to association with statements of public entities

a. And audit engagements of nonpublic entities

B. An accountant is associated when his/her name is used with his consent in a report, document, or other communication containing financial statements

1. Also with statements submitted to clients or others
2. Nonetheless, statements are management representations

a. And management is responsible for compliance with GAAP

3. Accountants may be associated with audited or unaudited statements

a. Statements are audited if sufficient audit procedures are performed

1) See SAS 2 (Section 509), "Reports on Audited Financial Statements"

b. Unaudited interim statements of public companies are reviewed based on SAS 24 (Section 722), "Review of Interim Financial Information"

c. Unaudited statements of nonpublic companies are issued per Statements on Standards for Accounting and Review Services (SSARS)

C. Accountants should issue an unaudited disclaimer on unaudited or unreviewed statements of public companies

1. The disclaimer may accompany or be on the statements
2. Each page of the statements should be marked "unaudited"
3. Accountant has no responsibility beyond reading for obvious material errors

    a. No mention should be made of any procedures that were performed

4. Accountant should not let his/her name be associated with unaudited statements presented in client documents

    a. Unless the statements are marked as "unaudited" and that "no opinion has been expressed"

5. If the unaudited statements of a public company are prepared on a comprehensive basis other than GAAP, modify identification of the statements in the standard disclaimer

    a. E.g., statements of assets and liabilities from cash transactions
    b. A footnote should explain the difference between the comprehensive basis and GAAP
    c. See SAS 14 (Section 621) "Special Reports"

6. If the accountant is not independent with respect to public company statements, a disclaimer indicating nonindependence is required

    a. Irrespective of any audit procedures that were performed
    b. No mention should be made of the reason for nonindependence

7. If the accountant believes the unaudited statements are not per GAAP, the accountant should

    a. Suggest appropriate revision
    b. If unsuccessful, modify the disclaimer to refer to the departure from GAAP--including effects

        1) Not practicable to remedy statement deficiencies in some cases, e.g., inadequate disclosure
        2) Then, explanation of the deficiency should be made e.g., when management has elected to omit subtantially all disclosures, report should clearly indicate such

    c. If client refuses to accept modified report, accountant should disassociate from statement

D. Reporting on unaudited statements when one period is audited

    1. When unaudited statements are presented in comparative form for SEC filings, mark statements unaudited

        a. And make no reference to them in the auditor's report

    2. In cases other than SEC filings, unaudited comparative statements should also be marked as unaudited

        a. Additionally, the report of the prior period should be reissued
        b. OR the current report should have a separate paragraph describing responsibility assumed on prior period statements indicating

            1) Service performed
            2) Date of prior report
            3) Description of material report modifications
            4) Explanation that the service was less than an audit

      c. If a nonpublic entity, the separate paragraph should describe the compilation or review undertaken

  3. When the current statements are unaudited and the comparative statements have been audited

      a. The current report should have a separate paragraph indicating

          1) The prior period statements were audited
          2) The date of the prior audit report
          3) Type of opinion expressed
          4) Reasons for other than unqualified report
          5) No audit procedures were performed after the date of the prior report

E. Negative Assurance

  1. If a disclaimer is issued, negative assurance should not be given

      a. I.e., negative assurance contradicts the disclaimer
      b. Unless permitted by other AICPA standards

          1) E.g., letters for underwriters

  2. Accountants may give negative assurance on statements which are part of a special acquisition engagement if

      a. Applicable requirements of letters for underwriters are met, SAS 1 Section 631

  3. SAS 35 (Au 622) "Special Reports Applying Agreed-Upon Procedures" should be followed when reporting upon the results of agreed-upon audit procedures

      a. The entity's financial statements should not accompany the special report

505 Reports on Comparative Financial Statements (SAS 15)

Supersedes para 315.11, 509.49, and 516.11-.12

A. The fourth standard of reporting applies to statements of prior periods presented for comparative purposes

  1. Continuing auditors should update their report to cover comparative statements
  2. Ordinarily date report on comparative statements as of completion of the most recent examination
  3. Standard report for two annual periods (changes from standard report recommended in SAS 2, para 7 are underlined)

> We have examined the balance sheets of ABC Company as of [at] December 31, 19X2 and 19X1, and the related statements of income, retained earnings, and changes in financial position for the years then ended. Our examinations were made in accordance with generally accepted auditing standards and, accordingly, included such tests of the accounting records and such other auditing procedures as we considered necessary in the circumstances.

In our opinion, the financial statements referred to above present fairly the financial position of ABC Company as of [at] December 31, 19X2 and 19X1, and the results of its operations and the changes in its financial position for the years then ended, in conformity with generally accepted accounting principles applied on a consistent basis.

4. The auditor should be alert for circumstances affecting prior year statements, audit reports, and disclosures in updating his report

B. The auditor may express an unqualified opinion on one period's statements and modify or disclaim on other periods' statements presented

1. All substantive reasons should be explained in a middle paragraph

a. Not required for a change in accounting principle (Section 509.29-.47)

2. Opinion paragraph should be appropriately modified

a. With reference to the explanatory paragraph

C. Revision of previous reports may be required if the auditor becomes aware of circumstances affecting the appropriateness of previous audit reports issued on comparative statements

1. Events which cause revision of previously issued audit reports

a. Subsequent resolution of an uncertainty

1) Updated report requires no modification

b. Discovery of an uncertainty that may affect prior period statements

1) May need to modify or to disclaim updated report

c. Subsequent correct restatement of prior period statements which were not in accord with GAAP

1) Updated report requires no modification but should explain restatement

2. All substantive reasons for revision of a previously issued report should be disclosed in a separate paragraph(s)

3. If the revised report is other than unqualified, the opinion paragraph should refer to the explanatory paragraph

4. The explanatory paragraph should disclose

a. Date of previous report
b. Type of opinion previously expressed
c. Circumstances calling for a changed report
d. The updated opinion differs from the previous opinion

D. Predecessor auditors normally can (but are not required to) reissue a report on comparative statements

1. At the request of the client to perform the service
2. After

a. Reading the current statements
b. Comparing statements previously issued with current format (i.e., current comparative statements)
c. Obtaining a representation letter from the successor auditor indicating

       1) Absence of knowledge of anything materially affecting statements reported on by predecessor

3. If predecessor has reason to believe events occurred which may affect the previously issued opinion,

    a. The auditor should inquire and perform procedures to determine whether the previously issued report needs to be revised

4. Unrevised reissued reports should be dated per the original report

    a. Revised reissued reports should be dual dated

5. No reference should be made to the successor auditor

E. If the predecessor's report is not presented, the successor's report should be modified

1. Successor's report should indicate

    a. Comparative statements were audited by other CPAs
    b. Date of their report
    c. Type of opinion expressed by predecessor
    d. Substantive reasons if not unqualified

2. If comparative statements are restated, disclose

    a. A predecessor previously reported on prior statements
    b. A review of the adjustments was made
    c. Footnote describing the adjustments
    d. Adjustments that were made are appropriate

509 Reports on Audited Financial Statements (SAS 2)

Para 49 superseded by SAS 15, now Section 505

A. Supersedes SAS 1 sections

1. 510.01-515.10 comprising discussion of the various types of opinions
2. 535.01-542.04 discussing

    a. Opinions on prior years' statements
    b. Circumstances requiring short-form departure
    c. Restrictions imposed by the client

3. 544.01 concerning lack of conformity with GAAP
4. 547.01-547.04 discussing uncertainties caused by possible future developments

B. Applies to a complete set of financial statements or an individual statement, e.g., a balance sheet

1. Does not apply to unaudited statements
2. Does not apply to special presentations (Section 621)
3. An unqualified opinion may be expressed on one statement and qualified opinion or disclaimer may be expressed on another

C. The first phrase in the opinion paragraph of the example short-form has been changed to "In our opinion, the financial statements referred to above present" from "the aforementioned financial statements present"

1. If a statement of changes in stockholders' equity accounts is presented, identify in the scope paragraph

    2. Report may be addressed to client company or board of directors or stock-holders

        a. To partners, proprietor, etc., if unincorporated

        b. To client if examinee is not client, i.e., examination of a company for a third party

D. Circumstances resulting in departure from short-form

    1. Scope of exam is restricted because necessary procedure(s) is (are) not carried out

        a. For example

            1) Timing of work
            2) Inability to obtain sufficient, competent evidential matter
            3) Inadequacy of accounting records

        b. Decision to qualify or disclaim is based on importance of omissions

            1) Nature, magnitude, potential effect
            2) Significance to statements is greater if they affect many statement items

        c. Observation of inventory and confirmation of receivables are commonly restricted

            1) If client-imposed, CPA should generally disclaim

        d. If the CPA reports on only one statement and audit procedures are not limited, the restriction (quite acceptable) is in reporting objectives, not audit scope

    2. Reference to the report of another CPA reflects division of responsibility and is not a qualification of opinion

        a. Disclosed in scope paragraph and referred to in opinion paragraph. (See Section 543 of SAS 1.)

    3. Departure from GAAP requires qualified or adverse opinion

        a. Materiality determines choice of adverse or qualified opinion

            1) Dollar magnitude, i.e., relative size
            2) Qualitative judgments

                a) Significance to operations
                b) Pervasiveness (number of items affected)
                c) Impact on statements taken as a whole

        b. Inadequate disclosure is a departure

            1) CPA should disclose in report, if practicable, and render qualified or adverse opinion

    4. Departure from a promulgated GAAP is covered by ethics rule 203

    "A member shall not express an opinion that financial statements are presented in conformity with generally accepted accounting principles if such statements contain any departure from an accounting principle promulgated by the body designated by Council to establish such principles which has a material effect on the statements taken as a whole, unless the member can demonstrate that due to unusual circumstances the financial statements would otherwise have been misleading. In such cases his report must describe the departure, the approximate effects thereof, if practicable, and the reasons why compliance with the principle would result in a misleading statement."

    a. If departure is justified, a middle paragraph(s) should describe the situation, effects, and reasons therefor

       1) No modification of opinion paragraph required

5. GAAP not consistently applied

    a. Requires report modification as to consistency (Section 546, SAS 1)

6. Uncertainties are matters which are <u>not</u> susceptible to reasonable estimation

    a. Estimates are commonly made of other items for which there <u>is</u> a basis for reasonable estimates

       1) Examples are asset lives, receivable collectibility, inventory value and warranty liability

       2) If the CPA disagrees with the client's determination and amount is material, render qualified or adverse opinion

    b. Conversely, uncertainties cannot be reasonably estimated and thus it is not known whether statements should be adjusted or in what amount

       1) Uncertainties with respect to specific matters may be isolated and understood

          a) Recovery of a deferred cost

          b) Specific litigation

       2) The impact of multiple uncertainties or complex uncertainties is often difficult to determine

          a) Recurring losses

          b) Deficiencies in working capital

          c) Violation of loan covenants

          d) Inability to obtain financing

    c. CPA should not estimate outcome of uncertainties for management

       1) CPA must determine whether to qualify

       2) Qualification unnecessary if probable effects are minimal

    d. If statements affected by uncertainties also violate GAAP, opinion should also be modified to so reflect

    e. The qualifying phraseology in the opinion paragraph should be the same regardless of the expected outcome of the uncertainty. The alternatives are

       1) Recognition in subsequent statements

       2) Adjustment of statements upon which uncertainty qualification was expressed

       3) No monetary effect on statements

7. Emphasis of a matter by CPA may be made in an unqualified opinion

    a. For example

       1) Client is a component of a larger entity

       2) Significant transactions with related parties

        3) Important subsequent events
        4) Matter affecting comparability

E. Unqualified opinion

  1. Statements present fairly

     a. Financial position
     b. Results of operations
     c. Changes in financial position

  2. In conformity with GAAP

     a. Including adequate disclosure

  3. Consistently applied
  4. After examination per GAAS

F. Qualified opinion

  1. States that "except for" or "subject to" qualification "the statements..." are qualified with respect to

     a. Scope

        1) Lack of sufficient competent evidential matter
        2) Restriction in scope of exam

     b. Or opinion

        1) Material violation of GAAP
        2) Material change in GAAP
        3) Significant uncertainties

     c. And disclaimer or adverse opinion not appropriate

  2. Do not modify opinion paragraph unless qualifying

     a. Reference to another CPA is not a qualification

  3. If unaudited material appears in statements (e.g., merger or subsequent event date) and identified as "unaudited," no reference is needed in report

     a. If unaudited data should have been audited, qualification or disclaimer is necessary

  4. All substantive reasons for qualification should be presented in a separate middle paragraph(s)

     a. Explanatory paragraph(s) should be referred to in the opinion paragraph
     b. Explanatory paragraph(s) requirement does not apply when opinion paragraph has been modified due to change in GAAP (consistency exception)

     c. The explanatory paragraph(s) should disclose effect of qualification problem on each statement

        1) If disclosures are made in a footnote, the explanatory paragraph may be shortened by referring to the footnote

     d. The explanatory paragraph(s) should explain whether the qualification arose because

        1) Client and CPA opinions differed
        2) An uncertainty existed

5. When qualification results from scope limitation or insufficient evidence, it should be described in

    a. Scope paragraph
    b. Opinion paragraph
    c. Explanatory paragraph

        1) Should not be explained in a footnote

6. Qualified opinions should contain the word "except" or "exception"

    a. Unless the qualification is due to an uncertainty and then "subject to" should be used

7. The wording for a qualification due to a scope limitation should indicate the potential effects of the limitation rather than the limitation itself

    a. Wording similar to, "In our opinion, except for the above mentioned scope limitation" should not be used

G. Adverse opinions state that statement(s), taken as a whole, do not present fairly in accordance with GAAP

    1. A separate paragraph of the report should disclose

        a. All substantive reasons for the opinion
        b. Effect on each of the individual statements--if not determinable, so state

    2. The opinion paragraph should refer directly to the separate explanatory paragraph(s)

        a. Reservations of noncompliance with GAAP concerning other matters not causing the adverse opinion should be disclosed

    3. Normally, no mention of consistency should be made in the adverse opinion

        a. If CPA has exceptions as to consistency, so state

H. Disclaimer indicates no opinion is expressed

    1. All substantive reasons for disclaimer should be disclosed in separate paragraph(s)

        a. Disclaimer is not appropriate when CPA believes violations of GAAP exist
        b. Any reservations about fair presentation should be disclosed

    2. If due to a significant scope limitation, a separate paragraph should explain the noncompliance with GAAS

        a. No reference should be made to procedures carried out

I. Piecemeal opinions may overshadow or contradict an adverse opinion or disclaimer and should not be issued

510   Expression of Opinion

511   Unqualified Opinion

512   Qualified Opinion

513   Adverse Opinion

514   Disclaimer of Opinion

515   Piecemeal Opinion

All superseded by SAS 2, now Sec. 509

516   Unaudited Financial Statements

517   Reporting when CPA is not Independent

518   Negative Assurance

All superseded by SAS 26, now Sec. 504

519   Reports on a Limited Review of Interim Financial Information

Superseded by SAS 36, now Section 722

530   Dating of Report

A.   Generally last day of fieldwork

1.   No responsibility after this date (except in SEC filings)

B.   Events occurring after fieldwork but before issuance of report

1.   If adjustment of accounts is made without disclosure, date last day of field work

2.   If event is disclosed, either

a.   Dual date

1)   Report is dated as of last day of fieldwork
2)   Subsequent event footnote dated later

b.   Report dated as of the subsequent event

1)   Responsibility extends to later date
2)   Extend procedures of Au 560.12 to this date

C.   Reissuance of report

1.   Use of original report date implies no further examination
2.   Subsequent events may require modification of statements, opinion, or notes. Dual date as above.

535   Opinions on Prior Year Statements

540   Circumstances Requiring Departure from Standard Report

541   Client Restrictions

All superseded by SAS 2, now Section 509

542   Other Conditions Restricting Scope

Para .01-.04 superseded by SAS 2, now Section 509

A. If CPA cannot satisfy himself as to beginning inventories with alternative procedures,

   1. Disclose limitations and qualify or disclaim

B. Long-term investments

   1. If material, CPA needs sufficient competent evidential matter
   2. When insufficient evidential matter exists, disclose and qualify or disclaim

543 Part of Examination Made by Other Independent Auditors

Para 18 superseded by SAS 7, now Section 315

A. Principal auditor

   1. CPA must decide whether his participation is sufficient to be principal CPA

      a. Materiality of his overall examination
      b. Knowledge of overall statements
      c. Importance of components examined by CPA to overall enterprise

   2. Principal auditor must decide whether to accept responsibility of other CPA

      a. If so, no mention is made in opinion
      b. If not, disclose work of other CPA and divide responsibility

   3. Other CPA remains responsible for his/her work in either case

B. Decision not to refer to other CPA

   1. No mention is made when CPA satisfied him/herself about other CPA's

      a. Independence
      b. Professional reputation
      c. Audit examination

   2. Usually the case when

      a. Other CPA is associated or correspondent CPA
      b. Other CPA retained and supervised by CPA
      c. CPA satisfied him/herself about other CPA's work
      d. Portion of statements examined by other CPA is not material

   3. Avoids misinterpretation by reader of degree of responsibility taken
   4. Possible additional procedures

      a. Visit other CPA and discuss audit
      b. Review other CPA's audit programs
      c. Review workpapers of other CPA
      d. Discuss matters with management of component examined by other CPA
      e. Perform supplemental procedures on component

C. Decision to refer to other CPA

   1. Possible reasons

      a. Impracticable to review other CPA's work or perform other procedures
      b. Component material part of overall statements

   2. Report should clearly indicate the divided responsibility in both paragraphs

3. Report should indicate the magnitude of other CPA's examination

    a. Dollar amounts or percentages of

        1) Total assets
        2) Total income
        3) Or other appropriate criteria

    b. If more than one other auditor, percentages covered may be stated in aggregate
    c. The other CPA may be named

        1) Only with his/her permission
        2) His/her report must be presented with principal report

4. Reference to other CPA is not a qualification

    a. Indicates divided responsibility

D. Procedures applicable to either method

  1. Make inquiries about professional reputation of other CPA

    a. AICPA, state society, local chapter, etc.
    b. Other CPAs
    c. Bankers and creditors
    d. Other

  2. Obtain representation from other CPA that s/he is independent per AICPA or SEC
  3. Ascertain that other CPA

    a. Knows statements and his/her report will be used by principal CPA
    b. Is familiar with GAAP and GAAS
    c. Is familiar with SEC rules if applicable
    d. Knows a review of intercompany transactions will be made by the principal CPA

  4. If CPA determines s/he can neither assume responsibility nor rely on work of other CPA, s/he should qualify or disclaim

    a. Reasons should be stated
    b. Magnitude of portion of statements affected disclosed

E. Long-term investments

  1. CPA is principal auditor when s/he uses audited statements of investee under the equity method

F. Qualifications in other CPA's report

  1. CPA must determine materiality of other CPA's qualification to CPA's opinion on overall statements

    a. If other report not presented and qualification not material, need not reference qualification
    b. If other CPA's report is presented, CPA may wish to explain disposition of other CPA's qualification

G. Restated statements following pooling

  1. Following pooling, CPA may express opinion on restated statements of prior periods

      a. If CPA cannot satisfy him/herself with respect to the restated statements opinion on only the combining of the statements is appropriate, i.e., given the individual company statements, the pooling method was properly applied

      b. No opinion should be expressed unless CPA formerly expressed opinion on one of the combining companies

  2. If CPA expresses an opinion on the compilation, s/he does not assume responsibility for work of other CPAs or restated statements

      a. CPA's review is directed toward math accuracy and compliance with GAAP

      b. CPA may inquire about:

          1) Elimination of intercompany transactions
          2) Combining adjustments and eliminations
          3) Adjustments to attain uniformity
          4) Manner of disclosure

544   Lack of Conformity with GAAP

Para .01 superseded by SAS 2, now Section 509

A. GAAP and first reporting standard equally applicable to statements of regulated companies (e.g., insurance and financial institutions)

B. If statements of regulated companies lack conformity with GAAP

  1. Qualified or adverse must be issued
  2. "An adverse opinion may be accompanied by an opinion on supplementary data which are presented in conformity with GAAP"
  3. A supplementary opinion may be expressed stating conformity with prescribed accounting

      a. Must be accompanied by qualified or adverse

545   Inadequate Disclosure

See SAS 21, now Section 435, for segment disclosure requirements

A. Information essential for fair presentation must be disclosed in statements or related notes

  1. When client does not adequately disclose, include information in middle paragraph, if practicable, and express qualified or adverse opinion

  2. Additional explanatory matter (not required for adequate disclosure) included in middle paragraph, does not constitute qualification (no modification of opinion paragraph)

B. Omission of funds statement

  1. If omission <u>not</u> approved by APB 19, qualify opinion

      a. Do not prepare funds statement to include in report

546   Reporting on Inconsistency

A. Change in principle

    1. Indicate nature of change

        a. Make concurrence explicit using phrase "with which we concur"

    2. If change requires retroactive treatment, state

        a. "Consistent after retroactive restatement"
        b. No mention if in year subsequent to change

    3. Change in principle not requiring restatement should be referred to as long as year-of-change statements are presented

        a. Not for change in beginning of first year presented

B. Changes not conforming to GAAP

    1. A change in principle should be based on the fact that

        a. New principle is within GAAP
        b. Method of change is according to GAAP
        c. Management justification is reasonable

    2. If the new principle or <u>method</u> of accounting change is <u>not</u> in accord with GAAP

        a. Qualified (as to both conformity and consistency), or
        b. Adverse if sufficiently material

    3. If change does not have reasonable justification

        a. Qualified opinion relating to:

            1) Conformity with GAAP
            2) Consistency of application

    4. Reporting in subsequent years after qualification for change

        a. CPA should continue to express reservation about the change as long as the period-of-change statements are presented

        b. If client continues to use unacceptable method, CPA should express qualified or adverse
        c. If change is accounted for prospectively when restatement or cumulative adjustment required, current results may be misstated

            1) Express qualified or adverse opinion

        d. If reasonable justification was not presented in.year of change, CPA should continue to express exception as long as the statements of the year-of-change are presented

C. Reports following a pooling

    1. Prior years' statements should be restated in year of pooling to provide comparability

        a. Lack of comparability results in inconsistency--qualify
        b. If single period statements are presented, pooling transaction and restated data should be disclosed in a footnote

D. First examination

    1. CPA should satisfy him/herself with respect to consistent application of GAAP

        a. Inadequate records or client limitations may preclude such satisfaction

        1) May result in balance sheet only opinion with no consistency phrase

    b. If prior statements and records were <u>not</u> in accordance with GAAP, the CPA may omit reference to consistency

E. Pro forma effects of accounting changes

    1. Pro forma effects of retroactive changes should be disclosed when single year statements are presented

547 Unusual Uncertainties

Superseded by SAS 2, now Section 509

550 Other Information in Documents Containing Audited Financial Statements (SAS 8)

A. This statement applies to

    1. Annual reports

        a. For owners
        b. Of charitable organizations distributed to public
        c. Filed with the SEC under the 1934 Act (e.g., 10-K)

    2. Not reports filed with the SEC in registration statements under the 1933 Act (initial offerings)
    3. Not other information on which auditor is engaged to express an opinion

B. The auditor's responsibility with respect to the other information is limited to financial information identified in the audit report

    1. No obligation to perform any audit procedures on other data
    2. Only to read to determine if material inconsistencies exist with the data (or its presentation) in the financial statements

C. If a material inconsistency exists, the auditor shall consider whether the statements and/or audit report need revision

    1. If no revision needed, the auditor should request that the other information be revised to eliminate the material inconsistency

    2. If the other information is not revised, the auditor should (depending on the circumstances)

        a. Insert explanatory paragraph in audit report
        b. Withhold use of report from client
        c. Withdraw from engagement

D. The auditor should discuss any material misstatements (in contrast to material inconsistencies) with the client

    1. The auditor may not have the expertise to assess the validity of some assertions

        a. Valid differences of opinion may exist

    2. The client should receive advice from others, e.g., legal counsel
    3. If a material misstatement of fact continues to exist, the auditor should

        a. Notify client in writing
        b. Consult legal counsel

551 Reporting on Information Accompanying the Basic Financial Statements in Auditor-Submitted Documents (SAS 29)

Supersedes SAS 1, Section 610

A. Statement provides guidance on reporting when auditor submits to client or others a document containing information in addition to the basic financial statements and auditor's standard report

B. Auditor's standard report covers the basic financial statements: balance sheet, statement of income, statement of retained earnings or changes in stockholders' equity, and statement of changes in financial position

  1. The following are considered part of basic financial statements

      a. Notes to financial statements
      b. Descriptions of accounting policies
      c. Schedules and explanatory materials

  2. For purpose of this statement, "basic financial statements" also include

      a. An individual basic financial statement, e.g., a balance sheet or statement of income
      b. Financial statements prepared on a comprehensive basis of accounting other than GAAP

C. Information covered by this statement is presented outside the basic financial statements and is not necessary for presentation in conformity with GAAP. Such information includes

  1. Consolidating information
  2. Historical summaries
  3. Statistical data
  4. Other material

D. When auditor submits a document containing audited financial statements, s/he has responsibility to report on all information included in the document

  1. If auditor's standard report is included in a client prepared document and auditor was not engaged to report on information accompanying basic financial statements, auditor's responsibility is covered in SAS 8 (Section 550) and other statements covering specific types of information, e.g., SAS 27 (Section 553)
  2. Auditor's report on information accompanying basic financial statements in auditor-submitted document has same objective as auditor's report on basic financial statement

      a. Describe character of examination
      b. Describe degree of responsibility taken

E. Guidelines to apply to auditor's report on information accompanying basic financial statements in auditor-submitted document

  1. State examination was made for purpose of forming opinion on basic financial statements taken as a whole
  2. Identify accompanying information
  3. State that accompanying information is presented for purposes of additional analysis and is not a required part of basic statements

4. Include an opinion on accompanying information or disclaimer if audit proce-
    dures not applied

    a. If an opinion is given, report should indicate that the accompanying
        information is fairly stated in all material respects as it relates to
        the basic financial statements taken as a whole

    b. An opinion may be expressed on portions of the accompanying information
        and a disclaimer given on the remainder

    c. If auditor disclaims an opinion on all or part of accompanying infor-
        mation, label information "Unaudited" or refer to auditor's disclaimer

5. Report on accompanying information may be added to auditor's standard report
    or may appear separately in auditor-submitted document

F. Additional reporting considerations

1. The measurement of materiality is the same as when forming an opinion on
    basic financial statements taken as a whole

    a. Accordingly, auditor need not apply procedures as extensive as would be
        necessary to express an opinion on information taken alone

2. If auditor concludes accompanying information is materially misstated, s/he

    a. Should propose revision to client, and
    b. If revision not accepted, audit report should be modified or the
        misstated information should be omitted

3. Auditor should consider the effect of any modifications in his/her standard
    report when reporting on accompanying information

    a. If a qualified opinion is issued on the basic financial statements, the
        impact on any accompanying information should be indicated

    b. If an opinion on basic statements is adverse or disclaimed, no opinion
        should be expressed on any accompanying information; any opinion would
        be similar to a piecemeal opinion, para AU 509.48 and para 621.12

4. Where client asks for inclusion in auditor-submitted document of non-
    accounting information and accounting information not directly related to
    basic financial statements, the auditor should generally disclaim an opinion
    unless records supporting the information were tested by auditor

G. When supplementary information required by the FASB is outside the basic
    statements

1. Opinion disclaimed unless the auditor is engaged to express an opinion on it
2. Report expanded, per para 553.08, if required information is omitted, de-
    parts from FASB guidelines, or auditor procedures prescribed by Section 553
    not applied

H. Consolidating information, if included, should be suitably identified and report
    should describe character of examination of consolidating information

1. If auditor was engaged to express an opinion only on consolidated financial
    statements and not on individual statements

    a. Auditor should be satisfied consolidating information is suitably
        identified (e.g., Consolidated Balance Sheet--December 31, 19X1, with
        Consolidating Information)

    b. Auditor should add to report a statement that consolidating information is fairly stated in all material respects in relation to consolidated financial statements taken as a whole

  2. If auditor was engaged to express opinion on both the consolidated financial statements and the individual financial statements

    a. Responsibility for the individual statements equal to that for consolidated statements

    b. Individual statements should include disclosures necessary for each to be presented in accordance with GAAP

I. Any comments describing procedures applied to specific financial statement items should be placed apart from other information accompanying the basic financial statements

  1. Should not contradict or detract from the scope description in the standard report

J. If more than one document containing the audited financial statements exists, the auditor must be satisfied that the basic financial statements in all such documents contain enough information for presentation in accordance with GAAP

  1. E.g., an auditor must be satisfied that the accompanying information in the auditor-submitted document will not support an allegation charging nondisclosure of information of which the auditor is aware in the client document

552 Reporting on Condensed Financial Statements and Selected Financial Data (SAS 42)

A. Provides guidance on reporting in a client prepared document which contains information derived from complete audited financial statements and reported as

  1. Condensed financial statements
  2. Selected financial data

B. Condensed financial statements do not contain sufficient detail to present financial position, results of operations, or changes in financial position in conformity with GAAP. Therefore

  1. Condensed financial statements should be read in conjunction with most recent complete financial statement
  2. Auditor should report on condensed financial statements in a different manner than s/he reports on complete financial statements

C. Auditor's report on condensed financial statements (CFS) when auditor has performed complete financial statement audit should indicate

  1. Complete financial statements have been examined and auditor has expressed an opinion thereon
  2. Date of auditor's complete financial statement report
  3. Type of opinion expressed
  4. Whether information in condensed financial statements is fairly presented in all material respects in relation to the complete financial statement from which it is derived

D. Auditor's report on selected financial data (SFD) should be limited to data derived from audited financial statements

  1. When SFD includes information not derived from audited financial statements, auditor should specifically identify data on which s/he is reporting

2. Auditor's report on SFD should indicate items "C.1.," "C.3.," and "C.4." above
3. When comparative SFD are presented and some of the data was derived from financial statements audited by another independent auditor

   a. Report should state that fact, and
   b. Auditor should not express an opinion on that data

E. When client prepares document which includes CFS or SFD, and

   1. Client document does not include

      a. Complete financial statements, or
      b. Statement referencing information filed with regulatory agency, and

   2. Client is required to file complete audited financial statements with regulatory agency, then

      a. Auditor should request client to either not include auditor's name in documents, or

         1) Include auditor's report on <u>condensed financial statements</u>
         2) Include a disclaimer of opinion in document which contains <u>selected financial data</u>

553 Supplementary Information Required by the FASB (SAS 27)

A. This SAS applies to audits where supplementary data required by the FASB are presented but not audited

   1. And also to voluntary disclosure of data if the data are required of other companies by the FASB

      a. E.g., constant dollar and current cost data by nonpublic companies
      b. Unless client indicates this SAS was not complied with or auditor disclaims

         1) Then, SAS 8 "Other Information in Documents Containing Audited Financial Statements" applies

B. The auditor is required to report on supplementary disclosures only when

   1. Supplementary data required by the FASB are omitted

      a. Auditor does not have to present the supplementary.data

   2. Material departure from FASB guidelines in data measurement or presentation
   3. Auditor is unable to perform prescribed procedures
   4. Also, if the supplementary data are not separated from the financial statements and are not marked as "unaudited," the audit report should be modified to disclaim on the supplementary data

C. Auditor's limited procedures for supplementary disclosures required by the FASB

   1. Determine whether the supplemental information is required in the circumstances
   2. Inquire of management whether supplemental disclosures

      a. Were measured and presented per FASB guidelines
      b. Whether measurement or presentation methods have changed
      c. Are based on significant assumptions or interpretations

  3. Compare the supplemental disclosures to

      a. Management's responses to the foregoing
      b. The audited statements
      c. Other information obtained during the audit

  4. Consider need to include representations in the written representation letter. (See SAS 19, "Client Representations.")

  5. Apply additional procedures required by other applicable SASs

  6. Make additional inquiries if the foregoing procedures indicate possible exceptions

*554 Supplementary Information on the Effects of Changing Prices (SAS 28)

A. SFAS 33 requires "public" entities which meet its size tests to present information on the effects of changing prices; other entities are encouraged to present this information

  1. Required information is presented as supplementary information in externally issued annual reports containing the primary financial statements of the entity

  2. Experimentation is encouraged; entities should develop techniques to fit their situations

B. Auditor inquiries of management per Section 553 relative to their judgments on measurement and presentation should pertain to

  1. Sources of information, including selection criteria, for latest and five most recent fiscal years

  2. Assumptions and judgments made in calculating constant dollar and current cost amounts, e.g., monetary versus nonmonetary classification

  3. The need to reduce measurements of inventory and of PP&E from historical cost/constant dollar amounts or current cost amounts to lower recoverable amounts

C. SFAS 33 also requires explanations of the supplementary information and discussions of its significance in light of the entity's circumstances

  1. Narrative explanations and discussions should be read by the auditor and compared with audited financial statements and required supplementary information

  2. Any inconsistency or misstatement unresolved through discussion with management should be described in the auditor's report on financial statements

*555 Supplementary Oil and Gas Reserve Information (SAS 45)

A. This statement gives guidance in applying the procedures specified in SAS 27

---

  *Review this section quickly as more detailed information is provided than normally asked on the CPA exam.

1. SFAS 69 requires disclosure of proved oil and gas reserve quantities, changes in reserves, a standardized measure of discounted net cash flows relating to reserves, and changes in standardized measure

2. Regulation S-X requires certain supplementary disclosures for SEC reporting firms

B. Determining above amounts requires expertise of a reservoir engineer

C. Auditor's inquiries should be directed at management's understanding of specific requirements of supplementary disclosure, including

1. Factors considered in arriving at reserve quantity information, e.g., quantities owned, domestic and foreign, net of others' interests

2. Items separately disclosed, e.g., reserves subject to long-term agreements with foreign countries where entity acts as producer

3. Factors considered in arriving at reserve value information to meet Regulation S-X requirements

D. Additionally, the auditor should apply the following procedures

1. Ask about qualifications of person who estimated reserve information
2. Compare recent production with earlier reserve estimates and ask about significant variation
3. Compare reserve quantity information with information used for depletion and amortization and ask about differences
4. Ask about methods and bases used to determine reserve value information including whether

   a. Prices used to develop future cash inflows from proved reserves are based on prices received at end of entity's fiscal year and are in accordance with contracts and regulations

   b. Entity's projections for nature and timing of future development of proved reserves and production rates are consistent with plans for development

   c. Estimates of future development and production costs are based on year-end costs and assumed continuation of existing economic conditions

   d. Future income tax expenses are computed using appropriate tax rates
   e. Future net cash flows have been properly discounted
   f. For full-cost firms, future costs of development coincide with depletion and amortization amounts
   g. Changes in standardized measure of discounted net cash flows are properly computed

5. Ask if bases and reserves are documented and if information is current

E. Additional inquiries may be necessary if information does not meet the guidelines of Section 553

1. Auditor may not be in a position to evaluate responses due to nature of oil and gas reserve information

   a. Limitation should be disclosed in report

*556 Supplementary Mineral Reserve Information (SAS 40)

A. This statement gives guidance in applying procedures specified in Section 553 (SAS 27)

B. SFAS 39 requires entities of certain size that have mineral reserves (except oil and gas) to disclose quantity and price information

C. The quality of an estimate of proved, or proved and probable, reserves depends on the availability, completeness and accuracy of data, as well as experience and judgment of a specialist

D. In applying procedures in Section 553 (SAS 27) auditor's inquiries should be directed to management's understanding of supplementary reserve information disclosures, including

1. Separate disclosure of

   a. Estimated quantities of mineral reserves used for cost amortization purposes
   b. Estimated physical units, or percentages, or significant mineral products in mineral product extracted
   c. Quantities of significant mineral product extracted and/or produced by milling or similar process
   d. Quantity of mineral reserves purchased or sold in place during year
   e. Average market price for each significant mineral product

2. Factors considered for determining reserve quantity information reported

   a. Reserves attributable to consolidated subsidiaries
   b. Proportionate share of reserves of proportionately consolidated investees

3. Separate disclosure of entity's proportional interest in reserves of investees accounted for by the equity method

E. Auditor's procedures should also include

1. Inquire as to

   a. Who made the estimates--mining engineer, geologist, or other specialist
   b. Whether methods and bases used for estimating reserve information are documented and reviewed on a current basis
   c. Method and bases used to calculate market price information disclosed and compare to appropriate sources

2. Compare

   a. Recent production to reserve estimates of significant property
   b. Reserve quantity information to corresponding depletion and amortization information
   c. Production information to corresponding information used to prepare financial statements
   d. Information concerning mineral reserves purchased or sold in place, to information used to prepare financial statements
   e. Make inquiries for any significant differences of the above comparisons

---

*Review this section quickly as more detailed information is provided than normally asked on the CPA exam.

F. Section 553 (SAS 27) indicates auditor should make additional inquiries if s/he believes information may not be presented within applicable guidelines

    1. Limitation will need to be reported if auditor cannot evaluate additional inquiries

560 Subsequent Events

Para .12d amended by SAS 12, now Section 337

A. Two types of events subsequent to balance sheet date and prior to reporting date

    1. Events that provide additional evidence about conditions that existed at the balance sheet date

        a. Adjust statements

            1) Events affecting realization of assets or settlement of estimated liabilities usually require adjustment

    2. Events arising after balance sheet date

        a. Disclose
        b. If significant, disclose with pro forma statements

            1) Sale of bond or stock issue
            2) Purchase of a business
            3) Litigation settlement (litigation based on a post-balance sheet event)
            4) Fire or flood loss
            5) Receivable loss (loss due to a post-balance sheet event)

        c. If extreme, a middle explanatory paragraph may be appropriate in the audit report

B. Reissued statements (subsequent to reporting date) in reports to regulatory agencies should not be adjusted unless adjustments are corrections of error or prior period adjustments per APB

    1. Same criteria apply to reissued comparative statements

C. Auditing procedures subsequent to year end and prior to report date

    1. Certain procedures are applied to transactions after year end

        a. To assure proper year-end cutoff
        b. To help evaluate asset and liability valuation

    2. In addition, the CPA should perform other procedures near completion of fieldwork to identify subsequent events

        a. Read latest interim statements

            1) Make comparison with other data

        b. Discuss with management

            1) Existence of contingent liabilities
            2) Significant changes in shareholders' equity items
            3) Statement items accounted for on tentative data
            4) Unusual adjustments in the subsequent period

        c. Read minutes of Board of Directors and other committees

            1) Make inquiries when minutes are not available

    d. Obtain lawyer's letter on

        1) Litigation
        2) Impending litigation, claims
        3) Contingent liabilities

    e. Management representation letter on subsequent events

561 Subsequent Discovery of Facts Existing at Report Date

A. Procedures for CPA who becomes aware of facts that may have existed at the date of his/her report which might have affected report

1. Consult with attorney regarding client confidential information
2. Applies to all statements reported on by CPAs

B. CPA has no obligation for additional procedures after report date unless s/he becomes aware of facts that may have existed at report date

1. Does not apply to events occurring after report date
2. Does not apply to resolution of contingencies disclosed in report

C. CPA should determine if subsequently discovered information is

1. Reliable and
2. Existed at date of report
3. If both reliable and existed at date of report

    a. Would report have been affected?
    b. Are persons still relying on the report?

        1) How long since the report was issued?

D. When CPA acts to prevent future reliance on his/her report

1. Statements should be revised and reissued if the effect of the subsequently discovered information can be determined promptly
2. If issuance of statements of a subsequent period is imminent, appropriate revision can be made in such statements
3. If effect cannot be promptly determined and it appears statements will be revised after investigation, persons relying on statements should be notified of facts known to CPA

    a. Client should disclose to regulatory body if appropriate

E. If client refuses to cooperate, CPA should notify each director and explain situation including following steps to be taken by the CPA

1. Notify client that CPA's report cannot be associated with statements
2. Notify regulatory agencies
3. Notify each person known by CPA to be relying on statements

    a. Regulatory authority if widely held

F. Guidelines for disclosure

1. If CPA makes satisfactory investigation

    a. Disclose nature of information and effect on report and statements
    b. Disclosure should be precise and factual and limited to "a." above

        1) No comment on conduct or motives

2. If client did not cooperate

    a. Details not necessary

    b. Indicate information has surfaced and client has not cooperated

610 Long-Form Reports

Superseded by SAS 29, Section 551

620 Special Reports

Superseded by SAS 14, Section 621

621 Special Reports (SAS 14)

Supersedes Section 620 of SAS 1

A. Special reports are appropriate for

    1. Statements prepared per a "comprehensive basis of accounting" other than GAAP

    2. Specific elements of statements

    3. Compliance with contractual or regulatory requirements related to audited statements

    4. Information on prescribed forms or prescribed audit reports

    5. Not

        a. Limited reviews of interim statements

        b. Forecasts, projections, feasibility studies

        c. Compliance with contractual or regulatory requirement unrelated to financial statements

B. Reports per a comprehensive basis of accounting other than GAAP

    1. GAAS applies to examinations of any statements

        a. Statements are presentations of financial data and explanatory notes based on accounting records per a comprehensive basis of accounting

            1) Includes the four basic statements, and

            2) Statements of assets and liabilities excluding shareholder equity

            3) Statements of revenue and expense

            4) Summaries of operations

            5) Statements of operations by product line

            6) Statements of cash receipts and disbursements

    2. A comprehensive basis of accounting (allowing issuance of a special report) must be one of the following

        a. Basis of accounting used to comply with government regulatory agency

        b. Basis of accounting used for tax purposes

        c. Cash receipts and disbursements and modified accrual method

        d. A definite set of criteria with substantial authoritative support applied to all material statement items

3. Reports on statements per a comprehensive basis of accounting other than GAAP

    a. Scope paragraph

        1) Statement identification
        2) Per GAAS

    b. Separate middle paragraph

        1) States, or preferably, refers to a statement note explaining basis
        2) Refers to a footnote describing difference between basis used and GAAP
        3) States basis is not per GAAP

    c. Opinion paragraph stating

        1) Statements present fairly per basis (otherwise disclose reasons)
        2) Consistently applied

4. Reports on one or more items in statements, e.g., rents, royalties, etc.

    a. All GAAS apply, except first and second standards of reporting

        1) First standard of reporting is applicable if report is per GAAP

    b. If audit is a special engagement to report on the specific item rather than a part of an overall audit

        1) Audit procedures may have to be extended due to interrelated nature of statement items
        2) The measure of materiality must be related to each individual element rather than statements as a whole

    c. A special report should not be issued on specific elements in statements upon which an adverse or disclaimer was issued, if tantamount to a piecemeal opinion

        1) Allowable only if element(s) reported on not major part of statements

            a) Special report should not accompany statements of entity

    d. Reports on specific elements should

        1) Identify specific elements examined
        2) State if examination was per GAAS (and a part of an overall exam, if so) and possibly audit procedures applied
        3) Identify basis of presentation, e.g., agreement, GAAP, etc.
        4) Describe significant interpretations
        5) Indicate fairness of presentation
        6) If applicable, consistency of applying basis of presentation

5. Special reports on statements per regulatory agency may only be issued if

    a. The report is to be filed only with the regulatory agency
    b. Or if additional distribution is approved by an AICPA pronouncement

6. Unless comprehensive basis of accounting other than GAAP is used, use standard audit report

    a. Modified for departures from GAAP

7. The following statement descriptions should only be used to describe statements per GAAP

    a. Balance sheet
    b. Statement of financial position
    c. Statement of income
    d. Statement of operations
    e. Statement of changes in financial position

8. If statements are not suitably titled, auditor should modify report to disclose this fact

C. Reports on compliance with contractual or regulatory requirements are required in some bond indentures, loan agreements, etc.

    1. May only require negative assurance in the auditor's short-form report, or
    2. A special report usually containing

        a. Negative assurance concerning requirements
        b. Statement whether examination per GAAS and report date

D. Reports on information in prescribed forms

    1. Schedules which prescribe wording of the auditor's report are frequently not acceptable

        a. E.g., assertions not compatible with the auditor's function
        b. Auditor should revise or rewrite report per professional standards

---

622 Special Reports--Applying Agreed-Upon Procedures to Specific Elements, Accounts, or Items of a Financial Statements (SAS 35)

Supersedes SAS 14, paras 15-17

A. Accountant may accept engagement whose scope is limited to applying to one or more specified elements, accounts, or items of a financial statement agreed-upon procedures that are insufficient to enable him/her to express an opinion on these elements, accounts, or items, provided

    1. Involved parties have a clear understanding of procedures to be applied **and**
    2. Distribution of report is restricted to named parties

B. Accountant may satisfy these requirements by meeting with named parties to discuss procedures to be applied

C. If accountant is unable to meet with named parties, s/he may apply one of following procedures

    1. Discuss the procedures with legal counsel or appropriate representative of parties
    2. Review relevant correspondence from parties
    3. Compare procedures to written requirements of a supervisory agency
    4. Distribute a draft of the report or a copy of client's engagement letter to the parties involved with a request for comments before report is issued

D. Effects on GAAS

    1. General standards and first standard of fieldwork apply
    2. All other standards are not applicable

E. Accountant's report on results of agreed-upon procedures should

    1. Indicate specified elements, accounts, or items to which procedures were applied
    2. Indicate intended distribution of report
    3. List procedures performed
    4. State accountant's finding
    5. Disclaim an opinion with respect to elements, accounts, or items
    6. State that the report relates only to item specified and not to entity's financial statements taken as a whole

F. Accountant may express negative assurance if s/he has no adjustments to propose to the specified elements, accounts, or items

631 Letters for Underwriters (SAS 38)

A. Overall issues

    1. The statement deals with the relationship of the CPA with the client and underwriters under the Securities Act of 1933

    2. Underwriters wish to perform a "reasonable investigation" of the information in registration statements (this is a defense under the 1933 Act)

        a. The criteria for a reasonable investigation are not clearly established
        b. Underwriters rely on a letter (comfort letter) from CPAs to assist

    3. When a CPA has audited the historical financial statements, s/he may give comfort in the letter with respect to the following

        a. The CPA's independence (explicitly stated)
        b. Compliance of audit with SEC requirements (explicitly stated)
        c. Unaudited statements in registration statement (negative assurance provided)
        d. Changes in statement items subsequent to latest statements (negative assurance provided)
        e. Tables, statistics, and other financial data (negative assurance provided)

    4. A CPA can give comfort only on matters in which his/her professional competence is substantially relevant

        a. The CPA, client, and underwriter should meet to agree on comfort letter content

    5. SEC usually accepts only unqualified or subject to audit reports (type of report issued on annual financial statements is disclosed in comfort letter)

B. Form of comfort letter

    1. Dates

        a. Closing date - securities delivered to underwriter (letter normally so dated)
        b. Cutoff date - last date of CPA's procedures related to comfort letter
        c. Effective date - securities registration becomes effective
        d. Filing date - securities registration filed (recorded) with SEC

    2. Addressee is client, underwriter, or both

3. Letter identifies statements, data examined, and registration statement; CPA's independence; and compliance with the SEC requirements in <u>separate</u> paragraphs

4. Letter should <u>not</u> repeat report on audited statements and should <u>not</u> provide negative assurance about opinion

C. Unaudited statements in registration statement (condensed financial statements and capsule information)

1. Agreed-upon procedures should be outlined

2. Do not use terms such as general review, limited review, test, or check

3. Negative assurance provided only if CPA has audited past annual statements or will audit them

D. Changes in statement items subsequent to latest statements

1. Do not make opinionated statements such as "<u>adverse</u> changes" or "nothing of interest arose"; make objective statements only

E. Tables, statistics, and other financial data

1. Comment only on matters in which CPA's competence has relevance (accounting related - typically under the internal accounting control system)

   a. One would not, for example, provide negative assurance with respect to square footage of facilities

F. Comfort letters should indicate CPA makes no representations concerning legal matters and that report is for underwriter

640   Reports on Internal Control

Superseded by SAS 30 (642)

641   Reports on IC Based on Criteria Established by Governmental Agencies

Superseded by SAS 30 (642)

642   Reporting on Internal Accounting Control (SAS 30)

Supersedes Sections 640 and 641

A. Statement describes

1. Procedures accountant should apply in various types of engagements undertaken to report on an entity's system of internal accounting control

2. Different forms of accountant's report to issue in connection with such engagements

B. Accountant may be engaged to report on entity's system of internal accounting control in several ways; accountant may be engaged to

1. Express an opinion on entity's system of internal accounting control on a specified date or for a specified period of time

2. Report on entity's system, for restricted use of management, specified regulatory agencies, or specified third parties, based solely on study and evaluation of internal accounting control made as part of audit of entity's

financial statements that is insufficient for expressing an opinion on system

3. Report on all or part of entity's system, for restricted use of management or specified regulatory agencies, based on regulatory agencies' guidelines

4. Issue other special-purpose reports on part or all of an entity's system for restricted use of management, regulatory agencies, or other specified parties

C. Accountant may also be involved with entity's system of internal accounting control in ways that do not involve reporting in accordance with this statement, e.g., consulting

1. In these circumstances, accountant may communicate results of engagement by letters, memoranda, and other less formal means solely for internal information of management

D. Expression of opinion on entity's system of internal accounting control

1. General considerations

a. Objectives of internal accounting control stated in section 320.28 are to provide management with reasonable assurance that assets are safe-guarded from unauthorized use and that financial records are reliable to permit preparation of financial statements; objectives are achieved when

1) Transactions are executed in accordance with management's authorization

2) Transactions are recorded as necessary to

a) Permit preparation of financial statements in conformity with GAAP and

b) Maintain accountability for assets

3) Access to assets permitted only in accordance with management's authorization

4) Recorded accountability for assets is compared to existing assets and all discrepancies resolved

b. Safeguarding of assets refers to protection against loss arising from errors and irregularities in processing transactions and handling related assets

1) Does not refer to losses stemming from management's operating decisions

c. Objective of reliability of financial records relates to financial statements issued to external users

d. Internal accounting control as it relates to estimates and judgments involves procedures to provide assurance that estimators review relevant information when making the required estimates and judgments

e. Inherent limitations exist which should be recognized in assessing the effectiveness of internal accounting control systems, e.g.

1) Projection of current evaluation of system to future periods is subject to risk that

a) Procedures may become inadequate because of changes in conditions, or

b) Degree of compliance with prescribed procedures may deteriorate

   f. Engagements to express opinion on internal accounting control and the study and evaluation of internal accounting control for an audit in accordance with GAAS differ in purpose and scope

     1) Auditor's study and evaluation of internal accounting control establishes basis for determining extent to which auditing procedures are to be restricted and assists in planning and performing examination

     2) In audit, auditor may decide not to rely on prescribed control procedures because

       a) Procedures are not satisfactory for his/her purposes, or
       b) Audit effort required to test compliance with procedures would exceed reduction in effort achieved by reliance

     3) Accordingly, study and evaluation of internal accounting control in an audit is generally more limited than that made in an engagement to express an opinion on the system of internal accounting control

     4) However, accountant's opinion of system of internal accounting control <u>does not</u> increase reliability of entity's audited financial statements

   g. Although scope of engagement to express opinion on system of internal accounting control differs from scope of audit, procedures are similar in nature

     1) Study and evaluation made in connection with engagement to express opinion on system may also serve as basis for reliance on internal accounting controls in determining audit tests

     2) Accountant need not apply procedures in audit that duplicate procedures applied for purpose of expressing opinion on entity's system of internal accounting control

   h. Auditor's opinion does not indicate compliance or noncompliance with Foreign Corrupt Practices Act; this is a legal determination

2. Study and evaluation for purpose of expressing an opinion on internal accounting control includes

   a. Planning scope of engagement in which auditor must consider

     1) Nature of entity's operations, e.g., volume of transactions and risk of asset misuse or misappropriation

     2) Overall control environment, e.g., organizational structure, communication methods, management's financial reports, management's supervision of system, and competence of personnel

     3) Extent of recent changes in operations or control procedures
     4) Relative significance of various classes of transactions
     5) Knowledge obtained in past engagements
     6) Which locations to study in multiple location firms
     7) Work performed by internal auditors (follow guidance in Section 322)
     8) Documentation of specific control objectives and related procedures

b. Reviewing design of system to secure information to judge whether control procedures are suitably designed to achieve objectives of internal accounting control, accountant should consider

    1) Flow of transactions through accounting system

        a) Identify classes of transactions, e.g., by cycle of activity
        b) Understand flow from authorization through execution

    2) Specific control objectives that relate to points in processing of transactions and handling of assets where errors or irregularities could occur

    3) Specific control procedures established to achieve specific control objectives

        a) Primary control procedures are applied at points where errors or irregularities could occur in the processing of transactions and the handling of assets (e.g., monthly bank account reconciliation)

        b) Secondary controls are those administrative controls which also help to achieve a specific internal accounting control objective (they are not a part of the processing of transactions or the handling of assets--e.g., comparison of actual to budgeted costs)

c. Testing compliance with prescribed procedures to provide basis for conclusions on application of prescribed procedures

    1) Nature and extent of compliance tests involve essentially same considerations as tests of compliance in audit

    2) In engagement to express opinion on a system as of a specified date, the period of time necessary for testing compliance varies with nature of control tested

    3) If management has changed its system of internal controls to correct weaknesses, accountant need not consider superseded controls

d. Evaluating results of review of the design of system and tests of compliance

    1) Accountant should identify weaknesses in system and evaluate whether they are material, either individually or in combination

    2) Weakness is material if condition results in more than a relatively low risk of errors or irregularities in amounts that would be material in relation to financial statements

    3) In evaluating an individual weakness, accountant should recognize that

        a) The amounts of errors or irregularities that may occur and remain undetected range from zero to gross amount of assets or transactions exposed to weakness

        b) The risk of errors or irregularities is likely to be different for the different possible amounts within that range (i.e., risk of errors or irregularities in amounts equal to gross exposure may be low, but risk of smaller amounts may be greater)

    4) In evaluating combined effect of individually immaterial weaknesses, accountant should consider

        a) Range of amount of errors or irregularities that may result during same accounting period from two or more individual weaknesses

        b) Probability that such combination of errors or irregularities would be material

    5) Evaluation of identified weaknesses is a subjective process that depends on such factors as nature of accounting process and assets exposed to weaknesses, overall control environment, experience and judgment of those making estimates, and extent that historical data are available

        a) Historical data provide more reasonable basis for estimating risk of errors than they do for estimating risk of irregularities

            1] Errors are unintentional, underlying causes tend to result in predictable level of occurrence

            2] Irregularities are intentional, underlying causes less predictable

3. Accountant should ordinarily obtain management's written representations that

  a. Acknowledge management's responsibility for establishing and monitoring the system of internal accounting control

  b. State that management has disclosed all material weaknesses

  c. Describe any irregularities by individuals having key roles in the system of internal accounting control

  d. State whether there were any changes since report date that would have a significant impact on the system and any changes by management to correct material weaknesses

4. Extent to which accountant documents engagement to express opinion on system of internal accounting control is a matter of professional judgment

  a. Documents prepared by entity to describe its system may be used by accountant in his working papers

5. Form of accountant's report

  a. Independent accountant may express opinion on a system of internal accounting control of any entity for which financial statements in conformity with GAAP, or any other criteria applicable to such statements, can be prepared

  b. Accountant's report expressing opinion on entity's system of internal control should contain

    1) Description of scope of engagement

    2) Date to which opinion relates

    3) Statement that establishment and maintenance of system is responsibility of management

    4) Explanation of broad objectives and inherent limitations of internal accounting control

> 5) Opinion on whether system taken as a whole was sufficient to meet broad objectives of internal accounting control

c. Report should be dated as of date of completion of fieldwork and be addressed to entity, board of directors, or stockholders

d. If study and evaluation discloses conditions that, individually or in combination, result in one or more material weaknesses, accountant should modify opinion paragraph of his/her report by

> 1) Describing material weaknesses
> 2) Stating whether they result from absence of control procedures or degree of compliance with them
> 3) Describing general nature of potential errors or irregularities that may occur as result of weaknesses
>
> 4) Accountant may also report to management other weaknesses even though they are not considered to be material

e. If a document that contains an accountant's opinion identifying a material weakness also includes statement by management asserting that cost of correction of weakness would exceed benefits of reducing risk of errors or irregularities, the accountant

> 1) Should not express any opinion on management's assertion
> 2) May disclaim an opinion on such assertion

f. Accountant should not mention corrective action implemented by management unless s/he is satisfied such procedures are suitably designed and being applied as prescribed

g. If study and evaluation of internal accounting discovers a material weakness and if opinion on system is issued in conjunction with examination of entity's financial statements

> 1) Accountant should indicate that opinion on internal control does not affect report on financial statements

h. Significant scope limitations caused by circumstances and/or client restrictions may require qualified opinion or disclaimer

> 1) If client-imposed, accountant should generally issue a disclaimer

i. Opinions which are formed, in part, by relying on another accountant's report should be referred to in describing scope and in expressing opinion (see Section 543)

j. If subsequent information becomes known to the accountant which might have affected the opinion, follow Section 561

E. Report on internal accounting control based solely on study and evaluation made as part of audit (even though it is not sufficient for expressing opinion on system taken as a whole)

1. Auditor may report in these circumstances, provided report

a. Indicates that it is solely for management, specified agency, or specified third party
b. Describes limited purpose of study and evaluation, and
c. Disclaims opinion on system of internal accounting control taken as a whole

2. If study and evaluation discloses material weaknesses, report should

    a. Describe weaknesses and

    b. State that they were considered in determining audit tests to be applied in examination of financial statements

3. Auditor may disclose immaterial weaknesses if comments on such weaknesses are clearly distinguished from material weaknesses

    a. If more immaterial weaknesses are reported to one group than to another, auditor must be able to defend his/her judgment to the group receiving fewer weaknesses in their report

4. Some reports on internal accounting control contain comments on additional matters (e.g., regulatory agency may require comments on specific parts of administrative control). Auditor should

    a. Modify language of report to

        1) Identify additional matters and distinguish them from internal accounting control

        2) Reasonably describe scope of review and tests concerning those matters

        3) Express appropriate conclusions

    b. Refer to contracts or regulations to determine extent of modification

5. Practice of submitting suggestions or comments concerning aspects of entity's internal accounting control to management by less formal means (e.g., letters and memoranda) is still encouraged

F. Reports based on criteria established by regulatory agencies

    1. Agency may set forth specific criteria for evaluation of adequacy of internal accounting control procedures for their purposes and may require report based on those criteria

    2. Criteria established by agency may be set forth in audit guides, questionnaires, or other publications

        a. Criteria may encompass specified aspects of internal accounting control, specified aspects of administrative control, or compliance with grants, regulations, or statutes

    3. For accountant to be able to issue report, criteria should be in reasonable detail and in terms susceptible to objective application

    4. Accountant's report should

        a. Clearly identify matters covered by study

        b. Indicate whether study included tests of compliance with procedures to be studied in engagement

        c. Describe objective and limitations of internal accounting control and accountant's evaluation of it

        d. State accountant's conclusions, based on agency's criteria, concerning adequacy of procedures studied, with exception concerning any material weaknesses

       e. State its specific purpose, e.g., for a grant, and that it should not be used for any other purpose

          1) If agency requires accountant to report on all conditions not in conformity with agency's criteria, accountant must do so regardless of materiality

          2) Accountant may report on immaterial items and make recommendations for corrective action even if not required by agency

   5. For purposes of these reports, a material weakness includes a

       a. Condition that results in more than a relatively low risk that errors or irregularities which are material in relation to applicable grant or program may occur and it is likely the condition will not be detected by employees in performance of their duties

       b. Condition in which lack of conformity with agency criteria is material in accordance with agency's guidelines for determining materiality

   6. Accountant is not responsible for comprehensiveness of agency's criteria

       a. However, s/he should report any relevant condition even if not covered by agency's criteria

G. Other special purpose reports

   1. Accountant may be engaged to issue special report for restricted use of management, another independent accountant, or other specified third parties

   2. Report may be on all or part of entity's system of internal accounting control or proposed system of internal accounting control

   3. Form of report in these circumstances is flexible; however, it should

       a. Describe scope and nature of accountant's procedures
       b. Disclaim opinion on whether system, taken as a whole, meets objectives of internal accounting control
       c. State accountant's findings
       d. Indicate that report is solely intended for management or specified third party

710 Filing under Federal Securities Statutes

Superseded by SAS 37, Section 711

711 Filing under Federal Securities Statutes (SAS 37)

A. Act of 1933 imposes responsibility on accountants (among others) for false or misleading statements if accountant has consented to having his/her name associated with statements in the registration statement

B. Accountant has defense against lawsuits regarding false or misleading statements if

   1. CPA had, after reasonable investigation, reasonable grounds to believe and did believe that statements were true and not misleading at the effective date of the registration statement
   2. Standard of reasonableness is that of a prudent man in the management of his own property

Ch 5/SAS   Sections 720, 721, and 722   355

C. Other federal statutes contain civil and criminal penalties, under certain conditions, for making or filing misleading statements with the SEC

D. Independent accountant should read the <u>experts section</u> of the prospectus to ascertain that his/her name is not used in a manner that infers greater responsibility than intended. The wording should not imply

   1. That the independent accountant prepared the report
   2. That the financials are not management's representations

E. When an independent accountant's report based on a review of interim financial information is included in a registration statement, prospectus that includes a statement about the independent accountant's involvement should emphasize that the review report is not a <u>report</u> or <u>part</u> of the registration statement as defined in Sections 7 and 11 of the Securities Act of 1933

F. Subsequent events procedures for 1933 Act

   1. CPA should extend his investigation from that of his report to the effective date or as close as possible

      a. CPA should ask client to keep him informed of registration progress
      b. CPA relies mainly on inquiries of client

         1) Read prospectus and relevant portions of registration statement
         2) Obtain written confirmation from managerial and accounting personnel about subsequent items not mentioned in registration statement

   2. CPA has not expressed opinion on unauditeds, but if s/he is aware of non-compliance with GAAP

      a. Insist upon revision
      b. Comment upon in his/her report
      c. Inquire of attorney about withholding opinion from registration statement

   3. Predecessor CPA also has subsequent event responsibility

      a. Read applicable portions of prospectus and registration statement
      b. Obtain representation letter from successor CPA about subsequent events

         1) If required, predecessor statements should be adjusted and commented upon in notes or report

720 Limited Review of Interim Financial Information

Superseded by SAS 24, Section 721

721 Review of Interim Financial Information (SAS 24)

Superseded by SAS 36, Section 722

722 Review of Interim Financial Information (SAS 36)

Supersedes SAS 24, Section 721

A. Provides guidance on nature, timing, and extent of procedures to be applied in a review of interim financial information and on reporting applicable to such engagements

      1. Includes both review of interim information presented alone and along with audited financials

B. Objective is to provide accountant with a basis for reporting whether material modifications should be made for such information to conform with GAAP. Objective is not to provide reasonable basis for opinion as in an audit.

      1. No opinion issued since review does not study and evaluate internal control and won't assure that accountant will become aware of all significant matters

C. Procedures affected by

      1. Timely nature of interim reporting, and
      2. Greater use of estimation than at year end

D. Nature of procedures

      1. Primarily inquiries and analytical review of procedures concerning significant accounting matters, i.e.

          a. Accounting system
          b. Significant changes in system of accounting control
          c. Identify and provide a basis for inquiry about related and independent items that appear unusual
          d. Compare results with preceding interim period, anticipated results and its relationship to predictive patterns
          e. Read minutes of meetings
          f. Read interim information to determine if it conforms with GAAP
          g. Read reports prepared by other accountants
          h. Inquire of officers and executives if they changed accounting procedures or if they applied GAAP in a consistent manner
          i. Events subsequent to interim date with material effect
          j. Obtain written representations from management concerning its responsibility for financial information

E. Timing of procedures

      1. Adequate planning
      2. Perform some work prior to interim date

F. Extent of procedures depends on

      1. Accountant's knowledge of accounting and reporting practices
      2. Accountant's knowledge of weaknesses in internal accounting control

          a. Changes in accounting system
          b. Changes in procedures from prior annual year end
          c. If weakness could prevent interim information from conforming with GAAP, determine if it represents a restriction on scope of engagement

      3. Accountant's knowledge of changes in nature and volume of activities or accounting changes
      4. Application of new or old accounting pronouncements
      5. Accounting records maintained at multiple locations

          a. Similar to making an examination of client's financial statements in accordance with GAAP

      6. Questions raised in performing other procedures

G. Accountant's report

   1. Use of auditor name permitted

      a. Unless scope restricted

   2. Include report in written communication
   3. Report should include

      a. Statement that review in accordance with AICPA standards
      b. Identification of information reviewed
      c. Description of interim review procedures
      d. Statement that an interim review is substantially less in scope than examination per GAAS, and that no opinion is expressed
      e. Statement on awareness of any material modifications needed for conformity with GAAP

   4. Dated as of completion of review
   5. Each page of information marked "unaudited"
   6. May refer to review of other accountants
   7. Circumstances requiring modification

      a. Departures from GAAP

         1) Describe nature and effects

      b. Inadequate disclosure
      c. Uncertainties and a lack of consistency do <u>not</u> require disclosure if properly disclosed in financial statements

H. Interim information accompanying audited financials

   1. Presented as supplementary information outside the statements, or
   2. Included as note to statements and marked "unaudited"
   3. Audit report not modified unless

      a. SEC required interim data omitted or not reviewed
      b. Interim data not appropriately marked "unaudited"
      c. Departure from GAAP in interim data not described in separate review report

730 Unaudited Replacement Cost Information (SAS 18)

Deleted by the Auditing Standards Board

901 Public Warehouses--Controls and Procedures for Goods Held

A. Public warehouse operations

   1. Types

      a. Terminal warehouse. Principal function is furnishing storage, but may provide packaging, etc. Usually stores a wide variety of goods.

      b. Field warehouse. Principal function is financing arrangement. It is usually established on premises of owner of goods and warehouseman's personnel are those of owner. Purpose is to allow warehouseman to take possession of goods and issue warehouse receipts to owner to be used as collateral for loans.

    c. Warehouses may also be classified as to physical configuration, e.g.

      1) Refrigerated
      2) Bulk

  2. Warehouse receipts

    a. Negotiable

      1) Article 7 of UCC
      2) Certain terms to provide for negotiation and transfer
      3) Goods may be surrendered by warehouseman only on basis of receipt

    b. Nonnegotiable

      1) Not required for withdrawal of goods
      2) Allows partial withdrawal

  3. Government regulation

    a. U.S. Warehouse Act
    b. U.S. Commodity Exchange
    c. Tariff Act of 1930

B. Warehouseman

  1. Internal controls

    a. Goods of others are not assets or liabilities, but contingent liability exists for

      1) Loss or improper release of goods
      2) Improper issuance of warehouse receipts
      3) Failure to maintain effective custody of goods

    b. Study and evalute accounting control and administrative control

      1) Administrative control relating to custodial responsibility

    c. Receiving, storing, delivering controls

      1) Receipts issued for goods stored
      2) Receiving reports for all goods stored
      3) Goods stored should be weighed, counted, etc.
      4) Goods stored separately unless fungible (interchangeable)
      5) Instruction that goods are released only on proper authorization; surrender of receipt if negotiable
      6) Limit access to storage area and control keys
      7) Periodic statements to owners asking for notification of discrepancies
      8) Stored goods counted periodically
      9) Regular inspection of perishable goods
     10) Protective devices: sprinklers, burglar alarms, etc.
     11) Goods released only on basis of authorized written instruction
     12) Counts per stock clerks checked by shipping clerks

    d. Warehouse receipts

      1) Prenumbered receipts and account for numbers
      2) Safeguard unused forms
      3) Receipt forms issued only to authorized persons
      4) Signer of receipts ascertains support of receiving reports

    5) Receipts prepared to deter alteration
    6) Limited number of signers

  e. Insurance

    1) Review amount and type of coverage

 2. Additional controls for field warehouses

  a. Controls at both central office and field warehouse
  b. Only nonnegotiable receipts issued from field warehouse
  c. Investigate and approve field arrangements

    1) Consider reputation and financial standing of depositor
    2) Prepare contract to meet requirements of depositor and lender
    3) Evaluate physical effectiveness of facilities
    4) Satisfy legal matters of field facilities lease
    5) Bonding of field employees
    6) Written instructions to field employees
    7) Maintenance of detail records at central office
    8) Examination of field facilities by central employees

 3. Procedures of CPA

  a. Study and evaluate accounting and administrative controls
  b. Test warehouseman's records of all goods held
  c. Test accountability under recorded outstanding warehouse receipts
  d. Observe physical counts and reconcile to records

    1) May not be possible if negotiable: then confirm with original holder

  e. Review insurance coverage

C. Controls and procedures for clients' goods stored at public warehouses

 1. Internal controls (by client)

  a. Consider reputation and financial standing of warehouseman
  b. Inspect physical facilities
  c. Inquire of warehouseman's control procedures
  d. Inquire of warehouseman's insurance
  e. Inquire of government licensing, inspection, etc.
  f. Review of warehouseman's statements and CPA report
  g. Physical count of stored goods
  h. Reconciliation of warehouseman's statements and owner's records

 2. Procedures of CPA (see Section 331)

Guide for a Review of a Financial Forecast (October 1980)

A. This guide provides guidance regarding the scope of the accountant's review of financial forecasts and describes procedures used to evaluate management's underlying assumptions and the appropriate presentation of the forecast

B. The objective of a review is to provide a basis for the accountant's report stating whether the forecast was properly prepared according to stated assumptions and whether the form complies with recommendations in Statement of Position 75-4

 1. Assumptions should provide reasonable support for the forecast

C. The following broad guidelines apply to a review of a financial forecast

1. Ordinarily, an engagement letter would be prepared stating the agreement between management and the accountant regarding the objectives of the review and the services to be provided
2. Work should be performed by persons with sufficient training and skill
3. The accountant should maintain an independence in mental attitude during the engagement (See Code of Professional Ethics)
4. The accountant should exercise due professional care
5. Work should be planned and supervised
6. The accountant should become knowledgeable of the forecasting process in order to determine the scope of the review
7. The accountant should acquire adequate supporting information as a basis for the report
8. The accountant should include a statement concerning whether s/he believes the financial forecast complies with AICPA guidelines and is based on assumptions that provide reasonable support for management's forecast

D. Factors determining the scope of the accountant's review include

1. An understanding of the business through review, inquiry, and/or consultation regarding

    a. Costs of operations and the availability of resources
    b. The entity's market segments
    c. Characteristics and practices of the industry (Refer to AICPA guides and industry publications)
    d. Past trends of the entity or similar entities, e.g., turnover of receivables, administrative policies

2. Previous forecasts which may indicate management's potential for forecasting effectively

    a. Does not determine reliability

3. The time period forecasted and the degree to which historical figures are included

4. Knowledge of the forecasting process through consultation with entity personnel, review of entity documents, and analysis of forecasting techniques

E. Procedures used in evaluating assumptions include

1. Determining whether management has identified the relevant key factors

    a. Investigate sensitive areas and consider the effect on the forecast of variations in factors, e.g., market and technological trends
    b. Analyze previous financial statements (including interim statements) which may highlight principal factors

2. Evaluating the support for assumptions

    a. The accountant should be able to conclude that the assumptions used in preparing the forecast are reasonable

        1) Assumptions need not be considered individually if they have no material effect on the forecast

    b. The accountant cannot determine that any outcome is most probable because of the uncertainty involved in forecasting

    c. The accountant should examine carefully assumptions that are material to forecasted amounts, highly uncertain or risky, or deviate from past trends

    d. In determining whether the assumptions have adequate support, the accountant should consider

        1) The adequacy of the information - internal and external - which gave rise to the assumptions, e.g., engineering studies

        2) Whether assumptions are consistent

        3) The reliability and comparability of the financial information and other data as a basis for assumptions

        4) The logic used in developing assumptions

        5) E.g., support could include obtaining key business ratios or obtaining from client's legal counsel a letter which covers the legality of any planned changes in production or marketing

F. When evaluating the preparation and presentation of the forecast, the accountant should provide reasonable assurance that the forecast

    1. Does, in fact, reflect management's assumptions, that are

        a. Consistent

        b. Translated with mathematical accuracy

    2. Uses accounting principles in accordance with GAAP and is consistent with accounting principles used in financial statements

    3. Complies with the guidelines in Statement of Position 75-4 regarding the disclosure of the assumptions and the presentation of the forecast

G. The accountant should obtain written representations from management that

    1. State management's estimates of the most probable financial position, results of operations, and changes in financial position for the forecasted period

    2. Acknowledge that the forecast is based on management's judgments given the present situation

H. The accountant should consider any historical data for the same period

    1. If it is used in the forecast, and that period is significant to the forecast, the accountant should make a review of the historical information

I. When using specialists for the review, follow the guidelines in SAS 11

J. Working papers for the review should indicate

    1. The work had been planned and supervised

    2. The forecasting process had been evaluated

    3. The assumptions that were used in forecasting and their origination

    4. Whether assumptions were sufficiently supported and the forecast was properly prepared and presented

Appendix - Definitions (Financial Forecasts)

A. A <u>financial forecast</u> represents the most probable financial position, results of operations, and changes in financial position for one or more future periods for an entity

1. <u>Entity</u> describes any unit, present or future, for which financial statements could be prepared according to GAAP or another comprehensive basis of accounting
2. <u>Most probable</u> indicates that the forecast is based on what management believes to be the most likely set of conditions and the most likely course of action
3. <u>Financial forecasts</u> are not the same as financial projections or feasibility studies

   a. A financial projection may not be based on the most likely set of assumptions
   b. A feasibility study analyzes a proposed course of action and may contain a forecast or may be used in preparation of a forecast

B. A <u>forecasting process</u>

1. Uses policies, procedures, methods, and practices to prepare, monitor, and update forecasts
2. Delineates the steps to be followed in preparing the forecast
3. Documents procedures, methods, and practices to be used in preparing the forecast

STATEMENTS ON STANDARDS FOR ACCOUNTING AND REVIEW SERVICES

SSARS 1 Compilation and Review of Financial Statements

Para 14a amended by SSARS 5, para 1
Para 17 amended by SSARS 5, para 2

A. This statement defines and sets standards for

1. Compilation of financial statements
2. Review of financial statements
3. Does not apply to

   a. Statements of publicly traded companies
   b. Preparing a working trial balance
   c. Assisting in adjusting the books of account
   d. Consulting on accounting, tax, and similar matters
   e. Preparing tax returns
   f. Providing bookkeeping or data processing services

      1) Unless the output is financial statements

   g. Processing financial data for clients of other CPAs
   h. Preparing financial forecasts

B. This statement applies to all unaudited engagements for nonpublic companies

1. Accountant's name cannot be associated with financial statements unless

   a. Auditor has compiled or reviewed the statements and the statements are accompanied by the accountant's report
   b. Statements are accompanied by an indication that statements were not compiled or reviewed by the accountant

2. Thus, accountants are precluded from merely typing or reproducing statements

Ch 5   SSARS 1   363

3. Accountants should establish an understanding with the client regarding the services to be performed

   a. Preferably in writing
   b. Provide that engagement cannot be relied on to disclose errors, irregularities, illegal acts, etc.
   c. Accountant will inform the entity of any exception coming to his attention

C. Compilation of financial statements

   1. "Presenting in the form of financial statements information that is the representation of management (owners) without undertaking to express any assurance on the statements"
   2. Accountants should understand accounting principles and practices of client industry

      a. May be obtained from AICPA guides, industry publications, etc.

   3. Accountants should understand the nature of client's business, accounting records, etc.
   4. Accountant is not required to make any inquiries or perform any other verification procedures
   5. Accountant should require client to correct any errors or omissions observed by the accountant

      a. Including misapplication of GAAP

   6. Before issuing a report, the auditor should read the compiled statements and check them for clerical accuracy
   7. Compiled statements should be accompanied by reports stating

      a. A compilation has been performed in accordance with standards established by AICPA
      b. A compilation is a presentation of statements that are a client representation
      c. The statements have not been audited or reviewed and no opinion or assurance is expressed on them
      d. Any procedures performed by the accountant should not be described in the report
      e. The date of completion of compilation should be date of the accountant's report
      f. Each page of the statement should be marked "See Accountant's Compilation Report"
      g. Accountant may issue a report on only one of the financial statements. See SSARS 3 for guidance where accountant is asked to compile statements in a prescribed form calling for a departure from GAAP.

      h. If financial statements do not have disclosures required per GAAP or other basis of accounting, indicate such in a separate paragraph of the report

         1) If only limited disclosures are made, label "Selected Information - Substantially All Disclosures Required by GAAP Are Not Included"

         2) See SSARS 3 for guidance when the financial statements are included in a prescribed form not requiring disclosures

        3) If accountant is not independent, the last paragraph of the accountant's report should disclose this lack of independence

            a) The reason for lack of independence should not be described

    i. If more than one service is rendered, issue report on highest level of service

D. Review of financial statements

    1. "Performing inquiry and analytical procedures that provide the accountant with a reasonable basis for expressing limited assurance that there are no material modifications that should be made to the statements in order for them to be in conformity with generally accepted accounting principles, or, if applicable, with another comprehensive basis of accounting."

        a. Does not assure detection of all items that would be disclosed in an audit

    2. Accountant needs sufficient knowledge of client industry and client company to perform inquiry and analytical procedures to provide a reasonable basis for expressing limited assurance on the statements

        a. Industry knowledge can come from AICPA guides, industry publications, etc.

        b. Accountant's knowledge of client business is ordinarily obtained through experience with client

    3. Accountant's inquiry and analytical procedures consist of

        a. Inquiries concerning client's accounting principles and practices

        b. Inquiries concerning client's procedures for recording, classifying, and summarizing accounting transactions

        c. Analytical procedures to identify unusual items and relationships

            1) Comparison of statements with prior periods
            2) Comparison of statements with anticipated results, e.g., budgets
            3) Study of predictable patterns of elements in the statements

        d. Inquiries concerning stockholders', board of directors', and other committee meetings

        e. Reading the statements to consider if they conform to GAAP

        f. Obtaining reports from other accountants, if any, who have audited or reviewed statements or significant components of the client

        g. Inquiries of person responsible for statements

            1) Whether statements are per GAAP or another comprehensive method of accounting
            2) Changes in the client's business activities or accounting methods
            3) Any exceptions concerning the other analytical procedures
            4) Subsequent events having a material effect on statements

    4. A review does not contemplate

        a. Study and evaluation of internal control
        b. Tests of accounting records, and
        c. Any other audit procedures
        d. However, additional procedures to achieve limited assurance are required if auditor finds mistakes, incomplete presentations, etc.

5. The working papers should contain

    a. Accountant's inquiry and analytical procedures
    b. Unusual matters arising in the review, including their disposition
    c. Possibly a representation letter from chief executive officer and chief financial officers

6. The report on a review of financial statements contains

    a. A review was performed per AICPA standards
    b. A review consists of inquiries and analytical procedures
    c. All information included in the statements is a representation of management
    d. A review is substantially less in scope than an audit

        1) No audit opinion is expressed

    e. The accountant is not aware of any deviations from GAAP
    f. Any other procedures performed by the accountant should not be described
    g. Date of completion of the inquiry and analytical procedures should be the date of the report
    h. Each page of the statements should be marked "See Accountant's Review Report"
    i. Use separate paragraph for modifying the standard report

E. Departures from GAAP

    1. Ask client to revise to comply with GAAP
    2. If not revised, modify report

        a. In separate paragraph with dollar effect of departure
        b. Or if sufficiently material, withdraw from engagement

    3. SSARS 3 provides guidance when the departure is called for by a prescribed form

F. Subsequent discovery of facts existing at date of report

    1. Consult with SAS 1, Section 561 for both compilation and review
    2. Consult an attorney

G. Supplemental information

    1. Accountant should clearly indicate responsibility being taken for supplementary data presented with the statements

        a. By explanation in the review report
        b. Or by a separate report on the other data

            1) Primary purpose of review is statement presentation per GAAP
            2) Other data are only supplementary

                a) Subjected to inquiry and analytical procedures
                b) No modifications to supplementary data are indicated

            3) Alternatively, supplementary data have not been subjected to review

                a) No assurance given by the accountant

H. Change from audit to review or compilation

    1. May be requested by client due to

        a. Changed client requirements
        b. Client misunderstanding
        c. Restriction on audit scope

    2. Auditor should consider

        a. Client reason and implications
        b. Additional effort to complete audit
        c. Additional cost to complete audit

    3. Client may have a reasonable basis for requesting change to compilation or review

        a. But may be motivated by a scope restriction to cover up misstatements, etc.
        b. Accountant should refuse review or compilation if client refuses

            1) Auditor correspondence with client attorney
            2) To sign a representation letter

        c. If audit is substantially complete, the switch to a review or compilation is questionable

    4. If audit engagement is changed, review or compilation report should not refer to

        a. The original engagement
        b. Any auditing procedures performed
        c. Any audit scope limitation

I. Review and compilation reports should cover prior year statements, if presented

J. Effective for reporting periods ending after 6/30/79

SSARS 2 Reporting on Comparative Financial Statements

Supersedes para 50 of SSARS 1

A. Accountants should issue appropriate report(s) covering each period presented as a comparative statement

    1. Comparative statements that have not been audited, reviewed, or compiled, should not be presented in columnar format

        a. They may be presented on separate pages clearly marked "no audit, review, or compilation undertaken," and "accountant assumes no responsibility"
        b. In transition to SSARS

            1) Accountants may reissue their SAS Section 516 or 517 disclaimer on comparative statements
            2) OR modify the accountant's report of the current period to explain the accountant's responsibilities on the comparative statements, i.e., in the last paragraph of the report
            3) OR comply with SSARS 1 standards with respect to the comparative statements

2. The report may be modified for one or more periods presented and unmodified for others

3. Compiled statements omitting most of the disclosures per GAAP should not be presented comparatively with statements containing the disclosures

4. Each page of the statements should state "See Accountant's Report"

B. Continuing accountant's standard report

1. If the same or higher level of service is rendered, the report(s) on comparative statements should be updated

   a. Audit review compilation
   b. Updated report is a reexpression of the same report

      1) OR modification thereof due to currently acquired information

2. If a lower level of service is rendered, the accountant should

   a. Provide a separate paragraph in the current report explaining responsibility for comparative statements
   b. OR reissue report on comparative statements

      1) I.e., use date of original report (dual date for any modification)

   c. Either way the accountant should state that no additional procedures have been applied to the comparative statements

3. Report on comparative statements changed due to GAAP departure

   a. The accountant may during the current period become aware of nonconformity with GAAP in prior statements
   b. The accountant's current report should include a separate paragraph stating

      1) Date of accountant's previous report
      2) Circumstances causing change in accountant's previous report
      3) When applicable, that the prior statements have been changed

C. Predecessor may reissue compilation or review report

1. Not required to, but may, based on agreement with client
2. Predecessor must determine if reissuance is appropriate based on

   a. Current vs. prior period statement format
   b. Newly discovered subsequent events
   c. Changes in the statements affecting the report

3. Predecessor should perform the following procedures

   a. Read current statements and successor's report
   b. Compare prior and current statements
   c. Obtain letter from successor stating successor knows of no problems with prior statements

      1) Predecessor cannot refer to letter in report

4. If anything comes to predecessor's attention that may affect the prior statements or his/her report, the predecessor should

   a. Make necessary inquiries and analytical review
   b. Perform any other necessary procedures

      c. Revise statements and report as appropriate

         1) Dual date report
         2) An explanatory paragraph may be added to explain restatement (not necessary for a change in accounting principle)

  5. Predecessor should not reissue report if all of the above cannot be satisfactorily completed

D. If the predecessor's report is not presented and the successor has not compiled or reviewed the statements,

  1. The successor should add a paragraph stating

      a. Prior (comparative) statements were compiled or reviewed by another accountant(s)
      b. Date of their report
      c. Description of disclaimer or limited assurance given
      d. Description of quotation of any modification

E. Other matters

  1. When current statements were compiled or reviewed and the comparative statements audited

      a. Issue compilation or review report on current year
      b. OR reissue audit report on prior period or add paragraph to current year's report stating

         1) Comparative statements were audited
         2) Date of audit report
         3) Type of opinion expressed
         4) Explanation of any modification of the audit report
         5) No audit procedures were performed after the date of the audit report

  2. When current statements are audited and the comparative statements compiled or reviewed, comply with SASs
  3. If current statements omit substantially all disclosures, and comparative statements are also presented without substantially all disclosures, <u>but</u> were previously reported on with the disclosures - an additional explanatory paragraph is required in the current year's report

  4. When companies change (public/nonpublic) status, report based on their current status

      a. E.g., do not reissue a compilation or review report on company that was nonpublic, but is now public

F. Effective for years ending after 11/29/79

  1. Application encouraged for years ending after 7/1/79

SSARS 3 Compilation Reports on Financial Statements Included in Certain Prescribed Forms

Amends SSARS 1 and SSARS 2

A. This Statement provides

  1. Guidance applicable to reports presented in a prescribed form

2. An alternative compilation report form when prescribed form or related instructions call for a GAAP departure by designating a non-GAAP measurement principle or not requesting GAAP disclosure

    a. Reference to GAAP in this statement includes, where applicable, a comprehensive basis of accounting other than GAAP

B. Prescribed form - any preprinted standard form designed or adopted by the party to which financial information is to be provided

    1. E.g., trade associations, banks, etc. (includes regulatory bodies, not involved in sale or trading of securities)

    2. Does not include forms designed or adopted by the client

C. Presumptions concerning prescribed forms

    1. Sufficient to meet the needs of the body designing or adopting
    2. No need to advise such bodies of GAAP departures required by the form

D. Guidance on Reports

    1. Departures from GAAP other than those required by prescribed form

        a. Follow guidelines in paras 39-41 of SSARS 1; suggested wording is

> However, I did become aware of a departure from generally accepted accounting principles that is not called for by the prescribed form or related instructions, as described in the following paragraph.

    2. Departures from requirements of prescribed form

        a. Treat as equivalent to a departure from GAAP

    3. Accountant should not sign preprinted report form that is not in conformance with SSARS 1 or 3

        a. Append an appropriate report to the prescribed form

SSARS 4 Communications between Predecessor and Successor Accountants

Amends SSARS 2, para 16

A. Statement gives guidance to a successor accountant who decides to communicate with predecessor accountant concerning acceptance of compilation or review engagement of nonpublic entity

    1. Requires predecessor to respond completely and promptly to such inquiries
    2. Also provides guidelines relative to additional successor inquiries

B. For purposes of this statement successor accountant refers to an accountant who has been invited to make (or has accepted) a proposal to compile or review

C. For purposes of this statement predecessor accountant refers to an accountant who has resigned or been notified of termination and who, as a minimum, compiled financial statements for the prior year

    1. Or for period ended within 12 months of date of the financial statements to be compiled or reviewed

D. Inquiries in conjunction with acceptance of an engagement

    1. Not required, but may do so if, for example

        a. Information concerning client, principals, and management is limited or appears to be in need of special attention

        b. Change in accountants occurs substantially after end of period for which financial statements are to be compiled or reviewed

        c. There have been frequent changes in accountants

    2. An accountant may not disclose confidential information without consent of client

        a. Except as permitted by AICPA Rules of Conduct

        b. Successor accountant should request client to

            1) Permit him/her to make inquiries
            2) Authorize predecessor to respond completely

        c. If client refuses to comply with request for inquiry, accountant should consider reasons for, and implications of, such denial as they relate to accepting the engagement

    3. May be oral or written and typically would include requests for information on

        a. Matters which might affect the integrity of management (owners)

        b. Disagreement about accounting principles or necessity of certain procedures

        c. If necessary, cooperation of management (owners) in providing additional or revised information

        d. Predecessor's understanding of reason for change in accountants

    4. Predecessor should respond promptly and completely to requests made in connection with engagements

        a. If due to unusual circumstances, response must be limited, accountant should so indicate

            1) E.g., unusual circumstances include pending litigation but do not include unpaid fees

E. Other inquiries

    1. May be made before/after acceptance of engagement to facilitate compilation or review

    2. Might include questions about prior periods' circumstances such as

        a. Deficiencies in underlying financial data

        b. Necessity of performing other accounting services

        c. Areas requiring inordinate time

    3. May include request for access to predecessor's working papers

        a. Successor should request client authorization

        b. Customary for predecessor to be available for consultation and provide certain of his/her workpapers

        c. Predecessor and successor should agree on which workpapers

            1) Will be available
            2) May be copied

    d. Generally predecessor should provide access to workpapers relating to

        1) Matters of continuing accounting significance
        2) Contingencies

    e. Predecessor may refuse for valid business reasons, including but not limited to unpaid fees

    f. If client is considering several successors

        1) Predecessor and working papers need not be made available until client names one as successor

    g. Successor should not reference report or work of predecessor in his/her report

        1) Except as expressly permitted by SSARS 2 or SAS 26 with respect to prior period financials

F. Predecessor accountant's financial statements

    1. If successor becomes aware of information indicating the need for revision of financial statements reported on by predecessor

        a. Request client to inform predecessor accountant
        b. SSARS 1, para 42 gives guidance to predecessor in determining appropriate course of action

    2. If client refuses to inform predecessor or successor is not satisfied with predecessor's actions

        a. Successor would be well advised to consult with attorney

SSARS 5 Reporting on Compiled Financial Statements

Amends SSARS 1, paras 14a and 17

(Outlines of amended paragraphs of SSARS 1 have been revised to reflect changes in SSARS 5)

CHAPTER SIX

BUSINESS LAW MODULES

The business law section of the CPA examination tests the candidate's:

1. Ability to recognize legal problems
2. Knowledge of legal principles with respect to the topics listed above
3. Ability to apply the legal principles to the problem situation in order to derive the textbook solution

Preparation for the business law section of the exam has one major advantage over the other sections: the boundaries of knowledge tested are clearly restricted to the topical content of the 16 business law modules, i.e., you only need to refer to one good text instead of a library of review materials. Refer to "Self-Study Program" in Chapter 1 for detailed suggestions on how to study the business law outlines in this volume and business law questions in Volume II. The basic procedure for each of the 16 business law modules is:

1. Work 10 to 15 multiple choice questions in Volume II to indicate your proficiency and familiarity with the type and difficulty of questions.

2. Study the outlines in this volume.

3. Work the remaining multiple choice questions in Volume II. Study the answer explanations of those you missed or had trouble with.

4. Work the essay questions in Volume II.

Answering Business Law Questions

    Law essay questions frequently differ from auditing and theory questions by requiring a conclusion, e.g.,

    Is the instrument in question negotiable commercial paper?

    Assuming the instrument is negotiable, does Meglo qualify as a holder in due course entitled to collect the full $3,000?

You must be prepared to begin your answer with an unequivocal yes or no followed by a period. Recognize that you are not used to this type of situation. Follow the solutions approach for essay questions as outlined in Chapter 3 with recognition that the unofficial answer is going to begin with Yes. or No. for these types of questions.

    Virtually all of these questions requiring conclusions also require "why" or "explain." Clearly, an unsupported yes or no will be worth little more than a blank answer. Always explain the legal principle(s) involved, and justify your application of the principle(s). Do not wander into other areas or deal with legal principles not specifically required by the question. Once again, "what will appear on the unofficial solution?"

    The AICPA Content Specification Outline of the coverage of business law, including the authors' frequency analysis thereof (last nine exams), appears on the following pages.

Sources of the Law

Law comes from two sources: statutes and common law. Common law is that which has evolved through court decisions. Decisions of higher courts are binding on lower courts in the same jurisdiction. Common law is applied where there is no statute covering the issue and also to help interpret statutes.

Most business law is regulated by the individual states and therefore may differ from state to state. The Uniform Commercial Code (UCC) has been adopted (sometimes with small changes) by all states except Louisiana, and also is law in the District of Columbia. The CPA exam tests the content of the 1972 Uniform Commercial Code (as amended). The UCC has caused both modernization of business law and uniformity among the states. Wherever applicable, the UCC is to be used on the CPA Examination. The UCC covers the following areas on the CPA Examination.

1.   Contracts - for Sales of Goods and Bulk Sales only
2.   Negotiable Instruments
3.   Secured Transactions
4.   Documents of Title
5.   Investment Securities

Most other areas are governed by individual state statutes and common law. Nevertheless, general rules of law can be stated for these areas and the rules provided herein are to be used on the CPA Examination. For some subjects, there are uniform acts, e.g., Uniform Partnership Act. These are not to be confused with federal law. They are uniform in that most states have enacted them as statutes either in their entirety or with small changes and therefore can be used as the general law in that area.

The areas covered by federal law are:

1.   Accountant's Legal Liability (as provided in the Securities Acts)
2.   Federal Securities Law
3.   Antitrust
4.   Bankruptcy
5.   Employer-Employee Relationship (except for Workman's Compensation)

AICPA CONTENT SPECIFICATION OUTLINE/FREQUENCY ANALYSIS[*]
BUSINESS LAW

	May 1980	Nov. 1980	May 1981	Nov. 1981	May 1982	Nov. 1982	May 1983	Nov. 1983	May 1984
I. The CPA and the Law									
A. Common Law Liability to Clients and Third Persons	-	-	3	- [1]	- [.50]	- [.50]	- [.25]	4	- [1]
B. Federal Statutory Liability									
1. Securities Acts	- [.50]	- [1]	1	-	-	- [.50]	- [.75]	2	-
2. Internal Revenue Code	- [.50]	-	1	-	-	-	-	2	-
C. Workpapers, Privileged Communication, and Confidentiality	-	-	1	-	- [.50]	-	-	2	-
Total MC	-	-	6	-	-	-	-	10	-
Total Essays	1	1	-	1	1	1	1	-	1
Actual Percentage[**] (AICPA 10%)	12%	10%	6%	10%	10%	10%	10%	10%	10%
II. Business Organization									
A. Agency									
1. Formation and Termination	-	2	1	3	-	1	-	1	1
2. Liabilities of Principal for Tort and Contract	-	1	-	1	1	-	1	1	1
3. Disclosed and Undisclosed Principals	-	2	2	-	1	-	-	1	1
4. Agency Authority and Liability	- [.50]	1	2	1	1	2	1	1	1
B. Partnerships									
1. Formation and Existence of Partnerships	-	2	- [.50]	2	2	-	1	1	-
2. Liabilities and Authority of Partners	- [.50]	2	- [.50]	3	2	- [.25]	1	2	-
3. Transfer of Partnership Interest	-	1	-	-	-	- [.25]	1	1	- [.50]
4. Dissolution and Winding Up	-	1	-	2	-	-	-	-	-
C. Corporations									
1. Formation	2	-	-	-	3	-	-	-	1
2. Purposes and Powers	1	-	-	-	-	-	-	-	-

[*]The classifications are the authors'.

[**]The Actual Percentage was calculated by adding the Total MC Questions to the points for each essay (which varied in weight until Nov. 1980, when all essays became worth 10 points), relating to this area (i.e., I, II, etc.) and dividing by 100 (total points available for all Business Law areas).

AICPA CONTENT SPECIFICATION OUTLINE/FREQUENCY ANALYSIS (CONTINUED)
BUSINESS LAW

	May 1980	Nov. 1980	May 1981	Nov. 1981	May 1982	Nov. 1982	May 1983	Nov. 1983	May 1984
3. Stockholders, Directors, and Officers	3	–	2	–	1	– [.25]	– [.50]	3	1
4. Financial Structure, Capital, and Dividends	1	– [.50]	5	–	–	– [.25]	– [.50]	1	2
5. Merger, Consolidation, and Dissolution	1	–	1	– [.25]	–	–	– [.25]	1	2
D. Other Forms									
1. Individual Proprietorships	–	–	–	–	–	–	–	–	–
2. Trusts and Estates	–	–	–	–	–	–	–	–	–
3. Joint Ventures	–	–	–	–	–	–	–	1	–
4. Associations	–	–	–	–	–	–	–	–	–
Total MC	8	12	13	12	11	3	5	14	10
Total Essays	1	.50	1	.25	–	1	1.25	–	.50
Actual Percentage (AICPA 15%)	20%	17%	23%	15%	11%	13%	18%	14%	15%

III. Contracts

	May 1980	Nov. 1980	May 1981	Nov. 1981	May 1982	Nov. 1982	May 1983	Nov. 1983	May 1984
A. Nature and Classification of Contracts	1	–	–	1	–	–	1	–	–
B. Offer and Acceptance	1 [.33]	– [1]	4	5	2	3	2	3	2 [.25]
C. Consideration	–	1	–	–	1 [.25]	2	1	2	1
D. Capacity, Legality, and Public Policy	–	–	–	–	–	1	–	– [.25]	1
E. Other Defenses									
1. Statute of Frauds	–	–	3	–	–	–	3	– [.50]	– [.25]
2. Statute of Limitations	–	–	–	1	–	–	–	–	–
3. Fraud	–	–	–	1	– [.50]	1	–	–	– [.25]
4. Duress	–	–	–	–	1	–	–	–	–
5. Misrepresentation	–	–	–	–	–	1	–	– [.25]	–
6. Mistake	–	–	–	1	–	–	1	–	1
7. Undue Influence	–	–	–	–	–	–	1	–	–
F. Parol Evidence Rule	–	–	2	–	–	1	2	–	–
G. Third-Party Rights	–	–	–	–	–	1	1	–	–
H. Assignments	–	–	–	1	–	2	1	–	–
I. Discharge, Breach, and Remedies	– [.33]	–	1	1	1 [.25]	2	3	1	1 [.25]
Total MC	2	1	10	11	5	14	16	6	6
Total Essays	.67	1	–	–	1	–	–	1	1
Actual Percentage (AICPA 15%)	10%	11%	10%	11%	15%	14%	16%	16%	16%

AICPA CONTENT SPECIFICATION OUTLINE/FREQUENCY ANALYSIS (CONTINUED)
BUSINESS LAW

	May 1980	Nov. 1980	May 1981	Nov. 1981	May 1982	Nov. 1982	May 1983	Nov. 1983	May 1984
IV. Debtor-Creditor Relationships and Consumer Protection									
A. Bankruptcy									
1. Voluntary and Involuntary Bankruptcy	2	-	2	- [.50]	2	2	2	- [.50]	1
2. Effects of Bankruptcy on Debtor and Creditors	2	- [.50]	3	-	2	1	1	-	3
3. Reorganizations	-	-	-	-	1	1	1	-	-
B. Suretyship									
1. Liabilities of Sureties and Cosureties	2	- [.25]	3	4	2	3	1	- [.50]	2
2. Release of Sureties	1	- [.25]	-	1	2	1	1	-	1
3. Subrogation and Contribution	2	-	1	1	-	1	1	-	1
C. Bulk Transfers									
1. Publication, Notification and Other Requirements	-	-	-	- [.50]	1	-	1	-	1
2. Rights of Pre-Sale Creditors	-	-	-	-	-	-	1	-	-
3. Rights of Post-Sale Creditors	-	-	-	-	-	-	1	-	-
4. Effects of Security Interests	-	-	-	-	-	1	-	-	-
D. Federal Consumer Protection Legislation									
1. Consumer Credit Protection Act	-	-	-	-	-	-	-	-	1
2. Magnuson-Moss Federal Warranty Act	-	-	-	-	-	-	-	-	-
3. Regulation of Deceptive Practices Pursuant to Section 5, Federal Trade Commission Act	-	-	-	-	-	-	-	-	-
Total MC	9	-	9	6	10	10	10	-	10
Total Essays	-	1	-	1	-	-	-	1	-
Actual Percentage (AICPA 10%)	9%	10%	9%	16%	10%	10%	10%	10%	10%
V. Government Regulation of Business									
A. Administrative Law									
1. Activities Subject to Regulation	-	-	-	-	-	-	-	-	-
2. Functions of Regulatory Agencies	-	-	-	-	-	-	-	1	-
3. Judicial Review of Agency Decisions	-	-	-	-	-	-	-	1	1

AICPA CONTENT SPECIFICATION OUTLINE/FREQUENCY ANALYSIS (CONTINUED)
BUSINESS LAW

	May 1980	Nov. 1980	May 1981	Nov. 1981	May 1982	Nov. 1982	May 1983	Nov. 1983	May 1984
B. Antitrust Law									
1. Price-Fixing and Other Concerted Activities	3	1 [.50]	3	2	4	- [.50]	1	2	- [.50]
2. Mergers and Acquisitions	-	-	-	1	1	-	1	2	-
3. Unfair Methods of Competition	-	-	-	-	-	-	-	1	-
4. Price Discrimination	-	-	-	1	-	-	1 [.50]	-	-
5. Sanctions	1	-	-	-	2	-	-	1	-
C. Regulation of Employment									
1. Equal Employment Opportunity Laws	-	1	-	-	-	-	-	1	-
2. Federal Unemployment Tax Act	-	-	-	-	-	-	-	1	-
3. Workmen's Compensation	-	1	1	-	-	2	1	-	1
4. Federal Insurance Contributions Act	2	1	1	1	-	-	1	1	1
5. Fair Labor Standards Act	-	-	1	-	1	2	-	-	-
D. Federal Securities Acts									
1. Securities Registration and Reporting Requirements	-	2	- [.67]	- [.75]	- [1]	1	-	-	2
2. Exempt Securities and Transactions	-	3	-	-	-	1	-	-	1
3. Insider Information and Anti-Fraud Provisions	-	-	-	-	-	2	-	-	1
4. Short-Swing Profits	-	-	-	-	-	-	-	1	1
5. Civil and Criminal Liabilities	-	-	-	-	-	-	-	2	1
6. Corrupt Practices	-	1	- [.33]	-	-	1	-	1	1
7. Proxy Solicitations and Tender Offers	-	-	-	-	-	- [.50]	- [.25]	-	-
Total MC	6	10	6	5	8	9	5	15	10
Total Essays	-	.50	1	.75	1	1	.75	-	.50
Actual Percentage (AICPA 15%)	6%	15%	16%	12%	18%	19%	13%	15%	15%
VI. Uniform Commercial Code									
A. Commercial Paper									
1. Types of Negotiable Instruments	1	-	-	-	1	3	-	- [.25]	3
2. Requisites for Negotiability	-	4	-	2	2	3	-	- [.25]	1
3. Transfer and Negotiation	-	-	-	2	2	2	-	-	2
4. Holders and Holders in Due Course	2	1	- [.50]	1	1	2	- [.25]	-	2
5. Liabilities, Defenses, and Rights	4	5	- [.50]	4	2	1	- [.25]	1	2
6. Discharge	1	-	-	-	1	-	-	-	-

AICPA CONTENT SPECIFICATION OUTLINE/FREQUENCY ANALYSIS (CONTINUED)
BUSINESS LAW

	May 1980	Nov. 1980	May 1981	Nov. 1981	May 1982	Nov. 1982	May 1983	Nov. 1983	May 1984
B. Documents of Title and Investment Securities									
1. Warehouse Receipts	–	–	–	2	1	–	1	–	1
	[.33]								
2. Bills of Lading	–	–	–	–	–	1	1	–	–
3. Issuance, Transfer, and Registration of Securities	–	1	–	–	2	–	2	1	–
C. Sales									
1. Contracts Covering Goods	2	2	2	1	–	2	1	3	1
	[.33]								
2. Warranties	1	–	2	–	–	1	2	2	3
				[.50]	[.50]				
3. Product Liability	1	–	–	–	–	–	–	2	–
4. Risk of Loss	1	–	1	–	–	1	–	3	2
							[.50]		
5. Performance and Obligations	2	3	–	–	–	–	–	1	2
					[.25]				
6. Remedies and Defenses	–	1	1	–	2	1	1	2	1
					[.25]				
D. Secured Transactions									
1. Attachment of Security Agreements	–	–	–	2	–	1	1	–	1
2. Perfection of Security Interests	–	4	–	2	2	4	2	–	1
			[.50]						
3. Priorities	–	–	–	–	–	–	1	–	1
			[.50]					[.50]	
4. Rights of Debtors, Creditors, and Third Parties	–	4	–	1	–	2	2	–	1
Total MC	15	25	6	17	16	24	14	15	24
Total Essays	.67	–	2	.50	1	–	1	1	
Actual Percentage (AICPA 25%)	24%	25%	26%	22%	26%	24%	24%	25%	24%

VII. Property, Estates, & Trusts

	May 1980	Nov. 1980	May 1981	Nov. 1981	May 1982	Nov. 1982	May 1983	Nov. 1983	May 1984
A. Real and Personal Property									
1. Distinctions Between Realty and Personalty	–	–	–	–	–	–	1	–	–
						[.50]			
2. Easements and Other Non-possessory Interests	1	–	–	–	–	–	1	–	–
								[.50]	
3. Types of Ownership	1	–	–	–	–	–	–	–	–
									[.50]
4. Landlord-Tenant	–	1	–	–	–	–	–	–	–
5. Deeds, Recording, Title Defects, and Title Insurance	–	1	1	–	2	–	2	–	–

AICPA CONTENT SPECIFICATION OUTLINE/FREQUENCY ANALYSIS (CONTINUED)
BUSINESS LAW

	May 1980	Nov. 1980	May 1981	Nov. 1981	May 1982	Nov. 1982	May 1983	Nov. 1983	May 1984
B. Mortgages									
1. Characteristics	-	-	2	-	1	-	1	-	-
	[.33]								
2. Recording Requirements	-	-	-	-	-	-	1	-	-
3. Priorities	-	-	-	-	1	-	1	-	-
				[.50]					
4. Foreclosure	-	-	-	-	-	-	1	-	-
	[.33]								
C. Administration of Estates and Trusts	5	5	3	4	3	-	-	-	-
								[.50]	[.50]
D. Fire and Casualty Insurance									
1. Coinsurance	-	-	-	1	1	-	1	-	-
						[.25]			
2. Multiple Insurance Coverage	1	1	-	-	-	-	-	-	-
						[.25]			
3. Insurable Interest	1	1	1	3	2	-	1	-	-
4. Life Insurance***	1	3	3	1	-	-	-	-	-
Total MC	10	12	10	9	10	-	10	-	-
Total Essays	.67	-	-	.50	-	1	-	1	1
Actual Percentage (AICPA 10%)	19%	12%	10%	14%	10%	10%	10%	10%	10%

***This classification has been added by the authors. Effective with the November 1983 exam, this area is no longer being tested.

CONTRACTS

Overview

Contracts is the most frequently tested topic in the business law section of the CPA exam. Candidates must understand both the classifications of contracts and the essential elements of a contract. One way to review contracts and emphasize their importance is by asking a series of questions:

1. Is there a contract? Why?
2. Is it enforceable? Why?
3. Has there been performance? Why?
4. If not, why?
5. Which party is at fault? Why?
6. What are the damages?

Note that there are two sets of contract rules to be learned. The first is the traditional common law contract rules which govern transactions involving the sale of land and the sale of services. The second set of contract rules is the Uniform Commercial Code which has replaced the common law in transactions involving the sale of goods. Goods per the code comprise personal property. Hence, if the subject of the contract is for the sale or purchase of personal property, the provisions of the Uniform Commercial Code, and not the common law, are applicable. Every examination will require the students to make this distinction.

The AICPA appears to emphasize questions on the formation of common law contracts and the formation of sales contracts. A large number of the questions require the candidate to make an immediate distinction whether UCC rules or common law rules are applicable. With the emphasis on contract formation, many questions test the rules of offers.

Another large number of questions test the question of enforceability. That is, there is heavy emphasis on the statute of frauds. A third grouping of questions concerns whether performance or a breach has occurred. Another grouping of questions concerns the rules of remedies.

The outline of contracts consists of the following sections.

Classification of Contracts
Essential Elements of a Contract
Reality of Consent
Assignment and Delegation
Third Party Beneficiary Contracts
Discharge of Contracts
Performance
Remedies
Statute of Limitations

Contracts Definitions

Contract. An agreement between parties creating an obligation for which the law provides a remedy for breach.

Consideration. An act, promise, or forbearance which is the bargained-for price to enter into an enforceable agreement. Consideration is legally sufficient if it is either a legal benefit to the promisor or a legal detriment to the promisee, or both.

Option. An agreement supported by consideration to hold an offer open for a certain length of time.

Parol Evidence Rule. A rule which excludes contradictory oral agreements or conversations entered into prior to and at the time an agreement is reduced to writing. The theory is that the writing incorporated all of the prior exchanges that the parties intended to be bound by. It does not exclude subsequent oral modifications to the contract.

Assignment. Assignment is the transfer by one person to another of a right that usually arises out of a contract. A transfer of the "the contract" or "all my rights under the contract," or an assignment in similar general terms is an assignment of rights, and unless the language or the circumstances indicate the contrary, it is also a delegation of the performance of the duties of the assignor. Acceptance of the assignment by the assignee constitutes a promise by him to perform those duties.

Novation. A substitution of one obligation for another with the agreement of the creditor, e.g., debtor B is substituted for debtor A and by agreement with creditor C, debtor A is discharged.

Third Party Beneficiary. A person who receives rights under a contract at the time of its making, because the primary parties to the agreement intend to confer legal rights on the beneficiary. If the motivation for conferring the rights on the beneficiary is to make a gift to the beneficiary, then the beneficiary is labeled a donee beneficiary. However, if the motivation is to pay an obligation owed to the beneficiary, the beneficiary is labeled a creditor beneficiary. A person who is in fact benefited but not intended to be benefited by the primary parties is called an incidental beneficiary and has no rights under the contract.

7

Recision. Rescission is the annulment of a contract whereby the parties are placed in a position as if there had been no contract.

Statute of Limitations. A bar to bringing an action after a prescribed period of time.

Anticipatory Breach. Where a party to a contract is so incapacitated as to not be able to perform, or who has announced an intent not to perform at the time for performance. Except in cases calling for the payment of money, a party to an otherwise valid contract may accept an anticipatory breach as being an immediate breach and seek damages.

Statute of Frauds. Designates which contracts must be in writing and signed by the party to be charged in order to be enforceable.

A. Classification of Contracts

1. Executory--a contract which has not yet been performed. Only promises have been given.

    a. Wholly executory when there has been no performance, e.g., each party has merely promised
    b. Partially executory when only part of contract is still unperformed, e.g., one party has performed and the other has not

2. Executed--a contract where all parties have completely performed and no obligation remains

3. Express--a contract whose oral or written terms are openly stated in clear language

4. Implied--a contract which is inferred by the conduct of the parties

    EXAMPLE: ABC Co. calls ACE Trucking to deliver some goods. ACE takes the goods and address of their destination. Nothing more is said. There is an implied contract that ACE will deliver the goods and ABC will pay.

5. Quasi-contract--a type of implied contract. It provides a remedy where one person has been unjustly enriched to the detriment of another.

    EXAMPLE: D falsely claims to be a pauper and obtains care at a home for the aged. A large estate is discovered at his death. The home may sue for the reasonable value of services rendered.

6. Bilateral--a contract in which a promise is given in exchange for a promise; e.g., I promise to pay you if you promise to act

7. Unilateral--a contract in which a promise on one side is given for an act on the other; e.g., I will pay you for your act

8. Valid--an enforceable contract which has all the elements necessary to create an obligation

9. Unenforceable--a contract which creates an obligation, but cannot be enforced by judicial proceedings; i.e., verbal contracts which are required by the Statute of Frauds to be in writing

10. Void--a contract which lacks one or more of the necessary elements of a contract. The promisor incurs no legal obligation.

11. Voidable--a contract in which one or both of the parties have the power to void the legal relationship. If affirmative steps are not taken to void, however, the contract will be enforceable.

12. Unconscionable--a contract, the terms of which are so unfair (one-sided) that it is presumed that no one would agree to them

13. Adhesion--offeror is in a position to say "take it or leave it." Such absence of negotiation sometimes leads to a finding of unconscionability

    a. Usually occurs when a large business entity requires its customers to use their standard form contract without allowing modification

14. Divisible--performance of contract is divided into two or more parts and the consideration is apportionable to each part

    a. In effect, independent agreements made at the same time

15. Entire--consideration is conditioned upon complete performance. Performance and consideration are not severable into parts.

16. Joint obligation--two or more parties promise to perform the obligation together. It must be enforced against both (all) of them together.

    EXAMPLE: A and B enter into a contract with P in which they "jointly" promise to build a house for P. If A and B do not finish the house, P must sue both A and B in one lawsuit in order to recover damages.

17. Joint and several obligation--two or more parties promise to perform the obligation and any one of them will accept liability for the entire performance. All or any one may be sued for the entire amount.

    EXAMPLE: A and B enter into a contract with P in which each promises individually to build a house for P. If A and B do not finish the house, P may sue either A or B (or both) for the full amount of damages.

B. Essential Elements of a Contract

    a) Agreement: offer and acceptance
    b) Consideration
    c) Legal capacity
    d) Legality of Object (Valid subject matter)
    e) Compliance with Statute of Frauds (Not generally considered to be an essential element but an important requirement of form as to enforceability)

1. Agreement--both parties consent to be bound

There must be a "meeting of the minds" on the terms of the contract. Use an objective test. That is, do the parties appear to have agreed and interpreted each other's negotiations as a reasonable person would?

a. Offer

    1) May be either written or oral

    2) Must be a clear intent to contract. Would a reasonable person take the offer seriously?

        a) Invitations to negotiate are not offers, e.g., price tags or lists, auctions, inquiries, ads

            1] <u>But</u> an ad for a limited quantity sold on a first-come basis may be an offer

        b) Promises made in jest or in excitement are not offers

        c) Statements of opinion or of intent are not offers

        EXAMPLE: A doctor tells a patient that he will fully recover in a couple of days, but it actually takes two weeks. This is a statement of opinion, not an offer.

        EXAMPLE: "I am going to sell my car for $400." This is a statement of intent, not an offer.

    3) The offer must be definite and certain as to what will be agreed upon in the contract

        a) Essential terms are parties, price, time for performance, subject matter (quantity and type)

        b) If unclear or open terms are clarified in subsequent negotiations, the contract will become valid

        c) See UCC Rules - The UCC will regard communications as offers if there is a clear intent even if all terms are not present

    4) Must be communicated to the offeree by the offeror or his/her agent. This means by the medium intended by the offeror, e.g., by mail, telegraph, phone, etc.

        a) An offeree may learn of a public offer, e.g., reward in any way. S/he merely needs knowledge of it.

    5) Mistaken offers. These involve errors in facts such as submitting a bid based on erroneous computations, errors in words or symbols such as typing mistakes, and errors in transmission such as by a telegraph operator.

        a) If the offeree knows or should know it is a mistake, then s/he cannot accept and form a valid contract

            1] E.g., the offeror's bid is unduly lower than the others

        b) If the offeree does not know or should not know it is a mistake, then acceptance forms a valid contract

            1] The offeror may be able to rescind by notifying the offeree before the offeree changes his/her position in reliance on the contract

EXAMPLE: A construction company submits an erroneous bid to replace an old wing in X's building. Even if X accepts the bid, the construction company may be able to rescind the contract if it notifies X of the error before X takes further action. However, if X demolishes the old wing in reliance on the bid, the contract cannot be rescinded.

    c) Mistakes in transmission of offer are deemed to be offeror's fault (risk) because he chose the transmitter

        1] Offeree is less likely to realize an error

        2] Offeror can recover from transmitter if performance was negligent

6) Offers are generally revocable by the offeror any time prior to acceptance by offeree. [see "b.2)b)" below]

    a) An auction is an invitation to negotiate. A bid is an offer. Falling of the hammer is acceptance.

        1] The offeror may revoke his offer prior to the falling of the hammer

        2] Offeree may reject even the highest bid unless the auction is "without reserve," then the highest bid must be accepted

b. Termination of an offer

1) Rejection by offeree

    a) Must be communicated to the offeror

    b) Rejection is effective when received by the offeror

        1] If the offeree sends a rejection and then an acceptance, the first received by the offeror is effective

    c) Counteroffer is a rejection

        1] Must be in the form of an offer

EXAMPLE: An offer is made to sell a car for $500 and a counteroffer is, "I'll give you $300."

        2] A mere inquiry or request for additional or different terms is not a counteroffer and does not terminate or affect offer

EXAMPLE: An offer is made to sell a car for $500 and an inquiry is, "Will you sell for $300?"

2) Revocation by offeror

    a) Generally, offeror may revoke offer at any time prior to acceptance by offeree. Revocation is effective when received.

EXAMPLE: X offers his car to Y stating that the offer will remain open for 10 days. However, on the 5th day Y receives from X a revocation of the offer. The offer would be terminated on the 5th day even though X stated that it would remain open for 10 days.

    b) If offeree learns (by any reliable means) that offeror has already sold subject of offer, the offer is revoked

    c) Public offers must be revoked by the same amount of publicity used in making offer

      EXAMPLE: Offer of reward for apprehension of arsonist in a newspaper makes headlines. It cannot be revoked by a small notice in the back of the newspaper.

    d) Options cannot be revoked because they are separate contracts, i.e., consideration has been paid for a promise to keep an offer open. See UCC Rules for firm offers by merchants concerning sale of goods.

    e) Part performance of a unilateral offer removes offeror's right to revoke for a reasonable time. See UCC Rules below.

  3) Lapse of time

    a) Offeror may specify period of time, e.g., one week
    b) If no time is specified, after a reasonable time
    c) Offeror may specify the happening of an event

      1] The offeree need not be informed of occurrence of event

  4) Death or insanity of offeror terminates offer

    a) Does not affect an option contract since it is already binding
    b) Death or insanity of offeree also terminates private (personal) offers since only offeree can accept

  5) Illegality

    a) The offer terminates if after making offer and before it is accepted, it becomes illegal

      EXAMPLE: X offers to rent to Y an upstairs floor for a cabaret. Before Y accepts, the city adopts a fire code making use of the premises illegal without substantial rebuilding.

  6) Bankruptcy or insolvency of either offeror or offeree
  7) Impossibility

    a) The offer terminates if after making offer and before it is accepted, performance becomes impossible

      EXAMPLE: X offers his car to Y for $500, but before Y agrees to the purchase, X's car is destroyed by fire.

c. Acceptance

  1) May be written or oral
  2) An offer may only be accepted by the person to whom it was directed

    a) Use an objective determination. To whom would a reasonable person believe it to be directed?
    b) Rewards can usually be accepted by anyone who knows of them

  3) Offeree must have knowledge of the offer and intend to accept

    a) If X sends an offer to Y, and Y then sends an acceptance to X, presumably Y had knowledge of the offer even if he did not read it

     b) If X makes an offer and Y accepts, Y will be presumed to have intended the acceptance since X will rely on it

     c) In a unilateral offer--such as a reward--the offeree cannot collect if he performed without knowledge of the offer, nor if he performed without intending to collect the reward

        EXAMPLE: Person gives information to clear his conscience while dying.

4) Acceptance must generally be in a form specified by the offer

     a) By a promise in a bilateral contract

        1] May be inferred from conduct
        2] Full performance in time allowed for acceptance is as acceptable as a promise to perform

     b) By performance of an act in a unilateral contract

        1] Part performance removes offeror's right to revoke offer, but offeree must fully perform to accept

     c) Acceptance in form of a promise must be communicated to the offeror. Offeror is deemed to be aware of the completion of an act unless there is no means for him/her to know.

5) Acceptance must be unequivocal and unconditional

     a) An acceptance which attempts to change terms of the offer is not an acceptance, but a rejection and counteroffer. Mere inquiry is not a counteroffer.
     b) A condition which does not change or add to the terms of the contract is not a counteroffer, i.e., a condition that is already part of the contract because of law, even though not expressed in previous negotiations
     c) See UCC rules below for different rules when sale of goods is involved

6) Silence is not acceptance unless

     a) The offer indicated that silence would constitute an acceptance, e.g., offer states "your silence is acceptance," and the offeree intended his/her silence as an acceptance. But if offeree does not intend to accept, such language has no effect, i.e., offeree is under no duty to reply, and offeror assumes such acceptance at his/her own risk.
     b) Offeree has taken the benefit of services or goods and exercised control over them when s/he had opportunity to reject them

        1] Statutes usually provide that unsolicited merchandise may be treated as a gift

     c) Through course of dealings or course of performance between the parties, silence is the mode of acceptance

7) Time of acceptance under common law

     a) Generally, acceptance must be sent by means specified by offer. If not specified, offeree may use same means as offeror or any other reasonable means

b) If acceptance is made by the specified means, or by the same means in the absence of instructions, the acceptance is effective when out of the offeree's possession and into the possession of the independent agency for transmission (constructive communication); e.g., when placed in mail or when telegram is sent

EXAMPLE: Offeror mails a written offer without stating the mode of acceptance. Offeree mails acceptance. Offeror, before receipt, calls offeree to revoke the offer. The contract exists because acceptance was effective when mailed and revocation of offer came too late.

c) Other methods of acceptance are considered effective when actually received by the offeror
d) A late acceptance is not valid. It is a counteroffer and a valid contract is formed only if the original offeror then accepts.
e) See UCC Rules below for different rules when sale of goods is involved

8) A lost or delayed acceptance is still valid. The offeror can protect him/herself by specifying the means of communication or that acceptance is only valid when received.
9) The offeree cannot retrieve an acceptance from the agency of communication. Once sent, it is final.

d. Once there is an offer and acceptance, a contract is formed

1) Minor details, e.g., closing details, can be worked out later
2) Formalization often occurs later

a) Statute of Frauds may require some writing (not necessarily the formal one) prior to enforcement

e. Uniform Commercial Code Rules

1) Remember the UCC applies almost entirely to the sale of goods (in the area of contracts), i.e., tangible personal property, not real property, service, or insurance contracts
2) A written and signed offer for the sale of goods, by a merchant, giving assurance that it will be held open for a specified time is irrevocable for that period

a) No consideration needed
b) If no time is specified, a reasonable time is inferred
c) In no case is the period to exceed three months
d) If the assurance is given on a form supplied by the offeree, it must be separately signed by the offeror

3) Unless otherwise indicated, an offer for the sale of goods shall be construed as inviting acceptance in any manner and by any medium reasonable in the circumstances

a) Acceptance will be effective when sent

4) Unequivocal acceptance of an offer for the sale of goods is not necessary under the Code

a) An acceptance containing additional terms is valid (unless the acceptance is expressly conditional upon the additional terms)

b) The additional terms are considered proposals to the offeror for additions to the contract

c) Between merchants, these additional terms become part of the contract unless:

1] Original offer precludes such
2] New terms materially alter the original offer
3] The original offeror gives notice of his objection within a reasonable time

5) Even if the writings do not establish a contract, conduct by the parties recognizing a contract will establish one

a) The terms will be those on which the writings agree and those provided for in the UCC where not agreed on, e.g., reasonable price, place of delivery

b) Often occurs when merchants send preprinted forms to each other with conflicting terms and forms are not read for more than quantity and price

6) An offer to buy goods for prompt shipment which is ambiguous as to intent is construed to invite acceptance, either by a prompt promise to ship or prompt shipment

7) With respect to a unilateral offer, beginning of performance by the offeree, i.e., part performance, will bind the offeror if followed within a reasonable time by a notice of acceptance

8) Even if terms are left open, a contract for the sale of goods will not fail for indefiniteness if there was intent to contract and a reasonable basis for establishing a remedy is available

a) Open price term--construed as reasonable price at time of delivery. Or parties can agree to allow third party to set price.

b) Open place of delivery term--seller's place of business if any; otherwise seller's residence or if identified goods are some place else, known to both parties at time of contracting, then at that place

c) Open time of shipment or delivery--becomes a reasonable time

d) Open time for payment--due at time and place of receipt of goods or at time and place of delivery of documents of title if any

1] If on credit, credit period begins running at time of shipment

2. Consideration--an act, promise, or forbearance which is offered by one party and accepted by the other as an inducement to enter an agreement

a. The test of consideration is the sufferance of a legal detriment by the performing party. The other party receives a legal benefit at the same time.

1) A legal detriment is suffered when a party does or binds himself to do something he is not legally obligated to do, or when he surrenders a legal right, e.g., a promise to pay money

2) Legal detriment does not have to be economic, e.g., giving up drinking, smoking, and swearing

b. Consideration must be bargained for. Parties must intend to suffer legal detriment.

   1) Acceptance of a gift or service does not mean one intends to return a gift or service

c. Mutuality of obligation. This means both parties must be bound or neither is. Each could maintain an action against the other for breach.

   1) If X and Y agree that X will buy all the sand he <u>wants</u> from Y, the contract is illusory because X need not buy anything

   2) But if X and Y agree that X will buy all his requirements for his established business from Y, the contract is valid since both are bound

d. Adequacy of consideration. The courts generally do not look into the fairness of the exchange.

   1) An exchange of unequal amounts of money or fungible goods is not enforceable

   2) Negligible consideration may not be adequate, e.g., nominal consideration such as $1

e. Forbearance to sue on claim is good consideration (legal detriment). The claim need not be valid if in good faith.

f. Past consideration (consideration for a prior act, forbearance, or agreement) is not sufficient for a new contract

g. Preexisting legal duty generally is not sufficient as consideration as no new legal detriment is suffered by performing a prior obligation

   1) Agreement to pay a lesser sum than already owed is unenforceable. But if debtor incurs a detriment in addition to paying, creditor's promise to accept lesser sum will be binding.

   EXAMPLE: X owes Y $1,000. Y agrees to accept $500 and X will also install Y's new furnace at no additional cost.

   2) Agreement to pay more to finish a job, such as building a house, is unenforceable unless unforeseen difficulties are encountered, e.g., an underground stream or marshy land under a house
   3) Agreement to pay a policeman to recover stolen goods is unenforceable
   4) Preexisting duty to third party gets the same results as preexisting duty to contracting party

   EXAMPLE: X promises to pay Y, a jockey, $50 to ride as hard as he can in the race. Y already owes his employer, Z, that duty so there is no consideration to enforce the agreement.

h. Moral obligation is generally not consideration except:

   1) Promise to pay or ratification of a voidable antecedent debt or promise to perform a voidable antecedent duty (e.g., ratification by infant upon reaching maturity)
   2) Promise to pay a debt barred by the Statute of Limitations. Acknowledgment or part payment coupled with an intent to pay implies a promise. Statutes may require writing.
   3) Promise to pay a debt barred by bankruptcy. Promise must adhere to strict rules stated in Bankruptcy Reform Act of 1978 concerning reaffirmations of dischargeable debts.

i. <u>Promissory estoppel</u> acts as a substitute for consideration and renders the promise enforceable. Promisor is estopped from asserting lack of consideration.

   1) Necessary elements

      a) Detrimental reliance on a promise
      b) Reliance is reasonable and foreseeable
      c) Damage results (injustice) if promise is not enforced

   2) Usually applied to gratuitous promises but trend is to apply to commercial transactions. At least recovery of expenses is allowed.

     EXAMPLE: A wealthy man in the community promises to pay for a new church if it is built. The church committee reasonably (and in good faith) relies on the promise and incurs the expenses.

     EXAMPLE: Uncle promises his nephew, who feels that college is too expensive, that he will pay for his education if the nephew obtains a degree. Nephew reasonably (and in good faith) relies on the promise and incurs the expenses.

j. Under the UCC, a contract (for sale of goods) may be modified orally or in writing without consideration

   1) Statute of Frauds is applicable if the contract as modified is within Statute

     EXAMPLE: X and Y enter in oral agreement whereby X agrees to pay $450 for a dryer. Due to a price increase experienced by Y, X subsequently agrees to pay $500 for the same dryer. This modification must be in writing to be enforceable because the contract as modified is within the Statute of Frauds. If as modified the sale price would have been $480, the oral modification would be enforceable.

   2) Parties can, in signed writing, exclude future modifications except when made in signed writing

3. Legal Capacity

a. An agreement between parties in which one or both lack the capacity to contract is void or in some cases voidable

b. Minors (persons under age 18 or 21)

   1) A minor may contract, but the agreement is voidable by him. The adult with whom he deals is held to the contract unless the minor disaffirms.

   2) A minor who disaffirms must return what is left of the consideration he received and may recover all of the consideration he gave

   3) A minor may disaffirm a contract at any time until a reasonable time after reaching majority. Failure to disaffirm within a reasonable time after reaching majority acts as ratification; e.g., one year is too long

   4) Disaffirmance is personal and unless he dies or becomes insane, disaffirmance must be by the infant

   5) A minor may ratify within a reasonable time after reaching the age of majority. Ratification prior to majority is not effective.

   6) A minor is liable for the reasonable value of necessaries furnished to him on a quasi-contract theory

        a) Minor may disaffirm the contract if it is executory, i.e., not com-
           pleted
        b) Necessaries include food, clothing, shelter, education, etc., con-
           sidering his age and position in life

    7) A minor usually is liable for his torts (civil wrongs), but this may
       depend on his age (above 14 commonly liable). Some states use this as a
       basis for holding a minor liable on a contract where he fraudulently
       misrepresents his age, but this is not the majority rule. (Parents are
       not liable for torts of minors unless they direct or condone certain
       conduct.)

  c. Incompetent persons

    1) An agreement by a person adjudicated insane is void from the beginning

        a) An insane person need not return the consideration

    2) If a contract is made before adjudication of insanity it may be
       voidable

        a) It will be valid provided there was no knowledge of insanity, the
           agreement is reasonable, and no advantage is taken of disabled par-
           ty's condition
        b) Where courts hold such agreements voidable, restitution is a con-
           dition precedent to disaffirmance

  d. Drunkard's legal capacity is determined by his ability to understand and by
    degree of intoxication
  e. Corporations contract through agents and are only limited by their charters
  f. Aliens generally have no disabilities

4. Legality of Object (Valid subject matter)

  a. An agreement is unenforceable if its subject matter is illegal or violates
    public policy

    1) If it becomes illegal after the offer but before acceptance, then the
       offer is terminated
    2) If it becomes illegal after acceptance, then the contract is discharged
       because of impossibility of performance
    3) If only partially illegal, i.e., an illegal clause, then the rest of
       the contract is enforceable if the clause is severable

  b. Either the consideration or the object of the contract may be illegal be-
    cause of statute or public policy
  c. When both parties are guilty (equal in guilt or legal fault called pari
    delicto), neither will be aided; i.e., if one party had already given some
    consideration, he will not get it back

    1) But if one party repudiates (repents) prior to performance, s/he may
       recover his/her consideration

       *EXAMPLE: X contracts to buy stolen goods from Y. If X pays Y but then
       repents and refuses to accept the stolen goods, X may recover the money
       he paid Y.*

  d. When one party is innocent (ignorant), s/he will usually be given relief

1) A member of a class of people designed to be protected by a statute is considered innocent; e.g., purchaser of stock issued in violation of blue-sky laws

e. Types of illegal contracts

1) Agreement to commit a crime or tort
2) In some states, contracts agreed to on Sunday, or to be performed on Sunday
3) Wagering contracts
4) Usury (contract for greater than legal interest rate)
5) Agreements to interfere with justice
6) Restraint of trade

   a) May be enforceable if ancillary to a contract and reasonable. See ANTITRUST.

7) Services rendered without a license when statute requires a license
8) Exculpatory clauses (party tries to relieve himself of liability for his own negligence) are against public policy

   EXAMPLE: Hospital requires patients to sign forms waiving liability for malpractice prior to admittance.

5. Conformity with the Statute of Frauds

a. Contracts required to be in writing and signed by the party to be charged

1) An agreement by an executor or administrator to answer for the debt of the decedent out of the estate of the executor, i.e., not out of the estate of the decedent
2) An agreement to answer for the debt or default of another (contract of guaranty)

   a) A secondary promise is within this section of the Statute of Frauds (required to be in writing)

      EXAMPLE: "If Jack doesn't pay, I will."

   b) A primary promise is not within this section of the Statute of Frauds

      EXAMPLE: "Let Jack have it, and I will pay."

   c) Guarantee of a del credere agent (see AGENCY) is not subject to the Statute of Frauds
   d) Promise of indemnity (will pay no matter whose fault, e.g., insurance) is not within the Statute
   e) Assignor's promise to assignee, guaranteeing obligor's performance is not within the Statute
   f) Oral joint debts are enforceable, e.g., A and B jointly purchase a bicycle
   g) Promise for benefit of promisor may be oral

      EXAMPLE: Promisor agrees to answer for default of X, because X is promisor's supplier and he needs X to stay in business to keep himself in business.

3) An agreement made upon consideration of marriage, i.e., antenuptial contract

    a) Contracts defining each spouse's rights and duties are becoming a major type of antenuptial contract
    b) Mutual promises to marry are not within the Statute

4) An agreement that cannot be performed within one year

    a) Time is measured from the date of making the contract, not counting the first day
    b) Concerned with when completion can be, not how long performance takes
    c) If the performance is contingent on something which could take place in less than one year, the agreement may be oral

    EXAMPLE: "I will employ you as long as you live." Promisor could possibly die in less than one year.

    d) But if the terms call for more than one year, it must be written even if there is a possibility of taking place in less than one year

    EXAMPLE: "I will employ you for 5 years." Death could shorten, but the terms control for the writing requirement under the Statute of Frauds.

    e) Cannot accelerate payment of a debt to get out of writing requirement
    f) Generally if on one side performance is complete but on the other side cannot be performed within the year, it is not within the Statute. This is especially true if performance has been accepted and all that remains is the payment of money (e.g., sale with payments spread over two years).

5) An agreement to sell land or any interest in land

    a) Includes fee simple estates, easements, leases longer than 1 year, contracts to mortgage, and contracts to sell real estate

    b) Part performance may satisfy the Statute but this requires:

        1] Possession of the land and
        2] Either part payment or making of improvements

    c) Under the UCC, sale of a growing crop is a sale of goods no matter who severs. But sales of timber, minerals, buildings and fixtures are sales of interests in land unless seller severs.

6) Agreement for the sale of goods for $500 or more is required to be in writing under the UCC

    a) Also, agreement for the sale of securities of any amount
    b) Agreement creating in the creditor a nonpossessory security interest in goods. See SECURED TRANSACTIONS.
    c) Agreement for the sale of intangibles over $5,000; e.g., patents, copyrights or contract rights
    d) Exceptions to the writing requirement

        1] Part performance makes the contract enforceable to the extent of performance (must be receipt and acceptance)

        2] Specially manufactured goods not suitable for sale in the ordinary course of seller's business if seller had made a substantial start in their manufacture before attempted repudiation of such agreement

        3] Contract is enforceable against the party who admits the contract in court. Enforceable to the extent admitted.

        4] Between merchants, if one party sends a written confirmation to another stating terms of an oral agreement, the other party must object within ten days to retain the protection of this section of the Statute of Frauds

b. No formal writing is required except that there must be some written note or memorandum signed by the party sought to be charged

  1) Any form will do, e.g., letter, telegram, receipt
  2) Need not be a single document, e.g., two telegrams
  3) Need not be made at same time as contract

    a) Must be made before suit is brought
    b) Need not exist at time of suit, i.e., may have been destroyed

  4) Should include such matters as:

    a) Identity of parties
    b) Description of subject matter
    c) Terms and conditions
    d) Consideration
    e) Signature

        1] Only needs signature or authenticating mark of party sought to be bound
        2] Signature need not be at end nor be in a special form so long as intent to authenticate existed; e.g., initials, stamp, printed letterhead, etc.

  5) Under the UCC a writing is adequate if it indicates a contract has been made between the parties and is signed by the one to be bound

    a) May omit material terms (e.g., price, delivery, time for performance) so long as quantity is stated. Reasonable terms will be inferred.

c. Noncompliance with the Statute of Frauds, i.e., failure to make a writing, will make the contract unenforceable

d. Promissory estoppel will prevent a party from asserting the Statute of Frauds as a defense if he has promised not to and the other party has relied on the promise to his detriment

e. Parol evidence rule. Written agreement intended by parties to be final and complete, i.e., an integration, may not be contradicted by prior or contemporaneous oral evidence

  1) Applies to written contracts even when not required under Statute of Frauds
  2) Evidence of integration often shown by a merger clause

EXAMPLE: "This agreement is complete; no other representations have been made."

3) Exceptions (party may present oral proof)

a) To show invalidity of contract, e.g., fraud, forgery, duress, mistake, failure of consideration

b) To show terms not inconsistent with the writing that the parties would not be expected to have included

EXAMPLE: Builder promises to use reasonable care not to damage nearby trees when building a house.

c) To explain the intended meaning of an ambiguity, proof cannot contradict terms in the contract but can explain them

d) Under the UCC, written terms may be supplemented or explained by course of dealing, usage of trade or course of performance

e) To show condition precedent--oral proof can be presented to show a fact or event must occur before agreement is valid

4) Does not apply to subsequent transactions, e.g., oral promises made after original agreement, or a separate and distinct oral agreement made at same time as a written contract

C. Reality of Consent--Mutual assent is essential to every agreement. If one of the following concepts is present, a contract may be void or voidable.

1. Fraud--must include the following elements

a. Misrepresentation of a material fact

1) Can be a total falsehood, series of truths not true together, physical concealment of defect

2) Silence is not a misrepresentation unless there is a duty to speak, e.g.,

a) Fiduciary relationship between parties
b) Seller of property knows there is a latent defect

3) Must be a statement of past or present fact

a) Opinion, e.g., of value, is not fact unless from an expert
b) Prophecy is not fact; e.g., "Next year you will make twice as much"
c) Dealers' talk, i.e., puffing, is not fact
d) Presently existing intention in the mind of the speaker is a fact

b. Intent to mislead--"scienter"

1) Need knowledge of falsity with intent to mislead
2) Reckless mistake or utter disregard for truth can be a substitute (constructive fraud)

c. Reasonable reliance by injured party

1) One who knows the truth or might have learned it by a reasonable inquiry may not recover

d. Resulting in injury to others

1) Giving rise to an action for damages by injured party

e. Remedies for fraud

1) If contract is voidable

a) Defrauded party may affirm agreement and sue for damages under tort of deceit, or if the party is sued on the contract then he may set up the fraud in reduction of the damages
b) Defrauded party may rescind contract
c) Once defrauded party affirms agreement, party cannot rescind contract

2) If contract is void

a) The defrauded party may sue for fraud and seek damages in tort

f. Fraud may occur

1) In the inducement

a) The misrepresentation occurs during contract negotiations
b) Creates voidable contract at option of defrauded party

EXAMPLE: A represents to B that his car has been driven 50,000 miles when in fact it has been driven for 150,000 miles. If B purchases A's car in reliance on this misrepresentation, fraud in the inducement is present, creating a voidable contract at B's option.

2) In the execution

a) Misrepresentation occurs in the actual form of the agreement
b) Creates a void contract

EXAMPLE: Larry Lawyer represents to Danny Dumb that Danny is signing his will, when in fact he is signing a promissory note payable to Larry. This promissory note is void because fraud in the execution is present.

2. Innocent misrepresentation

a. An innocent misstatement made in good faith, i.e., no scienter
b. Creates the right of rescission (cancellation) in the other party--to return both parties to their precontract positions

1) All benefits must be returned by both parties

3. Mistake--an act done under an erroneous conviction

a. Unilateral mistake generally is not grounds to rescind a contract unless:

1) Mistaken party is free of negligence
2) Other party knew of the mistake
3) Failure to read provisions of the contract before signing is generally no excuse
4) As to mistakes in computations, the general rule is that the contract is voidable if the mistaken party was not negligent and the amount of the error was so great that the other party should have known a mistake had been made

b. Mutual mistake (by both parties) generally makes a contract voidable

1) A contract may be reformed to comply with the intent of the parties if the mistake was made in reducing the agreement to writing

2) Where the parties are merely ignorant as to the value of the subject matter, the damaged party is not permitted to rescind

4. Duress--a contract entered into because of duress can be voided because of invalid consent

   a. Any acts or threats of violence against a party or a member of party's family, which in fact deprives the party of free will and causes him to agree, is duress
   b. Economic duress: contract is only voidable if one party puts the other in desperate economic condition

5. Undue influence--the mental coercion of one person over another which prevents understanding or voluntary action

   a. Usually occurs when a very dominant person has complete influence over a weaker person, sometimes older
   b. Also occurs through abuse of a fiduciary relationship, e.g., CPA, attorney, guardian, trustee, etc.

6. Unconscionable contract--an oppressive contract in which one party has taken a severe, unfair advantage of the other, usually because of the latter's absence of choice or poor education

   a. Under these circumstances a court may void the contract or reform the terms so as to be fair to both parties

      1) E.g., exclude an unconscionable clause or limit it

7. Hardship, bad economic conditions, or a bad deal are not conditions creating voidable contracts

   a. These are assumed to have been contemplated

8. Infancy, incompetency, and noncompliance with the Statute of Frauds may also create a voidable contract.

D. Assignment and Delegation

1. Generally, a party's rights in a contract are assignable and duties are delegable

   a. No consideration is needed for a valid assignment

      1) Gratuitous assignments are revocable

         EXAMPLE: A owes B a debt for services B performed for A, but B has been unable to collect because A has been in financial difficulty. B may gratuitously assign this debt to X if X can collect it. If A's financial position improves, B may revoke the assignment to X and collect the debt himself or assign it to another for consideration.

   b. Rights may be assigned without delegating duties, or duties may be delegated without assigning rights
   c. Partial assignments may be made, e.g., only assign part of one's rights such as the right to receive money
   d. A delegation of duties is not an anticipatory breach

      EXAMPLE: X Company contracted to deliver certain goods to Y. If X Company is low on these goods, it may delegate this duty to S Company, its subsidiary. It is not an anticipatory breach because X has not indicated that performance will not occur.

e. An assignment of a contract is taken to mean both assignment of rights and delegation of duties

f. Exceptions

1) Contract involving personal services, credit, trust, or confidence, e.g., an artist cannot delegate his duty to paint a portrait

   a) But a contractor building a house according to a blueprint can delegate his duty to someone qualified because no special skill is involved, just following a set of directions

   b) With permission, personal duties can be delegated

2) Provision of contract or statute prohibits assignment or delegation

   a) Trend is to look with disfavor on prohibitions against assignments where only a right to money is concerned

   b) The UCC makes prohibition against assignment of monetary rights ineffective

3) The assignment would materially change the risk or obligations of the other party

   a) E.g., insurance contract, requirement and output contracts, and contracts where personal credit is involved

4) Under common law, one cannot assign future rights in a future contract, i.e., a nonexisting contract, because these rights do not exist

   a) Can assign future rights in an existing contract

5) Under UCC all future rights are assignable whether in future contracts or existing contracts

2. An assignment generally extinguishes any rights of the assignor but a delegation does not relieve a delegant of his duties

   a. The assignee acquires the assignor's rights against the obligor and has the exclusive right to performance

   b. If an obligor has notice of the assignment, he may not pay the assignor without risk of also having to pay the assignee. If the obligor has no notice, he may pay the assignor and the assignee can recover from the assignor.

   c. Unless there is a novation, the delegating party is still liable if the delegatee does not perform

   1) A novation occurs when the three parties agree to replace the delegator (or assignor) with the delagatee (or assignee). It discharges the obligor and makes the delegatee fully liable.

      EXAMPLE: A sells a car to B and accepts payments over time. B sells the car to C who agrees to take over the payments. No novation unless A agrees to accept C and release B.

3. A party taking an assignment generally steps into the shoes of the assignor. He gets no better rights than the assignor had.

   a. The assignee is subject to any defenses the obligor could assert against the assignor

b. The assignee may recover from the assignor if the assignor causes the ob-
    ligor not to perform; e.g., the assignor does not perform his duties and
    the obligor asserts that as a defense

4. If an assignor makes more than one assignment of the same right, there are two
    rules to be applied depending upon the state

    a. Either the first assignee to give notice to the obligor prevails, or
    b. The first to obtain an assignment prevails
    c. Under the UCC, an assignee can perfect his assignment by filing a financing
        statement (see SECURED TRANSACTIONS)

        1) First to file prevails

E. Third-Party Beneficiary Contracts

1. Contracting parties enter into agreement intended to benefit third party(ies).
    There are three types of third-party beneficiaries.

    a. Creditor beneficiary--one party (the promisor) contracts with the debtor
        (the promisee) to pay a debt owed to the creditor (third-party benefi-
        ciary)

        *EXAMPLE: X owes C $100. X contracts with Y to paint Y's house if Y will
        pay C $100. C is a creditor beneficiary.*

        *EXAMPLE: Buyer assumes the seller's mortgage. Mortgagee is a creditor
        beneficiary.*

    b. Donee beneficiary--almost the same as a creditor beneficiary except the
        promisee's intent is to confer a gift upon the third-party through the prom-
        isor's performance

        *EXAMPLE: X contracts to buy Y's car if Y will deliver it to D, X's son. D
        is a donee beneficiary.*

    c. Incidental beneficiary--third party who receives an unintended benefit from
        a contract. He obtains <u>no</u> rights.

        *EXAMPLE: X and Y contract to build an apartment building. A, a nearby
        store owner, would benefit from increased business and is an incidental ben-
        eficiary.*

2. Only an intended beneficiary (creditor or donee) can maintain an action against
    contracting parties for nonperformance

    a. Intent of the promisee controls
    b. Creditor beneficiary can proceed against either contracting party

        *EXAMPLE: X owes C $100. X contracts with M to paint M's house if M will
        pay C $100. If X does not paint M's house, C may sue X because X still owes
        C $100. C may also sue M, because M now owes C $100 under the contract. C
        is a creditor beneficiary and can sue either party.*

    c. Donee beneficiary can proceed against the promisor only

        *EXAMPLE: X contracts to buy Y's car if Y will deliver it to D. If Y does
        not deliver the car, D may sue Y. However, D may not sue X because it was a
        gift from X, not an obligation.*

3. Until a third party has accepted the benefits of the contract, the parties may rescind and defeat his rights

    EXAMPLE: X owes C $100. X contracts with Y to paint Y's house if Y will pay C $100. X and Y may rescind the contract before Y pays C $100. Then there is no contract for C to enforce, however, C may still sue X for the $100 owed.

4. The promisor can assert any defenses against the third-party beneficiary that he has against the promisee

F. Discharge of Contracts

1. By performance. (See next section.)

2. By agreement: consideration is necessary, but often it is supplied by a promise for a promise, e.g., both parties agreeing to release other party of contractual obligation

    a. Under the UCC, no consideration is needed to modify a contract for the sale of goods
    b. Cancellation is the physical destruction of the document with the intent to destroy its legal effect
    c. Merger occurs when the party acquires a remedy or accepts a security of a higher nature

        EXAMPLE: A judgment is obtained on a contract; the obligation owed is that under the judgment.

        EXAMPLE: The giving of a promissory note in exchange for money owed on an open account.

    d. Mutual release is a subsequent agreement that the contract is no longer binding
    e. Mutual rescission involves dissolution of the contract and placing the parties, so far as possible, in the position they were in prior to making the contract
    f. A novation is an agreement among all parties whereby an initial agreement is discharged by the creation of a new agreement. May involve substitution of creditors, debtors or of obligations.

        EXAMPLE: A party purchases land and assumes a mortgage. The original mortgagor is still liable unless a novation has occurred.

    g. Partial discharge occurs when there is a modification of the contract

        1) There must be mutual assent
        2) There must be a writing if the original contract was in writing. Under the UCC, a writing is not needed to modify a written sale of goods, unless the contract requires such or the contract is under the Statute of Frauds as modified.
        3) Where the writing requirement is not met, an attempt to modify can operate as a waiver

    h. Accord and satisfaction. The accord is a substituted agreement giving, usually, easier terms. The satisfaction is performance. The claim may be disputed or not. Until satisfaction is begun, promisee may recover on old contract.

> *EXAMPLE: X sells a boat to Y who promises to pay in 30 days. Y fails. X and Y agree that Y will fix X's roof as satisfaction. Y is liable until he starts the roof repair.*

3. By Release or Covenant not to sue

    a. Release of one joint obligor releases the other(s) unless an express reservation of rights against the other(s) is made

        1) Reservation of rights is made by wording so in the release, e.g., "I release X but reserve all rights against Y"

    b. Covenant not to sue one joint obligor does not affect the other(s)

    > *EXAMPLE: X and Y are jointly liable to A. If A promises not to sue X, A may still sue Y. However, if A had released X from the obligation, Y would also be released.*

4. By performance becoming objectively impossible

    a. Performance becomes illegal
    b. Death of party where personal service is necessary
    c. Destruction of the subject matter without fault of promisor
    d. Bankruptcy of party
    e. Unanticipated and extreme difficulty will rarely excuse

        1) The UCC provides for discharge on the basis of commercial frustration in a sale of goods where performance is "made impracticable by the occurrence of a contingency the nonoccurrence of which was a basic assumption on which the contract was made"

        > *EXAMPLE: The sole source of supply for the object of the contract disappears. Both buyer and seller assumed the source would be available.*

        2) Discharge if the other party prevents performance (a breach of contract)

5. By breach of contract (failure to carry out the terms of the contract)

    a. Partial breach (minor breach). Injured party is not discharged but may sue.
    b. Total breach. Injured party discharged and may sue or rescind.

        1) Material breach. Failure to perform a term so essential that purpose of the parties is defeated.

    c. Anticipatory breach. Renunciation before performance is due.

        1) May sue at once, or
        2) Wait until time performance is due and then sue
        3) If other party has not changed position in reliance upon the repudiation, repudiating party can retract repudiation and perform at appointed time, thereby discharging their contractual obligation

        > *EXAMPLE: X agrees to convey and Y agrees to pay for land on April 1. On February 1, Y learns that X has sold to Z. Y may sue before April 1, or he may wait and sue on April 1.*

G. Performance

1. Duty to perform is absolute under a covenant to perform; e.g., "I will pay you $100 when you deliver the goods"

2. Duty to perform may depend upon a condition, which is a fact or event, the occurrence or nonoccurrence of which creates or removes the duty to perform

    a. Condition precedent is one which must occur before there is a duty to perform; e.g., "I will lend you $1,000 if your credit checks out"

    b. Condition subsequent is one which removes the preexisting duty to perform; e.g., "I will pay you for these goods unless I decide to return them"

    c. Conditions concurrent are mutually dependent upon performance at nearly the same time, e.g., delivery and payment for goods

    d. Satisfaction as a condition. Normally when a contract guarantees satisfaction, this means the agreement is performed when a reasonable person would be satisfied. However, if the agreement is expressly conditioned upon the personal satisfaction of one of the contracting parties, then performance does not occur until that party is actually satisfied.

        1) Objective satisfaction. Satisfaction of a reasonable man is enough, e.g., constructing a sidewalk.
        2) Personal satisfaction. Contracts involving personal tastes or judgment; e.g., painting a portrait.

3. Tender of performance is an offer to perform; e.g., offer to pay debt

    a. Necessary to put other party in breach if concurrent conditions

        EXAMPLE: X has contracted to buy goods from Y with delivery and payment to take place concurrently. X must offer the money to Y before Y has breached the contract for failure to deliver.

    b. Must comply with contract as to time, place, and manner (amount and kind)
    c. If tender of payment is refused, tender has the effect of:
        1) Stopping the running of interest
        2) Discharging any security

    d. If tender of performance other than payment is refused, it is a breach of contract and promisor is excused from performance

4. Under the doctrine of substantial performance, performance is satisfied if:

    a. There has been substantial performance, and
    b. Deviations are minor, and
    c. There has been a good faith effort to comply, and
    d. Damages for deviations are deducted from the price

5. Part payment when debtor owes more than one debt to the creditor

    a. Debtor may specify which debt payment applies to

        1) Otherwise, creditor can apply to either
        2) If neither specifies, law presumes application in order of maturity (oldest first). However, all unsecured debts are considered paid before secured debts, even if the secured debts are older.

H. Remedies

1. Rescission--annulment of contract and return of parties to precontract position. No suit for contract damages is then allowed.

   a. Often the remedy for a voidable contract

2. Restitution--return of consideration to the injured party

   a. Not available if a debt is owed or for a severable part of the contract
      which is complete

3. Specific performance--compels the performance promised. Used only when money
   damages will not suffice; e.g., when subject matter is unique, as in a contract
   for sale of land.

4. Injunction--compels an act by the party (positive injunction), or restrains an
   act (negative injunction)

5. Damages--Payment of money

   a. Purpose is to place injured party in as good a position as he would have
      occupied if contract had been performed

   b. Actual or compensatory damages are equal to the amount caused by the breach

      1) Lost profits are the difference between the contract price and the
         market price

         a) If market value is zero because of the breach, then damages are the
            full contract price

      2) Consequential and incidental damages are those reasonably foreseeable
         as a result of breach, e.g., spoilage of goods and expenses incurred in
         expectation of fulfillment of the contract such as traveling expenses

         a) These are recoverable

      3) Damages that are not foreseeable are not recoverable

   c. Punitive damages are generally not allowed

   d. Liquidated damages are damages that are known or certain in amount (fixed).
      Often determined by estimate and agreement beforehand and provided for in
      the contract.

      1) Excessive liquidated damages are penalties and not enforceable in court
      2) Reasonableness judged as of time contract was made

   e. Mitigation of damages. Party injured by breach must use reasonable care to
      minimize the loss.

      *EXAMPLE: One who receives perishables which are not the goods bargained
      for must take reasonable steps to prevent loss from spoilage.*

      *EXAMPLE: X contracts to fix Y's car. After X begins work, Y breaches and
      says "Stop." X cannot continue to work and incur more costs, i.e., put in
      more parts and labor.*

6. Quantum meruit is based upon the reasonable value of services rendered. This
   action is based on quasi-contract and not on the original agreement.

7. Accord and satisfaction--substitution and performance of a new agreement in place of an old agreement

8. Arbitration--resolution of dispute, outside of the judicial system, by a party agreed to by the disputing parties

I. Statute of Limitations

1. Bars suit if not brought within the statutory period

2. Statute begins to run from the time a cause of action accrues, e.g., breach

3. Running of the statute may be stopped (tolled) by:

    a. Disability of plaintiff to sue, e.g., insanity
    b. Defendant's absence from jurisdiction

4. Written promise to pay a debt, or a partial payment coupled with intent to pay remainder will start the running of the statute over again

5. Statute begins to run from the date of execution of a demand note

SALES

Overview

This topic is primarily concerned with Article 2 (sales) and Article 6 (bulk sales) of the Uniform Commercial Code (U.C.C.). The AICPA often requires the candidate to distinguish between the application of the common law of contracts and the U.C.C. Consequently, the candidate must recognize when the contract involves the sale of "goods" and then apply the U.C.C. to these agreements. Recently the AICPA has stated that the topic of product liability will be questioned more frequently in the future. Product liability concerns the seller's liability for defective products under the theories of negligence, strict liability and warranty. Other topics questioned in the sales area include:

> Firm Offer Rule
> Battle of Forms
> Modification of Pre-existing Contract
> Statute of Frauds
> Performance of Sales Agreement
> Remedies
> Identification
> Risk of Loss
> Bulk Sales
> Sale of Goods by Non-owner
> Entrusting
> Shipment Terms

Sales Definitions

Bulk Sale. Any transfer of a major part or all of the materials, supplies, or inventory of a transferor's business, i.e., not in the ordinary course of business.

Goods. All things (including specially manufactured goods) which are moveable at the time of identification to the contract for sale except money, investment securities, intangible property, contract rights, or accounts receivable. Goods also include the unborn young of animals, growing crops, and standing timber to be cut. Other things which are attached to realty such as minerals or buildings are considered goods if they are to be severed from the land by the seller.

Firm Offer. A written signed offer, by a merchant, giving assurance that it will be held open for a specified time is irrevocable for that period, not to exceed three months.

Battle of Forms. Between merchants, additional terms included in the acceptance become part of the contract unless
a. original offer precludes such; or
b. new terms materially alter the original offer; or
c. The original offeror gives notice of his objection within a reasonable time.

Merchant. A person who deals in the kind of goods being sold, or alternatively, who by occupation holds himself out as having superior knowledge and skills as to the goods involved in the transaction. Such knowledge or skill may be acquired through the employment of an expert.

Warranty. A warranty is a statement or representation, with reference to the character, quality, or title of goods, made by a seller of goods to the buyer which is given contemporaneously with and as part of the contract for sale.

Cover. The buyer's discretionary right to buy goods elsewhere when a seller wrongfully fails to deliver conforming goods required by the contract. The buyer may recover any additional costs from the breaching party so long as he acted in good faith and without unreasonable delay.

Cure. The seller's right to remedy nonconforming goods which have been shipped to the buyer prior to the date of final performance of the contract.

Merchantable. The goods are reasonably suitable for the purpose for which they were made and sold. They must also be a fair and average quality as established by the market place.

Entrusting. Transferring possession of goods to a merchant who deals in such goods gives the merchant the power to transfer all rights of the entruster to a good faith purchaser in ordinary course of business.

A.   Contracts for Sale of Goods

1.   Article 2 of the Uniform Commercial Code controls contracts for the sale of goods in almost all state jurisdictions

   a.   The tendency of the UCC is to find a contract obligation in cases where it is plainly the intent of the parties, even though some technical element of a contract may be missing. The intent of the UCC is to facilitate and expedite commercial transactions.

b. The express elements necessary for a sales contract are

  1) Parties
  2) Price - can be ommitted and contract will be enforced at a reasonable
      price
  3) Time for performance

    a) If not present, reasonable time is implied
    b) If agreement states time is of essence, then delay in performance is
        a material breach and nonbreaching party can terminate performance
        and sue for damages

  4) Subject matter

    a) Normally, quantity must be included before agreement is con-
        sidered enforceable

c. Open terms will not cause a contract for the sale of goods to fail for in-
    definiteness if there was an intent to contract and a reasonable basis for
    establishing a remedy is available. If the place of delivery is left open,
    the UCC provides that the seller's place of business shall be the proper
    place of delivery.

2. Definitions

  a. Merchant--see Sales Definitions
  b. Goods--all things which are moveable at the time and identified to the con
      tract for sale

    1) To be distinguished from investment securities and things in action,
        e.g., contracts, documents of title, commercial paper
    2) The goods must be both existing and identified for an interest to pass
        to the buyer
    3) Moveable distinguishes goods from real property

      a) A contract for the sale of oil, minerals, etc. is a sale of goods
          if they are to be severed by the seller or standing timber to be cut
          by either party

    4) Fungible goods--so similar that one unit is considered the equivalent
        of any other, e.g., bushel of U.S. No. 1 wheat or corn

  c. Firm offer--a written signed offer, by a merchant, giving assurance that it
      will be held open for a specified time is irrevocable for that period, not
      to exceed three months
  d. Battle of forms--between merchants, additional terms included in the
      acceptance become part of the contract unless

    1) Original offer precludes such, or
    2) New terms materially alter the original offer, or
    3) The original offeror gives notice of his objection within a reasonable
        time

  e. Bailment--bailor (usually owner of property) transfers temporary possession
      of personal property to bailee without transferring title

      *EXAMPLE: Herb borrows Ike's law notes to prepare for CPA exam. A bailment
      is created with Ike the bailor and Herb the bailee.*

  f. Consignment--a type of bailment where the bailee (consignee) is to sell the
      property for the owner (consignor)

g. Shipment terms
    1) C.O.D. shipments--collect on delivery
    2) F.O.B.--free on board. Means the seller will pay the freight and bear the risk of loss to the place named
        a) It will be a shipping contract if the place of shipment is named, i.e., buyer pays freight

           Example: Seller is in Dallas, buyer is in Chicago: F.O.B. Dallas.

        b) It will be a destination contract if the place of destination is named, i.e., seller pays freight

           Example: Seller is in Dallas, buyer is in Chicago: F.O.B. Chicago.

    3) F.A.S. vessel--free along side
        a) Seller must deliver goods along side the named vessel at his own risk and expense

    4) C.I.F.--cost, insurance, and freight included in price
        a) Seller puts goods in hands of a carrier and obtains insurance in buyer's name, who then has risk of loss

h. No arrival, no sale--seller ships but if goods do not arrive, contract fails and neither party is liable
i. Sale on approval--goods may be returned even if they conform to the contract

    1) Goods bought for use, e.g., consumer purchaser
    2) Seller retains title and risk of loss until acceptance
    3) Creditors of buyer cannot reach goods until buyer accepts

j. Sale or return--goods may be returned even if they conform to the contract

    1) Goods bought for resale, e.g., merchant buyer
    2) Seller retains title but buyer has risk of loss
    3) Creditors of buyer can reach the goods, unless notice of seller's interest is posted or filed as required

k. Document of title--any document which in the regular course of business is accepted as adequate evidence that the person in possession of the document is entitled to receive, hold and dispose of the document and the goods it covers
l. Bill of lading--a document of title which is issued by a private or common carrier in exchange for goods delivered to it for shipment. It may be negotiable or nonnegotiable.
m. Warehouse receipt--a document of title issued by a person engaged in the business of storing goods, i.e., a warehouseman. It acknowledges receipt of the goods, describes the goods stored, and contains the terms of the storage contract. It may be negotiable or nonnegotiable.

3. Passage of title

a. Once goods are identified to the contract, the parties may agree as to when title passes

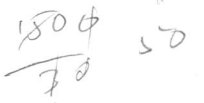

   b. Otherwise, title generally passes when the seller completes his performance with respect to physical delivery

      1) If a destination contract, title passes on tender at destination, i.e., buyer's place of business

      2) If a shipping contract, title passes upon the seller putting the goods in the possession of the carrier

   c. If seller has no duty to move the goods:

      1) Title passes upon delivery of documents of title

      2) If no document of title exists, title passes at the time and place of contracting if the goods are identifiable

      3) If goods not identified, there is only a contract to sell; no title passes

   d. Rejection of goods or a justified revocation of acceptance by buyer revests title in seller

4. Sale of goods by nonowner

   a. If seller has a void title (no title) to goods then bona fide purchaser acquires no title

   b. If seller has a voidable title to goods (i.e., seller obtained goods through fraud inducement) then bona fide purchaser receives good title

   c. Entrusting--transferring possession of goods to a merchant who deals in such goods gives the merchant the power to transfer all rights of the entruster to a good faith purchaser in ordinary course of business

    Example: A leaves a ring with B, a jeweler, to be cleaned. B sells the ring to C. C has good title to the ring and A would have to sue B for the loss.

5. Identification--occurs when the goods that are going to be used to perform the contract are shipped, marked or otherwise designated as such

   a. Identification creates a special property interest in the goods on behalf of buyer. This means buyer has:

      1) An insurable interest in the goods

      2) Right to inspect goods at reasonable time and at buyer's expense

      3) Right to sue for damages caused by any third party who wrongfully destroys or damages goods

      4) If within 10 days of buyer's first payment seller is insolvent, the right to demand goods upon offering full contract price

6. Risk of loss (unlike common law, does not depend on title under the UCC)

   a. Parties may agree as to who bears the risk, otherwise UCC rules apply

   b. If a breach of contract, the party in breach has the risk of loss unless the party not in breach has the goods fully insured

   c. If the goods are to be shipped by a carrier:

      1) And the seller must deliver the goods to a specified destination (destination contract), seller has risk of loss until duly tendered by carrier at destination

      2) And the seller is not required to deliver the goods to specified destination (shipping contract), buyer has risk of loss once goods are delivered to an appropriate carrier

d. If the goods are in possession of a bailee (e.g., public warehouse) and seller does not have to move them, risk of loss passes to buyer when

1) Buyer receives a negotiable document of title, or
2) Bailee acknowledges buyer's right to possession, or
3) Buyer receives a non-negotiable document of title or written direction to the bailee to deliver the goods. Buyer has reasonable time to present to bailee.

e. In a case not within "c." or "d.," risk passes to buyer on receipt if seller is a merchant. If he is not, risk passes on tender of delivery.

f. Sale on approval keeps the risk with the seller until goods are accepted by buyer

g. Sale or return puts the risk on the buyer until he returns the goods

h. Risk of loss can be covered by insurance. In general, party has an insurable interest whenever he can suffer damage

1) Buyer usually allowed an insurable interest when goods are identified to the contract
2) Seller usually has an insurable interest so long as he has title or a security interest

7. Product liability--a manufacturer or seller may be responsible when a product is defective and causes injury or damage to a person or property. There are three theories under which manufacturers and sellers may be held liable.

a. Negligence--the injured party must prove the defendant failed to exercise reasonable care (common law remedy)

Example: Negligent design, negligent packaging or inadequate instructions for use of product.

Example: A car manufacturer is negligent in a structural design and as a result, a driver of a car is severely injured. The driver may sue the manufacturer even though he did not contract with the manufacturer.

1) It is generally difficult to prove this type of negligence
2) Privity of contract (contractual connection between parties, e.g., buyer-seller) is not needed because the suit is not based on a contract
3) The negligence theory is being replaced in some states by strict liability

b. Strict liability--a manufacturer or seller may be held liable for injuries caused by a product because of its inherent danger without proving negligence. (Generally based on statutes.)

1) Injured party generally must show

a) Product was defective when it left hands of seller, and
b) The defect caused the injury, and
c) The defect caused the product to be unreasonably dangerous

2) Neither bad intent nor fault of the retailer or wholesaler need be found. They are liable merely for selling it in the defective condition received from the manufacturer. They may in turn sue the manufacturer.

3) Privity of contract is not needed because the suit is not based on a contract

a) Any user or consumer of the product who is injured may sue. In some instances, they can also recover for property damages.

c. Warranty liability--purchaser of a product may sue based on the warranties made

1) Warranty of title

a) Seller warrants good title, rightful transfer and freedom from any security interest or lien that the buyer has no knowledge of

Example: A seller of stolen goods would be liable to a buyer for damages.

b) Merchant warrants goods to be free of any rightful claim of infringement, e.g., patent or trademark, unless buyer furnished specifications to seller for manufacture of the goods

c) Can only be disclaimed by specific language or circumstances which give buyer reason to know he is receiving less than full title

1] Cannot be disclaimed by language such as "as is"

2) Express warranties

a) Any affirmation of fact or promise made by the seller to the buyer which relates to the goods and becomes part of the basis of the bargain creates an express warranty that the goods shall conform to the affirmation or promise

1] Sales talk, puffing, or a statement purporting to be merely the seller's opinion does not create a warranty

2] No reliance is necessary (need not be proven) on part of buyer
3] Must form part of the basis of bargain

a] Would include advertisements read by buyer
b] Normally would not include warranties given after the sale or contract was made

4] No intent to create warranty is needed on the part of the seller

b) Any description of the goods which is made part of the basis of the bargain creates an express warranty that the goods shall conform to the description

c) Any sample or model which is made part of the basis of the bargain creates an express warranty that the goods shall conform to the sample or model

d) It is not necessary to the creation of an express warranty that the seller use formal words such as "warranty" or "guarantee"

3) Implied warranties (a promise arising by operation of law)

a) Merchantability--goods are fit for the ordinary purpose for which goods of this type are used and will pass without objection in the trade. This warranty also guarantees that the goods are properly packaged and labeled. This warranty is implied if

1] The seller is a merchant with respect to goods of the kind being sold
2] Warranty is not modified or excluded

b) Fitness for a particular purpose

   1] This warranty is created when the seller knows of the particular use for which the goods are required and further knows that the buyer is relying on the skill and judgment of the seller to select and furnish suitable goods for this particular use

   EXAMPLE: A buyer relying upon a paint salesman to select a particular exterior house paint that will effectively cover existing siding.

   2] Buyer must actually rely on seller and cannot have superior knowledge
   3] The product is then warranted for the particular expressed purpose and the seller may be liable if the product fails to so perform
   4] Applicable both to merchants and nonmerchants

4) UCC, being consumer oriented, allows these warranties to extend to parties other than the purchaser even without privity of contract

   a) Extends to a buyer's family and also to guests in the home who may reasonably be expected to use and/or be affected by the goods and who are injured

   EXAMPLE: A dinner guest breaks a tooth on a small piece of metal in the food. Note that in food, the substance causing injury must be foreign, not something customarily found in it (bone in fish).

5) Disclaimers. Warranty liability may be escaped or modified by disclaimers (also available at common law without rules defining limits of disclaimers).

   a) A disclaimer inconsistent with an express warranty is not effective, i.e., a description of a warranty in a contract cannot be disclaimed
   b) Disclaimers must be clear and conspicuous
   c) A disclaimer of merchantability must use the word "merchantability" unless all implied warranties are disclaimed as in "e." below
   d) To disclaim the implied warranty of fitness for a particular purpose, the disclaimer must be in writing and conspicuous
   e) All implied warranties (including merchantability) can be disclaimed by language such as "as is" or "with all faults" which makes plain that there is no implied warranty
   f) If the buyer has had ample opportunity to inspect the goods or sample, there is no implied warranty as to any defects which ought reasonably to have been discovered
   g) Implied warranties may be excluded or modified by course of dealing, course of performance, or usage of trade

6) Magnuson-Moss Warranty Act (federal law)--purpose is to make written warranties more understandable and meaningful to consumer

   a) Applies to consumer products manufactured after January 3, 1975 and costing more than $10
   b) Only applies where written warranties are given

     c) Must be clear and conspicuous designation of either "full warranty" or "limited warranty"

         1] "Full"--seller must agree to repair defective part. If impossible, then consumer has choice of refund or replacement without charge. No time limit can be imposed in a "full" warranty.

         2] "Limited"--seller not making one of required guarantees needed for "full warranty." If limited time is the only limitation then can be labeled "full 6, 12, etc. month warranty."

     d) Warranty may not be conditioned upon the consumer's using a brand or trade name article or service in connection with the warranted goods

     e) If written warranties are given, Magnuson-Moss Act prohibits disclaimers (ineffective if used) or modification of implied warranties (except duration may be limited to that of the written warranty)

B. Remedies for breach of contract for sale of goods

1. In general, either party may, upon breach by the other, cancel the contract and terminate executory obligations. Unlike common law rescission, however, cancellation does not discharge a claim for damages.

2. A seller's duty to perform under a contract for sale is excused if performance as agreed has been made impracticable by the occurrence of a contingency, nonoccurrence of which was a basic assumption on which the contract was made

3. Either party may demand adequate assurance of performance when reasonable grounds for insecurity arise with respect to performance of the other party

    a. E.g., buyer falls behind in payments or seller delivers defective goods to other buyers

    b. Party may suspend performance while waiting for assurance

    c. Failure to provide assurance within a reasonable time, not to exceed 30 days, is repudiation of the contract

    d. Provision in contract, that seller may accelerate payment when he has a good faith belief that makes him insecure, is valid

4. Seller's remedies

    a. Seller has right to "cure" nonconformity, i.e., tender conforming goods

       1) Within original time of contract or

       2) Within reasonable time if seller thought nonconforming tender would be acceptable

       3) Seller must notify buyer of his intention to cure

    b. A seller may resell the goods if buyer breaches in acceptance

       1) May be a public or private sale

          a) If private, must give notice to buyer who breached, otherwise losses cannot be recovered

          b) In any event, good faith purchasers take free of original buyer's claims

2) If seller resells in a commercially reasonable manner, he may recover any loss on the sale from the buyer who breached, but he is not responsible to the buyer who breached for profits made on the resale

c. A seller may stop a shipment of any size in the hands of a carrier if the buyer is insolvent

1) He may stop only carloads, truckloads, or larger lots for repudiation or failure to pay by buyer
2) Seller must notify carrier in time so carrier can reasonably stop before delivery
3) Seller is liable to carrier for any damages
4) If the goods have negotiable documents of title, carrier (bailee) can demand surrender of them before returning goods

a) Bailee is under a duty to turn goods over to the holder of negotiable documents of title regardless of insolvency

5) If carrier has acknowledged buyer's right to goods, carrier has no right to stop

d. A seller may recover goods received by an insolvent buyer if demand is made within 10 days of receipt

1) However, if the buyer has made a written misrepresentation of solvency within 3 months before delivery, this 10-day limitation does not apply

2) If buyer is insolvent, seller may demand cash to make delivery

e. Seller may recover damages

1) If buyer repudiates agreement or refuses goods, seller may recover the difference between market price at time of tender and contract price, plus incidental damages, minus expenses saved due to buyer's breach

2) If the measure of damages stated above in "1)" is inadequate to place the seller in as good a position as performance would have, then the seller can sue for the lost profits, plus incidental damages, less expenses saved due to the buyer's breach

3) The seller can recover the full contract price when

a) The buyer has already accepted the goods
b) Conforming goods have been destroyed after the risk of loss has transferred to buyer
c) The seller is unable to resell the identified goods

f. Remedies for anticipatory breach (see Breach of Contract) apply here, i.e., sue at once or wait until time for performance

1) If breach by buyer comes during manufacture of goods, seller may

a) Complete goods and identify to contract, or
b) Cease and sell for scrap, or
c) Proceed in other reasonable manner

2) Any of the above must be done while exercising reasonable commercial judgment
3) Buyer who breaches is then liable for damages measured by whatever course of action seller takes

5. Buyer's remedies

   a. Buyer may reject nonconforming goods, either in entirety or any commercial unit, e.g., bale, carload, etc.

      1) Must do so in reasonable time and give notice to seller (failure may operate as acceptance)

         a) Buyer must have reasonable time to inspect even after physical acceptance

      2) Buyer must care for goods until returned
      3) If buyer is a merchant, he must follow reasonable instructions of seller, e.g., ship, sell

         a) Right to indemnity for costs

      4) If goods are perishable or threatened with decline in value, buyer must make reasonable effort to sell
      5) Buyer has a security interest in any goods in his possession to the extent of any payments made to seller and any expenses incurred

         a) He may sell the goods as a seller may in "3.b." above

   b. Buyer may accept nonconforming goods

      1) Buyer must pay at contract price but may still recover damages, i.e., deduct damages from price if he gives seller notice

      2) Buyer may revoke acceptance in a reasonable time if

         a) Accepted expecting nonconformity to be cured
         b) Accepted because of difficulty of discovering defect
         c) Accepted because seller assured conformity

   c. Buyer may recover damages measured by the difference between the contract price and the market value of the goods at the time buyer learns of the breach, plus any incidental damages and consequential damages

      1) Consequential damages are damages resulting from buyer's needs which the seller was aware of at the time of contracting

   d. Buyer has the right of cover

      1) Buyer can buy substitute goods from another seller. The buyer will still have the right to damages after engaging in "cover."

         a) Damages are difference between cost of cover and contract price, plus incidental and consequential damages
         b) Failure to cover does not bar other remedies

6. Statute of Limitations for sale of goods is 4 years

   a. An action for breach must be commenced within this period
   b. Parties may agree to reduce to not less than one year but may not extend it
   c. Statute of Limitations begins running when the contract is breached
   d. Breach of warranty occurs upon tender of delivery
   e. If warranty expressly extends to future performance, statute runs from time breach occurs or should have been discovered

C. <u>Bulk Sales</u>--covered by Article 6 of UCC

1. A bulk transfer is any transfer in bulk which is not made in the ordinary course of business, but which consists of a major part of the materials, equipment, or inventory of a business

    a. Covers enterprises whose principal business is the sale of merchandise, including those who manufacture what they sell

2. The purpose of Article 6 is to prevent defrauding of creditors, e.g., a merchant quickly sells out and leaves without paying creditors

    a. The exceptions from Article 6 generally are transfers which ordinarily would not give rise to the defrauding of creditors

        1) Security transfers, i.e., to give security for performance
        2) General assignments for benefit of all creditors
        3) Settlement of a lien or other security interest
        4) Sales by fiduciaries and judicial or public officials
        5) Transfers to a person with a known place of business in the state who becomes bound to pay the debts and who is solvent

        6) Transfers to new business that is merely a change in form of the old business (and assumes the debts of the old business)

3. A bulk transfer is valid if

    a. Transferee requires transferor to supply a list of existing creditors, and
    b. A schedule of property transferred is prepared, and
    c. Transferee either keeps the list and schedule for 6 months and permits inspection, or files them in a public office, and

    d. Notice is given creditors at least 10 days before possession of goods is taken or payment is made, whichever happens first

4. Failure to comply makes the sale ineffective against the seller's creditors. They may enforce their claims against the goods in possession of the buyer (transferee).

    a. A subsequent bona fide purchaser (one who takes from buyer for value and without knowledge) has valid title to the goods and is free of creditor's claims

NEGOTIABLE INSTRUMENTS
(COMMERCIAL PAPER)

Overview

Commercial paper coverage on the CPA exam includes the types of negotiable instruments, the concept and importance of negotiability, the requirements of negotiability, negotiation, the holder in due course concept, defenses, and the rights of parties to a negotiable instrument. The function of commercial paper is to provide a medium of exchange which is readily transferable like money and yet does not require present payment. In effect it creates credit, yet it is easier to transfer than contract rights and not subject to as many defenses as contracts are. To be negotiable, an instrument must

a. Be a writing signed by the maker or drawer;
b. Contain an unconditional promise or order to pay a sum certain in money;
c. Be payable on demand or at definite time;
d. Be payable to order or bearer;
e. Contain no other promise except the payment of money.

These requirements must be present on the face of the instrument. Instruments which do not comply with these provisions are non-negotiable and are transferable only by assignment. The assignee of a non-negotiable instrument takes it subject to all defenses.

Commercial paper (negotiable instruments) is a frequently and heavily weighted subject on the CPA exam. The central theme of the exam questions on negotiable instruments, whether in objective or essay form, is what is the liability of the primary parties under various factual circumstances and what is the liability of secondarily liable parties under certain fact situations. Similar questions in different form emphasize what are the rights of the holder against the primary party and secondary parties under certain sets of circumstances. Thus in reviewing this area of business law, emphasis should be placed upon the legal liability arising upon execution of negotiable commercial paper, the legal liability arising upon indorsements of various types, and the warranty of various parties upon transfer or presentment for payment. A solid understanding of the distinction between real and personal defenses is required. Also frequently tested is the relationship between a bank and its customers. understanding of the distinction between real and personal defenses is required. Also, frequently tested is the relationship between a bank and its customers and the negotiation of documents of title and investment securities.

Negotiable Instrument Definitions

Concept of Negotiability. A characteristic of a special class of contracts which permits a written obligation to pass freely from person to person as a substitute for money. A transferee of the instrument may obtain better rights than the transferor had if the transferee satisfies the requirements of being a holder in due course.

Words of Negotiability. Every negotiable instrument must be payable on its face to "order" or to "bearer" to be negotiable. These are the so-called magic words of negotiability.

Holder in Due Course. Any person who has possession of an instrument that was either drawn, issued, or indorsed to him, or to his order, or to bearer. Also, a holder in due course must take the instrument for value, in good faith, without notice of its being overdue or dishonored, or knowledge that any person has a defense against it or a claim to it. A holder in due course takes an instrument free from any personal defenses.

Personal Defenses. Defenses or claims between the original parties to the contract, such as absence or failure of consideration, nondelivery of completed instrument, fraud in the inducement, nondelivery of an incomplete instrument, conditional delivery of a completed instrument, payment before maturity, and prior discharge of a party.

Real Defenses. Defenses which go to the validity of the instrument at its inception and includes incapacity, duress, illegality, forgery, material alterations, fraud in the execution of the instrument, and discharge of the party in a bankruptcy or other insolvency proceeding.

Shelter Provision. A party acquiring a negotiable instrument from a holder in due course acquires the holder in due course status although the taker does not himself satisfy the requirements of being a holder in due course. This subsequent holder acquires all the rights of a holder in due course unless a party to any prior fraud or illegality affecting the instrument.

Issue. The first delivery of an instrument. Subsequent delivery of an instrument is called a transfer or negotiation.

Drawee. A person on whom a check or draft is drawn, e.g., a bank.

Drawer. Person who writes and signs a check or draft.

Maker. A person who writes and signs a note as a promise to pay.

Payee. A person to whom a check, draft, or note is made out.

Indorser. A person who signs the back of an instrument to transfer it.

Primary Liability. A maker of a note or an acceptor of a draft has primary liability because he has contracted or promised to pay the instrument according to its terms.

Secondarily Liable. Parties such as a drawer and indorsers promise to pay the instrument only upon dishonor and notice of its dishonor.

Presentment. Where a holder of an instrument makes a demand for acceptance or payment to a maker, acceptor, drawee, or other payor. It must be timely to be proper.

A. Negotiable Instrument

1. A contractual obligation which calls for the payment of money but at the same time provides a medium of exchange in lieu of money by allowing the exchange of funds in the form of a note, check, draft, etc.

   a. Most important concept is that a subsequent holder, by meeting certain requirements, can take an instrument free of most contractual claims or defenses on it

      1) Normally an assignee of a contract right is subject to defenses on the contract, e.g., nonperformance

         EXAMPLE: X Company entered into a contract to sell goods to Y Company. X Company assigned its contract right to payment for the goods to Z Company in payment of a debt. If the goods do not conform to the contract, Y Company can refuse to pay Z Company by asserting its defenses on the contract.

      2) But a holder in due course of a negotiable instrument would be free of most claims of the maker or promisor of a note against the payee

         EXAMPLE: X Company entered into a contract to sell goods to Y Company, but Y Company gave X Company a negotiable note before receiving the goods. X Company transferred the note to Z Company (who qualified as a HDC). Y Company must now pay on the note regardless of any contractual defenses against X Company.

   b. A nonnegotiable instrument can still be assigned as in a contract but the taker or holder is subject to all the defenses of prior parties

B. Types of Negotiable Instruments

1. A promissory note is a promise to pay a sum of money

   a. It is a two-party instrument: maker and payee
   b. The person promising to pay is the maker, and the person to be paid is the payee
   c. May be payable on demand or on a date
   d. May include provisions for collection fees, attorney's fees, interest, etc.

EXAMPLE: "I promise to pay to bearer $1,000 on July 4, 1980."

2. A draft is an order from one person directing another to pay a third person

    a. It is a three-party instrument: drawer, drawee and payee
    b. The person ordering payment is the "drawer"
    c. The person to whom the order is directed is the "drawee"
    d. The person to receive payment is the "payee"
    e. Drafts may be payable on sight (on demand) or within a certain time

EXAMPLE: "Bank, pay to bearer $1,000 in 30 days."

3. Checks are an order by the drawer directing a bank to pay money to the payee

    a. A type of draft
    b. Must be drawn on a bank
    c. Must be payable on demand (holder can ask for payment any time)

4. Certificates of deposit are written acknowledgments by a bank of receipt of money with a promise to repay

    a. A type of note

5. Trade acceptance is an order by a buyer directing some payor (bank) to pay seller

    a. Given to seller for a sale of goods
    b. Buyer must accept it by signing
    c. A type of draft

6. Other instruments which may be negotiable and have consequences similar to those of notes and drafts but which are not governed by this section (Articles 3 and 4 of UCC) and do not have holders in due course

    a. Letter of credit is an engagement by a bank in behalf of a customer (buyer) to honor demands for payment of seller upon compliance with specified conditions
    b. Bill of lading (document of title) is a receipt for the delivery of goods to a carrier. Goods are only released on surrender of it.

        1) Use same basic rules to determine who is a holder in due course and whether one exists (although called "holder to whom duly negotiated")
        2) Major difference is documents of title are not payable in money but rather in delivery of identified goods

    c. Investment security evidences an interest in property, an enterprise (stock), or an obligation, e.g., bond

        1) All are negotiable
        2) Issued in bearer form or registered, i.e., specific holder is registered
        3) "Bona fide purchaser" is the term used similar to a holder in due course

C. Requirements of Negotiability (all are required)

    a) Written and signed by the maker (note) or the drawer (draft)
    b) Unconditional promise or order to pay a sum certain in money
    c) Payable at a definite time or on demand

        d) Payable to order or to bearer
        e) Contains no other promise or obligation

1. Must be <u>written and signed</u> by the maker or drawer

   a. Writing is satisfied by handwriting, printing, typing, or any other reduction to physical form
   b. Signing is satisfied by any symbol intended to represent a signature

      1) Intent is the important factor
      2) May use own name or assumed name
      3) Rubber stamp, printing, or initials are accepted

   c. See AGENCY for signature by agent and liability thereon

2. Must contain an <u>unconditional promise or order</u> to pay a <u>sum certain</u> in money

   a. Unconditional means not subject to any conditions

      1) If payment depends upon (subject to) another agreement or transaction, then it is conditional and nonnegotiable

        a) It may state the consideration given for the underlying transaction, or that it arose out of a separate agreement
        b) If provision requires one to refer to something not within four corners of instrument to determine his rights, it is conditional and nonnegotiable

        EXAMPLE: "I promise to pay $100 to bearer if X completes his contract," is conditional and nonnegotiable.

      2) If payment is only to be from a certain source, then it is conditional and nonnegotiable. However, instrument is still unconditional if:

        a) It indicates a particular account that is to be debited (for bookkeeping purposes)
        b) By government, it can be limited to payment from a particular fund or source
        c) It is limited to entire assets of a partnership, association, trust, or estate

        EXAMPLE: "I promise to pay $100 to bearer only out of my account in Bank X," is conditional and nonnegotiable.

      3) If there are other promises or agreements, but payment is not dependent upon them, then it is still unconditional

        a) May state that it is secured
        b) May promise to maintain or protect collateral

   b. Promise or order is more than an acknowledgment or request
      1) A promise is an undertaking to pay
      2) An order is a direction to pay

   c. It is a sum certain even if it includes installments, possible discounts, interest rates, collection fees, and attorney's fees
      1) If not stated, interest runs from date of issue
      2) Even if no interest on note, judgment rate (specified by state statute) of interest runs from time of demand of payment

3) Sum certain if, at any time of payment, holder can determine the amount payable

d. Money is any accepted medium of exchange

   1) Foreign currency is acceptable

3. Must be payable at a <u>definite time or on demand</u>

   a. It is a definite time if payable:

      1) On a certain date, or
      2) X days after a certain date, or
      3) Within a certain time, or
      4) On a certain date subject to acceleration

         a) E.g., where a payment is missed, total balance may become due at once

      5) On a certain date subject to an extension of time, if:

         a) At the option of the holder
         b) At the option of the maker or drawer only if extension is limited to a definite amount of time

   b. It is not definite if payable on an act or event that is not certain as to time of occurrence, e.g., death
   c. On demand includes:

      1) Payable on sight
      2) Payable on presentation
      3) No time for payment stated

4. Document must be payable <u>to order</u> or <u>to bearer</u>. These are the magic words of negotiability.

   a. The instrument is payable to order if made payable to the order of:

      1) Any person, including the maker, drawer, drawee, or payee
      2) Two persons together or alternatively
      3) Any entity

   b. The instrument is also payable to order if it is payable to a person and his "assigns"
   c. The instrument is not payable to order if it is only payable to a person, e.g., "pay John Doe"

      1) Not negotiable
      2) It should be "pay to the order of John Doe" to be negotiable

   d. The instrument is payable to bearer if it is payable to:

      1) "Bearer"
      2) "Cash"
      3) "A person or bearer"

         a) But <u>not</u> to a person only, e.g., "pay to John Doe"

      4) "Order of bearer" or "order of cash"

   e. If payable both to order and to bearer, it is payable to order unless bearer words are typed or handwritten (not part of preprinted form)

f. The instrument cannot be made payable to persons consecutively, e.g., the maker cannot specify subsequent holders

g. Distinction between "order" or "bearer" is important for negotiation. See Negotiation.

D. Interpretation of Ambiguities in Negotiable Instruments

1. Contradictory terms

a. Words control over figures
b. Handwritten terms control over typewritten and printed terms
c. Typewritten terms control over printed (typeset) terms
d. If ambiguity exists as to whether a note or a draft, it can be treated as either
e. An instrument containing "I promise to pay" and signed by two persons results in joint and several liability for both

2. Omissions

a. Uncompleted instrument at time of signing is not enforceable until completed

   1) Holder may complete as authorized
   2) If completed without authority, it is treated as a material alteration. See Rights of a Holder in Due Course.
   3) Omits an essential date

      a) Essential if payment refers to it

         EXAMPLE: *"Pay X days after date."*

      b) If not essential, then enforceable and negotiable as a demand instrument

         EXAMPLE: *"Pay to bearer."*

b. Omission of statement of consideration does not affect negotiability (presumed)
c. Omission of where instrument is drawn or payable does not affect negotiability
d. If rate of interest is omitted when interest is provided for, use statutory judgment rate from the date of the instrument or the date of issue if undated
e. Seal is not needed

3. Others

a. Instrument may be postdated or antedated
b. Instrument may provide that by indorsing or cashing it, the payee acknowledges full satisfaction of debt
c. If an instrument is payable to order of more than one person:

   1) Either payee may negotiate or enforce it if payable to him in the alternative

      EXAMPLE: *"Pay $100 to the order of X or Y." Either X or Y may indorse it.*

   2) All payees must negotiate or enforce it if not payable to them in the alternative

EXAMPLE: "Pay $100 to the order of X and Y." Both X and Y must indorse it to obtain payment.

    d. Where instrument contains an extension of time provision

        1) The extension is limited to a period of time not longer than the original period if the provision does not specify otherwise
        2) A consent to extension embodied in the instrument binds those who sign it
        3) Holder may not extend time if maker or acceptor objects and tenders full payment

    e. Transferor and transferee may modify terms of a negotiable instrument as between them by a written agreement executed as part of the same transaction

        1) Affects subsequent transferees, except
        2) HDC not affected if he takes without notice

E. Negotiation

1. Mere "transfer" of an instrument is the transfer without the requirements of negotiation

    a. Transferee obtains only the rights the transferor had, i.e., any defenses against the transferor are good against the transferee

    b. Transferee may have the requirements fulfilled, i.e., indorsement, and become a holder of a negotiated instrument at that date

        1) An enforceable right of the transferee

2. "Negotiation" is the transfer of an instrument by the proper means so the transferee becomes a holder (necessary to be a holder in due course)

    a. Bearer paper is negotiated by mere delivery
    b. Order paper requires the party negotiating to indorse and deliver the instrument
    c. Indorsement must convey entire instrument or it is a partial assignment and not effective for negotiation

3. Indorsements

    a. Blank indorsement is the transferor's signature alone, and converts order paper to bearer paper, e.g., indorse a check by signing it

        1) Holder may write above the indorsement and convert it to a special indorsement

    b. Special indorsement is made to a specific person called an indorsee, e.g., on a check indorsed "payable to Smith, signed Jones"

        1) May only be further negotiated by payee's (Smith's) indorsement
        2) Notice that negotiability is not destroyed by an indorsement. The words "order" or "bearer" only need to be on the face of the instrument.

EXAMPLE: A check that is payable to the order of Clark on its face has the following indorsements on its back:

On its face this instrument is order paper, thus Clark's indorsement is needed for proper negotiation. When Clark signs blank indorsement this changes the instrument to bearer paper in Smithers' hands. Smithers can properly negotiate the check by mere delivery. When Smithers engages in a special indorsement this changes the check back to order paper in the hands of White.

   c. Restrictive indorsement restricts payment, e.g., "for deposit only" or "pay if X work is done"

     1) Subsequent transferees must comply with the indorsement or be sure it has been done
     2) Restrictions prohibiting further transfer are of no effect

   d. Qualified indorsement disclaims (contract but not warranty) liability if the instrument is dishonored, e.g., "without recourse"

     1) This has the effect of reducing the warranty of "no defense" to "no knowledge of any defense." (See <u>Liability</u>.)

4. Negotiation is effective even if it may be rescinded, e.g., made by a minor or obtained by fraud or duress

5. If a prior party reacquires an instrument, he may cancel any indorsement not necessary to his title, e.g., all those after his earlier indorsement

   a. He may further negotiate the instrument
   b. A party whose indorsement is stricken is discharged against all (has no further liability), even against a subsequent HDC

   c. If he renegotiates it without cancelling parties, the parties between his two indorsements are discharged to all except subsequent HDC

6. Use of another's name

   a. Indorsement is effective if payee named is not intended to have an interest in the instrument

EXAMPLE: Agent has authority to sign checks. He makes one out to a non-existent payee, indorses, and cashes it himself (fictitious payee exception).

EXAMPLE: Employee submits time card of nonexistent employee and drawer, in good faith, signs the check. Employee indorses and cashes it himself (fictitious payee exception).

EXAMPLE: Imposter represents himself as another. Drawer makes check out to this other person and imposter indorses and cashes it (imposter exception).

b. If the named payee was intended to have the instrument, then indorsement by another is forgery and not effective

   EXAMPLE: Payroll check is delivered to a rightful employee. The employee loses the check and the finder of the check indorses the employee's name on it.

c. Not fraudulent to use a name other than one's own if not for a fraudulent purpose

d. If payee's name is misspelled, he may indorse in proper spelling or in misspelling, but a taker for value may require both

F. Holder in Due Course

1. In general, a holder in due course (HDC) is a designation for a person who is entitled to payment on a negotiable instrument regardless of the payor's contractual claims

2. To be a holder in due course, a taker must:

   a. Be a holder (explained in Negotiation, just above)
   b. Take the instrument for value

      1) A holder gives value if he:

         a) Pays or performs the agreed consideration
         b) Acquires a security interest in the instrument, e.g., the holder takes possession of the instrument as collateral for another debt
         c) Gives another negotiable instrument
         d) Takes as a satisfaction of a previous existing debt

      2) A bank takes for value (has a security interest) to the extent that credit has been given for a deposit and withdrawn

         a) FIFO method is used to determine whether it has been withdrawn

         EXAMPLE: Y opens an account in X bank for $500 cash. Later Y deposits a $500 check. If Y withdraws $500, X bank has not yet given value for the check because the original $500 cash has been withdrawn under FIFO. However, if Y withdraws $1,000, X bank has given value for the check.

      3) An executory promise is not value unless it is irrevocable, e.g., contract

      4) Value does not have to be for full amount of instrument

         a) If less, HDC only to extent value given
         b) Purchase at discount is value for full face amount of instrument provided HDC took in good faith, as long as not too large a discount

         EXAMPLE: Purchase of a $1,000 instrument in good faith for $950 is considered full value, but purchase of the same instrument for $500 is not considered full value due to the grossly excessive discount.

   c. Take in good faith

      1) Adopts a subjective test of good faith ("empty head, pure heart theory"), rather than an objective test based on what might be commercially reasonable under the circumstances

d. Take without notice that it is overdue, has been dishonored, or that any person has a defense or claim to it

1) Holder has notice when he knows or has reason to know
2) Overdue

a) Domestic checks presumed overdue in 30 days
b) Acceleration of an instrument is notice

3) Defense or claim

a) So incomplete, irregular, or obvious signs of forgery
b) If purchaser has notice that any party's claim is voidable or that all parties have been discharged

4) There is no notice of a defense or claim if:

a) It is antedated or postdated
b) He knows that there has been a default in payment or interest

5) But one may acquire notice _after_ becoming a holder and giving value

a) I.e., once one is a HDC, acquiring notice does not end HDC status

G. Rights of a Holder in Due Course

1. A holder in due course takes free of all person's claims and defenses _except_:

a. He takes subject to all real and personal defenses of the person with whom he dealt

1) I.e., the special rights of a HDC do not apply between the HDC and the person from whom he acquired the negotiable instrument

b. He takes subject to real defenses
c. Federal Trade Commission has abolished the HDC rule (i.e., HDC will take subject to all defenses) in consumer credit sales where:

1) Third party takes consumer's note or installment contract in a retail sale
2) It only applies to consumer credit transactions
3) It does not apply where no credit is given, i.e., where consumer pays with a check
4) Purpose is to prevent a consumer from being required to pay on a negotiable instrument when he has a contractual claim against the seller

2. Real defenses generally exist when the instrument lacks legal validity at its inception. Real defenses that a HDC takes subject to are:

a. Forgery

1) Applies to signatures of makers, drawers, and indorsers
2) May be ratified and thereby not a defense
3) Includes authorized agents exceeding their authority
4) A forged signature creates no liability against the person whose signature it purports to be, but instead operates as the signature of the unauthorized signer
5) Exceptions

a) Fictitious payee rule - If the person signing the instrument on behalf of the maker or drawer, or supplying the name of the payee to the maker or drawer, intends the payee to have no interest in the instrument, then such person has the power to indorse the instrument in the payee's name and transfer good title to a holder in due course. This would not create a real defense on the instrument.

EXAMPLE: Hawkins, the assistant to the controller of a general partnership, told the controller that the firm owed Samuel $500. The alleged Samuel represented by Hawkins to be a creditor was a fictitious person. Relying upon Hawkins' statement, the controller signed the firm name to the check. Hawkins indorsed the check on its back, signing the name "Henry Samuel," and cashed it at a liquor store. The drawee bank can charge the firm's account since the partnership has no real defense because of the fictitious payee exception. Anyone could indorse this instrument with "Henry Samuel" and transfer good title to the check because Hawkins never intended that the payee have an interest in the check. (Fact situation found in Question 43 of November 1977 CPA Exam.)

b) Imposter exception - This exception occurs when an imposter induces the maker or drawer to issue the instrument to the imposter in the name of the person the imposter is representing himself to be. The indorsement of the imposter does not constitute a forgery.

EXAMPLE: Davidson bears a remarkable physical resemblance to Ford, one of the town's most prominent citizens. He presented himself one day at the Friendly Finance Company, represented himself as Ford, and requested a loan of $500. Accordingly, being anxious to please so prominent a citizen, the manager at Friendly delivered to Davidson a $500 check payable to Ford. When Davidson signs Ford's name on the back of the check this does not create the real defense of forgery because of the imposter rule. A holder in due course could enforce this instrument against Friendly. (Fact situation found in Question 47 of November 1978 CPA Exam.)

c) If person's negligence substantially contributes to the forgery that person is prevented from raising the defense of forgery.

EXAMPLE: Drawer has a signature stamp and leaves it lying around.

b. Material alterations of instrument

1) Alteration of amount, date, parties, etc.

a) If fraudulent, it discharges any party whose contract is thereby changed as against any other party other than a subsequent HDC

EXAMPLE: X makes a check payable to Y for $100. Y manages to change it to $1,000. X is no longer liable on the check to Y.

b) A subsequent HDC may enforce it according to its original tenor

EXAMPLE: If Y in the above example negotiates the $1,000 check to a HDC, the HDC may still enforce it against X for $100.

2) Also unauthorized completion

a) If fraudulent, it discharges any party whose contract is thereby changed as against any party other than a subsequent HDC

EXAMPLE: X writes a check for $100 but does not fill in to whom it is to be paid. Y steals this check and completes it as payable to Y. X is not liable on the check to Y.

b) A subsequent HDC may enforce it as completed

EXAMPLE: Y in the above example negotiates the check, which he made payable to himself, to a HDC. The HDC may enforce the check against X.

3) No defense if the drawer's or maker's negligence substantially contributed to the alteration or completion

EXAMPLE: Drawer leaves signed but uncompleted checks in his desk.

c. Fraud

1) Applies to the instrument itself

a) E.g., misrepresentation as to the character of or terms of the instrument

EXAMPLE: X writes a note payable to himself and induces Y, who cannot read, to sign it by telling Y that it is a receipt needed to win a prize.

2) Fraud as to the underlying consideration or inducement to give the instrument is a personal defense, i.e., it is not a real defense, and it cannot be asserted against a HDC

d. Void transaction (not voidable)

1) Caused by duress, illegality (e.g., usury), incapacity
2) Determined by state law, not UCC

e. Infancy unless for necessities
f. Discharge in bankruptcy or another discharge that the holder has notice of when he takes the instrument

EXAMPLE: Crossed out indorsements are notice that the parties crossed out are discharged. These crossed out parties have a real defense against a HDC.

3. A person who takes through a holder in due course acquires the same rights as a holder in due course due to <u>Shelter Provision</u>

a. A holder in due course (HDC) has the effect of "washing" the instrument

EXAMPLE: A HDC transfers a note to X who knows that the payee violated the terms of the contract under which the note was issued. X is not a HDC because he has notice of a defense on the note. However, X has the rights of a HDC because he took it after a HDC. The defense is personal and X may recover on the note from the maker.

b. Does not apply to holders who also held subject to the defense prior to the HDC, i.e., person who reacquires instrument

c. Does not apply to defenses arising by holders subsequent to the HDC

4. A person who is not a HDC and who has not taken through a HDC takes the instrument subject to all defenses and any party's claim

H. Liability of Parties

1. Maker of a note and acceptor of an instrument have primary liability, i.e., they promise to pay the instrument according to its tenor

    a. Acceptance is the drawee's signed engagement to honor it when presented

        1) By writing on the instrument; signature alone is good
        2) By certification (bank unconditionally promises to pay a check)

            a) Where a holder obtains certification of an instrument, the drawer and all prior indorsers are discharged
            b) Where a drawer obtains certification of an instrument, all prior indorsers are discharged but the drawer is not
            c) Bank has no obligation to certify

    b. Drawee is not liable at all until acceptance

        1) Holder cannot require a drawee to accept

            a) Refusal to accept is dishonor of the instrument

        2) Drawee is liable only to drawer if he does not accept

    c. Co-makers have joint and several liability, i.e., either one can be held liable for full amount
    d. No party is ever (contractually) liable until he signs the instrument in some manner

2. Drawer and indorsers are secondarily liable, i.e., they promise to pay only upon dishonor of the instrument and notice of the dishonor

    a. Either may sign "without recourse" and avoid this liability (but it may be difficult to transfer as such)
    b. Indorsers are liable in the order in which they signed, i.e., from bottom up

        1) Parties are only liable to subsequent holders or the payor
        2) May agree otherwise
        3) Practical effect is that the first solvent indorser will be held liable and he will in turn have to proceed against a prior indorser

        EXAMPLE: Maker of a note is insolvent and indorsers signed in the following order, from top to bottom: A, B, C, D. The holder of the note seeks payment. D is liable first, then C, then B, then A. If C and D are insolvent, B will be liable as the first solvent indorser.

    c. Any indorser makes the following <u>warranties</u> upon transfer and receipt of consideration

        1) Has good title or is authorized to receive payment by one who does
        2) All signatures are good
        3) No material alterations
        4) No defense of any party is good against him

            a) A transferor indorsing "without recourse" warrants only that he has no knowledge of any defense of any party that is good against him

        5) No knowledge of any insolvency proceeding against maker or drawer
        6) Transferor makes these warranties only to his transferee if he does not indorse. If he does he also makes them to all subsequent holders who take in good faith.

> Note: These warranties are one reason why an indorser who is held liable on the note can proceed against a prior indorser.

    d. Any unauthorized signature operates as signature of the unauthorized party and he may be held liable in the capacity in which he signed

3. Any person who obtains payment or acceptance and any prior transferor warrants to the payor, e.g., maker, drawee, that:

    a. He has good title or is authorized to receive payment by one who does
    b. He has no knowledge of forgery of maker's or drawer's signature

      1) HDC does not so warrant to maker or drawer with respect to maker's or drawer's own signature
      2) HDC does not so warrant to drawee if acting in good faith

    c. No material alterations

      1) HDC does not so warrant to maker or drawer

4. Accommodation party is liable in the capacity in which he has signed even if taker knows of his accommodation status

    a. Accommodation party is one who signs to lend his name to other party

    EXAMPLE: Father-in-law indorses a note for son-in-law so creditor will accept it.

    b. Accommodating maker is liable as a maker would be
    c. Accommodating indorser is liable as an indorser would be
    d. Indorsement that shows it is not in chain of title is notice of its accommodation character

    EXAMPLE: A check is payable to P. P indorses on the back, "Pay to the order of X, signed P." However X requires Y to sign as an accommodation indorser for P before X will take the check. If Y signs after P, it is out of order since X would normally sign after P. Therefore subsequent holders have notice that Y is an accommodation indorser.

      1) Notice of default need not be given to accommodation party

    e. The accommodation party has right of recourse against accommodated party if the accommodation party is held liable
      1) In effect, a surety

5. Guarantor adds words of guarantee to signature

    a. Payment guaranteed--if instrument not paid when due, he will pay
      1) Holder need not resort to any other party

    b. Collection guaranteed--if instrument not paid when due, he will pay only after a judgment is obtained and it cannot be collected, or if the acceptor is insolvent
    c. Presentment (defined in "2.a" on next page) and notice of dishonor not necessary

6. Agent is liable if:

    a. He signs in his name only (principal is not liable)

b. He signs in his name and names the principal but does not show he signed in a representative capacity (principal is also liable)

   EXAMPLE: Signed, "ABC company, John Doe."

c. He signs in his name showing a representative capacity but does not name the principal (principal is not liable)

   EXAMPLE: Signed, "John Doe, Agent."

d. Agent should sign "John Doe as agent for ABC Company" or similarly

I. Holding Parties Liable

1. Due presentment and due notice of dishonor are necessary to hold parties liable

    a. Delay of either one will discharge all indorsers

    b. Delay will only discharge drawer, acceptor, or maker if:

       1) Instrument is payable at a bank, and
       2) Bank becomes insolvent, and
       3) The drawer, acceptor, or maker assigns holder his right against the insolvent bank

    c. Protest may also be needed for foreign drafts (drawn or payable outside the U.S.)

       1) A formal attestation of dishonor by a U.S. consul
       2) Only limited use any more

2. Presentment

    a. A demand for acceptance or payment to maker, acceptor, drawee, or other payor
    b. May be made in person, by mail, or through a clearing house
    c. Must be made on or before the date it is payable or within a reasonable time if a demand instrument

       1) For drawer reasonable time is 30 days after date or issue, whichever is later
       2) For indorser reasonable time is 7 days after indorsement
       3) Must be at a reasonable hour--at bank during banking hours

    d. Payment or acceptance is due by the end of the business day following presentment but may be deferred by the person who is to pay (maker, acceptor, or drawee) for one business day

       1) Effect is that payment or acceptance must be made by the end of the next business day or there is dishonor

3. Notice of dishonor--dishonor occurs when acceptance or payment is refused after presentment

    a. Must be given to secondarily liable parties to hold them liable
    b. Must be given to each party one wishes to hold liable

       1) One notice operates for all who have rights against party notified

          EXAMPLE: Maker dishonors a note. The holder gives timely notice of the dishonor to all indorsers; A, B, and C who signed in order from top to bottom. If holder holds C liable, C may hold B liable. Holder's notice to B was effective for C also.

c. May be written, oral, or in any other reasonable manner. Effective if sent to last known address.

d. Notice must be given by:

1) Banks before midnight of the next banking day following receipt of item or receipt of notice of dishonor, whichever is later

2) Others before midnight of the third business day following dishonor or receipt of notice of dishonor

e. Notice to one partner is notice to all partners even if partnership is dissolved

f. Written notice is deemed to be received when sent (even though lost and never received)

EXAMPLE: A and B have indorsed a note. C presents it to maker for payment. Maker refuses to pay (dishonor). C notifies B of the dishonor within three days, but A is not notified for a week. C holds B liable. A cannot be held liable because he was not given timely notice of dishonor. B must resort to the maker.

4. Excused presentment and notice of dishonor

a. Delay of presentment and notice of dishonor is excused when party has no notice that instrument is due, e.g., acceleration without knowledge

b. Failure of presentment and notice of dishonor are excused when party to be charged (e.g., indorser) waives it

1) Waiver may be express or implied; either before or after presentment or notice is due

a) Waiver is express, if party to be charged writes, "I waive holder's failure to make presentment or to give notice of dishonor"

b) Waiver is implied if party to be charged pays

c. Failure of notice of dishonor is excused when party to be charged has dishonored it himself

d. Presentment is excused when obligor is dead or insolvent, or appears futile for other reasons

e. Waiver is often embodied in instrument itself and is binding on all parties

1) If only written above indorser's signature, it is only binding on that one indorser

5. Discharge of parties from liability

a. Upon discharge, a party is released from liability except:

1) A discharge is not effective against a subsequent HDC who does not have notice of the discharge when he takes the instrument

b. Discharge has already been stated with respect to:

1) Reacquisition and renegotiation--see <u>Negotiation</u> .

2) Fraudulent and material alteration--see <u>Rights of a Holder in Due Course</u>

3) Certification--see <u>Liability of Parties</u>

4) Delay in presentment and notice--see above

c. Discharge is also obtained

1) To the extent of payment or satisfaction to the holder

a) Cannot be made in bad faith, e.g., knowledge of theft of instrument

EXAMPLE: *Maker knows the instrument has been stolen from payee and payee's name forged. Maker is not discharged on the note if he pays a holder because payee may still collect from maker.*

b) Cannot be made in violation of restrictive indorsement

2) By making tender of full payment

a) Discharged to extent of subsequent liability for interest, costs and attorney's fees
b) Holder's refusal to accept tender discharges any party with recourse against party making tender

1] E.g., accommodation party of one making tender
2] E.g., indorsers are discharged from liability when maker tenders to holder

3) By cancellation, e.g., striking out another party's signature discharges the party whose signature is struck out

a) Holder may strike out any prior party's signature
b) No consideration needed

4) By renunciation, i.e., holder renounces rights against a particular party

a) Must be by a writing signed and delivered, or by surrendering the instrument to the party

5) Any person in position of a surety is discharged as in SURETYSHIP to the extent the holder releases, agrees not to sue, extends time, or impairs collateral, unless:

a) Holder preserves his rights against surety and surety's rights to recourse against others
b) Accommodation party and indorsers are in the same positions as sureties

6) Drawer and indorsers are discharged if holder assents to drawee's acceptance which varies the terms of the instrument

7) Any party may be discharged by an act or agreement with another party that would discharge a contract

a) Discharge is between those parties only

EXAMPLE: *A, B, C, and D have signed as indorsers. A may pay D $10 not to ever hold A liable. However B and C may still hold A liable if they are held liable first.*

J. Banks

1. Relationship between bank and depositor is debtor-creditor

a. Even though the depositor has funds in the bank, a payee cannot force a drawee to make payment. Banks are only liable to the drawer.
b. Only a drawer has an action against the bank-drawee for wrongfully dishonoring a check

2. Checks

   a. Banks are not obligated to pay on a check presented more than 6 months after date

      1) But they may pay in good faith and charge customer's account

   b. Even if a check creates an overdraft, a bank may charge customer's account

      1) In effect it is a loan

   c. Bank is liable to drawer for wrongful dishonor of a check

      1) Wrongful dishonor may occur if the bank in error believes funds are insufficient when they are sufficient

      2) Damages include consequential damages, e.g., damages resulting from nonpayment of the check

   d. Payment of bad checks, e.g., forged, altered, etc.

      1) Bank is liable to drawer for payment on bad checks unless drawer's negligence contributed

      2) Bank cannot recover from an innocent holder in due course to whom the bank paid on a bad check

      3) Drawer must inspect cancelled checks and inform bank promptly of any bad checks which were paid

   e. Oral stop payment is good for 14 days; written is good for six months and is renewable

      1) Stop-payment order must be given so as to afford the bank a reasonable opportunity to act on it

      2) Bank is liable to drawer if it pays after effective stop-payment order when drawer can prove that the bank's failure to obey the order caused drawer's loss. If drawer has no valid defense to justify dishonoring instrument then bank has no liability for failure to obey stop-payment order.

        EXAMPLE: Smith buys a T.V. set from the ABC Appliance Store and pays for the set with a check. Later in the day Smith finds a better model for the same price at another store. Smith telephones his bank and orders the bank to stop payment on the check. If the bank mistakenly pays Smith's check two days after receiving the stop order, the bank will not be liable since Smith could not rightfully rescind his agreement with ABC. Thus, Smith suffered no damages due to the bank's mistake. (Fact situation found in Question No. 5, November 1980 CPA Exam.)

      3) If drawer stops payment on the check, he is still liable to holder of check unless he has a valid defense (e.g., if holder qualifies as a holder in due course then drawer must be able to assert a real defense to free himself of liability)

   f. If depositor dies or becomes incompetent, bank may pay checks until it knows and then has a reasonable time to act

      1) May pay for 10 days after death even with knowledge, unless ordered to stop by an interested party, e.g., executor

g. Bank is entitled to a depositor's indorsement on checks deposited with the bank

   1) If missing, bank may supply

K. Transfer of Negotiable Documents of Title

1. The transfer of documents of title is governed by Article 7 of the UCC. The transfer of such documents is very similar to the transfer of negotiable instruments under Article 3 of the UCC.

2. Types of documents of title

   a. Bill of lading is a document issued by a carrier (a person engaged in the business of transporting or forwarding goods) evidencing receipt of the goods for transfer

   b. A warehouse receipt is a document issued as evidence of receipt of goods by a person engaged in the business of storing goods for hire

3. Form

   a. Negotiable. The document of title is negotiable if the face of the document contains the words of negotiability (order or bearer).

      1) Order document -- a document of title containing a promise to deliver the goods to the order of a named person. The person may be named on the face of the document or, if there are indorsements on the back of the document and the last indorsement is a special indorsement.

         a) Proper negotiation requires delivery of the document and indorsement by the named individual(s)

      2) Bearer document -- a document of title containing a promise to deliver the goods to bearer. "Bearer" may be stated on the face of the document or, if there are indorsements on the back of the document and the last indorsement is a blank indorsement.

         a) Proper negotiation merely requires delivery of the document

   b. Nonnegotiable (straight) documents of title are assigned, not negotiated. The assignee will never receive any better rights than the assignor had in the document.

      1) Indorsement of a nonnegotiable document neither makes it negotiable nor adds to the transferee's rights

4. Due negotiation. A document of title is "duly negotiated" when it is negotiated to a holder who takes it in good faith in the ordinary course of business without notice of a defense and pays value.

   a. Value does not include payment of a preexisting (antecedent) debt. This is an important difference from the value concept required to create a holder in due course under Article 3 of the UCC.

5. Rights acquired by due negotiation. A holder by due negotiation acquires rights very similar to those acquired by a holder in due course.

   a. These rights include:

        1) Title to the document
        2) Title to the goods
        3) All rights accruing under the law of agency or estoppel, including rights to goods delivered to the bailee after the document was issued, and
        4) The direct obligation of the issuer to hold or deliver the goods according to the terms of the document

  b. A holder by due negotiation defeats similar defenses to those defeated by a holder in due course under Article 3 of the UCC (personal but not real defenses)

  c. A document of title procurred by a thief upon placing stolen goods in a warehouse confers no rights in the underlying goods. This defense is valid against a subsequent holder to whom the document of title has been duly negotiated. Therefore, the original owner of the goods can assert better title to the goods than a holder who has received the document through due negotiation.

6. Rights acquired in the absence of due negotiation

  a. A transferee of a document, whether negotiable or nonnegotiable, to whom the document has been delivered, but not duly negotiated, acquires the title and rights which his transferor had or had actual authority to convey

7. Warranties transferred upon negotiation. A transferor for value warrants:

  a. That the document is genuine
  b. That he has no knowledge of any fact that would impair its validity or worth, and
  c. That his negotiation or transfer is rightful and fully effective with respect to the document of title and the goods it represents

L. Transfer of Investment Securities

1. The transfer of investment securities (stocks and bonds) are governed by Article 8 of the UCC. This Article states that investment securities are negotiable instruments. Consequently, the rules applicable to the transfer of investment securities are very similar to the rules contained in Article 3 of the UCC which governs the transfer of promissory notes, drafts, etc.

2. Proper negotiation of investment securities

  a. If no indorsements on the back of the certificate look to the face of the security

      1) If a registered security (names person entitled to the security) specified person must deliver and indorse
      2) If a bearer security only delivery of the security is needed

  b. If there are indorsements on the back of the certificate proper negotiation would be:

      1) Delivery if the last indorsement is a blank indorsement
      2) Delivery and indorsement by specified person if the last indorsement is a special indorsement

3. A bona fide purchaser (BFP) of an investment security is someone who:

    a. Receives the security through proper negotiation (delivery of a bearer security or delivery and indorsement of a registered security), and

    b. Gives value, and

    c. Takes in good faith and without notice of any adverse claim

4. A bona fide purchaser acquires the security free of most adverse claims such as fraud, duress, failure of consideration, theft of a bearer security, etc. This status is comparable to a holder in due course under Article 3 of the UCC.

5. A bona fide purchaser does not take the security free of theft of a registered security which would result in the claim of a forged indorsement. However, if the issuer (normally a corporation) transfers the registration of the security to the BFP based upon the unauthorized indorsement, the BFP has title to the security. The original owner of the security (the party the thief stole the instrument from) is also entitled to receive a new certificate from the issuer evidencing the security that was stolen.

EXAMPLE: Herb stole from Ike an unindorsed registered certificate of stock (an order certificate). Ike gave the issuing corporation notice of loss within a reasonable period of time. Herb, the thief, forges Ike's name to the certificate and then delivers it to Danny, a bona fide purchaser who pays value and takes the certificate without knowledge of the theft or forgery. Ike is still the owner of the shares, and Herb is liable to Ike for their value. If Danny surrenders the certificate to the issuing corporation which cancels it and issues a new one in Danny's name, Danny is now owner of the shares represented by the certificate registered in his name. However, Ike is entitled to receive from the corporation a new certificate for the same number of shares.

6. A purchaser who does not qualify as a bona fide purchaser receives the rights of his/her transferor unless the purchaser took part in creating the defense present or is trying to better his/her position by passing the security through the BFP (similar to the shelter provision under Article 3 of the UCC).

7. A transferor of a security for value

    a. Extends the following warranties:

        1) Transfer is effective and rightful, and

        2) The security is genuine and has not been materially altered, and

        3) S/he knows of no fact that might impair the validity of the security

    b. Is entitled to a reissued certificate of stock without giving further compensation to the issuer, if bona fide purchaser originally received a stock certificate containing an unauthorized signature of an employee of the issuer, who had been entrusted with the responsible handling of stock certificates.

SECURED TRANSACTIONS

Overview

A secured transaction is a legal method to give additional assurances to a creditor that he will be paid if the debtor is unable or unwilling to pay as promised. The creditor is "secured" by specifying certain property as an alternate source of payment (collateral). Secured transactions are possible only when goods are sold and delivered, services are rendered, or money is loaned in exchange for a promise to pay in the future. If some form of collateral is given as security for payment, the credit is said to be secured. However, where the credit is given on the debtor's unsupported promise to pay, the credit is said to be unsecured.

The mechanics of creation of a valid security interest are frequently tested with an emphasis on the particular rules with respect to who must sign the security agreement and the filing documents, where they must be filed, and the time limitations which are applicable to various steps in a secured transaction. Candidates are frequently asked to explain the rights between competing parties or to establish priorities among competing parties in the same collateral. Other common topics are the purchase money security interest, the impact of bankruptcy and the rights of a trustee in bankruptcy against the collateral, and the rights of the secured party upon default.

Secured Transactions Definitions

Security Interest. The interest obtained by the creditor in the property, either possessory or non-possessory, which secures the obligation to pay or perform.

Collateral. The property in which the security interest is retained.

Debtor. The party who owes the payment or obligation in the security agreement whether or not he owns the collateral.

Secured Party. The party in whose favor there is a security interest until a debt or other obligation is satisfied.

Security Agreement. The written agreement between the debtor and the creditor which invests the creditor with a security interest in the collateral. Must be signed by the debtor.

Purchase Money Security Interest. Where a seller retains an interest in the goods sold to a buyer to secure all or part of the purchase price, or where a creditor advances funds or incurs obligations to enable a debtor to acquire rights in or use of collateral. Purchase money security interests are given priority over other claimants under many circumstances.

Example: Purchaser wants to buy a new car. Bank finances the purchase. Purchaser signs an agreement which states that in the event of default Bank may recover the car. The car is the collateral; Bank is the secured party; Bank has a purchase-money security interest; purchaser is the debtor.

Attachment. Attachment is when the agreement between the parties creates a security interest in the collateral and not just against the debtor. Three things are required for the mechanics of attachment:

a. Security agreement between the parties;
b. Value given by the creditor; and
c. The debtor has rights in the collateral.

After-Acquired Property Agreement. A security agreement that provides the secured party will have liens on property acquired in the future, so long as the debt exists, without the necessity of a new security agreement.

Floating Lien. A security interest in constantly changing collateral such as inventory or other forms of after-acquired property.

Future Advances Clause. A provision in a present security agreement which is designed to provide the present collateral as security for additional advances of money or goods to be made in the future. Does not attach until value is given.

Perfection. The final step in a security transaction in which notice is given to other potentially interested parties by the filing of a financing statement, by the secured parties taking possession of the collateral, or by attachment alone.

Priority. A set of rules for determining the order of payment between conflicting security interests in the same collateral.

A. Article 9 of the UCC

1. Secured transactions are primarily controlled by Article 9. The exam is now testing the 1972 official text. This chapter reflects the 1972 official text.

   a. Article 9 is a complete rewrite of the law of secured transactions to accommodate today's business needs

   b. It creates uniformity in the method of securing an interest in collateral

2. Applicability

   a. To any transaction (regardless of its form) which is intended to create a security interest in personal (tangible or intangible) property or fixtures

      EXAMPLE: Manufacturers finance equipment or raw materials, wholesalers and retailers finance equipment and inventory, and consumers finance purchases by giving their creditors security in certain described personal property. Whatever the form, these agreements are all secured transactions under Article 9.

      1) Applies to security interests created by contract but not to statutory liens

         a) A statutory lien is one that arises by statute

            EXAMPLE: Liens granted by state law for sevices or materials, e.g., the artisan's lien given to a repairman who fixes personal property.

            EXAMPLE: A contractor can obtain a lien (mechanic's lien) on a house or other real property that he works on.

            EXAMPLE: A landlord can obtain a lien on the furnishings and effects of a defaulting tenant.

      2) Also does not apply to:

         a) Liens on real property interests (see Mortgages in PROPERTY)
         b) Security interests governed by federal statutes
         c) Assignment of wage claims
         d) Claims arising out of judicial proceedings

   b. Applies to leases and consignments of personal property if they are really intended as a security interest

      1) If actually a security interest, must comply with all aspects of Article 9 of UCC

      2) Lease is likely to be a security interest if at end of lease, lessee gets title or has option to purchase at nominal sum

   c. See "Types of Collateral" (below) for collateral covered by Article 9

3. Some pre-UCC terms are sometimes used on the exam. You should be familiar with them although the modern security interest replaces them all.

   a. Pledge--giving possession of personal property as collateral for an obligation

      1) Sort of a bailment

      2) This is still done but it is no longer called a pledge. Possession of collateral is one means of perfecting a security interest.

10

    b. Chattel mortgage--simply a mortgage on personal property (chattels)

       1) Like a real property mortgage, it allowed a security interest in personal property without the need for possession (a pledge)

       2) They were required to be filed or recorded in some public manner

    c. Conditional sale (also called retained title)--seller delivered possession to the buyer but did not deliver title until paid in full

B. Types of Collateral

1. Intangible personal property

    a. Instruments are negotiable and non-negotiable debt instruments and securities that evidence a right to payment of money and are transferable by indorsement and delivery

       1) Include drafts, notes, checks, certificates of deposit, bonds, and shares of stock

    b. Documents of title include bills of lading and warehouse receipts

       1) To be a document of title it must:

          a) Be issued by or addressed to a bailee, and
          b) Cover goods in bailee's possession

    c. Chattel paper is defined as one or more writings which taken together evidence both a monetary obligation and a security interest in specified goods

       1) Generally consists of conditional sales contracts, chattel mortgages, and retained title arrangements

    d. Accounts generally refer to accounts receivable which are not evidenced by an instrument or chattel paper

    e. General intangibles are personal property that may be used as commercial collateral and not included within any of the above four (4) classifications, e.g., copyrights, patents, goodwill, and literary rights

2. Tangible personal property (goods)

    a. Equipment consists of goods used or bought for use primarily in a business

       1) Generally covers all goods which are not inventory, farm products or consumer goods

    b. Farm products are crops, livestock, or supplies used or produced in farming

       1) Must be in possession of the debtor who is performing some farming operation

    c. Consumer goods are those used or bought for use primarily for personal, family, or household purposes

       1) Goods may be bought for personal use and then actually used as equipment

    d. Inventory constitutes items held for sale in the ordinary course of business operations

       1) Includes raw materials and goods consumed in a business, e.g., fuel

e. These classes are mutually exclusive. Goods cannot belong in two of these classes at the same time. The classification is determined by the dominant use of goods when the security interest arises.

EXAMPLE: CPA purchases stereo on credit giving seller a security interest. If the stereo (collateral) is placed at CPA's home it would be consumer goods. If placed in his office it would be equipment. If he transported the stereo back and forth, the dominant use must be determined.

3. Proceeds are whatever is received when collateral or proceeds are disposed of

EXAMPLE: Debtor sells or exchanges the collateral and receives new property, money, check or account receivable. Each of these is proceeds.

4. Fixtures are former personal property which has been attached to real property so as to become a part thereof

EXAMPLE: Heating or air conditioning systems, elevators, office machines, or appliances installed in a permanent manner.

C. Creation of Security Interest

1. The Code uses the term "attach" for the time when a security interest in collateral is created

   a. This is when it becomes enforceable against the debtor and against third parties who are aware of the security interest

   b. The secured party can obtain even better rights, against other secured creditors and against those who purchase the collateral from the debtor, by "perfecting." See next section.

2. A security interest attaches when the following all exist (in any order)

   a. There is a security agreement between the parties
   b. The secured party gives value
   c. The debtor has rights in the collateral

3. Security Agreement

   a. May be an oral agreement to convey a security interest if:

      1) The collateral is in the possession of the secured party

   b. Otherwise it must:

      1) Be written
      2) Show debtor's intent to convey a security interest
      3) Contain a description of the collateral

         a) Collateral must be identifiable from it

      4) Be signed by the debtor

   c. Financing statement (see "D.2.b." below) ordinarily will not suffice as a security agreement unless it meets the requirements of a security agreement

      1) Unlike a security agreement, a financing statement does not require that a conveyance of a security interest be shown

4. Value given may be any consideration that would support a contract

    a. Usually goods or money, e.g., delivery of equipment or a loan

    b. Includes a preexisting claim

5. Rights in the collateral

    a. The collateral must exist; therefore, a debtor has no rights in:

        1) Unborn livestock until conceived

        2) Fish until caught

        3) Crops until growing

        4) Oil or gas until extracted

        5) Contract rights or accounts until they exist

    b. The debtor must have an interest in the collateral

        1) Need not have title

        2) May be a right to possession

> *EXAMPLE: Consumer obtains a loan to buy a car. He signs a security agreement and is given the loan before he contracts to buy the car. The security interest does not attach until he actually buys the car.*

6. Future goods (after-acquired property) may also become part of collateral if the agreement contains an after-acquired property clause

> *EXAMPLE: An agreement states the collateral is all of debtor's office furniture now owned and hereafter acquired. As soon as the debtor acquires rights to other office furniture, the security interest will attach.*

    a. Only applies to consumer goods if:

        1) They are accessions, i.e., goods installed or attached to other goods covered by a security agreement, or

> *EXAMPLE: Creditor has a security interest in a car and the debtor puts new tires on the car. The new tires are covered by the security agreement.*

        2) Debtor acquires rights in the goods within 10 days after secured party gives value

> *EXAMPLE: Debtor buys a stereo under a security agreement with an after-acquired clause. Twelve days later debtor buys a T.V. from the same seller. The T.V. is not covered by the after-acquired clause and, therefore, does not become part of the collateral, whether or not debtor pays for it in full.*

    b. Applies to any other type of collateral. It is commonly used for inventory or accounts receivable, i.e., a floating lien.

        1) Liens on the changing inventory or accounts receivable

        2) Lien automatically attaches to the new inventory or accounts receivable as the old are sold or collected

> *EXAMPLE: Bank makes a loan to dealer and obtains a security interest in inventory of the dealer "Now possessed and hereafter acquired." As soon as the dealer acquires rights in new inventory, the security interest will attach.*

c. Security interest attaches automatically when the new property is acquired but not until then

7. Collateral may secure future advances by the secured party in addition to the present value given

a. Must be so stated in security agreement

   EXAMPLE: "This collateral is given in security for the loan made as of this date and all future obligations of debtor to this creditor." This security interest will automatically attach to secure the original obligation of the debtor and any future advance of money or delivery of goods on credit.

b. Security interest does not attach until the value (future advance) is given

   EXAMPLE: Debtor buys a stereo under a security agreement with a future advance clause. Later, debtor buys a T.V. without paying in full. The stereo is collateral for the payments on the T.V. as well as for payments on the stereo itself.

8. Proceeds from sale or exchange of secured goods are automatically covered by a security agreement unless otherwise stated

a. Security interest will continue in any identifiable proceeds

   EXAMPLE: Checks that have not been deposited, cash that has not been deposited or commingled, account receivable, or new property received in exchange for the collateral.

D. Perfecting a Security Interest

1. Perfection is a term used by the UCC to indicate compliance with a set of procedures which gives the party that perfects a security interest priority over other parties that also may claim the collateral

a. These other parties may be:

   1) Other secured creditors
   2) Persons who purchase the collateral from the debtor
   3) Trustees in bankruptcy
   4) Lien creditors, i.e., acquired a lien by judicial process

b. Accomplishing steps of perfection are not a substitute for the creation of a security interest. They are additional steps.

2. Perfection may be accomplished by:

a. Taking possession of the collateral

   1) For money, goods, instruments (securities, negotiable and non-negotiable debt instruments), and chattel paper

      a) Only method for money, negotiable instruments, and securities
      b) E.g., negotiable warehouse receipts entitle the possessor to the goods stored in the warehouse. The warehouse operator also has a lien on the goods for storage costs.
      c) For a non-negotiable document, perfect by issuing document in name of secured party, by notifying bailee, or by filing as to the goods (not the document)

2) Perfection is effective as long as possession lasts
3) While in possession, the secured party

   a) Must use reasonable care to preserve the property

   b) May keep profits from the property (e.g., stock dividends, newborn calf) as additional collateral, except that

      1] Money must be remitted to the debtor or applied to the obligation

4) The debtor (owner)

   a) Must bear any accidental loss to the collateral provided the secured party has used reasonable care

      1] Each party has an insurable interest in the collateral

   b) Is liable for reasonable expenses, e.g., taxes, insurance of the collateral

b. <u>Filing</u> a financing statement (written notice filed in public records)

1) For all collateral except money and instruments (they must be possessed)

   a) Only method for contract rights, accounts and other intangibles (because there is nothing to possess)

2) Financing statement must:

   a) Give names of both parties
   b) Contain addresses of both
   c) Identify type of or describe collateral

      1] Unlike description in security agreement, it need not identify the specific collateral. It must merely identify the type of collateral.

   d) Be signed by the debtor (secured party need not sign)

      1] Amendments must be signed by both parties

   e) The security agreement may suffice if it complies with the above

      1] But a copy of it must be filed as below

3) Filing

   a) By statute, usually in county recorder's office, Secretary of State, or both

      1] Financing statement covering fixtures, timber to be cut, or minerals must also be filed in real estate records

   b) Has the functional purpose of giving notice to the public of creditor's security interest in the collateral

   c) Lasts for five years and may be continued for another five years (by a continuation statement)

   d) Upon full payment to the creditor, debtor may request a release from the creditor, which the debtor can then file (termination statement)

1] Secured party must file a termination statement within one month after there is no secured obligation or commitment to make future advances in the case of a financing statement covering consumer goods

2] Failure of the secured party to provide termination statement within one month in the case of consumer goods or within 10 days of written demand subjects him to $100 penalty and liability for any loss caused to debtor

4) Filing may be done anytime, even before the security agreement is made. But perfection does not occur until all requirements are met.

EXAMPLE: Bank is going to finance the inventory of a car dealer who is beginning business. They immediately file a financing statement. When the inventory arrives they sign a security agreement. Perfection occurs when the security agreement is signed.

5) Perfection is ineffective if financing statement is improper or if it is filed in wrong place

6) Upon the request of any person, the filing officer (a public official) shall issue his certificate showing:

a) Whether a financing statement is on file naming a particular debtor
b) When it was filed
c) The names and addresses of the secured parties
d) A uniform fee is charged for this service
e) A copy of the financing statement is also available for a fee

7) The secured party is only under an obligation to furnish information on the indebtedness and the security interest on request of the debtor

a) Third parties are limited to the information on file unless secured party willingly gives more information

c. Attachment alone--In several situations, perfection is accomplished simply by the attachment of the security interest without further action, i.e., automatic perfection without either possession or filing. (See "Creation of Security Interest," "C.")

1) For purchase money security interest in consumer goods

a) Except for motor vehicles. They are perfected by a lien on certificate of title which is filed with the state.

b) Not effective against a bona fide purchaser for value who buys the goods for his own personal, family, or household use unless secured party files

EXAMPLE: Dealer sells goods to A that are consumer goods in A's hands (e.g., washer and dryer for family use). When the dealer's security interest attaches, it is also perfected without the need to file. If A sells the washer to his neighbor for family use, the neighbor takes free of the dealer's security interest if neighbor was unaware of the security interest. A second-hand goods dealer who bought from A would be subject to the dealer's interest. If the original dealer had perfected by filing in addition to perfection by attachment alone, dealer would be protected against all parties (neighbor and dealers).

2) Temporary perfection for

   a) Proceeds of collateral for 10 days where interest in original collateral was perfected and proceeds are of type that cannot be perfected by filing or by filing in same place as original collateral

      1] If proceeds are of same type as original collateral, they are automatically perfected if original collateral was

      EXAMPLE. Debtor sells equipment for a promissory note. Secured creditor has temporary perfection for ten days in the note.

      EXAMPLE: Debtor trades equipment in on new equipment. New equipment is perfected if old equipment was. No temporary perfection is needed.

   b) Instruments and negotiable documents for 21 days to the extent new value is given under an existing written security agreement

3. Field warehousing

   a. A device frequently used to obtain a security interest in inventory

      1) Where the secured party wants the added security of possession
      2) The inventory is kept on the debtor's premises but under the control of the secured party
      3) Warehouse receipts are issued by the warehouseman or secured party. Warehouse receipts:

         a) Acknowledge receipt of the goods
         b) Describe goods
         c) Contain terms of storage contract
         d) Can be negotiable or nonnegotiable

      4) It is less expensive than renting an outside warehouse and makes the goods more accessible to the debtor when it is in effect a floating lien on the inventory

   b. The secured party must have dominion and control over the security

      1) A separate room or warehouse on the debtor's premises is used
      2) All the locks are changed
      3) It is posted showing the secured party's possession
      4) An employee of the secured party or an independent warehouseman controls access to the goods
      5) Temporary relinquishment of control is permissible to allow for exchange of collateral (a revolving type of collateral arrangement)

         a) If the secured party temporarily gives up control without receiving other collateral, he runs the risk of losing his priority in this interval

   c. Secured party can also file a financing statement as to the goods

4. Consignments

   a. The 1972 amendments to Article 9 of the UCC set forth the procedures a consignor must follow in order to prevail against his consignee's creditors

b. These procedures must be complied with even though a True Consignment (essentially an agency relationship between consignor and consignee) exists. A true consignment is present when:

   1) Consignor retains title to goods; and
   2) Consignee has no obligation to buy the goods; and
   3) Consignor has a right to all proceeds

   EXAMPLE: Manufacturer gives possession of goods to a marketing representative for the purpose of selling goods on commission.

c. To perfect his/her interest, a consignor must:

   1) Comply with applicable local law by posting a sign on the consignee's premises disclosing the consignor's interest in the goods or
   2) Establish that the consignee is generally known as selling goods owned by other individuals or
   3) File a financing statement under Article 9 and give notice to the consignee's creditors who have perfected security interests in the same type of goods

      a) Notice must contain description of the goods to be delivered and be given before the consignee receives possession of goods

E. Order of Priorities

1. The UCC provides rules for determining priorities between conflicting security interests in the same collateral (knowledge of other security interests is immaterial)

   a. Purchase-money security interest has priority over all other security interests if it is perfected when debtor receives possession or within 10 days

   EXAMPLE: A has perfected a security agreement against specifically described personal property of B. The agreement contains an "after-acquired" property clause. If C sells goods to B on credit and retains a security interest, there is a conflict between A's and C's security interest in the same collateral. If the goods which C sold to B are not inventory in B's hands, then C's security interest will prevail over A's if C perfects when B receives possession or within 10 days after.

   1) If inventory, no 10-day leeway is allowed for perfection to have priority

      a) Party with purchase-money security interest must give notice to other secured party
      b) Party with purchase-money security interest must perfect prior to debtor's taking possession

   EXAMPLE: If the goods (in the example above) furnished by C were inventory goods in B's hands, then C must notify A that a purchase-money security interest in inventory of B is to be acquired and C must perfect by filing before delivering possession to B.

   2) Knowledge of preexisting security interest has no effect

   b. If both interests are perfected, the priority is established by the order or date of either filing or perfection

      1) The first to either perfect or to file has priority as long as there is no interruption in the period after filing or perfection

      2) Immaterial which attached first or whether filing preceded attachment

  c. If none is perfected, then by order of attachment

  d. Perfected interest over unperfected interest and secured interest over an unsecured interest

2. Purchasers of collateral from debtor

  a. Purchaser takes free of an unperfected security interest if he takes for value and without notice of the unperfected security interest

      1) Purchaser of inventory goods in ordinary course of business takes free of any security interest even if he knows of security interest

        EXAMPLE: B enters S's store to make purchases from S for value and with no unusual arrangement. Even though bank has a valid perfected security interest in all of S's inventory, B's purchases are no longer subject to the bank's interest. B's knowledge of the bank's interest is immaterial. Note that the bank may have an interest in the proceeds of the B-S transaction.

  b. Purchaser takes free of a perfected security interest if:

      1) Secured party authorizes sale

        a) When security interest is in a dealer's inventory and is a floating lien, authority to sell can be presumed

      2) Purchaser buys from dealer of goods in ordinary course of business, even if he knows of any security interest

        a) Must not have knowledge that sale is in violation of the security agreement. (Warning: a filed financing statement may be deemed to give the purchaser such knowledge even if he does not read it.)

      3) Purchaser of consumer goods who buys from any seller for consumer use, for value, and without notice of security interest

        a) But the secured party retains priority against a purchaser of consumer goods if he filed a financing statement

          1] Seller obtains a perfected purchase money security interest in consumer goods without filing upon the sale, since perfection occurs upon attachment. But seller must file to be protected against all parties.

      4) Holder in due course of a negotiable instrument is not affected by any security interest

3. Lien creditor, e.g., repairman or contractor

  a. Has priority over an unperfected security interest

      1) Knowledge of security interest is immaterial

b. Has priority over a security interest perfected after attachment of the lien

c. A security interest perfected before the lien attaches has priority over the lien, to the extent advances under the security interest are made:

1) Before the lien arises, or
2) Within 45 days after the lien arises, or
3) Without knowledge of the lien, or
4) Under a commitment entered into without knowledge of the lien

EXAMPLE: ABC Credit Co. loans $500 to D and takes a security interest in D's car. The security agreement has a future advance clause. Later a mechanic acquires a lien on D's car. After the lien arises, ABC loans another $500 to D based on the original security interest. ABC has priority over the mechanic for the first $500 loaned to D. The mechanic has priority over ABC as to the second $500 unless the second loan was made within 45 days after the lien arose, without the knowledge of the lien or under a commitment entered into without knowledge of the lien.

d. Lien by statute or implied in law (not by judgment or court order) has priority over a prior perfected security interest unless state statute expressly provides otherwise

EXAMPLE: A person such as a repairman, in the ordinary course of business, furnishes services or materials with respect to goods subject to a security interest. The repairman (artisan lien) has priority.

EXAMPLE: A contractor obtains a mechanic's lien when he does work on a house and is not paid. A mechanic's lien has priority over the mortgagee.

4. Trustee in bankruptcy as a lien creditor

a. Trustee has the rights of a lien creditor from the date of filing of petition in bankruptcy

1) So he has priority over a security interest perfected after date of filing petition

b. Trustee also takes the position of any existing lien creditor

1) So if an existing lien creditor has obtained execution of a lien before a security interest was perfected, trustee has priority over that security interest

a) Trustee will also void the actual lien if it was made within 4 months of filing of petition in bankruptcy and bankrupt was insolvent at the time

c. Perfecting a security interest can also be a preference (see Bankruptcy) if it meets the requirement and trustee can void it

EXAMPLE: An existing security interest is later perfected during the four-month period. This gives it a preference over other secured creditors.

d. If the creditor has perfected a security interest and the trustee cannot use one of the above means to take priority, then the creditor takes the property and it does not become part of the bankrupt estate

5. After-acquired property

a. Perfection when debtor acquires (no attachment until debtor has rights in it)

b. If two parties have an after-acquired clause, first to have filed financing statement on original collateral has priority

c. Purchase-money security interest has priority if it perfects within 10 days (except if inventory) [see "E.1.a.1)" above]

6. Future advances

a. If a security interest is perfected by filing or possession, a future advance is secured with same priority in collateral as the original advance

b. Otherwise priority is determined from the time the future advance was made

7. Proceeds are deemed filed for or perfected at the time original collateral was filed for or perfected

8. Fixtures and accessions

a. Perfected security interest in fixtures must be filed in real estate records to have priority over a party with encumbrance on the real property

1) First to file has priority
2) No filing is needed in the real estate records for readily removable factory or office machines or readily removable replacements of domestic appliances which are consumer goods if they are perfected before becoming fixtures

b. Perfected purchase money security interest in fixtures before they are attached to real property has priority over an existing recorded encumbrance if:

1) Secured party filed in real estate records before attachment to real property or within 10 days thereafter

c. Security interest in accessions perfected before they are installed has priority over all claims of interest to the whole

1) Accessions are goods installed in or affixed to other goods; e.g., a new motor installed in an old car

d. Security interest in accessions perfected after they are installed only has priority over subsequent claims of interest to the whole

F. Remedies on Default

1. If collateral consists of claims, e.g., receivables, the secured party has the right of collection from third parties

a. Secured party must notify third party
b. Secured party must account for any surplus and debtor is liable for any deficiency
c. Secured party may deduct his reasonable expenses
d. Secured party may collect on claims before default if so agreed with debtor

2. Secured party may retain collateral already in his possession or may take possession from debtor

   a. May do so himself if he can without breach of the peace
   b. Otherwise, he must use judicial process
   c. Security agreement may require the debtor to assemble the collateral at a convenient place for the secured party

   d. Secured party has same duties to take reasonable care of collateral in his possession as when he perfects by possession

3. If secured party proposes to satisfy obligation by retaining the collateral, he must

   a. Send written notice to debtor and if debtor objects within 21 days, secured party must sell collateral

   b. If not consumer goods, then he must also notify other secured parties (who have sent written notice of their interest) and if they object within 21 days, secured party must sell collateral

   c. Can only retain consumer goods if debtor has paid less than 60 percent of the purchase price or obligation

      1) If 60 percent or more has been paid, the collateral must be sold unless debtor waives his right to sale, in writing, signed after default occurs

4. Secured party may sell collateral

   a. May be a public or a private sale
   b. Must use commercially reasonable practices
   c. Must sell within a commercially reasonable time
   d. Must notify debtor before sale unless collateral is perishable, threatens to decline in value, or is type sold on a recognized market

      1) Must also notify other secured parties (who have sent written notice of their interest) unless collateral consists of consumer goods

   e. Secured party may buy at any public sale and also at a private sale if collateral is:

      1) Type sold on recognized market, or
      2) Has a widely distributed standard price quotation

   f. Proceeds must be applied in this order:

      1) Secured party's reasonable expenses
      2) Debt secured by collateral
      3) Other secured debt of subordinate secured parties

   g. Debtor is entitled to any surplus and is liable for any deficiency

5. Debtor has right to redeem collateral before secured party disposes of it by tendering:

   a. Entire debt, and
   b. Secured party's reasonable expenses

BANKRUPTCY

Overview

The overall objective of bankruptcy law is to allow honest insolvent debtors to surrender most of their assets and obtain release from their debts. A secondary purpose is to give creditors fair opportunity to share in the debtor's limited assets in proportion to their claims.

Bankruptcy is tested primarily with objective questions. These questions emphasize administration of the bankrupt's estate, allowable claims, nonallowable claims, and claims not discharged by bankruptcy. Also tested are the priorities with respect to distribution of assets, the eligibility of the bankrupt for discharge, and the effect of discharge. These materials reflect the bankruptcy law as stated in the Bankruptcy Reform Act of 1978.

Bankruptcy Definitions

Trustee. A person elected by the creditors (or appointed by the judge) to assemble, collect, administer, and liquidate the bankrupt's estate.

Preferential Transfers. Transfers by insolvent debtor to creditors as payment for antecedent debts. Trustee may set aside such transfers if they occur within previous 90 days.

Insolvency in the "equity sense". Debtor is unable to pay debts as they become due.

Insolvency in the "bankruptcy sense". Liabilities exceed fair market value of all assets.

Priorities. The order in which unsecured debts of the bankrupt are payable:

a. Administration costs.
b. Claims arising in ordinary course of debtor's business after bankruptcy petition is filed.
c. Wages of bankrupt's employees $2,000 maximum each accrued within 90 days before petition in bankruptcy was filed.
d. Contributions to employee benefit plans arising from services performed within the prior 180 days, limited to $2,000 per employee and reduced by amount received as wages preference.
e. Consumer deposits for undelivered goods or services limited to $900 per individual.
f. Taxes (federal, state, and local).
g. General (unsecured) creditors.

Secured creditors pursue their claims against the collateral.

Provable Claim. One that may be asserted and allowed against a bankrupt's estate. Allowed claims are entitled to share pro rata in the distribution of assets.

A. Alternatives to Bankruptcy Proceedings

1. Creditors may choose to do nothing

   a. Expense of collection may exceed what creditors could recover if

      1) Much property is secured or mortgaged
      2) Exemptions may be high, i.e., amount the debtor may keep after bankruptcy proceedings

   b. Creditors may expect debtor to pull through
   c. Tax deduction is available for bad debts if uncollectibility of debt established
   d. Creditors may simply extend the time when payment is due

2. Grab law

   a. Creditors may rush to satisfy their claims individually through legal proceedings
   b. Methods

       1) Obtain legal judgments against debtor
       2) Seize and sell property
       3) Attach liens to property
       4) Garnish debts owed to debtor
       5) Recover property fraudulently conveyed to a third person, e.g., given to relative to put beyond creditors' reach

  c. May result in bankruptcy proceedings

       1) Especially if some creditors do not fare well and are dissatisfied
       2) Liens, preferential transfers, and fraudulent conveyances may be set aside

3. Assignment for the benefit of creditors

  a. Provided for the benefit of creditors
  b. Debtor voluntarily transfers all of his assets to an assignee (or trustee) to be sold for the benefit of creditors

  c. Assignee takes legal title

       1) Debtor must cease all control of assets
       2) Assignment is irrevocable

  d. No agreement between creditors is necessary
  e. Dissatisfied creditors may file a timely petition in bankruptcy and assignments may be set aside

4. Creditors' committee

  a. Submission of business and financial affairs by the debtor to the control of a committee of creditors
  b. Creditors' committee is given management of assets or business but not necessarily title
  c. Not as severe as assignment because assets not liquidated
  d. Nevertheless, it is similar to assignment for benefit of creditors

5. Composition with creditors

  a. Creditors agree to accept less than is due, i.e., a percentage of their claims, in full satisfaction of the debt

  b. Must have consideration

       1) The creditors' mutual promises to accept less than full amount

          a) Must have more than one creditor because one creditor is not bound by promise to accept less, but if more than one creditor, their mutual promises bind them
          b) All the creditors need not agree unless the agreement so states

       2) Debtor pays (pro rata) creditors

  c. Creditors who do not agree are not bound
  d. Dissatisfied creditors may be able to force debtor into bankruptcy

6. Receiverships

  a. This provides for the general administration of a debtor's assets by a court appointee for the benefit of all parties

B. Chapter 7 Voluntary Bankruptcy Petitions

1. A voluntary bankruptcy petition is a formal request by the debtor for an order of relief

    a. The petition is filed with the court along with a list of the debtor's assets and liabilities
    b. Debtor need not be insolvent. He merely needs to state that he has debts.
    c. The debtor is automatically given an order of relief upon filing of petition

2. Any person, partnerships, or corporation may file a bankruptcy petition with the exception of a

    a. Governmental unit -- may file under Chapter 9
    b. Railroad
    c. Insurance company
    d. Banking corporation
    e. Building and loan association
    f. Credit union

C. Chapter 7 Involuntary Bankruptcy Petitions

1. An involuntary bankruptcy petition may be filed with the bankruptcy court by the creditors requesting an order for relief

2. Requirements to file petition

    a. If there are fewer than twelve creditors, a single creditor may file the petition as long as his claim aggregates $5,000 in excess of any security he may hold

        1) Claims must not be contingent as to liability

    b. If there are twelve or more creditors, then at least three must sign the petition and they must have claims which aggregate $5,000 in excess of any security held by them

        1) Claims must not be contingent as to liability

    c. Creditors who file in bad faith may be assessed damages (actual and punitive) by the court

3. Exempt from involuntary bankruptcy are

    a. Persons (individuals, partnerships, or corporations) owing less than $5,000
    b. Farmers -- if 80% of their income comes from farming operations
    c. Governmental units, railroads, insurance companies, banks, savings and loan associations, and charitable corporations

    d. Charitable organizations

4. Bankruptcy not available (voluntarily or involuntarily) for deceased person's estate

    a. But once bankruptcy has begun, it is not stopped if bankrupt (debtor) dies

5. An order of relief will be granted if the requirements for filing are met, and

   a. The petition is uncontested; or
   b. The petition is contested; and

      1) The debtor is generally not paying his/her debts as they become due; or
      2) During the 120 days preceding the filing of the petition, a custodian was appointed or took possession of substantially all of the property of the debtor

      EXAMPLE: Debtor assigns his property for the benefit of his creditor.

D. Chapter 7 Bankruptcy Proceedings

1. Take place only in a federal district court.   (Bankruptcy is a federal law.)

   a. An order of relief must be granted
   b. Court appoints interim trustee
   c. Filing petition automatically stays (suspends) other legal proceeding against debtor's estate until bankruptcy case is over or until court orders otherwise

      EXAMPLE: Mortgage foreclosure by savings and loan will be suspended against debtor.

2. First creditors' meeting

   a. Debtor furnishes a schedule of assets, their locations, and a list of creditors

      1) Claims of omitted creditors who do not obtain actual notice of the bankruptcy proceedings within the 6 month period in which creditors must file claims are not discharged

   b. Creditors must be given 20 days notice
   c. Called within 25-45 days after order for relief
   d. Claims are deemed allowed unless objected to, in which case the court will determine their validity

      1) Contingent and unliquidated claims are estimated

   e. Trustee may be elected in Chapter 7 proceeding. If no election requested by creditors, interim trustee appointed by Court continues in office.

      1) Creditor voting for election of trustee requires a majority as to the amount of claims being voted and the voting creditors must represent 20% of all claims entitled to vote

         a) Secured creditor can only vote to extent claim exceeds collateral
         b) Creditors who are not allowed to vote include

            1] Relatives (of an individual debtor)
            2] Officers, directors, and stockholders (of a corporate debtor)

3. Trustee -- the representative of the estate

   a. Court appoints an interim trustee until creditors elect one
   b. Permanent trustee may be elected at first creditors' meeting

      1) Often creditors do not find it worthwhile to attend the creditors' meeting and the interim trustee will remain as trustee

c. Duties -- to collect, liquidate, and distribute the estate, keeping accurate records of all transactions

    1) Creditors have six months to file claims in Chapter 7 case

d. The Estate which the trustee represents consists of any property presently owned (or received) by the debtor within six months after petition for bankruptcy -- by bequest, devise, inheritance, property settlement with spouse, divorce decree, or life insurance

    1) Property acquired, other than by methods listed above, by debtor after filing is "new estate" and not subject to creditors' claims in bankruptcy proceeding

    2) Exemptions -- debtor is entitled

        a) To keep any interests in joint tenancy property if those interests are exempt under other nonbankruptcy law, and

        b) The option of choosing either certain necessaries permitted by the state law where the petition is filed (state exemptions) or the federal exemptions (unless the particular state involved has enacted legislation to eliminate federal exemptions)

            1] Typical state exemptions (limited in monetary value) include

                a] Small amount of money
                b] Residence
                c] Clothing
                d] Tools of trade
                e] Insurance, or

            2] Allowable federal exemptions include

                a] $7,500 equity in a residence
                b] $1,200 equity in a car
                c] $750 in books and tools of one's trade
                d] $200 per item qualifying of consumer goods (for personal, family, or home use)
                e] $500 in jewelry
                f] Social security and alimony
                g] Prescribed health aids
                h] The unused portion of $7,500 homestead exemptions (item a]) can be used to protect any type of property including cash

e. Powers of trustee

    1) Trustee may take any legal action necessary to carry out duties

        a) Trustee may utilize any defense available to the debtor against third parties
        b) Trustee may continue or cease any legal action started by the debtor for the benefit of the estate

    2) Trustee must within sixty days of the order for relief assume or reject any executory contract, including leases, made by the debtor

    a) Any not assumed are deemed rejected

    b) Rejection of a contract is a breach of contract and the injured party may become an unsecured creditor

3) Trustee may set aside liens (those which arise automatically under law)

    a) Becomes effective when bankruptcy petition is filed or when debtor becomes insolvent

    b) Is not enforceable against a bona fide purchaser when the petition is filed

    c) Is enforceable against landlord for rent

4) Trustee may set aside transfers made within one year prior to the filing of the bankruptcy petition if

    a) The transfer was made with intent to hinder, delay, or defraud any creditor. The debtor need not be insolvent at time of transfer. Or

    b) Debtor received less than a reasonably equivalent value in exchange for such transfer or obligation and the debtor

        1] Was insolvent at the time, or became insolvent as a result of the transfer

        2] Was engaged in business, or was about to engage in a transaction, for which debtor's property was unreasonably small capital

        3] Intended or believed it would incur debts beyond its ability to pay them as they matured

    c) If the fact that the transfer was a fraudulent conveyance was the only grounds for avoiding the transfer; once avoided by trustee, transferee that gave value in good faith has a lien on property transferred to the extent of value given

5) Trustee may also set aside <u>preferential transfers</u> of property to a creditor made within the previous 90 days while insolvent in the "bankruptcy sense"

    a) Preferential transfers are those made for antecedent debts which enable the creditor to receive more than he would have otherwise under a Chapter 7 liquidation proceeding

    b) The Bankruptcy Act presumes that the debtor is insolvent during the 90 days prior to the date the petition was filed

    c) Preferential transfers made to insiders within the previous 12 months may be set aside if creditor, at the time the preference was made, had reasonable cause to believe the debtor was insolvent

        1] Insiders are relatives, officers, directors, controlling stockholders of corporations, or general partners of partnerships

        2] If preference occurred within the period between 90 days prior to the filing of the petition and 1 year before the filing, the trustee has the burden of proving that debtor was insolvent in "bankruptcy sense" (no presumption) and that insider/creditor had reason to believe the debtor was insolvent at the time of the transfer

EXAMPLE: One year ago Herb purchased a car on credit from Ike. Thirty days before filing for bankruptcy, Herb, while insolvent, makes a payment to Ike concerning the auto. This is a preference. If Ike were Herb's brother, this payment would have been a preference if it had occurred 120 days before the filing of the petition with Ike knowing that Herb was insolvent when payment was made (insider preference).

    d) Exceptions to trustee's power to avoid preferential transfers

       1] A substantially contemporaneous exchange between creditor and debtor whereby debtor receives new value

EXAMPLE: Herb while insolvent purchases a car for cash from Ike within 90 days of filing a petition in bankruptcy. The trustee could not avoid this transaction because Herb, the debtor, received present (i.e., new) value, the car, for the cash transferred to Ike, the creditor. This is not a voidable preference.

       2] A payment made by debtor in the ordinary course of business not later than 45 days after such debt was incurred is not a preference

       3] A security interest given by debtor to acquire property that is perfected within 10 days after such security interest attaches

  f. Trustee may sue or be sued

  g. Trustee makes interim reports to the court and makes a final accounting of the administration of the estate

E. Claims

1. Property rights -- where claimant has a property right, property is turned over to claimant, because not considered part of debtor's estate

  a. Reclamation is a claim against specific property by a person claiming it to be his

EXAMPLE: A person rented a truck for a week and in the meantime he becomes bankrupt. The lessor will make a reclamation.

  b. Trust claim is made by beneficiary for trust property when the trustee is bankrupt

EXAMPLE: Trustee maintains a trust account for beneficiary under a trust set up in a will. Trustee becomes bankrupt. The trust account is not part of trustee's estate. The beneficiary may claim the trust account as his property.

  c. Secured claim when debtor has a security interest, e.g., mortgage, in property or security interest under Article 9 of UCC

    1) As long as trustee does not successfully attack the security-- basically, security interest must be without defects to prevail against trustee (i.e., perfected security interests)

    2) Secured status may be achieved by subrogation, e.g., surety is subrogated to creditor's collateral

    d. Set-offs are allowed to the extent the bankrupt and creditor have mutual debts whether unsecured or not

2. Filing of claims

    a. All claims must be filed within six months after the first creditors' meeting

    b. Claims must

       1) State consideration for claim
       2) Be signed by creditor
       3) Be under oath
       4) State security held
       5) List payments on claim
       6) State that claim is just

3. Claims are deemed allowed unless an objection is made

    a. Contingent and unliquidated claims may be estimated

4. Claims below are not allowed if an objection is made

    a. Unenforceable claims (by law or agreement)
    b. Unmatured interest as of date of filing bankruptcy petition
    c. Claims which may be offset
    d. Property tax claim in excess of the property value
    e. Insider or attorney claims in excess of reasonable value of services
    f. Alimony, maintenance, and support claims for amounts due after bankruptcy petition is filed (they are not dischargeable)

    g. Landlord's damages for lease termination in excess of any unpaid rent and the greater of

       1) One year's rent, or
       2) 15% of the remaining lease not to exceed 3 years rent

    h. Damages for termination of an employment contract in excess of one year's wages
    i. Certain employment tax claims

5. Priority of claims (be sure to know)

    a. Property rights, e.g., secured debts

       1) Technically, they are not a part of the priorities because they never become part of the bankrupt estate. But practically, the validity of the property right must be determined and they are the first claims to be satisfied. (Any amount owed to the creditor in excess of the secured debt claim is settled as unsecured, see "b.7)" below.)

    b. Unsecured claims are payable in order, or prorated at each level

       1) Administration costs

          a) Includes attorney, accountant, and trustee fees

       2) Claims arising in ordinary course of debtor's business after bankruptcy petition is filed
       3) Wages of bankrupt's employees ($2,000 maximum each) accrued within 3 months before the petition in bankruptcy was filed

4) Contributions to employee reduced benefit plans within the prior 180 days, limited to $2,000 per employee, reduced by amount received as wage preference

5) Consumer deposits for undelivered goods or services limited to $900 per individual

6) Taxes (federal, state, and local)

7) General (unsecured) creditors

F. Discharge of a Bankrupt

1. A discharge is the release of a debtor from all his debts not paid in bankruptcy except those not dischargeable

    a. Granting an order of relief to an individual is an automatic application for discharge

    b. Corporations and partnerships cannot receive a discharge

2. A debtor must be adjudged an "honest debtor" to be discharged

3. Acts that bar discharge of all debts

    a. Improper actions during bankruptcy proceeding

        1) Making false claims against the estate

        2) Making any false entry in or on any document of account relating to bankrupt's affairs

        3) Concealing property

        4) Transfer of property after filing with intent to defeat the law

        5) Received money for acting or not acting in bankruptcy proceedings

        6) These acts are also punishable by fines and imprisonment

    b. Failed to satisfactorily explain any loss of assets

    c. Refused to obey court orders

    d. Removed or destroyed property within twelve months prior to the filing of the petition

    e. Destroyed, falsified, concealed, or failed to keep books of account or records unless such act was justified under the circumstances

    f. Been discharged in bankruptcy proceedings within the past six years

G. Debts Not Discharged by Bankruptcy

1. Taxes within three years of filing bankruptcy petition

2. Liability for obtaining money or property by false pretenses

3. Willful and malicious injuries to a person or property of another

4. Alimony, separate maintenance, or child support

5. Unscheduled debts unless creditor had actual notice of proceedings, i.e., where bankrupt failed to list creditor and debt

6. Those created by fraud while acting in a fiduciary capacity

7. Governmental fines or penalties imposed within prior 3 years

8. Educational loans of a governmental unit or nonprofit institution which became due within prior 5 years
9. Those from a prior bankruptcy proceeding in which the debtor waived discharge or was denied discharge

H. Revocation of Discharge

1. Discharge may be revoked if bankrupt committed fraud during bankruptcy proceedings

   EXAMPLE: *A bankrupt conceals assets in order to defraud creditors.*

2. Must be applied for by an interested party within one year of discharge

   a. Interested party is someone affected, e.g., creditor who never received payment

I. Reaffirmation

1. Debtor promises to pay a debt that will be or has been discharged. The code makes it difficult to reaffirm a dischargeable debt.

   a. Reaffirmation of a dischargeable debt to be enforceable must satisfy four conditions

      1) The agreement must have been made before the granting of a discharge
      2) The debtor has 30 days after the date the agreement becomes enforceable to rescind the agreement
      3) The court must have held the discharge hearing and the debtor must have attended and received the appropriate warnings from the court
      4) Concerns only individual debtors seeking reaffirmation of an unsecured consumer debt. The court must approve the agreement.

J. Debts Adjustment Plans - Chapter 13

1. To be eligible debtor must

   a. Have regular income, and
   b. Owe unsecured debts of less than $100,000, and
   c. Owe secured debts of less than $350,000

2. Initiated when debtor files voluntary petition in bankruptcy court

   a. Creditors may not file involuntary petition under Chapter 13
   b. Petition normally includes composition or extension plan

      1) Composition -- see "A.5."
      2) Extension -- provides debtor up to three years (five years if court approves) for payments to creditors

   c. Filing of petition stays all collection and straight bankruptcy proceedings against debtor
   d. Debtor has exclusive right to propose plan

      1) If debtor does not file plan, creditors may force debtor into involuntary proceeding under Chapter 7

    e. Plan will be confirmed or denied by court without approval of creditors

        1) However, unsecured creditors must receive as much as they would get under Chapter 7

    f. Court must appoint trustee in Chapter 13 cases

    g. Debtor engaged in business may continue to operate that business subject to limitations imposed by court

    h. Completion of plan discharges debtor from debts covered

    i. If composition were involved, then discharge bars another discharge for six years unless debtor paid 70% of debts covered

K. Business Reorganization - Chapter 11

1. Goal is to keep financially troubled firm in business. It is an alternative to liquidation under Chapter 7 (straight bankruptcy).

2. Can be initiated by debtor (voluntary) or creditors (involuntary)

3. Available to individuals, partnerships, or corporations including railroads. All other entities ineligible to be debtors under Chapter 7 are ineligible under Chapter 11.

4. If involuntary, same requirements must be met as needed to initiate a Chapter 7 involuntary proceeding. (See "C.2.")

5. Creditors' committee is selected from unsecured creditors after court accepts petition and grants order for relief

    a. Duties include

        1) Determine if business should continue to operate

        2) Determine if court should be asked to appoint a trustee or examiner

        3) Conduct an investigation of the debtor's financial affairs

        4) Generally consult with the debtor or trustee in the administration of the case

6. A trustee may be appointed "for cause" or "in the interest of creditors"

    a. Cause shall include fraud, dishonesty, incompetence, or gross mismanagement

    b. Trustee may be appointed only upon request of a party of interest and after notice and hearing

7. Unless the court orders otherwise, the debtor may continue to operate the business

8. If debtor does not submit plan within 120 days of order of relief, creditor may then file reorganization plan

9. Once confirmed plan is a binding contract between debtor and creditor concerning financial rehabilitation of the firm

SURETYSHIP

Overview

Suretyship is a broad legal term describing relationships where one person agrees to be answerable for the debt or default of another person. Suretyship is a form of security so that if the primary (principal) debtor is unable or unwilling to perform, the creditor has an immediate and direct remedy against the surety rather than against an insolvent, deceased, incapacitated, or reluctant debtor. Thus, suretyship allows creditors to insure themselves against the principal debtor's defenses of lack of capacity, death, bankruptcy, or inability to pay. However, the undertaking of a surety is not absolute. The surety may defend against payment of the debt or obligation by asserting any of its available defenses.

Suretyship is more frequently tested by objective questions than by essay questions on the examination. The questions emphasize first the identification and characteristics of the suretyship relationship such as formation, consideration, and capacity. Second, they emphasize the various rights of the parties involved in the suretyship agreement. Third, they emphasize the distinction between surety and guarantor. The last major group of questions concerns the surety's defenses.

Suretyship Definitions

Characteristics of Guarantee. Often used as a synonymous term for suretyship but is technically different in that the guarantor promises (after the debt is created) to pay if the debtor cannot or does not. Since this is a separate contract, separate consideration from that supporting the contract of the principal debtor is required.

Guarantor of Collection. A conditional guarantor who becomes secondarily liable for the debt or performance of another in contrast to a surety who is primarily liable with the debtor. The creditor must give notice of the debtor's default, and must exercise "due diligence" in enforcing his remedies against the principal debtor and exhaust these remedies by reducing his claim against the debtor to judgment and showing the judgment remains unsatisfied (unpaid) before the guarantor of collection's obligation arises.

Right of Contribution. The right of contribution arises among co-sureties when one co-surety, in performance of debtor's obligation, pays more than his proportionate share of the total liability, and thereby entitles the co-surety to compel the other co-sureties to compensate him for the excess amount paid (i.e., contribution from the other co-sureties for their respective pro rata share of liability).

Subrogation. The surety who pays the debt owed to the creditor succeeds to the rights of the creditor against the debtor and can recover from the debtor in the same manner the creditor was entitled. The surety acquires the identical claim or right the creditor possessed against the obligor. Thus, a surety who pays "steps into the shoes" of the creditor.

Suretyship Characteristics. A surety is a person who promises to be answerable for the debt, default, or miscarriage of another by assuring performance upon the debtor's default. A surety has primary liability to creditors and is legally answerable without being given notice of debtor's default or demand on the due date.

A. Nature of Suretyship

1. A suretyship contract is a relationship whereby one person agrees (promises) to be answerable for debt, default, or miscarriage of another by assuring performance upon debtor's default
   a. Surety agrees with creditor to satisfy obligation if principal debtor does not
   b. Surety's promise is made to creditor
   c. Purpose of a suretyship agreement is to protect creditor by providing creditor with added security for obligation and reduce creditor's risk of loss

   EXAMPLE: In order for X to obtain a loan from Bank, M (who has a good credit standing) promises to Bank that he will pay debt if X defaults.

2. Suretyship agreements involve three parties
   a. Creditor is obligee of debt owed by principal debtor and one to whom surety is bound to satisfy upon debtor's default (Bank in above example)
   b. Principal debtor is primary obligor who has ultimate liability for debt owed to creditor (X in above example)

    c. Surety is party who promises to perform upon default of principal debtor (M in above example)

        1) Surety technically has primary liability to creditor because creditor need not first attempt to collect from debtor; surety is simply liable if debtor does not perform. Also, surety is liable without creditor giving surety notice of debtor's default. (Compare to conditional guarantor--"B.2." below.)

3. Co-sureties exist when two or more sureties are bound to answer for same obligation or debt of principal debtor

    EXAMPLE: M and N promise Bank that they will pay X's debt if he defaults.

    a. Co-sureties share loss between them as agreed; if no agreement, they share in proportion to amount each has personally guaranteed

4. Subsurety is one who guarantees surety's performance (i.e., a surety for a surety on same debt)

    EXAMPLE: M (principal surety) agrees to pay Bank if X defaults, and N (subsurety) agrees to pay Bank if M does not.

    a. Principal surety is primarily liable and bears entire burden of performance, with subsurety in effect acting as a surety for principal surety

5. A suretyship contract can be created without knowledge of principal debtor

    EXAMPLE: Son applies to Bank X for a loan. Without son's knowledge, father promises Bank X to answer for his son's debt if the son defaults. Father is a surety.

6. Typical suretyship arrangements

    a. Seller of goods on credit requires buyer to obtain a surety to guarantee payment of goods purchased
    b. Bank requires owners or directors of closely held corporation to act as sureties for loan to corporation
    c. In order to transfer a check or note, transferor may be required to obtain a surety (accommodation indorser) to guarantee payment. (See Liability of Parties in NEGOTIABLE INSTRUMENTS.)
    d. Where a party sells real property and purchaser expressly assumes seller's mortgage on property (i.e., promises to pay mortgage debt). Seller becomes surety and purchaser is principal debtor.

7. Third-party beneficiary contract vs. suretyship contract

    a. A third-party beneficiary contract is one in which third party receives benefits from agreement made between promisor and promisee, although third person is not party to contract

    EXAMPLE: Father says: "Ship goods to my son and I will pay for them." This describes a third-party beneficiary contract, not a suretyship arrangement. Father is not promising to pay the debt of another, but rather engaging in an original promise to pay (i.e., a debtor) for goods creditor delivers to son.

8. Indemnity contract vs. suretyship contract

    a. An indemnity contract is contract between two parties (whereas surety relationship is tripartite) whereby indemnitor makes a promise to a potential debtor, indemnitee, (not to creditor as in suretyship arrangement), to indemnify and reimburse debtor for payment of debt or for loss that may arise in future. Indemnitor pays because it has assumed risk of loss, not because of any default by principal debtor as in suretyship arrangement.

EXAMPLE: Under terms of standard automobile collision insurance policy, insurance company agrees to indemnify automobile owner against damage to his/her car caused by collision.

B. Guarantor

1. Surety and guarantor are for most part synonymous, but there are some distinctions arising in their initial creation

   a. A surety is usually bound with principal debtor by same instrument, executed at same time and on same consideration, although it is not necessary

   b. Contract of guarantor is generally created separately from the primary "debtor-creditor" contract, it is a separate undertaking, in which principal debtor does not join. It is usually entered into after that of principal debtor, and is founded on a separate consideration (due to two distinct agreements) from that supporting contract of principal debtor.

   c. Surety is usually liable to pay creditor if debtor does not pay

      1) Normally, a creditor can immediately sue surety upon debtor's default (i.e., no further action by creditor against principal debtor is necessary; notice to surety of principal debtor's default is not required)

      2) Most other guarantors are liable in same manner as a surety, as described above

2. Conditional guarantors -- liability is dependent upon some condition, beyond mere default of principal debtor, in guarantee agreement

   a. Commonly guarantor's liability will be conditioned on creditor first attempting to collect from debtor himself and guarantor being given notice of principal debtor's default (i.e., a guarantor of collection)

   b. Guarantor of collection is one who becomes secondarily liable for debt or performance of another in contrast to surety who is primarily liable with principal debtor

   c. Creditor must exercise "due diligence" in enforcing his/her remedies against principal debtor and exhaust these remedies by reducing his/her claim against debtor to judgment and showing judgment remains unsatisfied (unpaid) before guarantor of collection's obligation arises

   d. Failure of creditor to give guarantor of collection notice of principal debtor's default or failure of creditor to use "due diligence" in exercising his remedies against debtor will create defense to guarantor's liability. (See Surety's Defenses "G." below.)

3. In this outline, term "surety" will include guaranty, except for conditional guaranty, which, as aforementioned, is distinct and which will be specifically identified where referred to hereinafter

C. Contracts

1. Generally, suretyship and guaranty contracts are required to meet general provisions of contracts. For legally binding suretyship or guaranty arrangement to

exist, all requisite elements to establish a legally enforceable contract must be present. (See Essential Elements of a Contract in CONTRACTS.)

2. Promise of a surety is not binding without consideration

   a. Normally, consideration (e.g., loan or sale of goods) given by creditor to debtor is extended to surety such that separate consideration is not needed to support suretyship contract. Consideration supporting principal debtor's promise to creditor also supports surety's promise, since surety's promise is generally given as inducement to creditor to confer benefit upon principal debtor.

      1) If surety's undertaking arises at same time creditor extends a loan or makes a sale of goods to principal debtor (i.e., suretyship contract is contemporaneous with primary contract), surety does not need to receive separate consideration beyond that supporting principal debtor's contract because consideration supporting principal contract is deemed to also support suretyship contract

      2) Where creditor has extended credit prior to surety's promise, or surety's promise is given after debtor is legally obligated to perform (i.e., surety's undertaking is entered subsequent to principal contract), independent consideration is required to support surety's promise

3. Because of nature of surety and guaranty contracts ("promises to answer for the debt, default, or miscarriage of another") they fall within the Statute of Frauds and must be in writing to be enforceable. (See Statute of Frauds in CONTRACTS.)

   a. Writing must be signed by surety and contain statement of surety's promise
   b. An agreement is not within Statute of Frauds if surety's promise is made for his/her own benefit ("main purpose" or "leading object" rule)

      1) This rule is invoked when main object of surety is to serve some pecuniary interest of his/her own

         EXAMPLE: *S agrees to answer for debt or default of X because X is S's supplier and S needs X to stay in business to keep himself in business.*

      2) Therefore, surety's oral promise is binding whenever its primary purpose is to benefit surety rather than principal debtor

      3) A del credere agent's guarantee of collection of accounts falls within this "main purpose" rule. A del credere agent sells goods on credit to purchasers in behalf of his/her principal and assumes, generally for a higher commission, obligation to pay his/her principal what purchasers fail to pay

         a) Although del credere agent's guaranty is promise to answer for debt of another, it is considered as having been given primarily for his own benefit, and therefore, not within the Statute of Frauds

4. Capacity to act as surety

   a. Any individual that possesses general capacity to contract
   b. Corporations cannot be sureties unless in furtherance of their business or expressly allowed in their articles of incorporation (otherwise considered Ultra vires act)

c. Partnerships may act as sureties unless partnership agreement expressly prohibits it from entering into suretyship contracts

d. An individual partner has no authority to bind partnership as surety 1) unless it is in furtherance of partnership business, 2) is expressly authorized in articles of copartnership, or 3) copartners expressly authorize such action by unanimous consent

D. Accommodation (Gratuitous) Surety vs. Compensated Surety

1. Compensated surety is one who assumes potential liability inherent in suretyship relationship for a fee

2. Accommodation surety is one who acts as surety without benefit of being compensated for assumption of such risk (i.e., a noncompensated surety)

3. Does not affect co-suretyships even if one surety is compensated and one is not

4. Sometimes law presumes that compensated surety assumes risks that noncompensated surety would not assume because compensated surety is paid for his/her promise

a. Ambiguities are generally construed in favor of accommodation sureties and more strictly against compensated sureties

b. Upon alteration of contract affecting debtor's duties, greater increase in risk in surety's undertaking is needed to discharge a compensated surety than an accommodation surety. (See Surety Defenses "G.3.f." below.)

E. Creditor's Rights

1. Against principal debtor

a. Creditor has right to receive payment or performance specified in contract with principal debtor

b. Creditor may proceed immediately against debtor upon default, subject to any agreement in contract

c. When debtor has more than one debt outstanding with same creditor and makes a part payment, debtor may give instructions as to which debt the payment is to apply

1) If debtor gives no instructions, creditor is free to apply part payment to whichever debt s/he chooses; fact that one debt is guaranteed by surety and other is not makes no difference in absence of instructions by debtor

2) Does not affect risk to surety and is not defense of surety

EXAMPLE: If debtor owes two debts to creditor and surety only guaranteed one, creditor may apply a payment from debtor to one not guaranteed (absent instructions by debtor) and surety is not released.

2. Against surety

a. Creditor may proceed immediately against surety upon principal debtor's default

1) Unless contract requires, it is not necessary to give surety notice of debtor's default

2) Since surety is immediately primarily liable, he can be sued without creditor first attempting to collect from debtor (i.e., without demand first being made upon debtor)

3. Against guarantor of collection
    a. A guarantor of collection's liability is conditioned on creditor notifying guarantor of debtor's default and creditor first attempting to collect from debtor
    b. Creditor must first exercise "due diligence" in enforcing his remedies against debtor and exhaust these remedies by reducing his claim against debtor to judgment and showing judgment remains unsatisfied (unpaid) before guarantor of collection's liability arises (i.e., guarantor of collection is secondarily liable for another's debt)

4. Against security (collateral) held by surety
    a. Creditor has an equitable interest in collateral held by surety even if both principal debtor and surety are solvent
    b. Surety must retain collateral as trustee for benefit of creditor
        1) Surety must retain, safeguard, and refrain from legally impairing collateral
        2) Surety must not release (give back) collateral to principal debtor before debt or performance is satisfied
    c. Creditor may gain equitable relief before default to prevent surety from wasting, releasing, or otherwise impairing collateral
    d. After principal debtor's default, creditor may resort to collateral held by surety to satisfy debt
        1) If creditor does resort to collateral, any excess collateral or amount realized by its disposal over debt amount must be returned to principal debtor
        2) If collateral is insufficient to satisfy debt, creditor may proceed against surety or debtor for balance due (deficiency)
    e. Creditor is not required to use collateral; creditor may instead proceed immediately against surety on his/her promise
        1) If surety pays, surety is subrogated to creditor's rights in collateral and is entitled to collateral
    f. If principal debtor pays obligation, collateral must be returned to debtor along with any income earned thereon

5. Against security (collateral) held by creditor
    a. Creditor may satisfy debt with any collateral of debtor's that s/he holds in his possession
    b. Upon default, creditor need not resort to collateral pledged; instead, s/he may proceed immediately against principal debtor or surety for payment
        1) If debtor pays, collateral must be returned to debtor along with any income earned thereon
        2) If surety pays, surety is subrogated to creditor's rights in collateral and is entitled to collateral
    c. If creditor does resort to collateral, any excess collateral or amount realized by its disposal over debt amount must be returned to principal debtor
        1) If collateral is insufficient to satisfy debt, creditor may proceed against surety or debtor for balance due (deficiency)

d. If both debtor and surety provide collateral and creditor elects to resort to collateral, s/he must first exhaust principal debtor's collateral for satisfaction of debt before resorting to surety's collateral

e. Creditor owes duty of care to retain and safeguard collateral

    1) If creditor voluntarily releases, destroys, or otherwise impairs collateral he holds, s/he reduces surety's obligation by that amount. (See Surety's Defenses "G.3.c." below.)

F. Surety's Rights

1. When the debt or obligation for which surety has given his/her promise has become due and before surety pays creditor

    a. Surety may request creditor to proceed first against debtor

        1) Creditor is not required to do so and his/her failure to try to enforce debt against debtor will not discharge surety's obligation

    b. Surety may request creditor to resort first to collateral if surety can show collateral is seriously depreciating in value, or if surety can show undue hardship will otherwise result

    c. Exoneration

        1) Surety may bring suit in equity and obtain judicial decree to compel debtor to pay obligation owed to creditor

        2) Surety must show that debtor has assets sufficient to satisfy debt that debtor is wrongfully holding

        3) Exoneration is not available if creditor demands prompt performance from surety upon debtor's default

2. When debt or obligation for which surety has given his/her promise has become due and after surety pays or performs obligation owing to creditor

    a. Surety is entitled to right of reimbursement from debtor

        1) May recover only actual payments to creditor in satisfaction of debt

        2) Surety is entitled to resort to collateral s/he holds or which is held by creditor as satisfaction of right of reimbursement

        3) Surety's payment of debt or performance of obligation after having received notice of principal debtor's valid defense against creditor will cause surety to lose right of reimbursement. (Surety's payment is considered voluntary.)

    b. Subrogation

        1) Surety who pursuant to his/her contractual undertaking fully satisfies obligation of debtor to creditor succeeds to rights of creditor against debtor (i.e., "stands in shoes of creditor") and can recover from debtor in same manner creditor was entitled

        2) Surety acquires identical claims or rights creditor possessed against principal debtor, permitting surety to assert rights s/he otherwise could not assert

            a) Where debtor has pledged collateral, surety succeeds to it if creditor has not resorted to collateral (i.e., surety is subrogated to creditor's rights in collateral)

        b) If debtor is adjudged to be bankrupt, surety is subrogated to rights of creditor's priority in bankruptcy proceeding

     3) Creditor has duty to take legal measures to effect surety's right of subrogation (e.g., assign rights against principal debtor or release all rights to collateral held as security)

  c. Right of contribution exists among co-sureties. (See "H.3." below.)

G. Surety's Defenses

1. Surety may exercise any defense on contract which would be available to debtor except for debtor's personal defenses

  a. Breach or failure of performance by creditor
  b. Impossibility or illegality of performance
  c. Failure of consideration
  d. Creditor obtains debtor's promise by fraud, duress, or misrepresentation
  e. Statute of Limitations

2. Surety may take advantage of his/her own contractual defenses

  a. Fraud or duress

     1) If creditor obtains surety's promise by fraud or duress, contract is voidable at surety's option

        EXAMPLE: Creditor forces X to sign suretyship agreement at threat of great bodily harm.

     2) Fraud by principal debtor on surety to induce a suretyship agreement will not release surety if creditor has extended credit in good faith

        a) But if creditor had knowledge of debtor's fraudulent representations, then surety may avoid liability

        EXAMPLE: Y asked Ace to act as surety on a loan from Bank. In order to induce Ace to act as surety, Y made fraudulent representations concerning its financial position to Ace. This fraud by Y will not release surety, Ace, if the creditor, Bank, had no knowledge of the fraud and extended credit in good faith. But if Bank had knowledge of Y's fraudulent representations, then Ace has a good defense and can avoid liability.

  b. Suretyship contract itself is void due to illegality
  c. Incapacity of surety (e.g., surety is a minor)
  d. Failure of consideration for suretyship contract

     1) However, when surety's and principal debtor's obligations are incurred at same time, there is no need for any separate consideration beyond that supporting principal debtor's contract; if surety's undertaking is entered into subsequent to debtor's contract, it must be supported by separate consideration. (See "C.2." above.)

  e. Suretyship agreement is not written as required per Statute of Frauds
  f. Statute of Limitations as to creditor's right to recover from surety

     1) Statute of Limitations is measured from date of default by principal debtor or when default should reasonably have been discovered by a diligent creditor, and bars action against surety if not commenced within statutory period

   a) Length of time varies by state

g. Surety may set-off any claims that s/he has against creditor, even if they do not arise out of surety obligation

h. If creditor fails to notify surety of any material facts within creditor's knowledge concerning debtor or his/her ability to perform, surety may assert this as a defense to avoid liability (i.e., concealment)

   1) Material facts are those facts pertaining to risk assumed by surety such that surety may not have assumed obligation had s/he been aware of these facts because they cause an increase in surety's risk

   EXAMPLE: Creditor's failure to report to surety that debtor has defaulted on several previous occasions.

   EXAMPLE: Creditor's failure to report to surety that debtor submitted fraudulent financial statements to surety to induce suretyship agreement.

3. Acts of creditor or debtor materially affecting surety's performance

   a. Release of principal debtor from liability by creditor without consent of surety will also discharge surety's liability

      1) But surety is not released if creditor specifically reserves his/her rights against surety
      2) Courts construe release of debtor while retaining rights against surety as a covenant not to sue debtor
      3) If debtor's release was obtained by fraud or duress, surety is only discharged to extent that s/he has been prejudiced

   b. Release of surety by creditor

      1) Does not release principal debtor since his/her obligation is not affected by surety's release

   c. Release, surrender, destruction, or impairment of collateral by creditor before or after debtor's default will release surety to extent of value of collateral released, surrendered, destroyed, or impaired

   d. Proper performance by debtor or satisfaction of creditor through collateral will discharge surety

   e. Tender of performance by debtor or surety and refusal by creditor will discharge surety

      1) If tender of performance is prior to time debt or obligation is due, creditor need not accept and surety is not released

      2) However, such tender of performance does not release principal debtor if contractual duty consists of obligation to pay money, it only terminates accrual of interest on debt; if debtor's contractual duty is anything other than obligation to pay money, then such tender of performance would also release debtor

   f. A material alteration or variance in terms and conditions of contract subsequent to surety's undertaking is a defense for surety if it increases risk of surety's undertaking

      1) Substitution of debtors (i.e., a change in identity of principal debtor or a delegation of principal debtor's obligation to another party)

      2) Change or modification in duties of principal debtor

3) Legally binding extension of time, without surety's consent

a) Compensated surety is normally not discharged, but is entitled to have his/her obligation reduced by extent of loss due to extension of time

4) A legally enforceable variance in amount, place, time, or manner of principal debtor's payments

5) Surety can consent to any alteration and thereby waive his defense

6) Modern trend is such that an accommodation (noncompensated) surety is completely discharged if creditor does anything that varies surety's risk. However, a compensated surety is discharged only if creditor actually causes a binding material increase in risk, and then surety is discharged only to extent of increased risk. (See "D.4." above.)

7) Surety is not released if creditor modifies principal debtor's duty or alters terms of contract and such modification can only be beneficial to surety (i.e., decreases surety's risk)

EXAMPLE: Creditor reduces interest rate on loan to principal debtor from 12% to 10%.

8) In order to release surety, there must be an actual alteration or variance in terms of contract and not an option or election that principal debtor can exercise under express terms of original agreement which surety has guaranteed

EXAMPLE: Tenant and landlord entered into a two year leasing agreement which expressly contained an option for an additional year which could be exercised by tenant, with X acting as surety on lease contract. If tenant exercises this option, X still remains bound as surety.

4. Following are not defenses of surety

a. Personal defenses of principal debtor

1) Death of debtor or debtor's lack of capacity
2) Insolvency (or discharge in bankruptcy) of debtor

a) Possibility of debtor's insolvency is a primary reason for engaging in a surety arrangement

3) Personal debtor's set-offs

a) Unless debtor assigns them to surety

b. Creditor did not give notice to surety of debtor's default or creditor did not first proceed against principal debtor

1) Unless a conditional guarantor. (See "B.2." above.)

c. Creditor does not resort to collateral

H. Co-sureties

1. Co-sureties exist when there is more than one surety for same obligation of principal debtor to same creditor

a. It does not matter that co-sureties do not know of each other or that they become sureties at different times; they need only share same burden

b. Each surety is bound to answer for same debt and shares in burden upon default of debtor

c. Co-sureties need not be bound for same amount; they can guarantee equal or unequal amounts of debt

    1) Collateral need not be held equally

2. Co-sureties are jointly and severally liable to creditor

   a. Creditor can proceed against both sureties jointly or against each one individually to extent (amount) surety has assumed liability by personally guaranteeing obligation

   b. If creditor sues both sureties, s/he may recover in any proportion from each, but may only recover total amount of debtor's obligation

   c. If creditor proceeds against a co-surety individually, surety's liability is limited to amount for which s/he agreed to be surety

   d. If creditor proceeds against a co-surety individually, surety held liable can proceed against other co-sureties for their proportionate share of liability

3. Right of contribution exists among co-sureties

   a. Right of contribution arises when co-surety, in performance of debtor's obligation, pays more than his/her proportionate share of total liability, and thereby entitles co-surety to compel other co-sureties to compensate him/her for excess amount paid (i.e., contribution from other co-sureties for their pro rata share of liability)

4. Co-sureties are only liable in contribution for their proportionate share

   a. Co-surety's pro rata share is proportion that each surety's risk (i.e., amount each has personally guaranteed) bears to total amount of risk assumed by all sureties

$$\left(\frac{\text{Dollar amount individual co-surety personally guaranteed}}{\text{Total dollar amount of risk assumed by all co-sureties}}\right)$$

   EXAMPLE: X and Y are co-sureties for $5,000 and $10,000, respectively, of a $10,000 debt. Each is liable in proportion to amount each has personally guaranteed. Since X guaranteed $5,000 of debt and Y guaranteed $10,000 of debt, then X is individually liable for 1/3 ($5,000/$15,000) of debt and Y is individually liable for 2/3 ($10,000/$15,000) of debt. Debtor defaults on $3,000 of debt. X is liable for $1,000 (1/3 x $3,000) and Y is liable for $2,000 (2/3 x $3,000). Although creditor may recover $3,000 from either, each co-surety has right of contribution from other co-surety.

5. Each co-surety is entitled to share in any collateral pledged (either held by creditor or other co-surety) in proportion to co-surety's liability for debtor's default

   EXAMPLE: If in above illustration, co-surety Y held collateral pledged by debtor worth $900, both co-sureties X and Y would be entitled to share in collateral in proportion to their respective liabilities. X would be entitled to 1/3 ($5,000/$15,000) of $900 collateral, or $300; and Y would be entitled to 2/3 ($10,000/$15,000) of $900 collateral, or $600.

6. Discharge or release of one co-surety by creditor results in a reduction of liability of remaining co-surety

    a. Remaining co-surety is released to extent of released co-surety's pro rata share of debt liability (unless there is a reservation of rights by creditor against remaining co-surety)

    b. This reduction in remaining co-surety's liability can also be stated as extent to which his/her right to contribution has been adversely affected (i.e., amount remaining co-surety would have been able to recover from co-surety, under his right of contribution, had co-surety not been discharged or released)

        EXAMPLE: A and B are co-sureties for $4,000 and $12,000, respectively, on a $12,000 debt. If creditor releases co-surety A, co-surety B is released to extent of co-surety A's liability. Each is liable in proportion to amount each has personally guaranteed. Since A guaranteed $4,000 of debt and B guaranteed $12,000 of debt, then A is individually liable for 1/4 ($4,000/$16,000) of debt and B is individually liable for 3/4 ($12,000/16,000) of debt, i.e., $9,000. Therefore, co-surety B is released of A's pro rata liability of $3,000 (1/4 x $12,000), and only remains a surety for $9,000 ($12,000 - $3,000) of debt.

7. A co-surety is not released from his/her obligation to perform merely because his/her co-surety refuses to perform. However, upon payment of full obligation, co-surety can demand a pro rata contribution from his nonperforming co-surety.

I. Surety Bonds

1. An acknowledgment of an obligation to make good the performance by another of some act, duty, or responsibility

    a. Usually issued by companies which for a stated consideration (fee) assume risk of performance by bonded party

    b. Performance of act, duty, or responsibility by bonded party discharges surety's obligation

2. Construction bonds (performance bonds) are given by surety to a landowner guaranteeing builder's obligation to perform construction

    a. If builder fails to perform, surety can be held liable for damages, but not specific performance

3. Fidelity bonds are form of insurance that protects an employer against losses sustained by dishonest employees (i.e., guarantees faithful performance of duties by employee)

    a. Any significant change in the employee's duties may serve to release surety bonding company from its obligation

4. Judicial bonds are those given in connection with judicial proceedings (e.g., bail bonds)

5. Official bonds are those given to government to guarantee faithful performance of duties by a public official (e.g., executors, guardians)

6. Surety bonding company retains right of subrogation against each of bonded parties

AGENCY

Overview

Agency is a relationship where one person is employed or appointed to act for another and subject to their control and includes independent contractors, employees, or servants. In a more narrow sense, the term is used to describe the principal and agent relationship. Agency is a fiduciary relationship in which one party (agent) voluntarily acts as a business representative of another (principal) in entering into contracts (with third parties). The law of agency is concerned with the rights, duties, and liabilities of these three parties as a result of the relationships between them. Over time the law has developed a body of legal principles to deal with the liability of the employer for the wrongs (torts) of all employees. Thus agency law involves the subject matter of torts as well as contracts.

Agency law is also important because a corporation, as a legal entity, can function and enter into contracts only through agents. Moreover, the law of partnership is to a large degree a special application of agency principles. Agents are classified according to the manner of their appointment, by the functions they perform, and by the authority they possess. The usual rules of capacity of parties are applicable to agency relationships, and as a general rule no particular formalities are required to create an agency.

The CPA exam emphasizes the creation of the agency relationship including ratification, the undisclosed principal relationship, unauthorized acts or torts committed by the agent within the course and scope of the agency relationship and principal's liability for agent's unauthorized contracts. While the above seem to be the most frequently tested topics in the objective questions, other topics that are tested regularly include termination of agency by operation of law, notice of termination, duties of the agent and principal to each other, etc.

Agency Definitions

Agency. An arrangement between two persons whereby one, called an agent, agrees to act for and be subject to the control of another, called a principal, in business transactions with third persons.

Independent Contractor. One employed to do some particular job using his own judgment and method, i.e., not subject to the control of the employer except as to results.

Agency by Estoppel. An agency arising when a principal, by conduct, clothes an agent with apparent authority which reasonably induces a third person to deal with such a person as an agent.

Implied Authority. Authority to do those acts which are usually or customarily done in conducting transactions such as the agent is authorized to transact. Also authority to do those acts which are reasonably necessary to carry out the agent's express authority.

Undisclosed Principal. An agency relationship where the agent appears to be acting in his own behalf. The third party has no knowledge that the agent is in fact acting as agent for a principal which the agent has failed to disclose.

Respondeat Superior. A doctrine whereby a principal or employer is held legally liable for any tort committed by his agent or employee, even though the act was not expressly authorized. The tort must be committed while the agent or employee is acting within the course and scope of his employment relationship.

A. Characteristics

1. Agency is a relationship by consent (agreement) between two parties, whereby one party (agent) agrees to act on behalf of the other party (principal). A contract is not required.

    a. Agent is subject to the continuous control of the principal

    b. Agent is a fiduciary and he must act for the benefit of the principal

    c. An agent can be used for other purposes, e.g., to perform physical acts, but we are primarily concerned with agents that agree to act for the principal in business transactions with third parties

    d. Agent's specific authority is determined by the principal but generally an agent has authority:

       1) To perform legal acts for the principal
       2) More specifically, to bind the principal contractually with third parties

2. Servant distinguished from an agent

  a. Servant is a type of agent
  b. Servant is subject to control of his physical conduct by master

      1) Master is a type of principal and is called such when the agent is a servant
      2) Agent is subject to a lesser and a more general control, i.e., what to do and when to do it, but not control of physical conduct
      3) Servant is usually employed for manual service, e.g., sales clerk
      4) Master is generally liable for servant's torts if committed within course and scope of employment relationship

3. Independent contractor distinguished from an agent

  a. Not subject to control of employer
  b. Not subject to regular supervision as a servant (or employee)
  c. Employer seeks the results only and contractor controls the methods

    EXAMPLE: A builder of homes has only to produce the results.

  d. Generally, employer is not liable for torts committed by independent contractor

      1) Unless independent contractor is employed to do something imminently or inherently dangerous, e.g., blasting

  e. Independent contractor may also be an agent in certain cases

    EXAMPLE: A public accounting firm represents a client in tax court.

4. Types of agents

  a. General--one who has broad power to act for the principal in various types of transactions

      1) Principal may be liable for unauthorized acts which similar general agents are authorized for

  b. Special--appointed for a limited purpose or a specific task

      1) If s/he performs unauthorized acts, principal is less likely to be liable than if s/he were a general agent

  c. Gratuitous--agrees to act without expectation of compensation

      1) Is not bound to perform, but once started must perform duties in non-negligent manner
      2) Not subject to as high a degree of care as a compensated agent

  d. Subagent--one appointed by an authorized agent to perform for the agent

    EXAMPLE: P hires A to manage a branch office and tells A to hire anyone he needs. If A hires X as an assistant, X is a subagent of P.

      1) If first agent is authorized only to employ for principal, then second agent is an agent of the principal, not a subagent

EXAMPLE: P asks A to hire 5 people to work in P's branch office. Those hired by A are agents of P, not agents of A.

   2) If first agent has no authority to employ, second agent will be an agent to first agent and not a subagent of principal

EXAMPLE: P hires A to manage a branch office but tells A not to hire anyone, that P will supply anyone needed. If A hires X as an assistant, X is an agent of A's, not a subagent of P.

5. Examples of agents--usually special agents

  a. Agency coupled with an interest -- agent has an interest in the subject matter of the agency: either a property interest or a security interest

    1) E.g., mortgagee with right to sell property on default of mortgagor
    2) Principal cannot terminate the agency

  b. Attorney--practices law for a number of persons
  c. Auctioneer--agent for seller of property. Once property sells, s/he acts as agent for both buyer and seller.
  d. Broker--special agent acting for either buyer or seller in business transactions, e.g., real estate broker
  e. Del credere--a sales agent who, prior to the creation and as a condition of the agency, guarantees the accounts of the customers to his/her principal (if the customers fail to pay)

    1) Guarantee is not within the Statute of Frauds, i.e., it is not required to be in writing

  f. Exclusive--only agent the principal may deal with for a certain purpose during life of the contract, e.g., real estate broker who has sole right to sell property except for personal sale by principal

  g. Factor--commercial agent employed to sell goods

    1) Factor has possession of goods and may sell in the factor's own name

  h. Promoter--commonly used to designate person who attempts to form a corporation

    1) Generally held personally liable for preincorporation contracts with third parties, even if corporation does come into being
    2) See CORPORATIONS for promoter's liability

6. Types of principals

  a. Disclosed--when the third party knows or should know the agent is acting for a principal and who the principal is

    1) Principal becomes a party to authorized contracts made by the agent in the principal's name

EXAMPLE: Signed, "John Doe as agent for Tom Thumb, principal." Therefore, only Tom Thumb is liable on the contract.

  b. Partially disclosed--when the third party knows or should know the agent is acting for a principal but does not know who the principal is

    1) Both the agent and the principal become parties to the contract

EXAMPLE: Signed, "John Doe as agent."

    c. Undisclosed--when the third party has no notice that the agent is acting for a principal

        1) Both agent and principal become parties to all authorized contracts if the agent so intended to act for principal

            EXAMPLE: Signed, "John Doe."

B. Methods of Creation

1. Appointment

    a. Express--by agreement between the principal and agent. No formalities necessary.

        1) Generally needs to be written for compensated agent to purchase or sell real estate

    b. Implied--created by conduct of principal showing the intention that the relationship exists

        1) This conduct is usually, but not necessarily, directed toward the agent and must cause the agent to reasonably believe it is the principal's intention

2. Estoppel--principal is not allowed to deny agency relationship when s/he causes third party to believe it exists

    a. Imposed by law rather than by agreement
    b. The third party must rely to his/her detriment on this appearance of agency before the principal is estopped from denying it

        EXAMPLE: A, not an agent of P, in P's presence, bargained with X to buy goods for P. If P remains silent, he will not be able to deny the agency.

3. Representation--principal represents to third party that someone is his/her agent.

    a. Creates apparent (ostensible) authority
    b. Does not require reliance by third party
    c. Directed toward third party causing third party to believe (as opposed to implied appointment when agent is led to believe)

        EXAMPLE: Principal writes to a third party that A is his agent and has authority. Even if A has no actual authority, he is an agent by representation.

4. Necessity--when a situation arises which makes it a matter of public policy to presume an agency relationship, e.g., in an emergency to contract for medical aid

5. Ratification--approval after the fact of an unauthorized act done by an agent or one not yet an agent

    a. By affirming the act or by accepting the benefits of the act
    b. Other party to the contract can withdraw before principal ratifies
    c. Ratification is effective retroactively back to time of agent's act
    d. Ratification is not retractable
    e. Requirements to be valid

1) Act must be one that would have been valid if agent had been authorized, i.e., lawful and delegable

   a) Torts can be ratified, but not crimes

2) Principal must have been in existence and competent when the act was done

3) Principal must have capacity when he ratifies

4) Agent must have purported to act on behalf of the one who later ratifies

5) Principal must be aware of all material facts

6) Act must be ratified in its entirety, i.e., cannot ratify the beneficial part and refuse the rest

   EXAMPLE: Receptionist has no authority to contract for X Company but signs a service contract on behalf of X Company. Officers of X Company make use of service contract. The receptionist's act is ratified.

C. Authority

1. Actual authority

   a. Express--consists of all authority expressly given by the principal to his/her agent

   b. Implied--authority that can be reasonably implied from express authority and from the conduct of the principal. See Methods of Creation.

      1) E.g., agent drives principal's car. Principal acquiesces by not objecting, so agent has implied authority to do it again.

      2) E.g., principal ratifies unauthorized act. Depending on circumstances, agent may have implied authority to do similar act.

      3) Includes authority reasonably necessary or usual to carry out express authority. E.g., authority to drive car home when s/he has authority to buy it.

2. Apparent (ostensible) authority -- third party(ies) must have reasonable belief based on principal's representations. Principal has clothed agent with apparent authority to do acts customary to one in the relationship of an agent to the principal.

   a. E.g., an agent insofar as third persons are concerned can do what the predecessor did or what agents in similar positions in the general business world are deemed authorized to do for their principals

   b. Secret limitations have no effect

      EXAMPLE: Principal makes agent manager of his store but tells him not to purchase goods on his own. Agent has apparent authority to purchase as similar managers would.

   c. Apparent authority exists only for those who know of principal's representations whether directly or indirectly

   d. Agent has apparent authority after termination of agency until those with whom the agent has dealt are given actual notice, others constructive notice

1) Notice may come from any source

3. Estoppel--not true authority, but an equitable doctrine to protect a third party who has detrimentally relied, by estopping the principal from denying the existence of authority

a. Often indistinguishable from effects of apparent authority or ratification

1) Estoppel may be applied where other doctrines technically won't work

b. Only creates rights in the third party(ies)

*EXAMPLE: A sells P's race horse to T in P's behalf. P did not give author-
ity, but since the race horse continues to lose races, P does not object.
When the horse begins to win races, P claims A never had authority to sell.
If A does not have apparent authority and if P did not technically ratify, P
can be estopped from denying the authority on equitable grounds.*

D. Capacity To Be Agent or Principal

1. Principal must be able to give legal consent

a. If act requires some legal capacity, e.g., legal age to sell land, then
principal must meet this requirement or agent cannot legally perform even if
s/he has capacity. Capacity cannot be increased by appointment of an
agent.

b. Infant (person under age of majority, i.e., 18 or 21) can, in most jurisdictions, appoint an agent

1) If not to secure necessities, the appointment can be voided at the
infant-principal's option

c. Insane person's agreements are voidable if made before s/he is judicially
found insane and void if made after the judicial determination

d. Marriage is not a bar for either spouse to be a principal or agent for the
other

e. Partnerships have all the partners as agents who, in turn, may appoint
other agents

f. Corporations, being artificial persons, must act entirely through agents

g. Unincorporated associations are not legal entities and therefore cannot
appoint agents

1) Individual members will be responsible as principals if they appoint an
agent

2. An agent must merely have sufficient mental and physical ability to carry out
instructions of his/her principal

a. Can bind principal even if agent is a minor or legally unable to act for
himself

b. Corporations, unincorporated associations, and partnerships may act as
agents

c. A mental incompetent or an infant of tender years may not be an agent

E. Obligations and Rights

1. Principal's obligations to agent

a. Compensate agent as per agreement, or, in the absence of an agreement, pay a reasonable amount for the agent's services
b. Guarantee agents reasonable expenses and indemnify agent against loss or liability for duties performed at the principal's direction which are not patently illegal
c. Not to discredit agent, nor interfere with his/her work
d. Inform agent of risks, e.g., physical harm, pecuniary loss
e. Only duty to subagent is indemnification. Agent has duties of principal to subagent.
f. May have remedies of discharging agent, restitution, damages, and accounting, or an injunction

2. Agent's obligations to principal

a. Agent is a fiduciary and must act in the best interest of the principal and with complete loyalty
b. Carry out instructions of principal exercising reasonable care and skill

   1) Cannot appoint subagent or delegate nonmechanical duties unless authorized, necessary, or customary

c. To account to the principal for profits and everything which rightfully belongs to the principal and not commingle funds
d. To indemnify principal for any damage wrongfully caused principal, e.g., tort while in course of employment
e. Give any information to principal which s/he would want or need to know
f. Duty not to compete or act adversely to principal

   1) Includes not acting for oneself unless principal knows and acquiesces

g. After termination, must cease acting as agent

   1) May still have duty not to reveal secrets of principal

3. Principal's liability to third parties

a. Disclosed or partially disclosed principal is liable on contracts and conveyances

   1) Where agent has actual authority, implied authority, apparent authority, or contract is later ratified
   2) Also held liable for any representations made by agent with authority to make them
   3) Principal not liable where third party has any notice that agent is exceeding his actual authority

b. Undisclosed principal is similarly liable unless

   1) Third party holds agent responsible (third party has choice)
   2) Agent has already fully performed contract
   3) Undisclosed principal is expressly excluded by contract
   4) Contract is a negotiable instrument

      a) Only fully disclosed (in instrument) principal is liable on a negotiable instrument

      c. If a writing is required under Statute of Frauds, principal will only be liable if agent signs

      d. Principal has his/her own personal defenses, e.g., lack of capacity, and defenses on the contract, e.g., nonperformance by the third party

          1) Principal does not have agent's personal defenses, e.g., right of set-off where third party owes agent debt

      e. Notice to agent is considered notice to the principal except where notice was given to agent before the formation of the agency relationship

          1) If agent is acting against interest of principal, i.e., in collusion with third party, then this third party's notice to agent is not notice to principal

      f. Principal is not liable for agent's crimes (violations of statutes) unless s/he was a party to the crime or acquiesced in commission

      g. Principal is liable for servant's torts committed within course and scope of employment (Doctrine of Respondeat Superior)

          1) A tort is a personal or civil wrong. Not under contract and not criminally prosecuted, although some actions may be both torts and crimes.

               EXAMPLE: A breaks T's arm. This is a tort and T may sue A for damages. A may also be prosecuted for criminal negligence. T may also hold A's principal (P) liable for the damages if he can prove that A was acting for P (in furtherance of P's interest) when T was injured.

          2) Servant need not be following instructions

              a) Rule applies even if servant/agent violated principal's instructions in committing tort

          3) Principal is only liable for agent's (who is not a servant) torts if s/he is doing an act within his/her authority

              a) Very little difference from liability for servant. On exam, can use course of employment rule for agents

          4) Of course, agent is still liable to third parties if they choose to sue him/her rather than the principal

          5) Contributory negligence, i.e., third party's negligence, is generally a defense for both the agent and his/her principal

              a) Some jurisdictions have adopted comparative negligence which means that the amount of damages is determined by comparing each party's negligence

4. Agent's liability to third parties

      a. Agent is liable on contract when

          1) Principal is undisclosed or partially disclosed

               a) Agent is not relieved from liability until principal performs or third party elects to hold principal liable

          2) S/he contracts in his/her own name

          3) S/he guarantees principal's performance and principal fails

      4) S/he signs a negotiable instrument and does not sign in a representative capacity and does not include the principal's name (undisclosed principal)

      5) S/he knows principal does not exist or is incompetent

         a) Liable even if third party also knows

      6) S/he knowingly acts without authority

  b. Agent is not liable when

      1) Principal is disclosed and agent signs all documents in representative capacity

      2) Principal ratifies unauthorized act

      3) Third party elects to hold partially disclosed or undisclosed principal liable

  c. Agent has his/her personal defenses, e.g., right of offset if third party owes him/her debt, and defenses on the contract, e.g., nonperformance by the third party

      1) Agent does not have principal's personal defenses, e.g., lack of capacity

  d. Agent is liable if s/he does not deliver property received from third party for principal

  e. Agent is liable for his/her own crimes and torts

5. Third parties' liability to principal and agent

  a. Third party has no contractual liability to agent unless:

      1) Agent is a party to the contract, i.e., undisclosed or partially disclosed principal, or

      2) Agent has an interest in the contract, e.g., agent invests in the contract

  b. Third party is liable to disclosed, partially disclosed, and undisclosed principals

      1) Third party has personal defenses against principal, e.g., lack of capacity, and defenses on the contract, e.g., nonperformance by principal

      2) Against undisclosed principal, third party also has personal defenses against agent

F. Termination of Principal-Agent Relationship

1. Acts of the parties

  a. By agreement

      1) Time specified in original agreement, e.g., agency for one year

      2) Mutual consent

      3) Accomplishment of objective, e.g., agency to buy a piece of land

  b. Principal may revoke or agent may renounce

      1) Party that terminates may be liable to other for breach of contract

      2) If either party violates duties, the other may terminate relationship without being in breach

      3) If agency was gratuitous, no breach

        4) Exception: Principal does not have power to revoke agency coupled with an interest [see "F.2.b.2)" below]

  c. Notice of termination is required (see "F.3." below)

2. By operation of law

  a. If subject of agreement becomes illegal or impossible

  b. Death or insanity of either party

        1) Principal's estate is not liable to agent or for contracts made by agent after principal's death except as provided by statute

        2) Exception is an agency coupled with an interest

        EXAMPLE: If mortgagee has power to sell the property to recover his loan, this authority to sell as mortgagor's agent is not terminated by mortgagor's death.

  c. Bankruptcy of principal terminates the relationship

        1) Bankruptcy of agent does not affect unless agent's solvency is needed for performance

  d. If terminated by operation of law no notice need be given

3. Third parties must be given notice if terminated by acts of the parties

  a. Otherwise, agent may still be able to bind principal by apparent authority

  b. Constructive notice, e.g., publishing in a newspaper, is sufficient to third parties who have not previously dealt with agent

  c. Actual notice, e.g., orally informing or sending a letter, must be given to third parties who have previously dealt with agent unless third party learns of termination from another source

PARTNERSHIP LAW

Overview

The Uniform Partnership Act is the uniform statute adopted by most states and is the basis for partnership questions on the exam. A partnership is an association of two or more persons to carry on a business as co-owners for profit. For most purposes, the partnership is not considered a separate entity, but a specialized form of agency. The major areas tested on partnerships are the characteristics of a partnership, comparisons with corporations, the rights and liabilities of the partnership itself, the rights, duties, and liabilities of the partners among themselves and to third parties, and the rights of various parties, including creditors, upon dissolution.

Partnership Definitions

Voluntary Association.   A relation imposed by law. The intent to be partners is not required, merely associating in such a way that the court finds that the parties are partners.

Partnership by Estoppel.   When persons hold themselves out to third parties as partners and such third parties change their positions in reliance upon the assumed partnership existence. Courts may then hold that a partnership exists under the doctrine of estoppel.

Partners' Authority.   Every partner is an agent of the partnership and an agent of every other partner. Thus the acts of every partner are binding if they are within the apparent scope of the partnership business. A partner's authority to bind other partners or the partnership to third parties may be expressed, implied, or apparent.

Partnership Property.   All property originally contributed to the partnership or subsequently acquired by the partnership. Partnership property also includes undivided profits, capital, goodwill, and partnership name.

Joint Liability.   Partners in a partnership are jointly liable on all debts and contract obligations of the partnership and must all be sued in the course of one law suit.

Joint and Several Liability.   Partners are jointly and severally liable for torts committed by a partner or an employee of the partnership in the course of the partnership business. Thus all can be sued in one law suit or they may be each sued separately.

Limited Partnership.   One formed pursuant to the Uniform Limited Partnership Act (not recognized at common law). A limited partnership consists of one or more general partners by whom the business is conducted, and one or more limited partners who contribute capital but who do not take part in management decisions. Limited partners cannot hold themselves out as general partners and are not liable for the debts of the partnership beyond the amount they contribute.

A. Nature of Partnerships

1. A partnership is an association of two or more persons to carry on a business as co-owners for profit

    a. To carry on a business includes almost every trade, occupation, or profession

        1) It does not include passive co-ownership of property, e.g., joint tenants of a piece of land

    b. Co-ownership of the "business" (and not merely of assets used in a business) is the most important element in determining whether a partnership exists. Each partner has a proprietary interest in the business.

        1) Co-ownership of property (including capital) is one element
        2) The most important and necessary element of co-ownership (and thereby partnership) is profit sharing

            a) Need not be equal and need not include loss sharing, although it usually does and is so presumed

1
4

      b) Receipt of a share of profits is prima facie evidence of a partnership unless it was payment for debt, interest on a loan, consideration for the sale of a business, or wages

   3) The other necessary element of co-ownership is joint control

      a) Each partner has an equal right to participate in management. May be contracted away to a managing partner.

  c. Purpose must be to make a profit

   1) Therefore non-profit associations such as religious groups, fraternal groups, and labor unions are not partnerships

2. The partnership relationship is completely voluntary and creates a fiduciary relationship between partners

  a. Partnership relationship is based on contract but arrangements may be quite informal

  b. Nevertheless, agreement can be inferred from conduct, e.g., allowing someone to share in management and profits may result in partnership even though actual intent to become partner is missing

  c. Fiduciary relationship arises because each partner is an agent for partnership and for each other in partnership business

3. In general, partnerships are governed by the Uniform Partnership Act (UPA) and by agency law

  a. UPA is a codification of the old common law and enunciates formation, rights, duties, liability, etc.

   1) Most aspects may be changed by agreement; e.g., rights and duties between partners by agreement among them, liability to third parties by agreement with them

   2) Also helps determine when a partnership exists

  b. Agency law also governs because partners are agents. Much of this is incorporated in the UPA.

4. Generally, any person (entity) who has the capacity to contract (see CONTRACTS) may become a partner

  a. Corporations can, but see CORPORATIONS for problems with excessive delegation of management

  b. Minors can, but contract of partnership is voidable (see CONTRACTS). Nevertheless, a minor's investment in the partnership is subject to creditor's claims.

  c. Partnerships can become partners

  d. Trustees can, if acting prudently (see TRUSTS AND ESTATES)

5. Common characteristics of partnerships

  a. Limited duration; when partner dies, partnership terminates

  b. Transfer of ownership requires agreement

  c. Not a distinct separate entity for many purposes, e.g., liability and taxation

  d. Unlimited liability of partners for partnership debts

  e. Ease of formation, can be very informal

        1) Thereby freedom from much government regulation

   f. Since partners are personally liable for debts, partnership may obtain credit more easily than a corporation given same financial condition

        1) A theoretical distinction. Practically, a corporation will either be:

           a) Large or sound enough to warrant availability of credit, or
           b) One or more stockholders or directors will be asked to assume personal liability

B. Types of Partnerships and Partners

1. Trading partnership engages in business of buying and selling goods for profit

   a. May include service businesses where goods are bought and sold with service, e.g., plumbers

2. Nontrading partnership is not engaged in commercial business of buying and selling

   EXAMPLE: Public accounting firm or other professional association

3. Limited partnership is a special statutory relationship consisting of general partners and limited partners. The limited partners only contribute capital and are only liable to that extent, analogous to shareholder.

   a. See end of this section for detailed Limited Partnership rules

4. General partner is one who shares in the management of the business and has unlimited liability

5. Limited partner is one who does not take part in the management process and whose liability is limited to his capital contribution

6. Silent partners have no voice in management, but share unlimited liability and are disclosed

7. Dormant partner is an inactive partner with right to management participation (although seldom used), but who is undisclosed; once disclosed has some liability as general partner

8. Ostensible partner is one who holds himself out as a partner or other partners represent him as a partner to third persons. If not actually a partner, he becomes a partner by estoppel.

C. Formation of Partnership

1. By agreement, express or implied

   a. Partnership relationship can be implied by the acts of the parties
   b. Partnership may be used to hold "partners" liable if third parties are led to believe a partnership exists

2. Creation of a partnership may be very informal, either oral or written

   a. Writing may be required under the Statute of Frauds, e.g., forming partnership for longer than one year

3. Under the Uniform Partnership Act, anyone who receives a share of profits is presumed to be a partner. This is, however, a rebuttable presumption.

4. Articles of copartnership (Partnership Agreement). Not legally necessary, but a good idea to have. Following are some typical provisions:

    a. Parties involved (partners)
    b. Name of partnership
    c. Duration
    d. Purposes
    e. Rights and duties, including profit and loss sharing, property management, etc.
    f. Dissolution procedures and rights

D. Partner's Rights

1. Partnership agreement, whether formal or informal, would be controlling

    a. Secondly, partner's intent inferred from conduct is controlling
    b. Lastly, the following rules are determinative of partner's rights

2. Partnership interest

    a. Refers to the partner's right to share in profits and return of contribution on dissolution
    b. Is considered personal property

        1) Even if the partnership property is real estate

    c. Does not include specific partnership property, merely right to use it for partnership purposes
    d. Freely assignable without other partner's consent

        1) Assignee is not substituted as a partner without consent of all other partners
        2) Assignee does not receive right to interfere in management, to have an accounting, to inspect books, etc., he simply receives assigning partner's share of profits
        3) Assignor remains liable as a partner
        4) Does not cause dissolution unless assignor also retires (withdraws)

    e. If partner withdraws, selling his interest back to the partnership:

        1) He loses all partner's rights and interests in the partnership
        2) If sold on time (installments), he is merely a creditor of the partnership
        3) He may continue to be partner by estoppel if he fails to give notice

3. Partnership property

    a. Includes:

        1) Property acquired with partnership funds unless different intent is shown
        2) Capital contributed by partners, e.g., cash, land, building, fixtures, securities. Contribution is determined by objective intent.
        3) Partnership profits before the profits are distributed
        4) Goodwill, partnership name, etc.

b. All partners have equal rights to the partnership property

   1) Even if title is in name of one partner

c. Not assignable nor subject to attachment individually, only by a claim on the partnership

   1) All partners can agree and assign property
   2) Any partner can assign or sell if for apparently carrying on the business of the partnership in the usual way

d. Each partner has an insurable interest in partnership property

e. Upon partner's death, his estate is only entitled to the deceased partner's interest in partnership, not specific property

   1) Partnership may have to be liquidated to settle his estate
   2) Life insurance often carried to avoid liquidation

f. May not be conveyed to point of making partnership insolvent. Such would be a fraudulent conveyance.

   1) Insolvency is determined by adding net assets of all general partners to net assets of partnership
   2) Includes a conveyance to a partner even if he promises to pay partnership debts

4. Participate in management

a. Right to participate equally in management

   1) Ordinary business decisions by a majority vote
   2) Unanimous consent needed to make fundamental changes

b. Power to act as an agent for partnership in partnership business

c. Also has right to inspect books and have full knowledge of partnership affairs

5. Share in profits

a. Profits and losses are shared equally unless agreement specifies otherwise

   1) Even if contributed capital is not equal
   2) E.g., agreement may specify in proportion to contributed capital
   3) E.g., agreement may specify one partner to receive greater share of profits for doing more work, while losses still shared equally

6. Other monetary rights

a. Indemnification for expenses incurred on behalf of the partnership
b. Interest on loans and extra advances to partnership

   1) No interest on capital contributions unless in partnership agreement

c. Indemnification by partnership for partnership expenses paid by a partner or contribution (by other partners) for expenses paid in excess of one's share

   EXAMPLE: Partner A pays the taxes on the land owned by the partnership. Partner A should be indemnified from the partnership cash account or one-third each from Partners B and C if the partnership is unable to pay.

d. No right to salary for work performed because this is a duty

   1) Common for partners to agree to pay salaries, especially if only one or two do most of the work

7. Nonmonetary rights between partners

   a. Fiduciary conduct

      1) Partners cannot gain personally from partnership transactions without agreement by other partners
      2) Any wrongly derived profits must be held by partner as trustee for others
      3) Must not compete with partnership
      4) May participate in other business as long as it is not competition
      5) Must abide by partnership agreement

   b. Exercise of reasonable skill

      1) Consultation with partners may avoid liability for hasty decisions

   c. Formal accounting of partnership affairs

      1) A comprehensive investigation of partnership transactions and decision on rights of partners
      2) Available when agreement provides for, or when partner is excluded from partnership business, or when some other irregularity occurs

   d. May sue partners or partnership in only limited situations

      1) Usually must petition for a formal accounting and dissolution

E. Relationship to Third Parties

1. Partners are agents of the partnership. See AGENCY for types of authority and how it is created.

   a. Can bind partnership to contracts with third parties

      1) Even where no actual authority, can bind partnership where there is apparent authority

   b. Partnership is liable for partner's torts committed in course and scope of business and for partner's breach of trust, i.e., misapplication of third party's funds

      EXAMPLE: A partner takes a third party's money on behalf of the partnership to invest in government bonds. Instead he uses it himself to build an addition onto his home.

   c. Partners usually have authority to buy and sell goods, receive money, and pay debts

      1) No authority to make the partnership a surety or guarantor

   d. Partnership is not liable for acts of partners outside of express, implied, or apparent authority

      EXAMPLE: A partner of a hardware store attempts to buy some real estate in the name of the partnership. Here apparent authority does not exist.

      1) Traditionally only a partner of a trading partnership had apparent authority to issue negotiable instruments and take out loans

         a) Partner of a non-trading partnership may have authority, if readily within apparent authority.

         EXAMPLE: An attorney issues a negotiable instrument to buy law books for his law firm's library.

2. Third parties should be aware that for certain acts, unanimous consent of the partners is needed

   a. Admission of a new partner
   b. Assignment of partnership property

      1) If title is only in name of one partner, innocent third party could get good title from this one partner because there is no notice that it is partnership property

   c. Disposition of partnership goodwill
   d. Make the partnership a surety or guarantor
   e. Admit to claim against partnership in court
   f. Submit a partnership claim to an arbitrator or a referee
   g. Any act making it impossible to carry on the business

3. Partner's liability is personal, i.e., extends to all his personal assets, not just investment in partnership, for all debts and liabilities of the partnership

   a. Partners are jointly liable on contracts, debt, and other obligations

      1) Joint liability means all partners must be sued together. Cannot sue only one.
      2) Partnership assets must be exhausted before partner's individual assets can be reached
      3) Release of one partner releases all
      4) Since majority vote rules, all partners are liable even if they did not vote or objected to the action

   b. Partners are jointly and severally liable for torts and breaches of trust (see "E.1.b." above)

      1) Several liability means a party may sue just one partner (any one) for the full amount
      2) Party has choice whether to sue one or all parties. If one partner has enough assets, he will be sued severally for simplicity.
      3) Partnership assets need not be exhausted first. Partnership need not even be sued.
      4) Release of one does not release others from liability

   c. Partners may agree not to hold a partner liable among themselves but they cannot prevent him being held personally liable by third parties

   d. Partners are not criminally liable unless they personally participate in some way or statute prescribes liability to all members of management, e.g., antitrust laws, environment regulation or sale of alcohol to a minor

e. New partners coming into a partnership are liable for existing debts only to the extent of their capital contributions

    1) Unless new partners assume personal liability for old debts

f. Partners withdrawing or dead (then their estates) may be liable for subsequent liabilities (by estoppel) unless notice of withdrawal or death is given to third parties

    1) Actual notice to creditors who previously dealt with partnership
    2) Constructive, e.g., published, notice is sufficient for others

F. Termination of a Partnership

1. Termination occurs when the winding up (often called liquidation) of partnership affairs is complete

    a. First, dissolution must occur--when the partners stop carrying on a business together
    b. Second, winding up takes place--the process of settling of partnership
    c. Lastly, termination occurs--winding up completed, i.e., partnership no longer exists

2. Voluntary dissolution can occur by agreement of the partners

    a. Prior agreement, e.g., partnership agreement

        1) Specified term of existence may have been reached
        2) Particular undertaking may have been accomplished
        3) Expulsion of a partner from business if so provided for in agreement

            a) If not provided for in agreement, partnership can be voluntarily dissolved and a new one formed without unwanted partner

    b. Present agreement of all partners

        1) Admittance of a new partner. But for all practical purposes nothing happens, e.g., no liquidation.
        2) All may agree to dissolution and to end the business

3. Involuntary dissolution

    a. Withdrawal of a partner

        1) If agreement specifies a term of existence or a particular undertaking, withdrawing partner will be in breach of contract if his withdrawal is prior to agreed time
        2) If no agreed length of partnership, any partner can terminate at any time

    b. Death of a partner

        1) Executor may require an accounting and payment to estate of decedent's interest

    c. Bankruptcy of a partner or partnership
    d. Subject matter of partnership business becomes illegal
    e. By decree of court in such cases as:

1) Partner is declared insane
2) Partner continually or seriously breaches partnership agreement
3) Partnership can only be operated at a loss with no view to profit in the future

4. Rights of partners in dissolution

   a. Where the cause of dissolution is not a violation of the partnership agreement (e.g., a dissolution upon expiration of specified partnership term)

      1) No partner has a claim or cause of action against any other partner for any loss sustained in the dissolution
      2) Each partner has right to have partnership assets applied to discharge of his/her liabilities, and balance distributed to partners in accordance with their respective interests

   b. Where the dissolution is caused by an act in violation of the partnership agreement (e.g., a partner's electing to dissolve a partnership for a fixed term prior to the expiration thereof; consequently, this would not be relevant to a partnership at will)

      1) The other ("innocent") partners are accorded certain rights in addition to those listed above; the right to damages, the right to purchase business (continue partnership business in firm name), and the right to wind up partnership affairs and arrange for distribution of assets
      2) The partnership interest of the partner that caused wrongful dissolution will be valued without taking goodwill into consideration

5. Dissolution can be avoided in most of the above cases by provision in partnership agreement

   a. Cannot be avoided if a court decrees
   b. Cannot be avoided where subject matter becomes illegal or where partnership is bankrupt

6. At dissolution, and during winding up

   a. Partners have no actual authority to act for partnership except as is necessary to wind up
   b. Partners are still liable to creditors
   c. Partners are responsible for distributing assets and satisfying creditors

7. Distribution priority (different from limited partnerships; see "G.10.")

   a. Creditors
   b. To partners for liabilities other than capital
   c. To partners for capital contributions
   d. To partners as to profits

   EXAMPLE: The partnership of Herb, Ike, and Bucky was dissolved. The partnership had liquid assets of $260,000 and liabilities of $240,000, of which $210,000 is owed to outside creditors and $30,000 is owed to Herb for a loan Herb made to the partnership. The capital contributions were: Herb, $20,000 and Ike, $15,000. Profits and losses are to be shared according to the following ratio: Herb, 50%; Ike, 30%; and Bucky, 20%.

The order of distribution of firm assets of a general partnership would be as follows: First, the outside creditors are satisfied, $210,000.

Second, Herb receives $30,000 representing his loan to the firm. Third, capital contributions are returned to Herb ($20,000) and Ike ($15,000). This results in a $15,000 deficit [$260,000 - ($210,000 + $30,000 + $20,000 + $15,000)]. The partners must contribute toward this deficiency according to the loss sharing ratio. Therefore, Herb must contribute $7,500 (50% x $15,000), Ike must contribute $4,500 (30% x $15,000), and Bucky must contribute $3,000 (20% x $15,000). Thusly, in the final result, Herb receives a net distribution of $42,500 [($30,000 + $20,000) - $7,500], Ike receives a net distribution of $10,500 ($15,000 - $4,500), and Bucky must contribute $3,000.

If Bucky is personally insolvent, the other partners (Herb and Ike) are liable in the <u>relative</u> proportion in which they share in the profits: Herb, $1,875 ($3,000 x 50%/80%) and Ike, $1,125 ($3,000 x 30%/80%). Therefore, Herb and Ike must reduce their net distributions by these respective amounts.

8. Partners are personally liable to partnership for any deficits in their capital accounts and to creditors for insufficiency of partnership assets

   a. Partners must contribute toward this deficiency according to loss sharing ratio, always same as profit sharing ratio unless agreed otherwise

   b. Priority between partnership creditors and partner's personal creditors (called marshalling of assets rule)

      1) Partnership creditors have first priority to partnership assets, any excess goes to personal creditors

      2) Usually, personal creditors have first priority to personal assets, any excess goes to partnership creditors. However, the Bankruptcy Reform Act of 1979 revised this so that the Trustee in bankruptcy of a partnership is entitled to share pro rata with unsecured creditors of a partner.

9. If business is continued after dissolution, a new partnership is formed and old creditors become creditors of the new partnership

   a. No name change is required, e.g., a retired partner's name may be used in the partnership name

10. Partners can bind the other partners and the partnership on contracts until third parties who have known of the partnership are given notice of the dissolution

    a. Actual notice must be given to third parties who have dealt with the partnership prior to dissolution

    b. Constructive notice, e.g., notice in newspaper, is adequate for third parties who have only known of the partnership

G. Limited Partnerships

1. Regulated by state statutes based on Uniform Limited Partnership Act - ULPA

   a. These statutes must be complied with for limited partner status, otherwise partners are general partners

1) Without statutes, no limited partnership can exist

b. In certain cases state "blue sky" laws (anti-fraud laws for sale of securities) must be complied with because limited partnership interests are considered securities

    1) E.g., where large number of limited partnership interests are offered to the public

c. If limited partnership interests are offered for sale in more than one state, the Securities Act of 1933 will have to be complied with (See FEDERAL SECURITIES LAW)

2. Must have at least one general partner

    a. Manage and conduct partnership business
    b. General partnership rules apply to them
    c. Liability cannot be limited

3. Limited partners (one or more are required to have a limited partnership)

    a. Contribute capital only

        1) May be cash or property
        2) Cannot consist of services
        3) May not withdraw capital so as to impair any creditor's status

            a) Need sufficient partnership property to pay all creditors before partners can withdraw capital

    b. Liability is limited to capital contributed

        1) Personal assets cannot be reached

    c. Has creditor status for loans to partnership

        1) See distribution of assets (see "G.10." below)

    d. Cannot take part in any management or control of the partnership

        1) Limited partner status lost if he or she becomes active in management

            a) Becomes liable as if general partner and is personally liable for partnership debts

        2) Can lend money and transact business with the partnership

            a) May not hold partnership property as collateral

        3) Has no apparent authority (as defined in AGENCY)

    e. Can inspect books and require an accounting
    f. Owes no fiduciary duty to partnership

        1) May own interest in competing business

    g. Can be a limited partner and a general partner at the same time

        1) Has rights and powers, and is subject to all restrictions of a general partner
        2) Has rights against other partners with respect to contributions as a limited partner

4. Limited partnerships must file (with state) a certificate of limited partnership

    a. Public information
    b. A formal proceeding is required for formation and amendments
    c. Contains information about the partnership, partners, contributions, profit sharing, rights, etc.
    d. Without filing, partnership will be considered a general partnership

5. A person who erroneously believes he is a limited partner, e.g., error in filing certificate, may avoid liability as a general partner by

    a. Renouncing his interest in the profits or other compensation immediately upon learning of the mistake

6. The firm name cannot contain the name of a limited partner unless he is also a general partner

    a. Firm name need not disclose fact that it is a limited partnership

7. Additional limited partners may be admitted if requirements for amendment are met

    a. To admit any new partner, there must be unanimous written consent by present partners

        1) Can be in original agreement

    b. Substitution of limited partners must meet same requirements
    c. Certificate must be amended

8. Death, insanity, bankruptcy, or retirement of a general partner dissolves the partnership unless the other general partners continue it

    a. Death, insanity, bankruptcy, or retirement of a limited partner does not dissolve the partnership unless there are no more partners

9. Limited partner's interest

    a. As in general partnership, refers to limited partner's right to share of profits and return of contribution on dissolution
    b. It is personal property
    c. Freely assignable without consent of other partners

        1) Assignee is not substituted as a limited partner unless all others agree to the substitution

            a) And certificate is amended

        2) Assignee has no right to inspect books, obtain an accounting, etc.

10. Distribution (priority, order) of assets on dissolution

    a. Creditors, including limited partners who are creditors
    b. Limited partners' profits and compensation by way of income on contributions
    c. Limited partners' capital contributions
    d. General partners' claims such as loans
    e. General partners' profits
    f. General partners' capital contributions

CORPORATIONS

Overview

A corporation is an artificial being which is created by or under law and which operates under a common name through its elected management. It is a legal entity, separate and distinct from its shareholders. The corporation has the authority vested in it by statute and its corporate charter. Exam questions frequently request the candidate to relate the characteristics and advantages of the corporate form over other forms of business organization. Advantages include limited liability, ease of transferability, continuity of existence, separate entity, ease of financing, centralized management, etc.

Basic to preparation for the exam on corporation law is to understand the procedure necessary to incorporate and to begin corporate business, the liabilities of a promoter who organizes a new corporation, the liability of shareholders for subscriptions, the liability of the corporation with respect to preincorporation contracts made by the promoter, the fiduciary relationship of the promoter to the stockholders and to the corporation, the various circumstances under which a stockholder may be liable for the debts of the corporation, the rights of shareholders concerning payment of dividends, the rights and duties of officers, directors, and other agents or employees of the corporation to the corporation, to stockholders, and to third persons, and the procedures necessary to merge, consolidate, or otherwise change the corporate structure.

Corporation Definitions

Promoter.   Person who forms a new corporation by complying with legal requirements, arranges capitalizations, and begins the business.

De Jure Corporation.   A corporation formed in full compliance with all mandatory provisions of an incorporation statute.

De Facto Corporation.   A corporation formed without full compliance (as to some material aspect) with all mandatory provisions of an incorporation statute. Substantial compliance and the exercise of corporate powers are required.

Corporation by Estoppel.   Not a de jure or de facto corporation, but the rule operates to prevent third parties from denying the existence of a corporation and seeking to sue the stockholders after having dealt with them as a corporation.

Pierce the Corporate Veil.   When courts disregard the corporation and hold the stockholders individually liable. This occurs when the corporate entity is used to perpetrate a fraud, or is found to be merely an agent or instrumentality of its stockholders.

Preemptive Right.   Stockholders may subscribe to all newly authorized issues of stock in sufficient amount to maintain present equity, i.e., their proportionate share of ownership. Preemptive rights may be contracted away in the corporate charter.

Ultra Vires.   Acts beyond the scope of corporate powers which may be a defense to enforcement of corporate acts in some cases. The ultra vires doctrine is unfavored by the courts as a corporate defense except in clear cases. Directors are personally liable for ultra vires acts which they approved.

Merger.   The combination of two or more corporations where one or more is dissolved and one remains in existence. The surviving corporation receives all assets and is subject to all liabilities of the merged corporations. Merger usually requires two-thirds stockholder approval with dissenting stockholders being paid fair market value for their shares.

Consolidation.   Where two or more corporations combine to form a newly created corporation in which all assets and all liabilities are acquired by the new company. Consolidation usually requires two-third shareholder approval with dissatisfied shareholders being paid fair value for their stock.

A.   Characteristics and Advantages of Corporate Form
1.   Limited liability

a. Generally a shareholder in a corporation risks only a sum equal to the amount of his investment. Liability for corporate affairs does not extend to his personal assets.

2. Transferability of interest

a. A share or interest in a corporation is represented by stock and can be freely bought, sold or assigned with little effect on the operations of the company

3. Continuous life

a. Unlike a partnership, a corporation is not terminated by the death of a shareholder, or his incapacity. It is customary to regard a corporation as perpetual, and it continues to exist until dissolved, merged, or otherwise terminated, entirely independent of the misfortunes of its shareholders.

4. Separate entity

a. A corporation is a legal entity in itself and is treated separately from its stockholders

   1) A corporation can take, hold, and convey property
   2) It can contract in its own name with its shareholders or third parties
   3) It can sue and be sued

5. Financing

a. Easy to raise capital in large amounts by issuance of stock or other securities, e.g., bonds
b. Flexibility because it can issue a number of classes of stock and bonds to suit its needs and investor demands

6. Corporate management

a. Corporations can employ management personnel who are experts in their fields of business
b. Persons who manage corporations are not necessarily shareholders
c. The management of a corporation is usually vested in a board of directors elected by the shareholders

B. Disadvantages of Form

1. Taxation

a. Tax burdens may be heavier than on individuals operating sole proprietorship because of federal "double taxation"

   1) Corporate taxation up to 46%
   2) Distributed earnings taxed to shareholders
   3) Subchapter S status can alleviate

b. Many states have a state corporate income tax

2. Costs of incorporating, because must meet formal creation requirements

3. Formal operating requirements must be complied with

a. Procedural and administrative details to be complied with
b. Continuing governmental supervision
c. Some states allow less formal operating requirements for small, closely held corporations

4. Traditionally most professionals could not practice under the corporate form, but many states now allow professional corporations in which personal liability is retained for professional acts

C. Types of Corporations

1. Domestic corporation is one which operates and does business within the state in which it was incorporated

2. Foreign corporation is one doing business in any state except the one in which it was incorporated

    a. Foreign corporations are not exempt from the requirements and administrative details of domestic corporations
    b. A corporation does business in a state when there are continuous transactions, i.e., not an isolated transaction

3. Municipal corporation is any county, town, school district, village, city or other division of the state established by the state legislature with powers of local government

4. Public corporation is created as an agency of state for governmental purposes including municipal corporations

5. Quasi-public corporation serves the public in general but may constitute a collection of private shareholders, i.e., public utility

6. Private corporation is one organized for nongovernmental purpose and can be either a stock or nonstock corporation

    a. Nonstock corporation is one with members of organization instead of shareholders. Likely to be nonprofit.

    b. The CPA exam emphasizes private stock corporations

7. Professional corporations are ones under state laws which allow professionals to incorporate, e.g., doctors, accountants, attorneys

    a. Shares may only be owned by the licensed professionals
    b. Retain personal liability for their professional acts
    c. Obtain other corporation benefits, e.g., limited liability for corporate debts, pension and profit-sharing benefits

8. Closely held corporation is one whose stock is owned by a limited number of persons usually with restrictions on the transfer of stock to keep it out of the hands of outsiders

    a. Informal administration of the corporation permitted, e.g., missing regular board of directors meeting

9. De facto corporation has been formed in fact but has not properly been formed under the law

    a. Usually defective because of some small error

        1) There must have been a good faith attempt to form
        2) There must have been at least an attempt to substantially comply with the incorporation statute

            EXAMPLE: An organization filed all the necessary papers but did not pay the filing fee.

b. It is necessary that there has been exercise of corporate power by this group

EXAMPLE: The organization in the example above is completely idle, holds no organizational meeting, and transacts no business in the corporate name. It is not even a de facto corporation.

c. Shareholders in a de facto corporation still have limited liability to third parties

1) If de facto incorporation is not achieved, the stockholders are treated as partners

d. A de facto corporation may only be challenged by the state directly (quo warranto proceeding) and may not be challenged by third parties

10. De jure corporation has been formed correctly in compliance with the incorporation statute

11. Corporation by estoppel is a term used in equity to prevent injustice when an organization has not qualified as either a de jure or a de facto corporation but has held itself out as one or has been recognized as being a corporation

EXAMPLE: Purchaser who makes a promissory note payable to a "corporation" cannot refuse to pay on the grounds that the "corporation" does not exist.

EXAMPLE: "Corporation" owes a debt to a supplier. The "corporation" cannot avoid the obligation by claiming that it is not a valid corporation.

D. Formation of Corporation

1. Promoter is the person(s) who forms the corporation, arranges the capitalization, and begins the business

a. Promoter handles the issuing of the prospectus, promoting stock subscriptions, and drawing up the charter
b. Position of promoter is a fiduciary relationship to the corporation, and the promoter is not permitted to act against the interest of the corporation in any manner

1) Does not prevent personal profit if fully disclosed

c. Promoter is not an agent of the corporation, because the corporation is still not in existence
d. Any agreements (preincorporation contracts) made by the promoter are not binding on the future corporation until adopted after the corporation comes into existence

1) If the corporation does not come into existence or does not adopt the contracts:

a) Promoter is not liable if he specified he was not contracting individually, but in name of proposed corporation (actually no contract in these cases)
b) Otherwise promoter is personally liable on contract. Adoption by corporation does not relieve promotor, novation required.

> 2) The corporation may explicitly or implicitly adopt the promoter's actions

   e. In the absence of a statute or charter provision the corporation is not liable to the promoter for his services unless later approved by the corporation

2. Authority to grant corporate charters is vested in the states

   a. Charters are granted by the states subject to the right of the state to repeal, amend, or alter the charter within constitutional limitations

3. Incorporation

   a. Incorporator must generally be an adult (age 18 or 21), a natural person, and a United States citizen. This, however, varies from state to state, (trend is to allow corporation to be an incorporator)

   b. Articles of incorporation (charter) are filed with the state. They contain:

> 1) Proposed name which cannot be the same or closely resemble the name of another corporation so as to be misleading
> 2) Purpose of corporation. The purpose is usually drafted as broadly as possible.
> 3) Powers of corporation. Also drafted broadly.
> 4) The amount of capital stock authorized and the types of stock to be issued
> 5) Location of home offices and principal place of business
> 6) Duration. In the absence of a specific statement, corporation existence is deemed to be perpetual.
> 7) Temporary directors (may be incorporators) and incorporators
> 8) Original stock subscribers
> 9) Designation of agent for service of process

   c. First shareholders' meeting

> 1) Stock certificates issued to shareholders
> 2) Resignation of temporary directors and election of new
> 3) Adoption of bylaws--the rules governing the operation of the corporation, e.g.:
>
>> a) Duties and authority of officers
>> b) Notice, time, place of meetings (directors' and shareholders')
>> c) Rules for issuance and transfer of securities

   d. At same meeting or a subsequent meeting, directors:

> 1) Elect officers
> 2) Adopt or reject preincorporation contracts
> 3) Begin business of corporation

E. <u>Corporate Financial Structure</u>

1. Definitions

   a. Authorized stock--that permitted in articles of incorporation, e.g., amount and types

   b. Unissued stock--authorized but not yet issued

   c. Issued stock--authorized and delivered to shareholders

d. Outstanding stock--issued and not repurchased by the corporation, i.e., it is still owned by shareholders

e. Treasury stock--issued but not outstanding, i.e., corporation repurchased it. There are special rules for treasury stock.

    1) The shares are not votable and do not receive dividends
    2) Corporation does not recognize gain or loss on transactions with its own stock
    3) Must be purchased with surplus, i.e., not legal capital
    4) May be resold without regard to par value

f. Cancelled stock--treasury stock that is cancelled:

    1) No longer issued or outstanding
    2) Makes room for more stock to be issued

g. Par value or stated value--amount stated on the shares

    1) The stock must be issued for this amount or more
    2) May subsequently be traded for any amount

h. Legal capital or stated capital or capital stock--number of shares issued times par value (or stated value)

    1) Dividends may not be declared or paid out of it
    2) Must be kept in corporation as a buffer for creditors

i. Paid-in surplus--amount paid for stock on issuance which is greater than par or stated value

j. Contributed capital--total amount paid for stock on issuance, i.e., stated capital plus paid-in surplus

k. Earned surplus (retained earnings)--total net profits retained by the corporation during its existence

    1) Reduced by any dividends paid out in prior years

l. Surplus--Includes earned surplus and paid-in surplus

    1) Also same as net assets less legal capital

2. Classes of stock

a. Common stock usually gives each shareholder one vote per share and is entitled to dividends if declared by the directors

    1) Has no priority over other stock for dividends
    2) Shareholders entitled to share in final distribution of assets
    3) Votes may be apportioned to shares in other ways, e.g., 1 vote per 10 shares
    4) Nonvoting common stock may be issued if provided for in the articles of incorporation

b. Preferred stock is given preferred status as to liquidations and dividends, but dividends are still discretionary

    1) Usually nonvoting stock
    2) Dividend rate is generally a fixed rate
    3) Cumulative preferred means that if a periodic dividend is not paid at the scheduled time, the obligation continues and accumulates; and must be satisfied before common stock may receive a dividend

        a) Noncumulative preferred means that if the dividend is passed, it will never be paid (i.e., the obligation to pay ceases)

        b) Held to be implicitly cumulative unless different intent shown

    4) Participating preferred participates further in corporate earnings left after a fixed amount is paid to preferred shares. The participation with common shares is generally on a fixed percentage basis.

  c. Callable (or redeemable) stock may be redeemed at a fixed price by the corporation. This call price is fixed in the articles of incorporation or may be subject to an agreement among the shareholders themselves.

  d. Convertible preferred gives the owner the option to convert the preferred stock to common stock at a fixed exchange rate

3. Marketing of stock

  a. May be subject to state "blue sky" laws or the Federal Securities Act. See FEDERAL SECURITIES LAW.

  b. Stock subscriptions are contracts to purchase a given number of shares in an existing corporation or one to be organized

    1) Subscription to stock is an offer to buy and is not binding until accepted by the corporation

    2) The subscriber may revoke his offer at any time prior to incorporation because the corporation cannot accept until it exists

        a) But if subscription is a contract among subscribers then it cannot be cancelled without consent of other subscribers--whether subscription is with corporation or other subscribers usually determined on basis of whether solicitation was from public or limited group

        b) Under the Model Incorporation Act, followed by many states, stock subscriptions are irrevocable for six months

    3) Once accepted, the subscriber becomes liable:

        a) For the purchase, and

        b) As a corporate shareholder

    4) An agreement to subscribe in the future is not a subscription

  c. Watered stock

    1) Stock is said to be watered when the cash or property exchanged is less than par value or stated value

        a) No-par stock cannot be watered as long as issue amount is reasonable

    2) Stock must be issued for consideration equal to the par or stated value

        a) No-par stock may be issued for consideration that the directors determine to be reasonable

    3) Creditors of the corporation may recover from the stockholders the amount of water in their shares; i.e., the amount the stockholders would have paid to the corporation had they paid the full amount required (i.e., par value less amount paid)

            a) If the corporation becomes insolvent
            b) Subsequent purchaser of watered stock is not liable unless he had
                knowledge thereof
    d. Consideration

        1) Consists of cash, property, services performed

            a) Directors' duty to set value on property received

        2) Executory promises are not good consideration, e.g.:

            a) Promise to perform services is not good
            b) Promise to pay is not good
            c) Promissory note is not good (whether negotiable or not)
4. Bonds

    a. Evidence of debt of the corporation. The owner of a bond is not an owner
        of the corporation but a creditor.
    b. Interest is paid on the debt at fixed intervals, and at a designated time,
        the principal is repaid
    c. Types

        1) Bearer--holder of the bond is entitled to the interest
        2) Convertible--convertible into common stock
        3) Debenture--unsecured
        4) Income--interest payable only if and when income is earned
        5) Registered--owner registered with corporation is entitled to the
            interest

F. Powers of Corporation

1. Types of corporate power

    a. Inherent power is that power which is necessary for corporate existence,
        e.g., power to contract
    b. Express powers are set out in the charter and bylaws at the time corpora-
        tion is organized
    c. Implied powers are those which are necessary to carry out the express powers
        and the purpose of the incorporation

        EXAMPLE: Open a checking account.

    d. Acts within the corporation's implied or express power are intra vires and
        outside are ultra vires

2. Corporations generally have the particular power to:

    a. Acquire their own shares (treasury stock) out of available surplus accord-
        ing to state laws
    b. Acquire shares of other corporations
    c. Make charitable contributions

        1) Political contributions are usually not allowed
        2) Contributions to change laws are a valid business purpose, e.g., ref-
            erendum measure

    d. Guarantee obligations of others only if in reasonable furtherance of cor-
        porations' business

       1) Does not allow indorsement for accommodation purposes only

  e. Become a partner only if expressly stated in charter or statute

       1) The problem with becoming a partner is that a corporation is to be managed by its board of directors and they cannot delegate this duty. In a partnership, all partners manage.

  f. To buy, own, hold, and sell real and personal property
  g. To contract through its agents in the name of the corporation
  h. To sue and be sued in its own name
  i. To have exclusive use of its corporate name in the jurisdiction
  j. To have a corporate seal

G. Liabilities of Corporations

1. Crimes

  a. Corporations are liable for crimes they are capable of committing, i.e., antitrust, but not murder
  b. Punishment generally consists of fines or forfeiture, although recently directors have been faced with prison sentences for crimes of the corporation

2. Torts

  a. Corporations are liable for the damages resulting from torts committed by their officers, directors, agents, or employees within the course and scope of their corporate duties

    EXAMPLE: Fraudulent deceit of a customer.
    EXAMPLE: Employee assaults a complaining customer.

  b. The defense that the tort occurred in connection with ultra vires acts is not valid

3. Ultra vires acts

  a. Illegal and ultra vires acts are not the same

       1) Illegal acts are acts in violation of statute of public policy

         EXAMPLE: False advertising.

       2) Whereas ultra vires acts are merely beyond the scope of the corporate powers, i.e., a legal act may be ultra vires

         EXAMPLE: Although legal to become a surety, the articles of incorporation may not allow it.

  b. The state and stockholders have the right to object to ultra vires acts. A competitor does not.
  c. An ultra vires contract will be upheld to the extent of performance by both sides

       1) Directors or officers may be sued by shareholders on behalf of the corporation or by the corporation itself if there are damages to the corporation

  d. An ultra vires contract that is wholly executory, i.e., no performance on either side is void and neither party can enforce it

e. If partially or fully performed on one side, then other side is estopped from raising <u>ultra</u> <u>vires</u> as a defense without being liable for damages

4. <u>Acts of officers</u>

a. Corporation is liable for authorized acts
b. Even if not authorized, if the act is of the type customarily delegated to such an officer, the corporation is liable
c. Corporations are generally liable on contracts made by their agents within the course and scope of corporate authority

1) Corporations are not obligated to perform illegal contracts
2) Preincorporation contracts must be adopted before there is liability

H. <u>Officers and Directors of Corporations</u>

1. Directors are elected by the shareholders. Officers are retained by the board of directors.

a. Directors elected at annual meeting
b. Term of office is usually 1 year

2. Directors' duties and powers

a. Generally to guide policies of company. They are generally in charge of a company's operations.

1) Power to discharge their duties

b. Must comply with statutes, articles of incorporation, and bylaws
c. Select officers
d. Declare dividends. May not abuse discretion.
e. A director as an individual has no power to bind the corporation. Must act as a board member at a duly constituted meeting of the board.

1) Must hold directors' meetings at times designated in the charter
2) May not vote by proxy

a) Majority vote of those present is needed for most business decisions (a quorum)
b) Some statutes require a majority vote of total directors to make business decisions

3) Action may be taken by the board with no meeting

a) Unless prohibited by articles of incorporation or by corporate bylaws, and
b) There must be unanimous written consent by the board members to the action to be taken

f. May delegate some authority, e.g., day to day or routine matters, to an executive committee

1) Composed of members of the board of directors

g. Directors are not entitled to compensation unless so provided in articles, bylaws, or by a resolution of the board passed before the services are rendered

1) May be reimbursed for expenses incurred on behalf of corporation
2) Entitled to compensation if acting in role as employee

3. Director's liability

    a. The general rule is that directors must exercise ordinary care and due diligence in performing the duties entrusted to them by virtue of their positions as directors. Trend is toward increased liability.

        1) Business judgment rule--As long as director is acting in good faith he will not be liable for errors of judgment unless he is negligent

        2) Directors are chargeable with knowledge of the affairs of the corporation

            a) Normally may rely on reports of officers

    b. Directors only liable for negligence if their action was the proximate cause of the corporation's loss

    c. Directors have a fiduciary relationship to the corporation

        1) Owe fiduciary duties of loyalty and due care to the corporation

        2) If directors engage in business transactions with the corporation, director must make full and complete disclosure to the board

            a) Transaction must be fair and equitable

            b) Cannot vote on this issue as a director

    d. Directors are personally liable for <u>ultra vires</u> acts of the corporation unless they specifically dissented

        EXAMPLE: Loans made to stockholders by a corporation.
        EXAMPLE: Dividends that impair capital.

    e. See FEDERAL SECURITIES LAW for insider trading, e.g., short-swing profits

4. Officers

    a. An officer of the corporation is one of its agents and can bind the corporation by his individual acts if within the scope of his authority

        1) The corporation is not bound by the acts of an agent beyond the scope of authority

        2) President usually has authority in transactions that are part of usual and regular course of business

            a) No authority for extraordinary transactions

            b) Rules of estoppel are applicable; e.g., corporation may not claim president had no authority if he acted as if he did

        3) Acts of officers may be ratified by board

    b. Officers and directors may be the same persons

    c. Officers are selected by the directors for a fixed term under the bylaws

        1) If a term is not definite, it is governed by the directors

    d. Officers have a fiduciary relationship with the corporation and are limited in business transactions as are directors

5. Indemnification of directors and employees

    a. A corporation has the power to indemnify any employee or director who is sued in a criminal or civil action if he acted in good faith and for what he reasonably believed to be the best interests of the corporation. The only exception is when it is proved the person engaged in misconduct in the performance of his/her duty to the corporation.

I. Stockholders' Rights

1. Types of Stockholders

    a. Stockholder in equity is one for whose benefit stock is held by another

        EXAMPLE: Beneficiary of a trust that holds stock is a stockholder in equity.

    b. Stockholder at law is a person who holds the stock directly

    c. Stock can be acquired by original issue, by purchase from another stockholder, or by purchase of treasury stock

2. Stockholders' rights commence:

    a. At the time the corporation accepts a subscription

    b. At time of payment and delivery of certificates in a contract to purchase

    c. Between corporation and new stockholder when registration is changed on corporate books

3. Right to a stock certificate

4. Right to transfer stock by indorsement and delivery or by separate assignment

    a. Stock certificates are negotiable instruments

      1) No holders in due course, but if properly indorsed, a thief may give good title

      2) If indorsement is forged, corporation will bear the loss against a purchaser in good faith if it has issued a new certificate

        EXAMPLE: X steals stock certificate from Y, forges Y's indorsement, submits it to the corporation for a new certificate, and transfers the new certificate to P, a purchaser in good faith. P will get to keep the certificate as a valid stockholder and the corporation will be liable to Y for the value of the shares.

    b. Corporation registers the transfer and issues new shares to transferee

    c. Limitations on transfer may be imposed, but they must be reasonable

      1) UCC requires that any restrictions must be plainly printed on the certificate to be effective against third party

      2) These limitations are most often imposed in closely held corporations

        EXAMPLE: Existing shareholders of the corporation may have first option to buy.

5. Right to vote for: election of directors, amendment of bylaws and charter, decision to dissolve the corporation, and any other fundamental corporate changes

    a. Governed by the charter and the class of stock owned

    b. Trustee votes shares held in trust

    c. Stockholders do not vote on how to manage the corporation. Management is entrusted to the board of directors.

    d. Cumulative voting may be required, i.e., a person gets as many votes as he has shares times the number of directors being elected

        EXAMPLE: 100 shares x 5 directors is 500 votes.

      1) Gives minority shareholders an opportunity to get some representation by voting all shares for one or two directors

     e. Can vote by proxy--an assignment of voting rights

        1) See FEDERAL SECURITIES LAW for proxy solicitation
        2) Shareholder may give up his voting power and place it irrevocably in the hands of others as in a voting trust

     f. The directors have the power to amend or repeal the bylaws unless reserved to the shareholders by the articles of incorporation

     g. Amendment of the articles of incorporation and approval of fundamental corporate changes such as a merger, consolidation, or sale of all assets requires only majority approval by shareholders

6. Right to dividends

     a. Shareholder generally has no inherent right to dividends unless they are declared by the board of directors

        1) Power to declare is discretionary based on the board's assessment of business needs
        2) When there is a surplus together with available cash, the shareholders may be able to compel declaration of dividends on the grounds that board's refusal to declare a dividend is in bad faith or its refusal is unreasonable so as to constitute an abuse of director discretion

     b. Dividends are normally payable to stockholders of record on a given date
     c. Dividend becomes a debt to the corporation when declared

        1) Generally cannot be revoked once declared

     d. Cannot be paid out of legal capital. See Director's Liability, "H.3."

        1) Some states allow payment out of paid-in surplus and some do not
        2) Earned surplus (retained earnings) is always a proper source

     e. Stock dividends also cannot be paid out of legal capital

        1) They must be paid out of retained earnings
        2) They increase legal capital

7. Right of stockholders to inspect books and records exists in common law and may be provided for by statute

     a. These books and records include minute books, stock certificate books, stock ledgers, general account books
     b. Must have a purpose reasonably related to his interest as shareholder, e.g., to communicate with other shareholders

        1) Not to compete with corporation

     c. Corporation may be subject to fines for refusal
     d. Directors, as opposed to shareholders, have an absolute right of inspection
     e. May bring his accountant or attorney along

8. Preemptive right

     a. This is the right to subscribe to new issues of stock (at FMV) so that a stockholder's ownership will not be diluted without the opportunity to maintain it

       EXAMPLE: Corporation has one class of common stock. Stockholder A owns 15%. A new issue of the same class of stock is to be made. Stockholder A has the right to buy 15% of it.

   b. This is the right of first refusal and applies to issuances of new stock of the same class or series that the shareholder owns
   c. Usually only applies to common stock, not preferred
   d. Not for treasury stock
   e. There is no preemptive right to purchase stock at par value
   f. This right may be denied by the charter

9. Stockholders' right to sue

   a. Stockholder can sue in his own behalf where his interests have been directly injured, e.g.:
       1) Denial of right to inspect records
       2) Denial of preemptive right

   b. Stockholders can sue on behalf of the corporation, i.e., a derivative suit
       1) In cases where a duty to the corporation is violated and corporation does not enforce, e.g.:
           a) Director violates his fiduciary duty to corporation
           b) Illegal declaration of dividends
           c) Fraud by officer on corporation
       2) Must first demand that directors sue in name of corporation and then may proceed if they refuse
           a) Suit may be barred if directors make good faith business judgment that the suit is not in the corporation's best interests
       3) Damages go to corporation
       4) Plaintiff must be a shareholder of record

10. Right to a pro rata share of distribution of assets on dissolution after creditors have been paid

J. Stockholder's Liability

1. Generally stockholder's liability is limited to his paid-in capital

2. May be liable to creditors for:

   a. Original issue stock sold at a discount (below par value). See watered stock discussion.
   b. Unpaid balance on no-par stock
   c. Dividends paid which impair capital
       1) If the corporation is insolvent

K. Substantial Change in Corporate Structure

1. Mergers

   a. This is the union of two corporations where one is absorbed into the other
       1) One is dissolved and the other remains in existence
       2) Survivor corporation issues its own shares to the shareholders of the other corporation

   b. The remaining corporation (possessor) gets all assets but is subject to all liabilities of the merged corporation
   c. Merger usually requires a two-thirds stockholder approval

          1) This minimum percentage is specified in state statutes, but the articles of incorporation can require a greater percentage

    d. Dissenting shareholders are paid FMV for their shares

          1) It is called the right of appraisal

    e. See ANTITRUST

2. Consolidations

    a. This is the joining of two or more corporations into a single new corporation different from any of the components
    b. All assets and liabilities are acquired by the new company
    c. Consolidations, like mergers, are strictly controlled by state statutes
    d. Dissatisfied shareholders in a merger or consolidation may dissent and assert appraisal rights, thereby receiving the FMV of their stock

3. Sale of substantially all assets

    a. One corporation may buy all the assets of another corporation
    b. Requires approval of the shareholders of the selling corporation
    c. For protection of creditors

          1) Fraudulent conveyances are illegal
          2) See SALES, Bulk Sales

    d. Also see ANTITRUST

4. Reorganization

    a. The rearrangement and revamping of a corporation's capital and asset structure with as little effect as possible upon creditors. It is an alternative to bankruptcy and forced liquidation.
    b. Reorganization can be:

          1) Voluntary
          2) Forced by Federal Bankruptcy Act

L. Dissolution

1. Dissolution is the termination of the corporation's status as a legal entity

    a. Liquidation is the winding up of affairs and distribution of assets
    b. Dissolution does not finally occur until liquidation is complete

2. Voluntary dissolution

    a. By expiration of time stipulated in charter

          1) Rare, usually perpetual existence

    b. Merger or consolidation
    c. Filing a certificate with the state to surrender charter

          1) By incorporators prior to issuance of shares
          2) Written consent of all stockholders
          3) Resolution at stockholders' meeting
          4) Usually requires two-thirds vote

    d. Judicial proceedings in bankruptcy by filing voluntary petition

3. Involuntary

   a. By the state because:

      1) Fraud in original application for legal existence
      2) Failure to pay taxes for long period
      3) No business activity
      4) Other substantial injury to public
      5) State may only suspend corporation's right to do business

4. Creditors must be given notice of the dissolution or the corporation will remain liable on its debts
5. Dissolution does not result from:

   a. Sale of all assets
   b. Appointment of receiver
   c. Assignment for benefit of creditors

ANTITRUST AND GOVERNMENT REGULATION

Overview

The CPA exam questions on antitrust are concerned with the preservation of competition and its application. Therefore candidates must be familiar with the basic provisions of the Sherman Act, the Clayton Act, the Robinson-Patman Act, the Federal Trade Commission Act, and their application in specific business situations. It should be emphasized that the underlying rationale of the antitrust laws is that society will be best served by the preservation of free competitive markets. Therefore any action, either hostile, or friendly, that undermines competition in the marketplace for any service or product, is generally a violation of the antitrust laws. Also the authority for the regulation of competion by the federal government requires that interstate commerce must be affected for the various acts to be applicable. However, most businesses are covered by the antitrust laws because they compete or deal with businesses that do engage directly in interstate commerce.

Antitrust Definitions

Sherman Act. The original antitrust legislation of the United States which provides that **every** contract, combination in the form of a trust or otherwise, or conspiracy in restraint of trade or commerce among the states or with foreign nations is declared illegal. Every person who shall monopolize, or attempt to monopolize, or combine or conspire with another person or persons to monopolize any part of trade or commerce among the several states, or with a foreign nation, shall be deemed guilty. Exemptions to this Act are those industries affected with a public interest and regulated by other government agencies such as the power industry, banking, insurance, airlines, radio, television, union activities, agricultural cooperatives, and exporters.

Rule of Reason. Rather than making a literal interpretation of the Act which would strike down each and every restraint, the United States Supreme Court has applied a reasonableness test in ascertaining illegality in many situations. In effect, the rule of reason permits the court to examine the reasons for the defendant business engaging in the activites which appear to be in violation of the Sherman Act.

Per Se Illegality. Opposite of rule of reason. The Supreme Court has ruled that in certain kinds of restraint there can be no reasonable explanation. Therefore, such acts will be held per se (in and of itself) illegal. Classic examples of per se violations of the antitrust laws are price-fixing, division of markets, division of customers, etc.

Federal Trade Commission Act. An act passed by Congress in 1914 which created the Federal Trade Commission and empowered it to identify any anticompetitive behavior that should be prohibited as an unfair method of competition, and to proceed against violators of the Sherman and Clayton Acts.

Clayton Act. An act, passed by Congress in 1914 to supplement and augment the Sherman Act by specifically outlawing certain practices that had been ruled by the courts to not be barred by the Sherman Act. The Clayton Act was also directed to anti-competitive conduct in its incipiency state. The Act was amended in 1950 by the Celler-Kefauver Amendment which made the statute much more stringent in the regulation of mergers.

Price Discrimination. Price differences to purchasers which are not based on differences in the grade, quality, quantity of the commodity sold, or in differences in the cost of selling, transportation, etc. Price cuts may be made to meet lawful competition, but not to substantially lessen competition or to create a monopoly.

Tying Sales or Arrangements. Where the purchaser or lessee of goods is required to buy or lease certain other articles sold or leased by the same seller in order to obtain the desired article.

Robinson-Patman Act. An antitrust act passed by Congress in 1936 for the purpose of greatly expanding the original prohibition against price discrimination which was contained in the Clayton Act. The Act makes it unlawful for any person engaged in interstate commerce to discriminate in price between purchasers of commodities of like grade and quality. Also prohibited are the paying or receiving of brokerage commissions, or discounts or rebates to customers which result in price discrimination.

A. General

1. The purpose of federal antitrust laws is to promote the production and distribution of goods and services in the most economical and efficient manner by preserving free, competitive markets

   a. Also promotes fairness and gives consumer a wider choice

2. Regulation (for our concerns) is by federal law, so interstate commerce must be affected before the activity is regulated

   a. If only intrastate (within state) commerce is <u>affected</u>, then federal government has no power to regulate

   b. The test is whether there is a substantial economic effect on interstate commerce

      1) Even if a business is only carried on within a state it may substantially affect interstate commerce if it

         a) Competes or deals with businesses that do business among several states, or

         b) Purchases or sells a substantial amount of products that come from or wind up in interstate commerce

         c) No fixed dollar volume is required

            EXAMPLE: Wholesale liquor dealers in a state agree to divide the state market among them. This agreement is purely intrastate but it reduces the chances for out-of-state distillers to enter the local market and therefore the agreement affects interstate commerce.

3. If the contract in restraint of trade is illegal, it is unenforceable by the parties, in addition to possible criminal or civil penalties and injunctions

   a. Vertical restraints are agreements between parties from different levels of the distribution chain (i.e., between manufacturer and retailer)

   b. Horizontal restraints are agreements between parties of the same level of the distribution chain (i.e., between two restraints or two manufacturers)

4. Some contracts in restraint of trade <u>are</u> legal and enforceable

   a. Seller of a business agrees not to compete with the buyer

      1) Only valid if for a reasonable time and a reasonable geographic area and if a proper business interest is sought to be protected

         a) Reasonable time is what is fair under the circumstances to protect buyer, e.g., 1 year or even 5 years sometimes, but not forever

         b) Reasonable area would be where the business is conducted, e.g., neighborhood. If business is statewide, then restriction can be for whole state.

            EXAMPLE: Seller of a bakery covenants not to compete in the immediate locality for five years. This is a reasonable area and length of time.

   b. Similarly, partners and employees can covenant not to compete with partnership or employer while relationship lasts and for a reasonable time thereafter and within a reasonable area

   c. Buyer or lessee of property may covenant not to use it in competition with, or to the injury of the seller or lessor

  1) Same standards of reasonableness apply

5. Exceptions to the antitrust laws

   a. Labor unions unless they join with businesses and act in violation
   b. Patents are a 17-year monopoly
   c. Copyrights are a monopoly for the author's life plus 50 years
   d. Trademarks are a 20-year monopoly with an indefinite number of renewals
   e. Regulated industries are regulated by government agencies because competition is not practical

      1) E.g., utilities, telephone, transportation, radio
      2) However, antitrust laws are applicable to regulated enterprises when dealing with mergers

   f. Municipalities and state agencies, unless they join with a business and act in violation

B. <u>Sherman Act of 1890</u>

1. Contracts, combinations, and conspiracies in restraint of trade are illegal

   a. Only unreasonable restraints are illegal (Rule of Reason)

      1) Determined on a case by case basis

   b. <u>Per Se</u> violations

      1) <u>Per se</u> violations are unreasonable as a matter of law; they do not have to be proven unreasonable
      2) Not justifiable, nor defendable

   c. Generally applies to horizontal restraints, i.e., among competitors

      1) Price fixing (agreement) is a <u>per se</u> violation

         a) Whether it actually affects prices or not
         b) Whether the fixed price is fair or not (presumed unfair)
         c) Dollar volume is unimportant. The existence of any price fixing agreement is illegal.
         d) An actual agreement is not necessary if the parties have a tacit understanding and adhere to it
         e) Includes quantity limitations and minimum, maximum, buying, and selling prices
         f) Does not include government regulated prices

         EXAMPLE: Two hotels, in order to maintain their standards of quality, agree not to rent rooms below some price which is both fair to the public and under which they can still maintain their standard of quality. This agreement is illegal and not justifiable.

      2) Joint boycotts, i.e., group agreements not to deal with another, are <u>per se</u> violations

         a) Does not include individual refusals to deal with someone as long as not part of an attempt to monopolize

      3) Horizontal territorial limitations is a <u>per se</u> violation

         EXAMPLE: Two competitors agree not to sell in each other's section of the city.

    d. Vertical territorial limitations (i.e., franchising agreements) where franchisee receives an exclusive right to sell in a specific territory but is precluded from selling in any area are no longer <u>per se</u> violations but presently only illegal if unreasonable (Rule of Reason).

       EXAMPLE: A distributor requires dealer to sell only in X suburban area.

    e. Vertical resale price maintenance is illegal, i.e., seller sets a minimum or maximum price to which the buyer must adhere when s/he resells

2. Formation of, or the attempt to form a monopoly is illegal

    a. Monopoly is the power to exclude competition and/or to control prices

      1) Percentage share of the market is a determining factor

        a) Various cases have held from 60% to 90% of a market may constitute monopolistic power

        b) A much lower percentage will suffice if the charge is attempting to monopolize rather than holding monopoly power

      2) The relevant market consists of the product market and the geographic market

        a) Product market consists of commodities reasonably interchangeable by consumers

          EXAMPLE: In a case involving a cellophane wrapping manufacturer, the product market was flexible wrapping material.

        b) Geographic market is the area in which the defendant and competitors sell the product

          EXAMPLE: A geographic market for a major beer brewer is national while for a taxi company it is very local.

    b. It must be an unreasonable monopolistic tendency

      1) Therefore, the high percentages above are required to constitute a monopoly

      2) If no intent, or monopoly is thrust on defendant then not illegal

        a) There must not be any predatory or coercive conduct

          EXAMPLE: There are several hotels in a town. Business drops and all but one close. The remaining hotel has taken no action to get the others to close. Although the remaining hotel has a monopoly it was thrust upon the hotel and is therefore not illegal.

3. Sanctions (not mutually exclusive, both civil and governmental prosecution available)

    a. Injunctions, forced divisions, forced divestiture (by individuals, corporations, or government)

      1) Government may seize property shipped in interstate commerce and violating party forfeits it

    b. Criminal penalties (by government)

   1) Individuals--maximum fine of $100,000 and/or up to 3 years in jail for
       each offense
   2) Corporations--maximum fine of $1 million

c. Treble damages (by individuals and corporations)

   1) I.e., actual damages, e.g., loss of profits, multiplied by 3
   2) Plus attorney fees and court costs
   3) Instituted to encourage private parties to enforce the antitrust laws

C. Clayton Act of 1914

1. Supplemented the Sherman Act to prohibit a corporation from acquiring the stock
    of a competing corporation (merger) where the effect might substantially lessen
    competition or tend to create a monopoly

    a. Acquisitions tending to create a monopoly are violations

       1) No actual monopoly need be created
       2) To cope with monopolistic trends in their incipiency
       3) Applies where there is a reasonable likelihood the merger or acquisi-
           tion will substantially lessen competition
       4) As under the Sherman Act, use the percentage of market (product and
           geographic) test

    b. Celler-Kefauver Amendment of 1950 added the prohibition of the acquisition
        of assets of another corporation where the effect might lessen competition

       1) Thus both asset and stock acquisitions are covered
       2) Includes vertical mergers (sellers-buyers) and conglomerate mergers
           (e.g., not in same industry) as well as horizontal mergers (com-
           petitors)

           EXAMPLE: A shoe manufacturer buys out one of its retailers. This is a
           vertical merger.
           EXAMPLE: A shoe retailer buys out another shoe retailer. This is a
           horizontal merger.
           EXAMPLE: A pen manufacturer buys out a clothing retailer. This is a
           conglomerate merger.

    c. Suit may be brought both before or after completion of the merger

       1) E.g., preliminary injunction to prevent violation
       2) E.g., forced divestiture anytime after completion of a merger if com-
           petitor threatened

    d. Under "failing company doctrine," a merger that is anticompetitive may be
        allowed if

       1) The acquired company is failing, and
       2) There is no other willing purchaser whose acquisition of the company
           would reduce competition less

2. Besides mergers, the Clayton Act prohibits the following arrangements if they
    substantially lessen competition

a. Price discrimination between different purchasers

   1) See Robinson-Patman Act

b. Interlocking directorates

   1) Applies to a director sitting on boards of two or more competing corporations, one of them with shareholders' equity of more than $1 million

c. Tying arrangements

   1) Occurs where seller forces buyer to take one or more other products as a condition to acquiring the desired product

      EXAMPLE: A manufacturer of a very popular line of jeans requires its retailers to also stock the manufacturer's line of shirts in order to obtain the jeans.

   2) Only applies to sales and leases, not consignments
   3) Practically, it is a per se violation because seller is usually in a monopolistic position if s/he can force other products onto a buyer

      a) An exception is granted a new business with a risky future. This justification disappears as the business becomes established.

d. Exclusive dealing arrangements

   1) Occurs where seller requires buyer to buy only seller's products, i.e., may not deal in the commodities of a competitor

      EXAMPLE: A sporting goods manufacturer requires its retailers not to sell its competitors' goods.

   2) A violation if a substantial dollar amount or substantial percentage of the market is involved, e.g., $500,000 or 20%

      a) Then presumed to be anticompetitive, i.e., a per se violation

3. Judicial standards for Clayton Act violations

   a. If competition is not lessened, it is not illegal
   b. Quantitative considerations

      1) Sales volume of product, in dollars
      2) Control of the market, e.g., percentage share

   c. Qualitative considerations

      1) Strength of competitors
      2) Ease of entry into industry by newcomers

4. Sanctions

   a. Injunctions, forced divisions, forced divestitures (by individuals, corporations, or government)
   b. No criminal penalties
   c. Treble damages (by individuals, corporations)

D. Federal Trade Commission Act of 1914

1. Created the Federal Trade Commission (FTC)

   a. FTC has authority to enforce most of the antitrust laws

    b. FTC has exclusive authority to enforce this Act's prohibitions, i.e., individuals may not enforce

    c. FTC has authority to determine what practices are unfair or undesirable

2. Prohibits unfair methods of competition and deceptive practices

    a. FTC has exclusive authority under this Act and can determine what is unfair

    b. FTC may stop unfair and deceptive practices in their incipiency, i.e., before an actual violation occurs, as well as after a violation occurs

> *EXAMPLE: An oil company agreed with a tire company that the oil company would promote the sale of the tire company's accessories to the oil company's independent dealers. There was no tying or overt coercion in these promotions to the independent dealers, but the dominant position of the oil company over its dealers created strong potential for stifling competition. The agreement was therefore an unfair method of competition.*

    c. Unfairness standards

        1) Cause of substantial injury to competitors or consumers
        2) Offends public policy
        3) Oppressive or unscrupulous practices

3. Sanctions

    a. Cease and desist orders (by FTC only). Judicial review available.

        1) Civil penalty of $5,000 for each violation
        2) Each day of continued violation is separate offense
        3) FTC may also use cease and desist orders for the Sherman Act and Clayton Act

    b. No criminal penalties

    c. No damages

E. Robinson-Patman Act of 1936

1. Amended the Clayton Act to expand control in the area of price discrimination

    a. Also makes buyers (in addition to sellers) liable for price discrimination

2. Prohibits

    a. Discrimination as to price between purchasers of goods of like quality and grade

        1) If the effect is to substantially lessen competition or tend to create a monopoly
        2) Or if the effect is to injure or prevent competition by competitors or customer's competitors
        3) Covers purchases only, not leases or consignments
        4) Includes price discrimination between different geographical areas unless based on cost

    b. Special discounts, rebates, or commissions, e.g., brokerage fees, to customers

        1) Services, e.g., advertising, not allowed either unless on a proportionate basis to all customers
        2) To prevent favoritism to purchasers of quantity
        3) Illegal per se

    c. Buyers also are prohibited from knowingly inducing or receiving a discrimination in price or service

3. Price (differential) discrimination is allowed if

    a. It can be directly related to lower costs caused by production and sales in quantity, i.e., functional

        1) This cost differential must be proven, reliance on the general assumption that larger quantities are cheaper is not accepted

    b. Price discrimination is to meet lawful competition

        1) If a competitor has a low price, this may be met
        2) Only to keep old customers, not to gain new ones
        3) Competitor's price must be lawful, i.e., price discrimination cannot be met with price discrimination

    c. There is no substantial lessening of competition nor injury of competition

4. Sanctions

    a. Injunctions (by individual, corporations, government)
    b. Criminal penalties--maximum fine of $5,000 and/or 1 year in jail
    c. Treble damages (by individuals, corporations)

F. Summary and Application

1. Contracts, combinations, or conspiracies in restraint of trade are illegal

    a. Use rule of reason--only unreasonable restraint of trade is illegal
    b. Generally applies to horizontal restraints although it may apply to vertical restraints, e.g., resale price maintenance
    c. Evidence of conspiracy will be used if an actual agreement to restrain trade cannot be proven

        1) E.g., conscious parallelism (simultaneous price changes by competitors after discussion of a plan) is evidence of price fixing
        2) Price leadership (absent a plan) is not evidence of restraining trade

2. Monopolization or the attempt to monopolize is illegal

    a. Monopoly is the power to exclude competition and/or to control prices

        1) Use percentage of market share test

    b. Applies to unreasonable monopolistic tendency

        1) Substantial market shares and predatory or coercive actions

3. Mergers are illegal if the effect may substantially lessen competition or tend to create a monopoly

    a. Applies to corporations only
    b. Applies to asset and stock acquisition
    c. Applies to vertical mergers, horizontal mergers, and conglomerate mergers
    d. The U.S. Department of Justice has promulgated merger guidelines (1982 Department of Justice Merger Guidelines) in order to inform the public of its view of the factors and considerations to be taken into account in ascertaining whether a merger is potentially unlawful

        1) The guidelines state that mergers should not be permitted to create or enhance "market power" or to facilitate its exercise

2) "Market power" is the ability of one or more firms to profitably maintain prices above competitive levels for a significant period of time

3) The merger guidelines are essentially quantitative in nature, based on both product market and geographical market share sizes

4) Market concentration is a function of the number of firms in a market and their respective market shares

5) The more concentrated the industry, the greater the likelihood that one firm, or a small group of firms, could successfully exercise market power

6) In evaluating mergers, the Department will consider both the post-merger market concentration and the increase in concentration resulting from the merger

e. "Failing company doctrine" is a defense

1) If the acquired company is failing
2) And there is no better purchaser available in the eyes of antitrust law

4. Interlocking directorates are illegal if they could cause an anticompetitive effect

a. Person sitting as director on boards of 2 or more competing corporations
b. One corporation must have shareholders' equity greater than $1 million

5. Price discrimination is illegal if the effect is to substantially lessen competition, tend to create a monopoly, or injure competition

a. Applies to goods of like quality and grade
b. Applies to purchases only, not leases or consignments
c. Buyer is also prohibited from knowingly inducing or receiving a discriminated price
d. Defenses are proving lower costs from quantity and meeting of lawful competition

6. Resale price maintenance is not allowed
7. Per Se violations

a. Price fixing

1) Includes quantity limitations and minimum, maximum, buying and selling prices
2) Price is presumed to be unreasonable and unfair
3) Does not include government regulated prices

b. Joint boycotts

1) Does not include an individual refusal to deal with another unless part of an attempt to monopolize

c. Territorial limitations

1) Between competitors
2) Between buyer and seller

a) Vertical territorial limitations are no longer per se violations
b) Such agreements are only illegal if unreasonable (rule of reason applicable)

d. Tying arrangements

       1) Where buyer must take one or more other products in order to get the desired product
       2) Does not apply to consignments
       3) Only illegal per se if substantial, e.g., $500,000

  e. Exclusive dealing requirements

       1) Where buyer may not deal in products of seller's competitors
       2) Only illegal per se if substantial amounts involved

  f. Granting special discounts, rebates, or commissions to avoid price discrimination prohibition

8. To enforce

  a. Interstate commerce must be involved
  b. Affected agreements are unenforceable
  c. Injunctions, forced divisions or divestitures may be obtained by individuals, corporations, or government
  d. Government may seize goods involved in antitrust violation if shipped in interstate commerce

       1) Violator forfeits goods

  e. FTC can issue cease and desist orders
  f. Treble damages to individuals and corporations
  g. Criminal penalties

       1) Individuals--under Sherman Act only, maximum fine of $100,000 and/or 3 years imprisonment
       2) Corporations--under Sherman Act only, maximum fine of $1 million
       3) Directors, officers, and agents of corporations--under all antitrust laws, maximum fine of $5,000 and/or 1 year imprisonment

9. Trade associations, business groups, etc.

  a. Generally, corporations or individuals cannot avoid liability for violation of the antitrust laws by having the plan made or executed by a trade association or the like

G. Administrative Law

1. Administrative law is law concerning powers and procedures of administrative agencies. An administrative agency is created when executive or legislative branch of government delegates some of its authority and responsibility to appropriate group of persons.

2. Functions of regulatory agencies

  a. When Congress initially creates an administrative agency, it delegates certain rulemaking (legislative), administering and regulating (executive), and adjudicative (judicial) functions to agency

  b. Administrative agencies combine duties and responsibilities of legislative, executive, and judicial branches of government

  c. Administrative agencies are able to promulgate rules, employ their policing powers to insure compliance, render judgments, and impose penalties or remedies as prescribed by law if violations have occurred

d. The functions of administrative agencies are generally described as

1) Administering
2) Rulemaking
3) Adjudicating
4) Investigating
5) Prosecuting
6) Advising
7) Supervising

e. Reasons why legislature formulated administrative agencies

1) Impossible for legislative branch to legislate in sufficient detail to cover all aspects of a problem. In many areas, it is necessary to have agency develop detailed rules and regulations to carry out legislative policy.
2) Impossible for courts to handle all disputes and controversies that may arise
3) To refer problem or area to experts for solution, since expertise is required to develop sound policies and proper decisions
4) Administrative agencies provide needed continuity and consistency in formulation, application, and enforcement of rules and regulations

f. Creation of an administrative agency occurs when legislature enacts legislation establishing agency and broadly defining its powers

3. Activities subject to regulation

a. There are several broad areas where administrative process of law making and enforcement is prevalent

1) Utilities

a) Federal Power Commission

2) Transportation

a) Interstate Commerce Commission
b) Federal Aviation Administration
c) National Highway Traffic Safety Administration

3) Communications

a) Federal Communications Commission

4) Finance

a) Securities and Exchange Commission
b) Federal Reserve Board

5) Energy

a) Federal Energy Regulatory Commission
b) Nuclear Regulatory Commission

6) Employment Practices

a) Equal Employment Opportunity Commission

7) Health and Safety

a) Occupational Safety and Health Administration
b) Food and Drug Administration

4. Judicial review of agency decisions

    a. Important set of controls on administrative behavior which arise from court review of agency action (or inaction)

    b. Through process of judicial review, courts scrutinize agency action and check agency interpretation and implementation of regulatory programs

    c. Functions of judicial review

        1) To assure that agency is acting in accord with will of political branches, as expressed in enabling legislation and jurisdictional limits contained in relevant statutes

        2) To provide process of reasoned decision making, requiring agencies to produce supporting facts and reasoned explanations

        3) To provide essential supplement to political controls on administration

        4) To enhance acceptability of administrative decisions by providing independent check on their validity

    d. Means of obtaining judicial review

        1) Most statutes creating federal agencies indicate procedure for obtaining judicial review of agency decisions

        2) Where there is no statutory provision for judicial review, party seeking review must resort to one of following common law writs

            a) Injunction and declaratory judgment--used to declare action illegal and to enjoin occurrence

            b) Mandamus--available to compel agency to perform duty owed party
            c) Certiorari--review administrative decisions in state courts
            d) Habeas corpus--review restriction on individual freedom

    e. Standing required to seek judicial review

        1) Persons adversely affected by an administrative decision may wish to obtain judicial review of the decision in federal court

        2) Party who seeks judicial review of an administrative decision must have standing to do so

        3) Party may establish standing if s/he has a personal stake in outcome of the case

        4) Personal stake can be demonstrated by person suffering legal wrong because of agency action, or adversely affected or aggrieved by agency action

        5) The party must show that s/he falls within "zone of interests" protected or regulated by relevant statute

            a) To determine applicable "zone of interests," court must examine purpose of the statute and ascertain whether party falls within the class Congress intended to protect or regulate

        6) Even where the party has established a personal stake, and is found to be within "zone of interests" protected by statute, standing will be denied unless injury is "fairly traceable" to administrative action in question

    f. Proper forum of relief

        1) Party who has suffered harm as a result of agency action and has satisfied requirements of standing may nonetheless be denied judicial review if court is not proper forum of relief

        2) Court will not review an administrative decision if

            a) Party's claim is not yet "ripe" for review

                1] Ripeness doctrine is designed to avoid litigating in the abstract--i.e., before actual application of the administrative policy to the party

                2] Court must consider two factors in determining whether an administrative decision is ripe for review

                    a] "Fitness of the issues" for immediate review, and
                    b] "Hardship to the party(ies)" that would result if court withheld review

            b) Agency has primary jurisdiction

                1] Judicial review may be denied where agency, rather than court, has jurisdiction to conduct initial trial of the case

                2] If relevant statute is unclear as to proper forum, "doctrine of primary jurisdiction" may be applied to give agency initial jurisdiction over matter

                    a] In such a case, party must first seek relief through agency, although agency's decision will then be subjected to judicial review

            c) Party has not yet exhausted available administrative remedies

                1] This is designed to protect integrity of administrative process and to avoid unnecessary litigation

        3) Final Order Rule--Judicial review is usually not available for rulings of agency that are not "final." Thus, various decisions of agency made during course of adjudication or rulemaking are not immediately reviewable; rather party must await agency's final determination of case.

5. Scope of judicial review

    a. Extent of reviewing court's power to set aside agency findings and judgments depends upon whether particular issue is question of law or question of fact

        1) Question of law--Agencies often decide questions of law in both rulemaking and adjudication

            a) Questions of law include such determinations as

                1] Whether agency had jurisdiction over matter
                2] Whether procedure used was appropriate
                3] Statutory interpretation that does not significantly involve facts of case

            b) Scope of review--Law questions are theoretically subject to full review under a "rightness" test. Court will determine correctness of agency's interpretation and may freely substitute its own judgment for that of agency, i.e., the court need not defer to agency's determination.

2) Question of fact--Questions of fact involve determinations that can be made without any knowledge of applicable law

    a) Scope of review--Judicial review of factual determinations made by agency is limited

        1] Extent of limitation depends upon standard of review that is used. In most cases, standard of review is "substantial evidence," whereby a court will not set aside an agency decision if it is supported by substantial evidence.

    b) Therefore, fact questions are reviewed under a "reasonable" test such that court defers to agency's determination if agency had a rational basis to support conclusion

    c) A broader scope of judicial review is permitted where agency findings of fact affected a claimant's constitutional rights. Reviewing court has the power to make an independent judgment with respect to agency findings of "constitutional" facts.

b. Scope of review for administrative rules

    1) Basic function of administrative agencies is legislative act of rule-making. Administrative rules are classified as

        a) Legislative (substantive)--fills gap in statute
        b) Interpretive--represents agency's view as to how statute or prior legislative rule should be interpreted

    2) Review of legislative rules--Legislative rules generally have force of law, and they carry a strong presumption of validity. Court may invalidate a legislative rule only if agency erred on question of law or if rule was arbitrary, capricious, or an abuse of discretion.

        a) Actions by an administrative agency must not be <u>Ultra Vires</u>, i.e., outside scope of power delegated to the agency. If agency acts outside this area, it is unconstitutionally exercising power.

    3) Review of interpretive rules--Reviewing court is free to substitute its own judgment for that of the agency on any questions of law involved

c. Scope of review for discretionary actions--Where administrative action is found to be completely within discretion of the agency, it is not reviewable at all. However, agency action or findings that represent an abuse of discretion may be set aside by courts.

H. <u>Federal Consumer Protection Legislation</u>

1. Consumer Credit Protection Act has been federal law since 1968

    a. Truth in Lending Act is major part of Consumer Credit Protection Act

        1) Purposes of act are to inform consumers of cost and conditions of credit extended to them and to regulate issuance and use of credit cards

        2) Transactions covered by Act include

            a) Consumer credit transactions not exceeding $25,000
            b) All real estate credit extended for consumer purposes
            c) Loans to businesses and governmental entities are exempt from Act

3) Creditors covered by Act include any individual or business who regularly extends credit to consumers (i.e., doctors, dentists, financial institutions, department stores, etc.)

4) Requirements of Act demand that creditor disclose

   a) Finance charge in dollar terms
   b) Annual percentage rate of interest charged
   c) Disclosures must be clear, conspicuous, and written

5) Act does not set maximum or minimum charges for credit. These are set by state usury laws.

6) Requirements of Act concerning issuance and use of credit cards

   a) Credit cards may only be issued as response to applications for or renewal of an accepted credit card

   b) Credit card holder's liability for unauthorized use (lost/stolen card) is limited to $50. However, if card holder voluntarily transfers card to a friend, with limits on its use, and the friend violates these limits, $50 limitation does not apply.

7) Real estate credit transactions

   a) Act provides for cooling off period that allows borrower to cancel loan within 3 business days after entering into it if his/her home is collateral for the loan. This cooling off period applies to second mortgages, but not to mortgage used to buy the home.

   b) Cooling off period also applies to the cancellation of mechanics' liens that result from repairs to home by craftsman if cancelled within 3 days of creation of contract

8) Act also regulates credit advertising

9) Penalties include criminal sanctions and fines up to $5,000 and prison up to one year. Also, civil remedies allowing consumer to sue violator and recover twice the amount of finance charge (not less than $100 or more than $1,000) plus court costs and reasonable attorney's fees.

b. Fair Credit Reporting Act is another portion of Consumer Credit Protection Act

   1) Purpose of Act is to ensure dissemination of accurate, current credit information about consumers
   2) Act covers credit information used to acquire a job, insurance, or credit
   3) If consumers are denied credit, they have right to demand of credit agency that provided reports any information in these reports relied upon by denying creditor. However, consumer does not have a right to report itself.
   4) Consumer can force credit agency to correct any mistake made in credit report
   5) FTC enforces this Act and consumers are allowed to sue violators for damages, reasonable attorney's fees, and court costs

c. Equal Credit Opportunity Act (ECOA) is part of Consumer Credit Protection Act

   1) Equal Credit Opportunity Act places requirements on financial institutions and other firms extending credit on regular basis

2) Lenders must make credit available to all credit-worthy customers without regard to an applicant's sex, marital status, national origin, race, religion, color, or age

3) Equal Credit Opportunity Act covers

   a) Any person who regularly extends, renews, or continues to give credit

      EXAMPLE: *Department stores, banks, and savings and loan associations.*

   b) Anyone who regularly arranges for credit extension, renewal, or continuation

      EXAMPLE: *Realtors and automobile dealers.*

4) Equal Credit Opportunity Act preserves lenders' rights to reject loan applicants because they are not worthy of credit

   a) Act does not require lenders to make loans
   b) Act limits the basis for which creditors can turn down loan applicants

5) The ECOA requires creditor to notify an applicant of its actions on credit application within thirty days of receiving completed application

6) The ECOA requires creditors to be specific in telling credit applicants why they are denied credit

7) ECOA can be enforced by private parties or administrative agencies

   a) Private parties may sue wrongdoer

      1] Damages, punitive damages, and injunctions are possible remedies

   b) Several federal administrative agencies have power to enforce ECOA

d. Fair Credit Billing Act is a part of Consumer Credit Protection Act

   1) Fair Credit Billing Act establishes a way for consumers to act upon credit card billing errors

      a) Applies only to credit cards, not to other billing arrangements
      b) If consumer sends a written billing complaint to creditor within sixty days of receiving allegedly erroneous bill, that creditor must acknowledge consumer's complaint within thirty days

         1] Consumer's complaint to credit card issuer must be written

      c) Credit card issuer must either explain alleged error in writing or correct error within two billing cycles

         1] But in no case more than ninety days after receiving credit card holder's complaint

   2) Fair Credit Billing Act allows retailers who accept credit cards to offer discounts to cash customers

      a) This recognizes the service fee merchants pay to credit card companies
      b) Act forbids merchants who honor credit cards to raise retail prices for card holders over what cash customers pay
      c) Act does not require discounts for cash customers

e. The Fair Debt Collection Practices Act is part of Consumer Credit Protection Act

   1) Fair Debt Collection Practices Act's purpose is to end abusive, deceptive, and unfair debt collection practices by debt collectors

      a) Act does not permit debt collectors to use unjust means to collect debts

      b) Debt collector may not harass, oppress, or abuse any person in collection efforts

         EXAMPLE: Using threats of violence to anyone or anyone's property or reputation. Using obscene or profane language. Advertising the debtor's debt.

      c) Act does not cancel consumer debts

   2) Only personal, family, and household debts are covered by Fair Debt Collection Practices Act

      EXAMPLE: If Herb buys a stereo on credit for home use, his debt is a consumer debt covered by the Act.

      a) Fair Debt Collection Practices Act does not protect business debtors

         EXAMPLE: If Ike buys stereo on credit to play music in waiting room of his doctor's office, debt is not a consumer debt because stereo is used for business purposes.

   3) Fair Debt Collection Practices Act describes a debt collector as anyone other than creditor (or creditor's attorney) who regularly collects debts for others

      a) Act does not apply to creditors who collect their own debts or to creditor's attorney's collection efforts

   4) Debt collector may contact a debtor in person or by mail, telephone, or telegram

      a) Contact may not occur at inconvenient or unusual hours, or at inconvenient or unusual places, unless debtor agrees

   5) Debt collector must stop contacting a debtor if the debtor says to do so in writing

   6) Debt collector may notify debtor that some specific action may be taken (i.e., suing debtor to collect), but only if debt collector or creditor usually takes such action

   7) Debt collectors may contact any person to locate a debtor

      a) The practice of trying to locate debtors is called "skip tracing"

      b) Debt collectors may tell people they contact only that they want to locate debtor; not that debtor owes money

   8) Within five days after debt collector first contacts debtor, debt collector must send debtor written notice telling

      a) Amount debtor owes

      b) Who creditor is, and

      c) What debtor should do if debtor believes money is not owed

      9) Debt collector may not contact debtor if debtor sends a letter within thirty days after first being contacted saying that no money is owed

        a) However, a debt collector may start to collect again if debtor is sent proof of the debt

      10) If creditor violates Fair Debt Collection Practices Act, debtor may sue creditor or may complain to Federal Trade Commission

2. Magnuson-Moss Warranty Act (see Sales Module "Contract for Sale of Goods," "A.7.c.6)")

3. Practices pursuant to Section 5 of Federal Trade Commission Act--under Section 5, FTC is authorized to stop unfair or deceptive acts or practices that influence, inhibit, or restrict consumers unfairly in their purchasing decisions. FTC has prohibited following practices

  a. Deceptive advertising consists of misleading or false statements concerning product

    1) Bait advertising (bait and switch)--Store advertises very low price on item to lure customers into store. Then salesperson tries to switch consumer to more expensive item. Bait advertising exists if seller

      a) Refuses to show advertised item, or
      b) Fails to have adequate quantities, or
      c) Fails to provide advertised item within reasonable time, or
      d) Encourages employees not to sell item

    2) FTC may force seller to engage in additional advertising to correct misconception created by deceptive advertisement

  b. Mail order sales--FTC has ruled that seller of mail order merchandise must ship ordered item promptly (within 30 days) after receiving the order. This rule exempts C.O.D. orders.

  c. Door-to-door solicitation sales--Concerning the sale, purchase, or rental of consumer goods or services with purchase price of $25 or more, FTC makes it an unfair trade practice for any door-to-door seller not to furnish a buyer with notice of fact that buyer has 3 days to cancel the sale

    1) Door-to-door seller must provide buyer with completed notice of cancellation form
    2) Sales not covered by this regulation are

      a) Sales of realty, insurance, or securities
      b) Sales made entirely by phone or mail
      c) Sales where buyer first contacted seller and asked seller to come to buyer's home

  d. Limitation of holder in due course (HDC) rule in consumer credit transactions--Holder in due course rule allows HDC to cut off all personal defenses of maker of promissory note. (See Negotiable Instruments Module "Rights of Holder in Due Course," "G.") FTC effectively abolished HDC doctrine in most consumer credit transactions.

    1) FTC rule requires that any consumer credit contract contain a conspicuous notice that any holder of contract is subject to all claims and defenses that consumer could assert against seller. This destroys possibility of subsequent holder of contract (and promissory note) being a HDC.

EXAMPLE: Prior to FTC rule, Danny buys a TV from Mutt Appliances on credit and signs promissory note payable to Mutt. Mutt immediately negotiates note to bank. TV does not work properly, and Danny learns that Mutt has gone out of business. Danny stops making payments on note. Bank sues him, and Danny asserts defenses of breach of warranty. Bank, as HDC, will defeat Danny's defense and collect note. However, if same example occurred presently, bank would not collect note because under FTC rule, bank will acquire no better rights than Mutt, the seller.

2) FTC rule does not apply to

    a) Transactions where business, instead of a consumer is purchaser
    b) Real property transactions
    c) Transactions where payment is made by check
    d) Credit card purchases

FEDERAL SECURITIES LAW

Overview

The Securities Act of 1933, as amended and the Securities Exchange Act of 1934, as amended are tested on the exam. Included are the scope of the 1933 Act, registration requirements, exempt securities, exempt transactions, and the liability of the various parties involved in making a public offering of securities. The purpose of the 1933 Act is to evaluate a security offering and to prevent fraud. The basic prohibition of the 1933 Act is that no sale of a security shall occur in interstate commerce without registration and without furnishing a prospectus to prospective purchasers unless the security or the transaction is exempt from registration.

The 1934 Act includes coverage of corporate reporting requirements, anti-fraud provisions, broker-dealer registration, disclosure of insider information, and short-swing profits. The purpose of the 1934 Act is the establishment of the Securities Exchange Commission and to assure fairness in the trading of securities subsequent to issuance. The basic scope of the 1934 Act is to require periodic reports of financial and other information concerning registered securities, regulate the solicitation of proxies, prohibit manipulative and deceptive devices in both the sale and purchase of securities, provide for periodic reports of insiders who trade in the corporation's securities, and provide for the corporation to recover short-swing profits by corporation insiders. The exam nearly always includes a question on Federal Securities Regulation; however, this is frequently combined with accountant's liability or is included within a question concerning corporation law.

Federal Securities Regulation Definitions

Security. A very broad term under the 1933 Act denoting stocks, bonds, promissory notes, and any other instrument, contract, or arrangement in which a person invests money with the expectation of earning a return through the efforts of persons other than himself.

Securities Exchange Commission. The government agency comprising five commissioners and its staff which was created to administer and enforce the Federal Securities Laws. The Commission interprets the acts, conducts investigations, adjudicates violations, and performs a rule-making function to implement the acts.

Registration under 1933 Act. The process of filing (prior to original issuance of securities) a registration statement which includes financial statements and all other relevant information about the registrant's properties, business, directors, principal officers, together with a prospectus. Unless amended or related to a self-registration, the prospectus, if filled out properly, will become effective on the twentieth day after the filing and is a public document. Full details of the securities being issued, its relation to the registrant's other securities, and the intended purpose of the proceeds of the issue must be included.

Prospectus. Any notice, circular, advertisement, letter, radio or TV statement which offers a security for sale and which must be given to every prospective purchaser of the security prior to or concurrently with the transmission of the security to that purchaser.

Registration Under 1934 Act. The filing of periodic statements with the SEC and the applicable stock exchange. All securities traded on a national security exchange and over-the-counter securities that are held by 500 or more owners must be registered if the issuer has more than $3 million in gross assets. Securities that may be exempted from the requirements of the 1933 Act may still be regulated by the 1934 Act.

Issuer. An issuer is a corporation, partnership, other association, or legal person who issues, or proposes to issue or sell, any new security.

Insider. The 1934 Act requires that every person who owns (directly or indirectly) more than 10% of any class of any nonexempt registered equity security, or who is a director or an officer of the issuer of such security, shall file a disclosure with the SEC. Also, further disclosure on a monthly basis is required of any changes in stock ownership. Insiders are liable to the issuer for all profit from the purchase or sale of securities held for less than six months.

Rule 10b-5 (1934 Act). Makes it unlawful to use the mails or any instrumentality of interstate commerce or any national securities exchange to defraud any person or make any false statement or omission of a material fact in connection with the purchase or sale of any security or in a report to the SEC. Violators of Rule 10b-5 may be liable for criminal penalties or for damages to the defrauded investors. Rule 10b-5 is not limited to securities subject to the Act, but applies to any sale of any security if interstate commerce is used. Under Rule 10b-5 the plaintiff must establish scienter, i.e., intent to deceive, manipulate, or defraud, or reckless conduct that is highly unreasonable.

A. <u>Securities Act of 1933</u> (Generally applies to initial issuances of securities)

1. Purposes of Act are to provide investors with full and fair disclosure of all material information relating to issuance of securities and to prevent fraud or misrepresentation

   a. This is accomplished by requiring

      1) A registration statement to be filed with the Securities and Exchange Commission (SEC) before either a public sale or an offer to sell securities in interstate commerce

         a) This is the fundamental thrust of the Act

      2) Prospectuses to be provided to investors with or before the sale or delivery of the securities

         a) This is to provide the public with the information provided to the SEC in the registration statement

      3) And by providing civil and criminal liabilities for failure to comply with these requirements and for misrepresentation or fraud in the sale of securities even if not required to be registered

   b. SEC does not evaluate the merits or value of securities

      1) SEC can only compel complete disclosure
      2) In theory, the public can evaluate the merit of the security when provided with complete disclosure

   c. The major items you need to know are

      1) That a registration statement and a prospectus are usually required
      2) What transactions are exempt from registration
      3) What the liability is for false or misleading registration statements
      4) What securities are exempt from registration

2. Definitions

   a. Security--any note, stock, bond, certificate of interest, investment contract, etc., or any interest or instrument commonly known as a security

      1) Includes limited partnership interests
      2) Includes rights and warrants to subscribe for the above
      3) Investment contract is a security when profits are to come from the efforts of others

   b. Restricted Security--a security acquired directly or indirectly from the issuer or affiliate in a transaction or chain of transactions not involving a public offering or a security acquired from the issuer that is subject to the sale limitations of regulation. See Exempt transactions.

      1) Unless Rule 144 (below) applies, a restricted security must be registered before resale
      2) Rule 144 states that if the seller holds for 2 years, sells through a broker, and the aggregate sales during preceding 3 months involve either 1% or less of the outstanding shares or less than the average weekly volume traded during the preceding four weeks, then the security can be resold without registration

   c. Person--individual, corporation, partnership, unincorporated association, business trust, government

d. Controlling person--has power, direct/indirect, to influence the management and/or policies of an issuer, whether by stock ownership, contract, position, or otherwise

EXAMPLE: A 51% stockholder is a controlling person by virtue of a majority ownership.

EXAMPLE: A director of a corporation also owns 10% of that same corporation. By virtue of the stock ownership and position on the board of directors, he has a strong voice in the management of the corporation. Therefore, he is a controlling person.

e. Issuer--every person who issues or proposes to issue any security

  1) Includes a controlling person

f. Underwriter--any person who has purchased from an issuer with a view to the public distribution of any security or participates in such an undertaking

  1) Includes any person who offers or sells for an issuer in connection with the distribution of any security
  2) Does not include a person who sells or distributes on commission for an underwriter (i.e., dealers)
  3) Remember, an issuer includes a controlling person

g. Dealer--agent, broker, or principal who spends either full or part time in the business of dealing or trading securities issued by another person

h. Sale--every contract for sale or disposition of a security for value (consideration)

  1) Offer to sell--every attempt to dispose of a security for value
  2) Includes neither preliminary negotiations nor agreements between an issuer and an underwriter
  3) Under Rule 145, the issuance of securities as part of a business reorganization (e.g., merger or consolidation) constitutes a sale and must be registered unless the issue qualifies as an exemption to the 1933 Act

i. Registration statement--the statement required to be filed with the SEC before an initial sale of securities in interstate commerce

  1) Includes any amendment, report, or document filed as part of the statement or incorporated therein by reference

j. Prospectus--any notice, circular, advertisement, letter, or communication offering any security for sale

  1) May be a written, radio, or television communication
  2) After the effective date of the registration statement, communication (written or oral) will not be considered a prospectus if

    a) Prior to or at same time, a written prospectus was also sent, or
    b) If it only states from whom a written prospectus is available, identifies the security, states the price, and who will execute orders for it (i.e., tombstone ad)

  3) Preliminary prospectus may be sent during the waiting period (i.e., time interval between the time of first filing with the SEC and the effective date), if so identified and states that it is subject to completion and amendment

    a) These statements must be made in red ink ("red herring" prospectus)

3. Registration requirements

    a. Registration is required under the Act if

        1) The securities are to be offered, sold, or delivered in interstate commerce or through the mails

           a) Interstate commerce means trade, commerce, transportation, or communication (e.g., telephone call) of securities among the several states or territories of the U.S.

        2) Unless it is an exempted security or exempted transaction

    b. Issuer has the primary duty of registration

        1) Any person who sells unregistered securities that should have been registered may be liable to a purchaser, unless the transaction is exempt

    c. Registration statements are public information
    d. Information required, in general

        1) Names of issuer, directors, officers, general partners, underwriters, large stockholders, counsel, etc.
        2) Description of property, business, and capitalization of issuer
        3) Description of the security to be sold and use to be made by issuer of proceeds
        4) Information about management of issuer
        5) Financial statements certified by an independent accountant
        6) Risks associated with the securities

    e. Prospectus is also filed as part of the registration statement

        1) Generally must contain the same information as the registration statement, but it may be condensed or summarized

    f. The registration statement and prospectus are examined by SEC

        1) Amendments are almost always required by SEC
        2) SEC may issue stop-order suspending effectiveness of registration if statement appears misleading
        3) Otherwise registration becomes effective on the 20th day after filing (or on the 20th day after the filing of an amendment)

           a) 20 days is called the waiting period

        4) It is unlawful for the company to offer or sell the securities prior to approval (effective registration date)

           a) Except for preliminary prospectuses

    g. Applies to both corporate and noncorporate issuers
    h. Registration covers a single distribution, so a second distribution must also be registered
    i. State "Blue Sky" laws must also be complied with (see "C." on page 548)

4. Exempt securities (need never be registered)

    a. Securities of governments, banks, quasi-governmental authorities (e.g., local hospital authorities), building and loan associations, farmers' co-ops, and railroads

        1) Public utilities are not exempt

b.   Commercial paper, e.g., note, draft, check, etc., with a maturity of nine months or less

   1) Must be for commercial purpose and not investment

c.   Securities of nonprofit religious, educational, or charitable organizations
d.   Certificates issued by a receiver or trustee in bankruptcy
e.   Insurance and annuity contracts
f.   Security exchanged by issuer exclusively with its existing shareholders

   1) No commission is paid
   2) Both sets of securities must have been issued by the same person

   EXAMPLE: A stock split is an exempt transaction under the 1933 Act and thus, the securities need not be registered at time of split.

5. Exempt transactions

a.   Intrastate issues--securities offered and sold only within one state

   1) Issuer must be a resident of the state and doing 80% of business in the state and must use at least 80% of the sale proceeds in connection with business operations in the state
   2) All offerees and purchasers must be residents of the state
   3) For 9 months after the last sale by the issuer, resales can only be made to residents of the state

   EXAMPLE: A regional corporation in need of additional capital makes an offer to the residents of the state in which it is incorporated to purchase a new issue of its stock. The offer expressly restricts sales to only residents of the state and all purchasers are residents of the state.

b.   Small issues (Regulation A)--issuances up to $1,500,000 may be exempt if

   1) There is a notice filing with the SEC
   2) An offering circular (containing financial information about the corporation and descriptive information about the offered securities) is provided to the offeree. Financial statements in the offering circular need not be audited.

c.   Casual sales--transaction by any person other than an issuer, underwriter, or dealer

   1) Generally covers sales by individual investors on their own account
   2) May be a transaction by a broker on a customer's order

      a) Does not include the solicitation of these orders

   3) Does not apply to sales by controlling persons (see "2.d." above)

d.   Regulation D establishes three exemptions in Rules 504, 505, and 506

   1) Rule 504 exempts an issuance of securities up to $500,000 sold in a 12-month period to any number of investors

      a) No general offering or solicitation is permitted
      b) The securities are restricted as to resale
      c) No specific disclosure is required

   2) Rule 505 exempts issuance of up to $5,000,000 in a 12-month period

      a) No general offering or solicitation is permitted

       b) Permits sales to 35 unaccredited investors and to unlimited number of accredited investors

       c) Accredited investors are banks, insurance companies, and persons with net worth exceeding $1,000,000 or having an annual income of $200,000 for two most recent years or make purchases of more than $150,000 of securities where the purchaser's total purchase price does not exceed 20% of the purchaser's net worth at the time of sale

       d) If purchased solely by accredited investors, no specific disclosure needed

       e) If nonaccredited investor purchases, audited statements and information similar to Form S-18 must be supplied

       f) Securities must be held for two years

   3) Rule 506 allows private placement of unlimited amount of securities

       a) Permits sales to unlimited number of accredited investors. (See "5.d.2)c)" above.)

       b) Permits sales to 35 purchasers that are not accredited investors but who must be sophisticated investors (individuals with knowledge and experience in financial matters or represented by such an individual)

       c) No general offering is permitted

       d) Resale is restricted

       e) If nonaccredited investor purchases, audited statements and information similar to Form S-18 must be supplied

EXAMPLE: A growing corporation is in need of additional capital and decides to make a new issuance of its stock. The stock is only offered to 10 of the president's friends who regularly make financial investments of this sort. They are interested in purchasing the stock for an investment and each of them is provided with the type of information that is regularly included in a registration statement.

 e. Post-registration transactions by dealer, i.e., dealer is not required to deliver prospectus

   1) If the transaction is made at least 40 days after first date security was offered to the public, or

   2) After 90 days if it is issuer's first public issue

   3) Does not apply to sales of securities that are a leftover part of an allotment from the public issue

6. Criminal, civil, and administrative liabilities

 a. In general, the issuer or any person who sells unregistered securities that should have been registered may be liable for his/her actions

   1) But the thrust of the criminal and civil liabilities is for misrepresentation and fraud whether or not the security is required to be registered

 b. Civil liability

   1) Purchaser of a security issued under a registration statement containing a false statement or omission of a material fact may sue

       a) Every signer of the registration statement

       b) All directors or partners of the issuer

    c) Underwriters

    d) Experts for authorized statements, e.g., accountants, attorneys, appraisers

2) Liability may not be avoided by disclaimer

3) Purchaser need not prove reliance on the registration statement unless

    a) Purchase of security was after issuer had made an earning statement (covering at least 12 months after effective date of registration) available to security holders

4) Most of the burden of proof is shifted to the defendant. But the "due diligence" defense provides that no person, other than the issuer, shall be liable where s/he can prove that

    a) As regards to parts of the registration statement not purporting to be made upon the authority of an expert, s/he had, after reasonable investigation, a reasonable belief that the statements were true and did not contain any omission of material fact

    EXAMPLE: Underwriter exercised reasonable care in his/her examination and investigation of the statements.

    b) As regards to parts of the registration statement purporting to be made upon the authority of an expert other than him/her, s/he had no reasonable grounds to believe and did not believe that the expert's statements were untrue or contained any omissions of material fact

    EXAMPLE: An attorney relies on a CPA's work as a foundation for his statements.

    c) As regards to parts of the registration statement made upon his authority as an expert, he had, after reasonable investigation, reasonable grounds to believe that the statements were true and did not contain any omission of material fact

    EXAMPLE: CPA performs an audit in a reasonable manner and discovers no irregularities.

5) Damages are the difference between price paid and

    a) Value of security when suit is brought, or

    b) Price security sold at, if before suit, or

    c) Price sold at after suit, if damages are less than in "a." above

    d) Never to exceed the price at which offered to public

    e) Underwriter is never liable for more than s/he underwrites, i.e., if s/he doesn't underwrite whole issue

6) Seller of a security is liable to purchaser

    a) If interstate commerce or the mails are used, and

    b) If registration is not in effect and should be, or

    c) If an untrue statement is made or omission of a material fact

    d) For amount paid, plus interest, less any income received

7) Statute of Limitations

    a) One year after the false statement or omission is discovered, or with reasonable diligence should have been found

    b) In no event can the action be commenced more than three years after the security was offered to the public

c. Criminal liability

    1) If a person intentionally makes an untrue statement or omits a material fact in the registration statement, or willfully violates the SEC Act or Regulation

    2) If a person uses interstate commerce or the mails to fraudulently sell any security

    3) Injunctions are available

    4) Maximum fine of $10,000 and/or up to 5 years imprisonment

    5) Exemptions not applicable here

        a) I.e., penalties available if fraudulent means used to sell security exempted from registration

d. Administrative action

    1) Suspension or revocation of broker-dealer registration

    2) Suspend or revoke registration of security (stop-order)

B. Securities Exchange Act of 1934 (Generally applies to subsequent trading of securities)

1. Purposes of the Act

a. Federally regulate securities exchanges and securities traded thereon

b. Require adequate information be provided in various transactions

c. Regulate the use of credit in securities transactions

d. Prevent unfair use of information by insiders

e. Prevent fraud and deceptive practices

2. Each of the following are required to register with the SEC if they use interstate commerce or the mails

a. National securities exchanges

b. Brokers and dealers (must register whether or not members of an exchange)

c. Dealers in municipal securities

d. Securities that are traded on any national securities exchange must be registered

e. Over-the-counter and other equity securities traded in interstate commerce and having assets of more than $1 million and 500 or more holders of record (stockholders) as of the last day of the issuer's fiscal year

    1) Equity securities--stock, rights to subscribe to, or securities convertible into stock. Not ordinary bonds.

f. Exempt securities

    1) Obligations of the U.S. government, guaranteed by, or in which the U.S. government has an interest

    2) Obligations of a state or political subdivision, or guaranteed thereby

        a) Municipal securities traded by broker or dealer are not exempt

    3) Industrial development bonds

3. Issuers of registered securities must file the following reports with the SEC

a. Current reports (Form 8-K) of certain material events such as a change in corporate control, revaluation of assets, or a change in the amount of issued securities

        1) Filed within 10 days of the close of the month in which events took place

    b. Quarterly reports (Form 10-Q) must be filed for each of the first three fiscal quarters of each fiscal year of the issuer

        1) Not required to be certified

    c. Annual reports (Form 10-K) must be certified by an independent public accountant

    d. These reports are not to be confused with reports to shareholders

4. Credit rules for brokers, dealers, banks, and members of exchanges

    a. The Federal Reserve Board regulates the maximum amount of credit (margin) that brokers, dealers, and banks may extend to purchasers of securities

        1) Guidelines vary from 50% to 100%
        2) Does not apply to exempt securities

    b. May borrow for business only through

        1) A bank that is a member of the Federal Reserve System, or
        2) A bank agreeing to follow the same procedures as members of the Federal Reserve System

    c. May not lend customer's securities without written consent
    d. May not hypothecate any customer's securities

        1) I.e., pledge without giving up possession or subject to a lien
        2) May do so to the extent a customer is indebted on the security

        EXAMPLE: Broker holds customer's securities for him. In order to make an investment of his own, broker needs collateral for a loan. He pledges his customer's securities as collateral. This is hypothecation and a violation of the Act unless the customer is indebted to the broker on these securities.

    e. Member of an exchange may not transact for his/her own account, except

        1) Odd-lot dealers--those who deal with lots less than units traded on exchange

        EXAMPLE: Certain shares are traded in 100-share units. An odd-lot dealer might execute a customer's order for 80 shares and he will have to take the other 20 shares himself.

        2) Specialist--one who deals with limited price orders and also deals for himself

        EXAMPLE: A specialist receives an order to buy 80 shares at price X. Only if the price is down to X will he buy 100 shares: 80 shares for his customer at price X, and 20 shares for himself.

5. Proxy solicitations

    a. Proxy--grant of authority by a shareholder to someone else to vote his shares at a meeting
    b. Proxy solicitation provisions apply to solicitation (by any means of interstate commerce or the mails) of holders of securities required to be registered under the 1934 Act

   c. Proxy statement must be sent with the proxy solicitation and must contain

      1) Disclosure of all material facts concerning matters to be voted upon
      2) Purpose is for fairness in corporate action and election of directors

   d. Requirements of the proxy itself

      1) Shall indicate on whose behalf the solicitation is made
      2) Provide a space to date it
      3) Identify clearly and impartially each matter to be acted on
      4) Means to choose approval or disapproval of each matter, e.g., yes or no

   e. Other inclusions in proxy material

      1) Proposals by shareholders which are a proper subject for shareholders to vote on
      2) Financial statements for the last two years, certified by an independent accountant, if

         a) Solicitation is on behalf of management, and
         b) It is for an annual meeting at which directors are to be elected

   f. The proxy statement, proxy itself, and any other soliciting material must be filed with SEC
   g. Brokers are required to forward proxies for customers' shares held by the broker
   h. Incumbent management is required to mail proxy materials of insurgents to shareholders if requested and expenses are paid by the insurgents

6. Regulation of insiders and insiders' profits

   a. Purpose is to prevent unfair use of information by insiders for their own benefit
   b. Insider--officers and directors of issuer and beneficial owners of more than 10% of any class of issuer's equity securities

      1) Beneficial ownership

         a) Securities owned by oneself, and
         b) Securities in spouse's name, minor children's name, or relative's name who shares the same home
         c) Securities in trust to which insider has a right

   c. Insiders must file, with the SEC and the national exchange involved, a report of

      1) The amount of equity securities of such issuer of which he is the beneficial owner, and
      2) The change in his ownership that occurs in any month

         a) No monthly report needed if no change occurs

   d. Insiders are liable to the company (issuer) for any profit from the purchase and sale of equity securities held for less than six months (short-swing profits)

      1) Insider must give the profit to the issuer

         a) Losses do not offset gains
         b) The purchase (used in determining gain) may be before or after the sale

EXAMPLE: A director purchases 100 shares of stock at $100 per share. Three months later he sells these same 100 shares of stock at $90 per share. Two months thereafter he purchases 100 more shares at $85 per share. He is liable to the company for $500 of short-swing profits. By comparing the sale and the second purchase, there is a $5 per share profit. The fact that there was a loss by comparing the first purchase and the sale is not taken into account.

2) If the purchase and sale are six months or more apart, there is no liability

   a) Time is the important test, intent does not count

      EXAMPLE: An officer purchases stock on January 15. He then sells the stock at a gain on July 16. Since the holding period was 6 months and 1 day, the officer is not liable to the corporation for the profit.

3) Two-year statute of limitations from date of sale
4) Exemptions

   a) Odd-lot transactions
   b) Transactions involving market value of $10,000 or less

5) Insiders who pass confidential information on to others would be liable under anti-fraud provisions

   a) Therefore cannot give tips to friends

e. Unlawful for insiders to sell securities of issuer if

   1) They do not own it--"short sale"

      EXAMPLE: A sale made (with delivery to occur later) with the expectation that the price will drop and the security can be purchased and delivered at a net gain.

   2) They own it but do not deliver it--"sale against the box"

      EXAMPLE: A sale made (with delivery to occur later) with the expectation that the price will drop and the security can be purchased and delivered at a net gain. However, the insider does own stock which he can deliver on the sale if the price does not drop as expected.

f. Anyone who acquires more than 5% of the ownership (beneficial) of a class of registered securities must report to

   1) Issuer, and
   2) Exchange security is traded on, and
   3) SEC
   4) Report must include

      a) Identity of persons involved
      b) Whether purpose is to acquire control
      c) Whether any major change is planned if control is obtained
      d) Number of shares owned
      e) Tender offers if planned

   5) If a tender offer is involved in acquiring more than 5% of a security, the purchaser must file the above report with the SEC and give similar information to the shareholders beforehand

a) Tender offer--offer to buy shareholder's stock in a planned take-over of the company

7. Anti-fraud provisions--very broad scope

a. Unlawful to manipulate prices and create appearance of active trading, e.g.,

1) Wash sales--purchase and sale at about the same time by one person (not good faith transactions by brokers)

2) Matched orders--one person sells and the other buys
3) Series of transactions to affect price or give appearance of active trading for the purpose of inducing trading by others

4) Induce purchase or sale by circulating information that market operations may affect price or by use of false or misleading statements

5) Whether or not securities are exempt

b. Unlawful to use any manipulative or deceptive devices in the purchase or sale of securities

1) This applies to all securities, whether registered or not (as long as either the mails, interstate commerce, or a national stock exchange is used)

2) Includes any act, practice, or scheme which operates a fraud or deceit upon any person

3) Most importantly, it is unlawful to make any false statement of a material fact or omission of a material fact necessary to make the statement not misleading

a) The basic test of materiality is whether a reasonable man would attach importance to the fact in determining his choice of action in the transaction

EXAMPLE: A broker offers to sell a stock and omits to tell the purchaser that the corporation is about to make an unfavorable merger.

b) Deliberate intent to deceive or reckless conduct is required; negligence is not enough
c) This applies to any seller, buyer, or person who lends his/her name to statements used in the buying and selling of the securities

d) This liability also applies to accountants. See ACCOUNTANT'S LEGAL LIABILITY.

4) Would apply to an insider who buys or sells on inside information until it is disseminated to the public

c. SEC urges affirmative disclosure of material information affecting the issuer and securities

1) No statutory duty to do so
2) Must forego trading if one has such knowledge

a) Includes insiders and anyone with knowledge, e.g., accountant, attorney
b) May not tip information to others, nor may tipees trade the securities

8. Civil and criminal liabilities

    a. Civil liability

        1) Any person who willfully participates in the manipulation of security prices may be liable to anyone who buys or sells a security at a price that is thereby affected

        2) Any person who makes a false or misleading statement with respect to any material fact in any application, report, or document is liable to

            a) Any person who purchased or sold the security at a price affected thereby, provided

                1] S/he relied on the statement, and
                2] S/he did not know it was false or misleading

            b) The person who made the statement can avoid liability if he proves

                1] S/he acted in good faith, and
                2] S/he had no knowledge that the statement was false or misleading

            c) See "B.7.b.3)" above for materiality and intent to deceive requirements

    b. Criminal liability

        1) Willful violations of the Act, regulations, or rules
        2) Willfully making false or misleading statements with respect to any material fact in any application, report, or document

        3) Maximum fine of $10,000 and/or up to 5 years imprisonment

    c. Administrative action

        1) Suspension or revocation of license or registration
        2) Suspend trading of stock

C. State "Blue Sky" Laws

1. These are state statutes regulating the issuance and sale of securities. They contain anti-fraud and registration provisions as in the Federal Acts.

    a. They are called "Blue Sky" laws because they were first enacted to prevent investors from being sold "a piece of the sky", i.e., a worthless security

2. Must be complied with in addition to federal laws

3. If registered under 1933 Act, frequently all that is needed is to file same documents with state

    a. Exemptions from federal laws are not exemptions from state laws

4. If privately placed without registration, filings may be subject to "merit" review by state commissions

D. Foreign Corrupt Practices Act of 1977

1. It is a criminal offense to offer a bribe to a foreign official, foreign political party, or foreign political candidate for the purpose of obtaining, retaining, or directing business to any person

   a. Applies to any U.S. business enterprise including

     1) Companies required to register with the SEC under the Exchange Act of 1934
     2) Domestic business organizations, e.g., corporation, partnership, association, business trust, sole proprietorship

   b. Penalties

     1) SEC registrants and domestic concerns (other than an individual)--up to $1,000,000 fine
     2) Individuals, officers, directors, stockholders, or agents who carry out the violation--up to $10,000 fine and/or up to 5 years imprisonment

       a) The business enterprise may not reimburse this fine

2. Companies must maintain accurate books and records and a system of internal accounting controls

   a. Applies only to companies required to register with the SEC under the Exchange Act of 1934
   b. Note that this part of the Act must be complied with even if there is no foreign activity. It is a catchall provision which may be used against any SEC registrant.
   c. The books and records must in reasonable detail accurately and fairly reflect the transactions and dispositions of the assets
   d. A system of internal accounting controls must be devised and maintained which is sufficient to provide reasonable assurances that

     1) Transactions are executed in accordance with management's general or specific authorization
     2) Transactions are recorded as necessary

       a) To permit preparation of financial statements in accordance with GAAP or any other criteria applicable to such statements, and

       b) To maintain accountability for assets

     3) Access to assets is permitted only in accordance with management's general or specific authorization
     4) The recorded accountability for assets is compared with the existing assets at reasonable intervals and appropriate action is taken with respect to any differences

   e. Penalties are a maximum fine of $10,000 and/or up to 5 years imprisonment

ACCOUNTANT'S LEGAL LIABILITY

Overview

The exam tests knowledge of the accountant's civil liability under common law to clients and to third parties. This common law civil liability is based on either contract or tort theory. In addition, the accountant's civil and criminal liability imposed by the Federal Securities Acts of 1933 and 1934 is tested.

The standard of conduct imposed upon accountants is similar to that imposed upon other professional persons. That is, accountants are expected to possess an average degree of learning and skill as do other accountants and to exercise reasonable care in the application of their profession. Thus the law imposes upon the accountant the generally accepted standards of competence and care as have developed within the profession.

Primary to this liability is that the accountant must fully perform his contractual agreement with the client as set out in a carefully drafted engagement letter or agreement. In addition, the accountant is expected to adhere to generally accepted accounting principles, generally accepted auditing standards, and court decisions which have specified the accountant's contractual and tort liability.

In recent years, objective and essay questions have been of the two-step variety requiring first that the candidate understand the facts as they relate to the legal situation, and secondly, that the facts be combined with the law to arrive at an answer which parallels what one would expect a court to reach in similar circumstances.

The following definitions are important for understanding an accountant's legal liability. Be sure that you understand:

1. The distinction between ordinary and gross negligence.
2. The distinction between fraud and constructive fraud.
3. The distinction between a third party primary beneficiary and a foreseen third party.[1]
4. The meaning(s) of the term scienter.

Throughout the following outline we use the term "accountant." Some CPA questions have also used the terms independent accountant, CPA and auditor instead of the term accountant.

Accountant's Legal Liability Definitions

Privity. Privity between an accountant and others denotes a mutual legal relationship to each other by virtue of being parties to the same contract. Thus to have privity with an accountant, a person must be the actual client or be an intended user or beneficiary of the work to be done by the accountant under the contract. (Note: The Securities Acts of 1933 and 1934 each eliminate the necessity of privity as a condition for an accountant's liability to certain persons.)

Ordinary Negligence (or sometimes simply called "negligence"). The failure of an accountant to do that which an ordinary, reasonable, prudent accountant would do under the same or similar circumstances.

Gross Negligence. Lack of even slight care, indicative of reckless disregard for fact.

Contributory Negligence. Contributory negligence is a defense to an action for negligence in which the defendant accountant seeks to prove that the client's damages were also the result of the client's failure to exercise reasonable care under the existing circumstances. It is not a defense available to an accountant under the Securities Act.

Fraud. Actual fraud constitutes an intentional misrepresentation of a material fact for the purpose of deceiving another person which causes harm to the victim as a result of reliance thereon.

Constructive Fraud. Where the court finds fraud even in the absence of intended wrong, based on gross negligence or willful indifference by the performing party showing a reckless disregard for the truth.

Scienter. Most frequently defined as the intent to deceive, mislead or convey a false impression (note that this is a fraud type definition). In certain jurisdictions scienter is defined as lack of knowledge of the truth or reckless disregard for the truth (a gross negligence type of definition).

Third Party Primary Beneficiary. An **identified** third party for whose **express** benefit the audit is undertaken. Example: An accountant performs an audit knowing that the Valley State Bank has required the audit for purposes of granting a loan to the client. Valley State Bank is a third party primary beneficiary.

Foreseen Third Party. Similar to a third party primary beneficiary except that the auditor need not be aware of the third party's specific identity. Examples:

---

[1]This distinction is from R. James Gormley, <u>The Law of Accountants and Auditors, Rights, Duties and Liabilities</u> (Warren, Gorham & Lamont, 1981), Ch. 6.

1.   An accountant performs an audit of a client knowing that the client will use the audited financial statements to help obtain a bank loan from a bank which is unidentified at this point.

2.   Several lenders whose loan agreement requires an audit.

Privileged Communication. An ethics notion that all conversations or other communications between an accountant and client may not be disclosed by the accountant without the client's consent. Generally, privileged communications are not sanctioned by law.

Therefore privilege is not a valid ground for an accountant's refusing to testify when required to by legal process except in those states where privileged communications statutes have been enacted.

Working Papers. Notes, memoranda, drafts, computations, figures, data and copies, etc., that an accountant accumulates when doing professional work or services for a client. Working papers are owned by the accountant and should be retained as evidence to establish the nature, extent, and propriety of the services rendered.

18

A. Common Law Liability to Clients

1. General nature of liability and responsibility to client

   a. Generally the basis of the relationship of an accountant to his/her client is that of an independent contractor (see AGENCY)
   b. Liability is usually based on breach of contract (point "2." below) or failure to exercise due care (point "3." below)
   c. The duty to perform an audit is not delegable because it is a contract for personal services. See CONTRACTS, Assignment and Delegation.
   d. Partners in accounting firms are liable for the acts, e.g., negligence of their employees, if in the course of employment (see AGENCY)
   e. Insurance

      1) Accountants' malpractice insurance covers their negligence
      2) Fidelity bond protects the client from the accountant's fraud
      3) Client's insurance company is subrogated to client's rights (i.e., has same rights of recovery of loss against accountant as client)

   f. Privileged communications between accountant and client

      1) Do not exist at common law so must be created by statute

         a) Only a few states have privileged communications

      2) To be considered privileged, an accountant-client communication must:

         a) Be located in a jurisdiction where recognized
         b) Have been intended to be confidential at time of communication
         c) Not be waived by the client

      3) If considered privileged, valid grounds exist for the accountant to refuse to testify in court concerning these matters

      4) Code of Professional Ethics prohibits disclosure of confidential client data unless:

         a) Client consents
         b) To comply with GAAS and GAAP
         c) To comply with enforceable subpoena (e.g., courts where privilege not recognized)
         d) Quality review under AICPA authorization
         e) Responding to AICPA or state trial board

        5) Working papers

           a) Owned by accountant in absence of statute or agreement to contrary
           b) Papers (audit and other) cannot be transferred to another without client consent
           c) Retention by accountant is for evidence of nature and extent of services
           d) Accountant must keep information in papers confidential
           e) Must produce, upon an enforceable subpoena, to a court or government agency

2. Liability to clients for breach of contract

    a. If accountant fails to carry out the terms of the contract s/he is in breach and subject to a suit for money damages
    b. Accountant is not under a duty to discover fraud except when:

        1) His/her negligence prevents discovery (i.e., a "normal" audit would have detected fraud)
        2) In cases of a special purpose defalcation audit, failure to exercise the care of a reasonable person under the circumstances

    c. When a major breach (e.g., no substantial service performed) accountant is not entitled to compensation

        1) Does not apply to minor errors, inaccuracies
        2) Accountant is not entitled to compensation if s/he does not finish the audit or if s/he finishes late where time was of the essence and, therefore, client receives no benefit

    d. Where accountant is entitled to compensation, client may be able to offset damages or loss caused by breach against compensation

    e. No punitive damages for breach

    f. Client must not interfere or prevent accountant from performing

3. Liability for failure to exercise due care (tort liability for negligence)

    a. Based on an accountant's failure to exercise due professional (reasonable) care

        1) Liable to client for ordinary negligence
        2) Need not be intentional
        3) Limited to losses that use of reasonable care would have avoided

    b. Quality of work required is basically that standard expected of an accountant performing his/her work with reasonable care

        1) The accountant is not liable for an honest error in judgment as long as s/he has acted with reasonable care
        2) What is reasonable care in any given circumstance is guided by:

           a) Contract with client
           b) GAAP and GAAS
           c) Court decisions
           d) State and federal statutes

    c. In most cases, liability for negligence will not be mitigated by contributory negligence of the client. One exception is the case in which the client has restricted the accountant's investigation. This is contributory negligence on the part of the client and <u>may</u> limit auditor liability.

      d. Clients will frequently sue based both on breach of contract and for failure to exercise due professional care

4. Liability for fraud

      a. May arise in two ways

          1) <u>Intentional</u> act of deceit by the accountant (actual fraud)
          2) Gross negligence showing a reckless disregard for the truth (constructive fraud)

             EXAMPLE: An accountant performing an audit omits a vital procedure, such as performing a bank reconciliation, to save time. Although this is intent, it is not an intentional act of deceit (fraud). It is a reckless disregard for the truth.

      b. Punitive damages can be awarded for fraud or constructive fraud

B. <u>Common Law Liability to Third Parties (Nonclients)</u>.

1. Parties that may sue

      a. Anyone may sue under common law

2. Proof Requirements

      a. Plaintiff (third party) must prove damages were incurred
      b. Plaintiff must prove there was a material misstatement or omission on the financial statements
      c. Plaintiff must prove reliance on the financial statements and that such reliance led to the damages
      d. Minimum degree of deficiency in accountant behavior necessary to be proven

          1) Primary beneficiary--Plaintiff must prove ordinary negligence, gross negligence <u>or</u> fraud
          2) Foreseen third party-- Court decisions unclear at this point. Traditionally plaintiff must prove either gross negligence or fraud. However, in some cases ordinary negligence has been held to be sufficient.
          3) Other third parties--Plaintiff must prove gross negligence or fraud

3. Damages

      a. In addition to actual damages incurred, punitive damages may be allowed for claims based on gross negligence or fraud

C. <u>Statutory Liability to Third Parties--Securities Act of 1933</u>

1. General Information on Securities Act of 1933

      a. Covers the regulation of sales of securities registered under 1933 Act

          1) The Act requires registration of initial issuances of securities with the SEC
          2) Section 11 makes it unlawful for registration statement (usually Form S-1) to contain untrue <u>material</u> fact or to omit a <u>material</u> fact

             a) Material fact--One about which an average prudent investor should be informed

        b) Most potential accountant liability occurs because registration statement (and prospectus) includes audited financial statements

        c) Accountant legal liability arises for untrue material fact or omission of material fact in registration statement (or prospectus)

        d) Act does not include periodic reports to SEC or annual reports to stockholders

     3) Plaintiff need not be the initial purchaser of the security

2. Parties that may sue

    a. Purchasers of registered securities

     1) Purchaser generally must prove the specific security was offered through the registration statement

3. Proof Requirements

    a. Plaintiff (purchaser) must prove damages were incurred

    b. Plaintiff must prove there was a material misstatement or omission on the financial statements included in the registration statement

    c. Plaintiff <u>need not</u> prove reliance on the financial statements

     1) Exception--Plaintiff must prove reliance if s/he purchased security after firm issued an earnings statement covering at least 12 months subsequent to effective date of registration statement

    d. If "a." and "b." above are proven, it is a <u>prima facie</u> case (sufficient to convict the CPA unless rebutted) and shifts the burden of proof to accountant who may escape liability by proving:

     1) "Due Diligence" That is, after a reasonable investigation, the accountant had reasonable ground to believe that the statements were true and there was no material misstatement

       NOTE: Although the basis of liability is not negligence under Section II, an accountant guilty of ordinary negligence (or gross) will probably not be able to establish "due diligence"

     2) Plaintiff knew the financial statements were incorrect when the investment was made

     3) Lack of causation. The loss was due to factors other than the misstatement or omission.

4. Damages

    a. Difference between amount paid and market value at time of suit

    b. If sold, difference between amount paid and sale price

    c. Damages cannot exceed price at which the security was offered to public

    d. Plaintiff cannot recover decrease in value after the suit is brought

     1) Accountant is given benefit of any increase in market value during suit

5. Statute of limitations

    a. Action must be brought against accountant within one year from discovery (or when discovery should have been made) of false statement or omission

    b. Action must be brought within three years after security is offered to the public

D. Statutory Liability to Third Parties--Securities Exchange Act of 1934

1. General Information on Securities Exchange Act of 1934

    a. The Act regulates securities sold on national stock exchanges

        1) This includes securities traded over-the-counter and other equity securities having more than $1 million in total assets and held by 500 or more persons at the end of a fiscal year

    b. The Act requires each company to furnish to the SEC an annual report (Form 10K)

        1) Includes financial statements (not necessarily the same as an annual report to shareholders) attested to by an accountant

        2) Accountant civil liability comes from 2 sections--10 (and Rule 10b5) and 18

            a) Section 10 (and Rule 10b5)--Makes it unlawful to:

                1] Employ any device, scheme or artifice to defraud
                2] Make untrue statement of material fact or omit material fact
                3] Engage in act, practice or course of business to commit fraud or deceit in connection with purchase or sale of security

            b) Section 18--Makes it unlawful to make false or misleading statement with respect to a material statement unless done in "good faith"

2. Parties who may sue

    a. Purchasers _and_ sellers of registered securities

3. Proof requirements--Section 10 (and Rule 10b5)

    a. Plaintiff (purchaser or seller) must prove damages were incurred
    b. Plaintiff must prove there was a material misstatement or omission on information released by the firm

        1) This information may, for example, be in form of audited financial statements in report to stockholders or in Form 10K

    c. Plaintiff must prove reliance on the financial information
    d. Plaintiff must prove the existence of _scienter_

        1) E.g., an accountant guilty of "only" ordinary negligence would not be liable

4. Proof requirements--Section 18

    a. Plaintiff (purchaser or seller) must prove damages were incurred
    b. Plaintiff must prove there was a material misstatement or omission on a report (usually form 10K) filed with SEC
    c. Plaintiff must prove reliance on form 10K (this, in the past, has limited the number of cases under Section 18)
    d. If "a.", "b." and "c." are proven, the burden of proof is shifted to the accountant who may escape liability by proving that s/he acted with "good faith"

        1) Although the basis of liability here is not in negligence, an accountant who has been grossly negligent typically will not be able to establish "good faith"

        2) An accountant who has been guilty of ordinary negligence will probably be able to establish "good faith"

5. Damages

    a. Generally the difference between amount paid and market value at time of suit

    b. If sold, difference between amount paid and sale price

    c. Damages may not exceed investor's actual damages

6. Statute of Limitations

    a. Section 10 (Rule 10b5)--Varies by state (because all liability is implied in this section)

    b. Section 18--Action must be brought within 1 year after discovery of facts and within 3 years after cause of action

E. Summary of Accountant's Civil Liability[1]

THE INDEPENDENT AUDITOR'S CIVIL LIABILITY—AN OVERVIEW

	Law						
	Common				1933 Act	1934 Act	
		Third Parties			Section 11	Section 10	Section 18
Elements of Proof	Client	Primary Beneficiary	Foreseen	Ordinary	Stock Purchasers	Stock Purchasers and Sellers	Stock Purchasers and Sellers
Resultant Damages	P	P	P	P	P	P	P
Material Misstatement or Omission	P	P	P	P	P	P	P
Justifiable Reliance	P	P	P	P	D[a]	P	P
Minimum Degree of Auditor Deficiency or Behavior	P(N)	P(N)	P(N or GN)	P(GN)	D(DD)	P(GN)	D(GF)

P = Burden of proof rests with plaintiff.

D = Burden of proof rests with defendant.

N = Ordinary negligence.

GN = Gross negligence.

DD = Due diligence. This term includes the auditor's ability to show good faith in the conduct of the audit and no knowledge of the material misstatement.

GF = Good faith. Auditor must prove s/he had not acted with scienter.

a = Defendent may escape liability by proving plaintiff knew of error (omission) before purchase. Plaintiff must prove reliance if an earnings statement covering at least 12 months subsequent to registration was available when security was purchased.

F. Criminal Liability

1. Sources of Liability

    a. Securities Act of 1933 (Section 24)

    b. Securities Exchange Act of 1934 (Section 32)

    c. Various other federal statutes (e.g., Federal Mail Fraud Statute, Federal Wire Fraud Statute, Federal False Statement Statute)

    d. Various state laws

---

[1] Schultz, J. J., Jr., and K. Pany, "The Independent Auditor's Civil Liability--an Overview," *The Accounting Review* (April, 1980), p. 320 (adapted).

2. General Proof Requirements
    a. Prosecution must prove that defendent realized s/he was performing a wrongful act or
    b. Defendent deliberately closed his/her eyes to facts s/he had a duty to see
3. Examples of Possible Criminal Actions

    a. CPA aids management in a fraudulent scheme
    b. CPA covers up prior year financial statement misstatements
4. Criminal Violations of Internal Revenue Code

    a. For willfully preparing false return (perjury)
    b. For willfully assisting others to evade taxes (tax evasion)

G. Applications

1. Direct contractual liability

    a. Accountant is liable for failure to carry out contract
        1) Substantial breach

            a) May not be entitled to compensation, e.g., work was so negligently performed that client cannot use it
            b) May be liable to client for damages, e.g., the contract stated time was of the essence and accountant did not meet deadline

        2) Minor breach

            a) Liable to client for damages, e.g., minor inaccuracies in final product

        3) Client must not prevent accountant from performing
    b. Client is liable to accountant for breach

        1) E.g., wrongful discharge
        2) Liable for lost profits--see CONTRACTS, Remedies
2. Liability from audit

    a. Failure to discover irregularities, e.g., shortages, defalcations, or other fraud
        1) No duty to discover in normal audit (i.e., unless specifically contracted for)
        2) Only liable if negligence or fraud caused accountant not to discover
            a) Failure to follow up upon discovery of something amiss or circumstances indicating presence of fraud is negligence

                EXAMPLE: Not to investigate missing invoices.
            b) Liable to client for negligence or fraud

                EXAMPLE: Accountant discovers an indication of fraud and does not report this to the client.
    b. Reliance on other auditor's work

        1) Liable for other auditor's work if no mention is made of him
        2) Not liable for other auditor's work if the audit report clearly indicates divided responsibility
        3) Cannot rely on unaudited data, must qualify or disclaim opinion

    c. Inadequate disclosure

        1) E.g., no mention in the financial statements of inadequate insurance or loans to officers
        2) Relieved of liability if a qualified opinion or disclaimer is issued

    d. Subsequent events and subsequent discovery

        1) Generally not liable on the audit report for effect of events subsequent to last day of fieldwork

            a) Unless report is dated as of the subsequent event
            b) Liability extends to the effective date of registration for reports filed with the SEC

        2) Liable if subsequently discovered facts that existed at report date indicate statements were misleading unless

            a) Immediate investigation is conducted, and
            b) Prompt revision of statements is possible, or
            c) SEC and persons known to be relying on statements are notified by client or CPA

3. Liability from preparation of unaudited financial statements

    a. Financial statements are unaudited if:

        1) No auditing procedures have been applied
        2) Insufficient audit procedures have been applied to express an opinion

    b. Failure to mark each page, "unaudited"
    c. Failure to issue a disclaimer of opinion
    d. Failure to inform client of any discovery of something amiss

        1) E.g., circumstances indicating presence of fraud

4. Liability for reports and documents filed with SEC

    a. For any false or misleading statements, including omission of a material fact

        1) Unless accountant had, after reasonable investigation, reasonable grounds to believe and did believe that statements were true and not misleading at the effective date of the registration statement. Due diligence defense requires evidence from external sources and verification of information received from officers and directors.

        2) Willful omission or misstatement gives rise to criminal liability

    b. For subsequent events up to the effective date of the registration under the 1933 Act

        1) Auditor must extend his review from the date of his report to the effective date of registration

H. Liability of Income Tax Return Preparers (1976 and 1978 Revenue Acts, 1982 Tax Equity and Fiscal Responsibility Act)

1. Definitions

    a. Preparer - an individual who prepares for compensation, or who employs one or more persons to prepare for compensation, a return, or a substantial portion of a return, under Subtitle A of the Internal Revenue Code, or a claim for refund. Subtitle A of the Internal Revenue Code covers <u>income</u> tax returns; as such, the preparer of an excise tax return, a gift tax return, or an estate tax return is not considered a preparer subject to the requirements and penalties described below.

    1) A preparer need <u>not</u> be enrolled to practice before the Internal Revenue Service. Preparation of tax returns is not included under the concept of "practice before the IRS."

b. Compensation - must be received and can be implied or explicit [e.g., a person who does his neighbor's return and receives a gift has not been compensated. An accountant who prepares the individual return of the president of a company, for which he performs the audit, for no additional fee as part of a prior agreement <u>has</u> been compensated (implied)].

2. Requirements

a. Preparer must sign returns done for compensation

    1) Must be a manual signature
    2) Include preparer's identification number and address

b. Returns and claims for refund must contain the identification number of the preparer and the identification number of that preparer's employer or partnership, if any

c. Preparer must provide a finished copy of the return or refund claim to the taxpayer before or at the time when s/he presents a copy to her/him for signing

d. Employers of income tax preparers must retain information on all preparers employed by them as follows:

    1) Name
    2) Taxpayer identification number
    3) Principal place of work

e. Preparer must either keep a list of those for whom returns were filed with the following information, or copies of the actual returns, for a minimum of three years

    1) Name
    2) Taxpayer identification number
    3) Taxable year
    4) Type of return or claim for refund filed

3. Preparer penalties

a. The general period for assessing preparer penalties is three years; however, there is no statutory limitation for preparer fraud

b. Negligent or intentional disregard for the "rules and regulations" which results in an understatement of the taxpayer's liability is subject to a $100 penalty

    1) The rules and regulations include the Internal Revenue Code, the Treasury Regulations, and Revenue Rulings
    2) A reasonable position that is disclosed in the return and is taken contrary to the existing rules and regulations in good faith is <u>not</u> considered to be negligence or intentional disregard
    3) The preparer bears the burden of proof

c. Willful disregard for the "rules and regulations" resulting in an understatement of the taxpayer's liability is subject to a $500 penalty

   1) There is no limitation for assessing the penalty for willful disregard of the "rules and regulations"

d. Additional penalties related to the requirements imposed upon a tax return preparer

   1) Failure to furnish the taxpayer with a copy of the return or claim for refund. A $25 penalty per failure.
   2) Failure to retain copies of the returns for at least three years, or a list of clients. A $50 penalty per failure subject to a maximum of $25,000.
   3) Failure to sign a return. A $25 penalty per failure.
   4) Failure to include social security number or employer identification number. A $25 penalty per failure.
   5) Failure by an employer to prepare and make available a list of preparers. Subject to a penalty of $100 or $5 per item missing from the list.
   6) The preparer indorsing or negotiating a refund check issued to the taxpayer is subject to a $500 penalty per occurrence

e. Promoting abusive tax shelters, etc.

   1) Any person who

      a) Organizes and/or participates in the sale of any interest
      b) Makes a statement with respect with respect to the allowability of deduction or credit, or
      c) Makes a gross valuation overstatement as to any material matter

   2) Such person shall pay a penalty equal to the greater of $1,000 or 10% of the income to be derived by such person from the activity

f. Penalties for aiding and abetting understatement of tax liability

   1) Any person who assists in the preparation of a document under the internal revenue laws knowing that such information will be used in connection with a material matter and that the information will result in an understatement of the tax liability will be subject to a $1,000 penalty unless the understatement applies to the liability of a corporation where the penalty is $10,000

g. Fraud and false statements

   1) Any person who

      a) Willfully subscribes to a return, statement, or other document which is verified by a written declaration that is made under the penalties of perjury, and which s/he does not believe to be true and correct as to every material matter; or

      b) Willfully aids, counsels, advises, etc. in the fraudulent preparation of such documents

   2) Such person is guilty of a felony and upon conviction shall be fined not more than $100,000 ($500,000 in the case of a corporation) or imprisoned not more than 3 years, or both, together with the costs of prosecution

h. Disclosure or use of information by preparers of returns

1) Any preparer who discloses any information furnished to him/her for the preparation of a return or uses the information for any purposes other than to prepare such a return is guilty of a misdemeanor

2) Such preparer shall be fined no more than $1,000, or imprisoned not more than one year, or both, plus payment of the costs of prosecution

4. An injunction can be sought by the IRS to prohibit an income tax preparer from engaging in the following practices

a. Actions subject to disclosure requirement penalties and understatement of liability penalties
b. Actions subject to criminal penalties under the Code
c. Misrepresentation of the preparer's eligibility to practice, experience, or education as an income tax preparer
d. Guaranteeing the payment of a tax refund or allowance of a tax credit
e. Other actions of a fraudulent or deceptive nature that substantially interfere with proper administration of the Internal Revenue Law

EMPLOYER-EMPLOYEE RELATIONSHIPS

Overview

Questions on this topic are based on the Fair Labor Standards Act, the Federal Social Security Act, typical state workmen's compensation laws, and equal employment opportunity laws. In effect, these laws supplement the law of agency in that certain benefits are owed to the employee by the employer based upon their employment relationship. The emphasis of these questions is on the impact these laws have on employer-employee relationships.

The Fair Labor Standards Act questions emphasize which workers are covered by the Act and the nature of the Act's requirements, regulations, and scope. The Federal Social Security Act questions relate to the coverage and benefits of the respective programs and to the federal tax treatment of the contributions and benefits. The workmen's compensation questions emphasize the theory and purpose underlying workmen's compensation laws, typical coverage, and the respective rights of the employer and employee under a claim. The topic of equal employment opportunity laws was scheduled to be tested for the first time on the November 1983 examination.

In recent years, several multiple choice questions on the topic of employer-employee relationships have appeared on each examination. While this topic is not heavily weighted, the questions usually test memorization of the rules, such that the candidate should know and understand most of the information set out in the outline below.

Employer-Employee Relationship Definitions

Employee. One who is employed to render services and whose performance is subject to the physical control or right to control by employer, not only as to the result to be accomplished by work but also to the details and means by which the result is to be performed.

Fair Labor Standards Act. A federal act which regulates minimum wages, maximum hours of employment and overtime pay, child labor standards, and equal pay in business engaged in interstate commerce.

Workmen's Compensation. An employee is entitled to workmen's compensation, without regard to fault, for any injury or disease sustained by the employee which arises out of and in the course of employment, unless it is self-inflicted, incurred as a result of intoxication, or participation in a mutual altercation.

A. Fair Labor Standards Act

1. Fair Labor Standards Act is one of several federal statutes regulating relationship between employer and employee. Act regulates minimum wages, maximum hours of employment and overtime pay, child labor standards, and equal pay. Act's provisions relate to businesses engaged in interstate commerce.

   a. It is also called Wages and Hours Law
   b. Administered and enforced by U.S. Department of Labor's Wage and Hour Division

2. Coverage

   a. Provisions are applicable to an employee if either

      1) Employee works in interstate commerce or produces goods for interstate commerce, or
      2) Employee works for a private business engaged in interstate commerce (self-employed or unpaid family workers excluded)

      3) Interstate commerce (involving more than one state) or business which affects interstate commerce is necessary for federal laws to apply, otherwise only state laws apply

   b. Exemptions

      1) Exemptions are per particular labor standards. See following sections.
      2) But may still be covered under state law

3. Maximum Hour and Overtime Pay Provision

    a. Employees must be paid at a rate not less than time and one-half their regular rate for hours worked in excess of 40 hours per week

        1) May not average work weeks together; each work week must be treated separately
        2) No overtime required for working more than 8 hours per day

            a) However, often required by state laws and union contracts

    b. Act does not set maximum number of hours that an employee can work in a given day or week

4. Minimum Wages Provision

    a. Minimum hourly wage as of Jan. 1, 1984 is $3.35 (expected to remain at $3.35 through 1985)
    b. State minimum wage is applicable if higher than federal minimum wage established by Act
    c. May be paid in a form other than cash, e.g., where employer furnishes meals, lodging, or similar items
    d. Minimum wage requirement may be satisfied by methods of compensation other than an hourly wage rate as long as other method equals or exceeds minimum wage rate

        1) E.g., piecework, commission, salary

    e. Not excused by being in an area of low or high unemployment

5. Equal Pay Provision

    a. Equal Pay Act of 1963 enacted as amendment to Fair Labor Standards Act
    b. Prohibits discrimination in wages on basis of sex
    c. For complete discussion see Equal Employment Opportunity Laws ("D.3." below)

6. Following categories of employees are exempt from coverage of Maximum Hour and Overtime Pay Provision only

    a. Agricultural employees
    b. Seamen
    c. Taxicab drivers
    d. Household servants who reside in the household
    e. Announcers, news editors, and chief engineers of certain radio and television studios
    f. Hospital employees if agree in advance to the following condition

        1) A work period consisting of 14 consecutive days may be substituted for 7-day work week. Therefore, overtime pay provision is applicable where hospital employee works in excess of 80 hours in a 14-day work period.

7. Following categories of employees are exempt from coverage of both Maximum Hour/Overtime Pay Provision and Minimum Wage Provision

    a. Amusement and recreational business employees with seasonal workloads
    b. Persons employed in forestry and fishing industry
    c. Casual babysitters
    d. Executive, administrative, or professional employees
    e. Outside salespersons
    f. Employees of railroads, express companies, and water, motor, and air carriers

g. Also partial exemptions for

1) Learners
2) Apprentices
3) Students
4) Messengers
5) Handicapped persons

8. Child Labor Provisions

a. Child Labor Provisions prohibit employment of "oppressive child labor"
b. Employment of a child under 16 is considered oppressive and is prohibited except for

1) Employment in agriculture outside school hours
2) Child actors
3) Children under 16 employed by a parent in a nonhazardous occupation
4) Newspaper delivery

c. Employment of minors between 16 and 18 in jobs determined to be hazardous or detrimental to their health or well-being is oppressive and is prohibited

9. Enforcement Provisions

a. Illegal to ship or sell goods in interstate commerce by any person/business with knowledge that such goods were produced in violation of Fair Labor Standards Act
b. Criminal sanctions are available of fine or imprisonment for willful violations
c. Employees injured by violation may bring a civil suit against employer
d. Injunctions available to restrain future violations of Act (issued only by appropriate federal court order)
e. The Secretary of Labor has power to

1) Issue subpoenas compelling attendance by a witness and the production of records by employer
2) Conduct investigations regarding practices subject to the Act
3) Issue a wage order which requires employer to pay wages found to be due and owing under the Act

B. Federal Social Security Act

1. Social insurance programs under Act cover old-age, survivor's and disability insurance, hospital insurance (Medicare), and unemployment insurance

a. Old-age, survivor's, disability, and hospital insurance programs are financed out of taxes paid by employers, employees, and self-employed under provisions of Federal Insurance Contributions Act and Self-Employment Contributions Act
b. Unemployment insurance programs are financed out of taxes paid by employers under both state and federal unemployment insurance laws

2. Coverage under Social Security Act is mandatory

a. A person may not elect not to be covered
b. Nor may a person give up his/her rights in exchange for money or other benefits
c. All employees are covered, whether part-time or full-time

3. Federal Insurance Contributions Act (FICA)

a. Imposes social security tax on employees, self-employed, and employers
b. Social security tax applies to compensation received which is considered to be "wages"
c. Tax rates are same for both employer and employee

    1) Tax rate for employer <u>and</u> employee is 7.00 percent for 1984 (7.05 percent for 1985). A cre<u>dit</u> of .3 percent of covered wages is allowed to employees for 1984 only.

        a) Paid only on the first $37,800 of wages in 1984*
        b) Employee must pay tax on earnings up to this base amount ($37,800), but is entitled to refund if tax is paid on amount in excess of base amount (i.e., FICA withholding exceeds the amount required by law to be withheld)

            1] This may happen when employee works for two separate employers at same time

    2) Tax rate and base amount dollar limitation are subject to change as Social Security Act is amended by Congress

d. It is employer's duty to withhold employee's share of FICA from employee's wages and remit both this amount and employer's equal share to government

    1) Employer is required to match FICA contributions of employees on a dollar-for-dollar basis
    2) If employer neglects to withhold, employer may be liable for both employee's and employer's share of taxes, i.e., to pay double tax (100% penalty)
    3) Employer is required to furnish employee with a written statement of wages paid and FICA contributions withheld during calendar year

e. Neither pension plans nor any other programs may be substituted for FICA coverage

4. Self-Employment Contributions Act*

a. Self-employed persons are required to report their own taxable earnings and pay required social security tax
b. Self-employment income is net earnings from self-employment
c. Applicable to first $37,800 of self-employment income at a net rate of 11.3 percent for 1984 (net rate of 11.8 percent for 1985)
d. The $37,800 is reduced by any wages received in tax year

    1) Because FICA will be paid on wages

5. Unemployment Insurance (Federal Unemployment Tax Act)

a. Tax is used to provide unemployment compensation benefits to workers who lost their jobs and cannot find replacement work
b. Federal unemployment tax must be paid if employer employs one or more persons covered by act <u>or</u> pays wages of $1,500 or more during any calendar quarter
c. Tax paid to federal government on only first $7,000 of wages at a rate of 3.5 percent for 1984 (6.2 percent for 1985)
d. Must also pay a state unemployment tax

---

*Amount for 1985 has not yet been set by Congress.

1) An employer is entitled to a credit against his/her federal unemployment tax for state unemployment taxes paid (maximum 2.7 percent credit for 1984 and maximum 5.4 percent credit for 1985)

2) State unemployment tax may be raised or lowered according to number of claims against employer

3) If an employer pays a low state unemployment tax because of a good employment record, then s/he is entitled to an additional credit against its federal unemployment tax based on difference between

   a) His/her tax rate, and
   b) Highest state tax rate (or 2.7 percent for 1984 and 5.4 percent for 1985 if state rate is higher)

6. Coverage under Social Security Act

   a. Must be an "employee"
   b. Services rendered must be "employment"
   c. Compensation received must be "wages"

7. Definitions

   a. Wages--all compensation for employment

      1) Include

         a) Money wages
         b) Other forms of compensation
         c) Servicemen's base pay
         d) Bonus and commissions
         e) Vacation and dismissal allowances
         f) Tips paid in cash if greater than $20

      2) Exclude

         a) Wages greater than $37,800*
         b) Travel expenses
         c) Employee medical and hospital expenses paid by employer
         d) Employee insurance premiums paid by employer
         e) Payment to employee retirement plan by employer

   b. Employee--person whose performance is subject to physical control or right to control by employer

      1) Required to comply with directions and details of where, when, and how work is to be performed
      2) Partners, self-employed persons, and independent contractors are not covered by unemployment compensation provisions since they are not "employees." They are covered as self-employed persons for old-age, survivor's, and disability insurance program purposes.

      3) Officers and directors of corporations are "employees" if they perform services and receive remuneration for these services from corporation

   c. Employer--one who employs services of others
   d. Employment--all service performed by an employee for person employing him

      1) Must be continuing or recurring work

   e. Self-employment--carrying on a trade or a business either as an individual or in a partnership

---

*Amount for 1985 has not yet been set by Congress.

       1) Can be both employed (in one job) and self-employed (another business), but must meet requirements of a trade or business, i.e., not a hobby, occasional investment, etc.

8. Old-age, survivor's, and disability insurance benefits

   a. Availability of benefits depends upon attainment by individual of "insured status"

      1) A certain length of working time ("quarters of coverage") is required to obtain insured status
      2) Employees and self-employed persons will receive one quarter of coverage for each $370 of earnings in a year, up to a maximum of four quarters per year
      3) A person is "fully insured" when s/he has been credited with either

         a) Forty quarters of coverage, or
         b) One quarter of coverage each year from age 21 until death or retirement

      4) A person is "currently insured" when s/he has been credited with at least six quarters of coverage during 13-quarter period ending with his/her death, disability, or retirement

   b. An individual who is "fully insured" is eligible for following benefits

      1) Survivor benefits for widow or widower and dependents
      2) Benefits for disabled worker and his/her dependents
      3) Old-age retirement benefits payable to retired worker and dependents

         a) Retirement age to receive full benefits is 65

      4) Lump-sum death benefits

   c. An individual who is "currently insured" is eligible for following benefits

      1) Limited survivor benefits
      2) Benefits for disabled worker and his/her dependents
      3) Lump-sum death benefits

   d. Amount of benefits depends upon

      1) Average monthly earnings, and
      2) Relationship of beneficiary to retired, deceased, or disabled worker

         a) E.g., husband, wife, child, grandchild--may be entitled to different benefits

9. Reduction of social security benefits

   a. Early retirement (results in reduced benefits)
   b. Returning to work after retirement can affect social security benefits

      1) Earnings, after retirement, which exceed an annual limitation results in reduced benefits of $1 in benefits for each $2 of earnings above a specified amount of annual earnings

         a) A person age 70 or older will not suffer a reduction in retirement benefits

      2) Income from savings, investment, insurance, or royalties do not affect benefits

3) Income from a limited partnership is considered investment income rather than self-employment income

10. Federal income tax treatment

   a. Benefits are recovered on a tax-free basis when received by individual (i.e., excluded from gross income)
   b. Since social security benefits are not included in gross income, employee's social security tax payments cannot be deducted from gross income
   c. Employer's portion of social security tax payments is deductible from his/her gross income

11. Unemployment benefits

   a. Eligibility for and amount of unemployment benefits are governed by state laws
   b. Does not include self-employed
   c. Generally available only to persons unemployed through no fault of their own; however, not available to seasonal workers if paid on a yearly basis, e.g., professional sports player in off-season
   d. One must have worked for a certain period of time and/or earned a certain amount of wages

C. Workmen's Compensation Acts

1. Workmen's compensation is a form of strict liability whereby employer is liable to employee for injuries or diseases sustained by employee which arise out of and in course (scope) of employment

2. Purpose

   a. To give employees certainty of benefits with little difficulty and no expense for job-related injuries or diseases

      1) Previously, employee had to sue employer for negligence to receive any benefits in form of damages
      2) Employee usually cannot waive his/her right to benefits

   b. Puts burden where it can be afforded, i.e., cost is passed on as an expense of production to be borne by employers (industry)

   c. No fault need be shown. Payment is automatic upon satisfaction of requirements.

      1) Removes employer's common law defenses of

         a) Assumption of risk--employee assumed risk of injury upon consenting to do work
         b) Negligence of a fellow employee (fellow servant doctrine)--employer could avoid liability by proving it was another employee's fault
         c) Contributory negligence--injured employee was also negligent

3. Regulated by the states

   a. Except that federal government employees are covered by a federal statute
   b. Each state has its own statute

4. Generally, there are two types of statutes

   a. Elective statutes (rapidly disappearing under threat of federal intervention)

        1) Employer may accept or reject provisions of statute

        2) If employer rejects, s/he loses three common law defenses (see "C.2.c.1)" above) against an employee's common law suit for damages

        3) Most employers accept workmen's compensation provisions, since loss of these common law defenses seriously impairs an employer's overall legal defense when an employee sues for damages

  b. Compulsory statutes (strong trend)

        1) Require that all employers within coverage of statute provide benefits

        2) Majority of states has compulsory coverage

5. Insurance required to provide benefits

  a. Employer may obtain an insurance policy

        1) Either with a state fund or a private company

  b. In lieu of an insurance policy, an employer may assume liability for workmen's compensation claims but must show proof of financial responsibility to carry own risk--i.e., self-insurance

6. Legislative scope

  a. Workmen's compensation coverage extends to all employees who are injured on job or in course (scope) of employment

        1) During an authorized time;

        2) In an authorized geographical location; and

        3) While acting in furtherance of employer's business purpose

  b. Coverage does not extend to employee while traveling to or from work

  c. Out of state work may be covered if it meets above mentioned criteria

  d. Although all states have a workmen's compensation law, not all employees are covered

        1) Exemptions

            a) Agricultural workers

            b) Domestic workers

            c) Casual employees, i.e., employment not in usual course of business or not regular

            d) Public employees (less frequently exempted than others)

            e) Employers who employ below a fixed number of people, e.g., four or five (half the states--no exemption)

  e. Must be an employee; coverage does not extend to independent contractors

  f. Most workmen's compensation laws extend coverage to minors

7. Legal action for damages

  a. Employers covered by workmen's compensation insurance are generally exempt from lawsuits by employees

  b. Acceptance of benefits under workmen's compensation laws by an employee is in lieu of an action for damages against employer and such a suit is barred

        1) Employer assumes a definite liability (strict liability) in exchange for employee giving up his/her common law rights to sue employer for damages

        2) When employee is covered by workmen's compensation law, his/her sole remedy against employer is that which is provided for under appropriate workmen's compensation act (exclusivity of remedy)

c. Employee is entitled to workmen's compensation benefits without regard to fault

1) Negligence or even gross negligence of injured employee is not a bar to recovery
2) Employee's negligence plays no role in determination of amount of benefits awarded
3) However, injuries caused by intentional self-infliction, participation in mutual altercation, or intoxication of employee do constitute a bar to recovery

d. When employer fails to provide workmen's compensation insurance or when employer's coverage is inadequate, injured employee may sue in common law for damages, and employer cannot resort to usual common law defenses. (See "C.2.c.1)" above.)

8. Actions against third parties

a. Employee's acceptance of workmen's compensation benefits does not bar a suit against a third party whose negligence caused injury

1) If employee sues and recovers from third party, employer (or its insurance carrier) is entitled to compensation for workmen's compensation benefits paid to employee

a) Any recovery in excess of workmen's compensation benefits received belongs to injured employee

b. If employee accepts workmen's compensation benefits, employer (or its insurance carrier) is subrogated to right of employee against a third party whose negligence caused injury

1) Therefore, if employee elects not to sue third party, employer (or its insurance carrier) obtains employee's right of action against third person

9. Claims

a. Normally administered by a state compensation board or commission
b. Employers are required to report all injuries to compensation board
c. Employees are required to give prompt notice of injury

1) Employee usually has thirty days to notify employer, and from sixty days to two years to file a claim with state compensation board

2) Time period normally begins to run from time injury is first noticed rather than from time of accident

3) In some states, failure to file claim on time may bar employee's recovery. In other states, failure to file claim on time will bar recovery only if delay has been prejudicial to employer.

10. Benefits

a. Medical

1) Provides for medical care to an injured or diseased employee

a) Normally unlimited with regard to time and dollar amount limitations

b. Disability

1) This is a partial wage continuation plan whereby employee is paid a percentage of his regular weekly wage subject to a maximum amount and maximum number of payments

c. Death

1) Various plans and schedules provide payments to widow and minor children

a) May be discontinued upon remarriage of widow or children reaching majority (usually 18)

d. Special provisions

1) Normally, statutes call for specific scheduled payments for loss of a limb or an eye
2) Also, if employee's injury is of a nature which prevents his returning to his occupation, plan may pay cost of retraining to prepare him for another occupation (rehabilitation)

e. Normally not subject to waiver by employee

D. Equal Employment Opportunity Laws

1. 1964 Civil Rights Act, Title VII, and Equal Employment Act of 1972 (which amends Title VII of 1964 Civil Rights Act)

a. Establish legal foundations to provide equal employment opportunity
b. It shall be unlawful employment practice for any employer or "person"

1) To fail or refuse to hire or to discharge any individual, or otherwise to discriminate against any individual with respect to compensation, terms, conditions, or privileges of employment because of such individual's race, color, religion, sex, or national origin

2) To limit, segregate, or classify his/her employees or applicants for employment in any way which would deprive or tend to deprive any individual of employment opportunities or otherwise adversely affect his status as employee, because of such individual's race, color, religion, sex, or national origin

c. Employers and "persons" covered

1) Public or private employers conducting business in an industry which affects interstate commerce having at least fifteen employees working for twenty or more weeks in current or preceding calendar year
2) Labor unions having at least fifteen members
3) Employment agencies
4) Joint labor-management committees for apprenticeship and training
5) Federal, state, and local governmental agencies

d. Defenses available

1) An employer is allowed to discriminate on basis of sex, national origin, or religion of any individual where sex, national origin, and/or religion are bona fide occupational qualifications (BFOQ) reasonably necessary for normal conduct of employer's business

EXAMPLE: Baptist church refusing to hire a Lutheran minister.

> *EXAMPLE: Male health club refusing to hire a female locker room attendant.*

   a) Omission of race and color from this exception may mean that Congress does not feel these two factors are ever bona fide occupational qualifications

2) Employers who are working under government security programs can deny employment to individuals because of their inability to obtain security clearance
3) Employers can establish different standards, compensation, terms, or conditions of employment if they are applied pursuant to a bona fide seniority or merit system, or a system which measures earnings by quantity and quality of production, or if they result from fact that employees work in different locations
4) Employer can give and act upon results of any professionally developed ability test (valid in statistical sense and in terms of content and construct) provided that such test, its administration, or action upon results is not designed, intended, or used to discriminate because of race, color, religion, sex, or national origin

e. Equal Employment Opportunity Commission (EEOC) was created to administer and enforce law

1) EEOC has following powers

   a) Receive and investigate complaints
   b) Require production of documentary evidence
   c) Examine and copy evidence
   d) Instigate and sustain informal conciliation proceedings
   e) Subpoena and examine witnesses under oath
   f) Sue an alleged violator
   g) File a civil suit in federal district court
   h) Issue and publish interpretations of Title VII of Civil Rights Act

2) EEOC has following remedies available for its use

   a) Reinstate employees to their prior employment
   b) Award back pay to employees
   c) Hire, reinstate, or promote victim of discriminatory practice
   d) Obtain an injunction to restrain future violations of law
   e) Exercise any other relief for a person "injured" as a result of a violation of law

2. Pregnancy Discrimination Act of 1978

a. Amended 1964 Civil Rights Act, Title VII, to define term "sex" to include pregnancy and pregnancy disabilities

b. Prohibits employers from discriminating against women workers based on pregnancy, childbirth, or related medical conditions. (See "D.1.b." above.)

1) Constitutes unlawful sex discrimination under Title VII of Civil Rights Act
2) Law covers unmarried as well as married pregnant women

   c. Coverage provisions

     1) Employers with health or disability plans must cover pregnancy, child-birth, and related medical conditions in same manner that other conditions are covered

     2) Employer cannot force a pregnant woman to stop working until her baby is born, provided she is capable of performing her duties properly

     3) Employer cannot specify how long a leave of absence must be taken after childbirth

3. Equal Pay Act of 1963

   a. Enacted as an amendment to Fair Labor Standards Act. (See "A.5." above.)

   b. Prohibits employers from discriminating on basis of sex in paying wages for equal work performed

     1) Equal wages must be paid for equal work on jobs requiring equal skills, effort, and responsibility to be performed under similar working conditions

   c. Amount of pay may be differentiated on basis of

     1) A system which measures earnings by quantity or quality of production
     2) Seniority system
     3) Merit system
     4) Differential based on any factor other than sex

     EXAMPLE: Shift differential--people who work on night shift may be paid more than people who work on day shift.

   d. Any wage differential based on sex must be remedied by raising lower wage rate; an employer is not permitted to reduce wage rate of any other employee to comply with equal pay provisions

   EXAMPLE: Employee X (a male worker) is paid $10/hour for work performed. Employee Y (a female worker) is paid $8/hour for doing the same job under similar working conditions. To remedy such discrimination, and to comply with the equal pay provisions, the employer must raise employee Y's pay rate to $10/hour.

   e. Equal Pay Act initially interpreted and enforced by Department of Labor, but responsibility for law was given to EEOC

4. Age Discrimination in Employment Act (1967), as amended in 1978

   a. It shall be unlawful employment practice for any employer or "person"

     1) To fail or refuse to hire, to discharge any individual, or otherwise to discriminate against persons with respect to compensation, terms, conditions, or privileges of employment because of such individual's age

     2) To limit, segregate, or classify employees or applicants for employment in any way which would deprive or tend to deprive any individual of employment opportunities or otherwise adversely affect his status as employee because of such individual's age

       a) Applies to persons between 40 and 70 years of age
       b) Promotes employment of older persons based on their abilities rather than on age

b. Same employers and "persons" covered under 1964 Civil Rights Act, Title VII, are covered under this act. (See "D.1.c." above.)

c. 1978 amendments to Age Discrimination in Employment Act prohibit mandatory retirement before age 70 for most workers employed by private business with at least twenty employees

d. Defenses available

    1) Law allows an employer to discriminate on basis of age when

        a) A certain age is a bona fide occupational qualification or requirement reasonably necessary for usual conduct of employer's business

        EXAMPLE: Movie production company refusing to hire a 55 year old man for an actor's role requiring a teenager.

        b) Treatment accorded employee is pursuant to terms of a bona fide seniority system or employee benefit plan (e.g., a layoff, pension, promotion, or insurance plan)

PROPERTY

Overview

Property is anything capable of being owned, i.e., the rights related to the ownership of things that society will recognize and enforce. Property is classified as real, personal, tangible, intangible, and public or private. Protection of property and settlement of disputes concerning property is a major function of the legal system.

Generally property as a topic is tested with multiple choice questions. The candidate should be able to distinguish between personal and real property and between tenancies in common, joint tenancies, and tenancies by the entirety. The candidate also should understand that any instrument given primarily as security is a mortgage and be able to distinguish between the legal results arising from "assumption" of a mortgage and taking one "subject to" a mortgage. Other questions concerning mortgages frequently require basic knowledge of the concepts of novation, suretyship, subrogation, redemption, and purchase money mortgages.

Questions on deeds usually distinguish between the legal implication of warranty deeds, quitclaim deeds, and special warranty deeds. Both mortgages and deeds must be publicly recorded, and the questions frequently require the candidate to identify a priority, discuss estoppel, and explain constructive notice. The most important topics under landlord and tenant are the Statute of Frauds, quiet enjoyment, the effect of a sale of leased property, assignment, destruction of the premises, remedies of the parties, and the various kinds of notices for termination of leases.

Property Definitions

Real Property. Land and things attached to the land in a permanent manner (includes crops and fixtures).

Personal Property. Anything capable of ownership that is not classified as real property.

Fixtures. Property which has changed its character from personal into real by virtue of having been attached to realty with the intent to make it a permanent attachment. Most fixtures are real property. Trade fixtures, fixtures used in a business, are readily detachable, e.g., barber chair, and are personal property.

Joint Tenancy. Concurrent ownership of property by two or more persons under an arrangement whereby the interest of a deceased tenant passes to the surviving joint tenants and not to the decedent's heirs. (Right of Survivorship.)

Tenancy in Common. Concurrent ownership of property by two or more persons under an arrangement whereby the interest of a deceased tenant in common passes to the deceased's heirs and not to the other tenants in common.

Warranty Deed. Contains unconditional promises by the grantor that he has title to the land he is conveying (or has authority to convey for the owner). Also warranted is that property is free from all encumbrances except for those that have been disclosed, that the grantee shall be assured of quiet enjoyment, and that the grantor will defend the grantee's title against claims by other persons.

Quitclaim Deed. A deed whereby the grantor conveys whatever interest in the subject land that the grantor owns, but makes no warranty of title.

Purchase Money Mortgage. A mortgage created concurrently with the sale of land and delivered by the buyer to the seller to secure the unpaid balance of the purchase price.

Assumption of Mortgage. A buyer who purchases mortgaged property and assumes the mortgage becomes personally liable on the mortgage. The seller also remains liable on the mortgage unless released by the mortgagee (which is called a novation).

Subject To. A buyer who purchases mortgaged property and only takes subject to the mortgage, does not personally become liable on the mortgage. However the mortgagee may foreclose and sell the property to pay the mortgage if he is not paid otherwise.

A. General Concepts

1. Personal property may be either

   a. Tangible--subject to physical possession

   > EXAMPLE: *An inventory of automobiles is tangible property.*

   b. Intangible--not subject to physical possession but subject to legal ownership

   > EXAMPLE: *Contractual rights to receive payments for automobiles that have been sold are intangible personal property.*

2. Gift

This is no longer being tested effective November, 1983.

3. Bailment

This is no longer being tested effective November, 1983.

4. Fixtures--an item that was originally personal property, but which is affixed to real property in a relatively permanent fashion such that it is considered to be part of the real property

   a. There are several factors which must be applied in determining whether personal property which has been attached to real property is a fixture (realty)

      1) Affixer's objective intent as to whether property is to be regarded as personalty or realty

         a) In general, a court will hold that an item is a fixture if it were the intention of the parties that it becomes part of the real property

         b) If the intent is clear, then this becomes the controlling factor in the determination of whether an item is a fixture or not

         c) This intent can be determined from various factors

            1] The intention of the parties as expressed in the agreement
            2] The nature of the article affixed
            3] The relationship of the parties (i.e., the affixer and the owner of the real property)

      2) The method and permanence to which the item is physically attached (annexed to the real property)

         a) If the item cannot be removed without material injury to the real property, it is generally held that the item has become part of the realty (i.e., a fixture)

      3) Adaptability of use of the personal property for the purpose for which the real property is used

         a) If the personal property is necessary or beneficial to the use of the real property, the more likely the item is a fixture

         b) But if the use or purpose of the item is unusual for the type of realty involved, it might be reasonable to conclude that it is personalty, and the affixer intends to remove the item when s/he leaves

      4) The property interest of that person in the real property at the time of the attachment of the item

   b. A trade fixture is an item installed (affixed) by a tenant in connection with a business s/he is conducting on the leased premises

     EXAMPLE: A tenant who is leasing the premises for use as a grocery store installs a refrigeration unit on the property. This refrigeration unit is integral to the conducting of business for which the tenant occupies the premises and therefore qualifies as a trade fixture.

      1) The personal property must be brought onto the leased business premises for the purpose of conducting and engaging in the trade or business for which the tenant occupies the premises

2) Trade fixtures remain personal property, giving the tenant the right to remove these items upon expiration of the lease

    a) But the tenant's right is limited to the extent that his/her action of removing the fixture may not materially damage the realty. If the item is so affixed onto the real property that removing it would cause substantial damage, then it is considered part of the realty.

B. Interests in Real Property

1. Present interests

    a. Fee simple absolute--complete and perpetual ownership

        1) Undivided ownership
        2) Highest estate in law (has the most ownership rights)
        3) May be restricted by easements, mortgages, state laws, etc.
        4) May be transferred inter vivos (while living), by intestate succession (without will), or by will (testate at death)

        5) Most private residences are fee simple absolute estates although they are commonly subject to mortgage

    b. Fee simple defeasible

        1) Fee simple determinable--upon the happening of the stated event the estate automatically reverts to the grantor

        EXAMPLE: Conveyance to the holder of an interest was, "to A as long as A uses it for church purposes." The interest will revert back to the grantor or his heirs if the property is not used for church purposes.

        2) Fee simple subject to condition subsequent--upon the happening of the stated event the grantor must take affirmative action to divest the grantee of the estate

        EXAMPLE: Conveyance to the holder of the interest was "to A, but if liquor is ever served on the premises, the grantor has right to re-enter the premises." The grantor has power of termination so as to repossess the premises.

    c. Life interest--an interest whose duration is usually measured by the life of the holder but may be measured by life of some other person

    EXAMPLE: Conveyance of land, "to A so long as he shall live."

        1) Upon termination (death), the property reverts to the grantor or his heirs, or to a named remainderman
        2) Usual life interest can be transferred by deed only, i.e., not by a will because it ends on death
        3) Holder of a life interest is entitled to ordinary use and profits of land but he may not commit waste (injure interests of remainderman)

            a) Must maintain property (in a reasonable state of repair), pay taxes on it, and pay the interest on a mortgage
            b) May not damage it such as by cutting all the trees or by extracting all the minerals
            c) May take profits, e.g., minerals, to the extent the grantor did before conveying or to the extent grantor contemplated them to be taken

    d.   Leaseholds--see Landlord-Tenant at end of PROPERTY module

2. Future interest (the holder of the interest has the right or possibility of possession in the future)

    a.   Reversion--future interest is left with transferor or his heirs at the end of transferee's estate

        1) Usually kept when conveying a life interest or an interest for a definite period of time

            EXAMPLE: *X conveys, "to Y for life" or "to Y for 10 years." X has a reversion.*

    b.   Remainder--future interest is in a third party at the end of transferee's estate

           EXAMPLE: *X conveys, "to Y for life, remainder to Z and his heirs."*

3. Concurrent interest--two or more persons (co-tenants) have undivided interests and concurrent possessory rights in real or personal property

    a.   Tenancy in common

        1) A concurrent interest with no right of survivorship
        2) Interest passes to heirs or devisees
        3) Unless stated otherwise, multiple grantees are presumed to be tenants in common

    b.   Joint tenancy (with right of survivorship)

        1) A concurrent interest with all rights of ownership going to the surviving joint tenants
        2) Most states have statutes which allow property to be put in a joint tenancy simply by express declaration (may have to use the term "joint tenancy with right of survivorship" and not as tenants in common)

    c.   Tenancy by the entirety

        1) Joint interest held by husband and wife
        2) It is presumed when both spouses' names appear on title document
        3) To transfer, both must convey
        4) Each spouse has a right of survivorship
        5) Divorce creates a tenancy in common

    d.   Rights and duties

        1) Each has the right to possess all portions of the property
        2) Joint tenant and tenant in common may convey their individual interest

            a) Tenancy in common--co-tenant may convey his individual interest in the whole but cannot convey a specific portion of the property

            b) Joint tenancy--as above, a specific portion of the property may not be conveyed. Transferee becomes a tenant in common (no right of survivorship) with other co-tenants. Co-tenants who did not convey remain joint tenants with right of survivorship.

        3) Co-tenants may terminate by judicial partition
        4) Co-tenants must contribute to taxes, repairs, etc.
        5) Creditors may compel partition to satisfy debts

4. Powers of appointment--power or authority to dispose of property or an interest in property

a. Holder of a power of appointment may either

    1) Exercise the power; recipients of the property or interest are appointees, or

    2) Not exercise the power; recipients of the property or interest are takers in default

    EXAMPLE: In his will, H gives W the power of appointment over a ranch he owns. H also provides that if W does not exercise this power by the time W dies, the ranch shall go to H's first child.

b. Types of powers

    1) General--holder of power may appoint anyone including himself

    2) Special--holder of power may only appoint from a specific group

    EXAMPLE: In his will, H gives W, his wife, a power of appointment over his ranch. H further provides that W only give this ranch to one of their children.

5. Easement--one person's right to make use of another's land

a. Types

    1) Easement appurtenant is an easement which involves two parcels of land

        a) The easement or right benefits one parcel (the dominant land) and burdens the other parcel (the servient land)

        EXAMPLE: The right to cross land to get to other land.

    2) Easement in gross is a personal right to use another's land and <u>not</u> connected to a second piece of land

    EXAMPLE: The owner gives a friend the right to hunt on his land.

b. Classes of easements

    1) Affirmative easement allows positive acts on the servient estate, the most common class of element

    EXAMPLE: The right to hunt.

    2) Negative easement deprives the owner of the servient estate of some right

    EXAMPLE: The right to light deprives the owner of a servient estate from building too high and shutting off the light to the dominant estate.

c. Formation

    1) By express grant or by reservation in a grant of land

    2) By necessity--right of access where no other way to reach land

    3) By prescription--adverse use of land, e.g., a path, by third parties. Similar to adverse possession. Necessary elements are

        a) Hostile or adverse use of, not permissive

        b) Open and notorious, not secretive

        c) Continuous and without interruption, i.e., never been stopped

        d) For the period of prescription (by state statute), e.g., 10 years

            1] Anytime use is stopped by owner or agent, period starts over again

d. Conveyance

    1) Easements appurtenant follow the land, the sale of either the dominant or servient tract does not affect the easement

    2) Easements in gross are not assignable (to other than the owner of the servient land) unless it was within the expectations of the parties on formation

      EXAMPLE: The right to hunt given to an individual is probably not assignable.

      EXAMPLE: The right to hunt given to a club probably is assignable because the expectation was for a large amount of use.

      a) Commercial easements are more commonly assignable because of expected use

6. License--allows one person permissive use (usually revocable) of the property of another
7. Profit--right to take something from another's land, e.g., timber, minerals, water

  a. Formation by grant or by prescription
  b. Cannot be apportioned (subleased) if it would increase the burden on the land

C. Adverse Possession

1. Possessor of land may acquire title if he holds for the statutory period

  a. The statutory period is the running of the Statute of Limitations. Varies by state from 5 to 20 years.
  b. The statute begins to run upon the taking of possession. The true owner must commence legal action before the statute runs or the adverse possessor obtains title.
  c. Successive possessors may tack (cumulate the required time together)

    1) Each possessor must transfer to the other. One cannot abandon or the statute begins over again for the next possessor.

  d. Disabilities of the true owner toll the statute, e.g., insanity, minority

    1) Disability must be present when cause of action first arises (when claimant takes possession). Disabilities arising while the statute is running do not affect.
    2) True owner of a future interest, e.g., a remainder, is not effected by adverse possession

      EXAMPLE: X dies and leaves his property to A for life, remainder to B. A pays little attention to the property and a third party acquires it by adverse possession. When A dies, B is entitled to the property regardless of the adverse possession.

2. Necessary elements

  a. Open and notorious possession

    1) Means type of possession that would give reasonable notice to anyone of claim of dominion

   b. Hostile possession

       1) Must act as an owner (not subordinate) or indicate intentions of owner-
           ship
       2) Color of title satisfies this requirement. When possession is taken
           under good faith belief in a defective instrument or deed purporting to
           convey the land.

       3) Does not occur when possession started permissively or as co-tenants
       4) Not satisfied if possessor acknowledges other's ownership

           a) Must claim the right to the land

   c. Actual possession

       1) Possession of land consistent with its normal use, e.g., farm land must
           be farmed

   d. Continuous possession

       1) Need not be constant, but may not be intermittent. Possession as norm-
           ally used.

   e. Exclusive possession

       1) The possession must be to the exclusion of all other persons

D. Contracts for Sale of Land

1. Generally precede transfers of land. Often includes escrows. (See "E.5.d.")

   *EXAMPLE: An earnest money agreement. The purchaser puts the money down to
   show his seriousness while he investigates the title (marketability) and
   arranges for a mortgage.*

   a. Generally, agreement must

       1) Be in writing and signed by the party to be bound
       2) Identify land and parties
       3) Identify purpose
       4) Contain terms or promises
       5) Contain purchase price

   b. Assignable unless prohibited in contract

2. If not expressed, there is an implied promise that seller will provide a
    marketable title

   a. A marketable title is one reasonably free from doubt. Does not contain
       such defects as breaks in the chain of title, outstanding liens, or de-
       fective instruments in the past (chain of title).

       1) Zoning restrictions do not make a title unmarketable

   b. Agreement may provide for marketable or "insurable" title

       1) Insurable title is one which a title insurance company will insure
           against defects, liens, and invalidity

   c. If title is not marketable, purchaser may

       1) Rescind and recover any down payment
       2) Sue for damages
       3) Sue for specific performance with a reduction in price

3. Risk of loss before deed is conveyed, e.g., if house burns who bears the burden?

    a. General rule is purchaser bears the risk of loss, subject to terms of the contract
    b. Courts might look to who has the most ownership rights and benefits, i.e., who would be owner in equity court? Normally the buyer.
    c. Either party can insure against a risk of loss

E. Conveyance by Deed

1. Warranty deeds contain the following covenants (unconditional promises)

    a. Title. Grantor has title of land he is conveying.
    b. Right to convey. Grantor has authority to convey.
    c. Free from encumbrances. Land is not burdened by any encumbrances, e.g., easements except as disclosed in the deed.
    d. Quiet enjoyment. Neither grantor nor third party with rightful claim will disturb grantee's possession.
    e. Further assurance. Grantor will procure any further documents to perfect title.
    f. General warranty. Grantor will defend title against claims by other parties.
    g. The first three are only breached at the time of conveyance. The rest cannot be breached until possession is interfered with.

2. Bargain and sale deed

    a. Generally, only convenants that grantor has done nothing to impair title, e.g., he has not created any encumbrances
    b. Does not warrant against prior (before grantor's ownership) impairments

3. Quitclaim deed conveys only whatever interest in land the grantor has. No warranty of title is made by grantor.

    a. It is insurable, recordable, and mortgagable as with any other deed

4. Clauses of a deed

    a. Premises clause includes

        1) Date
        2) Name of grantor and grantee
        3) Purpose of conveyance
        4) Consideration

    b. Granting clause contains

        1) Words of conveyance
        2) Description of the land

    c. Habendum or "to have" clause setting forth estate conveyed
    d. Reddendum clause contains any reservations, e.g., easements
    e. Covenants and warranties of title
    f. Signature, seal, and attestation of witnesses

5. There must be delivery for the deed to be effective. Intent is important. There must be an intent on the part of the grantor to pass title (convey) to the grantee.

a. Possession of the deed by grantee raises a presumption (rebuttable) of delivery

b. Possession of the deed by grantor raises a presumption (rebuttable) of no delivery

c. A recorded deed raises a presumption (rebuttable) of delivery

d. A deed given to a third party to give to the grantee upon performance of a condition is a delivery in escrow

    1) Escrow agent is an intermediary between the two parties. He holds the deed until the grantee pays him the money, then gives the deed to the grantee and the money to the grantor.

    2) Where grantor dies while deed is in escrow, upon performance by the grantee the date of delivery relates back to the time of delivery to escrow so there can be a valid delivery

6. Recording a deed gives constructive notice to the world (as a matter of law) of the grantee's ownership

a. Protects grantee (new owner) against subsequent purchasers

    EXAMPLE: X sells land to Y. Y records his deed. Later X sells land to Z. Z loses as against Y because Y recorded the deed giving constructive notice of the prior sale.

b. Deed is valid between immediate parties without recording

c. Most recording statutes are of either the notice type or the race-notice type

    1) Notice type--a subsequent purchaser (bona fide) who takes without notice of the first sale has priority

        a) I.e., if a grantee does not record immediately, he may lose his priority

    2) Race-notice--subsequent purchaser (bona fide) who takes without notice and records first, has priority

d. Notice refers to actual knowledge of prior sale and constructive knowledge, i.e., one is deemed to be aware of what is filed in the records

e. To be a purchaser, one must give value which does not include antecedent debts (as it does in SECURED TRANSACTIONS and NEGOTIABLE INSTRUMENTS)

7. Title insurance--generally used to insure that title is good and to cover the warranties by seller. Without title insurance purchaser's only recourse is against the grantor and he may not be able to satisfy the damages.

a. Standard insurance policies generally insure against all defects of record and defects the grantee may be aware of, but not defects disclosed by survey and physical inspection of premises

b. Title insurance company is liable for any damages or expenses if there is a title defect or encumbrance that is insured against

    1) Certain defects may not be insured by the title policy

F. Mortgages

1. Definition--nonpossessory lien on real property to secure the performance of an obligation, usually a debt

a. Obligation or debt is usually evidenced by a promissory note which is incorporated into the mortgage

b. Purchase-money mortgage is created when the seller takes a mortgage from the buyer at the time of sale

1) Or the lender furnishes the money with which the property is purchased

c. A mortgage may be given to secure future advances

d. A mortgage is an interest in real property and must be in writing, signed, etc. (must satisfy Statute of Frauds)

2. Rights

a. Mortgagor (owner, debtor) retains possession and the right to use the land

1) May transfer the land encumbered by the mortgage

b. Mortgagee (creditor) has a lien on the land and may assign the mortgage to third parties or foreclose on the land to satisfy the debt

1) Even if mortgagor transfers the land, it is still subject to the mortgage if it has been properly recorded

c. If the mortgagor defaults on payment of the note, the mortgagee may resort to the land for payment

1) A foreclosure sale
2) Requires judicial action
3) Mortgagee must return any excess proceeds from the sale to the mortgagor
4) If proceeds from the sale are insufficient to pay note, the mortgagor is still indebted to the mortgagee for the deficiency

a) A grantee, of the mortgagor, who assumed the mortgage would also be liable for the deficiency but one who took subject to the mortgage would not be personally liable

d. Mortgagor may usually save land after default by paying entire balance due (redemption) within a statutory period after foreclosure

1) Often may reinstate mortgage by making up default before foreclosure
2) Clauses of schemes which seek to bar right of redemption are against equity and ineffective

3. Mortgage may be recorded and receives the same benefits as recording a deed or recording an assignment of Contract. (See also Perfection by Filing in SECURED TRANSACTIONS.)

a. Gives constructive notice of the mortgage

1) But mortgage is effective between mortgagor and mortgagee and third parties, who have actual notice, without recording

b. Protects against subsequent mortgagees (priority of mortgage), purchasers, or other takers

c. Recording statutes are generally similar to (or the same ones) those used in recording deeds. See above.

d. First mortgagee to obtain a mortgage and to record it will have priority over all subsequent mortgagees subject to special rights of purchase, money security interests, and certain statutory liens (i.e., mechanic's or construction lien)

e. If the first mortgagee does not record, a subsequent mortgagee who records will have priority if he did not have notice of the first mortgage

    1) If he had notice, he cannot get priority in most jurisdictions

4. When mortgaged property is sold the buyer may

  a. Assume the mortgage

    1) If "assumed," the buyer becomes personally liable (mortgage holder is third-party beneficiary)

    2) The seller remains primarily liable unless released (novation) by mortgage holder

      a) But between the seller and buyer, the buyer has primary responsibility and the seller has the rights and responsibilities of a surety

    3) Normally the mortgage holder's consent is needed due to "due on sale clauses"

      a) Terms of mortgage may permit acceleration of principal or renegotiation of interest rate upon transfer of the property

  b. Take subject to the mortgage

    1) If taken "subject to" the buyer accepts no liability for the mortgage and the seller is still primarily liable

      a) Buyer may pay the mortgage and the mortgage holder must accept

    2) Mortgage holder may still foreclose on the property even in the hands of the buyer

      a) Buyer has no right against seller concerning the mortgage subject to terms of contract or conveyance

    3) Mortgage holder's consent not needed unless stipulated in mortgage and in no event can consent be unreasonably withheld, unless a "due on sale clause" is present

5. Termination of mortgage

  a. Payment of obligation

    1) Mortgage holder then gives owner a satisfaction of mortgage (receipt)

  b. Merger may occur

    1) When the title to the land and the mortgage are owned by the same person unless there is evidence of intent to the contrary

  c. If no payment is made for a statutory period after becoming due, the debt and lien will be unenforceable (running of the statute of limitations)

  d. If the mortgagor (debtor) tenders payment when due and mortgage holder refuses, the mortgage will terminate (and the debt becomes unsecured) and no additional interest will accrue

6. Deed of Trust--also a nonpossessory lien on real property to secure a debt

  a. Like a mortgage, debtor retains possession of the land and creditor has a lien on it

  b. Legal title is given to a trustee to hold

    1) Upon default, trustee may sell the land for the benefit of the creditor

    2) Unlike a mortgage, no judicial action is needed for the sale

c. Debtor has no right to redeem the land after the sale

    1) He can reinstate the deed of trust by making up the default before sale

7. Sale on Contract

a. Unlike a mortgage or a deed of trust, the seller retains title to the property

b. Purchaser takes possession and makes payments on the contract

c. Purchaser gets title when debt fully paid

d. If purchaser defaults on payments, s/he may forfeit the contract, or it may be foreclosed like a mortgage

    1) Seller keeps the money received and keeps the property

    2) If purchaser has paid a substantial amount on the contract, courts may allow the contract to be reinstated or allow the purchaser to pay off the whole contract price so as to not forfeit the property

e. Remember in bankruptcy, the trustee has 60 days to assume or reject executory contracts. If a seller on contract becomes bankrupt, the trustee may reject the contract, sell the property, return the contract purchaser's payments, and keep the profit from appreciation of market value.

G. Landlord Tenant

1. Definition--a relationship which arises from contracting for the possession of real property for some period of time

a. A lease is a contract and a conveyance

    1) Contract is the primary source of rights and duties

    2) May be oral if less than one year

    3) Lease is actually personal property

b. Landlord is the lessor and has the ownership interest called reversion

c. Tenant is the lessee and has a possessory interest

2. Types of leaseholds

a. Period-to-period

    1) Lease is for a fixed time such as a month or year but it continues from period-to-period until proper notice of termination is given

    2) Notice of termination must be given in the same amount of time as the rent or tenancy period (i.e., if tenancy is from month-to-month then the landlord or tenant must give at least one month's notice)

b. Definite period of time (called lease for years)

    1) Lease is for a fixed amount of time, e.g., lease of two years or six months

    2) Lease ends automatically at date of termination

c. Holdover by tenant after definite term with express or implied approval of landlord creates a period-to-period lease

3. Landlord's covenants (promises) and tenant's rights

a. Landlord's covenants are independent of tenant's rights; therefore, landlord's breach does not give tenant the right to breach

b. Right to possession. Landlord must make premises available to tenant.

        1) But if third party is wrongfully possessing premises, e.g., a holdover tenant, then it is tenant's duty to remove him in most states

c. Quiet enjoyment. Neither the landlord nor a third party with a valid claim will evict the tenant unless there has been a breach of the lease.

d. Fitness for use. Premises are fit for human occupation, i.e., warranty of habitability.

e. Tenant may assign or sublease unless prohibited or restricted in lease

        1) An assignment is the transfer by the lessee of his entire interest reserving no rights

           a) Assignee is in privity of contract with landlord and landlord may proceed against him for rent and breaches

           b) Assignor (lessee) is still liable to landlord unless there is a novation or release

        2) A sublease is the transfer by lessee of less than his entire interest; e.g., for three months during summer, then lessee returns to it in the fall

           a) Lessee (sublessor) is still liable on the lease
           b) Landlord has no privity with sublessee and can take no action against him for rent, but certain restrictions of original lease run with the land and are enforceable against sublessee

           c) Sublessee can assume obligations in the sublease and be liable to pay the landlord

f. Subject to lease terms trade fixtures attached by tenant may be removed if

        1) Removed on or before date of termination and
        2) Can be removed without substantial damage to premises

g. Tenant can use premises for any legal purpose unless lease restricts

4. Tenant's duties and landlord's rights

a. Rent. Due at end of term or period of tenancy unless otherwise agreed in lease.

        1) No right to withhold rent even if landlord is in breach (unless so provided by lease or by statute)
        2) Nonpayment gives landlord the right to sue for it or to bring an eviction suit or both

b. Tenant has obligation to make ordinary repairs. Lease or statute may make landlord liable.

        1) Structural repairs are landlord's duty
        2) Where landlord is liable for repairs, tenant may not withhold rent for landlord's breach

c. If tenant wrongfully abandons, landlord may

        1) Do nothing and sue for rent as it becomes due, or
        2) Rerent premises and hold lessee liable for damages if landlord has given lessee notice of rerenting, or
        3) Rerent or take possession without giving notice to lessee, but lessee's liability ceases

    d. If tenant wrongfully retains possession after termination, landlord may

        1) Evict tenant, or
        2) Treat as holdover tenant and charge with fair rental value, or
        3) Tenancy becomes one of period-to-period, and tenants are liable for rent the same as in the expired lease

    e. Landlord may terminate lease if tenant breaches

        1) A survival clause makes tenants continue to be liable for rent after termination if their breach caused termination subject to landlord's duty to mitigate his damage

5. Termination

    a. Expiration of lease
    b. Proper notice in a tenancy from period-to-period
    c. Surrender by lessee and acceptance by lessor
    d. Death of tenant terminates lease except for a lease for a period of years

        1) Death of lessor does not terminate the lease

    e. Eviction

        1) Actual eviction--ousting directly
        2) Constructive eviction--allowing conditions which make the property un- usable if landlord is liable for the condition of the premises (e.g., a leaking roof)

    f. Transfer of property does not affect tenancy

        1) New owner cannot rightfully terminate lease unless old owner could have, e.g., breach by tenant
        2) Buyer has notice of tenant's presence and rights because possession is a notorious fact

    g. Generally, damage to or destruction of the leased premises does not ter- minate lease or excuse tenant from paying rent where lease includes land and building(s), but where lease is of an office, floor, apartment, etc., destruction may terminate lease unless agreement provides otherwise

H. Governmental Restrictions on Use of Land

1. Zoning

    a. Municipal regulation of the building on and use of land in accordance with planned development
    b. Regulations include

        1) Height, number of stories, and size of buildings
        2) Density of population, e.g., single or multiple family dwellings
        3) Uses of land or structures, e.g., manufacture, retail business, res- idential

    c. Purpose is to plan the development and use of a municipality to make it a more attractive and livable place and to encourage the most appropriate use of land

2. Environmental Policies

a. Both state and federal laws
b. Generally require a determination of whether a project will have a significant adverse effect upon the environment balanced against the benefit derived
c. There must be some governmental action before the laws apply, e.g., public projects or issuance of building, development, or use permits to private parties

3. Other restrictions

a. Air pollution controls
b. Water pollution controls
c. Noise statutes

4. Condemnation (eminent domain)

a. Governmental authorities may condemn private property for public use
b. Government must pay a just compensation for it

INSURANCE

Overview

Insurance is a contract whereby, for a stipulated consideration called a premium, one party, called the insurer, undertakes to compensate the other, called the insured, against risks of loss on specified property, etc., by specified risk or perils. Stated otherwise, insurance is the distribution of the cost of risk over a large number of individuals subject to the same risks to reimburse the few who actually suffer loss from the risk. Basically, insurance is limited to providing protection against the risk of loss arising from a happening of events over which the insured has little control. Insurance contracts, like others, require agreement, consideration, capacity, legality, compliance with the Statute of Frauds, and delivery. Some of the more important concepts of insurance involve the identification of insurable interests, subrogation, standard clauses, and assignment of insurance contracts.

Primary emphasis on the exam is placed upon knowledge of fire and casualty insurance relating to the operation of a business. The questions are closely divided between multiple choice and essay, with perhaps the majority being multiple choice. While the coverage of insurance principles is broadly tested, the AICPA emphasizes insurable interest, multiple insurance coverage, subrogation, and knowledge of the most common standard clauses.

Insurance Definitions

Insurable Interest in Property. Must exist at the time the loss occurs. Every person has an insurable interest in the property of others, if that person has potential liability or loss in the event of its destruction. Under the Uniform Commercial Code a buyer acquires an insurable interest in goods by identification of the goods to the contract and a seller retains an insurable interest in goods so long as title to, or any security interest in, the goods remains.

Assignment of Insurance. Liability, fire, and other property insurance is deemed a personal contract and is nontransferable except by agreement of the insurance company. Proceeds from an insurance claim are assignable even if policy prohibits.

Subrogation. The right of the insurer to stand in the shoes of the insured after payment of loss. Thus the insurance company is able to recover from any person legally liable for the loss.

Co-insurance. A standard clause in property fire insurance which requires property to be insured up to a given percentage (usually 80%) of its FMV in order to recover loss in full (up to the face of the policy). If the property is insured for less than the fixed percentage of FMV, the insured must bear a proportionate part of the loss.

$$\text{Recovery} = \text{actual loss} \times \frac{\text{amount of insurance}}{\text{co-insurance \% × FMV of prop}}*$$

---

*At time of loss

A. General Considerations

1. Insurance is the distribution of the cost of risk over a large number of individuals subject to the same risk, in order to reimburse the few who actually suffer from the risk

2. Insurance is designed to protect against the large unexpected losses, not small everyday losses

    a. This is one reason for the $50 or $100 deductible clause in auto-collision insurance

3. Rates are based on past losses. There must be a large number of risks to provide an accurate average loss.

4. Insurance is not supposed to be gambling. Therefore, only those who may suffer loss from the risk may insure and only to the extent that loss may occur. (See Insurable interest below.)

    a. Indemnity is the purpose of insurance

5. Intentional acts of the insured usually are not insurable, e.g., fire by arson, liability for assault and battery

    a. Negligence or carelessness is insurable and is generally not a defense of the insurer
    b. Negligence of an insured's employees is also covered

6. Self-insurance is the periodic setting aside of money into a fund to provide for possible losses

    a. Not true insurance, because it is not a distribution of risk; it is preparation to meet possible losses
    b. Advantage is the saving if losses are small or nonexistent
    c. Disadvantages are the possibility of loss before a sufficient reserve is created and the possibility of losses greater than the cost of regular insurance premiums

7. Insurers

    a. Most insurers have incorporated due to conditions of the business
    b. Stock companies--typical corporation with capital stock and shareholders
    c. Mutual companies--no capital stock. Policyholders are the capital contributors and are actually the shareholders.

    d. Mixed companies--issue capital stock and ordinary policies of stock companies. Also issue participating policies (entitled to share in surplus).

B. Insurance Contract

1. Similar to a common law contract. Must contain all the essential elements, i.e., agreement, legality, capacity, and consideration

    a. Minors are often allowed, by statute, to take out insurance policies

2. Generally a unilateral contract where the insured prepays the premiums and the insurer promises to indemnify the insured against loss

3. Insurance is generally binding at the time of unconditional acceptance of the application and communication of this to the insured

    a. The application is the offer, and issuance of the policy is acceptance
    b. A company agent (as opposed to an independent agent) usually has power to issue a temporarily binding slip which obligates the insurer during the interim before issuance of the policy
    c. Physical delivery of the written policy is not necessary
    d. Insurer may require conditions to be met before the policy becomes effective, e.g., pay a premium

        1) A general agent may accept a policy for the insured

4. Policy is voidable at option of insurer (because assent was not real in law) if there is

    a. Concealment--the insured failed to inform the insurer at the time of application of a fact material to the insurer's risk

        EXAMPLE: An applicant for auto insurance is unable to drive and does not so inform the insurer.

1) Any matter specifically asked by insurer is by law material and failure to disclose or a misleading answer is concealment

2) Need not disclose facts learned after making the contract

b. Material misrepresentation by insured, e.g., nonexistent subject matter

1) Representation acceptable if substantially true, e.g., value of subject matter does not have to be exact

c. Breach of warranty. A warranty is a representation incorporated in the policy. It constitutes a condition precedent to the liability of the insurer and generally is presumed to be material (therefore, does not have to be proved material as do misrepresentations and concealments).

EXAMPLE: An applicant for fire insurance warrants that a night watchman will be on duty at night at all times to check for fire. If he is not and a loss occurs, this may release the insurer.

5. Statute of Frauds does not require the insurance contract to be in writing because it may fall within the one-year rule (but usually is required by state statutes)

6. Insurable interest

a. There must be a relationship between the insured and the insured event so that if the event occurs the insured will suffer substantial loss

b. In property, there must be both a legal interest and a possibility of pecuniary loss

1) Legal interest may be ownership or a secured interest, e.g., general creditors do not have an insurable interest but judgment lien creditors and mortgagees do

2) The insurable interest need not necessarily be present at the inception of the policy so long as it is present at the time of the loss

3) One can insure only to the extent one has an insurable interest, e.g., mortgagee can insure only the amount still due

4) Contract to purchase or possession of property can give an insurable interest, e.g., bailee has insurable interest

5) UCC expands the instances when an insurable interest exists. See Overview.

EXAMPLE: Owners, partners, lessees, mortgagees, bailees, and judgment lien creditors.

C. Subrogation

1. This is the right of the insurer to step into the shoes of the insured as to any cause of action relating to a third party whose conduct caused the loss

EXAMPLE: While driving his car, X is hit by Y. If X's insurance company pays X, the insurance company is subrogated to X's claim against Y.

a. Applies to accident, automobile collision, and fire policies

2. A general release of a third party, who caused the loss, by the insured will release the insurer from his obligation

EXAMPLE: While driving his car, X is hit by Y. Y talks X into signing a statement that X releases Y from all liability. X will not be able to recover on his insurance. X's insurance company is released when Y is released.

   a. Because the insurer's right of subrogation has been cut off
   b. A partial release will release the insurer to that extent

D. Accident Insurance

1. Accident insurance indemnifies the insured against expense, suffering, and loss of time resulting from personal injury or property damage

E. Automobile Insurance

1. Insures against loss or damage to an automobile from collision, theft, wind-storm, and fire, and also covers damage and personal injury caused to others

   a. Collision usually has a deductible amount which the insured must pay

2. Some states have new forms of no-fault insurance. Generally, this means that each vehicle owner's insurance pays his own expenses regardless of fault. Legal action is not permitted until property damage and personal injury exceed a fixed threshold.

F. Fidelity or Guaranty Insurance

1. Insures against loss from dishonesty of employee or persons in position of trust. (See SURETYSHIP.)

G. Liability Insurance

1. Insurer agrees to protect insured against liability for accidental damage to persons or property

   a. Usually includes duty to defend in a law suit brought by third parties
   b. Intentional wrongs not covered, e.g., fraud
   c. Insurer has no rights against the insured for causing the loss because this is what the insurance is to protect against

2. Common types

   a. Automobile--see above
   b. Personal liability--broad category that may cover almost any situation depending on coverage in insurance contract

     EXAMPLE: A person accidentally injures another while participating in a sport.

     EXAMPLE: A client falls and injures himself in his accountant's office.

   c. Malpractice--a form of personal liability

     1) Used by accountants, doctors, lawyers
     2) Protects against liability for harm caused by errors or negligence in work
     3) Does not protect against intentional wrongs, e.g., fraud

H. Life Insurance

This area is no longer being tested effective November, 1983.

I. Fire Insurance (See also Theory and Practice Module 26, Fixed Assets.)

1. Generally covers direct fire damage and also damage as a result of fire such as smoke, water, or chemicals

    a. Does not cover damage from a friendly fire, e.g., smoke from a fire in a fireplace
    b. Covers hostile fires, i.e., those not intended or those that have left the intended burning spot

2. Blanket policy applies to a class of property which may be changing (inventory) rather than a specific piece of property (specific policy)

3. Valued policy predetermines value of property which becomes the face value of the policy

    a. Unvalued policy (open) is one wherein the value of the property is determined at time of loss but there is a maximum amount of the policy

4. Recovery

    a. Under an open policy (unvalued) the insured recovers the FMV (determined at date of loss) of the property destroyed
    b. A valued policy pays the face of the policy for a total loss
    c. Always limited, at maximum, to face value of the policy
    d. For partial destruction, the actual damage is recovered

5. Coinsurance clause

    a. The insured agrees to maintain insurance equal to a specified percentage of the value of his property. Then when a loss occurs, the insurer only pays a proportionate share if the insured has not carried the specified percentage.

    EXAMPLE: Insured owns a building valued at $100,000. He obtains 2 insurance policies for $20,000 each and they both contain 80% coinsurance clauses. There is a fire and his loss is $40,000. He will only collect $20,000 on his insurance. See formula below.

    b. Formula

    $$\text{Recovery} = \text{Actual Loss} \times \frac{\text{Amount of Insurance}}{\text{Coinsurance \% X FMV of Property*}}$$

6. Pro rata clause

    a. Someone who is insured with multiple policies can only collect, from each insurer, the proportionate amount of the loss

        1) Proportion is the amount insured by each insurer to the total amount of insurance

---

* At time of loss

> *EXAMPLE: Insured incurs a loss due to fire on property and is entitled to a $10,000 recovery. The property is covered by two insurance policies, one for $8,000 from Company A and one for $12,000 from Company B. Consequently, total insurance coverage on the property was $20,000. Company A will be liable for 40% ($8,000/$20,000) of fire loss, i.e., $4,000 (40% x $10,000). Company B will be liable for 60% ($12,000/ $20,000) of fire loss, i.e., $6,000 (60% x $10,000).*

7. Proof of loss

   a. Insured must give insurer a statement of the amount of loss, cause of loss, etc.
   b. Must be done within a time period, e.g., 60 days

      1) Failure to comply will excuse the insurer's liability unless performance is made impracticable, e.g., death of insured

8. After destruction of property, creditors may treat the insurance proceeds as any other asset of the insured. Secured creditors have an interest in the proceeds without a special agreement to that effect.

9. Mortgagor and mortgagee have insurable interests, and mortgagees usually require insurance for their protection

10. Fire policies are usually not assignable because of the risk

    a. I.e., danger that new owner would not be reliable, e.g., record of arson
    b. Even if property is sold, there can be no assignment of insurance without insurer's consent
    c. A claim against an insurer may be assigned, e.g., house burns and insurance company has not yet paid

TRUSTS AND ESTATES

Overview

This topic includes the administration of a decedent's estate and the administration of a trust.

An estate is the legal entity which comes into existence on a person's death for the purpose of succeeding to the property of the decedent, to establish liability for payment of debts of the decedent, and to distribute any remaining property. The estate is administered in accordance with the decedent's will or the intestate statutes. An executor or administrator is approved by the court and empowered to act for the estate and carry out its responsibilities. An executor or administrator may engage the necessary legal, accounting, and other services. Adequate records must be kept to show proper disposition of the assets of the estate. At the conclusion of an estate, an accounting is generally rendered and the judicial settlement is secured in probate court, thereby closing the estate.

A trust arises where one person holds legal title to certain property for the use and benefit of another. In other words, in a trust, the legal and equitable title are split so that one called a trustee holds legal title for the benefit of another person, called a beneficiary. A trust is administered by a trustee who must perform the duties imposed by law and by the trust instrument and is personally liable if he does not follow these requirements.

The most frequently tested topic in estates and trusts is allocation of trust principal and income. Candidates should be thoroughly familiar with this distinction, e.g., between cash dividends and stock dividends. Also tested are the rights of beneficiaries to a trust with particular emphasis on the distinction between the rights of income beneficiary and the residual beneficiary, the duties of an administrator or executor of an estate as well as the duties of a trustee.

Trust and Estate Definitions

Intestate Succession. Where no valid will has been executed by a decedent, his property will be distributed in accordance with the applicable state statutes. In contrast, a deceased person leaving a will is said to be testate.

Executor. A person appointed by a testator (subject to confirmation by probate court) to carry out the directions and requests in the will and to dispose of the property according to the will and probate court after death.

Administrator. A person appointed by a court to administer the estate of a person who died without a will or whose executor cannot or will not serve.

Trust Income. Proceeds received from the use of trust property are treated as income to be used for the benefit of income beneficiaries and includes interest, cash dividends, rent, royalties, etc. Ordinary expenses are chargeable against trust income. These include insurance premiums on a property, interest expense, income and property taxes, and cost of repair of trust property.

Trust Corpus (Principal). Changes or increases in the value of trust property itself are treated as corpus for the benefit of the remainderman and include stock dividends, stock splits, insurance proceeds, and capital gains. Extraordinary expenses, however, such as costs incurred in sale or purchase of trust property and cost of improvements made by the trustee where the improvements will last longer than the income beneficiary's interest are decreases in trust corpus.

A. Estates

1. The execution and validity of a will is not considered within the competency of a CPA, i.e., a lawyer would have to be consulted. Therefore, only some general information regarding wills which pertains to administration of estates will follow.

    a. The emphasis on the CPA exam is now on administration of estates and trusts
    b. Preparation of tax returns and schedules used to render an accounting are within a CPA's competence and are routinely done by CPA firms

2. Definitions

    a. Will--the legal declaration of a person's intent which he wills or desires to be performed after his death

        1) Generally involves the disposition of property
        2) Person who makes a will--testator or testatrix

    b. Estate--a legal entity holding title to a person's property after his death

        1) It also must pay the decedent's debts
        2) It is administered by an executor or administrator (see next section)
        3) Arises by operation of law

    c. Testate--a person is said to die testate if there is a valid will in existence

        1) The estate will pass to beneficiaries by the terms of the will

    d. Intestate--a person is said to die intestate if there is no will or if the will is held invalid

        1) The estate will pass by intestate succession, i.e., state statute prescribes rules of distribution of an estate

    e. Legacy (bequest)--gift of personal property under a will

        1) Specific legacy is a gift of a specified item

             EXAMPLE: Decedent willed his car specifically to his son.

            a) If the specific item does not exist when the testator dies, the beneficiary gets nothing

        2) General legacy is a gift out of the general assets of the estate

             EXAMPLE: Decedent willed $100 to his son.

            a) As long as the estate is not insolvent, the beneficiary will receive general legacies

    f. Devise--gift of real property under a will

        1) Same rules apply as to legacies, above

    g. Residue--the remainder of an estate after all other gifts have been made

        EXAMPLE: "I hereby give ...to...and the rest of my estate to A."

        1) Its value is undetermined until an appraisal and inventory of the estate is made and all other gifts have been made or accounted for

3. Validity of a will

    a. Testator/testatrix must have capacity when s/he executes (makes) it, i.e., legal age and sound mind
    b. It must be signed and witnessed

        1) Except where handwritten wills are permitted

    c. It only is effective on the testator's/testatrix's death
    d. It is revocable and amendable during testator's/testatrix's life

B. Administration of Estates

1. Definitions

    a. Executor/executrix--the personal representative named in a will

    b. Administrator--person appointed by the court to administer the estate when there is no will or if the executor named in a will cannot or will not serve

2. The administrator or executor/executrix is a fiduciary and must act accordingly to carry out the wishes of the testator/testatrix or the statutory scheme

    a. Responsible for collecting all debts, paying all expenses, and generally carrying out the distribution to those entitled

        1) May sell assets to pay debts; personal property must be sold before real property (unless otherwise directed by a will)

        2) May contract and engage services, e.g., attorneys, accountants, appraisers

    b. Personally liable if he fails to execute his/her duties

    c. Must not commingle the estate with his/her own property

    d. Must keep an accounting of all assets and their disposition

3. The petition for probate must be filed in the proper court supervising distribution, usually called probate court

    a. This is necessary prior to distribution of the estate

    b. Petition consists of a statement of the approximate value of the estate and the names, ages, residence, and relationship of the heirs of the decedent

    c. Filed with the petition is generally a sworn statement, by the original witnesses to the will, that the will being submitted is valid

    d. All executed copies of the will must be presented to the court before they can be admitted to probate

4. The administrator or executor/executrix files an inventory of the estate for appraisal

    a. Taxes are also assessed

5. Creditors are given notice and they must file their claims within statutory time period

6. Distribution of estate

    a. By the terms of the will if there is one and to the extent it provides for the assets

    b. A surviving spouse, under the concept of statutory share, has the right to denounce the provision made in the will for him/her and elect instead a stated share (normally 1/3) of the decedent's estate

    c. By intestate succession when there is no will or if the will does not provide for the entire estate. Laws vary from state to state but generally the following order applies:

        1) Surviving spouse and children

        2) Other lineal descendents (grandchildren)

        3) Ascendents (parent, grandparents)

        4) Collaterals (brothers and sisters)

    d. Abatement--a process of determining the distribution of the estate when it is insufficient to satisfy all debts and gifts

        1) Debts and administration expenses are paid first, taking from (in order)

            a) Intestate property (property not provided for in the will)
            b) Residue
            c) General devises or legacies
            d) Specific devises or legacies

        2) Any remaining assets are distributed in the reverse order of above until they run out

7. The administrator or executor must render an accounting to the court to close the estate after all assets are distributed

    a. The accounting contains an inventory of all assets and debts of the estate, disposition of the debts, expenses of the estate, and distribution of the remaining assets

C. <u>Trusts</u>

1. Definition--a trust is a fiduciary relationship wherein one person (trustee) holds legal title to property for the benefit of another (beneficiary). Legal and equitable (beneficial) title are separated.

    a. Trustor/testatrix or settlor is the person who creates the trust

        1) Settlor can make him/herself either the trustee or beneficiary (not both), but, of course, s/he does not need to be either

    b. Trustee holds the legal title to the property for the beneficiary(ies), manages the property, and distributes the income to the beneficiary(ies) if so provided in the trust agreement

        1) The trustee is a fiduciary to beneficiaries

            a) Duty of loyalty; s/he may take no personal advantage from his/her position

        2) Power to do what is necessary to fulfill the terms of trust
        3) Duty to manage with reasonable intelligence and skill (as a prudent person)

            a) Must make complete accounting to beneficiary
            b) Must keep trust assets separate from personal assets
            c) May not delegate his control although s/he may seek advice from others, e.g., attorneys, accountants

        4) Trustee must invest trust assets as a prudent person would to preserve (not necessarily enlarge) corpus

            a) May not speculate
            b) Existence of speculative investments in the trust does not authorize trustee to retain them
            c) Must diversify investments
            d) Investment in a partnership would probably not be a prudent investment because of the potential liability
            e) Terms of the trust instrument may limit or enlarge the trustee's investment power

5) Personally liable on contracts

    a) Trustee is not liable where contract specifically states that he is contracting in a representative (fiduciary) capacity for the trust and it identifies the trust

    b) Merely signing as a trustee does not relieve him/her from liability

    c) If held personally liable, s/he may receive indemnification from the trust if the contract were properly made in his/her role as trustee

  c. Beneficiaries have an equitable interest

    1) They can require a trustee to carry out the terms of the trust and to act properly, e.g., sue for mismanagement, conversion, waste, etc.

    2) Commonly there are one or more beneficiaries who receive the income of the trust for life and then a remainderman (also a beneficiary) who gets the trust property upon termination

2. Creation requires:

  a. Intent to create a trust

    1) Writing is necessary for the transfer of real property to a trust

  b. Trustee

    1) If trustee does not have legal capacity or refuses to perform, court will appoint one

  c. Beneficiary
  d. Trust property (corpus or res)
  e. Trust purpose (any lawful purpose)
  f. Duration must be limited so as not to violate the rule against perpetuities

    1) This rule requires that a trust cannot (by its terms) last longer than a life in being plus 21 years or it will fail

      EXAMPLE: A forms a trust. The terms of this trust state that the income is to go to his son, B, for life unless B has a child, in which case the property will be distributed to this child at the age of 21.

    2) Purpose is to prevent title to property from being tied up for too long a period of time

3. Inter vivos trust is created by the settlor while living

  a. Transfer in trust is the transferring of property by a settlor to a trustee for the benefit of another
  b. Declaration of trust is when the settlor declares him/herself trustee for a beneficiary

    1) In a declaration of trust, no transfer of property is necessary

4. A testamentary trust is set up in the testator's/testatrix's will to have property transferred in trust after the death of the settlor

5. An active trust is one wherein the trustee has some specific duties to perform

  a. A passive trust is one requiring no duties of the trustee and title will pass to beneficiary

6. Charitable trust--a trust that has as its object some recognized social benefit, e.g., furthering education, religion, relief to poor

  a. Valid even if indefinite as to time and beneficiaries
  b. <u>Cy pres</u> (i.e., as near as possible) doctrine is used by courts to carry out
     general intent when specific instructions are impossible

7. Totten trusts

  a. Totten trust pertains to a bank savings account which the depositor opens
     as "John Smith in trust for Sam Smith"
  b. The trust is revocable by the depositor simply by withdrawing the money
  c. Funds may be used during depositor's life in any manner
  d. Totten trusts become irrevocable at depositor's death

8. Implied trusts

  a. Resulting trust arises when:

     1) Either the beneficial interest(s) fail(s)

        *EXAMPLE: An income beneficiary is named but a remainderman is not
        named. At the end of the trust the beneficial interest will fail.*

        a) Trustee then holds for settlor or settlor's heirs, or

     2) Title to property is taken (with consent) in the name of one who did
        not furnish the consideration

        *EXAMPLE: Prominent politician purchases some land but does not want
        his name associated with it. A business associate holds the land in his
        name for the politician.*

  b. Constructive trust arises to prevent injustice when property is wrongfully
     acquired

     *EXAMPLE: A conveys property to B but C fraudulently changes conveyance to
     his name. C is deemed to hold the property in trust for B.*

9. Clifford trust

  a. A trust having a duration of 10 or more years and
  b. Involves transfer of property to <u>irrevocable</u> trust
  c. Such a trust qualifies as a bona <u>fide transferee</u> of property for purposes of
     shifting income from the settlor (creator) to trust or its beneficiaries

  d. A transfer to an irrevocable trust for a shorter duration (less than 10
     years) will not qualify to shift income of the property

10. Termination

  a. Fulfillment of terms of trust
  b. Revocation by settlor only if s/he reserved a power of revocation

     1) Otherwise s/he cannot revoke

  c. Agreement by settlor and <u>all</u> beneficiaries
  d. Failure of trust purpose

     *EXAMPLE: A creates a trust, the income of which is to put his son, B,
     through school. B dies at an early age. The purpose of the trust has
     failed and the trust will terminate.*

D. Allocation of Principal and Income

1. This has been the most frequently tested topic in estates and trusts

2. Governed by the Uniform Principal and Income Act

    a. Most states have adopted it directly or with minor variations
    b. Apply these rules to both estates and trusts

3. Principal includes:

    a. Original trust property
    b. Proceeds and gains from sale of property, including insurance received on destruction of property
    c. New property purchased with principal or proceeds from principal
    d. Stock dividends and stock splits (cash dividends are income)
    e. Reserve for depreciation

4. Payable from principal are expenses affecting principal, e.g.,

    a. Principal of loans
    b. Litigation over trust property
    c. Permanent improvements
    d. Costs incurred in the purchase or sale of trust property

5. Income includes profits from trust principal, e.g.,

    a. Rent
    b. Interest
    c. Cash dividends
    d. Royalties

6. Payable from income are ordinary and operating expenses, e.g.,

    a. Interest
    b. Insurance premiums
    c. Taxes
    d. Repairs
    e. Depreciation expense is not payable from income but it is an income expense

7. Annuities are allocated between principal and income

8. Trustee is liable to income beneficiary and remainderman for confusion or commingling of assets

    a. CPA is likely to be consulted to determine the amount of money to go to the income beneficiary and the amount to go to the remainderman

E. Federal Estate Tax

The federal estate tax is a tax imposed on the right to transfer property by death. It is an excise tax levied upon the value of property transferred at death. The gross estate is composed of all property to the extent of the interest therein of the decedent at the time of his/her death.

The estate tax is computed on the basis of a taxable estate, which is the gross estate as reduced by various allowable deductions. Primary among these deductions from the gross estate is the "marital deduction," which has been tested most recently in Business Law.

Marital deduction--is allowed without limitation (unlimited) for the FMV of property passing to a surviving spouse.

a. A terminable interest granted to surviving spouse will not generally qualify for marital deduction
b. If the executor/executrix elects, the fair market value of qualified terminable interest property, commonly known by the acronym "Q-tip" (i.e., property placed in trust with income to surviving spouse for life and remainder to someone else at surviving spouse's death), is eligible for the marital deduction if the income from the property is paid at least annually to spouse and the property is not subject to transfer during the surviving spouse's lifetime

Further explanation of federal estate tax is provided in Module 44, Gift and Estate Taxes (GETX).

F. Real Estate Investment Trusts (REITS)

1. Real Estate Investment Trust Act

a. Authorized by Congress in 1960
b. Permits organization of unincorporated association to invest in real estate
c. Association need not pay corporate income taxes

2. Provisions to be met:

a. 100 or more certificate holders during each year
b. 5 or fewer holders must not own more than 50% of certificates
c. Trustees must have centralized control
d. Owners must have limited liability and free transferability of shares
e. Major portion of income must be rents from real property or gains on sale of real property
f. Must pay at least 90% of taxable income to certificate holders each year

3. Failure to meet provisions

a. Trust taxed as if corporation

4. Tax treatment

a. Ordinary income and capital gains pass through to investors
b. Depreciation and other losses do not pass through

5. Trust must comply with applicable SEC securities registration laws

CHAPTER SEVEN

ACCOUNTING PRACTICE AND ACCOUNTING THEORY

This chapter is very brief because Chapters 8 through 13 discuss topics common to and tested on both practice and theory.

Chapter 8   ARB, APB, and FASB Pronouncements
Chapter 9   Financial Accounting Review
Chapter 10 Cost and Managerial Accounting Review
Chapter 11 Quantitative Methods
Chapter 12 Governmental Accounting
Chapter 13 Taxes (tested only on practice)

Accounting Practice vs. Accounting Theory

Accounting practice tests application of accounting knowledge in a computational sense, i.e., problem solving. Also required is a knowledge of GAAP including all of the authoritative pronouncements, and industry practices where authoritative pronouncements do not exist. Most of the practice problems require problem solutions; some of the multiple choice questions only require specification of an accounting principle.

Accounting theory includes explanation and conceptual justification of accounting practices including GAAP; however, some theory multiple choice and essay questions require only regurgitation of authoritative pronouncements.

Condition Candidates

If you are preparing for either Accounting Practice or Accounting Theory only, you can still use this book effectively. The topical nature of the material tested in accounting practice does\not significantly differ from that tested in accounting theory (with the exception of income taxes). It is the nature of the questions that differs, i.e., problematic vs. conceptual. We believe that in order to assure yourself of success on the remaining section of the exam you must understand both the "why" (conceptual justification) and the "how" (problem solving) of the problems. The table on the next page illustrates the difference in emphasis to be followed in your preparation program.

Examination in Accounting Practice	Examination in Accounting Theory
• Work multiple choice questions from both theory and practice	• Work multiple choice questions from both theory and practice; ignore income taxes and questions requiring extensive computations
• Work problems from prior accounting practice exams	• Work essay questions from prior theory exams
• Briefly review the pronouncements in Chapter 8	• Study the outlines of the pronouncements in Chapter 8; in-depth knowledge is required

Preparing for Accounting Practice

First, become acquainted with the nature of the practice exam including the type and breadth of questions. Review the relative frequency of areas tested as compiled on the Content Specification outlines which follow.

Relatedly, you should evaluate your competency by working 10 to 20 multiple choice questions from each of the Modules 23-44 in this volume. This diagnostic routine will acquaint you with the specific nature of the questions tested on each topic as well as indicate the amount of study required per topic. You should work toward a 65% correct response rate as a minimum on each topic (65% is suggested as an across-the-board minimum because the multiple choice questions are graded on a curve and presumably you will do better than 65% on many topics). See discussion of self study programs and examination grading in Chapter 1 and Chapter 2.

Second, study the content of Chapters 8 through 13 emphasizing the mechanics of each topic such as inventory pricing, consolidations, equivalent units of production, etc. Use simple examples, journal entries, and diagrams to put a handle on the basic concepts underlying each topic. You may have to refer to your textbooks or other sources listed in Chapter 1 for topics with which you have had no previous exposure.

Third, work actual CPA practice problems from recent exams in this volume under examination conditions. Refer back to Chapter 3 and restudy the solutions approach for practice problems.

CPA practice problems are more involved and longer than typical problems found on undergraduate accounting examinations. CPA problems require special skills that are usually not developed in undergraduate accounting programs. You must develop these skills before the examination by applying the methodology in Chapter 3 on "live" CPA problems.

Fourth, work all of the objective questions in this volume including a review of the questions answered in your diagnostic self-evaluation.

Preparing for Accounting Theory

First, utilize the multiple choice questions in Volume II per the discussion of the first and fourth points just above, under "Preparing for Accounting Practice." Practice and theory multiple choice questions are very similar in scope and difficulty per topic. Candidates should be aware that the information in Modules 40-44, dealing with taxes, is not tested in accounting theory.

Second, emphasize the basic principles and objectives underlying accounting, e.g., revenue and expense recognition rules, etc. Study APB Statement No. 4 and introductory material in Chapters 8 through 13 which explains the basic concepts of each topic.

Third, read carefully the "Basic Accounting Theory" section which begins on page 616 in Chapter 8. This section integrates APB Statement 4 and SFACs 1-3. Note below how some chapters of Statement 4 have been supplanted by an SFAC:

APB Statement 4 Chapter	SFAC
1. Purpose and Nature of Statement	SFAC 1
2. Environment of Financial Acctg.	SFAC 1
3. Objectives of Financial Acctg.	SFAC 1, SFAC 2
4. Basic Elements of Financial Acctg.	SFAC 3
Basic Features of Financial Acctg.	SFAC 3*
5. GAAP - Pervasive Principles	
6. GAAP - Broad Operating Principles	
7. GAAP - Detailed Accounting Principles	
8. Financial Accounting in the Future	

*Only partially supplants Statement 4

Fourth, compare and contrast the basic concepts of financial, quantitative methods, etc., to the detailed rules for all of the specific topics. You want to understand the specific topics within the framework of the general models or rules, e.g., relating inventory valuation rules to the general theory of income recognition.

Fifth, practice the solutions approach for essay questions on recent CPA theory questions. Most CPA candidates have little experience with accounting essay questions; undergraduate accounting examinations generally consist of short problems. Be careful not to underemphasize writing out complete solutions to essay questions. Do not wait until the examination to develop answering techniques.

Sixth, recognize the value of the keyword outline (prepared in the exam margin). Practice it while answering old examination questions, and perhaps more

importantly, orient your study habits to the keyword outline approach. As you review material, think of it in "outline" or "list" form. For example, in outlining
the six pervasive principles from APB Statement 4, you can remember them by the
first letters of each principle forming IRI-USA. (See APB Statement No. 4, page
677.) While you should use the keyword outline to organize your answer, your answer
has to be written out for the grader. LISTS OF KEYWORDS, EVEN IN OUTLINE FORM, ARE
NOT ACCEPTABLE TO THE AICPA.

Seventh, get yourself in good physical and mental condition. Theory, tested on
Friday afternoon from 1:30 to 5:00, will follow 16 hours of practice, auditing, and
law examination. Commit yourself to stay and to work until 5:00 p.m. It is very
easy to get up and leave an hour early.

The AICPA Content Specification Outline of the coverage of financial accounting
in the Examinations in Accounting Practice and Accounting Theory including the
authors' frequency analysis thereof (last nine exams), appears on the following
pages.

The outlines for the other areas covered on the accounting practice and accounting theory exams have been placed in the chapters to which they apply.

Summary of Accounting Practice and Accounting Theory Exam Coverage

AICPA target percentage allocation of areas covered on Accounting Practice and
Accounting Theory exams:

		Practice		Theory	
		Target**	Present***	Target**	Present***
*Ch. 8-9	Financial Accounting	55%	55%	75%	75%
Ch. 10-11	Cost-Managerial and Quantitative Methods	15%	15%	15%	15%
Ch. 12	Governmental and Nonprofit	10%	10%	10%	10%
Ch. 13	Income Taxes	20%	20%	n/a	n/a
TOTAL		100%	100%	100%	100%

*Content outlines of financial accounting appear on the six following pages.
Outlines of other areas appear in the chapters in which these areas are reviewed.

**Was effective with the May 1984 exam.
***Coverage of May 1984 exam.

AICPA CONTENT SPECIFICATION OUTLINE/FREQUENCY ANALYSIS*

Financial Accounting

I. Presentation of Financial Statements or Worksheets

Practice

	M 80	N 80	M 81	N 81	M 82	N 82	M 83	N 83	M 84
A. Balance Sheet	–	–	–	–	–	–	[.5]	–	–
B. Income Statement	–	–	–	–	– [1]	–	– [.5]	–	–
C. Statement of Changes in Financial Position									
1. Statement Presentation**	2	– [1]	4	2	–	1 [1]	3	–	– [1]
2. Working Capital Computations**	–	–	3	2	–	–	–	1	–
D. Statement of Owners' Equity	–	–	–	–	–	–	–	[.5]	[.5]
E. Consolidated Financial Statements or Worksheets									
1. Pooled Companies	1	– [.5]	–	2	–	1	–	–	1
2. Purchased Companies	1 [.5]	1	–	–	–	1	1 [1]	–	1
3. Corrections	–	–	–	–	–	–	–	–	–
4. Eliminations	– [.5]	– [.5]	–	–	–	–	1	–	–
5. Intangibles – Goodwill	1	–	–	–	–	–	–	–	–
F. Disclosures in Notes to the Financial Statements	–	–	–	–	–	–	–	–	–
G. Supplementary Statements	–	2	1	–	–	–	–	–	–
Total Multiple Choice Questions	5	3	8	6	–	3	4	2	2
Total Problems	1	2	–	–	1	1	1	1.5	1.5
Actual Percentage ***	12.5%	21.5%	4%	3%	10%	11.5%	12%	16%	16%

(AICPA 15%)

Theory

No Comparable Theory Section

II. General Concepts, Principles, Terminology, Environment, and Other Professional Standards

Practice

No Comparable Practice Section

Theory

	M 80	N 80	M 81	N 81	M 82	N 82	M 83	N 83	M 84
A. Authority of Pronouncements (substantial authoritative support – GAAP)	–	–	–	–	–	–	–	–	–
B. Departures from Generally Accepted Accounting Principles	–	–	–	–	–	–	–	–	–
C. Conceptual Framework	–	–	–	–	3	3	4	2	2
D. Basic Concepts and Accounting Principles									
1. Asset and Liability**	–	–	–	1	–	–	–	–	–
2. Revenue and Expense**	–	1	2	4	–	– [.25]	1	1	1
3. Other**	2	3	3	1	1	–	–	–	–
E. Nonmonetary Transactions Concepts	1	1	–	–	1	–	–	–	–
F. Working Capital – Current Assets and Current Liabilities (terminology)	–	1	–	–	–	–	–	–	–
G. Comparative Financial Statements	–	–	–	–	–	–	–	–	–
H. Consolidated Financial Statements	1	–	–	– [.5]	1	2	–	–	– [.67]
I. Historical Cost, Constant Dollar, Current Cost, and Other Accounting Concepts	2	1 [1]	–	2	3	3	2	1	2
Total Multiple Choice Questions	6	7	5	8	9	8	7	4	5
Total Essays	–	–	1	.5	–	.25	–	–	.67
Actual Percentage ***	6%	7%	15%	13%	9%	10.5%	7%	4%	11.7%

(AICPA 15%)

* The classifications are the authors'

** These classifications have been added by the authors

*** The "actual percentage" is a measure of the relative coverage of the specific areas (i.e., I,II, etc.) on each Accounting Practice or Theory exam. This relative weight includes **both** multiple choice questions and essays/problems presented in that area.

AICPA CONTENT SPECIFICATION OUTLINE/FREQUENCY ANALYSIS*

Financial Accounting

III. Measurement, Valuation, Realization, and Presentation of Assets in Conformity with GAAP

	Practice									Theory								
	M 80	N 80	M 81	N 81	M 82	N 82	M 83	N 83	M 84	M 80	N 80	M 81	N 81	M 82	N 82	M 83	N 83	M 84
A. Cash	1	–	–	1	1	–	1	–	1	–	–	–	–	–	–	–	–	–
B. Marketable Securities and Investments																		
1. Marketable Equity Securities	–	1	–	1	–	1	2	–	1	1	1	–	1	–	–	–	1	1
							[1]							[.25]				[.33]
2. Other Securities	–	–	–	–	–	–	–	–	–	–	–	–	–	–	–	–	–	–
3. Investment in Bonds	–	–	–	–	–	–	1	–	–	–	–	–	–	–	–	1	–	1
4. Investment in Stocks	1	–	1	2	1	–	–	–	1	1	2	–	–	–	1	1	1	–
			[.25]											[.25]				
5. Sinking and Other Funds	–	–	–	–	1													
C. Receivables and Accruals																		
1. Accounts and Notes Receivable	2	1	2	–	–	–	–	–	–	1	–	–	–	–	–	–	1	–
								[.33]										
2. Affiliated Company Receivables	–	–	–	–	–	–	–	–	–	–	–	–	–	–	–	–	–	–
3. Discounting of Notes	–	–	–	–	1	–	2	–		–	–	–	1	–	–	–	1	1
															[.25]			
4. Installment Accounts	–	–	–	–	–	–	–	–		–	–	–	–	–	–	–	–	–
5. Interest and Other Accrued Income	–	–	–	–	–	–	–	–		–	–	–	–	–	–	1	–	–
								[.34]										
6. Allowance for Doubtful Accounts	–	–	–	1	–	–	–	1	–	–	–	–	–	–	1	–	–	–
	[.33]						[.5]								[.25]			
7. Lease Receivable — Lessor**	–	–	–	–	–	–	–	–	–	–	1	–	–	–	2	1	–	–
			[.25]							[.5]			[.67]					
D. Inventories																		
1. Acquisition Costs	–	–	–	1	2	–	–	1	–	–	1	–	–	–	–	–	1	–
				[.5]								[.6]						[.33]
2. Costing Methods	–	1	2	2	–	–	–	1	2	1	1	–	1	–	2	–	1	–
				[.5]		[.5]				[.33]		[.2]			[.25]			
3. Valuation Methods	1	–	1	1	1	1	–	2	2	1	–	–	1	1	1	–	1	–
										[.17]		[.2]				[.25]	[.25]	[.67]
E. Property, Plant, and Equipment																		
1. Acquisition Costs	1	1	2	–	2	–	1	–	2	1	–	1	–	–	–	–	1	–
					[.33]						[.5]						[.5]	
2. Additions and Betterments	–	–	–	–	–	–	1	–	1	–	–	–	–	–	1	–	–	–
											[.25]							
3. Depreciation, Amortization and Depletion	1	1	–	1	1	–	–	–	1	–	–	–	–	1	–	1	–	–
						[.17]												
4. Insurance	–	–	–	1	1	1	–	1	–	–	–	–	–	–	–	–	–	–
5. Involuntary Conversion	–	–	–	1	–	–	–	–	–	–	–	–	–	–	–	–	–	–
6. Leasehold Improvements	–	–	–	–	1	–	1	–	–	–	–	–	–	–	–	–	–	–
7. Maintenance and Repairs	–	–	–	–	1	–	–	1	–	–	–	–	–	–	–	–	–	–
8. Obsolescence and Write-Downs	–	–	–	–	–	–	–	–	–	–	–	–	–	–	–	–	–	–
9. Rearrangements and Moving Costs	–	–	–	–	–	–	–	1	–	–	–	–	–	–	–	–	–	1
10. Disposition	–	–	–	–	–	–	–	–	–	–	–	–	–	–	–	–	–	–
																	[.5]	
11. Capitalized Interest**	–	–	1	1	–	–	1	–	–	–	–	–	–	–	–	–	–	–
F. Capitalized Leased Assets — Lessee**																		
1. Acquisitions Costs	–	–	–	1	–	–	–	–	–	–	1	–	–	1	–	–	–	1
2. Amortization	–	–	–	–	–	–	–	–	–	–	–	–	–	–	–	–	–	1
G. Intangibles																		
1. Acquisition Costs	–	–	–	–	1	–	–	–	–	–	–	1	–	–	–	–	–	–
						[.25]												
2. Amortization	1	1	–	1	1	–	–	–	–	–	1	–	–	–	–	–	1	–
						[.25]												
3. Intangibles Carried as Investments (equity method)	–	–	–	–	–	–	–	–	–	–	–	–	–	–	–	1	–	–
H. Prepaid Expenses and Deferred Charges																		
1. Prepaid Expenses	–	–	–	–	–	1	–	–	–	1	–	–	1	–	–	1	–	1
2. Deferred Income Taxes	–	–	–	–	–	–	–	–	1	–	–	–	–	–	–	–	–	–
															[.25]			
3. Deferred Pension Costs	–	–	–	–	–	–	–	–	1	–	–	–	–	–	–	–	–	–
Total Multiple Choice Questions	8	6	9	14	14	5	9	8	15	7	8	2	6	3	8	9	7	6
Total Problems/Essays	.33	–	.5	1	–	1	1	1	.67	1	.75	1	.67	.75	.5	.5	1.25	1.33
Actual Percentage***	7.3%	3%	9.5%	17%	7%	12.5%	14.5%	14%	14.2%	17%	16%	12%	13%	10%	13%	14%	19.5%	19.3%
					(AICPA 10%)									(AICPA 15%)				

AICPA CONTENT SPECIFICATION OUTLINE/FREQUENCY ANALYSIS*

Financial Accounting

IV. Valuation, Recognition, and Presentation of Liabilities in Conformity with GAAP

	Practice									Theory								
	M 80	N 80	M 81	N 81	M 82	N 82	M 83	N 83	M 84	M 80	N 80	M 81	N 81	M 82	N 82	M 83	N 83	M 84
A. Payables and Accruals																		
1. Accounts and Notes Payable	—	—	—	—	—	1	1	—	—	—	—	—	1	—	—	—	—	1
2. Accrued Employees' Costs	—	—	—	—	—	—	1	2	1	—	—	—	—	—	—	—	—	— [.33]
3. Interest and Other Accrued Expenses	—	—	1	1	—	1	1	1	—	—	1	—	—	—	—	—	1	1
4. Accrued Pension Expense	—	—	—	—	— [.13]	1	—	—	—	—	—	—	—	—	1	—	—	—
5. Taxes Payable	—	—	—	—	—	—	—	—	—	—	—	—	—	—	—	—	—	—
6. Guarantees and Warranties	1	—	2	—	—	—	—	—	1	—	—	—	—	—	—	—	—	—
7. Deposits and Escrows	—	—	—	—	—	—	1	—	—	—	—	—	—	—	—	1	—	—
B. Deferred Revenues																		
1. Unperformed Service Contracts	—	—	1	—	—	1	1	—	1	1	—	—	—	—	—	—	—	—
2. Subscriptions or Tickets Outstanding	—	—	—	—	— [.13]	—	—	1	—	—	—	—	—	—	—	—	—	—
3. Installment Sales	—	—	—	—	—	—	—	—	—	—	—	—	—	—	—	—	—	—
4. Sales and Leaseback	—	—	—	—	—	—	1	—	—	—	—	—	—	—	—	—	—	—
C. Deferred Income Tax Liabilities																		
1. Equity Method of Accounting for Investments	—	—	—	—	—	—	1	—	—	—	—	—	—	—	—	—	—	—
2. Depreciation of Plant Assets	—	1	1	—	— [.80]	—	—	—	1	—	—	—	—	—	—	1	—	1
3. Long-Term Construction Contracts	—	—	—	—	—	—	—	—	—	—	—	—	—	— [.13]	—	—	—	—
4. Other Timing Differences	—	—	—	—	—	—	—	2	—	1	—	—	—	1 [.62]	—	—	—	1
D. Capitalized Lease Liability — Lessee																		
1. Measurement at Present Value	—	—	—	1	1	2	2	2	1	— [.25]	—	1 [.33]	—	—	—	2 [.67]	—	1
2. Amortization	—	—	—	—	—	—	—	—	—	—	—	—	—	—	—	—	—	— [.33]
E. Bonds Payable																		
1. Issue of Bonds	1	—	1	1	—	—	—	1	1	—	— [.10]	2	—	3 [.33]	—	—	1	— [.5]
2. Issue Costs	—	—	—	—	—	—	—	—	—	—	—	—	—	—	—	—	1	—
3. Amortization of Discount or Premium	—	—	—	—	1	—	1	2	—	—	— [.3]	—	—	—	— [.33]	1	1	— [.25]
4. Types of Bonds	—	—	—	—	—	—	—	—	—	—	— [.2]	—	—	—	—	—	—	—
5. Conversion of Bonds	—	—	—	—	—	—	1	—	1	—	—	—	—	—	— [.33]	—	1	—
6. Detachable Stock Warrants	1	1	—	—	—	2	1	—	—	—	— [.2]	—	—	—	—	—	1	—
7. Retirement of Bonds					(See VI.E.3)									(See VI.E.3)				
F. Long-Term Notes Payable	—	—	—	3	—	—	—	—	—	—	—	—	—	—	—	—	—	—
G. Contingent Liabilities and Commitments	—	—	—	—	—	—	—	—	—	—	—	—	—	—	—	—	—	—
Total Multiple Choice Questions	3	2	9	3	2	8	12	11	7	2	1	3	1	4	1	7	4	5
Total Problems/Essays	—	—	—	—	.25	.80	—	—	—	.25	.8	—	.33	.75	1	—	1	1.08
Actual Percentage***	1.5%	1%	4.5%	1.5%	3.5%	12%	6%	5.5%	3.5%	5%	9%	3%	4%	12%	11%	7%	14%	15.8%
				(AICPA 5%)										(AICPA 10%)				

AICPA CONTENT SPECIFICATION OUTLINE/FREQUENCY ANALYSIS*

Financial Accounting

V. Ownership Structure, Presentation, and Valuation of Equity Accounts in Conformity with GAAP

	Practice									Theory								
	M 80	N 80	M 81	N 81	M 82	N 82	M 83	N 83	M 84	M 80	N 80	M 81	N 81	M 82	N 82	M 83	N 83	M 84
A. Preferred and Common Stock																		
1. Issued	—	—	—	1	—	1	—	—	—	—	—	—	—	—	—	1	—	—
	[.17]										[.25]							
2. Outstanding	—	—	—	—	—	—	—	—	—	—	—	—	—	—	—	—	—	—
3. Legal Capital	—	—	—	—	—	—	—	—	—	—	—	—	—	—	—	—	—	—
4. Retirement of Stock	—	—	—	—	—	—	1	—	—	—	—	—	—	—	—	—	—	—
5. Book Value Per Share	—	—	2	—	1	1	—	—	—	—	—	—	1	—	—	—	—	—
								[.17]										
6. Classification	—	—	—	—	—	—	—	—	—	—	—	—	—	—	—	—	—	—
B. Additional Paid-In Capital	—	—	—	—	—	—	—	—	—	—	—	1	3	1	1	—	1	1
											[.25]							
C. Retained Earnings Statement and Dividends							[.33]											
1. Prior Period Adjustments	—	1	—	—	—	—	1	—	—	—	—	—	1	—	1	—	—	1
																	[.2]	
2. Net Income	—	1	—	—	—	—	—	—	—	—	—	—	—	—	—	—	—	—
3. Cash Dividends	1	—	—	—	—	—	—	—	—	—	—	—	—	—	—	—	—	—
											[.25]							
4. Property Dividends	—	—	—	1	—	1	—	1	—	—	—	—	—	—	—	—	1	—
5. Liquidating Dividends	—	—	—	—	—	—	—	—	—	—	—	—	—	—	—	—	—	—
6. Stock Dividends and Splits	—	2	1	3	—	1	1	—	—	1	—	1	—	1	—	—	1	1
	[.17]										[.25]						[.2]	
7. Appropriations of Retained Earnings	—	—	—	—	—	—	—	—	—	—	—	—	—	—	—	1	—	—
D. Treasury Stock and Other Contra Accounts																		
1. Cost Method	1	2	1	1	—	1	—	—	—	—	—	1	—	1	—	1	1	1
	[.33]																[.2]	
2. Par Value Method	1	—	—	—	—	—	1	—	—	—	—	—	—	—	—	1	—	—
3. Restrictions on Acquisitions of Treasury Stock	—	—	—	—	—	—	—	—	—	—	—	—	—	—	—	—	—	—
E. Stock Options, Warrants, and Rights	—	—	—	—	—	—	—	—	—	—	—	2	1	2	—	1	1	1
	[.33]			[.5]						[.5]								
F. Reorganization and Change in Entity																		
1. Incorporation of an Unincorporated Enterprise	—	—	—	—	—	—	1	—	—	—	—	—	—	—	—	—	—	—
2. Business Combinations					(See IE.1.&2.)									(See VIII.D.)				
3. Quasi-Reorganization	—	2	1	—	—	—	—	—	—	—	—	—	—	—	—	1	—	—
4. Bankruptcy	—	—	—	—	—	—	1	—	—	—	—	—	—	—	—	—	—	—
G. Partnerships																		
1. Formation	—	—	—	1	—	—	1	—	—	—	—	—	—	—	—	—	—	—
2. Admission, Retirements, and Dissolution	3	—	—	3	—	2	2	—	—	—	—	—	—	—	—	—	—	—
				[.5]														
3. Profit or Loss Distribution and Other Special Allocations	—	—	—	—	—	—	—	—	—	—	—	—	—	—	—	—	—	1
Total Multiple Choice Questions	6	8	5	10	1	7	8	2	—	1	—	6	5	5	6	2	5	6
Total Problems/Essays	1	—	—	.5	.5	—	—	.5	—	.5	1	—	—	—	—	.6	—	—
Actual Percentage*	13%	4%	2.5%	10%	5.5%	3.5%	4%	6%	0%	6%	10%	6%	5%	5%	6%	8%	5%	6%
				(AICPA 5%)									(AICPA 5%)					

AICPA CONTENT SPECIFICATION OUTLINE/FREQUENCY ANALYSIS*

Financial Accounting

VI. Measurement and Presentation of Income and Expense Items, Their Relationship to Matching and Periodicity, and Their Relationship to GAAP

	Practice									Theory								
	M 80	N 80	M 81	N 81	M 82	N 82	M 83	N 83	M 84	M 80	N 80	M 81	N 81	M 82	N 82	M 83	N 83	M 84
A. Sales or Revenue																		
1. Cash	—	—	—	—	—	—	—	—	—	—	—	—	—	—	—	—	—	—
2. At Time of Sale	—	—	—	—	—	—	1	—	1	—	—	—	—	—	—	—	—	—
(bracket)	[.33]																	
3. At Completion of Production	—	—	—	—	—	—	—	—	—	—	—	—	—	—	—	—	—	—
(bracket)		[.5]																
4. During Production (percentage-of-completion)	1	—	1	—	1	—	—	1	1	1	1	—	1	—	1	2	—	1
(bracket)		[.5]									[.5]						[1]	
5. Installment Method or Cost Recovery	—	—	—	—	1	—	—	—	1	—	—	—	—	—	—	—	—	—
(bracket)	[.33]				[.25]													
6. Equity in Earnings of Investee	—	1	—	—	—	—	1	—	—	—	—	—	—	—	—	—	1	—
(bracket)			[.17]											[.25]				
7. Interest	3	2	—	3	2	1	—	—	3	—	—	—	—	—	—	—	—	—
(bracket)			[.25]							[.25]								
8. Dividends	—	—	—	—	1	—	1	—	1	—	—	—	—	—	—	—	—	—
(bracket)			[.17]															
9. Royalties	—	—	—	—	—	—	1	—	1	—	—	—	—	—	—	—	—	—
10. Rent	—	1	—	—	1	—	2	—	—	—	—	—	—	—	1	2	—	—
(bracket)			[.25]															
11. Disposal of Assets and Liquidation of Liabilities	—	—	—	3	—	—	1	—	—	—	—	1	—	—	—	—	—	—
(bracket)											[.25]							
12. Foreign Exchange	—	—	—	—	—	—	—	—	—	—	1	—	—	—	—	—	1	—
B. Cost of Goods Sold	—	—	—	1	1	—	1	—	—	—	—	—	1	2	—	—	—	—
(bracket)																	[.5]	
C. Expenses																		
1. General and Administrative	—	—	—	—	—	—	—	—	1	—	—	—	1	—	—	—	—	—
2. Selling	—	—	—	—	—	—	—	—	—	—	—	—	—	—	—	—	—	—
3. Financial (interest)	—	—	—	—	1	—	—	—	—	—	—	—	1	1	—	—	—	—
(bracket)									[.17]									
4. Depreciation, Amortization, and Depletion	—	—	3	4	1	—	2	2	1	1	—	2	—	1	—	3	1	1
5. Research and Development	—	—	1	1	1	—	—	1	1	—	1	—	—	—	1	—	—	—
6. Foreign Exchange	—	—	—	—	—	—	—	—	—	—	—	—	—	—	—	—	—	—
7. Bad Debts	1	1	—	—	1	1	—	—	1	—	2	—	—	—	—	1	—	1
(bracket)														[.25]				
8. Royalties	—	—	—	—	1	—	—	—	—	—	—	—	—	—	—	—	—	—
9. Rent	—	—	—	—	—	—	—	—	1	—	—	—	1	—	—	—	—	—
(bracket)			[.25]							[.25]								
10. Compensation	1	—	2	1	—	1	1	—	1	—	—	—	1	—	1	—	—	—
(bracket)																		[.33]
11. Unusual Gains or Losses	—	1	1	1	—	—	—	3	—	—	—	1	—	—	1	—	—	1
(bracket)								[.16]						[.25]				
12. Capital Lease Expenses**	1	—	—	1	—	—	—	—	2	—	—	—	—	—	—	—	—	—
(bracket)			[.25]															
13. Pension Costs**	—	—	1	—	—	—	2	1	1	—	—	—	—	—	1	2	1	—
(bracket)						[.13]												[.34]
D. Provision for Income Tax																		
1. Current	1	—	1	—	—	—	2	1	1	—	—	—	—	—	—	—	—	—
2. Deferred	—	—	1	1	2	—	1	1	1	—	—	—	—	—	—	—	—	—
(bracket)						[.2]											[.25]	
3. Interperiod Allocation**	—	—	—	—	—	—	—	—	—	1	—	—	1	—	1	1	—	1
E. Recurring Versus Nonrecurring Transactions and Events																		
1. Discontinued Operations	—	2	1	1	—	1	—	1	1	—	—	—	1	—	—	—	1	—
(bracket)														[.25]				
2. Extraordinary Items	—	—	1	1	1	—	2	—	1	1	1	1	—	—	—	—	—	—
(bracket)																	[.2]	
3. Debt Extinguishment or Restructure**	—	2	1	1	—	3	2	2	2	1	—	—	1	1	—	1	2	—
(bracket)											[.2]							[.25]
F. Accounting Changes	—	1	2	—	1	2	1	3	3	—	—	2	—	1	—	—	—	—
(bracket)			[.25]															
G. Earnings Per Share	3	2	3	—	1	2	1	1	2	—	1	2	2	1	1	1	—	1
(bracket)				[.5]						[.5]					[.25]			
Total Multiple Choice Questions	11	13	19	19	17	11	21	18	28	6	6	10	11	6	8	13	7	6
Total Problems/Essays	.67	1	1.5	.5	.38	.2	—	—	.33	.75	.95	—	—	.5	.75	.7	1.25	.92
Actual Percentage*	12.2%	16.5%	24.5%	14.5%	12.3%	7.5%	10.5%	9%	17.3%	13%	15%	10%	11%	11%	15.5%	20%	19.5%	15.2%
					(AICPA 15%)									(AICPA 20%)				

AICPA CONTENT SPECIFICATION OUTLINE/FREQUENCY ANALYSIS*

Financial Accounting

VII. Other Financial Topics

	Practice M 80	N 80	M 81	N 81	M 82	N 82	M 83	N 83	M 84	Theory M 80	N 80	M 81	N 81	M 82	N 82	M 83	N 83	M 84
A. Accounting Policies	−	−	−	−	−	−	−	−	−									
B. Nonmonetary Transactions	−	1	1	2	− [.25]	−	1	3	1									
C. Interim Financial Statements	1	1	1	1	−	−	1	1	−									
D. Historical Cost, Constant Dollar Accounting, and Current Cost	1	−	1	2	1	−	1	1	1									
E. Loss or Gain Contingencies	1	1	1	1	1 [.37]	2	1	−	2									
F. Segments and Lines of Business	1	−	1	−	1	1	−	1	1			No Comparable						
G. Long-Term Contracts	−	−	−	−	−	1	−	−	−			Theory Section						
H. Employee Benefits	−	−	−	−	− [.25]	−	−	−	−									
I. Analysis of Financial Statements	2	4	4	2	2	2	2	2	1									
J. Development Stage Enterprises	−	−	−	−	−	−	−	−	−									
K. Personal Financial Statements	−	−	−	−	−	−	−	−	1									
L. Translation of Foreign Statements**	1	1	1	−	1	−	−	2	1									
Total Multiple Choice Questions	7	8	10	8	6	6	6	10	8									
Total Problems	−	−	−	−	.87	−	−	−	−									
Actual Percentage***	3.5%	4%	5%	4%	11.7%	3%	3%	5%	4%									

(AICPA 5%)

VIII. Other Financial Topics

	Practice M 80	N 80	M 81	N 81	M 82	N 82	M 83	N 83	M 84	Theory M 80	N 80	M 81	N 81	M 82	N 82	M 83	N 83	M 84
A. Statement of Changes in Financial Position										5	2	2	1	2	2	2	2	2
B. Accounting Policies										3	1	2	−	1	1	−	−	−
C. Accounting Changes																		
1. Principle										− [.17]	−	−	− [.5]	1	− [.25]	2	−	1
2. Estimate										− [.17]	−	−	− [.25]	1	1	−	− [.25]	−
3. Entity										− [.17]	−	−	− [.25]	−	−	−	1	−
D. Business Combinations										2	−	1	1 [.5]	3	2	1	2	−
E. Interim Financial Statements			No Comparable							−	1	1	1	1	1	−	1	−
F. Loss or Gain Contingencies			Practice Section							1	− [.5]	2	2	2	1	−	1 [1]	1
G. Segments and Lines of Business										2	2	1	1	−	−	1	−	1
H. Long-Term Contracts										−	−	1	−	1	−	−	−	−
I. Employee Benefits										2	1 [1]	1	1	1	−	−	1	−
J. Analysis of Financial Statements										2	−	2	1	− [1]	1 [.25]	1 [.2]	− [.25]	1
K. Development Stage Enterprises										−	−	−	−	−	−	−	−	−
L. Translation of Foreign Statements**										2	1	1	1	−	−	−	−	1
Total Multiple Choice Questions										19	8	14	9	13	9	7	8	7
Total Essays										.5	.5	1	1.5	1	.5	1.2	.5	−
Actual Percentage***										24%	13%	24%	24%	23%	14%	19%	13%	7%

(AICPA 10%)

CHAPTER EIGHT
ARB, APB, AND FASB PRONOUNCEMENTS

The AICPA was formed as the American Association of Public Accountants in 1887, changing its name to American Institute of Accountants in 1917. The name was again changed to American Institute of Certified Public Accountants in 1957. The Institute is a voluntary professional association which regulates the public accounting profession internally and represents the profession to the business community, government, and society in general.

Promulgation of Accounting Principles

The Institute's first "pronouncement" effort came in reaction to the threat of punitive federal legislation after the 1929 stock market crash. The Institute formed the Committee on Cooperation with Stock Exchanges, which sought ways to improve corporate reporting. The Committee's report, Audits of Corporate Accounts, coined the term "accounting principles" and a standard short-form report. The Committee also recommended 5 accounting principles which were adopted by the Institute's membership. They appear in Chapter 1A of ARB 43.

The Securities Acts of 1933 and 1934 resulted in the SEC and its power to specify the form and content of financial statements (i.e., accounting principles). The SEC, noting tremendous lack of uniformity in accounting principles, threatened to promulgate accounting rules, etc., if the Institute failed to exercise leadership in narrowing areas of inconsistency in accounting practices. The Committee on Accounting Procedure was formed by the Institute in 1939 to perform this function.

The Committee on Accounting Procedure (CAP) promulgated 51 Accounting Research Bulletins (ARB). ARB 43 is a rewrite of ARBs 1--42. The Committee on Accounting Procedure was superseded in 1959 by the Accounting Principles Board (APB) which issued 31 Opinions and 4 Statements. The APB was an Institute committee as was the Committee on Accounting Procedure.

APB Opinions constitute generally accepted accounting principles and must be complied with by companies in their financial statements. APB Statements are more advisory in nature and do not carry the official status of Opinions. In 1973, the APB was superseded by the Financial Accounting Standards Board.

The Financial Accounting Standards Board (FASB) is an independent agency comprised of seven full-time board members and a substantial research staff. The FASB issues Statements of Financial Accounting Standards (SFAS) and also interpretations of existing ARBs, APBs, and FASBs. In 1978, a new series of pronouncements, Statements of Financial Accounting Concepts (SFAC), which are similar in nature and scope to APB Statements, was initiated. SFACs do not establish GAAP.

As implied above, the Institute's efforts in the promulgation of accounting principles, rules, etc., has come from government impetus. Six periods of public criticism of accounting principles and their promulgation are evident:

1. Post-1929 market crash resulting in the Committee on Cooperation with Stock Exchanges

2. Latter 1930s when multitudes of alternative practices were discovered through SEC disclosure requirements resulting in the Committee on Accounting Procedure

3. Post World War II when rapid inflation was not reflected in the accounts resulting in the rewrite of ARBs 1-42 into ARB 43

4. Mid-50s when a general dissatisfaction with the acceptability of alternative accounting practices resulted in the APB

5. Late 60s when the APB came under intense criticism for its compromise positions on controversial topics resulting in the FASB

6. Mid-70s when the U.S. Senate Subcommittee on Reports, Accounting and Management (Metcalf Committee) issued its staff report, "The Accounting Establishment." The outcome of this latest critical evaluation of the profession is not yet evident.

Basic Accounting Theory

The foundation of financial accounting is generally accepted accounting principles (GAAP). As defined in APB Statement No. 4, GAAP encompasses "the conventions, rules, and procedures necessary to define accepted accounting practice at a particular time. The standard of 'generally accepted accounting principles' includes not only broad guidelines of general application, but also detailed practices and procedures." In practice, GAAP has come to include SFASs, FASB

Interpretations, APB Opinions, ARBs and SEC releases. These are the pronouncements to which practitioners look when determining if financial statements fairly present financial position, results of operations, and changes in financial position.

Although GAAP is the current basis for financial reporting, it does not constitute a cohesive body of accounting theory. Generally, SFASs and the other authoritative pronouncements have been the result of a problem-by-problem approach. The pronouncements have dealt with specific problems as they occur and are not predicated on an underlying body of theory.

Theory can be defined as a coherent set of hypothetical, conceptual, and pragmatic principles forming a general frame of reference for a field of inquiry; thus, accounting theory should be the basic principles of accounting rather than its practice (which GAAP describes or dictates). Accounting has a definite need for a conceptual theoretical structure. Such a structure is necessary if an authoritative body such as FASB is to promulgate consistent standards. A body of accounting theory should be the foundation of the standard-setting process, and should provide guidance where no authoritative GAAP exists.

There have been efforts to develop such a frame of reference. Notable early attempts include ARS No. 1 (The Basic Postulates of Accounting) and ARS No. 3 (A Tentative Set of Broad Accounting Principles for Business Enterprises) issued in 1961 and 1962. In 1966, the American Accounting Association issued A Statement of Basic Accounting Theory (ASOBAT). These three endeavors were largely ignored by the authoritative standard-setting bodies. In 1970, APB Statement 4 was released, based in part on ARS Nos. 1 and 3. Being a product of the APB, it is generally considered to be a more influential document than its predecessors. It can be thought of as the "official" accounting theory in areas where more recent guidelines have not yet been issued.

The current attempt to develop accounting theory began with the conceptual framework project. In 1976, FASB issued Tentative Conclusions on Objectives of Financial Statements of Business Enterprises, and later the same year, Conceptual Framework for Financial Accounting and Reporting: Elements of Financial Statements and Their Measurement. These two pronouncements led to the establishment of Statements of Financial Accounting Concepts, of which four have been issued. The purpose of this series is "to set forth fundamentals on which financial accounting and reporting standards will be based." In other words, the SFACs are the FASB's attempt to organize a framework that can serve as a reference point in formulating SFASs.

Definition of Accounting. Before discussing "accounting theory" further, it is important to understand what accounting is. APB Statement 4 defines accounting as "...a service activity. Its function is to provide quantitative information, primarily financial in nature, about economic entities that is intended to be useful in making economic decisions--in making reasoned choices among alternative courses of action." Financial accounting and reporting is the subset of accounting which most of the theoretical work discussed above is concerned with. "Financial reporting includes not only financial statements but also other means of communicating information that relates, directly or indirectly, to the information provided by a business enterprise's accounting system--that is, information about an enterprise's resources, obligations, earnings, etc." (SFAC 1). It is important to note that not all informational needs are met by accounting or financial reporting. The following diagram from a FASB Invitation to Comment, Financial Statements and Other Means of Financial Reporting describes the information spectrum:

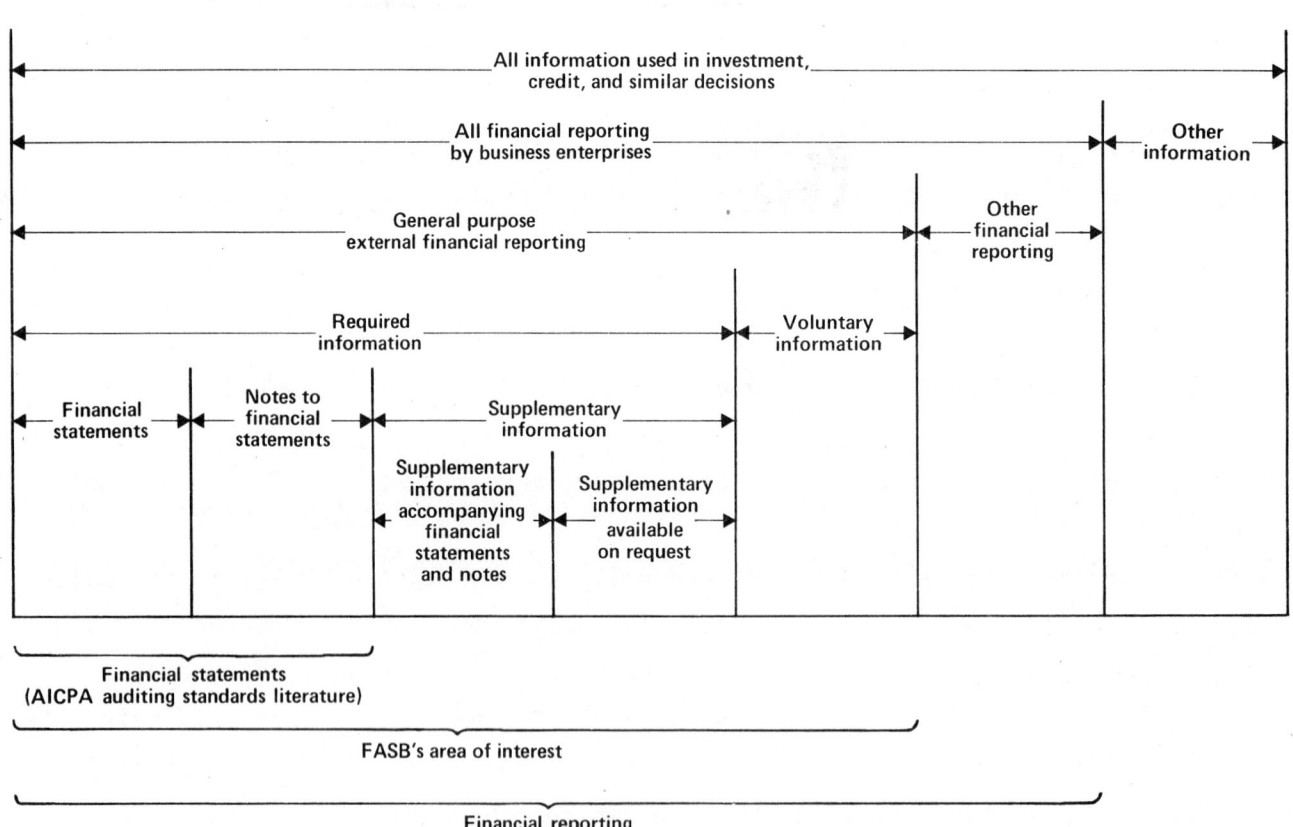

Components of the Conceptual Framework. The components of the conceptual framework for financial accounting and reporting include objectives, qualitative characteristics, elements, recognition, measurement, financial statements, earnings, funds flow, and liquidity. The relationship between these components is illustrated in the following diagram, also from <u>Financial Statements and Other Means of Financial Reporting</u>:

In the diagram below, components to the left are more basic and those to the right depend on components to their left. Components are closely related to those above or below them.

Conceptual Framework
For Financial Accounting and Reporting

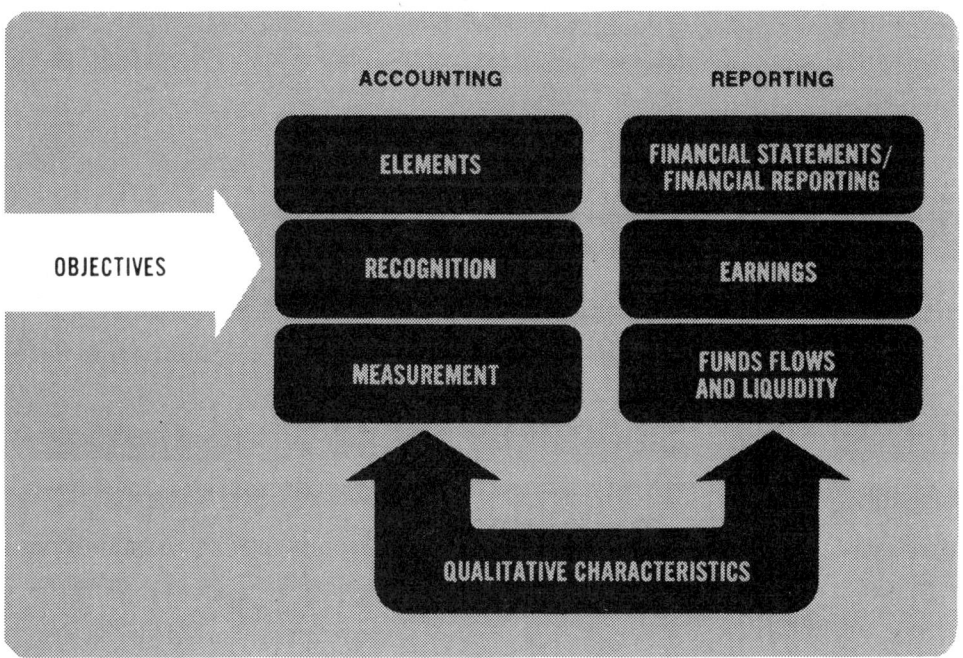

The most basic component of the conceptual framework is the objectives. The objectives underlie the other phases and are derived from the needs of those for whom financial information is intended. The objectives provide a focal point for financial reporting by identifying what types of information are relevant.

The qualitative characteristics also underlie most of the other phases. They are the criteria to be used in choosing and evaluating accounting and reporting policies.

Elements of financial statements are the components from which financial statements are created. They include assets, liabilities, equity, investments by owners, distributions to owners, comprehensive income, revenues, expenses, gains, and losses.

In order to be included in financial statements, an element must meet criteria for recognition and possess a characteristic which can be reliably measured.

Finally, reporting or display considerations are concerned with what information should be provided, who should provide it, and where it should be displayed. How the financial statements (financial position, earnings, and funds flow) are presented is the focal point of this part of the conceptual framework project.

Objectives of Financial Reporting. (See outline of SFAC 1 on page 743). Remember, objectives of financial reporting underlie the conceptual framework. They are the basis upon which a body of theory is established. The objectives described in SFAC 1 have not been verified by any empirical process, but they are an attempt by FASB to provide a foundation for a cohesive set of interrelated concepts.

The objectives focus on users of financial information. They are derived from "the needs of external users who lack the authority to prescribe the information they want and must rely on information management communicates to them." The external users who are emphasized in the objectives are actual and potential investors and creditors. These users are particularly interested in the amounts, timing and relative uncertainty of future cash flows, whether they be return of capital, interest, dividends, etc.

Three basic objectives are listed in SFAC 1. The objectives state that financial reporting should provide 1) information useful in investment and credit decisions, 2) information useful in assessing cash flow prospects (amount, timing, and uncertainty), and 3) information about enterprise resources, claims to those resources, and changes therein. A focal point in SFAC 1 is information about earnings and earning power. Earnings are a major cause of changes in resources. Despite the emphasis on cash flows, earnings are to be computed on the accrual basis, because accrual accounting "provides a better indication of an enterprise's present and continuing ability to generate favorable cash flows than information limited to the financial effects of cash receipts and payments."

Qualitative Characteristics. (See outline of SFAC 2 on page 744). The qualitative characteristics also underlie the conceptual framework, but in a different way. While the objectives provide an overall basis, the qualitative characteristics establish criteria for selecting and evaluating accounting alternatives which will meet the objectives. In other words, information must possess the qualitative characteristics if that information is to fulfill the objectives.

SFAC 2 views these characteristics as a hierarchy of accounting qualities, as represented in the diagram below:

A HIERARCHY OF ACCOUNTING QUALITIES

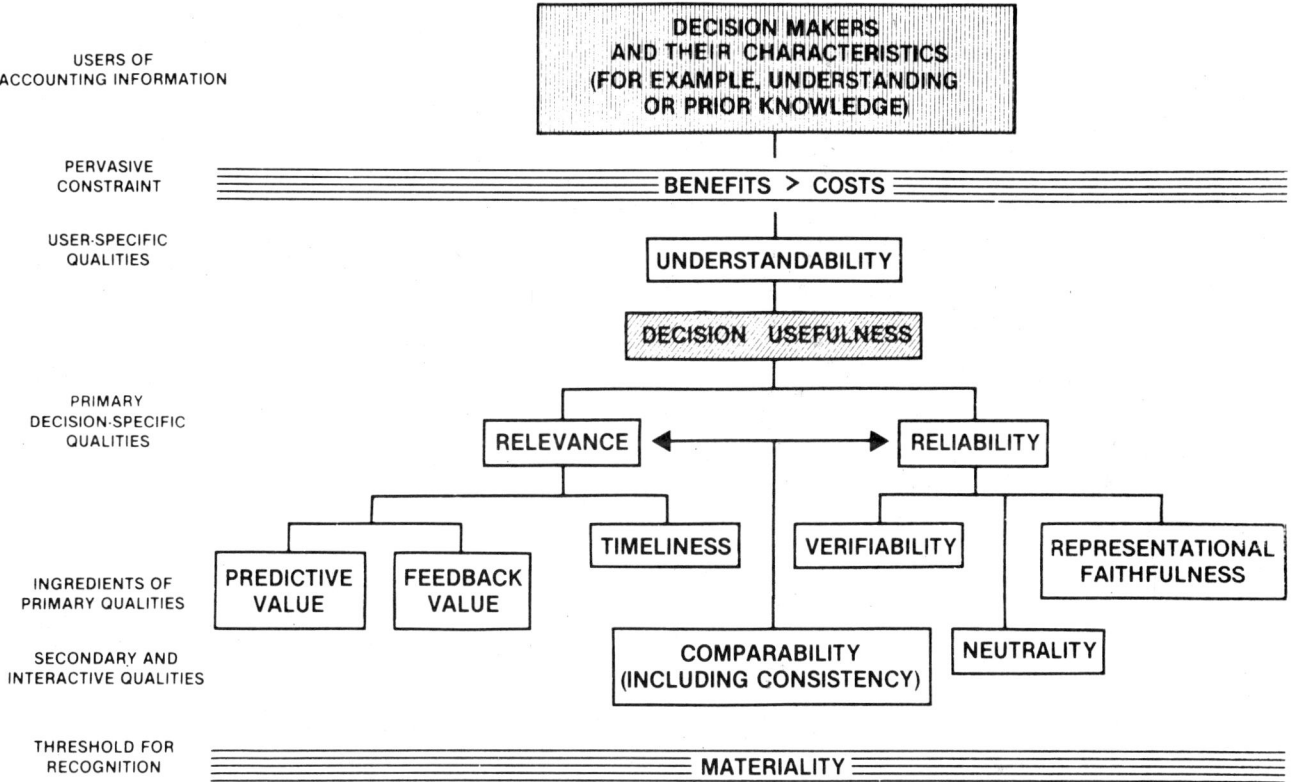

The diagram reveals many important relationships. At the top and bottom are constraints. If information falls outside these constraints, it would not be reported although it may possess some qualitative characteristics. Thus, information is not disclosed if the costs of disclosure outweigh the benefits, or if the information is not material enough to influence users.

The first two qualities in the hierarchy (understandability and decision usefulness) are not qualities relating solely to information. They also depend on qualities of particular decision makers. The usefulness and understandability of information depends on the knowledge and ability of those using it. SFAC 1 states that "financial information is a tool, and like most tools, cannot be of direct help to those who are unable or unwilling to use it or who misuse it."

The primary qualities that accounting information should possess are relevance and reliability. As the chart indicates, each of these is broken down into three components. Comparability is a secondary quality which interacts with relevance and reliability to enhance usefulness of information.

Accounting information is relevant if it has the "capacity to make a difference" in a decision. To be relevant in an investment or credit decision, information must help users form predictions about future cash flows (refer to objectives). This can occur through predictive value (improving capacity to predict) or feedback value (confirmation or correction of prior predictions). Of course, in order to be relevant, information must be available before it loses its capacity to affect decisions (timeliness).

Information is reliable if it is reasonably free from error and bias, and faithfully represents what it claims to represent. Reliability consists of verifiability, representational faithfulness, and neutrality.

The secondary qualities of comparability and consistency become important when assessing cash flows of different enterprises or of the same enterprises over different periods. Comparability of information enables users to identify similarities in and differences between two enterprises, while consistency (unchanging policies and procedures from period to period) does the same between periods for each enterprise.

Basic Elements. (See outline of SFAC 3 on page 745). Elements of financial statements are the ten basic building blocks from which financial statements are constructed. These definitions are based upon the objectives of SFAC 1. They are intended to assure that users will receive decision-useful information about enterprise resources (assets), claims to those resources (liabilities and equity), and changes therein (the other seven elements). In order to be included in the statements, an item must qualify as an element, meet recognition criteria, and be measurable.

The meaning of financial statement elements depends on the conceptual view of earnings which is adopted. Two basic views are the asset-liability view and the revenue-expense view. Under the asset-liability view, earnings are measured by the change (other than investments or withdrawals) in the net economic resources of an enterprise during a period. Therefore, definitions of assets and liabilities are the key under this view, and definitions of revenues, expenses, gains, and losses are secondary and are based on assets and liabilities.

The revenue-expense view holds that earnings are a measure of an enterprise's effectiveness in using its inputs to obtain and sell outputs. Thus, definitions of revenues and expenses are basic to this view, and definitions of assets, liabilities and other elements are derived from revenues and expenses.

Rather than review the definitions of all ten elements (contained in the outline of SFAC 3 on page 745, let us examine one definition in more detail. "Assets are probable future economic benefits obtained or controlled by a particular entity as a result of past transactions or events." This definition is based on the objectives and qualities of SFAC 1 and 2. The overall thrust of the objectives-- predicting and evaluating future cash flows--is reflected in the phrase "probable future economic benefits." "Control by a particular entity" is crucial if reporting an item as an asset is to have decision usefulness (or relevance). The quality of reliability is assured by the phrase "as a result of past transactions." Information is more verifiable, valid, and neutral (the components of reliability) if based on past transactions. A similar analysis can be applied to liabilities, equity, investments by owners, distributions to owners, comprehensive income, revenues, expenses, gains and losses.

SFAC 3 also defines some other concepts in addition to the ten elements. Especially important among these 11 additional concepts are accrual accounting, realization, recognition, and matching. Realization and recognition will be addressed by FASB later in the conceptual framework project. The definition of accrual accounting is important because SFAC 1 stated that accrual accounting should be used since it provides a better indication of future cash flows than the cash basis. This is true because accrual accounting records transactions with cash consequences (involving future cash flows) as they occur, not when the cash actually moves. Matching is referred to in most accounting literature as a principle, or fundamental law, of accounting. SFAC 3 refers to matching as a concept, but it will probably be established as a principle when FASB discusses the recognition and measurement phases of the conceptual framework project.

Some other basic "features" of accounting (also known as assumptions) were defined in APB Statement 4 (see outline on page 677). Especially important among these features are accounting entity, going concern, periodicity, monetary unit, and substance over form.

Recognition and Measurement. Recognition principles establish criteria concerning when an element should be included in the statements, while measurement principles govern the valuation of those elements. This is a crucial phase of the conceptual framework project which has not yet been discussed in a SFAC. Therefore,

this discussion will be based on earlier accounting literature including APB Statement 4.

An important issue to be resolved by FASB in this area is that of capital maintenance. Two basic concepts of capital maintenance (financial and physical) can be
used to separate return on capital (earnings) from return of capital (capital recovery). Remember, any capital which is "used up" during a period must be returned
before earnings can be recognized. In other words, earnings is the amount an entity
can distribute to its owners and be as well off at the end of the year as at the beginning.

One way "well-offness" can be measured is in terms of financial capital. This
concept of capital maintenance holds that the capital to be maintained is measured
by the amount of cash (possibly restated into constant dollars) invested by owners.
Earnings may not be recognized until the dollar investment in net assets, measured
in units of money or purchasing power, is returned. The financial capital maintenance concept is the traditional view which is reflected in most present financial
statements.

An alternative definition of "well-offness" is expressed in terms of physical
capital. This concept holds that the capital to be maintained is the physical productive capacity of the enterprise. Earnings may not be recognized until the current replacement costs of assets with the same productive capabilities of the assets
used up are returned. The physical capital maintenance concept supports current
cost accounting which must be used in some disclosures by certain entities (see SFAS
33). Again, the physical productive capacity may be measured in nominal or constant
dollars.

A simple example can further clarify the two capital maintenance concepts.
Suppose an enterprise invests $10 in an inventory item. At year end, the enterprise
sells the item for $15. In order to replace the item at year end, they would have
to pay $12 rather than $10. To further simplify, assume the increase in replacement
cost is due to specific price changes, and there is no general inflation.

The financial capital concept would maintain that the firm is as well off once
the dollar investment ($10) is returned. At that point, the financial capital is
maintained and the remaining $5 is return on capital, or income. The physical capi-
tal concept maintains that the firm is not as well off until the physical capacity
(a similar inventory item) is returned. Therefore, the firm must reinvest $12 to be
as well off. Then physical capital is maintained, and only the remaining $3 is re-
turn on capital or income.

As the previous discussion of capital maintenance indicates, FASB must decide which attribute will be measured (historical cost or current cost) and what unit of measure will be used (unadjusted dollars or dollars restated for changes in purchasing power). Refer to the section on inflation accounting (Chapter 9, Mod 30 of this volume) for further discussion.

APB Statement 4 (see outline on page 677) discussed six pervasive principles of accounting and three modifying conventions. Some or all of these principles may be established by FASB as recognition and measurement criteria, although Statement 4 does emphasize historical cost, unadjusted dollar accounting.

Three basic principles (or more depending on their coverage) will have to be established in the recognition and measurement area of the conceptual framework project. These principles will probably be concerned with cost, revenue, and matching. A cost principle will have to establish an appropriate valuation basis for financial statement elements (including the attribute to be measured and the unit of measure). A revenue principle will govern the measurement of revenue and the timing of its recognition. A matching principle should determine how expired costs, or expenses, should be associated with recognized revenues.

With respect to a cost principle, the alternatives available to FASB in this area can be found in the following table from the conceptual framework discussion memorandum. The table, which describes possible attributes of assets and liabilities which could be measured, is an excellent study aid for accounting theory.

ATTRIBUTES OF ASSETS AND LIABILITIES

Attribute	Assets	Liabilities
1. Historical cost/historical proceeds	Initially, the amount of cash (or its equivalent) paid to acquire an asset (historical cost); subsequent to acquisition, the historical amount may be adjusted for amortization.	Initially, the amount of cash (or its equivalent) received when an obligation was incurred (historical proceeds); subsequent to incurrence, the historical amount may be adjusted for amortization.
2. Current cost/current proceeds	Amount of cash (or its equivalent) that would have to be paid if the same asset were acquired currently (current cost) 2.1 The "same asset" may be an identical asset ("current reproduction cost" or "current cost of replacement in kind") 2.2 The "same asset" may be an asset with equivalent productive capacity ("current replacement cost")	Amount of proceeds that would be obtained if the same obligation were incurred currently (current proceeds)

Attribute	Assets	Liabilities
3. Current exit value in orderly liquidation	Amount of cash that could be obtained currently by selling the asset in orderly liquidation (current market value)	Cash outlay that would be required currently to eliminate the liability (current market value)
4. Expected exit value in due course of business	Amount of cash (or its equivalent) into which asset is expected to be converted in due course of business less direct costs necessary to make that conversion (this attribute of accounts receivable and inventories has customarily been referred to as "net realizable value")	Amount of cash (or its equivalent) expected to be paid to eliminate liability in due course of business including direct costs necessary to make those payments (nondiscounted amount of expected cash outlays)
5. Present value of expected cash flows	Present value of future cash inflows into which asset is expected to be converted in due course of business less present value of cash outflows necessary to obtain those inflows. Rate of discount may be: 5.1 Historical rate 5.2 Current rate 5.3 Other rate (for example, average expected rate or weighted average cost of capital)	Present value of future cash outflows to eliminate liability in due course of business including cash outflows necessary to make those payments. Rate of discount may be: 5.1 Historical rate 5.2 Current rate 5.3 Other rate (for example, average expected rate or incremental borrowing rate)

Reporting or Display. This facet of the conceptual framework is very dependent on the components previously discussed. Once the elements are defined, and it is determined when to recognize them and how to measure them, FASB must decide how they will be displayed in the financial statements. The concern is with what information will be provided, who should provide it, and where it should be displayed.

The information spectrum discussed earlier describes the available display options. Information can be formally incorporated in the financial statements (financial position, earnings, and funds flow), or in the notes to the financial statements. Other display alternatives are: required supplementary information (either accompanying the financial statements or available on request), or voluntary information.

Many of the important considerations in this area have been discussed in the accounting literature under the topic of disclosure. Most likely, a disclosure principle of some sort will later be adopted by FASB. Generally, it is felt that full disclosure is satisfied when the financial statements contain information sufficient to make them useful and not misleading. In other words, no relevant accounting information should be omitted. Qualitative characteristics such as relevance and reliability and the constraint of materiality are important in this area.

An example of the types of reporting and display alternatives available to FASB can be seen in the earnings statement:

Disclosure of reasons for past changes in revenues
Disclosure of reasons for past changes in expenses
Classification of expenses as fixed or variable
Detail of revenue and expense breakdowns
Information to be disclosed concerning irregular earnings
Types of separate supporting schedules
Restatement of prior year earnings
Inclusion of tables, graphs, or narration
Highlighting of certain groupings and relationships (e.g., gross margin or contribution margin)
Summarization of past performance
Disclosure of key ratios
Forecasting of future earnings

Similar alternatives can be developed for other forms of financial reporting.

STATUS OF ARBs, APBs, AND SFASs

The table on the following pages indicates whether ARBs, APBs, and SFASs have been superseded, modified, etc., by subsequent ARBs, APBs, or SFASs. You may wish to cross out superseded sections, paragraphs, etc., in original pronouncements and to cross reference them to superseding pronouncements. This will preclude the possibility of your studying superseded or amended material.

Each of the outlines in this chapter is referenced to the section where it is found in the FASB's Accounting Standards - Current Text (beginning with the June 1, 1983 Edition the Current Text is divided into two volumes: General Standards and Industry Standards), McGraw-Hill Book Company. These references appear in parentheses right after the original pronouncement reference.

Accounting Research Bulletins

ARB 43

Chapter 1B	Amended by APB 6 para 12, 13
Chapter 2A	Para 3 amended by APB 20
Chapter 2B	Superseded by APB 9
Chapter 3A	Para 6g amended by APB 21 para 16 Para 7 amended by SFAS 78 Para 8 amended by SFAS 6 Para 10 amended by APB 6 para 14
Chapter 3B	Superseded by APB 10 para 7
Chapter 4	Para 14 amended by APB 20

Chapter 5	Amended by APB 17 Para 10 superseded by APB 16 Para 8, 10 amended by SFAS 44
Chapter 6	Superseded by SFAS 5
Chapter 7A	Para 10 superseded by ARB 46
Chapter 7B	Para 6 amended by APB 6 para 16
Chapter 7C	Superseded by APB 16
Chapter 8	Superseded by APB 9
Chapter 9B	Superseded by APB 6 para 17
Chapter 9C	Para 11-13 amended by APB 11
Chapter 10A	Para 19 amended by SFAS 16
Chapter 10B	Superseded by APB 11
Chapter 11B	Para 8 amended by APB 11 Para 9 amended by SFAS 16
Chapter 12	Para 7, 10-22 superseded by SFAS 8 Para 5 amended by SFAS 8
Chapter 13A	Superseded by APB 8
Chapter 13B	Amended by APB 25
Chapter 14	Superseded by SFAS 13
Chapter 15	Superseded by APB 26
ARB 44	Superseded by ARB 44 (revised)
ARB 44(revised)	Para 4, 5, 7, 10 amended by APB 11 Para 9 revised by APB 6 para 20
ARB 47	Superseded by APB 8
ARB 48	Superseded by APB 16
ARB 49	Superseded by APB 15
ARB 50	Superseded by SFAS 5
ARB 51	Para 7-8 superseded by APB 16 Para 10 amended by SFAS 58 Para 16 superseded by APB 23 Para 17 amended by APB 11 Para 19-21 amended by APB 18

Accounting Principles Board Opinions

APB 2	Amended by APB 4
APB 3	Superseded by APB 19
APB 5	Superseded by SFAS 13
APB 6	Para 12c and 22 superseded by APB 16 Para 15 superseded by APB 17 Para 18 superseded by SFAS 8 Para 19 superseded by APB 26 Para 21 and 23 superseded by APB 11

APB 6 Appendix A	Superseded by Rule 203, Code of Professional Ethics
APB 7	Superseded by SFAS 13
APB 8	Amended by para 6, APB 12 Amended by SFAS 36, 74
APB 9	Para 6 amended by APB 13 Para 7 amended by para 9, APB 12 Para 18 modified by SFAS 16 Para 23, 24 deleted by SFAS 16 Para 20-22, 29 superseded by APB 30 Para 25 superseded by APB 20 Part II superseded by APB 15
APB 10	Para 2-4 superseded by APB 18 Para 5 superseded by APB 16 Para 8-9 superseded by APB 14
APB 11	Para 6 modified by APB 28 Para 38, 39, and 41 superseded by APB 23 Para 40 superseded by SFAS 9 Para 49, refer to APB 16 Para 57 amended by SFAS 37
APB 12	Para 11-15 superseded by APB 14
APB 15	Para 13 amended by APB 20 and APB 30 Para 33 amended by SFAS 55 Suspended for nonpublic enterprises by SFAS 21
APB 16	Para 99 amended by SFAS 10 Para 88 amended by SFAS 38 Para 96 amended by SFAS 79
APB 17	Amended by SFAS 2, 44, 72
APB 18	Para 15 superseded by SFAS 13 Para 19 superseded by APB 23 Para 19m amended by SFAS 58
APB 20	Footnote 9 deleted by SFAS 16 Para 16 amended by SFAS 32 Para 27 amended by SFAS 73 Para 34 amended by SFAS 58
APB 22	Para 13 amended by SFAS 2 and SFAS 8
APB 23	Para 2 amended by SFAS 9
APB 26	Amended by para 10, SFAS 15 Para 2, 3(a), 3(c), 19, 21 amended by SFAS 76
APB 27	Superseded by SFAS 13
APB 28	Amended by SFAS 3
APB 30	Does not affect APB 11 para 45, 61, or APB 16 para 60 Amended by SFAS 4, 44 Para 25 amended by SFAS 16
APB 31	Superseded by SFAS 13

Statements on Financial Accounting Standards

SFAS 1	Superseded by SFAS 8
SFAS 4	Para 8 and footnote 2 amended by SFAS 64
SFAS 5	Para 20 amended by SFAS 11
SFAS 8	Superseded by SFAS 52
SFAS 9	Superseded by SFAS 19
SFAS 13	Para 5b amended by SFAS 23 Para 5m superseded by SFAS 17 Para 8 amended by SFAS 26 Para 14 and 17 amended by SFAS 22 Para 5, 12, 16 and 18 amended by SFAS 29
SFAS 14	Suspended for nonpublic enterprises by SFAS 21 Para 4, 73, and footnote 15 deleted by SFAS 18 Para 41 amended by para 7b of SFAS 18 Para 7 amended by SFAS 24 Para 39 amended by SFAS 30
SFAS 19	Amended by SFAS 25 to permit full costing Paras 48-59 superseded by SFAS 69
SFAS 20	Superseded by SFAS 52
SFAS 32	Appendix A and/or B amended by SFAS 42, 56, 65, 67
SFAS 33	Supplemented by SFAS 39, 40, 41, 46, and 54 Para 51(b), 52(b), and 53(a) superseded by SFAS 69 Amended by SFAS 70
SFAS 34	Para 8 and 9 amended by SFAS 42 Para 9, 10, and 20 amended by SFAS 58 Para 10, 13, and 17 amended by SFAS 62
SFAS 35	Para 30 amended by SFAS 59, 75
SFAS 39	Amended by SFAS 69

FASB Interpretations Update

    FASB Interpretations, in contrast to Statements of Financial Accounting Standards (SFAS), are issued periodically to interpret an existing pronouncement. The FASB Interpretations are generally very narrow (specific) in comparison to SFASs, which amend or supersede existing pronouncements and establish GAAP in new areas. The FASB Interpretations issued to date and respective pronouncements interpreted are listed below. A summary of each interpretation is presented following the outline of the pronouncement interpreted. They are set apart in boxes only to separate them from the SFAS outlines. Those interpretations marked with an asterisk are not included because the authors feel that they are too specialized for the CPA exam.

Interp. No.	Pronouncement Interpreted	Interp. No.	Pronouncement Interpreted
1.	APB 20	19.	SFAS 13
2.	Superseded by SFAS 15	20.	APB 20
3.	APB 8	21.	SFAS 13
4.	SFAS 2	22.*	APBs 11 and 23
5.	Superseded by SFAS 7	23.	SFAS 13
6.	SFAS 2	24.	SFAS 13
7.	SFAS 7	25.	APB 2, 4, 11, 16
8.	SFAS 6	26.	SFAS 13
9.*	APB 16 and 17	27.	SFAS 13, APB 30
10.	SFAS 12	28.	APB 15, 25
11.	SFAS 12	29.	APB 23, 24
12.*	SFAS 12	30.	APB 29
13.	SFAS 12	31.	APB 15, Interpret. 28
14.	SFAS 5	32.	APB 2, 4, 11
15.	Superseded by SFAS 52	33.	SFAS 34
16.	SFAS 12	34.	SFAS 5
17.	Superseded by SFAS 52	35.	APB 18
18.	APB 28	36.	SFAS 19
		37.	SFAS 52

FASB Technical Bulletins

The FASB Technical Bulletins, unlike the foregoing forms of pronouncements, do not establish GAAP. These bulletins are interpretive in nature and provide answers to questions received by the FASB. Because of their limited applicability, we have not generally included summaries of Technical Bulletins in the following pages. However, in instances where we believe the Bulletins have widespread applicability making their requirement(s) prime candidates to be tested on the exam, we have included summaries following the pronouncements to which they apply.

FASB Technical Bulletin	Applicable Pronouncement
TB 83-1	APB 11

Study Program for the Accounting Pronouncements

Outlines of the unsuperseded official accounting pronouncements are presented in chronological order in this chapter. Effective dates of pronouncements are omitted unless they are a current implementation problem. You should:

1. Study through the outlines before studying Chapter 9, Financial Accounting
   a. The outlines presume prior study of the pronouncements
   b. If the outlines are your first contact with the pronouncements:
      1) Read the outline for an overview of the pronouncement
      2) Read the pronouncement
      3) Study the outline

    c. Please note that many of the recent SFASs are of such a specialized nature that the authors do not feel they will be tested in depth (denoted by a "†"). The outlines of these pronouncements should only be perused to get a general sense of their requirements

2. As you study Chapter 9, Financial Accounting:

    a. Return to this chapter to review appropriate pronouncements

    b. Each Chapter 9 study module contains references back to relevant pronouncements

        1) Examples, journal entries, etc., for the pronouncements are presented in Chapter 9

    c. SFASs that deal only with disclosure requirements are not covered in Chapter 9

3. <u>Required disclosures</u>. It is almost impossible to memorize all the required disclosures. A good approach is to take the position of a financial analyst: What data would you want to know? Utilizing this approach, you only have to memorize any exceptions, i.e., items you would not normally think a financial analyst would be interested in.

ACCOUNTING RESEARCH BULLETINS

ARB 43--Chapter 1A (A31, B50, C08, C23, R36, R70, R75)* Rules Adopted by Membership

Five rules recommended by the Committee on Cooperation with Stock Exchanges in 1934. The last rule is from another 1934 Institute committee.

1. Profit is realized at the point of sale unless collection is not reasonably assured.

2. Capital (paid-in) surplus should not be charged with losses or expenses, except in quasi-reorganizations.

3. Retained earnings of subsidiary created prior to acquisition is not part of consolidated retained earnings. This does not apply to poolings.

4. If it is possible to show treasury stock as an asset, dividends cannot be income.

5. Receivables from officers, employees, and affiliates must be separately disclosed.

6. Par value of stock issued for assets cannot be used to value the assets if some of the stock is subsequently donated back to the corporation.

Chapter 1B (C23) Profits or Losses on Treasury Stock   (Revised by APB 6, para 12)

Profits on treasury stock are not income and should be reflected in capital surplus.

Chapter 2A (F43) Comparative Financial Statements   (Cross referenced to APB 20)

Comparative statements enhance the usefulness of financial statements and should be presented.

---

*The references in parentheses are from the <u>FASB Accounting Standards - Current Text</u>, Volume II, McGraw-Hill Book Company.

Chapter 3A (B05) Current Assets and Current Liabilities
(Amended by APBs 6, 21 and SFAS 6)

Chapter 3A contains the definitions and eamples of current assets and liabilities. See SFAS 6 for refinancing short-term debt.

A. Current assets are "cash and other assets or resources commonly identified as those which are reasonably expected to be (1) realized in cash, (2) sold, or (3) consumed during the ordinary operating cycle of the business."

    1. Cash available for current operations (para 4)
    2. Inventories
    3. Trade receivables
    4. Other receivables collectible in one year
    5. Installment, deferred accounts, and notes receivable
    6. Marketable securities available for current operations
    7. Prepaid expenses

B. Current liabilities are "obligations whose liquidation is reasonably expected to require the use of existing resources properly classifiable as current assets or the creation of other current liabilities during the ordinary operating cycle of the business."
    1. Trade payables
    2. Collections received in advance of services
    3. Accruals of expenses
    4. Other liabilities coming due in one year
    5. Note that liabilities not using current assets for liquidation are not current liabilities, e.g., bonds being repaid from a sinking fund

C. Operating cycle is "average time intervening between the acquisition of materials or services entering this process and the final cash realization."

Chapter 4 (I78) Inventory Pricing

Contains 10 statements outlining inventory valuation.

    1. Inventory consists of tangible personal property

        a. Held for sale in ordinary course of business
        b. In process of production for such sale
        c. To be currently consumed in the production of such goods

    2. Major objective of inventory valuation is proper income determination

        a. Matching of costs and revenues

    3. Primary basis is cost. Cost includes all expenditures to bring article to existing condition and location.

        a. Direct or variable costing is not acceptable

    4. Cost may be determined under any flow assumption. Use method which most clearly reflects income

    5. Departure from cost to market required when utility is not as great as cost

    6. Market means current replacement cost subject to:

    a. Market should not exceed net realizable value (sales price less selling and completion costs)

    b. Market should not be less than net realizable value less normal profit

7. Lower of cost or market may be applied to individual items or the inventory as a whole. Use method which most clearly reflects income.

8. Basis for stating inventories and changes therein should be consistent and disclosed

9. Inventories may be stated above cost in exceptional cases

    a. No basis for cost allocation, e.g., meatpacking
    b. Disposal assured and price known, e.g., precious metals

10. Purchase commitment loss should be recognized in the same manner as inventory losses

Chapter 7A (Q15) Quasi-Reorganization

(Amended by ARB 46)

Describes what is permitted before and after quasi-reorganization.

A. Procedure in readjustment

  1. A clear report should be made to shareholders to obtain consent for the proposed restatements of assets and shareholders' equity
  2. Write-down of assets should not go below fair value
  3. If potential losses exist, provide for maximum probable loss
  4. When determined, amounts should be written off first to retained earnings and then to capital surplus

    a. A consolidated group should make write-offs such that all consolidated retained earnings are eliminated before any consolidated capital surplus is charged

B. Procedure after readjustment

  1. After readjustment, accounting should be similar to that appropriate for a new company
  2. A new, dated retained earnings account should be created

    a. Dated for 10 years. See ARB 46.

  3. Capital surplus arising from the reorganization is similar to any other capital surplus and should not be charged with losses

Chapter 7B (C20) Stock Dividends and Stock Splits

A. <u>Dividend</u>--evidence given to shareholders of their share of accumulated earnings which are going to be retained in the business

B. <u>Split</u>--stock issued to increase number of outstanding shares to reduce market price and/or to obtain a wider distribution of ownership

C. To the recipient, splits and dividends are not income. Dividends and splits take nothing from the property of the corporation and add nothing to the property of the recipient.

      1. Upon receipt of stock dividend or split, recipient should reallocate cost of shares previously held to all shares held

D. Issuer of a stock dividend (issuance is small in relation to shares outstanding and consequently has no apparent effect on market price) should capitalize retained earnings equal to the fair market value of shares issued

      1. Unless retained earnings are capitalized, retained earnings thought to be distributed by the recipient will be available for subsequent distribution

      2. Where distribution is so large it may materially affect price (a split), no capitalization is necessary other than required by law

          a. Some jurisdictions require that the par value of splits be capitalized, i.e., changes in par value are not permitted

      3. For closely held corporations, there is no need to capitalize retained earnings other than to meet legal requirements

      4. Issuances less than 20-25% of previously outstanding shares are dividends. Issuances greater than 20-25% of previously outstanding shares are splits.

Chapter 9A Depreciation and High Costs

Chapter 9 considers the problem of charging current income for depreciation of facilities acquired at lower price levels.

A. Recognition of the problem of providing for replacement of plant during price level increases

      1. The cost of material and labor are in current dollars while productive facility costs are in deflated dollars
      2. CAP disapproves immediate write-down of plant by depreciation charges believed to represent abnormal costs resulting from increasing price levels
      3. If inflation should proceed so far that historical cost loses significance, restatement of historical costs in depreciated dollars may be necessary

B. The problem of replacing plant during periods of increasing price levels should be met by financial management

      1. Stockholders, employees and the general public should be informed that plant replacement must be made out of present profits

Chapter 9B Depreciation on Appreciation (Superseded by APB 6, para 17)

Chapter 9C (D40) Emergency Facilities: Depreciation and Amortization
(Amended by APBs which were later either amended or superseded)

(The provisions of this pronouncement are not relevant to the CPA exam.)

Chapter 10A (T10) Real and Personal Property Taxes

Accounting for personal and real property taxes which vary in time of determination and collection from state to state.

A. In practice, the dates below have been used to apportion taxes between accounting periods

1. Assessment date
2. Beginning of fiscal period of taxing authority
3. End of fiscal period of taxing authority
4. Lien date
5. Date of tax levy
6. Date tax is payable
7. Date tax is delinquent
8. Period appearing on tax bill

B. The most acceptable basis is a monthly accrual on the taxpayer's books during the fiscal period of the taxing authority

1. At year end, the books will show the appropriate prepayment or accrual
2. An accrued liability, whether known or estimated, should be shown as a current liability
3. On income statement, property taxes may be charged to operating expense, deducted separately from income, prorated among accounts to which they apply, or combined with other taxes (but not with income taxes)

Chapter 11A (Co5) Cost-Plus-Fixed-Fee Contracts (CPFF)

A. When should CPFF revenues be included in the contractor's income statement?

1. Revenue may be credited to income based on partial performance if realization is reasonably assured

   a. Based on delivery of finished units is generally acceptable
   b. Per contract terms if representative of performance

B. What amounts are included in sales?

1. Reimbursable costs for manufacture and delivery of products
2. Fees for contracts involving services

C. What is proper balance sheet classification?

1. Unbilled costs and fees are receivables rather than inventory but should be shown separately

D. What is proper balance sheet disclosure of items related to CPFF?

1. Offsetting of advances on CPFF contracts against CPFF receivables is acceptable only if provided by contract and that treatment is expected in the normal course of transactions. Offsets should be clearly disclosed.

Chapter 11B (Co5) Renegotiation of Government Contracts

(The provisions of this pronouncement are not relevant to the CPA exam.)

Chapter 11C (Co5) Terminated Defense Contracts

(The provisions of this pronouncement are not relevant to the CPA exam.)

Chapter 12 Foreign Operations and Exchange (Superseded by SFAS 8)

Chapter 13B (C47) Stock Option Compensation Plans (Also see APB 25)

Cost of services received for compensation paid in stock options should be included in operations.

A. Compensation may arise when the corporation agrees to issue common stock to an employee at a stated price

  1. Other options may result in employee obligations such as continued employment

B. Stock options do not result in compensation if:

  1. Stock options are offered at a reasonable amount to raise capital
  2. Stock options are offered at a reasonable amount to induce wider holdings by employees

C. Alternative dates of measurement are when:

  1. Option plan is adopted
  2. Option is granted
  3. Grantee performs required conditions
  4. Grantee may first exercise option
  5. Grantee exercises option
  6. Grantee disposes of stock

D. Date of grant is the most reasonable date

  1. Considering the date of grant as a contract, it is the date value is determined
  2. Date of grant is date corporation foregoes alternative use
  3. In "C." above, "1." and "6." are not relevant

E. Compensation is excess of fair value over option price. APB 25 states the quoted market price or best estimate of fair market value is fair value.

F. Compensation cost should be spread over the period of service covered by the option contract

  1. Cash and compensation are equal to consideration for the stock when exercised (amount credited to stock and paid-in capital)

G. Disclosure should be made annually of:

  1. Number of shares under option
  2. Option price
  3. Number of shares exercisable
  4. Number of shares and price of options exercised

ARB 44 (D40) (Revised) Declining Balance Depreciation

A. Declining balance depreciation (and sum-of-the-years' digits) is systematic and rational

  1. When revenue earning power is greater in earlier periods of use
  2. When maintenance charges increase with age

B. Where accelerated depreciation is used for tax purposes but not for book purposes, accounting recognition should be given to deferred taxes

1. If accelerated depreciation is used for tax purposes and not for book purposes by a regulated company that does not recognize deferred taxes, disclosure should be made
2. Some regulatory bodies allow provisions for deferred taxes and some do not

    a. If provisions for deferred taxes are not allowed, the presumption is that regulated rates will be increased as depreciation savings are no longer available
    b. Thus, the regulatory body affects the proper matching of costs and revenues

ARB 45 (Co4) Long-term Construction Contracts

Discusses accounting for multiple period projects.

A. The percentage-of-completion method recognizes income as work progresses

1. Recognized income is to be that percentage of estimated income based on:

    a. (Incurred costs to date)/(Total expected costs) known as cost-to-cost measure
    b. Other measure of progress based on work performed, e.g., engineering or architectural estimate

2. Costs, for percentage-of-completion estimate, might exclude materials and subcontracts, especially in the early stages of a contract

    a. Avoids overstating the percentage-of-completion

3. If a loss is estimated on the contract, the <u>entire loss</u> should be recognized currently
4. Current assets include costs and income (loss) in excess of billings. Current liabilities include billings in excess of costs and income (loss).

    a. Contracts should be separated into net assets and net liabilities
    b. Contracts should not be offset on the balance sheet

5. Advantages of percentage-of-completion are periodic recognition of income and reflection of the status of the contract
6. The principal disadvantage is the reliance on estimates

B. The completed-contract method recognizes income when the contract is complete

1. General and administrative expenses can be allocated to contracts

    a. Not necessary if many projects are in process
    b. No excessive deferring of costs

2. Provision should be made for <u>entire amount of any expected loss</u> prior to job completion
3. An excess of accumulated costs over related billings is a current asset. An excess of accumulated billings over related costs is a liability (current in most cases)

    a. Balance sheet accounts are determined as in "A.4.a. & b."
    b. Recognized losses "B.2." reduce accumulated costs

    4. The advantage of the completed-contract method is that it is based on final results, and its primary disadvantage is that it does not reflect current performance

C. The percentage-of-completion method is recommended when total costs and percent of completion can be reasonably estimated

D. Disclosure should be made of extraordinary commitments by contractors which would not be financed by current billings

ARB 46 (Q15) Discontinuance of Dating Retained Earnings

Retained earnings subsequent to a quasi-reorganization should be dated for a period of 10 years. Thus, the fact that a reorganization took place is disclosed for 10 years.

ARB 51 (B50, C20, C51, R70) Consolidated Financial Statements (Also see APB 16)

A. Consolidated statements present financial statements of a parent and subsidiaries, as if the group were a single company for the benefit of the parent's stockholders and creditors

B. The general condition for consolidation is over 50% ownership of subsidiaries

    1. Subsidiaries which are a temporary investment (in reorganization, in bankruptcy, etc.) should not be consolidated
    2. Large indebtedness to bondholders should not preclude consolidation

C. Consolidation policy should be dictated by the need to make the statements meaningful in the circumstances, which implies adequate information without overburdening the reader

    1. Consolidated statements for a number of companies with heterogeneous operations may be preferable to a large number of separate statements
    2. It may be more useful not to consolidate some subsidiaries when their operations are entirely different than that of the consolidated group, e.g. a finance company subsidiary of a group of manufacturing companies

D. A difference in fiscal periods should not preclude consolidation

    1. Differences of 3 months are acceptable if one discloses material intervening events
    2. Differences in excess of 3 months should be consolidated on the basis of interim statements of the subsidiary

E. Consolidation policy should be disclosed by headings or footnotes

F. Intercompany balances and transactions should be eliminated in consolidated statements

    1. Intercompany gains and losses on assets remaining in the group should be eliminated (eliminate entire gross profit or loss even on transactions with minority interest subsidiaries)
    2. Companies in a regulated industry are allowed to recognize profit on intercompany sales

        a. E.g., when a subsidiary manufactures facilities for the parent or other subsidiaries

     b. The intercompany profit should constitute a reasonable rate of return on the investment

G. Retained earnings of subsidiaries at the acquisition date should not appear in the consolidated statements

H. When a parent purchases a subsidiary in several blocks of stock, the subsidiary's retained earnings should be determined by the step method (apply equity method to subsidiary retroactively)

I. When a subsidiary is purchased in midyear, subsidiary operations may be included in the consolidated income statement for the year and then the operating results prior to acquisition would be deducted

    1. As an alternative for a subsidiary purchased in midyear, post acquisition operations can be included in the consolidated income statement
    2. For midyear disposals, omit operations from the consolidated income statement and include equity in subsidiary's operations to disposal as a separate item in the income statement

Note: "G." through "I." pertain only to acquisitions accounted for as purchases per APB 16.

J. Subsidiaries' stock held by the parent should not be treated as outstanding in the consolidated balance sheet

K. If subsidiary losses eliminate the minority interest, charge any further minority interest losses to the parent's interest. If subsequent earnings arise, give parent's interest credit for minority interest losses previously absorbed.

L. When subsidiaries capitalize earnings subsequent to acquisition for stock dividends, such should not be reflected in the consolidated statements

    1. These are undistributed consolidated earnings
    2. Reverse the amounts pertaining to the parent's ownership

M. Sometimes combined, as distinguished from consolidated financial statements, are appropriate for commonly owned companies and are prepared as are consolidated statements

N. Parent company statements are sometimes required to inform creditors and preferred stockholders adequately. Dual column presentation of parent and consolidated statements is possible.

ACCOUNTING PRINCIPLES BOARD OPINIONS

APB 1 (D40) New Depreciation Guidelines

A. An interpretive opinion relating to a 1962 IRS release that revised recommended guidelines for service lives of assets

B. The opinion recommended companies attempt to adjust financial accounting asset service lives to conform with tax service lives (assuming that the tax service lives approximated the actual service lives)

APB 2 (I32) and 4 (I32) Accounting for the Investment Credit

The investment credit, a tax credit, is equal to a specified percentage of certain assets purchased. The tax credit, subject to limitations, reduces income tax payable during the year of purchase.

A. The APB considered three alternative accounting treatments

1. Subsidy to taxpayer's capital which was rejected, because the investment credit was thought to be an income item
2. Tax expense reduction (flow through) in year of asset purchase which was rejected in APB 2

    a. It was accepted in APB 4, because many firms and the SEC accepted this method after APB 2
    b. The argument for this treatment is that the tax savings is in year of purchase, because of the decision to purchase in that year

3. Cost reduction (deferral) which was accepted in APB 2 and APB 4. The APB supported the original adoption of this method because

    a. Earnings arise from use of facilities, not acquisition
    b. And ultimate realization is dependent on future use (otherwise it is recapturable)

B. The credit can be netted against the asset or shown as a deferred credit account. Carryforwards and carrybacks are allowable due to maximum annual credits, permitted by IRS.

1. Carrybacks should be shown as a receivable
2. Carryforwards should not be shown in the accounts until the credit becomes allowable, i.e., income is earned

---

FASB INTERPRETATION NO. 25 ACCOUNTING FOR AN UNUSED INVESTMENT TAX CREDIT
Does not permit recognition of investment tax credit (ITC) in advance of realization except to the extent it would be realized if tax liability was based on accounting income. Also, unused ITC acquired in a business combination cannot be recognized as an asset.

FASB INTERPRETATION NO. 32 APPLICATION OF PERCENTAGE LIMITATIONS IN RECOGNIZING INVESTMENT TAX CREDIT
The percentage limitation in determining income tax payable which can be offset in the with-and-without computation is the statutory rate for the computation year.

APB 2 Addendum - Accounting Principles for Regulated Industries

A. GAAP apply to regulated industries: utilities, common carriers, insurance companies, etc.

B. Differences may arise in the application of GAAP due to the rate making process. For instance, if a rate making body requires deferral of a cost normally expensed, the presumption is that the rate making body will allow the company to recover those costs in the future. Thus, it is properly deferrable.

C. Financial statements of regulated companies issued for financial reporting purposes should conform to GAAP

D. Auditors should comply with GAAS per regulated companies as per unregulated
    companies

APB 3 Statement of Sources and Application of Funds (Superseded by APB 19)

APB 5 Leases in Statements of Lessees (Superseded by SFAS 13)

APB 6 (B05, C23, D40, I60) Status of Accounting Research Bulletins

A. ARB 43, Chapter 1B Treasury Stock

1. An excess of purchase price of treasury stock, purchased for retirement or
    constructive retirement, over par or stated value may be allocated between
    capital surplus and retained earnings

    a. The charge to capital surplus is limited to all capital surplus from
        treasury stock transactions and retirements of the same issue and a pro
        rata portion of all other capital surplus of that issue

    b. Also, capital surplus applicable to fully retired issues may be charged

2. Alternatively, losses may be charged entirely to retained earnings
3. All gains on retirement of treasury stock go to capital surplus
4. When the decision to retire treasury stock has not been made, the cost of
    such is a contra shareholders' equity item. Losses may only be charged to
    capital surplus from treasury transactions and retirements of the same
    issue.
5. Some state laws prescribe accounting for treasury stock. These laws are to
    be followed where they are at variance with this APB. Disclose all statu-
    tory requirements concerning treasury stock such as dividend restrictions.

B. ARB 43, Chapter 3A Current Assets and Liabilities

Unearned interest, finance charges, etc. included in receivables should be deducted from the related receivable.

C. ARB 43, Chapter 7B Stock Dividends and Splits

States "the shareholder has no income solely as a result of the fact that the
corporation has income," but does not preclude use of the equity method.

D. ARB 43, Chapter 9B Depreciation on Appreciation

Fixed assets should not be written up to appraisal or market values. If foreign
subsidiaries have such write-ups, the write-ups are normally eliminated at consolidation. However, when write-ups have occurred, depreciation should be computed on the written-up amounts.

E. ARB 44 Revised Declining Balance Depreciation

Proper disclosure is necessary when a company, subject to rate-making regulation, uses accelerated depreciation for tax purposes, another method for financial reporting and does not provide for deferred taxes.

APB 7 Accounting for Leases of Lessors (Superseded by SFAS 13)

APB 8 (P15, A06) Pension Plans

Central problem is the annual charge to operations.

A. Pension plan, "an arrangement whereby a company undertakes to provide its re-
    tired employees with benefits that can be determined or estimated in advance
    from the provisions of a document . . . or from the company's practices."

    1. Applies to unfunded, insured, trust fund, defined contribution, defined
        benefit, deferred compensation plans, but not to profit sharing or plans
        whereby only selected employees receive pensions

        a. Actuarial assumptions: factors used to resolve uncertainties (e.g.,
            mortality rates, employee turnover, compensation levels, earnings on
            investments, etc.)

        b. Actuarial cost method: technique used by actuaries to determine costs
            of pension plan benefits

        c. Actuarial gains and losses: the effects on actuarially calculated pen-
            sion cost of: (1) deviations between actual experience and the actuarial
            assumptions used; or, (2) changes in actuarial assumptions as to future
            events

        d. Fund: assets accumulated to pay benefits

        e. Funded: the cumulative amount of pension cost that has been paid to a
            funding agency

        f. Interest: the return earned or to be earned on funds invested or to be
            invested to provide for future pension benefits [e.g., interest, divi-
            dends, rents, realized and unrealized gains (losses)]

        g. Normal cost: annual cost of a pension plan determined by a particular
            actuarial cost method

        h. Past service cost: cost assigned to periods prior to the inception of a
            pension plan under a particular actuarial cost method

        i. Pay-as-you-go: pension costs recognized only when benefits are paid to
            retired employees. (Note: this is not an acceptable method for deter-
            mining pension expense under APB 8.)

        j. Prior service cost: cost at a valuation point (after inception) as-
            signed to all prior periods. May arise as a result of an amendment to
            the plan, e.g., increase in benefits. Includes past service costs.

        k. Terminal funding: funding for each employee is made at retirement
            (Note: same as "i" above)

        l. Vested benefits: benefits not contingent on continued employment.
            Equal to the present value of all future payments to present and retired
            employees at a particular point in time.

B. All pension costs should be charged to income. Past service costs should not be
    charged to retained earnings.

    1. The maximum charge is the sum of:

        a. Normal cost
        b. Ten percent of past service costs until fully amortized
        c. Ten percent of changes in prior costs due to amendments to the plan

      d.   Interest on the cumulative difference between amounts expensed and amounts funded

  2.   The minimum charge is:

      a.   Normal cost
      b.   Interest on unfunded prior costs, i.e., on all unfunded amounts
      c.   A provision for vested benefits

  3.   The provision for vested benefits is the amount to reduce an excess of vested benefits over the sum of:

      a.   Pension fund
      b.   Plus balance sheet accruals
      c.   Minus any balance sheet deferred charges
      d.   The "excess" must decrease by 5% per year

C.   The difference between the amount funded (paid) and the annual provision should appear as either accrued or deferred pension cost on the balance sheet. In the event vested benefits exceed the pension fund and accrual, the accrual should be increased to the amount of vested benefits with a corresponding debit to deferred pension cost.

D.   Actuarial cost methods result in varying charges to income. Actuarial methods must be rational and systematic resulting in reasonably stable annual provisions. They include:

  1.   Accrued benefit methods in which the annual charge to income is the present value of increases in future payments due to the additional year of service. The charges increase per year because the employee is getting closer to retirement (shorter period to discount) and other factors such as increasing salary levels.

      a.   Unit credit method

  2.   Projected benefit method is a more level method of expensing pension plan benefits. Computations are based on projected payouts.

      a.   Entry age normal
      b.   Individual level premium
      c.   Aggregate method
      d.   Attained age normal

E.   Actuarial gains and losses arise because of errors in previously made forecasts of appreciation on investments, vesting rates, salary rates, etc. Actuarial gains and losses should not be recognized in one period. They should be spread or averaged over a 10 to 20 year period.

  1.   An alternative is to make an adjustment of prior service cost (implies at least 10 years of amortization remains)
  2.   Actuarial gains and losses should be recognized immediately if they arise from a single occurrence not related to the pension plan or ordinary business operations, e.g., a plant closing. Another example is a purchase of a business wherein the gain or loss adjusts the purchase price; immediate recognition is not acceptable in a pooling.

F.   All employees reasonably expected to receive benefits should be included in the cost calculations after allowing for turnover

G. Companies with more than one plan can use different actuarial cost methods, or can treat them as one plan

H. Defined contribution plans state that benefits will only be paid from stipulated contributions. In such cases, the contribution is the expense. If a defined contribution plan has defined benefits, the provision should be based on the defined benefits.

I. Insured funds should be accounted for as any other plan which may cause differences between funded amounts and annual provisions. In some plans, however, net premiums paid may be the appropriate annual provision.

J. The APB assumes funded plans. Annual provisions should be increased by interest on prior period provisions not funded, or be decreased by interest on overfunded amounts.

K. Deferred tax accounting is appropriate when pension expense per books and per tax return differ

L. The following disclosures should be made in the financial statements

1. Statement that a plan exists and who is covered
2. Statement of accounting and funding policies
3. Annual provision for pension cost
4. Nature and effect of significant matters that affect comparability such as changes in accounting methods [e.g., treatment of actuarial gains (losses)]
5. See SFAS 36 for additional disclosures required for defined benefit plans

M. Upon change of pension plan accounting method (actuarial cost method, treatment of actuarial gains and losses, amortization of prior costs, etc.), all adjustments must be carried forward prospectively and none retroactively, i.e., no charges to retained earnings

> FASB INTERPRETATION NO. 3 ACCOUNTING FOR THE COST OF PENSION PLANS SUBJECT TO THE EMPLOYEE RETIREMENT INCOME SECURITY ACT OF 1974
> ERISA does not change minimum-maximum calculations of APB 8, but may change amount of expense recognized. Changes should affect expense prospectively, not retroactively.

APB 9 (I17, CO8) Reporting the Results of Operations (Part II superseded by APB 15)

A. APB 9 ended the then-acceptable alternatives of current-operating and all-inclusive concepts of income statements

1. The current-operating concept presented only normal operation items in the income statement; extraordinary items were taken to retained earnings

2. The all-inclusive concept required all P&L items be included in the income statement; no P&L items were taken directly to retained earnings

B. APB 9 designated a new format in which all normal, operating items would be presented at the top of the income statement resulting in "net income before extraordinary items"

1. "Net income before extraordinary items" is followed by extraordinary items resulting in "net income"

C. "Prior period adjustments" are excluded from the income statement and constitute adjustments of beginning retained earnings disclosed at the top of the retained earnings statement

1. Beginning retained earnings are adjusted by "prior period adjustments" resulting in "restated beginning retained earnings"

2. "Restated retained earnings" is then adjusted for net income and dividends which results in ending retained earnings

D. See SFAS 16 for description of prior period adjustments

E. Prior period adjustments should be disclosed in the period of adjustment

1. The effect on each prior period presented should be disclosed including restated income taxes
2. Disclosure in subsequent periods is not normally required
3. Historical summary data should also be restated and disclosed in the period of adjustment

F. The APB also reaffirmed earlier positions that the following should not affect determination of net income

1. Transactions in the company's own stock
2. Transfers to or from retained earnings
3. Quasi-reorganization adjustments

APB 10 (A35, C16, I24, I28, R75) Omnibus Opinion--1966

A. Discounting tax allocation accounts

While Accounting Research Study No. 9 Interperiod Allocation of Corporate Income Taxes recommended present value discounting of long-term deferral accounts, deferred taxes should not be accounted for on a discounted basis

B. ARB 43, Chapter 3B   Working Capital

1. Offsetting of liabilities and assets in the balance sheet is not acceptable unless a right of offset exists
2. Most government securities are not designed to be prepayment of taxes and thus may not be offset against tax liabilities. Only where an explicit prepayment exists may an offset be used

C. Liquidation Preference of Preferred Stock

For preferred stock, disclose:

1. Involuntary liquidation value when it considerably exceeds par value
2. Aggregate or per share amounts to call or redeem
3. Aggregate and per share dividend arrearages when cumulative

D. Installment Method of Accounting

Revenues should be recognized at the point of sale unless receivables are in doubt. Then the installment or cost recovery method may be used.

APB 11 (I17, I24, I28, I37) Accounting for Income Taxes

A. Applicability

1. Does not apply to regulated industry companies described in the Addendum to APB 2
2. APB emphasizes that Opinions apply only to material items

B. Timing differences are transactions which affect taxable income in periods different from when they affect book income

   1. Timing differences originate in one period and reverse in a subsequent period
   2. For example, a company may recognize a gain in period of sale per books and recognize the gain in subsequent periods, e.g., when sales price is collected, per taxable income

C. Interperiod tax allocation is required which results in the recognition of tax effects in the period in which the related transactions are recognized per books. In "B.2." above, the tax expense associated with the gain would be recognized per books in the period the gain was recognized even though the tax liability would accrue as the sales price was collected.

   1. The deferred method of interperiod tax allocation, required by APB 11, emphasizes the tax effect of the timing difference when they originate. Deferred taxes are determined at the time the timing differences originate.

      a. Transactions reducing taxes currently payable are treated as deferred credits
      b. Transactions increasing taxes currently payable are treated as deferred charges
      c. Amortization of the deferred taxes is based on the transactions producing the deferrals

   2. The liability method, not advocated by the APB, accrues or defers the amount that is expected to be taken into taxable income, i.e., the expected tax rate is used to compute the accrual or deferral

      a. Computations are tentative
      b. Deferrals and accruals are subject to adjustment based on changes in tax rates

   3. The net of tax method, not allowed by the APB, nets the deferral or accrual (computed under the deferral or liability method) against the related asset or liability giving rise to the timing difference

   4. Partial allocation, not advocated by the APB, applies interperiod tax allocation to timing differences which will reverse in a relatively short period, e.g., five years

      a. Partial allocation would apply to installment sales and long-term contracts resulting in timing differences
      b. Partial allocation does not apply to timing differences which result in an indefinite postponement of tax payments. For example, use of accelerated depreciation for tax purposes and straight-line for book purposes, i.e., <u>comprehensive allocation.</u>

   5. Interperiod tax allocation is not applied to permanent timing differences

      a. Permanent differences are income or expense items appearing in book income but never in tax income or vice versa
      b. An example is interest income on municipal securities

   6. In computing the tax effects of a year

      a. Deferred taxes arising from transactions of this period may be recognized at current rates and reversal of deferred taxes should be done at rates existing at the beginning of the year in the deferral accounts

       1)   Or the net changes in the deferred accounts may be made at the prevailing rates

      b.   No recognition of reversals of timing effects should be made if no provision was originally made

D.   Operating losses may be carried forward or backward, i.e., deducted from future or past earnings for tax credit

   1.   Loss carrybacks should be recognized in the period of loss. It may also be appropriate to amortize existing net deferred tax credits.

   2.   Loss carryforwards should not be recognized until they are realized (income is earned in the future) unless realization is assured beyond any reasonable doubt

      a.   The loss resulted from an identifiable, isolated, and nonrecurring loss
      b.   And future taxable income is virtually certain to be large enough to offset the carryforward

   3.   When net deferred tax credits exist and a loss carryforward is not recognized, the net deferred tax credits should be amortized by the lesser of:

      a.   Tax effect of the loss carryforward
      b.   Normal amortization of the net deferred tax credits

   4.   If the operating loss credit is recognized in the future, the deferred tax credits amortized should be reinstated at current rates

   5.   When loss carryforward credits are recognized in subsequent periods, they are reported as extraordinary items

   6.   When a loss carryforward is recognized in the year of loss, existing deferred tax credit accounts are amortized in future years

      a.   The tax credit for the year of loss is computed with the expected tax rate at the time of realization. If subsequent changes take place in the tax rate, the asset account and tax expense should be adjusted in the year of change.

   7.   The rules covering operating loss carrybacks and carryforwards apply to other unused tax items carried forward and backward

E.   Intraperiod (TRA vs. TER) tax allocation requires the allocation of period tax expense to:

      a.   Income before extraordinary items
      b.   Extraordinary items
      c.   Prior period adjustments
      d.   Direct entries to other shareholder equity accounts

   1.   The income tax expense associated with income before extraordinary items should be determined independent of the tax consequences of the other items
   2.   The tax consequences of an operating loss should be associated with the operating loss when an operating loss occurs

F.   Financial statement disclosures

   1.   On the balance sheet, net current deferrals and net noncurrent deferrals should be disclosed (See SFAS 37)

a. Refunds of past taxes or offsets to future taxes arising from carry-forwards and carrybacks should be classified per definitions of current items ARB 43, Chapter 3A

b. Deferred taxes are not an element of shareholders' equity

2. The tax expense of the current period should be broken down into:

a. Taxes payable
b. Timing difference effects
c. Operating loss effects

3. Other required disclosures include:

a. Operating loss carryforwards not yet recognized and their expiration dates
b. Material amounts of other unused deductions or credits
c. Explanations of significant variations between book and tax income

---

FASB TECHNICAL BULLETIN 83-1 ACCOUNTING FOR THE REDUCTION IN THE TAX BASIS OF AN ASSET CAUSED BY AN INVESTMENT CREDIT

In accordance with AICPA Interpretation 8 a basis difference for tax and book purposes is generally treated as a permanent difference. However, section 205 of the Tax Equity and Fiscal Responsibility Act of 1982 (TEFRA) provides the taxpayer with the option of either reducing the allowable ITC or reducing the depreciable basis by 1/2 of the ITC taken. The reduction in the basis caused by the latter option is considered to be a timing difference. Accordingly, deferred taxes should be provided for a reduction in the tax basis of an asset in the year that the related investment credit is recognized as a credit to income tax expense.

The foregoing is applicable to only the flow-through method of accounting for the investment tax credit. The deferral method of accounting for the credit is not materially affected by the change and, therefore, not addressed by the bulletin.

APB 12 (C08, C38, D40, I69, V18) Omnibus Opinion--1967

A. Allowance or contra accounts (allowance for bad debts, accumulated depreciation, etc.) should be deducted from assets or groups of assets with appropriate disclosure

B. Disclosure of depreciable assets should include:

1. Depreciation expense for the period
2. Balances of major classes of depreciable assets by nature or function
3. Accumulated depreciation either by major class or in total
4. Description of method(s) of depreciation by major classes of assets

C. Deferred compensation contracts should be accounted for in compliance with APB 8 Accounting for the Cost of Pension Plans

1. The cost of these plans should be accrued over the period of active employment from the time the contract is entered into or the effective date of APB 12
2. When a plan calls for the option of a deferred annuity or minimum payment at death, the cost should be based on the deferred annuity

D. Changes in the separate shareholder equity accounts in addition to retained earnings and changes in number of equity securities must be disclosed in the year of change

1. In separate statements
2. Or the financial statements
3. Or the notes

APB 13 Amends APB 9 <u>Reporting the Results of Operation</u> to apply to commercial banks.

<u>APB 14 (D10, C08) Convertible Debt and Debt Issued with Stock Warrants</u>

A. Convertible debts are those securities which are convertible into common stock of the issuer or affiliate. Terms generally include:

1. Lower interest rate than on ordinary debt
2. Initial conversion price greater than the common price at time of issuance
3. A conversion price which does not decrease except to protect against dilution

B. While there are arguments to account for the debt and equity characteristics separately, the APB has concluded no proceeds of a convertible issue should be attributed to the conversion factor

1. Primary reasons are:

    a. The inseparability of the debt and conversion features
    b. The practical difficulties of valuing the conversion feature

C. When debt is issued with detachable purchase warrants, the debt and warrants generally trade separately and should be treated separately

1. The allocation of proceeds should be based on relative market value at date of issuance
2. Any resulting debt discount or premium should be accounted for as such

D. Separate valuation of debt and warrants is applicable where the debt may be used as consideration when exercising the warrants. Separate valuation is <u>not</u> acceptable where the debt must be tendered to exercise the warrants (i.e., the warrants are, in essence, nondetachable).

<u>APB 15 (E09, C16) Earnings per Share</u>   (only applies to publicly held companies per SFAS 21)

A. Earnings per share information must be presented on the face of the income statement for the following income elements:

1. Income from continuing operations (APB 30)
2. Income before extraordinary items and/or cumulative effect of an accounting change
3. Cumulative effect of change in accounting principle (APB 20)
4. Net income
5. It is desirable, but not required, for:

    a. Discontinued operations (APB 30)
    b. Extraordinary items

B. Simple capital structures

1. No potentially dilutive securities exist, e.g., no convertible bonds or preferred, no options or warrants, no contingent share agreements, etc.

2. If potentially dilutive securities exist, then dilution from these securities is less than 3% in the aggregate

  a. Dilution is defined as a reduction of EPS on outstanding weighted
      average common shares
  b. Antidilutive securities are not figured in the 3% test above because
      these securities either increase EPS on weighted average common shares
      outstanding or a loss per these shares is reduced

C. Complex capital structures
  1. Contain potentially dilutive securities, e.g., convertible debt and pre-
      ferred, options, contingent shares, e.g., which in the aggregate dilute EPS
      based upon outstanding common shares by 3% or more and require a dual pre-
      sentation of EPS
  2. Primary Earnings Per Share (PEPS) is based upon outstanding common and those
      securities substantially equivalent to common stock having a dilutive
      effect

    a. Common stock equivalents (CSE) are defined as, "a security which is not,
        in form, a common stock, but which usually contains provisions to enable
        its holder to become a common stockholder and which, because of its
        terms and the circumstances under which it was issued, is in substance
        equivalent to a common stock." (Para 25). Securities which either are
        CSE or have the potential to be are:

        1) Convertible debt and preferred stock
        2) Stock options and warrants
        3) Participating securities and two class common
        4) Contingent issuances

    b. Convertible securities are determined to be or not to be CSE at issu-
        ance

        1) Convertible securities are CSE if their yield rate, at issuance, is
            less then 2/3 of the then existing bank prime rate of interest*

        2) Convertible securities subsequently issued or outstanding with the
            same terms as other CSE are CSE

    c. Options and warrants are CSE at all times. The assumption of exercise,
        however, is not made until the exercise price is below the market price
        for substantially all of the last 3 months of the year.

    d. Contingent issuances are CSE if shares issued depend merely upon the
        passage of time or, if contingency is based upon maintenance or attain-
        ment of earnings levels and the earnings level is currently attained

  3. Fully Diluted Earnings Per Share (FDEPS) is a pro forma presentation of the
      maximum dilution of EPS based upon outstanding common shares by including
      all contingent issuances individually having a dilutive effect as of the
      beginning of the period

    a. FDEPS includes dilutive CSE, and
    b. FDEPS also includes the dilutive effects of securities which are not
        CSE
D. Computational Guidelines
  1. For both simple and complex capital structures, the following procedures
      apply:

*Amended by SFAS 55 to read: "then existing average Aa corporate bond yield."

a. Compute the weighted average of common shares outstanding. Treasury shares should be excluded as of date of repurchase.

b. EPS data for all periods presented should be retroactively adjusted for all splits and dividends, even those subsequent to the period being presented

c. For stock issued in purchase combinations, use weighted average from date of combination. For pooling combination, shares assumed outstanding the entire period regardless of when issued.

d. The claims of senior securities (nonconvertible preferred dividends) should be deducted from income prior to computing EPS. Dividends on cumulative preferred are deducted whether or not declared, while dividends on noncumulative preferred are deducted only if declared.

e. EPS figures should be based upon consolidated income figures after consolidating adjustments and eliminations

2. For complex capital structures, these additional procedures apply for PEPS and FDEPS:
   a. The "if converted" method is used to adjust EPS on outstanding common shares for dilutive convertible securities

   1) The convertible securities are considered to have been converted at the beginning of the period (or at issuance if later) increasing the denominator of EPS

   2) For convertible bonds, the interest savings net of tax is added to the numerator of EPS

   3) For convertible preferred, the preferred dividends deducted in arriving at EPS are not deducted, thereby, increasing the numerator. There is no tax effect because dividends are not an expense.

   4) If convertible preferred is antidilutive, then the computational guidelines for nonconvertible preferred apply.

   b. The "treasury stock" method is used to adjust EPS on outstanding common shares for dilutive options and warrants, i.e., those for which the exercise price is below the market price

   1) The options and warrants are assumed to be exercised at the beginning of the period (or the date the options and warrants were issued if later). The shares assumed issued increase the denominator of EPS

   2) The hypothetical proceeds are used to purchase treasury stock at the average price over the year for PEPS and at the end of year price, if higher, for FDEPS. This has the effect of decreasing the denominator but not to the extent increased in "1)" directly above.

      a) No more than 20% of the common stock outstanding at the end of the period may be treated as repurchased. The shares over 20% are added to the denominator

      b) If options and warrants for more than 20% of the common shares exist, then the excess hypothetical funds due to the 20% limitation should be considered to reduce long-term debt or to be invested in interest bearing securities. The resulting interest savings (on debt) or earnings (on securities) are added to the numerator net of tax

   3) No retroactive adjustment should be made to EPS figures for options and warrants as a result of market price changes

c. When convertible securities require payment of cash at conversion, they are considered options. The "if converted" method is used for the conversion and the "treasury stock" method is applied to the cash proceeds.

d. Contingent issuances dependent on certain conditions being met

    1) Maintenance or attainment of earning levels

        a) If level is currently attained, include shares in both PEPS and FDEPS

        b) If earnings level is not currently attained, do not include shares in PEPS calculation, but do include them in FDEPS, if dilutive, after adjusting numerator to specified earnings level

        c) If the contingency agreement expires without issuance of additional stock, the contingency should be excluded from the last period and the contingency should be retroactively removed from earlier periods

    2) Market price of stock at future date (applies to both PEPS and FDEPS)

        a) EPS should reflect number of shares issuable at year-end price

        b) Prior EPS figures should be retroactively adjusted for changes in shares issuable due to market price changes

    3) If contingent stock issuances are contingent on both market price and earnings levels, EPS adjustments should be based on both conditions

e. Computation guidelines for participating securities and two class common are not presented because of their relative unimportance insofar as the CPA exam is concerned

f. No antidilutive securities should be included in either PEPS and FDEPS

E. Disclosure Guidelines

  1. Captions for the income statement

    a. For simple capital structures--Earnings Per Common Share

    b. For complex capital structures

      1) Primary--Earnings per common and common equivalent share

      2) Fully diluted--Earnings per share assuming full dilution

  2. Additional disclosures for complex capital structure EPS

    a. A schedule explaining the EPS figures should be presented disclosing common stock equivalents, underlying assumptions, and number of shares issued upon conversion, warrants, etc.

    b. If potential dilution exists in any of the periods, both PEPS and FDEPS should be presented for all periods

      1) Gives the reader understanding of the trend in potential dilution

      2) If earnings of a prior period presented have been restated, the EPS data should be revised and effect of restatement in EPS should be disclosed in year of restatement

    c. Supplementary EPS figures should be presented when:

      1) Conversions during or after the period would have affected PEPS. Note that PEPS should not be retroactively adjusted for conversions

      2) Sale of common or common equivalents and the proceeds are used to retire debt, preferred, etc.

3. For both simple and complex capital structures, as the case may be, the financial statements should summarize the rights or equity issues outstanding

   a. Dividend and liquidation preferences
   b. Participation rights
   c. Call prices and dates
   d. Conversion or exercise prices and dates
   e. Sinking fund requirements
   f. Unusual voting rights

FASB INTERPRETATION NO. 31   TREATMENT OF STOCK COMPENSATION PLANS IN EPS COMPUTATIONS

When computing EPS, exercise proceeds from stock options include amount to be paid by employees and amounts of related compensation not yet expensed. Compensation expense previously recognized is excluded. If alternative plans available, use same plan to compute EPS as was used to compute compensation expense.

APB 16 (B50) Business Combinations
(Para 96 amended by SFAS 79)

Both pooling and purchase accounting are applicable to business combinations but not as alternatives. No part purchase, part pooling.

A. A combination meeting all of the following criteria is a pooling; all others are purchases

1. Combining companies. Independent ownerships are combined to continue previously separate operations (para 46).

   a. "Each of the combining companies is autonomous and has not been a subsidiary or division of another corporation within two years before the plan of combination is initiated."

     1) Plan is initiated when announced publicly to stockholders
     2) A new company meets criterion as long as it is not a successor to a nonindependent company
     3) A previously owned company divested due to government order is exempted from this criterion

   b. "Each of the combining companies is independent of the other combining companies."

     1) No more than 10% of any combining company is held by any other combining company(ies)

2. Combining of Interest. Combination by exchange of stock (para 47).

   a. "The combination is effected in a single transaction or is completed in accordance with a specific plan within one year after the plan is initiated."

     1) Must be completed in a year unless governmental proceeding or litigation prevent completion in one year

   b. "A corporation offers and issues only common stock with rights identical to those of the majority of its outstanding voting common stock in exchange for substantially all of the voting common stock interest of another company at the date the plan of combination is consummated."

1) Cash may be distributed for partial shares but not pro rata to all stockholders
2) 90% of stock outstanding at consummation must be acquired by issuing corporation. The following shares are excluded from the shares considered acquired at consummation.

   a) Stock acquired before plan was initiated and still owned
   b) Stock acquired, other than by issuing its own, between initiation and consummation
   c) Outstanding after consummation
   d) Shares of the issuing company held by a combining company are converted into an equivalent number of shares of the combining company and are deducted from the shares considered acquired at consummation

3) When more than 2 companies are combined, the criteria must be met for each of them
4) An issuing company may acquire equity securities of the combining company other than common by any means except those issued for the combining company's stock within the prior two years (which must be acquired with common stock)

c. "None of the combining companies changes the equity interest of the voting common stock in contemplation of effecting the combination either within two years before the plan of combination is initiated or between the dates the combination is initiated and consummated; changes in contemplation of effecting the combination may include distributions to stockholders and additional issues, exchanges, and retirements of securities."

   1) Normal dividend distributions (as determined by past dividends) are permitted

d. "Each of the combining companies reacquires shares of voting common stock only for purposes other than business combinations, and no company reacquires more than a normal number of shares between the dates the plan of combination is initiated and consummated."

   1) Normal treasury stock acquisitions (as determined by past acquisitions) are permitted
   2) Acquisition by other combining companies is the same as treasury stock acquisition

e. "The ratio of the interest of an individual common stockholder to those of other common stockholders in a combining company remains the same as a result of the exchange of stock to effect the combination."

   1) No stockholder denies or surrenders his potential share in the issuing corporation

f. "The voting rights to which the common stock ownership interests in the resulting combined corporation are entitled are exercisable by the stockholders; the stockholders are neither deprived of nor restricted in exercising those rights for a period."

   1) For example, stock cannot be put in a voting trust

g. "The combination is resolved at the date the plan is consummated and no provisions of the plan relating to the issue of securities or other consideration are pending."

        1) No contingent future issuances or other consideration (including through a trustee)

        2) Later settlement of contingencies at the date of consummation is permitted

3. Absence of Planned Transactions (para 48)

   a. "The combined corporation does not agree directly or indirectly to retire or reacquire all or part of the common stock issued to effect the combination."

   b. "The combined corporation does not enter into other financial arrangements for the benefit of the former stockholders of a combining company, such as a guaranty of loans secured by stock issued in the combination, which in effect negates the exchange of equity securities."

   c. "The combined corporation does not intend or plan to dispose of a significant part of the assets of the combining companies within two years after the combination other than disposals in the ordinary course of business of the formerly separate companies and to eliminate duplicate facilities or excess capacity."

B. Application of Pooling Method

1. Assets and liabilities are aggregated after adjusting all the accounts to conform to a uniform set of methods. The accounting changes are made retroactively, and prior periods statements restated.

2. Stockholder equities are combined also. If the par or stated value of the new corporation exceeds that of all the combining companies, the excess should be taken first from combined paid-in capital, and then from retained earnings.

   a. If a combining corporation has a deficit, it should not be eliminated before the combination but rather closed to the combined retained earnings

   b. An issuing corporation using its treasury stock to effect a combination should account for it first as retired and then reissued

   c. An investment in stock of an issuing company by a combining company is considered retired in the combination

        1) Issuing company stock is considered treasury stock

3. The first combined income statement should be reported as if the pooling had taken place at the beginning of the period, i.e., restate pooling to beginning of period to report a year of combined operations

   a. The effects of intercompany transactions, on current assets and liabilities, revenues, and cost of sales during the interim period prior to the combination, should be eliminated

        1) Per share effects of nonrecurring transactions on long-term assets and liabilities should be disclosed (they need not be eliminated)

   b. The balance sheet and other statements restated at the beginning of the period should be disclosed as being retroactively combined individual company statements

   c. Revenue, extraordinary items, and net income of each of the combining companies for the interim period prior to the pooling should be disclosed in the notes to the financial statements

4. The costs of a pooling are expensed as incurred

5. A pooling should be reported when consummated

    a. Statements of combining companies should be issued as the pooling is being initiated with disclosure of the pooling

    b. An issuing corporation should record stock paid for in cash at cost, and stock acquired by issuing stock at the proportionate share of the net book value of the acquired company

        1) Until the pooling method is known to be appropriate, the investment and income account should reflect proportionate income of the acquired company

        2) After pooling is consummated, retroactively restate statements on pooling basis

6. The notes of a combined company in the period of pooling should disclose:

    a. Name and description of pooled companies

    b. Pooling accounting was used

    c. Description and number of shares issued

    d. Details of operations of separate companies for period prior to pooling included in first year's operation

    e. Accounting adjustments to achieve uniform accounting methods

    f. Explanation of change in retained earnings caused by change in fiscal year

    g. Reconciliation of individual company operating results to combined results

C. Application of the Purchase Method

1. The standard historical cost principles are applied to purchase accounting

    a. Use fair value of property given or fair value of property received whichever is more clearly evident

    b. Cost of specific assets should be based on relative market value

    c. Nature of asset and not acquisition determines subsequent accounting (amortization)

2. The acquiring corporation is the one retaining the larger portion of the voting rights of the combined corporation

3. The cost of a company includes direct costs of acquisition but not indirect and general expenses

4. Additional payments to be made, contingent on future earnings and/or security prices, should be disclosed but not recorded as a liability

    a. If contingency payments are made because of attainment of specified earnings levels, the additional payment is considered an increase in the cost of the subsidiary (usually results in debits to goodwill)

    b. If contingency payments are made due to attainment of specified security price levels, the cost of the acquired company is not affected. Rather the amount originally recorded as consideration in acquisition should be reduced by the contingency payment (usually results in decreasing paid-in capital).

    c. If contingency payments are based on both security prices and earnings, the payment should be separated and accounted as in "a." and "b."

  d. Interest or dividends on contingency distributions paid to an escrow agent should be added to the cost of the acquisition when the contingency is resolved

  e. Tax savings from imputed interest in contingent issuances reduces the value of contingent consideration if based on earnings and increases capital recorded for contingent consideration if based on security prices

5. The acquiring corporation should allocate the cost of the acquired company to assets and liabilities acquired. Independent appraisals may be used.

  a. Marketable securities--net realizable value
  b. Receivables--present value after allowance and collection costs
  c. Finished goods and work-in-process inventories--net realizable value less normal profit
  d. Raw materials--replacement costs
  e. Plant--replacement cost if to be used and at net realizable value if to be sold
  f. Intangible assets (identifiable)--appraisal values
  g. Other assets--appraisal values
  h. Payables--current values
  i. Accruals (pensions, warranties, etc)--present values

6. The acquiring company should recognize the accrual of interest on assets and liabilities recorded at present values

  a. Previously recorded goodwill of the acquired company should not be recorded by the acquiring company
  b. The acquiring company should retroactively adjust goodwill for unrecognized tax loss carryforwards of an acquired company as they are recognized

7. The differences between the recorded and the tax base asset amounts are not timing differences
8. The value assigned to net assets should not exceed cost

  a. If the cost of the net assets acquired exceeds the net revised asset values, the excess should be recorded as goodwill

  b. If the net revised asset value exceeds costs, the excess should be credited, pro rata, to all noncurrent assets except marketable securities

    1) If a credit (negative goodwill) continues to exist after all noncurrent assets except marketable securities are written down to zero, the excess is a deferred credit and should be taken to income systematically and rationally
    2) No negative goodwill should be added directly to shareholders' equity at acquisition

9. The date of acquisition is the date assets are received and securities issued

  a. If a date other than when assets are transferred is considered the effective date, the interest effects of the exchange of consideration and income earned by the acquired should be recognized

10. The notes of the acquiring company in the year of purchase should include:

    a. Name and description of acquired company
    b. Acquisition was a purchase
    c. Period that acquired results of operations are consolidated
    d. Cost of acquired and shares issued
    e. Plan of amortization and goodwill
    f. Contingent payments

11. Pro forma results of operations of the current and immediate prior period (no other prior periods) should reflect operations of the combination including:*

    a. Revenue
    b. Income before extraordinary items
    c. Net income
    d. EPS

*Pro forma results in financial statements no longer required of nonpublic enterprises per SFAS 79

APB 17 (I60) Intangible Assets
(R&D references amended by SFAS 2)

A. Costs of intangible assets acquired from others should be recorded as assets

1. Expenditures to develop or maintain goodwill should be expensed when the intangibles:

    a. Are not specifically identifiable
    b. Have indeterminant lives
    c. Are related to the enterprise as a whole

2. Cost of an unidentifiable intangible is cash or fair value disbursed, or present value of liabilities assumed
3. Cost of an unidentifiable intangible (acquired with a group of assets) should be determined per APB 16

B. Intangibles should be amortized systematically over years benefited in view of the following factors:

1. Legal, regulatory, or contractual provisions
2. Provisions for renewal or extension
3. Obsolescence, demand, competition, etc.
4. Life expectancies of employees
5. Expected actions of competitors
6. Benefits may not be reasonably projected
7. Composite of many individual factors

C. Straight line amortization should be used unless another method is more appropriate

1. Cost should be amortized over the life of each individual asset
2. Period of amortization should not exceed forty years
3. The method and period should be disclosed

D. Periodic review of amortization policies should be undertaken, and required changes should be made prospectively but not to exceed forty years after acquisition

E. While goodwill cannot be disposed of apart from other assets, the appropriate portion of goodwill should be considered disposed when a substantial group of related acquired assets are sold

APB 18 (I82) The Equity Method for Investments

A. The equity method is to be used for all domestic and foreign unconsolidated subsidiaries

 1. The equity method is also to be reflected in parent only statements for subsidiaries
 2. The APB reaffirms that subsidiaries leasing property to the parent or affiliates should be consolidated

B. The equity method should be used for corporate joint ventures

C. The equity method should also be applied to investments where less than 50% ownership is held but the investor can exercise significant influence over operating and financing policies of the investee

 1. Twenty percent (20%) or more ownership should lead to presumption of substantial influence, unless there is evidence to the contrary

 2. Conversely, less than 20% ownership leads to the presumption of no substantial influence unless there is evidence to the contrary

 3. The 20% test should be based on voting stock outstanding and disregard common stock equivalents

 4. The following procedures should be used in applying the equity method

    a. Intercompany profits should be eliminated
    b. Difference between cost and net assets acquired should be accounted for per APB 16 and APB 17
    c. The investment account and investor's share of investee income should be presented as single amounts in investor statements with the exception of "d." below
    d. Investor's share of extraordinary items and prior period adjustments of investee should be so presented in statements of investor
    e. Investee capital transactions should be accounted for as are subsidiary capital transactions in consolidated statements
    f. Gains on sale of investment are the difference between selling price and carrying value
    g. When investee and investor fiscal periods do not coincide, use most recent investee statement and have consistent time lag
    h. Losses, not temporary in nature, of investment value should be recognized by investor
    i. Investor's share of investee loss should not be recorded once investment account is written to zero. Subsequent income should be recognized after losses not recognized are made up.
    j. Investor's share of investee's earnings should be computed after deducting investee's cumulative preferred dividends declared or not
    k. If an investor's holding falls below 20%, discontinue applying the equity method but make no retroactive adjustment
    l. When an investor's holding increases from a level less than 20% to a level equal to or greater than 20%, the investment account and retained earnings of the investor should be adjusted retroactively to reflect balances as if the equity account had been used (step by step method). They are prior period adjustments.

5. Statements of investors applying the equity method should disclose:

    a. Investees and percentages held

        1) Accounting policies followed
        2) Treatment of goodwill, if any

    b. Aggregate market value of investment (not for subsidiaries)
    c. When investments are material to investor, summarized information of assets, liabilities, and results of operations of investee may be necessary
    d. Conversion of securities, exercise of warrants, or issuances of investee's common stock which significantly affects investor's share of investee's income

---

FASB INTERPRETATION NO. 35 CRITERIA FOR APPLYING THE EQUITY METHOD OF ACCOUNTING FOR INVESTMENTS IN COMMON STOCK Interprets APB 18.
Investors owning between 20 and 50 percent of an investee may not be able to exercise significant influence over the investee's operating and financial policies. The presumption of significant influence stands until overcome by evidence to the contrary, such as: (1) opposition by the investee, (2) agreements under which the investor surrenders shareholder rights, (3) majority ownership by a small group of shareholders, (4) inability to obtain desired information from the investee, (5) inability to obtain representation on investee board of directors, etc. Whether contrary evidence is sufficient to negate the presumption of significant influence is a matter of judgment requiring a careful evaluation of all pertinent facts and circumstances, in some cases over an extended period of time. Application of this interpretation resulting in changes to or from the equity method shall be treated per APB 18, para 19l and 19m.

APB 19 (F40, C08) Statement of Changes in Financial Position

A. Objectives of funds statement are:

    1. Summarize financing and investing activities
    2. Complete disclosure of changes in financial position

B. Funds can mean cash or working capital

C. Funds statement should be present when both the income statement and balance sheet are presented

D. The "all financial resources" concept is required, i.e., investing activities not affecting cash or working capital must be included

E. The title is Statement of Changes in Financial Position

F. Extraordinary items* should be disclosed separately when reporting the results of operations

    1. Statement may begin with income or loss before extraordinary items* and adjusted for nonworking capital items, or
    2. Statement may deduct expenses requiring working capital from revenues providing working capital

    *Author's note: In view of APB 30 (redefining extraordinary items), and APB 20 (requiring cumulative effect treatment) extraordinary items should read as "nonoperating items."

3. After "1." or" 2.," the resulting working capital should be called "working
    capital provided from operations exclusive of extraordinary items*"

    *Author's note: In view of APB 30 (redefining extraordinary items), and APB
    20 (requiring cumulative effect treatment) extraordinary items should read
    as "nonoperating items."

G. The statement should either disclose in appropriate detail, the changes in cur-
    rent items, or

    1. If the working capital approach is used, a supplementary schedule of changes
        in current items should be presented

H. Beyond working capital or cash provided by operations, the statement should
    disclose:

    1. Outlays for noncurrent assets
    2. Proceeds of sale of assets not in normal course of business
    3. Conversion of debt or preferred to common
    4. Issuance or assumption of debt
    5. Dividends

I. Working capital or cash per share figures can be misleading and should be played
    down

APB 20 (A06, A35) Accounting Changes

Prescribes accounting for three types of accounting changes and correction of an
error in prior periods' financial statements. Both should be reported to facilitate
analysis and understanding of the financial statements.

A. Changes in principle

    1. Changes of principles should not be made unless to a preferable principle

        a. When the APB expresses a preference or rejects a principle, this is a
            justification for change
        b. Burden of justification for other changes rests on entity proposing
            change

    2. Special changes require retroactive adjustment of prior period statements

        a. Special changes include:

            1) From LIFO to any other inventory method
            2) Change in accounting for long-term contracts
            3) Change to or from full cost method in extractive industries.

        b. Nature and justification should be disclosed. Also, disclose effect on
            income before extraordinary items, net income, and per share amounts for
            all periods presented.

    3. For all other changes do not retroactively adjust prior periods

        a. Apply new method to current year
        b. The cumulative effect of the change on beginning retained earnings, as
            if the new principle had always been followed, should be presented on
            the income statement between extraordinary items and net income

            1) The cumulative effect should be net of tax effects

  c. The effect of the change in principle, on income before extraordinary items and net income, should be disclosed for the period of change

  d. The pro forma effect of retroactive application of the change should be shown on the face of the income statement as a separate section

   1) Net income before extraordinary items and net income should be retroactively computed
   2) PEPS and FDEPS should be presented for each income figure
   3) The restatement should be net of tax effects <u>and</u> nondiscretionary items (bonuses, royalties, etc.)

  e. A change in amortization method of assets is not considered a change in principle if only applied to new assets

   1) Disclose change and effect on income figures in year of change
   2) If new method is applied to old assets, it is a change in principle
  f. If pro forma amounts cannot be calculated, disclose reasons
  g. If the cumulative effect cannot be computed, disclose reasons and effect of change on current year's income figures
  h. A one time exemption exists for companies first issuing statements for:
   1) Additional equity capital
   2) Securities registration
   3) Business combination

B. Changes in estimate

 1. A change in estimate should be disclosed in the period of change if it affects that period only

  a. Disclosure should be made in future periods if it affects future periods
  b. A change in estimate that is recognized by a change in principle should be accounted for as a change in estimate

   1) For example, change from estimating salvage value to ignoring salvage value based on expected benefits

 2. Disclosure of changes in estimates should include effect on:

  a. Income before extraordinary items
  b. Net income
  c. Related per share amounts

C. Change in accounting entity

 1. Financial statements should be restated for all prior periods
 2. The nature and reasons of change should be explained in year of change
 3. Effect of changes on income figures and per share amounts should be disclosed for all periods presented

D. Correction of an error in prior statements

 1. Prior period adjustment
 2. Nature of error and effect on the income figures and per share amounts should be disclosed in the period the error is discovered

E. This opinion requires above rules to be applied to data presented in the <u>historical summary</u> and <u>highlighted data</u> of the annual report

FASB INTERPRETATION NO. 1   ACCOUNTING CHANGES RELATED TO THE COST OF INVENTORY
Changes in the cost composition of inventory is an accounting change and must
conform to APB Opinion 20, including justification for the change. Preferably
should be based on financial reporting objectives rather than tax-related benefits.

FASB INTERPRETATION NO. 20   REPORTING ACCOUNTING CHANGES UNDER AICPA STATEMENTS
OF POSITION
Accounting changes, to comply with an AICPA Statement of Position (SOP), should
be accounted for as specified by the SOP. If the SOP does not specify a method
of change, the entity must follow APB Opinion 20.

APB 21 (I69) Interest on Receivables and Payables
Accounting for receivables and payables whose face value does not approximate their
present value.

A. Applies to receivables and payables except:

1. Normal course of business receivables and payables maturing in less than one
    year
2. Amounts not requiring repayment in the future (will be applied to future
    purchases or sales)
3. Security deposits and retainages
4. Customary transactions of those whose primary business is lending money
5. Transactions where interest rates are tax affected or legally prescribed,
    e.g., municipal bonds and tax settlements
6. Parent-subsidiary transactions
7. Estimates of contractual obligations such as warranties

B. Notes exchanged for cash are recorded at face amount (presumption that face
    amount = present value)

1. If unstated rights or privileges are exchanged in issuance of note for
    cash, adjust cash payment to obtain present value of the cash and un-
    stated rights

C. Notes exchanged for goods or services in arm's-length transaction are recorded
    at face amount (presumption that face amount = present value)

1. Presumption not valid if note is:

    a. Noninterest bearing
    b. Stated interest rate is unreasonable
    c. Face amount of the note differs materially from sales price of goods or
        services

2. When presumption not valid, record note at fair value of goods or services

    a. Compute implicit rate [rate that discounts the future value (face of
        note plus cash interest, if any) to fair value of goods and services]
        for interest expense/revenue recognition

3. When no established market price for goods and services exists, record
    note at its fair market value

    a. Compute implicit rate [rate that discounts the future value (face of
        note plus cash interest, if any) to fair value of note] for interest
        expense/revenue recognition

4. When no fair market value exists for goods and services or note, record note at approximation of market value

   a. Use <u>imputed</u> rate to compute present value of (and discount on) note

   b. Imputed rate should approximate the rate an independent borrower and lender would negotiate in a similar transaction. Consider:

     1) Credit standing of issuer
     2) Restrictive covenants
     3) Collateral
     4) Payment and other terms
     5) Tax consequences to buyer and seller
     6) Market rate for sale or assignment
     7) Prime rate
     8) Published rates of similar bonds
     9) Current rates charged for mortgages on similar property

D. Discount or premium should be amortized by the interest method (constant rate of interest on the amount outstanding)

   1. Other methods may be used if the results are not materially different from those of the interest method

E. Discount or premium should be netted with the related asset or liability and <u>not</u> shown as separate asset or liability

   1. Issue costs should be reported as deferred charges

APB 22 (A10) Disclosure of Accounting Policies

A. Accounting policies can affect reported results significantly and the usefulness of the financial statements depends on the user's understanding of the accounting policies adopted by the reporting entity. Disclosure of accounting policies are:

   1. Essential to users
   2. Integral part of financial statements
   3. Required for one or more financial statements
   4. Required for not-for-profit entities
   5. Not required for unaudited interim statements

     a. If no change in accounting policy has occurred

B. Disclosure should include accounting principles and methods of applying them if material to reported amounts

   1. Generally, disclosure pertinent to recognition of revenue and expense
   2. Specifically, disclosure pertinent to:

     a. Selection from existing alternatives
     b. Principles peculiar to a particular industry
     c. Unusual or innovative applications

   3. Examples

     a. Consolidation method
     b. Depreciation methods
     c. Amortization of intangibles
     d. Inventory pricing

       e. R&D references amended by SFAS 2
       f. Translation of foreign currencies
       g. Long-term contract accounting
       h. Franchising and leasing activities

    4. Accounting policy disclosure should not duplicate disclosures elsewhere in the statements

       a. The disclosure of accounting policies may refer to details elsewhere, e.g., footnotes

C. Particularly useful is a separate <u>Summary of Significant Accounting Policies</u> preceding the notes

    1. Or as the initial note

APB 23 (I42) Accounting for Income Taxes--Special Areas

A. Undistributed earnings of subsidiaries

    1. Undistributed earnings should be presumed to be distributed in the future

       a. Tax effect may be based on assumptions such as the earnings were distributed currently and all tax benefits <u>were</u> taken
       b. Operating loss tax effects should be recognized in accordance with APB 11

    2. No tax need be accrued when sufficient evidence exists that the subsidiary will reinvest the undistributed earnings indefinitely or remit them tax free

       a. Parent should have specific evidence of the above, such as past experience and definite future programs

    3. If taxes have been accrued on undistributed earnings and it becomes apparent the earnings will not be remitted, adjust the deferred account, and adjust current tax expense (not an extraordinary item)

       a. If taxes have not been accrued and it becomes apparent the earnings will be distributed, accrue taxes as a current expense (not extraordinary)

    4. If a change in the investment results in:

       a. Change from subsidiary status to APB 18 status, follow APB 24

          1) If taxes on the subsidiary's undistributed earnings have not been accrued, accrue them when investee ceases to be a subsidiary

       b. Accrued taxes on undistributed earnings should be recognized upon disposition of a subsidiary or part thereof

    5. If a parent does not accrue taxes on subsidiaries' undistributed earnings

       a. The intention to reinvest permanently or receive tax free should be declared
       b. The cumulative amount of undistributed earnings on which taxes were not accrued should be disclosed

B. Investments in long-term corporate joint ventures follow the same rules for tax accruals on undistributed earnings for subsidiaries in "A" above, including required disclosures

C. Bad debt reserves of savings and loans. (This section is not included, because the authors feel that it is too specialized for the CPA exam.)

D. Policyholder's surplus of stock life insurance companies. (See note to "C" above.)

> FASB INTERPRETATION NO. 29 REPORTING TAX BENEFITS REALIZED ON DISPOSITION OF INVESTMENTS IN CERTAIN SUBSIDIARIES AND OTHER INVESTEES
> Covers accounting for tax benefits due to differing tax basis and book basis of investees at time of the sale. Investors should report such tax benefits realized upon disposition of an investee or subsidiary in the same manner as the gain or loss on the disposition is reported (e.g., an extraordinary item, disposal of a segment, etc.). Gains (losses) should be reported net of the tax effect.

APB 24 (I42) Accounting for Income Taxes (on equity investments)

A. Taxes should be accrued on undistributed earnings of investments in investees where "significant influence" can be exercised by the investor (APB 18)

   1. Unlike subsidiaries where control is possible, "significant influence" cannot guarantee absence of distributions
   2. Tax accruals should be based on the particular circumstances, e.g., use of ordinary or capital gains rates

B. Changes in investment. If an investment becomes a subsidiary (over 50%) or significant influence ceases (less than 20%), previously accrued taxes should not be recognized unless the investee's distributions exceed earnings subsequent to change in ownership level.

   1. Accrued taxes on undistributed earnings should be recognized upon sale of an investment or part thereof

APB 25 (C47) Accounting for Stock Issued to Employees

Redefines "measure of compensation" in ARB 43, Chapter 13B and prescribes accounting for "variable factor" plans and tax benefits related to stock issue plans.

A. No compensation is recognized for noncompensatory plans. Four noncompensation characteristics must be present.

   1. Substantially all full time employees may participate
   2. Stock is offered to employees equally or based on salary
   3. Time permitted for exercise of option is reasonable
   4. Discount from market is not greater than would be in an offer to sell stock to shareholders

B. All other plans are compensatory

   1. Compensation is the quoted market price less the amount the employee is required to pay

      a. If unavailable, use best estimate of market value

   2. The measurement date for determining compensation is the first date on which both of the following are known

      a. Number of shares the individual may receive
      b. Option price, if any

3. Note that the corporation recognizes compensation cost unless the employee must pay at least the market price (at measurement date)

C. Special rules in applying the measurement principle

1. Cost of treasury stock distributed in an option plan does not determine compensation cost. Use market value unless:

   a. Treasury stock is acquired during period, and
   b. Is awarded to employees shortly thereafter

2. Measurement date is not changed, because of provision that termination of employment reduces shares available

3. Measurement date may be year-end rather than date of individual award if:

   a. Award is provided by formal plan
   b. And plan designates factors to determine award
   c. And the award pertains to current service

4. Renewing or extending option establishes a new measurement date

5. Transferring stock to a trustee does not result in a new measurement date unless the transfer provides that the stock:

   a. Will not revert to corporation
   b. And terms to employee will not be changed
   c. And will not be granted to another employee

6. Measurement date for convertible securities is date the ratio of conversion is known

   a. Compensation is based on the higher value of:

      1) Original security, or
      2) Security into which original is convertible

7. Cash paid to an employee to settle an earlier award measures compensation cost

8. If option plans are combination of more than one plan, compensation should be measured for each of the parts

   a. If employee has a selection of alternatives, compensation on cost should be measured for the alternative most likely to be chosen

D. Compensation expense should be recognized as an expense in periods employee performs services

1. If an employee performs services for several periods prior to stock issuance, compensation expense should be accrued

   a. If the measurement date is after the grant date, the compensation should be accrued based on the current market price of stock

2. If stock is issued prior to when some of the services are performed, compensation expense should be deferred to those periods as a contra shareholder's equity item

3. Any adjustments of estimates regarding option plans should be done prospectively

   a. If an employee fails to exercise an option, compensation expense recognized in earlier periods should reduce compensation expense of the present period

E. Issuing corporation usually deducts (for tax purposes) the amount an employee reports as ordinary income in the year the employee includes the income in gross income

    a. The allowable deduction may differ from the related compensation expense

    b. The deduction may be allowable in a different period from when the compensation expense is recognized

  1. Deferred taxes should be recorded for timing differences

    a. The reduction in tax expense in a period (for future anticipated deduction) should not exceed the tax reduction of the related compensation expense of the period. Additional tax deductions may be available, because amounts employees report as ordinary income from stock issuances may exceed the related compensation expense recorded by the company in prior periods.

  2. The difference between the tax expense reduction (based on compensation expense, see "a." above) and the tax deduction should be netted to paid-in capital in excess of par value

    a. A reduction in paid-in capital is limited to paid-in capital arising from stock issuances under option plans

> **FASB INTERPRETATION NO. 28 ACCOUNTING FOR STOCK APPRECIATION RIGHTS AND OTHER VARIABLE STOCK OPTION OR AWARD PLANS**
> Changes in the market value of the stock between the date of the grant and the measurement date (the date both the number of shares and the option price are known) are adjustments to compensation expense in the period the market value of the stock changes. Stock appreciation rights are common stock equivalents for computing EPS, unless they are payable only in cash.

APB 26 (D14) Early Extinguishment of Debt*
(Amended by SFAS 76)

*Note: SFAS 76 has expanded coverage of APB 26 to all extinguishments of debt, whether early or not. Consequently, in this outline, references to the term "early" have been deleted.

A. Definitions (para 3)

  1. Extinguishment of debt. SFAS 76 defines transactions that should be recognized as an extinguishment of debt by the debtor.

  2. Net carrying amount. "Amount due at maturity, adjusted for unamortized premium, discount, and cost of issuance."

  3. Reacquisition price. "Amount paid on extinguishment, including a call premium and miscellaneous costs of reacquisition. If early extinguishment is achieved by a direct exchange of new securities, the reacquisition price is the total present value of the new securities."

  4. Refunding. Replacement of debt with other debt.

B. Retirement is usually achieved by use of liquid assets

  1. Currently in existence
  2. From sale of equity securities
  3. From sale of debt securities
  4. Creation of an irrevocable trust (see outline of SFAS 76)

C. Prior to APB 26

   1. Nonrefunding extinguishments were current losses and gains

   2. Gains and losses on refunding transactions were:

      a. Amortized over the life of the old issue (no longer permissible)

      b. Amortized over the life of the new issue (no longer permissible)

      c. Currently recognized in income

D. A <u>difference</u> between <u>reacquisition price</u> and <u>net carrying amount</u> of the extinguished debt should be recognized in the year of extinguishment as a separate item

   1. Gains and losses should not be amortized to future years

   2. Gains and losses are extraordinary (except on purchases to satisfy sinking fund requirements that an enterprise would have to meet within one year of extinguishment date). See SFAS 4 and 64.

E. The gains and losses on extinguishment of convertible debt should also be recognized currently. See "D." above.

APB 27 <u>Disclosure of Lease Commitments by Lessees</u>
(Now in SFAS 13-Codified)

APB 28 (I73) <u>Interim Financial Reporting</u>
(Amended by SFAS 3, FASB Interpretation 18)

PART I Application of GAAP to Interim Periods

A. APB faced basic question about interim periods

   1. Are interim periods basic accounting periods?

   2. Are interim periods integral parts of the annual period?

B. The APB decided interim periods are an <u>integral part of an annual period</u>

   1. Certain GAAP must be modified for interim reporting to better relate the interim period to the annual period

   2. These modifications follow

C. Revenue should be recognized on the same basis as for the annual period

D. Costs directly associated with revenue should be reported as in annual periods with the following <u>exceptions</u>:

   1. Estimated gross profit rates may be used to estimate inventory. Disclose method used and significant adjustments to reconcile to later physical inventory

   2. When LIFO base period inventories are liquidated during the interim period but are expected to be replaced by the end of the annual period, cost of sales should be priced at normal rather than at base period costs

   3. Declines in inventory market values, unless temporary, should be recognized. Subsequent recovery of market value should be recognized as a gain in the subsequent period.

   4. Unanticipated and unplanned standard cost variances should be recognized in the respective interim period

E. The objective of reporting all other costs is to obtain fair measure of operations for the annual period. These expenses include:

   1. Direct expenditures--salaries
   2. Accruals--vacation pay
   3. Amortization of deferrals--insurance

F. These costs should be applied in interim statements as follows:

   1. Charge to income as incurred, or based on time expiration, benefit received, etc. Follow procedures used in annual reports.
   2. Items not identified with specific period are charged as incurred
   3. No arbitrary assignment
   4. Gains and losses of any interim period that would not be deferred at year-end cannot be deferred in the interim period
   5. Costs frequently subjected to year-end adjustments should be anticipated in the interim periods

      a. Inventory shrinkage
      b. Allowance for uncollectibles, quantity discounts
      c. Discretionary year-end bonuses

G. Seasonal variations in above items require disclosure and one may add twelve-month reports ending at the interim date for current and preceding years

H. The best estimate of the annual tax rate should be used to provide taxes on a year-to-date basis (also see FASB Interpretation 18)

   1. The best estimate should take investment credits, capital gains, etc. into account, but not extraordinary items
   2. Tax effects of losses in early portion of the year should not be recognized unless realization is assured beyond a reasonable doubt, e.g., an established pattern of loss in early periods

      a. When tax effects of losses in early periods are not recognized, no taxes should be accrued in later periods until loss credit has been used

I. Extraordinary items should be disclosed separately and recognized in the period that they occur

   1. The materiality of extraordinary items should be determined in relation to expected annual income
   2. Effects of disposals of a segment of a business are not extraordinary items, but should be disclosed separately
   3. Extraordinary items should not be prorated over remainder of the year
   4. Contingencies should be disclosed in the same manner as required in annual reports

J. Each interim report should disclose any change in accounting principle from:

   1. Comparable period of prior year
   2. Preceding periods of current year
   3. Prior annual report

K. Reporting these changes

   1. APB 20 should be complied with, including restatement provisions
   2. A change in accounting estimate, (including effect on estimated tax rate) should be accounted for in period of change and disclosed in subsequent periods if material

3. Changes in principle, requiring cumulative effect, should be calculated for the effect on beginning annual retained earnings

   a. The cumulative effect should be reported in the first interim period (by restatement if necessary, see SFAS 3)
   b. Previously reported interim information should be restated
   c. Changes should be made in first period whenever possible
   d. Items not material to annual results, but material to interim results, should be disclosed separately in the interim reports

PART II Required Interim Disclosures by Publicly Traded Companies

A. Minimum disclosure includes:

1. Sales, provision for taxes, extraordinary items, cumulative effect of principle changes, and net income
2. PEPS and FDEPS
3. Seasonal revenue, costs, and expenses
4. Significant changes in estimates of taxes
5. Disposal of a business segment and extraordinary items
6. Contingent items
7. Changes in accounting principles and estimates
8. Significant changes in financial position

B. When summarized interim data are reported regularly, the above should be reported for the:

1. Current quarter
2. Current year to date or last 12 months with comparable data for the preceding year

C. If fourth quarter data are not separately reported, disclose in annual report

1. Disposal of business segment
2. Extraordinary, unusual, and infrequent items
3. Aggregate year-end adjustments

D. The APB encourages interim disclosure of financial position and funds flow data

1. If not disclosed, significant changes therein should be disclosed

---

FASB INTERPRETATION NO. 18 ACCOUNTING FOR INCOME TAXES IN INTERIM PERIODS
Tax on income from continuing operations for an interim period is based on estimated annual effective rate, which reflects anticipated tax planning alternatives. Expense of interim period is (year-to-date income) X (estimated rate) less (expense recognized in prior interim periods). Tax effect of special items (below continuing operations) computed as they occur. Tax benefits of losses are only recognized when realization is assured beyond a reasonable doubt.

APB 29 (N35, C11) Accounting for Nonmonetary Transactions

A. Definitions (para 3)

1. Monetary assets and liabilities. "Assets and liabilities whose amounts are fixed in terms of units of currency by contract or otherwise. Examples are cash, short or long-term accounts and notes receivable in cash, and short or long-term accounts and notes payable in cash."

2. Nonmonetary assets and liabilities. "Assets and liabilities other than monetary ones. Examples are inventories; investments in common stocks; property, plant and equipment; and liabilities for rent collected in advance."

3. Exchange. "A reciprocal transfer between an enterprise and another entity that results in the enterprise's acquiring assets or services or satisfying liabilities by surrendering other assets or services or incurring other obligations."

4. Nonreciprocal transfer. "Transfer of assets or services in one direction, either from an enterprise to its owners (whether or not in exchange for their ownership interests) or another entity or from owners or another entity to the enterprise. An entity's reacquisition of its outstanding stock is an example of a nonreciprocal transfer."

5. Productive assets. "Assets held for or used in the production of goods or services by the enterprise. Productive assets include an investment in another entity if the investment is accounted for by that method. Similar productive assets are productive assets that are of the same general type, that perform the same function or that are employed in the same line of business."

B. APB 29 does not apply to:

1. Business combinations
2. Transfer of nonmonetary assets between companies under common control
3. Acquisition of nonmonetary assets with capital stock of an enterprise
4. Stock dividends and splits, issued or received

C. APB 29 does apply to:

1. Nonreciprocal transfers with owners. Examples are distributions to stockholders

   a. Dividends
   b. To redeem capital stock
   c. In liquidation
   d. To settle rescission of a business combination

2. Nonreciprocal transfer with other than owners. Examples are:

   a. Contribution to charitable institution
   b. Contribution of land by governmental unit to a business

3. Nonmonetary exchange. Examples are exchanges of:

   a. Property exchanged for dissimilar property
   b. Property exchanged for similar property
   c. Productive assets

D. Nonmonetary transactions should generally be accounted for as are monetary transactions

1. Cost of a nonmonetary asset is the fair value of the asset surrendered to obtain it

    a. The difference between fair value and book value is a gain or loss
    b. Fair value of asset received, if clearer than that of asset given, should value transaction

2. Fair value should <u>not</u> be used to recognize gains unless fair value is determinable within reasonable limits
3. Fair value should <u>not</u> be used to recognize gains when exchange is not the culmination of an earnings process, e.g.:

    a. Exchange of property held for sale for similar property
    b. Exchange of similar productive assets

E. If a nonmonetary exchange, not a culmination of the earnings process, contains boot, the gain should be limited to the ratio (boot ÷ total consideration received) X the gain (total consideration received minus total consideration given)

   1. Firm paying boot should <u>not</u> recognize any gain

F. Liquidation distributions to owners should <u>not</u> be accounted for at fair value if a gain results (loss may be recognized)

   1. Use historical cost
   2. Other nonreciprocal distributions to owners should be accounted for at fair value if fair value:

       a. Is objectively measurable
       b. Would be clearly realizable if sold

G. Fair value should be determined in reference to:

   1. Estimated realizable values in cash transactions of similar assets
   2. Quoted market prices
   3. Independent appraisals
   4. Estimated fair value of that received in exchange
   5. Other evidence

H. Timing differences between taxable and book income arising from nonmonetary exchanges should be recognized in the usual manner

I. Nonmonetary transaction disclosures should include:

   1. Nature of the transactions
   2. Basis of accounting
   3. Gains and losses recognized

FASB INTERPRETATION NO. 30 ACCOUNTING FOR INVOLUNTARY CONVERSIONS OF NON-MONETARY ASSETS TO MONETARY ASSETS
When involuntary conversions of nonmonetary assets (e.g., fixed assets) to monetary assets (e.g., insurance proceeds) occur, the difference between the asset's cost and the monetary assets received should be reported as a gain or loss. If an unknown amount of monetary assets are to be received in a later period, gain (loss) is estimated per SFAS 5. Could be extraordinary per APB 30.

APB 30 (E09, I13, I17, I22) Reporting the Results of Operations
(Amended by SFAS 4)

A. Discontinued operations definitions

1. Segment of a business. "A component of an entity whose activities represent a separate major line of business or class of customer. A segment may be in the form of a subsidiary, a division or a department, and in some cases a joint venture or other nonsubsidiary investee, provided that its assets, results of operations, and activities can be clearly distinguished, physically and operationally and for financial reporting purposes, from the other assets, results of operations, and activities of the entity." (para 13)

2. Measurement date. "Date on which the management having authority to approve the action commits itself to a formal plan to dispose of a segment of the business, whether by sale or abandonment." (para 14)

3. Disposal date. "Date of closing the sale if the disposal is by sale or the date that operations cease if the disposal is by abandonment." (para 14)

B. The results of discontinued operations should be disclosed separately after income from continuing operations and before extraordinary items

1. Any estimated loss from disposal of discontinued operations should be reported with the results of discontinued operations
2. A gain on disposal should be recognized when realized
3. An example from APB 30 follows

```
Income from continuing operations before
     income taxes ...............................$XXXX

Provision for income taxes .......................  XXX
     Income from continuing operations ...........            $XXXX

Discontinued operations (Note_____):
     Income (loss) from operations
          of discontinued Division X
          (less applicable income
          taxes of $_____) .......................$XXXX

     Loss on disposal of Division X,
          including provision of $____ for
          operating losses during phase-out
          period (less applicable income
          taxes of $_____)........................ XXXX       XXXX
                         Net Income                           $XXXX
```

C. "Income (loss) from operations" is calculated from beginning of period to measurement date

D. "Gain (loss) on disposal" is calculated on the measurement date based on:

1. Net realizable value
2. Less costs directly associated with disposal

   a. Includes adjustments directly related to the disposal (e.g., severance pay, additional pension expense, relocation expenses)
   b. Does not include costs of normal business activities (e.g., write-down of A/R or inventories)

3. Plus (minus) estimated income (loss) from operations subsequent to measurement date (i.e., during phase-out period)

 a. Income limited to amount of loss otherwise recognizable from the disposal
 b. Limited to those estimates which can be projected with reasonable accuracy
 c. Limited, in the usual case, to disposals to be completed in less than one year

E. Additional disclosures for disposal of a segment

 1. Identity of segment
 2. Expected disposal date
 3. Expected manner of disposal
 4. Description of assets and liabilities remaining at balance sheet date
 5. Income or loss from operations and proceeds

F. Extraordinary items are <u>both</u> unusual and infrequent

 1. <u>Unusual nature.</u> "The underlying event or transaction should possess a high degree of abnormality and be of a type clearly unrelated to, or only incidentally related to, the ordinary and typical activities of the entity, taking into account the environment in which the entity operates."(para 20)

    a. Special characteristics of the entity

       1) Type and scope of operations
       2) Lines of business
       3) Operating policies

 2. <u>Infrequency of occurrence.</u> "The underlying event or transaction should be of a type that would not reasonably be expected to recur in the foreseeable future, taking into account the environment in which the entity operates."
    (para 20)

 3. Example of extraordinary presentation (para 11)

    Income before extraordinary items .... $XXX
    Extraordinary items (less applicable income
     taxes of $_____) (Note_____) XXX
    Net income .... $XXX

 4. Examples of gains and losses that are <u>not</u> generally extraordinary

    a. Write-downs or -offs of receivables, inventories, R&D, etc.
    b. Translation of foreign exchange including major devaluations
    c. Disposal of a segment of a business
    d. Sale of productive assets
    e. Effects of strikes
    f. Accruals on long-term contracts

 5. Extraordinary items should be classified separately if material on an individual basis

 6. Adjustments to prior estimates of losses on disposal of segments are not prior period adjustments, unless they meet criteria presented in APB 9

7. Gains or losses which are unusual or infrequent but not both, should be disclosed separately (but not net of tax) in the income statement or notes

APB 31 Disclosure of Lease Commitment by Lessees   (Superseded by SFAS 13)

APB STATEMENTS

Statements are not Opinions and are issued as special reports for the information and assistance of interested parties.

APB Statement 1

APB position that Accounting Research studies 1 and 3 contained "recommendations in part of a speculative and tentative nature." This is of little concern for CPA candidates.

APB Statement 2 (Supplanted by SFAS 14)

APB Statement 3 (Supplanted by SFAS 33)

APB Statement 4

Basic Concepts and Accounting Principles Underlying Financial Statements

    a. Purpose and Nature of the Statement
    b. The Environment of Financial Accounting
    c. Objectives of Financial Accounting and Financial Statements
    d. Basic Features and Basic Elements of Financial Accounting
    e. GAAP--Pervasive Principles
    f. GAAP--Broad Operating Principles
    g. GAAP--Detailed Accounting Principles
    h. Financial Accounting in the Future

A. Purpose and nature

  1. Provides a basis for better understanding of the broad fundamentals of financial accounting
  2. Provides a basis for guiding the future development of ·financial accounting
  3. The statement:

    a. Discusses nature, environment, limitations, etc. of financial accounting
    b. Lists the objectives of financial accounting
    c. Describes GAAP

  4. The nature is descriptive rather than prescriptive

B. The environment of financial accounting

1. Accounting "is a service activity. Its function is to provide quantitative information, primarily financial in nature, about economic entities that is intended to be useful in making economic decisions."   (para 9)

2. Uses and users of financial accounting

   a. Users with direct interests:

      1) Owners
      2) Creditors and suppliers
      3) Potential owners, creditors, and suppliers
      4) Management
      5) Taxing authorities
      6) Employees
      7) Customers

   b. Users with indirect interests:

      1) Financial analysts and advisors
      2) Stock exchanges
      3) Lawyers
      4) Regulatory and registration authorities
      5) Financial press
      6) Trade associations
      7) Labor unions

   c. Financial accounting data may be prepared for common or special needs of users

3. Organization of economic activity

   a. Production
   b. Income distribution
   c. Exchange
   d. Consumption
   e. Saving
   f. Investment
   g. Specialization and complexity within these functions imply

      1) Continuous activity resulting in accounting allocations between time periods
      2) Joint and intertwined activities leading to arbitrary allocations
      3) Dynamic activity wherein outcomes often differ from prior expectations

4. Individual business enterprise

   a. Economic resources

      1) Productive resources owned by enterprise
      2) Contractual rights to productive resources
      3) Products: finished and in-process
      4) Money
      5) Claims to receive money
      6) Ownership interests in other enterprises

   b. Economic obligations

             1) To pay money
             2) To provide goods and services

      c. Residual interest = Resources - obligations
      d. Classification of events

         1) External events

            a) Transfers of resources or obligations

               (1) Exchanges
               (2) Nonreciprocal transfers between:

                  (a) Enterprise and owners
                  (b) Enterprise and nonowners

            b) Other external events, changes in market values, etc.

         2) Internal events

            a) Production
            b) Casualties

   5. Measuring economic activity

      a. Historical cost
      b. Current replacement cost
      c. Current selling price
      d. Present value basis
      e. Note each of the above has at least some current usage

C. Objectives of financial accounting and financial statements

   1. General objectives (Supplanted by SFAC 1)
   2. Qualitative objectives (Supplanted by SFAC 2)

D. Basic features and basic elements

   1. Basic features

      a. Accounting entity--circumscribed area of interest
      b. Going concern--entity is viewed as continuing operations
      c. Measurement of economic resources and obligations--primary objective
      d. Time periods--specified periods shorter than business life
      e. Measurement in terms of money--monetary attributes
      f. Accrual--measurement as incurred, not on receipts and payments
      g. Exchange price--measurements primarily based thereon
      h. Approximation--required by complex and joint activities
      i. Judgment--necessarily involved
      j. General purpose financial information--accounting serves many users
      k. Fundamentally related financial statement--based on the same data
      l. Substance over form--legal form may differ from economic substance
      m. Materiality--only concerned with significant items

   2. Basic elements (Supplanted by SFAC 3)

E. Pervasive principles

   1. <u>Initial recording of assets and liabilities.</u> Assets and liabilities are recorded at the exchange price when acquired or incurred.

2. <u>Realization</u>. Revenue is recognized when the earning process is complete or <u>nearly</u> complete and an exchange has taken place.

3. <u>Associating cause and effect</u>. Expenses directly associated with revenue are recognized with revenue (product costs).

4. <u>Systematic and rational allocation</u>. Lacking direct association with revenue, some multiperiod costs are allocated to periods based on expected benefits in a systematic and rational manner.

5. <u>Immediate recognition</u>. Some costs are recognized in the current period.

6. <u>Unit of measure</u>. U.S. dollar is the unit of measure. No changes in purchasing power are recognized.

7. <u>Modifying conventions</u>
   a. Conservatism
   b. Emphasis on income
   c. Application of judgment by the accounting profession as a whole

F. Broad operating principles

The broad operating principles are not listed here. You may wish to refer directly to them in Chapter 7 of APB Statement 4. They are further detail of the pervasive principles listed in "E." above.

The series of operations carried out in accounting are listed below.

1. <u>Selecting</u> the events
2. <u>Analyzing</u> the events
3. <u>Measuring</u> the effects
4. <u>Classifying</u> the measured effects
5. <u>Recording</u> the measured effects
6. <u>Summarizing</u> the recorded effects
7. <u>Adjusting</u> the records
8. <u>Communicating</u> the processed information

G. Detailed accounting principles

Chapter 8 points out that there exists a large body of practices and procedures, but does not enumerate them.

H. Financial accounting in the future. (Supplanted by Conceptual Framework Project)

STATEMENTS ON FINANCIAL ACCOUNTING STANDARDS

SFAS 1 Disclosure of Foreign Currency Translation Information (Superseded by SFAS 8)

SFAS 2 (R50) Accounting for Research and Development Costs (R&D)

A. Establishes accounting standards for R&D costs with objective of reducing alternative practices. In summary, all R&D costs are expensed except intangible assets purchased from others and tangible assets that have alternative future uses (which are capitalized and depreciated or amortized as R&D expense).

   1. SFAS 2 specifies:

      a. R&D activities
      b. Elements of R&D costs
      c. Accounting for R&D costs
      d. Required disclosures for R&D

   2. SFAS 2 does not cover:

      a. R&D conducted for others under contract
      b. Activities unique to extractive industries

   3. Amends APB 17 to exclude R&D

      a. APB 22 is amended so as not to state that R&D accounting disclosure is commonly required

B. R&D Activities

   1. Research is "planned search or critical investigation aimed at discovery of new knowledge with the hope that such knowledge will be useful in developing a new product or service or a new process or technique in bringing about a significant improvement to an existing product or process."

   2. Development is "the translation of research findings or other knowledge into a plan or design for a new product or process or for a significant improvement to an existing product or process whether intended for sale or use."

   3. R&D examples

      a. Laboratory research to discover new knowledge

         1) Seeking applications for new research findings

      b. Formulation and design of product alternatives

         1) Testing for product alternatives
         2) Modification of products or processes

      c. Preproduction prototypes and models

         1) Tools, dies, etc. for new technology
         2) Pilot plants not capable of commercial production

      d. Engineering activity until product is ready for manufacture

4. Exclusions from R&D

   a. Engineering during an early phase of commercial production
   b. Quality control for commercial production
   c. Troubleshooting during commercial production breakdowns
   d. Routine, ongoing efforts to improve products
   e. Adaption of existing capability for a specific customer or other requirements
   f. Seasonal design changes to products
   g. Routine design of tools, dies, etc.
   h. Design, construction, startup, etc. of equipment except that used solely for R&D
   i. Legal work for patents or litigation
   j. Items "a-h" above are normally expensed; "i" is capitalized

C. Elements of R&D costs

  1. Materials, equipment, and facilities

   a. If acquired for a specific R&D project and have no alternative use
   b. If there are alternative uses, costs should be capitalized

    1) Charge to R&D as these materials, etc., are used

  2. Salaries, wages, and related costs
  3. Intangibles purchased from others are treated as materials, etc. in "1." above

   a. If capitalized, amortization is covered by APB 17

  4. R&D services performed by others
  5. A reasonable allocation of indirect costs

   a. Not general and administrative costs not clearly related to R&D

D. Accounting for R&D

  1. Expense R&D as incurred

E. Disclosure requirement

  1. Total R&D expensed per period

FASB INTERPRETATION NO. 4 APPLICABILITY OF SFAS 2 TO BUSINESS COMBINATIONS ACCOUNTED FOR BY THE PURCHASE METHOD
Acquisition cost should be assigned to all identifiable assets including intangibles which were the result from R&D. Subsequent to purchase, account for assets related to R&D per SFAS 2 including write-off of those intangibles having no alternative future use.

FASB INTERPRETATION NO. 6 APPLICABILITY OF SFAS 2 TO COMPUTER SOFTWARE
Computer software costs, if incurred for R&D, are treated as any other R&D costs.

SFAS 3 (I73) Reporting Accounting Changes in Interim Financial Statements
(Supersedes para 27 of APB 28)
(Amends para 31 of APB 28)

A. For cumulative effect changes made during the first interim period, include the cumulative effect of the change on beginning retained earnings in income of the first interim period

1. The new principle is used in the first period

B. For cumulative effect changes made in other interim periods, restate the previous interim periods using the newly adopted principle

1. Also include the cumulative effect on beginning (of the fiscal year) retained earnings in the results of the first interim period

a. When prechange interim periods are subsequently presented (e.g., for comparative purposes), use restated figures

C. Required disclosures for cumulative changes in interim reports

1. Nature and justification of change in interim period of change
2. The effect of the change on income from operations and net income (and related per share amounts) in period of change

a. Also for prechange interim periods

3. EPS figures on a pro forma retroactively adjusted basis as in para 19-25 of APB 20 in period of change

a. To provide comparability with prior years' interim periods

4. The same disclosures described in "2." and "3." above in period of change

a. For year-to-date statements
b. For 12 months-to-date statements

5. For subsequent interim periods (after the change), the effect of the change on the earnings and EPS figures for that period

D. For changes (principally to LIFO) where the effect on beginning retained earnings and pro forma amounts cannot be determined, explain reason for omitting such. (See para 11 of SFAS 3.)

1. If change is made in other than first interim period, restate prior interim periods

E. If a publicly traded company made a fourth quarter change and does not issue a fourth quarter report or explain the change in the annual report, the required dislosures shall be made in a footnote to the financial statements

SFAS 4 (D14, I17) Reporting Gains and Losses from Extinguishment of Debt
(Amends APB 30)
(Amended by SFAS 64)

A. Gains and losses from debt extinguishment are to be classified as extraordinary items (net of tax effect)

1. Does not apply to purchases of debt to satisfy sinking fund requirements that an enterprise would have to meet within one year of extinguishment date. (See also SFAS 64.)

a. Such gains and losses must be disclosed as a separate item

B. Disclosures required in statements or notes

1. Description of transaction and source of funds
2. Tax effect
3. Per share amount of gain or loss (net of tax)

SFAS 5 (C59, I50, R70) Accounting for Contingencies (Supersedes Chapter 6, ARB 43) (Supersedes ARB 50)

A. Contingency is "an existing condition, situation, or set of circumstances involving uncertainty as to possible gain or loss to an enterprise that will ultimately be resolved when one or more future events occur or fail to occur."

1. Definitions

a. Probable - Future events are likely to occur
b. Reasonably possible - Chance of occurrence is more than remote, but less than likely
c. Remote - Chance of occurrence is slight

2. Loss contingency examples

a. Receivable collection
b. Product warranty obligations
c. Risk of property losses by fire, explosion, etc.
d. Asset expropriation threat
e. Pending, threatened, etc., litigation
f. Actual or possible claims and assessments
g. Catastrophe losses faced by insurance companies

1) Including reinsurance companies

h. Guarantees of indebtedness of others
i. Banks' obligations under "standby letters of credit"
j. Agreements to repurchase receivables, related property, etc. that have been sold

B. Estimated loss from contingencies shall be accrued and charged to income when:

1. It is probable (at balance sheet date) that an asset has been impaired or liability incurred
2. And the amount of loss can be reasonably estimated

C. Loss contingency disclosures

1. Nature and amount of material items
2. Nonaccrued loss contingencies for which a reasonable possibility of loss exists

a. Disclose nature of contingency
b. Estimate possible range of loss

1) Or state estimate cannot be made

3. If a loss contingency develops after year end, but before the statements are issued, disclosure of the nature of the contingency and amount may be necessary

a. If a year-end contingency results in a loss before issuance of the statements, disclosure (possibly pro forma amounts) may be necessary

4. Disclose nature and amount of the following loss contingencies (even if remote)

    a. Guarantees of others' debts
    b. Standby letters of credit by banks
    c. Agreements to repurchase receivables

5. Government-regulated entities accruing loss contingencies prior to rules in "B." (above) must disclose:

    a. Accounting policy, nature of accrual, and basis of estimation
    b. Amount of related liability or asset valuation accounts

D. General, unspecified risks are not contingencies

E. Appropriation of RE for contingencies shown within shareholders' equity is not prohibited

1. Cannot be shown outside shareholders' equity
2. Contingency costs and losses cannot be charged to appropriation

F. Gain contingency accounting remains in effect as stated in ARB 50

1. Normally not reflected in accounts until realized
2. Adequate disclosure should be made without misleading implications of likelihood of realization

G. Other required disclosures per ARB and APB pronouncements remain in effect

---

FASB INTERPRETATION NO. 14   REASONABLE ESTIMATION OF THE AMOUNT OF LOSS
A range of the amount of a loss is sufficient to meet the criteria of SFAS 5 that the amount of loss be "subject to reasonable estimate." When one amount in the range is a better estimate, use it: otherwise, use the minimum of the range and disclose range.

FASB INTERPRETATION NO. 34   DISCLOSURE OF INDIRECT GUARANTEES OF INDEBTEDNESS OF OTHERS
Interprets SFAS 5 by defining the meaning of "indirect guarantee of the indebtedness of another." These are agreements which obligate one entity under conditions in which the funds are legally available to the second entity's creditors and these creditors may enforce the second entity's claims against the first entity.

SFAS 6 (B05) Classification of Short-term Obligations Expected to be Refinanced
Modifies para 8 of Chapter 3A, ARB 43

A. Short-term obligations per para 8 of ARB 43, Chapter 3A, shall be classified as a current liability unless:

1. Enterprise intends to refinance the obligation on a long-term basis
2. AND the intent is supported by ability to refinance (either "a." or "b.")

    a. Post balance sheet issuance of long-term debt or equity securities
    b. Financing agreement that clearly permits refinancing on a long-term basis

        1) Does not expire or is not callable for one year
        2) No violation of the agreement exists at the balance sheet date or has occurred to date

3. The amount of the short-term obligation excluded from current liability status should not exceed the:

    a. Net proceeds of debt or securities issued
    b. Net amounts available under refinancing agreements

        1) The enterprise must intend to exercise the financing agreement when the short-term obligation becomes due

---

FASB INTERPRETATION NO. 8 CLASSIFICATION OF A SHORT-TERM OBLIGATION REPAID PRIOR TO BEING REPLACED BY A LONG-TERM SECURITY
Short-term obligations that are repaid after the balance sheet date but before funds are obtained from long-term financing are to be classified as current liabilities at the balance sheet date. The reason is that current assets were used to satisfy the liabilities.

SFAS 7 (De4) Accounting and Reporting by Development Stage Companies

A. A company, division, component, etc., is in the development stage if:

1. Substantially all efforts are devoted toward establishing the business, or
2. Principal operations are underway but have not produced significant revenues

B. Example activities of development stage companies

1. Financial planning
2. Raising capital
3. Exploring or developing natural resources
4. R&D
5. Establishing sources of supply
6. Acquiring property, plant, equipment, etc.
7. Personnel recruitment and training
8. Developing markets
9. Production start-up

C. No special accounting standards apply to development stage companies

1. Report revenue in the income statement as in normal operations
2. Expense costs as one would for a company in normal operations
3. Capitalize costs as one would for a company in normal operations

    a. Determine cost recoverability within entity for which statements are being prepared

D. Development stage company statements include:

1. A balance sheet

    a. With cumulative net losses termed "deficit accumulated during development stage"

2. An income statement with revenues and expenses

    a. Also disclose cumulative expenses and revenues from the inception of the development stage

3. A statement of changes in financial position

    a. Also disclose cumulative amounts from inception

4. Statement of owner's investment including:

    a. Dates of issuance and number of shares, warrants, etc.

    b. Dollar amounts must be assigned to each issuance

       1) Dollar amounts must be assigned for noncash consideration

    c. Dollar amounts received for each issuance or basis for valuing noncash consideration

5. Identification of statements as those of a development stage company

6. During the first period of normal operations, notes to statements should disclose that company was, but is no longer, in the development stage

    a. Development stage statements presented for comparative purposes subsequent to development stage need not include above disclosures peculiar to development stage companies

---

FASB INTERPRETATION NO. 7 APPLYING SFAS 7 IN FINANCIAL STATEMENTS OF ESTAB-LISHED OPERATING ENTERPRISES
Allows parent or equity method investor companies to defer some development stage company costs which would have to be expensed by the development stage company. Costs may be deferred if recoverable within the entire entity.

SFAS 8 Accounting for the Translation of Foreign Currency Transactions and Foreign Currency Financial Statements (Superseded by SFAS 52)

SFAS 9 Accounting for Income Taxes - Oil and Gas Producing Companies (Superseded by SFAS 19)

SFAS 10 (B50) Extension of "Grandfather" Provisions for Business Combinations (Amends para 99 of APB 16)

A. Para 99 of APB 16 exempted companies with certain intercorporate investments from pooling criteria in APB 16 for a period of five years (expiring October 31, 1975)

B. The FASB eliminates the time limitation and thus allows the grandfather provisions in para 99 to continue

SFAS 11 Accounting for Contingencies - Transition Method (Supersedes para 20 of SFAS 5)

(The authors feel that this statement is no longer relevant to the CPA exam. It dealt with changing over to SFAS 5 when that statement was issued.)

SFAS 12 (I89) Accounting for Certain Marketable Securities

A. Marketable equity securities shall be carried at the lower of aggregate cost or market

1. Determined at the balance sheet date
2. An excess of aggregate cost over market is carried in a valuation (contra) allowance account
3. "Marketable" means prices are readily available on a national market or in the over-the-counter market (quotations included from at least 3 dealers) but not restricted stock
4. "Equity" means ownership shares or right to acquire (sell) common or preferred shares, e.g., put and call options

   a. Does not include treasury stock, convertible bonds, or redeemable preferred stock

B. The carrying amount (lower of aggregate cost or market) of current and noncurrent portfolios shall be determined separately

1. In an unclassified balance sheet, marketable equity securities shall be considered noncurrent
2. Portfolios (current and noncurrent) of consolidated entities not following specialized accounting practices for marketable securities shall be consolidated to determine carrying amount

   a. Portfolios of investees accounted by the equity method shall not be consolidated

      1) The investment in the investee may be a marketable equity security

3. If the classification (current vs. noncurrent) changes, security is transferred at the lower of cost or market

   a. If market is lower, the write-down is considered a realized loss
   b. And the market value becomes the new cost basis

C. Realized gains and losses are included in income in the period they occur

1. Changes in the valuation account for the current portfolio are also included in income each year
2. The accumulated changes in the valuation account for the noncurrent portfolio are separately disclosed in the equity section of the balance sheet, i.e., not taken to income until realized

   a. The debit is titled "Net unrealized loss in noncurrent marketable equity securities and its balance sheet presentation is similar to treasury stock under the cost method"
   b. Applies to statements not classified as current-noncurrent

D. Required disclosures for marketable equity securities

1. As of each balance sheet, aggregate cost and market value of marketable securities

   a. Each segregated as to current and noncurrent when so presented on the balance sheet
   b. Identification of which is the carrying amount

2. As of the latest balance sheet (segregated as to current and noncurrent)

   a. Gross unrealized gains for all marketable securities
   b. Gross unrealized losses for all marketable securities

3. For each period an income statement is presented

    a. Net realized gain or loss
    b. Basis on which cost was computed to determine the gain or loss
    c. The change in the valuation allowance account included in income (pertains to the current portfolio)
    d. The change in the valuation account included in the equity section of the balance sheet (pertains to the noncurrent portfolio)

4. Financial statements are not adjusted for realized gains or losses occurring after the balance sheet date

    a. Significant net realized and net unrealized gains or losses occurring after the balance sheet should be disclosed

E. A permanent decline in market value is a realized loss (even for entities with no current-noncurrent classification)

    1. No write-up for subsequent cost recoveries

F. Unrealized gains and losses, whether realized in income or included in the equity section, are timing differences

    1. The tax effect on an unrealized loss should be recognized only if it is reasonably certain it will be realized

Part II   Industries having specialized accounting practices with respect to marketable equity securities. (This section is not included because the authors feel that it is too specialized for the CPA exam.)

SFAS 12 is interpreted by FASB Interpretations 10, 11, 13 and 16. These are summarized below.

FASB INTERPRETATION NO. 10   APPLICATION OF SFAS 12 TO PERSONAL FINANCIAL STATEMENTS

Marketable equity securities included in personal financial statements are to be shown at the lower of aggregate cost or aggregate market value in the cost column.

FASB INTERPRETATION NO. 11   CHANGES IN MARKET VALUE AFTER THE BALANCE SHEET DATE

Post-balance-sheet-date market value declines in marketable equity securities may indicate a permanent decline had occurred at the balance sheet date. Any such permanent decline is recognized as loss in period it occurs. Loss measured by difference between cost and market value at balance sheet date. New adjusted cost not to be increased if market value increases.

FASB INTERPRETATION NO. 13   CONSOLIDATION OF A PARENT AND ITS SUBSIDIARIES HAVING DIFFERENT BALANCE SHEET DATES

Aggregate each subsidiary's marketable equity securities' cost and market value existing at the subsidiaries' balance sheet dates and combine them with the parent's aggregate cost and aggregate market value. Disclose net realized and unrealized gains or losses of both parent and subsidiaries arising between balance sheet dates and the date consolidated statements are issued.

FASB INTERPRETATION NO. 16 CLARIFICATION OF DEFINITIONS AND ACCOUNTING FOR MARKETABLE EQUITY SECURITIES THAT BECOME NON-MARKETABLE
Make the "marketable" determination at the balance sheet date. Restricted stock not marketable unless qualifies for sale within one year. Three quotations needed for over-the-counter stock (use first quotation available after year-end). If status changes, recognize excess of cost over market value as loss.

SFAS 13 (L10, C51) Accounting for Leases (Supersedes APB 5, 7, 27, 31, and para 15 of APB 18)

(The outline below is based on the comprehensive restatement as of May 1980 which includes SFAS 17, 22, 23, 26, 27, 28, and 29 and Interpretations 19, 21, 23, 24, 26 and 27.)

Applies to agreements for use of property, plant, and equipment, but not natural resources and not for licensing agreements such as patents and copyrights.

The major issue in accounting for leases is whether the benefits and risks incident to ownership have been transferred from lessor to lessee. If so, the lessor treats the lease as a sale or financing transaction and the lessee treats it as a purchase. Otherwise, the lease is accounted for as a rental agreement.

The following terms are given specific definitions for the purpose of SFAS 13.

Inception of the lease--the date of the written lease agreement or commitment wherein all principal provisions have been fixed and no principal provisions remain to be negotiated

FMV-- the transaction price in an arm's-length transaction to include volume and trade discounts and the consideration of prevailing market conditions. If the lessor is a manufacturer or dealer, ordinarily the seller's market price will be used. In other cases, the FMV will ordinarily be cost.

Bargain purchase option--option to purchase leased asset at substantially less than FMV when, at the inception of the lease, the exercise of the option appears reasonably assured

Lease term--the fixed, noncancelable term of the lease plus all renewal terms when renewal is reasonably assured. Note: the lease term should not extend beyond the date of a bargain purchase option.

Minimum lease payments--payments to be made during the lease term including: a bargain purchase option payment, guaranteed residual value, penalties for failure to renew, and other similar payments. Note: minimum payments do not include executory costs and payments for excessive use of the leased asset.

Interest rate implicit in the lease--the interest rate that applies when the discounted present value of the minimum lease payments and the unguaranteed salvage value is equal to the FMV of the leased asset (less any investment tax credit retained by the lessor)

Lessee's incremental borrowing rate--the interest rate that the lessee would have to pay to borrow over a similar term the funds necessary to purchase the asset

Initial direct costs--directly associable costs of negotiating and consummating completed leasing transactions, e.g., commissions, legal fees, and credit investigations. Compensation paid to salespersons, in addition to commissions and compensation of other employees for time spent in completed leasing activities, should also be included in initial direct costs. Compensation for time spent in negotiating leases that are not consummated are not included in initial direct costs. In addition, no portion of allocated supervisory and administrative overhead such as rent and facilities costs should be included as an initial direct cost. These are classified as indirect costs.

Contingent rentals--increases or decreases in lease payments which result from changes occurring subsequent to the inception of the lease; except that the pass-through of increases in the cost of construction and acquisition, or provisions that are dependent only on the passage of time should be excluded from contingent rentals. A contingency based on a price level index is a contingent payment and the computation of minimum lease payments should be based on the index applicable at the inception of the lease.

A. Classification of leases by lessees. Leases that meet one or more of the following criteria are capital leases, all other leases are operating leases.

   1. Lease transfers ownership (title) to lessee during lease term
   2. Lease contains a bargain purchase option

        Note: "3." and "4." do not apply if lease begins in last 25% of asset's life.

   3. Lease term is 75% or more of economic useful life of property
   4. Present value of minimum lease payments equals 90% or more of FMV of the leased property less lessor investment tax credit

        a. Present value is computed with lessee's incremental borrowing rate, unless lessor's implicit rate is known and is less than lessee's incremental rate (then use lessor's implicit rate)
        b. FMV is cash selling price for sales-type lease; lessor's cost for direct financing of lease. (If not recently purchased, estimate FMV.)

B. Classification of leases by lessors

   1. Sales-type leases provide for a manufacturer or dealer profit, i.e., FMV of leased property is greater than lessor cost or carrying value

        a. Sales-type leases must meet one of the four criteria for lessee capital leases ("A.1." to "A.4." above) and both of the following two criteria

            1) Collectibility is reasonably predictable, and
            2) No important uncertainties regarding costs to be incurred by lessor exist, such as unusual guarantees of performance. Note estimation of executory expenses such as insurance, maintenance, etc., are not considered.

        b. Renewals at the end of a lease term of a sales-type or direct financing lease may be accounted for as a sales-type lease if the criteria are otherwise satisfied. Renewals during the term of an existing lease may not be accounted for as a sales-type lease and would be accounted for as a direct financing lease if the criteria are otherwise satisfied.

   2. Direct financing leases must meet same criteria as sales-type leases (just above) but do not include a manufacturer's or dealer's profit

3. Leveraged leases are described below in "J."
4. Operating leases are all other leases which have not been classified as sales-type, direct financing, or leveraged

C. Lease classification is determined at the inception of the lease

1. If changes in the lease are subsequently made which change the classification, the lease should be considered a new agreement and reclassified and accounted for as a new lease. Exercise of renewal options, etc., are not changes in the lease.
2. Changes in estimates (e.g., economic life or residual value) or other circumstances (e.g., default) do not result in a new agreement but accounts should be adjusted and gains or losses recognized
3. If all lease provisions are fixed at inception, all determinations are to be estimated at inception

   a. The estimates are used to determine the classification and the accounting for the lease
   b. Unless the lease term begins after the inception and the lease payments remain to be determined by formula, no reclassification should be made on the basis of changes occurring after inception and before the lease begins
   c. When a lease begins after the inception and lease payments remain to be determined by formula (i.e., adjustments will be necessary because of changing conditions), the following provisions apply:

      1) The amounts finally estimated are used to determine the classification and the accounting for the lease
      2) The residual value may also be affected, and
      3) The lessee's incremental borrowing rate and estimated economic life of the asset originally estimated would both be affected

4. At the time of inception, sales-type leases involving real estate are subject to the additional requirements that a sale of the same property would have to meet for full and immediate profit recognition under the AICPA Industry Accounting Guide applicable to sales of real estate. If these additional requirements are not satisfied, the lease that would otherwise have been accounted for as a sales-type lease will be classified as an operating lease.
5. Lease classification shall not be changed as a result of a business combination

D. Accounting and reporting by lessees

1. Record capital leases as an asset and liability

   a. Leased asset shall not be recorded in excess of FMV. If the present value of the lease payments is greater than the FMV, the leased asset and related liability are recorded at FMV and the effective interest rate is thereby increased.
   b. Recognize interest expense using the effective interest method
   c. If there is a transfer of ownership or a bargain purchase option, the amortization period is the economic life of the asset. Otherwise, amortize assets to the expected residual value at the end of the lease term.

2. Rent on operating leases should be expensed on a straight line basis unless another method is better suited to the particular benefits and costs associated with the lease

3. Lessees must revalue their lease liability due to changes in a lease agreement arising from refunding related tax-exempt debt and recognize a gain or loss thereon in the period of refunding in accordance with SFAS 4

4. When a lessee purchases a leased asset that has been capitalized, any difference between the purchase price and the lease obligation is an adjustment to the asset carrying value but immediate recognition of a loss is not prohibited

5. Disclosures by lessees include:

    a. General description of leasing arrangement including:

        1) Basis of computing contingent payments

        2) Existence and terms of renewal or purchase options and escalation clauses

        3) Restrictions imposed by the lease agreement such as limitations on dividends and further leasing arrangements

    b. Capital lease requirements

        1) Usual current/noncurrent classifications

        2) Depreciation should be separately disclosed

        3) Future minimum lease payments in the aggregate and for each of the five succeeding fiscal years with separate deductions being made to show the amounts representing executory cost and imputed interest

        4) Total minimum sublease rentals to be received in the future under noncancelable subleases

        5) Total contingent rental actually incurred for each period for which an income statement is presented

    c. Operating lease - remaining noncancelable term in excess of one year requirements

        1) Future minimum lease payments in the aggregate and for each of the five succeeding fiscal years

        2) Total minimum sublease rentals to be received in the future under noncancelable subleases

    d. All operating leases

        1) Present separate amounts for minimum rentals, contingent rentals and sublease rentals

        2) Rental payments for leases with a term of a month or less may be excluded

E. Accounting and reporting by lessors

1. Sales-type leases

    a. Lease receivable is charged for the gross investment in the lease (the total net minimum lease payments plus the unguaranteed·residual value). Sales is credited for the present value of the minimum lease payments.

b. Cost of sales is the carrying value of the leased asset plus any initial direct costs less the present value of the unguaranteed residual value. Note that in a sales-type lease, initial direct costs are deducted in full in the period when the sale is recorded.

c. Recognize interest revenue using the effective interest method

d. At the end of the lease term, the balance in the receivable account should equal the guaranteed residual value or the renewal penalty, if any

e. Contingent rental payments are reported as income in the period earned

f. Due to changes in a lease agreement arising from refunding tax-exempt debt, lessors (usually governmental or quasi-governmental agencies) must make adjustments for changes in minimum payments, estimated salvage value, and interest rates, with any gain or loss recognized in the period of refunding

g. A decline in residual value which is not temporary must be recognized as a loss in the period in which the estimate is changed

2. Direct financing leases

a. Accounting is similar to sales-type lease except that no manufacturer's or dealer's profit is recognized

b. Lease receivable is charged for the gross investment in the lease, the asset account is credited for the net investment in the lease (cost to be acquired for purpose of leasing) and the difference is recorded as unearned income. Neither sales nor cost of goods sold is reported.

c. Initial direct costs are charged against income as incurred, but in the case of a direct financing lease, unearned income equal to the initial direct costs is recognized in the same period. This affects (i.e., lowers) the effective rate of interest to be used.

d. The remaining requirements are the same as those for the sales-type lease

3. Operating leases

a. Leased property is to be included with or near property, plant and equipment on the balance sheet and lessor's normal depreciation policies should be applied

b. Rental revenue should be reported on a straight line basis unless another method is better suited to the particular benefits and costs associated with the lease

c. Initial direct costs should be deferred and allocated over the lease term in proportion to the recognition of rental income

4. Participation by third parties

a. The sale (or assignment) of a lease (or property leased) accounted for as a sales-type or direct financing lease does not affect original accounting classification

   1) Profit (loss) is recognized at sale or assignment
   2) If sale is with recourse, recognized profit (loss) is deferred and spread over lease term in a systematic manner

b. Sale of property subject to an operating lease is not treated as a sale if substantial ownership risks are retained, e.g., in case of default, a commitment to acquire the leased property

    c. If sale of property subject to an operating lease is not recorded as a sale, transaction is accounted for as a borrowing, i.e., proceeds received are accounted for as a liability

5. Lessor disclosures when leasing is a predominant activity

    a. A general description of leasing arrangements

    b. Sales-type and direct financing lease disclosure

        1) Components of net investment in leases

            a) Future minimum payments less executory costs and allowance for bad debts
            b) Unguaranteed residual values
            c) Unamortized initial direct costs
            d) Unearned income

        2) Future minimum lease payments for each of next five years
        3) The amount of initial direct costs offset against unearned income on direct financing leases
        4) Contingent rentals earned for each period presented

    c. Operating lease disclosures

        1) Cost of property in total and by major property category and total accumulated depreciation
        2) Minimum noncancelable rentals in aggregate and for each of the five succeeding years
        3) Total contingent rentals for each income statement presented

F. Real estate leases

1. If land lease only - standard criteria to determine whether capital or operating; only include transfer of ownership and bargain purchase option

2. Leases involving both land and buildings

    a. If the lease transfers title or has bargain purchase option

        1) Lessee apportions present value of payments between land and building based on relative fair market values (considered separate leases)

            a) Building amortized per normal policy
            b) No amortization of land

        2) Lessor accounts as single lease-- sales-type, direct financing--as appropriate

    b. If the lease does <u>not</u> transfer title or have bargain purchase option

        1) And land is less than 25% of total FMV, both lessor and lessee account for lease as a single unit per all of the above rules

            a) Including capitalization if 75% economic life based on the building or the 90% FMV criterion is met

        2) And land is more than 25% of total FMV, both lessor and lessee shall account for the land and building portion of the lease separately per basic lease rules

        a) Lessee's incremental borrowing rate and land FMV determine land portion of payment (and thus building portion also)

        b) Land requires operating lease due to lack of title transfer

3. If land-with-building lease also includes equipment, account for equipment portion separately

4. When costs and FMV are determinable for leases involving only part of a building, account in same manner as entire building

    a. If FMV is not determinable for lessee, use only "75% of economic life" criterion to determine whether to capitalize and amortize

    b. If cost or FMV is not determinable for lessor, then treat as operating

    c. Leases of facilities such as terminal space from a governmental unit generally have an indeterminate economic life and should be classified as operating leases

G. Related party leases shall be accounted for as unrelated party leases except when terms have been significantly affected by relationship

1. Nature and extent of related party leasing must be disclosed
2. See ARB 51 and APB 18 for consolidated or investor-investee transactions
3. Leasing subsidiaries must be consolidated

H. Sale-leasebacks

1. Lessee (seller) accounts for the gain (loss) as follows:

    a. Any loss (when FMV < book value) on the sale should be recognized immediately

    b. Gain is deferred unless:

        1) Seller relinquishes the right to substantially all (PV of reasonable rentals $\leq$ 10% of fair value of asset sold) of the remaining use of the property sold--then separate transactions, and entire gain is recognized

        2) Seller retains more than a minor part, but less than substantially all (PV of reasonable rentals are > 10% but < 90% of fair value of asset sold) of the remaining use--then gain on sale is recognized to the extent of the excess of gain over the present value of minimum lease payments (operating) or the recorded amount of the leased asset (capital)

    c. If the gain is deferred:

        1) Defer and amortize sale profit over lease term proportionate to amortization (rental payments), if a capital lease (operating lease)

2. Lessor records as a purchase and a direct financing or operating lease

I. Accounting for subleases

1. The original lessor makes no adjustment for the typical sublease
2. If effectively a new agreement, record cancellation and new lease
3. The original lessee when relieved of primary liability, records a gain or loss when removing the capital lease asset and liability and secondary liability is accounted for per SFAS 5

    4. If the original lessee is not relieved of primary liability, the original lessee also becomes a lessor and follows the above rules

J. Leveraged leases are accounted for similarly to direct financing leases by lessor (lessee accounts as any other lease)

    1. They differ from direct financing leases as lessor finances leased asset with nonrecourse debt, i.e., substantial leverage exists. This causes the lessor's "net investment in lease" to decrease (possibly to a negative figure) and then increase over the lease.

    2. Compute the implicit rate of return on the original investment for each year the "net investment in lease" is positive

    3. The original entry to record a leveraged lease is:

        Lease receivable (net of nonrecourse loan principal and interest)
        Investment credit receivable
        Residual value of leased asset
            Cash investment in leased asset
            Unearned income

    4. The tax effect of pretax lease income (loss) is recognized annually

    5. Disclose deferred taxes, pretax income, tax effect, investment credit, etc., of leveraged leases separately

*SFAS 14 (S20) Financial Reporting for Segments of a Business Enterprise
(Cross-referenced to SFAS 18, 24, and 30.)

A. This SFAS requires disclosures about:

    - Enterprise operations in different industries
    - Foreign operations and export sales
    - Major customers

    1. The disclosures are required for all complete annual statements per GAAP including comparative presentations

        a. Applies only to publicly held companies per SFAS 21
        b. Does not apply to interim statements per SFAS 18

    2. The purpose of the disclosures is to assist statement users in appraising past and future performance of the enterprise

B. Segment information shall be based on the accounting bases used in consolidated rather than separate company statements

    1. For example, a segment, if a consolidated subsidiary, may have assets valued differently (because of goodwill allocation) for consolidation purposes than for separate company statements

    2. Segment data is not required for unconsolidated subsidiaries and equity method investees. However, disclose industries and geographic areas.

    3. Certain intercompany eliminations, normally eliminated for consolidation purposes, are included (not eliminated) in segment reporting, e.g., inter-segment sales and cost of sales

C. Definitions

---

    *Refer to diagrams on pages 699 and 701 as you study this outline.

C. Definitions

1. <u>Industry segment</u> "component of a business enterprise engaged in providing a product or service . . . primarily to unaffiliated customers"

2. <u>Segment revenue</u> includes revenue from unaffiliated customers and intersegment sales (use company transfer prices to determine intersegment sales)

3. <u>Operating profit (loss)</u> segment revenue less all operating expenses

    a. Operating expenses include expenses relating to both unaffiliated customer and segment revenue

    b. Operating expenses not directly traceable to segments shall be allocated thereto on a reasonable basis

    c. Intersegment purchases are priced at company transfer price

    d. Excludes general corporate revenues and expenses, income taxes, extraordinary items, interest expense, etc.

4. <u>Identifiable assets</u> those directly associable or used by the segment

    a. Includes an allocated portion of assets used jointly with other segments, goodwill, asset valuation accounts

    b. Excludes assets used by central administration

    c. Exclude investments (loans) in other segments

        1) Exception: not excluded from financial segments

D. To determine reportable segments

1. Identify individual products and services
2. Group products and services into segments
3. Select segments significant to enterprise

E. Grouping products

1. None of the established systems are necessarily suitable

    a. SIC-Standard Industrial Classification

    b. ESIC-Enterprise Standard Industrial Classification

2. A firm's profit centers are the starting point for determining segments

    a. Profit centers are the smallest units of activity for which revenue and expense data are accumulated

    b. Disaggregation may be required if profit centers cross industry lines

3. Segmentation on a worldwide basis is desirable but may not be practicable

    a. When impracticable, segment domestic and any practicable foreign operations

        1) Consider remaining foreign operations as a single segment

F. Each industry segment is significant if one or more of the following is true for the latest period

    a. Revenue is 10% or more of combined revenue (revenue includes intersegment revenue)

    b. Operating profit or loss is 10% or more of the greater of:

        1) Combined profit of all segments with profit, or

        2) Combined loss of all segments with loss

    c. Identifiable assets exceed 10% or more of combined identifiable assets of all segments

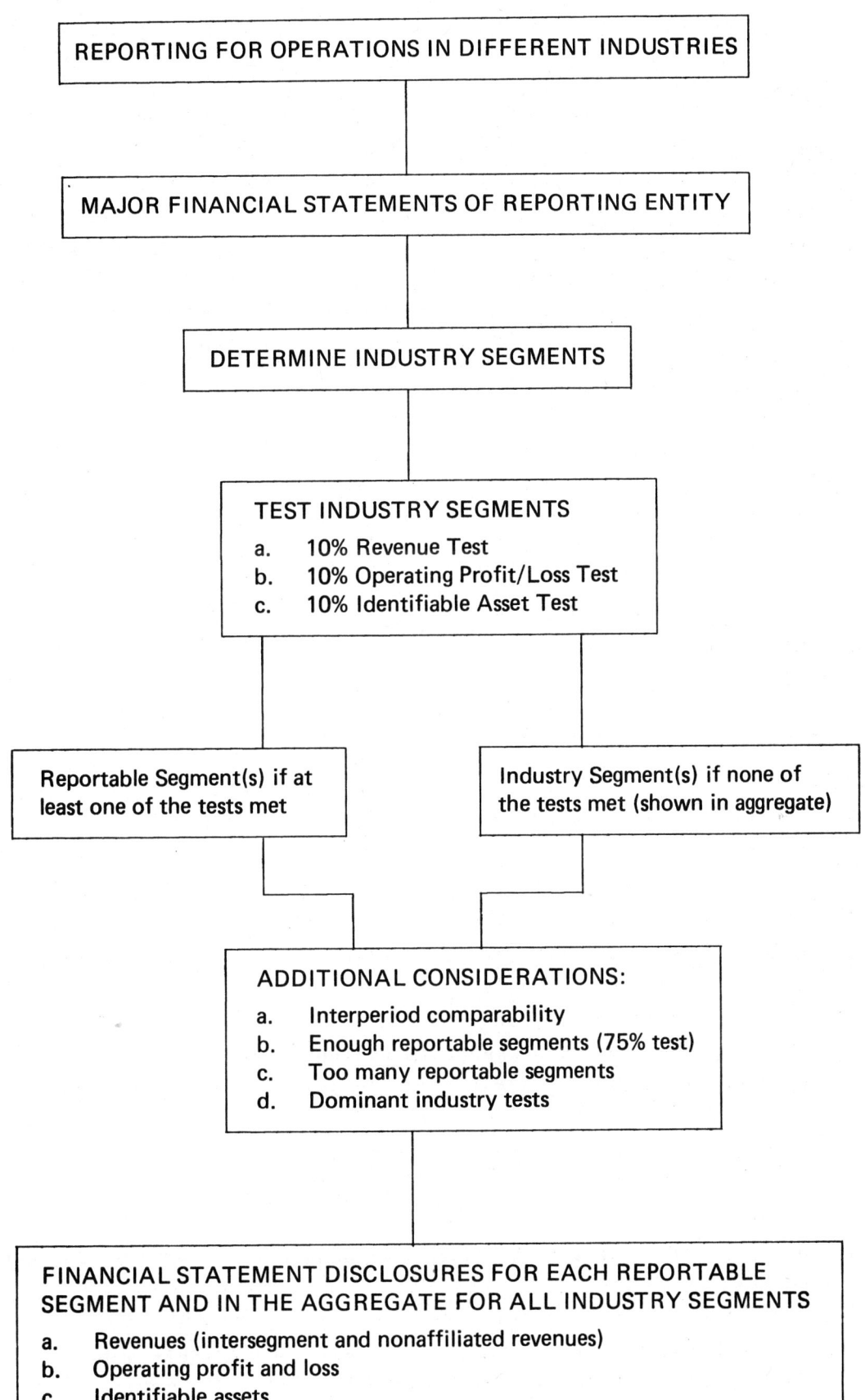

REPORTING FOR OPERATIONS IN DIFFERENT INDUSTRIES

MAJOR FINANCIAL STATEMENTS OF REPORTING ENTITY

DETERMINE INDUSTRY SEGMENTS

TEST INDUSTRY SEGMENTS
a. 10% Revenue Test
b. 10% Operating Profit/Loss Test
c. 10% Identifiable Asset Test

Reportable Segment(s) if at least one of the tests met

Industry Segment(s) if none of the tests met (shown in aggregate)

ADDITIONAL CONSIDERATIONS:
a. Interperiod comparability
b. Enough reportable segments (75% test)
c. Too many reportable segments
d. Dominant industry tests

FINANCIAL STATEMENT DISCLOSURES FOR EACH REPORTABLE SEGMENT AND IN THE AGGREGATE FOR ALL INDUSTRY SEGMENTS
a. Revenues (intersegment and nonaffiliated revenues)
b. Operating profit and loss
c. Identifiable assets

    d.   Revenue, operating profit, and identifiable assets of unsegmented
         foreign operations (due to impracticability) are included in combined
         figures for above tests

1.   A segment, not normally reported separately, may have abnormally high
     operating profit (loss) or revenue in one period

     a.   If useful, report separately
     b.   If not useful, report as in past and disclose

2.   The combined sales to nonaffiliated customers of segments reporting sepa-
     rately must be at least 75% of total sales to nonaffiliated customers

     a.   If not, additional segments must be identified as reportable segments

3.   The number of reportable segments probably should not exceed 10

     a.   Combine closely related segments if number of segments becomes
          impracticable

4.   No segment information need be disclosed if 90% of revenue, operating profit
     (loss), and identifiable assets are in a single industry, and

     a.   No other segment meets any of the 10% tests

G.   Information is to be presented for each reportable segment and in aggregate for
     the remaining segments not reported separately; disclose effect of any changes

     1.   Sales to unaffiliated customers and intersegment sales separately for each
          income statement presented

          a.   Use company transfer prices to price sales

     2.   Operating profit (loss) for each income statement presented (see "C.3."
          above)

          a.   Disclose unusual or infrequently occurring items
          b.   Additional measures of income may be disclosed consistently

     3.   Carrying amount of identifiable assets. Also for each segment:

          a.   Aggregate depreciation, depletion, and amortization
          b.   Capital expenditures
          c.   Equity in vertically integrated unconsolidated subsidiaries and equity
               method investees

H.   Segment information may be presented:

          a.   In the body of the statements (with appropriate explanatory disclosure)
          b.   Entirely in the notes
          c.   In a separate schedule to the statements (references as a part of the
               statements)

     1.   Revenue, profit, and asset data should be reported in dollars

          a.   Corresponding percentages are acceptable

     2.   Segment revenue, profit, and asset data should be reconciled to overall
          consolidated figures

I.   Foreign operations and export sales

     1.   Foreign operation revenue, operating profit, and identifiable assets (as per
          segments) shall be disclosed if either:

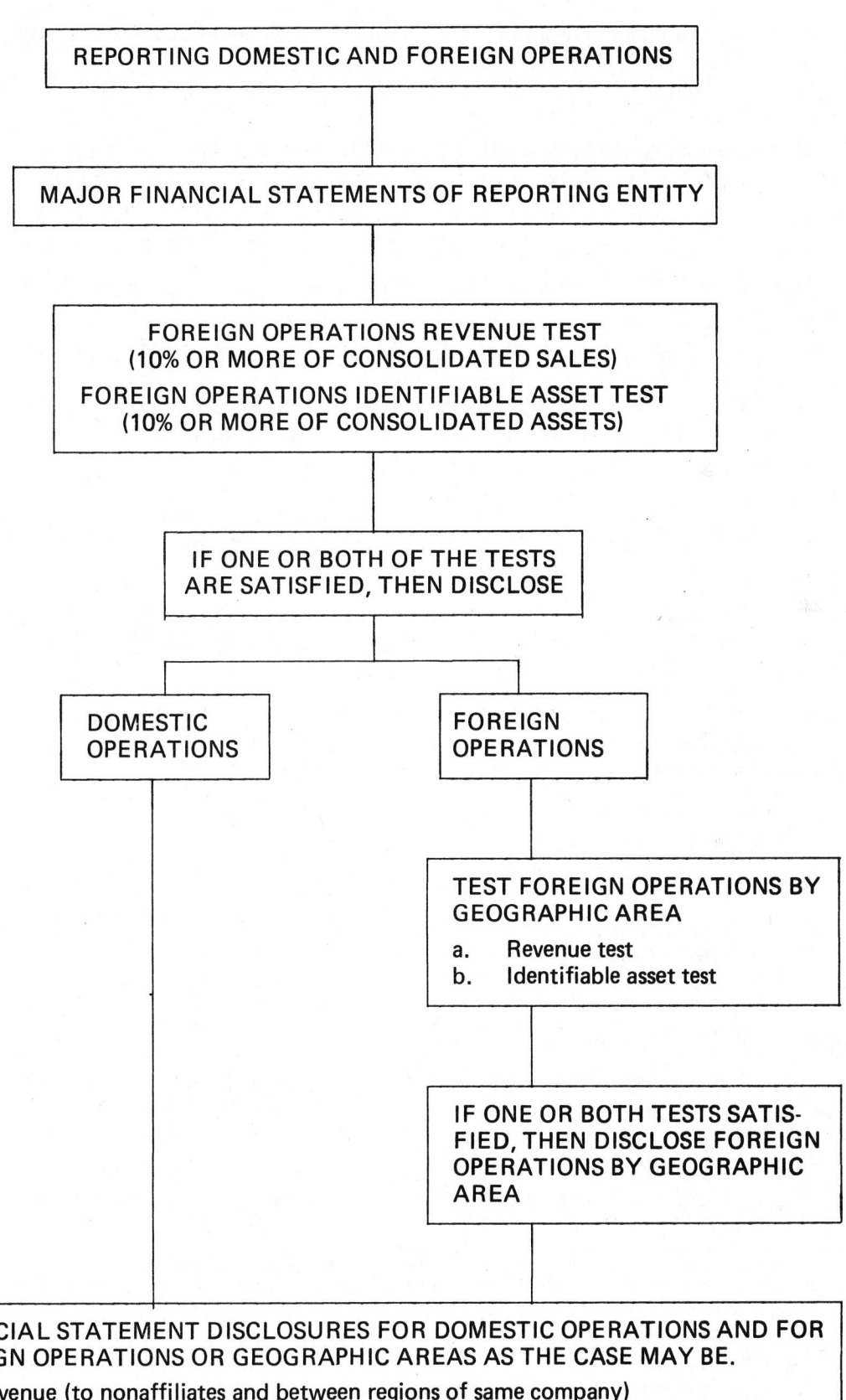

REPORTING DOMESTIC AND FOREIGN OPERATIONS

MAJOR FINANCIAL STATEMENTS OF REPORTING ENTITY

FOREIGN OPERATIONS REVENUE TEST
(10% OR MORE OF CONSOLIDATED SALES)
FOREIGN OPERATIONS IDENTIFIABLE ASSET TEST
(10% OR MORE OF CONSOLIDATED ASSETS)

IF ONE OR BOTH OF THE TESTS
ARE SATISFIED, THEN DISCLOSE

DOMESTIC
OPERATIONS

FOREIGN
OPERATIONS

TEST FOREIGN OPERATIONS BY
GEOGRAPHIC AREA

a.   Revenue test
b.   Identifiable asset test

IF ONE OR BOTH TESTS SATIS-
FIED, THEN DISCLOSE FOREIGN
OPERATIONS BY GEOGRAPHIC
AREA

FINANCIAL STATEMENT DISCLOSURES FOR DOMESTIC OPERATIONS AND FOR
FOREIGN OPERATIONS OR GEOGRAPHIC AREAS AS THE CASE MAY BE.

a.   Revenue (to nonaffiliates and between regions of same company)
b.   Operating profit/loss information
c.   Identifiable assets

    a. Foreign operation revenue to unaffiliated customers is 10% or more of consolidated revenue

    b. Foreign operation identifiable assets are 10% or more of consolidated assets

2. The foreign operation diclosures shall be further broken down by significant foreign geographic areas and in aggregate for insignificant areas

3. Disclose export sales in aggregate and by geographic area if sales to unaffiliated customers are 10% or more of consolidated sales

J. Disclose amount of revenue to each customer accounting for 10% or more of revenue

1. Disclose similarly if 10% or more revenue is derived from sales to domestic government agencies or foreign governments
2. Identify segment making sales
3. Required even if segmented data or foreign operation data are not required

K. Restate segment data for comparative purposes when:

1. Statements as a whole have been retroactively restated
2. A change has occurred in grouping segments or foreign operations

SFAS 15 (D22) Accounting by Debtors and Creditors for Troubled Debt Restructurings
(Supersedes FASB Interpretation No. 2 and amends APB 26 to exclude troubled debt restructurings from APB 26)

A. Troubled debt restructurings occur when a creditor is compelled to grant relief to a debtor due to the debtor's inability to service the debt. This SFAS prescribes accounting for such debt restructurings if:

1. By creditor-debtor agreement
2. Imposed by a court
3. Also includes repossessions and foreclosures
4 But not changes in lease agreements

    a. Nor legal actions to collect receivables
    b. Nor quasi-reorganizations

PART I Accounting by Debtors

A. If a debtor transfers assets to settle fully a payable, recognize a gain on restructuring equal to the book value of the payable less FMV of assets transferred

1. Estimate asset value by cash flows and risk if FMV cannot be determined
2. The difference between asset FMV and carrying value of the assets transferred is a gain or loss in disposition of assets per APB 30

B. If a debtor issues an equity interest to settle fully a payable, account for equity issued at FMV

1. Excess or carrying value of payable over equity FMV is a gain on restructuring

C. A debtor having the terms of troubled debt modified should account for the restructure prospectively, i.e., no adjustment of the payable

   1. Recompute the new effective rate of interest based on the new terms

      a. Total cash payments to be paid, less carrying value of payable is the interest

      b. Amortize the payable by the interest method (APB 21) using the new interest rate

   2. Exception is if restructured terms require total cash payments (including interest) which are less than the carrying value of the payable, write down the payable to the total cash to be paid

      a. Include contingent payments in calculation; this precludes recognizing a gain currently and interest expense later

      b. Recognize gain on the write-down

      c. All future cash payments reduce the payable, i.e., no interest expense is recognized

D. If restructured by partial settlement (assets and/or equity issuance) and modified terms:

   1. First account for asset and/or equity issuance per above

   2. Then account for modified terms per above

E. Related matters

   1. A repossession or foreclosure is accounted for per the above

   2. Gains from restructuring debt are aggregated and, if material, are an extraordinary item (see SFAS 4)

   3. Contingent payments on restructured debt shall be recognized per SFAS 5 (i.e., its payment is probable and subject to reasonable estimate)

   4. Legal fees on debt restructuring involving equity issuance reduce the amounts credited to the equity accounts

      a. All other direct costs of debt restructuring reduce gain or are expenses of the period if there is no gain

F. Disclosures by debtors

   1. Description of major changes in debt of each restructuring

   2. Aggregate gain on debt restructuring and related tax effect

   3. Aggregate net gain or loss in asset transfers due to restructuring

   4. EPS amount of aggregate gain in restructuring net of tax effect

PART II Accounting by Creditors (not applicable to receivables at market per specialized industry practices, e.g., bonds held by a mutual fund).

A. Assets (including equity interest in debtor) received as full payment are recorded at FMV

   1. Loss recognized (per APB 30) for excess of carrying value of receivable over asset FMV

   2. Account for assets received, e.g., depreciation, etc., as if purchased for cash

B. Creditors having terms of receivable restructured, account for the restructure prospectively, i.e., no adjustment of the receivable

1. Recognize excess of total cash to be received over carrying value of the receivable as interest per the interest method (APB 21)
2. Exception is if total payments to be received (including interest) are less than the carrying value of the receivable
   a. Write receivable down to total cash to be received and recognize the loss
      1) Consider contingency payments to be received if probable and subject to estimate
      2) If interest rates can fluctuate, use rate at time of restructuring to determine total cash to be received
   b. All future cash payments reduce carrying value of the receivable, i.e., no interest income

C. If a creditor's receivable is restructured by both receipt of assets and modification of terms, account for each portion of the restructure per the above

1. First, receivable is reduced by FMV of assets received

D. Related matters

1. A repossession or foreclosure is accounted for per the above.
2. If an adequate valuation account has already been established for the receivable being restructured, the loss can be charged to the valuation account
3. Contingent interest is not recognized until both the contingency is removed and it is earned.
   a. Not recognized, however, if it reduced loss as in "B.2.a.1)" above
4. Legal fees and other direct costs of restructuring are expensed as incurred
5. Receivables from sale of assets arising from debt restructure are accounted for per APB 21
   a. Difference between the carrying value of the receivable and the FMV of the assets received is a gain or loss

E. Disclosures by creditors for each category of restructured "reduced earnings" receivables

1. Aggregate recorded investment, and
   a. Gross interest income per original terms
   b. Interest income recognized during period
   c. Required only if currently yielding less than "market"
2. Amount of commitments to lend additional funds to debtors requiring restructuring

F. Substitution or addition of debtors is generally a modification of terms (relative to full payment)

SFAS 16 (A35, C59, I17, I73) Prior Period Adjustments (Supersedes para 23 and 24 of APB 9)
(Amends inconsistent references to APB 9 in APBs 20, 30, and SFAS 5)

A. All P&L items are included in the determination of net income except the two following items which are prior period adjustments

1. Correction of an error in statements of a prior period
2. Realized tax benefits of preacquisition operating loss carryforwards of purchased subsidiaries

B. An exception exists for interim reporting regarding certain adjustments relating to prior interim periods of the current year

    1. These "adjustments" (affecting prior interim periods of the current fiscal year) are settlements or adjustments of:

        a. Litigation or similar claims
        b. Income taxes
        c. Renegotiation proceedings
        d. Utility revenue per the rate-making process

    2. These "adjustments" must also:

        a. Be material to operating income, trends in income, etc.
        b. All or part of the adjustment is specifically identified with specified prior interim periods of the current fiscal year
        c. Not subject to reasonable estimation prior to the current interim period, e.g., new retroactive tax legislation

    3. When these "adjustments" occur after the first interim period and affect prior interim periods of the current year:

        a. Include applicable portion of the "adjustment" in the current interim period
        b. Restate prior interim periods of current fiscal year reflecting an applicable portion of the "adjustment"
        c. Include portion of "adjustment" applicable to prior fiscal periods in first interim period of current year
        d. In interim period of adjustment, disclose effect of "adjustment" for each period affected

            1) Operating income
            2) Net income
            3) EPS

SFAS 17 (L10) Accounting for Leases -- Initial Direct Costs
(Now in SFAS 13--Codified through May 1980)

SFAS 18 (S20) Financial Reporting for Segments of a Business Enterprise --   Interim Financial Statements
Deletes para 4 of SFAS 14

A. Para 4 of SFAS 14 required interim financial statements (prepared per GAAP) to report segment information that is required in annual statements

B. This SFAS eliminated the required reporting of segment information in interim statements as required by SFAS 14

    1. If interim segment information is presented, it should be per SFAS 14
    2. The FASB has interim financial reporting on its agenda as a major project

†SFAS 19 (Oi5) Financial Accounting and Reporting by Oil and Gas Producing Companies
(Supersedes SFAS 9)

Author's Note: This SFAS has been amended by SFAS 25 to suspend the requirement that oil and gas producers follow the successful efforts method of accounting. After the FASB issued this SFAS, the SEC took the position that a new method, "reserve recognition accounting," was to be developed. In the interim, the SEC is accepting the full costing method as well as the successful efforts method (see the outline of SFAS 25).

Thus, this SFAS continues to be in effect for those oil and gas producers using the successful efforts method. It also is in effect as to income tax allocation ("K." below) and production payments classified as debt ("J." below).

A. Definitions

1. Proved reserves -- quantities of oil and gas which are reasonably certain to be recovered in the future from known reservoirs under existing economic and operating conditions

2. Proved developed reserves -- reserves which can be recovered through existing wells and with existing equipment and operating methods. Additional recoveries expected from improved recovery techniques are includable only if proven by a test project.

3. Proved undeveloped reserves -- those expected to be recoverable from new wells on undrilled acreage or from recompletion of existing wells with reasonable certainty, i.e., adjacent productive units on successful tests of recompletion techniques

4. Field -- area of a single or multiple reservoirs grouped or related to the same geological structure or stratigraphic condition

5. Reservoir -- underground formation containing a natural accumulation of produceable oil or gas

6. Exploratory well -- well drilled outside a proved area or to a previously untested depth with the purpose of determining whether oil or gas reserves exist, i.e., not to develop proved oil or gas reserves discovered by previous drilling

7. Development well -- a well in a proved area for the purpose of extracting oil or gas

B. The costs of the wells, equipment, and proved properties are amortized as the oil and gas reserves are produced

1. Amortization costs plus production costs become the cost of the oil and gas produced

2. Unproven properties are evaluated annually, with a contra account and loss recorded as necessary

3. Costs not resulting in the acquisition of an asset (e.g., studies, carrying unproven land) are expensed as incurred

---

†This outline is not a comprehensive treatment of the respective SFAS. The authors feel this pronouncement is probably too specialized to warrant extensive coverage on the CPA Examination; however, candidates are advised to be familiar with the basic concepts put forth in the outline. Outlines of other pronouncements to which this note applies are similarly identified (†).

C. Acquisition costs (purchase, lease) of unproven or proven property are capitalized

   1. Reclassify unproven to proven when reserves are discovered; amortize using
       units-of-production method

D. Exploration costs are incurred in identifying prospective production areas.
Costs of studies expensed as incurred. Drilling costs capitalized if successful, expensed if not.

E. Development costs are incurred in developing proved reserves and are capitalized

   1. Exploration ("D." above) and developmental costs amortized based on proven
       developed reserves using units-of-production method

   2. If well is abandoned, allocate remaining cost to other wells

F. Production costs are incurred in getting oil and gas ready for shipment from
field and are treated as product costs, as are amortization of "B.," "C.," and
"D."

G. Costs of support equipment and facilities are capitalized and depreciated over
useful life as exploration, development, or production costs

H. Joint oil and gas costs allocated to oil and gas based on energy content, not
sales value

I. Balance sheet date conditions may be evaluated using subsequent information

J. A conveyance is transfer of an oil, gas, or operating interest in property.
Many are, in effect, borrowings repayable in cash or equivalent and are accounted for as debt.

K. In accounting for income taxes, interperiod tax allocation should be used

---

FASB INTERPRETATION 36   ACCOUNTING FOR EXPLORATORY WELLS IN PROGRESS AT THE END
OF A PERIOD.   INTERPRETS SFAS 19.
When a determination is made before issuing financial statements for a period
that an exploratory well or exploratory-type stratigraphic test well that was
in progress at the end of that period has not found proved reserves, costs incurred on the well through the end of the reporting period shall be charged to
expense of that period. Financial statements previously issued shall not be
retroactively restated.

SFAS 20 Accounting for Forward Exchange Contracts (Superseded by SFAS 52)

SFAS 21 (E09, S20) Suspension of the Reporting of EPS and Segment Data by Nonpublic
Enterprises

A. This Statement suspends APB 15 and SFAS 14 applicability to nonpublic companies

   1. APB 15 requires EPS presentations and disclosures
   2. SFAS 14 requires segment data disclosures
   3. Nonpublic companies are those whose securities do not trade in a public
       market

       a. Companies are considered public when they have to file registration
           statements on initial offerings
       b. Mutuals and cooperatives are considered nonpublic

B. If EPS and/or segment data are presented

       a. APB 15 and/or SFAS 14 must be complied with

SFAS 22 (L10) Changes in the Provisions of Lease Agreements Resulting from
Refundings of Tax-Exempt Debt
(Now in SFAS 13--Codified through May 1980)

SFAS 23 (L10) Inception of the Lease
(Now in SFAS 13--Codified through May 1980)

SFAS 24 (S20) Reporting Segment Information in Financial Statements That Are
Presented in Another Enterprise's Financial Report
(Amends para 7 of SFAS 14)

A. SFAS 14 "Financial Reporting for Segments of a Business Enterprise" required
    segment information for investees (subsidiaries, joint ventures, and equity
    method investees) when their complete set of statements was presented with con-
    solidated statements

    1. SFAS 21 "Suspension of the Reporting of Earnings Per Share and Segment
        Information by Nonpublic Enterprises" suspended the requirement with respect
        to separately issued statements of nonpublic investees

B. This SFAS deletes the requirement of segment information for financial state-
    ments of consolidated investees which are issued with the consolidated state-
    ments

    1. SFAS 14 still applies to statements of unconsolidated investees which are
        presented in the same financial report and are not exempted by SFAS 21

†SFAS 25 (Oi5) Suspension of Certain Accounting Requirements for Oil and Gas
Producing Companies
(Amends SFAS 19)

A. After SFAS 19 was issued, which required the successful efforts method of
    accounting, the SEC allowed oil and gas producers to use either successful
    efforts or full costing while a new method of "reserve recognition accounting"
    is being developed. Thus this SFAS rescinds the successful efforts require-
    ment. Both full costing and successful efforts are considered acceptable, with
    disclosure of method used.

B. Provisions in SFAS 19 retained

    1. Changes to meet SFAS 19 successful efforts requirements or to the full
        costing method specified by the SEC, should be by retroactive restatement

    2. Income tax allocation for oil and gas producers
    3. The requirement that production payments payable in cash or its equivalent
        be accounted for as debt

SFAS 26 (L10) Profit Recognition on Sales-Type Leases of Real Estate
(Now in SFAS 13--Codified through May 1980)

SFAS 27 (L10) Classification of Renewals or Extensions of Existing Sales-Type or
Direct Financing Leases
(Now in SFAS 13--Codified through May 1980)

SFAS 28 (L10) Accounting for Sales with Leasebacks
(Now in SFAS 13--Codified through May 1980)

SFAS 29 (L10) Determining Contingent Rentals
(Now in SFAS 13--Codified through May 1980)

SFAS 30 (S20) Disclosure of Information about Major Customers
(Amends para 39 of SFAS 14)

A. SFAS 14 required disclosure of sales to domestic government agencies in aggregate and sales to foreign government agencies in aggregate if either exceeded 10% of total sales

    1. Identity of customer need not be disclosed, but segment making sales should be disclosed

B. This SFAS changes the disclosure requirement to apply to the federal government, a state government, a local government, or a foreign government

    1. Rather than domestic or foreign government sales in aggregate
    2. I.e., each governmental unit is treated as a separate customer as are commercial enterprises
    3. The 10% of total sales criteria continues

SFAS 31 (I42) Accounting for Tax Benefits Related to U.K. Legislation Concerning Stock Relief
(This statement is not included because the authors feel that it is too specialized for the CPA exam.)

SFAS 32 (A06) Specialized Accounting and Reporting Principles and Practices in AICPA Statements of Position and Guides on Accounting and Auditing Matters
(Amends para 16 of APB 20)

A. The FASB has agreed to take over responsibility for specialized accounting and reporting practices in AICPA Statements of Position, Accounting Guides, and Auditing Guides

    1. The plan is to review the SOPs and Guides and to expose and issue SFASs

        a. Following the FASB's "due process" procedures

    2. Until each is reviewed, some may consider the SOPs and Guides "without force"
    3. Accordingly, the FASB has designated certain SOPs and Guides as "preferable" for justifying an accounting change per APB 20

        a. Thus, the FASB has given the SOPs and Guides status without establishing them as standards per Ethics Rule 203

            1) I.e., they are considered within GAAP

        b. The FASB excluded coverage of the Guide "Audits of State and Local Governmental Units" and related SOPs as the jurisdiction over governmental accounting is currently in question
        c. Also excluded were a few Guides and an SOP not covering financial reporting topics

            1) E.g., audit, EDP, and financial forecast topics

SFAS 33 (C27) Financial Reporting and Changing Prices

A. This SFAS requires certain supplementary constant dollar (price level adjusted) and current cost (current value) data to be disclosed by:

1. Public companies (consolidated if applicable)[**]
2. That, at the beginning of the year, have per GAAP either:

    a. Over $125 million in inventory and property, plant, and equipment (PP&E) before depreciation
    b. Or over $1 billion in total assets (after depreciation)

3. Except the current cost disclosures are not required for:

    a. Unprocessed natural resources
    b. Income producing real estate

B. The constant dollar and current cost disclosures are to be presented as supplementary data

1. For primary statements in annual reports

    a. Not for interim statements nor for segment information
    b. And not for separate company statements presented with consolidated statements

2. The supplementary disclosures do not affect the primary statements
3. And are not required of pooled companies in the year of pooling that meet the above size criteria due only to the pooling

C. A five year summary of certain data is also required

1. Net sales and other operating revenues
2. Constant dollar information

    a. Income from continuing operations
    b. Per share income from continuing operations
    c. Net assets at year end

3. Current cost information

    a. Income from continuing operations
    b. Per share income from continuing operations
    c. Net assets at year end
    d. Increases or decreases in the current cost amounts of inventory and PP&E, net of inflation

4. Other information

    a. Purchasing power gain or loss in net monetary items
    b. Cash dividends declared per common share
    c. Market price per common share at year end
    d. Consumer Price Index for each year as used for constant dollar calculations (either average-for-year or year-end Consumer Price Index)

D. Constant dollar (price level adjusted) disclosures

1. The minumum requirement is to restate the income statement (from continuing operations) in constant dollars, i.e., a statement format

---

[**]Amended by SFAS 54 to add: "except for investment companies."

a. Or adjust primary (historical cost) income from continuing operations to constant dollar income, i.e., a reconciliation format

b. Either way, the following items or their effect should be disclosed

   1) Cost of goods sold
   2) Depreciation, depletion, amortization
   3) Reduction of inventory and PP&E to recoverable amounts, if lower

c. Also the following should be disclosed in constant dollars (at recoverable amounts if lower) - note in the reconciliation format above only their effect would be disclosed

   1) Inventory
   2) PP&E
   3) Cost of goods sold
   4) Depreciation, depletion, and amortization

d. Also the purchasing power gain or loss on net monetary items should be disclosed

2. Or all of the financial statements may be restated in constant dollars

a. The purchasing power gain or loss on net monetary items is not a component of income from continuing operations

   1) Present it after income from continuing operations

E. Constant dollar measurements

1. Use Consumer Price Index (CPI) for all urban consumers

a. Which is published by the U.S. Bureau of Labor Statistics

2. Use average-for-year CPI for the year if only minimum disclosures are made

a. If statements are recast use average-for-year or year-end CPI
b. For the five-year summary, use:

   1) Average-for-year dollars
   2) Year-end dollars
   3) Base-year dollars

c. If CPIs are unpublished when needed, they may be estimated based on published forecasts or extrapolation from recent CPIs

3. Convert items into constant dollars by multiplying historical cost by the TO/FROM ratio

a. TO (the numerator) is the price index in year you are converting to
b. FROM (the denominator) is the price index in year you are converting from, i.e., the index existing at the time of original purchase

4. If inventory or PP&E is reduced to recoverable amounts if lower, the reduction is an expense in computing constant dollar income
5. Foreign currency items shall be translated to U.S. dollars per GAAP before conversion to constant dollars
6. Purchasing power gain or loss on monetary items:

a. End-of-year dollars: restate beginning net monetary items and increase or decrease in net monetary items to end-of-year dollars

   1) Compare with actual end-of-year net monetary items for gain or loss

   b. Average-for-year dollars: convert beginning, ending, and changes in net
       monetary items to average-for-year dollars

       1) Compare beginning, adjusted for changes, with ending for gain or
           loss

F. Current cost (current value) disclosures

   1. Income from continuing operations similar to that for constant dollars,
       i.e., in either a statement or reconciliation format (see "D.1.a." above)

       a. At a minimum, the following shall be reflected at current cost (or
           recoverable amount if related assets are also reflected at recoverable
           amount)

           1) Cost of goods sold
           2) Depreciation/amortization

   2. Current cost of inventory and PP&E at the current year end
   3. Changes in current cost of inventory and PP&E during the current year

       a. Both before and after the effects of inflation
       b. This change in current costs is not a component of income from con-
           tinuing operations

   4. Alternatively, all of the statements may be restated to current cost/
       constant dollar amounts

       a. Items other than cost of goods sold and depreciation/amortization may be
           shown at historical cost

           1) Adjusted at either year-end or average-for-year CPI

G. Current cost measurements

   1. Current cost of inventory is the current cost of purchasing or manufactur-
       ing, whichever is applicable

       a. Or recoverable amount if lower

   2. Current cost of PP&E is current cost of acquiring same service potential (or
       recoverable amount, if lower)

       a. I.e., the same operating costs and output
       b. Three valuation methods

           1) Current cost of new asset less depreciation
           2) Cost of comparable used asset
           3) Adjusting new asset cost for differences in:

               a) Useful life
               b) Output capacity
               c) Nature of service
               d) Operating costs

       c. Convert foreign asset prices at current exchange rate
       d. Assets may be priced individually or by category
       e. In summary, there are several approaches to determine current costs

           1) Indexation (application of price indices to original cost)

               a) Externally generated by class of goods
               b) Internally generated by class of goods

2) Direct pricing

    a) Current invoices

    b) Vendors' price quotations

    c) Current standard manufacturing costs

3. The income tax expense for current cost/constant dollar statements shall be the same as income tax expense on the primary statements, i.e., no adjustment is made

    a. No allocation of income tax expense is made between income from continuing operations and changes in the current cost of inventory and PP&E

4. Changes in current cost of inventory and PP&E are the differences between the current costs at entry dates and exit dates

    a. Entry dates are the later of the beginning of the year or date of acquisition

    b. Exit dates are the earlier of date of use, sale, etc., or year end

5. Changes in current costs are to be reported both before and after eliminating the effect of inflation

    a. Use average-for-year CPI

        1) Year-end CPI may be used if comprehensive current cost/constant dollar statements are prepared

H. Other items

1. All constant dollar and current cost items shall be stated at "recoverable amounts" if lower than the respective constant dollar or current cost figure

    a. If an asset is to be sold, the recoverable amount is net realizable value

        1) Selling price less disposal costs and completion costs

    b. If an asset is to be held, the recoverable amount is determined by discounting future cash flows from the asset

2. If there is no material difference between constant dollar income and current cost income, the current cost disclosures are not required for that year

    a. A footnote explanation is required

3. If depreciation is allocated to cost of sales and other functional expenses, aggregate constant dollar depreciation and aggregate current cost depreciation should be disclosed

4. Additional required disclosures

    a. Principal types of information used to calculate current cost data

    b. Differences between depreciation methods, estimates, etc., used for constant dollar and current cost calculations and for historical cost depreciation

    c. Exclusion of any income tax expense or allocations in the primary statements from constant dollar and current cost calculations

SFAS 34 (I67, I69) Capitalization of Interest Cost
(Para 8 and 9 amended by SFAS 42)
(Para 9, 10, and 20 amended by SFAS 58)

A. Interest costs, when material, incurred in acquiring the following types of assets, shall be capitalized

1. Assets constructed or produced for a firm's own use

   a. Including construction by others requiring progress payments

2. Assets intended for lease or sale that are produced as discrete projects

   a. E.g., ships and real estate developments

3. But not on:

   a. Routinely produced inventories
   b. Assets ready for their intended use
   c. Assets not being used nor being readied for use
   d. Land, unless it is being developed, e.g., as a plant site, real estate development, etc.

4. The objective of interest capitalization is to:

   a. Better reflect the acquisition cost of assets
   b. Better match costs to revenues in the period benefited

5. Capitalized interest shall be treated as any other asset cost for depreciation and other purposes

6. Required interest cost disclosures

   a. Total interest cost incurred
   b. Interest capitalized, if any

B. Amount of interest to be capitalized.

1. Conceptually, the interest that would have been avoided if the expenditures had not been made

2. Based on the average accumulated expenditures on the asset for the period

   a. Includes payment of cash, transfer of other assets, and incurring interest-bearing liabilities
   b. Reasonable approximations are permitted

3. Use the interest rates incurred during period

   a. First, the rates on specific new borrowings for the asset
   b. Second, a weighted average of other borrowings

      1) Use judgement to identify borrowings

4. Interest cost capitalized in any period cannot exceed interest cost incurred in that period

   a. On a consolidated basis for consolidated statements
   b. On an individual company basis for individual company statements

5. Capitalized interest should be compounded

C. Interest capitalization period

1. Begins when all the following three conditions are present

a. Asset expenditures have been made
b. Activities to ready asset for intended use are in progress

   1) Includes planning stages

c. Interest cost is being incurred

2. If activities to ready asset for intended use cease, interest capitalization ceases

   a. Not for brief interruptions that are externally imposed

3. Capitalization period ends when asset is substantially complete

   a. For assets completed in parts, interest capitalization on a part of the asset ends when that part is complete
   b. Capitalize all interest on assets required to be completed in entirety until entire project is finished

4. Interest capitalization continues if capitalized interest raises cost above market values

   a. Reduction of asset cost to market value is a separate accounting transaction

---

FASB INTERPRETATION NO. 33 APPLYING FASB STATEMENT NO. 34 TO OIL AND GAS PRO-
DUCING OPERATIONS ACCOUNTED FOR BY THE FULL COST METHOD
It clarifies which assets of oil and gas producing operations qualify for
capitalization of interest.

SFAS 35 (Pe5) Accounting and Reporting by Defined Benefit Pension Plans
(Para 30 amended by SFAS 59)

A. Covers all defined benefit pension plans (including those with death, disability, etc., benefits)

   1. Governmental, private, ERISA, non-ERISA, etc.
   2. But not terminated plans
   3. Also excludes government social security plans
   4. Does not mandate financial statements (preparation, distribution, or certification)

B. Establishes GAAP for pension plans

   1. Accounting principles not covered in this statement may apply
   2. Financial accounting standards in this statement are unique to defined benefit pension plans

C. Primary objective of pension plan statements: provide information to indicate ability of plan to pay accumulated benefits to participants. This requires information about:

   1. Resources available to pay benefits and stewardship thereof
   2. Participants' accumulated benefits
   3. Results of the plan's financial transactions
   4. Other factors affecting plan's ability to pay benefits

D. Pension plan financial statements include:

1. Statement of Net Assets available for benefits
2. Statement of Changes in Net Assets available for benefits
3. Information regarding the present value of accumulated benefits

    a. As of a benefit valuation date at beginning or end of plan year

4. Information of significant changes in accumulated benefits
5. Clarifications

    a. Information in present value of accumulated benefits and net assets available must be presented as of the same date
    b. Information on changes in net assets available and changes in present value of accumulated benefits must be presented for the same period.

6. Disclosure of the present value of accumulated plan benefits and changes therein may be disclosed in statement or footnote form

E. Net assets available for benefits shall be presented so as to permit assessment of the plan's resources available for payment to participants

1. The accrual basis of accounting shall be used
2. Contributions receivable from employers and participants

    a. Including amounts due by formal commitment

        1) If approved by employer's governing body
        2) Based on consistent prior pattern
        3) If an employer's tax deduction is taken prior to the report date

3. Fund investments are presented at their current value

    a. Based on market values, sales of similar assets, cash flows, etc.
    b. If financed by an insurance company, use amount reported OR amount that would be reported on ERISA's 5500 (C).
    c. Enough detail should be presented to identify the types of investments

4. Operating assets are presented at cost less the accumulated depreciation (e.g., buildings, equipment, etc.)

F. Changes in net assets minimum disclosure

1. Net change in current value of investments held at year end

    a. By major class of investment further segregated into those with and without quoted prices in an active market

2. Investment income, exclusive of "1." above
3. Contributions from employers (broken down into cash and noncash items)
4. Contributions from participants (including those collected by sponsor)
5. Contributions from other sources (disclose source)
6. Benefits paid
7. Payments to insurance companies for contracts not included in plan assets
8. Administrative expenses

G. Actuarial present value of accumulated plan benefits are those attributable to employee service prior to the benefit valuation date

1. Expected to be paid to:

    a. Retired or terminated employees or their beneficiaries
    b. Beneficiaries of deceased employees
    c. Present employees or their beneficiaries

2. Plan provisions apply to accumulated benefit measurement

    a. If the benefit accruing to each year of service is not specified, use:

        1) Ratio of years worked to years required for vesting
        2) OR ratio of years worked to total expected years to be worked

3. Measurement rules for accumulated benefits

    a. Based on employees' pay and service history as of benefit valuation date

    b. Projected service is only pertinent to:

        1) Increased benefits provided for length of service
        2) Early retirement benefits
        3) Death and disability benefits

    c. Automatic benefit increases, e.g., cost of living
    d. Exclude benefits from insurance contracts not included in plan assets
    e. Exclude plan amendments after the benefit valuation date
    f. Assume future compensation is unchanged in projecting Social Security benefits (SS benefits may affect the amount of pension benefits)

4. Actuarial present value is determined by adjusting accumulated benefits for:

    a. Time value of money
    b. Probability of payment

        1) Death, disability, withdrawal, retirement

5. Assume an ongoing plan

    a. Assumed rates of return should equal expected rates
    b. Rates of return should be consistent with inflation rates used for cost of living adjustments
    c. Administrative expenses can be reflected by:

        1) Adjusting expected rate of return (disclose)
        2) Discounting expected future cash payments

6. Separate disclosure of the present value of:

    a. Vested benefits of retired participants
    b. Other vested benefits
    c. Nonvested benefits

7. Also disclose employees' accumulated contributions, if any

    a. And interest rate thereon, if any

H. Changes in actuarial present value of accumulated plan benefits

1. Changes in actuarial assumptions are considered changes in estimates
2. If significant, individually or in aggregate, disclose factors affecting changes in actuarial present value, including:

    a. Plan amendments
    b. Changes in the nature of the plan
    c. Changes in actuarial assumptions

I. Other required disclosures

1. Assumptions to determine investment current values
2. Assumptions to determine accumulated benefit present values

    a. Assumed rate of return
    b. Inflation rate
    c. Retirement ages
    d. Changes in any assumptions

3. Also, the following, if applicable

    a. General description of the plan

        1) E.g., vesting and benefit provisions

    b. Significant changes in the plan agreement
    c. Priority order of participant claims and benefits guaranteed by PBGC (Pension Benefit Guarantee Corporation)
    d. Funding policy and compliance with ERISA
    e. Annuity contract with insurance companies
    f. Tax status if there is no exemption certificate
    g. Individual investments over 5% of total assets
    h. Real estate transactions with sponsor, employer, or employee organizations
    i. Subsequent events

J. Averages or other approximation methods are acceptable if results do not differ materially from results required in this statement.

SFAS 36 (P15) Disclosure of Pension Information
(Amends para 46 of APB 8)

A. To improve uniformity and comparability, employers shall make the following disclosures about their defined benefit pension plans:

1. Actuarial present value of vested accumulated plan benefits
2. Actuarial present value of nonvested accumulated plan benefits
3. Net assets available for benefits
4. The assumed rates of return used for the above
5. The date as of which the benefit information was derived

B. Clarifications

1. The valuation of the above is per SFAS 35
2. The disclosures shall be as of the most recent benefit information date
3. Data may be reported in total, separately, or in most useful subaggregation
4. If the above date is not available, the employer shall disclose the excess, if any, of vested benefits (present or actuarial value) over sum of:

    a. Pension fund
    b. Plus balance sheet accrual
    c. Less balance sheet prepayment of deferral

SFAS 37 (I28) Balance Sheet Classification of Deferred Income Taxes
(Amends para 57 of APB 11)

A. APB 11, para 57 required that deferred income tax debits and credits be accorded the same balance sheet classification as the asset or liability to which they relate

1. Para 57 does not cover the situation where a timing difference is <u>not related</u> to an asset or liability

B. This statement specifies that a deferred income tax charge or credit is related to a specific asset or liability if a decrease in the asset or liability balance results in a reversal of the timing difference

1. If related, classification (current or noncurrent) is the same as the related asset or liability

   a. E.g., a deferred tax credit which originated from using a different depreciation method on the tax return than on the books reverses during the periods when book depreciation is greater than tax depreciation

2. If not related, classification (current or noncurrent) is determined by the date the timing difference is expected to reverse

   a. E.g., A deferred tax credit which originated from changing inventory methods from LIFO to FIFO will decrease by 10% each year as permitted by the IRS, rather than as the inventory decreases

C. The requirement of "offsetting" or "netting" current debits against current credits and noncurrent debits against noncurrent credits remains in effect (para 57, APB 11)

SFAS 38 (B50, C59) Accounting for Preacquisition Contingencies of Purchased Enterprises
(Amends para 88 of APB 16)

A. This statement describes accounting for contingencies of an acquired enterprise that existed prior to the date on which a business combination accounted for as a purchase was consummated

1. In essence, the acquiring entity may assign final valuations to the acquired assets and liabilities up to one year after the combination occurs

B. Definitions

1. Preacquisition contingency - Contingency (asset, asset impairment, or liability) which is acquired from another enterprise in a business combination accounted for by the purchase method

2. Allocation period - Period of time necessary to identify and measure the assets purchased and liabilities assumed. This period ends when the acquiror has secured all known and available information. Typically, this period should not extend beyond one year of the date the combination was consummated.

C. Portion of total purchase price allocated to a preacquisition contingency other than the potential tax benefit of a loss carryforward (para 49, APB 11 and para 88, APB 16) is measured as follows:

1. If fair value is determinable during the "allocation period," use fair value as the basis of allocation
2. If fair value is not determinable during the "allocation period," use criteria of SFAS 5 and FASB Interpretation 14

D. Adjustment resulting from a preacquisition contingency made subsequent to the "allocation period" is a determinant of net income in the later period

†SFAS 39 (C27) Financial Reporting and Changing Prices: Specialized Assets - Mining and Oil and Gas
(Supplements SFAS 33)

A. SFAS 33 provided that entities which presented supplementary information on a current cost basis before December 25, 1980 (rather than postponing the first presentation one year) could measure mineral resource assets (assets that are directly related to, and get value from, all extracted minerals) at historical cost adjusted by a specific or general price index (historical cost/constant dollar)

B. This statement requires measurement of mineral resource assets and related expenses at current cost or lower recoverable amount (same basis required by SFAS 33 for PP&E and related expenses)

    1. Disclose information used in measurement

C. It also requires disclosure of information about quantities, production, and selling prices of mineral resources other than oil and gas reserves

†SFAS 40 (C27) Financial Reporting and Changing Prices: Specialized Assets - Timberland and Growing Timber
(Supplements SFAS 33)

A. SFAS 33 provided that entities which presented supplementary information on a current cost basis before December 25, 1980 (rather than postponing first presentation one year) could measure timberlands and growing timber at either historical cost/constant dollar amounts or at current cost or lower recoverable amounts

B. This statement extends the above interim provision indefinitely while the Board works with advisory task group for forest products industry to find improved measurement of specific price effects on timberlands

†SFAS 41 (C27) Financial Reporting and Changing Prices: Specialized Assets - Income-Producing Real Estate
(Supplements SFAS 33)

A. SFAS 33 provided that entities which presented supplementary information on a current cost basis before December 25, 1980 (rather than postponing first presentation one year) could measure income-producing real estate at either historical cost/constant dollar amounts or at current cost or lower recoverable amounts

B. This statement extends the above interim provision indefinitely while the Board works with advisory task group for the real estate industry to find improved measurement of specific price effects on income-producing real estate

SFAS 42 (I67) Determining Materiality for Capitalization of Interest Cost
(Amends SFAS 34)

A. Paras 8 and 9 of SFAS 34 were interpreted by some as establishing new tests of materiality

    1. Seemed to allow measurements of the income effect of interest capitalization by a pro forma prospective or retroactive computation while ignoring the current year's effect

B. This statement eliminates the misinterpreted language in para 8 (last two sentences) and para 9 (reference to para 8)

SFAS 43 (C44) Accounting for Compensated Absences

A. This statement addresses the accounting for future sick pay benefits, holidays, vacation benefits and other like compensated absences

B. Accrual of a liability for future compensated absences is required if <u>all</u> of the conditions listed below exist

   1. Obligation of employer to compensate employees arises from services already performed
   2. Obligation arises from vesting or accumulation of rights
   3. Probable payment of compensation
   4. Amount can be reasonably estimated

C. Above criteria require accrual of a liability for vacation benefits; however, other compensated absences typically do not require accrual of a liability

   1. In spite of the above criteria, accrual of a liability is not required for accumulating nonvesting rights to receive sick pay benefits because amounts are typically not large enough to justify cost

SFAS 44 (I17, I60) Accounting for Intangible Assets of Motor Carriers
(Amends para 8 and 10, Chapter 5, ARB 43. Interprets APB 17 and 30)

(This pronouncement deals with a one-time problem: how to account for interstate operating rights of motor carriers when that industry was deregulated. Therefore, the outline is not included in this volume.)

SFAS 45 (Fr3) Accounting for Franchise Fee Revenue

A. Definitions

   1. <u>Franchisee</u> - party who has been granted business rights
   2. <u>Franchisor</u> - party who grants business rights
   3. <u>Area franchise</u> - agreement transferring franchise rights within a geographical area permitting the opening of a number of franchise outlets

   4. <u>Bargain purchase</u> - franchisee is permitted to purchase equipment or supplies at a price significantly lower than fair value

   5. <u>Continuing franchise fee</u> - consideration for continuing rights granted by the agreement (general or specific) during its life

   6. <u>Franchise agreement</u> - essential criteria:

      a. Contractual relation between franchisee and franchisor
      b. Purpose is distribution of a product, service, or entire business concept
      c. Resources contributed by both franchisor and franchisee in establishing and maintaining the franchise
      d. Outline of specific marketing practices to be followed
      e. Creation of an establishment that will require and support the full-time business activity of the franchisee
      f. Both franchisee and franchisor have a common public identity

   7. <u>Initial franchise fee</u> - consideration for establishing the relationship and providing some initial services
   8. <u>Initial services</u> - variety of services and advice; e.g., site selection, financing and engineering services, advertising assistance, training of

personnel, manuals for operations, administration and recordkeeping, bookkeeping and advisory services, quality control programs

B. Franchise fee revenue from individual sales shall be recognized when all material services or conditions relating to the sale have been substantially performed or satisfied by the franchisor

    1. Substantial performance means:

        a. Franchisor has no remaining obligation or intent to refund money or forgive unpaid debt

        b. Substantially all initial services have been performed

        c. No other material conditions or obligations exist

    2. If a large initial franchise fee is required and continuing franchise fees are small in relation to future services, then a portion of the initial franchise fee shall be deferred and amortized over the life of the franchise

C. Initial franchise fees relating to area franchise sales shall be accounted for in a similar manner to individual franchise sales

    1. If franchisor's substantial obligations depend on number of individual franchises established, revenue shall be recognized in proportion to the initial mandatory services provided

D. If franchise fee includes a portion for tangible property, the portion applicable to the tangible assets shall be based on the fair value of the assets, and may be recognized before or after the revenue from initial services

E. Continuing franchise fees shall be reported as revenue as the fees are earned and become receivable from the franchise. Related costs shall be expensed as incurred.

F. If franchisee is given right to make bargain purchases, then a portion of the initial franchise fee shall be deferred and accounted for as an adjustment of the selling price when franchisee purchases equipment or supplies

G. Direct franchise costs shall be deferred until related revenue is recognized

    1. These costs should not exceed anticipated revenue less estimated additional related costs

H. Accounting for repossessed franchises

    1. If franchisor refunds fee, previously recognized revenue is accounted for as a reduction of revenue in current period

    2. If franchisor does not refund fee, previously recognized revenue is not adjusted

        a. Provide for estimated uncollectible amount

        b. Consideration retained for which revenue was not previously recognized should be recognized as revenue in current period

I. Disclosure of all significant commitments and obligations that have not yet been substantially performed are required

        a. Notes to the financial statements should disclose whether the installment or cost recovery method is used

        b. Initial franchise fees shall be segregated from other franchise fee revenue if significant

<u>†SFAS 46 (C27) Financial Reporting and Changing Prices: Motion Picture Films</u>
(Supplements SFAS 33)

A. This statement requires enterprises that present information on a current cost basis to <u>combine with that information</u> measures of motion picture films and related expenses, at either historical cost/constant dollar amounts or at current cost or lower recoverable amounts

<u>SFAS 47 (C32) Disclosure of Long-Term Obligations</u>

A. This statement requires that a firm disclose

  1. Commitments under unconditional purchase obligations that are associated with suppliers (financing arrangements)
  2. Future payments on long-term borrowings and redeemable stock

B. <u>Unconditional purchase obligations</u> are obligations to transfer funds in the future for fixed or minimum amounts of goods or services at fixed or minimum prices

  1. Unconditional purchase obligations that have all the following character-istics must be disclosed; they are not recorded on the balance sheet

    a. Is noncancelable or cancelable only:

      1) Upon occurrence of a remote contingency, or
      2) With permission of another party, or
      3) If a replacement agreement is signed between same parties
      4) Upon penalty payment such that continuation appears reasonably assured

  2. Was negotiated as part of arranging financing for the facilities that will provide the contracted goods
  3. Has a remaining term greater than one year

C. Disclosure of those unconditional purchase obligations <u>not recorded</u> on the balance sheet shall include:

  1. Nature and term of the obligation
  2. Amount of the fixed and determinable portion of the obligation as of the most recent balance sheet in the aggregate and if determinable for each of the next 5 years
  3. Description of any variable elements of the obligation
  4. Amounts purchased under the obligation(s) for each year an income statement is presented
  5. Encourages disclosing imputed interest to reduce the obligation to present value using:

    a) Effective interest rate, or if unknown
    b) Purchaser's incremental borrowing rate at the date the obligation was entered into

D. This statement <u>does not change</u> the accounting for obligations that <u>are recorded on the balance sheet</u>, nor does it suggest that disclosure is a substitute for accounting recognition. For <u>recorded</u> obligations, the following information should be disclosed for each of the next five years.

  1. Aggregate amount of payments for unconditional obligations that meet criteria for balance sheet recognition
  2. Combined aggregate amount of maturities and sinking fund requirements for all long-term borrowings

3. Amount of redemption requirements for all issues of capital stock that are redeemable at fixed or determinable prices on fixed or determinable dates

SFAS 48 (R75) Revenue Recognition When Right of Return Exists
(Extracts from AICPA Statement of Position (SOP) 75-1)

A. Specifies accounting for sales in which a product may be returned for refund, credit applied to amounts owed, or in exchange for other products

1. Right is specified by contract or is a matter of existing practice
2. Right may be exercised by ultimate customer or party who resells product to others
3. Not applicable to service revenue, real estate or lease transactions, or return of defective goods

B. Recognize revenue from right of return sales only if all of the following conditions are met

1. Price is substantially fixed or determinable at date of sale
2. Buyer has paid or is unconditionally obligated to pay
3. Obligation is not changed by theft, destruction, or damage of product
4. Buyer has "economic substance" apart from seller (i.e., sale is not with a party established mainly for purpose of recognizing sales revenue)
5. Seller has no significant obligation for performance to directly cause resale of product
6. Amount of future returns can be reasonably estimated

C. If all of the conditions in "B." above are met, record sales and cost of sales and

1. Reduce sales revenue and cost of sales to reflect estimated returns
2. Accrue expected costs or losses in accordance with SFAS 5

D. If any condition in "B." above is not met, do not recognize sales and cost of sales until either:

1. All conditions are subsequently met, or
2. Return privilege has substantially expired

E. Factors which may impair ability to make a reasonable estimate of returns include:

1. Susceptibility of product to significant external factors (e.g., obsolescence or changes in demand)
2. Long period of return privilege
3. Absence of experience with similar products or inability to apply such experience due to changing circumstances (e.g., marketing policies or customer relationships)
4. Absence of large volume of similar transactions

F. Reference to SOP 75-1 is deleted from SFAS 32, Appendix A

G. Effective for fiscal years beginning after 6/15/81; earlier application is encouraged

1. Accounting changes to conform with the statement shall be applied retroactively with disclosure of effect on sales, income before extraordinary items, net income, and related per-share amounts

2. If restatement of all years presented not practicable:

a. Restate as many consecutive years as practicable
b. Include cumulative effect in income of earliest year restated with proper disclosure

SFAS 49 (D18) Accounting for Product Financing Arrangements
(Extracts from AICPA Statement of Position (SOP) 78-8)

A. Establishes accounting and reporting standards for product financing arrangements by requiring treatment as a borrowing rather than as a sale

1. This statement does not alter any requirement of SFAS 48, nor does it apply to transactions for which sales revenue shall be accorded current recognition in accordance with that statement
2. Requirements of Addendum to APB 2 govern application of this statement to firm's operations that are regulated for rate making purposes on individual-company-cost-of-service basis

B. In product financing arrangements, a sponsor (entity which is financing its inventory)

1. Sells product to another entity and agrees to repurchase the product, or
2. Arranges for another entity to purchase product on a sponsor's behalf and agrees to purchase product, or
3. Controls disposition of product that has been purchased by another entity using the type of arrangement in either "1." or "2." above

C. Other typical, but not necessary, characteristics of such agreements are:

1. Entity that purchases product was established for that purpose or is an existing trust, nonbusiness organization, or credit grantor
2. Financed product is to be used or sold by sponsor
3. Financed product is stored in sponsor's premises
4. Debt of purchasing entity is guaranteed by sponsor

D. The standards established (see "E." below) apply to agreements described in "B." above which meet both of the following criteria

1. Sponsor is required to purchase product at specified prices; a predetermined sponsor price is present in agreements that:

a. Include resale price guarantees for products sold to third parties
b. Give sponsor option to purchase with significant penalty if option is not exercised
c. Provide option for other entity to require sponsor purchase

2. Payments to other entity are set by the financing agreement and sponsor's payments will be modified, as necessary, to cover fluctuations in purchasing and holding costs (including interest) incurred by other entity

E. Standards of accounting and reporting for sponsors

1. If agreement meets description of "B.1.":

a. Liability is recorded when proceeds received
b. No sale is recorded
c. Financed inventory is not removed from balance sheet

2. If agreement meets description of "B.2.":

a. Asset (inventory) and related liability are recorded when purchased by other entity

3. Shall account for financing and holding costs as they are incurred by the other entity in the same manner as such costs are normally accounted for

   a. Interest costs shall be treated separately in accordance with SFAS 34

SFAS 50 (Re4) Financial Reporting in the Record and Music Industry[†]

A. License fee is recognized as revenue when license agreement is, in substance, an outright sale and collection of fee is reasonably assured

B. Licensee may pay minimum guarantee (MG) in advance. Licensor reports MG as liability initially, then amortizes liability to revenue as license fee is earned.

C. Royalties paid to artists are expensed when record is sold. Advance royalties, under certain conditions, are recorded as asset and subsequently expensed as royalty is earned.

D. Cost of record master incurred by record company shall be reported as asset or expense dependent upon past performance and current popularity of artist

SFAS 51 (Ca4) Financial Reporting by Cable Television Companies[†]

A. Prematurity Period--cable television system is partially under construction and partially in service

B. During prematurity period, a portion of the programming and other system costs associated with that portion of system under construction may be capitalized

C. Interest cost capitalization during prematurity period is calculated on average qualifying assets (see SFAS 34)

D. Initial hookup fees are recognized as revenue to extent of direct selling costs with remainder deferred and then amortized to income

E. Initial installation costs are capitalized and depreciated

SFAS 52 Foreign Currency Translation (Supersedes SFAS 8, SFAS 20, and SFAS Interpretations 15 and 17)

A. Primary objectives of foreign currency translation

   1. Should provide information disclosing effects of rate changes on enterprise cash flows and equity
   2. Should also provide information in consolidated statements as to financial results and relationships of individual consolidated entities measured in their respective functional currencies in accordance with U.S. GAAP

B. Functional currency is the currency of the primary economic environment in which a foreign entity operates (i.e., the environment in which the entity generates and spends cash)

   1. A foreign entity's assets, liabilities, revenues, expenses, gains, and losses shall be measured in that entity's functional currency

2. The functional currency could be the currency of the country in which the entity operates if the entity is a self-contained unit operating in a foreign country

    Example: An entity (1) whose operations are not integrated with those of the parent, (2) whose buying and selling activities are primarily local, and (3) whose cash flows are primarily in the foreign currency.

3. There may be several functional currencies if there are many self-contained entities operating in different countries

4. The functional currency might be the U.S. dollar if the foreign entity's operations are considered to be a direct and integral part of the U.S. parent's operations

    Example: An entity (1) whose operations are integrated with those of the parent, (2) whose buying and selling activities are primarily in the parent's country and/or the parent's currency, and (3) whose cash flows are available for remittance to the parent.

5. Functional currency for a foreign entity, once determined, shall be used consistently unless it is clear that economic facts and circumstances have changed

    a. If a change is made, do not restate previously issued financial statements

6. If a foreign entity's bookkeeping is not done in the functional currency, the process of converting from the currency used for the books and records to the functional currency is called remeasurement

    a. Remeasurement is intended to produce the same result (e.g., balances for assets, expenses, liabilities, etc.) as if the functional currency had been used for bookkeeping purposes

    b. In highly inflationary economies (cumulative inflation over a 3-year period is $\geq$ 100%), the remeasurement of a foreign entity's financial statements shall be done as if the functional currency were the reporting currency (i.e., the U.S. dollar)

7. The functional currency (if not the U.S. dollar) is translated to the reporting currency (assumed to be the U.S. dollar) by using appropriate exchange rates (see item "C." below)

    a. If the functional currency is the U.S. dollar, there is no need to translate (if the books and records are maintained in U.S. dollars)

C. The translation of foreign currency financial statements (those incorporated in the financial statements of a reporting enterprise by consolidation, combination or the equity method of accounting) should use a current exchange rate if the foreign currency is the functional currency

1. Assets and liabilities - exchange rate at the balance sheet date is used to translate the functional currency to the reporting currency

2. Revenues (expenses) and gains (losses) - exchange rates when the transactions were recorded shall be used to translate from the functional currency to the reporting currency

      a. Weighted averages for exchange rates may be used for items occurring numerous times during the period

   3. Translation adjustments will result from the translation process if the functional currency is a foreign currency

      a. Translation adjustments are not an element of net income of the reporting entity

      b. Translation adjustments are accumulated and reported as part of the reporting entity's owners' equity

      c. Accumulated translation adjustments remain part of owners' equity until the reporting entity disposes of the foreign entity.

          1) In period of disposal, these adjustments are reported as part of the gain (loss) on sale or liquidation

D. <u>Foreign currency transactions</u> are those which are denominated (fixed) in other than the entity's functional currency

   1. Receivables and/or payables, which are fixed in a currency other than the functional currency, may result in transaction gains (losses) due to changes in exchange rates after the transaction date

   2. Transaction gains or losses generally are reported on the income statement in the period during which the exchange rates change

   3. Deferred taxes may have to be provided for transaction gains or losses which are realized for income tax purposes in a time period different than that for financial reporting

E. <u>A forward exchange contract</u> represents an agreement to exchange different currencies at a specified future rate and at a specified future date

   1. A forward exchange contract is accounted for like a foreign currency transaction

   2. Gains (losses) on forward contracts (except those noted in "4." below) are disclosed on the income statement during the period in which the spot rates change

      a. <u>Spot rate</u> is the rate for immediate delivery of the currencies exchanged

   3. Discounts (premiums) on forward contracts are accounted for separately from the gains or losses noted in "2." above.

      a. Discounts (premiums) generally are amortized and charged to income during the life of the forward contract

   4. Gains (losses) on a forward contract that is intended to hedge an identifiable foreign currency commitment should be deferred until the transaction date

      a. Losses should not be deferred if deferral leads to the recognition of losses in later periods

F. Financial statement disclosures required:

   1. Aggregate transaction gain (loss) that is included in the entity's net income

   2. Analysis of changes in accumulated translation adjustments which are reported as part of the entity's owners' equity

   3. Significant rate changes subsequent to the date of the financial statements including effects on unsettled foreign currency transactions

---

FASB INTERPRETATION NO. 37   ACCOUNTING FOR TRANSLATION ADJUSTMENTS UPON SALE OF PART OF AN INVESTMENT IN A FOREIGN ENTITY
If an enterprise sells part of its ownership interest in a foreign entity, a pro rata portion of the accumulated translation adjustment component of equity attributable to that investment shall be recognized in measuring the gain (loss) on the sale.

---

†SFAS 53 (Mo6) Financial Reporting by Producers and Distributors of Motion Picture Films

A. Revenue from sale (license) of motion picture exhibition rights to theaters is recognized on exhibition dates

B. License agreement for television program material is considered as sale of a right or a group of rights. Revenue is recognized, dependent upon certain conditions, when the license period begins.

C. Film production costs and exploitation costs (includes advertising and cost of prints that clearly benefit future periods) are capitalized and amortized to expense using specialized method

D. Inventory valuation of film is lower of:

1. Unamortized production and exploitation costs, or
2. Net realizable value

E. Balance sheet classifications are specified in pronouncement

†SFAS 54 (C27) Financial Reporting and Changing Prices: Investment Companies
(Amends SFAS 33)

A. For investment companies, information required by SFAS 33 is, in part, either not relevant or already provided in primary financial statements

1. Remainder is readily determinable by financial statement readers

B. Therefore, investment companies are not required to provide SFAS 33 disclosures and supplemental information

SFAS 55 (E09) Determining Whether a Convertible Security is a Common Stock Equivalent
(Amends para 33 of APB 15)

A. APB 15 used bank prime interest rate in cash yield test for determining common stock equivalents (CSEs)

1. Convertible securities were CSEs if cash yield was less than two-thirds of bank prime interest rate at time of issuance

B. Recent bank prime interest rates have been volatile and often higher than long-term interest rates

1. Classification of some convertible securities as CSEs was contrary to the intent of APB 15

C. Therefore, in the cash yield test, "bank prime interest rate" is replaced by "average Aa corporate bond yield"

SFAS 56 (A06, Co4) Designation of AICPA Guide and Statement of Position (SOP) 81-1 on Contractor Accounting and SOP 81-2 Concerning Hospital-Related Organizations as Preferable for Purposes of Applying APB Opinion 20
(Amends SFAS 32)

A. SFAS 32 designates, as "preferable," those accounting principles which are contained in the AICPA Statements of Position (SOPs) and AICPA Guides (Accounting and Auditing) listed in Appendix A of SFAS 32

B. The guide and SOPs listed below are added to the list of Appendix A of SFAS 32

    1. Audit and Accounting Guide for Construction Contractors
    2. SOP 81-1, Accounting for Performance of Construction-Type and Certain Production-Type Contracts
    3. SOP 81-2, Reporting Practices concerning Hospital-Related Organizations

SFAS 57 (R36) Related Party Disclosures

A. Definitions

    1. Affiliate - Party that controls, is controlled by, or is under common control with another enterprise, directly or indirectly

    2. Control - Power to direct or cause direction of management through owner-ship, contract, or other means

    3. Immediate family - Family members whom principal owners or management might control/influence or be controlled/influenced by

    4. Management - Persons responsible for enterprise objectives who have policy-making and decision-making authority

        a. E.g., board of directors, chief executive and operating officers, and vice-presidents
        b. Includes persons without formal titles

    5. Principal owners - Owners of more than 10% of a firm's voting interests

        a. Includes known beneficial owners

    6. Related parties - Affiliates, equity method investees, employee benefit trusts, principal owners, management or any party that can significantly influence a transaction

B. Financial statements shall include disclosures of material transactions between related parties except:

    1. Compensation agreements, expense allowances, and other similar items in the ordinary course of business
    2. Transactions which are eliminated in the preparation of consolidated/com-bined financial statements

C. Disclosures of material transactions shall include:

    1. Nature of relationship(s)
    2. Description of transaction(s), including those assigned zero or nominal accounts
    3. Dollar amount of transactions for each income statement period and effect of any change in method of establishing terms

4. Amounts due to/from related parties, including terms and manner of settlement

D. Representations concerning related party transactions shall not imply that terms were equivalent to those resulting in arm's-length bargaining unless such statement can be substantiated

E. When a <u>control</u> relationship exists, disclose such relationship even though no transactions have occurred

SFAS 58 (I67) Capitalization of Interest Cost in Financial Statements that Include Investments Accounted for by the Equity Method
(Amends para 9, 10, and 20 of SFAS 34)

A. Investments (equity, loans, and advances) in investees accounted for by equity method

1. Shall be considered qualifying assets of the investor (including parent company and consolidated subsidiaries) up to point when planned principal operations begin
2. Once operations begin, current or subsequent investment in that investee shall not be considered qualifying assets
3. Account for capitalized interest in some manner as other differences between investment cost and book value of net assets acquired (APB 18)

B. For parent company and subsidiaries, only the qualifying assets appearing in the consolidated balance sheet shall be eligible for interest capitalization

C. If an investee which was not consolidated in the past is consolidated, do not restate capitalized interest costs

†SFAS 59 (Pe5) Deferral of the Effective Date of Certain Accounting Requirements for Pension Plans of State and Local Governmental Units
(Amends SFAS 35)

(This statement is not relevant to the CPA exam; it merely changes the effective date of SFAS 35 for pension plans of governmental entities.)

†SFAS 60 (I42) Accounting and Reporting by Insurance Enterprises

A. Applies to insurance enterprises (except mutual life insurance enterprises, assessment enterprises, and fraternal benefit societies)

B. Insurance contracts are classified as:

1. Long-Duration Contracts

a. Policy expected to remain in force for extended period. Includes whole-life, annuity, guaranteed renewable term life, endowment, annuity, title insurance
b. Premiums recognized as revenue when due from policyholders
c. Liability for future policy benefits = PV of benefits to be paid - PV of premiums to be received

2. Short-Duration Contracts

    a. All contracts not classified as long-duration. Includes property and liability contracts

    b. Premiums recognized as revenue over contract life or period of risk

    c. Claim costs and estimates of insured events that have occurred but not been reported are recognized when insured event occurs

C. Direct costs associated with acquisition (issuance or renewal) of contracts are capitalized and then amortized to expense in proportion to premium revenue recognized

    1. Includes commissions, underwriting and policy issue personnel salaries, medical and inspection fees

    2. Unamortized acquisition costs are classified as assets

D. Investments by insurance enterprises

    1. Common and nonredeemable preferred stock reported at market

    2. Bonds and redeemable preferred stock reported at amortized cost

    3. Mortgage loans reported at outstanding principal or amortized cost

    4. Real estate reported at depreciated cost

E. Gains (losses) on investments

    1. Realized gains (losses)

        a. Reported net of tax

        b. Reported below operating income on income statement

    2. Unrealized gains (losses)

        a. Reported net of tax

        b. Included in stockholders' equity

†SFAS 61 (Ti7) Accounting for Title Plant

A. Applies to enterprises that use a title plant in their operations. Includes title insurance enterprises, title abstract enterprises, and title agents.

    1. Title Plant includes information pertaining to all matters affecting title to parcels of land in a specific geographical area

B. Direct costs of constructing title plants incurred before title plant can be used to perform title searches must be capitalized

    1. Do not depreciate capitalized costs unless value has been impaired

C. After operations begin, costs of doing title searches and maintaining title plant are expensed when incurred

†SFAS 62 (I67) Capitalization of Interest Cost in Situations Involving Certain Tax-Exempt Borrowings and Certain Gifts and Grants
(Amends para 10, 13, and 17 of SFAS 34)

A. Requires capitalization of net interest cost involving acquisition of qualifying assets financed with proceeds of externally restricted tax-exempt borrowings

    1. Net interest cost = interest cost of borrowing - interest earned on temporary investment of proceeds

        a. Applicable only from date of borrowing until assets ready for intended use

B. Does not permit capitalization of interest cost on assets acquired with gifts and grants whose use is restricted by the donor or grantor

    1. Interest earned from temporary investment of these gifts or grants are considered additions to the gift or grant

†SFAS 63 (Br5) Financial Reporting by Broadcasters

A. Broadcaster--an entity or an affiliated group of entities that transmits radio or television program material

B. Program material exhibition rights acquired under a license agreement are accounted for as a purchase of rights by the licensee (broadcaster)

C. Licensee reports asset and liability for rights acquired and obligations incurred at either present value (per APB 21) or gross amount of liability

    1. Reported when license period begins and all of the following are met:

        a. Cost is known or reasonably determinable
        b. Licensee has accepted program material
        c. Program is available for first showing

    2. The alternative that permits recording the asset and liability "gross" apparently resulted from a compromise by members of the FASB

D. Establishes reporting standards for barter transactions and network affiliation agreements

SFAS 64 (D14) Extinguishments of Debt Made to Satisfy Sinking-Fund Requirements
(Amends para 8 and footnote 2 of SFAS 4)

A. Gains (losses) on extinguishment of debt made to satisfy sinking-fund requirements which would need to be met within one year of extinguishment date do not require extraordinary item classification

B. Means used to achieve the extinguishment (cash, noncash) does not affect the resultant classification of gains (losses)

†SFAS 65 (Mo4) Accounting for Certain Mortgage Banking Activities

A. Applies to mortgage banking activities whether performed by mortgage banking enterprises, commercial banks, or thrift institutions

B. Mortgage loans or mortgage-backed securities (mortgage instruments) held for sale are reported at lower of cost or market

    1. Changes in the valuation allowance are included in that period's net income
    2. Purchase discounts shall not be amortized to interest revenue
    3. Mortgage instruments shall be segregated to determine market value (i.e., residential, commercial, committed, uncommitted)

4. Mortgage instruments transferred to long-term investment classification are transferred at lower of cost or market
5. Permanent impairment of long-term investment requires reduction to expected collectible amount

    a. No recovery of write-down until sale, maturity, or other disposition

C. Mortgage instruments transferred under formal or informal repurchase agreements are:

1. Accounted for as collateralized financing arrangement
2. Reported by transferor as being held for sale

D. Sales price of mortgage instruments is adjusted if stated servicing fee rate differs materially from current (normal) servicing fee rate

E. Balance sheet classification shall distinguish between mortgage instruments which are:

1. Held for sale
2. Held as long-term investments

SFAS 66 (Rel) Accounting for Sales of Real Estate

A. Other than retail land sales

1. Use the full accrual method if the following criteria are satisfied

    a. Sale is consummated
    b. Buyer's initial and continuing investments demonstrate a commitment to pay for the property
    c. Seller's receivable is not subject to future subordination
    d. Risks and rewards of ownership have been transferred

2. When the criteria are not met and dependent upon the particular circumstance, use one of the following methods

    a. Installment method
    b. Cost recovery method
    c. Deposit method
    d. Reduced profit method
    e. Financing, leasing, or profit-sharing arrangement rather than a sale

B. †Retail land sales

1. Use full accrual method of accounting when all of the following criteria are satisfied

    a. Refund period has expired
    b. Cumulative payments of principal and interest are ≥ 10% of contract sales price
    c. Seller's land sales receivables are collectible--20% down payment indicates collectibility
    d. Seller's receivable is not subject to subordination other than subordination by an individual lot buyer for home construction purposes
    e. Seller has no significant remaining obligations for construction or development

2. When these criteria are not met and dependent upon the particular circumstance, use one of the following methods

    a. Percentage-of-completion method
    b. Installment method
    c. Deposit method

†SFAS 67 (Re2) Accounting for Costs and Initial Rental Operations of Real Estate Projects

A. Establishes accounting and reporting standards for acquisition, development, construction, selling, and rental cost associated with real estate projects

B. Preacquisition costs (e.g., cost of surveying) are capitalized if certain conditions are met

    1. They become project costs when property is purchased
    2. They are expensed when it's probable that the property will not be acquired

C. Taxes and insurance are capitalized only until property is substantially complete and ready for intended use

D. Rental project being developed changes from nonoperating to operating when:

    1. Substantially completed and available for occupancy, or
    2. Tenant improvements are completed, or
    3. No later than one year from cessation of major construction activities

E. When property changes to operating status:

    1. Only development and construction cost should be capitalized
    2. Amortization of all capitalized costs should begin

F. If real estate is abandoned, capitalized costs related thereto shall be expensed

G. Costs incurred to rent or sell real estate projects are capitalized if certain conditions are met

SFAS 68 (R55) Research and Development Arrangements

A. Establishes accounting for enterprise's obligation under arrangement in which R&D is funded by others

B. Obligation to repay any of the funds provided by other parties regardless of the outcome of the R&D is a liability which shall be estimated and recognized

    1. Obligation may be written, contractual, or presumed (because of surrounding conditions)
    2. Charge R&D costs to expense as incurred

C. Obligation for contract to perform R&D for others arises (no liability recorded) when financial risk associated with R&D has been transferred because repayment of any funds provided by other parties depends solely on the results

D. Loan or advance made by enterprise to other parties should be expensed if repayment depends solely on R&D results having future economic benefits

    1. Classify as R&D expense unless related to some other function (advertising, marketing, etc.)

E. Financial statement disclosure

1. For arrangements in "B" and "D" above, follow SFAS 2 disclosure
2. For arrangements in "C" above:

   a. Terms of significant agreements under R&D arrangements as of the date of each balance presented
   b. Amount of compensation earned and costs incurred under R&D arrangements for each period for which income statement is presented

†SFAS 69 (C27, C51, I73, Oi5, S20) Disclosures About Oil and Gas Producing Activities
(Amends and supersedes SFAS 19, paras 48-59; SFAS 25, paras 4-9; SFAS 33, paras 51-53)

A. Both publicly traded and other enterprises engaged in oil and gas production shall continue to disclose:

1. Method of accounting for costs incurred in those activities
2. Manner of disposing of capitalized costs relating to these activities

B. Publicly traded enterprises with significant oil and gas producing activities shall make additional disclosures when issuing complete financial statements

1. Enterprise has significant activities if one of three tests is met

   a. Revenues from oil and gas production activities are > 10% of enterprise's combined revenues (sales to unaffiliated customers and sales or transfers to enterprise's other operation) of all of enterprise's industry segments
   b. Results of operations for oil and gas production activities are > 10% of greater of:

      1) Combined profit of all segments showing an operating profit or
      2) Combined loss of all segments showing an operating loss

   c. Identifiable assets test as defined in FASB 14, para 10

2. Disclosures are not required in interim report unless event causes a significant change in reserve quantities disclosed in latest annual report

C. Required disclosures include:

1. Net quantities of proved oil and gas reserves shall be shown as of beginning and end of year
2. Aggregate capitalized costs pertaining to oil and gas producing activities and aggregate related accumulated depreciation
3. Costs related to oil and gas activities (property acquisition, exploration, and development) whether capitalized or expensed
4. Results of operations in aggregate and for each geographic area for which reserve quantities are disclosed
5. Standardized measure of discounted future net cash flows relating to proved oil and gas reserve quantities

SFAS 70 (C27) Financial Reporting and Changing Prices: Foreign Currency Translation
(Amends SFAS 33)

A. If U.S. dollar is the functional currency for all of entity's significant operations, reporting of supplementary information concerning changing prices remains as per SFAS 33

B. If functional currencies other than U.S. dollar are used for significant part of an entity's operations

    1. Entity is not required to report historical cost information measured in units of constant purchasing power for either current or prior years, if current cost information is disclosed for those years

    2. Entities that have insignificant amounts of inventory and property, plant, and equipment may continue to use constant dollar information as a substitute for current cost information

C. Operations for which functional currency is not U.S. dollar should first measure current cost amounts and increases (decreases) therein in functional currency and then translate these into U.S. dollar equivalents

    1. Adjustments made to current cost information to reflect effects of general inflation shall be measured either:

        a. After translation using the U.S. CPI(U) (translate-restate method), or
        b. Before translation using the functional currency general price level index (restate-translate method)
        c. Same method must be used for operations measured in functional currency other than U.S. dollar and for all periods presented
        d. Method used shall be disclosed

†SFAS 71 (Re6) Accounting for the Effects of Certain Types of Regulation

A. Statement provides guidance in preparing general purpose financial statements for public utilities and certain other regulated companies

    1. Type of regulation usually allows rates (prices) to be set at levels intended to cover costs of providing services and cost of capital (interest costs and earnings on shareholders' investments)

B. Revenues intended to cover some costs are provided either before or after costs are incurred

    1. If revenue is provided for incurred costs to be recovered in future, costs are capitalized
    2. If revenue is provided for expected future costs, receipts are recognized as liabilities

C. Requires recognition of certain allowable costs as assets and increases in net income

    1. If allowable costs include an allowance for cost of funds (including debt and equity components) used during construction, capitalize and increase net income by amount used for rate-making purposes instead of following SFAS 34
    2. If allowable costs include reasonable intercompany profits, such profits should not be eliminated in entity's financial statements

D. These companies do not record deferred income taxes if:

    1. Current tax benefits (costs) of timing differences are passed through to customers in current prices, and

    2. It is probable that any resulting taxes payable in future years will be recovered through future rates

E. If deferred taxes not recognized, disclose cumulative net amounts of timing differences for which deferred taxes not recorded

F. Expected refunds of revenue collected in prior years should be charged to income in period in which those refunds are first recognized

G. Leases should be classified in accordance with SFAS 13

---

†SFAS 72 (B50, Bt7, I60) Accounting for Certain Acquisitions of Banking or Thrift Institutions
(Amends APB 17 and FASB Interpretation 9)

A. Applies to the acquisition of a commercial bank, savings and loan association, mutual savings bank, credit union, or similar institution accounted for by purchase method

B. Combination in which there is an excess of fair value of liabilities assumed over fair value of tangible and identifiable intangible assets

    1. Amortize such excess [unidentifiable intangible assets (UIA)] using interest method over period no longer than that used for amortizing discount on long-term interest bearing assets acquired

C. Subsequent sale or liquidation of large portion or separable group of assets

    1. If operating assets, UIA attributable to those assets is included in cost of assets sold

    2. If interest-bearing assets and benefits of UIA are significantly reduced, charge reduction of UIA to income

D. Established accounting treatment of regulatory financial assistance granted to enterprise

---

†SFAS 73 (A06, A35) Reporting a Change in Accounting for Railroad Track Structures
(Amends APB 20, para 20)

A. Changes from retirement-replacement-betterment (RRB) accounting to depreciation accounting should be reported by restating financial statements of all prior periods presented

    1. RRB accounting treats expenditures as follows:

        a. Initial track structure cost--capitalized and not expensed until retirement

        b. Replacement track structure cost--expensed unless a betterment

        c. Betterment structure cost--difference between current cost of new track structure acquired and current cost of like track structure is capitalized and not expensed until retirement

SFAS 74 (C45, P15) Accounting for Special Termination Benefits Paid to Employees

A. Establishes accounting for employers offering for short periods of time special termination benefits to employees (e.g., early retirement benefits)

B. Requires employer to recognize liability and expense when following conditions are both met

1. Employees accept offer
2. Amount can be reasonably estimated

C. Amount recognized includes

1. Lump-sum payments
2. Present value of any expected future payments

D. Employee termination under special termination benefit arrangements may affect employer's previously accrued expenses or other employee benefits (e.g., pension benefits)

1. Include these effects, if reliably measurable, in measuring termination expense

SFAS 75 (Pe5) Deferral of the Effective Date of Certain Accounting Requirements for Pension Plans of State and Local Governmental Entities
(Supersedes SFAS 59)

(This statement is not relevant to the CPA exam; it indefinitely suspends the effective date of SFAS 35 for pension plans of governmental entities.)

SFAS 76 (D14, L10) Extinguishment of Debt
(Amends APB 26)

A. Statement provides guidance to debtors as to what shall be considered an extinguishment of debt for financial reporting purposes

1. Amends APB 26 by

a. Referring to standards in this statement
b. Making it apply to all extinguishments of debt, whether early or not, except for

1) Convertible debt
2) Troubled debt restructurings

2. Other situations excluded from scope of statement

a. Redeemable preferred stock
b. Debt with variable terms

B. Debt shall be considered extinguished for financial reporting purposes in following circumstances:

1. Debtor pays creditor and is relieved of all obligations relative to that debt

a. Includes reacquisition of outstanding debt securities in securities markets, regardless of whether securities are cancelled or held as treasury bonds

2. Debtor is legally released from being primary obligor under the debt either judicially or by creditor <u>and</u> it is probable that debtor will not be required to make future payments relative to that debt under any guarantees

3. Debtor places cash or other assets in irrevocable trust

   a. Trust is to be used for sole purpose of satisfying scheduled payments of both interest and principal of a specific obligation

   b. Only remote possibility exists that debtor will be required to make future payments with respect to that debt

   c. In this situation, debt is extinguished even though debtor is <u>not</u> legally released from being primary obligor

C. Requirements regarding nature of assets held by irrevocable trust

1. Trust is restricted to owning only monetary assets that are essentially risk-free as to amount, timing, and collection of interest and principal

2. Monetary assets must be denominated in currency in which debt is payable. For debt denominated in U.S. dollars, essentially risk-free monetary assets are limited to

   a. Direct obligations of U.S. government
   b. Obligations guaranteed by U.S. government
   c. Securities backed by U.S. government obligations as collateral under arrangement by which interest and principal payments on collateral flow to holder (the trust) of security

      1) Securities that can be paid prior to scheduled maturity are not essentially risk free as to the timing of collection of interest and payment; they do not qualify for ownership

3. Monetary assets held by trust must provide cash flows that approximately coincide with the timing and amount of scheduled interest and principal payments on debt being extinguished

D. Accounting for costs related to placing assets in trust

1. If trust assets will be used to pay any related costs, those costs should be considered in determining amount of funds required by trust

2. If debtor incurs obligation to pay any related costs, debtor shall accrue liability for those probable payments in period debt recognized as extinguished

E. If debt is considered extinguished under provisions of B.3., following shall be disclosed so long as debt remains outstanding

1. General description of transaction
2. Amount considered extinguished at end of period

SFAS 77 (L10, R20) Reporting by Transferors for Transfers of Receivables with Recourse

A. Statement establishes financial accounting reporting standards by transferors for transfers of receivables with recourse that purport to be sales of receivables

1. Also applies to

    a. Transfers of specified interests in particular receivable or pool of receivables that provide for recourse (participation agreement)
    b. Factoring agreements that provide for recourse
    c. Sales or assignments with recourse of leases or property subject to leases accounted for as sales-type or direct financing leases

2. Does not address accounting and reporting

    a. By transferees
    b. Of loans collateralized by receivables for which receivables and loans are reported on borrower's balance sheet

    c. For exchanges of substantially identical receivables or other assets

B. Definitions

    1. Current (normal) servicing fee rate--rate charged for comparable agreements covering like receivables
    2. Net receivables--gross amount of receivables, including finance and service charges and fees owed by debtor included in recorded receivables, less related unearned finance and service charges and fees

    3. Probable adjustments--adjustments for (a) estimated bad debt losses and related costs of collections and repossessions per SFAS 5 (b) estimated effects of prepayments (c) defects in elgibility of transferred receivables (e.g., defects in legal title)
    4. Recourse--right of transferee to receive payment from transferor (a) nonpayment of debtors when due (b) effects of prepayments (c) adjustments from defects in elgibility of transferred receivables

C. Transfer of receivables with recourse is recognized as sale if all three of following are met

    1. Transferor surrenders control of future economic benefits embodied in receivables
    2. Transferor's obligation under recourse provisions can be reasonably estimated
    3. Transferee cannot require transferor to repurchase receivables except pursuant to recourse provisions

D. If transfer qualifies as recognizable sale

    1. All probable adjustments in connection with recourse obligations to transferor shall be accrued in accordance with SFAS 5

    2. Gain (loss) shall be recognized, measured by difference between

        a. Sales price, adjusted for accrual for probable adjustments, and
        b. Net receivables

    3. If receivables are sold with servicing retained by transferor, the sales price shall be adjusted to provide for normal servicing fee in each subsequent period in those cases in which either

        a. Stated servicing fee rate differs materially from normal servicing fee rate, or
        b. No servicing fee is specified

4. Sales price may be subject to change during receivable term because of floating interest rate provision

   a. Estimate sales price using appropriate market interest rate at transfer date

   b. Subsequent changes in interest rates from rate used at transfer date shall be considered changes in estimate of sales price (not interest cost or interest revenue)

   c. Effect reported in income in period interest rate changes in accordance with APB 20, para 31

E. If any of the conditions in C. is not met, the amount of proceeds from transfer of receivables shall be reported as liability

F. For transfers of receivables with recourse reported as sale, transferor shall disclose

1. Proceeds received during each period for which income statement is presented
2. Balance of receivables transferred that remain uncollected at date of each balance sheet presented (if available)

SFAS 78 (B05) Classification of Obligations That Are Callable by the Creditor
(Amends ARB 43, Chapter 3A)

A. Statement specifies that the current liability classification is also intended to include

1. Obligations that, by their terms, are due on demand or will be due on demand within one year (or operating cycle, if longer) from balance sheet date, even though liquidation may not be expected within that period

2. Long-term obligations that are or will be callable by creditor either because

   a. Debtor's violation of debt agrement provision at balance sheet date makes obligation callable <u>or</u>

   b. Violation, if not cured within grace period, will make obligation callable

B. Callable obligations in "A.2." should be classified current unless one of the following conditions is met

1. Creditor has waived or subsequently lost right to demand prepayment for more than one year (or operating cycle, if longer) from balance sheet date

2. For long-term obligations containing grace period within which debtor may cure violation, it is probable violation will be cured within that period

   a. If obligation meets this condition, the circumstances shall be disclosed

C. This statement does <u>not</u> modify SFAS 6 or 47

SFAS 79 (B50) Elimination of Certain Disclosures for Business Combinations by Non-Public Enterprises
(Amends APB 16, para 96)

A. Disclosures of pro forma results of operations for business combinations accounted for using <u>purchase</u> method no longer required for <u>nonpublic</u> enterprises

STATEMENTS OF FINANCIAL ACCOUNTING CONCEPTS (SFAC)

These are a new series of pronouncements to set forth financial accounting and reporting objectives and concepts. The objectives and concepts will be used by the FASB to develop financial accounting and reporting standards and by practitioners in areas where promulgated GAAP does not exist. The new SFAC pronouncements will not establish GAAP as contemplated by Rule 203 of the AICPA Code of Professional Ethics, i.e., they will be similar in authority to APB Statements.

SFAC 1 Objectives of Financial Reporting by Business Enterprises

A. Financial accounting concepts are fundamentals on which standards of financial accounting and reporting are based

1. I.e., do not establish GAAP

a. And do not come under AICPA ethics rule 203

2. Defines financial accounting concepts broader than financial statements and other data

B. Environmental context of objectives

1. Financial reporting provides information for making business and economic decisions
2. The United States is a market economy

a. Dominated by investor owned enterprises
b. Even though the government generates economic statistics

C. Characteristics and limitations of information

1. Primarily financial (quantitative) in nature
2. Limited to individual business enterprises
3. Based on approximated measures, i.e., estimates
4. Largely limited to past transactions, i.e., historically based
5. Just one source of users' data base
6. Must conform to cost-benefit rationale

D. Potential users and their interests

1. "Owners, lenders, potential investors, suppliers, creditors, employees, management, directors, customers, financial analysts and advisors, brokers, underwriters, stock exchanges, lawyers, economists, taxing authorities, regulatory authorities, legislators, financial press and reporting agencies, labor unions, trade associations, business researchers, teachers and students, and the public."
2. Users are generally interested in cash flow generation

a. Amounts, timing, and uncertainties

3. Many external users lack authority to prescribe information

a. E.g., absentee owners, customers, etc.

E. General purpose external financial reporting

1. To satisfy informational needs of external users who lack authority to prescribe data they desire

  2. Focuses on external users

    a. Management may prescribe data for their needs

  3. Directed primarily at investors and creditors

    a. Which results in data of likely usefulness to others

F. Objectives of financial reporting

  1. "Financial reporting should provide information that is useful to present and potential investors and creditors and other users in making rational investment, credit, and similar decisions."

  2. "Financial reporting should provide information to help present and potential investors and creditors and other users in assessing the amounts, timing, and uncertainty of prospective cash receipts from dividends or interest and the proceeds from the sale, redemption, or maturity of securities or loans."

  3. "Financial reporting should provide information about the economic resources of an enterprise, the claims to those resources (obligations of the enterprise to transfer resources to other entities and owner's equity), and the effects of transactions, events, and circumstances that change resources and claims to those resources."

    a. Economic resource, obligation, and owners' equity data permit assessment of:

      1) Liquidity and solvency
      2) Financial strength

    b. Funds flow data is important
    c. Earnings performance data permit assessment of future performance

      1) Thus, primary focus of reporting is on earnings

    d. Management stewardship and performance is reported on
    e. Management explanation and interpretation is important

SFAC 2 Qualitative Characteristics of Accounting Information

A. Purpose is to examine the characteristics that make accounting information useful and establish criteria for selecting and evaluating accounting alternatives

  1. Guidance needed by both FASB and individual accountants
  2. The usefulness of accounting information must be evaluated in relation to decision making
  3. Based on objectives of financial reporting (SFAC 1)

B. The hierarchy of accounting qualities

  1. User-specific qualities (not inherent in information)

    a. Understandability
    b. Newness

2. Decision-specific qualities (necessary for usefulness)

   a. Relevance - "capacity" of information to "make a difference" in a decision

     1) Timeliness - being available while able to influence decisions
     2) Predictive value - improves decision makers' capacity to predict
     3) Feedback value - enables users to confirm or correct prior expectations

   b. Reliability - freedom from error and bias and faithful representation of what is claimed to be represented

     1) Verifiability - secures a high degree of consensus among independent measurers
     2) Representative faithfulness - agreement between data and resources or events represented (validity)
     3) Neutrality - freedom from bias toward a predetermined result

3. Secondary and interactive qualities

   a. Comparability between enterprises
   b. Consistency in application over time

4. Constraints

   a. Materiality - information should not be provided if below the user's threshold for recognition
   b. Costs and benefits - benefits derived from disclosure must exceed associated costs

SFAC 3 Elements of Financial Statements of Business Enterprises

A. Statement contains definitions of financial statement elements

  1. Definitions of elements provide a significant first test in determining if an item qualifies for inclusion in the financial statements

   a. Possessing the characteristics of a definition of an element is a necessary but not a sufficient condition for including an item in the financial statements

   b. To qualify for inclusion in the financial statements an item must:

     1) Meet recognition criteria, e.g., revenue recognition tests
     2) Possess a relevant attribute which can be measured reliably, e.g., historical cost/historical proceeds

   c. The additional conditions for inclusion under "b." are subjects of future SFACs

B. Assets are probable future economic benefits controlled by a particular entity as a result of past transactions or events

  1. Characteristics of assets

   a. Probable future benefit by contribution to future net cash inflows
   b. Entity can obtain and control access to benefit
   c. Transaction or event leading to control has already occurred

  2. Asset continues as an asset until collected, transferred, used, or destroyed
  3. Valuation accounts are part of related asset

C. Liabilities are probable future sacrifices of economic benefits, arising from present obligations of a particular entity which result from past transactions or events

   1. Characteristics of liabilities

      a. Legal, equitable, or constructive duty to transfer assets in future
      b. Little or no discretion to avoid future sacrifice
      c. Transaction or event obligating enterprise has already occurred

   2. Liability remains a liability until settled or discharged
   3. Valuation accounts are part of related liability

D. Equity is the residual interest in the assets of an entity that remains after deducting liabilities; in a business enterprise, the ownership interest

   1. Characteristics of equity

      a. The source of distributions by an enterprise to its owners
      b. No unconditional right to receive future transfer of assets; depends on future profitability
      c. Inevitably affected by enterprise's operations and circumstances affecting the enterprise

   2. Transactions or events that change owner's equity include revenues and expenses; gains and losses; investments by owners; distributions to owners; and, changes within owners' equity (does not change amount)

E. Investments by owners are increases in net assets resulting from transfers by other entities of something of value to obtain ownership

F. Distributions to owners are decreases in net assets resulting from transferring assets, rendering services, or incurring liabilities by the enterprise to owners

G. Comprehensive income is the change in equity of an entity during a period from transactions and other events of nonowner sources, i.e., all equity amount changes except investment and distributions

   1. Term "comprehensive" income is used instead of earnings because the board is reserving "earnings" for a component part of comprehensive income yet to be determined
   2. Concept of capital maintenance or recovery of cost is needed in order to separate return on capital from return of capital
   3. Financial capital maintenance concept vs. physical capital maintenance concept

      a. Financial capital maintenance - objective is to maintain purchasing power
      b. Physical capital maintenance - objective is to maintain operating capacity

   4. Comprehensive income is return on financial capital
   5. Characteristics, sources and components of comprehensive income include:

      a. Cash receipts (excluding investments) less cash outlays (excluding distributions) over the life of an enterprise

         1) Recognition criteria and choice of attributes to be measured affect timing, not amount

b. Specific sources of income are

1) Transactions between enterprise and nonowners
2) Enterprise's productive efforts
3) Price changes, casualties, and other interactions with environment

c. <u>Earnings process</u> is the production and distribution of goods or services so firm can pay for goods and services it uses and provide return to owners

d. Peripheral activities may also provide income

e. Components of comprehensive income

1) Basic components - revenues, expenses, gains and losses
2) Intermediate components result from combining basic components

f. Display considerations (e.g., items included in operating income) are the subject of another SFAC

H. <u>Revenues</u> are increases in assets or decreases in liabilities during a period from delivering goods, rendering services, or other activities constituting the enterprise's central operations

1. Characteristics of revenues

a. Accomplishments of the earning process
b. Actual or expected cash inflows resulting from central operations
c. Inflows reported gross

I. <u>Expenses</u> are decreases in assets or increases in liabilities during a period from delivery of goods, rendering of services, or other activities constituting the enterprise's central operations

1. Characteristics of expenses

a. Sacrifices involved in carrying out the earnings process
b. Actual or expected cash outflows resulting from central operations
c. Outflows reported gross

J. <u>Gains (losses)</u> are increases (decreases) in equity from peripheral transactions of an entity excluding revenues (expenses) and investment by owners (distribution to owners)

1. Characteristics of gains and losses

a. Result from peripheral transactions and circumstances which may be beyond control
b. May be classified according to sources or as operating and nonoperating
c. Change in equity reported net

K. Accrual accounting and related concepts include

1. <u>Transaction</u> - an external event involving transfer of something of value between two or more entities
2. <u>Event</u> - a happening of consequence to an enterprise (internal or external)
3. <u>Circumstances</u> - a set of conditions developed from events which may occur imperceptibly and create possibly unanticipated situations
4. <u>Accrual accounting</u> - recording "cash consequence" transactions as they occur rather than with movement of cash; deals with process of cash movement instead of beginning or end of process (per para 44 of SFAC 1)

a. Based on cash and credit transactions, exchanges, price changes, changes in form of assets and liabilities

5. Accrual - recognizing revenues and related asset increases and expenses and related liability increases as they occur; expected future cash receipt or payment
6. Deferral - recognizing a liability for cash receipt or an asset for cash payment with expected future revenue or expense; past cash receipt or payment
7. Allocation - process of assigning or distributing an amount according to a plan or formula

    a. Includes amortization

8. Amortization - process of systematically reducing an amount by periodic payments or write-downs
9. Realization - process of converting noncash resources and rights into money; refers to sales of assets for cash or claims to cash

    a. Realized - identifies revenues or gains or losses on assets sold
    b. Unrealized - identifies revenues or gains or losses on assets unsold

10. Recognition - process of formally recording an item in the financial statements

    a. Major difference between accrual and cash basis accounting is timing of recognition of income items

11. Matching - simultaneous recognition of revenues and expenses which are related directly or jointly to the same transactions or events

SFAC 4 Objectives of Financial Reporting by Nonbusiness Organizations

(The outline of SFAC 4 can be found at the end of Chapter 12, Governmental and Nonprofit Accounting.)

CHAPTER NINE

FINANCIAL ACCOUNTING REVIEW

INTRODUCTION

This chapter is written to help you review intermediate and advanced accounting (financial accounting) for both the practice and theory sections of the exam. The AICPA Content Specification Outline of the coverage of financial accounting in the Examinations in Accounting Practice and Accounting Theory, including the authors' frequency analysis thereof (last nine exams), appears in Chapter 7.

The chapter is organized along the lines of the traditional intermediate and advanced accounting texts. The topics are arranged per the eleven financial modules (on the previous pages). You will be referred to Chapter 8 frequently to review the outline of AICPA pronouncements on the particular topic being discussed. These outlines can be located easily be referring to the headings identifying the pronouncements which appear at the top of each page in Chapter 8. At first consideration, presentation might appear more comprehensive if the outlines of APBs, SFASs, etc., were integrated in this chapter rather than presented separately in Chapter 8. Separate presentation, however, allows separate study of the pronouncements and also precludes confusion with the editorial views of the authors.

The objective is to provide you with the basic concepts, journal entries, and formulas for each topic and subtopic. Hopefully you will be able to expand, adapt, and apply the basics to specific problem situations as presented in multiple choice questions, theory essay questions, and practice problems appearing on the exam. Keep in mind the importance of working all three types of questions under exam conditions as you study the basics set forth in this chapter. Refer to Volume II for multiple choice questions, essay questions, and practice problems on each of the financial accounting topics.

As you work through this chapter, remember that there are many possible series of journal entries and account titles that can be used in accounting for a specific type of economic transaction, e.g., consignments. Reconcile the approach illustrated in this chapter with the approach you studied as an undergraduate (or appeared in your intermediate or advanced text).

MISCELLANEOUS FINANCIAL TOPICS

A. Basic Concepts

This miscellaneous financial topics module includes the basic financial statements except the Statement of Changes. It also includes revenue and expense recognition rules, accounting changes, interim reporting, segment reporting, etc. The relevant accounting pronouncements are indicated in the discussion complete with cross references to outlines of the pronouncements in Chapter 8. (Note these outlines appear in the following sequence: ARBs, APBs, APB Statements, SFASs, and SFACs. The page headers in Chapter 8 identify the sources of the pronouncements outlined on those pages.) Turn to each outline as directed and study the outline while reviewing the related journal entries, computations, etc.

1. History of Accounting

The double entry system as we know it was developed during the Renaissance in Southern Europe. The first known writing on the topic was by Luca Pacciolo in 1494. This system of balancing accounts, including real and nominal accounts, has been used by businesses from then to now: from simple joint trading ventures to multinational companies. The point is that accounting is a well-accepted versatile language of business.

2. Income Determination

The primary objective of accounting is to measure income. Income is a measure of management's efficiency in combining the factors of production into desired goods and services.

Efficient firms with prospects of increased efficiency (higher profits) have greater access to financial capital and at lower costs. Their stock usually sells at higher price-earnings ratio than the stock of a company with less enthusiastic prospects. The credit rating of the prospectively efficient company is probably higher than the prospectively less efficient company. Thus, the "cost of capital" will be lower for the company with the brighter outlook, i.e., lower stock dividend yield rates and/or lower interest rates.

The entire process of acquiring the factors of production, processing them, and selling the resulting goods and services produces revenue. The acquisition of raw materials is part of the revenue-producing process as is providing warranty protection.

Under accrual basis accounting, revenue is generally recognized at the point of sale (ARB 43, Chapter 1A, Rule 1) or as service is performed. The point of sale is when title passes: generally when shipped, if FOB shipping point and when received, if FOB destination.

Three exceptions exist to the general revenue recognition rule: during production, at the point where production is complete, and at the point of cash collection. The table below identifies the criteria applicable to each basis, the appropriate accounting method, and the reasons for using that basis.

Recognition basis/source of GAAP	Accounting method	Criteria for use of basis	Reason(s) for departing from sale basis
• **Point of sale** ARB 43 (Ch 1A, Rule 1)	• Transactions approach (sales basis)	• Exchange has taken place • Earnings process is (virtually) complete	— — — —
• **During production basis** ARB 45	• Percentage-of-completion	• Long-term construction,* property, or service contract • Dependable estimates of extent of progress and cost to complete • Reasonable assurance of collectibility of contract price	• Availability of evidence of ultimate proceeds • Better measure of periodic income • Avoidance of fluctuations in revenues, expenses, and income
• **Completion-of-production basis** ARB 43 (Ch 4, St. 9)	• Net realizable value	• Immediate marketability at quoted prices • Unit interchangeability • Difficulty of determining costs	• Known or determinable revenues • Inability to determine costs and thereby defer expense recognition until sale
• **Cash collection basis** APB 10	• Installment and cost recovery method	• Absence of a reasonable basis for estimating degree of collectibility	• Level of uncertainty with respect to collection of the receivable precludes recognition of gross profit before cash is received

*Note that the "completed contract" method for construction contracts is not a departure from the sale basis.

Source: Adapted from Henry R. Jaenicke, *Survey of Present Practices in Recognizing Revenues, Expenses, Gains, and Losses,* FASB, 1981.

Under accrual accounting, expenses are recognized as related revenues are recognized, i.e., (product) expenses are matched with revenues. Some (period) expenses, however, cannot be associated with particular revenues and are recognized as incurred.

1) Product costs are those which can be associated with particular sales, e.g., cost of sales. Product costs attach to a unit of product and become an expense only when the unit to which they attach is sold. This is known as associating "cause and effect."
2) Period costs are not particularly or conveniently assignable to a product. They become expenses due to the passage of time by:

   a) Immediate recognition if the future benefit cannot be measured, e.g., advertising

b) Systematically and rationally if benefits are produced in certain
   future periods, e.g., asset depreciation

Thus, income is the net effect of inflows of revenue and outflows of expense during
a period of time. The period in which revenues and expenses are taken to the income
statement (recognized) is determined by the above criteria.

Cash basis accounting, in contrast to accrual basis accounting, recognizes income when cash is received and expenses when cash is disbursed. Cash basis accounting is subject to manipulation, i.e., cash receipts and expenses can be switched
from one year to another by management. Another reason for adopting accrual basis
accounting is that economic transactions have become more involved and multi-period.
An expenditure for a fixed asset may produce revenue for years and years.

3. Accruals and Deferrals

Accrual--accrual basis recognition precedes (leads) cash receipt/expenditure

   Revenue--recognition of revenue earned, but not received
   Expense--recognition of expense incurred, but not paid

Deferral--cash receipt/expenditure precedes (leads) accrual basis recognition

   Revenue--postponement of recognition of revenue; cash is received, but
            revenue is not earned
   Expense--postponement of recognition of expense; cash is paid, but ex-
            pense is not incurred

A deferral postpones recognition of revenue or expense by placing the amount in
liability and asset accounts. Two methods are possible for deferring revenues and
expenses depending on whether real or nominal accounts are originally used to record
the cash transaction.

Deferrals of Expense

	Expense method			Asset method		
When paid	Insurance expense	xx		Prepaid insurance	xx	
	Cash		xx	Cash		xx
Year end	Prepaid insurance	xx		Insurance expense	xx	
	Insurance expense		xx	Prepaid insurance		xx
Reverse	Yes			No		

Deferrals of Revenue

	Revenue method			Liability method		
When received	Cash	xx		Cash	xx	
	Rent revenue		xx	Unearned rent		xx
Year end	Rent revenue	xx		Unearned rent	xx	
	Unearned revenue		xx	Rent revenue		xx
Reverse	Yes			No		

Accruals do not have two methods, but can be complicated by failure to reverse adjusting entries (also true for deferrals).

Accruals

	Expense			Revenue	
Adjustment	Wages expense	xx		Interest receivable	xx
	Wages payable		xx	Interest revenue		xx
Reverse	Yes			Yes	

4. Reversing Entries

Entries are reversed for bookkeeping expediency. If accruals are reversed, the subsequent cash transaction is reflected in the associated nominal account. If accruals are not reversed, the subsequent cash transaction must be apportioned between a nominal and real account.

Cash	(amount received)
Revenue	(earned in current period)
Revenue Receivable	(accrual at last year end)

Alternatively, adjustments may only be made to the real accounts at year end. For example: given no reversing entries and all interest received being credited to interest revenue, the adjusting entry is to adjust the beginning unearned income to ending unearned income.

The solutions approach is to use a T-account analysis of the appropriate real and/or nominal accounts. For example, in the case of interest revenue accounts, you should construct T-accounts for interest revenue, interest receivable, and unearned interest revenue.

5. Asset Valuation

Generally, assets are valued at their historical cost, but alternatives exist and are used.

a. Historical cost--cost when purchased is an objectively measured figure, but may be out of date due to rising price levels and changing market value

b. Replacement cost--cost to replace which may be hard to measure due to changes in technology and other factors. The lower of cost or market rule for inventory defines market as replacement cost (subject to maximum and minimum limits). For further discussion, see Module 25.

c. Market value--hypothetical selling price which may be hard to value due to the absence of an arm's-length transaction with payments in currency. Certain investments are to be valued at market value when less than cost. See outline of SFAS 12.

d. Constant dollar and current cost adjusted--adjusted for changes in the purchasing power of the dollar and for changes in specific prices. For further discussion, see outline of SFAS 33 and Module 30.

e. Discounted cash flow--estimate of current values based on the present value of estimated future cash flows. Requires estimates of both future cash flows and appropriate discount rates. See Nonroutine Decisions, Module 37.

6. Installment Sales

Revenue is recognized as cash is collected. Thus, revenue recognition takes place at the point of cash collection rather than the point of sale. Installment sale accounting can only be used where "collection of the sale price is not reasonably assured" (APB 10, para 12).

Under the installment sales method, gross profit is deferred to future periods and recognized proportionately to collection of the receivables. Installment receivables and deferred gross profit accounts must be kept separate by year, because the gross profit rate usually varies from year to year.

EXAMPLE:

Year	Sales	Cost of Sales	Collections of Year 1	Collections of Year 3
1	300,000	225,000*	80,000	--
2	0	0	120,000	--
3	200,000	160,000**	100,000	100,000

* 25% gross profit rate   ** 20% gross profit rate

To record sale	Year 1		Year 2		Year 3	
Install A/R-1	300,000		--		--	
Install A/R-3	--		--		200,000	
Install sales		300,000		--		200,000
To record cash receipt						
Cash	80,000		120,000		200,000	
Install A/R-1		80,000		120,000		100,000
Install A/R-3		--		--		100,000
To defer gross profit						
Install sales	300,000		--		200,000	
Install cost of sales		225,000		--		160,000
Deferred install GP-1		75,000		--		--
Deferred install GP-3		--		--		40,000
To recognize gross profit						
Deferred install GP-1	20,000[1]		30,000[2]		25,000[3]	
Deferred install GP-3	--		--		20,000[4]	
GP realized on install method		20,000		30,000		45,000

[1](25% x 80,000)   [3](25% x 100,000)
[2](25% x 120,000)   [4](20% x 100,000)

7. Repossession of Installment Sales

On repossession, the repossessed asset should be accounted for at its FMV or net realizable value less selling profit. The related receivable and deferred gross profit must be written off and the resulting gain or loss recognized. For example, the goods sold in year 1 above were repossessed in year 3 when they had a FMV of $60,000 because the year 3 payment had not been made (note this transaction and entry are not reflected in the entries above).

Repossessed inventory	$60,000	
Deferred install. GP-1	25,000	
Loss on repossession	15,000	
Install A/R-1		$100,000

8. Cost Recovery Method

The cost recovery method is similar to the installment sales method in that gross profit on the sale is deferred. The difference is that no profit is recognized until the cumulative receipts exceed the cost of the asset sold. For example, in the installment sales example, the entire profit from year 1 sales ($75,000) would be recognized in year 3. Profit on year 3 sales will be recognized in year 4 to the extent that in year 4 cash collections on year 3 sales exceed $60,000 (160,000 - 100,000). The cost recovery method is used when the uncertainty of collection is so great that even use of the installment method is precluded.

9. Sales Basis Criteria for Selected Transactions

Under GAAP, specific rules have been developed which are stated in the form of conditions which must be met before it is acceptable to recognize profit from "a sale in the ordinary course of business." Unfortunately, these rules represent a patchwork set of criteria for applying the sales basis of revenue recognition. This patchwork set of criteria contains many inconsistencies either in the results obtained or in the rationale justifying the criteria. The table on the following page summarizes the criteria which have been devised for applying the sales basis to selected transactions involving the sale of assets.

10. Franchise Agreements

SFAS 45 (see outline) provides that the initial franchise fee be recognized as revenue by the franchisor **only** upon substantial performance of their initial service obligation. The amount and timing of revenue recognized depends upon whether the

Recognition issue/ source of GAAP	Factors to be considered before recognizing revenue on the sale basis	Conditions that cause recognition to be delayed beyond time of sale
• Sale with a right of return SFAS 48	• Whether economic substance of the transaction is a sale or a financing arrangement • Determination of sales price • Probability of collection of sales price • Seller's future obligations • Predictability of returns	• Sales price not fixed or determinable • Payment excused until product is sold • Payment excused if property stolen or damaged • Buyer without separate economic substance • Seller's obligation to bring about resale of the property • Inability to predict future returns
• Product financing arrangement SFAS 49	• Whether risks and rewards of ownership are transferred	• Agreement requires repurchase at specified prices or provides compensation for losses
• Real estate sale SFAS 66	• Probability of collection • Seller's continued involvement • Whether economic substance of the transaction is a sale of real estate or another type of transaction, such as a service contract	• Inadequate buyer investment in the property • Seller's continuing obligations, such as participation in future losses, responsibility to obtain financing, construct buildings, or initiate or support operations
• Retail land sale SFAS 66	• Probability of collection • Likelihood of refunds • Likelihood of seller's meeting obligations	• Recision period not over • Inadequate buyer investment • Collection not predictable • Completion of improvements not assured
• Sales-type lease SFAS 13	• Transfer of benefits and risks of ownership • Probability of collection • Predictability of future unreimbursable costs	• Inability to meet conditions specified above for real estate sales • Inability to meet specified conditions (four criteria) indicating transfer of benefits and risks of ownership • Collectibility not predictable • Uncertainty about future unreimbursable costs
• Sale of receivables with recourse SFAS 77	• Control of receivables • Terms under recourse provisions • Predictability of collections and related costs	• Control of receivables not surrendered • Obligation under recourse provisions not reasonably estimable • Repurchase of receivables required by other than recourse provisions
• Nonmonetary exchange APB 29	• Completion of earning process	• Exchanges of similar inventory or productive assets
• Sale-leaseback transaction SFAS 13	• Substance of the transaction • Portion of property leased back • Length of leaseback period	• All sale-leaseback transactions are financing transactions and not sales transactions unless leaseback covers only a small part of the property or is for a short period of time

Source: Adapted from Henry R. Jaenicke, *Survey of Present Practices in Recognizing Revenues, Expenses, Gains, and Losses*, FASB, 1981.

contract contains bargain purchase agreements, tangible property, and whether the continuing franchise fees are reasonable in relation to future service obligations. Direct franchise costs are deferred until the related revenue is recognized.

11. Service Sales Transactions

Service sales transactions are transactions in which the seller performs acts for the buyer as the principal result of the sale. Examples of service sales include accounting, architecture, engineering, mortgage banking, garbage removal, and legal services. These types of transactions can present difficulties in deciding when revenue should be recognized and when costs should be expensed.

There are four methods of service revenue recognition (specific performance, completed performance, proportional performance, and collection) which base recognition of revenue and related costs on the extent of the seller's performance of specified acts; three types of costs are associated with service sales transactions:

1) Initial Direct Costs are directly associated with negotiating and consummating service agreements
2) Direct Costs can be clearly identified with services performed
3) Indirect Costs are all costs which do not fall into the first two categories

The following diagram describes the four methods.

Service sales method	Comparable product sales method	When appropriate	Revenue recognized	Expense recognized Indirect	Direct	Initial direct
Specific Performance	Point of Sale	Service consists of one act	When act takes place	As incurred	Deferred until revenue recognized; then expense	Deferred until revenue recognized; then expense
Completed Performance	Completed-Contract	More than one act; only last act is significant	When last act takes place	Same as above	Same as above	Same as above
Proportional Performance	Percentage of Completion	More than one relatively equal act	1. Equal amount for each act; 2. By ratio of direct costs for each act; or 3. On a straight-line basis over length of contract	Same as above	As incurred	Proportionately with revenue
Collection	Installment Sales and Cost Recovery	Uncertainty of collectibility	As cash is collected	Same as above	As incurred	As incurred

Source: Adapted from "Accounting for Certain Service Transactions," *FASB Invitation to Comment* (Stamford, Conn.: FASB, 1978), p. 20.

B. Error Correction

Accountants must be in a position to anticipate, locate, and correct errors in their functions of systems and procedures design, controllership, and attestation. Errors which are discovered in the same year that they are made are corrected by:

1) Determining the entry that was made
2) Determining the correct entry
3) Reversing the incorrect entry(ies)
4) Making the correct entry

Errors in classification, e.g., sales expense instead of R&D expense, affect only one period. Nonsystematic errors in adjusting entries, e.g., an error in ending inventory of one period, affect two periods and are known as self-correcting (counterbalancing) errors. For example, overstating ending inventory of period A will overstate the income of period A and understate that of period B. Other errors will affect the income of several periods such as misrecording the cost of a long-lived asset, i.e., depreciation will be misstated for all periods.

When an error is discovered in a period subsequent to the period when the error occurred, an entry must be made to correct the accounts as if the error had not been made. For example, assume the entry to accrue wage expense in the amount of $500 is omitted on 12/31/78. The errors that would be caused by such an omission may be categorized as follows:

	1978	1979	1980
Expense	Understated	Overstated	Correct
Income	Overstated	Understated	Correct
Wages Payable	Understated	Correct	Correct
Retained Earnings	Overstated	Correct	Correct

If the company follows the policy of reversing adjusting entries for accruals, then correction of the error any time during 1979 will require:

Adjustment to correct error	500	
Wage expense		500

The adjustment account, when closed to retained earnings, will correct for the 1/1/79 overstatement in retained earnings due to the overstatement of 1978 income. The credit to wage expense will reduce the expense account for 1979 to an amount equal to 1979 wages.

If the error were discovered in 1980, no entry would be required since the error self-corrects during 1979. The 1980 balances would be the same with or without the error.

The requirements of error analysis questions vary considerably. When asked for the effect of errors, be careful to determine the effect rather than the correction; they are opposite. The effect of revenue overstatement on income is over or plus, while the correction to income is to minus. Also distinguish between correcting/adjusting entries (which can be made in the accounts to correct the current period) and "worksheet entries" which adjust amounts reported in prior periods, i.e., journal entries are not recorded to correct nominal accounts of prior periods.

Correction of errors meets the criteria for prior periods' adjustments per SFAS 16. They should be reported as adjustments to beginning retained earnings of single-year statements, and to retained earnings of the earliest year presented in comparative statements for the error effects prior to the earliest year presented. Adjustments to the comparative years should be made to reflect retroactive application of the prior period adjustments.

The analysis of inventory errors in a periodic inventory system is facilitated by setting up a statement of cost of goods sold. Items which are correct are indicated "OK," while items which are incorrect are listed as overstated (over) or understated (under). In the example below, year A will be the error year and year B will be the following year assuming the error is not corrected. Case #1 will be an overstatement of the ending inventory and Case #2 will be the understatement of both the ending inventory and purchases.

	Case #1 (Overstatement of EI)		Case #2 (Understatement of EI and PUR)	
	A	B	A	B
Beginning inventory	OK	Over	OK	Under
+ purchases	OK	OK	Under	Over
Goods available for sale	OK	Over	Under	OK
Ending inventory	Over	OK	Under	OK
Cost of goods sold	Under	Over	OK	OK
Income	Over	Under	OK	OK
Retained earnings	Over	OK	OK	OK
Accounts payable	OK	OK	Under	OK

A = year of error;   B = year subsequent to error.

C. Accounting Changes

Changes in accounting principle (or the method of applying them) must be justified by those who (firm's management) make the change unless they are made in order to comply with a FASB position. Study the outline of APB 20 and also see the two tables on pages 766 and 767.

Five special changes require retroactive restatement of all periods presented as if the new method had been used in all prior periods. These five special changes are:

1) From LIFO to another inventory method
2) Change in method of accounting for long-term contracts
3) Change to or from the full cost method of accounting for exploration costs in the extractive industries
4) Any change made by a company first issuing financial statements for the purpose of obtaining additional equity capital or affecting a combination or registering securities (APB 20, para 29)
5) Change mandated by an authoritative pronouncement

Retroactive restatement means redoing all statements presented as if they were prepared according to the new accounting principle (or prepared correctly if correction of an error). Also restate statements of changed entities, i.e., changes in accounting entities such as poolings.

All other changes are accounted for by the "cumulative effect" method:

1) Computing the effect of the change on retained earnings at the beginning of the year in which the change is made

2) Using the new principle in the current year

3) Reporting the effect of the new method on beginning retained earnings less tax effects as "cumulative effect on prior years of new accounting method (described), net of tax" to be presented as the last item in the income statement, i.e., after extraordinary items and before net income

4) Presenting comparative years' data as previously reported

5) Recomputing the following income and EPS data for all periods presented as if the new method had been applied retroactively, and disclosing on the face of the income statement after EPS data. These items come after normal EPS disclosures per APB 15.

PRO FORMA AMOUNTS ASSUMING RETROACTIVE APPLICATION OF NEW METHOD

Income before extraordinary items	xxxx	xxxx
PEPS	x	x
FDEPS	x	x
Net income	xxxx	xxxx
PEPS	x	x
FDEPS	x	x

6) The above formats which disclose the effect of retroactive application of the new principle should reflect nondiscretionary items .as well as tax effects

   a) Nondiscretionary items, e.g., royalty contracts and executive bonus agreements, are those items that would have also changed income upon retroactive change to the new accounting method

7) A possible exception is a change in inventory method to LIFO because the cumulative effect may not be determinable. For changes to LIFO no recognition is given to any cumulative effect associated with the change. The base year inventory for all subsequent LIFO calculations is the opening inventory in the year LIFO is adopted.

The following example is taken from para 42 and 43 of APB 20. Assume a change in 1979 from accelerated to straight-line depreciation. The following figures describe the:

1) Depreciation effect per year (increase in income)
2) Depreciation (direct) effect net of tax (constant 50%)
3) Nondiscretionary item effect net of tax, incentive compensation at 10% of pretax accounting income (decrease in income)
4) Pro forma amounts, direct and nondiscretionary items net of tax

Year	Excess of Accelerated Depreciation Over Straight-Line Depreciation	Direct Less Tax Effect	Nondiscretionary Item, Net of Tax	Pro Forma
Prior to 1975	$20,000	$10,000	$ 1,000	$ 9,000
1975	80,000	40,000	4,000	36,000
1976	70,000	35,000	3,500	31,500
1977	50,000	25,000	2,500	22,500
1978	30,000	15,000	1,500	13,500
Total at beginning of 1979	$250,000	$125,000	$12,500	$112,500

Example income statements, EPS disclosures, and pro forma retroactive disclosures are presented below for 1979 and 1978.

	1979	1978
Income before extraordinary item and cumulative effect of a change in accounting principle	$1,200,000	$1,100,000
Extraordinary item (description)	(35,000)	100,000
Cumulative effect on prior years (to December 31, 1978) of changing to a different depreciation method	125,000	
Net Income	$1,290,000	$1,200,000

Per share amounts--
Earnings per common share--assuming no dilution:

	1979	1978
Income before extraordinary item and cumulative effect of a change in accounting principle	$1.20	$1.10
Extraordinary item	(0.04)	0.10
Cumulative effect on prior years (to December 31, 1978) of changing to a different depreciation method	0.13	
	$1.29	$1.20

Earnings per common share--assuming full dilution:
Income before extraordinary item and cumulative

effect of a change in accounting principle	$1.11	$1.02
Extraordinary item	(0.03)	0.09
Cumulative effect on prior years (to December 31, 1978) of changing to a different depreciation method	0.11	
Net Income	$1.19	$1.11

Pro forma amounts assuming the new depreciation
method is applied retroactively--

Income before extraordinary item	$1,200,000	$1,113,500
Earnings per common share--assuming no dilution	$1.20	$1.11
Earnings per common share--assuming full dilution	$1.11	$1.04
Net Income	$1,165,000	$1,213,500
Earnings per common share--assuming no dilution	$1.17	$1.21
Earnings per common share--assuming full dilution	$1.08	$1.13

Special points to note about the preceding example include:

1) The 1979 income before extraordinary items of $1,200,000 is the same pro forma as in the income statement, because the new accounting method was used in 1979
2) The 1979 net income differs between the income statement and pro forma by the cumulative effect not included in the pro forma
3) Both the 1978 income figures differ between the income statement and pro forma by $13,500 (depreciation less tax effects and nondiscretionary items)
4) Remember the cumulative effect follows extraordinary items
5) Review the format and title of the pro forma presentation of retroactive application
6) Review the EPS presentation (in compliance with APB 15)

1. Changes in Accounting Estimates

Account for changes in estimates of useful lives, salvage value, collectibility of receivables, etc., prospectively, i.e., no retroactive restatement. For example, if the useful life of an asset is increased from 10 years to 15 years during year 6, amortize the remaining book value over years 6 through 15 (assume no salvage value).

SUMMARY OF ACCOUNTING FOR ACCOUNTING CHANGES AND ERROR CORRECTION

	Reporting on financial statements						Recording in books	
	Footnote disclosures		Effect on income before X-items, NI, EPS		Statement disclosures			
	Nature of item	Justification*	Current yr. only	All periods presented	Retroactive treatment: previous financial statements restated	Cumulative effect treatment: pro formas shown for all years	Direct dr./cr. to retained earnings	Cumulative effect account
ACCOUNTING CHANGES								
In Principle								
General-change in principle or method of application from one acceptable GAAP to another. (Change from unacceptable GAAP is correction of error.)	X	X	X			X		X
Special								
• LIFO to another method	X	X		X	X		X	
• Change in method of accounting for long-term construction contracts.								
• Change to or from "full cost" method of accounting in the extractive industries.	X	X			X		X	
Special Exemptions for closely held corporation when it changes principles before its initial public offering.	X				X		X	
FASB Mandated Examples: equity method, R&D costs, inflation accounting.	X			X	X		X	
In Estimate ** Natural occurrence because judgment is used in preparation of statements. New events, more experience, and additional information affect earlier good faith estimates.	X	X		X***				
In Reporting Entity *** Includes consolidated or combined statements in place of individual statements, change in group of subsidiaries for which consolidated statements are prepared, change in companies included in combined statements, and business combination accounted for as a pooling of interests.	X	X		X	X			
ERROR CORRECTION Mathematical mistakes, mistakes in applying principles, oversight or misuse of available facts, change from unacceptable to acceptable GAAP.	X			X	X		X	

*Should clearly explain why the newly adopted accounting principle is preferable.

**Change in estimate effected by a change in principle is accounted for as a change in estimate.

***For material changes affecting more than just the current year.

D. Financial Statements

SUMMARY OF APB OPINIONS AND FASB STANDARDS PERTAINING TO THE INCOME STATEMENT[a]

Type of Situation	Criteria	Examples	Placement on Financial Statements
Extraordinary items	Material; unusual; nonrecurring (infrequent).	Gains or losses resulting from casualties, an expropriation, or a prohibition under a new law.[b]	Separate section in the income statement entitled extraordinary items. (Shown net of tax)
Material gains or losses, not considered extraordinary	Material; character typical of the customary business activities; unusual or infrequent but not both.	Write-downs of receivables, inventories; adjustments of accrued contract prices; gains or losses from fluctuations of foreign exchange; gains or losses from sales of assets used in business.	Separate section in income statement above income before extraordinary items. (Not shown net of tax)
Prior period adjustments and accounting changes that require restatement	Material corrections of errors applicable to prior periods or accounting changes required or permitted by an FASB Statement or an APB Opinion to be handled retroactively.	Corrections of errors; retroactive restatements per *APB Opinion No. 20* or other authoritative pronouncements.	Adjust the beginning balance of retained earnings. (Shown net of tax)
Changes in estimates	Normal, recurring corrections and adjustments.	Changes in the realizability of receivables and inventories; changes in estimated lives of equipment, intangible assets; changes in estimated liability for warranty costs, income taxes, and salary payments.	Change in income statement only in the account affected. (Not shown net of tax)
Changes in principle[c]	Change from one generally accepted principle to another.	Changing the basis of inventory pricing from FIFO to average cost; change in the method of depreciation from accelerated to straight-line.	Cumulative effect of the adjustment is reflected in the income statement between the captions extraordinary items and net income. (Shown net of tax)
Discontinued operations	Disposal of a segment of a business constituting a separate line of business or class of customer.	Sale by diversified company of major division which represents only activities in electronics industry. Food distributor that sells wholesale to supermarket chains and through fast-food restaurants decides to discontinue the division that sells to one of two classes of customers.	Shown in separate section of the income statement after continuing operations but before extraordinary items. (Shown net of tax)

[a]This summary provides only the general rules to be followed in accounting for the various situations described above. Exceptions do exist in some of these situations.
[b]Material gains and losses from extinguishment of debt and tax benefits of loss carryforwards are considered extraordinary, even though criteria for extraordinary items may not be met.
[c]The general rule per *APB Opinion No. 20* is to use the cumulative effect approach. However, all the recent FASB pronouncements require or permit the retroactive method whenever a new standard is adopted for the first time.

This Summary is reprinted from Kieso and Weygandt, *Intermediate Accounting*, 4th Edition, John Wiley and Sons, 1983, with permission.

Combined Statement of Income and Retained Earnings
For the Year Ended December 31, 19X4

Sales		$2,482
Cost of goods sold (see schedule A)		1,489
Gross margin on sales		993
Operating expenses		
Selling expenses	$ 220	
Administrative expenses	255	475
Income from operations		518
Other revenues/gains (expenses/losses)		
Interest revenue (expense)	(40)	
Gain on sale of investment in ABC Company	100	
Gain on translation of foreign currencies	20	80
Income from continuing operations before provision for		
income taxes		598
Provision for income taxes		239
Income from continuing operations		359*
Discontinued Operations:		
Loss from operations of discontinued Division Z (less applica-		
ble taxes of $466)	699**	
Loss on disposal of Division Z including operating losses dur-		
ing phase-out period (less applicable taxes of $67)	100**	799
Loss before extraordinary items and effect of accounting changes		(440)*
Extraordinary loss from earthquake (less applicable income taxes of $30)		45**
Cumulative effect on prior years of retroactive application of		
new depreciation method (less applicable income taxes of $80)		120*
Net loss		(605)*
Retained Earnings, January 1, 19X4	2,000	
Prior period adjustment:		
Correction of depreciation error (less applicable income		
taxes of $28)	42	
Adjusted Retained Earnings, January 1, 19X4		1,958
Total		1,353
Deduct Dividends:		
Preferred stock	40	
Common stock	30	70
Retained Earnings, December 31, 19X4		$1,283

Note:
1. Assumes a tax rate of 40% on applicable items
2. Asterisk (*) indicates where earnings per share (EPS) amounts would be necessary. In the case of a double asterisk (**) they are optional and/or need not be shown on the face of the income statement.
3. Footnote explanation would also be required for many of the above events and transactions.

Schedule A

Cost of Goods Sold

Merchandise inventory, January 1, 19X4			$ 461
Purchases		$1,989	
Less: purchase discounts	$ 19		
purchase returns and allowances	128	147	
Net purchases		1,842	
Freight and transportation in		38	1,880
Total merchandise available for sale			2,341
Less merchandise inventory, December 31, 19X4			852
Cost of goods sold			$1,489

1. Income and Retained Earnings Statement Formats

Turn to the outline of APB 9 and APB 30. Income statements may be prepared using a multiple step or single step form. The multiple step form is illustrated on the previous page. This statement is a combined statement of income and retained earnings. Note that the retained earnings statement begins with prior period adjustments (see outline of SFAS 16).

2. Discontinued Operations

As shown on the above income statement, the "Discontinued Operations" section consists of two components. The first one, "Income (Loss) from Operations," is disclosed for the current year only if the decision to discontinue operations is made after the beginning of the fiscal year for which the financials are being prepared. In the diagram below, the "Income (Loss) from Operations" component is determined for the time period designated by "A"--the period from the beginning of the year to the date the decision is made to discontinue a segment's operations (measurement date). The second component, "Gain (Loss) on Disposal" may consist of two elements:

1) Income (Loss) from operations during the phase-out period (the period between the measurement date and disposal date), and

2) Gain (Loss) from disposal of segment assets

The "Gain (Loss) on Disposal" component is determined for the time period designated "B" in the diagram below.

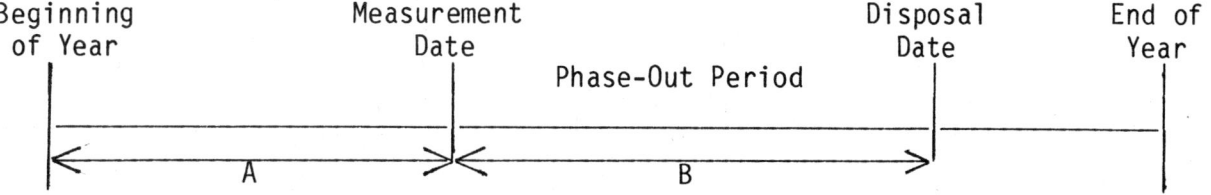

There are special rules for situations in which the disposal date occurs in the year after the measurement date. The problem is one of estimating the unrealized "Gain (Loss) on Disposal" for that part of the phase-out period which is in the following year and comparing it to the actual "Gain (Loss) on Disposal" that has already been realized at the end of the preceding year for which the financials are being prepared. Two rules apply to this situation:

1) A realized "Loss on Disposal" may be increased by an estimated loss or it may be reduced by an estimated gain (but only to zero), or

2) A realized "Gain on Disposal" may be reduced by an estimated loss but cannot be increased due to an estimated gain

The diagram below depicts the relationships discussed above.

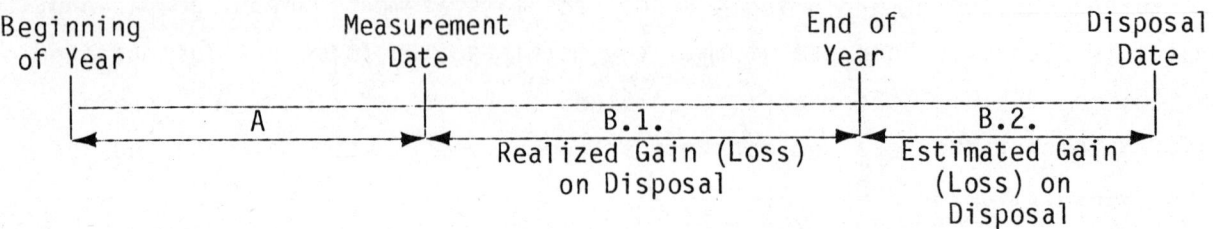

To find the year-end gain (loss), compare the amounts for "B.1." and "B.2." using the rules stated above.

EXAMPLE:

Facts	*Analysis*
A. Loss from Operations from beginning of year to the measurement date, $699, net of taxes of $466	Reported as first component of discontinued operations
B. 1. Realized loss from operations from measurement date to end of current year, $400, net of taxes of $267.	Reported as second component of discontinued operations: $400 loss realized during phase-out period minus the $300 estimated *net* gain to be realized in the next period (estimated gain·on disposal less the estimated loss from operations)
2. Estimated loss from operations from year end to disposal date, $200, net of taxes of $133. Estimated gain from disposal of assets during next year, $500, net of taxes of $333.	

The presentation of this case in the financials is shown in the combined statement of income and retained earnings shown above.

When "discontinued operations" are disclosed in a comparative income statement, the income statement presented for each previous year must be adjusted retroactively to enhance comparability with the current year's income statement. Accordingly, the revenues, cost of goods sold, and operating expenses (including income taxes) for the discontinued segment are removed from the revenues, cost of goods sold, and operating expenses of continuing operations and are netted into one figure, i.e., "Income (Loss) from Operations." The following excerpt from a comparative income statement shows the proper disclosure (19X3 figures assumed):

	19X4	19X3
Discontinued operations:		
Loss from Operations of discontinued Division Z net of applicable taxes	$699	$820
Loss on Disposal of assets of discontinued Division Z, including loss during phase-out period, net of applicable taxes	$100	--

3. <u>Balance Sheets</u>

Balance sheets or statements of financial position present assets, liabilities, and residual (shareholders' equity). The balance sheet reports the effect of transactions at a point in time, whereas:

1) Income statements
2) Statements of retained earnings
3) Statements of changes in financial position

report the effect of transactions over a period of time.

Balance sheets are generally presented in one of three formats:

Distinction between current and noncurrent assets and liabilities is almost universal.

> Current assets--"cash and other assets or resources commonly identified as those which are reasonably expected to be realized in cash or sold or consumed during the normal operating cycle of the business."   (ARB 43, Chapter 3A, para 4)

> Current liabilities--"obligations whose liquidation is reasonably expected to require the use of existing resources properly classifiable as current assets or the creation of other current liabilities" (during the normal operating cycle of the business).   (ARB 43, Chapter 3A, para 7)

Note current assets include those expected to be:

1) Realized in cash
2) Sold
3) Consumed

Current liabilities are those expected to:

1) Use current assets
2) Create other current liabilities

The operating cycle is the average time between acquisition of materials and final cash realization. Review the outline of ARB 43, Chapter 3A.

4. <u>Other Financial Statement Concepts</u>
   a. Accounting policies must be set forth as the initial footnote to the statements. Disclosures are required of:

      1) Accounting principles used when alternatives exist
      2) Principles peculiar to a particular industry
      3) Unusual or innovative applications of accounting principles

      Turn to the outline of APB 22. Additional disclosures required for specific situations are specified at the end of almost every official pronouncement, e.g., APBs and SFASs. Study these disclosure requirements by assuming you are a financial analyst analyzing the statements: What would you want disclosed? Note any required disclosures that are not "common sense."

b. Accounting for development-stage companies is per GAAP except additional disclosure of cumulative (from inception) losses, revenues, expenses, funds, flow items, are disclosed in the income statement and statement of changes. Study the outline of SFAS 7.

c. Accounting by oil and gas producing companies including property acquisition, exploration, development, and production of oil is specified per SFAS 19. Property acquisition cost, successful exploratory well costs, and production well costs are capitalized and charged to production. Unsuccessful exploratory well costs are expensed per successful efforts accounting. The full cost is also permitted (see outline of SFAS 25). Also interperiod tax allocation ignoring effects of statutory depletion (which is considered a permanent difference) is now required. Study the outline of SFAS 19.

E. Interim Reporting

The term interim reporting is used to describe financial reporting for periods of less than one year, generally quarterly financial statements. The primary purposes of interim reporting are to provide information which is more timely than is available in annual reports, and to highlight business turning points which could be "buried" in annual reports.

There are two basic conceptual approaches to interim reporting: the discrete view and the integral view.

    Discrete view--each interim period is a separate accounting period; interim period must stand on its own; same principles and procedures as for annual reports; no special accruals or deferrals.

    Integral view--each interim period is an integral part of an annual period; expectations for annual period must be reflected in interim reports; special accruals, deferrals, and allocations utilized.

APB 28 (see outline) adopted the integral view.

APB 28 consists of two parts. Part one does not require issuance of interim financial statements, but does prescribe accounting standards to be used in preparing such statements. Part two sets forth minimum disclosures to be included in interim financial reports.

The table below summarizes the accounting standards set forth in part one of APB 28.

Income statement item	General rule	Exceptions
Revenues	Same basis as annual reports	None
Cost of goods sold	Same basis as annual reports	1. Gross profit method may be used to estimate CGS and ending inventory for each interim period 2. Liquidation of LIFO base-period inventory, if expected to be replaced by year end, should not affect interim CGS 3. Temporary declines in inventory market value need not be recognized 4. Planned manufacturing variances should be deferred if expected to be absorbed by year end
All other costs and expenses	Same basis as annual reports	Expenditures which **clearly benefit** more than one interim period may be allocated among periods benefitted, e.g., annual repairs, property taxes
Income taxes	(Year-to-date income) x (estimated annual tax rate), less (expense recognized in previous quarters)	None
Discontinued operations	Recognized in interim period as incurred	None
Extraordinary items	Recognized in interim period as incurred Materiality is evaluated based upon expected annual results	None
Change in accounting principle	Retroactive—same as annual reports Cumulative effect—if change made in first quarter, report cumulative effect in first quarter's results. If change made in 2nd or 3rd quarter, report cumulative effect only in 6 or 9 month summary	None

The disclosures required in part two of APB 28 are summarized in the pronouncement outline. A key disclosure item for interim reporting is the seasonal nature of the firm's operations. This disclosure helps prevent misleading inferences and predictions about annual results.

APB 28 as interpreted by FASB Interpretation 18 requires that income tax expense be estimated each period using an estimated annual effective tax rate (see FASB Interpretation 18). The example on the following page illustrates the application of this requirement.

	(a)	(b)	(c) Estimated	(d)=(b)x(c)	(e)	(f)=(d)-(e)
Qtr.	Quarterly income before income taxes	Year-to-date income before income taxes	annual effective tax rate	Year-to-date income tax expense	Previous quarters' expense	Current quarter's expense
1	$100,000	$100,000	40%	$ 40,000	$ 0	$ 40,000
2	150,000	250,000	42%	105,000	40,000	65,000
3	300,000	550,000	46%	253,000	105,000	148,000
4	200,000	750,000	45%	337,500	253,000	84,500

In the above chart, columns (a) and (c) are assumed to be given. Column (b) is obtained by accumulating column (a) figures. Column (e) is either 1) the preceding quarter's entry in column (d), or 2) the cumulative total of previous quarters in column (f).

F. Segment Reporting

SFAS 14 (see outline) sets forth financial reporting standards for segments of a business enterprise. Four different types of segment information must be disclosed:
1) Different industries
2) Foreign operations and geographic areas
3) Export sales
4) Major customers

The purpose of segment disclosure is to assist investors and lenders in assessing the future potential of an enterprise. Consolidated statements give the user the overall view (results of operations, financial position, and changes thereof). However, trends, opportunities, risk factors, etc., can get lost when data for a diversified company are merged into consolidated statements. Consolidated statements refer to the primary statements of the reporting entity. They are not limited to the statements of parent and subsidiaries (the conventional meaning of the term consolidated statements). Segment disclosure, as required by SFAS 14, breaks out this useful, more detailed information from the consolidated statements.

Different industries. Certain disclosures must be made for significant industry segments. An industry segment sells a related group of products primarily to unaffiliated customers for a profit. An industry segment is significant (reportable) if it satisfies at least one of the following three 10% tests:

Revenues--10% or more of combined segment revenue (including intersegment revenue)

Operating profit or loss--10% or more of the greater of: combined profit of segments reporting profit, or combined loss of segments reporting loss

Identifiable assets--10% or more of combined segment identifiable assets

The key disclosures for reportable segments are sales to unaffiliated customers, intersegment sales, operating profit or loss, and identifiable assets, all reconciled to consolidated amounts. Other disclosures include depreciation, depletion and amortization expense, and capital expenditures.

Operating profit or loss is unaffiliated revenue and intersegment revenue, less all operating expenses, including common costs (operating expenses incurred for the benefit of more than one segment). Common costs are generally allocated based on relative revenue or profit before allocation. General corporate revenues and expenses (interest, taxes, X/O items, etc.) are not allocated. Similarly, identifiable assets used by more than one segment are allocated to those segments, but general corporate assets (cash and marketable securities) are not allocated.

There are some limitations to the number of segments which are to be reported. There must be enough segments reported so that at least 75% of unaffiliated revenues is shown by reportable segments (75% test). Also, the number of reportable segments should not be so large (10 is a rule of thumb) as to make the information less useful. When a reportable segment is excluded or a nonreportable segment included, appropriate disclosure must be made.

The following example illustrates the three 10% tests (revenues, operating profit or loss, and identifiable assets) and the 75% test.

Segment	Unaffiliated revenue	Intersegment revenue	Total revenue	Operating profit (loss)	Identifiable assets
A	90	90	180	20	70
B	120		120	10	50
C	110	20	130	(40)	90
D	200		200	0	140
E	330	110	440	(100)	230
F	380		380	60	260
Total	1230	220	1450	(50)	840

Revenues test: (10%)(1450) = $145
  Reportable segments: A, D, E, F

Operating profit or loss test: (10%)(140) = $14
  Reportable segments: A, C, E, F
  [Note: Operating loss (140) is greater than operating profit, 90]

Identifiable assets test: (10%)(840) = $84
  Reportable segments: C, D, E, F

Reportable segments are those which pass at least one of the 10% tests. Segments A, C, D, E, and F are reportable in this example.

75% test: (75%)(1230) = $922.50

Segments A, C, D, E, and F have total unaffiliated revenue of $1,110, which is greater than $922.50. The 75% test is satisfied; no additional segments need be reported.

Foreign operations, geographic areas, and export sales. Information must be disclosed for foreign operations in general, or geographic areas specifically, if at least one of the following two 10% tests are met:

Revenues (unaffiliated): 10% or more of consolidated revenue
Identifiable assets: 10% or more of consolidated total assets

The key disclosures are sales to unaffiliated customers, inter-area sales, operating profit or loss, and identifiable assets, all reconciled to consolidated amounts. This information is disclosed for foreign operations in total if there are no reportable geographic areas, or for each reportable geographic area. Domestic operations are also disclosed.

Disclosure is also required if sales to unaffiliated customers outside the U.S. are equal to or exceed 10% of consolidated revenue. Note this disclosure is required independently of that for foreign operations and geographic areas.

Major customers. Certain disclosures are made concerning major customers if the following 10% test is met:

Revenues: If 10% or more of consolidated revenue comes from a single customer, the enterprise must disclose this fact in addition to the amount of such revenues, and the industry segment making the sales.

Practice and theory multiple choice questions on segment reporting have emphasized industry segments (more specifically, operating profit or loss, the 10% tests, and allocation of common costs). Essay questions have emphasized definitions (industry segment, revenue, operating profit and loss, identifiable assets) the 10% tests, the 75% test and the rule of thumb for maximum number of segments. There have been no segment reporting practice problems.

G. Personal Financial Statements (SOP 82-1)

Personal financial statements may be prepared for an individual, husband and wife, or family. Personal financial statements (PFS) consist of:

1) Statement of financial condition--presents estimated current values of assets, estimated current amounts of liabilities, estimated income taxes and net worth at a specified date
2) Statement of changes in net worth--presents main sources of increases (decreases) in net worth

Assets and liabilities, including changes therein, should be recognized using the accrual basis of accounting. Assets and liabilities should be listed by order of liquidity and maturity, not a current/noncurrent basis.

In PFSs, assets should be presented at their estimated current value. This is an amount at which the item could be exchanged assuming both parties are well informed, neither party is compelled to buy or sell, and material disposal costs are deducted to arrive at current values. <u>Liabilities</u> should be presented at the lesser of the discounted amount of cash to be paid or the current cash settlement amount. Income taxes payable should include unpaid income taxes for completed tax years and the estimated amount for the elapsed portion of the current tax year. Also, PFSs should include the estimated income tax on the difference between the current value (amount) of assets (liabilities) and their respective tax bases as if they had been realized or liquidated. The table below summarizes the methods of determining "estimated current values" for assets and "estimated current amounts" for liabilities.

Assets and liabilities	Discounted cash flow	Market price	Appraised value	Other
• Receivables	X			
• Marketable securities		X		
• Options		X		
• Investment in life insurance				Cash value less outstanding loans
• Investment in closely held business	X		X	Liquidation value, multiple of earnings, reproduction value, adjustment of book value or cost
• Real estate	X		X	Sales of similar property
• Intangible assets	X			
• Future interests (nonforfeitable rights)	X			
• Payables and other liabilities	X			Discharge amount if lower than discounted amount
• Noncancellable commitments	X			
• Income taxes payable				Unpaid income tax for completed tax years and estimated income tax for elapsed portion of current tax year to date of financial statements
• Estimated income tax on difference between current values of assets and current amounts of liabilities and their respective tax bases				Computed as if current value of assets and liabilities had been respectively realized or liquidated considering applicable tax laws and regulations, recapture provisions and carryovers

Business interests which comprise a large portion of a person's total assets should be shown separately from other investments. An investment in a separate entity which is marketable as a going concern (e.g., closely held corporation) should be presented as one amount. If the investment is a limited business activity, not conducted in a separate business entity, separate asset and liability amounts should be shown (e.g., investment in real estate and related mortgage). Of course, only the person's beneficial interest in the investment is included in their PFS.

WORKING CAPITAL

Working capital is the excess of current assets over current liabilities. Turn back to Chapter 3A of ARB 43 which defines current assets and current liabilities. This study module reviews the accounting for all current assets (except inventory which is presented in the next module), current liabilities, and the Statement of Changes in Financial Position.

Cash is generally easy to account for and is usually under a strong system of internal control. Unrestricted cash available for general use is presented as the first current asset.

1) Cash set aside for special uses is usually disclosed separately. The entry to set up a special fund is:

          Special cash fund   xx
              Cash   xx

2) Cash restricted as to use, e.g., not transferable out of a foreign country, should be disclosed separately, but not as a current asset if it cannot be used in the next year (this is true of special funds also)

3) Imprest (petty) cash funds are generally included in the total cash figure, but unreimbursed expense vouchers are excluded. The fund is set up by:

          Petty cash   xx
              Cash   xx

When petty cash is paid out by the custodian, the custodian obtains a receipt for the expenditure (expense voucher). Periodically, the fund is replenished by reimbursing the custodian for the expense vouchers in the fund.

          Expenses, etc.   xx
              Cash   xx

Any difference between the sum of the expense vouchers and the amount of cash needed to return the fund to its original balance will be debited or credited to the cash over and short account. Note that once the fund is set up, no entries are made to the petty cash account unless the fund is changed in amount or eliminated.

When the petty cash account is not fully reimbursed at year end, i.e., not at its original balance, an adjusting entry is needed to record the expenses paid from the fund which have not yet been recorded. This adjusting entry is later reversed.

          Expenses   (unreimbursed expenses at year end)
              Petty cash   (same)

A. Bank Reconciliations

Bank reconciliations are prepared by bank depositors when they receive their monthly bank statements. The reconciliation is made to determine any required adjustments to the cash balance. Two types of reconciling items are possible.

1) Reconciling items not requiring adjustment on the books (type A)
2) Reconciling items requiring adjustment on the books (type B)

There are three type A reconciling items. They do not require adjusting journal entries.

1) Outstanding checks
2) Deposits in transit
3) Bank errors

All other reconciling items (type B) require adjusting journal entries. Examples of type B reconciling items include:

1) Unrecorded returned nonsufficient funds (NSF) checks
2) Unrecorded bank charges
3) Errors in the cash account
4) Unrecorded bank collections of notes receivable

Two types of formats are used in bank reconciliations.

Format 1	Format 2
Balance per bank	Balance per bank
+(-) A adjustments	+(-) A adjustments
Correct cash balance	+(-) B adjustments
	Balance per books
Balance per books	+(-) B adjustments
+(-) B adjustments	Correct cash balance
Correct cash balance	

Type A and B adjustments can be either added or subtracted depending upon the type of format and the nature of the item.

Reconciling items must be analyzed to determine whether they are included in (1) the balance per bank, and/or (2) the balance per books. If they are included in one, but not the other, an adjustment is required. For instance, the $1,800 deposit in transit in the following example is included in the balance per books but not in the balance per bank. Thus it must be added to the balance per bank to reconcile to the correct cash balance. Deposits in transit do not require an adjusting journal entry. Analyze all reconciling items in this manner, but remember, only journalize type B reconciling items.

Sample Bank Reconciliation (Format 1)

Per bank statement	$4,702
Deposits in transit	1,800
Outstanding checks	(1,200)
Bank error	50
Correct cash balance	$5,352
Per books	$5,332
Service charges	(5)
Note collected by bank	150
Customer's NSF check	(170)
Deposit of July 10 recorded as $749 instead of $794	45
Correct cash balance	$5,352

Note that the balance per bank and balance per books each are reconciled directly to the corrected balance.

B. Adjusting Journal Entries

All of the items in the per books section of a bank reconciliation (type B) require adjusting entries. The entries for the above example appear below.

Miscellaneous expense	5		A/R	170	
Cash		5	Cash		170
Cash	150		Cash	45	
Notes receivable		150	A/R (or sales)		45

C. Four-Column Cash Reconciliation

Unlike the bank reconciliation above, which is as of a specific date, a four-column cash reconciliation, also known as a "proof of cash," reconciles bank and book cash balances over a specified time period. A proof of cash consists of four columns: beginning of the period bank reconciliation, receipts, disbursements, and end of the period bank reconciliation. Thus, the proof of cash cross-foots as well as foots.

Sample Proof of Cash (Format 2)

	Bank Reconciliation June 30, 1983	Receipts	Disbursements	Bank Reconciliation July 31, 1983
Balance per bank statement	$3,402	$25,200	$23,900	$4,702
Deposits in transit				
June 30, 1983	1,610	(1,610)		
July 31, 1983		1,800		1,800
Outstanding checks				
June 30, 1983	(450)		(450)	
July 31, 1983			1,200	(1,200)
Service charges			(5)	5
Note collected by bank		(150)		(150)
Customer's NSF check			(170)	170
Deposit of July 10 recorded as $749 instead of $794		(45)		(45)
Bank error			(50)	50
Balance per books	$4,562	$25,195	$24,425	$5,332

Note that there are no type B reconciling items in the beginning reconciliation column. This is because the $4,562 has been adjusted when the June bank statement was reconciled. Notice that figures appearing in the center columns have unlike signs if they are adjacent and like signs if they are not adjacent to amounts in the side columns.

The purpose of the proof of cash is to disclose any irregularities, such as un-recorded disbursements and receipts within a month, which would not be detected by a bank reconciliation. For example, if the center two columns each required a nega-tive $1,000 to make the top line reconcile with the bottom line, there may be un-recorded receipts and deposits of $1,000.

D. Receivables

Accounts receivable should be disclosed in the balance sheet at net realizable value by source, e.g., trade, officer, etc. Officer, employee, and affiliate com-pany receivables should be separately disclosed (ARB 43, Chapter 1A). Unearned interest and finance charges should be deducted from gross receivables (APB 6, para 14).

E. Anticipation of Sales Discounts

Cash discounts are generally recognized as expense when cash payment is received within the discount period. As long as cash discounts to be taken on year-end re-ceivables remain constant from year to year, there is no problem. If, however, discounts on year-end receivables fluctuate, a year-end allowance can be set up or sales can be recorded net of the discounts. The entries to record sales at net are shown below in comparison to the sales recorded gross.

		Sales at net	Sales at gross
1)	Sale	A/R (net) Sales (net)	A/R (gross) Sales (gross)
2)	Cash receipt within discount period	Cash (net) A/R (net)	Sales disc. (disc.) Cash (net) A/R (gross)
3)	Cash receipt after discount period	Cash (gross) A/R (net) Disc. not taken (disc.)	Cash (gross) A/R (gross)

If a sales discount allowance method is used, the entry below is made with the gross method entries. The entry should be reversed.

Sales discounts   (expected disc. on year-end A/R)
    Allowance for sales disc.   (expected disc. on year-end A/R)

Similarly, when using the "net method," an entry should be made to pick up discounts not expected to be taken on year-end receivables. Generally, however, these latter adjustments are not made, because they are assumed to be about the same each period.

F. Bad Debts Expense

There are two approaches to bad debts.

1) Direct write-off method
2) Allowance method

Under the direct write-off method, bad debts are considered an expense in the period in which they are written off.

Bad debts expense   (uncollectible A/R)
    A/R   (uncollectible A/R)

The allowance method seeks to estimate the amount of uncollectible receivables, and establishes a contra valuation account (allowance for bad debts) for the amount estimated to be uncollectible. The adjusting entry to set up the allowance is:

Bad debts expense   (estimated)
    Allowance for bad debts   (estimated)

The entry to write-off bad debts is:

Allowance for bad debts   (uncollectible A/R)
    A/R   (uncollectible A/R)

There are two methods to determine the annual charge to bad debts expense.

1) Annual sales
2) Year-end A/R

For example, charging bad debts expense for 1% of sales is based on the theory that bad debts are a function of sales; this method emphasizes the income statement.

Charging bad debts on year-end A/R is based on the theory that bad debts are a function of A/R collections during the period; this method emphasizes the balance sheet. A bad debts percentage can be applied to total A/R or subsets of A/R. Often an aging schedule is prepared for this purpose. An A/R aging schedule classifies A/R by their age, e.g., 30, 60, 90, 120, etc., days overdue.

When bad debt expense is estimated as a function of sales, any balance in the allowance account is ignored in making the adjusting entry. When the expense is estimated based on outstanding receivables, the expense is the amount needed to adjust the allowance account so that A/R minus the allowance equals the net realizable value of accounts receivable. The balance in the allowance account is ignored in the first case but is an integral part of the calculation in the second case. Net accounts receivable is the balance in accounts receivable less the allowance for bad

debts. Also remember that net receivables <u>do not change</u> when a specific account is
written off since both accounts receivable and the allowance account are reduced by
the same amount.

G. <u>Pledging, Assigning, Selling A/R</u> (see outline of SFAS 77)

Sometimes businesses cannot wait for the cash flow from the normal collection of
A/R. In some cases, A/R may be pledged to secure a loan. The A/R pledged serve as
collateral in case of default. At the balance sheet date, the amounts of A/R
pledged should be disclosed either parenthetically or in the notes.

Assignment of A/R is a procedure where more formal rights in the A/R are given
(assigned) to the lender. The assignor (debtor) still collects on the A/R assigned,
but remits the proceeds to the lender. Generally, the amount of A/R assigned is
greater than the cash received from the assignee (creditor) so as to cover finance
charges and uncollectible accounts. The journal entries for both the assignor and
the assignee follow.

		Assignor	Assignee

1)	Cash is advanced for less than total A/R assigned	A/R assigned
		   A/R
			Note receivable
			   Finance revenue
			   Cash

		Cash Finance charge Note payable	
2)	Cash is collected and remitted to finance company	Cash A/R assigned	

		Note payable
		   Cash
			Cash
			   Note receivable

3)	A/R are written off	Allowance for
		  doubtful accounts
		   A/R assigned	

4)	Remainder of A/R are collected and note paid	Cash A/R assigned	

		Note payable
		Interest expense
		   Cash
			Cash
			   Note receivable
			   Interest revenue

		A/R A/R assigned	
5)	Financial statement presentation	A/R assigned x Note payable <u>(x)</u> Equity in A/R assigned x	Note receivable (x)

Note that the assignor offsets the liability with the asset to which it relates.
This is not generally allowed, but an exception is made due to the contractual

connection between the assigned A/R and their obligation, the notes payable. The assigneee also discloses either parenthetically or in a footnote the amount of the assigned A/R securing the loan.

Sales (factoring) of accounts receivable usually results in collection of the receivables by the factor. In most factoring transactions, the factor buys A/R without recourse. The entry for selling A/R without recourse is:

>   Factor's margin
>   Receivable from factor
>   A/R

If the cash is drawn prior to the average due date of the A/R factored, interest or a finance charge will be levied when the cash is advanced. The entry for cash advances will thus, most likely, take the following form:

>   Cash
>   Finance charge
>   Receivable from factor

The factor's margin provides a margin of protection against sales returns, allowances and disputed accounts. As sales returns and allowances are approved, the following entry is made on the books of the seller.

>   Sales returns and allowances
>   Factor's margin

When all of the amounts have been collected by the factor, the balance in the factor's margin account is returned to the seller. The balance in factor's margin will be reported as a current asset on the balance sheet.

In some cases, the factor may buy A/R with recourse. Per SFAS 77, these conditions must be met for the transfer of A/R to be considered a sale:

1) Surrender of A/R control by the transferor
2) Obligation of transferor is estimable
3) Repurchase of A/R by transferor is limited to recourse provisions

If these are met, the difference between the selling price and the receivables transferred is recognized as a gain (loss). If any of the above conditions is not met, the transaction is viewed as a loan collateralized by A/R, and the amount of the proceeds should be reported as a liability.

H. Discounting Notes Receivable

Notes are simply formal receivables with a written promise to pay and may be negotiable and/or interest bearing. Traditionally, notes receivable have been accounted for independently of accounts receivable. Aside from accruing interest revenue, etc., the common transaction involving notes receivable is discounting them, i.e., selling them (usually with recourse). The entry to record N/R discounting with recourse is:

    Cash   (cash proceeds)
    Interest inc. or exp.   (plug)
         N/R discounted   (face value)

To calculate cash proceeds:

1) Compute maturity value of the note. Face value plus (face value X contract interest rate for number of days of note).

2) Compute discount, i.e., bank interest. Maturity value X bank interest or discount rate for days remaining to maturity date.

3) Subtract discount from maturity value. Note that the bank is lending the maturity value, i.e., the amount to be collected at the maturity date.

   EXAMPLE: 60 days, 9%, $1,000 note discounted with the bank when 30 days remain to maturity. Bank interest rate is 8%.

1. $\frac{60}{360}$ X $\frac{9}{100}$ X $1,000 + $1,000 = $1,015   Maturity Value

2. $\frac{30}{360}$ X $\frac{8}{100}$ X $1,015 = $6.77   Bank Interest Charge

3. $1,015 - $6.77 = $1,008.23   Cash Proceeds

"N/R discounted" is a contra N/R account which discloses the contingent liability. If notes are sold "without recourse," there is no contingent liability; it is essentially a sale and the credit in the entry above would be to "notes receivable." At the maturity date (when the note is honored or dishonored), the following entry is recorded to recognize that the contingency is resolved:

    N/R discounted   (face)
         N/R   (face)

If the note is dishonored:

    A/R   (maturity value + penalty)
         Cash   (maturity value + penalty)

This entry is made in addition to eliminating the contingent liability (N/R discounted). The A/R is from the maker who dishonored the note.

The contingent liability may also be disclosed by footnote or parenthetically. "N/R" instead of "N/R discounted" would be credited when the note is discounted (i.e., no contingent liability account is used).

I. Short-Term Investments

Short-term or temporary investments, a current asset, ordinarily consists of marketable debt securities and marketable equity securities. To be considered a temporary investment a security must be:

1) Readily marketable
2) Intended to be converted into cash within one year or the operating cycle, whichever is longer

Securities held for control, to maintain a business relationship or for long-term price appreciation are specifically excluded from this category.

The cost of debt securities includes brokerage fees and taxes, but accrued interest (on debt securities) at the date of purchase must be segregated as a separate asset. The selling price is considered net of brokerage fees, etc. If there have been numerous purchases of the same security, then some flow assumption is necessary at the time of sale. Specific identification, FIFO, and weighted average are acceptable for financial reporting. For tax purposes, FIFO is required unless specific identification has been used.

J. Marketable Equity Securities

The accounting for marketable equity securities is governed by SFAS 12 (see the outline and related FASB Interpretations). Equity securities so covered include common, preferred, and other capital stock warrants, rights, and call options. Treasury stock, redeemable preferred stock and convertible bonds are excluded.

The cost of an equity security includes the purchase price and all costs incidental to acquisition such as brokerage commissions and taxes. Subsequent to acquisition, SFAS 12 specifies that the carrying value of these securities must be the lower of the aggregate cost or market value of the portfolio as determined on the balance sheet date.

SFAS 12 specifies that the excess of aggregate cost over aggregate market value must be carried in a separate "valuation allowance" account. The purpose of this account is to allow the securities to be adjusted to their net realizable value at the balance sheet date. SFAS 12 requires that realized gains and losses, as well as changes in the valuation allowance for short-term equity securities, be used in the calculation of net income. Thus, unrealized losses and their recoveries due to the year-end adjustment of the valuation allowance account are to be reported in net income. In no case may the recovery exceed the balance in the allowance account. In other words, the recovery is limited to the extent to which previous losses were recognized.

At the end of the year an adjusting entry is made to change the balance in the valuation allowance account to the balance dictated by the aggregate cost/aggregate market comparison.

For example, consider the three-security portfolio (current) below for the years 1983 and 1984.

| Security | 1983 (Yr. of Purchase) | | | 1984 | | |
	Cost	Market	Allowance	Cost	Market	Allowance
A	8,000	10,000	2,000	8,000	6,000	(2,000)
B	20,000	16,000	(4,000)	20,000	25,000	5,000
C	30,000	12,000	(18,000)	30,000	15,000	(15,000)
	58,000	38,000	(20,000)	58,000	46,000	(12,000)

Since the aggregate cost exceeds market in 1983, the year-end adjustment is as follows:

Unrealized loss on marketable securities   20,000
        Allowance for excess of cost over market   20,000

The unrealized loss would appear as other expense on the income statement and ultimately be closed out to retained earnings. The allowance account (not closed out) would be deducted from the securities account on the balance sheet date and remain unchanged until the next balance sheet date.

In 1984, two items should be noted. First, aggregate cost still exceeds market, so the allowance account is still necessary. Second, the allowance balance needed is $12,000, while the present balance of $20,000 remains in the general ledger from last year. Thus, a recovery of an unrealized loss of $8,000 is recorded to reduce the allowance account to $12,000. The securities would be presented in the 1984 balance sheet at their fair market value of $46,000.

Allowance for excess of cost over market   8,000
        Recovery of unrealized loss on
            marketable securities   8,000

Note that the reversal of the writedown ($8,000) is treated as a recovery, instead of as an unrealized gain, since it is considered a change in the estimate of an un-realized loss. It would appear on the income statement in other revenues, while the allowance account would appear as before.

If instead the aggregate market value had been $62,000 (i.e., greater than cost), the above entry would have been for $20,000, the entire balance in the allow-ance account. This would reduce its balance to zero, and the securities would be shown on the balance sheet at cost.

Realized gains (losses) result from the actual sale of the securities and are treated in the traditional manner, with the gain (loss) as the difference between the cost of the security and its selling price. Disposition of securities does not affect the valuation account. At the end of the year, the aggregate cost and market values of the remaining securities are compared in determining the valuation balance.

For classified balance sheets, equity securities should be grouped into two portfolios - a current and a noncurrent portfolio. If unclassified balance sheets are prepared, all marketable equity securities are treated as noncurrent.

For noncurrent equity securities, a separate comparison of aggregate cost and aggregate market is also made each year in the same manner as for current securities. It is important to note, however, that the unrealized losses or their recoveries due to the adjustment of the valuation allowance for noncurrent assets do not go to the income statement. Instead, the balance in the unrealized loss account appears in the equity section of the balance sheet reducing owner's equity (similar to the treatment accorded to treasury stock). The unrealized loss account is reduced only as the balance needed in the allowance account becomes smaller. Thus, as the market value of the noncurrent portfolio increases to cost, the allowance is debited and the unrealized loss account is credited. Changes in value of noncurrent marketable equity securities do not appear in income until actually realized.

If a decline in value takes place for long-term equity securities and the decline is viewed as not being temporary, then the cost basis of the security is written down to a new cost basis. The write-down is permanent and is considered realized.

SFAS 12 also provides that if security is moved from the current to the noncurrent portfolio, or vice versa, a realized loss may be recognized on the transfer. If the market value of the transferred security is less than its cost, the market value becomes the new cost at the time of transfer and the loss is considered realized.

K. Marketable Debt Securities

SFAS 12 is not applicable to debt securities. ARB 43 prescribes cost as the carrying value for debt securities unless two conditions have occurred. The two conditions which necessitate a switch to lower of cost or market are when:

   1) The decline in the value of debt securities is substantial, and
   2) The decline in market value is not due to a temporary condition

Thus, debt securities are carried at cost or at lower of cost or market depending upon whether the conditions specified above have occurred. Note that the lower of cost or market treatment is not automatically applied as it is for marketable equity securities.

The premium or discount on long-term debt securities is amortized. On short-term debt securities, amortization is generally ignored. Investor accounting for debt securities is discussed in Module 29, Section "B.3."

L. Current Liabilities

"Obligations whose liquidation is reasonably expected to require the use of existing resources properly classifiable as current assets, or the creation of other current liabilities." (ARB 43, Chapter 3, para 7)

Related Liability Definitions:

Determinable Liabilities - the amount of cash and time of payment are known and reasonably precise. Such liabilities are usually evidenced by written contracts but may also arise from implied agreements or imposed legal statutes. Examples include notes payable and liabilities for various taxes.

Contingent Liabilities - such obligations may exist but are dependent on uncertain future events (uncertainties could include unsettled litigation or proposed government action). These liabilities (loss contingencies) should only be recorded on the books if:

    a) It is possible to obtain a reasonable estimate of the loss, and
    b) It is probable at the balance sheet date that the loss has been incurred and information prior to the date the financial statements are issued does not change this assessment

Examples of contingent liabilities might include unsettled lawsuits and warranty obligations. For information on accounting for contingencies, see outline of SFAS 5.

M. Examples of Current Liabilities (as they fall within the above definition)

1. Trade accounts and notes payable

2. Loan obligations - including current portions of long-term debt. This is not true if the current portion of long-term debt will not require the use of current assets, e.g., be paid from a sinking fund which is not classified as current.

3. Short-term obligations expected to be refinanced cannot be reclassified as noncurrent liabilities unless there is both an intent and an ability to refinance. See the outline of SFAS 6.

4. Dividends payable - cash dividends are a liability when declared. They cannot be rescinded.

5. Accrued liabilities - adjusting entries to reflect our use of goods or services before we pay for them. We will pay in future periods even though we have incurred the expense in this period, e.g., interest, payroll, rent expenses.

         Expense account   xx
              Liability (usually current) account   xx

6. Payroll - there are two entries to record payroll. The first records the employee's payment and our deductions on behalf of the employee. The second is to record the employer's taxes.

Payroll expense	(gross pay)
Payroll payable, cash	(net pay)
Income taxes payable	xx
FICA taxes payable	xx
Union dues payable	xx
Medical insurance payable	xx

Payroll tax expense	xx
FICA taxes payable	xx
Federal unemployment tax payable	xx
State unemployment tax payable	xx

7. Property taxes. See the outline of ARB 43, Chapter 10A. Generally, there is a monthly accrual for property taxes over the fiscal period of the taxing authority. If taxes are payable at the end of the tax authority's fiscal period, the monthly accrual would be:

Property tax expense	xx
Property tax payable	xx

    If the taxes were paid at the beginning of the period, the entry to record the prepayment would be followed by monthly entries to expense the prepayment.

Prepaid property taxes	xx		Property tax expense	xx
Cash		xx	Prepaid property taxes	xx

    If taxes are due, but not paid at the beginning of the year, the liability should be recorded and the deferred charge expensed over the fiscal year of the taxing body.

Deferred property taxes	xx		Property tax expense	xx
Property tax payable		xx	Deferred property taxes	xx

8. Bonus arrangements

Bonus expense	xx
Bonus payable	xx

    Set up equations to describe the terms of the bonus agreement. The general forms of the equations follow:

    $$B = P(NI - B - T)$$
    $$T = R(NI - B)$$
    $$B = \text{bonus}$$
    $$P = \text{bonus or profitsharing rate (10\%)}$$
    $$NI = \text{net income (\$150,000)}$$
    $$T = \text{taxes}$$
    $$R = \text{tax rate (40\%)}$$

EXAMPLE: *Work through the above equations using the data in parentheses.*

$$T = .40(150,000 - B)$$
$$T = 60,000 - .4B$$
$$B = .10(150,000 - B - T)$$
$$B = .10(150,000 - B - 60,000 + .4B)$$
$$B = 15,000 - .1B - 6,000 + .04B$$
$$1.06B = 9,000$$
$$B = \$8,491$$

9. Premium plans - companies offering premiums, e.g., towels, knives, and other prizes, to promote their products often have premium liability for outstanding coupons. The expense should be recorded in the period of the sale and be based on the estimated redemption rate.

    Premium plan expense   xx
        Premium plan liability   xx

    As coupons are redeemed for premiums the liability is paid.

    Premium plan liability   xx
        Premiums   xx

10. Advances from customers - record as deferred revenue and recognize as revenue when earned

    Cash   xx   Deferred revenue   xx
        Deferred revenue   xx   Revenue   xx

11. Warranties - estimated future warranty costs which are both probable and reasonably estimable are recorded as an expense in the period in which the related sales are made. This application of the matching process creates a current liability to which future warranty expenditures should be charged.

    Warranty expense   xx   Warranty liability   xx
        Warranty liab.   xx   Cash, inventory, etc.   xx

    If the costs are either not probable or not estimable, the warranty costs are not expensed until actually incurred, which is the only method acceptable for tax purposes.

N. Statement of Changes in Financial Position (APB 19)

The objective of the Statement of Changes in Financial Position is to disclose the financing and investing activities of a business enterprise. These statements may be prepared using a "working capital" or a "cash" basis. Since the trend in corporate reporting is to use the "cash" basis, candidates should be sure to review preparation of cash basis statements as thoroughly as they review working capital basis statements. The statement is prepared by explaining the change in working capital in terms of changes in all of the noncurrent accounts.

Looking at the balance sheet and equations below, it can be seen that the net change in working capital over a period of time must be equal to the net change in all noncurrent accounts.

CA	CL

Any increases use working capital	Noncurrent Assets	Noncurrent Liabilities and Shareholders' Equity	Any increases provide working capital
Any decreases provide working capital	Total Assets _____	Total Credits _____	Any decreases use working capital

$$A = L + SE$$
$$CA + NCA = CL + NCL + SE$$
$$\Delta CA + \Delta NCA = \Delta CL + \Delta NCL + \Delta SE \qquad (\Delta = change)$$
$$\Delta CA - \Delta CL = -\Delta NCA + \Delta NCL + \Delta SE$$
$$(one figure) = (changes in all noncurrent accounts)$$

O. Procedural Steps

1. Calculate the change in working capital
2. Determine "working capital provided by operations" (used by operations if a loss)

   a. Add all nonworking capital charges, e.g., depreciation, back to income before nonoperating items
   b. Deduct from income all nonworking capital credits, e.g., investment credit amortization

3. Analyze all changes in working capital accounts in terms of working capital provided and working capital applied

   a. Include all nonworking capital financing and investing activities not affecting working capital, e.g., exchange of bonds for land, in a special section of the statement (all financial resources concept)

4. Prepare the formal statement
5. Prepare a subsidiary schedule disclosing the details of the change in working capital, i.e., a schedule disclosing changes in individual current assets and current liabilities

Elaboration of Step 2. If income before nonoperating items is taken as the starting point for determining working capital from operations, then certain items must be added or deducted to obtain flows of working capital.

Since some items of revenue and expense do not contribute to income as a net provider of working capital, deductions from revenue that did not require the use of working capital must be added back. In essence, adding these items back eliminates them from the statement. Since the items did not use working capital and were subtracted in determining income, it is proper to eliminate them by adding them.

Items to be added back include depreciation, amortization of intangibles, amortization of discount on bonds payable, losses recognized on investments carried per the equity method, bad debt expense on <u>long-term</u> receivables, and any increase in noncurrent deferred tax liability. Note each of these items is charged against income but does not decrease working capital.

Items to be deducted from income to convert income to a statement of working capital flows include all revenues and income which did not provide working capital. Common examples include income recognized on investments carried per the equity method, decreases in the deferred tax liability, and amortization of the premium on bonds payable.

Finally, gains (losses) on fixed assets and long-term investments require adjustment, since the working capital received is not measured by the gain (or loss), i.e., a fixed asset with a book value of $10, sold for $15 in cash, provides $15 in working capital but is reported as only a $5 gain on the income statement. The $15 is shown as a separate item on the statement and the $5 gain is subtracted (eliminated) from income. Losses on asset disposals are added back to income. See Statement Format below.

P. <u>Statement Format</u>

COMPANY X
Statement of Changes in Financial Position
Year Ended December 31, 19X1

Working capital provided
    Operations
        Income before nonoperating items   xx
        + Charges not using WC   x
        - Revenues not producing WC   <u>x</u>   <u>x</u>   xx
    Decreases in noncurrent assets   xx
    Increases in noncurrent liabilities & shareholders' equity   <u>xx</u>
        Total working capital provided   <u>xxx</u>

Working capital applied
    Increases in noncurrent assets   xx
    Decreases in noncurrent liabilities & shareholders' equity   <u>xx</u>
        Total working capital applied   <u>xx</u>
Increase (decrease) in working capital   <u>xx</u>

Investing activities not affecting working capital
    Noncurrent assets for noncurrent liabilities and
      shareholders' equity   <u>xx</u>

    Noncurrent liabilities and shareholders' equity for
      noncurrent assets   <u>xx</u>

Schedule of Changes in Working Capital

	Now	Then	Change
Current assets	xx	xx	xx
Current liabilities	xx	xx	<u>xx</u>
Change in working capital			<u>xx</u>

Q. Example

Net income was $15,000. Fixed assets costing $5,000 with a book value of $2,000 were sold for $4,000. Investments costing $5,000 were used to retire $5,000 of bonds outstanding.

	Year 2	Year 1
Cash	17,000	14,000
Accounts receivable	6,000	7,000
Investments	17,000	22,000
Fixed assets	22,000	17,000
	62,000	60,000
Accounts payable	4,000	7,000
Bonds payable	5,000	10,000
Common stock	20,000	20,000
Retained earnings	28,000	19,000
Accumulated depreciation	5,000	4,000
	62,000	60,000

1. Change in working capital

	Year 2	Year 1	Change
Cash	17,000	14,000	+3,000
A/R	6,000	7,000	-1,000
A/P	4,000	7,000	+3,000
	Net change in working capital		+5,000

2. Working capital provided by operations

Net income	$15,000
Gain on sale of fixed assets	- 2,000
Net income from operations	13,000
Depreciation expense*	+ 4,000
Working capital provided	17,000

*Net credit increases in accumulated depreciation of $4,000 after a $3,000 debit from sale of fixed assets.

Asset cost	$5,000
Book value	-2,000
Accum. depr.	3,000

3. Analysis of changes in working capital account

   a. Investments decreased by $5,000 as they were exchanged for bonds outstanding (all financial resources concept)

   b. Fixed assets increased by $5,000 after $5,000 of assets were sold. Thus, $10,000 of fixed assets were purchased.

   c. The decrease of $5,000 in bonds payable is explained in "a."

   d. Common stock had no change

   e. Retained earnings increased $9,000 after net income of $15,000, indicating a dividend of $6,000

4. Formal statement

HEADING

Working capital provided
    Net income $15,000
        Add (deduct) items not affecting WC
            Gain on sale   (2,000)
            Depreciation expense   4,000 $17,000
    Sale of assets   4,000
        Total working capital provided $21,000

Working capital applied
    Dividends paid $ 6,000
    Purchase of fixed assets   10,000
        Total working capital applied $16,000
Increase in working capital $ 5,000

Financing and investing activities not affecting working capital
    Exchange of investments to retire bonds payable $ 5,000

5. Schedule of Changes in Working Capital
   Appears in "1." on previous page.

The above problem may also be solved using the "T-account approach." This method provides a quick, systematic, and sure-fire way to accumulate the information necessary to prepare the statement. The changes in working capital are explained using the noncurrent accounts.

The first step under this approach is to calculate the change in working capital (see "1." above). This is used as the "bottom line" figure in the statement.

Next, set up T-accounts for each of the noncurrent accounts and enter their respective beginning and ending balances. Also set up T-accounts for working capital and working capital provided by operations.

```
        Working Capital                         WC—Operations
       5,000 |                           (1) 15,000 |
  (2)  4,000 |                                      |  2,000 (2)
             |  6,000 (6)                (5)  4,000 |
  (7) 17,000 | 10,000 (4)                    19,000 |  2,000
      21,000 | 16,000                               | 17,000 (7)
             |  5,000 Increase in WC        19,000  | 19,000
      ───────────────
      21,000 | 21,000


      Investments              Fixed Assets               Accum. Depr.
   22,000 |                 17,000 |                             |  4,000
          |  5,000 (3)             |  5,000 (2)        (2)  3,000 |
          |              (4) 10,000 |                            |  4,000 (5)
   ───────                 ─────────                   ──────────────
   17,000 |                 22,000 |                             |  5,000


    Bonds Payable              Common Stock              Retained Earnings
          | 10,000                    | 20,000                   | 19,000
  (3) 5,000 |                         |                          | 15,000 (1)
   ───────                  ──────────                 (6)  6,000 |
          |  5,000                    | 20,000                    | 28,000
```

After this is done, analyze the events that affect working capital, distinguishing between items which affect working capital from operations and working capital in general.

1. Net income was the major source of working capital provided by operations and, therefore, is debited to that account. The corresponding credit is to retained earnings, since net income is closed to retained earnings at the end of the year.

2. Fixed assets with an original cost of $5,000 and a book value of $2,000 were sold for $4,000, resulting in a $2,000 ordinary gain. The journal entry would be:

Working capital (cash)	4,000	
Accumulated depr.	3,000	
Fixed assets		5,000
WC - operations (gain)		2,000

3. Investments were used to retire a portion of the bonds payable. Although this transaction did not involve working capital, it (and any others like it) is presented in the Statement of Changes under the all financial resources concept.

After all events have been analyzed, a verification of the ending balances in each of the noncurrent accounts may yield other transactions.

4. In order for the ending balance of fixed assets to balance, an additional $10,000 of fixed assets must have been purchased during the year.

5. An analysis of the accumulated depreciation account reveals a credit of $4,000 which is needed to reconcile the ending balance. This indicates depreciation expense was $4,000 in year 2. Working capital provided by operations is the debit since depreciation expense reduced net income, but had no effect on working capital and thus must be added back.

6. In order to balance the retained earnings account, a $6,000 debit is required, implying that, in year 2, a dividend of $6,000 was declared.

7. After all of the noncurrent accounts are balanced, the balance in the working capital provided by operations account is transferred to the working capital account. Netting the working capital account yields a $5,000 debit balance, which matches the initial calculation of the change in working capital. This represents the increase in working capital during year 2.

The final step is the preparation of the statement. Both the postings into the working capital accounts and the postings resulting from the application of the all financial resources concept make up the line items of the statement. The formal Statement of Changes and Schedule of Changes would appear as before (see "4." and "5." in previous example).

R. Cash Format

As mentioned under "N." above, a switch to the cash format for the Statement of Changes has been made by many companies. Presumably, this change will also be reflected in CPA exam coverage. On a cash format, the change in cash is explained in terms of the changes in all of the other balance sheet accounts.

1) In addition to the changes in all noncurrent accounts, changes in current accounts (other than cash) are sources and uses of cash. They are presented as part of "cash provided (used, if a loss) by operations."

2) Because the changes in all current accounts are presented in the statement itself, no subsidiary schedule of changes in working capital is required

The following diagram may facilitate the adjustments to income for statement of changes on a cash basis. The diagram is simply an expanded balance sheet equation.

	Current Assets	+	Fixed Assets	=	Current Liabilities	+	Long-Term Liabilities	+	Income	Income Adjustment to Convert to Cash Flow
1)	Increase			=					Increase	Decrease
2)	Decrease			=					Decrease	Increase
3)				=	Increase				Decrease	Increase
4)				=	Decrease				Increase	Decrease

Under the cash basis we are trying to explain why <u>cash</u> changed. If we start with net income, it must be recognized that certain changes in income occur because of changes in current assets and current liabilities, not because of changes in cash. To determine cash flows we must adjust the income number to remove those income flows which resulted from noncash events. Whether we add or subtract, the change in the account balance can be read from the last column in the table above.

For example, using Row 1, a credit sale would increase accounts receivable and income, but does not affect cash. It must be removed from the income statement to convert to a cash flow statement. The last column indicates that the increase in a current asset balance must be deducted from income to obtain cash flow.

Similarly, an increase in a current liability, Row 3, must be added to income to obtain cash flows (e.g., accrued wages are on the income statements as an expense, but they do not require cash - the increase in wages payable must be added back to get this noncash flow expense off the statement).

The cash basis solution to the problem above is:

```
Cash provided
    Operations
        Net income                  $15,000
        Gain on sale                - 2,000
        Depreciation expense        + 4,000
        Decrease in A/R             + 1,000
        Decrease in A/P             - 3,000      $15,000
    Sale of assets                                4,000

        Total cash provided                     $19,000

Cash applied
    Dividends paid                  $ 6,000
    Purchase of fixed assets         10,000      $16,000
Net increase in cash                            $ 3,000

    Financing and investing activities not affecting cash
        Exchange of investments to retire bonds payable   $ 5,000
```

The "T-account approach" may also be used in solving a Statement of Changes problem on a cash basis. The methodology is the same as discussed in "Q.," except that the T-accounts for working capital are not necessary. Instead, T-accounts for cash provided by operations and for cash are used.

S. Solutions Approach Example

The following problem is presented as an example of the solutions approach applied to a Statement of Changes problem. To obtain the maximum benefit, study the problem, ignoring the felt tip pen markings. As you reread the problem, work through the solutions approach as illustrated.

First, glance over the problem noting that the changes in balance sheet accounts during the calendar year 1983 are presented (not beginning and ending balances but the differences). Six paragraphs of additional information regarding transactions during 1983 are also presented.

Second, study the requirements. They are very straightforward: a statement of changes in financial position and a schedule of changes in working capital for 1983. Also note that the working capital format (in contrast to the cash format) is required.

Next, visualize the solution format. The statement of changes is a listing of the sources of working capital and the uses of working capital, the difference being the change in working capital during the year. The schedule of working capital is just the detail of the change in working capital, i.e., the change in the balance of each working capital account.

Third, determine the steps to your solution. One approach is to complete the
schedule of changes in working capital to determine the overall change in working
capital for the year (the figure you are working to in the statement of changes,
i.e., your check figure). Next you need to analyze the changes in each of the noncurrent accounts in the balance sheet during 1983 to determine the sources and uses
of working capital. As part of this analysis you need to determine the working
capital provided by operations. Upon completion of these analyses you will be able
to prepare the final solution.

As part of this solution step, you should do a quick mental review of accounting principles and procedures applicable to the statement of changes. Recall that
APB 19 requires the "all financial resources" concept, i.e., reporting changes in
noncurrent accounts that do not result in working capital flows during the year.

You may wish to refresh your understanding of the statement of changes in
financial position. It explains the change in net working capital during the period
in terms of changes in all of the noncurrent accounts.

Fourth, study the text of the problem preparing intermediary solutions as you
proceed.

1. Work through the balance sheet noting which accounts are current assets and
    which are current liabilities. Note: an increase in current assets is an
    increase in working capital, but an increase in current liabilities is a
    decrease in working capital.

2. Prepare the schedule of changes in working capital

Cash	+	$ 50,000
Receivables	+	76,000
Inventories	+	37,000
Prepaid expenses	+	1,000
Payables	+	55,500
Notes payable	+	15,000
Accrued expenses	−	33,000
Net increase		$201,500

3. Become conversant with each of the noncurrent accounts before reading the
    additional information. This makes you more efficient in analyzing the
    additional information.

4. Read through each of the six paragraphs of additional information noting
    their effect on the statement of changes

    a. The $172,300 of net income is a base figure for computing working
        capital provided by operations. Add income statement items not using
        working capital, e.g., depreciation, and deduct income statement items
        not producing working capital, e.g., amortization of deferred revenues.

    b. The write-off of accounts receivable using the allowance account does
        not change the net accounts receivable or create a change in income.
        Thus, no adjustment is required.

Illustration of Solutions Approach

The following schedule showing net changes in balance-sheet accounts at December 31, 1983, compared to December 31, 1982, was prepared from the records of The Sodium Company. The statement of changes in financial position for the year ended December 31, 1983, has not yet been prepared.

[handwritten: 1983]

Assets	Net change increase (decrease)
Cash	*CA* $ 50,000
Accounts receivable, net	*CA* 76,000
Inventories	*CA* 37,000
Prepaid expenses	*CA* 1,000
Property, plant and equipment, net	64,000
Total assets	$228,000

[handwritten: PPE BB 45000 48000 63500 EB 60,500]

[handwritten: Acc. DEP BB 43,800 40,300 EB 3,500]

Liabilities	
Accounts payable	*CL* $(55,500)
Notes payable - current	*CL* (15,000)
Accrued expenses	*CL* 33,000
Bonds payable	(28,000)
Less: Unamortized bond discount	1,200
Total liabilities	(64,300)

[handwritten: STK 100,000 400,000 500,000]

Stockholders' Equity	
Common stock, $10 par value	500,000
Capital contributed in excess of par value	200,000
Retained earnings	(437,700)
Appropriation of retained earnings for possible future inventory price decline	30,000
Total stockholders' equity	292,300
Total liabilities and stockholders' equity	$228,000

[handwritten: PD. IN 40,000 160,000 200,000]

[handwritten: R.E. 560,000 30,000 172,300 DIV. 20,000 437,700]

[handwritten:
CA	CL
50,000	55,500
76,000	15,000
37,000	70,500
1,000	-33,000
+164,000	
37500	37,500
201,500 NET INCREASE	
]

Additional Information:

1. The net income for the year ended December 31, 1983, was $172,300. There were no extraordinary items. *[handwritten: 172,300 SOURCE]*

2. During the year ended December 31, 1983, uncollectible accounts receivable of $26,400 were written off by a charge to allowance for doubtful accounts.

3. A comparison of property, plant and equipment as of the end of each year follows:

	December 31, 1983	1982	Net increase (decrease)
Property, plant and equipment	$570,500	$510,000	$60,500
Less: Accumulated depreciation	224,500	228,000	(3,500)
Property, plant and equipment, net	$346,000	$282,000	$64,000

During 1983, machinery was purchased at a cost of $45,000. In addition, machinery that was acquired in 1976 at a cost of $48,000 was sold for $3,600. At the date of sale, the machinery had an undepreciated cost of $4,200. The remaining increase in property, plant and equipment resulted from the acquisition of a tract of land for a new plant site.

4. The bonds payable mature at the rate of $28,000 every year. *[handwritten: 28,000 USE]*

5. In January 1983, the Company issued an additional 10,000 shares of its common stock at $14 per share upon the exercise of outstanding stock options held by key employees. In May 1983, the Company declared and issued a 5% stock dividend on its outstanding stock. During the year, a cash dividend was paid on the common stock. On December 31, 1983, there were 840,000 shares of common stock outstanding.

6. The appropriation of retained earnings for possible future inventory price decline was provided by a charge against retained earnings, in anticipation of an expected future drop in the market related to goods in inventory. *[handwritten: N/A]*

Required:

a. *[handwritten: ①]* Prepare a statement of changes in financial position for the year ended December 31, 1983, based upon the information presented above. The statement should be prepared using a working capital format.

b. *[handwritten: ②]* Prepare a schedule of changes in working capital for the year 1983.

c. The fixed asset and accumulated depreciation accounts need to be analyzed separately. The T-account analysis below, of the fixed asset account, indicates working capital was used to purchase a $45,000 machine and land for $63,500. The sale of the old machine for $3,600 was a source of working capital (since the $3,600 is included as a separate source, the $600 loss, i.e., the book value was $4,200, must be added to income so as not to include the transaction twice). The T-account analysis of the accumulated depreciation account indicates 1983 depreciation of $40,300.

Fixed Assets				Acc. Dep.		
New machine	45,000		Old machine	43,800		
Old machine		48,000	1983 deprec.		40,300	
Land	63,500		Net decrease	3,500		
Net increase	60,500					

d. The bonds payable decreased by $28,000 which is a use of working capital. The related bond discount amortization, $1,200, is a charge in the income statement but does not use working capital. Therefore, bond discount must be added back to net income in the process of determining working capital provided by operations.

e. T-account analysis should be used to analyze the changes in common stock, paid-in capital, and retained earnings accounts. In January, stock with a par value of $100,000 was sold. This brought the shares outstanding to 800,000 ($10 par value), before the 5% stock dividend increased the number outstanding to 840,000. The increase of $200,000 in the premium account is made up of $40,000 in excess of par value from the sale of 10,000 shares and $160,000 from the stock dividend. Thus, $140,000 of working capital is provided by the sale of stock. The stock dividend is not a financing or investment transaction, and thus is not included within the "all financial resources" concept of APB 19.

Stock			Paid-in Capital			Retained Earnings		
Stock sale	100,000		Stock sale	40,000		Stock div.	560,000	
Stock dividend	400,000		Stock dividend	160,000		1983 income		172,300
1983 increase	500,000		1983 increase	200,000		Appropriation	30,000	
						Cash div.	20,000	
						1983 decrease	437,700	

f. The stock dividend resulted in a $560,000 debit to retained earnings. The appropriation of retained earnings (also not a financing or investment transaction) resulted in a debit of $30,000. If the $172,300 of 1983 income is subtracted from the $590,000 ($560,000 + $30,000) of debits, only a $417,700 decrease is obtained and a $437,700 decrease in retained earnings occurred. Thus, the difference of $20,000 is a cash dividend, as is implied in paragraph number five of the problem.

Fifth, prepare the solution. Remember that the statement should begin with a three-line heading: company name, statement title, and period covered. The sources of working capital as noted above should be listed first. Add depreciation and bond amortization to net income to determine working capital provided from operations.

After subtotalling the sources of working capital, list the uses of working capital per the above. The net change in working capital, $201,500, is the same as the figure previously determined as the net change in individual working capital items. The unofficial answer follows.

Sixth, when the changes per the statement of changes in financial position equal the change in working capital per the subsidiary schedule, you probably have a substantially correct solution. You should also include the T-account analyses prepared above as part of your solution.

If on the other hand, your change in working capital per the statement of changes does not equal the change per your subsidiary schedule, rework your subsidiary schedule and the statement of changes as time permits. Remember, do not go beyond the maximum time allowed. Also, you may find it better to go on and work another problem and come back and get a fresh start if time permits. If you are forced to turn in an incomplete or incorrect solution you probably are missing only one or two items (or you made a math error). Thus, you probably still scored 75% or better on the problem.

a.

The Sodium Company
Statement of Changes in
Financial Position
For the Year Ended December 31, 1983

Sources of working capital:

From operations:		
Net income		$172,300
Add: Charges not requiring an		
outlay of working capital:		
Depreciation	$ 40,300	
Amortization of bond dis-		
count	1,200	
Loss on sale of machinery		
(total proceeds shown below)	600	
Working capital provided from		
operations		214,400
Proceeds from sale of machinery		3,600
Proceeds from exercise of common		
stock options		140,000
Total sources of working capital		358,000

Uses of working capital:

Cash dividends on common stock	20,000
Purchase of machinery	45,000
Purchase of land	63,500
Decrease in bonds payable	28,000
Total uses of working capital	156,500
Increase in working capital during year	$201,500

b.

The Sodium Company
Schedule of Changes in Working Capital
For the Year Ended December 31, 1983

Increase in current assets:

Cash	$ 50,000
Accounts receivable	76,000
Inventories	37,000
Prepaid expenses	1,000
Total increase in current assets	164,000

Increase (decrease) in current liabilities:

Accounts payable	(55,500)
Notes payable—current	(15,000)
Accrued expenses	33,000
Net decrease in current liabilities	(37,500)
Increase in working capital during year	$201,500

INVENTORY

Inventory is used to designate those items of tangible personal property which are: (1) held for sale in the ordinary course of business, (2) in process of production for such sale, or (3) to be used currently in the production of items for sale (ARB 43). Inventory has financial significance because it affects both the income statement and the balance sheet; it is generally the primary source of revenues and represents a material asset. Because of the amount of the costs involved, inventory management is also an important topic and is tested on the exam. This issue is covered in Module 38 (Quantitative Methods). The primary accounting questions regarding inventory are:

1. Ownership of goods. Which items are to be included in inventory?
2. Cost. Which costs are to be assigned to inventory?
3. Cost flow assumption. Which cost flow assumption should be adopted?
4. Valuation. How should the market value of inventories be reflected?

The basic authoritative pronouncement covering inventories is ARB 43, Chapter 4; study the outline before proceeding through this module.

A. Determining Inventory and Cost of Goods Sold

Inventory value is a function of two variables:

1) The number of units
2) The pricing of the units

Item	No. of units	Price	Extension
A	3	$6	$18
B	4	7	28
C	5	8	40
		Total Value	$86

Inventory is determined by using one of two types of systems:

1) Periodic
2) Perpetual

Under the periodic system, inventory is counted periodically and then priced. The ending inventory is usually recorded in the cost of goods sold (CGS) entry.

Ending inventory	xx	
CGS	(plug)	
Beginning inventory		xx
Purchases		xx

CGS = Purchases - (the change in inventory). For example, if ending inventory decreases, all of the purchases and some of the inventory have been sold. If ending inventory increases, all of the purchases have not been sold.

Alternatively, the perpetual inventory system keeps a running total of the units on hand (and possibly their value) by recording all increases and decreases as they occur. When inventory is purchased, the inventory account, rather than purchases, is debited. As inventory is sold, the following entry is recorded:

CGS   (cost)
        Inventory   (cost)

B. Inventory Valuation and Cost-Flow Methods

1) Specific identification	10) Base stock
2) Weighted-average	11) Dollar-value LIFO
3) Simple average	12) Retail dollar-value LIFO
4) Moving average	13) Standard costs
5) Lower of cost or market	14) Direct costing
6) Gross profit	15) Market
7) Retail method	16) Cost apportionment by relative sales value
8) First-in, first-out	
9) Last-in, first-out	17) Long-term contracts

1. Specific Identification

Seller determines which item is sold. For example, a seller has four machines costing $260, $260, $180, $110 (the latter were purchased on sale). When seller sells a machine, s/he can sell any machine (and charge the appropriate amount to CGS). Significant dollar value items are frequently accounted for by specific identification.

2. Weighted-Average

Seller averages cost of all items on hand and purchased during the period. Items on hand and CGS are priced at this average cost. For example:

	Units	Cost
Beginning inventory	100	$200 (2.00 unit)
Purchase 1	150	315 (2.10 unit)
Purchase 2	50	85 (1.70 unit)
	300	$600

Weighted-average cost $600 / 300 = $2.00 unit

3. Simple Average

Seller does not weight average for units purchased or in beginning inventory, e.g., the above $2.00, $2.10, and $1.70 unit costs would be averaged to $1.93. The method is fairly accurate if all purchases, production runs, and beginning inventory quantities are equal.

4. Moving Average

Cost recalculated after every addition of merchandise if the addition is not priced at the average. In the weighted-average example if 50 items were sold before purchase 1 and purchase 2, the calculations would be:

	Units on hand	Purchases (at cost)	Sale (at cost)	Total cost	Inventory unit cost
Beginning inventory	100			$200	$2.00
Sale 1 (50 units)	50		$100	100	2.00
Purchase 1 (150 units)	200	$315		415	2.075
Sale 2 (50 units)	150		103.75*	311.25	2.075
Purchase 2 (50 units)	200	85		396.25	1.98**

```
 *   50 x $2.075
**   $396.25 / 200
```

Sales do not change the unit price, because they are taken out of inventory at the average price. Moving average may only be used in perpetual systems which account for changes in value with each change in inventory (and not in systems only accounting for units).

5. Lower of Cost or Market

"A departure from the cost basis of pricing the inventory is required when the utility of the goods is no longer as great as its cost" (ARB 43, Chapter 4, para 8)

Paragraph 9 of Chapter 4 states the lower of cost or market rule.

a. Determine market

Market is replacement cost limited to

1) Ceiling -- which is net realizable value (selling price less selling costs and costs to complete)
2) Floor -- which is net realizable value less normal profit

Note, if replacement cost is above net realizable value, market is net realizable value. Likewise, market is net realizable value minus normal profit if replacement cost is less than net realizable value minus normal profit.

b. Determine cost

Note that the floor and ceiling have nothing to do with cost.

c. Select the lower of cost or market for either each individual item or for inventory as a whole (compute total market and total cost, and select lower)

Lower of Cost or Market Example

Item	Cost	Replacement Cost	Selling Price	Selling Cost	Normal Profit
A	$10.50	$10.25	$15.00	$2.50	$2.50
B	5.75	5.25	8.00	1.50	1.00
C	4.25	4.75	5.50	1.00	1.50

Item A -- Market is replacement cost, $10.25, because it is between $10.00 (floor) and $12.50 (ceiling). Lower of cost or market is $10.25.

Item B -- Market is the floor, $5.50 ($8.00 - $1.50 - $1.00). Lower of cost or market is $5.50.

Item C -- Market is the ceiling, $4.50 ($5.50 - $1.00). Lower of cost or market is $4.25.

Observations about AICPA rule

1) The floor limitation on market prevents recognition of more than normal profit in future periods (if you use the market figure)

2) The ceiling limitation on market prevents recognition of a loss in future periods (if you use the market figure)

3) Cost or market applied to individual items will always be as low as and usually lower than cost or market applied to the inventory as a whole. They will be the same when all items at market or all items at cost are lower.

4) Once inventory has been written down there can be no recovery from the write-down until the units are sold. Recall that this differs from marketable securities where recoveries of prior write-downs are required to be taken into the income stream.

Methods of recording the write-down

If market is less than cost at the end of any period there are two methods available to record the market decline. The entry to establish the ending inventory can be made using the lower of cost or market figure. The difficulty with this procedure is that it overstates cost of goods sold by the amount of the market loss and thus fails to disclose the market loss separately.

An alternative treatment is to debit the inventory account for the actual cost (not market) of goods on hand, and then to make the following entry to give separate recognition to the market decline:

Loss due to market decline	xx	
Inventory		xx

These two alternatives are illustrated below for the following data:

Beginning inventory	$20
Purchases	80
Ending inventory (cost)	40
Ending inventory (market)	30

	Loss Hidden	Loss Disclosed
BI	$ 20	$ 20
+ Purchases	80	80
Goods available	100	100
- EI	30	40
CGS	70	60
Loss due to market decline	0	10

Notice that in both cases the total expense is $70, but that in the loss disclosed case full disclosure of the period's events is provided.

6. Gross Profit

Inventory is computed by reducing sales to cost of sales by deducting gross profit from sales. Comparison of cost of sales to purchases gives the change in inventory.

If the gross profit rate is 25% of sales and inventory is $30,000 at the beginning of period A, what are the ending inventories for consecutive periods A, B, and C?

Period	Sales	Purchases
A	$60,000	$40,000
B	70,000	50,000
C	80,000	60,000

A. Cost of sales is $45,000. A negative change in inventory of $5,000 reduces the inventory to $25,000.
B. Cost of sales of $52,500 reduces the inventory from $25,000 to $22,500
C. Cost of sales is $60,000 not changing inventory; it remains at $22,500

Conversion of gross profit rates on cost and retail.

Cost	Retail
1/2 (50%)	1/3 (33%)
1/3 (33%)	1/4 (25%)
1/4 (25%)	1/5 (20%)
1/5 (20%)	1/6 (16%)

Note that you just add one to the denominator of the gross profit rate on cost, if the numerator of the gross profit ratio is one [otherwise add the numerator to the denominator, e.g., 2/5 (40%); 2/7 (29%)]. Always be cautious about gross profit rates (on cost or retail).

7. Retail Method

Inventory is counted at retail value and then reduced to cost by a cost ratio. A "conservative" retail method adds markups, but not markdowns in determining the cost ratio, e.g.:

	Cost	Retail	
Beginning inventory	x	x	
+Purchases	x	x	
+Markups		x	
Goods available	x	xx	
−Sales		x	
−Markdowns		x	
Ending inventory		x	Multiplied by

$$\frac{COST}{RETAIL} \text{ ratio} = EI \text{ at cost}$$

The goods available ratio (x/xx) provides the cost ratio. The retail inventory method can be calculated to approximate FIFO, FIFO LCM, average, average LCM, LIFO, or LIFO LCM inventory methods. LIFO LCM is not acceptable for tax purposes. Which of these approximations is obtained depends upon the numbers which are used to calculate the COST/RETAIL ratio.

To obtain valuations at cost, the goods available at retail should include both markups and markdowns in the calculation of the percentage. To obtain LCM valuations, markdowns are excluded from the goods available at retail, thus inflating the denominator of the ratio and making the ratio smaller or more conservative.

The average cost ratio obviously would include the BI in the ratio, while a FIFO ratio ignores the BI and includes only the purchases in the calculation. The FIFO and average ratios may be dichotomized as shown below:

	Include BI	Exclude BI
Include markups and markdowns	Average cost	FIFO cost
Include markups but exclude markdowns	Average LCM	FIFO LCM

The FIFO or average retail EI is the EI at retail multiplied by the respective COST/RETAIL percentages. Remember that the average LCM calculation is frequently referred to as the conventional retail inventory method.

The LIFO calculation also uses the FIFO percentages if the inventory is increasing. The percentage is used to calculate the value of the incremental layer only - not the value of the whole inventory. The value of the incremental layer is added to the BI at cost to establish the EI at LIFO. If the EI at retail is less than the BI at retail, then the reduction in the LIFO inventory takes place at the COST/RETAIL ratio of the BI.

The following example which assumes no additional markups or markdowns, will illustrate the LIFO calculations.

	Cost	Retail
BI	$20	$ 40
Purchases	30	90
		$130
Sales		80
EI at retail		$ 50

Since the EI at retail has increased, the BI is still unused under a LIFO assumption and a new layer of $10 at retail has been added to the inventory. Since the layer was established from purchases of the current period, the FIFO percentage of 30/90 is used to convert the $10 retail layer to the new cost layer of $3.33. The EI at LIFO will be $20 + 3.33, or $23.33.

If the EI at retail had been $30, not $50, then the EI at cost would have been $30 x (20/40), or $15. The purchases of the current period would be irrelevant since it is assumed they are all sold and cannot be in inventory.

8. First-In, First-Out (FIFO)

The goods received earliest are sold first.

       in   ⟶   goods   out   ⟶

In a period of rising prices, cost of goods sold is made up of the earlier, lower-priced goods resulting in a larger profit (relative to LIFO). The ending inventory is made up of more recent purchases and thus is at a more current value (relative to LIFO) on the balance sheet. It should be noted that this cost-flow assumption may be used even when it does not match the physical flow of goods.

9. <u>Last-In, First-Out (LIFO)</u>

The goods received last are sold first.

Thus, the cost of goods sold is relatively current (resulting in the matching of current costs with sales). Again, this cost-flow assumption might not parallel the physical flow of goods.

LIFO is widely adopted, because it is acceptable for tax purposes, i.e., in periods of rising prices it reduces tax liability due to the lower reported income. LIFO smoothes out fluctuations in the income stream relative to FIFO, because it matches current costs with current revenues. Its disadvantages are that it results in large profits if inventory decreases and early layers are included in cost of sales. If LIFO is used for tax purposes, it must be used for financial reporting. Inventory layers may be added using the (1) earliest acquisition costs, (2) weighted-average unit cost for the period (unit LIFO method), or (3) latest acquisition costs.

LIFO may be applied individually to each item in inventory or it may be applied to inventory items grouped into pools. The inventory items in each pool must be <u>identical</u>. Once the pool is established, increases or decreases in inventory are determined by comparing the total number of units in the pool at the beginning of the period with the total number of units at the end of the period.

The advantage of using LIFO pools is that the company can make slight changes in the composition of its product without having to worry about liquidating the LIFO layers (matching old costs against current revenue). In addition, it lessens the accounting cost of applying the LIFO method. The disadvantage of using LIFO pools occurs because most companies are constantly changing their mix of products and production methods. These changes can result in new items being carried in inventory which are not identical to the inventory items in existing pools. Under these circumstances, the income tax regulations require that a new inventory pool be created to accommodate the new items. This results in additional expenditures of time and money. Furthermore, the addition of new items to inventory may indicate that the company is no longer using (purchasing) the items in the existing pools. If this is the case, a liquidation of LIFO layers can occur which will cause old costs (from the liquidated layers) to be matched against current revenues.

For example, a firm manufactures wooden desks and groups all types of wood used in manufacturing the desks into one inventory pool. The beginning inventory pool contained the following items:

Item	Number of Board Feet	Price Per Board Foot	Total Cost	
Oak	100	$10	$1,000	
Walnut	100	20	2,000	
Pine	200	5	1,000	
	400		$4,000	($10 [4000/400] per board foot)

At the end of year 1, the pool contained the following:

Item	Number of Board Feet	Price Per Board Foot	Total Cost
Oak	105	$15	$1,575
Walnut	95	25	2,375
Pine	210	8	1,680
	410		$5,630

Since the ending inventory increased by 10 board feet, a LIFO layer has been added.

As stated above, new LIFO layers can be costed at any of three methods. For this example we will assume that the weighted-average cost of the current year purchases was $13.

Year 1 ending inventory would be:

	Number of Board Feet		LIFO Cost Per Board Foot	Total Cost
Beginning inventory layer	400	x	$10	$4,000
Year 1 layer	10	x	13	130
	410			$4,130

Because of the increased cost of wood in year 2, the firm decides to change from making all wood desks to manufacturing steel desks trimmed with either oak or walnut. As a result of this decision, no more pine will be purchased and lesser amounts of oak and walnut will be carried in inventory.

At the end of year 2, the pool contained the following:

Item	Number of Board Feet	Price Per Board Foot	Total Cost
Oak	40	$16	$ 640
Walnut	50	26	1,300
	90		$1,940

Year 2 ending inventory would be:

	Number of Board Feet		LIFO Cost Per Board Foot	Total Cost
Beginning inventory layer	90	x	$10	$900

Therefore, because of a change in product composition, old inventory costs will be matched against current revenues in the income statement of year 2. Under the LIFO pooled approach, steel could not be included in the existing LIFO pool because it is not identical to the wood.

10. Base Stock

The base stock method is based on the theory that a minimal level of inventory is a "permanent" investment, i.e., it must be continually maintained. This "permanent" investment is then carried at its historical cost. The effect, in a period of rising prices, is to understate inventory (like LIFO). Some companies use this method for accounting purposes; however, base stock was ruled unconstitutional by the Supreme Court in a tax case in the mid-Thirties.

11. Dollar-Value LIFO

To apply LIFO, a firm must keep track of the number of original units and the number of units in each layer (increases by year since original purchase), and their respective prices. The cost of such recordkeeping for retail stores with numerous items (e.g., 5¢ & 10¢ stores) would far outweigh the ensuing tax benefits. A possible solution to this problem is dollar-value LIFO. Dollar-value LIFO prices "dollars of inventory" at "price levels" rather than pricing units of inventory at unit prices. The inventory is divided into different "pools" of similar items (in terms of interchangeability, type of material, or similarity in use) rather than identical items as under regular LIFO. As a result, a broader range of goods may be included in each pool, thus making it more difficult to erode previous LIFO layers.

Always remember that the individual layers in a dollar-value LIFO inventory are valued as follows:

$$\begin{array}{ccc} \$ \\ \text{value} \\ \text{LIFO} \end{array} = \begin{array}{c} \text{Inventory at} \\ \text{base prices} \end{array} \times \begin{array}{c} \text{Conversion} \\ \text{price index} \end{array}$$

In applying dollar-value LIFO, manufacturers develop their own indexes while retailers and wholesalers use published figures. In computing the conversion price index, the double extension technique is used, named so because each year the ending inventory is extended at both base-year prices and current-year prices. The index, computed as follows, measures the change in the inventory cost since the base year.

$$\frac{\text{EI at current prices}}{\text{EI at base-year prices}} = \begin{array}{c} \text{Conversion} \\ \text{price index} \end{array}$$

To illustrate the computation of the index, assume products A and B have base-year costs of $3 and $5 respectively, and at the end of the year, product A costs $3.20 and B, $5.75 with 2,000 and 800 units on hand respectively. The index for the year is 110%:

	End of Year Cost	÷	Base-Year Cost	=	Index
Product A	2,000 @ $3.20 = $ 6,400		2,000 @ $3 = $ 6,000		
Product B	800 @ $5.75 = $ 4,600		800 @ $5 = $ 4,000		
	$11,000	÷	$10,000	=	110%

Steps in dollar-value LIFO

1) Compute the conversion price index
2) Subtract the beginning inventory at base-year prices from the ending inventory at base-year prices to determine the

   a) New layer of inventory added, or
   b) The sale of inventory from existing layers (LIFO liquidation)

3) Determine value of new layer (if there is an increase at base-year prices) to be added or value of layers remaining (if there is a decrease at base-year prices)

For example, if the beginning inventory for year 3 was $110,000 at base-year prices (LIFO base of $100,000 + the $10,000 layer added in year 2) and the ending inventory was $125,000 at base-year prices, the increment in year 3 at base-year prices would be $15,000. This $15,000 increment would be valued at 120% (assumed) or $18,000. Thus, the base base and other layers would be valued at the "conversion price index" existing when the layers came into existence.

Base-Year Prices	x Index	= Extension
Year 1 (base) $100,000	1.00	$100,000
Year 2 layer 10,000	1.10	11,000
Year 3 layer 15,000	1.20	18,000
Ending inventory $125,000		$129,000

If the ending inventory at base-year prices decreases, the decrease is not valued at the current "conversion price index," but rather at the "conversion price index" when the layer came into existence.

For example, if the base-year ending inventory value at the end of year 4 in the above diagram were $105,000 in total, the inventory value would be $105,500. This would be a liquidation situation and the inventory would consist of remaining old layers including the LIFO base.

Base-Year Prices	x Index	= Extension
Year 1 (base) $100,000	1.00	$100,000
Year 2 layer 5,000	1.10	5,500
Ending inventory $105,000		$105,500

In solving problems where conversion price index numbers are given, the ending inventory is often given in total current-year dollars. In these cases, it is necessary to find the ending inventory at base-year prices by dividing the ending inventory by the conversion price index.

12. Retail Dollar-Value LIFO

This method couples the retail method with dollar-value LIFO. The dollar-value LIFO records are counted and maintained at retail with the conversion to cost by a COST/RETAIL ratio being made as a final step.

Retail dollar-value LIFO involves five steps which are enumerated below

a. Count the EI at current retail price and convert it to base period retail prices
b. Determine the BI at base period retail prices
c. Subtract "b" from "a" to determine the real change in inventory measured in terms of base period retail prices
d. If the inventory has increased, convert the real change in inventory at base year's retail prices to the real change in inventory at current year's retail prices by multiplying the quantity in "c" by the conversion price index
e. Determine the cost of the new layer by multiplying the quantity in "d" by the COST/RETAIL ratio for the current period

This new layer will be added to the BI at cost to establish the EI at cost. The following example will illustrate these steps:

		Cost	Retail
1)	BI	$26,900	$40,000

2) EI -- counted at ending retail prices = $44,100
3) COST/RETAIL ratio on current year purchases = 80%
4) The price level has increased from 100 to 105 during the year

The previously described steps are as follows for the above data:

a. $44,100 ÷ 1.05 = $42,000
b. $40,000
c. $42,000 - $40,000 = $2,000
d. $2,000 x 1.05 = $2,100
e. New layer at cost = $2,100 x 80% = $ 1,680
   BI at cost   26,900
   EI at LIFO cost $28,580

If the EI counted at ending retail prices had been $31,500, and all other data remained unchanged the previously described steps would yield the following:

a. $31,500 ÷ 1.05 = $30,000
b. $40,000
c. $30,000 - $40,000 = ($10,000)
d. $10,000 x 1.00 = $10,000
e. $10,000 x 26,900/40,000 = $ 6,725
   BI at LIFO   26,900
   Decrease in LIFO
     inventory   - 6,725
   EI at LIFO $20,175

Thus the decline in inventory cost is measured at the retail prices of the period when the BI (or liquidated layer) was established and converted using the COST/RETAIL ratio of the period when it was established (here it is assumed to be the beginning ratio of $26,900/$40,000).

13. Standard Costs

Standard costs are predetermined costs in a cost accounting system, generally used for control purposes. Inventory may be costed at standard only if variances are reasonable, i.e., not large. Large debit (unfavorable) variances would indicate inventory (and cost of sales) were undervalued, whereas large credit (favorable) variances would indicate inventory is overvalued.

14. Direct (Variable) Costing

Direct costing is not an acceptable method for valuing inventory (ARB 43, Chapter 4, para 5). Direct costing considers only variable costs as product costs and fixed production costs as period costs. In contrast, absorption costing considers both variable and fixed manufacturing costs as product costs. See Module 35 (Planning, Control, and Analysis) for further discussion.

15. Market

    Inventory can be valued at market when market is lower than cost. Occasionally, this will be above cost.

    a. Precious metals with a fixed market value
    b. Items such as in meatpacking where costs cannot be allocated and

        1) Quoted market prices exist
        2) Goods are interchangeable, e.g., agricultural commodities

16. Cost Apportionment By Relative Sales Value

    Basket purchases and similar situations require cost allocation based on relative value. For example a developer may spend $400,000 to acquire land, survey, curb and gutter, pave streets, etc. for a subdivision. Due to location and size, the lots may vary in selling price. If the total of all selling prices were $600,000, the developer could cost each lot at 2/3 (400/600; cost retail ratio) of its selling price.

17. Long-Term Construction Contracts. (See outline of ARB 45.)

    Long-term contracts are accounted for by the

    a. Completed-contract method--recognition of contract profit at contract completion. All costs are deferred until completion and then matched to revenues.

    b. Percentage-of-completion--recognition of contract profit during construction based on expected total profit and estimated progress in the current period

       In practice, various procedures are used to measure the extent of progress toward completion under the percentage-of-completion method, but the most widely used one is cost-to-cost which is based on the assumed relationship between a unit of input and productivity. Under cost-to-cost, the profit to recognize in the current period can be determined by the following formula:

$$\text{Profit formula} = \left(\frac{\text{Cost to date}}{\text{Total expected cost}} \times \text{Expected profit} \right) - \text{profit recognized in previous periods}$$

    The ledger account titles used in this discussion are unique to long-term construction contracts. In practice, there are numerous account titles for the same item (e.g., "billings on LT contracts" vs. "partial billings on construction in process") and various methodology for journalizing the same transactions (e.g., separate revenue and expense control accounts in lieu of "income on LT contracts"). The following example has been simplified to highlight the main concepts.

    EXAMPLE: Assume a $500,000 contract which requires three years to complete and incurs a total cost of $405,000. The following data pertain to the construction period.

		Year 1	Year 2	Year 3
Cumulative costs incurred to date		$150,000	$360,000	$405,000
Estimated costs yet to be incurred at year end		300,000	40,000	--
Progress billings made during year		200,000	200,000	100,000
Collections of billings		175,000	200,000	125,000

		Percentage of Completion		Completed Contract	
Year 1 Costs	Construction in progress	150,000		150,000	
	Cash		150,000		150,000
Year 1 Progress billings	Accounts receivable	200,000		200,000	
	Billings on LT contracts		200,000		200,000
Year 1 Cash collected	Cash	175,000		175,000	
	Accounts receivable		175,000		175,000
Year 1 Profit recognition*	Construction in progress	16,667		none	
	Income on LT contract		16,667		
Year 2 Costs	Construction in progress	210,000		210,000	
	Cash		210,000		210,000
Year 2 Progress billings	Accounts receivable	200,000		200,000	
	Billings on LT contracts		200,000		200,000
Year 2 Cash collected	Cash	200,000		200,000	
	Accounts receivable		200,000		200,000
Year 2 Profit recognition**	Construction in progress	73,333		none	
	Income on LT contract		73,333		
Year 3 Costs	Construction in progress	45,000		45,000	
	Cash		45,000		45,000
Year 3 Progress billings	Accounts receivable	100,000		100,000	
	Billings on LT contracts		100,000		100,000
Year 3 Cash collected	Cash	125,000		125,000	
	Accounts receivable		125,000		125,000
Final profit*** recognition	Billings on LT Contracts	500,000		500,000	
	Const. in progress		495,000		405,000
	Income on LT contract		5,000		95,000

$*\dfrac{150,000}{450,000}$ X $50,000 = $16,667 $**(\dfrac{360,000}{400,000}$ X 100,000) - 16,667 = $73,333

$***(\dfrac{405,000}{405,000}$ X 95,000) - 90,000 = $5,000

Summary of Accounts Used in Construction Accounting
(No loss expected or incurred)

Balance Sheet			*Income Statement*

Construction in Progress

(a)	(d)
(e)	(f)

A/P, Materials, etc.

	(a)

Income on LT Contracts

	(d)
	(e)
	(f)

Accounts Receivable

(b)	(c)

Billings on LT Contracts

(d)	(b)
(f)	

Explanation of Journal Entries

Both Methods	*Completed-Contract Method*	*Percentage-of-Completion Method*
(a) To record accumulated costs	(d) To record income upon completion	(e) To record recognition of interim income
(b) To record progress billings		(f) To record completion of project
(c) To record cash collections		

The "construction in progress" account is a cost accumulation account similar to "work in process" for job order costing, except that the percentage-of-completion method includes interim profits in the account. The "billings on LT contracts" account is similar to an unearned revenue account. The "construction in progress" account should be netted against the "billings on LT contracts" account on a project-by-project basis, resulting in net current assets and/or net current liabilities. Under the percentage-of-completion method in the above example, a net current asset of $50,000 [($150,000 + $16,667 + $210,000 + $73,333) - ($200,000 + $200,000)] would be reported at the end of year 2. A net current liability of $40,000 would result under the completed contract method [($200,000 + $200,000) - ($150,000 + $210,000)] for the same year.

Balance Sheet Classification*

Method Used	*Current Asset*	*Current Liability*
Both methods	projects where CIP at year-end** > billings	projects where billings > CIP at year-end**
Completed-contract		Estimated loss on uncompleted contract

*Evaluate and classify on a project-by-project basis.
Construction in progress including income (loss) recognized, **if percentage-of-completion method.

Contract Losses. In any year when a percentage-of-completion contract has an expected loss, the amount of the loss reported in that year is the total expected loss plus all profit previously recognized. For example, if the expected costs yet to be incurred at the end of year 2 were $148,000, the total expected loss is $8,000 [$500,000 - ($360,000 + $148,000)] and the total loss reported in year 2 would be $24,667 ($8,000 + $16,667). Similarly, under the completed-contract method, total expected losses are recognized as soon as they are estimated. The loss recognized is similar to that for percentage-of-completion except the amount is for the expected loss only ($8,000) because interim profits have not been recorded. Journal entries and a schedule (for percentage-of-completion) follow.

Journal entry at end of year 2	Percentage-of-Completion	Completed Contract
Loss on uncompleted LT contracts	24,667	8,000
Construction in progress	24,667	--
Estimated loss on uncompleted contract (reported as a current liability)	--	8,000

Profit or Loss Recognized on Contract
(Percentage-of-Completion Method)

	Year 1	Year 2	Year 3
Contract Price:	$500,000	$500,000	$500,000
Estimated Total Costs:			
Costs incurred to date	$150,000	$360,000	$504,000*
Estimated cost yet to be incurred	300,000	148,000	–
Estimated total costs for the three-year period, actual for year 3	$450,000	$508,000	$504,000
Estimated total income (loss) for three-year period, actual for year 3	$ 16,667	$ (8,000)	$ (4,000)
Income (loss) previously recognized	–	16,667	(8,000)
Amount of estimated income (loss) recognized in the current period, actual for year 3	$ 16,667	$ (24,667)	$ 4,000

*assumed

ARB 45 recommends the use of percentage-of-completion when estimates of cost to complete and of the extent of progress toward completion are dependable; otherwise use the completed-contract method. The advantage of percentage-of-completion is periodic recognition of income and the disadvantage is dependence on estimates. The advantage of the completed-contract method is that it is based on results, not estimates, and the disadvantage is that current performance is not reflected and income recognition may be irregular.

C. Losses on Purchase Commitments

Purchase commitments (PC) result from formal contracts to purchase specific quantities of goods at fixed prices in the future. When there is a decline in market value below the contract price at the balance sheet date and the contracts are noncancellable, an unrealized loss has occurred and, if material, should be recorded in the period of decline.

Estimated loss on PC	(excess of PC over mkt.)
Accrued loss on PC	(excess of PC over mkt.)

If further declines in market value are estimated to occur before delivery is made, the amount of the loss to be accrued should be increased to include this additional decline in market value per SFAS 5. The loss is taken to the income statement; the accrued loss on PC is a liability account and shown on the balance sheet.

When the item(s) is subsequently purchased:

Purchases	xx	
Accrued loss on PC		xx
Cash		xx

If a partial or full recovery occurs before the inventory is purchased, the accrued loss account would be reduced by the amount of the recovery. Likewise, an income statement account, "Recovery on Loss of PC," would be credited.

D. Items To Include in Inventory

Goods shipped FOB shipping point which are in transit should be included in the inventory of the buyer since title passes to the buyer when the carrier receives the goods. Goods shipped FOB destination should be included in the inventory of the seller until the goods are received by the buyer. The more complicated UCC rules concerning transfer of title should be used for the law portion, not the practice portion, of the exam. (See Module 8, Sales.)

E. Consignments

Consignors consign their goods to consignees who are sales agents of the consignors. Consigned goods remain the property of the consignor until sold. Therefore, any unsold goods (including a proportionate share of freight costs incurred in shipping the goods to the consignee) must be included in the consignor's inventory. The UCC rules concerning consignments should be used for the law portion, not the practice portion, of the exam. (See Module 10, Secured Transactions.)

FIXED ASSETS

Fixed assets are those expenditures for tangible property which will be used for a period of more than one year. Their cost, therefore, is deferred to future periods in compliance with the matching principle. All of the costs to get the assets in the existing condition and location are capitalized, e.g., cost of negotiations, sales taxes, finders fees, shipment, installation, breaking in, etc.

A. Capitalization of Interest

SFAS 34 (see outline and SFAS 58 and 62 also) requires the capitalization of interest as part of the cost of certain assets. Only assets which require a period of time to be prepared for use qualify for interest capitalization. These include assets constructed for sale produced as discrete projects (e.g., ships) and assets constructed for a firm's own use. For example, a building purchased by an entity would not qualify, but one constructed over a period of time would. Other assets that do not qualify include those in use or ready for use and ones not being used in the earnings activities of a firm (e.g., idle land). Inventories routinely manufactured or repetitively produced in large quantities do not qualify, even if a long maturation period is involved (e.g., tobacco and whiskey).

Only interest costs actually incurred during construction are eligible for capitalization, including amounts resulting from the amortization of any discount, premium, or issue costs. No imputed cost of equity capital is included. The amount to be capitalized is:

$$\left(\begin{array}{c}\text{Average accumulated expenditures}\\\text{during construction}\end{array}\right) \text{ X } \left(\text{Interest Rate}\right) \text{ X } \left(\begin{array}{c}\text{Construction}\\\text{Period}\end{array}\right)$$

The interest rate used is the rate on specific borrowings for the asset, or a weighted average of other borrowings when a specific rate is not available. Capitalized interest should be compounded. This is usually accomplished by including the interest capitalized in a previous period in the calculation of average accumulated expenditures of subsequent periods. Furthermore, noninterest bearing payables (e.g., trade payables and accruals) are excluded in determining these expenditures. In practice, both the weighted average interest rate and the average accumulated expenditures have been computed on the following bases: monthly, quarterly, semi-annual, and annual. The interest capitalization period begins when, and continues as long as, all three of the following conditions are met:

2 6

1) Expenditures for the asset have been made
2) Activities necessary to get the asset ready for its intended use are in progress
3) Interest cost is being incurred

The period ends when the asset is substantially complete. Brief interruptions and delays do not suspend interest capitalization, while suspension of the activities will. In no case should the amount capitalized exceed the interest actually incurred.

As an example, assume a company has been constructing an asset which qualifies for interest capitalization. By the beginning of July, $3,000,000 had been spent on the asset; an additional $800,000 was spent during July. During the month, the company had the following debt outstanding:

1) A loan of $2,000,000 specifically for financing the asset. Interest of 1% per month ($20,000).
2) A note payable of $1,500,000. Interest of 1 1/2% per month ($22,500).
3) Bonds payable of $1,000,000. Interest of 1% per month ($10,000).

The amount of interest to be capitalized during July is computed below:

Average accumulated expenditures

($3,000,000 + $3,800,000) ÷ 2 = $3,400,000

Interest cost capitalized

$2,000,000 x 1%	=	$20,000	
1,400,000 x 1.3%*	=	18,200	
$3,400,000		$38,200	interest capitalized

*Average rate on other borrowings:

$$\frac{\$22,500 + \$10,000}{\$1,500,000 + \$1,000,000} = 1.3\%$$

Journal Entry:

Asset	38,200	
Interest Expense		38,200

Note that the specific rate is used when available, but an average rate on other borrowings is used for any expenditures ($1,400,000) above the specific amount borrowed ($2,000,000). Interest on expenditures made to acquire land on which a building is to be constructed qualify for interest capitalization. The capitalization period begins when activities necessary to construct the building commence and ends when the building is substantially complete. Interest so capitalized becomes part of the cost of the building. Thus, it is charged to expense as the building is depreciated.

Frequently, the funds borrowed to finance the construction project are temporarily invested until needed. Per FASB Technical Bulletin 81-5, the interest revenue earned on these funds must be recognized and may not be offset against the interest expense to be capitalized.

B. Self Construction Costs

All direct costs (labor, materials, and variable overhead) should be capitalized. A controversy exists, however, with regard to the capitalization of fixed overhead. Proponents call for charging assets under construction with their fair share of fixed overhead; not to do so would penalize the operating results of the present period, they argue.

The argument against allocating fixed overhead to self constructed assets is that the cost of the assets is only the incremental cost. This is quite correct if the asset is constructed when operations are less than at full capacity, i.e., the asset construction does not prevent normal production from taking place.

Gains and losses on self construction (by comparison of construction costs with outside costs) are not normally recognized. In the case, however, that the cost of self construction exceeds the market value (replacement cost from an outside source) by a material amount, a writedown should be taken.

C. Nonmonetary Exchanges

Study the outline of APB 29. Nonmonetary exchanges are generally to be recorded at fair market value (of asset given up or asset received if "more clearly evident") with gains (losses) recognized. There are some exceptions. Accounting for nonmonetary exchanges is summarized below:

Situation	Accounting Method
A. Fair value is determinable	
1. Dissimilar assets 2. Similar assets	Fair value method

a. Economic loss
      b. Economic gain (no boot received)
      c. Economic gain (boot received)
	Fair value method
	Book value method
	Hybrid method

B. Fair value not determinable	Book value method

One important point to note is that under all methods, in all situations, losses are recognized in full. The special accounting methods apply only to certain gains.

Situation A-1. Dissimilar assets. When dissimilar assets are exchanged, it is assumed that the earnings process is complete. Normal accounting procedures are followed. The asset received is recorded at the fair value of the asset surrendered, and any gain (loss) is recognized. For example, assume a company trades a machine with a fair market value (FMV) of $12,000 (cost, $10,000; accumulated depreciation, $3,000) for land.

Land	$12,000	(FMV)
Accumulated depreciation	3,000	
Machine	$10,000	
Gain on exchange	5,000	(FMV-NBV)

    Situation A-2(a). Similar assets (loss). When similar assets are exchanged, it is assumed that the earnings process is <u>not</u> complete, and gains are <u>not</u> recognized. However, a conservative approach is taken and <u>losses are recognized</u> in full. Therefore, in a loss situation, the asset received is recorded at fair value. For example, assume a machine with a FMV of $5,000 (cost, $10,000; accumulated depreciation, $3,000) is traded for a similar machine.

Machine (new)	$5,000	(FMV)
Accumulated depreciation	3,000	
Loss on exchange	2,000	(NBV-FMV)
Machine (old)	$10,000	

    Situation A-2(b). Similar assets (gain, no boot received). Gains are not generally recognized when similar assets are exchanged because the earnings process is not complete. The asset received is recorded at the book value of the asset relinquished. For example, assume a machine with a FMV of $12,000 (cost, $10,000; accumulated depreciation, $3,000) is traded for a similar machine.

Machine (new)	$7,000	
Accumulated depreciation	3,000	
Machine (old)	$10,000	

There are two ways to compute the amount at which the new machine is recorded.

    1) Net book value of the machine given up ($10,000 - $3,000)
    2) FMV of new machine ($12,000) less gain not recognized ($5,000)

Also note that if boot is <u>paid</u>, the same procedure is followed.

    Situation A-2(c). Similar assets (gain, boot received). When similar assets are exchanged and boot is received, part of the gain realized is recognized. The logic is described below:

Given	Received	Transaction is	Gain is
Old asset	New asset	Part exchange	Partially <u>not</u> recognized
	Cash	Part sale	Partially recognized

The portion of the gain recognized is the portion relating to the "sale" part of the transaction, i.e., the portion which relates to the boot.

$$\left(\frac{\text{Boot}}{\text{Boot + FMV of Asset Received}} \right) \left(\text{Total Gain} \right) = \text{Gain Recognized}$$

For example, assume a machine with a FMV of $12,000 (cost, $10,000; accumulated depreciation, $3,000) is traded for a similar machine and $4,000 cash:

Cash	$4,000	
Machine (new)	4,667	
Accumulated depreciation	3,000	
Machine (old)		$10,000
Gain on exchange		1,667

The total gain realized is $5,000 ($12,000 FMV of old machine less $7,000 NBV given up). However, only the portion relating to the boot is recognized:

$$\left(\frac{\$4,000}{\$4,000 + \$8,000*}\right)\left(\$5,000\right) \quad = \quad \underline{\$1,667}$$

*[$12,000 FMV of old machine less $4,000 cash (boot) received]

There are two ways to compute the amount at which the new machine is recorded:

1) Net book value of machine given up, less cash received, plus gain recognized

   $7,000 - $4,000 + $1,667 = $4,667

2) FMV of new machine ($8,000) less gain not recognized ($3,333)

Situation B. Fair value not determinable. When the fair values of the assets exchanged are not determinable, a gain (loss) cannot be computed. Therefore, the book value method is used. The asset received is recorded at the book value of the asset relinquished, and no gain (loss) is recognized.

D. Purchase of Groups of Fixed Assets

   Cost should be allocated based on relative market value as in inventory.

   $$(\text{cost of all assets acquired}) \ \text{x} \ \frac{\text{Market value of A}}{\text{Market value of all assets acquired}}$$

   EXAMPLE: Purchase of Asset 1 with a FMV of $60,000, Asset 2 with a FMV of $120,000, and Asset 3 with a FMV of $20,000 all for $150,000 cash.

	FMV	Relative FMV	x	Total Cost	=	Allocated Cost
Asset 1	$ 60,000	60/200		$150,000		$45,000
Asset 2	120,000	120/200		150,000		90,000
Asset 3	20,000	20/200		150,000		15,000
Total FMV	$200,000					

   Journalized:

Asset 1	$45,000	
Asset 2	90,000	
Asset 3	15,000	
Cash		$150,000

E. Capital Versus Revenue Expenditures

Capital expenditures and revenue expenditures are charges that are incurred after the acquisition cost has been determined and the related fixed asset is in operation.

Capital expenditures are not normal, recurring expenses; they benefit the operations of more than one period. The cost of major rearrangements of assets to increase efficiency is an example of a capital expenditure.

Revenue expenditures are normal recurring expenditures. However, some expenditures that meet the test for capital expenditures are expensed because they are immaterial, e.g., less than $50.

Expenditures to improve the efficiency or extend the asset life should be capitalized and charged to future periods. A subtle distinction is sometimes made between an improvement in efficiency and an extension of the asset life. Some accountants feel improvements in efficiency should be charged to the asset account, and improvements extending the asset life should be charged to the accumulated depreciation account. The rationale is that improvements extending the asset life will need to be depreciated over an extended period of time, requiring revision of depreciation schedules.

The chart on the following page summarizes the appropriate treatment of expenditures related to fixed assets.

F. Depreciation

Depreciation is the annual charge to income for asset use during the period. This is simply a means of spreading asset costs to periods in which the assets produce revenue. Essentially, the "depreciation base" is spread over the asset's useful life (period during which it produces revenue). The objective is to match asset cost with revenue produced. The depreciation base is cost

> plus installation costs
> running in costs
> removal costs
> etc.
> less salvage value

The useful life can be limited by:

1) Technological change
2) Normal deterioration
3) Physical usage

COSTS SUBSEQUENT TO ACQUISITION OF PROPERTY, PLANT, AND EQUIPMENT

Type of Expenditure / Characteristics	Normal Accounting Treatment			
	Expense When Incurred	Capitalize		Other
		Charge to Asset	Charge to Accum. Deprec.	
1. Additions				
• Extensions, enlargements, or expansions made to an existing asset		X		
2. Repairs and Maintenance				
a. Ordinary				
• Recurring, relatively small expenditures				
1. Maintain normal operating condition	X			
2. **Do not** add materially to use value	X			
3. **Do not** extend useful life	X			
b. Extraordinary (major)				
• Not recurring, relatively large expenditures				
1. Primarily increase the use value		X		
2. Primarily extend the useful life			X	
3. Replacements and betterments				
• Major component of asset is removed and replaced with the same type of component with comparable performance capabilities (replacement) or a different type of component having superior performance capabilities (betterment)				
a. Book value of old component is known				• Remove old asset cost and accum. deprec. • Recognize any loss (or gain) on old asset • Charge asset for replacement component
b. Book value of old component is **not** known				
1. Primarily extends useful life			X	
2. Primarily increases the use value		X		
4. Reinstallations and Rearrangements				
• Provide greater efficiency in production or reduce production costs				
1. Material costs, benefits extend into future accounting periods		X		
2. No measureable future benefit	X			

The first two indicate depreciation is a function of time whereas the third indicates depreciation is a function of the level of activity. Other depreciation methods include retirement, replacement, group, composite, etc.

Depreciation methods based on time are:

1) Straight-line
2) Accelerated

    a) Declining balance (DB)

       1] Most common is double-declining balance (DDB)

    b) Sum-of-the-years'-digits (SYD)

3) Present value

    a) Sinking fund
    b) Annuity

Straight-line and accelerated depreciation are illustrated by the following example: $10,000 asset, 4-year life, $2,000 salvage value.

Year	Straight line	DDB	SYD
1	$2,000	$5,000	$3,200
2	$2,000	$2,500	$2,400
3	$2,000	$ 500	$1,600
4	$2,000	--	$ 800

Straight line $$\frac{\$10,000 - \$2,000}{4}$$

DDB   Twice the straight line rate (2 X 25%) times the net book value at beginning of each year, but not below salvage value (salvage value is not deducted for depreciation base).

SYD   4/10*, 3/10, 2/10, 1/10 of ($10,000 - $2,000).

$$\frac{*n(n + 1)}{2} = \frac{4 \times 5}{2} = 10$$

Physical usage depreciation is based on activity, e.g., machine hours, or output, e.g., finished widgets.

$$\frac{\text{Annual}}{\text{depreciation}} = \frac{\text{Current activity or output}}{\text{Total expected activity or output}} \times \text{Depreciation base}$$

EXAMPLE: A machine costs $60,000. The machine's total output is expected to be 500,000 units. If 100,000 units are produced in the first year, $12,000 of depreciation would be incurred (100/500 x $60,000).

Note that physical usage depreciation results in a varying charge, i.e., not constant. Also physical usage depreciation is based on asset activity rather than expiration of time.

Present value depreciation is a depreciation method wherein the rate of return on investment remains constant. Utilities and other rate-regulated industries may benefit by constant rates of return.

$$\frac{\text{NI from asset}}{\text{Book value of asset}}$$

Assuming a constant cash flow from the asset, the depreciation charge must be increasing in nature, because the book value of the asset is decreasing. Two methods involving time value of money formulas (annuity and sinking fund) may be used to compute PV depreciation. Both methods result in the same depreciation; one is computed by the present value of annuity formula and the other is computed with the future value of an annuity formula.

Note that increasing depreciation charges is contrary to straight-line and ac-celerated depreciation as illustrated by the following graph.

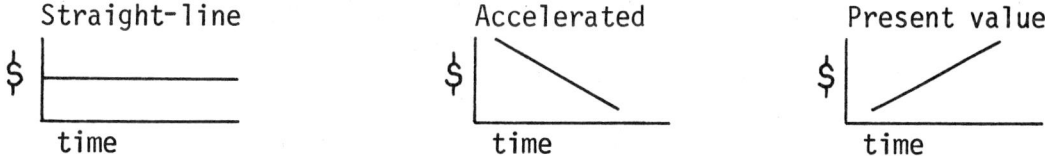

Accelerated depreciation is justified by:
  1) Book value approximates market value
  2) Increased productivity when asset is new
  3) Increasing maintenance charges with age

Little justification, however, can be given for present-value depreciation other than from a capital budgeting and rate regulation viewpoint.

Retirement depreciation is a method wherein the cost of an asset is charged to expense the period in which it is retired. Replacement depreciation is a method wherein the original cost is carried in the accounts and cost of replacement is ex-pensed in the period of replacement.

Composite (group) depreciation averages the service life of a number of prop-erty units and depreciates the group as if it were a single unit. The term "group" is used when the assets are similar; "composite" when they are dissimilar. The depreciation rate is the following ratio.

$$\frac{\text{Sum of SL depreciation of individual assets}}{\text{Total asset cost}}$$

Thus composite depreciation is a weighted average of a group of assets - usually of a similar nature, expected life, etc.

EXAMPLE: Three types of assets (A, B, and C) are depreciated under the composite method.

Asset Type	Asset Cost	Salvage Value	Depreciation Base	Useful Life (Yrs.)	SL Annual Depreciation
A	$ 45,000	$15,000	$ 30,000	5	$ 6,000
B	90,000	50,000	40,000	4	10,000
C	145,000	25,000	120,000	3	40,000
	$280,000	$90,000	$190,000		$56,000

$$\text{Depreciation or composite rate} = \frac{\$56,000}{\$280,000} = 20\%$$

Composite life = 3.39 years ($190,000 ÷ $56,000)

Note that the composite life is the depreciation base divided by the annual depreciation. Depreciation is recorded until the book value of the composite group is depreciated to the salvage value of the then remaining assets. As assets are retired the composite group salvage value is reduced. Also note that gains and losses are not recognized on disposal, i.e., gains and losses are netted into accumulated depreciation. This latter practice also affects the length of time required to reduce the book value (cost less accumulated depreciation) to the group salvage value. The entry to record a retirement is:

Cash, other consideration	(amount received)
Accumulated depreciation	(plug)
Asset	(original cost)

Changes in Depreciation. The exam frequently tests changes in depreciation due to changes in expected useful life and salvage value. Make the change prospectively from the beginning of the year in which the change in estimate is made. The procedure for straight-line depreciation is:

1) Divide the periods remaining (from the beginning of the year of change) into
2) The remaining depreciation base, i.e., undepreciated cost to date less revised salvage value

Fractional Year Depreciation. Many conventions exist for accounting for depreciation for midyear asset acquisitions. They include:

1) A whole year's depreciation in year of acquisition and none in year of disposal
2) One-half year's depreciation in year of acquisition and year of disposal
3) Depreciation to nearest whole month in both year of acquisition and year of disposal

CPA exam questions generally specify the convention to be followed. If not, select a convention reasonable in the circumstances and provide an explanation to the grader.

G. Other Disposals

             Cash   (amount received)
             Accumulated depreciation   (old asset)
                 Old asset   (cost)
                 Gain or loss   (loss)   (gain)

Do not forget to depreciate disposed assets up to the point of disposal. Also, recognize the need to write off fully depreciated assets that are retired.

             Accumulated depreciation   (cost)
                 Old asset   (cost)

In addition, recognize that the carrying (book) value of fixed assets may have to be either removed or reduced due to an impairment of value resulting from obsolescence or other economic influences. If technological changes result in total obsolescence (permanent impairment) of a machine (due to either a change of technology in the machine itself or in the product it makes if usable only in making that product), the machine should be removed from the accounts.

             Accumulated depreciation   xxx
             Loss due to impairment   xxx
                 Obsolete asset   xxx

If technological change results in a partial impairment of the fixed asset, the machine should be written down by increasing accumulated depreciation.

             Loss due to impairment   xxx
                 Accumulated depreciation   xxx

H. Depletion

Depletion is "depreciation" of natural resources. The depletion base is the total cost of the property providing the natural resources. This includes all development costs such as exploring, drilling, excavating, and other preparatory costs.

The depletion base is usually allocated by the ratio of extracted units over the total expected recoverable units.

$$\frac{\text{Units extracted}}{\text{Total expected recoverable units}} \times (\text{Depletion base})$$

The unit depletion rate is frequently revised due to the uncertainties surrounding the recovery of natural resources. The revised unit rate in any year takes the following form:

$$\frac{\text{orig. cost + add'l. cost incurred - resid. value - depletion taken in previous yrs.}}{\text{units withdrawn currently + estimated units recoverable at year end}}$$

Note that the adjustment is being made prospectively, i.e., the remaining unde-
pleted cost is being expensed over the remaining recoverable units.

A distinction should be made between the full-cost and successful efforts
(direct write-off) methods of handling natural resource development cost. The full-
cost method capitalizes development costs of unproductive expenditures, e.g., a dry
oil well, and the successful efforts method expenses the unproductive expenditure in
the year of incurrence.

The full-cost concept is based on the premise that 100 holes are going to have
to be drilled to obtain 40 producing wells and therefore the cost of 40 productive
wells is the cost of drilling 100 holes. The full-cost concept can be applied to a
40-acre development area, a multiple-state oil basin, or an entire continent. SFAS
19 required that the cost of unsuccessful exploratory wells be expensed, i.e.,
successful efforts, but SFAS 25 also permits the full-cost method.

I. Insurance (see also Business Law: Module 21, Insurance)

When an insured loss occurs, an insurance loss account should be set up and
charged for all losses. These losses include decreases in asset value, earned
insurance premiums, etc. The account should be credited for any payments from the
insurance company. The remainder is closed to P & L.

Coinsurance is a contractual requirement that the insured maintain a certain
level of insurance, e.g., 80%. In the event the insured does not maintain the required amount, the insured becomes a coinsurer to the extent that the required
insurance is not carried.

A coinsurance provision is applicable only to partial destruction of the insured
property. When the property is totally destroyed, the coinsurance provision has no
relevance and indemnification will be the lower of "1)" or "2)" below.

For example, if the insured has $100,000 of FMV, a $60,000 policy requiring 80%
insurance, and a $32,000 loss, the coinsurance limitation is $24,000 (60,000/80,000
x $32,000). The other two limitations (indemnification is the lower of the three)
are:

1) Amount of loss
2) Face of policy

When multiple policies exist, they share responsibility in proportion to their face
amounts.

Example: Market value $200,000, loss $60,000.

Policy	Coins	Face	Loss Proration	Coins Limitation	Lowest of last 3 col.
1	--	10,000	6,000	--	6,000
2	70%	40,000	24,000	17,143*	17,143
3	80%	30,000	18,000	11,250**	11,250
4	90%	20,000	12,000	6,667***	6,667
		100,000	60,000		41,060

$$* \quad \frac{40,000}{140,000} \times 60,000 \qquad ** \quad \frac{30,000}{160,000} \times 60,000 \qquad *** \quad \frac{20,000}{180,000} \times 60,000$$

The formula to remember for computing the coinsurance limitation when there are multiple policies is:

$$\frac{\text{Face of Policy}}{\substack{\text{Greater of Aggregate Insurance} \\ \text{Coverage of All Companies } \underline{or} \\ \text{Coinsurance Requirement}}} \quad X \quad \text{Loss}$$

<u>Cash Surrender Value of Life Insurance</u>. Another noncurrent investment is cash surrender value of life insurance policies when the company is beneficiary (rather than insured employees). The entry to record insurance premiums that increase cash surrender value is:

Insurance expense	(plug)
Cash surrender value	(increase in CSV)
Cash	(total premium)

Cash surrender value is then a noncurrent asset unless the company plans to cash the policy, e.g., next period the policy is going to be cashed in.

During the first few years of a policy, no cash surrender value may attach to the policy. If so, all of the insurance premium would be expense.

J. <u>Intangible Assets (APB 17)</u>

Intangible assets are nonphysical assets. Intangible assets normally include only noncurrent intangibles, e.g., accounts receivable are not considered intangibles. Examples of intangible assets include copyrights, leaseholds, organizational costs, trademarks, franchises, patents, and goodwill. These intangibles may be categorized according to the following characteristics:

1) Identifiability. Separately identifiable or lacking specific identification.

2) Manner of acquisition. Acquired singly, in groups, or in business combinations; or developed internally.

3) Expected period of benefit. Limited by law or contract, related to human or economic factors, or indefinite or indeterminate duration.

4) Separability from enterprise. Rights transferable without title, salable, or inseparable from the entire enterprise. See the outline of APB 17.

Acquisition and Amortization of Intangibles. Purchased intangibles should be recorded at cost, which represents the potential earning power of the intangible at time of acquisition. Internally developed intangibles are recorded at the cost of development, unless the intangible:

1) Is not specifically identifiable
2) Has an indeterminate life, or
3) Is not separable from the enterprise (such as goodwill)

If one of the above criteria is present, all costs of development are expensed because measurement of the asset and association of costs with future benefits is difficult.

Intangible assets should be amortized by crediting the intangible account directly (contra accounts are not used).

```
            Amortization expense          xx
                Intangible asset              xx
```

Intangibles are normally amortized on a straight-line basis, although any systematic and rational approach is acceptable. Amortization is over the intangible's useful life, which may be less than its legal life. In no case is the useful life to exceed forty years. Factors to consider in determining useful life are listed in the outline of APB 17.

Goodwill is recorded only when an entire business is purchased because internally developed goodwill is not specifically identifiable, has an indeterminate life, and is not separable from the enterprise. Purchase of goodwill as a part of acquiring a business is discussed in the Investments and Consolidations module.

Intermediate texts typically discuss methods to estimate goodwill. These calculations are to be used only for valuing a business to be bought or sold. The calculation is not made to write up goodwill on the books of an existing business. Methods typically discussed include:

1) Some multiple, e.g., 3, of earnings. If earnings were 5,000, the business would be valued at $15,000.

2) Some multiple, e.g., 3, of excess earnings. If the excess earnings were 1,000, goodwill would be valued at $3,000.

3) Capitalization of excess earnings, e.g., at a 20% return rate. If excess earnings were $1,000, goodwill would be $5,000, i.e., what amount should be invested given a 20% interest rate to earn $1,000/year? $5,000. It is found by dividing the earnings by the interest rate.

$$\text{Earnings} = \text{Interest Rate} \times \text{Investment}$$
$$\text{Investment} = \frac{\text{Earnings}}{\text{Interest Rate}}$$

4) Capitalization of earnings, e.g., at a 20% return rate. If earnings were $5,000, the business would be valued at $25,000 per the above formula.

The problem with valuing excess earnings is that the procedure requires specification of (1) the normal earnings rate, and (2) the level of investment. For example, given $5,000 earnings, an investment of $40,000 and 10% normal return on investment, what are the excess earnings? $1,000.

($5,000 - $40,000 x .10)

Remember My Dear Aunt Sally (MDAS) - always multiply and divide first (order makes no difference), and then add and subtract (order makes no difference).

K. Deferred Charges

Expenditures of a prepayment nature that benefit several future periods, i.e., are not prepaid expenses, are sometimes categorized as deferred charges rather than intangibles. Examples are organizational costs and bond issue costs. These types of costs should be amortized to the periods benefited. Even though organizational costs theoretically benefit an indefinite number of future periods, they are usually amortized over a relatively short period of time, e.g., 5 years.

L. Research and Development Costs (SFASs 2 and 68)

SFAS 2 (see outline) requires R&D costs to be expensed as incurred except for intangibles or fixed assets purchased from others having alternative future uses. These should be capitalized and amortized over their useful life. Thus the cost of patents and R&D equipment purchased from third parties having a market value may be deferred and amortized over the asset's useful life. Internally developed R&D may not be deferred.

Finally, R&D done under contract for others is not required to be expensed per SFAS 2. The costs incurred would be matched with revenue using the completed-contract or percentage-of-completion method.

DEFERRED TAX

APB 9 and APB 11 require in<u>tra</u>period tax allocation. APB 11 requires <u>inter</u>-period tax allocation. APB 23 presumes undistributed earnings of subsidiaries will be distributed and thus accrual of taxes is required unless evidence exists that the undistributed earnings will not be distributed (then accrual of the taxes is not required). APB 24 requires interperiod tax allocation on undistributed earnings of equity method investees (20%-50% ownership). FASB Interpretation 22 refused to extend the interperiod tax allocation exemptions to railway roadbeds and tunnel borings. FASB Interpretation 29 requires certain tax benefits realized on disposition of investments in investees to be reported as part of the related gain or loss. SFAS 37 clarifies the basis for classification of deferred income taxes on the balance sheet. Finally, Technical Bulletin 83-1 provides guidance concerning the difference in the accounting and tax depreciation of an asset when an entity elects to reduce its tax basis.

Study the outlines in Chapter 8 of each of these pronouncements along with studying this module: APBs 2, 4, 11, 23, 24; SFAS 37; and FASB Technical Bulletin 83-1.

A. Investment Tax Credit

The investment tax credit reduces taxes by a specified percentage in the year in which qualifying property is placed into service. This percentage is based upon whether the qualifying property is 3-year or 5-year property; and, if the entity elects to reduce the basis of the property or the allowable investment credit. (See Mod 40, page 1173 for computational details.) The accounting issue is whether the tax credit is a reduction of the cost of the qualifying property, deferral method; or whether it is a reduction in the tax expense in the year placed in service, flow-through method. Both methods are permitted by APB 4.

The immediate recognition (also known as "flow-through") method reduces the tax expense and the tax liability by the amount of the credit in the year the asset is placed in service. Under this method, if the entity elects to reduce the allowable amount of the credit, there are no accounting implications; however, if the entity chooses to reduce the basis of the asset, there exists a timing difference which will reverse as the asset is depreciated and/or when the asset is sold. According to FASB Technical Bulletin 83-1, deferred taxes should be provided for this basis reduction in the year in which the related investment credit is recognized as a reduction in income tax expense.

EXAMPLE: *Company X purchased machinery in 1983 that qualified for investment tax credit of $10,000. The machinery is depreciated over a 5-year period. X Company's taxable and book income before taxes was $250,000. X Company has a 40% effective tax rate and accounts for investment credit on the flow-through method.*

The tax expense for 1983 is computed as follows:

Currently payable:		
Taxable income	$250,000	
x Effective rate	x .40	
Gross tax	$100,000	
Less: investment credit	10,000	
Current expense		$90,000
Deferred expense:		
Investment tax credit	$10,000	
x Basis reduction percentage	x .50	
Basis reduction	$ 5,000	
x Effective rate	x .40	
Deferred expense		2,000
Total income tax expense		$92,000

The entry required to record the tax expense for 1983 would be

Income tax expense	92,000	
Deferred income taxes		2,000
Income taxes payable		90,000

Use of the flow-through method in cases where the taxpayer elects to reduce the asset's basis will always *result in a deferred item.*

The deferral method requires crediting an account which is classified on the balance sheet as either (1) a deferred credit or (2) a contra asset account for the amount of the investment tax credit. Unlike the flow-through method, no accounting implications are imposed by the decision of the entity to reduce the basis or reduce the allowable credit. The deferred credit is amortized over the life of the asset, i.e., the tax credit is considered a reduction in asset cost.

Referring to the above example, if the deferral method had been used the following entries would be recorded:

Income tax expense	100,000	
Income tax payable		100,000
Income tax payable	10,000	
Deferred investment tax credit		10,000
Deferred investment tax credit	2,000*	
Income tax expense		2,000

*This amount is the annual portion of the deferred credit (i.e., 10,000 ÷ 5-year life).

B. Intraperiod Tax Allocation

Income taxes are to be allocated within an accounting period to continuing operations, discontinued operations, extraordinary items, and prior period adjustments.

EXAMPLE:
$400,000	income from continuing operations	
(30,000)	expropriation -- extraordinary item	
(20,000)	loss from operations of discontinued division	
70,000	underfooted sales journal last year--prior period adj.	
$420,000	taxable income	

Assuming a 40% tax rate on all transactions, the journal entry that might be made to record the above tax expenses and credits is:

Continuing operations tax expense	$160,000	
Prior period adjustment tax expense	28,000	
Expropriation tax credit		12,000
Discontinued division loss tax credit		8,000
Taxes payable		168,000

The above entry would be made if all of the above accounts appeared in the ledger. Whether or not the above entry is made, only $160,000 tax expense should be charged to ordinary operations. The net prior period adjustment should be $42,000; net expropriation loss should be $18,000; net discontinued operations loss should be $12,000.

C. Interperiod Tax Allocation

The problem of interperiod allocation arises because timing differences exist in the revenues and expenses for financial reporting purposes and for tax purposes. APB 11 requires that the income tax applicable to the income recognized currently on the income statement be estimated and accrued without regard to the timing of the payment of the tax. The objective of interperiod allocation is to match tax expense with the related income as recognized for accounting purposes.

EXAMPLE: *Percentage-of-completion for accounting (reporting) purposes, and completed contract for tax purposes with percentage-of-completion income of $40,000, $50,000, and $70,000 in years 1, 2 and 3.*

	Tax Allocation			No Tax Allocation		
	1	2	3	1	2	3
Income	40,000	50,000	70,000	40,000	50,000	70,000
Tax Exp.	20,000	25,000	35,000	0	0	80,000
NI	20,000	25,000	35,000	40,000	50,000	(10,000)

The need for tax allocation is illustrated by the above example. When tax allocation is not followed, tax expense equals tax payable, and the ability of the user to compare income numbers across time or to make inferences about the future is limited. Interperiod allocation accrues the tax expense as the income is earned.

Interperiod allocation is only required for timing differences. A timing difference occurs when the period in which an item of revenue is taxable or an expense is deductible for tax purposes differs from the period when the item is recognized for financial reporting. The item will appear on both sets of books, but at different times.

A permanent difference affects only book income or only taxable income, but not both. For example, interest on municipal bonds is not included in taxable income but is included in book income, and amortization of consolidated goodwill is deducted in computing book income but not deductible in computing taxable income.

> EXAMPLE: *During the first year of operations, a corporation did not receive any income. At year end, the only income-related items were Rent Receivable of $500, and Interest Receivable on tax free bonds of $100. The tax books (cash basis) would show $0 income and $0 tax payable. The accounting books would show (assuming a tax rate of 40%) tax expense of $200 (40% of $500). The tax is not accrued on the interest. It is a permanent difference that will never be taxed. The expense is measured by asking the question: How much tax will ever be paid on the income currently reported on the financial books?*

The concept of interperiod tax allocation is very simple under the "deferred" method (required by APB 11 in preference to liability and net of tax methods). Debit tax expense for accounting income (adjusted for permanent differences) times the tax rate. Credit taxes payable for taxable income times the tax rate. The difference is debited or credited, as the need may be, to "deferred taxes."

        Tax expense   (tax rate x accounting income)
        Deferred taxes   (dr. or cr. to balance)
            Taxes payable   (tax rate x tax income)

The following entries would be made for the completed/percentage-of-completion contract example presented above.

Year 1

     Tax expense   20,000
         Deferred taxes   20,000

Year 2

     Tax expense   25,000
         Deferred taxes   25,000

Year 3

     Tax expense   35,000
     Deferred taxes   45,000
         Taxes payable   80,000

D. Loss Carryforwards and Carrybacks

Operating losses of a particular period can be carried back to the 3 immediate past periods' income resulting in a tax credit. Losses may also be carried forward for 15 years to offset income if income arises in any of those 15 years. Companies may at the time of the loss elect to carry forward only.

Loss carrybacks occur when losses in the current period are carried back to periods in which there was income. Loss carrybacks result in tax refunds in the loss period and thus should be recognized in the year of the loss.

```
Tax refund receivable      (based on tax credit due to loss)
     Tax loss credit           (same)
```

The tax loss credit would be closed to income in the year of the loss and act to decrease the loss. It is not treated as an extraordinary item.

Tax loss carryforwards are generally not recognized in the year the loss occurs. APB 11 requires that in normal circumstances the carryforward should not be recognized until it is realized, i.e., it should be recognized in the subsequent period when income exists and creates a current receivable from the government. When treated in this manner, the carryforward is an extraordinary item in the year it is realized.

Under unusual circumstances (when the carryforward is assured beyond any reasonable doubt), loss carryforwards can be recognized in the year of the loss (para 47, APB 11). If the loss carryforward qualifies for this treatment, it is treated as a normal operating item and not as an extraordinary item.

For example, assume the income reported in the first three years of operations is $30,000, ($35,000), and $100,000. The tax rate is 30%. The normal entry to be made in year 2 will record only the carryback:

```
Tax refund receivable        9,000
     Tax loss credit                      9,000
```

The credit will appear before extraordinary items as a reduction of the operating loss.

In year 3, the $5,000 which could not be carried back will be carried forward to obtain a $1,500 reduction in tax payable during year 3. The entry to record taxes in year 3 is:

```
Tax expense               30,000
     Tax reduction --
          carryforward                 1,500
     Tax payable                      28,500
```

The tax reduction of $1,500 will be reported as an extraordinary item.

If the carryforward had met the criteria of para 47, the entry in year 2 would have been:

Tax refund receivable	$9,000	
Deferred tax loss carryforward (asset)	1,500	
Tax loss credit		$10,500

The full credit of $10,500 would have appeared before extraordinary items in year 2.

E. Complicating Factors in Tax Allocation

The above overview of tax allocation ignored the effects of the changing complex series of tax rates, i.e., surcharge exemptions, special tax rates, tax credits, and operating losses. While the above examples assumed one tax rate applies to the net effect of the tax-book, originating-reversing, timing difference, there are two possible major complications.

   1) The tax rate may vary over the difference between tax income and book income due to surcharges, credits, etc.

   2) APB 11 allows reversing timing differences to be computed based on the rates in existence when the differences originated as an alternative to the current rate.

The first issue is usually resolved on the CPA exam by specification of one effective tax rate. In practice the adjustment of deferred taxes is computed by determining tax expense and tax liability in separate computations utilizing the effects of applicable surcharges, credits, operating loss carryovers, etc. The difference between the two is the adjustment of deferred taxes.

The second issue, repeated, is APB 11 (para 37), which permits originating deferred tax credits to be computed at current rates and reversing credits at rates existing when the credits originated. This is obviously more complicated than applying the current rate to the change in the deferred credits during the year.

The computations to determine the effect of the timing difference reversals at the rates existing when the differences originated can be based on individual items or groups of similar items, e.g., all installment sales, all assets depreciated by accelerated depreciation, etc. If done individually each item resulting in a timing difference must be kept track of to determine the amount and timing of reversals. If done by group, the originating timing differences in the current period times the current tax rate can be compared with the reversing timing differences of earlier periods multiplied by the then-existing rates. The difference is an adjustment to deferred taxes.

An example which illustrates the use of different tax rates for originating and reversing timing differences follows. Assume that, for Company M, the only difference between pretax accounting income and taxable income is the result of using straight-line depreciation for financial reporting and ACRS for the tax return.

Assume that Company M purchases fixed asset A on January 1, year 1, for $15,000. Asset A qualifies as 3-year recovery property with a useful life for book purposes of 5 years and no salvage value. Company M elects to reduce the allowable ITC percentage in lieu of reducing the basis (discussed earlier in this module) for all assets. On January 1 of each of the next 4 years fixed assets B, C, D, and E are each purchased for $15,000. All of these qualify as 3-year recovery property, have a useful life of 5 years, and have no salvage value. The following schedule indicates the depreciation expense for each of the 5 years for financial and tax reports.

Schedule Showing Financial and Tax Depreciation Expense

Asset	Year 1 Book	Year 1 Tax	Year 2 Book	Year 2 Tax	Year 3 Book	Year 3 Tax	Year 4 Book	Year 4 Tax	Year 5 Book	Year 5 Tax
A	$3,000	$3,750	$3,000	$5,700	$3,000	$5,550	$3,000	$ --	$3,000	$ --
B			3,000	3,750	3,000	5,700	3,000	5,550	3,000	--
C					3,000	3,750	3,000	5,700	3,000	5,550
D							3,000	3,750	3,000	5,700
E									3,000	3,750
Depr. Exp.	$3,000	$3,750	$6,000	$9,450	$9,000	$15,000	$12,000	$15,000	$15,000	$15,000

Timing differences:

	Year 1	Year 2	Year 3	Year 4	Year 5
Originating	$750	$3,450	$6,000	$6,000	$6,000
Reversing	-0-	-0-	-0-	3,000	6,000
Net Changes	$750	$3,450	$6,000	$3,000	$ -0-

Note that, for each asset, tax depreciation for the first 3 years of estimated useful life exceeds book depreciation. The deferred tax effects of these differences are referred to as originating timing differences. The deferred tax effects result from multiplying the tax rate times the differences noted above. Note also that, for each asset, book depreciation exceeds tax depreciation for the last 2 years of useful life. The deferred tax effects of these differences are referred to as reversing timing differences. In order to calculate deferred taxes for the differences in the example, the income tax rates are assumed to be 46% for years 1 and 2 and 48% for years 3 through 5.

Deferred taxes can be calculated by applying either the gross change or the net change methods. The gross change method uses the current year's tax rate for determining the deferred tax effects of originating timing differences. However, this method requires the use of historical tax rates for the reversing timing differences (i.e., the rates in existence when the differences originated). The application of this method to timing differences given in the example produce the following:

	Years				
	1	2	3	4	5
Timing differences:					
Originating	$750(.46) = $345	$3,450(.46) = $1,587	$6,000(.48) = $2,880	$6,000(.48) = $2,880	$6,000(.48) = $2,880
Reversing	0	0	0	$3,000(.46) = $1,380	$6,000(.46) = $2,760
Deferred Tax Credits for Year	$345	$1,587	$2,880	$1,500	$120

An alternative to the gross change method is the net change method. This method uses the current year's tax rate for both originating and reversing timing differences. To illustrate this alternative, the deferred tax credits for the five years are:

	Years				
	1	2	3	4	5
Net changes from schedule	$750	$3,450	$6,000	$3,000	$-0-
Deferred tax credits	$345	$1,587	$2,880	$1,440	$-0-

The deferred tax credits for years 1 and 2 result from a 46% tax rate while the deferred tax credits for years 3 - 5 result from a 48% tax rate. The primary advantage of the net change method is its simplicity.

One additional reversal issue concerns APB 23 and APB 24. APB 23, which deals with long-term investments of greater than 50%, allows a corporation to assume that the timing difference (the undistributed income since date of acquisition) will reverse in the form of a dividend or in the form of a capital gain--or that it will not reverse at all. Obviously the tax expense and deferred tax liability recorded when the difference originates will be a function of which of the three assumptions above is made.

APB 24, dealing with long-term investments between 20 and 50 percent, requires the investor to assume reversal either in the form of a dividend or capital gain. Again the entry to be made will depend upon the assumed form the reversal takes.

To illustrate the application of APBs 23 and 24, assume the Parent Company owns 70% of the outstanding common stock of Subsidiary Company and 30% of the outstanding common stock of Investee Company. Additional data for Subsidiary and Investee Companies for the year 1980 are as follows:

	Investee Co.	Subsidiary Co.
Net Income	$50,000	$100,000
Dividends Paid	20,000	60,000

F. Income Tax Effects from Investee Co. (APB 24)

The pretax accounting income of Parent Company will include equity in investee income equal to $15,000 ($50,000 times 30%). Parent's taxable income, however, will include dividend income of $6,000 ($20,000 times 30%), and a credit of 85% of the $6,000, or $5,100, will also be allowed for the dividends received. This 85% dividends received deduction is a permanent difference between pretax accounting and taxable income and is allowed for dividends received from domestic corporations in which the ownership percentage is less than 80%. A 100% credit (dividends received deduction) is allowed for dividends received from domestic corporations in which the ownership percentage is 80% to 100%. As discussed in APB 24, the originating timing difference results from Parent's equity ($9,000) in the Investee's undistributed income of $30,000. The amount of the deferred tax credit in 1980 depends upon the expectations of Parent Co. as to the manner in which the $9,000 of undistributed income will be received. If the expectation of receipt is via dividends, then the timing difference is 15% of $9,000 or $1,350, and the deferred tax credit for this originating timing difference in 1980 is the current tax rate times $1,350. If the expectation of receipt, however, is through future sale of the investment, then the timing difference is $9,000, and the deferred tax credit is the current capital gains rate times the $9,000.

The entries below illustrate these alternatives. A tax rate of 40% is used for ordinary income, and a rate of 25% is used for capital gains. Note that the amounts in the entries below relate only to Investee Company's incremental impact upon Parent Company's tax accounts.

	Expectations for Undistributed Income	
	Dividends	Capital Gains
Income tax expense	900	2610
Deferred taxes	540[b]	2250[c]
Income taxes payable	360[a]	360[a]

[a]Computation of income taxes payable:

Dividend income -- 30%($20,000)	$6,000
Less: 85% dividends received deduction	(5,100)
Amount included in parent's taxable income	$ 900
Tax liability -- 40%($900)	$ 360

ᵇComputation of deferred tax credit (dividend assumption):
   Originating timing difference:

Parent's share of undistributed income -- 30%($30,000)	$9,000
Less: 85% dividends received deduction	(7,650)
Originating timing difference	$1,350
Deferred tax credit -- 40%($1,350)	$ 540

ᶜComputation of deferred tax credit (capital gain assumption):

Originating timing difference - Parent's share of undistributed income -- 30%($30,000)	$9,000
Deferred tax credit -- 25%($9,000)	$2,250

G. Income Tax Effects from Subsidiary Co. (APB 23)

The pretax accounting income of Parent will also include equity in subsidiary income of $70,000 (70% of $100,000). Note also that this $70,000 will be included in pretax consolidated income if Parent and Subsidiary consolidate. For tax purposes, Parent and Subsidiary cannot file a consolidated tax return because the minimum level of control, i.e., 80%, is not present. Consequently, the taxable income of Parent will include dividend income of $42,000 (70% of $60,000) and there will be an 85% dividends received deduction of $35,700. The originating timing difference discussed in APB 23 results from Parent's equity ($28,000) in the subsidiary's undistributed earnings of $40,000. The amount of the deferred tax credit in 1980 depends upon the expectations of Parent Company as to the manner in which this $28,000 of undistributed income will be received. The same expectations can exist as previously discussed for Parent's equity in Investee's undistributed earnings, i.e., through future dividend distributions or capital gains. In addition, however, if the Parent can demonstrate that its share of the Subsidiary Company's earnings will be permanently reinvested by Subsidiary, then APB 23 states that no timing difference exists, and therefore, no deferred tax credits arise. Note that this alternative does not exist for stock investments between 20% and 50%.

The entries below illustrate these alternatives. Tax rates of 40% for ordinary income and 25% for capital gains are assumed. Note that the amounts in the entries below relate only to Subsidiary Company's incremental impact upon Parent Company's tax accounts.

	Expectations for Undistributed Income		
	Dividends	Cap. Gains	Reinvested
Income tax expense	4,200	9,520	2,520
Deferred taxes	1,680[b]	7,000[c]	-0-
Income taxes payable	2,520[a]	2,520[a]	2,520[a]

[a]Computation of income taxes payable:

Dividend income -- 70% ($60,000)	$42,000
Less: 85% dividends received deduction	(35,700)
Amount included in Parent's taxable income	6,300
Tax liability -- 40% ($6,300)	$ 2,520

[b]Computation of deferred tax credit (dividend assumption):

Originating timing difference:

Parent's share of undistributed income -- 70% ($40,000)	$28,000
Less: 85% dividends received deduction	(23,800)
Originating timing difference	$ 4,200
Deferred tax credit -- 40% ($4,200)	$ 1,680

[c]Computation of deferred tax credit (capital gain assumption):

Originating timing difference -- Parent's share of undistributed income -- 70% ($40,000)	$28,000
Deferred tax credit -- 25% ($28,000)	$ 7,000

If a parent company owns 80% or more of the voting stock of a subsidiary, and parent consolidates the subsidiary for both financial and tax reports, then no timing differences exist between pretax consolidated income and taxable income. If, in the circumstances noted above, consolidated financial statements are prepared but a consolidated tax return is not, then it should be noted that a dividends received deduction of 100% is allowed. Accordingly, the timing difference between pretax consolidated income and taxable income is zero if the parent assumes the undistributed income will be realized in dividends.

The diagram on the next page illustrates the accounting and income tax treatment of the undistributed investee/subsidiary earnings by corporate investors under different levels of ownership.

SUMMARY OF TIMING DIFFERENCES OF INVESTEES AND SUBSIDIARIES

Level of Ownership Interest

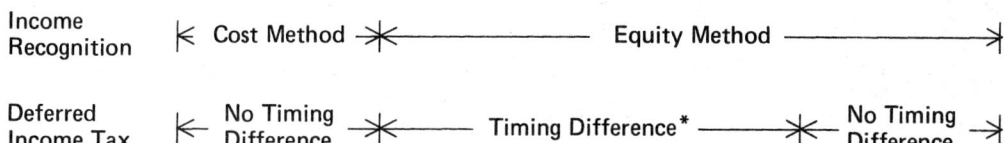

| 0% | <20% | 50% | ≥80% | 100% |

Accounting

Income
Recognition

Deferred
Income Tax

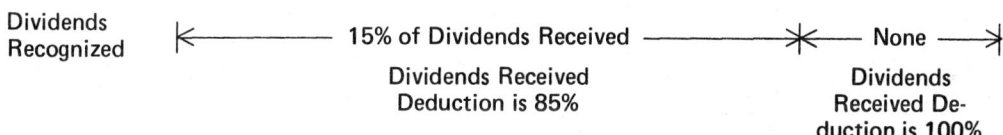

Income Tax

Dividends
Recognized

*Recognition of Timing Differences

Ownership level ≥ 20% ≤ 50%: timing difference **must** be accounted for.
Ownership level > 50%: timing difference must **normally** be accounted for, unless management intends to reinvest the
  subsididary's earnings indefinitely into the future.

STOCKHOLDERS' EQUITY

Stockholders' equity is the residual of assets minus liabilities, i.e., net assets. Due to the number of fraudulent manipulations involving stocks, many states have legislated accounting for stockholder equity transactions and they are controlled to some degree, e.g., conditions under which dividends may be paid.

Common stockholders' equity consists of two major categories: contributed capital and retained earnings. Retained earnings are either appropriated or unappropriated. Contributed capital consists of paid-in and donated. Paid-in consists of paid-in excess and legal capital. Legal capital is the par or stated value of stock. An outline of stockholders' equity follows.

Contributed capital

- Paid-in, e.g., common and preferred stock

  - Legal -- par, stated, no par
  - Paid-in excess of par
  - Paid-in from other transactions

    - Treasury stock
    - Retirement of stock
    - Stock dividends recorded at market
    - Stock warrants detachable from bonds
    - Lapse of stock purchase warrants
    - Conversion of convertible bonds recorded at market value of the stock
    - Any other gain on the company's own stock transactions

- Donated capital

Retained earnings

- Appropriated
- Unappropriated

Contra stockholders' equity items (deducted after contributed capital and retained earnings above are totaled)

- Treasury stock (cost method)
- Unrealized losses on long-term equity securities (SFAS 12, para 11)
- Deferred compensation costs if by issuance of stock to employees (APB 25, para 14)
- Some unrealized foreign currency translations (see SFAS 52 paras 13, 18, and 19; may also increase SE)

A. Common Stock

The entry to record the issuance of common stock is:

```
Cash                        (amount received)
     Common stock                (par or stated value)
     Paid-in excess              (forced)
```

If stock is sold for less than par, a discount account is debited.

Very little stock is issued at a discount because of the resulting potential liability to the original purchaser for the difference between the issue price (when less than par) and par which in many states is legal capital. This liability has been avoided by use of stated value and no par stock, but is mainly avoided by establishing par values below market.

Control accounts are occasionally used to control unissued stock. At authorization:

```
Unissued common stock           (total par or stated value)
     Common stock authorized         (same)
```

At issuance:

```
Cash                            (cash received)
     Unissued common stock          (par or stated value)
     Paid-in excess                 (forced)
```

The credit balance in the authorized account is the total available for issuance. The debit balance in the unissued account is the amount not issued. Thus, authorized (cr) - unissued (dr) = issued (cr). The unissued account is an offset account to the authorized account.

No-par stock is occasionally issued, i.e., no par or stated value exists. All of the proceeds from issuance of no-par stock are credited to "common stock."

Stock issued for services or assets should be valued at FMV.

```
Legal expenses          (FMV)
Assets                  (FMV)
     Common stock            (par)
     Paid-in excess          (forced)
```

Costs of registering and issuing common stock are generally netted against the proceeds, i.e., reduce "paid-in excess." An alternative method is to consider stock issue costs an organizational cost.

B. Preferred Stock

As implied, preferred stock has preferential rights: most commonly the right to receive dividends prior to common stockholders. Generally the dividend payout is specified, e.g., 7% of par. Additional possible features:

1) Participating -- share with common stockholders in dividend distributions after both preferred and common stockholders receive a specified level of dividend payment

   a) Participation with common stockholders in dividends is usually specified in terms of a percentage of legal capital. For example, 7% preferred receive 7% of their par value in dividends before common stockholders receive dividends. Fully participating preferred would receive the same percentage dividend as common stockholders if the common stockholders received over a 7% (of par value) dividend.

2) Cumulative -- dividends not paid in any year (dividends in arrears) must be made up before distributions can be made to common stockholders

   a) Dividends in arrears are not a liability until declared. They should be disclosed parenthetically or in the footnotes.

3) Convertible -- preferred stockholders have an option of exchanging their stock for common stock at a specified ratio

   a) Conversion is usually accounted for at book value

Preferred stock	(par converted)
Preferred paid-in accounts	(related balances)
Common stock	(par)
Paid-in excess	(forced)

   b) If market value is used, common stock and paid-in excess are credited for the market value, usually resulting in a large debit to retained earnings. (Plug figure in the journal entry.)

4) Callable -- the corporation has the option to repurchase the preferred stock at a specified price

   a) If called, no gain or loss is recognized. Gains are taken to a paid-in capital account; losses are charged to retained earnings

Preferred stock	(par)
Preferred paid-in accounts	(related balances)
Retained earnings	(if dr. needed)
Cash	(amount paid)
Paid-in from preferred	
retirement	(if cr. needed)

Any of the above features present in a preferred stock issuance should be disclosed parenthetically in the balance sheet next to the account title.

C. Stock Subscriptions

   Stock (common/preferred) can be subscribed by investors. A receivable is established and "stock subscribed" credited. When the total subscription price is received, the stock (common/preferred) is issued.

At subscription:

Cash	(any cash received)
Subscription receivable	(balance)
Stock subscribed	(par)
Paid-in excess	(subscription price > par)

Cash receipt and issuance:

Cash	(balance)
Subscriptions receivable	(balance)
Common stock subscribed	(par)
Stock*	(par)

   *Unissued common stock, if unissued and authorized accounts are
   being used.

Upon default of subscription agreements, depending on agreement, the amount paid to

date may be:

   1) Returned to subscriber
   2) Kept by company
   3) Held to cover any losses on resale and balance returned

If returned:

Stock subscribed
Paid-in excess
Cash
Subscriptions receivable

If kept by the company, no cash would be paid and "paid-in from subscription de-

fault" credited instead of cash.

    If held to cover any losses on resale, a "refundable subscription deposit" lia-

bility would be credited instead of cash. If the stock were resold at less than the

original subscription price, the difference would be debited to "refundable sub-

scription deposit."

Cash	(payment)
Refundable subscription deposit	(forced)
Stock	(par)
Paid-in excess	(amount from original sale)

The balance in the refundable subscription account would be paid (possibly in an

equivalent number of shares) to the original subscriber.

D. Treasury Stock Transactions

    A firm's own stock repurchased on the open market is known as treasury stock.

Treasury stock is <u>not</u> an asset, as a firm may not own shares of itself. Instead it

is treated as a reduction of stockholders' equity.

Two methods of accounting for treasury stock exist: par value and cost. Under the cost method, treasury stock is debited for the cost of treasury stock. Any gain (loss) is recognized at the point of resale. Gains are credited to "paid-in capital from treasury stock transactions." Losses should be charged first to "paid-in capital from treasury stock (TS) transactions" or "paid-in capital from stock retirement" to the extent that either of these exists for that class of stock. The remainder of any loss is to be charged to retained earnings. In essence a one-transaction viewpoint is used, as the firm is treated as a middle "person" for the transfer of stock between two shareholders.

Under the par value method, all capital balances associated with the treasury shares are removed upon acquisition. Any excess of treasury stock cost over par value is accounted for by charging "paid-in capital from common stock" for the amount in excess of par received when the shares were originally issued. Any excess of the cost of acquiring the treasury stock over the original issue cost is charged to retained earnings. If treasury stock is acquired at a cost equal to or less than the original issue cost, "paid-in capital from common stock" is charged (debited) for the original amount in excess of par and "paid-in capital from treasury stock" is credited for the difference between the original issue price and the cost to acquire the treasury stock. When the treasury stock is resold, it is treated as a typical issuance, with the excess of selling price over par credited to "paid-in capital from common stock." Note that the par value method takes on a two-transaction viewpoint. The purchase is treated as a "retirement" of the shares, while the subsequent sale of the shares is treated as a "new" issue.

> EXAMPLE: *100 shares ($50 par) are originally sold at $60, reacquired at $70, and subsequently resold at $75.*

Cost method			Par value method		
Treasury stock	7,000		Treasury stock	5,000	
Cash		7,000	Paid-in capital--		
			common stock	1,000	
			Retained earnings	1,000	
			Cash		7,000
Cash	7,500		Cash	7,500	
Treasury stock		7,000	Treasury stock		5,000
Paid-in capital--			Paid-in capital--		
treasury stock		500	common stock		2,500

If the shares had been resold at $65:

Cost method		Par value method	
Cash	6,500	Cash	6,500
*Retained earnings	500	Treasury stock	5,000
Treasury stock	7,000	Paid-in capital--	
		common stock	1,500

  *"Paid-in capital--treasury stock" or "paid-in capital--retired stock" of that
  issue would be debited first to the extent it exists.

Note that total stockholders' equity is not affected by the method selected; only
the allocation among the equity accounts is different.

E. Retirement of Stock

   Formal retirement or constructive retirement (purchase with no intent of reissue) of stock is handled very similarly to treasury stock. When formally retired:

> Common stock
> *Paid-in excess
> *Retained earnings
>   *Treasury stock
>
> *Assuming a loss on the retirement of treasury stock

   1) "Paid-in from treasury stock transactions" may be debited to the extent
       it exists
   2) A pro rata portion of all paid-in capital existing for that issue, e.g.,
       if 2% of an issue is retired, up to 2% of all existing paid-in capital
       for that issue may be debited

Alternatively, the entire or any portion of the loss may be debited to retained
earnings. Any gains are credited to a "paid-in from retirement" account.

F. Dividends

   1. At the date of declaration, an entry is made to record the dividend
       liability

> Retained earnings (Dividends)
>   Dividends payable

   2. No entry is made at the date of record. Those owning stock at the date of
       record will be paid the previously declared dividends.

       a. The stockholder records consist of:

           1) General ledger account
           2) Subsidiary ledger

               a) Contains names and addresses of stockholders

           3) Stock certificate book

   b. Outside services: usually banks

       1) Transfer agent issues new certificates, cancelling old, and
           maintains stockholder ledger
       2) Registrar validates new certificates and controls against over-
           issuance
       3) Functions are now becoming combined

3. At the payment date, the liability is paid

    Dividend payable
        Cash

4. Property dividends are accounted for as cash dividends. They are recorded
    at FMV of the asset transferred with a gain (loss) recognized on the dif-
    ference between the asset's BV and FMV at disposition (see APB 29).

    a. Except for rescission of prior business combinations

5. Liquidation dividends (dividends based on other than earnings) are a return
    of capital to stockholders and should be so disclosed. Paid-in capital is
    usually debited rather than retained earnings. Common stock cannot be
    debited because it is the legal capital which can only be eliminated upon
    corporate dissolution.

6. Scrip dividends are issuance of promises to pay dividends in the future
    (and may bear interest) instead of cash

        Retained earnings   xx
            Scrip dividends payable   xx

    Scrip dividends are a liability which is extinguished by payment

        Scrip dividends payable   xx
        Interest expense (maybe)   xx   xx
            Cash

7. Unlike cash and property dividends, stock dividends are not a liability
    when declared. They can be rescinded as nothing is actually being dis-
    tributed to stockholders except more stock certificates. Current assets
    are not used to "pay" the dividend.

    a. After stock dividends, shareholders continue to own the same proportion
        of the corporation
    b. At declaration

        Retained earnings   (FMV of shares)
            Stock dividend distributable   (par)
            Paid-in excess of par   (plug)

    c. At issuance

        Stock dividend distributable   xx
            Common stock   xx

    d. Charge retained earnings for FMV of stock dividend if less than 20%-25%
        increase in stock outstanding

        1) Not required if closely held company

G. Stock Splits

Stock splits change the number of shares outstanding and the par value per share. Par value is reduced in proportion to the increase in the number of shares. The total par value outstanding does not change and no charge is made to retained earnings. If legal requirements preclude changing the par or stated value, charge retained earnings only for the par or stated value issued.

STOCK DIVIDENDS AND SPLITS: SUMMARY OF EFFECTS

	Total S.E.	Par Value Per Share	Total Par Outstanding	R.E.	Legal Capital	Additional Paid-In Capital	No. of Shares Outstanding
Stock Dividend < 20 - 25% of Shares Outstanding	N/C	N/C	+	Decrease By Market Value Of Shares Issued	+	+	+
Stock Split Effected in Form of Dividend > 20 - 25% of Shares Outstanding	N/C	N/C	+	Decrease By Par Value of Shares Issued	+	N/C	+
Stock Split	N/C	Decrease Proportionately	N/C	N/C	N/C	N/C	+

N/C = No Change

Prepared by Professor John R. Simon, Northern Illinois University

H. Appropriations of Retained Earnings (Reserves)

An entry to appropriate retained earnings restricts the amount of retained earnings that is available for dividends.

```
        RE (or Unappropriated RE)
            Reserve for RE (or Appropriated RE)
```

It is important to note, however, that the restriction of retained earnings does not necessarily provide cash for any intended purpose. The purpose is to show that assets in the amount of the appropriation are not available for dividends. SFAS 5 requires that when a reserve is no longer needed it must be returned directly to unappropriated retained earnings by reversing the entry that created it.

I. Stock Options

Study ARB 43, Chapter 13 B, and APB 25 before studying this section.

Compensation is generally measured by the dollar value difference between the option price and the market price if the option price is below the market price.

For financial reporting purposes, compensation is measured on the measurement date -- that date on which both the number of shares the individual employee is entitled to and the option or purchase price are known. The measurement date is usually, though not always, the grant date.

Many options are granted at a price equal to or greater than the market price when the option is granted for a fixed number of shares. Thus, there is no compensation expense and no journal entry involving compensation expense is recorded. Disclosure, however, as to the options outstanding, is required. When the employee acquires stock under these circumstances, the corporation debits cash for the option price, and credits cash for par and paid-in capital.

If the measurement date is the grant date and deferred compensation is recorded, it is amortized over the periods in which the employee provides the services for which the option contract is the reward. For example, an option is granted to a corporate officer to purchase 100 shares of $1 par common at $52 when the market price is $58. The entry to record the granting of the option is:

```
Deferred compensation expense     600           (a contra paid-in capital account)
     Stock options outstanding         600          (a paid-in capital account)
```

Deferred compensation is subtracted from stock options outstanding in the paid-in capital section of owners' equity to indicate the net contributed services on any date -- i.e., on the grant date nothing has yet been contributed by the option holder, and this would be measured by ($600 - $600 = 0). As the employee provides services to earn the option, an entry is made assigning compensation expense to periods (assume a 5 year period):

```
          Compensation expense              120
               Deferred compensation exp.          120
```

When the option is exercised, cash is received and stock is issued as reflected in the following entry (assume exercise after the 5 year period):

```
     Cash                                5,200          (option price)
     Stock options outstanding           600
          Common stock                        100          (par)
          Additional paid-in capital        5,700          (plug)
```

If the options are forfeited due to the employee(s) failing to fulfill an obligation, e.g., staying with the company, compensation expense is credited in the year of forfeiture. The amount credited reflects the total compensation expense previously charged to the income statement for the employee(s) who forfeited the options. In the example, assume the officer leaves the company in year 3, two years before the options can be exercised. The following entry is made in year 3:

```
Stock Options Outstanding       600
     Deferred Compensation Expense   360
     Compensation Expense            240
```

In the example above, the grant date and the measurement date coincide. If the measurement date follows the grant date, it is necessary to assume compensation expense based on the market values of the common stock that exist at the end of each period until the measurement date is reached. For example, assume that on 1/1/80, a company grants an option to purchase 100 shares of common stock at 90% of the market price at 12/31/82 and that the compensation period is 4 years. Note that at 1/1/80, the number of shares is determinable, but the option price is unknown. The market values of the common are as follows:

```
12/31/80                $10
12/31/81                 13
12/31/82                 15
```

The following entries for compensation expense are recorded:

	1980	1981	1982 and 1983
Compensation expense	25	35*	45*
Stock Options Outstanding	25	35	45

1980: [($10 - 9) x 100 shares] ÷ 4 = $25
1981: ($13 - 11.70) x 100 shares = ($130 - 25) ÷ 3 = $35
1982: ($15 - 13.50) x 100 shares = ($150 - 60) ÷ 2 = $45 for 1982 and 1983

Note that the market value of the stock at the end of the 1980 and 1981 is used as an estimate of the market price of the stock at 12/31/82.

A time line depicting the actual and estimated compensation expense would appear as follows:

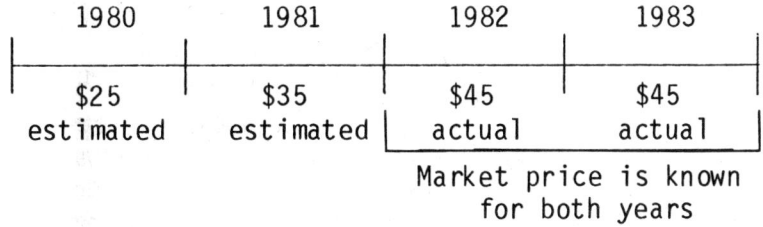

*Results from change in estimate

J. Stock Appreciation Rights

Study the summary of FASB Interpretation No. 28 on page 699 in conjunction with study of this section.

Stock appreciation rights (SARs) allow employees to receive stock or cash equal in amount to the difference between the market value and some predetermined amount per share for a certain number of shares. SARs allow employees to receive share appreciation without having to make a cash outlay as is common in stock option plans.

For financial reporting purposes, compensation expense is the excess of market value over a predetermined amount. Compensation expense is recorded in each period prior to exercise based on the excess of market value at the end of each period over a predetermined amount. Compensation expense is adjusted up or down as the market value of stock changes before the measurement date (which is the exercise date). Therefore, compensation expense could be credited if the stock's market value drops from one period to the next.

For example, assume a company grants 100 SARs, payable in cash, to an employee on 1/1/81. The predetermined amount for the SAR plan is $50 per right, and the market value of the stock is $55 on 12/31/81, $53 on 12/31/82, and $61 on 12/31/83. Compensation expense recorded in each year would be:

		Total Expense	-	Exp. Previously Accrued	=	Current Expense
1981	100 ($55-$50) =	$ 500	-	$ 0	=	$500
1982	100 ($53-$50) =	$ 300	-	$500	=	($200)
1983	100 ($61-$50) =	$1100	-	$300	=	$800

The total expense recognized over the 3-year period is $1100 [100($61-$50)]. Journal entries would be:

<table>
<tr><td>1981 and 1983</td><td></td><td>1982</td><td></td></tr>
<tr><td>Compensation Expense</td><td>$500/$800</td><td>Liability under SAR Plan</td><td>$200</td></tr>
<tr><td>   Liability under SAR Plan</td><td>$500/$800</td><td>   Compensation Expense</td><td>$200</td></tr>
</table>

If the SARs were to be redeemed in common stock, Stock Rights Outstanding (a paid-in capital account) would replace the liability account in the above entries.

The above example assumes no service or vesting period, which is a period of time until the SARs become exercisable. If the above plan had a 2-year service period, 50% of the total expense would be recognized at the end of the first year, and 100% at the end of the second year and thereafter until exercise. The compensation would be accrued as follows:

1981	($ 500)(50%)	= $ 250	- $ 0	=	$250
1982	($ 300)(100%)	= $ 300	- $250	=	$ 50
1983	($1100)(100%)	= $1100	- $300	=	$800

K. Earnings Per Share for Simple Capital Structures

In reviewing earnings per share, we recommend that candidates work through this section before reading the outline of APB 15.

A corporation is said to have a simple capital structure when (1) there are no potentially dilutive securities, or (2) if potentially dilutive securities are present, their aggregate effect on earnings per share (EPS) based upon weighted average common shares outstanding is less than (<) 3%. In this calculation, all antidilutive securities (those that would individually increase EPS based upon outstanding common shares) are disregarded.

In the simple capital structure situation, the calculation of EPS can be stated as follows:

$$\text{Earnings Per Common Share} = \frac{\text{Net Income - Applicable Preferred Dividends}}{\text{Weighted Average Number of Common Shares Outstanding}}$$

The following example will illustrate the application of this formula.

Numerator Information		Denominator Information	
a. Net Income	$100,000	a. Common shares outstanding 1-1-80	100,000
b. Extraordinary loss (net of tax)	30,000	b. Shares issued for cash 4-1	20,000
c. 6% Preferred Stock, $100 par, 1,000 shares issued and outstanding	100,000	c. Shares issued in 10% stock dividend declared in July	12,000
		d. Shares of treasury stock purchased 10-1	10,000

When a corporation reports discontinued operations, an extraordinary item and/or cumulative effect of an accounting principles change, earnings per share information is required for the following income elements:

1) Income from continuing operations
2) Income before extraordinary item and/or cumulative effect of a change in principle
3) The cumulative effect of the change in principle (net of tax) and
4) Net income

Reporting EPS on these four income elements is required regardless of whether the capital structure is simple or complex. In the example, earnings per share information is required for the second and fourth income elements.

When calculating the amount of the numerator the claims of senior securities (i.e., preferred stock) should be deducted to arrive at the earnings attributable to common shareholders. In the example, the preferred stock is cumulative. Thus, regardless of whether or not the board of directors declares a preferred dividend, holders of the preferred stock have a claim of $6,000 (1,000 shares x $6 per share) against 1980 earnings. Therefore, $6,000 has to be deducted from the numerator to arrive at the net income attributable to common shareholders. Note that this $6,000 would have been deducted for noncumulative preferred only if a dividend of this amount had been declared.

To summarize, at this point, the EPS calculations look as follows:

Earnings per common share:
On income before extraordinary item
$$\frac{\$130,000 - 6,000}{\text{Common Shares Outstanding}}$$

On net income
$$\frac{\$100,000 - 6,000}{\text{Common Shares Outstanding}}$$

The numerator of the EPS calculation covers a particular time period such as a month, a quarter, or a year. It is, therefore, consistent to calculate the average number of common shares which were outstanding during this same time period. The calculation below in Table I illustrates the determination of weighted average common shares outstanding. Note that for stock dividends the number of shares is adjusted retroactively for the shares which were outstanding prior to the dividend. Stock splits are handled in identical fashion.

TABLE I

Dates	Number Common Shares Outstanding	Months Outstanding	Fraction of Year	Shares x Fraction of Year
1-1 to 4-1	100,000 + 10% (100,000) = 110,000	3	¼	27,500
4-1 to 10-1	110,000 + 20,000 +10% (20,000) = 132,000	6	½	66,000
10-1 to 12-31	132,000 − 10,000 = 122,000	3	¼	30,500
Weighted average of common shares outstanding				124,000

In the weighted average computation, an additional problem is created if common shares are issued in a business combination during the year. If the combination is accounted for as a purchase, the common shares are weighted from the date of issuance. If the pooling method is used the shares are considered to be outstanding for the entire year, regardless of the date the pooling was consummated. Other complications in the weighted average calculation are posed by actual conversions of

debt and preferred stock to common during the year and by exercise of warrants and
options. These situations are introduced in the example presented for a complex
capital structure in the next section.

To complete the simple capital structure EPS example, the weighted average
number of common shares determined in Table I is divided into the income elements
previously computed to arrive at the following:

Earnings per common share:
On income before extraordinary item
$$\frac{\$130,000 - 6,000}{124,000 \text{ common shares}} = \$1.00$$

On net income
$$\frac{\$100,000 - 6,000}{124,000 \text{ common shares}} = \$.76$$

Reporting a $.24 loss per share due to the extraordinary item is optional. These
EPS numbers should be presented on the face of the income statement.

L. Earnings Per Share for Complex Capital Structures

By definition, complex capital structures are those which contain securities
which have the potential if assumed converted, if assumed exercised, etc. to reduce
or dilute earnings per share. If the aggregate reduction in EPS based upon the
weighted average of common shares outstanding is $\geq$ 3%, then a dual presentation of
EPS is mandated by APB 15--both primary EPS and fully diluted EPS must be disclosed.
Primary EPS is based upon outstanding common shares and dilutive common stock equivalents (CSE), while fully diluted EPS is based upon outstanding common shares, dilutive CSEs, and dilutive securities which are not CSEs. A CSE is a security which,
in form, is not a common stock but which, in substance, is accounted for as if it
were a common stock.

It is very important to note that in order to determine if dilution is $\geq$ 3%, EPS
based upon the weighted average number of common shares outstanding must be
calculated. If the dilution is immaterial (< 3%), then EPS based upon common shares
outstanding is reported on the face of the income statement as if the capital structure were simple. Otherwise, if the dilution is material, ($\geq$ 3%), then the dual
presentation noted above is required.

The following two independent examples will illustrate the procedures necessary
to calculate primary and fully diluted EPS. For both examples, assume net income is
$50,000, and the weighted average of common shares outstanding is 10,000.

In the first example, assume the following additional information with respect
to the capital structure:

a) 4% nonconvertible, cumulative preferred stock, par $100, 1,000 shares
issued and outstanding the entire year

b) Options and warrants to purchase 1,000 shares of common stock at $8 per share. The average market price of common stock during the year was $10 and the closing market price was $12 per share. The options and warrants were outstanding all year.

The capital structure in the example is complex because of the presence of the options and warrants. The preferred stock is not convertible; therefore, it is not a potentially dilutive security.

The first step in the solution of this problem is the determination of the EPS on the weighted average of common shares outstanding. This calculation appears as follows:

$$\frac{\text{Net Income - Preferred Dividends}}{\text{Weighted Average of Common Shares Outstanding}} = \frac{\$50,000 - 4,000}{10,000 \text{ shares}} = \$4.60$$

For purposes of this discussion, the EPS on weighted average common shares is referred to as the "benchmark" EPS. The "benchmark" EPS is used to determine if the 3% test is satisfied. In other words, if either primary or fully diluted EPS is $\leq$ $4.46 ($4.60 x 97%), a dual presentation of EPS is required. Note, also, that preferred dividends are deducted to arrive at net income applicable to common stock. When preferred is cumulative, this deduction is made whether or not dividends have been declared.

The calculation of primary EPS is based upon outstanding common stock and dilutive common stock equivalents. In the example, the options and warrants are the only potentially dilutive security. Options and warrants are considered to be common stock equivalents at all times. Consequently, the only question that must be resolved is whether or not the options and warrants are dilutive. For the primary computation, this question is resolved by comparing the average market price per common share of $10 with the exercise price of $8. If the average market price is > the exercise price, the effect of assuming the exercise of options and warrants is dilutive. However, if the average market price is $\leq$ the exercise price, the effect of assuming the exercise of options and warrants would be antidilutive, i.e., EPS would stay the same or increase. In the example, the options and warrants are dilutive ($10 > $8).

The method used to determine the dilutive effects of options and warrants is called the "treasury stock" method. In this example, all of the options and warrants are assumed to be exercised at the beginning of the year (the options and warrants were outstanding the entire year) and that the cash received is used to reacquire shares (treasury stock) at the average market price. The computation below illustrates the "treasury stock" method in the primary computation.

Proceeds from assumed exercise of options and warrants (1,000 shares x $8)	$8,000
Number of shares issued	1,000
Number of shares reacquired ($8,000 ÷ $10)	800
Number of shares assumed issued and not reacquired	200 *

Primary EPS can now be calculated, as follows, including the effects of applying the "treasury stock" method.

$$\frac{\text{Net Income - Preferred Dividends}}{\substack{\text{Weighted Average of Common Shares} \\ \text{Outstanding + Number of Shares not} \\ \text{Acquired with Proceeds from Options} \\ \text{and Warrants}}} = \frac{\$50,000 - 4,000}{10,200 \text{ shares}} = \$4.51$$

Note the incremental effects of the treasury stock method; there was no effect on the numerator of the EPS calculation while there were 200 shares added to the denominator. Note also that the options and warrants are dilutive. EPS is reduced from $4.60 to $4.51.

The calculation of fully diluted EPS is based upon outstanding common stock, dilutive CSEs, and other dilutive securities. This example does not contain any other dilutive securities. The options and warrants are the only potentially dilutive security in the example, and it has been shown that these securities are dilutive CSEs. However, the application of the "treasury stock" method differs for fully diluted EPS if the closing market price is higher than the average market price. When this occurs, use the closing market price in applying the "treasury stock" method.

---

*An alternative approach that can be used to calculate this number for primary EPS is demonstrated below:

$$\frac{\text{Ave. Mar. Price - Exer. Price}}{\text{Average Market Price}} \times \substack{\text{Number of} \\ \text{Shares un-} \\ \text{der Option/} \\ \text{Warrants}} = \text{Shares not Reacquired}$$

$$\frac{\$10 - 8}{\$10} \times 1,000 \text{ shares} = 200 \text{ shares}$$

The computation below illustrates this difference

Proceeds from assumed exercise of options and warrants (1,000 shares x $8)	$8,000
Number of shares issued	1,000
Number of shares reacquired ($8,000 ÷ $12)	667
Number of shares assumed issued and not reacquired	333

Fully diluted EPS can now be calculated, as follows:

$$\frac{\text{Net Income} - \text{Preferred Dividends}}{\substack{\text{Weighted Average of Common Shares Outstanding} \\ + \text{ Number of Shares not Acquired with Proceeds} \\ \text{of Options and Warrants}}} = \frac{\$50,000 - 4,000}{10,333 \text{ shares}} = \$4.45$$

Since fully diluted EPS satisfies the 3% test (the "benchmark" $4.60 x 97% = $4.46), a dual presentation of EPS is required (primary EPS = $4.51 and fully diluted = $4.45). Table II summarizes the calculations made for the first example involving complex capital structures.

TABLE II

Computations of Primary and Fully Diluted Earnings Per Share

Items	EPS on outstanding common stock (the "benchmark" EPS) Numerator	Denominator	Primary Numerator	Denominator	Fully Diluted Numerator	Denominator
Net income	$50,000		$50,000		$50,000	
Preferred div.	(4,000)		(4,000)		(4,000)	
Common shares outstanding		10,000 shs.		10,000 shs.		10,000 shs.
Options and warrants				200		333
Totals	$46,000 ÷	10,000 shs.	$46,000 ÷	10,200 shs.	$46,000 ÷	10,333 shs.
EPS	$4.60		$4.51		$4.45	

Before proceeding to the second example, note that the alternative approach to the calculation of the number of shares for the "treasury stock" method described on the previous page may also be used in the fully diluted calculation. The 333 shares that could not be reacquired are computed as follows:

End of Period Market Price (if higher)

$$\frac{\text{End of Period Market Price (if higher) - Exercise Price}}{\text{End of Period Market Price (if higher)}} \times \frac{\text{Number of Option/}}{\text{Warrant Shares}} = \frac{\text{Shares Not}}{\text{Reacquired}}$$

$$\frac{\$12 - 8}{\$12} \times 1,000 \text{ shares} = 333 \text{ shares}$$

For the second example, assume the following additional information about the capital structure (net income of $50,000 and common shares of 10,000 as in previous example):

a) 8% convertible debt, 200 bonds each convertible into 40 common shares. The bonds were outstanding the entire year. The average Aa corporate bond yield was 10% at the date the bonds were issued. The income tax rate is 40%. The bonds were issued at par ($1,000 per bond). No bonds were converted during the year.

b) 4% convertible, cumulative preferred stock, par $100, 1,000 shares issued and outstanding. Each preferred share is convertible into 2 common shares. The preferred was outstanding the entire year, and the average Aa corporate bond yield at the date the preferred was issued was 10%. The preferred was issued at par. No preferred stock was converted during the year.

The capital structure is complex in this example because of the presence of the two convertible securities.

The first step in the solution of this example is the calculation of EPS based upon weighted average of common shares outstanding. This "benchmark" EPS is the same as it was for the first example, i.e. $4.60. Again, a dual presentation of EPS will be required if either primary or fully diluted EPS ≤ $4.46 ($4.60 x 97%).

The next step is the computation of primary EPS. Unlike options and warrants, convertible securities are not automatically CSEs. A cash yield test must be performed on each convertible security to determine its CSE status. If the cash yield (cash to be received annually as interest or dividends divided by the issue price) at date of issuance of the convertible security is < 2/3 of the average Aa corporate bond yield (SFAS 55), the convertible security is a CSE; otherwise, it is not a CSE. Keep in mind that securities which fail the cash yield test can still affect the fully diluted EPS.

In the present example, the convertible bonds are not common stock equivalents because the cash yield at date of issuance of 8% is larger than 6.7% (2/3 x 10%). On the other hand, the convertible preferred is a CSE because its cash yield of 4% is less than 6.7%. The primary computation will include the convertible preferred if it is dilutive.

To determine the dilutive effect of the preferred stock, an assumption (called the "if converted" method) is made that all of the preferred stock is converted at the earliest date that it could have occurred during the year. In this example, the date would be January 1. The effects of this assumption are twofold. One, if the preferred is converted, there will be no preferred dividend of $4,000 for the year; and, two, there will be an additional 2,000 shares of common outstanding during the year (the conversion rate is 2 common for 1 preferred). Primary EPS is computed, as follows, reflecting these two assumptions:

$$\frac{\text{Net Income}}{\substack{\text{Weighted Average of Common Shares} \\ \text{Outstanding + Shares Issued upon} \\ \text{Conversion of Preferred}}} = \frac{\$50,000}{12,000 \text{ shares}} = \$4.17$$

The convertible preferred is dilutive because it reduced EPS from $4.60 to $4.17. Furthermore, primary EPS is lower than $4.46 ($4.60 x 97%). This means that a dual presentation of EPS is required.

Fully diluted EPS includes the dilutive effects of CSEs and other dilutive securities. In the example, the convertible bonds are assumed to have been converted at the beginning of the year. The effects of this assumption are twofold. One, if the bonds are converted, there will be no interest expense of $16,000 (8% x $200,000 face value); and, two, there will be an additional 8,000 shares (200 bonds x 40 shares) of common stock outstanding during the year. One note of caution, however, must be mentioned; namely, the effect of not having $16,000 of interest expense will increase income, but it will also increase tax expense. Consequently, the net effect of not having interest expense is $9,600 ($16,000 minus 40% x $16,000). Fully diluted EPS is computed, as follows, reflecting the dilutive preferred and the effects noted above for the convertible bonds.

$$\frac{\text{Net Income + Interest Expense (net of tax)}}{\substack{\text{Weighted Average of Commmon Shares Outstanding} \\ \text{+ Shares Issued upon Conversion of Preferred} \\ \text{and Conversion of Bonds}}} = \frac{\$50,000 + 9,600}{20,000 \text{ shares}} = \$2.98$$

The convertible debt is dilutive. Both the convertible bonds and preferred reduced EPS from $4.60 to $2.98. Table III summarizes the computations made for the second example.

The income statement disclosures for EPS, as a result of the second example, would be as follows:

Earnings per common and common equivalent shares (see note X) $4.17
Earnings per share assuming full dilution   2.98

Note X would state the assumptions made in determining both primary and fully diluted EPS numbers.

TABLE III

Computations of Primary and Fully Diluted Earnings Per Share

Items	EPS on outstanding common stock (the "benchmark" EPS)		Primary		Fully Diluted	
	Numerator	*Denominator*	*Numerator*	*Denominator*	*Numerator*	*Denominator*
Net income	$50,000		$50,000		$50,000	
Preferred div.	(4,000)					
Common shares outstanding		10,000 shs.		10,000 shs.		10,000 shs.
Conversion of preferred				2,000		2,000
Conversion of bonds					9,600	8,000
Totals	$46,000 ÷	10,000 shs.	$50,000 ÷	12,000 shs.	$59,600 ÷	20,000 shs.
EPS	$4.60		$4.17		$2.98	

In the two examples, all of the potentially dilutive securities were outstanding the entire year and no conversions or exercises were made during the year. If a potentially dilutive security were not outstanding the entire year, then the numerator and denominator effects would have to be "time-weighted." For instance, suppose the convertible bonds in the second example were issued during the current year on July 1. If all other facts remain unchanged, fully diluted EPS would be computed as follows:

$$\frac{\text{Net Income + Interest Expense (net of tax)}}{\substack{\text{Weighted Average of Common Shares Outstanding} \\ \text{+ Shares Issued upon Conversion of Preferred} \\ \text{and Conversion of Bonds}}} = \frac{\$50,000 + 1/2(9,600)}{10,000 + 2,000 + 1/2(8,000)} = \$3.43$$

The convertible debt is dilutive whether or not it is outstanding the entire year or for part of a year.

If actual conversions or exercises take place during a period, the common shares issued will be outstanding from their date of issuance and, therefore, will be in the weighted average of common shares outstanding. These shares are then weighted from their respective times of issuance. For example, assume that all the bonds in the second example are converted on July 1 into 8,000 common shares. Several important effects should be noted, as follows:

1) The weighted average of common shares outstanding will be increased by (8,000)(.5) or 4,000. Income will increase $4,800 net of tax, because the bonds are no longer outstanding.

2) The "if converted" method is applied to the period January 1 to July 1 because it was during this period that the bonds were potentially dilutive. The interest expense, net of tax, of $4,800 is added to the income, and 4,000 shares (.5 of 8,000) are added to the denominator.

3) Interestingly, the net effect of items 1 and 2 is the same for the period whether these dilutive bonds were outstanding the entire period or converted during the period.

It is also important to note that, in the second example, the preferred stock and bonds were both issued at par. This was done to facilitate the determination of cash yield. If, however, the convertible preferred and/or the convertible bonds were issued at amounts other than par, then cash yield would be determined at issuance as follows:

1) Preferred $= \dfrac{\text{Annual Dividend}}{\text{Amount Received at Issuance}} = $ Cash yield %

2) Bonds $\quad = \dfrac{\text{Annual Cash Interest}}{\text{Amount Received at Issuance}} = $ Cash yield %

The cash yield for each issue is then compared with 2/3 of the average Aa corporate bond yield rate at date of issue to determine if the security is a CSE. Also, when convertible debt is issued for a premium or a discount the interest expense net of taxes must be computed after giving effect to premium or discount amortization.

The topics discussed in the calculation of EPS for simple and complex capital structures have touched upon the major issues which should be understood. For topics or issues not explained in the example, e.g., the 20% limitation on purchase of shares in the treasury stock method, antidilutive conversions, etc., the reader is advised to study an intermediate accounting textbook and to examine the interpretation of APB 15.

M. Corporate Bankruptcy

The going concern assumption is one of the basic principles underlying the primary financial statements (Balance Sheet, Income Statement and Statement of Changes in Financial Position). However, this assumption of continued existence is threatened in corporations that are in severe financial trouble. A range of alternative actions is available to a company before it enters bankruptcy such as seeking extensions on due dates of debt, restructuring its debt, or allowing a court-appointed trustee to manage the corporation. These pre-bankruptcy options are presented in the following modules:

Creditor's agreements--Module 11, Bankruptcy
Quasi-reorganizations--Next section in this module
Troubled debt restructurings--Module 29, Present Value, Section C

Bankruptcy is the final legal act for a company. In bankruptcy, the accounting and financial reporting must present the information necessary for the liquidation of the business. The <u>Statement of Affairs</u> is prepared to present the current market values of the assets and the status of the various categories of the equity interests of the corporation.

The accountant must provide a prioritization of the creditors' claims against the net assets of the corporation. The legal rights of each creditor are determined by the terms of the credit agreement it has with the company and by the National Bankruptcy Act.

The Statement of Affairs classifies assets in the following order of priority (highest to lowest):

1) Assets pledged with fully secured creditors--assets having a fair valuation equal to or greater than the debts they serve as collateral for

2) Assets pledged with partially secured creditors--assets having a fair valuation less than their associated debts

3) Free assets--uncommitted assets available for remaining equity interests

The equity interests are classified in the following order (highest to lowest):

1) Preferred claims--these claims have priority as specified in the Bankruptcy Act

2) Fully secured creditors--these are claims which should be fully covered with the realizations from the assets pledged to the claims

3) Partially secured creditors--these are claims which may not be fully covered by the realizations of the pledged assets for these claims; the amount of the uncovered claims goes to the unsecured creditors category

4) Unsecured creditors--these are claims that have no priority and do not have any collateral claims to any specific assets

5) Stockholders' Equity--this represents any residual claim

The historical cost valuation principles used in a balance sheet assume a going concern assumption. As a business enters bankruptcy, the liquidation values of the assets become the most relevant measures. In addition, anticipated costs of liquidation should be recognized. The Statement of Affairs begins with the present book values of the company's assets in order to articulate with the balance sheet. After relating the projected proceeds from the liquidation of the assets to the various equity interests, the statement concludes with the estimated dollar amount of unsecured claims that cannot be paid (estimated deficiency).

> *EXAMPLE: The Vann Corporation's Balance Sheet for December 31, 1982 is shown below. The corporation is entering bankruptcy and expects to incur $6,000 of costs for the liquidation process. The estimated current values of the assets are determined and the various equity claims are prioritized. The Statement of Affairs for Vann Corporation is presented on page 869.*

The Vann Corporation
Balance Sheet
December 31, 1982

Assets

Cash	$ 1,500
Marketable Securities	10,000
Accounts Receivable (net)	18,000
Merchandise Inventory	41,000
Prepaid Expenses	2,000
Land	6,000
Building (net of depreciation)	65,000
Machinery (net of depreciation)	21,000
Goodwill	10,000
	$174,500

Equities

Accounts Payable	$ 30,000
Notes Payable	37,000
Accrued Wages	6,500
Mortgages Payable	45,000
Capital Stock ($10 par)	100,000
Retained Earnings (deficit)	<44,000>
	$174,500

N. Quasi-Reorganization (ARB 43, Chapter 7A)

The purpose of quasi-reorganization is to allow companies to avoid formal bankruptcy proceedings through an informal proceeding. The procedure is applicable for a situation where a going concern exists except for overvalued assets and a possible deficit. The overvalued assets result in high depreciation charges and losses or lower net income. The deficit precludes payment of dividends.

The procedure is applicable during a period of declining price levels (normally associated with decreased economic activity), such as the Thirties.

The procedures involve:

1) Proper authorization including from stockholders and creditors where required
2) Revaluation of assets to current values
3) Elimination of any deficit by charging paid-in capital

   a) First capital surplus
   b) Second capital stock

The Vann Corporation
Statement of Affairs
December 31, 1982

ASSETS

Book Values		Estimated Current Values	Amount Available to Unsecured Claims
	(1) Assets Pledged with Fully Secured Creditors:		
$ 6,000	Land	$12,000	
65,000	Building	41,000	
		$53,000	
	Less Mortgages Payable	45,000	$ 8,000
	(2) Assets Pledged with Partially Secured Creditors:		
10,000	Marketable Securities	$12,000	
	Notes Payable	37,000	
	(3) Free Assets		
1,500	Cash	1,500	
18,000	Accounts Receivable (net)	14,000	
41,000	Merchandise Inventory	22,500	
2,000	Prepaid Expenses	0	
21,000	Machinery	13,200	
10,000	Goodwill	0	51,200
	Estimated amount available		59,200
	Less: creditors with priority		(14,500)
	Net estimated amount available to unsecured creditors (81 cents on the dollar)		44,700
	Estimated deficiency to unsecured creditors		10,300
$174,500			$55,000

EQUITIES

Book Values			Amount Unsecured
	(1) Creditors with Priority		
$ 0	Estimated Liquidation Expenses (accounting, legal and other costs of liquidation process)	$ 8,000	
6,500	Accrued Wages	6,500	
		$14,500	
	(2) Fully Secured Creditors		
45,000	Mortgages Payable	45,000	
	(3) Partially Secured Creditors		
37,000	Notes Payable	37,000	
	Less Marketable Securities	12,000	25,000
	(4) Unsecured Creditors		
30,000	Accounts Payable		30,000
	(5) Stockholders' Equity		
100,000	Capital Stock		
(44,000)	Retained Earnings (deficit)		
$174,500			$55,000

To write down assets: here the adjustments are taken directly to retained earnings. An alternative is to use an intermediary account such as "adjustment account" which would later be closed to retained earnings.

Retained earnings	(writedown)
Assets	(writedown)

To eliminate the deficit

Paid-in capital	(deficit)
Retained earnings	(deficit)

In many cases, paid-in capital in excess of par value will be insufficient, and the par or stated value of the capital stock must be reduced to eliminate the deficit.

Existing paid-in capital	(amount on the books)
Capital stock	(total reduction in par)
Retained earnings	(deficit)
Paid-in capital from quasi-reorganization	(forced figure)

The paid-in capital arises from reducing the par or stated value from, for example, $100 to $50 rather than to $59.415. The $59.415 would come from dividing the shares outstanding into the retained earnings deficit.

ARB 46 requires retained earnings to be dated for 10 years (less than 10 years justified under exceptional circumstances) after a quasi-reorganization takes place. Disclosure similar to "since quasi-reorganization of June 30, 1977," would be appropriate.

O. Stock Rights

Generally, before additional stock is offered to the public, stock rights are issued to existing shareholders to prevent involuntary dilution of their voting rights (e.g., the preemptive privilege). The stock rights, evidenced by warrants, indicate the number and price at which the shares may be purchased. At issuance, the issuer makes only a memorandum entry. Upon exercise, the following entry is made:

Cash	(proceeds)
Common stock	(par)
Paid-in capital	(plug)

Information relating to stock rights outstanding must be disclosed. Detachable stock rights issued with preferred stock are treated like those on bonds (see Module 29, section "B.6."). Treatment of stock rights by recipients is discussed in Module 33, section "E."

PRESENT VALUE

A. Fundamentals

This module includes the basics of time value of money factors (TVMF) and non-current liabilities and other accounts requiring present values, e.g., investments in bonds. The three major application topics are bonds payable and bond investments, pensions, and leases. After completing the sections on bonds payable and bond investments study the outline of APB 21, Interest on Receivables and Payables.

1. Time Value of Money Formulas

The concepts of time value of money are essential for successful completion of the CPA exam. TVMF concepts are central to capital budgeting, leases, pensions, bonds, and other topics. You must understand the mechanics as well as the concepts. After studying the next few pages, work the multiple choice questions entitled Fundamental Concepts.

There are four basic time value of money formulas: A = Dollar amount, i = Interest rate, and n = Number of periods.

1) Future value of an amount $A(1+i)^n$

2) Present value of a future amount $\dfrac{A}{(1+i)^n}$

3) Future value of an annuity $A\left[\dfrac{(1+i)^n - 1}{i}\right]$

4) Present value of a future annuity $A\left[\dfrac{1 - (1+i)^{-n}}{i}\right]$

2. Future Value of an Amount (amount of $1)

The future value of an amount is the amount that will be available at some point in the future if an amount is deposited today and earns compound interest for "n" periods. The most common application is savings deposits. For example, if you deposited $100 today at 10%, you would have $110 at the end of the first year, $121 at the end of the second year, etc.

Formula: FV amount = $A(1+i)^n$

EXAMPLE:

A = $100, i = 10%
End of first year $100(1.10)
End of second year $100(1.10)^2 or $100(1.21)

The compounding feature allows you to earn interest on interest. In the second year of the example you earn $11 interest: $10 on the original $100 and $1 on the first year's interest of $10.

3. Present Value of a Future Amount (present value of $1)

The present value of a future amount is the amount you would pay now for an amount to be received "n" periods in the future given an interest rate of "i". A common application would be the proceeds you would lend today for a noninterest-bearing note receivable in the future. For example, if you were lending money at 10%, you would lend $100 for a $110 note due in one year or for a $121 note due in two years.

Formula:
$$PV \text{ amount} = A(1+i)^{-n} \text{ or } \frac{A}{(1+i)^n}$$

EXAMPLE:

$110 note due in 1 year $\dfrac{\$110}{1.10}$

$121 note due in 2 years $\dfrac{\$121}{(1.10)^2}$

The present value of $1 is the inverse of the future value of $1. Thus, given a future value of $1 table, you have a present value of $1 dividing each value into 1.00. Look at the present value of $1 and future value of $1 tables on the next page. The future value of $1 at 10% in 5 years is 1.611. Thus, the present value of $1 in 5 years would be 1.00 ÷ 1.611 which is .621 (check the table). Conversely, the future value of $1 is found by dividing the present value of $1 into 1.00, e.g., 1.00 ÷ .621 = 1.611.

4. Compounding

When interest is compounded more frequently than once a year, multiply "n" times the number of times compounded annually and divide "i" by the number of times compounded annually. For example, if the 10% were compounded semiannually, the amount of $1.00 at the end of 1 year would be $110.25 $[(1.05)^2]$ instead of $110.00. The extra $.25 is 5% of the 5.00 interest earned in the first half of the year.

5. Time Value of Money Factor (TVMF) Tables

Look over the tables below. You should be able to tell the type of table by the time value of money factors.

Future Value (Amount) of $1

n	6%	8%	10%	12%	15%
1	1.060	1.080	1.100	1.120	1.150
2	1.124	1.166	1.210	1.254	1.323
3	1.191	1.260	1.331	1.405	1.521
4	1.262	1.360	1.464	1.574	1.749
5	1.338	1.469	1.611	1.762	2.011

Present Value of $1

n	6%	8%	10%	12%	15%
1	.943	.926	.909	.893	.870
2	.890	.857	.826	.797	.756
3	.840	.794	.751	.712	.658
4	.792	.735	.683	.636	.572
5	.747	.681	.621	.567	.497

Future Value (Amount) of an Ordinary Annuity of $1

n	6%	8%	10%	12%	15%
1	1.000	1.000	1.000	1.000	1.000
2	2.060	2.080	2.100	2.120	2.150
3	3.184	3.246	3.310	3.374	3.473
4	4.375	4.506	4.641	4.779	4.993
5	5.637	5.867	6.105	6.353	6.742

Present Value of an Ordinary Annuity of $1

n	6%	8%	10%	12%	15%
1	.943	.926	.909	.893	.870
2	1.833	1.783	1.736	1.690	1.626
3	2.673	2.577	2.487	2.402	2.283
4	3.465	3.312	3.170	3.037	2.855
5	4.212	3.993	3.791	3.605	3.352

6. Future Value of an Ordinary Annuity

The future value of an ordinary annuity is the amount available "n" periods in the future as a result of the deposit of an amount (A) at the end of every period 1 through "n." Compound interest is earned at the rate of "i" on the deposits. The common application is a bond sinking fund. A deposit is made at the end of the first period and earns compound interest for n-1 periods (not during the first period, because the deposit is made at the end of the first period). The next to the last payment earns one period's interest, i.e., n - (n-1) = 1. The last payment earns no interest, because it is deposited at the end of the last (nth) period. Remember that in the FUTURE AMOUNT OF AN ORDINARY ANNUITY TABLE, all of the factors for any "n" row are based on one less interest period than the number of payments.

Formula:

$$FV \text{ annuity} = A(1+i)^{n-1} + A(1+i)^{n-2} + \ldots + A(1+i) + A = A\left[\frac{(1+i)^n - 1}{i}\right]$$

EXAMPLE:

Value of an annuity (i=.10) of $100/year at the end of three years, i.e., three payments, the first being made at end of the first period.

$$FV \text{ annuity} = \$100(1.10)^2 + \$100(1.10) + \$100 (1.00) = \$331.$$

7. Present Value of an Ordinary Annuity

The present value of an ordinary annuity is the value today, given a discount rate, of a series of future payments. A common application is the capitalization of lease payments by either lessors or lessees. Payments "1" through "n" are assumed to be made at the end of years "1" through "n," and are discounted back to the present.

Formula:

$$PV \text{ annuity} = \frac{A}{1+i} + \frac{A}{(1+i)^2} + \ldots + \frac{A}{(1+i)^{n-1}} + \frac{A}{(1+i)^n} = A\left[\frac{1-(1+i)^{-n}}{i}\right]$$

EXAMPLE:

Present value of an annuity (i=.10) of $100/year at the end of each year for three years.

$$PV \text{ annuity} = \frac{\$100}{1.10} + \frac{\$100}{1.10^2} + \frac{\$100}{1.10^3}$$

$$\$248.68 = 90.91 + 82.64 + 75.13$$

EXAMPLE application:

Assume a 5 year lease of equipment requiring payments of $1,000 at the end of each of the five years, which is to be capitalized. If the discount rate is 8%, the present value is $3,993 ($1,000 x 3.993).

8. Distinguishing a Future Value of an Annuity from a Present Value of an Annuity

Sometimes confusion arises in distinguishing between the future value (amount) of an annuity and the present value of an annuity. These two may be distinguished by determining whether the total dollar amount in the problem comes at the beginning (e.g., cost of equipment acquired for leasing) or at the end (e.g., the amount needed to retire bonds) of the series of payments as illustrated below.

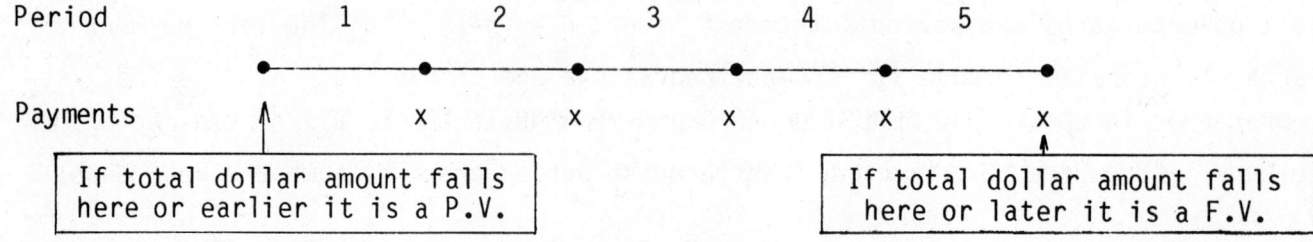

Remember: if the amount given or to be computed comes at the end of the series of payments, it is a <u>future value</u> of annuity situation. If the amount given or to be computed comes at the beginning of the series of payments, it is a <u>present value</u> of annuity situation.

9. Annuities Due

In some cases, the payments or annuities may not conform to the assumptions inherent in the annuity tables. For example, the payments might be made at the beginning of each of the five years instead of at the end of each year. This is an annuity due (annuity in advance) in contrast to an ordinary annuity (annuity in arrears). Both annuity due and ordinary annuity payments are represented by the "x's" in the illustration below:

Period	1	2	3	4	5

Annuity   x   x   x   x   x

Annuity Due   x   x   x   x   x

For a future value of annuity due situation, it is necessary to (a) find the TVMF for n + 1 periods and to (b) subtract 1.00. It is necessary to add "1" to "n" because the row of factors for each "n" in the ordinary annuity table has one less interval (interest period) than the number of payments. It is necessary to subtract 1.00 from the factor found on the n + 1 line in the table, because that factor will contain one more payment (1.00) than is actually being made. Finding the n + 1 factor and subtracting 1.00 gives a factor which includes compound interest for the additional period.

The TVMF of the present value of an annuity due is found by (a) finding the n - 1 factor in the ordinary annuity table and (b) adding 1.00 to that factor. It is necessary to use the n - 1 factor because the present value of annuity due has one less discount period than the number of payments. It is necessary to add 1.00 to the factor, because there is a payment at the beginning of period 1. If the payments in the 5 period lease example just above were made at the beginning of the period, the present value would be:

$$3.312 + 1.000 = 4.312$$
$$4.312 \times \$1,000 = \$4,312$$

The present value of the first payment which is made today is $1,000, i.e., the TVMF is 1.00. The remaining four payments comprise an ordinary annuity for four periods

as you can see on the above diagram. Always use time diagrams to analyze applications of annuities. Finally, notice that the present value of the annuity due in
the above example is $319 greater than the present value of the ordinary annuity,
because the payments are moved closer to the present.

10. TVMF Applications

The basic formula to use is:

FV or PV = TVMF x Amount

If an annuity is involved, the amount is the periodic payment or deposit; if not, it
is a single sum. Note that FV or PV is determined by 3 variables: time, interest
rate, and payment. TVMF represents two variables: time and interest rate. The
tables usually have the interest rate on the horizontal axis and time on the vertical axis. The above formula may also be stated:

$$\text{Amount} = \frac{\text{FV or PV}}{\text{TVMF}}$$

For example, if we need to accumulate $12,210 in five years to repay a loan, we
could determine the required annual deposit with the above formula. If the savings
rate were 10%, we would divide the FV ($12,210) by the TVMF of the future value of
annuity, n=5, i=.10 (6.105) and get $2,000. Thus, $2,000 deposited at the end of
each of five years earning 10% will result in $12,210. This formula may also be
used to find future values of an amount, present values of amounts, and annuities in
the same manner.

Another variation of the formula is:

$$\text{TVMF} = \frac{\text{FV or PV}}{\text{Amount}}$$

For example, we may be offered to choose between paying $3,312 in cash or $1,000 a
year at the end of each of the next four years. We determine the interest rate by
dividing the annual payment into the present value of the annuity to obtain the TVMF
(3.312) for n=4. We then find the interest rate which has the same or similar TVMF
(in this case 8%).

Alternatively, using the above formula, we may know the interest rate but not
know the number of payments. Given the TVMF, we can determine "n" by looking in the
TVMF table under the known interest rate. Remember the TVMF reflects two variables:
time and interest rate.

The table presented below summarizes the relationships between present value, future value and TVMFs for different cash flow timings.

SUMMARY OF TIME VALUE OF MONEY FACTORS (TVMF)

- Future value factor = (FV)   • Interest rate = i
- Present value factor = (PV)   • Number of periods or rents = n

A.   Future Value of 1.000

   1.   Future Value   =   Present Value x TVMF (FV)

   2.   TVMF (FV)   = $\dfrac{\text{Future Value}}{\text{Present Value}}$

   3.   Present Value   = $\dfrac{\text{Future Value}}{\text{TVMF (FV)}}$

B.   Present Value of 1.000

   1.   Present Value   =   Future Value x TVMF (PV)

   2.   TVMF (PV)   = $\dfrac{\text{Present Value}}{\text{Future Value}}$

   3.   Future Value   = $\dfrac{\text{Present Value}}{\text{TVMF (PV)}}$

C.   Future Value of an Ordinary Annuity of 1.000

   1.   Future Value of Annuity   =   Rent x TVMF (FV)

   2.   Rent   = $\dfrac{\text{Future Value of Annuity}}{\text{TVMF (FV)}}$

   3.   TVMF (FV)   = $\dfrac{\text{Future Value of Annuity}}{\text{Rent}}$

       a.   "i" unknown, or
       b.   "n" unknown

D.   Present Value of an Ordinary Annuity of 1.000

   1.   Present Value of Annuity   =   Rent x TVMF (PV)

   2.   Rent   = $\dfrac{\text{Present Value of Annuity}}{\text{TVMF (PV)}}$

   3.   TVMF (PV)   = $\dfrac{\text{Present Value of Annuity}}{\text{Rent}}$

       a.   "i" unknown, or
       b.   "n" unknown

E.   Annuities Due
   1.   Relationships are the same as those for ordinary annuities (C and D above).
   2.   Ordinary annuity table factors must be modified
       a.   TVMF (FV)   = $\text{TVMF}_{n+1} - 1.000$
       b.   TVMF (PV)   = $\text{TVMF}_{n-1} + 1.000$

F.   Alternative Terminology
   1.   Ordinary Annuity = Annuity in Arrears
   2.   Annuity Due = Annuity in Advance

11. Notes Receivable and Payable

Notes should be recorded at their present values (see outline of APB 21).
Upon receipt or issuance of a note, record the net value of the note receivable or
payable (i.e., note plus or minus premium or discount) at:
1. Cash received or paid
    a. Assumes no other rights or privileges
2. Established exchange price of property or services received or provided
    a. If not determinable, determine present value with imputed interest rate
Record interest revenue (on notes receivable) or interest expense (on notes payable)
as the effective rate of interest times the net receivable or payable during the
period.

For example, if a $10,000 noninterest-bearing note due in 3 years is issued for
a machine and the appropriate interest rate is 10%, the present value of the note is
$7,510 (or if the market value of the machine were $7,510, the discount rate would
be 10%). The entry to record the acquisition can be at net or gross (gross is preferable).

Note recorded at gross			Note recorded at net		
Machine	7,510		Machinery	7,510	
Discount on note pay	2,490				
Note payable		10,000	Note payable		7,510

At the end of the first year:

Interest expense	751		Interest expense	751	
Discount on note pay		751	Note payable		751
[10% of $7,510]					

At the end of year two:

Interest expense	826		Interest expense	826	
Discount on note pay		826	Note payable		826
[10% of $8,261 ($7,510 + $751)]					

At the end of year three:

Interest expense	909		Interest expense	909	
Discount on note pay		909	Note payable		909
[10% of $9,087 ($8,261 + $826)]					
Note payable	10,000		Note payable	10,000	
Cash		10,000	Cash		10,000

Understand that the entries would be the opposite for notes receivable except there
would be interest revenue rather than expense.

Another variation would be an interest-bearing note which had a present value different from the face value, because the stated rate of interest was too low or high (i.e., like bond discount and premium). The only difference is the cash (interest) received or paid.

1) Record the note at present value

2) Record interest revenue or expense at the effective rate of interest times the net book value of the note (face ± premium or discount)

3) Record cash received or paid (it is the stated interest rate times the face value)

4) Record the difference between the amount paid (received) and the amount of interest expense (revenue) as an adjustment to the premium or discount

5) Example entry (entry for creditor would have opposite entry)

> Interest expense   (effective rate times
>   net book value)
> Note premium or discount   (plug)
>   Cash   (amount paid: contract
>   rate times face value)

B. Bonds

1. Bonds Payable and Bond Investments

Investment in bonds and bonds payable are discussed together to contrast their treatment. Accounting for investments in bonds (short-term) was discussed briefly in Module 24 (Short-Term Investments), Section I.

Bonds generally provide for periodic fixed interest payments at a contract rate of interest. At issuance, or thereafter, the market rate of interest for the particular type of bond may be above, the same, or below the contract rate. If the market rate exceeds the contract rate, the bond value will be less than the maturity value. The difference (discount) will make up for the contract rate being below the market rate.

Conversely, when the contract rate exceeds the market rate, the bond will sell for more than maturity value to bring the effective rate to the market rate. When the contract rate equals the market rate, the bond will sell for the maturity value.

The market value of a bond is equal to the maturity value and interest payments discounted to the present. You may have to refer to the discussion of time value of money concepts in the previous section before working with the subsequent material. Finally, when solving bond problems, candidates must be careful when determining the number of months to use in the calculation of interest and discount/premium amortization. For example, candidates frequently look at a bond issue with an interest date of September 1 and count three months to December 31. This error is easy to make because candidates focus only on the fact that September is the ninth month instead of also noting whether the date is at the beginning or end of the month.

2. Bond Valuation Example

$10,000 in bonds, semiannual interest at 6% contract rate, maturing in 6 years, and market rate of 5%.

    1) Find present value of maturity value. Discount $10,000 back 12 periods at 2 1/2% interest. (Semiannual compounding is going to be required to discount the semiannual payments so it is also assumed here.)

$$\$10,000 \times \left(\frac{1}{(1.025)}\right)^{12}$$

        $10,000 x .7436 = $7,436

    2) Find the present value of the annuity of twelve $300 interest payments

        $300 PV $_{12|.025}$

        $300 x 10.26 = $3,078

    3) Today's value is $10,514 (7,436 + 3,078)

The $514 premium is to be recognized over the life of the bond issue. It is a reduction of interest expense on the books of the issuer and a reduction of interest revenue on the books of the investor. Amortization is to be by the interest, or present value basis. (See outline of APB 21.)

3. Journal Entries

The issuer's books will be illustrated at gross (including a premium or discount account) and the investor's books will be illustrated at net (no discount or premium account). The investor may record the bonds either net or gross, but the issuer records at gross. In the past, CPA examination problems and solutions have followed the net method on the books of the investor.

		Issuer			Investor	
1)	Issue and Acquisition	Cash	10,514		Bond invest	10,514
		Bonds pay		10,000	Cash	10,514
		Bond prem		514		
2)	First int payment	Interest exp	300		Cash	300
		Cash		300	Interest rev	300
3)	Premium-- Amortization	Bond prem	37.15*		Interest rev	37.15
		Interest exp		37.15	Bond invest	37.15*

*Interest receipt (payment) minus effective interest = 300 - 262.85 = 37.15
 Effective interest = net book value times effective rate = 10,514 x .025 = 262.85

Subsequent interest payments are recorded like entry 2 shown above. The amount of subsequent amortization (entry 3 above) changes. Interest to be recorded under the interest method is always computed by:

Effective Interest Rate x Net Book Value

This formula is true of all applications of the interest method. The effective rate of interest times net book value is the actual interest revenue or expense for the period. The difference between the actual interest and the amount received or paid is the amortization. The amortization table below shows the effective interest amounts and premium amortizations for the first four periods.

Period	3% cash interest	2½% effective interest	Decrease in book value	Book value of bonds
0				$10,514.00
1	$300(a)	$262.85(b)	$37.15(c)	10,476.85(d)
2	300	261.92	38.08	10,438.77
3	300	260.97	39.03	10,399.74
4	300	259.99	40.01	10,359.73

(a) 3% x $10,000   (c) $300 − $262.85
(b) 2½% x $10,514.00   (d) $10,514.00 − $37.15

Since the interest is paid semiannually, interest (including premium amortization) is recorded every six months. The journal entries for periods 2, 3, and 4 are:

	Issuer			Investor		
Period 2	Interest expense	261.92		Cash	300.00	
	Bond premium	38.08		Interest rev		261.92
	Cash		300.00	Bond invest		38.08
Period 3	Interest expense	260.97		Cash	300.00	
	Bond premium	39.03		Interest rev		260.97
	Cash		300.00	Bond invest		39.03
Period 4	Interest expense	259.99		Cash	300.00	
	Bond premium	40.01		Interest rev		259.99
	Cash		300.00	Bond invest		40.01

Notice that the interest (revenue and expense) decreases over time. This is because the net book value (which is also the present value) is decreasing from the maturity value plus premium to the maturity value. Thus, the effective rate is being multiplied times a smaller amount each 6 months.

Also, note that the change in interest each period is the prior period's premium amortization times the effective rate. For example, the interest in period 3 is $.95 less than in period 2, and $38.08 of premium was amortized in period 2. The effective rate of 2.5% (every 6 months) times $38.08 is $.95. Thus, if the interest changes due to the changing level of net book value, the change in interest will be equal to the change in net book value times the effective rate of interest.

Another complication may arise if the year end does not coincide with the interest dates. In such a case, an adjusting entry must be made. The proportional share of interest payable or receivable should be recognized along with the amortization of discount or premium. The amortization of discount or premium should be straight-line within the amortization period.

> EXAMPLE: Assume that in the above example, both issuer and investor have reporting periods ending 3 months after the issuance of the bonds.

	Issuer			Investor	
Entries on the closing date	Interest expense	150		Interest receivable	150
	Interest payable		150	Interest revenue	150
	Bond premium	18.57		Interest revenue	18.57
	Interest expense		18.57	Bond investment	18.57

Reverse at beginning of new period and make regular entry at next interest payment date.

If bonds are sold (bought) between interest dates, premium/discount amortization must be computed for the period between sale (purchase) date and last (next) interest date. This is accomplished by straight-lining the six-month amount which was calculated using the effective interest method.

> EXAMPLE: The investor sold $5,000 of bonds in the above example, two months after issuance, for $5,250 plus interest.
>
> 1. The bond premium which must be amortized to the point of sale ($5,000 for 2 months) is 1/2 x 1/3 x $37.15 or $6.19.
>
> | Interest revenue | $6.19 | |
> |---|---|---|
> | Investment | | $6.19 |
>
> 2. The sale is recorded. The investment account was $5,257 before amortization of $6.19. The cash received would be $5,250 plus $50 interest (1/2 x 1/3 x $300). The loss is a forced figure.
>
> | Cash | $5,300 | |
> |---|---|---|
> | Loss | $ .81 | |
> | Interest revenue | | $ 50.00 |
> | Investment | | $5,250.81 |
>
> 3. Check the interest revenue recorded ($50.00 - $6.19) to the interest earned: $5,257 x 2 1/2% x 1/3 (which equals $43.81).

Costs incurred in connection with issuing bonds should be classified as a deferred charge and amortized on a straight-line basis over the life of the bonds.

4. Comparison of Effective Interest and Straight-Line Amortization Methods

Although APB 21 requires use of the effective interest method for determining interest on receivables and payables, the straight-line method may be used if the result obtained is not materially different from that obtained using the effective interest method.

Several recent CPA exam questions have asked candidates to compare the dollar amount of interest revenue (expense) and the interest rate obtained under each method. The table below summarizes the relationships which are obtained under both methods when a note is issued at: (1) a premium and (2) a discount.

	Effective Interest Method			Straight-Line Method		
Note Is- sued At:	(a) Effective Interest Rate	x (b) Carrying (Book) Value	= (c) Amount of Interest In- come (Expense)	(d) Cash Interest	± (e) Discount (Premium) Amortization	= (f) Amount of Interest
(1) Discount	Constant	Increasing	Increasing	Constant	Constant	Constant
(2) Premium	Constant	Decreasing	Decreasing	Constant	Constant	Constant

In the above chart, the three columnar headings under each method are written in the form of an equation. Under the effective interest method, the dollar amount of interest revenue (expense), column (c), is derived by multiplying the effective rate (a constant percentage), column (a), by an increasing (decreasing) carrying value, column (b), resulting in an increasing (decreasing) dollar amount of interest, column (c).

Under the straight-line method, the dollar amount of interest revenue (expense), column (f), is the dollar amount of cash interest (nominal or stated rate times the face of the note), column (d) plus (minus) the discount (premium) amortization, column (e). When the constant dollar amount of interest revenue (expense) is related to an increasing (decreasing) carrying value the result is a decreasing (increasing) interest rate which is, essentially, an "accounting" or "book" interest rate. This rate is the result of using an arbitrary method (straight-line) which ignores the economic facts of the situation. The effective interest method gives recognition to the economic facts by using the rate (effective) which resulted from the bargaining of the parties to the note.

When the note is a bond, this may involve many parties (i.e., the market) and the effective rate is referred to as the "market" or "yield" rate.

5. Convertible Bonds (See outline of APB 14)

Bonds are frequently issued with the right to convert the bonds into common stock. When issued, no value is apportioned to the conversion feature. Two approaches are possible to account for bond conversions: valuing the transaction at cost (book value of the bonds) or valuing at market (of the stocks or bonds, whichever is more reliable). At market, assuming market value exceeds book value, the entries would be:

Issuer		Investor	
Loss on redemption	(plug)	Stock invest	(mkt)
Bonds payable	(book value)	Invest in bonds	(carrying value)
Bond premium	(book value)	Gain on conver-	
Common stock	(par)	sion	(plug)
Paid-in excess of par	(mkt-par)		

On the issuer's books, the debit (credit) to the loss (gain) account (ordinary) would be for the difference between the market value of the stock (bonds) and the book value of the bonds. The conversion is treated as the culmination of an earnings process; thus the loss (gain) should be recognized. The bonds and the related accounts must be written off, and paid-in excess of par is credited for the excess of the market value of the stock (bonds) over the stock's par value. On the investor's books, the gain (loss) would also be the difference between the market value of the stock (bonds) and the book value of the bonds. Remember in both cases that the accrued interest and discount or premium amortization must be recorded prior to the conversion.

Conversion under the cost method would result in debits to bonds payable and bond premium (or a credit to bond discount) equal to the book value of the bonds, and credits to common stock and paid-in excess of par equal to the book value. In practice, conversions are usually recorded at book value. Note that under this method no gain (loss) is recorded, as no gain (loss) should result from an equity transaction.

6. Debt Issued with Detachable Purchase Warrants

APB 14 (see outline) requires the proceeds of debt issued with detachable stock purchase warrants to be allocated between the debt and stock warrants based on relative market values. Example: units of one bond and one warrant (to buy 10 shares of stock at $50/share) are issued for $1,030. Thereafter, warrants trade at $40 and the bonds at $960. The relative market value of the warrants is 4% (40/1,000) and the relative market value of the bonds is 96% (960/1,000). Thus 41.20 (.04 x 1,030) of the issue price is assigned to the warrants.

Cash	1,030.00	
Bond discount	11.20	
Bonds payable		1,000.00
Paid-in capital--stock warrants		41.20

If one warrant were subsequently exercised:

Cash	500.00	
Paid-in capital--stock warrants	41.20	
Common stock		(par of 10 shs)
Paid-in excess		(plug)

The example could have indicated the current market value of the stock, e.g., $54, rather than the relative market values. In such a case, one would value the warrants based on the difference between option price and market price, e.g., [$54 (market) - $50 (option)] x 10 shares = $40 value for the warrants.

Notice the effect of requiring allocation of the cash received to the stock warrants. The final effect is to increase interest costs on the bond issue by reducing the premium or increasing the discount.

7. <u>Extinguishment of Debt</u> (see outlines of APB 26 and SFAS 76)

Debt is considered extinguished whenever the debtor pays the creditor and is relieved of all obligations relating to the debt. Typical examples of this are the calling of a bond by the debtor, requiring the bondholder to sell the bond to the issuing corporation at a certain date and stated price, and the open market repurchase of a debt issue. Refunding of debt (replacement of debt with other debt) is also considered an extinguishment. However, troubled debt restructures (situations where creditors agree to grant relief to debtors) and debt conversions initiated by the debt holders are not. Additionally, when the debtor is legally released from being the primary obligor of the debt either judicially or by the creditor and it is probable the debtor will make no further payments on it, the debt is considered extinguished.

All gains (losses) resulting from the extinguishment of debt should be recognized in the period of extinguishment. The gain (loss) is the difference between the bond's reacquisition price and its net book value [face value minus (plus) any unamortized discount (premium) and issue costs]. The rule is not affected by the reissuance of debt before or after the refunding. Furthermore, this rule applies to convertible bonds when reacquired with cash. The gain or loss is extraordinary (see SFASs 4 and 64).

Loss or gain	xx	xx
Bonds payable	xx	
Bond premium	xx	
Unamortized issue costs		xx
Bond discount		xx
Cash		xx

Debt may also be extinguished through defeasance, whereby the debtor places cash or essentially risk-free monetary assets (e.g., government and government guaranteed debt obligation) into an irrevocable trust used solely to service the interest and principal payments of a debt issue. The timing and amounts of the cash flows provided by the monetary assets used must approximately coincide with the scheduled interest and principal payments of the debt being extinguished. The entry required is as above, except that "Marketable debt securities" is credited instead of "Cash" when used. Prior to recording the extinguishment, the securities are revalued to FMV and an ordinary gain (loss) is recorded. Consequently, two different gains (losses) may be recorded in a defeasance using securities. The first results from the revaluation of the securities to FMV (ordinary in nature), and the second from the difference between the FMV of the securities placed in the trust and the net book value of the debt (extraordinary).

C. Debt Restructure

SFAS 15 (see outline) prescribes accounting for situations where creditors are compelled to grant relief (i.e., restructure debt) to debtors. Two types of re-structure are described.. The first is a settlement of the debt at less than the carrying amount and the second is a continuation of the debt with a modification of terms; accounting is prescribed for both debtors and creditors.

Debtors--If the debt is settled by the exchange of assets, an extraordinary gain is recognized for the difference between the carrying amount of the debt and the consideration given to extinguish the debt. If a noncash asset is given, a sepa-rate, ordinary gain or loss is recorded to revalue the noncash asset to FMV as the basis of the noncash asset given. Thus, a two-step process is used: (1) revalue the noncash asset to FMV and (2) determine the restructuring gain. If stock is is-sued to settle the liability, record the stock at FMV.

If the debt is continued with a modification of terms, it is necessary to compare the total future cash flows of the restructured debt (both principal and stated interest) with the prestructured carrying value. If the total amount of future cash flows is greater than the carrying value, no adjustment is made to the carrying value of the debt; however, a new effective interest rate must be computed. This rate makes the present value of the total future cash flows equal to the present carrying value of debt (principal and accrued interest). If the total future cash flows of the restructured debt are less than the present carrying value, the current debt should be reduced to the amount of the future cash flows and an extraordinary gain should be recognized. No interest expense would be recognized in subsequent periods when only principal is repaid.

If the restructuring consists of part settlement and part modification of payments, first account for the part settlement per the above, and then account for the modification of payments per the above.

Creditors--The accounting for restructurings is very similar to debtors, only in reverse or mirror-image form.

1) Assets received in full settlement are recorded at FMV

   a) Excess of receivable over asset FMV is an ordinary loss
   b) Subsequently account for the assets as if purchased for cash

2) Modification of payments results in reduction of future interest revenue. No recognition of loss in current period.

   a) Unless total future interest and principal receipts are less than book value of receivable

      1] Then write receivable down to total cash to be received and recognize no interest revenue in the future

      2] Note that this procedure is in contrast to the general doctrine of recognizing losses when they are evident. The prescribed procedure defers the loss (by not recognizing interest revenue in the future).

3) Part settlement and part modification of payments restructurings are accounted for per the above

   a) First as to the settlement portion
   b) Second as to the modification of terms

The following examples will further illustrate accounting for troubled debt restructures.

Example 1: Settlement of Debt--Debtor company transfers land in full settlement of its loan payable.

    Loan Payable (5 years remaining)
       (includes accrued interest of $10,000) $100,000

    Land: Book Value $70,000, Fair Value $80,000

Debtor:			Creditor:	
1. Land	10,000	1. Land	80,000	
Gain on trans-			Loss on settlement	20,000
fer of assets	10,000		Loan receivable	100,000
2. Loan	100,000			
Land		80,000		
Extraordinary				
Gain on settle-				
ment of debt		20,000		

Example 2: Restructure Gain/Loss Recognized--Assume the interest rate on above loan is 5%. Interest rate is reduced to 4% and principal and accrued interest at date of restructure are reduced to $80,000.

Future cash flows (after restructuring):

Principal	$80,000
Interest (5 years x $80,000 x 4%)	+16,000
Total cash to be received:	$96,000

Amount prior to restructure:

($90,000 principal + $10,000 accrued interest)	-100,000
Gain/Loss to be recognized	$ 4,000

        Debtor gain (extraordinary)
        Creditor loss (ordinary)

Debtor:		Creditor:	
Beginning of Year 1		**Beginning of Year 1**	
Loan payable	4,000	Loss on restructure	
Extraordinary gain		of debt	4,000
on restructure of		Loan receivable	4,000
debt	4,000		
End of Year 1-5		**End of Year 1-5**	
Loan payable	3,200	Cash	3,200
Cash	3,200	Loan receivable	3,200
(Note: No interest expense recorded in this case)			
End of Year 5		**End of Year 5**	
Loan payable	80,000	Cash	80,000
Cash	80,000	Loan receivable	80,000

Example 3: Restructure No Gain/Loss Recognized--Assume $100,000 is reduced to $85,000. The interest rate of 5% is reduced to 4%.

Future cash flows (after restructuring):

Principal	$ 85;000
Interest (5 years x $85,000 x 4%)	17,000
Total cash to be received	$102,000

Amount prior to restructure:

($90,000 principal + $10,000 accrued interest)	-100,000
Interest expense/revenue	$ 2,000
over 5 years	

In Example 3, a new effective interest rate must be computed so PV of future pay-ments = $100,000. A trial and error approach would be used. For the exam, you need to be prepared to describe this process and the entries, but not to make such a com-putation.

<table>
<tr><td colspan="3">Debtor:</td><td colspan="3">Creditor:</td></tr>
<tr><td colspan="3">End of Year 1-5</td><td colspan="3">End of Year 1-5</td></tr>
<tr><td>Loan payable</td><td>xxxx</td><td></td><td>Cash</td><td>3,400</td><td></td></tr>
<tr><td>Interest expense</td><td>xxx</td><td></td><td> Loan receivable</td><td></td><td>xxxx</td></tr>
<tr><td> Cash</td><td></td><td>3,400</td><td> Interest revenue</td><td></td><td>xxx</td></tr>
<tr><td colspan="3">End of Year 5</td><td colspan="3">End of Year 5</td></tr>
<tr><td>Loan payable</td><td>85,000</td><td></td><td>Cash</td><td>85,000</td><td></td></tr>
<tr><td> Cash</td><td></td><td>85,000</td><td> Loan receivable</td><td></td><td>85,000</td></tr>
</table>

(Note: x's equal different amounts each year based on effective interest rate com-puted)

(Note: x's equal different amounts each year)

To summarize the two basic situations:

1)   Settlement of Debt: the debtor transfers assets or grants an equity interest to the creditor in full satisfaction of the claim. Both debtor and creditor account for the fair values of assets transferred and equity interest granted. A gain or loss is recognized on the asset transferred. The debtor recognizes a gain and the creditor recognizes a loss for the difference between the recorded value of the debt and the fair values accounted for.

2)   Restructuring of the Debt: the terms of the debt are modified in order to reduce or defer cash payments that the debtor is obligated to make to the creditor, but the debt itself is continued. Both debtor and creditor account for the modification of terms as reductions in interest expense and interest revenue respectively, from the date of restructuring until maturity. Gains and losses will generally not be recognized unless the total future cash payments specified by the new terms are less than the recorded amount of the debt. Then the creditor (debtor) would recognize a loss (gain) for the difference. The creditor's loss is considered ordinary and the debtor's gain extraordinary.

Refer to the outline of SFAS 15 for the disclosure requirements.

D. Pensions

Mastery of the material related to accounting for employer pension plans re-quires a thorough knowledge of the accounting concepts, an understanding of the rel-evant terminology and disclosure requirements, and a working of the computational and recording aspects. Concepts and terminology are developed in ABP 8 and required disclosures are specified in SFAS 36. Therefore, the outline of these pronounce-ments should be reviewed before working through this section.

1. Pension Example

Assume an employee is 50 years old when his company adopts a pension plan. The employee can retire at 65 and receive $5,000 at the end of each year thereafter (his first payment is due one year after reaching 65). This $5,000 figure was determined on the basis of $250/year for each of the 20 years the employee has worked for the company, prior to the adoption of the plan.

Likewise, the employee's annual pension benefit will increase $250/year each additional year he works, e.g., the annual benefit will increase to $5,250 as a result of the next year of work. Assuming the employee works to age 65, the annual benefit will be $8,750.

2. Past Cost

If the employee is expected to live to receive 11 payments (from mortality tables), the amount of cash the company would need on hand at age 65 to cover the pension payments, based on work to age 50 (inception of the plan), is the present value of the annuity to be paid. The present value of an annuity of eleven payments of $5,000 at 6% interest rate (expected earnings rate of the pension fund) is:

$$\$5,000 \times 7.89 = \underline{\$39,450}$$

$39,450 is represented by the vertical distance at age 65 on the pension diagram. As the diagram indicates, the fund earns interest (upward slant) from 65 to 66 and pays $5,000 at the end of the first period and so on until the fund is depleted after 11 payments.

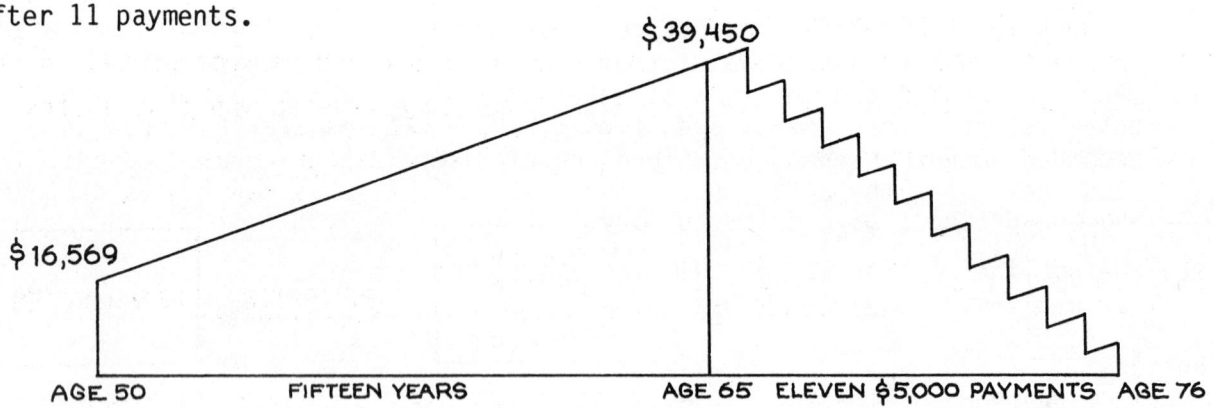

The amount required in the fund at the plan's inception is the discounted present value of the $39,450 required at age 65. The present value of $39,450 due in 15 years is:

$$\$39,450 \times .42 = \underline{\$16,569}$$

The $16,569 is the measure of past cost associated with the employee, and must be amortized over 10 years or longer. These types of calculations in a real pension plan are complicated by expected values, expected age at death, employee turnover, fund earnings rate, and other such actuarial factors.

3. Normal Cost

Because of the employee's service from age 50 to age 51, the employee will "earn" an annuity of $250 for 11 years after retirement. The present value of this annuity is the normal cost of this year, age 50-51. The present value of a $250 annual annuity for 11 years at 6% is:

$$\$250 \times 7.89 = \underline{\$1,972.50}$$

This amount must then be discounted back to the current period, age 50-51.

$$\$1,972.50 \times .44 = \underline{\$867.90}$$

The $867.90 is the normal cost for the current year, age 50-51. Note that the present value of the $250 annuity was discounted back 14 periods and the same amount would be discounted back only 13 periods for the next year, age 51-52.

$$\$1,972.50 \times .47 = \underline{\$927.07}$$

For year 3, age 52-53 (12 periods) the calculation would be:

$$\$1,972.50 \times .50 = \underline{\$986.25}$$

Normal annual pension cost under accrued benefit methods result in increasing charges to income, because as the time to retirement decreases, there is less time to earn interest on each annual deposit.

The critical determinants of the pension calculations can be represented in the diagram below which shows the entity's contributions to a trustee who distributes the benefits to the pensionees.

*Contribution is determined by an actuary based on actuarial assumptions and funding requirements required by the ERISA Act of 1974.

PENSION COST TIME LINE

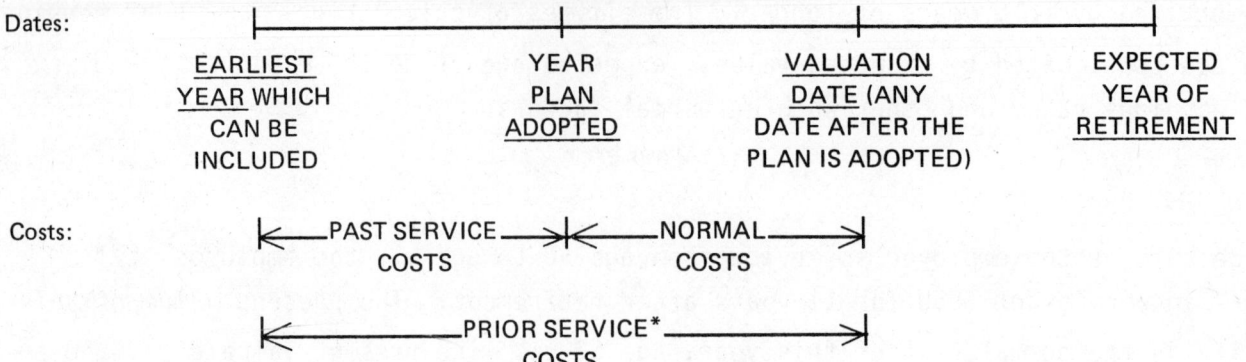

*Prior service costs are normal costs plus past service costs plus amendments for all periods prior to actuarial valuation date.

4. Minimum and Maximum

The determination of the amount to be reported as pension expense is governed by upper and lower limits which are defined in APB 8. Do not confuse the minimum and maximum with the accounting methods. They are a floor and a ceiling. These limits are calculated according to the following rules:

MINIMUM

      1. Normal cost

  + 2. Interest on unfunded amounts - to the extent that past and normal costs have not been deposited, the amount that should have been on deposit through the current period should be compared to the amount that was on deposit through the current period and this difference should be multiplied by the appropriate interest rate

  + 3. A provision for vested benefits, when applicable (see discussion on the following page)

MAXIMUM

      1. Normal cost

  + 2. 10% of the past service costs as computed at the inception of the plan until fully amortized

  + 3. 10% of the prior service costs arising from actions subsequent to the inception of the plan

 +/- 4. Interest equivalents on the difference between the amounts expensed and the amounts funded in prior years

      Interest equivalents are only computed on the difference between 1) the amount expensed to date, and 2) the amount funded to date. If funding in prior years exceeded the actuarially determined expense, the interest equivalent on the excess funding is deducted to determine the maximum. If funding in prior years was less than the actuarially determined expense, then interest on the prior years' expense will be added to determine the maximum (see the following numerical examples for an illustration of this adjustment).

5. Journal Entries

The entries for pension expense vary because of the different expense recognition/cash flow possibilities that exist. The amount of expense must be determined by an acceptable actuarial cost method and is bounded by the previously described maximum and minimum. The cash flows for pensions are controlled by the Employee Retirement Income Security Act (ERISA) of 1974. ERISA requires the funding of normal cost, at least 1/30 of past service costs of any new plan (1/40 for plans existing when the Act came into existence) and at least 1/15 of any prior service cost.

If the expense per APB 8 and the cash flow requirements (ERISA) are the same, the entry is:

> Pension expense*
>   Cash

If the expense is greater than the amount funded, then the entry should be:

> Pension expense*
>   Cash
>   Pension liability

If the expense is less than the amount funded, then the entry should be:

> Pension expense*
> Deferred pension costs
>   Cash

> *APB 8 uses the word provision.

Please note that if the amount funded equals the amount expensed (entry one above) every period, there will never be a related asset or liability on the balance sheet of the employer.

6. Vested Benefits

Vested benefits are those benefits which are earned by employees irrespective of continued employment. Vested benefits in excess of the current pension liability and amounts previously paid to the fund should be recorded as a liability and deferred charge.

> Deferred pension costs
>   Pension liability

Note the minimum pension expense requires a provision for vested benefits. Per para 17a of APB 8, the excess of vested benefits over:

1) Pension fund
2) Plus the balance sheet liability
3) Minus balance sheet deferred charges

must decrease by 5% per year. If it does not decrease by 5%, the pension charge
must be increased so as to result in the required 5% decrease.

The sum of the fund, plus liability, minus deferred charge, is a proxy for the
expense to date, i.e., the cash credits, plus liability credits, less deferred
charge debits, equals the expense debits.

Pension expense	(normal, past, interest costs)
Deferred pension charge	(pension liab. credit not expensed)
Cash	(amount paid to pension fund)
Pension liability	(expense not paid)

7. Pension Examples

The following examples are useful to illustrate the entries for pensions and the
calculations of the maximum and minimum amounts. For both examples assume the
following information:

Pension costs are determined by an acceptable actuarial method:

   a. The normal cost is $10,000 per year
   b. The past service cost is $60,000 as of the start of year 1
   c. The appropriate interest rate is 6%

EXAMPLE 1--Assume that the funding of the past service cost will be accomplished by equal annual payments for a 15 year period. For accounting purposes the
firm has decided to amortize the past service cost over a 20 year period. The calculations for year 1 and year 2 are as follows:

YEAR 1

	(a) Annual Amount	(b) Principal Balance	(c) Interest 6% x (b)	(d) Principal Reduction (a) - (c)	(e) Ending Balance (b) - (d)
n = 15	$6,179*	$60,000	$3,600	$2,579	$57,421
n = 20	$5,231**	$60,000	$3,600	$1,631	$58,369

*$6,179 = $60,000/9.71   **$5,231 = $60,000/11.47
(9.71 is the Present Value Factor for an ordinary annuity of 15 periods at 6%; 11.47
is the Present Value Factor for an ordinary annuity of 20 periods at 6%)

YEAR 2

n = 15	$6,179	$57,421	$3,445	$2,734	$54,687
n = 20	$5,231	$58,369	$3,502	$1,729	$56,640

Year 1--Tentative pension expense: $10,000 normal cost + $5,231 20-year amortization. Cash outflows: $10,000 normal cost + $6,179 15-year funding.

Minimum:
   normal costs $10,000
\+   interest on unfunded amount   3,600   (6% x $60,000)
                                   $13,600

Maximum:
   normal costs $10,000
\+   10% past service costs   6,000   (10% x $60,000)
\+   interest equivalents   -   (first year - no difference between
                                 $16,000 amounts expensed and funded in prior
                                             years)

∴ Tentative expense of $15,231 is acceptable.

    <u>Year 2</u>--Tentative expense: $10,000 normal cost + $5,231 20-year amortization -
$57 interest reduction of 6% of deferred charge balance* = $15,174

    *Because the employer is funding the past service cost more rapidly than would
be indicated by the 20-year amortization schedule, there is a "surplus" accumulation of $948 (6,179 - 5,231) which is generating interest of $57 ($948 x 6%)
that reduces the tentative expense of the current period.

Cash outflows: $10,000 normal cost + $6,179 15-year funding

Minimum:
   normal costs $10,000
\+   interest on unfunded amount   3,445   (6% x $57,421)
                                     $13,445

Maximum:
   normal costs $10,000
\+   10% past service costs   6,000
\-   interest equivalents   (57)   6%($15,231 expensed - $16,179 funded)
                                 $15,943

∴ Tentative expense of $15,174 is acceptable.

    The journal entries to record the expense and payments during the first two
years would be as follows:

	Year 1		Year 2	
Pension expense	15,231		15,174	
Deferred pension cost	948		1,005	
Cash		16,179		16,179

    <u>EXAMPLE 2</u>--Assume that the <u>funding</u> of the past service cost will be accomplished
by equal annual payments for a 22 year period. For accounting purposes the firm has
decided to <u>amortize</u> the past service cost over a 16 year period.

YEAR 1

	(a) Annual Amount	(b) Principal Balance	(c) Interest 6% x (b)	(d) Principal Reduction (a) - (c)	(e) Ending Balance (b) - (d)
n = 16	$5,935*	$60,000	$3,600	$2,335	$57,665
n = 22	$4,983**	$60,000	$3,600	$1,383	$58,617

*$5,935 = $60,000/10.11   **$4,983 = $60,000/12.04

(10.11 is the Present Value Factor for an ordinary annuity of 16 periods at 6%; 12.04 is the Present Value Factor for an ordinary annuity of 22 periods at 6%)

YEAR 2

n = 16	$5,935	$57,665	$3,460	$2,475	$55,190
n = 22	$4,983	$58,617	$3,517	$1,466	$57,151

Year 1--Tentative pension expense: $10,000 normal cost + $5,935 16-year amortization. Cash outflows: $10,000 normal cost + $4,983 22-year amortization.

Minimum:

	normal costs	$10,000	
+	interest on unfunded amount	3,600	(6% X $60,000)
		$13,600	

Maximum:

	normal costs	$10,000	
+	10% past service costs	6,000	(10% x $60,000)
+/-	interest equivalents	-	(first year - no difference between
		$16,000	amount expensed and funded in prior years)

∴ Tentative expense of $15,935 is acceptable.

Year 2--Tentative pension expense: $10,000 normal cost + $5,935 16-year amortization + $57 interest addition of 6% of deferred credit balance* = $15,992

*Because the employer is funding the past service cost less rapidly than would be indicated by the 16-year amortization schedule, there is a "reduced" accumulation of $952 ($4,983 - $5,935) which is not available to earn the required interest of $57 ($952 x 6%) and thereby the tentative expense of the current period is increased.

Cash outflow: $10,000 normal cost + $4,983 22-year amortization

Minimum:

	normal costs	$10,000	
+	interest on unfunded amount	3,517	(6% X $58,617)
		$13,517	

Maximum:

	normal costs	$10,000	
+	10% past service costs	6,000	
+	interest equivalents	57	6%($15,935 expensed - $14,983 funded)
		$16,057	

∴ Tentative expense of $15,992 is acceptable.

The journal entries to record the expense and payments during the first two years would be as follows:

	Year 1		Year 2	
Pension expense	15,935		15,992	
Pension liability		952		1,009
Cash		14,983		14,983

E. Leases

The major issue in accounting for leases is whether the financial impact of the lease agreement should be included in the main body of the financial statements. A lease is a contract which specifies the terms of an exchange transaction between the contracting parties. When it is deemed that the lease arrangement is in <u>substance</u> an installment sale, the economic impact of the lease contract will be emphasized over the <u>legal form</u> of the agreement. This focus is clearly stated in SFAS 13 para 60 as follows:

> "A lease that transfers substantially all of the benefits and risks incident to ownership of property should be accounted for as the acquisition of an asset and the incurrence of an obliga- tion by the lessee and as a sale or financing by the lessor."

1. Study Program for Leases

1) Review the material in this module so that you will be familiar with the major concepts and applications in the leasing area.

2) After you have developed a solid base of understanding, you should review the outline of SFAS 13 as comprehensively restated in May 1980.

3) The discussion of accounting for leases is structured to follow the lease classification matrix listed below.

Lessor	Lessee
Operating................Operating	
Direct Financing...........Capital	
Sales-type	
Leveraged	

a. Operating Lease, Lessor and Lessee

If the lease agreement is not classified as capital, direct financing, sales-type, or leveraged, then it is considered to be an operating lease. For accounting purposes, operating leases are regarded as rental agreements which do not affect the reporting of assets and equities in the main body of the financial statements. The lessor would continue to carry the leased property as an asset and rental revenues and related expenses would be included in the lessor's calculation of net income.

Similarly, the lessee would not report leased assets or equity claims in the financial statements and rental expense would be included in the lessee's calculation of net income. Rental revenue (expense) should be recognized by the lessor (lessee) on a straight-line basis unless another method more reasonably reflects the pattern of services rendered.

b. Direct Financing Lease, Lessor

A direct financing lease is an arrangement whereby the lessor (e.g., bank) agrees to purchase an asset (e.g., airplane) and lease it to the lessee (e.g., airlines). The agreement is initiated because the lessee does not want (or is unable) to purchase the asset outright. The lessor determines the schedule of lease payments and terms based on its required rate of return.

A lease is considered to be a direct financing lease from the point of view of the lessor if the following conditions are all satisfied:

1) Any one of the four criteria specified in para 7 of SFAS 13 are satisfied

   a) The lease transfers title to the lessee
   b) The lease contains a bargain purchase option
   c) The lease term is 75% or more of useful life and the lease is not first executed within the last 25% of the original useful life
   d) The present value of minimum lease payments is 90% or more of the net of the fair market value of the asset reduced by the investment credit retained by the lessor

2) The following two additional criteria are both satisfied:

   a) Collectibility of minimum lease payments is predictable and
   b) There are no important uncertainties concerning costs yet to be incurred by the lessor under the lease; and

3) The FMV of the leased asset at the inception of the lease is approximately equal to the cost or carrying amount of the asset

Direct financing leases result in interest revenue only for the lessor. There is no selling or dealer's profit from this type of lease. The difference between the asset cost and the total payments to be received by the lessor is interest revenue, earned over the life of the lease. Alternative methods of recording the lease transaction are shown below.

Lease receivable (gross)		Lease receivable (net)
Asset	-or-	Asset
Unearned interest revenue		

In addition, SFAS 13 specifies the following considerations and definitions:

- The gross investment in the lease equals the minimum lease payments (lease receivable) plus any unguaranteed residual value. No residual value is assumed to accrue to the value of the lessor if the lease transfers ownership or contains a bargain purchase option.

- Unearned revenue must be amortized to produce a constant periodic rate of return on net investment, i.e., the effective interest method.

- At the termination of the lease, the balance in the receivable should equal the unguaranteed residual value, assuming title is not transferred and there is no bargain purchase option.

- Initial direct costs should be charged against revenue as incurred, and a portion of the unearned interest income equal to the initial direct costs should be recognized as income in the same period.

Numerical Example 1:

Lease Information

1) A three year lease is initiated on 1/1/X1 for equipment costing $131,858 with an expected useful life of five years. FMV at 1/1/X1 of equipment is $131,858.

2) Three annual payments are due to the lessor beginning 12/31/X1. The property reverts back to the lessor upon termination of the lease.

3) The unguaranteed residual value at the end of year 3 is estimated to be $10,000

4) The lessor is to receive a 10% return (implicit rate)

5) The lease payments and unguaranteed residual value have a PV equal to $131,858 (FMV or asset) at the stipulated discount rate

6) The annual payment to the lessor is computed as follows:

PV of residual value = $10,000 x .7513 = $7,513
PV of lease payments = $131,858 - $7,513 = $124,345

$$\text{Annual payment} = \frac{\$124,345}{PV_{3,.10}} = \frac{\$124,345}{2.4869} = \$50,000$$

Lease Classification

This is a direct financing lease because criterion "b.1)d)" (90% test) is satisfied and FMV equals cost. Assume criteria "b.2)a)" and "b.2)b)" are satisfied.

Accounting for Lease

1) The following table illustrates the effective interest method

Date	Cash Receipt	Interest Revenue (10%)	Reduction in Net Invest	Net Investment
1/1/X1				$131,858
12/31/X1	$50,000	$13,186	$36,814	95,044
12/31/X2	50,000	9,504	40,496	54,548
12/31/X3	50,000	5,452	44,548	10,000

Note: The current and noncurrent balance sheet amounts can be taken directly from the amortization table. For example, at 12/31/X1, the lease receivable of $95,044 is $40,496 current and $54,548 noncurrent.

2) The lease may be recorded at the beginning of year 1 by the lessor under either the net or gross methods. The gross method is illustrated below.

3) In the amortization table above, the net investment in lease is the difference between gross investment and unearned interest revenue

<table>
<tr><td colspan="2"><u>Initial entry</u></td><td colspan="2"><u>Year 2</u></td></tr>
<tr><td>Lease receivable</td><td>160,000</td><td>Cash</td><td>50,000</td></tr>
<tr><td>   Equipment</td><td>   131,858</td><td>   Lease receivable</td><td>   50,000</td></tr>
<tr><td>   Unearned interest</td><td>   28,142</td><td></td><td></td></tr>
<tr><td></td><td></td><td>Unearned interest</td><td>9,504</td></tr>
<tr><td colspan="2" align="center"><u>Year 1</u></td><td>   Interest revenue</td><td>   9,504</td></tr>
<tr><td>Cash</td><td>50,000</td><td></td><td></td></tr>
<tr><td>   Lease receivable</td><td>   50,000</td><td colspan="2" align="center"><u>Year 3</u></td></tr>
<tr><td>Unearned interest</td><td>13,186</td><td>Cash</td><td>50,000</td></tr>
<tr><td>   Interest revenue</td><td>   13,186</td><td>   Lease receivable</td><td>   50,000</td></tr>
<tr><td></td><td></td><td>Unearned interest</td><td>5,452</td></tr>
<tr><td></td><td></td><td>   Interest revenue</td><td>   5,452</td></tr>
</table>

4) When the asset is returned the lessor makes the following entry:

Equipment	10,000	
Lease receivable		10,000

c. <u>Sales-Type Lease, Lessor</u>

Sales-type leases arise when a manufacturer or dealer (e.g., aircraft manufacturer, car dealership) leases an asset which otherwise might be sold outright for a profit. The lessor's profit consists of two components: (1) gross profit in year of sale, and (2) unearned interest revenue to be earned over the lease term using the effective interest method. The diagram below compares and contrasts direct financing leases with sales-type leases.

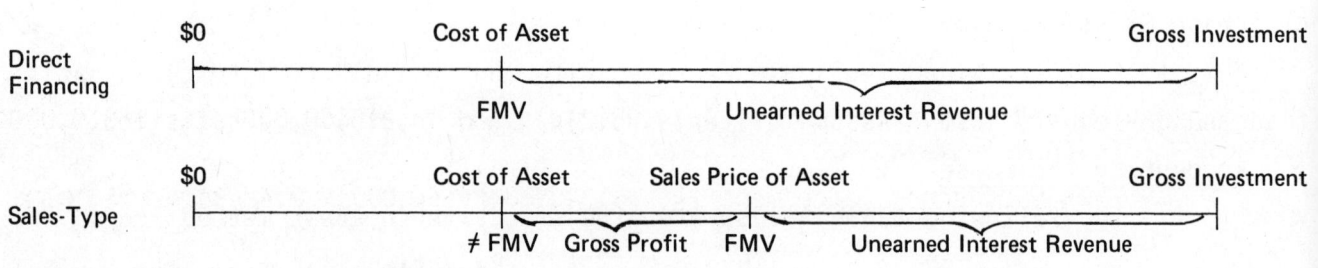

Prepared by Professor John R. Simon, Northern Illinois University.

A lease is considered to be a sales-type lease from the point of view of the lessor if the same conditions as for a direct financing lease are satisfied, except:

1) The PV of the minimum lease payments plus the unguaranteed residual value is <u>greater than</u> the cost or carrying value of the leased asset

In addition, SFAS 13 specifies the following considerations and definitions:

1) Sales price will equal the PV of the minimum lease payments (which does <u>not</u> include unguaranteed residual value)

2) Cost of goods sold equals the cost or carrying amount of the leased property minus the present value of any unguaranteed residual value to the lessor. Thus, cost of goods is the net amount transferred: the cost of the asset initially transferred less what will be returned (which is the unguaranteed residual value).

3) Any initial direct costs are charged against income as an operating expense in the year the lease is recorded

Numerical Example 2:

Lease Information

Assume same information as in previous example except:
1) The cost of the equipment is $100,000
2) The lease payments and unguaranteed residual value have a PV greater than the $100,000 cost at the stipulated discount rate

Lease Classification

This is a sales-type lease since criterion "1.d." (90% test) is satisfied and the cost of the asset is less than the PV of the minimum lease payments. Assume criterion "2.a." and "2.b." are satisfied.

Accounting for Lease

1) The gross investment is: $160,000 (3 payments of $50,000 plus a $10,000 residual)

The PV of gross investment is: $131,858 [($50,000 x 2.4869) + ($10,000 x .7513)]

The unearned interest revenue is: $28,142 ($160,000 - $131,858)
Sales are: $124,345 ($131,858 - $10,000 x .7513)
CGS is: $92,487 ($100,000 - $10,000 x .7513)

2) The entry to record the lease may be made under either the net or gross method

Net			Gross		
Lease receivable	131,858		Lease receivable	160,000	
Cost of goods sold	92,487		Cost of goods sold	92,487	
Sales		124,345	Sales		124,345
Inventory, FA, etc.		100,000	Inventory, FA, etc.		100,000
			Unearned interest		28,142

At the end of year 1, the following entry(ies) would be made:

Cash	50,000		Cash	50,000	
Interest revenue		13,186	Lease receivable		50,000
Lease receivable		36,814			
			Unearned interest	13,186	
			Interest revenue		13,186

The interest revenue will be recognized at 10% of the outstanding net investment each period. At termination the lease receivable will have a balance of $10,000 which is the unguaranteed residual value. If the asset is returned to the lessor (although it may be purchased by the lessee), the following entry is made:

Machinery	10,000	
Lease receivable		10,000

d. Leveraged Lease, Lessor

Lessors account for leveraged leases as though they were financing leases. Lessees account for leveraged leases as any other lease (operating/capital). Leveraged leases are those that include significant financing from a creditor (third party to the normal lessor-lessee relationship).

The primary distinction for accounting purposes is that the lessor's investment goes from positive to negative (due to early years' depreciation and investment credits) and finally back to positive (due to depreciation reversals) prior to becoming zero at the end of the lease. The issue, then, is how to recognize the interest revenue (especially when the net book value is negative). Per SFAS 13, the implicit rate of return is computed (and recognized) only in years when the lessor's "net investment in the lease" is positive.

e. Capital Leases, Lessee

A lease is considered to be a capital lease from the point of view of the lessee if any one of the four criteria specified in para 7 of SFAS 13 are satisfied (i.e., transfer of title, bargain purchase, 75% of useful life, 90% of net FMV). If the lease is classified as a capital lease, the lessee must record an asset and a liability based on the present value of the minimum lease payments as follows:

Leased asset	
Lease obligation	(PV of payments)

In addition, SFAS 13 specifies the following considerations and definitions:

1) Minimum lease payments are payments to be made during the lease term including: a bargain purchase option payment, guaranteed residual value, penalties for failure to renew, and other similar payments. Note, minimum payments do not include executory costs and payments for excessive use of the leased asset.

2) The lessee's incremental borrowing rate should be used unless the implicit rate in the lease is lower and it is practical for the lessee to gain knowledge of the lessor's implicit rate. Leased assets should not be recorded at greater than FMV.

3) The lease term does not extend beyond the date of a bargain purchase option but includes bargain renewal periods, periods when the lessor has the option to renew or extend, periods during which the lessee guarantees the debt of the lessor and periods in which a material penalty exists for failure to renew.

4) The cost of the leased asset should be depreciated over the lease term to the expected residual value to the lessee unless the lease transfers ownership or contains a bargain purchase option. If ownership transfers or if a bargain purchase option is included, then depreciate over the estimated useful life of the asset.

5) In allocating the cash payments to the reduction of the obligation and to interest expense, the effective interest method (APB 21) should be used.

6) When the lease terminates, the balance in the obligation account should equal the bargain purchase option price, a guaranteed residual value or a termination penalty.

7) Leased assets and obligations should be disclosed as such in the balance sheet. The obligation should be separated into current and noncurrent components.

Numerical Example 3:

Lease Information

1) Lease is initiated on 1/1/X1 for equipment with an expected useful life of three years. The equipment reverts back to the lessor upon expiration of the lease agreement.

2) Three payments are due to the lessor in the amount of $50,000 per year beginning 12/31/X1. An additional sum of $1,000 is to be paid annually by the lessee for insurance.

3) Lessee guarantees a $10,000 residual value on 12/31/X3 to the lessor

4) Irrespective of the $10,000 residual value guarantee, the leased asset is expected to have only a $1,000 salvage on 12/31/X3

5) The lessee's incremental borrowing rate is 10%. (Lessor's implicit rate is unknown)

6) The present value of the lease obligation is:

PV of guaranteed residual value = 10,000 X .7513 ≐   7,513
PV of annual payments   = 50,000 X 2.4869 = 124,345
                                                     131,858

Lease Classification

This lease is for the entire economic life of the asset. Since criterion "b.1)c)" (75% test) is satisfied, the lease is accounted for as a capital lease by the lessee. Criterion "b.1)d)" (90% test) is also satisfied.

Accounting for Lease

1) Note that executory costs (e.g., insurance, property taxes, etc.) are not included in the present value calculations

2) The entry to recognize the lease is:

    1/1/X1   Leased equipment   131,858
                    Lease obligation   131,858

3) The entries to record the payments and depreciation are:

	12/31/X1	12/31/X2	12/31/X3
Insurance expense	1,000	1,000	1,000
Lease obligation*	36,814	40,496	44,548
Interest expense*	13,186	9,504	5,452
Cash		51,000	51,000 51,000
Depreciation expense**	43,619	43,619	43,620
Accumulated depreciation		43,619	43,619 43,620

*Refer to the amortization table in the direct financing lease discussion.
**(130,858 ÷ 3 years)

4) The 12/31/X3 entry to record the guaranteed residual value payment (assuming salvage value = estimated residual value = $1,000) and to clear the lease related accounts from the lessee's books is:

        Lease obligation   10,000
        Accumulated Depreciation   130,858
            Cash   9,000
            Leased Equipment   131,858

Remember that leased assets are amortized over the life of the lease unless title transfers or a bargain purchase option exists--then over the useful life of the leased asset. At the end of the lease, the balance of the lease obligation should equal the guaranteed residual value, the bargain purchase option price, or a termination penalty. To illustrate, consider the example below.

Numerical Example 4:

Lease Information

1) A three year lease is initiated on 1/1/X1 for equipment with an expected useful life of five years

2) Three annual $50,000 payments are due the lessor beginning 1/1/X1

3) The lessee can exercise a bargain purchase option on 12/31/X3 for $10,000. The expected residual value at 12/31/X5 is $1,000.

4) The lessee's incremental borrowing rate is 10% (lessor's implicit rate is unknown)

Lease Classification

Although the lease term is for only 60% of the asset's useful life, the lessee would account for this as a capital lease because it contains a bargain purchase option [criterion "b.1)b)"].

Accounting for Lease

1) The present value of the lease obligation is:

PV of bargain purchase option = $10,000 x .7513 = $ 7,513
PV of annual payments   = $50,000 x 2.7355 = 136,775
                                                   $144,288

2) The following table summarizes the liability amortization

Date	Cash Payment	Interest Expense	Reduction in Obligation	Lease Obligation
1/1/X1				$144,288
1/1/X1	$50,000		$50,000	94,288
1/1/X2	50,000	$9,429	40,571	53,717
1/1/X3	50,000	5,372	44,628	9,089
12/31/X3		911*		10,000
12/31/X3	10,000		10,000	-0-

*Rounding error of $2

> Note: This is an annuity due with cash payments on 1/1 and interest expense accruals on 12/31.

3) The entry to record the lease is:

1/1/X1 Leased equipment   144,288
            Lease obligation   144,288

4) The entries to record the payments, interest expense, depreciation expense, and the exercise of the bargain purchase are:

		19X1		19X2		19X3	
1/1	Lease obligation	50,000		40,571		44,628	
	Accrued interest payable or interest expense*			9,429		5,372	
	Cash		50,000		50,000		50,000
12/31	Interest expense	9,429		5,372		911	
	Accrued int. payable		9,429		5,372		
	Lease obligation						911
12/31	Depreciation expense**	28,658		28,658		28,658	
	Accumulated depreciation		28,658		28,658		28,658
12/31	Lease obligation					10,000	
	Cash						10,000

*If 12/31 accruals are reversed
**(143,288 ÷ 5 years)

2. Other Considerations

To supplement the review of accounting for leases presented above, the following topics have been selected for further discussion:

a. Residual Value
b. Initial Direct Costs
c. Lessee's Fair Market Value Limitation
d. Sale-leaseback
e. Disclosure Requirements

a. Residual Value--Residual value can be unguaranteed or guaranteed. Some lease contracts require lessees to guarantee residual value to lessors. The lessee can either buy the leased asset at the end of the lease term for the guaranteed residual value or allow the lessor to sell the leased asset (with the lessee paying any deficiency or receiving any excess over the guaranteed residual value).

Guaranteed residual value is considered a "minimum lease payment" and is reflected in the lessor's lease receivable account and the lessee's lease payable account. At the end of the lease term, the receivable and payable on the respective lessor and lessee books should be equal to the guaranteed residual value. Both lessor and lessee consider the guaranteed residual value a final lease payment.

The lessee should depreciate the asset to the expected residual value, not the guaranteed residual value. Thus, the actual cost of using the asset is charged to operations over the useful life of the asset.

The present value of the unguaranteed residual value should be included in the lessor's net investment in the lease unless the lease transfers title to the leased asset or there is a bargain purchase option. The unguaranteed residual value is the estimated residual value of the leased asset at the end of the lease (if a guaranteed residual value exists, the unguaranteed residual value is the excess of estimated value over the guaranteed residual value).

At the end of the lease, the lessor's receivable account should be equal to the unguaranteed residual value. The lessor must review the estimated residual value annually and recognize any decreases as a loss. No upward adjustments of the residual value are permitted.

The lessee should amortize the leased asset over the life of the lease unless the lease transfers title or has a bargain purchase option. If the lease transfers title or has a bargain purchase option, the lessee should amortize the asset cost less estimated residual value over its useful life.

b. Initial Direct Costs--Initial direct costs are those costs directly associated with negotiation and consummation of leases. These costs include commissions, legal fees, credit investigations, document preparation, etc. Thus, initial direct costs are only incurred by lessors.

Initial direct costs of direct financing and sales-type leases are accounted for differently. In sales-type leases, initial direct costs are charged to operations in the year the sale is recorded. In direct financing leases, initial direct costs are expensed as incurred, <u>but</u> equal amounts of unearned lease revenue are recognized in the same period. Thus, the interest revenue in subsequent periods is decreased because a new effective rate schedule must be computed. In operating leases, initial direct costs are capitalized and subsequently amortized to expense in proportion to the recognition of rental revenue (which is usually straight-line).

c. <u>Lessee's Fair Market Value Limitation</u>--A lessee would normally record a capital lease (leased asset and related liability) at the present value of the minimum lease payments. In determining present value the lessee discounts the future payments using the lessee's incremental borrowing rate. Alternatively, the lessor's implicit rate is used if the lessee knows the lessor's implicit rate and if this rate is less than the lessee's incremental borrowing rate (using a lower interest rate increases the present value).

The amount recorded by the lessee, however, is limited to the FMV of the lease asset based on the evidence the lessee can obtain.

d. <u>Sales-leaseback</u>--These transactions may occur when the seller (lessee) has cash-flow or financing problems or because the tax advantages are beneficial. The seller (lessee) records a sale and an operating or capital lease. The buyer (lessor) records a purchase and a direct financing or operating lease.

Sale and Leaseback Transaction

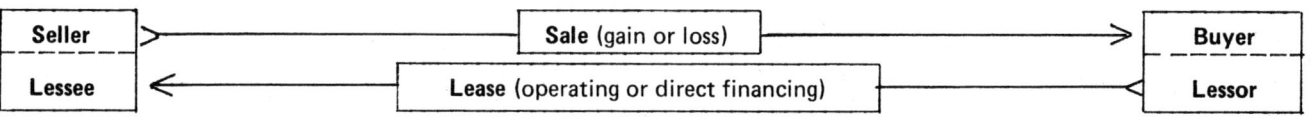

Source: Welsch, Zlatkovich, and Harrison, *Intermediate Accounting*, Sixth Edition, Richard D. Irwin, Inc., 1982, p. 693, with permission.

In a sale-leaseback transaction, there is a presumption that the sales price is inflated to produce a larger gain on the sale and a higher basis for depreciation. The inflated sales price is compensated for by inflated rental payments/receipts or interest expense/revenue. Because of this scenario, SFAS 13 requires any gain (loss) on the sale to be deferred and amortized

1) Over the lease term or economic life (use depreciation period rules) if the leaseback qualifies as a <u>capital lease</u>
2) In proportion to the rental payments if the leaseback is recorded as an <u>operating lease</u>

However, when the fair value of the property is less than its book value, a loss is recognized immediately for up to the difference between book value and fair value.

In some cases (i.e., profit on sale exceeds the total rentals under the leaseback), application of the general rule will result in negative rental expense. Refer to the outine of SFAS 13, Section "H," for the rules applicable to these special cases.

e. <u>Disclosure requirements</u>--The disclosures required of the lessor and lessee are very comprehensive and detailed. In essence, all terms of the leasing arrangement are required (i.e., contingent rentals, subleases, residual values, unearned interest revenue, etc.). For the details see the outline of SFAS 13 ("D.5." and "E.5."). There are, however, a couple of generic disclosure requirements. First, a <u>general description</u> of the leasing arrangement is required. Secondly, the minimum future payments to be received (paid) by the lessor (lessee) for each of the <u>five</u> <u>succeeding fiscal years</u> should also be disclosed. (A table summarizing the treatment of selected items in accounting for leases appears on the next page.)

TREATMENT OF SELECTED ITEMS IN ACCOUNTING FOR LEASES

| | Lessor | | Lessee | |
	Operating	Direct Financing and Sales-Type	Operating	Capital
Initial Direct Costs	Capitalize and amortize over lease term in proportion to rent revenue recognized (normally S.L. basis)	Direct financing: Expense in period incurred, and Match with equal amount of interest revenue, and Compute a new effective interest rate for remaining unearned interest. Sales-type: Expense in period incurred	N/A	N/A
Investment Tax Credit Retained by Lessor	N/A	Reduces FMV of leased asset for 90% test	N/A	Reduces FMV of leased asset for 90% test
Bargain Purchase Option	N/A	Include in: Minimum lease payments 90% test	N/A	Include in: Minimum lease payments 90% test
Guaranteed Residual Value	N/A	Include in: Minimum lease payments 90% test. Sales-type: Include PV in sales revenues	N/A	Include in: Minimum lease payments 90% test
Unguaranteed Residual Value	N/A	Include in: "Gross Investment in Lease" 90% test. Sales-type: Exclude from sales revenue Deduct PV from cost of sales	N/A	Not included in: Minimum lease payments 90% test
Contingent Rentals	Revenue in period earned	Not part of minimum lease payments; revenue in period earned	Expense in period incurred	Not part of minimum lease payments; expense in period incurred
Amortization Period	Amortize down to estimated residual value over estimated economic life of asset	N/A	N/A	[b]Amortize down to estimated residual value over lease term or estimated economic life
[a]Revenue (Expense)	Rent revenue (normally S.L. basis)	Direct financing: Interest revenue on net investment in lease (gross investment less unearned interest income). Sales-type: Dealer profit in period of sale (sales revenue less cost of leased asset). Interest revenue on net investment in lease	[c]Rent expense (normally S.L. basis)	Interest Expense and Depreciation Expense

[a]Elements of revenue (expense) listed for the above items are not repeated here (e.g., treatment of initial direct costs).

[b]If lease has automatic passage of title or bargain purchase option, use estimated economic life; otherwise, use the lease term.

[c]If payments are not on a S.L. basis, recognize rent expense on a S.L. basis unless another systematic and rational method is more representative of use benefit obtained from the property, in which case, the other method should be used.

INFLATION ACCOUNTING

Alternative reporting models which could provide a solution to the changing price dilemma are constant dollar accounting, current cost accounting, and current cost/constant dollar accounting. It is recommended that candidates work through this section before studying the outline of SFAS 33.

A. Constant Dollar Accounting

Constant dollar accounting is a method of reporting financial statement elements in dollars which have the same purchasing power. This method is often described as accounting in units of current purchasing power.

Purchasing power indicates the ability of a dollar to command goods and services. If the inflation rate during a given year for a group of items is 10%, then 110 end-of-year dollars are needed to purchase the same group of items which cost $100 at the beginning of the year. Similarly, a machine purchased at the beginning of that year for $1,000 would be presented in a year-end constant dollar balance sheet at a restated cost of $1,100. This represents the basic thrust of constant dollar accounting: the adjustment of historical data (nominal dollars) for changes in the general price level.

The adjustment of nominal dollar data is facilitated by the use of the Consumer Price Index, which reflects the average change in the retail prices of a wide variety of consumer goods. The adjustment is made by multiplying historical cost by the TO/FROM ratio:

$$\text{Historical cost (nominal dollars)} \times \frac{\text{Price level adjusting to}}{\text{Price level adjusting from}} = \text{Restated historical cost (constant dollar)}$$

For example, suppose an asset were purchased on 12/31/80 for $20,000 and the Consumer Price Index was 100 on 12/31/80, 110 on 12/31/81, and 120 on 12/31/82. Restatement for end-of-year balance sheets would be:

$$12/31/80 \qquad \$20,000 \times \frac{100}{100} = \$20,000$$

$$12/31/81 \qquad \$20,000 \times \frac{110}{100} = \$22,000$$

$$12/31/82 \qquad \$20,000 \times \frac{120}{100} = \$24,000$$

or

$$\$22,000 \times \frac{120}{110} = \$24,000$$

The preparation of constant dollar financial statements requires the classification of balance sheet items as either monetary or nonmonetary. Items are monetary if their amounts are fixed by statute or contract in terms of numbers of
dollars. Examples include cash, accounts and notes receivable, accounts and notes
payable, and bonds payable. By contract or statute these items are already stated
in current dollars and require no restatement. Nonmonetary items, on the other
hand, do require restatement to current dollars. Inventory, property, plant and
equipment, and unearned service revenue are examples of nonmonetary items. Under
some increasingly popular loan arrangements when the repayment of loan principal is
adjusted by an index, the receivable/payable is classified as a nonmonetary item.

The holding of a nonmonetary asset such as land during a period of inflation
need not result in a loss of purchasing power because the value of that land can
"flow" with the price level (hence, the need for restatement). However, if a monetary asset such as cash is held during a period of inflation with no interest,
purchasing power is lost because the cash will be able to purchase less goods and
services at year end than at the beginning of the year. This type of loss is simply
called a "purchasing power loss." If a firm's balance sheet included more monetary
liabilities than monetary assets throughout a given year, a purchasing power <u>gain</u>
would result, since the firm could pay its liabilities using cash which is 'worth
less' than the cash they borrowed.

A simple example can illustrate both the restatement process and the effect of
holding monetary assets. Assume that the Static Company has the following balance
sheet at the beginning of period 1.

Static Co.
Beginning of Period 1
Consumer Price Index = 100

Cash	$1,000	Common Stock	$2,000
Land	1,000		
	$2,000		$2,000

If the index increases to 110 by the end of year 1 and no transactions have taken
place, both the land and common stock would be restated to end-of-year dollars. But
in order to maintain the same level of purchasing power that was present at the beginning of the year, Static Co. should also have cash of $1,100 at year end. The
fact that the company held $1,000 cash throughout the year has resulted in a $100
purchasing power loss. The balance sheet at the end of period 1 would therefore be:

30

Static Co.
End of Period 1
Consumer Price Index = 110

Cash	$1,000	Common Stock	$2,200[b]
Land	1,100[a]	Retained Earnings	(100)[c]
	$2,100		$2,100

[a]$1,000 \times \frac{110}{100}$ [b]$2,000 \times \frac{110}{100}$ [c]Purchasing power loss $1,000 - ($1,000) $(\frac{110}{100})$

1. Constant Dollar Balance Sheet.

Preparation of a constant dollar balance sheet is an OBJECTIVE process. Monetary assets and liabilities need not be restated because they are already reported
in end-of-year dollars. All other assets, liabilities and owners equity accounts
(other than retained earnings) are restated in the same manner as were land and common stock in the Static Company example. Retained earnings is computed by adding
constant dollar net income including purchasing power gains/losses less any dividends (converted to end-of-year dollars) to the beginning balance of retained earnings.

The following data will serve to better illustrate a more complex balance sheet
restatement:

Equipment purchased 1/1/74	$60,000	Accumulated depreciation	$21,000
Equipment purchased 1/1/76	20,000	Accumulated depreciation	5,000
	$80,000		$26,000

Price indexes: 1/1/74, 100; 1/1/76, 120; 12/31/80, 150.

Adjustment to end-of-year dollars for a 12/31/80 balance sheet:

Equipment: $60,000 \times \frac{150}{100}$ = $ 90,000   Accumulated $21,000 \times \frac{150}{100}$ = $31,500
Depreciation:

$20,000 \times \frac{150}{120}$ = $\frac{25,000}{$115,000}$ $5,000 \times \frac{150}{120}$ = $\frac{6,250}{$37,750}$

2. Constant Dollar Income Statement.

Income statement items must also be restated to end-of-year dollars when constant dollar statements are prepared. For example, the depreciation expense related
to the equipment purchased on 1/1/74 in the previous illustration would have to be
multiplied by 150/100 in order to be properly stated on a constant dollar income

statement for 1980. Similarly, all other revenue and expense items must be adjusted, as the following example illustrates:

Huskie Company
Historical Cost Income Statement
1980

Sales	$100,000
less Cost of Goods Sold	(50,000)
Gross Margin	50,000
less Depr. Expense	(10,000)
Other Operating Expenses	(25,000)
Net Income	$15,000

Sales and operating expenses incurred evenly throughout year. Inventory sold during year purchased in first quarter. Depreciation expense related to building purchased 1/1/70. Indexes:

1/1/70	100
First quarter, 80	180
1980 average	190
12/31/80	200

Huskie Company
Constant Dollar Income Statement
1980

Sales	$(100,000 \times \frac{200}{190})$	105,263
less Cost of Goods Sold	$(50,000 \times \frac{200}{180})$	(55,556)
Gross Margin		49,707
less Depr. Expense	$(10,000 \times \frac{200}{100})$	(20,000)
Other Operating Expenses	$(25,000 \times \frac{200}{190})$	(26,316)
Income before Purchasing Power Gain (Loss)		3,391

Notice that before the above income statement would be complete, the purchasing power gain or loss on net monetary items would have to be computed and included in the statement.

The computation of purchasing power loss in the Static Company example was rather simple since only one monetary item and no transactions were involved. The calculations become a little more difficult in more complex situations. The basic format is as follows:

1) Determine all monetary items at the beginning and end of the year
2) Subtract monetary liabilities from monetary assets to determine "net monetary items"
3) Determine what the amount of year-end net monetary items would be if they were nonmonetary items

    a) Restate beginning net monetary items to year-end dollars
    b) Add all sources of monetary items (restated)
    c) Deduct all uses of monetary items (restated)

  4) Compare the "as if" amount from #3 with the actual year-end net monetary
     items

    a) "As if" > actual ---- Purchasing power loss
    b) "As if" < actual ---- Purchasing power gain

Notice that if a firm has more monetary liabilities than monetary assets, the amount
of net monetary items would be negative. Step #4 above would still apply. For
example, assume "as if" = ($10,000), and "actual" = ($20,000). A purchasing power
loss would result because ($10,000) > ($20,000).

   A segment of the unofficial solution to a May 1970 CPA examination problem is
adapted below to illustrate calculation of purchasing power gain or loss.

Purchasing power gain or loss	Historical or Nominal $'s	To/ From	Constant $'s 12/31/79
Indexes: 1/1/79, 100;			
Average 1979, 103			
12/31/79, 104			
Net monetary items--12/31/78	$ 445,000	104/100	$ 462,800
Add: Sales	1,900,000	104/103	1,918,447
	$2,345,000		$2,381,247
Deduct:			
Purchases	1,840,000		
Operating expenses & interest	215,000		
Purchase of marketable securities	400,000		
Acquisitions of equipment	150,000		
	2,605,000	104/103	2,630,291
Net monetary items--historical	$ (260,000)		
Net monetary items--historical --restated to 12/31/79 ("as if")			(249,044)
Net monetary items--12/31/79 (actual)			(260,000)
Purchasing power loss ("as if" > actual)			$ (10,956)

   Note that the left hand column of numbers is a funds flow statement where funds
are defined as net monetary items. It includes some items from the income statement
which affect net monetary assets (such as sales) but not others (e.g., depreciation) which have no effect on net monetary items. Also note that this example is
simplified--all sources and uses occurred evenly throughout the year (same restatement ratio used). A more realistic example might have some changes occurring evenly
throughout the year, and some occurring at specific points during the year (requiring different restatement ratios).

B. Current Cost Accounting

Current cost accounting is a method of valuing and reporting assets, liabilities, revenues, and expenses at their current cost at the balance sheet date or at the date of their use or sale.

It is important to distinguish between constant dollar and current cost accounting. Constant dollar accounting is concerned only with changes in the unit of measure--from nominal dollars to units of general purchasing power. Current cost accounting discards historical cost as a reporting model. The following matrix from APB Statement No. 3, Appendix D, illustrates the different reporting options.

	Unit of Measure	
Relationship measured	Nominal (Unadjusted) Dollars	Constant Dollars
Historical Cost	1	2
Current Cost	3	4

1) <u>Historical Cost/Nominal Dollars.</u> The original cost of the asset or liability and generally no changes in specific prices or the general price level are recorded.

2) <u>Historical Cost/Constant Dollars.</u> Original cost is reported but measured in dollars of equal purchasing power. Changes in specific prices are generally not recorded.

3) <u>Current Cost/Nominal Dollars.</u> The relationship measured is no longer historical cost, but current cost. The effect of changes in the general price level is not separated from the effect of changes in specific value.

4) <u>Current Cost/Constant Dollar.</u> The relationship measured is current cost, but the measuring unit is restated dollars. Changes in both the general and specific price levels are separately recorded.

Both constant dollar and current cost accounting are based in part on the theory of <u>capital maintenance</u>, which measures income by the difference in net assets (adjusted for owner investments and withdrawals) at two points in time. In other words, income is not recognized unless net assets are maintained.

Two basic concepts of capital maintenance (financial and physical) can be used to separate return on capital (earnings) from return of capital (capital recovery). Remember, any capital which is "used up" during a period must be returned before earnings can be recognized. In other words, earnings is the amount an entity can distribute to its owners and be as well off at the end of the year as at the beginning.

One way "well-offness" can be measured is in terms of financial capital. This concept of capital maintenance holds that the capital to be maintained is measured by the amount of cash (possibly restated into constant dollars) invested by owners.

Earnings may not be recognized until the dollar investment in net assets, measured in units of money or purchasing power, is returned. The financial capital maintenance concept is the traditional view which is reflected in most present financial statements.

An alternative definition of well-offness is expressed in terms of physical capital. This concept holds that the capital to be maintained is the physical productive capacity of the enterprise. Earnings may not be recognized until the current replacement costs of assets with the same productive capabilities as the assets used up are returned. The physical capital maintenance concept supports current cost accounting which must be reported in some disclosures by certain entities (see SFAS 33). Again, the physical productive capacity may be measured in nominal or constant dollars.

A simple example can further clarify the two capital maintenance concepts. Suppose an enterprise invests $10 in an inventory item. At year end, the enterprise sells the item for $15. In order to replace the item at year end, it would have to pay $12 rather than $10. To further simplify, assume the increase in replacement cost is due to specific price changes, and there is no general inflation.

The financial capital concept would maintain that the firm is as well-off once the dollar investment ($10) is returned. At that point, the financial capital is maintained and the remaining $5 is return on capital, or income. The physical capital concept maintains that the firm is not as well-off until the physical capacity (a similar inventory item) is returned. Therefore, the firm must reinvest $12 to be as well-off. Then physical capital is maintained and only the remaining $3 is return on capital, or income.

1. Current Cost/Nominal Dollar Balance Sheet.

Preparation of a current cost/nominal dollar balance sheet is fairly simple--for each item, the current cost is reported. Common stock is reported at the same amount as in conventional historical cost statements, and retained earnings is computed by adding to the beginning balance current cost net income less any dividends (already stated at current cost) declared during the year. No constant dollar adjustments are made.

2. Current Cost/Nominal Dollar Income Statement.

Preparation of a current cost/ nominal dollar income statement is more complicated, and an understanding of certain basic current cost concepts is necessary.

<u>Current cost income from continuing operations</u> is sales revenue less expenses on a current cost basis. <u>Realized holding gains</u> (the difference between current cost and historical cost of assets consumed) are then added to arrive at <u>realized income</u>, which will always be equal to historical cost net income. Finally, <u>unrealized holding gains</u> (increases in the current cost of assets held throughout the year) are included to result in <u>current cost net income</u>.

An example should help clarify these terms. Bell Co. went into business on 1/1/80. 1980 sales revenue was $200,000 and purchases totaled $150,000. Inventory with a historical cost of $100,000 was sold when its current cost was $160,000. Ending inventory (historical cost, $50,000) had a year-end current cost of $80,000. No other revenue was realized or expenses incurred during 1980. Historical and current cost income statements for 1980 are presented below:

Bell Company
Income Statements

Historical Cost/
Nominal Dollar Basis   **Current Cost/Nominal Dollar Basis**

Sales	$200,000	Sales		$200,000
less C.G.S.	(100,000)	less C.G.S.		(160,000)
		Cur. Cost Income from Cont. Oper.		40,000
		Realized Holding Gains (160,000 - 100,000)		60,000
Net Income	$100,000 ⟷	Realized Income		100,000
		Unrealized Holding Gains (80,000 - 50,000)		30,000
		Current Cost Net Income		$130,000

1980 journal entries for Bell Company in current cost system would be as follows:

a) Inventory   150,000
        Cash   150,000

b) Inventory   90,000
        Realizable
        Holding Gain   90,000

c) Cash   200,000
        Sales Revenue   200,000

d) Cost of Goods Sold   160,000
        Inventory   160,000

e) Realizable Holding Gain   90,000
        Realized Holding Gain   60,000
        Unrealized Holding Gain   30,000

In general, sales and some expense amounts (salaries, rent, etc.) will be the same under historical and current cost systems. However, whenever an expense represents the use or consumption of an asset whose current cost has changed since its acquisition (as with the inventory in the Bell Co. example), that expense must be expressed at the current cost of the asset when used. Realized holding gains are computed by comparing the current cost of assets when used or consumed with their historical cost. Unrealized holding gains for the period are determined by identifying changes in the current cost of assets held throughout the year (not used or consumed). Notice that the holding gains do not reflect changes in the general purchasing power. In other words, the holding gains are not reported net of general inflation when the reporting model is current cost/nominal dollar.

C. Current Cost/Constant Dollar Accounting

Current cost/constant dollar accounting is a method of accounting based on measures of current cost in terms of dollars which have the same general purchasing power. This method discards both historical cost (in favor of current cost) and nominal dollars as the unit of measurement (in favor of units of general purchasing power). One key point concerning current cost/constant dollar accounting: it attempts to separate both the effects of general inflation and changes in specific prices (measuring holding gains net of inflation).

The following two cases highlight differences in the various reporting models:

CASE FACTS

Date	Event	Historical Cost	Current Cost	Case 1 Price Index	Case 2 Price Index
1/1/80	Purchase of marketable security	$1,000	$1,000	100	100
12/31/80	Preparation of financial statements (Information pertains to marketable security)	1,000	1,600	120	180

Comparative Analysis

Reporting Model	Income Statement Case 1	Income Statement Case 2	Balance Sheet Case 1	Balance Sheet Case 2
Historical Cost/Nominal Dollar	-0-	-0-	$1,000	$1,000
Historical Cost/Constant Dollar (a)	-0-	-0-	$1,200	$1,800
Current Cost/Nominal Dollar (b)	$600	$600	$1,600	$1,600
Current Cost/Constant Dollar (c)	$400	($200)	$1,600	$1,600

Supporting Computations

Case 1	Case 2
(a) $\$1,000 \times \frac{120}{100}$	$\$1,000 \times \frac{180}{100}$
(b) $\$1,600 - \$1,000$	$\$1,600 - \$1,000$
(c) $\$1,600 - \$1,000 \times \frac{120}{100}$	$\$1,600 - \$1,000 \times \frac{180}{100}$

1) Note that generally, no gains or losses are recognized under historical cost/nominal dollar or historical cost/constant dollar because the securities have not been sold; changes in current cost ignored (except in lower of cost or market).

2) Balance sheet amounts for historical cost/nominal dollar and historical cost/constant dollar are both historical cost; only difference is restatement into constant dollar.

3) Gains and losses recognized in the last two alternatives due to changes in current cost. Amounts differ when nominal or constant dollars are used as measuring unit.

4) All balance sheet amounts are expressed at current cost under the last two alternatives.

1. Current Cost/Constant Dollar Balance Sheet.

All assets and liabilities are stated at current cost, as in a current cost balance sheet. Common stock would be adjusted to end-of-year dollars, while retained earnings will be equal to the beginning balance plus current cost/constant dollar net income less any dividend restated to end-of-year dollars.

2. Current Cost/Constant Dollar Income Statement.

First, the current cost income statement is restated to end-of-year dollars. Then, both realized and unrealized holding gains must be computed net of inflation (as shown previously in Cases 1 and 2). Finally, a purchasing power gain or loss on net monetary items is computed in the same fashion as was done in constant dollar accounting.

D. SFAS 33

SFAS 33 requires disclosure of supplementary constant dollar and current cost information by certain corporations (see outline). Disclosure requirements include: (1) constant dollar income; (2) purchasing power gain or loss on net monetary items; (3) current cost income; (4) current cost amounts for inventory and property, plant and equipment; and (5) holding gains (net of inflation) on inventory and property, plant and equipment. The statement makes no distinction between realized and un-realized holding gains.

There are two major differences between the requirements of FASB and the pre-ceding discussion of reporting models. First, no comprehensive presentation of con-stant dollar or current cost information is required*; only separate requirements such as those listed above are mandatory. Second, all constant-dollar and current cost information is reported in average-for-the-year dollars rather than end-of-the-year dollars. In other words, wherever a year-end price index would have been used, an average-for-the-year index is used instead. This approach makes constant dollar computations much simpler. Current cost data is also stated in average costs for the year.

Each of the supplementary disclosure requirements are described in the following paragraphs. These requirements are cross referenced to Schedules A and B (taken from SFAS 33) on page 923.

1. <u>Historical cost/constant dollar income from continuing operations</u>.

The FASB assumes all revenues and expenses, other than depreciation and cost of goods sold, were <u>incurred evenly</u> throughout the year. Therefore, no restatement is necessary to express these items in average-for-the-year dollars. Cost of goods sold and depreciation expense are restated using the same process described for con-stant dollar statements, except that these items are restated to average-for-the-year dollars.

2. <u>Purchasing power gain or loss on net monetary items</u>.

Purchasing power gain or loss is computed exactly as described earlier with the same exception: average-for-the-year dollars are used rather than end-of-year dol-lars. The following example contrasts the two methods:

Net monetary items 1/1/80	$100,000	1/1/80 price index	100
Sales	700,000	1980 average index	140
Purchases	(400,000)	12/31/80 price index	200
Expenses	(150,000)	Sales, purchases, expenses occurred	
		evenly throughout the year	
Dividends	(100,000)	Dividends declared on 12/31/80	
Net monetary items 12/31/80	$150,000		

*Although SFAS 33 does not require a comprehensive set of financial statements adjusted for changing prices, it does not prohibit firms from disclosing this information. If a complete set of financials is prepared they can be prepared in either average or end-of-year prices and/or dollars.

The guidelines from SFAS 33 for classification of items as monetary or nonmonetary are shown in Schedule D (taken from SFAS 33), page 924.

Purchasing Power Loss
End-of-Year Dollars

	Historical Cost/ Nominal Dollars		Index	Constant Dollars End-of-Year
Net monetary items 1/1/80	$100,000	x	200/100	$ 200,000
Add Sales	700,000	x	200/140	1,000,000
Deduct:				
Purchases	(400,000)	x	200/140	(571,429)
Expenses	(150,000)	x	200/140	(214,286)
Dividends	(100,000)	x	200/200	(100,000)
Net monetary items, 12/31/80	$150,000			
Net monetary items, restated ("as-if")				314,285
Net monetary items, historical				150,000
Purchasing power loss ("as if" > actual)				$ 164,285

Purchasing Power Loss
Average-for-the-Year Dollars

	Historical Cost/ Nominal Dollars		Index	Constant Dollars Average-for-the-Year
Net monetary items, 1/1/80	$100,000	x	140/100	$140,000
Add Sales	700,000	x	140/140	700,000
Deduct:				
Purchases	(400,000)	x	140/140	(400,000)
Expenses	(150,000)	x	140/140	(150,000)
Dividends	(100,000)	x	140/200	(70,000)
Net monetary items, 12/31/80	$150,000			
Net monetary items, restated ("as-if")				220,000
Net monetary items, historical	150,000	x	140/200	105,000
Purchasing power loss ["as if" > actual (restated)]				$115,000

An important point to remember is that the purchasing power gain or loss on net monetary items is <u>not</u> an element of income from continuing operations.

3. <u>Current Cost Income from Continuing Operations</u>.

The FASB requires that only cost of goods sold and depreciation expense be expressed at current cost. All other items are expressed as in a historical cost income statement.

4. <u>Current Cost Amounts for Inventory and Property, Plant and Equipment</u>.

The FASB requires presentation of the current cost of these items, <u>restated to average-for-the-year dollars</u>. This restatement is necessary for a presentation consistent with other items presented.

5. <u>Holding Gains or Losses (net of inflation)</u>.

   Holding gains or losses need only be computed on inventory, cost of goods sold, property, plant and equipment, and depreciation expense. The holding gains or losses, net of inflation are computed by comparing current cost (restated to average dollars) with historical cost (restated to average dollars). For example, if land were acquired for $100,000 when the price index was 100, had a current cost of $300,000 at year end when the price index was 200, and the average-for-the-year index was 150, the FASB holding gain would be computed as follows:

$$\text{Current cost, restated} \quad -- \quad (\$300,000)(\tfrac{150}{200}) \quad = \quad \$225,000$$

$$\text{Historical cost, restated} \quad -- \quad (\$100,000)(\tfrac{150}{100}) \quad = \quad \underline{150,000}$$

$$\text{Holding gain, net of inflation} \qquad\qquad\qquad\qquad \underline{\$\ 75,000}$$

Please note that the $75,000 holding gain is not to be included in income from continuing operations.

   Schedule C (taken from SFAS 33), page 924, illustrates the five year disclosure requirement. While these requirements apply only to large companies, the FASB encourages experimentation by all companies in the area of changing prices. The FASB requires the disclosure of both constant dollar and current cost information "to provide a basis for studying the usefulness of the two types of information." In the future the FASB may require more or less information on one or more of the discussed reporting models.

SCHEDULE A*
STATEMENT OF INCOME FROM CONTINUING
OPERATIONS ADJUSTED FOR CHANGING PRICES

For the Year Ended December 31, 1980
(In (000s) of Average 1980 Dollars)

Income from continuing operations, as reported in the income statement		$ 9,000
Adjustments to restate costs for the effect of general inflation		
Cost of goods sold	(7,384)	
Depreciation and amortization expense	(4,130)	(11,514)

---

*This illustration, which shows a reconciliation format, and Schedule B on the following page, which shows the same numbers in a statement format, are acceptable alternatives.

(1) Loss from continuing operations adjusted for general inflation		(2,514)
Adjustments to reflect the difference between general inflation and changes in specific prices (current costs)		
Cost of goods sold	(1,024)	
Depreciation and amortization expense	(5,370)	(6,394)
(3) Loss from continuing operations adjusted for changes in specific prices		$(8,908)
(2) Gain from decline in purchasing power of net amounts owed		$ 7,729
(4) Increase in specific prices (current cost) of inventories and property, plant, and equipment held during the year*		$ 24,608
Effect of increase in general price level		18,959
(5) Excess of increase in specific prices over increase in the general price level		$ 5,649

*At December 31, 1980 current cost of inventory was $65,700 and current cost of property, plant, and equipment, net of accumulated depreciation was $85,100.

SCHEDULE B
STATEMENT OF INCOME FROM CONTINUING OPERATIONS ADJUSTED FOR CHANGING PRICES

For the Year Ended December 31, 1980
(In (000s) of Dollars)

	As Reported in the Primary Statements	Adjusted for General Inflation	Adjusted for Changes in Specific Prices (Current Costs)
Net sales and other operating revenues	$253,000	$253,000	$253,000
Cost of goods sold	197,000	204,384	205,408
Depreciation and amortization expense	10,000	14,130	19,500
Other operating expense	20,835	20,835	20,835
Interest expense	7,165	7,165	7,165
Provision for income taxes	9,000	9,000	9,000
	244,000	255,514	261,908
(1) & (3) Income (loss) from continuing operations	$ 9,000	$(2,514)	$(8,908)
(2) Gain from decline in purchasing power of net amounts owed		$ 7,729	$ 7,729
(4) Increase in specific prices (current cost) of inventories and property, plant, and equipment held during the year*			$ 24,608
Effect of increase in general price level			18,959
(5) Excess of increase in specific prices over increase in the general price level			$ 5,649

*At December 31, 1980 current cost of inventory was $65,700 and current cost of property, plant, and equipment, net of accumulated depreciation was $85,100.

SCHEDULE C
FIVE-YEAR COMPARISON OF SELECTED
SUPPLEMENTARY FINANCIAL DATA ADJUSTED FOR EFFECTS OF CHANGING PRICES
(In (000s) of Average 1980 Dollars)

	Years Ended December 31,				
	1976	1977	1978	1979	1980
Net sales and other operating revenues	265,000	235,000	240,000	237,063	253,000
Historical cost information adjusted for general inflation					
Income (loss) from continuing operations				(2,761)	(2,514)
Income (loss) from continuing operations per common share				$ (1.91)	$ (1.68)
Net assets at year end				55,518	57,733
Current cost information					
Income (loss) from continuing operations				(4,125)	(8,908)
Income (loss) from continuing operations per common share				$ (2.75)	$ (5.94)
Excess of increase in specific prices over increase in the general price level				2,292	5,649
Net assets at year end				79,996	81,466
Gain from decline in purchasing power of net amounts owed				7,027	7,729
Cash dividends declared per common share	$ 2.59	$ 2.43	$ 2.26	$ 2.16	$ 2.00
Market price per common share at year end	$ 32	$ 31	$ 43	$ 39	$ 35
Average consumer price index	170.5	181.5	195.4	205.0	220.9

SCHEDULE D
MONETARY VS. NONMONETARY ITEMS
Assets

Item	Monetary	Nonmonetary	Requires Analysis
Cash on hand, demand deposits, time deposits	X		
Foreign currency and claims to foreign currency	X		
Securities:			
Common stock (equity method not used)		X	
Preferred stock (convertible or participating), convertible bonds			X
Other preferred stock or bonds	X		
Accounts and notes receivable, allowance for doubtful accounts	X		
Mortgage loans	X		

Item	Monetary	Nonmonetary	Requires Analysis
Inventories		X	
Loans to employees	X		
Prepaid expenses			X
Long-term receivables	X		
Refundable deposits	X		
Advances to unconsolidated subsidiaries	X		
Equity in unconsolidated subsidiaries		X	
Pension and other funds			X
Property, plant and equipment and accumulated depreciation		X	
Cash surrender value of life insurance	X		
Purchase commitments (portion paid on fixed price contracts)		X	
Advances to supplier (not on fixed price contracts)	X		
Deferred income tax charges	X		
Patents, trademarks, goodwill and other intangible assets		X	
Deferred life insurance policy acquisition costs	X		
Deferred property and casualty insurance policy acquistion costs		X	

Liabilities

Item	Monetary	Nonmonetary	Requires Analysis
Accounts and notes payable, accrued expenses payable	X		
Accrued vacation pay			X
Cash dividends payable	X		
Obligations payable in foreign currency	X		
Sales commitments (portion collected on fixed price contracts)		X	
Advances from customers (not on fixed price contracts)	X		
Accrued losses on purchase commitments	X		
Deferred revenue			X
Refundable deposits	X		
Bonds payable, other long-term debt, and related discount or premium	X		
Accrued pension obligations			X
Obligations under warranties		X	
Deferred income tax credits	X		
Deferred investment tax credits		X	
Life or property and casualty insurance policy reserves	X		
Unearned insurance premiums		X	
Deposit liabilities of financial institutions	X		

E. Foreign Currency Translation

The rules for the translation of foreign currency into U.S. dollars apply to two major areas:

1) Foreign currency transactions which are denominated in other than a company's functional currency (e.g., exports, imports, loans) and

2) Foreign currency financial statements of branches, divisions, subsidiaries, and other investees which are incorporated with the financial statements of a U.S. company by combination, consolidation, or the equity method

The objectives of translation are:

1) To provide information relative to the expected economic effects of rate changes on an enterprise's cash flows and equity and

2) To provide information in consolidated statements relative to the financial results and relationships of each individual foreign consolidated entity as reflected by the functional currency of each reporting entity

The first objective influences the rules for the translation of foreign currency transactions, while both objectives influence the rules for the translation of foreign currency financial statements. After working through this module, read through the outlines of SFAS 52 and SFAS 70.

F. Translation of Foreign Currency Statements

Assume that a U.S. company has a 100% owned subsidiary in West Germany. The subsidiary's operations consist of leasing space in an office building. Its balance sheet at December 31, 1982 and its income statement for 1982 are presented below:

West German Company
Balance Sheet
December 31, 1982

Assets	Deutsche marks	Liabilities and Owners' Equity	Deutsche marks
Cash	60	Accounts Payable	100
Accounts Receivable (Net)	100	Mortgage Payable	200
Land	200	Common Stock	100
Building	500	Retained Earnings	360
Less Accumulated Depr.	(100)		
Total Assets	DM 760	Total Liabilities and Owners' Equity	DM 760

West German Company
Income Statement
For Year Ended December 31, 1982

Revenues	DM 260
Operating Expenses (includes depreciation expense of 20 DM)	160
Net Income	DM 100

In addition to the information above, the following data are also needed for the translation process:

1) Transactions involving land, building, mortgage payable, and common stock were all effected in 1977.
2) No dividends were paid during 1982.
3) Exchange rates for various dates follow:

    1DM = $.30 in 1977
    1DM = $.40 average for 1977 to 1982
    1DM = $.50 at beginning of 1982
    1DM = $.55 at end of 1982
    1DM = $.53 weighted average for 1982

If the U.S. company wants to present consolidated financial statements which include the results of its West German subsidiary, the financial statements of the West German company must be translated into U.S. dollars. However, before this can be accomplished, the management of the U.S. company must determine the functional currency of its West German subsidiary. SFAS 52 defines an entity's functional currency as ". . . the currency of the primary economic environment in which the entity operates; normally, that is the currency of the environment in which an entity primarily generates and expends cash." The decision concerning the functional currency is important because, once determined, it should be used consistently, unless it is clear that economic facts and circumstances have changed. The selection of the functional currency is dependent upon an evaluation of several factors. These factors include the following:

1) Cash flows (Do the foreign entity's cash flows directly affect the parent's cash flows and are they immediately available for remittance to the parent?)

2) Sales prices (Are the foreign entity's sales prices responsive to exchange rate changes and to international competition?)

3) Sales markets (Is the foreign entity's sales market the parent's country or are sales denominated in the parent's currency?)

4) Expenses (Are the foreign entity's expenses incurred in the parent's country?)

5) Financing (Is the foreign entity's financing primarily from the parent or is it denominated in the parent's currency?)

6) Intercompany transactions (Is there a high volume of intercompany transactions between the parent and foreign entity?)

If the answers to the questions above are predominantly yes, the functional currency would be the reporting currency of the parent, i.e., the U.S. dollar. On the other hand, if the answers to the questions were predominantly no, the functional currency would be the foreign currency. In the example described previously, the DM would be the functional currency if the answers were no. Note that the functional currency does not necessarily have to be the local currency of the foreign country when the answers to the questions are negative. In other words, it is possible for a foreign currency other than deutsche marks to be the functional currency of our West German company, e.g., Swiss francs or Italian lira could be the functional currency. However, assume these other possibilities are not alternatives in the example mentioned previously.

If the circumstances indicate the DM to be the functional currency, SFAS 52 mandates the current rate method for the translation of the foreign currency financial statements. This technique is illustrated below for the West German financial statements shown previously.

Balance Sheet
(Deutsche mark is Functional Currency)

	DM	Exchange Rates	U.S. Dollars
Assets:			
Cash	60	.55	33
Accounts Receivable (Net)	100	.55	55
Land	200	.55	110
Building (Net)	400	.55	220
Totals	DM 760		$418
Liabilities and Owners' Equity:			
Accounts Payable	100	.55	55
Mortgage Payable	200	.55	110
Common Stock	100	.30	30
Retained Earnings	360	see income statement	157
Translation Adjustments	--		66
Totals	DM 760		$418

Combined Income and Retained Earnings Statement

	DM	Exchange Rates	U.S. Dollars
Revenues	260	.53	$137.80
Operating Expenses (including 20 DM of depreciation expense)	160	.53	84.80
Net Income	100		53.00
Retained Earnings at 1/1/82	260	.40	104.00
Retained Earnings at 12/31/82	DM 360		$157.00

The following points should be noted from the illustration of the translation process:

a) All assets and liabilities are translated using the current rate at the balance sheet date. All revenues and expenses should be translated at the rates in effect when these items are recognized during the period. Due to practical considerations, however, weighted average rates can be used to translate revenues and expenses.

b) Owners' equity accounts are translated by using historical exchange rates. Common stock was issued in 1977 when the exchange rate was 1DM = $.30. The beginning balance of retained earnings for 1982 was accumulated when the weighted average exchange rate was 1DM = $.40.

c) Translation adjustments result from translating all assets and liabilities at the current rate, while owners' equity is translated by using historical rates and income statement items are translated by using weighted average rates. The translation adjustments balance is reported in the owners' equity section of the consolidated balance sheet.

d) The translation adjustments credit of $66 is calculated as follows (note the items below are the only ones not translated at the current rate):

Common Stock	100 DM (.55 - .30) =	$25
Retained Earnings 1/1/82	260 DM (.55 - .40) =	39
Net Income for 1982	100 DM (.55 - .53) =	2
	Translation Adjustment	$66

The illustration of the current rate technique assumed the DM to be the functional currency. Assume, however, that the circumstances were evaluated by the U.S. company, and the U.S. dollar was chosen as the functional currency. Under this alternative, SFAS 52 requires the foreign currency financial statements to be remeasured into U.S. dollars. According to SFAS 52, the ". . . remeasurement process is intended to produce the same result as if the entity's books of record had been maintained in the functional currency." If the U.S. dollar is the functional currency, the remeasurement of foreign currency financial statements into U.S. dollars makes translation unnecessary. The remeasurement process is illustrated below for the West German subsidiary. Note that the remeasurement process is similar to the temporal method of translation which was recommended in SFAS 8, the predecessor of SFAS 52.

Balance Sheet
(U.S. Dollar is Functional Currency)

	DM	Exchange Rates	U.S. Dollars
Assets:			
Cash	60	.55	33
Accounts Receivable (Net)	100	.55	55
Land	200	.30	60
Building (Net)	400	.30	120
Totals	DM 760		$268
Liabilities and Owners' Equity:			
Accounts Payable	100	.55	55
Mortgage Payable	200	.55	110
Common Stock	100	.30	30
Retained Earnings	360	see income statement	73
Totals	DM 760		$268

One significant difference between remeasurement and the temporal method is the translation of deferred taxes. Deferred taxes are now considered monetary and would be translated by using the current rate. Under SFAS 8, they were considered non-monetary and were translated by using historical rates.

Combined Income and Retained Earnings Statement

	DM	Exchange Rates	U.S. Dollars
Revenues	260	.53	$137.80
Expenses (exclusive of depreciation)	140	.53	$ 74.20
Depreciation	20	.30	6.00
Total Expenses	160		$ 80.20
Foreign Exchange Loss	--	--	10.60
Net Income (Loss)	100		$(47.00)
Retained Earnings at 1/1/82	260		26.00
Retained Earnings at 12/31/82	DM 360		$ 73.00

The following observations should be noted about the remeasurement process:

a) Assets and liabilities which have historical cost balances are translated by using historical exchange rates. Monetary assets and monetary liabilities, on the other hand, are translated by using the current rate at the balance sheet date.

b) Revenues and expenses that occur during a period are translated, for practical purposes, by using the weighted average exchange rate for the period. Revenues and expenses that represent allocations of historical balances (e.g., depreciation) are translated by using historical exchange rates.

c) The foreign exchange loss of $10.60 is reported on the consolidated income statement. The loss is the result of the remeasurement process which assumes the U.S. dollar is the functional currency.

d) The calculation of the loss is the result of the rules employed in the remeasurement process. In mechanical terms, the foreign exchange loss is the amount needed to make the debits equal the credits in the West German Company's U.S. dollar trial balance. Note this technique below:

	DM DR	DM CR	Exchange Rates	U.S. Dollars DR	U.S. Dollars CR
Cash	60		.55	33	
Accounts Rec. (Net)	100		.55	55	
Land	200		.30	60	
Building (Net)	400		.30	120	
Accounts Payable		100	.55		55
Mortgage Payable		200	.55		110
Common Stock		100	.30		30
Retained Earnings (1/1/82)		260			26
Revenues		260	.53		137.80
Expenses	140		.53	74.20	
Depreciation Exp.	20		.30	6	
TOTALS	DM 920	DM 920		$348.20	$358.80
Foreign Exchange Loss				10.60	
TOTALS				$358.80	$358.80

The significant points to remember about the West German illustration are summarized below:

1) Before foreign currency financial statements can be translated into U.S. dollars, a decision has to be made regarding the functional currency.

2) If the functional currency is the foreign currency, the current rate method is used to translate to U.S. dollars. All assets and liabilities are translated by using the current rate at the balance sheet date. Owners' equity is translated by using historical rates while revenues (and gains) and expenses (and losses) are translated at the rates in existence during the period when the transactions occurred. A weighted average rate can be used for items occurring numerous times throughout the period. The translation adjustments (debit or credit) which result from the application of these rules are reported in owners' equity.

3) If the functional currency is the reporting currency (the U.S. dollar), the foreign currency financial statements are remeasured into U.S. dollars. All foreign currency balances are restated to U.S. dollars using both historical and current exchange rates. Foreign currency balances which reflect prices from past transactions (e.g., inventories carried at cost, prepaid insurance, property, plant and equipment, etc.) are translated by using historical rates while foreign currency balances which reflect prices from current transactions (e.g., inventories and marketable equity securities carried at market, etc.,) are translated by using the current rate. Monetary assets and liabilities are translated by using the current rate. (Deferred taxes are translated by using the current rate.) Foreign exchange gains/losses that result from the remeasurement process are reported on the income statement.

The above summary can be arranged in tabular form as shown below:

Functional Currency	Functional Currency Determinants	Translation Method	Reporting
Local currency of foreign company[a]	a. Operations not integrated with parent's operations b. Buying and selling activities primarily in local currency c. Cash flows not immediately available for remittance to parent	Current Rate (All assets/liabilities translated using current rate; revenues/expenses use weighted average rate; equity accounts use historical rates)	Translation adjustments are reported in equity section of consolidated balance sheet. Analysis of changes in accumulated translation adjustments disclosed via footnote.
U.S. Dollar	a. Operations integrated with parent's operations b. Buying and selling activities primarily in U.S. and/or U.S. dollars c. Cash flows immediately available for remittance to parent	Remeasurement (Monetary assets/liabilities use current rate; historical cost balances use historical rates; revenues/expenses use weighted average rates and historical rates, the latter for allocations like depr. exp.).	Foreign exchange gain/loss is reported on the consolidated income statement

[a]The functional currency could be a foreign currency other than the local currency. If this is the case, the foreign currency statements are first remeasured in the functional currency before they are translated to U.S. dollars using the current rate method.

Before proceeding to foreign currency transactions, a few comments concerning the translation of foreign currency financial statements in highly inflationary economies should be made. If the cumulative inflation rate $\geq$ 100% over a three year period in a foreign country, the foreign currency statements of a company located in that country are remeasured into the reporting currency, i.e., the U.S. dollar. In other words, it is assumed the reporting currency is the functional currency. The flowchart on the next page summarizes the requirements of SFAS 52 with respect to foreign currency financial statements.

FOREIGN CURRENCY FINANCIAL STATEMENTS

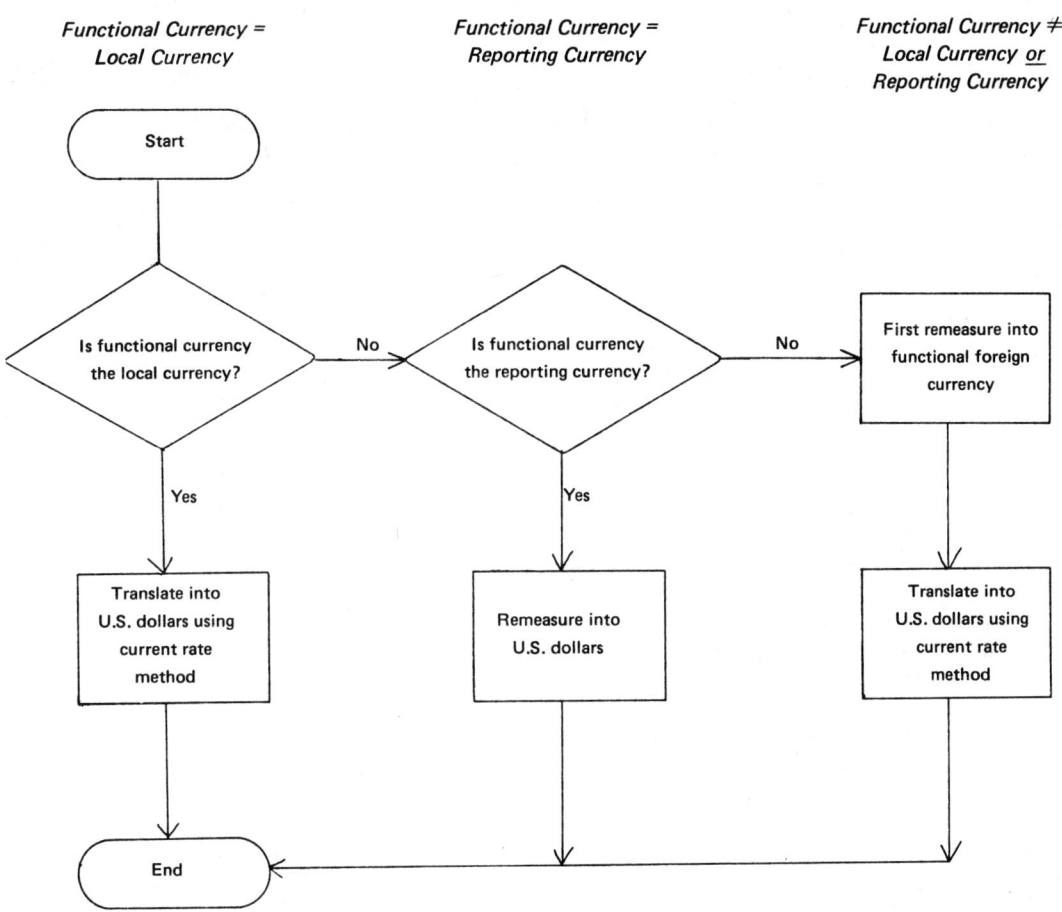

G. Translation of Foreign Currency Transactions

A foreign currency transaction, according to SFAS 52, is a transaction ". . . denominated in a currency other than the entity's functional currency." Denominated means that the balance is fixed in terms of the number of units of a foreign currency regardless of changes in the exchange rate. When a U.S. company buys or sells to an unrelated foreign company, and the U.S. company agrees either to pay for goods or receive payment for the goods in foreign currency units, this is a foreign currency transaction from the point of view of the U.S. company (the functional currency is the U.S. dollar). In these situations, the U.S. company has "crossed currencies" and directly assumes the risk of fluctuating foreign exchange rates of the foreign currency units. This exposed foreign currency risk may lead to recognition of foreign exchange gains or losses in the income statement of the U.S. company, as defined in SFAS 52. If the U.S. company pays or receives U.S. dollars in import and export transactions, the risk which occurs as the result of fluctuating foreign exchange rates is borne by the foreign supplier or customer, and there is no need to apply the procedures outlined in SFAS 52 to the transaction reported in U.S. dollars on the U.S. company's books, i.e., as part of stockholders' equity.

The following example will illustrate the terminology and procedures applicable to the translation of foreign currency transactions. Assume that U.S. Company, an exporter, sells merchandise to a customer in West Germany on December 1, 1982, for 10,000 deutsche marks (DM). Receipt is due on January 31, 1983, and U.S. Company prepares financial statements on December 31, 1982. At the transaction date (December 1, 1982), the spot rate for immediate exchange of foreign currencies indicates that 1 DM is equivalent to $.50. This quotation is referred to as a direct quotation since the exchange is stated in terms of a direct translation of the currency in which the debt is measured. To find the U.S. dollar equivalent of this transaction, simply multiply the foreign currency amount, 10,000 DM, by $.50 to get $5,000. Occasionally, spot rates are quoted indirectly (e.g., $1 is equivalent to 2 DM). In the example used, since $1 is equivalent to 2 DM, the foreign currency amount would be divided by 2 to get the U.S. dollar amount of $5,000 if an indirect quotation were used.

At December 1, 1982, the foreign currency transaction should be recorded by U.S. Company in the following manner:

    Accounts Receivable - West Germany $5,000
        Sales $5,000

The accounts receivable and sales are measured in U.S. dollars at the transaction date using the spot rate at the time of the transaction. While the accounts receivable is measured and reported in U.S. dollars, the receivable is denominated or fixed in DM. This characteristic can result in foreign exchange gains or losses if the spot rate for DM changes between the transaction date and the date the transaction is settled.

If financial statements are prepared between the transaction date and the settlement date, the FASB requires that receivables and liabilities denominated in a currency other than the functional currency be restated to reflect the spot rates in existence at the balance sheet date. Assume that, on December 31, 1982, the spot rate for DM is 1 DM = $.52. This means that 10,000 DM are worth $5,200, and that the accounts receivable denominated in DM are increased by $200. The following journal entry should be recorded as of December 31, 1982:

    Accounts Receivable - West Germany $200
        Foreign Currency Transaction Gain $200

Note that the sales account, which was credited on the transaction date for $5,000, is not affected by changes in the spot rate. This treatment exemplifies the "two-transaction" viewpoint adopted by the FASB. In other words, making the sale is the result of an operating decision, while bearing the risk of fluctuating spot rates is the result of a financing decision. Therefore, the amount determined as sales revenue at the transaction date should not be altered because of a financing decision to wait until January 31, 1983, for payment of the account. The risk of a foreign exchange loss can be avoided either by demanding immediate payment on December 1 or by entering into a forward exchange contract to hedge the exposed asset (accounts receivable). The fact that U.S. Company, in the example, did not act in either of these two ways is reflected by requiring the recognition of foreign currency transaction gains or losses on this type of transaction. These gains or losses are reported on the U.S. Company's income statement as financial (nonoperating) items in the period during which the exchange rates changed.

It is also important to note that reporting transaction gains or losses before the transaction is settled results in reporting unrealized gains or losses. This is an exception to the conventional realization principle which normally applies. This practice also results in a temporary timing difference between pretax accounting income and taxable income. This is due to the fact that foreign exchange gains and losses do not enter into the determination of taxable income until the year they are realized. Thus, interperiod tax allocation adjustments are required.

To complete the previous illustration, assume that on January 31, 1983, the foreign currency transaction is settled when the spot rate is 1 DM = $.51. Note that the account receivable is valued at $5,200 at this point. The receipt of DM and their conversion into dollars should be journalized as follows:

Foreign Currency	$5,100	
Foreign Currency Transaction Loss	$ 100	
Accounts Receivable - West Germany		$5,200
Cash	$5,100	
Foreign Currency		$5,100

The net effect of this foreign currency transaction was to receive $5,100 from a sale which was measured originally at $5,000. This realized net foreign currency transaction gain of $100 is reported on two income statements--a $200 gain in 1982 and a $100 loss in 1983.

It was stated previously that foreign currency transaction gains and losses on assets and liabilities, which are denominated in a currency other than the functional currency, can be hedged if the U.S. Company enters into a forward exchange contract. In the example, the U.S. Company could enter into a forward exchange contract on December 1 to sell 10,000 DM for a negotiated amount to a foreign exchange broker for future delivery on January 31, 1983. This forward contract is a hedge against the exposed asset position created by having accounts receivable denominated in DM.

The negotiated rate referred to above is called a futures or forward rate. In most cases, this futures rate is not identical to the spot rate at the date of the forward contract. The difference between the futures rate and the spot rate at the date of the forward contract is referred to as a discount or a premium. Any discount or premium must be amortized over the term of the forward contract, generally on a straight-line basis. The amortization of discount or premium is reflected in a separate revenue or expense account, not as an addition or subtraction to the foreign exchange gain or loss amount. Under this treatment it is important to observe that no net foreign exchange gains or losses result if assets and liabilities denominated in foreign currency are completely hedged at the transaction date.

To illustrate the preceding discussion, consider the following additional information for the example previously covered:

> On December 1, 1982, U.S. Company entered into a forward exchange contract to sell 10,000 DM on January 31, 1983 at $.505 per DM. The spot rate on December 1 is $.50 per DM.

The transactions which reflect the sale of goods and the forward exchange contract appear as follows:

Sale Transaction Entries				Forward Exchange Contract Entries (Futures Rate 1 DM = $.505)		
12-1-82 (spot rate 1 DM = $.50)						
Accounts Receivable –				Due from Exchange Broker	$5,050	
West Germany	$5,000			Due to Exchange Broker		$5,000
Sales		$5,000		Premium on Forward Contract		$ 50
12-31-82 (spot rate 1 DM = $.52)						
Accounts Receivable –				Foreign Cur. Trans. Loss	$ 200	
West Germany	$ 200			Due to Exchange Broker		$ 200
Foreign Currency Transaction Gain		$ 200		Premium on Forward Contract	$ 25	
				Financial Revenue		$ 25
				($25 = $50/2 months)		
01-31-83 (spot rate 1 DM = $.51)						
Foreign Currency	$5,100			Due to Exchange Broker	$5,200	
Foreign Cur. Trans. Loss	$ 100			Foreign Currency		$5,100
Accounts Receivable – West Germany		$5,200		Foreign Cur. Trans. Gain		$ 100
				Cash	$5,050	
				Due from Exchange Broker		$5,050
				Premium on Contract	$ 25	
				Financial Revenue		$ 25

The following points should be noted from the entries above:

1) The net foreign currency transaction gain/loss is zero. The account "Due from Exchange Broker" is fixed in terms of U.S. dollars and this amount is not affected by changes in spot rates between the transaction and settlement dates. The account "Due to Exchange Broker" is fixed or denominated in DM. The U.S. Company owes the exchange broker 10,000 DM, and these must be delivered on January 31, 1983. Because this liability is denominated in DM, its amount is determined by spot rates. Since spot rates change, this liability changes in amount equal to the changes in accounts receivable because both of the amounts are based on the same spot rates. These changes are reflected as foreign currency transaction gains and losses which net out to zero.

2) The "Premium on Forward Contract" is fixed in terms of U.S. dollars. This amount is amortized to a financial revenue account over the life of the forward contract on a straight-line basis.

3) The net effect of this transaction is that $5,050 was received on January 31, 1983, for a sale originally recorded at $5,000. The $50 difference was taken into income via amortization.

SFAS 52 does not require a forward exchange contract in order for a hedge to take place. For example, it is possible for a foreign currency transaction to act as an economic hedge against a parent's net investment in a foreign entity. Assume that an American parent company has a wholly owned British subsidiary which has net assets of 2 million pounds. The parent company can borrow 2 million pounds to hedge its net investment in the British subsidiary. Fluctuations in the exchange rate for pounds will have no net effect on the parent company because of the foreign currency transaction. Note that SFAS 52 requires that transaction gains/losses resulting from hedging net investments in foreign entities be reported on the balance sheet in the same way that translation adjustments are reported.

The financial statement disclosures required by SFAS 52 consist of the following:

1) Aggregate transaction gain (loss) that is included in the entity's net income.

2) Analysis of changes in accumulated translation adjustments which are reported as part of the entity's owners' equity.

3) Significant rate changes subsequent to the date of the financial statements including effects on unsettled foreign currency transactions.

H. Glossary

Discount or Premium on a Forward Contract

"The foreign currency amount of the contract multiplied by the difference between the contracted forward rate and the spot rate at the date of inception of the contract."

Foreign Currency Statements

"Financial statements that employ as the unit of measure a functional currency that is not the reporting currency of the enterprise."

Foreign Currency Transactions

"Transactions whose terms are denominated in a currency other than the entity's functional currency. Foreign currency transactions arise when an enterprise (a) buys or sells on credit goods or services whose prices are denominated in foreign currency, (b) borrows or lends funds and the amounts payable or receivable are denominated in foreign currency, (c) is a party to an unperformed forward exchange contract, or (d) for other reasons, acquires or disposes of assets, or incurs or settles liabilities denominated in foreign currency."

Foreign Currency Translation

"The process of expressing in the reporting currency of the enterprise those amounts that are denominated or measured in a different currency."

Forward Exchange Contract

"An agreement to exchange at a specified future date currencies of different countries at a specified rate (forward rate)."

Functional Currency

"An entity's functional currency is the currency of the primary economic environment in which the entity operates; normally, that is the currency of the environment in which an entity primarily generates and expends cash."

Local Currency

"The currency of a particular country being referred to."

Remeasurement

"If an entity's books and records are not kept in its functional currency, remeasurement into the functional currency is required. Monetary balances are translated by using the current exchange rate and nonmonetary balances are translated by using historical exchange rates. If the U.S. dollar is the functional currency, remeasurement into the reporting currency (the U.S. dollar) obviates translation."

Reporting Currency

"The currency in which an enterprise prepares its financial statements."

Transaction Gain or Loss

"Transaction gains or losses result from a change in exchange rates between the functional currency and the currency in which a foreign currency transaction is denominated. They represent an increase or decrease in (a) the actual functional currency cash flows realized upon settlement of foreign currency transactions and (b) the expected functional currency cash flows on unsettled foreign currency transactions."

Translation Adjustments

"Translation adjustments result from the process of translating financial statements from the entity's functional currency into the reporting currency."

RATIO ANALYSIS

Ratio analysis familiarity is often required on the CPA examination, especially on objective questions. Financial ratios are used to evaluate a particular firm against industry norms, e.g., a current ratio of 1:1 may be indicative of solvency problems for a company in an industry where experience has determined 2.5:1 to be a reasonable current ratio.

Financial ratios generally relate to solvency, operational efficiency, and also to profitability.

A. Solvency (Short-Term Viability)

   1) Acid, quick -- measures ability to pay current liabilities from cash and near-cash items

$$\frac{\text{Cash, Net Receivables, Marketable Securities}}{\text{Current Liabilities}}$$

   2) Current -- measures ability to pay current liabilities from cash, near-cash, and cash-flow items

$$\frac{\text{Current Assets}}{\text{Current Liabilities}}$$

B. Operational Efficiency

   1) Asset turnover -- indicates how efficiently an enterprise utilizes its assets

$$\frac{\text{Net Sales}}{\text{Total Assets}}$$

   2) Inventory turnover -- measures the number of times inventory was sold and reflects inventory order and investment policies

$$\frac{\text{Cost of Goods Sold}}{\text{Average Inventory}}$$

   3) Number of days supply in average inventory -- number of days inventory is held before sale; reflects on efficiency of inventory policies

$$\frac{365*}{\text{Inventory Turnover}}$$

   4) Receivable turnover

$$\frac{\text{Net Credit Sales}}{\text{Average Net Receivables}}$$

   5) Number of days sales in average receivables -- average length of outstanding receivables which reflects on credit and collection policies

$$\frac{365*}{\text{Receivable Turnover}}$$

6) Length of operating cycle -- measures length of time from purchase of inventory to collection of cash

> Number of Days   Number of Days
> Supply in Average + Sales in Average
> Inventory   Receivables

*Alternatively 300 or 360 may be considered the number of days in a year.

C. Leverage (Long-Term Risk)

1) Times interest earned -- measure of ability to pay interest costs

$$\frac{\text{Net Income + Interest Expense + Income Taxes}}{\text{Interest Expense}}$$

2) Debt ratio -- percent of assets financed by creditors. One minus the debt ratio equals the percent of assets financed by stockholders.

$$\frac{\text{Total Liabilities}}{\text{Total Assets}}$$

3) Debt to equity -- measures leverage

$$\frac{\text{Total Liabilities}}{\text{Common Stockholders' Equity}}$$

4) Leverage is the common stockholders' ability to profit from rates of return on assets which exceed the cost of liabilities. Conversely, rates of return below cost of liabilities magnify stockholders' losses.

EXAMPLE:

Leverage

Total assets $100,000	*Total liabilities $90,000*
	Shareholders' equity 10,000

Assume 5% average interest cost on all liabilities, i.e., interest expense is $4,500.

If net income, before interest expense, is $10,000 (10% return on assets), the return on shareholder equity is $5,500 (55%).

If net income, before interest expense, is $2,000 (2% return on assets), the return on shareholder equity is - $2,500 (-25%).

D. Profitability

1) EPS -- measures income per share of ownership

$$\frac{\text{Net Income Available to Common Stockholders, e.g., less pref. div.}}{\text{Average Shares Outstanding}}$$

2) Profit margin -- measures the percent of profit on each dollar of sales

$$\frac{\text{Net Income}}{\text{Net Sales}}$$

3) Rate of return on assets -- permits analysis of the components of return of assets (i.e., profit margin and asset turnover)

> Profit Margin x Asset Turnover

4) Common stock yield -- measures cash flow return on investment in common
stock

$$\frac{\text{Dividend Per Share}}{\text{Market Value Per Share}}$$

5) Book value of common stock (at a point in time) -- not a meaningful
measure as assets are carried at historical costs

$$\frac{\text{Common Stockholders' Equity}}{\text{Shares Outstanding}}$$

6) Rate of return on common stockholders' equity -- measures the return
earned on the stockholders' investment in the firm

$$\frac{\text{Net Income Available to Common Stockholders}}{\text{Common Stockholders' Equity}}$$

E. Common size financial statements are set forth as percentages in place of the
traditional dollar amounts, e.g., every item in the statements expressed as a
percent of sales. Common size statements permit relative efficiency of different sized companies to be compared and evaluated.

F. Other

Many ratios exist. You should be able to identify numerator and denominator by
their title, e.g., sales to fixed assets.

1) Price-earnings (an important ratio which determines the amount of
capital available through stock issuances)
2) Sales to fixed assets
3) Sales to owners' equity
4) Owners' equity to total liabilities
5) Fixed assets to long-term debt
6) Dividend payout ratio
7) Cash flow per share

Caution: Be careful to determine the appropriate dollar figure after you
understand the concept, e.g., accounts receivable, shares outstanding, etc.
Consider the following before settling on the amount.

1) Average or year end (e.g., shares outstanding)
2) Net or gross (e.g., receivables)
3) Before or after adjusting items (e.g., taxes, preferred dividends,
etc.)

Evaluate the purpose and usefulness of ratios in terms of the following
categories:

1) Solvency
2) Operational efficiency
3) Leverage
4) Overall profitability, value

PARTNERSHIP ACCOUNTING

Since several multiple choice questions (and occasionally a problem) appear on every accounting practice exam, you should review the following material carefully.

A. Partnership Formation

In partnership accounting the partners' capital accounts are the residual accounts, i.e., similar to shareholder equity in corporate accounting. The entry to record the capital investment of partners A and B is:

            Cash
                A Capital
                B Capital

All capital contributions, withdrawals, and P&L are closed to this account or an intermediary account "drawing." If drawing accounts were used, each partner would have one. The drawing account is a holding (nominal account like dividends) account in which capital contributions, withdrawals, and P&L are closed. Then the drawing account is closed to the capital account.

B. Distribution of Income and Loss

Unless specified otherwise in the articles of co-partnership, P&L is divided equally. Partnership P&L frequently is divided among partners based on:

(1)   Interest on investments
(2)   Salaries
(3)   Bonuses
(4)   Specified P&L sharing rates

The distribution agreement per the articles of co-partnership determines P&L distribution. In complex distribution schemes, allocations of P&L for interest, bonuses, etc., may result in a negative P&L balance to be allocated in the partners' P&L ratio.

> EXAMPLE: *Partnership P&L Distribution*
>
> *Partners receive 5% interest on beginning capital balances*
> *Partner B receives a $6,000 salary*
> *Partner C receives a 10% bonus after interest and salaries*
> *The P&L ratios are A -- 50%, B -- 30%, C -- 20%*

Assuming partnership net income of $18,250, the following distribution schedule would be prepared.

		A	B	C
P&L ratio		.50	.30	.20
Beginning capital balance		30,000	10,000	5,000
	Cumulative Distribution			
5% interest	2,250	1,500	500	250
Salary	8,250		6,000	
Bonus	9,250			1,000*
Remaining dist.	18,250	4,500	2,700	1,800
P&L dist.		6,000	9,200	3,050
Ending capital balances		36,000	19,200	8,050

*($18,250 - $8,250) x .10 = $1,000

Note that if the interest, salary, and bonus allocation had exceeded net income, the excess would have been deducted on the distribution schedule in the P&L ratio.

C. Changes in Ownership

Admissions of new partners can take place either through purchase directly from existing partners, or purchase from the partnership. Purchase directly from existing partner(s) (new partner pays old partner(s) directly) requires that partnership capital be relabeled. For example, if X purchases partner A's share of a partnership with the other partners' consent, simply relabel the capital account.

              A Capital
                  X Capital

If X would negotiate to purchase 1/3 of each of A, B, and C's capital accounts

              A Capital   (1/3 of A's capital)
              B Capital   (1/3 of B's capital)
              C Capital   (1/3 of C's capital)
                  X Capital   (1/3 of partnership capital)

Once again, the above examples assume that the new partner's partnership capital interest was purchased directly from the old partner(s). These examples reflect only the capital purchased; the P&L ratios would also be negotiated, but are not recorded in the double-entry system. P&L ratios are used only to allocate profit and loss.

Turning now to the admission of a new partner into the partnership, three general cases can occur. The new partner can purchase a capital balance:

    1) Equal to the purchase price
    2) Greater than the purchase price
    3) Less than the purchase price

Remember P&L ratios may be different from capital ratios and are not recorded.

If the capital balance is to be equal to the purchase price, simply debit cash and credit capital on the partnership books.

    Cash
        Capital -- new partner

If the capital account is not to equal the cash contribution, two methods are in use.

Goodwill method--The old partnership capital balance plus new partner's contribution is not equal to the new partnership capital, because goodwill is recorded. Thus, total assets (and total capital) are changed by more than the cash (or asset) contribution. Also, no adjustment is made between capital accounts as in the bonus method.

Bonus method--The old partnership capital balance plus new partner's contribution is equal to the new partnership capital. Adjustments are only made between partner's capital accounts.

Partnership Example: Total Old Capital ($60,000) for ABC Partnership

Partner	A	B	C
Capital	$10,000	$20,000	$30,000
P&L ratio	.40	.40	.20

Remember P&L ratios are independently negotiated and are not recorded on the books. They are only used to allocate P&L.

Case 1--Goodwill to the new partner

D is admitted to a 20% share of capital and P&L for $10,000.

Goodwill	5,000	
Cash	10,000	
D Capital		15,000

If D is to have a 20% share of capital, the old partners will have 80%. If $60,000 (old capital) equals 80%, $75,000 is 100%. Therefore, D's capital will be $15,000 made up of a $10,000 contribution and $5,000 goodwill.

Normally the new P&L ratios would be .32, .32, .16, and .20. Twenty percent was taken from each of the old partners' P&L ratios.

Case 2--Goodwill to old partners

D is to contribute $20,000 cash for a 20% share of capital and P&L. The plan is based on recognition that the net assets of the old partnership are worth $80,000.

Goodwill	20,000	
A Capital		8,000
B Capital		8,000
C Capital		4,000
Cash	20,000	
D Capital		20,000

Goodwill is allocated in the P&L ratio.

Goodwill: Revalue the Assets

Case 3--Bonus to the new partner

D is admitted to a 20% share in capital and P&L for $10,000. No goodwill is to be recorded.

Cash	10,000	
A Capital	1,600	
B Capital	1,600	
C Capital	800	
D Capital		14,000

Total new partnership net assets (capital) will be $70,000. D is to receive $14,000 for $10,000 cash. Allocate $4,000 of the old partners' capital in the P&L ratio to D.

Case 4--Bonus to the old partners

D is to be admitted to a 20% share of capital and P&L for $30,000. No goodwill is to be recorded.

Cash	30,000	
D Capital		18,000
A Capital		4,800
B Capital		4,800
C Capital		2,400

D is to receive 20% of $90,000 of new net assets for $30,000. The remainder ($12,000) is allocated to the old partners in their P&L ratios.

Note that the new partner's P&L share was assumed to be 20% above, but the entries would be the same no matter what D's P&L ratio was. Only subsequent P&L allocations would be affected.

To review, the bonus method and the goodwill method provide for the adjustment of capital accounts upon the admission of a new partner. The adjustment is made proportionately to the old partners' capital (as to their P&L ratios) and/or to the new partner's capital account.

1) The goodwill method provides for revaluation of assets to adjust the relative amounts in the capital accounts -- old capital to new capital

2) The bonus method provides for revaluation of relative amounts in the capital accounts by direct adjustment, e.g., debit or credit the old capital accounts and credit or debit the new partner's capital

Finally, both bonus and goodwill can be reflected in the admission of a partner by both adjusting the relative amounts in the old and new partners' capital accounts and recording goodwill.

Case 5--Bonus and goodwill to the old partners

D is to be admitted to a 20% share of capital and P&L for $30,000. It is agreed that the partnership is worth $75,000 prior to D's admission.

Goodwill	15,000	
A Capital		6,000
B Capital		6,000
C Capital		3,000

The partnership assets of $60,000 are revalued to $75,000 prior to D's admission.

Cash	30,000	
A		3,600
B		3,600
C		1,800
D		21,000

D receives a 20% interest in the new capital of $105,000 ($75,000 + $30,000) with the $9,000 bonus being allocated to the old partners in their P&L ratios.

The table below summarizes the goodwill and bonus situations discussed above.

When to Apply Goodwill Method	**When to Apply Bonus Method**

New Partnership Capital	$>$	Old Partners' Capital	$+$	New Partner's Asset Investment	New Partnership Capital	$=$	Old Partner's Capital	$+$	New Partner's Asset Investment

Which Partner(s) Goodwill is Recognized | **Which Partner(s) Receive Bonus**

- **New Partner's Goodwill**

  New Partner's Capital Credit $>$ New Partner's Asset Investment

  (The difference represents goodwill)

- **Old Partner's Goodwill**

  New Partner's Capital Credit $=$ New Partner's Asset Investment

  (Goodwill is allocated to old partners in their P/L Ratio)

- **New Partner**

  New Partner's Capital Credit $>$ New Partner's Asset Investment

  (The difference represents the bonus)

- **Old Partners**

  New Partner's Capital Credit $<$ New Partner's Asset Investment

  (The difference represents the bonus allocated to old partners in their P/L Ratio)

D. Partner Deaths and Withdrawals

Partner deaths or withdrawals are accounted for in the opposite manner to admissions of new partners. Partnership assets may be revalued through either the bonus or goodwill methods for the withdrawing or the estate of the deceased partner. In other words, the withdrawing partner's capital account must be adjusted to the amount the withdrawing partner is to receive.

The adjustment can be achieved by counter-adjustment to the remaining partners' capital accounts, i.e., the bonus method. For example, assuming the ABC partnership data on page 944 partner A may withdraw from the partnership for $16,000 per agreement with partners B and C.

```
        B Capital              4,000
        C Capital              2,000
            A Capital                      6,000

        A Capital             16,000
            Cash                          16,000
```

The $6,000 bonus to A is allocated to B and C in proportion to their P&L ratios i.e., a 4:2 ratio.

The adjustment to the withdrawing partner's capital account can also be accomplished by asset adjustment, i.e., the goodwill method. Again assuming A's receipt of $16,000 upon withdrawal from the ABC partnership

```
        Goodwill              15,000
            A Capital                      6,000
            B Capital                      6,000
            C Capital                      3,000

        A Capital             16,000
            Cash                          16,000
```

A's P&L share being 40%, $15,000 of goodwill is required for a $6,000 increase in A's capital.

$$\frac{40}{100}x = 6000$$
$$x = \frac{6000}{1} \times \frac{100}{40} = 15,000$$

E. Incorporation of a Partnership

Partnerships can be incorporated or partnership assets and liabilities can be sold to a corporation. In either case, partnership assets may be revalued to market before sale or incorporation.

In the case of the incorporation of a partnership, the following entries might take place.

First the assets are revalued. The revaluation gain might be recorded in a "revaluation account" which would later be closed to the capital accounts.

```
        Assets
            A Capital
            B Capital
            C Capital
```

Second, stock is issued. The detail of who owns what stock is kept in the stockholders ledger (a subsidiary ledger), not in the general ledger accounts.

```
        A Capital
        B Capital
        C Capital
            Common stock
            Paid-in excess (if any)
```

In the case where partnership assets and liabilities are sold to a corporation, the following entries might take place. It is assumed that cash is not transferred to the corporation. Two intermediary accounts, "revaluation account" and "due from corporation," are illustrated in the partnership entries.

Partnership	Corporation
Assets	
Revaluation account	
Revaluation account	
Capital accounts	
Due from corporation	Assets (except cash)
Liabilities	Liabilities
Assets (except cash)	Common stock
	Paid-in excess (if any)
Corporation stock	
Due from corporation	
Capital accounts	
Corporation stock	
Cash	

F. Partnership Liquidation

The two important things to know about partnership liquidations are the statement of partnership liquidation and installment cash distribution schedules. The statement of partnership liquidation is similar to a schedule you prepared to learn the double entry system in your elementary accounting course. The statement of partnership liquidation reports all the transactions incurred in the liquidation process.

Statement of Partnership Liquidation

	Cash	Other Assets	Liabilities	A(50%)	Capital B(30%)	C(20%)
Balances	5,000	75,000	45,000	12,000	17,000	6,000
Sale of assets	40,000	(60,000)		(10,000)	(6,000)	(4,000)
	45,000	15,000	45,000	2,000	11,000	2,000
Payment of liabilities	(45,000)		(45,000)			
	0	15,000	0	2,000	11,000	2,000
Sale of assets	10,000	(15,000)		(2,500)	(1,500)	(1,000)
	10,000	0	0	(500)	9,500	1,000
Distribution of A's deficit				500	(300)	(200)
	10,000	0	0	0	9,200	800
Final distribution of cash	(10,000)				(9,200)	(800)

Notice that A's $500 deficit is allocated to the remaining solvent partners' capital balances. The allocation is based on the relative P&L ratios of the remaining solvent partners: in this case, 3/5 and 2/5. A is liable to the partnership for this amount. If A is personally solvent and repays the $500, $300 will go to B and $200 to C.

To avoid possible liquidation payments to partners who may later have a deficit balance (i.e., a partner receives a liquidation payment but subsequently is liable to the partnership for a deficit in his account), a schedule of installment cash distributions should be prepared.

The schedule of installment cash distribution is prepared by determining the amount of loss required to eliminate each partner's account assuming the other partners are personally insolvent (cannot repay any deficit in their capital account). This is done on a schedule of possible losses. The loss required to eliminate a partner's capital account is determined by dividing the partner's P&L ratio into the partner's capital account (includes partner loans to the partnership and net of drawing). Partners' loans are included with partner's capital, because a right of offset exists between each partner's loan and capital accounts.

The following illustration of a schedule of possible losses is based on the example used in the statement of partnership liquidation.

Schedule of Possible Losses

	Total	A(50%)	B(30%)	C(20%)
Capital balances	$35,000	$12,000	$17,000	$ 6,000
Loss to eliminate A	24,000	(12,000)	(7,200)	(4,800)
		0	$ 9,800	$ 1,200
Additional loss to eliminate C	3,000*		(1,800)	(1,200)
			8,000	0
Additional loss to eliminate B	8,000		(8,000)	
	35,000			

*Allocated 60:40

In other words, a loss of $35,000 would eliminate all 3 partners. A loss of $27,000 would eliminate A and C. A loss of $24,000 would eliminate A. From this we can see that the first $8,000 after all liabilities should go to B (assumes the remaining $27,000 of assets are worthless). The next $3,000 should be allocated 60:40 to B and C (assumes the remaining $24,000 of assets are worthless).

A cash distribution schedule is usually prepared from the schedule of possible losses. The cash distribution schedule sets forth a cash distribution plan which precludes overpayment to insolvent partners. Note that the schedule below assumes all liabilities have been paid. If they had not, the first payments would be made to creditors other than partners, i.e., all creditors would be paid prior to partners' receiving any payment.

Cash Distribution Schedule

Partner		A	B	C
First	$ 8,000		100%	
Next	3,000		60%	40%
Next	24,000	50%	30%	20%
Any other		50%	30%	20%

An important point should be made about partners' drawing and loan accounts. They should be added (subtracted if dr. balance) to the partners' capital accounts before distributing possible losses. The cash is repaid according to the cash distribution schedule, and loans of any partner are assumed to be repaid with the first cash that partner receives according to the cash distribution schedule. Remember: loan balances are not repaid before allocating possible losses; a right of offset exists between partners' capital deficits and loans.

INVESTMENTS AND CONSOLIDATIONS

This module includes investments in stock in which the investor is presumed to exercise significant influence or control over the investee. There are investments generally involving 20% or more of the investee corporation's outstanding voting stock and are accounted for using APB 18. The module also presents stock dividends, stock splits and stock rights. Investments in marketable equity securities which do not give the investor the ability to exercise significant influence are accounted for by using SFAS 12. Discussion of those investments is included in Module 24 (Working Capital).

A. Concepts of Accounting and Investment Percentage

The accounting rules for investments in the stock of another corporation are generally based on the percentage of the voting stock obtained.

1. Investments of less than 20% of the outstanding stock

> SFAS 12 requires that "small" investments in marketable equity securities be carried at the lower of aggregate cost or market. Income is realized under the cost method when dividends are received. Discussion of these smaller investments (both current and noncurrent) is presented in the Working Capital module.

2. Investments between 20% and 50% of the outstanding stock

> At 20% or more ownership, the investor is presumed to be able to significantly influence the operating or financial decisions of the investee. Most investments in this range will result in significant influence; however, the 20% level is just a guide. FASB Interpretation 35 presents several examples in which an investor owning between 20% and 50% may not be able to exercise influence over the investee. An example of this is a situation in which the majority ownership is concentrated among a small group of investors who ignore the views of the minority investor. Additional examples are included in the summary of Interpretation 35, page 661. The equity method of accounting is used for investments resulting in significant influence. The few cases of investments in this range that do not provide significant influence are generally accounted for under the lower of aggregate cost or market method per SFAS 12.

3. Investments of more than 50% of the outstanding stock

> At more than 50% ownership, the investor has control because of its majority ownership of the voting stock. Most of these investments will require the preparation of consolidated financial statements.

The exhibit on the next page illustrates the major concepts of accounting for investments.

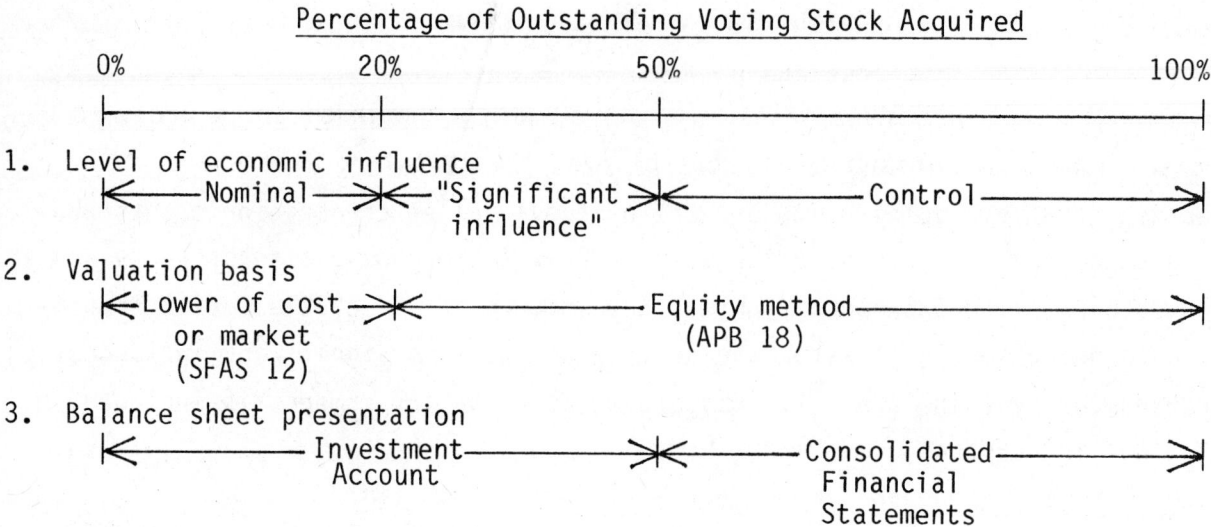

Several exceptions to these general concepts exist. These exceptions are noted in the following discussions.

B. Equity Method (APB 18)

APB 18 requires the use of the equity method when accounting for investments in which the investor has the ability to exercise significant influence over the operating and financial policies of the investee. APB 18 assumes that ownership of 20% or more of the outstanding stock will result in that ability. Exceptions to the use of the equity method (i.e., use the cost method) are related to an assessment of the investor's level of influence over the investee. The cost method should be used if the investment of more than 20% is judged to be temporary, if the investment is in a company operating in a foreign country which has severe restrictions on the operations of companies and on the transfer of monies to outside the country, and for other investments of more than 20% that do not result in significant influence.

The cost and equity methods differ in the treatment of the investment account and in the recognition of earnings from the investment. The cost method begins with recording the cost of the investment in the investment account. Income is recognized for the dividends which are distributed from earnings of the investee earned since the date the investor acquired the stock. Any dividends distributed by the investee which exceed the earnings since the acquisition date are classified as return of capital and recorded as a reduction of the investment account. No periodic amortizations or accruals are made to the investment account under the cost method.

The equity method also begins with recording the cost of the investment in the investment account but the cost and equity methods differ from this point on. A basic concept of the equity method is the reciprocal relationship formed between the investment account on the investor's books and the book values of the net assets on the investee's books. As changes in the investee's net assets occur (e.g., earnings, dividends, etc.), the investor will recognize the percentage of ownership share of that change in the investment account.

Another aspect of the equity method is the computation and eventual amortization of the difference between the cost of the investment and the book value of the acquired asset share at the investment date. The abundance of advanced accounting texts currently in print use an assortment of terms to describe the characteristics of this concept. For purposes of uniformity, the following underlined terms shall be used throughout this module:

Differential: the difference between the cost of the investment and the underlying book value of the net assets of the investee. This difference can be either positive or negative, as follows:

a) Excess of Cost over Book Value, which is generally attributable to:

1) Excess of fair value over book value, when the fair values of the investee's assets are greater than their book values, and

2) Goodwill, when the investee has high earnings potential for which the investor has paid more than the fair values of the other net assets

b) Excess of Book Value over Cost, which is generally attributable to:

1) Excess of book value over fair value, when the book values of the net assets of the investee are greater than their fair values, and

2) Excess of fair value over cost, when the cost of the investment is less than even the fair values of the investee's net assets. Some authors term this "negative goodwill".

The differential will be amortized to the investment account. Thus, similar to the amortization of bond investment premium or discount, the original investment in stock will approach the underlying book values of the investee's net assets held at the investment date.

EXAMPLE: Company A purchased 20 shares of B Company's 100 shares of common outstanding for $25,000. The book value of B's total net worth (i.e., stockholders' equity) at the date of the investment was $120,000. Any excess of cost over book value is due to goodwill to be amortized over 40 years.

Investment cost		*$25,000*
Book value of B Company	*$120,000*	
Percentage owned	*20%*	
Investor's share		*24,000*
Excess of cost over book value (due to goodwill)		*$ 1,000*

Amortization over 40 years
$1,000 ÷ 40 years = $25

An illustration of accounting just for the amortization is shown below. Other
adjustments to the investment account which are normally required are discussed
later in this module.

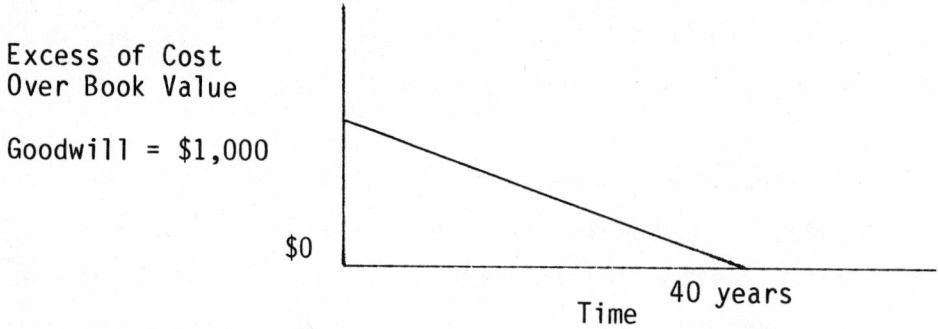

Excess of Cost
Over Book Value

Goodwill = $1,000

$0

Time   40 years

Under the equity method, the "Income from Investment" account is a parallel income statement account to the "Investment in Stock" balance sheet account. These
two accounts should include all the income recognitions and amortizations resulting
from the investment. Note that under the equity method, dividends received from the
investee are a reduction in the balance sheet account and are <u>not</u> part of the "Income from Investment" account.

Alternative levels of recording the results of intercompany transactions and
amortizations in both the investment and investment income accounts are used in
accounting practice. The alternatives are presented below:

1) Cost method--No intercompany transactions or amortizations are recognized in either the investment account or investment income account
   under this method.

2) "Partial" equity--Includes recognition of percentage share of income or
   loss, dividends, and any changes in the investment percentage. This
   method is often used for investments that will be consolidated. Thus,
   amortizations and other adjustments are made on the work sheets, not in
   the investment account.

3) "Full" equity--In addition to the factors above, this level includes the
   amortization of the differential between the investment cost and book
   value of the investment. This level also recognizes the effects of any
   intercompany transactions (e.g., inventory, fixed assets, and bonds) between the investor and investee corporations. APB 18 requires that all
   unconsolidated investments be reported in the financial statements using
   the "full" equity method.

*EXTENDED EXAMPLE: Assume the same facts for A Company and B Company as stated
above.   In addition, B Company earned $10,000 income for the year and paid
$6,000 in dividends.   There were no intercompany transactions.   If A Company
does <u>not</u> have significant influence over B Company, the investment would be
accounted for by the cost method.   If A Company can significantly influence
B Company, the equity method is used to account for and report the investment.
The appropriate entries are:*

	Cost Method		Equity Method	
1.	To record purchase of 20% interest			

Cost Method

1. To record purchase of 20% interest

		Equity Method	
Investment in Stock of B	$25,000	Investment in Stock of B	$25,000
Cash	$25,000	Cash	$25,000

2. To record percentage share of investee's reported income

Cost Method		Equity Method	
No Entry		Investment in Stock of B	$ 2,000
		Income from Investment	$2,000
		(20% x $10,000)	

3. To record percentage share of dividend received as distribution of income

Cost Method		Equity Method	
Cash	$1,200	Cash	$ 1,200
Dividend Income from Investment	$1,200	Investment in Stock of B	$1,200
(20% x $6,000)			

4. To record amortizations of goodwill in accordance with APB 18 using maximum period allowed by APB 17

Cost Method		Equity Method	
No Entry		Income from Investment	$ 25
		Investment in Stock of B	$ 25

The differences in the account balances under the equity vs. cost methods reflect the different income recognition processes and underlying asset valuation concepts of the two methods. The investment account balance under the cost method remains at the investment cost of $25,000, while under the equity method, the investment balance increases to $25,775. The $775 difference is the investor's share of the increase in the investee's undistributed earnings less the investor's amortization of the differential (excess of cost over the book value of the investment).

The amount of investment income to be recognized by the investor is also dependent upon the length of time during the year the investment is owned. For example, assume that A Company acquired the 20% interest on July 1, 1982, and B Company earned $10,000 of income ratably over the period from January 1, to December 31, 1982. The entry to record A Company's percentage share of B Company's income for the period of July 1 to December 31, 1982, would be:

Cost Method	Equity Method	
No Entry	Investment in Stock of B	$1,000
	Income from Investment	$1,000
	(20% x $10,000 x 6/12)	

The receipt of the $1,200 of dividends after the acquisition date would require additional analysis since the $1,200 dividend received is greater than the investor's share of the investee's income ($1,000) since acquisition. The difference of $200 ($1,200 - $1,000) is a return of capital under the cost method, and is recorded as follows:

Cost Method			Equity Method		
Cash	$1,200		Cash		$1,200
Dividend Income			Investment in		
from Investment	$1,000		Stock of B		$1,200
Investment in					
Stock of B		$ 200			

The amortization of goodwill will also be pro-rated to the time period the investment was held. The entry to record the partial year's amortization since the date of acquisition is:

Cost Method	Equity Method		
No Entry	Income from Investment	$12.50	
	Investment in Stock		
	of B		$12.50
	($1,000 ÷ 40 years = $25.00)		
	($25 x 6/12 = $12.50)		

When an investor changes from the cost to the equity method, the investment account must be adjusted retroactively and prior years' income and retained earnings must be retroactively restated. A change to the equity method would be made if an investor made additional purchases of stock and, for the first time, is able to exercise significant influence over the operating and financial decisions of the investee. Remember that APB 18 states that investments of 20% or more of the investee's outstanding stock carry the "presumption" that the investor has the ability to exercise significant influence. Therefore, in most cases, when an investment below 20% increases to above 20%, the investor will retroactively change from the cost method to the equity method.

The retroactive change to the equity method requires a prior period adjustment for the difference in the investment account and retained earnings account between the amounts that were recognized in prior periods under the cost method and the amounts that would have been recognized if the equity method had been used. In the full year investment example earlier, if A Company had previously accounted for its investment in B Company using the cost method and now begins applying the equity method because of the increased ability to significantly influence B Company, the change entry would be:

1911L

```
Investment in B Company              $775
    Retained Earnings                       $775
    ($775 = $2,000 - $1,200 - $25)
```

If the change is made at any time point other than the beginning of the fiscal period, the change entry would also include an adjustment to the period's "Income from Investment" account to record the difference between the cost and equity methods for the current period.

When an investor discontinues using the equity method because of an inability to influence the investee's financial and operating policies, no retroactive restatement is allowed. An example of this would be a disposal of stock resulting in a decrease in the percentage of stock owned from above 20% to below 20%. The earnings or losses that relate to the shares retained by the investor that were previously recognized by the investor should remain as a part of the carrying amount. However, if dividends received by the investor in subsequent periods exceed the investor's share of the investee's earnings for such periods, the excess should be accounted for as a return of capital and recorded as a reduction in the investment carrying amount.

A T-account is used to exhibit the major changes in the "Investment in Stock" account.

Investments in Stock

Original cost of investment	
Percentage share of investee's income since acquisition	Percentage share of investee's losses since acquisition
	Percentage share of dividends received
	Amortizations of excess of cost over book value
Amortizations of excess of book value over cost	
Increase above "significant influence" ownership - retroactive adjustment for change to equity	Disposals or sales of investment in stock

In addition to the above, several adjustments may be added if the "full equity" method is used. This method eliminates the effects of intercompany profits from transactions such as sales of inventory between the investor and investee corporations. This method is rarely required on the exam but candidates should briefly review these additions in association with the discussion of the elimination entries required for consolidated working papers presented later in this module.

Investments in Stock (continued)

Realized portion of intercompany profit from last period confirmed this period	Elimination of unrealized portion of intercompany profit transactions from current period

C. Equity Method and Interperiod Tax Allocation

Interperiod tax allocation may be required when the equity method is used. The difference between the income recognized using the equity method and the dividends received from the investee normally represent a timing difference item for which interperiod allocation is necessary. Note that companies are allowed to exclude 85% of the dividend income from investees. If an investor owns 80% or more of the investee's stock, the dividend exclusion is increased to 100%, i.e., no taxes are due on investee dividend distributions. The dividend exclusion (dividend received deduction) is a permanent difference.

APB 23 discusses the tax allocation criteria for investments of more than 50% of the outstanding stock and APB 24 presents the criteria for investments of less than 50% which are accounted for by the equity method. A discussion of tax allocation concepts and several examples are provided in Module 27, Deferred Taxes.

D. Stock Dividends and Splits

Do not record as income. The recipient continues to own the same proportion of the investee as before the stock split or dividend. The investor should make a memo entry to record the receipt of the additional shares and recompute the per-share cost of the stock.

E. Stock Rights

Investors in common stocks occasionally receive stock rights to purchase additional common stock below the existing market price. The investee company has probably issued the stock rights to satisfy the investor's preemptive right to maintain an existing level of ownership of the investee. It is possible to waive these preemptive rights in some jurisdictions.

Rights are issued below the existing market price to encourage the exercise of the rights, i.e., investor's use thereof resulting in acquisitions of additional shares of stock. The rights represent a possible dilution of investor ownership and should be recorded by allocating the cost of the stock between the market value of the rights and the market value of the stock. This is accomplished by applying the following ratio to the cost basis of the stock.

$$\frac{\text{Market value of right}}{\text{Market value of right} + \text{Market value of stock}}$$

The following entry is made to record the receipt of the rights.

Investment in stock rights
    Investment in common stock

The rights can be sold or exercised. The entry for exercise is

Investment in common stock
    Investment in stock rights
    Cash

If the stock rights lapse.

Loss on lapse of stock rights
    Investment in stock rights

F. Business Combinations

Many companies expand their operations by acquiring other businesses. The acquiring company may be seeking diversification of its business, a more stable supply of raw materials for its production, an increase in the range of products or services it offers, or any one of many other business reasons. The accounting issues of business combinations begin with properly recording and reporting the economic events of the date of business combination. Accounting subsequent to the combination is dependent on the alternatives selected at the combination date. Thus, as you study this section, you should fully understand how the combination is first recorded and reported before proceeding to events occurring after the combination date.

From a legal perspective, business combinations are classified into three categories as follows:

1. Merger--One company acquires the assets and liabilities of one or more other companies in exchange for stock, cash or other consideration. The acquiring company continues to exist as a separate legal entity, but the acquired company ceases to exist as a seperate legal entity, its stock is cancelled, and its books are closed. The separate assets and liabilities are recorded on the acquiring firm's books. (A Corp. + B Corp. = A Corp.)

2. Consolidation--A new firm is formed to issue stock in exchange for the stock of two or more combining or consolidating companies. The acquired firms normally cease to continue as separate legal entities, therefore, the new (acquiring) firm will record the separate assets and liabilities of the acquired firms. (A Corp. + B Corp. = C Corp.)

3. Acquisition--A company acquires a majority (> 50%) of the common stock of another company and each company continues its legal existence. The acquiring company (parent) will record an "Investment in Acquired Company's Stock" in the combination entry. (A Corp. + B Corp. = Consolidated Financial Statements of A and B)

Mergers and consolidations require 100% ownership of the acquired company but the acquisition business combination requires only a majority ownership of the outstanding stock. In addition, by maintaining the separate legal existence of the acquired company (B Corp.) and not cancelling its stock, the parent company (A Corp.) can retain greater flexibility in raising additional capital by using B Corp. shares as collateral for a loan or through the issuance of new shares of B Corp.

Financial statements for combinations which are in the legal forms of mergers and consolidations are prepared in the normal accounting process since all assets and liabilities are recorded on just one set of books. Accounting for an acquisition, however, results in an investment account on the acquiring company's books while the assets and liabilities are still recorded and shown on the books of the acquired company. Financial reporting for this combination generally requires the bringing together, or accounting consolidation, of the accounts from these two sets of books to prepare financial reports for the economic entity now formed between the parent and subsidiary companies.

G. Accounting for the Combination

Regardless of the legal form, there are only two accounting methods applied to any business combination--purchase or pooling. These two methods are mutually exclusive and the selection of the accounting method is determined by specific aspects of the facts surrounding the combination.

1. Purchase Accounting

Purchase accounting for a combination is similar to the accounting treatment used in the acquisition of any asset group. The fair market value of the consideration (cash, stock, debt securities, etc.) given by the acquiring firm is used as the valuation basis of the combination. The assets and liabilities of the acquired firm are revalued to their respective fair market values at the combination date. Any difference between the value of the consideration given and the fair market values of the net assets obtained is normally recorded as goodwill. The financial statements of the acquiring company reflect the combined operations from the date of combination.

2. The Pooling Method

The pooling method assumes a combining of stockholders' interests. The basis of valuation in pooling is the book value of the net assets on the books of the acquired company. Therefore, goodwill may <u>not</u> be created at the date of combination in a pooling combination. The financial statements of the acquiring company will include a restatement of all prior years' presented to include the operations and financial position of the pooled companies for all years presented.

APB 16 specified twelve criteria which must be met before a combination may be accounted for as a pooling of interests. Failure to meet any one of these twelve criteria will preclude a pooling treatment. A complete list of the criteria is provided in the outline of APB 16. The major criteria are: (a) the combining companies have ownership interests independent of each other and were not recently a subsidiary or division of any other company; (b) the combination is effected by a single transaction or in accord with a plan lasting not more than one year; (c) at least 90% of the voting ownership interests of the combinee company are acquired in exchange for the issuance of the combinor company's voting shares, and all shareholders have the same equity rights; and (d) no planned intent exists to segment the operations or acquired stockholders' interests after the combination date.

A recent issue of <u>Accounting Trends and Techniques</u> indicates that slightly less than 20% of the combinations made by its sample companies used the pooling method. Although its use has been declining, pooling accounting is still an accounting alternative for business combinations and has been examined on recent CPA exams.

H. A Company and B Company--Date of Combination

A presentation of the date of combination entries for purchase and pooling will be made in the next two sections of this module. We will be using a comprehensive example for these sections and the remaining parts of the discussion on consolidation accounting. The following balance sheets of A Company and B Company provide the foundation for further discussion. As you study the remainder of this module, be sure you understand where the numbers are being derived from.

A Company and B Company
Balance Sheets 1/1/82
(Immediately Before Combination)

	A Company	B Company
Assets		
Cash	$ 30,900	$ 37,400
Accounts Receivable	34,200	9,100
Inventories	22,900	16,100
Equipment	200,000	50,000
Less: Accumulated Depreciation	(21,000)	(10,000)
Patents	-0-	10,000
Total Assets	$267,000	$112,600
Liabilities and Equity		
Accounts Payable	$ 4,000	$ 6,600
Bonds Payable	100,000	-0-
Capital Stock ($10 par)	100,000	50,000
Additional Paid-in Capital	15,000	15,000
Retained Earnings	48,000	41,000
Total Liabilities and Equity	$267,000	$112,600

The concept of book value of the investment is a basic principle of accounting for business combinations and will be used in many different computations. Note that the book value of the net assets of B Company may be computed by two different methods:

1) Subtract the book value of the liabilities from the book values of the assets

$$\$112,600 - \$6,600 = \$106,000$$

2) Add the book values of the components of B Company stockholders' equity

$$\$50,000 + \$15,000 + \$41,000 = \$106,000$$

I. Date of Combination--Purchase Accounting

Purchase accounting uses fair market values of the net assets as the valuation basis for the combination. The difference between the value of the consideration given by the acquiring firm and the book value of the net assets obtained is the excess of cost over book value, or excess of book value over cost (referred to here as differential) of the net assets obtained. As discussed earlier, this differential has two components, as follows:

1) An amount representing an adjustment of the book values of the net assets up (or down) to their respective fair market values, and

2) An amount representing goodwill

Assume that our Company A purchased <u>all</u> the net assets of B Company. At the date of combination, the fair values of all the assets and liabilities were determined by appraisal, as follows:

B Company Item	Book Value (BV)	Fair Market Value (FMV)	Difference Between BV and FMV
Cash	$ 37,400	$ 37,400	$ -0-
Accounts Rec. (net)	9,100	9,100	-0-
Inventories	16,100	17,100	1,000
Equipment (net)	40,000	48,000	8,000
Patents	10,000	13,000	3,000
Accounts Payable	<6,600>	<6,600>	-0-
Totals	$106,000	$118,000	$12,000

The $12,000 is the difference between the book value and fair market values of B Company and is one component of the differential.

Four different cases displaying a range of total acquisition costs are presented below. The form of consideration paid to B Company by A Company is assumed to be cash but, under purchase accounting, it could be stock, cash, debentures or any other form of payment.

The allocation of the difference between cost and book value is a two-step process. First, the assets and liabilities must be valued at their respective fair market values and then any remainder is allocated to goodwill. Note that the differential may be positive or negative and that the net assets could have fair market values less than book values.

Case:	Case A	Case B	Case C	Case D
Consideration Paid:	$134,000	$118,000	$106,000	$100,000
Notes:	(> FMV)	(= FMV)	(< FMV)	(< FMV)
	(> BV)	(> BV)	(= BV)	(< BV)

Step 1) Compute the Differential

	Case A	Case B	Case C	Case D
Book Value	$106,000	$106,000	$106,000	$106,000
Investment Cost	134,000	118,000	106,000	100,000
Differential	$ 28,000	$ 12,000	-0-	<$ 6,000>

Step 2) Allocation of Differential

  a) Revaluation of net assets to fair market value

	Case A	Case B	Case C	Case D
FMV, net assets	$118,000	$118,000	$118,000	$118,000
-BV	106,000	106,000	106,000	106,000
Portion to net assets	$ 12,000	$ 12,000	$ 12,000	$ 12,000

b) Remainder (Excess of cost greater than fair value, or fair value greater than cost)

FMV, net assets	$118,000	$118,000	$118,000	$118,000
-Investment cost	134,000	118,000	106,000	100,000
Goodwill	$ 16,000	-0-	<$ 12,000>	<$ 18,000>

Step 3) Accounting for Goodwill and the Excess of fair value greater than cost.

APB 16 assumes the excess of cost greater than fair value is goodwill (Case A). This would be amortized in accordance with APB 17. If the fair value of the assets is greater than the investment cost, (Cases C and D), then APB 16 requires this excess to be proportionally applied to reduce the assigned values of the noncurrent assets acquired (except long-term investments in marketable securities). If these assets are reduced to zero value, any remaining excess of fair value over cost shall be established as a deferred credit.

Reallocations are required in Cases C and D because the fair values of the net assets are greater than costs, as follows:

Item	Assigned Values of Noncurrent Assets Acquired	Proportion	Excess of Fair Value Over Cost	Reallocation	New Assigned Value
Case C: Equipment	$48,000	$48,000/$61,000	<$12,000>	<$9,443>	$38,557
Patents	$13,000	$13,000/$61,000	<$12,000>	<$2,557>	$10,443
	$61,000			<$12,000>	
Case D: Equipment	$48,000	$48,000/$61,000	<$18,000>	<$14,164>	$33,836
Patents	$13,000	$13,000/$61,000	<$18,000>	<$ 3,836>	$ 9,164
	$61,000			<$18,000>	

Date of combination entries on A Company's books for the purchase-merger are:

	Case A	Case B	Case C	Case D
Cash	$37,400	$37,400	$37,400	$37,400
A/R	9,100	9,100	9,100	9,100
Inventories	17,100	17,100	17,100	17,100
Equipment (net)	48,000	48,000	38,557	33,836
Patents	13,000	13,000	10,443	9,164
Goodwill	16,000	-0-	-0-	-0-
A/Pay.	$ 6,600	$ 6,600	$ 6,600	$ 6,600
Cash	134,000	118,000	106,000	100,000

B Company would close its books and cease to operate as a separate entity.

If B Company maintained its separate legal status, the combination would be accounted for as a 100% acquisition. The date of combination entries on A Company's books for each of the four cases would be:

Investment in B Company	$134,000	$118,000	$106,000	$100,000
Cash		$134,000	$118,000	$106,000	$100,000

Consolidated financial statements would normally be prepared when acquisitions of more than 50% of outstanding stock are made. Consolidated statements are discussed later in this module.

Some candidates find that using value lines to display the features of purchase accounting helps to sort out the various concepts. Value lines are provided below for Cases A and D. You might want to do the value lines for Cases B and C.

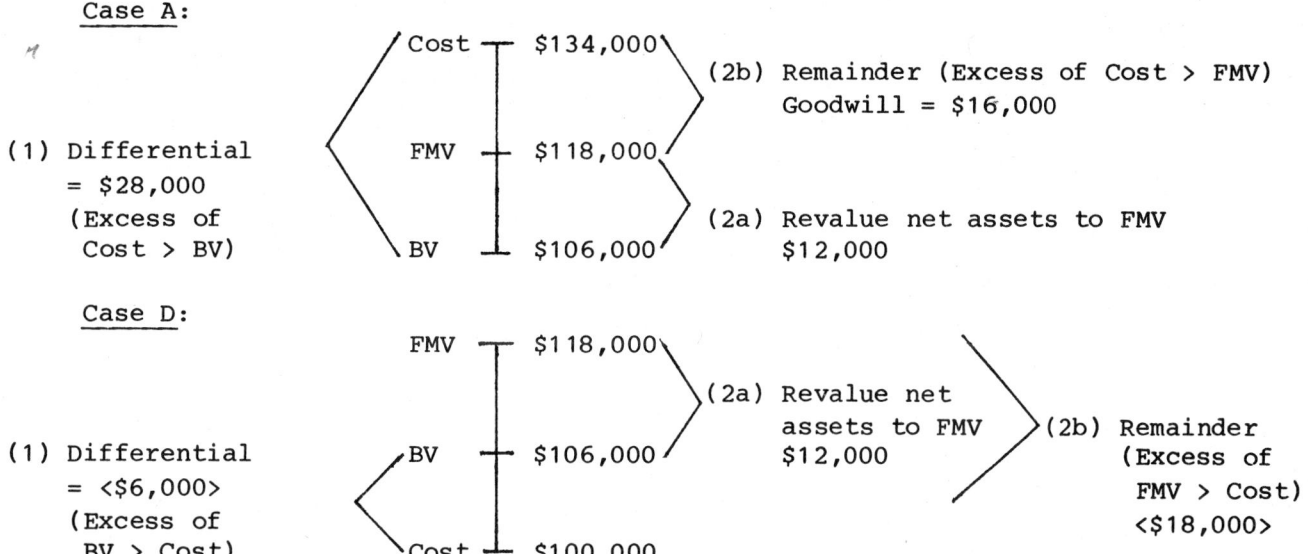

Case A:

Case D:

J. Date of Combination-Pooling Accounting

Pooling accounting requires a uniting of the stockholders' equities of the combining firms. A comparison of the par or stated value of the surviving company's common stock must be made with the total par or stated value of the common stock capital of the combining companies before combination. This process is often referred to as determining the "mix" of the pooled stockholders' equity and must be performed prior to making the date of combination entries. In determining the "mix" of pooled stockholders' equity, it is necessary to remember that under pooling the book value of the net assets is used to record the combination.

To illustrate this process, we will use the information from our comprehensive example of A Company and B Company. Note the companies have the following equity accounts immediately before the combination.

	A	B
Capital Stock ($10 par)	$100,000	$ 50,000
Additional Paid-in Capital	15,000	15,000
Retained Earnings	48,000	41,000
Totals	$163,000	$106,000

Pooling requires the continuation of at least $65,000 of contributed capital from B Company ($50,000 Capital Stock + $15,000 Additional Paid-in Capital). The "mix" of the contributed capital items in A Company's date of combination entry will be based on the par of the stock given up by A Company.

If the par of the stock issued by the issuer (Company A) is greater than the present par on the books of the combinee company (Company B), the following sequence should be used as each item is fully extinguished:

1) Total par value outstanding of combinee (Company B)
2) Additional paid-in capital of combinee (Company B)
3) Additional paid-in capital of issuer (Company A)
4) Retained earnings of combinee (Company B)
5) Retained earnings of issuer (Company A)

If the par issued is less than the present par on the books of the combinee, the excess of the prior par over the new par is added to Additional Paid-in Capital.

The company name in parentheses provides the company source for determining the amount of the entry.

1. Merger and consolidation legal forms

Case 1: Par value of common stock issued by A Company is $30,000. The entry on A's books would be as follows:

*Net Assets of B	$106,000	
Capital Stock (Co. A)		$30,000
Additional Paid-In Capital (Co. B)		35,000
Retained Earnings (Co. B)		41,000

*Note: The book values of B's specific assets and liabilities would be listed separately.

Case 2: Par value of common stock issued by A Company is $60,000. The entry on A's books would be as follows:

Net Assets of B	$106,000	
Capital Stock (Co. A)		$60,000
Additional Paid-in Capital (Co. B)		5,000
Retained Earnings (Co. B)		41,000

Case 3: Par value of common stock issued by A Company is $75,000. The entry on A's books would be as follows:

Net Assets of B	$106,000	
*Paid-in Capital (Co. A)	10,000	
Capital Stock (Co. A)		$75,000
Retained Earnings (Co. B)		41,000

*Note: This represents paid-in capital formerly associated with A Company's stockholders. If the par of the stock issued by A was > $80,000, the retained earnings credit above would have been reduced.

2. Acquisition legal form

If Company B is maintained as a separate legal entity, consolidated financial statements will have to be prepared. The combination entries will include an "Investment in B Stock" account rather than the specific net assets of Company B. The combination entry on A's books for Case 1 on the preceding page would be as follows:

Investment in Company B's Common Stock	$106,000	
Capital Stock (Co. A)		$30,000
Additional Paid-in Capital (Co. B)		35,000
Retained Earnings (Co. B)		41,000

Subsequent cases would be treated similarly based on the par of the stock issued. It is important to note that in 100% acquisitions, all of the final amounts and accounts in the consolidated financial statements would be the same as if the business combination were treated as a merger or consolidation.

APB 16 requires that pooled operations be reported for the first complete period reported. Thus, if the pooling took place in mid-period, the pooling method will have to be applied retroactively from the point of pooling to the beginning of the period. In addition, if comparative statements are presented, they must be restated on a combined basis to reflect the pooled firms. Intercompany transactions occurring before the date of combination should be eliminated when the pooling method is applied retroactively. Intercompany eliminations are explained later in this module.

K. Purchase and Pooling Combination Entries Reviewed

The following matrix provides a review of the combination entries of the surviving or investing firm for the three legal forms of combination (merger, consolidation, and acquisition) for which stock is given. The legal form is primarily dependent on whether the combined company, Company B in our examples, retains a separate, legal existence or transfers its assets and liabilities to Company A and cancels any remaining stock of Company B. The purchase versus pooling choice is independent of the legal form. Accounting for the combination (purchase or pooling) will be determined by the specific aspects of the combination transaction that are specified in APB 16. The items in parentheses are valuation bases or the company source for determining the dollar amount for the entry.

Purchase-Pooling Matrix

Accounting Method

Legal Form	Purchase	Pooling

1. Merger
(A Co. + B Co. = A Co.)
	Assets (FMV of B)
	  Liabilities (FMV of B)
	  Capital Stock (Co. A)
	  Add'l. PIC (Co. A)
		Assets (Book Value of B)
		  Liabilities (BV of B)
		  Capital Stock (Co. A)
		  Add'l. PIC (Co. B)
		  Retained Earnings (Co. B)

2. Consolidation
(A Co. + B Co. = C Co.)
	Assets (FMV of both A and B)
	  Liabilities (FMV of A and B)
	  Capital Stock (Co. C)
	  Add'l. PIC (Co. C)
		Assets (BV of both A and B)
		  Liabilities (BV of A and B)
		  Capital Stock (Co. C)
		  Add'l. PIC (both A and B)
		  Retained Earnings (both A and B)

3. Acquisition
(A Co. + B Co. = Consolidated Statements of A and B)
	Investment in B (FMV)
	  Capital Stock (Co. A)
	  Add'l. PIC (Co. A)
		Investment in B (BV)
		  Capital Stock (Co. A)
		  Add'l. PIC (Co. B)
		  Retained Earnings (Co. B)

L. Consolidated Financial Statements

An investment of more than 50% of the outstanding voting stock will normally require the preparation of consolidated financial statements. The complete consolidation process is presented in the next section of this module. The investment account will be eliminated in the consolidation working papers and will be replaced with the specific assets and liabilities of the investee corporation. Consolidation is generally required for investments of more than 50% of the outstanding voting stock except when:

1) The control is likely to be temporary
2) The investee is in legal reorganization or bankruptcy
3) The investee and investor operate in dissimilar industries (e.g., a bank and a manufacturing company)
4) The investee operates in a foreign country which has severe restrictions on the financial transactions of its business firms or is subject to material political or economic uncertainty

In these limited cases, the investment will be reported as a long term investment in an unconsolidated subsidiary on the investor's balance sheet with its balance determined by using the equity method except for some foreign subsidiaries which might be reported at cost because of operating restrictions imposed by the foreign country.

The concept of consolidated statements is that the resources of two or more companies are under the control of the parent company. Consolidated statements are prepared as if the group of legal entities were one economic entity group. Consolidated statements are presumed to be more meaningful for management, owners, and creditors of the parent company and they are normally required for fair presentation of the financially-related companies. Individual company statements should continue to be prepared for minority ownership and creditors of the subsidiary companies.

The accounting principles used to record and report events for a single legal entity are also applicable to a consolidated economic entity of two or more companies. The concept of the reporting entity is expanded to include more than one company, but all other accounting principles are applied in the same way as for an individual company. The consolidation process eliminates reciprocal items that are shown on both the parent and subsidiary's books. These eliminations are necessary to avoid double-counting the same items which would misstate the financials of the combined economic entity.

Consolidated financial statements are prepared from worksheets which begin with the trial balances of the parent and subsidiary companies. Eliminating worksheet entries are made to reflect the two separate companies' results of operations and financial position as one combined economic entity. The entire consolidation process takes place only on a worksheet; no consolidation elimination entries are ever recorded on either the parent's or subsidiary's books.

Consolidated Balance Sheets are typically prepared at the date of combination to determine the initial financial position of the economic entity. Any intercompany accounts between the parent and subsidiary must be eliminated against each other. In addition, the "Investment in Subsidiary's Stock" account from the parent's books will be eliminated against the reciprocal accounts of the subsidiary's stockholders' equity. The remaining accounts are then combined to prepare the consolidated balance sheet. The preparation of consolidated statements after the date of combination become a little more complex because the parent's and subsidiary's income statements may include reciprocal intercompany accounts which must be eliminated. The next section of the module will present an example of the preparation of a consolidated balance sheet at the date of combination for both purchase and pooling accounting. You should carefully review the date of combination consolidation process before proceeding to the preparation of consolidated statements subsequent to combination.

M. Date of Combination Consolidated Balance Sheet--Purchase Accounting

This example uses the numbers from the A Company and B Company presented on page 962. The discussion in the preceding sections assumed a 100% combination in which the parent acquired control of all the subsidiary's stock or net assets. For the remainder of the module, we will be assuming that the parent company (A Company) acquired a 90% interest in the net assets of the subsidiary company (B Company). The remaining 10% of the outstanding stock is held by third party investors referred to as the minority interest. In the illustrated problem, you will be able to review the determination of how minority interest is computed and disclosed on the consolidated financial statements. Note that only the "acquisition" legal form leads to the preparation of consolidated statements and includes less than 100% business combinations.

The assumptions for this illustration are:

1) On January 1, 1982, A Company acquires a 90% interest in B Company in exchange for 5,400 shares of $10 par stock having a total market value of $120,600
2) The purchase method of accounting is used for the combination
3) Any goodwill resulting from the combination will be amortized over a period of 10 years

The workpaper for a consolidated balance sheet at the date of acquisition is presented on page 971. The first two columns are the trial balances from the books of A Company and B Company immediately following the acquisition.

1. Investment Entry on A Company's books

The entry to record the 90% purchase-acquisition on A Company's books was:

Investment in Stock of B Company	$120,600	
Capital Stock		$54,000
Additional Paid-in Capital		66,600

(To record the issuance of 5,400 shares of $10 par stock to acquire a 90% interest in B Company.)

Although common stock is used for the consideration in our example, A Company could have used debentures, cash or any other form of consideration acceptable to B Company's stockholders to make the purchase combination.

A COMPANY AND B COMPANY CONSOLIDATED WORKING PAPERS

Purchase Accounting   **For Date of Combination — 1/1/82**

90% Interest

	A Company	B Company	Debit		Credit	Minority Interest	Consolidated Balances
			Adjustments and Eliminations				
Balance Sheet 1/1/82							
Cash	30,900	37,400					68,300
Accounts Receivable	34,200	9,100					43,300
Inventories	22,900	16,100	(b)	900			39,900
Equipment	200,000	50,000	(b)	9,000			259,000
Accumulated Depreciation	(21,000)	(10,000)			(b) 1,800		(32,800)
Investment in stock of B Company	120,600				(a) 120,600		
Difference Between Cost and Book Value			(a)	25,200	(b) 25,200		
Excess of Cost over Fair Value (Goodwill)			(b)	14,400			14,400
Patents		10,000	(b)	2,700			12,700
Total Assets	387,600	112,600					404,800
Accounts Payable	4,000	6,600					10,600
Bonds Payable	100,000						100,000
Capital Stock	154,000	50,000	(a)	45,000		5,000	154,000
Additional Paid-in Capital	81,600	15,000	(a)	13,500		1,500	81,600
Retained Earnings	48,000	41,000	(a)	36,900		4,100	48,000
Minority Interest						10,600	10,600 MI
Total Liabilities and Equity	387,600	112,600		147,600	147,600		404,800

2. Difference between Investment Cost and Book Value

   The difference between the investment cost and the parent company's equity in the net assets of the subsidiary is computed as follows:

Investment cost		$120,600
Book Value % at date of combination		
B Company's:		
Capital Stock	$ 50,000	
Additional Paid-in Capital	15,000	
Retained Earnings	41,000	
Total	$106,000	
Parent's share of ownership	x 90%	
Parent's share of book value		95,400
Excess of Cost over Book Value		$ 25,200

   This difference is due to several undervalued assets and to unrecorded goodwill. The allocation procedure is similar to that shown on page 963 for a 100% purchase; however, in this case, the parent company obtained a 90% interest and thus will recognize 90% of the difference between the fair market values and book values of the subsidiary's assets, not 100%. The allocation is presented as:

Item	Book Value (B.V.)	Fair Market Value (F.M.V.)	Difference Between B.V. and F.M.V.	Ownership Percentage	Percentage Share of Difference Between B.V. and F.M.V.
Cash	$ 37,400	$ 37,400	$ –0–		
Accounts Receivable (net)	9,100	9,100	–0–		
Inventories	16,100	17,100	1,000	90%	$ 900
Equipment	50,000	60,000	10,000	90%	9,000
Accumulated Depreciation	(10,000)	(12,000)	(2,000)	90%	(1,800)
Patents	10,000	13,000	3,000	90%	2,700
Accounts Payable	(6,600)	(6,600)	–0–		
Total	$106,000	$118,000	$12,000		

Amount of difference between cost and book value share allocated to revaluation of net assets	$10,800
Total differential	25,200
Remainder allocated to goodwill	$14,400

The equipment has a book value of $40,000 ($50,000 less 20% depreciation of $10,000). An appraisal concluded with a judgment that the equipment's replacement cost was $60,000 less 20% accumulated depreciation of $12,000 resulting in a net fair value of $48,000.

3. Elimination entries on workpaper

The basic reciprocal accounts are the investment in subsidiary account on the parent's books and the subsidiary's stockholder equity accounts. Only the parent's share of the subsidiary's accounts may be eliminated as reciprocal accounts. The remaining 10% portion is allocated to the minority interest. The entries below include documentation showing the company source for the information. Those aids will help you trace the numbers. The workpaper entry to eliminate the basic reciprocal accounts are:

```
(a) Capital stock--B Co.                            $45,000
      Additional Paid-in Capital--B Co.              13,500
      Retained Earnings--B Co.                       36,900*
      Differential                                   25,200
          Investment in Stock of B Co.-A Co.                     $120,600
      *($36,900 = 90% x $41,000)
```

Note that only 90% of B Company's stockholders' equity accounts are eliminated. Also, an account called "Differential" is debited in the workpaper entry. The Differential account is a temporary account to record the difference between the cost of the investment in B Company from the parent's books and the book value of the parent's interest (90% in our case) from the subsidiary's books.

The next step is to allocate the differential to the specific accounts by making the following workpaper entry:

```
(b) Inventory                                   $    900
      Equipment                                    9,000
      Patents                                       2,700
      Goodwill                                     14,400
          Accumulated Depreciation                            $ 1,800
          Differential                                         25,200
```

This entry reflects the allocations prepared in step 2 on the previous page and recognizes the parent's share of the asset revaluations.

The minority interest column is the 10% interest of B Company's net assets owned by outside, third parties. Minority interest must be disclosed because 100% of the book values of B Company are included in the consolidated statements although A Company controls only 90% of the net assets. An alternative method to "prove" minority interest is to multiply the net assets of the subsidiary times the minority interest share, as follows:

$$\frac{\text{Stockholders' Equity of B Company}}{\$106,000} \quad \text{x} \quad \frac{\text{Minority Interest \%}}{10\%} \quad = \$10,600$$

The $10,600 would be reported on the credit side of the consolidated balance sheet between liabilities and stockholders' equity.

The principle used to prepare the consolidated balance sheet is called the parent company concept. This is the method used most often on the CPA exam and also used in about ninety percent of actual cases of consolidations. An alternative approach is known as the entity concept. The two differ in the amount of the asset revaluations recognized on the consolidated balance sheet. Under the parent company concept, just the parent's share of the revaluation is shown and the minority interest is reported at its share of the subsidiary's book value. If the entity concept were used, the net assets of B Company would be included in the consolidated balance sheet at 100% of their fair values at the date of acquisition and minority interest would be reported at its share of the fair value of the sub. In our example, minority interest under the entity concept would have been:

$$\frac{\text{Total Fair Market Value}}{\text{of Net Assets of B Company}} \quad \text{x} \quad \frac{\text{Minority}}{\text{Percentage}}$$
$$\$118,000 \qquad\qquad \text{x} \qquad 10\% \quad = \$11,800$$

Our example does not include any other intercompany accounts as of the date of combination. If any existed, they would be eliminated to fairly present the consolidated entity. Several examples of other reciprocal accounts will be shown later in this module for the preparation of consolidated financial statements subsequent to the date of acquisition.

N. Date of Combination Consolidated Balance Sheet--Pooling Accounting

The preparation of a consolidated balance sheet for a pooling acquisition follows the basic principles discussed in the section on recording the pooling combination. Book values are reported as the basis of the net assets of the combined companies and the continuity of the acquired stockholders' equity is reflected in the carryforward of the capital "mix" from the values shown on the acquired company's books.

For purposes of this section, the following assumptions will be made:

1) On January 1, 1982, A Company acquired a 90% interest in B Company in exchange for 5,400 shares of $10 par value stock of A Company

2) All criteria for a pooling have been met and the combination is treated as a pooling of interests

The workpaper for a consolidated balance sheet at the date of combination is presented below. Note that the first two columns are trial balances of A Company and B Company immediately after the combination was recorded by A Company.

1. Investment entry recorded on A Company's books

The following entry was made by A Company to record its 90% acquisition-pooling of B Company:

Investment in Stock of B Company	$95,400	
Capital Stock, $10 par		$54,000
Additional Paid-in Capital		4,500
Retained Earnings		36,900

A COMPANY AND B COMPANY CONSOLIDATED WORKING PAPERS

Pooling Accounting
90% Interest

For Date of Combination -- 1/1/82

Balance Sheet 1/1/82	A Company	B Company	Adjustments and Eliminations Debit	Adjustments and Eliminations Credit	Minority Interest	Consolidated Balances
Cash	30,900	37,400				68,300
Accounts Receivable	34,200	9,100				43,300
Inventories	22,900	16,100				39,000
Equipment	200,000	50,000				250,000
Less Accumulated Depreciation	(21,000)	(10,000)				(31,000)
Investment in Stock of B Company	95,400			(a) 95,400		
Patents		10,000				10,000
Total Assets	362,400	112,600				379,600
Accounts Payable	4,000	6,600				10,600
Bonds Payable	100,000					100,000
Capital Stock	154,000	50,000	(a) 45,000		5,000	154,000
Additional Paid-in Capital	19,500	15,000	(a) 13,500		1,500	19,500
Retained Earnings	84,900	41,000	(a) 36,900		4,100	84,900
Minority Interest					10,600	10,600
Total Liabilities and Equity	362,400	112,600	95,400	95,400		379,600

The investment entry reflects the capital "mix" for a pooling of less than a 100% investment. The following schedule shows the mix for our 90% combination accomplished by the issuance of 5,400 shares of A Company's $10 par stock:

	B Company	A Company's Percentage Share	A's Share of B's Equity
Capital Stock	$ 50,000	90%	$45,000
Additional Paid-in Capital	15,000	90%	13,500
Retained Earnings	41,000	90%	36,900
	$106,000		$95,400

The $54,000 (5,400 shares x $10 par) in new capital issued by A Company represents $45,000 from B Company's Capital Stock and $9,000 of the $13,500 share of B Company's Additional Paid-in Capital. Note the remaining $4,500 of capital and $36,900 of B Company's Retained Earnings are carried over to A Company's books in the combination date entry. The $10,600 of B's capital that is not carried over to A will eventually be shown as Minority Interest on the Consolidated Balance Sheet.

2. Elimination entry on workpaper

Pooling accounting uses book values as a basis of valuation; therefore, no "differential" will ever occur in a pooling. The reciprocal accounts in a pooling consolidated balance sheet are the "Investment in Stock of B Company" account from the parent's books and the stockholders' equity accounts from the subsidiary's books. Again, note that only 90% of the equity of B Company is being eliminated; the 10% remainder will be recognized as minority interest. The workpaper elimination entry is:

(a) Capital Stock--B Co. $45,000
    Additional Paid-in Capital--B Co.   13,500
    Retained Earnings--B Co.   36,900*
        Investment in Stock of B Company--A Co. $95,400

    (*36,900 = 90% x $41,000)

The next section of the module will cover the preparation of consolidated financial statements subsequent to the date of acquisition. You should be sure you fully understand date of combination consolidations before proceeding.

0. Consolidated Financial Statements Subsequent to Acquisition

The concepts used to prepare subsequent consolidated statements are essentially the same as used to prepare the consolidated balance sheet at the acquisition date. The income statement and statement of retained earnings are added to reflect the results of operations since the acquisition date. Furthermore, some additional reciprocal accounts may have to be eliminated because of intercompany transactions between the parent and subsidiary corporations. Please note that the financial statements of a consolidated entity are prepared using the same accounting principles that would be employed by a single, unconsolidated enterprise. The only difference is that some reciprocal accounts appearing on both companies' books must be eliminated against each other before the two corporations may be presented as one consolidated economic entity. Your review should concentrate on the accounts and amounts appearing on the consolidated statements (amounts in the last column of the worksheet). This "end-result" focus will help provide the understanding of why certain elimination entries are necessary.

An expanded version of the consolidated worksheet is necessary if the income statement and retained earnings statement must also be prepared. A comprehensive format often called "the three statement layout" is an integrated vertical array of the income statement, the retained earnings statement, and the balance sheet. The net income of the period is carried to the retained earnings statement and the ending retained earnings is carried down to the balance sheet. If you are required to prepare just the consolidated balance sheet, then eliminating entries involving nominal accounts (income statement accounts and "Dividends Declared" account) would be made directly against the ending balance of retained earnings presented on the balance sheet.

The following discussion assumes the parent is using the partial equity method to account for the majority investment. Some firms may use the cost method during the period to record investment income because it requires fewer book adjustments to the investment account. In cases where the cost method is used during the period, one approach is to adjust the investment and investment income accounts to the equity method through an entry on the workpaper and the consolidation process may then be continued. Assuming that an income statement and retained earnings statement are being prepared in addition to the balance sheet, the general form of this entry is made on the workpapers:

Dividend Income (for income recognized using cost method)
Investment in Sub (% of undistributed income of sub)
Equity in Subsidiary's Income (for income recognized using equity
method)

Additional entries would be required to recognize the equity income in prior periods if the investment were owned for more than one period and to recognize the amortizations of any differential for all periods the investment was held. After these entries are made, the investment and equity in subsidiary's income accounts would be stated at equity and the consolidation process may continue. It is important to note that the formal consolidated statements will be the same regardless of the method used by the parent to account for the investment on its books. The concept of measurement used in the preparation of the consolidated statements is equivalent to the full equity method and the elimination process will result in statements presented under that concept.

P. Intercompany Transactions and Profit Confirmation

Three general types of intercompany transactions may occur between the parent and subsidiary companies. Intercompany transactions require special handling because the profit or loss from these events must be properly presented on the consolidated financial statements. The three types of intercompany transactions are: intercompany sales of merchandise; transactions in fixed assets; and, intercompany debt/equity transactions. These events may generate "unrealized profit" (also referred to as unconfirmed profit) which is a profit or gain shown in the trial balance from one of the company's books, but should not be shown in the consolidated financial statements. Intercompany bond transaction may require recognition of a gain or loss on the consolidated financials which is not in the trial balances of either the parent or subsidiary companies.

1. Intercompany inventory transactions

Unrealized profit in ending inventory arises through intercompany sales above cost that are not resold to third parties prior to year end. Thus, the profit on the selling corporation's books is overstated, because an arm's length transaction has not yet taken place. The inventory is overstated on the purchaser's books for the amount of the unrealized intercompany profit. An exhibit of the relationships is shown below:

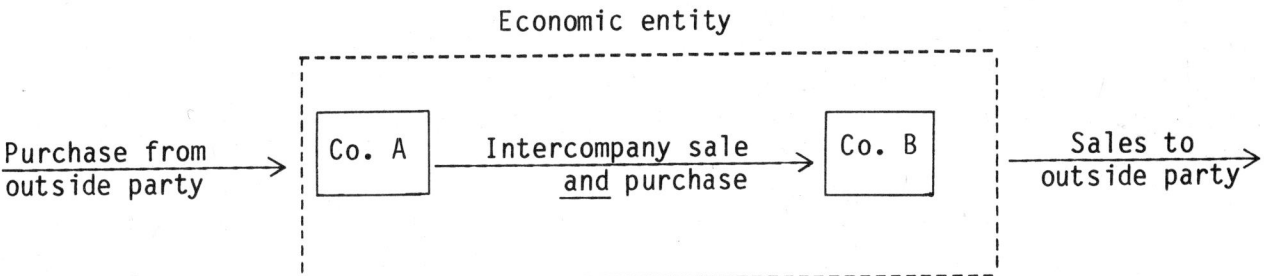

Economic entity

Purchase from outside party → Co. A — Intercompany sale and purchase → Co. B — Sales to outside party

Companies A and B are two separate legal entities and will each record the sale or purchase of goods. From a consolidated or economic entity viewpoint, however, the intercompany transaction is a transfer of assets which cannot result in revenue recognition until these goods are sold to a third party. Assuming a sale from Company A to Company B (a "downstream" intercompany sale), the sale income of Company A cannot be recognized until the goods are sold to third parties by Company B. In addition, the ending inventory of Company B is overstated by the amount of profit in the inventory acquired from Company A. Once intercompany sales have been sold to third parties' the earning process has been verified by an arm's-length transaction with third parties. Thus, recognition of previously unrecognized profit must be made at that time.

2. Intercompany fixed asset transactions

Unrealized profits on fixed assets arise through intercompany sales of fixed assets above undepreciated cost. From a consolidated viewpoint, the transaction represents the internal transfer of assets and no gain (loss) should be recognized. Therefore, any gain (loss) must be eliminated and the carrying value of the transferred asset must be returned to its initial book value basis. In subsequent periods, depreciation expense is overstated, because an overvalued asset is being depreciated on the books of the company showing the asset. This overstatement of depreciation must also be eliminated in the consolidation process.

3. Intercompany bond transactions

When one consolidated company buys bonds of another consolidated company, there are several reciprocal items to eliminate: investment in bonds and bonds payable, interest income and interest expense, and interest payable and interest receivable. Intercompany gains and losses cannot arise from direct intercompany bond purchases. The book value would be the same on both books and the interest accounts would be reciprocal. Note that APB 21 does not require the use of the effective interest method for debt transactions between parent and subsidiary companies. Straight line amortizations of premiums or discounts are often used in these instances.

Gains and losses on intercompany bond holdings may occur when:

a) Already outstanding bonds are purchased by a parent or sub
b) From a third party
c) For an amount different from the carrying value of the issuer

However, the bonds are still recorded as liabilities on the issuer's separate books and as an investment in bonds on the purchasing corporation's books. It is only from the consolidated position that these bonds may be viewed as being "retired". The eliminating entry is to recognize the gain (loss) on the consolidated "retirement of debt" in the year of intercompany bond purchase. This gain (loss) would normally be an extraordinary item in accordance with SFAS 4.

Q. Example of Subsequent Consolidated Financial Statements

The following information extends the basic example of A Company and B Company begun earlier in this module. The example illustrates the major consolidation concepts and procedures most likely to appear on the exam.

EXTENDED EXAMPLE

On January 1, 1982, A Company acquired 90% of the stock of B Company in exchange for 5,400 shares of $10 par stock having a total market value of $120,600.

The purchase method of accounting is used for the combination.

On January 1, 1982, B Company's assets and liabilities had the following book and fair values:

	Book Value	Fair Value	
Cash	$ 37,400	$ 37,400	
Accounts Receivable (net)	9,100	9,100	
Inventories	16,100	17,100	100
Equipment	50,000	60,000	10,000
Accumulated Depreciation	<10,000>	<12,000>	<2000>
Patents	10,000	13,000	3000
Accounts Payable	<6,600>	<6,600>	
	$106,000	$118,000	

Any cost in excess of the fair values of the net assets of B Company was attributable to expected future earnings of B Company and will be amortized over a period of 10 years.

Financial statement data of the two companies as of December 31, 1982 (the end of the first year after combination) are presented below.

- *During 1982, A Company sold merchandise to B Company that originally cost A Company $15,000 and the sale was made for $20,000. On December 31, 1982, B Company's inventory included merchandise purchased from A Company at a cost to B Company of $12,000.*

- *Also during 1982, A Company acquired $18,000 of merchandise from B Company. B Company uses a normal markup of 25% above its cost. A Company's ending inventory includes $10,000 of the merchandise acquired from B Company.*

- *B Company reduced its intercompany account payable to A Company to a balance of $4,000 as of December 31, 1982, by making a payment of $1,000 on December 30. This $1,000 payment was still in transit on December 31, 1982.*

- *On January 2, 1982, B Company acquired equipment from A Company for $7,000. The equipment was originally purchased by A Company for $5,000 and had a book value of $4,000 at the date of sale to B Company. The equipment had an estimated remaining life of 4 years as of January 2, 1982.*

- *On December 31, 1982, B Company purchased for $44,000, 50% of the outstanding bonds issued by A Company. The bonds mature on December 31, 1987 and were originally issued at par. The bonds pay interest annually on December 31 of each year and the interest was paid to the prior investor immediately before B Company's purchase of the bonds.*

The consolidated worksheet for the preparation of consolidated financial statements as of December 31, 1982, is presented on the next page.

The investment account balance at the statement date should be reconciled to ensure the parent company made the proper entries under the method of accounting used to account for the investment. As noted earlier, A Company is using the partial equity method, without amortizations. The amortizations of the excess of cost over book value will be recognized only on the worksheets. This method is the one typically followed on the CPA exam; however, be sure you determine the method used in the exam problem--don't assume! The "proof" of the investment account of A Company is:

A COMPANY AND B COMPANY CONSOLIDATED WORKING PAPERS
Year Ended December 31, 1982

Purchase Accounting
90% Owned
Subsequent, Partial Equity

	A Company	B Company	Adjustments and Eliminations Debit		Credit	Minority Interest	Consolidated Balances
Income Statements for year ended 12/31/82							
Sales	750,000	420,000	(a)	38,000			1,132,000
Cost of Sales	581,000	266,000	(b)	5,000	(a) 38,000		814,900
			(i)	900			
Gross Margin	169,000	154,000					317,100
Depreciation and interest expense	28,400	16,200	(i)	1,800	(d) 750		45,650
Other operating expenses	117,000	128,400	(i)	1,710			247,110
Net income from operations	23,600	9,400					24,340
Gain on sale of equipment	3,000		(d)	3,000			
Gain on bonds					(e) 6,000		6,000
Equity in Subsidiary's Income	8,460		(f)	8,460			
Minority Income (.10 x $7,400)						740	(740)
Net Income	35,060	9,400		58,870	44,750	740	29,600
Statement of Retained Earnings for Year Ended 12/31/82							
1/1/82 Retained Earnings							
A Company	48,000						48,000
B Company		41,000	(g)	36,900		4,100	
Add Net Income							
(from above)	35,060	9,400		58,870	44,750	740	29,600
Total	83,060	50,400				4,840	77,600
Deduct Dividends	15,000	4,000			(f) 3,600	400	15,000
Balance December 31, 1982	68,060	46,400		95,770	48,350	4,440	62,600
Balance Sheet 12/31/82							
Cash	45,300	6,400	(1)	1,000			52,700
Accounts Receivable (net)	43,700	12,100			(1) 1,000		50,800
					(c) 4,000		
Inventories	38,300	20,750	(h)	900	(b) 5,000		54,050
					(i) 900		
Equipment	195,000	57,000	(h)	9,000	(d) 2,000		259,000
Accumulated Depreciation	(35,200)	(18,900)			(d) 250		(57,950)
					(h) 1,800		
					(i) 1,800		
Investment in Stock of B Company	125,460				(f) 4,860		
					(g) 120,600		
Differential			(g)	25,200	(h) 25,200		
Goodwill			(h)	14,400	(i) 1,440		12,960
Investment in Bonds of A Company		44,000			(e) 44,000		
Patents		9,000	(h)	2,700	(i) 270		11,430
	412,560	130,350					382,990
Accounts Payable	8,900	18,950	(c)	4,000			23,850
Bonds Payable	100,000		(e)	50,000			50,000
Capital Stock	154,000	50,000	(g)	45,000		5,000	154,000
Additional Paid-in Capital	81,600	15,000	(g)	13,500		1,500	81,600
Retained Earnings (from above)	68,060	46,400		95,770	48,350	4,440	62,600
Minority Interest						10,940	10,940
	412,560	130,350		261,470	261,470		382,990

Investment in Stock of B Company

Original cost	$120,600		
% of B Company's income (90% x $9,400)	8,460	$3,600	% of B Company's dividends declared (90% x $4,000)
Bal (12/31/82)	$125,460		

Any errors will require correcting entries before the consolidation process is continued. Correcting entries will be posted to the books of the appropriate company; eliminating entries are <u>not</u> posted to either company's books.

The difference between the investment cost and the book value of the net assets acquired was determined and allocated in the preparation of the date of combination consolidated statements presented on page 980. For purposes of brevity, that process will not be duplicated here since the same computations are used in preparing financial statements for as long as the investment is owned.

The following adjusting and eliminating entries will be required to prepare consolidated financials as of December 31, 1982. Note that a consolidated income statement is required and, therefore, the nominal accounts are still "open". The number or letter in parentheses to the left of the entry corresponds to the key used on the work sheet.

Step 1: Complete the transaction for any intercompany items in transit at the end of the year.

(1) Cash $1,000
          Accounts Receivable $1,000

This <u>adjusting</u> entry will now properly present the financial positions of both companies and the consolidation process may be continued.

Step 2: Prepare the eliminating entries.

(a) Sales $38,000
          Cost of Goods Sold $38,000

Total intercompany sales of $38,000 include $20,000 in a downstream transaction from A Company to B Company and $18,000 in an upstream transaction from B Company to A Company.

(b) Cost of Goods Sold $5,000
          Inventory $5,000

The ending inventories are overstated because of the unrealized profit from the intercompany sales. The debit to cost of goods sold is required because a decrease in ending inventory will increase cost of goods sold to be deducted on the income statement. Supporting computations for the entry are:

	In Ending Inventory of	
	A Company	B Company
Intercompany sales not resold, at selling price	$10,000	$12,000
Cost basis of remaining intercompany merchandise		
From B to A (÷ 125%)	<8,000>	
From A to B (÷ 133 1/3%)		<9,000>
Unrealized profit	$ 2,000	$ 3,000

When preparing consolidated work papers for 1983 (the next fiscal period), an additional eliminating entry will be required if the goods in 1982's ending inventory are sold to outsiders during 1983. The additional entry will recognize the profit for 1983 that was eliminated as unrealized in 1982. This entry is necessary since the entry at the end of 1982 was made only on the worksheet. The 1983 entry will be:

Retained Earnings - B Comp. (1/1/83) $2,000
Retained Earnings - A Comp. (1/1/83)   3,000
    Cost of Goods Sold (1983) $5,000

(c) Accounts Payable $4,000
    Accounts Receivable $4,000

This eliminates the remaining intercompany receivable/payable owed by B Company to A Company. This eliminating entry is necessary to avoid overstating the consolidated entity's balance sheet. The receivable/payable is not extinguished and B Company must still transfer $4,000 to A Company in the future.

(d) Gain on Sale of Equipment $3,000
    Equipment $2,000
    Accumulated Depreciation   250
    Depreciation Expense   750

Eliminates the gain on the intercompany sale of the equipment, eliminates the overstatement of equipment, and removes the excess depreciation taken on the gain. Supporting computations for the entry are:

	Cost	At date of intercompany sale Accum. Depr.	1982 Depreciation Expense	End-of-period Accum. Depr.
Original basis (to seller-A Comp)	$5,000	<$1,000>	$1,000	<$2,000>
New basis (to buyer-B Comp)	7,000	-0-	1,750	< 1,750>
Difference	<$2,000>		<$ 750>	$ 250

If the intercompany sale had not occurred, A Company would have depreciated the remaining book value of $4,000 over the estimated remaining life of 4 years. However, since B Company's acquisition price ($7,000) was more than A Company's basis in the asset ($4,000), the depreciation recorded on the books of B Company will include part of the intercompany unrealized profit. The equipment must be reflected on the consolidated statements at the original cost to the consolidated entity. Therefore, the "write-up" of $2,000 in the equipment, the excess depreciation of $750, and the gain of $3,000 must be eliminated and the ending balance of accumulated depreciation must be shown at what it would have been if the intercompany equipment transaction had not occurred. In future periods, a retained earnings account will be used instead of the gain account; however, the other concepts will be extended to include the additional periods.

(e) Bonds Payable $50,000
      Investment in Bonds of A Company $44,000
      Gain on Extinguishment of Debt   6,000

This entry eliminates the book value of A Company's debt against the bond investment account of B Company. To the consolidated entity, this transaction must be shown as a retirement of debt even though A Company has the outstanding intercompany debt to B Company. SFAS 4 specifies gains or losses on debt extinguishment, if material, should be shown as an extraordinary item. In future periods, B Company will amortize the discount thereby bringing the investment account up to par value and a retained earnings account will be used in the eliminating entry instead of the gain account.

(f) Equity in Subsidiary's Income--A Co. $ 8,460
      Dividends Declared--B Co. $ 3,600
      Investment in Stock of B Company   4,860

This elimination entry adjusts the investment account back to its balance at the beginning of the period and also eliminates the subsidiary income account.

(g) Capital Stock--B Co. $45,000
   Additional Paid-in Capital--B Co.   13,500
   Retained Earnings--B Co.   36,900
   Differential   25,200
      Investment in Stock of B Co.--A Co. $120,600

This entry eliminates 90% of B Company's stockholders' equity at the beginning of the year, 1/1/82. Note that the changes during the year were eliminated in entry (f) above. The differential account reflects the excess of investment cost greater than the book value of the assets acquired.

(h) Inventory $ 900
   Equipment   9,000
   Patents   2,700
   Goodwill   14,400
      Accumulated Depreciation $ 1,800
      Differential   25,200

This entry allocates the differential (excess of investment cost over the book values of the assets acquired). Note that this entry is the same as the allocation entry made to prepare consolidated financial statements for January 1, 1982, the date of acquisition.

(i)

Cost of Goods Sold	$ 900	
Depreciation Expense	1,800	
Other Operating Expenses--		
Patent Amortization	270	
Other Operating Expenses--		
Goodwill Amortization	1,440	
Inventory		$ 900
Accumulated Depreciation		1,800
Patents		270
Goodwill		1,440

This elimination entry amortizes the revaluations to fair market value made in entry (h). The inventory has been sold and therefore becomes part of cost of goods sold. The remaining revaluation will be amortized as follows:

	Revaluation	Amortization Period	Annual Amortization
Equipment (net)	$ 7,200	4 years	$1,800
Patents	2,700	10 years	270
Goodwill	14,400	10 years	1,440

The amortizations will continue to be made on future work sheets. For example, at the end of the next year (1983), the amortization entry (i) would be as follows:

Differential	$4,410	
Depreciation Expense	1,800	
Other Operating Expenses--		
Patent Amortization	270	
Other Operating Expenses--		
Goodwill Amortization	1,440	
Inventory		$ 900
Accumulated Depreciation		3,600
Patents		540
Goodwill		2,880

The initial debit of $4,410 to differential is an aggregation of the prior period's charges to income statement accounts ($900 + $1,800 + $270 + $1,440). During subsequent years, some authors prefer reducing the allocated amounts in entry (h) for prior period's charges. In this case, the amortization entry in future periods would reflect just that period's amortizations.

This extended example has assumed the purchase method was used to account for the combination of A Company and B Company. As a result, the consolidated financial statements will include the parent company's share of the revaluations to fair market values of the subsidiary's net assets. A pooling, however, is based on book

values. No differential exists in pooling accounting and, thus, entry (g) above
would be different while entries (h) and (i) would not be made for a pooling. All
other eliminating entries would be the same. The basic elimination entry (g) for a
pooling, using the equity method of accounting for the investment, would be:

Capital Stock--B Co.	$45,000	
Additional Paid-in Capital--B Co.	13,500	
Retained Earnings--B Co.	36,900	
Investment in Stock of B Company		$95,400

R. Minority Interest

The parent company often acquires less than 100% (but more than 50%) of the
subsidiary's outstanding stock. Under either the purchase or pooling method the
consolidated financial statements will include all of the assets, liabilities,
revenues, and expenses of these less than wholly-owned subsidiaries. The percentage
of the stock not owned by the parent company represents the minority interest's
share of the net assets of the subsidiary. Minority interest will be a line item
deduction on the income statement for its portion of the subsidiary's income and,
under the parent company concept, will be shown on the consolidated balance sheet
after long-term debt but before stockholders' equity. The following procedures apply to cases of less than wholly-owned subsidiaries:

1) Only the parent's share of the sub's shareholders' equity is eliminated
    in the basic eliminating entry. The minority interest's share is pre-
    sented separately.

2) The entire amount of intercompany reciprocal items is eliminated. For
    example, all receivables/payables and sales/cost of sales with a 90%
    subsidiary are eliminated.

3) For intercompany transactions in inventory and fixed assets, the possi-
    ble effect on minority interest depends on whether the original trans-
    action affected the subsidiary's income statement. Minority interest is
    adjusted only if the subsidiary is the selling entity. In this case,
    the minority interest is adjusted for its percentage ownership of the
    common stock of the subsidiary. The minority interest is not adjusted
    for unrealized profits on downstream sales. The effects of downstream
    transactions are confined solely to the parent's (i.e., controlling)
    ownership interests.

The minority interest's share of the subsidiary's income is shown as a deduction
on the consolidated income statement since 100% of the sub's revenues and expenses
are combined although the parent company owns less than a 100% interest. For our
example, the minority interest deduction on the income statement is computed as follows:

B Company's reported income	$9,400
Less: unrealized profit on an upstream inventory sale	<2,000>
B Company's income for con- solidated financial purposes	$7,400
Minority interest share	10%
Minority interest on Income Statement	$ 740

The minority interest's share of the net assets of B Company is shown on the Consolidated Balance Sheet between liabilities and controlling interest's equity. The computation for the minority interest shown in the balance sheet for our example is:

B Company's capital stock, 12/31/82	$50,000	
Minority interest share	10%	$5,000
B Company's additional paid-in capital, 12/31/82	$15,000	
Minority interest share	10%	1,500
B Company's retained earnings, 1/1/82	$41,000	
Minority interest share	10%	4,100
B Company's 1982 income for consolidated purposes	$ 7,400	
Minority interest share	10%	740
B Company's dividends during 1982	$ 4,000	
Minority interest share	10%	<400>
Total minority interest, 12/31/82		$10,940

The remainder of the consolidation process is just work sheet techniques, as follows:

a) Take all income items across horizontally and foot the adjustments, minority interest, and consolidated columns down to the net income line.

b) Take the amounts on the net income line (on income statement) in the adjustments, minority interest, and consolidated balances columns down to retained earnings items across the consolidated balances column. Foot and crossfoot the retained earnings statement.

c) Take the amounts of ending retained earnings in each of the four columns down to the ending retained earnings line in the balance sheet. Foot the minority interest column and place its total in the consolidated balances column. Take all the balance sheet items across to consoli- dated balances column.

S. Subsequent Consolidated Balance Sheet Only

Consolidation exam problems generally require only the Consolidated Balance Sheet. In this case, the effects of all the income statement account balances will have been closed to the retained earnings accounts. You should carefully review the adjustments and eliminations that were made noting that the nominal accounts (income statement accounts and Dividends Declared account) would be replaced with the account "Retained Earnings". Thus, elimination entry "(a)" would not be required; entry "(b)" would be:

(b) Retained Earnings	$5,000	
Inventory		$5,000

Retained Earnings would be substituted for the nominal accounts in all other eliminating entries. A shortcut alternative to eliminating entries "(f)" and "(g)" is to use the ending balance of B Company's Retained Earnings as follows:

(f & g) Capital Stock--B Co.	$45,000	
Additional Paid-in Capital--B Co.	13,500	
*Retained Earnings--B Co.	41,760	
Differential	25,200	
Investment in Stock of B Co.--A Co.		$125,460

*($41,760 = 90% x $46,400 ending balance of B Company's Retained Earnings)

A worksheet for just the Consolidated Balance Sheet is presented on the next page. The adjusting and eliminating entries are keyed to the entries and entry explanations for the three-statement layout presented earlier. Several elimination entries have been combined and are shown as "(f/g)" or "(h/i)." Note that the final Consolidated Balance Sheet amounts are the same when only the balance sheet is being prepared as well as when all three statements are being prepared.

T. Consolidated Net Income and Consolidated Retained Earnings

In some cases, you may be asked just to determine the Consolidated Net Income (CNI) of the parent and subsidiary companies. A shorter, analytical approach may be used instead of the work sheet method. An analytical definition of CNI is exhibited for our example on the second page following this one.

If the "full" equity method had been used to account for the investment, all the adjustments to the parent company's income (see top of second page following) would have been reflected in the "Equity in Subsidiary's Income" account on the parent company's books. Under the "partial" equity method, only the equity accrual of $8,460 is shown in the Equity in Subsidiary's Income account. All other adjustments are made only on the consolidated work sheet.

A COMPANY AND B COMPANY CONSOLIDATED WORKING PAPERS
CONSOLIDATED BALANCE SHEET ONLY

Purchase Accounting
90% Owned
Subsequent, Partial Equity

December 31, 1982

	A Company	B Company	\<Adjustments and Eliminations\> Debit			Credit	Minority Interest	Consolidated Balance Sheet
Assets								
Cash	45,300	4,600	(1)	1,000				52,700
Accounts Receivable (net)	43,700	12,100			(1)	1,000		50,800
					(c)	4,000		
Inventories	38,300	20,750	(h/i)	900	(b)	5,000		54,050
					(h/i)	900		
Equipment	195,000	57,00	(h/i)	9,000	(d)	2,000		259,000
Accumulated Depreciation	(35,200)	(18,900)			(d)	250		(57,950)
					(h/i)	3,600		
Investment in Stock of								
B Company	125,460				(f/g)	125,460		
Differential			(f/g)	25,200	(h/i)	25,200		
Goodwill			(h/i)	12,960				12,960
Investment in Bonds								
of A Company		44,000			(e)	44,000		
Patents		9,000	(h/i)	2,430				11,430
Total	412,560	130,350						382,990
Liabilities and Stock-								
holder's Equity								
Accounts Payable	8,900	18,950	(c)	4,000				23,850
Bonds Payable	100,000		(e)	50,000				50,000
Capital Stock	154,000	50,000	(f/g)	45,000			5,000	154,000
Additional Paid-in Capital	81,600	15,000	(f/g)	13,500			1,500	81,600
Retained Earnings	68,060	46,400	(b)	5,000	(e)	6,000	4,440	62,600
			(d)	2,250				
			(f/g)	41,760				
			(h/i)	4,410				
Minority Interest							10,940	10,940
Total	412,560	130,350		217,410		217,410		382,990

        Parent company's net income from
          independent operations $26,600

± Parent company's share of subsidiary's
     equity income (loss) (equity accrual)
     (90% x $9,400--reported income of B Co.)   +   8,460
± Period's amortization of difference
     between cost and book value
     ($900--inventory; $1,800--equip.;
     $270--patent; $1,440--goodwill)   -   4,410
- Parent company's share of unrealized
     profit on intercompany transactions
     ($3,000--merchandise sale of A to B;
     $1,800--90% of sale of goods from B
     to A; $3,000--sale of equipment)   -   7,800
+ Parent company's share of realized
     profit on intercompany transactions
     ($6,000--bonds; $750--from elimination
     of excessive depr. on equip. sale from
     A to B)   +   6,750
   CNI   29,600

Consolidated Retained Earnings (CRE) may be determined once CNI is found. An analytical definition of CRE for our example is:

        Parent company's beginning
          Retained Earnings (1/1/82) $48,000

+ Consolidated net income for period   + 29,600

- Parent company's dividends to its
     shareholders (note: subsidiary's
     dividends to outside parties are
     a component of minority interest,
     not CRE)   - 15,000
   CRE $62,600

U. Changes in Ownership

Changes in the level of ownership of subsidiaries frequently occur through purchase or sale of the subsidiary's stock by the parent or changes in the sub's shares outstanding. If the subsidiary changes the number of shares outstanding (for example, through treasury stock transactions), the transaction may require an entry on the parent's books to maintain the parent's reciprocity in the net assets of the subsidiary.

For example, if the subsidiary, through treasury stock transactions, increases the relative book value owned by the parent, the increase must be recorded to maintain reciprocity between the investment account on the parent's accounting records and its equivalent stockholders' equity accounts in the subsidiary's books.

> Investment in sub
>   Paid-in capital

On the other hand, if the sub's treasury stock transactions decrease the parent's equity:

>   Paid-in capital
>   Investment in sub

When the parent's share of ownership increases through a purchase of additional stock, simply debit investment and credit cash for cost. A problem occurs with consolidated income statements when the change in ownership takes place in mid-period. Consolidated statements should be prepared based on the ending ownership level. For example, assume that A Company increased its ownership of B Company from 90% to 95% on October 1, 1982. The investment was acquired at book value of $5,452.50 (5% X [$50,000 C.S. + $15,000 A.P.I.C. + $44,050 R.E. at 10-1-82]). If the subsidiary earned its income of $9,400 evenly over the year, the consolidated net income should reflect a net of:

	90% x $9,400 x 12/12	= $8,460.00
+	5% x $9,400 x 3/12	= $ 117.50
	95%	$8,577.50

The interim stock purchase will result in a new account being shown on the Consolidated Income Statement. The account is <u>Purchased Preacquisition Earnings</u> which represents the percentage of the subsidiary's earnings earned, in this case, on the 5% stock interest from January 1, 1982 to October 1, 1982. The basic eliminating entries would be based on the 95% ownership as follows:

Equity in Subsidiary's Income--A Co.	$ 8,577.50	
Dividends Declared--B Co.		$ 3,600.00
Investment in Stock of B Company		4,977.50
Capital Stock--B Co.	47,500.00	
Additional Paid-in Capital--B Co.	14,250.00	
Retained Earnings--B Co.	38,750.00[*]	
Purchased Preacquisition earnings	352.50[**]	
Differential	25,200.00	
Investment in Stock of B Co.--A Co.		$126,052.50

[*](95% x $41,000 beginning 1982 balance   = $38,950)
  (less preacquisition dividend of 5% x $4,000 = <$200>)
  (Retained earnings available, as adjusted   = $38,750)
[**]($352.50 = 5% x $9,400 x 9/12)

Purchased Preacquisition Earnings is shown as a deduction along with Minority Interest to arrive at Consolidated Net Income. You should note that purchased preacquisition earnings are used only with interim acquisitions under the purchase accounting method; all poolings are assumed to take place at the beginning of the period regardless of when, during the period, the acquisition was actually made.

CHAPTER TEN

COST ACCOUNTING REVIEW

Cost and managerial accounting, as contrasted to financial accounting, produce data primarily for management decision making. Management needs data for:

1. Planning and controlling day-to-day operations, e.g., use of standard costs to evaluate production efficiency
2. Long-range planning and decision making, e.g., use of capital budgeting techniques in making decisions concerning investment projects

Another function is to determine inventory costs for financial reporting purposes. Determining inventory costs is the more traditional role of cost accounting.

The AICPA Content Specification Outline of the coverage of cost-managerial accounting in the Accounting Practice and Accounting Theory exams, including the authors' frequency analysis thereof (last nine exams), appears on the next page. Please note that part Q of the outline is covered in Mod 38. Also, note the number of topics that are tested with about the same frequency on every exam.

BASIC COST ACCOUNTING TERMINOLOGY

1. Managerial Accounting emphasizes data for managerial decisions in contrast to cost accounting which emphasizes determination of inventory costs

2. Planning is selecting goals, and choosing methods to attain the goals. Control is the implementation of the plans.

3. Line personnel have direct responsibility for attaining objectives, e.g., plant supervisor, foremen, and production workers. Staff personnel provide service to line functions, e.g., purchasing agents and maintenance personnel.

4. A budget is a quantification of the plan for operations. A flexible budget is a budget which is adjusted for changes in volume. Performance reports compare budgeted and actual performance.

5. Management by exception emphasizes material deviations from plans, e.g., variances in a performance report

6. Responsibility accounting assigns costs and/or revenues to responsibility centers

7. Controller generally implies a financial officer having responsibility for internal operations such as budgeting and the system of internal control. Treasurer generally implies a financial officer having responsibility for external reporting such as investor relations and the annual report.

8. Product costs are those that can be associated with the production of specific revenues, e.g., cost of sales. Product costs attach to a physical unit and become an expense in the period in which the unit to which they attach is sold. Product costs normally include direct labor, direct material, and factory overhead. Period costs cannot be associated (or matched) with specific revenues, e.g., advertising expenditures. Period costs become expenses as time passes.

9. Direct (prime) costs are easily traceable to specific units of production, e.g., direct labor and direct material. Indirect costs are not easily traceable to specific units of production, e.g., factory overhead.

AICPA CONTENT SPECIFICATION OUTLINES/FREQUENCY ANALYSIS*

Cost Accumulation, Planning, and Control

		Practice									Theory								
		M 80	N 80	M 81	N 81	M 82	N 82	M 83	N 83	M 84	M 80	N 80	M 81	N 81	M 82	N 82	M 83	N 83	M 84
A.	**Nature of Cost Elements**																		
	1. Direct Materials	–	–	–	–	–	2	1	–	–	–	–	1	1	–	–	–	–	1
	2. Direct Labor	–	–	–	–	–	2	1	1	–	–	–	1	–	–	–	–	1	–
	3. Overhead (actual, applied, and allocation methods)	–	–	1	–	1	2	–	–	–	– [1]	–	1	2	– [.5]	1	1	3	3
B.	**Job Order Costing**	–	– [.5]	1	–	1	1	5	–	– [.5]	1	–	1	1	1	1	–	–	–
C.	**Process Costing**	2 [1]	2 [.5]	2	1	2	2	4	2	–	1	2	2	2	1	1	– [.5]	2	1
D.	**Standard Cost and Variance Analysis**	3	3	3 [1]	4 [1]	3	2	1	4	– [1]	1	4	1	2	– [.5]	2	1	2	2
E.	**Joint Costing**	2	2	2	1	– [.17]	2	3	2	–	1	1	1	2	1	1	–	–	1
F.	**By-Product Costing**	–	–	–	–	– [.33]	–	–	–	–	–	1	1	–	–	1	–	–	–
G.	**Spoilage, Waste, and Scrap**	–	–	–	–	2	2	1	1	–	–	1	–	1	–	–	–	–	–
H.	**Absorption and Direct Costing**	–	1	1	–	2	3	2	2	–	–	1	1	1	2	– [.33]	1	1	1
I.	**Transfer Pricing**	–	–	–	–	–	–	–	2	–	–	–	–	–	–	–	–	–	–
J.	**Product Pricing**	–	–	–	–	–	–	–	–	–	–	–	–	–	–	–	–	–	–
K.	**Budgeting and Flexible Budgeting**	1	1	2	1	– [.5]	7	–	2	–	–	1	–	–	–	1	1	–	1
L.	**Breakeven and Cost-Volume-Profit Analysis**	3	2	3	4	2	4	– [1]	3	–	1	2	– [.5]	2	2	–	– [.5]	2	2
M.	**Gross Profit Analysis**	–	–	–	1	1	2	–	–	–	–	–	–	–	–	–	–	–	–
N.	**Differential Cost Analysis**																		
	1. Activity Levels	–	–	–	1	–	–	–	–	–	–	–	–	–	–	–	–	–	–
	2. Sunk Costs	1	1	–	1	1	2	–	–	–	1	1	–	–	–	–	–	–	1
	3. Contribution to Profit	1	1	1	1	1	2	–	2	–	–	–	–	–	–	–	–	–	–
	4. Uncertainty	–	–	–	–	–	–	–	–	–	–	–	–	–	–	–	–	–	–
	5. Time Periods	–	–	–	–	–	–	–	–	–	–	–	–	–	–	–	–	–	–
O.	**Capital Budgeting Techniques**																		
	1. Net Present Value	2	–	2	2	1	1	–	–	–	2	1	– [.08]	–	1	– [.33]	–	1	–
	2. Internal Rate of Return	–	2	1	–	1	1	–	1	–	–	–	– [.08]	1	1	– [.33]	–	1	1
	3. Payback Period	1	1	1	1	1	1	–	–	–	–	1 [.25]	–	–	–	–	–	–	–
	4. Accounting Rate of Return	1	1	–	1	–	1	1	1	–	–	– [.08]	–	–	–	–	–	–	–
P.	**Performance Analysis**																		
	1. Return on Investment	–	–	–	–	–	–	–	1	–	–	–	–	–	–	–	–	1	–
	2. Residual Income	–	–	–	–	–	–	–	1	–	–	–	–	–	–	–	–	–	–
	3. Controllable Revenue and Costs	–	–	–	–	–	–	–	–	–	–	–	–	–	1	–	–	–	–
Q.	**Quantitative Techniques for Planning and Control**																		
	1. Regression and Correlation Analysis	–	–	–	–	–	–	–	–	–	1	1	–	–	–	1	–	1	–
	2. Learning Curves	–	–	–	–	–	1	–	–	–	–	–	–	–	–	–	–	–	–
	3. Economic Order Quantity	2	1	–	–	–	–	1	1	–	–	1	–	1	–	1	1	–	–
	4. PERT/Cost	–	–	–	1	–	–	–	–	–	–	1	–	1	–	–	–	–	–
	5. Sensitivity Analysis	–	–	–	–	–	–	–	–	–	–	–	–	–	–	–	–	–	–
	6. Probability Analysis	–	1	–	–	1	–	–	1	–	–	–	–	1	–	–	–	–	–
	7. Linear Programming	1	1	–	–	–	–	–	1	–	–	1	–	1	1	–	–	1	1
Total Multiple Choice Questions		20	20	20	20	20	40	20	29	–	9	20	10	20	10	10	5	15	15
Total Problems/Essays		1	1	1	1	1	–	1	–	1.5	1	–	1	–	1	1	1	–	–
Actual Percentage**		20%	20%	20%	20%	20%	20%	20%	14.5%	15%	19%	20%	20%	20%	20%	20%	15%	15%	15%
						(AICPA 15%)									(AICPA 15%)				

*The classifications are the authors'

The "actual percentage" is a measure of the relative coverage of the specific areas (i.e., I, II, etc.) on each Accounting Practice or Theory exam. This relative weight includes **both multiple choice questions and essays/problems presented in that area.

10. <u>Direct material</u> is the cost of material directly and conveniently traceable to a product. Minor material items (nails, glue) are not deemed conveniently traceable. These items are treated as indirect material along with production supplies.

11. <u>Direct labor</u> is the cost of labor directly transforming a product. This theoretically should include fringe benefits, but frequently does not. This is contrasted with <u>indirect labor</u> which is the cost of supporting labor (e.g., material handling labor).

12. <u>Factory (manufacturing) overhead</u> normally includes indirect labor cost, supplies cost, and other production facility costs such as plant depreciation, taxes, plant supervisors' salaries, etc. It is comprised of all manufacturing costs less the sum of direct material and direct labor.

13. <u>Conversion costs</u> include direct labor and manufacturing overhead. They are the costs of converting direct material into finished product.

14. <u>Direct (variable) costing</u> considers all fixed manufacturing overhead as a period cost rather than a product cost. This system is contrasted with <u>absorption (full) costing</u> which considers fixed manufacturing overhead as a product cost. The treatment of fixed manufacturing cost as a period cost rather than a product cost is the only difference between direct costing and absorption costing. All other costs (i.e., variable manufacturing, fixed selling and variable selling) are treated the same under both systems. Direct costing is not acceptable per GAAP.

15. <u>Cost behavior patterns</u> are functional relationships between costs and volume. The independent variable, volume, is on the horizontal axis. The dependent variable, cost, is on the vertical axis.

16. <u>Fixed costs</u> do not vary with volume within the relevant range for a given period of time (usually 1 year), e.g., plant depreciation

17. <u>Variable costs</u> vary proportionately in total with volume throughout the relevant range, e.g., direct material

18. <u>Semi-fixed costs (or stepped costs)</u> are fixed over relatively short ranges of production levels, e.g., foremen's salaries. Fixed, variable, and semi-fixed costs are diagrammed below.

19. <u>Mixed costs (semi-variable)</u> are costs which have a fixed component and a variable component. The fixed and variable components are separated by using a scattergraph or the high-low method.

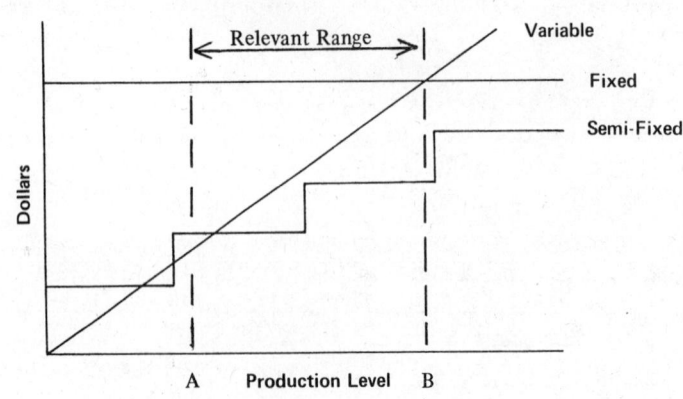

20. <u>Relevant range</u> is the operating range of activity in which cost behavior patterns are valid (A to B in the illustration). Thus, it is the production range for which fixed costs are fixed, i.e., if production doubles, an additional shift of salaried foremen would be added.

21. <u>Average cost</u> is the total cost divided by the number of units produced. Average variable cost remains constant. Average fixed cost decreases (increases) with increases (decreases) in the level of production as diagrammed below.

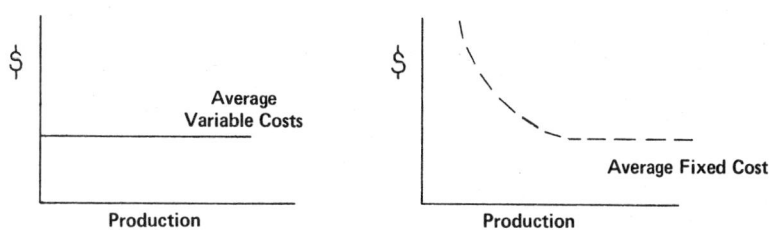

22. <u>Job-order costing</u> is a system for allocating costs to groups of unique products made to customer specification. <u>Process costing</u> is a system for allocating costs to homogeneous units of a mass-produced product.

23. <u>Direct materials inventory</u> includes cost of materials awaiting entry into the production system. <u>Work-in-process inventory</u> includes the cost of units being produced but not yet completed. <u>Finished goods inventory</u> includes the cost of units completed but unsold.

24. <u>Joint costs</u> are costs common to multiple products that emerge at a split-off point. <u>Joint costing</u> is a system of assigning joint costs to <u>joint products</u> whose sales values are relatively similar. When a joint product has insignificant sales value relative to the other products, it is called a by-product.

25. <u>Standard costs</u> are predetermined target costs. <u>Variances</u> are differences between standards and actual results.

26. <u>Controllable costs</u> can be affected by an individual or level of supervision during the current period, e.g., amount of direct labor per unit of production is usually under the control of a production foreman. Uncontrollable costs are those which cannot be affected by the individual in question, e.g., depreciation is not usually subject to the production foreman's control.

27. <u>Cost-volume-profit (CVP) analysis</u> is a planning tool used to analyze the effects of changes in volume, mix, selling price, variable expense, fixed expense, and profit

28. <u>Contribution margin</u> is revenue less all variable costs

29. <u>Nonroutine decisions</u> include contraction or expansion, make or buy, special orders, capital budgeting, etc. The following terminology is encountered in nonroutine decisions.

    a. <u>Sunk, past, or unavoidable costs</u> are committed costs which are not avoidable and are irrelevant to the decision process
    b. <u>Avoidable costs</u> are costs which will not continue if a department (or product) is terminated
    c. <u>Shutdown (committed) costs</u> are fixed costs that cannot be controlled by management within a 1 year time period

d. Discretionary (managed) costs are fixed costs whose level is set by current (within a 1 year time period) management decisions (e.g., advertising, research and development).
e. Relevant costs are future costs that will change as a result of a specific decision
f. Differential (incremental) cost is the difference in cost between two alternatives
g. Opportunity cost is the maximum income (savings) obtainable from the alternative use of a resource
h. Outlay (out-of-pocket) cost is the cash disbursement associated with a specific project

30. Capital budgeting is the planning and controlling of long-term capital outlays

COSTING SYSTEMS

The basic purpose of any costing system is to allocate the costs of production (direct materials, direct labor, and manufacturing overhead) to the units produced. This basic purpose of costing systems (job order, process) is discussed in this module.

A. Cost of Goods Manufactured

Regardless of which costing system is used, a cost of goods manufactured (CGM) statement is prepared to summarize the manufacturing activity of the period. CGM for a manufacturing firm is equivalent to purchases for a merchandising firm. Although it may take different forms, essentially the CGM statement is a summary of the direct materials and work-in-process (WIP) account.

$$BWIP + DM + DL + MOH - EWIP = CGM$$

A typical CGM statement is presented below.

Uddin Company
Cost of Goods Manufactured
Year Ended December 31, 1983

Direct materials:		
Inventory, Jan. 1	$ 23,000	
Purchases	98,000	
Materials available for use	121,000	
Inventory, Dec. 31	16,000	
Direct materials used		$105,000
Direct labor		72,000
Factory overhead:		
Indirect labor	$ 14,000	
Supplies	4,000	
Utilities	8,000	
Depreciation	13,000	
Other	3,000	42,000
Manufacturing costs incurred, 1983		219,000
Add work-in-process inventory, Jan. 1		25,000
Manufacturing costs to account for		244,000
Deduct work-in-process inventory, Dec. 31		30,000
Cost of goods manufactured (completed)		$214,000

The result of the CGM statement is used in the cost of goods sold (CGS) statement, as indicated below.

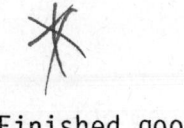

Uddin Company
Cost of Goods Sold
Year Ended December 31, 1983

Finished goods, Jan. 1	$ 40,000
Add cost of goods manufactured (completed), per statement above	214,000
Cost of goods available for sale	254,000
Deduct finished goods, Dec. 31	53,000
Cost of goods sold	$201,000

B. Cost Flows

Before discussing any particular costing system, it is important to understand the flow of costs through the accounts, as summarized in the diagram below.

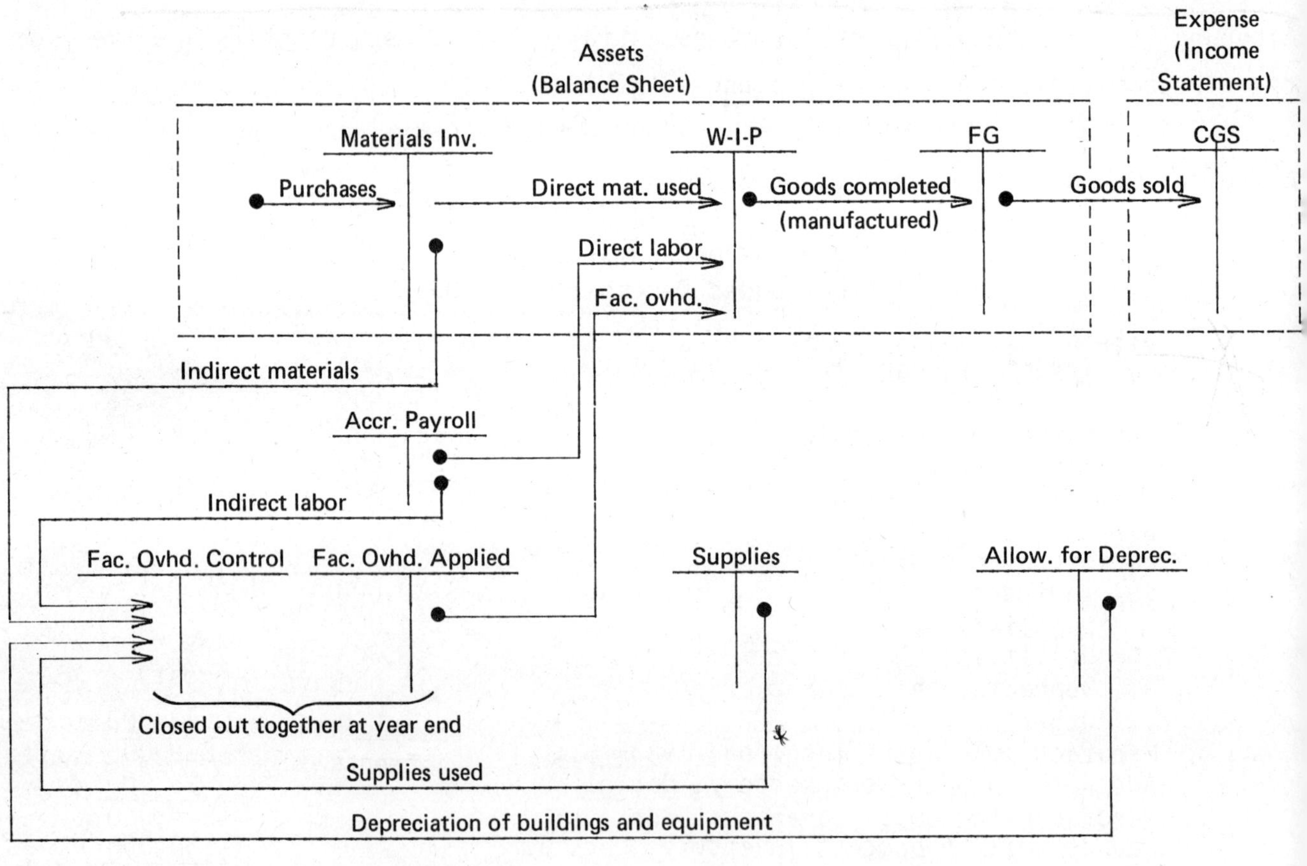

Assets (Balance Sheet) / Expense (Income Statement)

Materials Inv.	W-I-P	FG	CGS
Purchases → Direct mat. used	Goods completed (manufactured)	Goods sold	

Direct labor
Fac. ovhd.

Indirect materials

Accr. Payroll

Indirect labor

Fac. Ovhd. Control   Fac. Ovhd. Applied   Supplies   Allow. for Deprec.

Closed out together at year end

Supplies used

Depreciation of buildings and equipment

Analyze the diagram carefully before proceeding. The details will be explained further in the next few pages.

C. Job-Order Costing

Job-order costing is a system for allocating costs to groups of unique products. It is applicable to the production of customer-specified products such as the manufacture of special machines. Each job becomes a cost center for which costs are accumulated. A subsidiary record (job cost sheet) is needed to keep track of all unfinished jobs (work in process) and finished jobs (finished goods). Note that the total of unfinished job cost sheets will equal the work-in-process balance.

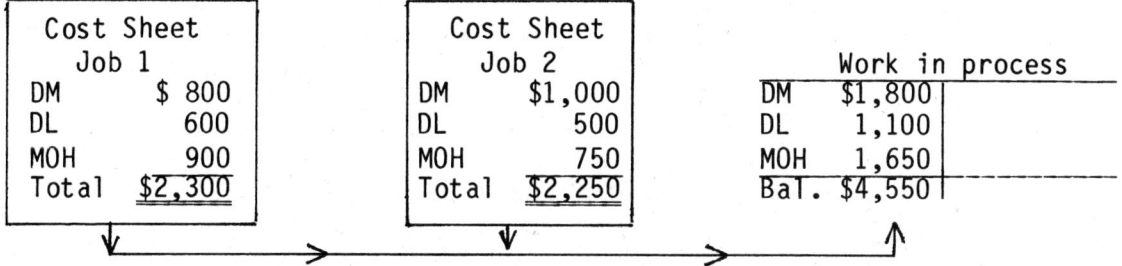

Job-order costing journal entries are presented below. The entries are similar to those made for process costing, which is also discussed in this module.

1. Materials and supplies are purchased.

Materials inventory	xx	
Accounts payable		xx

2. Materials and supplies are used.

Work in process (direct)	xx	
Factory overhead control (indirect)	xx	
Materials inventory		xx

3. The factory payroll is recorded.

Work in process (direct)	xx	
Factory overhead control (indirect)	xx	
Accrued payroll		xx

4. Other actual overhead costs are incurred.

Factory overhead control	xx	
Various accounts		xx

5. Overhead is applied to production.

Work in process	xx	
Factory overhead applied		xx

6. Specific jobs are completed.

Finished goods inventory	xx	
Work in process		xx

7. Specific jobs are sold.

Accounts receivable	xx	
Sales (sales price)		xx
Cost of goods sold	xx	
Finished goods inventory (cost)		xx

Note that whenever work in process is debited or credited in the above entries, the amount of the entry is the sum of the postings on the job-order cost sheets. The balances on the job-order cost sheets are also the basis for the entries transferring completed goods to finished goods inventory and transferring goods shipped to customers to cost of goods sold.

The work-in-process account is analyzed below:

Work in process

1. Beginning balance	
2. Direct materials used	
3. Direct labor used	5. Cost of goods manufactured (CGM)
4. Overhead applied	
6. Ending balance	

The total of items 1, 2, 3, and 4 ends up as either CGM (#5) or ending work in process (#6). A similar analysis can be performed on the finished goods account.

Finished Goods

1. Beginning balance	
2. Cost of goods manufactured	3. Cost of goods sold (CGS)
4. Ending balance	

The total of items 1 and 2 is allocated either to CGS (#3) or to ending finished goods (#4). Again we see the overall objective of the costing system--to allocate the costs of production to CGS (expense) and ending inventories (assets).

D. Accounting for Overhead

Accounting for manufacturing overhead is an important part of job-order costing and any other costing system. Overhead consists of all manufacturing costs other than direct materials and direct labor. The distinguishing feature of manufacturing overhead is that while it must be incurred in order to produce goods, it cannot be directly traced to the final product as can direct materials and direct labor. Therefore, overhead must be applied, rather than directly charged, to goods produced. The overhead application process is described below.

1) Overhead items are grouped by cost behavior, such as fixed and variable
2) The fixed and variable overhead costs are estimated for the forthcoming year (e.g., $500,000)
3) A denominator (activity) base is chosen (see discussion below). A common choice is direct labor hours.
4) The activity level is estimated for the forthcoming year (e.g., 80,000 hours)
5) A predetermined overhead rate is computed:

$$\frac{\text{Estimated overhead costs}}{\text{Estimated activity level}} = \frac{\$500,000}{80,000 \text{ hours}} = \$6.25/\text{hour}$$

6) As actual overhead costs are incurred, they are debited to factory overhead control (e.g., $400)

Factory overhead control (actual)	$400	
Various accounts		$400

7) As jobs are completed, the predetermined overhead rate is used to apply
    overhead to these jobs. For example, if job 17 used 52 direct labor
    hours, $325 of overhead (52 x $6.25) would be charged to work in process
    and entered on the job cost sheet.

    Work in process $325
        Factory overhead applied $325

A topic tested frequently on the CPA exam is the treatment of spoilage costs and
rework on defective units. In a job-order system, the costs of spoilage and defective units can be handled in two different ways. When spoilage is attributable to
general factory conditions, net spoilage costs are spread over all jobs by including
an "allowance for spoiled goods" in the predetermined overhead rate (i.e., estimated
spoilage costs are included in the numerator of the computation to derive the predetermined overhead rate). Alternatively, when spoilage is attributable to exacting
job specifications, net spoilage costs are charged to the specific jobs involved.
With this approach spoilage is not reflected in the predetermined overhead. Under
both methods, the proceeds from spoiled goods sold should be offset against the
total cost of goods produced leaving net spoilage costs to be accounted for by
either of the two methods described above. To compute the unit cost of goods produced on a given job, spoiled units would be excluded from output. However, defective units that have been reworked are included in good output. For example, assume
final inspection of Job 606 resulted in the production of 2,000 good units, 150
spoiled units, and 40 defective units. The defective units were reworked and the
spoiled units were sold. Output for the job would be 2,040 units (2,000 good units
plus 40 units reworked). Spoiled units are ignored.

The activity base should be chosen so that there is a causal relationship between the base and overhead costs. Examples of activity bases are:
   1) Direct labor hours   3) Machine hours
   2) Direct labor cost   4) Material cost
For example, overhead may result from (be a function of) hours worked regardless of
who works, which would mean that direct labor hours should be the activity base.
If, on the other hand, more overhead costs were incurred because of higher paid
employees, e.g., higher workmen's compensation costs, direct labor dollars might be
a more appropriate activity base.

When the activity level is estimated (step "D.4" above), a number of approaches
can be used, as illustrated in the diagram below:

Approach	Definition	Support
Theoretical capacity	Output is produced efficiently 100% of the time.	Little
	↓	
Practical capacity	ADJUSTED FOR: noncontrollable factors such as days off, down time, etc. Output is produced efficiently maximum percentage of time practical (75-85%).	Good guide for competitive pricing; highlights effect of idle capacity
	↓	
Normal volume	ADJUSTED FOR: long-run product demand. Average annual output necessary to meet sales and inventory fluctuations over 4-5 year period.	Based on expected results; stabilizes product costs from year to year
	↓	
Expected annual capacity	ADJUSTED FOR: current year fluctuations. Expected output for current year.	Based on expected results; aids current planning and control; costs product at close to actual costs

Note that theoretical capacity is larger than practical capacity, which is larger than normal volume. Expected annual capacity fluctuates above and below normal volume. Most firms use expected annual capacity which minimizes under or overapplied overhead. Use of normal volume results in more under or overapplied overhead, but these amounts balance out over a multi-year period. Use of practical capacity results in consistently underapplied overhead.

At year end overhead may be:

1) Overapplied--more is applied than incurred (i.e., credit balance in applied account exceeds debit balance in control account) because:

   a) Overhead costs were overestimated
   b) More than expected activity took place, and/or
   c) Actual production costs were less than expected

2) Underapplied--less overhead is applied than incurred (i.e., debit balance in control account exceeds credit balance in applied account) because:

   a) Overhead costs were underestimated
   b) Less than expected activity took place, and/or
   c) Actual production costs were more than expected

E. Disposition of Under and Overapplied Overhead

1) If the under or overapplied overhead is immaterial, it is frequently written off to cost of goods sold on grounds of expediency

Overhead applied (debit for balance)	xx	
Cost of goods sold (debit or credit to balance entry)	xx	
Overhead control (credit for balance)		xx

2) If the balance is material, then an adjustment must be made to all goods which were costed at the erroneous application rate during the current period. The goods with the incorrect costs will be in three accounts: Work-in-Process Inventory, Finished Goods Inventory, and Cost of Goods Sold.

The amount of adjustment to WIP will be calculated as follows:

$$\frac{\text{Overhead applied this period in WIP ending inventory}}{\text{Total overhead applied this period}} \text{ X } \begin{array}{l}\text{under or over-}\\\text{applied overhead}\end{array}$$

Similar calculation will be made for FG and CGS by substituting the overhead applied to these amounts in the numerator above.

The entry, then, to close the overhead accounts when overhead has been underapplied will be as follows:

Cost of goods sold	xx	
Finished goods inventory	xx	
Work-in-process inventory	xx	
Factory overhead applied	xx	
Factory overhead control		xx

The effect of this entry is to close the overhead accounts and to accurately state the cost of the units worked on during the current period.

Another topic often tested on the CPA exam is determining whether a cost is direct material or labor, or an overhead item. In general, if it is feasible to physically trace a production cost to the final product, it is direct. Otherwise, it is an indirect cost included in overhead. The table below shows some specific examples:

Production costs		Nonproduction costs
Direct (prime) costs	*Indirect (overhead) costs*	
Direct materials:	Indirect materials:	Supplies:
Steel	Factory supplies	Office supplies
Lumber	Machine oil	Advertising supplies
Automobile subassemblies		
Direct labor:	Indirect labor:	Payroll:
Machine operator	Factory janitor	Salesmen's salaries
Assembly line worker	Forklift operator	Administrative salaries
	Overtime and fringe benefits	
	Other:	Other:
	Factory depreciation	Warehouse depreciation
	Factory power	Office utilities
	Factory rent	Office rent
	Factory insurance	General insurance

F. Service Department Cost Allocation

A large firm will have several production departments, each of which may compute a separate predetermined overhead rate. A problem arises when a <u>service</u> department (maintenance, receiving, etc.) incurs costs and benefits multiple production departments.

Costs of these service departments must be allocated to production departments because all manufacturing costs must ultimately be traced to products. For example, the costs of the materials-handling cost center may need to be allocated to the production departments (and possibly other service departments). Apportionment of service department costs should be based on meaningful criteria such as:

1) Services provided
2) Services available
3) Benefits received
4) Equity

Examples of apportionment bases are:

1) Area for building costs
2) Usage for electricity

   a. Theoretical or practical capacity for fixed electric costs

3) Employees for cafeteria, personnel, and first aid
4) Usage for materials handling, maintenance, etc.

Service department costs can be allocated by:

1) Direct method
2) Step method

1. Direct Method

The direct method simply allocates the costs of each service department to each of the producing departments based on a relative level of the apportionment base. For example, if a service department had costs of $140,000, and Departments X and Y used 80% and 20% of the apportionment base, X and Y would be assigned $112,000 and $28,000 respectively. Note that the direct method ignores use of services by other service departments. For example, the direct method would ignore the fact that service Department A uses the services of service Department B as noted below.

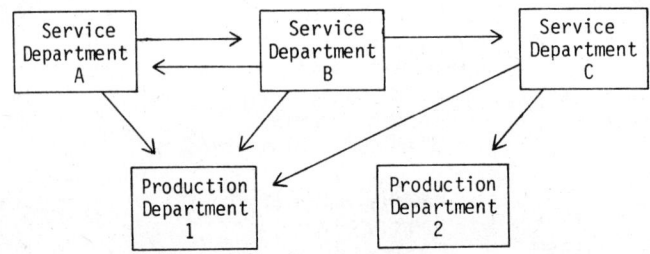

2. Step Method

The step method allocates service department costs to other service departments as well as production departments. The allocation process is:

a. Select the service department serving the most other service departments, e.g., Department B above

   1) When more than one service department services an equal number of service departments, select the department with the highest costs

b. Allocate the costs of the service department selected in "a." to the production departments and other service departments based on a relative level of the apportionment base as in the direct method

c. Costs of service departments are never allocated back to departments whose costs have already been allocated

Note that the step method ignores the fact that reciprocal services are used between some service departments.

> EXAMPLE: Assume that service Department A provides maintenance for the plant. Square footage has been determined to be the most appropriate apportionment base for purposes of allocating Department A costs. Service Department B provides cafeteria services for the plant. Number of employees has been selected as the apportionment base in Department B.

Departments

	Service		Production		
	A	B	1	2	Totals
Costs	$4,000	$6,000	$38,000	$42,000	$90,000
Sq. footage	3,000 ft.	1,000 ft.	4,000 ft.	5,000 ft.	13,000 ft.
No. of employees	300	200	400	300	1,200
Use of A	—	$\frac{1,000}{10,000}$ = 10%[a]	$\frac{4,000}{10,000}$ = 40%	$\frac{5,000}{10,000}$ = 50%	100%
Use of B	$\frac{300}{1,000}$ = 30%	—	$\frac{400}{1,000}$ = 40%	$\frac{300}{1,000}$ = 30%	100%

Direct Method--Allocate A's and B's costs directly to production departments 1 and 2.

	A	B	1	2
Costs prior to allocation	4,000	6,000	38,000	42,000
Allocation of A's costs*	(4,000)		1,778	2,222
Allocation of B's costs**		(6,000)	3,429	2,571
	0	0	43,207	46,793

*   4/9 and 5/9
** 4/7 and 3/7

$90,000

Step Method--Allocate B's costs (B has more costs than A) to Departments A, 1 and 2. Next allocate A's costs to Departments 1 and 2; you cannot allocate A's costs back to B, as B's costs have already been allocated.

	A	B	1	2
Costs prior to allocation	4,000	6,000	38,000	42,000
Allocation of B's costs*	1,800	(6,000)	2,400	1,800
Allocation of A's costs**	(5,800)		2,578	3,222
	0	0	42,978	47,022

*   3/10, 4/10, and 3/10
** 4/9 and 5/9

$90,000

G. Process Costing

Process costing, in contrast to job-order costing, is applicable to a continuous process of production of the same or similar goods, e.g., oil refining and

---

[a]Note that when calculating the usage of A by the departments served, the square footage occupied by Department A is irrelevant. In other words, only square footage occupied by the departments receiving allocations (B, 1, and 2) is considered. Usage of B is calculated similarly, ignoring the number of employees in Department B.

chemical production. Since there is no need to determine the costs of different groups of products because the product is uniform, each processing department becomes a cost center.

Process costing can be broken down into the steps listed below:

1) Visualize the physical flow of units
2) Compute equivalent units of production
3) Determine costs to allocate
4) Compute unit costs
5) Allocate total costs to:

    a. Cost of goods manufactured (completed)
    b. Cost of ending work in process

1. Flow of Units

The cost flow diagram shown under "B." above is the same for process costing except there will typically be several WIP accounts. When solving a process costing problem, it is helpful to visualize the physical flow of units, as illustrated in the diagram below.

Beginning WIP ─────────────▶ Good output and spoilage

Units started ─────────────▶ Ending WIP

Good output and spoilage can include units completed, normal spoilage, and/or abnormal spoilage.

2. Equivalent Units of Production (EUP)

An EUP is the amount of work equivalent to completing one unit from start to finish. In a process costing system, products are assigned costs periodically (usually monthly). At any one moment some units are incomplete which makes the EUP calculations necessary to allocate manufacturing costs between:

1) Goods finished during the period (cost of goods manufactured)
2) Ending work in process

The two primary EUP methods used for process costing are first-in, first-out (FIFO) and weighted-average (WA). In FIFO, beginning WIP is handled separately; equivalent units refer only to the work done in the current period. The weighted-average method "averages" work done last period (on this period's beginning WIP) and the current period's work when computing EUP. The EUP calculations are:

FIFO	WEIGHTED-AVERAGE
Work to complete beg. WIP	All units completed
+ Units started and completed	
+ Work to date on end. WIP	+ Work to date on end. WIP
Equivalent units (FIFO)	Equivalent units (WA)

Note that the FIFO computation includes only what is done this period on the beginning WIP, while the WA computation includes all work done on the beginning WIP. That is the only difference.

3. Simple Process Costing Example

Assume we begin with 800 units 25% complete for labor and overhead, and 100% complete for materials because they are introduced at the start of the process. We start 4,200 units. 4,000 units are completed, while 1,000 remain in ending WIP (20% complete for labor and overhead and 100% complete for materials). The costs are summarized in the following T-account.

Work in process

BWIP				
materials	$900			
labor + OH	840	$ 1,740	Goods finished $???	
Current				
materials	4,200			
labor + OH	14,000	18,200		
EWIP		$???		

First, the physical flow of units is diagrammed:

Beginning WIP	800 ———————	800 ———————→	4,000 Completed	
		3,200		
Started	4,200 ———————	1,000 ———————→	1,000 End WIP	
To Account for	5,000		5,000 Accounted for	

Second, equivalent units are computed. Both FIFO and WA are illustrated.

Materials

FIFO		WA	
Work to complete BWIP	0	Units completed	4,000
Started and completed	3,200		
Work on EWIP (1,000 x 100%)	1,000	Work on EWIP (1,000 x 100%)	1,000
EUP (FIFO)	4,200	EUP (WA)	5,000

Labor and Overhead

FIFO		WA	
Work to complete BWIP			
(800 x 75%)	600	Units completed	4,000
Started and completed	3,200		
Work on EWIP			
(1,000 x 20%)	200	Work on EWIP (1,000 x 20%)	200
EUP (FIFO)	4,000		4,200

The next step is the computation of unit costs. FIFO is basically current costs divided by current work, while WA is all costs divided by all work.

FIFO Current costs EUP (FIFO)			WA All costs EUP (WA)		

Materials:

$$\frac{\$4,200}{4,200} = \quad \$1.00$$

Materials:

$$\frac{\$900 + \$4,200}{5,000} = \quad \$1.02$$

Labor and overhead:

$$\frac{\$14,000}{4,000} = \quad \underline{\$3.50}$$

Labor and overhead:

$$\frac{\$840 + 14,000}{4,200} = \quad \underline{\$3.533}$$

Total $\underline{\$4.50}$ Total $\underline{\$4.553}$

The final step is to allocate total costs to units completed (4,000) and to ending WIP (1,000). Remember, in FIFO, beginning WIP is handled separately.

FIFO

Cost of units completed:
- Cost of BWIP $1,740
- Cost to complete BWIP
  (800 x 75% x $3.50) 2,100
- Cost of units started
  and completed
  (3,200 x $4.50) .... $\underline{14,400}$
                                          $\underline{\$18,240}$

Cost of ending WIP
- Materials
  (1,000 x $1.00) $1,000
- Labor + OH
  (200 x $3.50) .... $\underline{700}$
                                          $\underline{\$1,700}$

WA

Cost of units completed:
4,000 x 4.553 = $\underline{\$18,212}$

Cost of ending WIP
- Materials
  (1,000 x $1.02) $1,020
- Labor + OH
  (200 x $3.533) .... $\underline{707}$
                                          $\underline{\$1,727}$

Now the T-account can be filled in:

WIP (FIFO)	
$1,740	
$18,200	$18,240
$1,700	

WIP (WA)	
$1,740	
$18,200	$18,212
$1,728*	

*$1 adjustment due to rounding.

4. EUP for Material

In the above example, material was assumed to be added at the beginning of the process. Material is often added at different points in the process, e.g., 10%, 70%, or gradually during the process.

5. FIFO Work-in-Process Assumption

Notice that two groups of finished product are transferred out of work in process in the above FIFO example.

1) Product started last period and finished this period
2) Product started and finished this period

In many cases, however, there are multiple processing departments which require the FIFO assumption to be modified. If FIFO were strictly followed, the second processing department would have three groups of finished product.

1) Product started last period and finished this period
2) Product in the first incoming FIFO batch from the prior process
3) Product in the second incoming FIFO batch from the prior process

The third in a series of processing departments might have four groups of finished product priced differently; the fourth department five groups, etc. To overcome this potential bookkeeping nightmare, incoming material from a prior processing department is considered to be one batch (at one average cost).

6. Spoilage and Similar Items

The following terms are commonly used:

1) <u>Spoilage</u> - inferior goods either discarded or sold for disposal value
2) <u>Defective units</u> - inferior goods reworked and sold as normal product
3) <u>Waste</u> - materials lost in the manufacturing process
4) <u>Scrap</u> - material residue which has some salvage value

A major distinction is made between normal and abnormal spoilage.

a. Normal spoilage is the cost of spoiled units which are due to the nature of the manufacturing process, i.e., which occur under efficient operating conditions

1) Normal spoilage is a necessary cost in the production process and is, therefore, a <u>product cost</u>

b. Abnormal spoilage is the cost of spoiled units which were spoiled through some unnecessary act, event, or condition

1) Abnormal spoilage is a <u>period cost</u>, e.g., "loss on abnormal spoilage"
2) Abnormal spoilage costs should not be included in cost of goods sold

When abnormal spoilage occurs and some salvage value exists, the following entry is made:

Loss on abnormal spoilage	(forced)
Spoiled goods	(net realizable value)
Work in process	(costs applicable to the spoiled goods at point of removal)

If no salvage value exists, all of the applicable costs would be charged to the loss account.

If spoilage is normal and consistent, no special entry is needed for the spoilage. Total costs incurred are simply allocated to FG and EWIP, based on relative EUP in FG and EWIP. If the spoilage were not consistent from period to period, unit costs would vary unless spoilage costs were accounted for separately and run through the overhead account when spoilage did occur, e.g.:

Overhead   (cost of spoiled goods)
    EWIP   (same)

Thus, the cost of this spoilage, even though occurring irregularly, would be spread across a whole year's production.

Note, spoilage must be considered in EUP calculations if a separate entry is going to be made to remove spoilage costs (whether normal or abnormal) from the work-in-process account. For example, if spoilage is discovered at the 60% point in processing and 100 units of abnormal spoilage are discovered, 60 EUP have occurred. The amount of abnormal loss would be the cost of 60 EUP (processing) plus the materials added to 100 units of production up to the 60% point. Spoilage would not include the cost of materials added at the 75% point of production.

7. Process Cost Example Problem

The Dan Smith Chicken Factory processes chicken through two departments, the Cleaning Department and the Processing Department. Data relevant to these two departments for 1983 is given below.

Cleaning Department
Material (chicken) is added at the beginning of the process
Labor and overhead (conversion) costs are added continuously
No spoilage takes place in this department
There is no beginning work-in-process inventory. 10,000 units are started in production, 2,000 of which are in process at period-end, 75% complete
Material cost for 1983 = $5,000
DL&MOH → Conversion cost for 1983 = $2,470

Processing Department
Material added (coloring, packaging, etc.) is added at the end of the process
Labor and overhead (conversion) costs are added continuously
Work in process, January 1, 4,000 units; 20% complete
Work in process, December 31, 1,000 units; 60% complete
Units spoiled, considered normal 60 units
Units spoiled, considered abnormal 40 units
Assume spoilage is discovered at the end of the processing department following packaging
Material cost for 1983 = $660
Conversion cost for 1983 = $1,404
Work in process on January 1 has a cost of $4,480 ($3,200 transferred-in cost, $1,280 conversion cost)

a. FIFO Solution

Cleaning Department

Step 1 Visualize the physical flow of units.

Beginning WIP	0	0	8,000 Completed
		8,000	
Started	10,000	2,000	2,000 Ending WIP
To account for	10,000		10,000 Accounted for

Step 2   Calculate EUP.

	Materials	Conversion
Work to complete BWIP	0	0
Started and completed	8,000	8,000
Work to date on EWIP	2,000	1,500 (2,000 x 75%)
EUP (FIFO)	10,000	9,500

Step 3   Determine costs to allocate using a department T-account.

Cleaning Department

BWIP	$ 0	To processing 8,000	$?
Material	5,000	EWIP (2,000 1/2 complete)	?
Conversion costs	2,250		
Costs to allocate	$7,250		

Step 4   Calculate unit costs.

Material	$5,000/10,000	=	$.50 each
Conversion	$2,470/9,500	=	$.26 each
			$.76

Step 5   Allocate costs to finished goods and EWIP (no BWIP to worry about!).

Goods finished 8,000 @ .76		$6,080
EWIP		
2,000 @ $.50	$1,000	
1,500 @ $.26	390	1,390
Costs allocated		$7,470

The cost of production report for the cleaning department appears on page 1014. Note that the five steps in a process cost problem can be memorized using the mnemonic: PECUA (Physical Flow, Equivalent Units of Production, Costs to Allocate, Unit Costs, Allocate Costs).

Processing Department

Step 1   Visualize the physical flow of units.

Beginning WIP	4,000 ──4,000──►11,000	Good output and spoilage
	╱ 7,000 ╱	
Transferred in	8,000 ──1,000──►1,000	Ending WIP
To account for	12,000	12,000 Accounted for

Breakdown of good output and spoilage:

	──►10,900	Good units completed
11,000	──►60	Normal spoilage
	──►40	Abnormal spoilage

Step 2   Calculate EUP.

	Trans-in*	Materials	Conversion
Work to complete BWIP	0	4,000	3,200 (4,000 X 80%)
Started and completed (includes normal spoilage)	6,960[a]	6,960	6,960
Abnormal spoilage	40	40[b]	40
Work to date on EWIP	1,000	0[b]	600 (1,000 X 60%)
EUP (FIFO)	8,000	11,000	10,800

*Note: Units transferred in are treated the same as material added at the beginning of the process.

[a]10,900 completed + 60 normal spoilage - 4,000 BWIP

[b]Since materials are added at the end of the process, when the spoilage is discovered, spoilage has full materials while EWIP has yet to receive materials.

Step 3 Determine costs to allocate using a department T-account.

Processing Department

BWIP 4,000, 20%	Goods finished
From cleaning $3,200	Started last year 4,000 $?
Conversion 1,280 $ 4,480	Started this year 6,960 ?
	(includes normal
From cleaning 8,000 @ $.76 6,080	spoilage of 60)
Material 660	
Conversion 1,404	Abnormal spoilage 40 ?
Costs to allocate $12,624	EWIP (1,000, 60% complete)

Step 4   Calculate unit costs.

Transferred in (from cleaning)	$6,080/ 8,000	=	$.76
Material	$ 660/11,000	=	.06
Conversion	$1,404/10,800	=	.13
Total unit cost			$.95

Step 5   Allocate costs to finished goods, spoilage, and EWIP.

Goods finished

Started last year 4,000	$ 4,480
3,200 conversion EUP @ $.13	416
4,000 units of material @ $.06	240
	$ 5,136

Started this year 6,960		
6,960 @ $.95	6,612	CGM; transferred to finished
(Includes normal spoilage)	$11,748	goods

Spoilage 40 @ $.95	38	recognized as loss

EWIP

Transferred from cleaning			
1,000 @ $.76	$760		
Materials 0 @ $.06	0		
Conversion 600 @ $.13	78	838	remains in WIP account
Costs allocated		$12,624	

The entry to transfer the goods from the Cleaning Department to the Processing Department is

    WIP-Processing $6,080
        WIP-Cleaning $6,080

The cost of production report for the processing department appears on page 1015.

The entry to reflect the transfer out of the processing department and into finished goods will be

    FG $ 11,748
    Loss-Abnormal Spoilage   38
        WIP - Processing $ 11,786

b. Weighted-Average Solution

Cleaning Department

The weighted-average solution for the cleaning department is the same as the FIFO solution because there was no BWIP.

Processing Department

Step 1   Visualize the <u>physical flow</u> of units (same as Step 1 on page 1011).

Step 2   Calculate EUP.

	Trans in	Materials	Conversion
All units completed (includes normal spoilage)	10,960	10,960	10,960
Abnormal spoilage	40	40	40
Work to date on EWIP	1,000	0	600 (1,000 x 60%)
EUP (WA)	12,000	11,000	11,600

Step 3   Determine <u>costs to allocate</u> using a department T-account (same as Step 3 on <u>page 1012</u>).

Step 4   Calculate <u>unit costs.</u>

From cleaning	($3,200 + $6,080)/12,000	= $ .7733
Material	($0 + $660)/11,000	= .0600
Conversion	($1,280 + $1,404)/11,600	= .2314
		$1.0647

Cleaning Department
Costs of Production Report*
For the Year Ended December 31, 1983

Description	Total	Direct Materials	Conversion
Physical units to be accounted for			
Beginning inventory	-0-	-0-	-0-
Units started	10,000		
Units to be accounted for	10,000		
Equivalent units of production			
Transferred out	8,000	8,000	8,000
Ending inventory[a]	2,000	2,000	1,500
Units Accounted for	10,000	10,000	9,500

EQUIVALENT UNITS

Manufacturing costs (current)			
To Account for	$ 7,470	$ 5,000 $\div \underline{}$ =	$ 2,470 $\div \underline{}$ =
Cost per equivalent unit (.76 = .50 + .26)[b]	$ .76	$ .50	$ .26
Allocation of total costs			
Transferred out (8,000 X .76)	$ 6,080	$ 4,000	$ 2,080
Ending work in process (Mtls: 2,000 X .50) (Conv: 1,500 X .26)	$ 1,390	$ 1,000	$ 390
Total Cost Accounted for	$ 7,470	$ 5,000	$ 2,470

(EQUAL; SAME TOTAL)

---

[a]2,000 X percentage of completion
   (mtls., 100%; conversion, 75%)

[b].76 cannot be obtained by dividing $7,470 by equivalent units. It is simply
the sum of the two per unit amounts.

*Note: The production report using weighted-average and FIFO are the same since
there is no beginning inventory in this process.

Processing Department
Costs of Production Report, FIFO Method
For the Year Ended December 31, 1983

Description	Total	Trans. in	Direct Mtls.	Conv.
Physical units to account for				
Beginning inventory	4,000	-0-	4,000	3,200
Transferred in	8,000			
Units to be accounted for	12,000			
Equivalent units of production				
Abnormal spoilage	40	40	40	40
Normal spoilage	60	60	60	60
Completed & transferred out	10,900	6,900[a]	6,900[a]	6,900[a]
Ending work in process:	1,000			
Trans. (1,000 X 100%)		1,000		
Conv. (1,000 X 60%)				600
Units Accounted for	12,000			
Work completed during year				
in equivalent units		8,000	11,000	10,800
Manufacturing costs				
Beginning inventory	$ 4,480			
Current costs	8,144	$6,080 ÷ __ = __	$ 660 ÷ __ = __	$1,404 ÷ __ = __
Total costs to account for	$12,624			
Cost per equivalent unit[b]		$ .76	$ .06	$ .13

Allocation of costs	Total	Trans. In	Direct Mtls.	Conv.
Abnormal spoilage	$ 38.00	$ 30.40	$ 2.40	$ 5.20
(40 X eq. unit costs)				
Units completed				
Beginning WIP	4,480	3,200		1,280
To finish beg. WIP	656		240	416
(Mtls: 4,000 X .06)				
(Conv: 3,200 X .13)[c]				
Started & completed[d]	6,612	5,289.60	417.60	904.80
(6,960 X unit costs)				
Total cost of units				
completed	$11,748.00	$ 8,489.60	$ 657.60	$2,600.80
Ending work in process	838			
(Trans: 1,000 X .76)		760		
(Conv: 600 X .13)				78
Total costs accounted for	$12,624.00	$ 9,280.00	$ 660.00	$2,684.00

---

[a]Started and completed this period (10,900 completed less 4,000 BWIP).

[b]Current costs ÷ current period equivalent units.

[c]Beginning work in process was 20% complete. 80% of processing is added this period or 3,200 equivalent units X equivalent unit costs.

[d]Units started and completed includes normal spoilage of 60 units.

Processing Department
Costs of Production Report, Weighted-Average Method
For the Year Ended December 31, 1983

Description	Total	Trans. in	Direct Mtls.	Conv.
Physical units to account for				
Beginning inventory	4,000	4,000	4,000	4,000
Transferred in	8,000			
Units to be accounted for	12,000			
Equivalent units of production				
Abnormal spoilage	40	40	40	40
Normal spoilage	60	60	60	60
Completed & transferred out	10,900	6,900[a]	6,900[a]	6,900[a]
Ending work in process:	1,000			
Trans. (1,000 X 100%)		1,000		
Conv. (1,000 X 60%)				600
Total work done in equivalent units	12,000	12,000	11,000	11,600
Manufacturing costs				
Beginning inventory	$ 4,480	$ 3,200	$	$ 1,280
Current costs	8,144	6,080	660	1,404
Total costs	$12,624	$ 9,280	$ 660	$ 2,684
Cost per equivalent unit	$ 1.0647	$ .7733	$ .06	$ .2314

Allocation of costs	Total	Trans. in	Direct Mtls.	Conv.
Abnormal spoilage (40 X eq. unit costs)	$ 42.59	$ 30.93	$ 2.40	$ 9.26
Units completed[b] (10,960 X unit costs)	11,669.11	8,475.37	657.60	2,536.14
Ending work in process: (Trans. 1,000 X .7733) (Conv. 600 X .2314)	912.14	773.30		138.84
Total costs	$12,623.84*	$ 9,279.60	$ 660.00	$ 2,684.24

[a]Started and completed this period (10,900 completed less 4,000 BWIP).

[b]Units completed (10,960) includes normal spoilage of 60 units.

*Difference ($.16) due to rounding.

Step 5   Allocate costs to finished goods, spoilage, and EWIP.

Goods finished	(10,960 @ 1.0647)		$11,669 (Rounded)
Spoilage	(40 @ 1.0647)		43
EWIP			
From cleaning 1,000 @ .7733		773	
Conversion 600 @ .2314		139	912
Costs allocated			$12,624

Weighted-average resulted in more costs remaining in EWIP, because BWIP costs were much greater than the current period costs.

The cost of production report for the processing department appears on page 1016.

H. Joint Products

Joint products are two or more products produced together up to a split-off point where they become separately identifiable. They cannot be produced by themselves. For example, a steak cannot be produced by itself. Roasts, ribs, liver, hamburger, etc. are produced with steak. Other industries which produce joint products include:

1) Chemicals   3) Mining
2) Lumber   4) Petroleum

Joint products are said to have common, or joint costs until the split-off point. The split-off point is the point of production when the joint products can be individually identified and removed from the joint, or common process, i.e., they can be sold, processed further in alternative ways, etc. Costs incurred after the split-off point for any one of the joint products are called separable costs.

Common costs are allocated to the joint products at the split-off point, usually on the basis of sales value at the split-off point, hypothetical sales value after further processing, or some physical measure. The following example illustrates the sales value at split-off and hypothetical sales value after further processing methods. The sales value at split-off method must be used if a value at split-off exists.

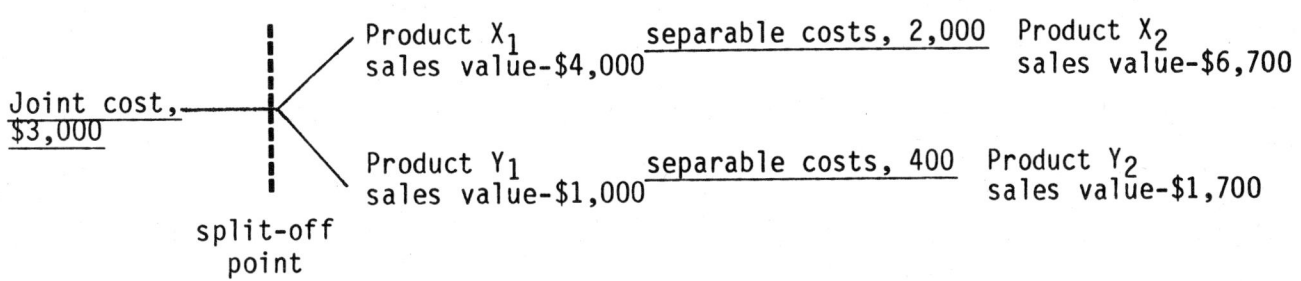

Joint cost, $3,000 — split-off point

Product X₁ sales value-$4,000 → separable costs, 2,000 → Product X₂ sales value-$6,700

Product Y₁ sales value-$1,000 → separable costs, 400 → Product Y₂ sales value-$1,700

Sales Value at Split-off

Product	Sales Value @ Split	Ratio	X	Joint Costs	=	Allocated Joint Costs
X_1	$4,000	$\dfrac{\$4,000}{\$5,000}$	X	$3,000	=	$2,400
Y_1	$1,000	$\dfrac{\$1,000}{\$5,000}$	X	$3,000	=	$ 600
Total	$5,000					$3,000

If the sales value at split-off were not available or one did not exist, we must use the hypothetical sales value after further processing method:

Hypothetical Sales Value After Further Processing

Product	Final Sales Value	-	Separable Costs	=	Hypothetical Sales Value	Ratio	X	Joint Costs	=	Allocated Joint Costs
X_2	$6,700	-	$2,000	=	$4,700	$\dfrac{\$4,700}{\$6,000}$	X	$3,000	=	$2,350
Y_2	$1,700	-	$ 400	=	$1,300	$\dfrac{\$1,300}{\$6,000}$	X	$3,000	=	$ 650
Total					$6,000					$3,000

Physical measures (units, pounds, etc.) generally are not used because of the misleading income statement effect. With an allocation based on pounds, steak would show a big profit while ground beef would be a consistent loser.

Joint cost allocation is performed for the purpose of inventory valuation and income determination. However, joint costs should be ignored for any internal decisions including the decision on whether to process a joint product further beyond the split-off point. The sell or process further decision should be based on incremental revenues and costs. If incremental revenue from further processing exceeds incremental costs, then process further. If incremental costs exceed incremental revenues, then sell without further processing. In the previous example both X_1 and Y_1 should be further processed.

Incremental revenue		-	Incremental cost	=	Advantage of Further Processing
X_1: $6,700 - $4,000 =	$2,700	-	$2,000	=	$700
Y_1: $1,700 - $1,000 =	$ 700	-	$ 400	=	$300

If X_1 could have sold for only \$5,500 after further processing, the incremental revenue (\$1,500) would not cover the incremental cost (\$2,000), and X_1 should not be further processed.

I. By-Products

By-products, in contrast to joint products, have little market value relative to the overall value of the product(s) being produced. Joint costs should never be allocated to a by-product. Instead, they should be valued at market or net realizable value and accounted for as a contra production cost.

By-product inventory	(Market value)
Work in process	(Same)

Rather than recognizing by-product market value as a reduction of production cost, it is sometimes recognized when sold and disclosed as:

1) Ordinary sales
2) Other income
3) Contra to cost of sales

PLANNING, CONTROL,
AND ANALYSIS

This module discusses a number of tools used internally for financial planning, control, and analysis. Included are the high-low method, CVP analysis, budgeting and flexible budgeting, direct (variable) and absorption (full) costing, product pricing, and responsibility accounting.

A. High-Low Method

Many of the tools discussed later require the separation of costs into their fixed and variable components (refer to the definitions of fixed, variable, and mixed costs under "Basic Cost Accounting Terminology" beginning on the second page of this chapter). One way of doing this is using the high-low method. This method is illustrated using the following observations for factory overhead costs (DLH = direct labor hours):

			Cost	
Month	DLH	Factory Rent	Factory Supplies	Maintenance
1	40,000	$50,000	$ 60,000	$115,000
2	45,000	50,000	67,500	110,000 (low)
3	76,000	50,000	114,000	158,000
4	60,000	50,000	90,000	135,000
5	75,000	50,000	112,500	170,000 (high)
6	75,000	50,000	112,500	145,000

When using the high-low method, you choose the highest <u>cost</u> observation and the lowest <u>cost</u> observation (<u>not</u> the high and low activity observations) from several recent periods. The difference in cost is divided by the difference in activity to obtain the variable cost. The fixed cost can then be computed at either the high or low level (same either way).

Application of the high-low method to segregate the mixed cost (maintenance) into its variable and fixed elements is illustrated below.

Cost item	Variable Rate Computation	Fixed Rate Computation
Maintenance	$\frac{\$170,000 - \$110,000}{75,000 - 45,000} = \underline{\$2/DLH}$	$\$170,000 - (75,000 \times \$2) = \underline{\$20,000}$ or $\$110,000 - (45,000 \times \$2) = \underline{\$20,000}$

Note that in the example above, factory rent is a fixed cost ($50,000 per month) while factory supplies is a variable cost ($60,000 ÷ 40,000 DLH = $1.50 per DLH each month).

While the high-low method is a rather crude technique compared to regression analysis, it is used often on the CPA Exam. More sophisticated techniques (such as regression analysis) are discussed in Module 38, "A.3."

B. Cost-Volume-Profit (CVP) Analysis

   Breakeven (CVP) analysis provides management with profitability estimates at all
levels of production in the relevant range (the normal operating range). Breakeven
or CVP analysis is based on the firm's profit function. Profit is a function of
sales, variable costs, and fixed costs.

Profit (NI) = Sales (S) - Fixed Costs (FC) - Variable Costs (VC)

When profit is zero   0 = S - FC - VC

S = FC + VC

Fixed costs are constant in the relevant range, but both sales and variable costs
are a function of the level of activity, i.e., production and sales. For example,
if widgets are sold at $2.00/unit, variable costs are $.40/unit, and fixed costs are
$20,000, breakeven is 12,500 units.

```
        X = units of production and sales to breakeven
  $2.00X = $.40X + $20,000
  $1.60X = $20,000
        X =  12,500 units (breakeven point)
```

   The cost-volume-profit relationship is diagrammed below.

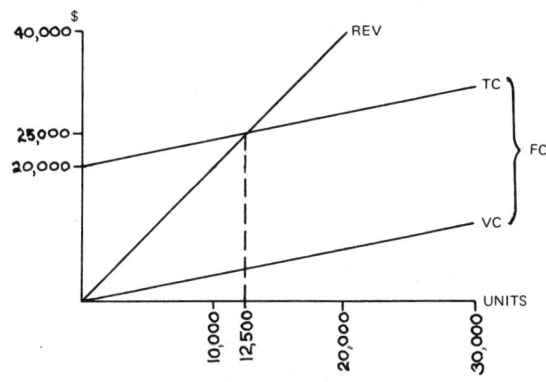

The breakeven point can be thought of as the amount of contribution margin (sales
minus variable costs) required to cover the fixed costs. In the previous example,
the unit contribution margin (CM) is $1.60 ($2.00-$.40). Thus, sales of 12,500
units are required to cover the $20,000 of fixed costs. This illustrates the
possibility of two shortcut approaches.

Shortcut 1

Units to breakeven = $\dfrac{\text{Fixed costs}}{\text{Unit CM}}$ = $\dfrac{\$20,000}{\$1.60}$ = 12,500 units

Shortcut 2

Dollars to breakeven =

$$\frac{\text{Fixed costs}}{\text{CM percentage}} = \frac{\text{Fixed costs}}{\dfrac{\text{CM per unit}}{\dfrac{\text{Selling price}}{\text{per unit}}}} = \frac{\$20,000}{\dfrac{\$1.60}{\$2.00}} = \frac{\$20,000}{80\%} = \underline{\$25,000 \text{ sales dollars}}$$

A number of variations on the basic CVP calculation are found on the CPA Exam. These are illustrated in the following paragraphs.

1. Target net income. Selling price is $2, variable cost per unit is $.40, fixed costs are $20,000, and desired net income is $5,000. What is the level of sales in units?

Equation→   Sales = VC + FC + NI
            $2X = $.4X + $20,000 + $5,000

Shortcut→ $\dfrac{FC + NI}{CM} = \dfrac{\$20,000 + \$5,000}{\$1.60}$

Solution→   <u>15,625 units</u>

2. Target net income-percentage of sales. Same facts, except desired net income is 30% of sales. What is the level of sales in units?

Equation→   Sales = VC + FC + NI
            $2X = $.4X + $20,000 + .30($2X)

Solution→   <u>20,000 units</u>

3. No per unit information given. Fixed costs are $20,000, and variable expenses are 20% of sales. What is the level of sales in dollars?

Equation→   Sales = VC + FC
            S = .2(S) + $20,000

Shortcut→ $\dfrac{FC}{CM\%} = \dfrac{20,000}{.8}$

Solution→   <u>$25,000 sales dollars</u>

4. Decision making. Selling price is $2, variable cost per unit is $.40, and fixed costs are $20,000. Purchasing a new machine will increase fixed costs by $5,000, but variable costs will be cut by 20%. If the selling price is cut by 10%, what is the breakeven point in units?

Equation→   Sales = VC + FC
            $1.8X = $.32X + $25,000

Shortcut→ $\dfrac{FC}{CM} = \dfrac{\$25,000}{\$1.48}$

Solution→   <u>16,892 units</u>

C. Breakeven: Multi-Product Firm

If a firm makes more than one product, it is necessary to use "composite" units to find the number of units of each product to breakeven. A "composite" unit consists of the proportionate number of units which make up the firm's sales mix. For example, assume that a firm has two products with the following selling prices and variable costs.

Product	Selling Price	Variable Costs	Contribution Margin
A	$.60	$.20	$.40
B	$.40	$.15	$.25

The sales mix consists of 3 units of A for every 2 units of B (3:2) and fixed costs are $34,000.

The first step is to find the "composite" contribution margin.

Composite contribution margin = 3($.40) + 2($.25) = $1.70

Next compute the number of composite units to breakeven.

$$\frac{\$34,000 \text{ fixed costs}}{\$1.70 \text{ composite contribution margin}} = \underline{20,000} \text{ composite units}$$

Finally, determine the number of units of A and B at the breakeven point by multiplying the composite units by the number of units of A(3) and the number of units of B(2) in the mix.

A: 20,000 x 3 = 60,000 units

B: 20,000 x 2 = 40,000 units

D. Assumptions of CVP Analysis

When applying CVP to a specific case and in interpreting the results therefrom, it is important to keep in mind the assumptions underlying CVP which are listed below.

1) Selling price does not change with the activity level
2) The sales mix remains constant
3) Costs can be separated into fixed and variable elements
4) Variable costs per unit are constant
5) Total fixed costs are constant over the relevant range
6) Material, labor, and overhead prices are unchanged
7) Productivity and efficiency are constant
8) Volume is the only factor which causes changes in cost
9) Activity will be in the relevant range where all assumptions are valid
10) Units produced = units sold

E. Budgeting

Budgeting is a plan of action for future operations. The most important functions of a budget are to coordinate the various functional activities of the firm and to provide a basis for control of the activities. The budget process begins with an estimate of sales and then proceeds systematically as outlined below.

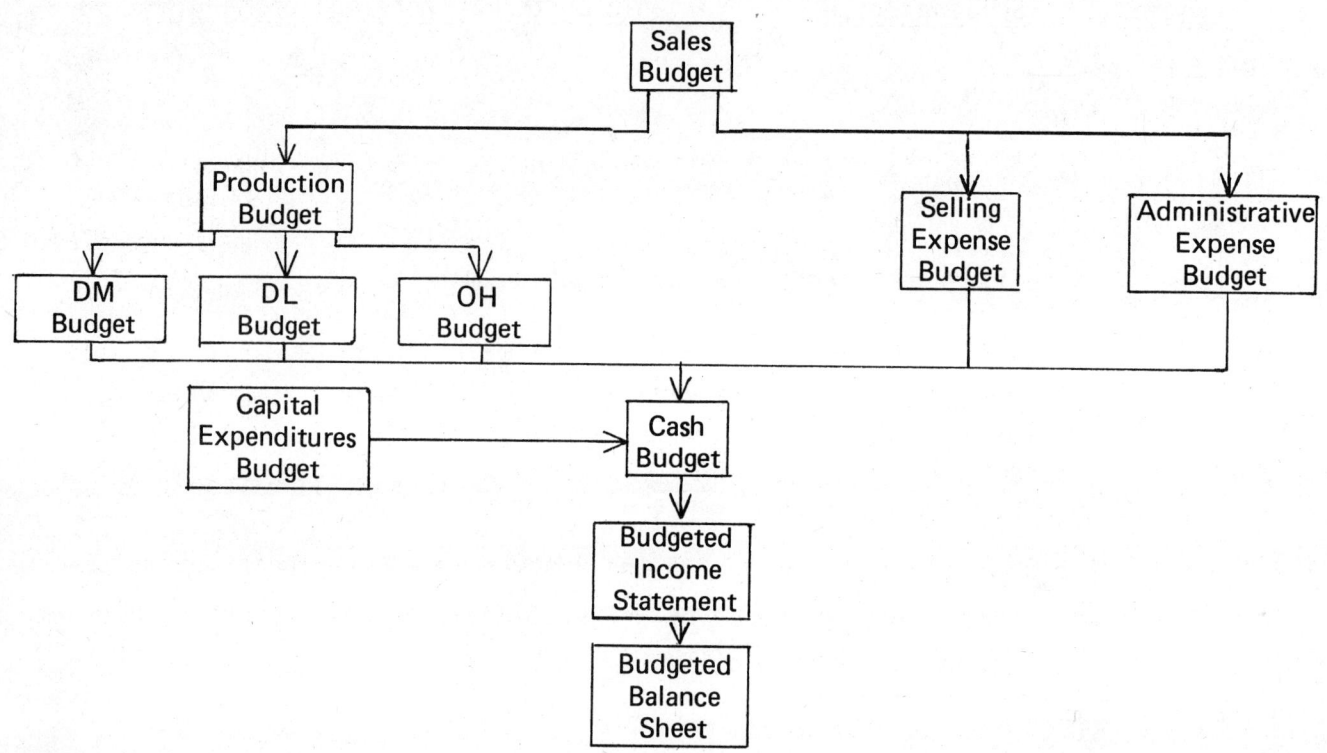

The basic formats of some of the key budgets are presented below.

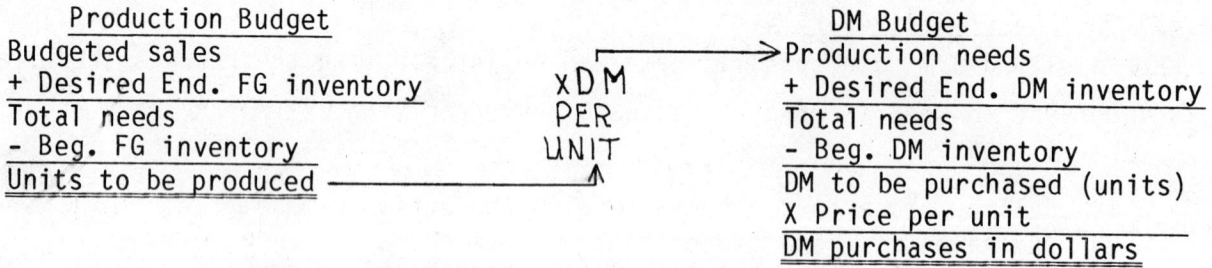

Note that before proceeding to the cash budget, DM purchases would have to be converted to payments for DM purchases, based on some payment schedule (e.g., 70% in month of purchase, 30% in month following).

<u>Cash Budget</u>
Beginning cash balance
+ <u>Receipts</u> (collections from customers, etc.)
Cash available
- <u>Payments</u> (materials, expenses, payroll, etc.)
Estimated cash balance before financing
± <u>Financing</u> (planned borrowing or short-term investing to bring cash to
                desired balance)
<u>Ending cash balance</u>

F. Flexible Budgets

A flexible budget is a budget adjusted for changes in volume. In the planning phase, a flexible budget is used to compare the effects of various activity levels on costs and revenues. In the controlling phase, the flexible budget is used to help analyze actual results by comparing actual results with a flexible budget for the level of activity achieved in the period (see Module 36, Standards and Variances).

Presented below is a sample flexible budget for overhead costs.

Factory Overhead
Flexible Budget

Direct labor hours	<u>18,000</u>	<u>20,000</u>	<u>22,000</u>
Variable factory overhead			
Supplies	$ 18,000	$ 20,000	$ 22,000
Power	99,000	110,000	121,000
Idle time	3,600	4,000	4,400
Overtime premium	1,800	2,000	2,200
Total ($6.80 per DLH)	$122,400	$136,000	$149,600
Fixed factory overhead			
Supervision	$ 15,000	$ 15,000	$ 15,000
Depreciation	32,000	32,000	32,000
Power	8,000	8,000	8,000
Property taxes	5,000	5,000	5,000
Insurance	1,500	1,500	1,500
Total	$ 61,500	$ 61,500	$ 61,500
Total overhead	$183,900	$197,500	$211,100

G. Direct (Variable) and Absorption (Full) Costing

Direct (variable) costing is a form of relevant costing. Direct costing considers fixed manufacturing costs as period rather than product costs. It is advocated because, in the short run, fixed costs are sunk costs and should be disregarded. Therefore, only variable manufacturing costs are inventoried. Direct costing is not acceptable as GAAP for external reporting, however.

Direct and absorption costing methods of accounting for fixed manufacturing overhead result in different levels of net income in most cases. The differences are timing differences, i.e., when to recognize the fixed manufacturing overhead as an expense.

1) In the period incurred--direct costing
2) In the period in which the units to which fixed overhead has been related are sold--absorption costing

The relationship between direct costing (DC) and absorption costing (AC) follows.

Sales = Production (no change in inventory)   No difference
Sales > Production (inventory decreases)   DC income greater than AC income
Sales < Production (inventory increases)   DC income less than AC income

EXAMPLE of direct costing: Production begins in period A with 5,000 units. Fixed manufacturing costs equal $5,000 and variable manufacturing costs are $1/unit. Sales were 4,000 units at $3/unit. In period B, production units and costs were the same as in period A. Sales were 6,000 units at $3/unit.

| | Direct costing | | Absorption costing | |
	Period A	Period B	Period A	Period B
Sales	$12,000	$18,000	$12,000	$18,000
Less costs	9,000	11,000	8,000	12,000
Profit	$ 3,000	$ 7,000	$ 4,000	$ 6,000

(a) $\dfrac{\$5,000 \text{ Fixed costs}}{5,000 \text{ Units}}$ X (1,000 Units E.I. - 0 Units B.I.)

(b) $\dfrac{\$5,000 \text{ Fixed costs}}{5,000 \text{ Units}}$ X (0 Units E.I. - 1,000 Units B.I.)

Both direct and absorption costing recognized $10,000 profit in periods A + B. Direct costing income in period A was less than absorption income, because production exceeded sales resulting in $1,000 of fixed costs being inventoried under AC that were expensed under DC.

| | Fixed | | Variable | | Total | |
	Period A	Period B	Period A	Period B	Period A	Period B
Direct	$5,000 *	$5,000*	$4,000	$6,000	$9,000	$11,000
Absorption	4,000	6,000	4,000	6,000	$8,000	12,000

*The same every period.

If the example included either variable or fixed selling costs, they would be deducted in total in the period in which they were incurred on both the direct and the absorption costing income statements. The format of the income statement changes under direct costing to reflect the alternate treatment given the fixed manufacturing costs and to emphasize contribution margin. The recommended format under direct costing follows:

Sales
- variable manufacturing costs
= manufacturing contribution margin
- variable selling and administrative expenses
= contribution margin
- fixed manufacturing, selling, and administrative expenses
= net income

Absorption costing can lead to two categories of errors in managerial decision making.

1) Absorption costing overstates the short-run costs of production by including fixed costs (the short-run costs of production may consist of only variable costs). Thus, management may choose not to produce when they should.

2) On the other hand, absorption costing defers fixed costs of production which decreases losses or increases income in periods when production exceeds sales. The result is that management may wish to produce at full capacity when demand is less than capacity to maximize absorption costing income. Remember, only absorption costing is acceptable GAAP.

In summary, variable costs are the only relevant costs in the short run.

H. Contribution Margin

The direct costing income statement shown above can be broken into further detail to emphasize controllability.

1) Variable manufacturing costs are deducted from sales to obtain manufacturing contribution margin.

2) Variable selling and administrative expenses are deducted from manufacturing contribution margin to obtain contribution margin.

3) Controllable fixed costs of various levels, e.g., division, department, etc., are deducted from contribution margin to obtain the segment contribution at that level.

4) Costs common to all operations are finally deducted to obtain income before taxes.

Example Contribution Approach Income Statement

	Total	Segment 1	Segment 2
Sales	$600	$350	$250
- Variable manufacturing costs	220	115	105
Manufacturing contribution margin	380	235	145
- Variable selling and admin. exp.	100	70	30
Contribution margin	280	165	115
- Controllable fixed costs	80	35	45
Controllable contribution	200	130	70
- Uncontrollable fixed costs	90	60	30
Segment contribution	110	$ 70	$ 40
- Unallocable costs	60*		
Income before taxes	$ 50		

*Not allocated to any segment of the firm. Examples include corporate office salaries and advertising for firm name.

If costs are not controllable by a subdivision (cost or profit center) of a firm, costs should not be allocated to the subdivision for evaluation or decision-making purposes (see Responsibility Accounting later in this module).

Contribution margin data can be used in a variety of situations, including:

1) Determination of which products to emphasize (see also Scarce Resources in Module 37)
2) Determination of which products should be retained and which should be eliminated (see also Nonroutine Decisions in Module 37)
3) Evaluation of mutually exclusive alternatives such as special orders, sales promotion plans, etc. (see also Nonroutine Decisions in Module 37)
4) Determination of sales level necessary to achieve desired profit (see CVP Analysis above)
5) Establishment of product prices (see also Product Pricing later in this module)
6) Evaluation of the effects of changes in revenues, costs and volume upon profit (see CVP Analysis above)
7) Understanding of the basic profit relationships of the firm (see CVP Analysis above)

I. Product Pricing

Product pricing requires the use of judgment by the cost accountant and the manager in order to maximize the entity's profits and increase shareholders' wealth. In order to find the combination of sales price and volume yielding the greatest profits, management needs to make many assumptions regarding customer preferences, competitors' reactions, economic conditions, cost structures, etc. Additionally, management must also look at their cost of capital in determining a desired rate of return. This rate of return will represent the desired minimum markup on the cost of goods. This concept is useful in that it recognizes the cost of funds; however, it ignores the complexity of pricing and the effect of changing prices on the amount of capital employed.

In maximizing shareholders' wealth, management must consider not only product costs but must also react to external changes, e.g., a competitor's price on a relatively undifferentiated product. However, costs usually are the starting point in determining prices. In the long-run, all costs, including fixed costs, must be considered. However, decisions involving short-range pricing, such as a special order, may be evaluated on the basis of contribution margin. The contribution margin approach considers all relevant variable costs plus any additional fixed costs needed for the new production level. (Other fixed costs are included in the costs of existing long-range products.)

Cost-plus pricing is a starting point for the pricing decision; prices are set at variable costs plus a percentage markup, or at full manufacturing cost plus a percentage markup. The percentage markup must cover fixed costs and profit (variable approach), or operating expenses and a profit (full cost approach). Consider the following example.

Annual sales--10,000 units

Manufacturing costs		Operating costs	
Fixed	$20,000	Fixed	$10,000
Variable	$3/unit	Variable	$2.50/unit

If price is set at variable cost plus 60% ($5.50 x 160%), or full manufacturing cost plus 76% ($5.00 x 176%), the selling price would be $8.80.

Finally, the use of "standard costs" that are attainable eliminates the effect of unusual efficiency/inefficiency on price. Implementing standard costs can also reduce clerical time and speed up the availability of cost figures for the pricing decision.

J. Responsibility Accounting

Responsibility accounting allocates those revenues and/or assets to responsibility centers which the manager of the responsibility center can control. If a manager is only responsible for costs, the area of responsibility under his/her control is called a cost center. Cost centers represent the most basic activities or responsibilities. Both production and service departments are cost centers representing activities and responsibilities (even though there may be more basic cost centers within production and service departments). The objective of responsibility accounting is to use cost data to evaluate those deemed responsible for the activities and/or decisions of a given cost center.

If the manager is responsible for both revenues and costs, the area of responsibility under his/her control is called a profit center. A contribution income statement similar to the one in the beginning of this module would be prepared for each profit center. Finally, if the manager is responsible for revenues, costs, and investment, the area of responsibility under his/her control is called an investment center.

K. Transfer Pricing

Decentralization of profit or investment centers requires pricing policies for transfers of goods or services between those profit centers. Basically, there are three transfer pricing alternatives: variable cost, full cost, and market price.

A transfer price based on <u>variable cost</u> is viable only when no external market exists for the product or there is idle capacity within the transferring division, because the opportunity cost is equal to zero.

A transfer price based on <u>full cost</u> includes the transferring division s fixed costs. A major problem with full cost transfer pricing is that a division charging full cost is not motivated to control costs. Therefore, a recipient division would be forced to absorb the inefficiencies of the transferring division. Because of this, the use of full cost for transfer pricing could lead to poor motivation and dysfunctional decision making.

A transfer price based on <u>market price</u> is justified if a competitive market exists for the product. However, if any costs can be avoided by selling internally, then the market transfer price should be reduced by these cost savings. A variation of market price is negotiated market in which the two divisions negotiate a transfer price with market price as the ceiling and variable cost as the floor.

Generally, in setting a transfer price, outlay[*] cost (cash outflows that are directly related to the production and transfer of goods or services) plus opportunity cost to the overall company should determine the transfer price.

> EXAMPLE: *Able Division of Cooke Company produces a machine part, 20% of which are sold to Base Division of Cooke Company and the remainder to outside customers. Corporate policy requires that all interdivisional sales and purchases be recorded at variable cost as a transfer price. Able Division's estimated sales and standard cost data for the year ending December 31, 19X1, based on full capacity of 100,000 units, are as follows:*

	Base	Outsiders
Sales	$ 800,000	$7,200,000
Variable costs	(800,000)	(3,200,000)
Fixed costs	(300,000)	(1,200,000)
Gross Margin	$(300,000)	$2,800,000
Unit Sales	20,000	80,000

> *Able has an opportunity to sell the above 20,000 units to an outside customer at a price of $70 per unit during 19X1 on a continuing basis. Base could purchase its requirements from an outside supplier at a price of $80 per unit.*

> *Note, when Cooke Company required variable costs to control the transfer price, Able Division would not want to transfer the machine part internally, since Able sustains a loss on the transfer. However, if Able were permitted to sell the 20,000 units to the outside customer, thereby forcing Base to purchase its requirements from an outsider, Cooke Company's overall income would decrease as shown on the following page.*

---

[*]Charles T. Horngren, <u>Cost Accounting: A Managerial Emphasis</u>, Fifth Edition (Englewood Cliffs, New Jersey: Prentice-Hall, Inc., 1982), p. 637.

Increase in revenue to Able ($70-$40)	*$ 30*
Increase in cost to Base ($80-$40)	*40*
Per unit effect	*$-10*
Units affected	*x 20,000*
Decrease in profit	*($200,000)*

Application of the transfer pricing formula that uses the outlay cost plus opportunity cost to the company as a whole is shown below.

Outlay cost (variable cost in this example)	*$40*
+ Opportunity cost (contribution sacrificed by not selling to outsider)	*30*
	$ 70

A transfer price of $70 would not change the overall income of Cooke Company; Able's gross margin would increase by $600,000 [20,000 units ($70-$40)] and Base's would decrease by the same amount. Note that if idle capacity existed the transfer price would be $40 [($40 outlay cost) + (-0- opportunity cost)].

L. Performance Analysis

As entities become more decentralized, it becomes necessary to evaluate each department or division in terms of profitability. The most popular measure for analyzing the profitability of a division is <u>return on investment</u> (ROI). ROI measures the relationship between a division's profit and the capital invested in the division.

$$\text{ROI} = \frac{\text{Net Income of Division}}{\text{Sales of Division}} \times \frac{\text{Sales of Division}}{\text{Total Assets of Division}}$$

$$= \frac{\text{Net Income of Division}}{\text{Total Assets of Division}}$$

A division may improve ROI by lowering its asset base while keeping income and sales constant, lowering expenses while keeping sales and assets constant or, increasing sales while keeping assets and net profit as a proportion of sales constant. Although ROI is quite popular as a performance evaluation measure, it can, at times, motivate a manager to reject a project which is profitable from the entire company's point of view, because it may lower the division's ROI and thus adversely affect the manager's performance evaluation.

EXAMPLE: Borke Company's cost of capital is 10%. One of Borke Company's division managers has the opportunity of investing in a project that will generate $45,000 of net income per year for eight years on an initial investment of $300,000. The division's current income is $250,000 from a total divisional asset base of $1,000,000. The manager should accept the project since it offers a 15% return and the company's cost of capital is 10%. Chances are the manager will reject the project since it will lower the division current ROI from:

$$\frac{250,000}{1,000,000} = 25\% \text{ to } \frac{250,000 + 45,000}{1,000,000 + 300,000} = 22.7\%$$

In this case the use of ROI has led to an incorrect decision.

An alternative method for evaluating divisional performance is the <u>residual income method</u>. Residual income is the net income of a division less the cost of capital on the division's assets. The division's residual income before the project would be $250,000 - (.10 x $1,000,000) = $150,000. Under the residual income approach a manager would be evaluated on how well s/he maximizes dollars of residual income instead of maximizing a profit percentage. Using the example above, the manager would have accepted the project under consideration since it would raise his/her residual income by [$45,000 - (.10 x $300,000)] = $15,000 per year.

STANDARDS AND VARIANCES

Standard costs are predetermined target costs which should be attainable under efficient conditions. The tightness, or attainment difficulty, of standard costs should be determined by the principles of motivation (e.g., excessively tight standards may result in employees feeling the standards are impossible to achieve; consequently, they may ignore the standards). Standard costs are used to aid in the budget process, pinpoint trouble areas, and evaluate performance. Standard costing will often result in lower bookkeeping costs than actual costing, because standard costing does not require actual department costs to be allocated to each unit produced in that department.

The tightness of standards are generally described by one of two terms. Ideal standards reflect the absolute minimum costs which could be achieved under perfect operating conditions. Currently attainable standards should be achieved under efficient operating conditions. Generally, currently attainable standards are set so they will be difficult, but not impossible, to achieve. Currently attainable standards are most often used since they are more realistic for budgeting purposes and are a better motivational tool than ideal standards.

Variances are differences between actual and standard costs. The total variance is generally broken down into subvariances to further pinpoint the causes of the variance.

A. Variance Analysis

In calculating the variances for direct material and direct labor the following symbols will be employed as defined.

AP: Actual price paid per unit of input, e.g., price per foot of lumber, per hour of labor, per ton of steel, etc.
SP: Standard price per unit of input
AQ: The actual quantity of input (feet, hours, tons, etc.) used in production
SQ: The standard quantity of input that should have been used for the good units produced

Variances can be computed using either the diagram approach (facilitates understanding), or the equation approach (quicker problem solving). Both approaches are discussed below.

B. Material Variances

The diagram for computing material variances is

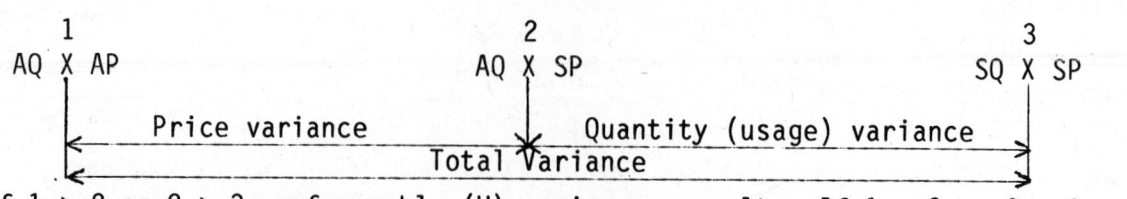

If 1 > 2 or 2 > 3, unfavorable (U) variances result. If 1 < 2 or 2 < 3, a favorable (F) variance is the result. The equation approach is:

    Price variance = (AP - SP) X AQ
    Quantity variance = (AQ - SQ) X SP

The only alternative allowed on the variances above concerns the material price variance. The price variance can be recognized when material is placed in production (as assumed in the previous discussion) or when material is purchased (which is desirable for early identification and control). If the price variance is to be recognized at the time of purchase, AQ (for the price variance _only_) becomes quantity _purchased_ rather than quantity _used_.

The materials price variance is generally considered to be the responsibility of the purchasing department, while the materials quantity variance is the responsibility of the production department.

C. Labor Variances

The computational form of the labor variances is similar to the calculation of material variances -- all that changes is that the price being used changes from price per pound of material to price per hour of labor, and the quantity changes from pounds, yards, etc., to hours. Therefore, the diagrams and equations are the same, although the terminology differs.

Material variance   Labor variance

    Price ─────────────────────────>   Rate
    Quantity ───────────────────────>   Efficiency

Labor rate and efficiency variances are usually the responsibility of the production department.

D. Overhead Variances

Overhead variances can be computed at different levels of sophistication. These levels are called 2-way, and 3-way analysis. Overhead variance analysis can be performed on a combined basis (more frequently seen on the CPA exam), or separately on fixed and variable overhead.

E. Overhead Analysis: 2-way

   2-way analysis provides more information as to why overhead was under or over-applied by bringing the flexible budget into consideration.

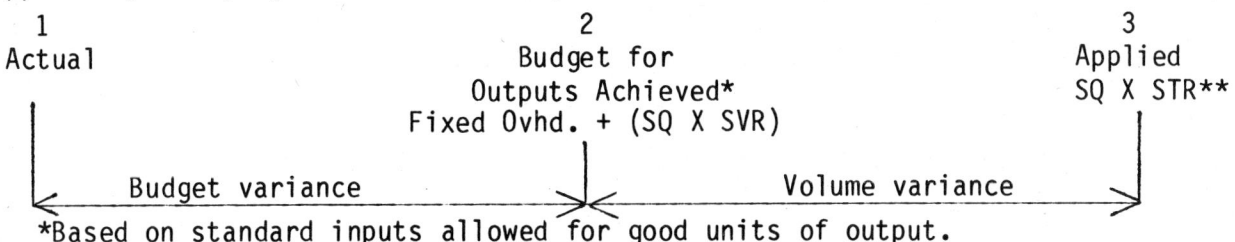

1
Actual

2
Budget for
Outputs Achieved*
Fixed Ovhd. + (SQ X SVR)

3
Applied
SQ X STR**

Budget variance

Volume variance

   *Based on standard inputs allowed for good units of output.

   **Standard total rate (STR) = standard variable rate (SVR) + standard fixed rate (SFR).

Again, if 1 > 2 or 2 > 3, the variances are unfavorable (U); if 1 < 2 or 2 < 3, the variances are favorable (F). When the overhead rate is based on direct labor hours, item 2 is simply the budgeted overhead based on <u>standard</u> direct labor hours (fixed cost, plus standard hours X standard variable rate). It is important to note that the standard variable rate for overhead is the variable rate computed for the flexible budget (by the high-low method, regression analysis, etc.). See the first page of Module 35, PLAN.

   The budget variance (also called the flexible-budget or controllable variance) arises when the amount spent on both fixed and variable overhead differs from the amount budgeted for the output achieved.

   The volume variance (also called the noncontrollable, activity, capacity, or de-nominator variance) is solely a <u>fixed</u> overhead variance. It is caused by under or over utilization of capacity. If actual output is less than (more than) denominator activity, an unfavorable (favorable) volume variance results. A shortcut for com-puting the volume variance is:

$$\left(\begin{array}{c} \text{Standard Fixed} \\ \text{Overhead Rate} \end{array}\right) \text{X} \left(\begin{array}{c} \text{Denominator} \\ \text{Volume} \end{array} - \begin{array}{c} \text{Standard Volume} \\ \text{for Output} \end{array}\right)$$

The denominator volume in the above formula would be the activity level (See Module 34, Section "D.") that is selected for determining the standard fixed overhead cost per unit (to be used in assigning fixed overhead costs to units produced). In other words, the denominator volume is the activity level used to set the predetermined fixed overhead rate for product-costing purposes.

F. Overhead Analysis: 3-way

   3-way analysis goes one step further by introducing the flexible budget for actual (not standard) volume.

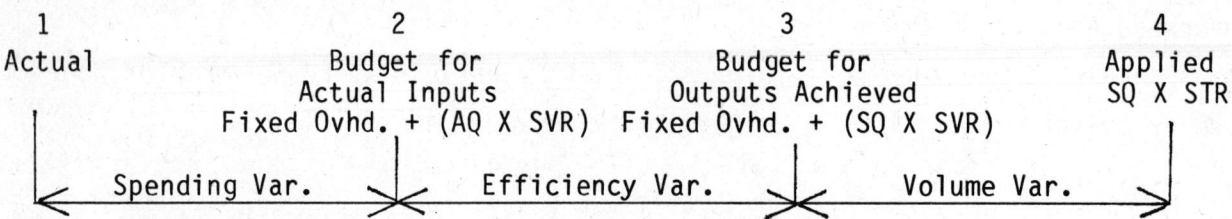

Again, smaller numbers to the left mean favorable variances, while smaller numbers to the right mean unfavorable variances.

The difference between 2 and 3 is that 2 is the flexible budget for <u>actual</u> direct labor hours, and 3 is the flexible budget for <u>standard</u> direct labor hours.

3-way analysis takes the budget variance and breaks it down into the spending and efficiency variances. The spending variance (also called the price variance) is caused by differences between the actual amount spent for fixed and variable overhead items, and the amounts budgeted based on actual direct labor hours.

The efficiency variance is solely a variable overhead variance. It is caused by more (less) variable overhead being incurred due to inefficient (efficient) use of labor hours.

G. Overhead Analysis by Cost Behavior

Often, CPA questions on overhead analysis concentrate on either fixed or variable overhead. 2-way and 3-way analysis can be summarized by cost behavior as follows:

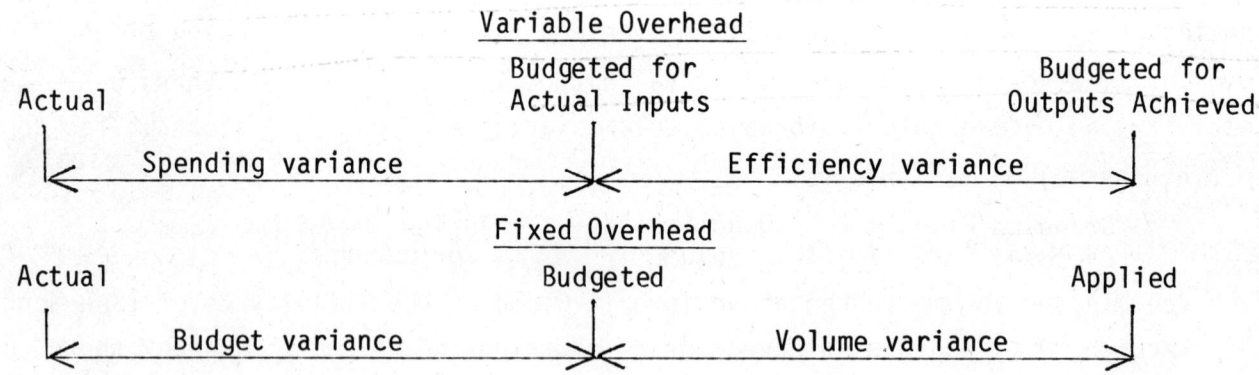

H. 4-Way Variances

A 4-way variance analysis may be undertaken by computing a fixed overhead efficiency variance, but generally it is felt this variance has little or no meaning. It would be computed by (AH - SH) X SFR.

I. <u>Journal Entries for Variances</u>

Variances are often computed and analyzed, but not entered into the accounts. If incorporated into the accounts, the standard amounts are entered into the inventory accounts. For example, when materials are purchased, SP is known but SQ is not known. Therefore, the materials account is debited for AQ X SP. When materials are used, SQ is also known, so work in process is debited for SQ X SP. Entries for materials and labor are presented below.

Materials	AQxSP		
Price variance	XXX(U)	or	XXX(F)
Accounts payable			AQxAP
WIP inventory	SQxSP		
Quantity variance	XXX(U)	or	XXX(F)
Materials			AQxSP
WIP inventory	SQxSP		
Rate variance	XXX(U)	or	XXX(F)
Efficiency variance	XXX(U)	or	XXX(F)
Accrued payroll			AQxAP

A(n) unfavorable (favorable) variance is recorded as a debit (credit) to the variance account. Overhead variances, while computed and analyzed monthly, would not normally be entered in the accounts. The total overhead variance, of course, is the difference between the balances in the Control and Applied accounts.

J. <u>Disposition of Variances</u>

If immaterial, variances are frequently written off to cost of goods sold on grounds of expediency (ARB 43 states that you may report inventories using standard costs if they are based on currently attainable standards). If material, the variances must be allocated among the inventories and cost of goods sold, usually in proportion to the ending balances.

K. <u>Analysis of Variance Example</u>

Standard costs and actual costs for direct materials, direct labor, and factory overhead incurred for the manufacture of 5,000 units of product were as follows:

Standard Costs	Standard Cost per unit	Actual Costs
Direct materials 2 lbs. @ $1.60 per lb.	$ 3.20	Materials 10,100 lbs. pur-
Direct labor 3 hours @ $2.50 per hour	7.50	chased @ $1.65 per lb.
Factory overhead on "normal capacity"		9,500 lbs. used in pro-
of 16,000 direct labor hours		duction
Variable 3 hours @ $1.50	4.50	Labor 15,400 hours worked
Fixed 3 hours @ $ .50*	1.50	@ $2.60 per hour
	$16.70	Overhead Cost
		Variable $22,800
		Fixed $ 8,100

*$8,000 budgeted fixed overhead costs ÷ by 16,000 direct labor hours

1. Material Variances

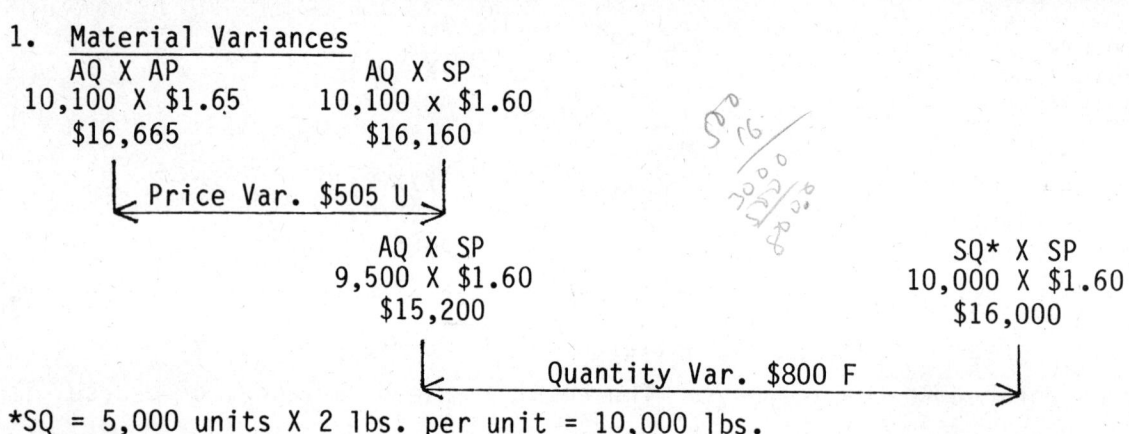

AQ X AP	AQ X SP
10,100 X $1.65	10,100 x $1.60
$16,665	$16,160

⌊ Price Var. $505 U ⌋

AQ X SP	SQ* X SP
9,500 X $1.60	10,000 X $1.60
$15,200	$16,000

⌊ Quantity Var. $800 F ⌋

*SQ = 5,000 units X 2 lbs. per unit = 10,000 lbs.

2. Labor Variances

AH X AR	AH X SR	SH* X SR
15,400 X $2.60	15,400 X $2.50	15,000 X $2.50
$40,040	$38,500	$37,500

⌊ Rate Var. $1,540 U ⌋ ⌊ Efficiency Var. $1,000 U ⌋

*SH = 5,000 units X 3 hours = 15,000 hours

3. Journal Entries

Raw Materials Inventory	$16,160	
Materials Price Variance	$505	
A/P		$16,665
WIP Inventory	$16,000	
Materials Quantity Variance		$800
Raw Materials		$15,200
WIP Inventory	$37,500	
Labor Rate Variance	$1,540	
Labor Efficiency Variance	$1,000	
Wages Payable		$40,040

Labor V = (AR-SP) AP
(2.60-2.50) 15,400

4. Overhead Variances (2-way and 3-way)

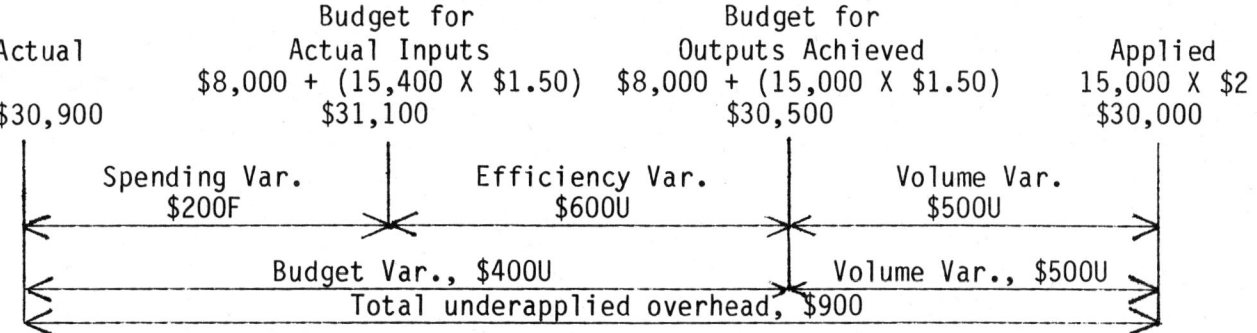

If the overhead variances are broken down by cost behavior, they are analyzed as follows:

5. Variable Overhead

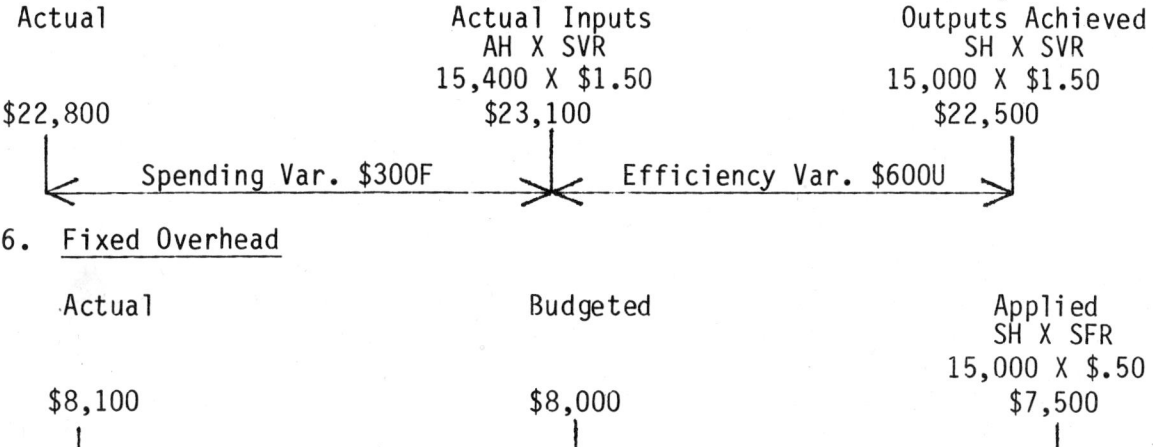

6. Fixed Overhead

L. Standard Process Costing

The discussion and examples in this module have assumed the use of standards and variances with a job-order costing system. When standards and variances are used with a process costing system, the allowable quantities of inputs (e.g., direct labor hours) are based on the equivalent units of output achieved during the current period. Therefore, the computation of equivalent units under standard process costing is the same as under FIFO.

M. Analysis of Variation in Gross Profit (AVGP)

An AVGP may be undertaken to isolate the factors causing an overall increase or decrease in a firm's gross profit between two periods. In performing the analysis, revenue and cost of goods sold are both analyzed by isolating three variances which explain the total variation in each.

The problem (with notation for analyzing revenue) is shown in the diagram below.

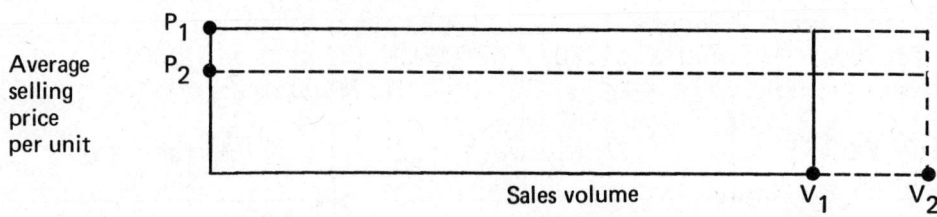

Note that, conceptually, it is the same analysis shown earlier for standard cost variances. In this problem, P_2 and V_2 are the average unit selling price and sales volume respectively, for the latest time period, and P_1 and V_1 are the average unit selling price and sales volume respectively, for one period earlier. The computation of the three variances for revenue are as follows:

1) Selling Price = $(P_2 - P_1) V_1$

2) Sales Volume = $(V_2 - V_1) P_1$

3) Selling Price-Sales Volume = $(V_2 - V_1) (P_2 - P_1)$

In solving these problems, the effect of each variable (price and volume) is determined by holding each variable (price and volume) constant while varying the other "1)" and "2)" above . Then the joint effect of the two variables is determined by multiplying the variation in one variable times the variation in the other. In the previous example, the following results would be obtained:

1) Selling Price: Unfavorable because $P_2 < P_1$

2) Sales Volume: Favorable because $V_2 > V_1$

3) Selling Price-Sales Volume: Unfavorable because $P_2 < P_1$, while $V_2 > V_1$

The total variation in revenue will be the sum of "1)", "2)", and "3)" above. Whether it is positive or negative is determined by the values of P_1 and V_1 and the magnitude of the changes in these two variables.

The same analysis would be done for cost of goods sold. The average production cost per unit would be used for P_1 and P_2 instead of the average unit selling price, but the quantities for production volume would be the same as those used for sales volume. The latter is an assumption used in doing the AVGP. Finally, the overall variation in gross profit would be the sum of the variation in revenue plus the variation in cost of goods sold.

NONROUTINE DECISIONS

The focus of this module is nonroutine decision making, which can be broken down into two broad categories, referred to here as short-term differential (relevant) cost analysis and capital budgeting decisions (or long-term differential cost analysis). The basic difference between these two categories is that capital budgeting decisions involve a large initial investment to be returned over a long-term period, while short-term differential cost decisions do not involve such an investment or such a long-term for the returns.

A. Short-Term Differential Cost Analysis

Differential cost decisions include:

1) Sell or process further (see also module 34)
2) Special order
3) Make or buy
4) Closing a department or segment
5) Sale of obsolete inventory
6) Scarce resources

These decisions would better be described as differential cost and revenue decisions, since basically the decision maker must consider differences in costs and revenues over various alternatives. All other things being equal, the alternative providing the greatest profits (or cost savings) should be chosen.

Three concepts are found in most differential cost decisions:

1) The only relevant costs or revenues are those expected future costs and revenues that differ across alternatives
2) All costs incurred in the past (past or sunk costs) are irrelevant, unless they have future tax ramifications
3) Opportunity cost, the income obtainable from an alternative use of a resource, must be considered

The table presented below summarizes the various differential cost decisions, and includes only quantitative factors. Qualitative factors may be equally important. For example, in the make or buy decision, qualitative factors include:

1) Quality of purchased part compared to manufactured part
2) Relationships with suppliers
3) Quickness in obtaining needed parts

Uncertainty also affects decision making. See the probability section in Module 38 for further discussion.

Decision	*Description*	*Decision guideline*
1. Sell or process further	Should joint products be sold at split-off or processed further?	Ignore joint costs. Process further if incremental revenue exceeds incremental cost.
2. Special order	Should a discount-priced order be accepted when there is idle capacity?	If regular sales are not affected, accept order when the revenue from the order exceeds the incremental cost. Fixed production costs are usually irrelevant.
3. Make or buy	Should a part be manufactured or bought from a supplier?	Choose lower-cost option. Fixed costs usually are irrelevant. Often opportunity costs are present.
4. Closing a department or segment	Should a segment of the company, such as a product line, be terminated?	Compare existing contribution margin with alternative. Consider any changes in future fixed costs.
5. Sale of obsolete inventory	Should obsolete inventory be re-worked or junked?	Cost of inventory is ignored. Choose alternative with greatest excess of future revenue over future cost.
6. Scarce resources	Which products should be emphasized when capacity is limited?	Determine scarce resource (e.g., machine-hours). Emphasize products with greatest contribution margin per unit of scarce resource.

An example of a differential cost decision (special order) is presented below, comparing the simpler, more efficient <u>incremental</u> approach with the equally effective but more cumbersome <u>total</u> approach. Unless a problem requires the total approach, use of the incremental approach will save valuable exam time.

> EXAMPLE: *Potts Co. manufactures cookware. Expected annual volume of 100,000 sets per year is well below full capacity of 150,000. Normal selling price is $40/set. Manufacturing cost is $30/set ($20 variable and $10 fixed). Total fixed manufacturing cost is $1,000,000. Selling and administrative expenses are expected to be $500,000 ($300,000 fixed and $200,000 variable). A catalog company offers to buy 25,000 sets for $27/set. No extra selling and administrative costs would be caused by the order, and acceptance will not affect regular sales. Should the offer be accepted?*

Incremental approach

Incremental revenue (25,000 X $27)	$675,000
Incremental cost (25,000 X $20)	(500,000)
Benefit of accepting order	$175,000

Total approach

		Without order		With order
Sales (100,000 X $40)		$4,000,000	[+(25,000 X $27)]	$4,675,000
less Variable costs:				
Man.	(100,000 x $20)	(2,000,000)	[+(25,000 X $20)]	(2,500,000)
Sell. and admin.	(100,000 x $2)	(200,000)		(200,000)
Contribution margin		1,800,000		1,975,000
less Fixed costs:				
Manufacturing		(1,000,000)		(1,000,000)
Sell. and admin.		(300,000)		(300,000)
Operating income		$ 500,000		$ 675,000

With either approach, operating income is increased by $175,000. Therefore the order should be accepted.

B. Capital Budgeting

Capital budgeting is a technique to evaluate long-term investments. The capital budgeting decision involves evaluation of an investment today in terms of the present value of future cash returns from the investment. The objective is to identify the most profitable or best investment alternative. The cash returns can take two forms depending on the nature of the project. If the project will produce revenue, the return is the difference between the cash revenues (inflows) and cash expenses (outflows). The return from projects which result in cost savings take the form of negative cash outflows (e.g., cash outflows for labor that are not made because a new machine is more efficient). Conceptually, the results of both types of projects are the same. The entity ends up with more cash by making the initial capital investment.

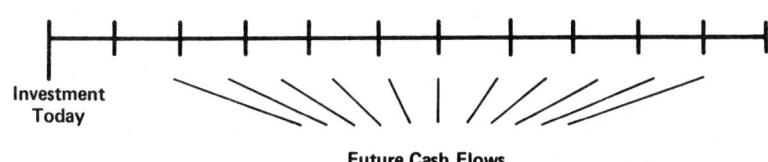

Investment
Today

Future Cash Flows

Two terms frequently used on the CPA exam are net cash flow (difference between future annual cash inflows and outflows) and after-tax net cash flow (net cash flow after tax expense).

The choice among alternative investing decisions can be made on the basis of several capital budgeting models: 1) Payback, 2) Net present value, 3) Internal (time-adjusted) rate of return, and 4) Accounting rate of return.

The <u>payback</u> method evaluates investments on the length of time until recapture (return) of the investment. For example, if a $10,000 investment were to return $2,500 a year, the payback period would be 4 years. If the payback period is to be computed after income taxes, it is necessary to deduct depreciation from the $2,500 to determine income taxes. Assuming a five-year life with no salvage value and a 40% income tax rate, the after-tax payback period would be computed as follows:

$2,500 - (40%)($2,500 - $2,000) = <u>$2,300</u>
$10,000 ÷ $2,300 = <u>4.35 years</u>

Note that the depreciation is <u>not</u> subtracted from the $2,500; only the income taxes which are affected by the depreciation deduction are subtracted.

This method ignores project profitability and the time value of money. The only redeeming aspects of the payback method are that it is an indicator of risk and liquidity. The shorter the payback period, the faster the investment is returned (liquidity) and the shorter the time the funds are at risk to changes in the environment.

The net present value method (NPV) calculates the present value of the future cash flows of a project and compares the present value of the cash flows with the investment outlay required to implement the project. The net present value of a project is defined as:

(The present value of future cash flows) minus (The required investment).

The calculation of the present value of the cash flows requires the selection of a discount rate (also referred to as the target or hurdle rate). The rate used should be the minimum rate of return that management is willing to accept on capital investment projects. The rate used should be no less than the cost of capital -- the rate management currently must pay to obtain funds. A project which earns exactly the desired rate of return will have a net present value of 0. A positive net present value identifies projects which will earn in excess of the minimum rate. For example, in a company desiring a minimum return of 6%, if an investment of $10,000 is to return $2,500 for five years, the present value of the cash flows is $10,530 ($2,500 x 4.212: 4.212 is the TVMF for the present value of an annuity, n = 5, i = 6%; see "Time value of money," Module 29). The net present value of $530 ($10,530 - $10,000) indicates the project will earn a return in excess of the 6% minimum desired. If the requirement were for a net-of-tax return of 6%, the net-of-tax cash flow of $2,300 computed in the previous section for the payback method would be multiplied by 4.212. This would result in a present value of $9,687.60 for the cash inflows, which is less than the $10,000 initial outlay. Therefore, this investment should not be made.

The internal (time-adjusted) rate of return method (IRR) determines the rate of discount at which the present value of the benefits will exactly equal the investment outlay. This rate is compared with the minimum desired rate to determine if the investment should be made. The internal rate of return is determined by setting the investment today equal to the discounted value of future cash flows. The discounting factor (rate of return) is the unknown. Using the above example,

$$PV \text{ (investment today)} = TVMF \times Cash \text{ Flows}$$
$$\$10,000 = TVMF \times \$2,500$$
$$TVMF = 4.00$$

The interest rate of a TVMF of 4.00 where n = 5 is approximately 8%. The after-tax rate of return is determined using the $2,300 after-tax cash inflow amount as follows:

$$\$10,000 = TVMF \times \$2,300$$
$$TVMF = 4.35$$

The interest rate of a TVMF of 4.35 where n = 5 is approximately 5%. CPA exam multiple choice questions in this area do not require finding the exact rate of return if the exact TVMF falls between two TVMFs given in a table. The choices are worded "less than 5%, but greater than 0%," "less than 7%, but greater than 5%," etc.

The relationship between the NPV method and the IRR method can be summarized as follows:

NPV	IRR
NPV > 0	IRR > Discount Rate
NPV = 0	IRR = Discount Rate
NPV < 0	IRR < Discount Rate

The internal rate of return method is based upon an important assumption when comparing investments of different lengths. The method implicitly assumes that the cash inflows from the investment with the shorter life can be reinvested at the same internal rate of return. For example, when comparing an investment in serial bonds yielding 9%, and single, fixed-maturity bonds yielding 8%, the internal rate of return method assumes that the serial bond repayments can be reinvested at 9%. If the serial bond repayments can only be reinvested at 6%, the 8% fixed-maturity bonds might be the better alternative.

The accounting rate of return method (ARR) computes an approximate rate of return which ignores the time value of money. It is computed as follows:

ARR = Expected increase in annual net income ÷ Average investment

Using the same example, the ARR before taxes is:

($2,500 - $2,000) ÷ ($10,000 ÷ 2) = 10%

The ARR after taxes is:

($2,300 - $2,000) ÷ ($10,000 ÷ 2) = 6%

Note that the numerator is the increase in net income, not cash flows, so depreciation is subtracted. The average investment is one-half the initial investment because the initial investment is depreciated down to zero by the end of the project. If a problem asked for ARR based on initial investment, you would not divide the investment by 2.

Two complicating factors often found on the CPA exam are <u>salvage value</u> and <u>uneven cash flows.</u> Salvage value affects all methods by changing the depreciation tax deduction. Also, in the NPV and IRR methods, the salvage value is a future cash inflow which must be considered.

Uneven cash flows mean that the payback formula cannot be used; net cash inflows must be accumulated until the investment is returned. For the NPV and IRR methods, each year's net cash inflow must be discounted separately using the present value of $1 table. Finally, when computing ARR the numerator becomes the <u>average</u> expected increase in annual net income.

The following chart summarizes the strengths and weaknesses of the capital budgeting methods.

Method	*Strengths*	*Weaknesses* **
Payback	1. Easy to understand and use	1. Ignores time value of money
	2. Emphasizes liquidity	2. Ignores cash flows after payback period
		3. Does not measure profitability
Net Present Value (NPV)	1. Emphasizes cash flows	1. Favors larger, longer projects
	2. Recognizes time value of money	2. Assumes no change in required rate of return
	3. Assumes discount rate is reinvestment rate*	
	4. Easy to apply	
Time Adjusted Rate of Return (IRR)	1. Emphasizes cash flows	1. Assumes IRR is the reinvestment rate*
	2. Recognizes time value of money	2. Favors shorter projects
	3. Computes true return of projects	
Accounting Rate of Return (ARR)	1. Easy to understand and use	1. Does not emphasize cash flows
	2. Ties in with income statement and performance evaluation	2. Ignores time value of money
		3. Misstates the true return of projects

*Note that assuming the discount rate is the reinvestment rate results in using the **same** reinvestment rate for projects of similar risk, while assuming the IRR is the reinvestment rate assumes higher reinvestment rates for projects with higher true returns, regardless of the risk involved.

**All methods share the weakness of assuming future cash flows are certain.

C. Sensitivity Analysis

The "certainty" weakness mentioned above can be offset somewhat by using sensitivity analysis. This type of analysis attempts to determine how calculations (such as NPV or IRR) will be affected if the various predictions are in error.

Examples of sensitivity analysis include

1) Determining how far net cash inflows would have to drop before NPV = 0 or before IRR = the required rate of return

2) Calculating NPV and IRR under pessimistic and optimistic cash flow estimates

3) Using a computer simulation to combine probabilistic estimates of cash flows into a probabilistic distribution of IRR

4) Determining how short useful life would have to be before NPV = 0 or before IRR = the required rate of return

CHAPTER ELEVEN

QUANTITATIVE METHODS

This chapter reviews managerial optimization models. Optimization models are specific math applications to certain classes of business problems, e.g., when to reorder inventory. The word "model" is used because the relationship between two or more variables is stated, e.g., inventory costs include costs of holding, ordering, stockouts, etc. This is in contrast to the examination of an entire business "system" which would involve many more variables and be more complex.

The word optimization is used because the objective of the model is to find an optimum action or level of activity in order to maximize income, production, etc. or to minimize costs, errors, etc. These optimization models have been developed to improve managerial efficiency in business and government. An alternative to optimizing is satisficing where merely an acceptable solution, not the best solution, is sought.

Quantitative methods questions appear on both practice and theory sections of the examination. Recent quantitative questions have been largely glossarial in nature, apparently based on the premise that practicing CPAs only need to recognize situations that can benefit from MAS specialists, i.e., the questions have become less computational and thus easier. An exception is the economic order quantity (EOQ) calculation which has been required on several examinations (you should memorize the formula). For the majority of questions, all that is required is knowledge of when, how, and why particular optimization models are used.

The presentation in this chapter is geared toward the types of quantitative questions currently appearing on the CPA exam (see AICPA Content Specification Outline for Cost-Managerial, Section Q, page 993).

A. Analyzing Cost Behavior

1. **High-Low Method.** The high-low method computes the slope based on the highest and lowest observations (See also "A.", Module 35.)

$$\text{Slope} = \frac{\text{Vertical distance between high and low points}}{\text{Horizontal distance between high and low points}}$$

This method may be inaccurate if the high and low points are not representative as illustrated in the following chart by the solid line.

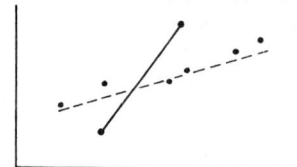

2. **Scattergraph Method.** The scattergraph method is a graphical approach to computing the relationship between two variables. The dependent variable is plotted on the vertical axis and the independent variable on the horizontal axis. A straight line is then drawn through the observation points which best describe the relationship between the two variables. In the graph above, the broken line illustrates the relationship. The slope of the line is "b" and the point where the line intercepts the vertical axis is "a" in the following discussion of "method of least squares." This method lacks precision, because by freely drawing the line through the points, it is possible to obtain a line that does not minimize the deviations of the points from the line.

3. **Regression Analysis.** Regression (least squares) analysis determines the functional relationship between variables. For example, you may wish to determine the relationship of electricity cost to level of activity. Based on activity levels and electricity charges of past months, the following chart (scattergram) might be prepared.

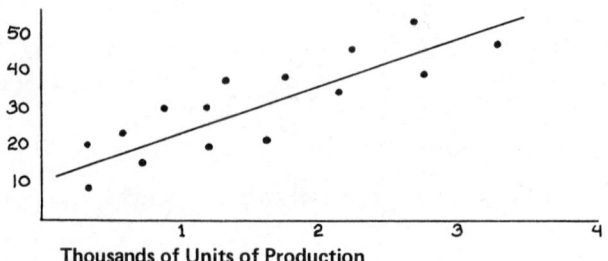

As production increases, electric costs increase. The relationship appears linear.
Linearity is an assumption underlying regression. If the power costs begin to fall
after 3,000 units of production, the relationship between electricity and production
would not be linear, and linear regression would not be appropriate.

The method of least squares fits a regression line between the observation
points such that the sum of the squared vertical differences between the regression
line and the individual observations is minimized. For example, in the above scattergram, there are 15 observations, and the sum of the squares of the vertical differences between each observation and the regression line is minimized. The regression line -- $Y = a + bx$ is determined by the "normal" equations:

$$\sum Y = na + b\sum X$$
$$\sum XY = a\sum X + b\sum X^2$$

Y = dependent variable, e.g., electricity costs
X = independent variable, e.g., level of production
a = Y intercept (where the regression line intersects the vertical axis)
b = slope of the regression line
n = number of observations, e.g., 15 in above example

The goodness of the least squares fit, i.e., how well the regression line fits
the observed data, is measured by the coefficient of determination (r^2); the proportion of squared variation between observed data. The better the line fits the observed data points, i.e., the closer the observed data points are to the line, the
closer r^2 will be to 1.00 -- r^2s of 90-99% are considered very good (small r^2
is used for simple regression; capital R^2 for multiple regression).

If the independent variable in regression analysis is time, it is said to be a
time series analysis. For example, annual car sales for the past 20 years may be
used to predict car sales for next year. Time series analysis is a form of trend
analysis which is widely used for sales forecasting.

If there is only one independent variable, the analysis is known as simple regression (as in the above example). Multiple regression consists of a functional
relationship with multiple independent variables, e.g., cost may be a function of
several variables.

4. Correlation Analysis. Correlation is the relationship between variables. If
the variables move with each other, they have a direct relationship (positive correlation) as in A. If the variables move in opposite directions, they have an
inverse relationship (negative correlation) as in B.

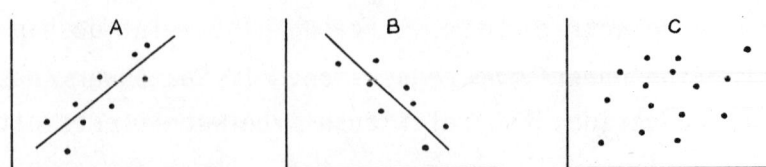

The degree and direction of correlation is measured from -1 to 1. The sign (negative or positive) describes whether the relationship is inverse or direct. The coefficient of correlation is measured by

$$\sqrt{\frac{\text{Amount of variation explained}}{\text{Total variation}}}$$

If all of the observations were in a straight line, all of the variation would be explained and the coefficient of correlation would be 1 or -1 depending upon whether the relationship is positive or negative. If there is no correlation, as in C above, the coefficient of correlation is 0.

Note that the coefficient of correlation is similar in concept to the coefficient of determination discussed above in "method of least squares." The coefficient of determination cannot have a negative value, as can the coefficient of correlation, because the coefficient of determination is based on squared deviations, i.e., if you square a negative number, the result is positive.

B. Learning Curves

Learning curves describe the efficiencies arising from experience because with experience comes increased productivity. Thus productivity increases with production size, but at a decreasing rate as diagrammed below.

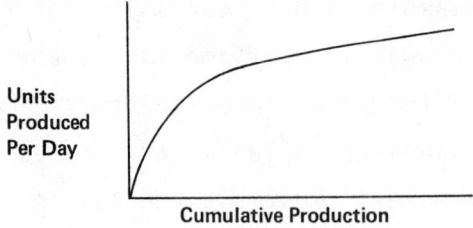

Learning curves are particularly acute at early stages of production, e.g., set-up and training costs. As production increases, experience produces less and less efficiencies until the curve becomes horizontal, at which point no increased efficiencies are possible.

Example Problem

The Green Company's new process will be carried out in one department. The production process has an expected learning curve of 80%. The costs subject to the learning effect for the first batch produced by the process were $10,000. Using the simplest form of the learning function, the cumulative average cost per batch subject to the learning effect after the 16th batch has been produced may be estimated as

   a. $3,276.80.
   b. $4,096.00.
   c. $8,000.00
   d. $10,000.00

Example Explanation

(1174,Q2,26)   (b)   An 80% learning curve indicates that the cost of a process reduced to an 80% level every time production is doubled. Thus, moving from the first batch to the second batch will result in a 20% cost savings, or the second batch will cost 80% of the first batch. The fourth batch will cost 80% of the second batch, and the eighth batch will cost 80% of the fourth batch, and the sixteenth batch will cost 80% of the eighth batch. The calculations follow below.

   (1)   10,000
   (2)   8,000
   (4)   6,400
   (8)   5,120
   (16)   4,096

C. Probability Analysis

In as much as business decisions are made in a probabilistic rather than a deterministic setting, expected value is a very important concept. Expected value is the <u>sum</u> of the <u>probability of each event occurring</u> times the <u>payoff of that event</u>. Example of expected value of the life of an asset:

Years of Life	Probability	X	Payoff	=	Expected Value
3	.20		3		.6
4	.30		4		1.2
5	.30		5		1.5
6	.10		6		.6
7	.10		7		.7
					4.6 years

The above example illustrates a discrete probability distribution, i.e., the probability that the life is either 3, 4, 5, 6, or 7 years but not 3.1 or 3.8 years. A continuous probability distribution is one that indicates the probability that any point on a continuous range of values, e.g., 3.181 or 4.44921 years, may occur. To compute the expected value of a continuous distribution of payoffs, one multiplies the integral of the probability function times the integral of the payoff function.

D. Inventory Models

A basic inventory model exists to assist in two inventory questions.

   1.   How much to order
   2.   When to reorder

How Much to Order. The amount to be ordered is known as the economic order quantity (EOQ). The EOQ minimizes the sum of the ordering and carrying costs. The total inventory cost function includes:

1. Carrying costs (which increase order size)

   a. Storage costs
   b. Interest costs
   c. Spoilage, etc.
   d. Insurance

   If x is the number of units received in each shipment, x ÷ 2 would be the average inventory. If k is the unit cost of holding one unit of inventory for one year, kx ÷ 2 is the annual inventory carrying cost.

2. Ordering costs (which decrease with order size)

   a. Transportation costs (carload rates)
   b. Administrative costs of purchasing and accounts payable costs of receiving and inspecting goods

   If a is the fixed cost of an inventory order, b is the variable cost of ordering, D is total demand per year, and (D/x) is the number of orders, the reorder cost is (a + bx) (D/x).

$$\text{Total cost (TC)} = kx/2 + (a + bx)(D/x)$$

$$TC = kx/2 + a\,D/x + bD$$

The EOQ formula is a common approach to determine order quantity. The formula is derived by setting the annual carrying cost equal to annual purchase cost or by differentiating the cost function with respect to order size. The formula is:

$$EOQ = \sqrt{\frac{2aD}{k}}$$

a = cost of placing one order
D = annual demand in units
k = annual cost of carrying one unit in inventory for one year
    (cost per unit of material X carrying cost percentage)

The EOQ can also be depicted in a graph as shown below. The EOQ is where the annual carrying costs and annual ordering costs intersect.

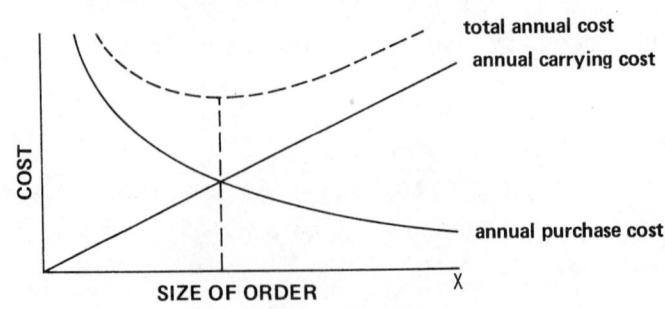

EXAMPLE: The following information relates to Huskie Company

Units required per year	3,000
Cost of placing an order	$ 40
Unit carrying cost per year	$ 6

Assuming that the units will be used evenly throughout the year, what is the economic order quantity?

A. 200
B. 300
C. 400
D. 500

Solution:

$$EOQ = \sqrt{\frac{2 \times a \times D}{k}} = \sqrt{\frac{2 \times \$40 \times 3,000}{\$6}} = 200 \text{ units}$$

The formula for the EOQ model can also be used to determine the optimal size of a production run. In these applications, "a" is the setup cost; "D" is the annual demand for the finished product and "k" is the variable manufacturing cost per unit times the carrying cost percentage.

Assumptions of the EOQ Model. The EOQ model was developed on the basis of several assumptions regarding the acquisition and use of inventory items. The assumptions which underlie the EOQ model are*:

1. Demand occurs at a constant rate throughout the year
2. Lead time on the receipt of orders is constant
3. The entire quantity ordered is received at one time
4. The unit costs of the items ordered are constant; thus there can be no quantity discounts
5. There are no limitations on the size of the inventory

The model is insensitive to minor violations of these assumptions. The square root sign makes the EOQ model relatively insensitive to input estimation errors. However, when there are serious violations, the EOQ model should be adapted or not used.

When to Reorder. When to reorder is a stockout problem, i.e., the objective is to order at a point in time so as not to run out of stock before receiving the inventory ordered but not so early that an excessive quantity of "safety" stock is maintained. The stockout problem is diagrammed below.

---

*Taken with permission from "Making EOQ Operational," unpublished manuscript by James A. Hendricks, Northern Illinois University and Cynthia D. Dailey, Peat, Marwick, Mitchell & Co.

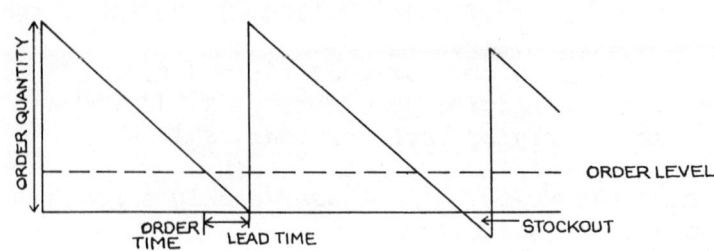

The vertical distance is the order size determined by the EOQ formula. The line sloping downward to the right represents the inventory as it is being used or sold. The horizontal broken line is the order point. The horizontal difference between the time the order is placed and received is the order lead time. Theoretically, it is desirable to have zero inventory when the inventory shipment is received. If the order point is so computed, there may be a stockout situation if:

1. Demand is greater than expected during the lead time or
2. The order time exceeds the lead time

A stockout is illustrated in the above graph on the second purchase. Safety stocks may be used to guard against stockout. Safety stocks are maintained by increasing the lead time. Both stockouts and safety stocks have costs associated with them. The typical cost elements comprising carrying costs of safety stock and stockout costs are listed below:

Carrying Costs of Safety Stock	Stockout Costs
a. Storage	1. Profit on lost sales
b. Interest	2. Customer ill will
c. Spoilage	3. Idle equipment
d. Insurance	4. Work stoppages
e. Property taxes	

Safety stocks decrease stockout costs but increase carrying costs. The amount of safety stock should be such as to minimize the sum of stockout and carrying costs as illustrated below.

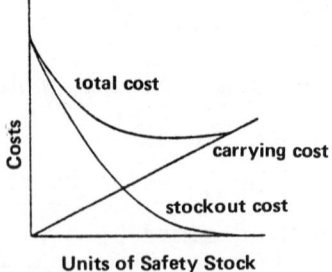

Units of Safety Stock

With a larger safety stock, the stockout costs will be smaller, but the carrying costs associated with the safety stock will be larger. The most common approach to setting the optimum safety-stock level is the probabilistic approach which looks at previous lead-time periods to see what the probabilities of running out of stock (a stockout) are for different assessed levels of safety stock. The following example illustrates this approach and shows how carrying costs and stockout costs behave as units of safety stock are increased.

EXAMPLE: The Polly Company wishes to determine the amount of safety stock to maintain for product D in order to minimize the sum of stockout costs and carrying costs. The following information is available:

Stockout cost	$80 per occurrence
Carrying Cost of Safety Stock	$ 3 per unit
Number of purchase orders	5 per year

What is the number of units of safety stock that will result in the lowest cost, given the four levels of safety stock and their related probability of being out of stock (columns 1 and 2 below)?

Solution: In order to answer the question it is necessary to compute the stockout costs and carrying costs for each of the four alternatives.

Unit Levels of Safety Stock	Probability of Being Out of Stock	Cost of Stockout	# of Orders Per Year	Stockout Cost[a]		Carrying Cost[b]	Total Cost[c]
20	.40	x $80	x 5 =	$160	+	$ 60	= $220
40	.20	x $80	x 5 =	80	+	120	= 200
50	.10	x $80	x 5 =	40	+	150	= 190
60	.05	x $80	x 5 =	20	+	180	= 200

Computations

[a]Probability of being out of stock x cost of stockout x number of orders per year

[b]Safety stock x cost ($3) of carrying one unit for one year

[c]Carrying cost + stockout cost

A safety stock of 50 units is optimal since it results in the lowest total cost.

When a safety stock is maintained, the order point is computed as follows:

Order point = (daily demand X days in lead time) + safety stock

If we assume in the Polly example that the average usage is 20 units per day and the lead time is 6 days, the order point would be computed as follows:

Order point = (20 X 6) + 50 = <u>170 units</u>

E. Network Problems

Network analysis is the methodology to determine the shortest or longest route
through a network or the maximum flow through a network. For example, the following
network problem appeared on the May 1971 examination (571,P5,19-23). This is a PERT
(Program Evaluation and Review Technique) example.

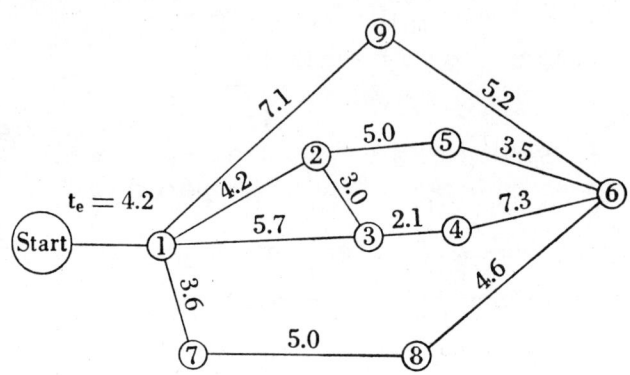

The formula for deriving the estimated time (t_e) for each activity (con-
necting line) is:

$$T_e = \frac{t_o + 4t_m + t_p}{6}$$

t_o = optimistic time; t_m = most probable time; t_p = pessimistic time

PERT attempts to:

1. Forecast the time of project completion
2. Monitor progress during work on the project
3. Identify parts of the project which are critical to timely completion

Maximum flow problems attempt to forecast maximum flow and to identify bottlenecks.

Pipeline, road, and air lane flows are examples of maximum flow problems.

Definitions:

1. Network -- graph of junction points (nodes) connected by lines (branches)
2. Connected -- all nodes are connected by branches
3. Oriented, directed -- source of flow, from origin (source) to destination
    (sink)
4. Critical Path -- path requiring the greatest amount of time (e.g.,1-2-3-4-6
    in the above example)
5. Slack Time -- excess time over budget that will not affect critical path
    time (e.g., 4.3 on path 1-9-6)
6. Tree -- connected graph containing no cycles
7. Example (PERT report format)

Event (Node)	Original Schedule	Earliest Time	Latest Time	Slack

F. Linear Programming

Linear programming is a technique to make optimal use of limited resources. Business applications of linear programming usually maximize profits or minimize costs. Conditions calling for the use of linear programming include:

1. Specification of a cost or revenue objective function. An objective function must be specified. Thus, one objective of maximizing or minimizing must be stated in a formula. For example, the profit on parts 1 and 2 might be $4 and $3 respectively.

$$Z = 4X_1 + 3X_2 \qquad X_1 = \text{Part 1}$$
$$Z = \text{Profit} \qquad X_2 = \text{Part 2}$$

   Parts X_1 and X_2 are the only possible output of a special foundry department and a special milling department.

2. The limited resources must be subject to alternative uses. For example, the special foundry can either produce part 1 or part 2, and the special milling department can finish either part 1 or part 2.

3. The alternative uses of the limited resources must be specified. For example, the foundry may pour 24 tons of casting a week. Part X_1 requires 2 tons and part X_2 requires 4 tons. Thus the casting department can pour $12X_1$ or $6X_2$ or any combination thereof.

$$2X_1 + 4X_2 \leq 24$$

   The milling department can produce 30 hours per week. Part 1 requires 4 hours, and part 2 requires 2 hours resulting in the following constraint.

$$4X_1 + 2X_2 \leq 30$$

The graphic solution appears on the next page.

First, you should draw the constraint lines. The foundry constraint was $2X_1 + 4X_2 \leq 24$. Thus, at best, the foundry can only produce $12X_1$ or $6X_2$ (see the graph) or any combination thereof. Foundry production can be at the level signified by any point beneath the foundry constraint line.

The milling constraint allows, at best, 7 1/2 X_1 or $15X_2$ (see the graph). Milling production can be at _any_ point under the milling constraint line, e.g., production of $12X_1$ and no X_2 is not a feasible solution. The area of feasible solution is signified by lines perpendicular to the constraint lines.

Next, the profit lines are drawn from the equation $Z = 4X_1 + 3X_2$. For example, a $24 profit would result from production of $6X_1$ _or_ $8X_2$ _or_ any linear combination thereof as represented by the broken line on the graph. To maximize profit, one wants to produce at a point on a profit line as far away from the origin as possible. The line farthest away from the origin but still intersecting the area of feasible solution is a $33 profit line (8 1/4 X_1 + 11X_2). A $36 profit line is also illustrated but doesn't fall within the area of feasible solutions. The optimal solution can be seen to be the intersection of the $33 profit line with the intersection of the foundry and milling constraints. The intersection has the coordinates $X_1 = 6$, $X_2 = 3$. Solution of the point of intersection of the foundry and milling constraints is found by setting the constraints equal to each other and solving for X_1 and Y_2. Multiply the milling equation by -2 and add it to the foundry equation.

Graphic Solution

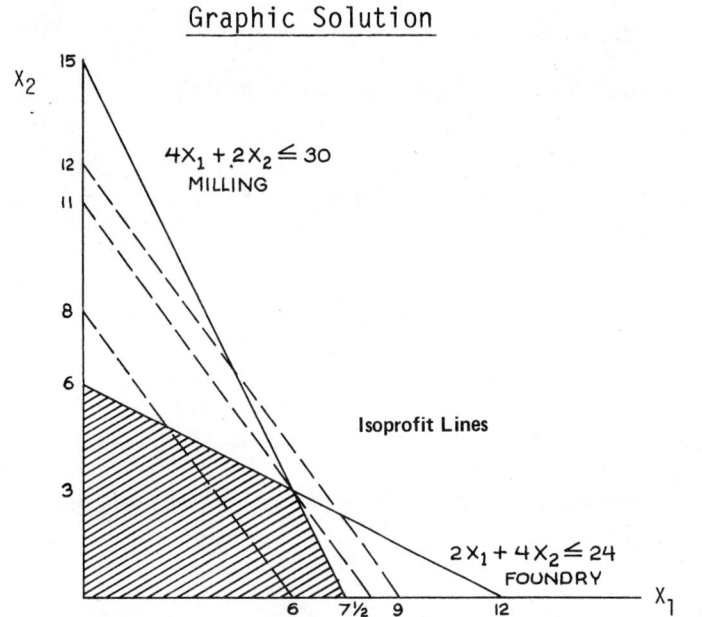

Mathematical Solution

$$4X_1 + 2X_2 = 30$$

$$2X_1 + 4X_2 = 24$$

$$-8X_1 - 4X_2 = -60$$

$$\overline{-6X_1 \qquad\qquad = -36}$$

$$X_1 = 6$$

$$X_2 = 3$$

$$Z = 4X_1 + 3X_2$$

$$Z = 24 + 9 = \underline{\underline{\$33}}$$

The graphic solution consists of 2 sets of lines: 1) constraint lines (solid) and profit lines (broken). It should be pointed out that the linear programming optimal solution will be at an extreme point, i.e., the intersection of constraint equations. In isolated cases, the profit line may have the same slope as a constraint line and the optimal solution would coincide with that particular constraint line over the distance that the constraint line was within the area of feasible solution.

G. Sensitivity Analysis

After a problem has been formulated into a mathematical model, it may be subjected to sensitivity analysis. This analysis uses a trial and error method in which the "sensitivity" of the solution to changes in any given variable or parameter is calculated. In linear programming problems, an application of "sensitivity" analysis is to test the range over which a constraint value may be changed without changing the optimal solution.

CHAPTER TWELVE

ACCOUNTING FOR GOVERNMENTAL AND OTHER
NONPROFIT ENTITIES

Module Number	Module Code	
39	GOV	Governmental Accounting

I. Governmental (State and Local) Accounting - 1061
   A. Fund Accounting - 1062
   B. Budgets and Their Impact upon the Accounting System - 1064
   C. Financial Statements for State and Local Governments - 1066
   D. Interim Financial Statements - 1067
   E. Governmental Funds - 1069
   F. Proprietary Funds - 1088
   G. Fiduciary Funds--Trust and Agency - 1090
   H. The GFA and GLTD Account Groups - 1093
   I. Interfund Transfers and Other Interfund Transactions - 1095
   J. State and Local Government Fund Review Checklist - 1098
II. Other Nonprofit Entities - 1099
   A. College and University Accounting - 1100
   B. Hospital Accounting - 1107
   C. Voluntary Health and Welfare Organizations - 1113
   D. SOP 78-10--Other Nonprofit Organizations - 1118
   E. Statement of Financial Accounting Concepts No. 4 - 1121

Questions on governmental and other nonprofit entities have appeared on all recent examinations. Questions have dealt with local government and various nonprofit organizations. These questions have fallen into four categories:

1) Multiple choice questions on the Theory exam either requiring identification of the local government fund in which to account for a specific type of transaction or identifying procedures in either local government or nonprofit organizations
2) Problems on the Practice exam involving journal entries in one or several local government funds
3) Problems on the Practice exam requiring the preparation of journal entries and/or operating statements for nonprofit organizations
4) Essay questions on the Theory exam requiring description of and rationale for various accounting concepts and practices

The AICPA Content Specification Outline of the coverage of governmental and nonprofit accounting in the Practice and Theory exams, including the authors' frequency analysis (last nine exams), appears on the next page.

---

*SFAC 4 refers to the other nonprofit entities discussed in this chapter as "Nonbusiness Organizations." An outline of this statement appears at the end of this chapter.

AICPA CONTENT SPECIFICATION OUTLINE/FREQUENCY ANALYSIS*

Not-For-Profit and Governmental Accounting

	Practice									Theory								
	M 80	N 80	M 81	N 81	M 82	N 82	M 83	N 83	M 84	M 80	N 80	M 81	N 81	M 82	N 82	M 83	N 83	M 84
A. Conceptual Framework (Theory Only)	—	—	—	—	—	—	—	—	—	—	—	—	—	—	—	—	—	—
B. Fund Accounting	[1]**	—	—	—	—	—	—	—	—	—	—	—	—	—	—	—	—	—
1. Fund Balance	—	—	—	—	—	—	—	—	1	2	1	—	[.25]	1	—	1	—	1
2. Estimated Revenues	—	—	—	—	—	—	—	—	1	—	—	1	[.25]	—	1	—	—	1
3. Appropriations	—	—	—	—	1	—	—	—	1	1	1	—	[.5]	1	—	—	1	1
4. Encumbrances	—	—	—	—	1	—	—	—	1	1	1	1	—	1	1	1	—	—
5. Reserve for Encumbrances	—	—	—	—	—	—	—	—	—	—	—	—	—	—	—	—	1	—
6. Revenues	—	—	—	—	—	—	—	—	—	—	—	—	—	—	1	2	—	—
7. Expenditures	—	—	—	—	—	—	—	—	1	—	1	1	—	—	2	—	1	—
C. Types of Funds and Fund Accounts																		
1. General Fund	—	—	[.5]	[1]	4	—	—	—	—	—	1	1	—	—	—	1	—	—
2. Special Revenue Funds	—	—	—	—	—	—	—	—	1	1	—	—	—	—	—	1	—	—
3. Debt Service Funds	—	—	—	—	2	—	—	—	1	—	1	—	—	1	1	—	1	—
4. Capital Projects Funds	—	[1]	—	—	2	—	—	—	—	1	1	1	—	—	—	—	—	1
5. Enterprise Funds	—	—	—	—	1	—	—	—	1	—	1	1	—	1	—	—	—	—
6. Internal Service Funds	—	—	[.5]	—	—	—	—	—	1	—	—	1	—	1	1	1	—	—
7. Trust and Agency Funds	—	—	—	—	—	—	—	—	—	1	—	1	—	—	—	1	—	—
8. Special Assessment Funds	—	—	—	—	—	—	—	—	—	—	—	—	—	1	—	1	—	—
9. General Fixed Asset Account Group	—	—	—	—	2	—	—	—	2	1	—	—	—	—	1	—	1	—
10. General Long-Term Debt Account Group	—	—	—	—	1	—	—	—	—	—	—	1	—	1	1	1	1	2
11. Endowment and Quasi-Endowment Funds	—	—	—	—	1	—	—	—	—	—	—	—	—	—	—	—	—	—
12. Restricted Funds	—	—	—	—	—	—	—	—	—	—	—	—	—	—	—	—	—	—
13. Nonrestricted Funds	—	—	—	—	—	—	—	—	—	—	—	—	—	—	—	—	—	—
14. Property Funds	—	—	—	—	—	—	—	—	—	—	—	—	—	—	—	—	—	—
D. Presentation of Financial Statements for Various Not-For-Profit and Governmental Organizations	—	—	—	—	—	—	—	—	—	—	—	—	—	—	—	—	1	2
E. Various Types of Not-For-Profit and Governmental Organizations																		
1. Local and State Governments	—	—	—	—	—	—	—	—	—	—	—	—	—	—	—	—	—	—
2. Educational Institutions	—	—	—	—	2	—	—	[1]	2	—	1	—	—	1	—	1	1	—
3. Hospitals	—	—	—	—	3	[1]	—	—	4	1	—	1	—	1	1	—	1	1
4. Charitable, Religious, and Other Organizations	—	—	—	—	—	—	[1]	—	3	1	1	—	—	—	—	—	—	1
Total Multiple Choice Questions	—	—	—	—	20	—	—	—	20	10	10	10	—	10	10	10	10	10
Total Problems/Essays	1	1	1	1	—	1	1	1	—	—	—	—	1	—	—	—	—	—
Actual Percentage***	10%	10%	10%	10%	10%	10%	10%	10%	10%	10%	10%	10%	10%	10%	10%	10%	10%	10%

(AICPA 10%)   (AICPA 10%)

*The classifications are the authors'

**Comprehensive problems

***The "actual percentage" is a measure of the relative coverage of the specific areas (i.e., I, II, etc.) on each Accounting Practice or Theory exam. This relative weight includes **both** multiple choice questions and essays/problems presented in that area.

The first part of this chapter is a discussion of state and local governmental accounting, and the second part outlines accounting for nonprofit entities, including colleges and universities, hospitals, voluntary health and welfare organizations, and other nonprofit organizations. Studying this chapter and solving the recent problems involving governmental and other nonprofit entities will prepare you for the examination.

I. GOVERNMENTAL (STATE AND LOCAL) ACCOUNTING

Governmental accounting has many similarities to commercial accounting. For example, governmental accounting uses the double-entry system, journals, ledgers, trial balances, financial statements, internal control, etc. Differences arise due to the objectives and environment of government. The major differences include:

1) The absence of a profit motive, except for governmental enterprises, such as utilities
2) A legal emphasis which involves restrictions both in the raising and spending of revenues
3) An inability to "match" revenues with expenses, as revenues are often provided by persons other than those receiving the services
4) An emphasis on accountability or stewardship of resources entrusted to public officials
5) The use of fund accounting
6) The recording of the budget in some funds
7) The use of modified accrual accounting rather than full accrual accounting in some funds

The organization now known as the National Council on Governmental Accounting* published Governmental Accounting, Auditing, and Financial Reporting (GAAFR) in 1968. This document was an authoritative source of GAAP for governmental entities. In 1974, the AICPA issued an audit guide, Audits of State and Local Governmental Units, which contained some modifications of the principles enumerated in the 1968 GAAFR. Additional amendments were contained in AICPA Statements of Position 75-3 and 77-2.

In 1979, the NCGA issued Statement 1: Governmental Accounting and Financial Reporting Principles, which was effective June 30, 1980. Statement 1 is a restatement and modification of the principles contained in the 1968 GAAFR and the AICPA publications. The AICPA then issued Statement of Position 80-2, also effective June 30,

---

*Established by the Municipal Finance Officers Association (MFOA) and other organizations.

1980, which stated that financial statements prepared in accordance with NCGA Statement 1 are in conformity with GAAP. Any materials in the 1974 Audit Guide that are in conflict with Statement 1 were superseded.

In addition to Statement 1, the NCGA has issued the following statements:

Statement	Subject
2	Grant, Entitlement, and Shared Revenue Accounting and Reporting by State and Local Governments
3	Defining the Governmental Reporting Entity
4	Accounting and Financial Reporting Principles for Claims and Judgments and Compensated Absences
5	Accounting and Financial Reporting Principles for Lease Agreements of State and Local Governments
6	Pension Accounting and Financial Reporting: Public Employee Retirement Systems and State and Local Government Employees
7	Financial Reporting for Component Units within the Governmental Reporting Entity

In addition, the NCGA has issued several interpretations dealing with various issues.

The most recent development is that the Financial Accounting Foundation has approved the formation of a Governmental Accounting Standards Board, which will have authority to establish principles for state and local governmental units. As of the date of this writing, the new GASB is in the process of formation.

A. Fund Accounting

Statement 1 contains twelve basic principles of accounting and reporting for governmental entities. Three of these principles deal specifically with fund accounting. These principles cover the:

1) Definition of a fund
2) Types of funds
3) Number of funds

Governmental financial activities should be carried out and accounted for through funds. A fund is defined in Statement 1 as:

A fiscal and accounting entity with a self-balancing set of accounts recording cash and other financial resources, together with all related liabilities and residual equities and balances, and changes therein, which are segregated for the purpose of carrying on specific activities or attaining certain objectives in accordance with special regulations, restrictions, or limitations.

A fund, then, is:

1) A fiscal and accounting entity

   a) Self-balancing set of accounts
   b) Transactions affecting assets, liabilities, and residual equity are
      recorded

2) Segregated

   a) Specific activities
   b) Attaining certain objectives

3) In accordance with

   a) Special regulations
   b) Restrictions
   c) Limitations

There are eight funds which are classified into three general types.

Governmental Funds   Proprietary Funds
   1) General   6) Internal Service
   2) Special Revenue   7) Enterprise
   3) Capital Projects   Fiduciary Funds
   4) Debt Service   8) Trust and Agency
   5) Special Assessment

Additionally, there are a General Fixed Asset Group of Accounts and a General Long-Term Debt Group of Accounts. These account groups are not funds because they do not have fiscal authority over resource inflows or outflows. Statement 1 contains three additional principles (discussed later) which cover accounting for fixed assets and long-term debt.

The major peculiarities of governmental accounting are reflected in the governmental funds rather than the proprietary funds or the fiduciary funds. In the governmental funds, the objective is providing services to the public. All of these funds are expendable, i.e., they are not concerned with preserving capital (capital maintenance) or measuring "net income" (matching). Rather, governmental funds are concerned with the availability of resources to provide services, and the emphasis is on working capital flows. Usually, only current assets and current liabilities are accounted for in the expendable funds (five governmental funds plus expendable trust and agency funds). Long-term debt in the Special Assessment Funds is an exception. Fixed assets and long-term liabilities of governmental funds are mostly accounted for in separate self-balancing groups of accounts.

The proprietary funds use accounting and reporting techniques similar to commercial enterprises. The accounting and reporting techniques of fiduciary funds depend on whether the Trust Fund is expendable or nonexpendable. Expendable Trust and Agency Funds are accounted for like governmental funds, while Nonexpendable and Pension Trust Funds are accounted for like proprietary funds.

The third basic principle in <u>Statement 1</u> dealing with fund accounting states that each governmental unit:

> should establish and maintain those funds required by law and sound financial administration. Only the minimum number of funds consistent with legal and operating requirements should be established, however, since unnecessary funds result in inflexibility, undue complexity, and inefficient financial administration.

B. <u>Budgets and Their Impact upon the Accounting System</u>

The NCGA, in one of its basic principles, states:

1) An annual budget(s) should be adopted by every governmental unit
2) The accounting system should provide the basis for appropriate budgetary control
3) Budgetary comparisons should be included in the appropriate financial statements and schedules for governmental funds for which an annual budget has been adopted

In accordance with the principle above, budgets should be prepared for each of the eight funds used by governmental units. This directive, by itself, does not differentiate governmental from commercial enterprises. What is different, however, is the inclusion of budgetary accounts in the formal accounting system for the governmental funds. Inclusion of the budgetary accounts facilitates the budget-actual comparison indicated in the NCGA principle. NCGA <u>Statement 1</u> indicates that inclusion of budgetary accounts would be "essential for the General, Special Revenue, and other annually budgeted governmental funds which have numerous types of revenues, expenditures, and transfers." In other cases, inclusion or exclusion would depend upon the circumstances. <u>The use of budgetary accounts is optional for the Debt Service, Capital Projects, or Special Assessment Funds.</u> CPA examination questions sometimes, but not always, include budgetary accounts for these three funds.

. Budgetary accounts (Estimated Revenues and Appropriations) are incorporated into governmental accounting systems to provide legislative control over receipts and disbursements and to provide an assessment of management's stewardship by facilitating a comparison of budget vs. actual. These budgetary accounts are <u>anticipatory asset</u> and <u>anticipatory liability</u> accounts even though they are temporary (nominal) accounts. The journal entries below illustrate the budgetary accounts used by the General and Special Revenue Funds.

Upon adoption of the estimated revenues and appropriations budgets (at the beginning of the period), the following entry is made and posted to the general ledger:

Estimated Revenues
    (individual items are posted
    to subsidiary revenues ledger)
	$1,000,000	(anticipated resources/
		revenues)

Appropriations
        (individual items are posted
        to subsidiary appropriations
        expenditure ledger)
	$ 980,000	(anticipated expenditures/
		liabilities)

Unreserved Fund Balance	$ 20,000	(surplus is anticipated)

"Unreserved Fund Balance" is an equity account. The credit (debit if a deficit budget), when posted, adjusts the account to its anticipated year-end balance and maintains the integrity of the double-entry system.

As actual resource inflows and outflows occur during the year, they are recorded in "Revenues" and "Expenditures" accounts, and the detail is posted to the revenues and appropriations subsidiary ledgers in order to facilitate budget vs. actual comparisons. In order to prevent the overspending of an item in the appropriations budget, an additional budgetary account is maintained during the year. This budgetary account is called "Encumbrances." When goods or services are ordered, appropriations (specific items in the subsidiary ledger) are encumbered (restricted) with the following entry.

Encumbrances (detail posted to the subsid- iary appropriations ledger)	$5,000 (cost estimate)
Reserve for Encumbrances	$5,000 (cost estimate)

"Reserve for Encumbrances" is a fund equity account (a reservation of fund balance). When the debit in the entry is posted, the amount that can still be spent (technically known as "Unencumbered Appropriations") for an individual item is reduced. Thereafter, when the goods or services ordered are received, the encumbrance entry is reversed and the actual resource outflow (Expenditures) is recorded.

Reserve for Encumbrances	$5,000
Encumbrances (detail posted to subsidiary ledger)	$5,000
Expenditures (detail posted to subsidiary ledger)	$5,200 (actual cost)
Vouchers Payable	$5,200 (actual cost)

The "Encumbrances" account does not represent an expenditure; it is a budgetary account which represents the estimated cost of goods or services which have yet to be received. In effect, the recording of encumbrances represents the recording of executory contracts, which is essential to prevent overspending of an appropriation (normally, an illegal act). Likewise, the account "Reserve for Encumbrances" is not a liability account; it is a reservation (restriction) of the fund balance. If encumbrances are outstanding at the end of a period, the reserve for encumbrances is reported in the fund balance section of the balance sheet (similar to an appropriation of retained earnings on a corporation's balance sheet).

At the end of the year, the following closing entries would be recorded, assuming actual revenues for the year totaled $970,000, actual expenditures for the year were $950,000, and encumbrances outstanding at year end were $20,000.

1. Unreserved Fund Balance $ 30,000
   Revenues $970,000
     Estimated Revenues $1,000,000

If revenues exceeded estimated revenues, unreserved fund balance would increase and, therefore, be credited. During the period, revenues are considered a contra estimated revenue account in the interim balance sheet.

2. Appropriations $980,000
      Unreserved Fund Balance $ 10,000
      Expenditures $950,000
      Encumbrances $ 20,000

If appropriations had been exceeded by expenditures and encumbrances (a violation of the budget), unreserved fund balance would decrease and, therefore, be debited. During the period, both expenditures and encumbrances are considered contra appropriations accounts in the interim balance sheet.

C. Financial Statements for State and Local Governments

GAAFR Statement 1 provides for two types of annual reports, the General Purpose Financial Statements, which include the minimum statements required for GAAP and a clean opinion, and the Comprehensive Annual Financial Report, which contains a great deal of detail that is helpful for many users. According to Statement 1, the Comprehensive Annual Financial Report (CAFR) includes the following:

A. Introductory Section (table of contents, letter of transmittal, etc.)
B. Financial Section

1. Auditor's Report
2. General Purpose Financial Statements

   a. Combined Balance Sheet - All Fund Types and Account Groups
   b. Combined Statement of Revenues, Expenditures, and Changes in Fund Balances - All Governmental Fund Types
   c. Combined Statement of Revenues, Expenditures, and Changes in Fund Balances - Budget and Actual - General and Special Revenue Fund Types (and similar governmental fund types for which annual budgets have been legally adopted)
   d. Combined Statement of Revenue, Expenses, and Changes in Retained Earnings (or Equity) - All Proprietary Fund Types

e. Combined Statement of Changes in Financial Position - All Proprietary Fund Types
f. Notes to the Financial Statements
3. Combining and Individual Fund and Account Group Statements and Schedules

C. Statistical Tables

The following page reflects the sample "Combined Statement of Revenues, Expenditures, and Changes in Fund Balances - All Governmental Fund Types and Expendable
Trust Funds" that is displayed in NCGA Statement 1. This statement is to be prepared in accordance with generally accepted accounting principles, even if the budget is prepared on a non GAAP basis (such as the cash basis). The "expenditures" in
this statement do not include the amounts encumbered but not yet received. On the
other hand, the Combined Statement of Revenues, Expenditures, and Changes in Fund
Balances--Budget and Actual ("2.c." above) is to be prepared on the budgetary basis.
The budgetary basis may differ from the GAAP basis in various ways. For example,
the cash basis of accounting may be assumed in the budget, and it is possible that
encumbrances will be included in the expenditures column, especially if outstanding
encumbrances do not lapse (carry over to the next fiscal year). If differences
exist between the budgetary and GAAP bases, a reconciliation must be provided either
on this statement or in the footnotes.

D. Interim Financial Statements

Statement 1, in one of its basic principles, states that governmental units
should prepare appropriate interim financial statements. Based upon the preceding
discussion relating to Governmental Funds, the interim financial reports should
disclose information concerning estimated vs. actual revenues, and appropriations
vs. expenditures. For example, the interim balance sheet below shows the
integration of budgetary information with actual.

City of Zee
General Fund
Interim Balance Sheet
At March 31, 1985

Cash		$xx	Vouchers Payable		$xx
Receivables (net of allowance			Appropriations	$xx	
for uncollectible			Less: Expenditures $xx		
accounts)		xx	Encumbrances xx	(xx)	
Estimated Revenue	$xx		Unencumbered Appropriations		xx
Less: Revenue	xx		Fund Balance:		
Unrealized Revenue		xx	Reserved for Encumbrances xx		
			Unreserved	xx	xx
Total		$xx	Total		$xx

Name of Governmental Unit

**Combined Statement of Revenues, Expenditures, and Changes in Fund Balances—
All Governmental Fund Types and Expendable Trust Funds
for the Fiscal Year Ended December 31, 19X2**

	Governmental Fund Types					Fiduciary Fund Type	Totals (Memorandum Only) Year Ended	
	General	Special Revenue	Debt Service	Capital Projects	Special Assessment	Expendable Trust	December 31, 19X2	December 31, 19X1
Revenues:								
Taxes	$ 881,300	$ 189,300	$ 79,177	$ —	$ —	$ —	$1,149,777	$1,137,900
Special assessments levied	—	—	—	—	240,000	--	240,000	250,400
Licenses and permits	103,000	—	—	—	--	—	103,000	96,500
Intergovernmental revenues	186,500	831,100	41,500	1,250,000	—	—	2,309,100	1,258,800
Charges for services	91,000	79,100	--	—	—	—	170,100	160,400
Fines and forfeits	33,200	—	—	—	—	—	33,200	26,300
Miscellaneous revenues	19,500	71,625	7,140	3,750	29,095	200	131,310	111,500
Total revenues	1,314,500	1,171,125	127,817	1,253,750	269,095	200	4,136,487	3,041,800
Expenditures:								
Current:								
General government	121,805	—	--	—	—	—	121,805	134,200
Public safety	258,395	480,000	—	—	...	—	738,395	671,300
Highways and streets	85,400	417,000	—	—	--	—	502,400	408,700
Sanitation	56,250	—	—	--	—	—	56,250	44,100
Health	44,500	—	—	—	—	—	44,500	36,600
Welfare	46,800	—	—	--	—	—	46,800	41,400
Culture and recreation	40,900	256,450	—	--	—	—	297,350	286,400
Education	509,150	—	—	—	—	2,420	511,570	512,000
Capital outlay	—	—	--	1,625,500	313,100	—	1,938,600	803,000
Debt service:								
Principal retirement	—	—	60,000	—	—	---	60,000	52,100
Interest and fiscal charges	—	—	40,420	--	28,000	—	68,420	50,000
Total expenditures	1,163,200	1,153,450	100,420	1,625,500	341,100	2,420	4,386,090	3,039,800
Excess of revenues over (under) expenditures	151,300	17,675	27,397	(371,750)	(72,005)	(2,220)	(249,603)	2,000
Other Financing Sources (Uses):								
Proceeds of general obligation bonds	—	—	—	900,000	—	—	900,000	—
Operating transfers in	—	—	—	64,500	10,000	2,530	77,030	89,120
Operating transfers out	(74,500)	—	—	—	—	—	(74,500)	(87,000)
Total other financing sources (uses)	(74,500)	--	—	964,500	10,000	2,530	902,530	2,120
Excess of revenues and other sources over (under) expenditures and other uses	76,800	17,675	27,397	592,750	(62,005)	310	652,927	4,120
Fund balances — January 1	202,500	151,035	182,813	357,350	293,075	26,555	1,213,328	1,209,208
Fund balances — December 31	$ 279,300	$ 168,710	$210,210	$ 950,100	$231,070	$26,865	$1,866,255	$1,213,328

The notes to the financial statements are an integral part of this statement.

Source: National Council on Governmental Accounting, NCGA Statement 1: Governmental Accounting and Financial Reporting Principles, p. 33 (reprinted with permission).

In addition to the balance sheet, interim reports showing detailed comparisons between estimated vs. actual revenues by source (e.g., taxes, licenses and permits), and appropriations vs. expenditures and encumbrances by function, department, and object of expenditure (e.g., public safety--police salaries) should be prepared. These statements should disclose year-to-date information and compare the current with the preceding year.

E. Governmental Funds

The 8 funds and 2 groups of accounts listed on page 1063 are discussed in this section. First, a complete explanation is provided of the General Fund. Second, the distinguishing accounts, entries, etc., of the other funds are presented. Before sitting for the exam, you need to obtain a thorough understanding of the General Fund and also learn the peculiarities of the other funds. Emphasis should be put on:

1) The purpose and nature of each fund
2) Account titles of the budgetary accounts
3) Other peculiar account titles and transactions
4) Fixed asset and long-term debt accounting
5) Accrual vs. modified accrual basis accounting
6) Interfund transactions and transfers
7) Financial statements applicable to each fund

Before individual funds are discussed, it is important to understand what is meant by accrual and the modified accrual basis of accounting. One of the basic NCGA principles states, "The modified accrual or accrual basis of accounting, as appropriate, should be used in measuring financial position and operating results." Accrual basis accounting is recognition of revenues in the accounting period the revenues are earned and recognition of expenses in the accounting period the expenses are incurred. In addition, revenues and expenses have to be measurable in order to be reported. The following funds should use full accrual accounting:

Proprietary Funds	Fiduciary Funds
Enterprise	Nonexpendable Trust
Internal Service	and Pension Funds

All of the funds which use accrual accounting (except Pension Trust Funds) are nonexpendable; i.e., an objective of each of the funds is to maintain capital. The modified accrual basis of accounting, on the other hand, recognizes:

1) Revenues in the accounting period in which they are both measurable and available to finance expenditures
2) Expenditures in the accounting period in which the liabilities are both measurable and incurred *

Revenues normally recognized on the accrual basis include property taxes (when available to finance current expenditures),** firm intergovernmental grants and revenues, interest on investments and delinquent taxes, other taxes collected and not yet released by intermediary governments, and regularly billed charges for services. Revenues normally recognized on the cash basis include sales taxes, licenses and permits, fines and forfeits, interest on deferred special assessments (when approximately offsetting interest expenditures on special assessment debt), parking meter receipts, etc. Revenue from special assessments should be recognized when the assessments are currently due.

There are four major exceptions to recognition of expenditures as they are incurred.

1) In Debt Service Funds, expenditures for interest on general long-term debt should represent that which is matured (due) and payable during the fiscal period. Expenditures (and the related liability) for unmatured interest (accrued interest) at the end of the year are not recorded.

2) In the Special Assessments funds, expenditures for interest on special assessment bonds secured by special assessment levies may be recorded only when matured and payable. Again, unmatured interest does not have to be recorded at the end of the year.

3) Inventories of materials and supplies may be considered expenditures either when purchased (purchases method) or when used (consumption method)

4) Expenditures for insurance and similar prepaid items may be recognized in the period of acquisition

The modified accrual basis is used in the following funds:

Governmental Funds	Fiduciary
General	Expendable Trust Funds
Special Revenue	Agency Funds
Capital Projects	
Debt Service	
Special Assessments	

All of the funds which use the modified accrual basis are expendable and do not, therefore, have a capital maintenance objective. Additional description of the modified accrual basis is provided in the discussion of specific funds.

---

*In those expendable funds in which the modified accrual basis is used, the term expenditures (an outflow of current resources) is used in lieu of expenses. This is because matching is not an objective of accounting in these funds.

**NCGA Interpretation 3 indicates that property tax revenue generally is available to finance current expenditures if collected during the current period or will be collected within 60 days after the end of the current period.

1. The General Fund

The General Fund is the most significant Governmental Fund. It accounts for all transactions not accounted for in any other fund. Revenues come from many sources (taxes, licenses and permits, fines and forfeits, charges for services, etc.), and the expenditures cover the major functions of government (public safety, highways and streets, education, etc.). An overview of the account structure for the General Fund is as follows:

	Nominal Accounts	
Balance Sheet Accounts	**Operating**	**Budgetary**
Current Assets (Dr.)	Revenues (Cr.)	Estimated Revenues (Dr.)
Current Liabilities (Cr.)	Expenditures (Dr.)	Appropriations (Cr.)
Fund Equity (Cr.)	Transfers (Dr. or Cr.)	Encumbrances (Dr.)
Reserved Fund Balance	Operating	Estimated Operating Transfers In (Dr.)
Unreserved Fund Balance	Residual Equity	Estimated Operating Transfers Out (Cr.)

The following represents an accounting cycle problem for the General Fund. Some of these entries have been illustrated previously.

a. Adoption of a budget where estimated revenues exceed appropriations by $60,000. (First year of existence for this governmental unit.)

Estimated Revenues (detail posted to subsidiary ledger)	$300,000	
Appropriations (detail posted to subsidiary ledger)		$240,000
Estimated Operating Transfers Out		$ 50,000
Unreserved Fund Balance		$ 10,000

b. Transfers to Debt Service Fund (for general long-term debt interest and principal payments) and Special Assessments Fund (for General Fund's share of a project) amount to $20,000 and $30,000 respectively.

Operating Transfers Out	$50,000	
Due to Debt Service Fund		$20,000
Due to Special Assessments Fund		$30,000

According to the NCGA principles, "Transfers should be recognized in the accounting period in which the interfund receivable and payable arises." The account "Operating Transfers Out" is a temporary account which is closed against the budgetary account "Estimated Operating Transfers Out" at the end of the year. The accounts "Due to -- Fund" are current liabilities. Note that the Debt Service and Special Assessments Funds would each record a receivable, as follows:

Debt Service		Special Assessments	
Due from General Fund	$20,000	Due from General Fund	$30,000
Operating Transfers In	$20,000	Operating Transfers In	$30,000

The "Operating Transfers" accounts are closed at the end of the year. It is important to note that the account "Operating Transfers Out" is not an expenditure account, and that the account "Operating Transfers In" is not a revenue account but is considered "Other Financing Sources (Uses)." For more discussion of interfund transactions and transfers, see the discussion on pages 1095 to 1099.

c. The property tax levy is recorded as revenues, under the modified accrual basis, when the tax levy is enacted by the governmental unit, if collections will be in time to finance expenditures of the current period. The tax bills amount to $250,000, and $20,000 is estimated to be uncollectible.

Property Taxes Receivable - Current	$250,000	
Allowance for Uncollectible Taxes - Current		$ 20,000
Revenues		$230,000

Under the modified accrual basis, revenues should be recorded in the period in which they are both measurable and available. NCGA Interpretation 3 requires that property taxes be recognized as a revenue if the taxes are:

1) Available - collected soon enough to pay liabilities of the current period (within 60 days of the end of the fiscal year)
2) To finance the budget of the current period

If the modified accrual criteria for recognition are not met, the property tax levy would be recorded with a credit to Deferred Revenues instead of Revenues.

If cash is needed to pay for expenditures before the property tax receivables are collected, it is not uncommon for governmental units to borrow on tax anticipation warrants. The receivable serves as security for this loan and, as taxes are collected, the anticipation warrants are liquidated, i.e., "Tax Anticipation Warrants Payable" is debited.

Note, also, the treatment of the allowance for uncollectible accounts. Expendable funds account for resource inflows (revenues) and resource outflows (expenditures). Expenses are not recorded. The allowance for uncollectible accounts represents an estimated reduction in a resource inflow and, accordingly, revenues are recorded net of estimated uncollectible taxes.

d. Revenues from fines, licenses, and permits amount to $40,000.

| Cash | $40,000 | |
| Revenues (detail posted) | | $40,000 |

Resource inflows from fines, licenses, permits, etc. are usually not measurable until the cash is collected. Sometimes, it is possible to measure the potential resource inflow; however, because the availability is questionable, revenues are recorded when cash is collected.

e. The state owes the city $25,000 for the city's share of the state sales tax. The amount has not been received at year end, but it is expected within the first few months of the next fiscal year.

| State Sales Tax Receivable | $25,000 | |
| Revenues (detail posted) | | $25,000 |

Sales taxes, income taxes, etc. are not accrued before collected by a governmental unit. However, once collected, it is appropriate for recipient governmental units to record the receivable and revenue. The amount due from the state is measurable, and it will soon be available to finance year-end liabilities which resulted from expenditures. Other firm commitments from the state or other governmental units for grants, etc. are also recorded.

f. Incurred liabilities for salaries, repairs, utilities, rent, and other regularly occurring items for $220,000.

Expenditures (detail posted)	$220,000
Vouchers Payable	$220,000

Note that all resource outflows authorized in the appropriations budget are debited to "Expenditures." It makes no difference whether the outflow is for a fire truck or for rent. Remember, expendable funds do not have a capital maintenance objective. Also, note that the encumbrance accounts were not used in this example. There is usually no need to encumber appropriations for items that occur regularly, and which possess a highly predictable amount--e.g., salaries, rent, etc. It should be pointed out, however, that there is no hard and fast rule for when to use encumbrances, and encumbrance policies do vary tremendously, i.e., from every expenditure being encumbered to virtually no expenditures being encumbered.

g. Ordered one police car; estimated cost is $7,000. One month later, ordered second police car; estimated cost is $6,500.

Encumbrances	$7,000
Reserve for Encumbrances	$7,000
Encumbrances	$6,500
Reserve for Encumbrances	$6,500

Recording encumbrances prevents overspending line-item appropriations. In the case of the police cars, assume the appropriations budget authorized $14,000 for police vehicles. After the first police car was ordered, the unencumbered appropriation for police vehicles was reduced to $7,000. This placed a dollar limit on what could be spent on the second car.

h. Police car ordered first was received; actual cost is $6,800.

Reserve for Encumbrances	$7,000
Encumbrances	$7,000
Expenditures	$6,800
Vouchers Payable	$6,800

In order to achieve accountability and control over fixed assets acquired by expendable funds, the following entry would be made in the General Fixed Assets (GFA) Group of Accounts:

Vehicles - Police Cars	$6,800
Investment in Fixed Assets - General Fund Revenues	$6,800

i. Property tax collections amounted to $233,000, payments to other funds amounted to $50,000 (see Item B), and payments of vouchers were $190,000.

Cash	$233,000	
Property Taxes Receivable - Current		$233,000
Due to Debt Service Fund	$ 20,000	
Due to Special Assessments Fund	$ 30,000	
Cash		$ 50,000
Vouchers Payable	$190,000	
Cash		$190,000
Allowance for Uncollectible Taxes - Current	$ 3,000	
Revenues		$ 3,000

The last entry above is required because the "Allowance for Uncollectible Taxes - Current" was overstated. Note that the estimate was $20,000 in entry "c." above. Tax revenues were estimated to be $230,000. Since property tax collections exceeded $230,000 for the current year, an increase in revenues is required.

j. Recorded $5,000 inventory of materials and supplies, reduced the allowance for uncollectible property taxes to $10,000, and reclassified uncollected property taxes to delinquent accounts.

Materials and Supplies Inventory*	$ 5,000	
Reserve for Inventory of		
Materials and Supplies		$ 5,000
Allowance for Uncollectible Taxes - Current	$ 7,000	
Revenues		$ 7,000
Property Taxes Receivable - Delinquent	$17,000	
Allowance for Uncollectible Taxes - Current	$10,000	
Allowance for Uncollectible Taxes -		
Delinquent		$10,000
Property Taxes Receivable - Current		$17,000

One of the reasons for recording the inventory of materials and supplies is to inform the preparers of the budget that items purchased during the year and charged to expenditures (Item "f.") are still unused. The account "Reserve for Inventory of Materials and Supplies" is a reservation of fund balance. In this respect, it is similar to "Reserve for Encumbrances."

The second entry adjusts the estimate of uncollectible property taxes. This is the result of collecting more property taxes than anticipated (see entries made in "c." and "i." above).

The third entry reclassifies property taxes receivable from current to delinquent at the end of the year. Generally, interest and penalty charges accrue

---

*The illustration covers the "purchase method" for materials and supplies. The "consumption method" is not covered in this illustration. Consult an advanced or governmental text for coverage of the latter method.

on the unpaid taxes from the date they become delinquent. If these items have
accrued at the end of a fiscal period, they would be recorded in the following
way:

Interest and Penalties Receivable on		
Delinquent Taxes	$xx	
Allowance for Uncollectible Interest		
and Penalties		$xx
Revenues		$xx

k. Appropriate closing entries are made.

Revenues	$305,000	
Unreserved Fund Balance		$ 5,000
Estimated Revenues		$300,000
Estimated Operating Transfers Out	$ 50,000	
Operating Transfers Out		$ 50,000
Appropriations	$240,000	
Expenditures		$226,800
Encumbrances		$ 6,500
Unreserved Fund Balance		$ 6,700
Reserve for Encumbrances	$ 6,500	
Reserve for Encumbrances - Prior Year		$ 6,500

Financial Statements. Under NCGA Statement 1, individual fund statements should
not be prepared that simply repeat information found in the combined or combining
statements but would be prepared to present individual fund budgetary comparisons
(not needed for the General Fund), to present prior year comparative data, or to
present more detailed information than is found in the combined or combining statements. The statements normally found in a CAFR for the General Fund are:

1) Balance Sheet (as part of the Combined Statement)
2) Statement of Revenues, Expenditures, and Changes in Fund Balances (as part
   of the Combined Statement--GAAP Basis)

3) Statement of Revenues, Expenditures, and Changes in Fund Balances--Budget
   and Actual (as part of the Combined Statement--Budgetary Basis)

4) Statement of Budgeted and Actual Revenues (in greater detail)
5) Statement of Budgeted and Actual Expenditures and Encumbrances (in greater
   detail)

The fourth and fifth statements may be combined.

The following balance sheet would represent the General Fund portion of the
Combined Balance Sheet:

City of X
General Fund
Balance Sheet
At June 30, 19XX

Assets			Liabilities and Fund Equity		
Cash		$33,000	Liabilities:		
Property Taxes Receivable - Delinquent	$17,000		Vouchers Payable		$36,800
			Fund Equity:		
Less: Allowance for Uncollectible Taxes - Delinquent	10,000	7,000	Reserved for Inventory of Materials and Supplies	$ 5,000	
State Sales Tax Receivable		25,000	Reserved for Encumbrances - Prior Year	6,500	
Inventory of Materials and Supplies		5,000	Unreserved Fund Balance	21,700	
			Total Fund Equity		$33,200
Total Assets		$70,000	Total Liabilities and Fund Equity		$70,000

Note the following points from the balance sheet:

1) The total fund equity is $33,200, but only $21,700 is unreserved. This $21,700 represents the appropriable component of total fund balance, i.e., the amount that can be used next period to help finance a deficit budget. The $21,700 represents unreserved net liquid resources.

2) The reason for crediting "Reserve for Inventory of Materials and Supplies" in item "j." previously should now be more meaningful. The inventory of materials and supplies is not a liquid resource which can be used to finance future expenditures. Consequently, if this asset is disclosed, it must be disclosed via a fund restriction.

3) The "Reserve for Encumbrances" which is disclosed on the balance sheet relates to the second police car which was ordered but not delivered at year end. When the car is received in the next period, the following journal entries would be made, assuming the actual cost is $6,600:

Expenditures - Prior Year	$6,600	
Vouchers Payable		$6,600
Reserved for Encumbrances - Prior Year	$6,500	
Unreserved Fund Balance	$ 100	
Expenditures - Prior Year		$6,600

In the General Fixed Assets Group of Accounts:

Vehicles - Police Cars	$6,600	
Investment in Fixed Assets - General Fund Revenues		$6,600

The following would be the General Fund Portion of the "Budget/Actual Combined Statement."

CITY OF X
GENERAL FUND
STATEMENT OF REVENUES, EXPENDITURES, AND CHANGES IN FUND
BALANCE - BUDGET AND ACTUAL
FOR YEAR ENDED JUNE 30, 19XX

	Budget	Actual	Variance Over (Under)
Revenues:			
. . . . . .	$300,000	$305,000	$ 5,000
. . .			
Expenditures:			
. . . . . .	240,000	226,800	(13,200)
. . .			
Excess of Revenues over Expenditures	$ 60,000	$ 78,200	$18,200
Other Financing Uses: Operating Transfers Out	(50,000)	(50,000)	-0-
Excess of Revenues over Expenditures and Other Financing Uses	$ 10,000	$28,200	$18,200
Fund Balance at Beginning of Year	-0-	-0-	-0-
Add Increase in Reserve for Inventory	5,000	5,000	-0-
Fund Balance at End of Year	$ 15,000	$33,200	$18,200

Note that the Statement ends with the total Fund Balance. An acceptable alternative for this Statement or for the Statement of Revenues, Expenditures, and Changes in Fund Balances would be to end with Unreserved Fund Balance. If this were done, the $6,500 Reserve for Encumbrances would be subtracted from the $28,200 in the "Actual" column to get the $21,700 Unreserved Fund Balance.

One additional point needs to be covered before going to Special Revenue Funds, i.e., how to account for the inventory of materials and supplies in the second or any subsequent year. Accordingly, assume that at the end of the second year, $4,000 of materials and supplies were unused. The adjusting entry would appear as follows:

Reserve for Inventory of Materials and Supplies $1,000
    Materials and Supplies Inventory $1,000

This entry, when posted, will result in a balance of $4,000 in the inventory and reserve accounts. Note the entry at the end of the first year established a $5,000 balance in these accounts. Thereafter, the inventory and reserve accounts are adjusted upward or downward to whatever the balance is at the end of the year.

1. ALTERNATE GAAFR BUDGET ENTRIES. The 1980 <u>GAAFR</u>, published by the MFOA, created a new method for handling the budgetary accounts when an annual budget is adopted. The procedures outlined in <u>GAAFR</u> are not required for GAAP but are presented below as an alternative means of handling the budgetary portions of the illustrative problem for the General Fund. Each transaction below has the same identifying letter as the same transaction in the illustrative General Fund problem.

a. Adoption of the budget.

ESTIMATED REVENUES CONTROL	$300,000	
APPROPRIATIONS CONTROL		$240,000
ESTIMATED OTHER FINANCING USES CONTROL		$ 50,000
BUDGETARY FUND BALANCE		$ 10,000

Note that all budgetary accounts are capitalized. Also note that the account "Budgetary Fund Balance" is a budgetary account. The equity account, "Unreserved Fund Balance," will not be affected until the end of the accounting period.

g. Ordered two police cars, one month apart.

ENCUMBRANCES CONTROL	$7,000	
FUND BALANCE RESERVED FOR ENCUMBRANCES		$7,000
ENCUMBRANCES CONTROL	$6,500	
FUND BALANCE RESERVED FOR ENCUMBRANCES		$6,500

These are both budgetary accounts. The equity account, "Reserve for Encumbrances," is not yet affected.

h. The first police car arrived, actual cost $6,800.

FUND BALANCE RESERVED FOR ENCUMBRANCES	$ 7,000	
ENCUMBRANCES CONTROL		$ 7,000
Expenditures	$ 6,800	
Vouchers Payable		$ 6,800

Note that "Expenditures" is not a budgetary account and, therefore, is not capitalized.

k. Appropriate closing entries are made.

FUND BALANCE RESERVED FOR ENCUMBRANCES	$ 6,500	
ENCUMBRANCES CONTROL		$ 6,500
Unreserved Fund Balance	$ 6,500	
Reserve for Encumbrances		$ 6,500
APPROPRIATIONS CONTROL	$240,000	
ESTIMATED OTHER FINANCING USES CONTROL	$ 50,000	
BUDGETARY FUND BALANCE	$ 10,000	
ESTIMATED REVENUES CONTROL		$300,000
Revenues	$305,000	
Expenditures		$226,800
Operating Transfers Out		$ 50,000
Unreserved Fund Balance		$ 28,200

The first and third closing entries simply close the budgetary accounts by reversing out the balances. The second closing entry adjusts the equity account, "Reserve for Encumbrances," from the beginning to ending balance by decreasing (in this case) Unreserved Fund Balance. The amount is $6,500, since there was no beginning balance in Reserve for Encumbrances. The fourth closing entry closes out the operating accounts to Unreserved Fund Balance.

2. Special Revenue Funds

Special Revenue Funds account for earmarked revenue as opposed to the many revenue sources which are accounted for in the General Fund. The earmarked revenue is then used to finance various authorized expenditures. For example, the proceeds from on-street parking meters might be placed in a Parking Meter Fund. The resources of this fund could be used for traffic law enforcement - traffic courts and police. Similarly, a city might place its share of the state's gasoline tax revenues into a State Gasoline Tax Fund, which could then be used to maintain streets. Note that a governmental unit has some discretion in terms of how many Special Revenue Funds it creates. Sometimes separate funds are required by law or grant requirements. Many federal and state grants, including revenue sharing, are reported in Special Revenue Funds.

The accounting for Special Revenue Funds parallels that of the General Fund. In terms of financial reporting, when a governmental unit has more than one Special Revenue Fund, the NCGA mandates combining fund reports for the Comprehensive Annual Financial Report.

A special problem relates to the receipt of grant proceeds and the recognition of revenues. NCGA Statement 2 indicates that a restricted revenue is not considered earned until the expenditure has taken place. The reasoning is that if the expenditure does not take place in accordance with grant guidelines, it will be necessary to return the grant proceeds. For example, if the City of X receives $100,000 in grant proceeds in 19X1, but expends those proceeds in FY 19X2, the entries for both years would be as follows:

19X1
```
     Cash                          $100,000
          Deferred Revenues                    $100,000
```

19X2
```
     Expenditures                  $100,000
          Cash                                 $100,000

     Deferred Revenues             $100,000
          Revenues                             $100,000
```

Of course, if the funds were expended in FY 19X1, the revenue would also be recognized in that year.

3. Capital Projects Funds

Capital Projects Funds account for the acquisition and use of resources for the construction or purchase of major, long-lived fixed assets, except for those which are financed by Special Assessment, Internal Service, and Enterprise Funds. Resources for construction or purchase normally come from the issuance of general long-term debt and from government grants (federal, state, and local).

Budgets (long-term capital budgets) for estimated resources and appropriations must be approved before the project can begin. However, unlike the operating budgets of General and Special Revenue Funds, the capital projects budget is not generally recorded formally in the accounts. The budget is generally not recorded because a Capital Projects Fund is usually established for each project, and the number of revenue and other financing sources and expenditure outlays is small. However, it is permissable to record the budget if so desired by the governmental unit.

The following transactions illustrate the entries encountered in the Capital Projects Fund.

a. City Council approved the construction of a new city hall at an estimated cost of $10,000,000. General obligation long-term serial debt was authorized for issuance in the face amount of $10,000,000.

No formal entry need be recorded for the project authorization, although a budgetary entry is permissible. Assume a "memorandum only" recording.

b. $10,000,000 in 8% general obligation serial bonds were issued for $10,100,000. Assume that the premium is transferred to a debt service fund for the eventual payment of the debt.

Cash	$10,100,000	
Proceeds of Bonds		$10,100,000
Operating Transfers Out	$ 100,000	
Cash		$ 100,000

Note the credit to "Proceeds of Bonds." This is an "Other Financing Source" on the operating statement, whereas the "Operating Transfers Out" is an "Other Financing Use." Both accounts are temporary accounts that are closed to Unreserved Fund Balance at year end.

The sale of bonds and the transfer require entries in the Debt Service Fund and the General Long-Term Debt Group of Accounts.

Debt Service Fund

Cash	$ 100,000	
Operating Transfer In		$ 100,000

General Long-Term Debt Group

Amount Available for Retirement of Bonds	$ 100,000	
Amount to be Provided for Retirement of Bonds	$4,900,000	
8% General Obligation Serial Bonds Payable		$5,000,000

These entries will be explained in more detail later.

c. The bond issue proceeds are temporarily invested in a Certificate of Deposit (CD) and earn $50,000. The earnings are authorized to be sent to the Debt Service Fund for the payment of bonds.

Capital Projects Fund			Debt Service Fund		
Investment in CD	$10,000,000				
Cash		$10,000,000			
Cash	$ 50,000				
Revenues		$ 50,000			
Operating Transfers Out	$ 50,000		Cash	$50,000	
Cash		$ 50,000	Operating Transfers In		$50,000

General Long-Term Debt Group

Amount Available for Retirement of Bonds	$50,000	
Amount to be Provided for Retirement of Bonds		$50,000

d. The lowest bid, $9,800,000, is accepted from a general contractor.

Encumbrances	$9,800,000	
Reserve for Encumbrances		$9,800,000

e. $2,000,000 of the temporary investments are liquidated.

Cash	$2,000,000	
Investment in CD		$2,000,000

f. Progress billings due to the general contractor for work performed amount to $2,000,000. The contract allows 10% of the billings to be retained until final inspection and approval of the building. The contractor was paid $1,800,000.

Reserve for Encumbrances	$2,000,000	
Encumbrances		$2,000,000
Expenditures	$2,000,000	
Contracts Payable		$2,000,000
Contracts Payable	$2,000,000	
Cash		$1,800,000
Contracts Payable - Retained Percentage		$ 200,000

The account "Contracts Payable - Retained Percentage" is a liability account. Note, also, that the fixed asset is not recorded in the Capital Projects

Fund because this fund is expendable and does not have a capital maintenance objective. The fixed asset is recorded in the General Fixed Asset Group of Accounts.

At this point (year end), note that construction in progress would be recorded in the GFA Group of Accounts, as follows:

Construction in Progress - City Hall	$2,000,000
Investment in General Fixed Assets - Capital	
Projects Fund - G.O. Bonds	$2,000,000

When the project is finished, "Construction in Progress" would be credited and "Buildings" would be debited.

g. Interest accrued on CD at the end of the year amounted to $40,000. This was authorized to be sent to the Debt Service Fund for the payment of debt.

Capital Projects Fund		Debt Service Fund	
Interest Receivable	$40,000		
Revenues	$40,000		
Operating Transfers			
Out	$40,000	Due From Other Funds	$40,000
Due to Other Funds	$40,000	Operating Transfers	
		In	$40,000

General Long-Term Debt Group	
Amount Available for Retirement of Bonds	$40,000
Amount to be Provided for Retirement of Bonds	$40,000

The interest is recognized because it is measurable and will soon be available to finance Debt Service Fund expenditures.

h. Closing entries for the Capital Projects Fund would appear as follows:

1)	Revenues	$ 90,000	
	Proceeds of Bonds	$10,100,000	
	Unreserved Fund Balance		$10,190,000
2)	Unreserved Fund Balance	$ 9,800,000	
	Encumbrances		$7,800,000
	Expenditures		$2,000,000
3)	Unreserved Fund Balance	$ 190,000	
	Operating Transfers Out		$ 190,000

NCGA Statement 1 requires that the totals for all Capital Projects Funds appear in the Combined Balance Sheet, the Combined Statement of Revenues, Expenditures, and Changes in Fund Balances, and the Combined Statement of Revenues, Expenditures, and Changes in Fund Balances--Budget and Actual. Combining Statements are required if the governmental unit has more than one Capital Projects Fund.

A "stand-alone" Statement of Revenues, Expenditures, and Changes in Fund Balances appears for the Capital Projects Fund example:

City of X
Capital Projects Fund
Statement of Revenues, Expenditures, and Changes
in Fund Balances
Year Ended June 30, 19XX

Revenues and Other Financing Sources:
   Revenues:
      Interest on Temporary Investments $ 90,000
   Other Financing Sources:
      Proceeds of General Obligation Bonds   10,100,000
      Total Revenues and Other Financing Sources $10,190,000
Expenditures and Other Financing Uses:
   Expenditures:
      Construction of City Hall   2,000,000
   Other Uses:
      Transfer to Debt Service Fund   190,000
      Total Expenditures and Other Financing Uses $ 2,190,000
Excess of Revenues and Other Financing Sources
 over Expenditures and Other Uses $ 8,000,000
Fund Balance at Beginning of Year   -0-
Deduct Reserve for Encumbrances   7,800,000
Unreserved Fund Balance at End of Year $ 200,000

Note that the above operating statement classified "Other Financing Sources" with "Revenues" and "Other Uses" with "Expenditures." This is an acceptable alternative to the format shown for the General Fund on page 1077.

At the beginning of the second year, the following entry would be made to reestablish the "Encumbrances" balance:

Encumbrances $7,800,000
   Unreserved Fund Balance $7,800,000

The purpose of this entry is to permit the recording of expenditures in the normal manner; i.e., reverse the encumbrances before recording the expenditures.

When the city hall project is finished, the Capital Projects Fund should be terminated. Assuming there are no cost overruns, the excess cash left in the fund upon project completion must be transferred to some other fund. This is called a residual equity transfer and is described along with other interfund transactions and transfers on pages 1096 to 1097. Finally, upon project completion, the GFA will record the fixed asset as follows:

City Hall $9,800,000
   Construction in Progress - City Hall $2,000,000
   Investment in General Fixed Assets - Capital
   Projects Fund - G.O. Bonds $7,800,000

4. Debt Service Funds

Debt Service Funds usually handle the repayment of general obligation long-term debt. This type of debt is secured by the good faith and taxing power of the governmental unit. Repayment of special assessment, internal service, and enterprise long-term debt is accounted for in these individual funds. Consequently, the type of debt for which the Debt Service Fund is established usually is the result of issuing general obligation bonds for capital projects. The Debt Service Fund is used to account for repayment of bond principal and the payment of interest.

The bond liability to be extinguished is not recorded in the Debt Service Fund until it matures. The purpose of this fund is to accumulate resources to liquidate general long-term debt. When the debt matures, it is transferred from the General Long-Term Debt (GLTD) Group of Accounts to the Debt Service Fund. Remember, when the bonds were sold to finance the city hall project, the liability was recorded in the GLTD Group of Accounts.

The Debt Service Fund often requires an annual operating budget for its estimated revenues, other financing sources, and appropriations. The resources usually come from an allocated portion of property taxes and from interfund transfers. The expenditures are made for matured bonds payable and for interest. Remember that Statement 1 permits governmental units to either record or not record the budget in the accounts of debt service funds. However, in the example which follows, the budget is recorded because of the importance of ensuring that funds are available for debt service payments.

Assume the City of X authorizes a Debt Service Fund for the general obligation serial bonds issued to finance the city hall project. The Debt Service Fund is also authorized to pay the 8% interest on the $10,000,000 of debt on August 1 and February 1. The fiscal year end is June 30. Note that the Debt Service Fund has received resources from the General and Capital Projects Funds. Transactions showing recognition and receipt of these resources were illustrated in the discussions of the General and Capital Projects Funds. They are repeated below as follows:

1)	Due From General Fund	$ 20,000	(Transaction "b."
	Operating Transfers In	$ 20,000	on page 1071)
2)	Cash	$ 20,000	(Transaction "b."
	Due from General Fund	$ 20,000	on page 1071)
3)	Cash	$100,000	(Transaction "b."
	Operating Transfers In	$100,000	on page 1080)
4)	Cash	$ 50,000	(Transaction "c."
	Operating Transfers In	$ 50,000	on page 1081)
5)	Due from Capital Projects Fund	$ 40,000	(Transaction "g."
	Operating Transfers In	$ 40,000	on page 1082)

Assume the bonds were issued on July 1. In addition, assume that $250,000 of
the bonds mature each six months, starting February 1.

a. The following entry records the budget for the first year.

Estimated Operating Transfers In	$200,000	
Estimated Revenues (portion of property taxes)	$850,000	
Appropriations (for two interest and one		
principal payment)		$1,050,000

b. The property tax levy contains an $870,000 portion allocable to the Debt Ser-
vice Fund. $20,000 of this amount is estimated to be uncollectible.

Property Taxes Receivable - Current	$870,000	
Allowance for Uncollectible Taxes - Current		$ 20,000
Revenues		$850,000

c. $840,000 of property taxes are collected during the year. The remainder of the
property taxes are reclassified as delinquent.

Cash	$840,000	
Property Taxes Receivable - Current		$840,000
Property Taxes Receivable - Delinquent	$ 30,000	
Allowance for Uncollectible Taxes - Current	$ 20,000	
Property Taxes Receivable - Current		$ 30,000
Allowance for Uncollectible Taxes - Delinquent		$ 20,000

Assuming that $40,000 of the tax collections are for the payment of principal
and the remainder is for the payment of interest, the following entry is
required in the General Long-Term Debt Group of Accounts:

Amount Available for the Retirement of Bonds	$ 40,000	
Amount to be Provided for the Retirement of Bonds		$ 40,000

d. The semi-annual interest is paid on August 1 and February 1. The following
entries are made twice each year.

Expenditures	$400,000	
Matured Interest Payable		$400,000
Matured Interest Payable	$400,000	
Cash		$400,000

Note that accrued interest from February 1 to June 30 need not be recorded.
This is an exception permitted by the modified accrual basis--unmatured interest
is not recorded in Debt Service Funds.

e. On February 1, the first $250,000 principal payment became due of which $200,000
was paid. The following entries would be made in the Debt Service Fund and
General Long-Term Debt Group of Accounts:

Debt Service Fund

Expenditures	$250,000	
Matured Bonds Payable		$250,000
Matured Bonds Payable	$200,000	
Cash		$200,000

General Long-Term Debt Group of Accounts

8% General Obligation Serial Bonds Payable	$250,000	
Amount Available for Retirement of Bonds		$250,000

If a bank were used as the fiscal agent, cash would first be transferred to a "Cash with Fiscal Agent" account, and payment would then be made from that account.

f. Appropriate closing entries are made based upon all information presented:

Operating Transfers In	$ 210,000	
Revenues	$ 850,000	
Appropriations	$1,050,000	
Estimated Revenues		$ 850,000
Expenditures		$1,050,000
Estimated Operating Transfers In		$ 200,000
Fund Balance		$ 10,000

The balance sheet for the Debt Service Fund would appear as follows:

City of X
Debt Service Fund
Balance Sheet
June 30, 19XX

Assets		Liabilities and Fund Equity	
Cash	$ 10,000	Liabilities:	
Due from Capital Projects Fund	40,000	Matured Bonds Payable	$ 50,000
Property taxes receivable--delinquent (net of $20,000 allowance for uncollectible taxes)	10,000	Fund Equity:	
		Fund Balance	10,000
Total Assets	$ 60,000	Total Liabilities and Fund Equity	$ 60,000

Note that the $10,000 Fund Balance equals the "Amount Available for Retirement of Debt" in the General Long-Term Debt Group of Accounts.

5. Special Assessment Funds

Special Assessment Funds account for the acquisition and use of resources for constructing capital improvements which are partially or fully paid by assessments levied against the owners of benefited property. The accounting for a Special Assessment Fund is similar to that of a Capital Projects Fund except the bond liability is recorded directly in the Special Assessment Fund. The following is an example of accounting for a special assessment project:

a. A special sidewalk project is authorized at a cost of $200,000. The city has agreed to transfer $30,000 of General Fund resources needed for the construction. Bonds with a face of $170,000 are issued at par. Special assessments totalling $170,000 are levied against the property owners, payable ratably over a ten-year period. The bonds mature in ten years and pay interest at 8% on September 1 and March 1. The following journal entries are recorded:

1) Budget is recorded in memorandum form (again, the budget might have been recorded formally).

2) Due from General Fund $ 30,000
        Operating Transfers In $ 30,000

This transaction was discussed previously in the section covering the General Fund.

3) Cash $170,000
        Bonds Payable $170,000

Note the bonds payable are recorded directly in this fund. These bonds are not general obligation debt. They are secured by the special assessments levied against the property owners. Accordingly, the GLTD Group of Accounts does not report this liability.

4) Special Assessments Receivable - Current $ 17,000
    Special Assessments Receivable - Deferred $153,000
        Revenues $ 17,000
        Deferred Revenues $153,000

Since Special Assessment Funds are governmental funds and use modified accrual accounting, revenues cannot be recognized until available to finance current period expenditures. One method, and the method followed in this review, is to recognize revenues as the assessments become current. This will result in a negative fund balance in many situations. This problem should be addressed soon by the GASB.

The deferred special assessments earn interest. The interest earned is used to service the interest on the bonds payable. The interest is recorded as revenue when received; accrued interest receivable does not have to be recorded (see discussion below).

5) On September 1 and March 1, the interest on the bonds is recorded as follows (entries recorded twice each fiscal year):

            Expenditures - Interest $ 6,800
                Interest Payable $ 6,800

            Interest Payable $ 6,800
                Cash $ 6,800

It is important to note that expenditures for interest do not have to be accrued from March 1 to June 30. This is an exception permitted by the modified accrual basis if the interest accrued is approximately offset by accrued interest earned on deferred special assessments.

b. Contracts are let for the construction of the sidewalks in the amount of $190,000. The sidewalks are completed at a cost of $191,000. The first installment of the special assessments is received:

1)	Encumbrances	$190,000
	Reserve for Encumbrances	$190,000
2)	Reserve for Encumbrances	$190,000
	Encumbrances	$190,000
3)	Expenditures - Sidewalks	$191,000
	Contracts Payable	$191,000
4)	Cash	$ 17,000
	Special Assessments Receivable - Current	$ 17,000

Note that the capital asset is not recorded in the Special Assessments Fund. It may be recorded in the GFA Group of Accounts as follows:

Improvements Other Than Buildings	$191,000
Investment in Fixed Assets - Special Assessments Fund Bonds	$161,000
Investment in General Fixed Assets - General Fund Revenues	$ 30,000

The Special Assessments Fund continues in existence until the special assessments have been collected and the bond liability is liquidated.

F. Proprietary Funds

Internal Service (formerly intragovernmental service) Funds are established to account for the provision of goods and services by one department of the government to other departments within the government on generally a not-for-profit (cost-reimbursement) basis. Internal Service Funds are budgeted through the budgets of the user departments. Internal Service Funds are normally established for the following types of activities--central garages, motor pools, central printing and duplicating, stores departments, etc. Enterprise Funds, on the other hand, account for activities by which the government provides goods and services which are (1) rendered primarily to the general public, (2) financed substantially or entirely through user charges, and (3) intended to be self-supporting. Enterprise Funds are usually established for public utilities, toll roads and bridges, transit systems, golf courses, etc.

Proprietary Funds use the accrual basis of accounting and are nonexpendable; capital is to be maintained. Revenues and expenses are recorded just as they would be in commercial enterprises. Fixed assets are recorded in Proprietary Funds, and depreciation expense is deducted from revenues. The GFA Group of Accounts does not account for fixed assets of Proprietary Funds. These funds also report their own long-term liabilities. The GLTD Group of Accounts is not used to report Proprietary

Fund long-term debt because the debt is secured by present and future Proprietary Fund resources.

When Proprietary Funds are initially established, a contribution or advance is usually received from the General Fund. A contribution is a residual equity transfer and would be recorded by the Internal Service or Enterprise Fund as follows:

```
Cash                                   xx
     Contribution from Government            xx
```

The contribution account is a permanent equity account on the balance sheet of a Proprietary Fund. It is equivalent to paid-in capital in a corporation. On the other hand, an advance from the General Fund is a long-term loan and would be recorded by the Internal Service or Enterprise Fund as follows:

```
Cash                                   xx
     Advance from General Fund               xx
```

The advance is a long-term liability on the Proprietary Fund's balance sheet and a long-term asset on the General Fund's balance sheet. According to NCGA Statement 2, "Grants, entitlements, or shared revenues received before the revenue recognition criteria have been met should be reported as Deferred Revenue, a liability account." A grant for a capital asset will be credited to "Contributed Capital," a subdivision of fund equity, as follows:

```
Equipment, etc.                        $100,000
     Contributed Capital-Capital Grants          $100,000
```

As the asset is depreciated, the following entry would normally be made:

```
Accumulated Amortization - Contributed
  Capital-Capital Grants               $10,000
     Accumulated Depreciation - Equipment        $10,000
```

In other words, the depreciation is charged directly to the capital account.

It is also important to note that Proprietary Funds do not formally record their operating budgets. Encumbrance accounting need not be used, and a retained earnings account, often with several reserves or appropriations, reflects the accumulated earnings to date. Other journal entries relating to Proprietary Funds will not be shown because of their similarity to entries for commercial enterprises.

The financial statements of Proprietary Funds include the following:

1) Balance Sheet
2) Statement of Revenues, Expenses, and Changes in Retained Earnings
3) Statement of Changes in Financial Position

Totals for Internal Service and Enterprise Funds would be presented in the combined statements. Where more than one Internal Service or Enterprise Fund exists, combining statements would be required.

G. Fiduciary Funds--Trust and Agency

Trust Funds are similar to Agency Funds in that each type of fund is used to account for monies held for others, trust funds generally being used when assets are held for substantial periods of time. Trust and Agency Funds do not generally record their budgets formally except for some expendable Trust Funds.

There are three types of Trust Funds: Expendable, Nonexpendable, and Pension. An Expendable Trust Fund is accounted for as a Governmental Fund--modified accrual basis. Nonexpendable and Pension Trust Funds are accounted for as Proprietary Funds--accrual basis. An example of an Expendable Trust Fund is a Bond Guarantee Fund wherein performance bonds are held. The bond is returned to the contractor upon satisfactory performance, or remitted to the appropriate fund if there is unsatisfactory performance. When the bond is received, fund balance is credited. Fund balance is debited when the bond is returned. Interest earned would be closed to the fund balance account.

Nonexpendable Trust Funds either permit earnings to be expended, e.g., Endowment Funds, or do not permit earnings to be expended, e.g., Loan Funds.

Example entries for a Loan Fund would appear as follows:

Cash	$5,000	(to record a residual equity transfer
Loan Fund Balance	$5,000	from some other fund, e.g. General Fund)
Loans Receivable	$4,000	
Cash	$4,000	
Cash	$3,600	Note: Interest revenues increase the
Loans Receivable	$3,000	fund balance available for future
Interest Revenue	$ 600	loans.
Interest Revenue	$ 600	
Loan Fund Balance	$ 600	

Example entries for a Nonexpendable Trust Fund (principal remains intact) whose earnings are transferred to an Expendable Trust Fund would appear as follows:

Cash	$10,000	(to record receipt of resources from
Endowment Fund Balance	$10,000	a donor)
Investments	$10,000	
Cash	$10,000	
Cash	$1,000	(to record earnings from invest-
Investment Revenue	$1,000	ments)
Transfer to Expendable Trust Fund	$1,000	(to record authorized transfer of
Due to Expendable Trust Fund/Cash	$1,000	earnings to the Expendable Trust Fund)
Investment Revenue	$1,000	(to record closing entry)
Transfer to Expendable Trust Fund	$1,000	

An important point to remember is that capital gains and losses are part of the Endowment Fund principal, i.e., they are not part of the expendable income. Example entries for the Expendable Trust Fund referred to above would appear as follows:

```
Due from Endowment Fund/Cash  $1,000     (to record interest transferred
   Transfer from Endowment Fund  $1,000  from Endowment Fund above)

Expenditures                   $ 900     (to record expenditures author-
   Cash                        $ 900     ized in the trust agreement)

Transfer from Endowment Fund   $1,000    (to record closing entry)
   Expenditures                     $ 900
   Fund Balance                     $ 100
```

Pension Trust Funds, on the other hand, have additional accounts and entries due to the complexities of pensions. Assume that contributions are received from the employees and the employer:

```
Cash                                    $20,000
   Contributions - Employees               $10,000
   Contributions - Employer                $10,000
```

When pensions become payable, the following entries are recorded:

```
Expenses                                $5,000
   Annuities Payable                        $5,000

Annuities Payable                       $5,000
   Cash                                     $5,000
```

Investment revenues are recorded as revenues and are closed at year end to appropriate reserve accounts.

```
Cash                                    $15,000
   Investment Revenue                       $15,000

Investment Revenue                      $15,000
   Reserve for Membership Annuities         $ 5,000
   Reserve for Employee Contributions       $ 5,000
   Reserve for Employer Contributions       $ 5,000
```

When active employees retire, balances are transferred from the reserves for active employees to the reserve for retired employees:

```
Reserve for Employee Contributions      $7,000
Reserve for Employer Contributions      $7,000
   Reserve for Membership Annuities         $14,000
```

Note the use of reserve accounts above. The "Reserve for Employees Contributions" represents the amounts contributed by active employees plus any interest accumulated on these contributions. The "Reserve for Employer Contributions" represents the employer's contributions plus any accumulated interest for active employees. The "Reserve for Membership Annuities" represents employee and employer contributions plus accumulated interest for retired employees.

Closing entries for the Pension Fund would be as follows:

Contributions - Employees	$10,000		
Contributions - Employer	$10,000		
Reserve for Employees Contributions		$10,000	
Reserve for Employer Contributions		$10,000	
Reserve for Membership Annuities	$ 5,000		
Expenses		$ 5,000	

Unfunded liabilities for defined benefit pension plans are generally disclosed in footnotes. Both the FASB and NCGA have recently issued statements regarding pension plan disclosure. Since these statements conflict in some ways, both statements have been postponed for state and local governmental units.

Agency Funds hold temporary deposits, such as employee wage withholdings, for subsequent payment. For example, if union dues had been withheld from employees for subsequent payment to the union, the following entries would be made in an Agency Fund:

Cash	xx	
Union Dues Payable		xx
Union Dues Payable	xx	
Cash		xx

In addition to the example above, another common use of Agency Funds is to hold property taxes. Property taxes are usually remitted to a county treasurer who places the monies in a county Tax Agency Fund. The taxes are held until such time they are remitted to each of the political subdivisions located within the county. Agency Funds have only assets and liabilities as accounts.

Financial statements required for Trust and Agency funds depend upon their measurement focus. Nonexpendable and Pension Trust Funds are often combined with the proprietary funds in the combined statements. Combining and individual fund statements would require:

1) Balance Sheet
2) Statements of Revenues, Expenses, and Changes in Fund Balances
3) Statement of Changes in Financial Position

Expendable Trust Funds normally are combined with the governmental funds in the combined statements. Combining and individual fund statements would include:

1) Balance Sheet
2) Statement of Revenues, Expenditures, and Changes in Fund Balances
3) Statement of Revenues, Expenditures, and Changes in Fund Balances (if an annual budget is adopted)

Agency Funds would appear in the Combined Balance Sheet and should have a Combining Statement of Assets and Liabilities.

H. The GFA and GLTD Account Groups

Throughout the discussion of Governmental Funds, entries in the General Fixed Asset and General Long-Term Debt Groups of Accounts were made when necessary. It is now important to review these two groups of accounts.

Investments in general fixed assets are not recorded in the governmental funds but in the General Fixed Asset Group of Accounts. These assets never cause depreciation to be recorded as a charge in the governmental funds. It is permissible to show accumulated depreciation in the GFA Group, but not required (and almost never done).

Investments in general fixed assets are not recorded in the Governmental Funds, but rather in the General Fixed Asset Group of Accounts.

General	Review Note: These are all expendable funds.
Special Revenue	Emphasis is on expendable resources to pro-
Capital Projects	vide goods and services. Each uses the modi-
Debt Services	fied accrual method.
Special Assessment	

Fixed assets are recorded in the funds shown below and not in the General Fixed Asset Group of Accounts. Depreciation is recorded on fixed assets in these funds (except on nonrevenue-producing property in Trust Funds):

    Internal Service
    Enterprise
    Nonexpendable Trust

The entries in the General Fixed Asset Group are very simple. Fixed assets are recorded at cost or fair market value, if donated. Debit the Fixed Asset Account purchased or constructed, e.g., land, building, etc., and credit Investment in Fixed Assets--(blank) Fund--Source.

Land	xx	
Building	xx	
Investment in General Fixed Assets--		
General Fund Revenues		xx

Uncompleted assets are recorded as "Construction in Progress" at year end, and are subsequently recorded as fixed assets when completed. When fixed assets are retired, simply reverse the entry in the General Fixed Asset Group of Accounts. Remember, normally depreciation is not recorded. Any cash received for the asset when sold is generally recorded in the General Fund with a credit to miscellaneous revenue, and the entry in the GFA Group recording the asset is reversed.

The governmental unit should present a schedule of its general fixed assets according to sources, as follows:

City of X
Schedule of General Fixed Assets by Sources
June 30, 19XX

General Fixed Assets:		Investment in General Fixed Assets from:	
Land	$x	General Fund Revenues	$x
Building	x	Special Revenue Fund Revenues	x
Improvements Other than		Capital Projects Funds:	
Buildings	x	General Obligation Bonds	x
Equipment	x	County Grants	x
Construction-in-Progress	x	Special Assessments	x
Total General Fixed Assets	$x	Total Investment in General Fixed Assets	$x

Other statements include:

1) Schedule of General Fixed Assets - By Function and Activity
2) Schedule of Changes in General Fixed Assets - By Function and Activity

The GLTD Group of Accounts records long-term debt from the following funds:

General
Special Revenue
Capital Projects

Long-term debt is carried in the following funds:

Special Assessment
Enterprise
Internal Service (possibly)
Nonexpendable Trust (possibly)

If long-term debt in one of these funds above is guaranteed by the General Fund, footnote disclosure should be made in the General Long-Term Debt Group of Accounts.

The entry to record long-term debt in the General Long-Term Group of Accounts is:

Amount to be Provided for Retirement of Bonds   xx
     Bonds Payable   xx

As monies are set aside for bond repayment (in the Debt Service Fund), the following entry is made:

Amount Available in Debt Service Fund   xx
     Amount to be Provided for Retirement of Bonds   xx

The entry to record retirement in GLTD is:

Bonds Payable   xx   (See disclosure of
     Amount Available for Retirement of Bonds   xx   Debt Service Fund
                                                                for entries made
                                                                in that fund)

Thus, entries are required when:

1) Debt is incurred
2) Monies are set aside for debt repayment
3) Debt is repaid

Remember that the GLTD group records transactions involving debt principal, not interest.

I. Interfund Transfers and Other Interfund Transactions

Assuming appropriate authorization, a governmental unit's resources can be shifted among the various funds of a governmental unit for a variety of reasons. In addition, certain transactions involve more than one fund. There are six types of interfund transactions:

1) Loans
2) Quasi-external transactions
3) Expenditure/expense reimbursement transactions
4) Residual equity transfers
5) All other transfers which are not of the residual equity type (operating transfers)
6) Transactions affecting more than one fund/group

The first type of resource movement described above, loans, results in a shift (temporary or long-term) of the resource cash from one fund to another fund. The creditor fund sets up a receivable while the debtor fund establishes a payable. The receivable/payable descriptions for a short-term loan are: Due from...Fund/Due to ...Fund Accounts.* As an example, suppose the General Fund, in order to alleviate a temporary cash flow problem, borrows $100,000 from the Enterprise Fund. The loan is to be paid in six months. The entries which would be made are:

General Fund		Enterprise Fund	
Cash	$100,000	Due from General Fund	$100,000
Due to Enterprise Fund	$100,000	Cash	$100,000

If interest is charged at 10% on this loan, the following entries would be made at the end of six months:

General Fund		Enterprise Fund	
Due to Enterprise Fund	$100,000	Cash	$105,000
Expenditures	$ 5,000	Interest Revenues	$ 5,000
Cash	$105,000	Due from General Fund	$100,000

Note the expenditure/revenue treatment of the interest above. This treatment leads directly to the next type of resource movement, i.e., from quasi-external transactions.

Quasi-external transactions are accounted for as if the transaction were between an individual fund and an entity external to the particular governmental unit, i.e., as revenue and expenditures/expenses in the affected funds. In the loan example, the interest paid is treated the same way it would have been had the General Fund borrowed the money from a bank, i.e., an expenditure. Similarly, the interest received is treated the same way it would have been had the Enterprise Fund lent the

---

*If the loan is long-term, "Due from...Fund" is changed to "Advance to...Fund" and "Due to...Fund" is changed to "Advance from...Fund."

money to an entity outside of the particular governmental unit, i.e., a revenue. Other examples which illustrate quasi-external transactions include the following:

1) The General or Special Revenue Fund's use of the services provided by Internal Service Funds, e.g., printing, data processing, motor vehicle, etc. services
2) The General or Special Revenue Fund's use of the services provided by enterprise funds, e.g., water and sewer, electricity, etc. services

To illustrate one of these transactions, suppose that General Fund personnel use motor vehicles owned by the Internal Service Fund. The latter fund's bill for these services amounts to $1,500. The following entries would be made:

General Fund		Internal Service	
Expenditures	$1,500	Due from General Fund/Cash	$1,500
Due to Internal Service Fund/Cash	$1,500	Billings to Departments	$1,500

The third type of interfund resource movement involves <u>reimbursement</u> for expenditures/expenses which were initially paid by one fund on behalf of some other fund. To illustrate, suppose that General and Special Revenue Fund personnel attend a conference together, for which the total cost is $10,000. The entire bill is paid by the General Fund, which results in a charge to expenditures for $10,000. However, suppose that $3,000 of the $10,000 was for Special Revenue Fund personnel. The Special Revenue Fund should reimburse the General Fund for the latter's expenditure of funds which relate to the Special Revenue Fund. The following entries would be made:

General Fund		Special Revenue Fund	
Due from Special Revenue Fund/Cash	$3,000	Expenditures	$3,000
Expenditures	$3,000	Due to General Fund/Cash	$3,000

As one last point, note that expenses, rather than expenditures, would be involved if the reimbursement affects Proprietary Funds, i.e., Internal Service and Enterprise Funds.

The fourth type of resource movement involves <u>residual equity transfers</u> between funds. Equity accounts are debited and credited in the paying and receiving funds, respectively. Typical examples which illustrate this type of transaction include the transfer of excess cash from the Capital Projects and Debt Service Funds to the General Fund. This transfer occurs at the conclusion of the capital project or when the general obligation debt has been fully paid and cash balances remain in these funds. The following journal entries would be made:

General Fund	Debt Service	Capital Projects Fund
Due from--Fund/Cash xx	Fund Balance	Unreserved Fund
Unreserved Fund	(Residual Equity	Balance (Residual
Balance (Residual	Transfer) xx	Equity Transfer) xx
Equity Transfer) xx	Due to General	Due to General
	Fund/Cash xx	Fund/Cash xx

Another example which illustrates a residual equity transfer is the contribution made by the General Fund to an Internal Service Fund or to an Enterprise Fund. These contributions, which help to establish operations, are equivalent to paid-in capital in the proprietary funds being established. The following journal entries show how these contributions would be recorded:

General Fund	Internal Use/Enterprise Funds
Unreserved Fund Balance	Due from General Fund/Cash xx
(Residual Equity Transfer) xx	Contribution from Government* xx
Due to--Fund/Cash xx	

Residual Equity Transfers are reported as adjustments of the beginning Fund Balance of a governmental fund. For example, in the statement on page 1068, a Residual Equity Transfer in the General Fund would be reported after the January 1 Fund Balance of $202,500 and would adjust the December 31 Fund Balance.

Operating transfers include all interfund transfers which are not residual equity transfers. As stated in the 1974 industry audit guide, "Frequently, statutes will not permit a direct allocation of a revenue source between two funds. Accordingly, it is necessary to have an annual transfer from the fund legally required to receive the revenue to a fund authorized to expend all or some portion of the revenue" (Audits of State and Local Governmental Units).

Generally, these resource transfers require payments from the General Fund to various other funds. It is essential to note that expenditure/expense and revenue accounts are not used to record or report these operating transfers. Instead, special "Operating Transfers Out" and "Operating Transfers In" accounts are used. These accounts are temporary accounts and are closed at the end of the fiscal year. Examples which illustrate this type of resource movement include the following:

1) The General Fund's transfer of resources to the Special Assessment Fund for the governmental unit's share of the project's cost
2) The General Fund's transfer of resources to the Capital Projects Fund for the governmental unit's share of the project's cost
3) The Capital Projects' transfer of resources, representing investment income, to the Debt Service Fund for debt repayment
4) The General Fund's transfer to a Debt Service Fund of resources for payment of debt principal and interest

---

*"Contribution from Government" is reported in the equity section of the balance sheet for Proprietary Funds.

J. STATE AND LOCAL GOVERNMENT FUND REVIEW CHECKLIST

	Governmental Funds					Proprietary Funds		Fiduciary Funds
	General	Special Revenue	Capital Projects	Debt Service	Special Assessment	Internal Service	Enterprise	Trust & Agency
Accounting basis	Modified Accrual	Modified Accrual	Modified Accrual	Modified Accrual	Modified Accrual	Accrual	Accrual	See p. 1090
Land, Buildings, Equipment, etc.	No	No	No	No	No	Yes depreciation also	Yes depreciation also	Yes See p. 1090
Long-term debt	No	No	No	No	Yes	Possibly	Yes	Possibly, See p. 1090
Budgetary Accounts Asset	Estimated Revenues	Estimated Revenues	None*	Estimated Revenues**	None*	None	None	None
Liability	Appropriations	Appropriations	None*	Appropriations	None*	None	None	None
Encumbrances	Yes	Yes	Yes	No	Yes	No	No	No

Nonfund Account Groups

General Fixed Asset Group

Land
Buildings
Etc.
Investments in fixed assets--(blank) Fund

General Long-term Debt

Amount to be provided for retirement of bonds
Amount available for retirement of bonds
Bonds Payable

*Not required, as a separate fund is set up for each project, i.e., revenues, expenditures, and encumbrances can be taken directly to fund balance. However the NCGA permits budgetary accounts.
**Estimated revenues relates to serial bond issues; Required Contributions and Required Earnings accounts would be used if term bonds were issued.

Journal entries for the first two examples would appear as follows:

		Special Assessment and	
General Fund		Capital Projects Funds	
Operating Transfers Out	xx	Due from General Fund/Cash	xx
Due to Capital Projects		Operating Transfers In	xx
Fund/Cash	xx	(Entry is made in each fund above)	

Operating transfers are classified as "Other Financing Sources/Uses" in the operating statements of governmental funds.

An example of <u>transactions affecting more than one fund or group of accounts</u> would be the example in this review of the construction of a new city hall. Entries were required in the Capital Projects and Debt Service Funds and the General Fixed Assets Group of Accounts. Review of interfund problems is necessary, as this type of question is common on the CPA exam.

II. OTHER NONPROFIT ENTITIES

In addition to governmental accounting, other nonprofit accounting entities have been tested on recent examinations. For example:

(577, T4) required a description of fund accounting; the distinction between accrual and modified accrual and which is used for a voluntary health and welfare organization; differences in accounting for voluntary health and welfare organizations and governmental units

(1177, Q4) required journal entries for 12 hospital transactions

(1178, Q5) required journal entries in a university's current unrestricted, current restricted, and endowment funds

(582, Q2) contained some multiple choice questions relating to colleges and hospitals

(1182, Q5) required a hospital's Statement of Revenues and Expenses and the necessary footnotes thereto

(583, Q5) required journal entries and an all-inclusive activity statement for a community sports club

(1183, Q4) required journal entries and a Statement of Changes in Fund Balances for the unrestricted and restricted current funds of a university

Most nonprofit CPA exam questions can be answered adequately based on a knowledge of governmental fund accounting and familiarity with certain aspects of the four types of nonprofit organizations. The four types of nonprofit organizations that have been tested and the current sources of GAAP are:

1) Colleges and Universities (AICPA <u>Audits of Colleges and Universities</u>, AICPA <u>Statement of Position 74-8</u>, National Association of College and University Business Officers, <u>College and University Business Administration</u>)

2) Hospitals (AICPA Hospital Audit Guide, 1972, AICPA Statement of Position 78-7, American Hospital Association, Chart of Accounts for Hospitals)

3) Voluntary Health and Welfare Organizations (AICPA Audits of Voluntary Health and Welfare Organizations, 1974)

4) Other Nonprofit Organizations (AICPA Statement of Position 78-10, contained in AICPA Audits of Certain Nonprofit Organizations, 1981)

In order to prepare for the possibility of nonprofit organizations on the CPA exam, candidates should become familiar with the fund structure, the statement formats, and the major unique accounting features of each of the four types of nonprofit organizations. In addition, candidates can use general accounting knowledge to answer many parts, using account titles given in the problems.

A. College and University Accounting

The Committee on College and University Accounting and Auditing of the AICPA states that:

> Service, rather than profits is the objective of an educational institution; thus, the primary obligation of accounting and reporting is one of accounting for resources received and used rather than for the determination of net income. Frequently, there is no relationship between the fees charged and the actual expenditures for program services (Audit of Colleges and Universities, p. 5).

This statement reflects the similarity between college and university accounting and that for the expendable, governmental funds for state and local governmental units.

The accounting and reporting for colleges and universities is done through funds. The fund groups below are usually maintained:

1) Current Funds

   a) Unrestricted
   b) Restricted

2) Loan Funds
3) Endowment and similar funds
4) Annuity and Life Income Funds
5) Plant Funds

   a) Unexpended
   b) Investment in Plant
   c) Funds for Retirement of Indebtedness
   d) Funds for Renewals and Replacements

6) Agency Funds

The accrual basis of accounting should be used for all fund groups. Encumbrance accounting is similar to that used by governmental units, i.e., reported as reservations of fund balance. The financial statements for colleges and universities include the following:

1) Balance Sheet (see following pages for example)
2) Statement of Current Funds Revenues, Expenditures, and other Changes
3) Statement of Changes in Fund Balances (see following pages for example)

A discussion of each of the fund groups is presented on the following pages.

Current Funds are those ". . . which are expendable for any purpose in performing the primary objectives of the institution, i.e., instruction, research, extension, and public service. . ." (Audits of Colleges and Universities, p. 13). Unrestricted current funds are only subject to the usual budgetary limitations, while restricted current funds are subject to provisions limiting their use. Examples of restricted funds are special purpose federal grants, legislative appropriations, private donations for a specific purpose, etc. Unrestricted current funds are internally designated in that a governing board determines how the resources are to be used. Restricted current funds are externally restricted because donors or other outside parties determine how the resources are to be used.

In addition, auxiliary enterprise activities (dormitories, cafeterias, bookstores, etc.) are accounted for in the current funds category and follow the accounting rules applicable to current funds rather than those of enterprise funds of governmental units.

Current funds follow accrual accounting, but do record budget entries and encumbrances. Depreciation is not recorded in the current funds, even for assets of auxiliary enterprises. Grants made to restricted funds are recognized as revenues only when earned, by incurring the expenditure, as was the case for local governmental units.

Loan Funds are those from which cash may be loaned to students, faculty, and staff. Interest revenues increase the fund balance and provide a larger asset base for subsequent loans. Assets consist of cash, temporary investments, and notes receivable (less a provision for uncollectibles).

Endowment Funds include endowment, term endowment, and quasi-endowment funds. Endowment funds are those in which the principal is required to be kept intact in perpetuity. The earnings from the investment of the principal are either expended or added to the principal, depending upon the wishes of the donor. If expended, these resources are transferred to the restricted current funds group and expenditures are made there according to the donor restrictions. Term endowment funds are treated as endowment until a certain event or condition has been met (e.g., time passage), and then all or part of the principal may be expended. Quasi-endowment funds are similar to endowment and term endowment funds. The difference lies in the

SAMPLE EDUCATIONAL INSTITUTION BALANCE SHEET

June 30, 19X2 and 19X1

Assets	19X2	19X1	Liabilities and Fund Balances	19X2	19X1
Current funds:			**Current funds:**		
Unrestricted:			Unrestricted:		
Cash	$ 210,000	$ 110,000	Accounts payable	$ 145,000	$ 115,000
Investments	450,000	360,000	Students' deposits	60,000	55,000
Accounts receivable	228,000	175,000	Due to other funds	158,000	120,000
Inventories, at LCM	118,000	100,000	Fund balance	643,000	455,000
Total unrestricted	1,006,000	745,000	Total unrestricted	1,006,000	745,000
Restricted:			Restricted:		
Cash	145,000	101,000	Accounts payable	14,000	5,000
Investments	315,000	325,000	Fund balances	446,000	421,000
Total restricted	460,000	426,000	Total restricted	460,000	426,000
Total current funds	$1,466,000	$1,171,000	Total current funds	$1,466,000	$1,171,000
Loan funds:			**Loan funds:**		
Cash	$ 30,000	$ 20,000	Fund balances:		
Investments	100,000	100,000	U.S. Govt. grants refundable	$ 50,000	$ 33,000
Loans to students, faculty and staff	553,000	382,000	University funds	633,000	469,000
Total loan funds	$ 683,000	$ 502,000	Total loan funds	$ 683,000	$ 502,000
Endowment and similar funds:			**Endowment and similar funds:**		
Cash	$ 100,000	$ 101,000	Endowment fund balance	$ 7,800,000	$ 6,740,000
Investments	13,900,000	11,800,000	Term endowment fund balance	6,200,000	5,161,000
Total endowment and similar funds	$14,000,000	$11,901,000	Total endowment and similar funds	$14,000,000	$11,901,000
Annuity funds:			**Annuity funds:**		
Cash	$ 55,000	$ 45,000	Annuities payable	$2,150,000	$2,300,000
Investments	3,260,000	3,010,000	Fund balances	1,165,000	755,000
Total annuity funds	$3,315,000	$3,055,000	Total annuity funds	$3,315,000	$3,055,000
Plant funds:			**Plant funds:**		
Unexpended:			Unexpended:		
Cash	$ 425,000	$ 530,000	Accounts payable	$ 200,000	$ 120,000
Investments	1,285,000	1,590,000	Fund balances	1,510,000	2,000,000
Total unexpended	1,710,000	2,120,000	Total unexpended	$1,710,000	$2,120,000
Renewal and replacement:			Renewal and replacement:		
Cash	110,000	94,000	Fund balances:		
Investments	150,000	286,000	Restricted	25,000	180,000
			Unrestricted	235,000	200,000
Total renewal & replacement	260,000	380,000	Total renewal & replacement	260,000	380,000
Retirement of indebtedness:			Retirement of indebtedness:		
Cash	50,000	40,000	Fund balances:		
Deposits with trustees	250,000	253,000	Restricted	185,000	125,000
			Unrestricted	115,000	168,000
Total retirement of indebtedness	300,000	293,000	Total retirement of indebtedness	300,000	293,000
Investment in plant:			Investment in plant:		
Land	1,600,000	1,690,000	Mortgages payable	3,390,000	3,410,000
Buildings and equipment	40,000,000	38,260,000	Net investment in plant	38,210,000	36,540,000
Total investment in plant	41,600,000	39,950,000	Total investment in plant	41,600,000	39,950,000
Total plant funds	$43,870,000	$42,743,000	Total plant funds	$43,870,000	$42,743,000
Agency funds:			**Agency funds:**		
Cash	$ 50,000	$ 70,000	Deposits held in custody for others	$ 110,000	$ 90,000
Investments	60,000	20,000			
Total agency funds	$ 110,000	$ 90,000	Total agency funds	$ 110,000	$ 90,000

Sample Educational Institution
Statement of Changes in Fund Balances
Year Ended June 30, 19—

	Current funds Unrestricted	Current funds Restricted	Loan funds	Endowment and similar funds	Annuity and life income funds	Plant funds Unexpended	Plant funds Renewals and replacements	Plant funds Retirement of indebtedness	Investment in plant
Revenues and other additions									
Unrestricted current fund revenues	$7,540,000	$ —	$ —	$ —	$ —	$ —	$ —	$ —	$ —
Expired term endowment—restricted	—	—	—	—	—	50,000	—	—	—
State appropriations—restricted	—	—	—	—	—	50,000	—	—	—
Federal grants and contracts— restricted	—	500,000	—	—	—	—	—	—	—
Private gifts, grants and contracts— restricted	—	370,000	100,000	1,500,000	800,000	115,000	—	65,000	15,000
Investment income—restricted	—	224,000	12,000	10,000	—	5,000	5,000	5,000	—
Realized gains on investments— unrestricted	—	—	—	109,000	—	—	—	—	—
Realized gains on investments— restricted	—	—	4,000	50,000	—	10,000	5,000	5,000	—
Interest on loans receivable	—	—	7,000	—	—	—	—	—	—
U.S. government advances	—	—	18,000	—	—	—	—	—	—
Expended for plant facilities (including $100,000 charged to current funds expenditures)	—	—	—	—	—	—	—	—	1,550,000
Retirement of indebtedness	—	—	—	—	—	—	—	—	220,000
Accrued interest on sale of bonds	—	—	—	—	—	—	—	3,000	—
Matured annuity and life income restricted to endowment	—	—	—	10,000	—	—	—	—	—
Total revenues and other additions	$7,540,000	$1,094,000	$141,000	$ 1,679,000	$ 800,000	$ 230,000	$ 10,000	$ 78,000	$ 1,785,000
Expenditures and other deductions									
Educational and general expenditures	4,400,000	1,014,000	—	—	—	—	—	—	—
Auxiliary enterprises expenditures	1,830,000	—	—	—	—	—	—	—	—
Indirect costs recovered	—	35,000	—	—	—	—	—	—	—
Refunded to grantors	—	20,000	10,000	—	—	—	—	—	—
Loan cancellations and write-offs	—	—	1,000	—	—	—	—	—	—
Administrative and collection costs	—	—	1,000	—	—	—	—	1,000	—
Adjustment of actuarial liability for annuities payable	—	—	—	—	75,000	—	—	—	—
Expended for plant facilities (including noncapitalized expenditures of $50,000)	—	—	—	—	—	1,200,000	300,000	—	—
Retirement of indebtedness	—	—	—	—	—	—	—	220,000	—
Interest on indebtedness	—	—	—	—	—	—	—	190,000	—
Disposal of plant facilities	—	—	—	—	—	—	—	—	115,000
Expired term endowments ($40,000 unrestricted, $50,000 restricted to plant)	—	—	—	90,000	—	—	—	—	—
Matured annuity and life income funds restricted to endowment	—	—	—	—	10,000	—	—	—	—
Total expenditures and other deductions	$6,230,000	$1,069,000	$ 12,000	$ 90,000	$ 85,000	$1,200,000	$300,000	$411,000	$ 115,000
Transfers among funds—additions/ (deductions)									
Mandatory:									
Principal and interest	(340,000)	—	—	—	—	—	—	340,000	—
Renewals and replacements	(170,000)	—	—	—	—	—	170,000	—	—
Loan fund matching grant	(2,000)	—	2,000	—	—	—	—	—	—
Unrestricted gifts allocated	(650,000)	—	50,000	550,000	—	50,000	—	—	—
Portion of unrestricted quasi-endowment funds investment gains appropriated	40,000	—	—	(40,000)	—	—	—	—	—
Total transfers	($1,122,000)	$ —	$ 52,000	$ 510,000	$ —	$ 50,000	$170,000	$340,000	$ —
Net increase/(decrease) for the year	$ 188,000	$ 25,000	$181,000	$ 2,099,000	$ 715,000	($ 920,000)	($120,000)	$ 7,000	$ 1,670,000
Fund balance at beginning of year	455,000	421,000	502,000	11,901,000	2,505,000	2,120,000	380,000	293,000	36,540,000
Fund balance at end of year	$ 643,000	$ 446,000	$683,000	$14,000,000	$3,220,000	$1,200,000	$260,000	$300,000	$38,210,000

Source: Reprinted from *College and University Business Administration*, Chapter 5:7, pp. 458–459, by permission of the National Association of College and University Business Officers.

control aspects. Quasi-endowment funds are controlled by the governing board of the college or university, not some external donor, and are unrestricted. It should be noted that an endowment must be under the control of the university to be recorded; a recent CPA exam question involved a trust established at a bank with the university as beneficiary. Only a memo entry was required.

Annuity and Life Income Funds, if not significant, are reported along with the endowment funds; otherwise, if material, they are reported separately. This fund group receives gifts or amounts from donors which constitute principal. In the case of life income funds, all earnings from the principal are usually paid annually to the donor while living. Upon the donor's death, the principal is transferred to some other fund group, e.g., current funds, endowment funds, etc., by the governing board. In the case of annuity funds, both the term and the amount or percentage of income to be transferred to the donor may be fixed. As a result, the accounting is more complex; an annuities payable liability account must be established equal to the present value of the future payments.

Plant Funds usually consist of four independent, balancing sections, each section consisting of a self-balancing set of accounts.

1) Unexpended Plant Funds which comprise funds restricted for physical plant expenditures
2) Investment in Plant which accounts for past expenditures in plant
3) Funds for the Retirement of Indebtedness which are similar to Debt Service Funds
4) Funds for Renewals and Replacements, used often by private colleges to accumulate resources on a long-term basis

When monies are set aside for plant acquisition, rehabilitation, etc., by other funds (e.g., current, endowment, annuity, etc.), the cash is accounted for in the Unexpended Plant Fund section. When monies are spent for plant acquisition, the investment is recorded in the Investment in Plant Fund section. Note that these sections of the Plant Fund are not directly parallel to any specific municipal funds. Liabilities may be recorded temporarily in the Unexpended Plant Fund section from the time monies are raised (e.g., sale of bonds) until expenditures are made to acquire physical facilities.

Agency Funds are used to account for funds not owned or controlled by the college or university but in the custody of the school, e.g., deposits, etc. They are quite similar to municipal agency funds.

Illustrative Transactions. Many entries for colleges and universities are similar to entries for state and local government. For example, the Revenues,

Expenditures, Encumbrances, and various reserve accounts are used in the Current Funds Group, although full accrual accounting is employed. Some entries that are different and relate to situations unique to colleges and universities are presented below.

a. Budget Entry. In the Current Funds Group, a budget for a fiscal year might appear as follows:

Unrestricted Current Funds		
Unrealized Revenues	$20,000,000	
Estimated Expenditures		$19,500,000
Unallocated Budget Balance		500,000

At year end, these accounts would all be closed out, in a manner similar to the GAAFR entries for state and local government.

b. Bad Debts. Unlike local government, where estimates of uncollectible receivables are considered to be deductions from revenues, colleges and universities normally debit expenditures. Assume that a college recorded tuition revenues of $10,000,000, of which $9,000,000 is collected in cash, and a 3% bad debt rate is used:

Unrestricted Current Funds		
Cash	$9,000,000	
Accounts Receivable - Student Fees	1,000,000	
Expenditures	30,000	
Revenues - Student Fees		$10,000,000
Allowance for Uncollectible Accounts		30,000

c. Summer School. If a session is offered in a term that is held during more than one fiscal year, GAAP requires that both revenues and expenditures be reported in the fiscal year in which most of the instruction takes place. In practice, this often means that revenues are deferred. For example, when summer session fees are collected for an institution that has a June 30 fiscal year end, the entry would be:

Unrestricted Current Funds		
Cash	$500,000	
Deferred Revenues		$500,000

In the new fiscal year, as the expenditures are recognized for faculty salaries and other purposes, the revenues would be recognized:

Deferred Revenues	$500,000	
Revenues		$500,000

d. Transfers - Mandatory and Nonmandatory. Assume that transfers are made from the Unrestricted Current Funds to the Plant Funds. $340,000 represents a mandatory transfer to the Funds for Retirement of Indebtedness for debt service repayment and

$170,000 represents a nonmandatory transfer to the Funds for Renewals and Replacements for future renovations:

Unrestricted Current Funds
Mandatory Transfer to Funds for Retirement of Indebtedness	$340,000	
Nonmandatory Transfer to Funds for Renewals and Replacements	170,000	
Cash		$510,000

Funds for Retirement of Indebtedness
Cash	$340,000	
Fund Balance		$340,000

Funds for Renewals and Replacements
Cash	$170,000	
Fund Balance		$170,000

Note how this transaction would be reported in the Statement of Changes in Fund Balances.

e. Grants for Current Purposes. Assume that a federal grant was received in the amount of $100,000 for cancer research. Of that amount, one half was expended this fiscal year, and the remainder will be expended in future years. Of the $50,000 expended this year, $10,000 represented indirect cost recoveries to the institution, and $40,000 was expended directly on the grant.

Restricted Current Funds
Cash	$90,000	
Fund Balance		$50,000
Revenues - Governmental Grants and Contracts		40,000

Expenditures - Governmental Grants and Contracts	40,000	
Cash		40,000

Unrestricted Current Funds
Cash	$10,000	
Revenues - Governmental Grants and Contracts - Indirect Cost Recovering		$10,000

It can be seen that Restricted Current Funds Revenues will always equal Expenditures.

f. Endowment Transactions. Assume that a wealthy alumnus contributed $1,000,000 in corporate stock to the institution, asking that the $1,000,000 be maintained, and that the proceeds be used for student scholarships. During the first year, $50,000 was received in dividends, and $40,000 was expended for scholarships.

Endowment Funds
<u>Investment in A Corporation Stock</u> $1,000,000
    Fund Balance - Income Restricted $1,000,000

Restricted Current Funds
<u>Cash</u> $50,000
    Revenues - Endowment Income $40,000
    Fund Balance - Restricted   10,000

Expenditures - Student Aid   40,000
    Cash   40,000

g. <u>Plant Fund Transactions.</u> Assume that a college borrows $2,000,000 to construct a small dormitory.

Unexpended Plant Funds
<u>Cash</u> $2,000,000
    Bonds Payable $2,000,000

Construction Work in Progress   2,000,000
    Cash   2,000,000

Bonds Payable   2,000,000
    Construction Work in Progress   2,000,000

Investment in Plant Funds
<u>Buildings</u> $2,000,000
    Bonds Payable $2,000,000

Further, assume that a total of $200,000 was paid for debt service for this project, including $100,000 for principal and $100,000 for interest:

Funds for Retirement of Indebtedness
<u>Fund Balance</u> $200,000
    Cash $200,000

Investment in Plant Funds
<u>Bonds Payable</u> $100,000
    Net Investment in Plant $100,000

Note that in all of the above entries, Revenues and Expenditures have been recorded only in the Unrestricted and Restricted Current Funds. Fund Balance is debited and credited for similar entries in the other funds, indicating that those transactions appear in the Statement of Changes in Fund Balances.

B. <u>Hospital Accounting</u>

Hospitals generally have fewer funds than municipalities and colleges and universities. Additionally, they use the accrual basis including depreciation (expenses are matched with revenues). To summarize, hospital accounting is more similar to profit-oriented financial accounting than to municipal or college and university accounting because hospitals are similar to a business (hospitals provide services based primarily on user fees as does a business enterprise). The

financial statements have separate sections for each type of fund. Hospital
statements include:

1) Statement of Revenues and Expenses (see following pages for example)
2) Balance Sheet (see following pages for example)
3) Statement of Changes in Fund Balance
4) Statement of Changes in Financial Position

Hospitals generally make a major distinction between unrestricted and restricted
funds. The balance sheet on page 1109 illustrates three categories of restricted
funds: Specific Purpose Funds, Plant Replacement and Expansion Funds, and Endowment
Funds. Each of these funds is accounted for essentially as a trust fund.

Unrestricted Funds. The unrestricted funds account for all of the unrestricted
assets of a hospital. All revenues and expenses of a hospital are reported in the
unrestricted funds. Full accrual accounting is used, and fixed assets are depreciated. The American Hospital Association proposes two types of unrestricted funds:
(1) the Operating Fund, and (2) Board Designated Funds. Board designated funds
account for assets set aside by the governing board, but the assets remain unrestricted.

An understanding of some of the unique features of hospital accounting can be
gained by looking at the Statement of Revenues and Expenses on page 1110. Patient
Service Revenues include all charges to all patients at the full rate, regardless of
the amount eventually paid. Allowances and Uncollectible Accounts represent revenue
deductions for bad debts, contractual adjustments by Medicare, Medicaid, Blue Cross,
etc., and employee discounts. Other Operating Revenues include amounts transferred
from restricted funds, purchase discounts, tuition from nursing students, cafeteria
and parking lot revenues, etc. Nonoperating Revenues include gifts, bequests, and
investment income.

Restricted Funds. As can be seen from the Balance Sheet on p. 1109, hospitals
report three types of restricted funds. Specific Purpose Funds contain assets that
have been restricted by granting agencies and other donors for current purposes.
When expenditures take place, the funds are transferred to the unrestricted funds,
where the amounts are recognized as other operating revenues and (normally)
operating expenses. Plant Replacement and Expansion Funds hold assets set aside by
donors for the future construction of hospital plant. When expended, the funds are
transferred to the unrestricted fund, where the assets are capitalized. Endowment
Funds hold assets that are invested, the proceeds of which are to be available for
either restricted or unrestricted purposes.

SAMPLE HOSPITAL BALANCE SHEET
December 31, 19——
(with Comparative Figures for 19——)

[in thousands]

Unrestricted Funds

	Current Year	Prior Year
Assets		
Current:		
Cash	$ 133	$ 33
Receivables	$ 1,382	$ 1,269
Less estimated uncollectibles	$ (160)	(105)
	1,222	1,164
Due from restricted funds	215	—
Inventories	176	183
Prepaid expenses	68	73
Total current assets	1,814	1,453
Other:		
Cash	143	40
Investments	1,427	1,740
Property, plant, and equipment	11,028	10,375
Accumulated depreciation	(3,885)	(3,600)
Net property, plant, and equip.	7,143	6,775
Total	$10,527	$10,008

	Current Year	Prior Year
Liabilities and Fund Balances		
Current:		
Notes payable to banks	$ 227	$ 300
Current long-term debt	90	90
Accounts payable	450	463
Accrued expenses	150	147
Advances from third parties	300	200
Deferred revenue	10	10
Total current liabilities	1,227	1,210
Deferred revenue—third-party reimbursement	200	90
Long-term debt:		
Housing bonds	500	520
Mortgage note	1,200	1,270
Total long-term debt	1,700	1,790
Fund balance	7,400	6,918
Total	$10,527	$10,008

Restricted Funds

	Current Year	Prior Year
Assets		
Specific purpose funds:		
Cash	$ 2	$ 1
Investments	200	70
Grants receivable	90	—
Total	$ 292	$ 71
Plant replacement and expansion funds:		
Cash	$ 10	$ 450
Investments	800	290
Pledges receivable, net of estimated uncollectible	20	360
Total	$ 830	$ 1,100
Endowment funds:		
Cash	$ 50	$ 33
Investments	6,100	3,942
Total	$ 6,150	$ 3,975

	Current Year	Prior Year
Liabilities and Fund Balances		
Specific purpose funds:		
Due to unrestricted funds	$ 215	
Fund balances:		
Research grants	15	30
Other	62	41
	77	71
Total	$ 292	$ 71
Plant replacement and expansion funds:		
Fund balances:		
Restricted by third-parties	$ 380	$ 150
Other	450	950
Total	$ 830	$ 1,100
Endowment funds:		
Fund balances:		
Permanent endowment	$ 4,850	$ 2,675
Term endowment	1,300	1,300
Total	$ 6,150	$ 3,975

Sample Hospital
Statement of Revenues and Expenses
Year Ended December 31, 19—
(with comparative figures for 19—)

	Current year	Prior year
Patient service revenue	$8,500,000	$8,000,000
Allowances and uncollectible accounts (after deduction of related gifts, grants, subsidies, and other income—$55,000 and $40,000)	(1,777,000)	(1,700,000)
Net patient service revenue	$6,723,000	$6,300,000
Other operating revenue (including $100,000 and $80,000 from specific purpose funds)	184,000	173,000
Total operating revenue	$6,907,000	$6,473,000
Operating expenses:		
Nursing services	2,200,000	2,000,000
Other professional services	1,900,000	1,700,000
General services	2,100,000	2,000,000
Fiscal services	375,000	360,000
Administrative services (including interest expense of $50,000 and $40,000)	400,000	375,000
Provision for depreciation	300,000	250,000
Total operating expenses	$7,275,000	$6,685,000
Loss from operations	$ (368,000)	$ (212,000)
Nonoperating revenue:		
Unrestricted gifts and bequests	228,000	205,000
Unrestricted income from endowment funds	170,000	80,000
Income and gains from board-designated funds	54,000	41,000
Total nonoperating revenue	$ 452,000	$ 326,000
Excess of revenues over expenses	$ 84,000	$ 114,000

Source: AICPA, *Hospital Audit Guide*, p. 42.

Illustrative Transactions. Entries in the unrestricted funds generally parallel entries for business enterprises. Revenues and expenses are recorded on the full accrual basis. Fixed assets and long-term debt are recorded directly in the Unrestricted Funds, and depreciation is recorded. Entries in the restricted funds record additions to and deductions from fund balance. Some entries that illustrate accounting for hospitals are presented below.

a. Unrestricted Revenues. Assume that $1,000,000 is received in cash from patients, an additional $1,000,000 is due from patients and third party payors, $100,000 is received from cafeteria sales, and $50,000 is received as an unrestricted gift.

Unrestricted Funds		
Cash	$1,150,000	
Accounts and Notes Receivable	1,000,000	
Patient Service Revenues		2,000,000
Other Operating Revenues		100,000
Nonoperating Revenues		50,000

b. Revenue Deductions. Assume that the estimated provision for bad debts is $70,000, contractual adjustments are $80,000, and charity services $40,000.

Unrestricted Funds		
Provision for Bad Debts	$70,000	
Contractual Adjustments	80,000	
Charity Services	40,000	
Allowance for Uncollectible Receivables		$ 70,000
Accounts and Notes Receivable		120,000

The three debit accounts are revenue deductions, as Patient Service Revenue is to be recorded at the total amount that would be charged to full paying patients.

c. Restricted Gifts and Grants. Assume that a hospital received $90,000 to conduct cancer research. When the funds are received, the following entry would be made:

Specific Purpose Funds		
Cash	$90,000	
Fund Balance		$90,000

Assume further that the funds are later expended for cancer research.

Specific Purpose Funds		
Fund Balance	$90,000	
Cash		$90,000
Unrestricted Funds		
Cash	$90,000	
Other Operating Revenues		$90,000
Other Services (Research)	90,000	
Cash		90,000

d. Fixed Asset Transactions. Assume that contributors gave $1,000,000 for a fund drive for a building addition. The funds would qualify as restricted gifts due to the intentions of the donor. Later, that amount plus $2,000,000 raised from the sale of bonds was used for the construction (on a turn-key basis) of a building addition.

Plant Replacement and Expansion Funds		
Cash	$1,000,000	
Fund Balance		$1,000,000
Fund Balance	1,000,000	
Cash		1,000,000
Unrestricted Funds		
Cash	$3,000,000	
Transfers from Restricted Funds		
for Capital Outlays		$1,000,000
Bonds Payable		2,000,000
Buildings	3,000,000	
Cash		3,000,000

    e. Endowment Fund Transactions. Assume that on the first day of a fiscal year,
a wealthy patron gave $1,000,000 in corporate stocks to the hospital with the
stipulation that half the proceeds be used for cancer research (restricted) and half
be used in accordance with the wishes of the Board of Trustees. During the first
year, $80,000 in dividends was received.

Endowment Fund

Cash	$1,000,000	
Fund Balance - Income Restricted		$500,000
Fund Balance - Income Unrestricted		500,000
Cash	$80,000	
Due to Specific Purpose Fund		$40,000
Due to Unrestricted Fund		40,000

Assume further that the $80,000 was transferred during the same fiscal year:

Endowment Fund

Due to Specific Purpose Fund	$40,000	
Due to Unrestricted Fund	40,000	
Cash		$80,000

Specific Purpose Fund

Cash	$40,000	
Fund Balance		$40,000

Unrestricted Fund

Cash	$40,000	
Nonoperating Revenues		$40,000

When the research expense takes place, the accounting would be identical to the
$90,000 shown above in subsection "c."

    An examination of these entries should indicate that all revenues, expenses, and
other transactions of substance take place in the unrestricted fund. The three
restricted funds are "holding" funds for monies restricted by donors and grantors.
As soon as those funds are expended, the transactions are recorded in the
unrestricted fund.

    A final note pertains to board designated funds. It was mentioned above that
the American Hospital Association recommends two unrestricted funds: operating and
board designated. If this practice is followed, the board designated fund would be
accounted for as illustrated for the restricted funds, but it would be classified as
unrestricted. An example of a board designated fund would be if the Board of
Trustees decided to set aside funds for future construction in an amount equal to
depreciation charges (i.e., "fund the depreciation").

C. Voluntary Health and Welfare Organizations

Voluntary health and welfare organizations perform voluntary services, e.g., Red Cross, Salvation Army, American Cancer Society, and local level counterparts. Their revenue is derived primarily from voluntary contributions from the general public. The following financial reports are required to be prepared:

1) Statement of Support, Revenues and Expenses, and Changes in Fund Balances (see following pages for example)
2) Statement of Functional Expenses
3) Balance Sheet (see following pages for example)

The following funds are recommended for voluntary health and welfare organizations:

1) Current Unrestricted Funds account for all resources used in the operations of the organization that are not restricted for special purposes by donors. Land, building, and equipment may be accounted for in separate funds. Unrestricted revenues are contributions, bequests, fees, dues, investment income, sale of services, etc. Expenditures are for program services and other expenses of the organization.

2) Current Restricted Funds account for resources available for specific current operations per donor or grantor specifications or restrictions. Restricted income may also come from grants, income from endowment funds, or other sources.

3) Land, Building, and Equipment Funds (Plant Funds) account for investment in fixed assets including unexpended resources contributed specifically for the use of replacing land, building, and equipment. Additionally, land, building, and equipment and the related obligations are included in the fund. Depreciation should be recorded on fixed assets, and gains or losses on sale of fixed assets should be included as income in the plant fund accounts. Adjustments to and from the Plant Fund and other funds should be recorded as direct reductions and additions to respective fund balances.

4) Endowment Funds are accounted for as other endowment funds. However, these Endowment Funds include only amounts that have been restricted by the donor. There are no quasi-endowments or legally unrestricted amounts included in voluntary health and welfare endowment funds. Income from restricted endowment funds should be transferred to the current restricted funds. Income from unrestricted endowment funds should be transferred to the current unrestricted fund. If restrictions on endowment fund principal lapse, the resources released should be transferred to unrestricted or special restricted funds.

5) Custodian Funds are in effect agency funds which account for assets owned by others, i.e., not the property of the voluntary health or welfare organization.

6) Loan and Annuity Funds are usually not significant to voluntary health and welfare organizations. If they are, they should be shown separately.

Voluntary Health and Welfare Service
Statement of Support, Revenue, and Expenses and Changes in Fund Balances
Year Ended December 31, 19X2
(with comparative totals for 19X1)

| | 19X2 | | | | | |
| | Current funds | | Land, building and equipment fund | Endowment fund | Total all funds | |
	Unrestricted	Restricted			19X2	19X1
Public support and revenue:						
Public support:						
Contributions (net of estimated uncollectible pledges of $195,000 in 19X2 and $150,000 in 19X1)	$3,764,000	$162,000	$ —	$ 2,000	$3,928,000	$3,976,000
Contributions to building fund		—	72,000	—	72,000	150,000
Special events (net of direct costs of $181,000 in 19X2 and $163,000 in 19X1)	104,000	—	—	—	104,000	92,000
Legacies and bequests	92,000	—	—	4,000	96,000	129,000
Received from federated and nonfederated campaigns (which incurred related fund-raising expenses of $38,000 in 19X2 and $29,000 in 19X1)	275,000	—	—	—	275,000	308,000
Total public support	$4,235,000	$162,000	$ 72,000	$ 6,000	$4,475,000	$4,655,000
Revenue:						
Membership dues	17,000	—	—	—	17,000	12,000
Investment income	98,000	10,000	—	—	108,000	94,000
Realized gain on investment transactions	200,000	—	—	25,000	225,000	275,000
Miscellaneous	42,000	—	—	—	42,000	47,000
Total revenue	$ 357,000	$ 10,000	$ —	$ 25,000	$ 392,000	$ 428,000
Total support and revenue	$4,592,000	$172,000	$ 72,000	$ 31,000	$4,867,000	$5,083,000
Expenses:						
Program services:						
Research	1,257,000	155,000	2,000	—	1,414,000	1,365,000
Public health education	539,000	—	5,000	—	544,000	485,000
Professional education and training	612,000	—	6,000	—	618,000	516,000
Community services	568,000	—	10,000	—	578,000	486,000
Total program services	$2,976,000	$155,000	$ 23,000	—	$3,154,000	$2,852,000
Supporting services:						
Management and general	567,000	—	7,000	—	574,000	638,000
Fund raising	642,000	—	12,000	—	654,000	546,000
Total supporting services	$1,209,000	—	$ 19,000	—	$1,228,000	$1,184,000
Total expenses	$4,185,000	$155,000	$ 42,000	—	$4,382,000	$4,036,000
Excess (deficiency) of public support and revenue over expenses	407,000	17,000	30,000	31,000		
Other changes in fund balances:						
Property and equipment acquisitions from unrestricted funds	(17,000)	—	17,000	—		
Transfer of realized endowment fund appreciation	100,000	—	—	(100,000)		
Returned to donor	—	(8,000)	—	—		
Fund balances, beginning of year	5,361,000	123,000	649,000	2,017,000		
Fund balances, end of year	$5,851,000	$132,000	$696,000	$1,948,000		

Source: AICPA, *Audits of Voluntary Health and Welfare Organizations*, pp. 42–43.

VOLUNTARY HEALTH AND WELFARE SERVICE
BALANCE SHEETS
December 31, 19X2 and 19X1

Assets	19X2	19X1	Liabilities and Fund Balances	19X2	19X1
		CURRENT FUNDS			
		Unrestricted			
Cash	$2,207,000	$2,530,000	Accounts payable	$ 148,000	$ 139,000
Investments:			Research grants payable	596,000	616,000
For long-term purposes	2,727,000	2,245,000	Contributions for future periods	245,000	219,000
Other	1,075,000	950,000	Total liabilities	989,000	974,000
Pledges receivable	475,000	363,000	Fund balances designated for:		
Inventories of ed. materials	70,000	61,000	Long-term investments	2,800,000	2,300,000
Accrued interest and receivables	286,000	186,000	Purchases of new equipment	100,000	—
			Research purposes	1,152,000	1,748,000
			Available for general activities	1,799,000	1,313,000
			Total fund balance	5,851,000	5,361,000
Total	$6,840,000	$6,335,000	Total	$6,840,000	$6,335,000

		Restricted			
Cash	$ 3,000	$ 5,000	Fund balances:		
Investments	71,000	72,000	Professional education	$ 84,000	$ —
Grants receivable	58,000	46,000	Research grants	48,000	123,000
Total	$ 132,000	$ 123,000	Total	$ 132,000	$ 123,000

LAND, BUILDING AND EQUIPMENT FUND

Assets	19X2	19X1	Liabilities and Fund Balances	19X2	19X1
Cash	$ 3,000	$ 2,000	Mortgage pay., 8% due 19XX	$ 32,000	$ 36,000
Investments	177,000	145,000	Fund balances:		
Pledges receivable	32,000	25,000	Expended	484,000	477,000
Land, buildings and equipment			Unexpended—restricted	212,000	172,000
less accumulated depreciation	516,000	513,000	Total fund balance	696,000	649,000
Total	$ 728,000	$ 685,000	Total	$ 728,000	$ 685,000

ENDOWMENT FUNDS

Assets	19X2	19X1	Liabilities and Fund Balances	19X2	19X1
Cash	$ 4,000	$ 10,000	Fund balance	$1,948,000	$2,017,000
Investments	1,944,000	2,007,000			
Total	$1,948,000	$2,017,000	Total	$1,948,000	$2,017,000

A look at the financial statements should help point out some unique features of voluntary health and welfare organization accounting. First, note that the operating statement includes a "total" column. This total is required and high-lights the fact that, unlike hospitals, these organizations may report revenues and expenses in all funds, except agency. Depreciation expense is normally reported in the land, building, and equipment fund. Full accrual accounting is required. Like all other nonprofit organizations, assets must be restricted by donors or others external to the organization before being classified as "Restricted" on the financial statements.

In the Statement of Support, Revenue, and Expenses and Changes in Fund Balances, note that "public support" and "revenue" are reported separately. "Public support" includes contributions, special events, legacies and bequests, and indirect support. Contributions include cash, investments, donated materials, or donated services. "Revenues" include internally generated resources including dues, investment income, and charges for services. Also, note that expenses are classified as between "program" and "supporting," giving the potential contributor an idea of where his/her money would be expended.

Illustrative Transactions. Unlike colleges and hospitals, voluntary health and welfare organizations may report revenues and expenses in any of their funds. Some illustrative entries that point out some of the unique features of these organizations follow.

a. Public Support and Revenues. Assume that a voluntary health and welfare organization reported the following: unrestricted cash donations, $50,000; unre-stricted pledges, $40,000; restricted pledges, $30,000, of which one half is designated by the donor for future periods; unrestricted special events, $25,000 (net of $15,000 costs); unrestricted membership dues, $10,000; investment income, $5,000; and a realized gain on endowment investments of $2,000. All pledges are subject to a 2% uncollectible rate.

Unrestricted Current Funds

Cash	$100,000	
Pledges Receivable	40,000	
Estimated Uncollectible Pledges Receivable		$ 800
Public Support - Contributions		89,200
Public Support - Special Events		40,000
Revenues - Membership Dues		10,000
Cost of Special Events	15,000	
Cash		15,000

Restricted Current Funds
Cash	$ 5,000	
Pledges Receivable	30,000	
Estimated Uncollectible Pledges Receivable		$ 600
Public Support - Contributions		14,700
Support and Revenue Designated for		
Future Periods		14,700
Revenues - Investment Income		5,000

Endowment Funds
Cash	$20,000	
Investments		$18,000
Revenues - Realized Gain on Investments		2,000

b. Expenses. Expenses for voluntary health and welfare organizations may be reported in any of the funds, although endowment funds normally report transfers to other funds. Expenses are recorded both by object and by function, so that the Statement of Functional Expenses may be prepared. Assuming that a voluntary health and welfare organization had three programs, the expenses for a given period might be reported (by function) as follows:

Unrestricted Current Funds
Public Health Education Expense	$100,000	
Public Health Research Expense	110,000	
Community Services Expense	50,000	
Management and General Expense	30,000	
Fund Raising Expense	15,000	
Cash		$300,000
Accounts Payable		5,000

Restricted Current Funds
Public Health Education Expense	$15,000	
Public Health Research Expense	20,000	
Community Services Expense	25,000	
Cash		$60,000

Assuming that $10,000 of the restricted expenses is from funds contributed in prior periods, the following entry would be required:

Restricted Current Funds
Support and Revenue Designated for Future		
Periods	$10,000	
Public Support - Contributions		$10,000

c. Fixed Assets and Depreciation. Fixed assets and depreciation transactions are recorded in the land, building, and equipment fund. The Fund Balance account in this fund is separated into two categories. The Fund Balance - Expended represents the net book value of the fixed assets not represented by indebtedness. The Fund Balance - Unexpended represents the assets available for future expenditure for plant.

Assume that equipment is purchased for $100,000, of which $50,000 is paid from funds on hand (which were "offset" by a $50,000 credit balance in Fund Balance - Unexpended), and $50,000 is borrowed:

Land, Building, and Equipment Fund

Equipment	$100,000	
Mortgage Notes Payable		$50,000
Cash		50,000
Fund Balance - Unexpended	50,000	
Fund Balance - Expended		50,000

Assume that $10,000 was later paid to retire part of the mortgage note:

Land, Building, and Equipment Fund

Mortgage Note Payable	$10,000	
Cash		$10,000
Fund Balance - Unexpended	10,000	
Fund Balance - Expended		10,000

Assume finally that depreciation expense for this equipment amounted to $5,000.

Land, Building, and Equipment Fund

Depreciation Expense - Equipment	$5,000	
Accumulated Depreciation - Equipment		$5,000
Public Health Education Expense	1,000	
Public Health Research Expense	1,000	
Community Services Expense	2,000	
Management and General Expense	500	
Fund Raising Expense	500	
Depreciation Expense - Equipment		5,000
Fund Balance - Expended	5,000	
Fund Balance - Unexpended		5,000

At year end, public support, revenues, and expenses of the land, building, and equipment fund are closed out to the Fund Balance - Unexpended account. The first and second entries above illustrate how expenses can be charged to both objects of expenditure and function.

D. SOP 78-10 "Accounting Principles and Reporting Practices for Certain Nonprofit Organizations"

The purpose of SOP 78-10 is to provide general accounting and reporting guidelines for all nonprofit entities other than those on which audit guides had previously been issued. The intent of this SOP is to state general principles for all nonprofit organizations rather than develop specialized techniques for each different type of nonprofit organization. Some examples of such nonprofit organizations are:

Cemetery organizations
Civic organizations
Fraternal organizations
Labor unions
Libraries
Museums
Other cultural institutions
Performing arts organizations
Political parties

Private elementary and secondary schools
Private and community foundations
Professional associations
Public broadcasting stations
Religious organizations
Research and scientific organizations
Social and country clubs
Trade associations
Zoological and botanical societies

Other organizations operating for the direct economic benefit of their member stockholders, e.g., mutual insurance companies, trusts, etc., are not covered by this SOP.

Financial statements required for these nonprofit organizations include:

1) Balance Sheet
2) Statement of Activity (see example)
3) Statement of Changes in Financial Position

A great deal of flexibility is permitted in the fund structure and in the reporting format for these nonprofit organizations. Fund accounting is permitted but not required. If fund accounting is used, the reporting format may show all accounts separately for each fund (as is done for colleges, hospitals, etc.), or the fund balance alone may have separate balances. Some additional features of accounting for other nonprofit organizations include:

1) Fund accounting is to be used
2) Only assets restricted by outside donors or grantors should be classified as "Restricted." Restricted assets are offset by a liability, "Deferred Revenues," until expended, so that the revenue and expense are recognized in the same accounting period.
3) Fixed assets should be capitalized and depreciated. Exceptions include art collections, rare books, cathedrals, and similar items.
4) Investments may be carried at market. Increases and decreases in market value of investments are recorded as revenues and expenses.
5) Capital grants are shown separately after an "Excess from Current Endeavors" line in the operating statement. See the Statement of Activity.
6) Restricted capital additions should be treated as deferred capital support until used
7) Enforceable pledges should be valued at their estimated realizable value and recorded as support revenue
8) Donated materials and investments normally are recorded at FMV when received, unless the intent is to quickly pass the item through to a grantee
9) Donated services are generally not recorded unless the service would normally be purchased by the reporting or a similar organization

Illustrative Transactions. As mentioned earlier, a great deal of flexibility is permitted in the recording and reporting of transactions for other nonprofit

Sample Performing Arts Organization
Statement of Activity
Years Ended June 30, 19X1, and 19X0

	19X1	19X0
Revenue and support from operations		
Admissions	$1,557,567	$1,287,564
Dividends and interest	21,555	2,430
Net realized gains and losses	54,700	18,300
Tuition	242,926	130,723
Concessions and other support	103,582	68,754
	1,980,330	1,507,771
Production costs	476,982	427,754
Operating expenses	797,044	685,522
Ballet school	473,658	301,722
Neighborhood productions	378,454	81,326
General and administrative expense	390,487	469,891
	2,516,625	1,966,215
Deficiency from operations	(536,295)	(458,444)
Donated services, materials, and facilities	—	8,000
Annual giving	150,379	78,469
Grants	702,368	678,322
Fund-raising costs	(35,743)	(50,454)
	817,004	714,337
Excess from current endeavors	280,709	255,893
Capital additions	11,221	18,250
Total increase in entity capital	$ 291,930	$ 274,143

organizations. A few transactions are illustrated below for a nonprofit organization that is choosing to report for the entire organization rather than by fund.

a. Revenue, Support, and Capital Additions. Assume that a nonprofit organization reported the following: dues received in cash, $30,000; unrestricted contributions received in cash, $50,000; snack bar sales, $15,000; contributions received for current capital additions, $10,000; contributions received for capital additions in the future, $60,000.

Cash	$165,000	
Revenues - Membership Dues		$30,000
Public Support - Contributions		50,000
Revenues - Snack Bar Sales		15,000
Capital Additions		10,000
Deferred Capital Support		60,000

The "Capital Additions" must be shown as a separate item after "Excess from Current Endeavors" on the Activity Statement. The "Deferred Capital Support" account is a liability.

b. Investment Transactions. Assume that a nonprofit organization received $20,000 in dividends for a given year, that investments were sold at a $15,000 loss, and that the remaining investments increased in market value by $10,000.

Cash	$20,000	
Revenues - Investment Income		$20,000
Cash	70,000	
Loss from Sale of Investments	15,000	
Investments		85,000
Investments	10,000	
Revenues - Unrealized Gain on		
Investments		10,000

Investments may be carried at market. If this is done, the unrealized gains and losses are reported in the same manner as realized gains and losses.

E. **SFAC 4 Objectives of Reporting by Nonbusiness Organizations**

    Recently the FASB issued <u>Statement of Financial Accounting Concepts No. 4: Objectives of Financial Reporting by Nonbusiness Organizations</u>. An outline of this statement is provided below. It should be noted that at this time the Board has deferred its decision on the applicability of these objectives to state and local governmental financial reporting. They are applicable, however, to all other nonprofit entities discussed in this module.

<u>Outline of Concepts No. 4</u>

1. Distinguishing characteristics of nonbusiness organizations

    a. Significant receipts of resources from providers who do not expect to receive proportionate economic benefits

    b. Operating purpose other than providing goods and services at a profit

    c. Absence of defined ownership interest

    d. Include most human services organizations, churches, foundations, private nonprofit hospitals, nonprofit schools

2. Environmental setting of objectives

    a. Objectives are affected by economic, legal, political, and social environment in which nonbusiness organizations function

    b. Environments of nonbusiness organizations and business enterprises are similar in that both produce and distribute goods and services and use scarce resources

    c. Environments of nonbusiness organizations are different in that noneconomic reasons are factors in decision to provide resources to many nonbusiness organizations as opposed to an anticipated return in the case of business organizations

    d. Objectives are also affected by characteristics and limitations of the kind of information financial reporting can provide

3. Users include

    a. Resource providers

        1) Directly compensated (lenders, suppliers, employees)

        2) Not directly compensated (members, contributors, taxpayers)

b. Constituents - those who use and benefit from organization's services
c. Governing and oversight bodies - those responsible for setting policies and overseeing
d. Managers - responsible for carrying out policies

4. Present and potential users share a common interest in information about

a. The services provided by the organization
b. The organization's efficiency and effectiveness in providing those services
c. The organization's ability to continue to provide those services

5. The objectives specify that financial reporting by nonbusiness organizations should

a. Provide information that is useful in making rational decisions about allocation of resources to the organization

1) Information should be comprehensible to those with a reasonable understanding of organization's activities

b. Provide information that is useful in assessing the organization's services and ability to continue providing services

1) Necessary for evaluation of past performance

c. Provide information that is useful in assessing management stewardship and performance

1) Effective and efficient use of organization's resources
2) Compliance with statutory, contractual, or other limitations

d. Provide information about economic resources, obligations, net resources, and changes therein

1) Enables identification of financial strengths and weaknesses
2) Helps evaluation of organization performance
3) Aids assessment of future ability to render services
4) Should include information on resource restrictions

e. Provide information about the performance of the organization during the period

1) Periodic measurement of changes in amount and nature of net resources

a) Amounts and kinds of inflows and outflows of resources
b) Identification of inflows and outflows of restricted resources
c) Measured by accrual accounting

2) Information about service efforts and accomplishments

a) How resources are used in providing different services
b) Goods or services produced and program results

f. Provide information about organization's liquidity

1) How cash is obtained and spent
2) Borrowing and repayment of borrowing

g. Include explanations and interpretations to aid understanding

CHAPTER THIRTEEN

TAXES

TAXES ON THE ACCOUNTING PRACTICE EXAMINATION

A minimum of 20% of the practice section of the examination tests federal income taxation. Prior to May 1980, this was accomplished by a problem containing a series of multiple choice questions in one practice section, and a long computational tax problem in the other practice section. However, beginning with the May 1980 examination, both tax problems have consisted solely of multiple choice questions.

Thus, it is likely that you will have two tax problems in the practice sections, each problem consisting of a series of 20 multiple choice questions. One series of multiple choice questions will test corporations and partnerships, while the other series of multiple choice questions will test individual taxation.

The multiple choice questions test detailed application of the Internal Revenue Code and tax regulations. Past coverage indicates that the tax law in effect during the preceding calendar year is tested. Thus, it would appear that the 1983 tax law will be tested on both 1984 examinations. This is important because some tax law changes are not effective until 1984. Moreover, as a practical matter, the examiners generally avoid testing candidates on recent tax law changes.

The AICPA Content Specification Outline of the coverage of taxes, including the authors' frequency analysis thereof (last nine exams), appears on the following pages. The frequency analysis should be used as an indication of the topics' relative importance on past Accounting Practice exams.

The summary tax outlines presented in this chapter begin by emphasizing individual taxation. Because of numerous common concepts, partnership and corporate taxation are presented later in terms of their differences from individual taxation (i.e., learn individual taxes thoroughly and then learn the peculiarities of partnership and corporate taxation). Interperiod and intraperiod tax allocation questions are presented in Module 27: Deferred Taxes.

The property transactions outline has been inserted between individual taxation and the partnership and corporate tax outlines because property transactions are common to all types of taxpayers, and generally play an important role within every tax problem, both PTAX and CTAX, as well as ITAX.

The next section outlines three basic federal income tax returns: 1040-Individual; 1065-Partnership; and 1120-Corporation. These outlines are an intermediary step between the simple formula outline (below) and the outlines of the detailed rules (continued on last page of content outlines).

AICPA CONTENT SPECIFICATION OUTLINE/FREQUENCY ANALYSIS*
TAXES

	May 1980	Nov. 1980	May 1981	Nov. 1981	May 1982	Nov. 1982	May 1983	Nov. 1983	May 1984
I. Federal Taxation--Individuals									
A. Inclusions for Gross Income and Adjusted Gross Income									
1. Reporting Basis of Taxpayer--Cash, Accrual, or Modified	-	-	-	-	-	-	1	2	-
2. Compensation for Services	-	-	-	-	-	-	-	-	-
3. Net Earnings from Self-Employment**	1	1	-	-	1	1	-	-	-
4. Interest	2	-	1	-	1	-	-	1	2
5. Rents and Royalties	1	1	1	1	-	-	1	-	-
6. Dividends	1	-	-	1	2	1	-	1	-
7. Alimony	1	1	1	2	-	-	1	-	1
8. Capital Gains and Losses	1	2	1	1	2	-	1	1	-
9. Miscellaneous Income	1	2	2	-	-	3	1	-	-
B. Exclusions and Other Deductions (including adjustments to arrive at Adjusted Gross Income)	-	2	1	2	2	5	3	1	6
C. Gain or Loss on Property Transactions									
1. Character	1	-	-	1	-	-	-	2	-
2. Recognition	-	2	1	-	1	2	1	2	2
3. Basis and Holding Period	-	1	-	-	1	3	2	1	2
D. Deductions from Adjusted Gross Income									
1. Zero Bracket Amount	-	-	-	-	-	-	-	1	-
2. Interest	1	2	1	-	1	-	1	-	-
3. Taxes	2	-	3	2	3	1	1	-	1
4. Contributions	2	-	1	1	1	1	1	-	-
5. Medical Expenses	2	1	1	1	2	-	-	1	1
6. Casualty Losses	1	2	1	1	-	-	1	1	1
7. Miscellaneous Deductions	-	1	-	3	-	-	-	3	1
E. Filing Status and Exemptions	2	1	2	-	2	-	3	1	2
F. Tax Determination									
1. Tax Computations	1	-	1	1	-	-	1	-	-
2. Tax Credits and Other Allowances	-	1	2	3	1	2	-	-	1

*The classifications are the authors'.

**These classifications have been added by the authors.

AICPA CONTENT SPECIFICATION OUTLINE/FREQUENCY ANALYSIS (CONTINUED)
TAXES

	May 1980	Nov. 1980	May 1981	Nov. 1981	May 1982	Nov. 1982	May 1983	Nov. 1983	May 1984
G. Statute of Limitations									
1. Claims for Refund	-	-	-	-	-	-	-	-	-
2. Assessments	-	-	-	-	-	1	1	-	-
H. Effect of Gift and Estate Taxation on Individuals	-	-	-	-	-	-	-	2	-
Total MC Questions	20	20	20	20	20	20	20	20	20
Total Problems	-	-	-	-	-	-	-	-	-
Actual Percentage*** (AICPA 10%)	10%	10%	10%	10%	10%	10%	10%	10%	10%

II. Federal Taxation--Corporations and Partnerships

	May 1980	Nov. 1980	May 1981	Nov. 1981	May 1982	Nov. 1982	May 1983	Nov. 1983	May 1984
A. Determination of Taxable Income or Loss									
1. Determination of Gross Income Including Capital Gains and Losses									
a. Sec. 1231 and Capital Gains and Losses**	2	2	1	2	1	3	1	2	2
b. Issuance of Stock (including treasury stock)**	1	1	2	-	-	-	1	1	-
2. Deductions from Gross Income									
a. Charitable Contributions**	1	1	1	-	1	1	1	-	1
b. Dividends Received**	2	1	-	1	1	1	-	1	-
c. Organization Expenditures**	1	1	1	-	1	-	-	1	1
d. Net Operating Loss**	1	1	1	1	-	1	1	2	-
e. Depreciation and Other**	3	1	3	2	1	2	-	1	2
3. Reconciliation of Taxable Income and Book Income	2	3	1	1	-	1	-	-	-
4. Reconciliation of Opening and Closing Retained Earnings	-	-	-	1	1	-	1	-	-
5. Consolidations	-	-	-	-	-	-	-	-	1

***The "actual percentage" is a measure of the relative coverage of the specific areas (i.e., I, II, etc.) on each Accounting Practice exam. This relative weighting includes <u>both</u> multiple choice questions and problems presented in that area.

AICPA CONTENT SPECIFICATION OUTLINE/FREQUENCY ANALYSIS (CONTINUED)
TAXES

	May 1980	Nov. 1980	May 1981	Nov. 1981	May 1982	Nov. 1982	May 1983	Nov. 1983	May 1984
B. Tax Determination									
1. Tax Computations	-	-	-	-	-	-	1	-	-
2. Tax Credits	-	1	1	1	2	1	-	1	-
C. Subchapter S Corporations	2	2	3	1	2	2	1	2	1
D. Personal Holding Companies	-	-	1	-	-	-	1	1	1
E. Accumulated Earnings Tax	1	-	-	-	1	-	1	1	1
F. Distributions	1	1	1	-	-	1	-	1	3
G. Tax-Free Incorporation	-	1	-	1	1	1	1	-	1
H. Reorganizations	-	1	1	1	2	1	-	-	1
I. Liquidations and Dissolutions	-	-	-	1	1	1	2	1	2
J. Formation of Partnership									
1. Contribution of Capital	-	-	-	-	1	-	-	-	-
2. Contribution of Services	-	-	-	1	1	-	-	1	1
K. Basis of Partner's Interest									
1. Acquired through Contribution	-	-	-	-	2	1	1	1	1
2. Interest Acquired from Another Partner	-	-	-	-	-	-	-	-	-
3. Holding Period of Partner's Interest	-	-	-	-	-	-	-	-	-
4. Adjustments to Basis of Partner's Interest	-	1	-	1	-	-	-	-	-
L. Basis of Property Contributed to Partnership	-	-	1	-	-	-	-	-	-
M. Determination of Partnership Ordinary Income	2	1	1	1	-	1	-	1	-
N. Determination of Partner's Taxable Income									
1. Partner's Distributive Share of Income	-	-	1	2	-	-	-	1	1
2. Elections Available to Partners (different reporting methods)	-	-	-	-	-	-	-	-	-
3. Deductibility of Losses from Partnership**	1	-	-	-	-	-	-	-	-

AICPA CONTENT SPECIFICATION OUTLINE/FREQUENCY ANALYSIS (CONTINUED)
TAXES

	May 1980	Nov. 1980	May 1981	Nov. 1981	May 1982	Nov. 1982	May 1983	Nov. 1983	May 1984
O. Accounting Periods of Partnership and Partners	-	-	-	-	-	-	-	-	-
P. Partner Dealing with Own Partnership									
1. Sales and Exchanges	-	-	-	1	1	1	-	-	-
2. Guaranteed Payments	-	-	-	-	-	-	-	-	-
3. H.R. 10 Plans	-	-	-	-	-	-	1	-	-
Q. Treatment of Liabilities	-	-	-	-	-	-	-	-	-
R. Distributions of Partnership Assets									
1. Current Distributions	-	-	-	-	-	-	-	-	-
2. Distributions in Complete Liquidations	-	-	-	-	-	-	-	-	-
3. Basis of Distributed Property	-	1	-	-	-	-	2	1	-
S. Termination of Partnership									
1. Change of Membership	-	-	-	-	-	-	2	-	-
2. Merger or Split-Up of Partnership	-	-	-	-	-	-	-	-	-
3. Sale or Exchange of Partnership Interest	-	-	-	1	-	1	1	-	-
4. Payments to a Retiring Partner	-	-	-	-	-	-	1	-	-
5. Payments to a Deceased Partner's Successor	-	-	-	-	-	-	-	-	-
Total MC Questions	20	20	20	20	20	20	20	20	20
Total Problems	-	-	-	-	-	-	-	-	-
Actual Percentage (AICPA 10%)	10%	10%	10%	10%	10%	10%	10%	10%	10%

Formula Outline for Individual Returns:
    Gross income
        less "above the line" deductions
    Adjusted gross income
        less excess itemized deductions (or add "unused zero bracket amount")
        less exemptions
    Taxable income
        times tax rates
        less tax credits
    Tax liability

OVERVIEW OF FEDERAL TAX RETURNS

The following overviews are taken from specific tax return forms. Problems requiring computation of taxable income require that you be familiar with the outlines below. The tax return outlines also help you "pull together" all of the detailed tax rules. The schedule and form identification numbers are provided for reference only; they are not tested on the examination.

Review, in detail, the outlines of the return forms presented below. The outlines will introduce you to the topics tested on the exam and their relationship to final "tax liability."

Form 1040 - Individuals

A. INCOME

1. Wages, salaries, tips, etc.
2. Interest (Sch. B)
3. Dividend income less exclusion (Sch. B)
4. Income other than wages, dividends, and interest (The gross income reported on the schedules below is already reduced by corresponding deductible expenses. Only the net income (or loss) is reported on Form 1040.)

   a. State and local income tax refunds
   b. Alimony received
   c. Business income or loss (Sch. C)
   d. Capital gain or loss (Sch. D)
   e. Supplemental gains or losses (Form 4797)
   f. Fully taxable pensions and annuities
   g. Other pensions, annuities, rents, royalties (Sch. E)
   h. Unemployment compensation
   i. Other

B. Less "above the line" deductions

1. Moving expenses (Form 3903)
2. Employee business expenses (Form 2106)
3. Payments to an individual retirement arrangement (IRA)(Form 5329)
4. Payments to a Keogh retirement plan
5. Forfeited interest penalty for premature withdrawals
6. Alimony paid
7. Deduction for a married couple when both work (Sch. W)
8. Disability income exclusion (Form 2440)

C. ADJUSTED GROSS INCOME

D. Less excess itemized deductions (Sch. A), including

1. Medical and dental expenses
2. Taxes
3. Interest expense
4. Contributions

     5. Casualty or theft losses
     6. Miscellaneous

E. Less exemptions ($1,000 each)

F. TAXABLE INCOME

     1. Find your tax in the tables, or
     2. Use tax rate schedules

G. Additional taxes

     1. Tax on accumulation distributions of trusts (Form 4970)
     2. Special 10-year averaging method (Form 4972)
     3. Lump-sum retirement plan distribution 10-year averaging (Form 5544)
     4. Penalty tax on premature distributions from a retirement plan

H. Less tax credits

     1. Political contribution credit
     2. Credit for the elderly (Sch. R & RP)
     3. Credit for child care expenses (Form 2441)
     4. Investment credit (Form 3468)
     5. Foreign tax credit (Form 1116)
     6. Targeted jobs credit (Form 5884)
     7. Residential energy credit (Form 5695)

I. TAX LIABILITY

J. Other taxes

     1. Self-employment tax (Sch. SE)
     2. Alternative minimum tax (Form 6251)
     3. Investment credit recapture (Form 4255)
     4. Social security tax on tip income (Form 4137)
     5. Uncollected social security tax on tips (Form W-2)
     6. Tax on individual retirement arrangements (Form 5329)

K. Less Payments

     1. Tax withheld on wages
     2. Estimated tax payments
     3. Earned income credit
     4. Amount paid with an extension
     5. Excess FICA paid
     6. Credit for federal tax on special fuels (Form 4136)
     7. Credit from a regulated investment company (Form 2439)

L. Amount overpaid or balance due

Form 1065 - Partnerships

A. INCOME

     1. Gross sales less returns and allowances
     2. Less cost of goods sold
     3. GROSS PROFIT
     4. Ordinary income from other partnerships and fiduciaries

      5. Nonqualifying dividends and interest
      6. Rents
      7. Royalties
      8. Net farm profit
      9. Ordinary gain or loss (may include depreciation recapture)
     10. Other

B. Less deductions

      1. Salaries and wages
      2. Guaranteed payments to partners
      3. Rents
      4. Interest expense
      5. Taxes
      6. Bad debts
      7. Repairs
      8. Depreciation
      9. Depletion
     10. Retirement plans
     11. Employee benefit program contributions
     12. Other

C. Ordinary income (loss)

D. Schedule K (on partnership return) and Schedule K-1 to be prepared for each individual partner

      1.   Ordinary income (loss)
      2.   Guaranteed payments
      3.   Interest from All-Savers Certificates
      4.   Dividends qualifying for exclusion
      5.   Net short-term capital gain (loss)
      6.   Net long-term capital gain (loss)
      7.   Net gain (loss) due to casualty or theft
      8.   Net gain (loss) from Section 1231 transactions
      9.   Other
     10.   Charitable contributions
     11.   Sec. 179 expense deduction
     12.a. Payments for partners to IRA
     12.b. Payments for partners to Keogh Plan
     12.c. Payments for partners to Simplified Employee Pension
     13.   Other
     14.   Jobs credit
     15.   Alcohol fuel credit
     16.   Credit for income tax withheld
     17.   Other
     18.a. Gross farming or fishing income
     18.b. Net earnings from self-employment
     18.c. Other

19.   Tax preference items
  a.   Accelerated depreciation on nonrecovery real property or
        15-year real property
  b.   Accelerated depreciation on personal property subject to a lease
  c.   Depletion (other than oil and gas)
  d.(1) Excess intangible drilling costs
  d.(2) Net income from oil, gas, or geothermal wells
  e.   Net investment income (loss)
  f.   Other
20.   Investment interest expense
21.   Type of income

Form 1120 - Corporations

A. Gross income

  1.   Gross sales less returns and allowances
  2.   Less cost of goods sold
  3.   GROSS PROFIT
  4.   Dividends
  5.   Interest
  6.   Gross rents
  7.   Gross royalties
  8.   Net capital gains
  9.   Ordinary gain or loss
  10. Other income

B. Less deductions

  1.   Compensation of officers
  2.   Salaries and wages (net of jobs credit)
  3.   Repairs
  4.   Bad debts
  5.   Rents
  6.   Taxes
  7.   Interest
  8.   Charitable contributions
  9.   Depreciation
  10. Depletion
  11. Advertising
  12. Pension, profit-sharing-plan contributions
  13. Employee benefit programs
  14. Other
  15. Net operating loss deduction
  16. Dividend received deduction

C. TAXABLE INCOME times tax rates

D. Less tax credits equals TAX LIABILITY

I. GROSS INCOME ON INDIVIDUAL RETURNS

This section outlines: (1) gross income in general, (2) exclusions from gross income, (3) items to be included in gross income, (4) tax accounting methods, and (5) items to be included in gross income net of deductions (e.g., business income, sales and exchanges).

A. **In General**

1. <u>Gross income</u> includes all income from whatever source derived, unless specifically excluded

    a. Includes all flow of wealth to the taxpayer

    b. Does not include a return of capital, e.g., if a taxpayer loans $6,000 to another and is repaid $6,500 at a later date, only the $500 difference is included in gross income

    c. The income must be <u>realized</u>, i.e., there must be a transaction which gives rise to the income

        1) Mere accretions in value of property are not income, e.g., value of one's home increases $2,000 during year. Only if the house is sold will the increase in value be realized.

        2) A transaction may be in the form of

            a) Actual receipt of cash or property

            b) Accrual of a receivable

            c) Sale or exchange

    d. The income must also be <u>recognized</u>, i.e., the transaction must be a taxable event, and not a transaction for which nonrecognition is provided in the Internal Revenue Code

        1) E.g., an exchange of certain types of property for like-kind property is specifically made a transaction in which the gain, although realized, will not be recognized. Nonrecognition transactions are listed in "Exclusions from Gross Income" (see on following page) and "Sales and Exchanges," (page 1181).

    e. An <u>assignment of income</u> will not be recognized for tax purposes

        1) If income from property is assigned, it is still taxable to the owner of the property

            a) E.g., X owns a building and assigns the rents to Y. X remains taxable on the rents, even though the rents are received by Y

        2) If income from services is assigned, it is still taxable to the person who earns it

            a) E.g., X earns $200 per week. To pay off a debt owed to Y, he assigns half of it to Y. $200 per week remains taxable to X.

2. Distinction between exclusions, deductions, and credits

    a. <u>Exclusions</u>--income items which are not included in gross income

        1) Exclusions must be specified by law. Remember, gross income includes all income except that specifically excluded.

2) Although exclusions are exempt from income tax, they may still be taxed, e.g., gifts may be subject to the gift tax

b. <u>Deductions</u>--amounts that are subtracted from income to arrive at adjusted gross income or taxable income

1) Deductions for adjusted gross income (above the line deductions)-- amounts deducted from gross income to arrive at adjusted gross income

a) Adjusted gross income is an important subtotal because it is used in the computation of some of the limitations on below the line deductions

2) Itemized deductions (below the line deductions)--amounts deducted from adjusted gross income to arrive at taxable income

c. <u>Credits</u>--amounts subtracted from the computed tax to arrive at taxes payable

B. <u>Exclusions from Gross Income</u> (not reported)

1. Payments received for <u>support</u> of minor children

a. Must be children of the parent making the payments
b. Decree of divorce or separate maintenance must specify the amount to be treated as child support, otherwise payments may be treated as alimony

2. <u>Property settlement</u> (division of capital) received in a divorce

3. <u>Annuities</u> and pensions are excluded to the extent they are a return of capital

a. Excluded portion of each payment is:

$$\frac{\text{Net Cost of Annuity}}{\text{Expected Total Annuity Payments}} \quad X \quad \text{Payment Received}$$

b. "Expected total annuity payments" is calculated by multiplying the annual return times:

1) The number of years receivable if an annuity for a definite period
2) A life expectancy multiple (from IRS tables) if an annuity for life

c. Once this exclusion ratio is determined, it remains constant, even if the annuitant outlives his life expectancy
d. If the annuity is an <u>employee annuity</u> and all the employee's cost can be recovered in the first 3 years of the annuity:

1) Then all annuity payments received are excluded until the employee's cost is recovered; thereafter,
2) All additional payments received are taxable

EXAMPLE: Mr. Jones retired on January 31, 1981 with a monthly pension of $200. He contributed $5,000 toward the cost of the employee pension. Since he will recover his $5,000 cost within 36 months, the payments will be treated as follows:

Year	Nontaxable	Taxable
1981	$2,200	$ -0-
1982	2,400	-0-
1983	400	2,000
1984	-0-	2,400

4
0

e. Dividends received before the annuity starting date are excluded

1) But they reduce the cost of annuity
2) They are included in income if they exceed the cost of the annuity

4. Life insurance proceeds (face amount of policy) are generally excluded if paid by reason of death

a. If beneficiary elects to receive the benefits in installments, use annuity exclusion ratio above using the face amount of policy as cost, i.e., only the interest will be included in income

1) If beneficiary is the decedent's surviving spouse, there is an exclusion of up to $1,000/year for such interest income

b. Life insurance dividends on unmatured policies are excluded as long as the dividends do not exceed the premiums paid
c. If a life insurance policy is purchased from another owner for valuable consideration, all proceeds in excess of cost are included in gross income

5. Certain employee benefits are excluded

a. Payment of death benefits by employer to employee's beneficiary

1) Exclusion not applicable to amounts to which employee had a non-forfeitable right before death
2) Limited to $5,000 per employee (not per beneficiary)

a) If more than 1 employer, limit is $5,000 total and must be allocated pro rata to all beneficiaries

b. Group-term life insurance premiums paid by employer (up to $50,000 of insurance coverage)

1) Exclusion not limited if beneficiary is the employer or a qualified charity

c. Premiums employer pays to fund an accident or health plan for employees are excluded
d. Accident and health benefits provided by employer are excluded if benefits are for

1) Disabled employee under age 65, retired as permanently and totally disabled (unable to do substantial gainful activity for at least 12 months)

a) Exclusion is limited to $100/week
b) Exclusion is reduced by adjusted gross income (before the exclusion) in excess of $15,000
c) This exclusion repealed for taxable years beginning after 1983

2) Permanent injury or loss of bodily function
3) Reimbursement for medical care of employee, his spouse, or dependents

a) Employee cannot take itemized deduction for reimbursed medical expenses
b) Exclusion may not apply to highly compensated individuals if reimbursed under a discriminatory self-insured medical plan

e. Meals or lodging furnished for the convenience of the employer on the employer's premises are excluded

       1) For the convenience of the employer means there must be a noncompensatory reason such as the employee is required to be on duty during this period

       2) In the case of lodging, it also must be a condition of employment

  f. Employer contributions to, and benefits derived from a group legal services plan are excluded through 1984

  g. Benefits for payment of tuition, fees, etc., derived from an employer's qualified educational assistance program, are excluded through 1983

  h. The value of transportation, between the employee's residence and place of employment, furnished under a qualified transportation plan is excluded through 1985

  i. Minor fringe benefits are excluded:

       1) Holiday presents (e.g., turkeys) but not cash or items easily convertible into cash

       2) Courtesy discounts to employees, but bargain purchases are not excluded

  j. Workmen's compensation is excluded

6. Accident and health insurance benefits derived from policies purchased by the taxpayer are excluded; but not excluded if the medical expenses were deducted in a prior year and the tax benefit rule applies

7. Compensation for damages resulting from personal or family injury

  a. Damages for slander of personal reputation are excluded from income; damages for slander of professional or business reputation are not excluded

  b. Damages for loss of property are excluded, except to the extent they exceed the basis of the property destroyed

  c. Damages for loss of profit or income are not excluded

  d. Punitive damages are not excluded, e.g., treble damages in antitrust recovery

8. Gifts, bequests, devises, or inheritances are excluded

  a. Income from property so acquired is not excluded, e.g., interest or rent

  b. "Gifts" from employer except for death benefits and holiday presents are generally not excluded

9. Dividends from taxable domestic corporations are excluded as follows:

  a. An individual may exclude up to $100 of dividends ($200 on a joint return). For example, if husband receives $80 of dividends and his wife receives $120 of dividends, the total exclusion would be $200 on a joint return.

       1) Dividends that do not qualify for the exclusion include dividends from:

          a) Foreign corporations   c) Money market funds
          b) Exempt organizations   d) Real estate investment trusts

  b. Beginning in 1982, an individual who chooses to participate in a public utility dividend reinvestment plan, to receive dividends in the form of common stock rather than cash, may elect to exclude up to $750 per year ($1,500 on a joint return) of the stock dividend

       1) The qualified dividend stock will have a zero basis

       2) If the dividend stock is sold within one year of distribution, the proceeds will be taxed as ordinary income

10. The receipt of <u>stock dividends</u> (or stock rights) is generally excluded from income (see page 1181 for basis and holding period); but, the FMV of the stock received will be included in income if the distribution

    a. Is on preferred stock
    b. Is payable, at the election of any shareholder, in stock or property
    c. Results in the receipt of preferred stock by some common shareholders, and the receipt of common stock by other common shareholders
    d. Results in the receipt of property by some shareholders, and an increase in the proportionate interests of other shareholders in earnings or assets of the corporation

11. Certain <u>interest income</u> is excluded

    a. Interest on obligations of a state or one of its political subdivisions (municipal bonds), the District of Columbia, and U.S. possessions is not taxable

       1) Not industrial development bonds in excess of $1,000,000 issued after 4/30/68
       2) Not arbitrage bonds (those used to acquire other obligations with a higher yield) issued after 10/9/69

    b. Interest on qualified scholarship funding bonds
    c. An individual is eligible for a lifetime exclusion of up to $1,000 ($2,000 on a joint return) of interest earned on <u>All-Savers Certificates</u> issued before 1983

       1) If any portion of the certificate is redeemed before maturity, the holder loses the exclusion for all interest earned on the certificate

       2) If any portion of the certificate is used as collateral for a loan, the holder is treated as having redeemed the certificate before maturity

12. <u>Scholarships</u> and <u>fellowships</u> are generally excluded but

    a. Not excluded if payments are compensation for past, present, or future services (unless required of all candidates for the degree)

    b. If recipient is not a candidate for a degree

       1) The grantor must be a tax-exempt organization or government agency, and
       2) The exclusion is limited to $300 times the number of months for which the grant is received (maximum of 36 months)

13. <u>Political contributions</u> received by candidates are excluded from income, but included if put to personal use

14. Rental value of parsonage or cash rental allowance for a parsonage is excluded by a minister

15. <u>Discharge of indebtedness</u> normally results in income to debtor, but may be <u>excluded</u> if

    a. A discharge of certain student loans
    b. A discharge of a corporation's debt by a shareholder (treated as a contribution to capital)
    c. The discharge is a gift
    d. A discharge of qualified business indebtedness and taxpayer elects to reduce basis of depreciable property by the amount excluded from income
    e. Debt is discharged in bankruptcy proceeding, or debtor is insolvent both before and after discharge

1) If debtor insolvent before but solvent after discharge of debt, income is recognized to the extent that the FMV of assets exceeds liabilities after discharge

2) The amount excluded from income in "e." on the preceding page must be applied to reduce tax attributes in the following order:

   a) NOL for taxable year and loss carryovers to taxable year
   b) Investment, jobs, and alcohol fuel credits
   c) Capital loss of taxable year and carryovers to taxable year
   d) Reduction of the basis of property
   e) Foreign tax credit carryovers to or from taxable year

3) Instead of reducing tax attributes in the above order, taxpayer may elect to first reduce the basis of depreciable property

16. <u>Lease Improvements.</u> Increase in value of property due to improvements made by lessee are excluded from lessor's income unless improvements are made in lieu of rent

C. Items to be Included in Gross Income

Gross income includes all income from any source except those specifically excluded. The more common items of gross income are listed below. Those items requiring a detailed explanation are discussed in the following pages.

1. Compensation for services, including wages, salaries, bonuses, commissions, fees and tips

   a. Also includes similar earned income from sources outside U.S.
   b. Room and board unless for employer convenience
   c. Life insurance premium except for group-term life insurance of $50,000 or less
   d. Employee expenses paid or reimbursed by the employer unless the employee has to account to the employer for these expenses
   e. Property received as compensation is included in income at FMV
   f. Bargain purchases by an employee from an employer are included in income at FMV less price paid

2. Gross income derived from business and professions
3. Distributive share of partnership or S corporation income
4. Gains derived from dealings in property, i.e., profits from the sale or exchange of real estate, securities, or other property
5. Interest including:

   a. Earnings from savings and loan associations, mutual savings banks, credit unions, etc.
   b. Interest on bank deposits, corporate or U.S. government bonds and notes

      1) Note that interest from U.S. obligations is included while interest on state and local obligations is excluded

   c. Interest on tax refunds
   d. Interest on state and local industrial development bonds in excess of $1,000,000 issued after April 30, 1968, or arbitrage bonds issued after October 9, 1969

6. Rents and royalties
7. Dividends (less up to $100 or $200 exclusion)

8. <u>Alimony and separate maintenance</u> payments

   a. Payments are included in gross income if made pursuant to (i.e., after) a decree of divorce or separate maintenance, or written separation agreement, and are

      1). Uncertain in amount or for an indefinite period (e.g., terminate upon death or remarriage, or change in economic status), or

      2) To be paid for more than 10 years (except annual payment for current and future years in excess of 10% of the principal sum)

         a) E.g., $150,000 is to be received over 15 years; $20,000 in each of the first 5 years and $5,000 in each subsequent year. Assuming payments are timely made, $15,000 in each of the first 5 years and $5,000 in each of the last 10 years is included in income as alimony. The remainder is excluded from income.

9. Social security, pensions, annuities (other than excluded recovery of capital)

   a. Beginning in 1984, a portion of social security benefits may be included in gross income if the recipient's AGI (before a for two-earner married deduction; and including tax-exempt interest) plus 50% of the benefits

      1) Exceeds a base amount of

         a) $32,000 for married individuals filing a joint return
         b) Zero for a married individual filing a separate return
         c) $25,000 for all other individuals

      2) Amount included in gross income is lesser of

         a) One-half of social security benefits, or
         b) One-half of the excess of the taxpayer's combined income (i.e., modified AGI plus 50% of benefits) over the base amount

   b. Lump-sum distributions from retirement plans

      1) Pre-1974 accumulations--treated as long-term capital gain
      2) Post-1973 accumulations--treated as ordinary income
      3) Recipient may qualify to elect 10-year averaging for ordinary income portion, or may elect to treat all accumulations as ordinary income subject to 10-year averaging

10. Income in respect of a decedent and from an interest in an estate or trust

    a. Income in respect of a decedent is income which a decedent did not receive before death, e.g., installment payments that are paid to estate after his death. Such income has the same character as it would have had if the decedent had lived.

11. Employer supplemental unemployment benefits or strike benefits from union funds
12. Fees, including those received by an executor, administrator, director, or for jury duty or precinct election board duty
13. Income from discharge of indebtedness unless specifically excluded p. 1138)
14. <u>Stock Options</u>

    a. An <u>incentive stock option</u> receives favorable tax treatment

       1) The option must meet certain technical requirements to qualify
       2) No income is recognized by employee when option is granted or exercised

3) If employee holds the stock acquired through exercise of the option at least 2 years from the date the option was granted, and holds the stock itself at least 1 year, the:

    a) Employee's realized gain will be long-term capital gain
    b) Employer receives no deduction

4) If the holding period requirements above are not met, the employee has ordinary income to the extent that the FMV at date of exercise exceeds the option price

    a) Remainder of gain is S-T or L-T capital gain
    b) Employer receives a deduction equal to the amount employee reports as ordinary income

b. A <u>nonqualified stock option</u> is included in income when received if option has a determinable FMV

1) If option has no ascertainable FMV when received, then income arises when option is exercised; to the extent of the difference between the FMV when exercised and the option price

2) Amount recognized (at receipt or when exercised) is treated as ordinary income to employee; employer is allowed a deduction equal to amount included in employee's income

c. An <u>employee stock purchase plan</u> which does not discriminate against rank and file employees

1) No income when employee receives or exercises option
2) If the employee holds the stock at least 2 years after the option is granted and at least 1 year after exercise, then:

    a) Employee has ordinary income to the extent of the lesser of:

        1] FMV at time option granted over option price, or
        2] FMV at disposition over option price

    b) Capital gain to the extent realized gain exceeds ordinary income

3) If the stock is not held for the required time, then:

    a) Employee has ordinary income at the time of sale for the difference between FMV when exercised and the option price

        1] This amount also increases basis

    b) Capital gain or loss for the difference between selling price and increased basis

15. <u>Prizes and awards</u> are generally taxable. They are excluded only if in recognition of civic, artistic, educational, scientific, or literary achievement and only if:

a. Recipient was selected without any action on his part, and
b. Recipient is not required to render additional future services

16. Recovery of bad debt is included in income to the extent the bad debt deduction provided a tax benefit in prior year

a. If the "reserve method" is used for bad debts, recovery is credited to the reserve account and excluded from income

17. Embezzled or other illegal income

18. Refund of state or local taxes is included in income if the taxes were deducted in a prior year and resulted in a tax benefit

19. Gambling winnings

20. Unemployment compensation is included in income to the extent of the lesser of:

    a. Unemployment compensation, or

    b. 1/2 the excess of AGI (including unemployment compensation and excludable disability income, and before the "marriage penalty deduction") over:

        1) $12,000 if single taxpayer, or
        2) $18,000 if taxpayer filing joint return, or
        3) $-0- if married taxpayer not filing joint return

> EXAMPLE: Taxpayer is single and received $5,000 of unemployment compensation during 1983. His AGI (excluding the unemployment compensation) was $15,000. $4,000 of the unemployment compensation will be included in gross income (i.e., lesser of (1) $5,000, or (2) 1/2 [($15,000 + $5,000) - $12,000]).

D. Tax Accounting Methods

Tax accounting methods often affect the period in which an item of income or deduction is recognized. Note that the classification of an item is not changed, only the time for its inclusion in the tax computation.

1. Cash method or accrual method is commonly used

    a. Cash method recognizes income when first received or constructively received; expenses when paid out

        1) Constructive receipt means that an item is unqualifiedly available without restriction (e.g., interest on bank deposit is income when credited to account)

        2) Not all receipts are income:

            a) Loan proceeds
            b) Recovery of capital

        3) Not all payments are deductible:

            a) Loan repayment
            b) Expenditures benefiting future years (fixed assets) must be capitalized, and depreciated as under accrual accounting

    b. Accrual method recognizes income when the "right to receive payment" has occurred; expenses when the "obligation to pay" has occurred

        1) Accrual method must be used for purchases and sales when inventories are required to clearly reflect income

        2) Accrual method differs somewhat from that used in financial accounting (see "2." following)

2. Special rules regarding methods of accounting

    a. Rents and royalties received in advance are included in gross income in the year received under both the cash and accrual methods

> EXAMPLE: In 1983, a landlord signs a 5-year lease. During 1983, he receives $5,000 for that year's rent, and $5,000 as advance rent for the last year (1987) of the lease. All $10,000 will be included in income for 1983.

b. No advance deduction is generally allowed accrual method taxpayers for estimated or contingent expenses; the obligation must be "fixed and determinable"
c. Alimony, medical services, and charitable contributions are deductible only in the year paid (see CORPORATIONS for an exception regarding charitable contributions)

3. The installment method of reporting income was substantially changed by the Installment Sales Revision Act of 1980

a. The installment method is now required, unless taxpayer makes a negative election to report the full amount of gain in year of sale
b. The amount to be reported in each year is determined by the formula:

$$\frac{\text{Gross Profit of Entire Sale}}{\text{Total Contract Price}} \times \text{Amount Received in Year}$$

1) Contract price is the selling price reduced by the amount of any indebtedness which is assumed or taken subject to by the buyer, to the extent not in excess of the seller's basis in the property

EXAMPLE: Taxpayer sells property with a basis of $80,000 to buyer for a selling price of $150,000. As part of the purchase price, buyer agrees to assume a $50,000 mortgage on the property and pay the remaining $100,000 in 10 equal annual installments together with adequate interest.

The contract price is $100,000 ($150,000 – $50,000); the gross profit is $70,000 ($150,000 – $80,000); and the gross profit ratio is 70% ($70,000 ÷ $100,000). Thus, $7,000 of each $10,000 payment is reported as gain from the sale.

EXAMPLE: Assume the same facts as above except that the seller's basis is $30,000.

The contract price is $120,000 ($150,000 – mortgage assumed but only to extent of seller's basis of $30,000); the gross profit is $120,000 ($150,000 – $30,000); and the gross profit ratio is 100% ($120,000 ÷ $120,000). Thus, 100% of each $10,000 payment is reported as gain from the sale. In addition, the amount by which the assumed mortgage exceeds the seller's basis ($20,000) is deemed to be a payment in year of sale. Since the gross profit ratio is 100%, all $20,000 is reported as gain in the year the mortgage is assumed.

2) Use of the installment method does not change the character of the income to be reported

a) E.g., ordinary income, Sec. 1231 gain, capital gain, etc.
b) If the gain is subject to Sec. 1245 or 1250 recapture, the gain on each installment is ordinary income until the entire recapture is made

4. Special methods are allowable for contracts that are not completed within the year they are started

a. Percentage-of-completion method recognizes income each year based on the % of the contract completed that year
b. Completed-contract method recognizes income only when the contract is completed

E. Business Income and Deductions

1. Gross income for a business includes sales less cost of goods sold plus other income. In computing cost of goods sold:

    a. Inventory is generally valued at (1) cost, or (2) market, whichever is lower
    b. Specific identification, FIFO, and LIFO are allowed
    c. If LIFO is used for taxes, it must also be used on books
    d. Lower of cost or market cannot be used with LIFO

2. All ordinary (customary and not a capital expenditure) and necessary (appropriate and helpful) expenses incurred in a trade or business are deductible

    a. Business expenses that violate public policy (fines or illegal kickbacks) are not deductible
    b. Business expenses must be reasonable

        1) E.g., if salaries are excessive (unreasonable compensation) they may be disallowed as a deduction to the extent unreasonable
        2) Reasonableness of compensation issue generally arises only when the relationship between the employer and employee exceeds that of the normal employer-employee relationship (i.e., employee is also a shareholder)
        3) Use test of what another enterprise would pay under similar circumstances

    c. Entertainment expenses must be directly related or associated with the active conduct of a trade or business

        1) Adequate records must be maintained to substantiate the amount of expense, i.e., who, when, where, why (the 4 Ws)

            a) Receipts must be maintained for all lodging expenditures and for other expenditures of $25 or more except transportation expenditures where receipts are not readily available

        2) No deduction is generally allowed for expenses with respect to an entertainment, recreational, or amusement facility

            a) Entertainment facilities include yachts, hunting lodges, fishing camps, swimming pools, etc.
            b) If the facility is used for a business purpose, the related out-of-pocket expenditures are deductible even though depreciation, etc. of the facility is not deductible
            c) Proportional part of membership fees paid to social, athletic, luncheon, sporting, or country clubs is deductible if club is used more than 50% for business, and then only the portion attributable to directly related use is deductible

                EXAMPLE: A taxpayer paid dues of $500 to a country club. During the year, he used the club 30 days for personal use, 25 days for entertainment directly related to his business, 35 days for business meals, and 10 days for entertainment associated with his business. Since the club was used more than 50% for business purposes (70 of 100 days), he can deduct the part of his dues that is directly related (including busines meals) to his business use of the club.

                $500 \dfrac{25 + 35}{100} = \$300.$

    d. Deductions for business gifts are limited to $25 per recipient each year

        1) Advertising and promotional gifts costing $4 or less are not so limited

2) Gifts of tangible personal property costing $400 or less are deductible if awarded to an employee for length of service, productivity, or safety achievement
3) Gifts of tangible personal property costing $1,600 or less are deductible if awarded to an employee under a qualified plan for length of service, productivity, or safety achievement

   a) Plan must be written and nondiscriminatory
   b) Average cost of all items awarded under the plan during the tax year must not exceed $400

e. <u>Bad debts</u> are generally deducted in the year they become worthless

1) There must have been a valid "debtor-creditor" relationship
2) A <u>business</u> bad debt is one that is incurred in the trade or business of the lender

   a) Deductible against ordinary income (toward AGI)
   b) Deduction allowed for partial worthlessness

3) Business bad debts may be deducted either by the specific charge-off method or by the reserve method

   a) Under the <u>specific charge-off method</u>, a deduction is allowed when a specific debt becomes partially or totally worthless

   b) Under the <u>reserve method</u>, a deduction is allowed for a reasonable addition to the reserve

      1] Generally, a percentage (i.e., determined by dividing average net bad debt losses by average receivables) is applied to the ending balance of accounts receivable to determine the required reserve at the end of the year. The bad debt deduction represents the amount necessary to bring the reserve up to the required balance.
      2] Individual bad debts are charged against the reserve, not gross income

   c) A bad debt deduction is available for accounts or notes receivable only if the amount owed has already been included in gross income for the current or a prior taxable year. Since receivables of a <u>cash method</u> taxpayer have not yet been included in gross income, the <u>receivables</u> cannot be deducted when they become uncollectible.

4) A <u>nonbusiness</u> bad debt (not incurred in trade or business) can only be deducted

   a) If totally worthless
   b) As a short-term capital loss

5) Guarantor of debt who has to pay, takes same deduction as if the loss was from a direct loan

   a) Business bad debt if guarantee related to trade, business, or employment
   b) Nonbusiness bad debt if guarantee entered into for profit but not related to trade or business

f. Expenses may exceed income resulting in a deductible loss if the activity is engaged in for profit

1) Expenses of an activity not engaged in for profit (a hobby) are deductible if they are

   a) Allowable anyway, e.g., interest, taxes, casualty losses
   b) Operating expenses, but not to exceed gross income from the hobby reduced by interest, taxes, and casualty losses

2) An activity is presumed to be for profit if it produces profit in 2 or more years out of 5 consecutive years (2 out of 7 years for horses)

3. Net operating loss (NOL)

   a. A net operating loss may occur even if an individual is not engaged in a separate trade or business (e.g., a NOL created by a personal casualty loss)

   b. NOLs incurred after 1975 may be carried back 3 years and carried forward 15 years to offset profits in other years

      1) Carryback is first made to the third preceding year
      2) May elect not to carryback and only carryforward 15 years

   c. To compute the NOL, begin with the loss using all income items and deductions (including the zero bracket amount)

      1) Then reduce this loss by adding back

         a) Any NOL carryover or carryback from another year
         b) Deduction for LTCG
         c) Excess of capital losses over capital gains

            1] Excess of nonbusiness capital losses over nonbusiness capital gains even if overall gains exceed losses

         d) Personal exemptions ($1,000 per exemption)
         e) Excess of nonbusiness deductions (usually itemized deductions) over nonbusiness income

            1] The ZBA is treated as a nonbusiness deduction
            2] Contributions to a self-employed retirement plan are considered nonbusiness deductions
            3] Casualty losses (even if personal) are considered business deductions
            4] Dividends are nonbusiness income; salary and rent are business income

      2) Any remaining loss is a NOL and must be carried back first, unless election is made to carryforward only

4. Limitation on deductions for business use of home. To be deductible:

   a. A portion of the home must be used exclusively and regularly as the principal place of business or as a meeting place for patients, clients, or customers

      1) Exclusive use rule does not apply to a place of regular storage of business inventory or a day-care center
      2) If an employee, the exclusive use must be for the convenience of the employer

   b. Deduction is limited to the excess of gross income over deductions otherwise allowable for taxes, interest, and casualty losses

EXAMPLE: Taxpayer uses 10% of his home exclusively for business purposes. Gross income from his business totaled $750, and he incurred the following expenses:

	Total	10% Business
Interest	$4,000	$400
Taxes	2,500	250
Utilities, insurance	1,500	150
Depreciation	2,000	200

Since total deductions for business use of the home are limited to business gross income, the taxpayer can deduct the following for business use of his home: $400 interest; $250 taxes; $100 utilities and insurance; and $-0- depreciation. Operating expenses such as utilities and insurance must be deducted before depreciation.

5. Loss deductions incurred in a trade or business, or in the production of income are limited to the amount a taxpayer has "at risk"

    a. Applies to all activities except:

        1) The holding of real estate

        2) The leasing of personal property by a closely held corporation (5 or fewer individuals own more than 50% of stock)

    b. Applies to individuals and closely held regular corporations

    c. Amount "at risk" includes:

        1) The cash and adjusted basis of property contributed by the taxpayer, and

        2) Liabilities for which the taxpayer is personally liable; excludes non-recourse debt

    d. Excess losses can be carried over to subsequent years (no time limit) and deducted when the "at risk" amount has been increased

    e. Previously allowed losses will be recaptured as income if the amount at risk is reduced below zero

6. Contributions to retirement plans

    a. Corporations are entitled to a deduction for contributions made

        1) See CORPORATIONS, page 1214

    b. Self-employed individuals deduct contributions to a Keogh plan or IRA as an above the line deduction separately from the computation of business income

        1) See "contributions to certain retirement plans," page 1154

F. Depreciation, Depletion, and Amortization

    Depreciation is an allowance for the exhaustion, wear and tear of property used in a trade or business, or of property held for the production of income. The Economic Recovery Tax Act of 1981 substantially changed accounting for depreciation through the advent of the Accelerated Cost Recovery System (ACRS) which has essentially replaced useful-life concepts with shorter recovery periods.

1. For property placed in service prior to 1981, the basis of property reduced by salvage value would be recovered over its useful life using the straight-line, declining balance, or sum-of-the-years'-digits method. Whether an accelerated method of depreciation could be used depended on the classification and useful life of the property, and whether it was new or used when acquired.

2. Accelerated Cost Recovery System (ACRS)

   a. ACRS is mandatory for most depreciable property placed in service after 1980. Taxpayers will continue to use facts and circumstances or Class Life Asset Depreciation Range (CLADR) for property placed in service prior to 1981.

   b. Salvage value is completely ignored under ACRS

   c. Unlike prior law, the method of cost recovery and the recovery period are the same for both new and used property under ACRS

   d. Recovery property includes all property other than land, intangible assets, and property the taxpayer elects to depreciate under a method not expressed in terms of years (e.g., unit of production or income forecast methods). Recovery property is divided into four basic recovery period classes:

      1) 3-year property--This class consists of tangible personal property (Sec. 1245 property) with a class life of four years or less (primarily autos and light-duty trucks), personal property used in research and experimentation, and certain special tools

      2) 5-year property--This class consists generally of machinery and equipment and includes all personal property not in other classes

      3) 10-year property--This class includes certain public utility property and short-lived real property (class life of less than 13 years)

      4) 15-year property--This class consists of real property and certain public utility property

   e. The recovery deduction is determined by using a table of percentages which incorporates certain accelerated methods

      1) The cost recovery tables for personal property are based on the half-year convention which assumes all recovery property is placed in service in the middle of a taxable year. The cost recovery tables for real property are based on the month the property is placed in service.

      2) For each year, a statutory percentage is taken from the table and applied to the unadjusted basis of the recovery property

      3) No recovery deduction is allowed for personal property in the year in which the property is disposed of or retired. A recovery deduction for real property is allowed based on the month of disposition.

      4) A taxpayer may instead elect to use the straight-line method (using the half-year convention for personal property) to recover cost over the recovery period or a longer period

         a) This election applies to all property, within a property class, placed in service during the taxable year (except 15-year real property which is a property-by-property election)

b) The straight-line election and choice of recovery period is irrevocable for each year's acquisition

*EXAMPLE: Assume that in December, 1981 a taxpayer purchased a new
truck (3-year property) for $10,000, and used machinery (5-year
property) for $20,000.*

ACRS Percentages

Recovery year	Applicable % for property class	
	3-year	5-year
1	25%	15%
2	38%	22%
3	37%	21%
4	--	21%
5	--	21%

Using percentages from the table above, his cost recovery deductions
would be as follows:

	1981	1982	1983	1984	1985	Total
Truck	$2,500	$3,800	$3,700	--	--	$10,000
Machinery	$3,000	$4,400	$4,200	$4,200	$4,200	$20,000

*If the taxpayer had instead elected to use the straight-line method
(using a half-year convention) and a 3-year recovery period for the
3-year property, his recovery deductions for the truck would be:*

	1981	1982	1983	1984	1985	Total
Truck	$1,667	$3,333	$3,333	$1,667	--	$10,000

f. Starting in 1982, a taxpayer may annually elect to treat the cost of
qualifying depreciable property as an expense rather than a capital expenditure:

1) Annual cost that may be expensed is $5,000 for 1983, $7,500 for 1984 and
1985
2) No ITC is available for expensed portion of cost

*EXAMPLE: Taxpayer purchases a truck for $20,000 in 1983 to use in his
business. He elects to deduct $5,000 as his Sec. 179 expense election.
The cost of the truck ($20,000) is reduced by $5,000 so that its adjusted basis for ACRS depreciation and the investment tax credit is
$15,000.*

g. For property placed in service after 1982, recoverable basis must be reduced by 50% of the regular ITC, by 50% of the business energy ITC, by 50%
of the credit for certified historic structure, and by 100% of the rehabilitation credit on property not qualifying as a certified historic
structure

1) A taxpayer may elect a reduced regular ITC instead of reducing the basis of property by 50% of the regular ITC (see "Election to reduce credit," page 1174)

EXAMPLE: If the truck and machinery in the previous example were instead acquired in 1983, the cost would be reduced by 50% of the regular ITC.

			Truck	Machinery
Cost			$10,000	$20,000
Less:	1/2 ITC of $600		- 300	
	1/2 ITC of $2,000			- 1,000
Basis			$ 9,700	$19,000

Using percentages from the table, cost recovery deductions would then be:

1983	1984	1985	1986	1987	Total
$2,425	$3,686	$3,589	--	--	$ 9,700
$2,850	$4,180	$3,990	$3,990	$3,990	$19,000

3. Depletion

a. Depletion is allowed on timber, minerals, oil and gas, and other exhaustible natural resources or wasting assets

b. There are 2 basic methods to compute

1) Cost method divides the adjusted basis by the total number of recoverable units and multiplies by the number of units sold (or payment received for, if cash basis) during the year

a) Adjusted basis is cost less accumulated depletion (not below zero)

EXAMPLE: Land cost $10,050,000 of which $50,000 is the residual value of the land. There are 1,000,000 barrels of oil recoverable. If 10,000 barrels were sold, cost depletion would be ($10,000,000 ÷ 1,000,000 barrels) x 10,000 = $100,000.

2) Percentage method uses a specified percentage of gross income from the property during the year

a) Deduction may not exceed 50% of the taxable income (before depletion) from the property

b) May be taken even after costs have been recovered and there is no basis

c) May be used for domestic oil and gas wells by "independent producer" or royalty owner; cannot be used for timber

d) The percentage is a statutory amount and generally ranges from 5% to 20% depending on the mineral

4. Amortization is allowed for several special types of capital expenditures

a. A corporation's or partnership's organizational expenses can be amortized over 60 or more months

1) Otherwise deductible only when corporation or partnership is dissolved

b. Amounts incurred for investigation and start-up of an active trade or busi-
    ness (other than organizational expenditures of a corporation or partner-
    ship) can be amortized over 60 or more months beginning with the month in
    which business begins

    1) Otherwise only deductible when the business is sold or terminated

c. Pollution control facilities can be amortized over 60 months if installed
    on property that was placed in operation prior to 1976

    1) The pollution control investment must not increase output, capacity, or
        the useful life of the asset

d. Rehabilitation expenditures for low income housing made through 1983 can be
    amortized over 60 months

    1) Limited to $20,000 per unit ($40,000 per unit for certified programs)

e. Patents and copyrights may be amortized over their useful life

    1) 17 years for patents; life of author plus 50 years for copyrights
    2) If become obsolete early, deduct in that year

f. Research and experimental expenses may be amortized over 60 months or more

    1) Alternatively may be expensed at election of taxpayer if done so for
        year in which such expenses are first incurred or paid

II. "ABOVE THE LINE" DEDUCTIONS

"Above the line" deductions are taken from gross income to determine adjusted
gross income. Adjusted gross income is important, because it may affect the amount
of allowable charitable contributions, medical expense, and casualty loss deductions. The deductions which reduce gross income to arrive at adjusted gross income
are:

1) Business deductions of a self-employed person (see Business Income and
    Deductions, page 1144)
2) Long-term capital gains (60%) deduction (discussed in Capital Gains and
    Losses, page 1190)
3) Losses from sale or exchange of property (discussed in Sales and Ex-
    changes and in Capital Gains and Losses, pages 1181 and 1188)
4) Employee business expenses:

    a) Reimbursed expenses
    b) Transportation and travel expenses
    c) Outside salesman expenses

5) Moving expenses
6) Deductions attributable to rents and royalties
7) Contributions to self-employed retirement plans and IRAs
8) Penalties for premature withdrawals from time deposits
9) Alimony payments
10) Deduction for two-earner married couples

A. <u>Employee Business Expenses</u> (only 3 categories)

1. <u>Reimbursed expenses</u> are deductible "above the line" if the reimbursement is included in gross income

   a. If travel and transportation expenses or outside salesman expenses exceed the reimbursement, the excess can be deducted "above the line." Other non-reimbursed expenses are "below the line" deductions.

   b. Reimbursements do not have to be included in income and the reimbursed expenses are not deducted if an employee adequately "accounts" to the employer

      1) Employee must submit a report describing each element of the expense

         a) Remember the 4 Ws: who, when, where, and why; plus the amount
         b) Receipts must be maintained for all lodging expenditures and for other travel and entertainment expenditures of $25 or more, except transportation expenditures whose receipts are not readily available

      2) Per diem and per mile arrangements satisfy this, e.g., reimbursement not in excess of $44 per day and 20.5¢ per mile

2. <u>Transportation</u> and <u>travel expenses</u> are deductible "above the line" even though not reimbursed

   a. Deductible transportation expenses:

      1) Include local transportation expenses between two job locations
      2) Exclude commuting expenses between residence and job

   b. Deductible travel expenses are those incurred while temporarily "away from tax home" overnight including meals, lodging, transportation, and expenses incident to travel (clothes care, etc.)

      1) Travel expenses to and from domestic destination are fully deductible if business is the primary purpose of trip
      2) Food and lodging are only deductible if away from home overnight
      3) Automobile expenses include gas, oil, repairs, tires, insurance, interest, taxes, parking, tolls, etc.

         a) Prorate costs between business and personal use
         b) Alternatively, taxpayer can use standard mileage rate of 20.5¢/mile for first 15,000 business miles, and 11¢/mile in excess of 15,000 (plus parking and tolls)

   c. The expense of a foreign/personal business trip must be allocated between business and pleasure

      1) No allocation is required if the trip is reimbursed, was less than 7 days, or less than 25% of trip was personal

   d. Expenses of attending conventions outside the North American area (i.e., U.S., its possessions, Canada, Mexico, and certain Central American and Caribbean nations) are deductible only if:

      1) The meeting is directly related to taxpayer's trade or business, and
      2) It is as reasonable to hold the meeting outside the North American area as in it

a) Up to $2,000 of expenses of attending a convention aboard a cruise ship are deductible per year if directly related to business or income-producing activity, the ship is U.S. registered, and all ports of call are in U.S. or its possessions

3. Outside salesman expenses--all business expenses of an employee who principally solicits business for his employer while away from the employer's place of business are deductible "above the line"

B. Moving expenses are deductible "above the line"

1. The distance between the former residence and new job (d_2) must be at least 35 miles farther than from the former residence to the former job (d_1). (i.e., $d_2 - d_1 \geq 35$ miles).

   a. If no former job, new job must be at least 35 miles from former residence

2. Employee must be employed at least 39 weeks out of the 12 months following the move

   a. Self-employed individual must be employed 78 weeks out of the 24 months following the move (in addition to 39 weeks out of first 12 months)

3. Deductible expenses are:

   a. Travel expenses for family to move
   b. Costs of moving household goods and personal assets
   c. Costs of househunting including transportation, meals, and lodging
   d. Temporary living expenses during any 30-day period after obtaining employment
   e. Residence sale and purchase related expenses, e.g., real estate commissions

      1) "c." and "d." are limited to $1,500
      2) "c.", "d.", and "e." are limited to $3,000

C. Expenses attributable to property held for the production of rents or royalties are deductible "above the line"

1. Rental of vacation home

   a. If there is any personal use, the amount deductible is:

      1) $\dfrac{\text{No. of Days Rented}}{\text{Total Days Used}} \times \text{Total Expenses} = \text{Amount Deductible}$

      2) Personal use is by taxpayer, or any other person to whom a fair rent is not charged

   b. If used as a residence, amount deductible is further limited to rental income less deductions otherwise allowable for interest, taxes, and casualty losses

      1) Used as a residence if personal use exceeds greater of 14 days or 10% of number of days rented
      2) Neither these limitations nor those in "1)" (above) apply if rented or held for rental for a continuous 12 month period with no personal use

      EXAMPLE: *Use house as a principal residence and then begin to rent in June. As long as rental continues for 12 consecutive months, limitations do not apply in year converted to rental.*

c. If used as a residence (above) and rented for less than 15 days per year, then income therefrom is not reported, and rental expense deductions are not allowed

EXAMPLE: Taxpayer rents his condominium for 120 days for $2,000 and uses it himself for 60 days. The rest of the year it is vacant. His expenses are:

Mortgage interest	$1,800
Real estate taxes	600
Utilities	300
Maintenance	300
Depreciation	2,000
	$5,000

Taxpayer may deduct the following expenses:

	Rental Expense	Itemized Deduction
Mortgage interest	$1,200	$ 600
Real estate taxes	400	200
Utilities	200	-0-
Maintenance	200	-0-
Depreciation	-0-	-0-
	$2,000	$ 800

Taxpayer may not deduct any depreciation because his rental expense deductions are limited to rental income when he has made personal use of the condominium in excess of the 14-day or 10% rule.

D. Contributions to Certain Retirement Plans

1. <u>Self-employed</u> individuals (sole proprietors and partners) may contribute to a qualified retirement plan (called H.R.-10 or Keogh Plan)

a. For 1983, the maximum contribution and deduction is the lesser of:

   1) $15,000, or 15% of earned income
   2) If AGI (exclusive of payments to the plan) is $15,000 or less, an individual <u>may</u> make a minimum payment (not subject to the above percentage limitation) up to the lesser of

      a) $750, or
      b) 100% of earned income

b. For 1984, the maximum contribution and deduction is the lesser of

   1) $30,000, or 25% of earned income
   2) Beginning in 1984, the definition of "earned income" includes the retirement plan deduction (i.e., earnings from self-employment must be reduced by the retirement plan contribution for purposes of determining the maximum deduction). To simplify the computation, multiply earnings from self-employment by 20%.

EXAMPLE: A CPA has earnings from self-employment of $140,000 for 1984. The maximum that can be deducted for contributions to the CPA's self-employed retirement plan for 1984 would be $140,000 x 20% = $28,000 [i.e., ($140,000 - $28,000) x 25% = $28,000].

c. Contributions made up until the due date of the tax return (including extensions) are deemed to be made for the taxable year for which the tax return is being filed, if taxpayer so specifies

2. Contributions to an <u>Individual Retirement Account</u> (IRA)

   a. All individuals, whether or not included in an employer's plan or a self-employed plan, may contribute to an IRA

   b. Maximum deduction is lesser of

      1) $2,000, or
      2) 100% of compensation

   c. For taxpayer with nonworking spouse, a <u>spousal IRA</u> may be established in addition to taxpayer's IRA. Then the maximum contribution allowed as a deduction on a joint return is lesser of

      1) $2,250, or
      2) 100% of taxpayer's compensation
      3) However, the deduction for either the taxpayer's IRA or the spouse's IRA can't exceed $2,000

   d. Contributions made up until the due date of the tax return (including extensions) are deemed to be made for the taxable year for which the tax return is being filed, if taxpayer so specifies

3. An employer's contributions to an employee's <u>simplified employee pension plan</u> are deductible up to the lesser of 15% of compensation, or $15,000 for 1983 (25% of compensation or $30,000 for 1984)

   a. The employee includes the contributions in income and then takes an offsetting deduction from income
   b. In addition, the employee may set up an IRA

E. Penalties for <u>Premature Withdrawals</u> from Time Deposits

1. Full amount of interest is included in gross income

2. Forfeited interest is then subtracted "above the line"

F. <u>Alimony</u> or separate maintenance payments are deducted "above the line"

1. Paid pursuant to a

   a. Decree of divorce or separate maintenance
   b. Written separation agreement
   c. Decree for support

2. Includes periodic payments or installment payments of a lump-sum to be paid over a period of more than 10 years except annual payment for current and future years exceeding 10% of the principal-sum

3. Child support is not alimony, nor are

   a. Lump-sum cash or property settlements
   b. Nonrequired payments or payments not arising from divorce or separation

4. If both alimony and child support are called for, and less is paid than required; payments are first applied to child support, then to alimony

G. A deduction is allowed for <u>two-earner married couples</u> who file a joint return. The deduction is <u>10%</u> of the lower spouse's earned income of up to $30,000 for 1983 and later years.

III.   ITEMIZED DEDUCTIONS FROM ADJUSTED GROSS INCOME

Excess itemized deductions reduce "adjusted gross income." They are sometimes referred to as "below the line" deductions because they are deducted from adjusted gross income. Excess itemized deductions along with personal exemptions reduce adjusted gross income to taxable income.

Itemized deductions are only deducted to the extent they exceed the "zero bracket amount." Therefore the deduction is for <u>excess itemized deductions</u>. The <u>zero bracket amount</u> is based on the filing status of a taxpayer (below) and is built into both the tax tables and tax schedules.

Filing Status	Zero Bracket Amount
a) Single or head of household	$2,300
b) Married, filing jointly; or surviving spouse	$3,400
c) Married, filing separately	$1,700

The major itemized deductions are outlined below. It should be remembered that some may be deducted "above the line" if they are incurred by a self-employed taxpayer in a trade or business, or for the production of rents or royalties.

A.   Medical and Dental Expenses

1. Medical and dental expenses paid by taxpayer for himself, spouse, or dependent (relationship, support, and citizenship tests are met) are deductible in year of payment, if not reimbursed by insurance, employer, etc.

2. Computation

    a. For 1983, all medicines are included as medical expenses to the extent in excess of 1% of adjusted gross income. Beginning in 1984, the 1% of AGI floor is eliminated. However, only prescribed medicine and insulin are deductible.

    b. Remaining medical expenses are deducted to the extent in excess of <u>5%</u> of adjusted gross income, including:

       1) The balance of medicines after the 1% limitation in "a."

       2) All other deductible medical expenses, including medical insurance premiums

    EXAMPLE: Ralph and Alice Jones, who have Adjusted Gross Income of $20,000, paid the following medical expenses: $700 for hospital and doctor bills (above reimbursement), $250 for prescription medicine, and $600 for medical insurance. Assuming the same facts for both 1983 and 1984, the Joneses would compute their medical expense deduction as follows:

	1983	1984
Prescribed medicine	$250	$250
Less 1% of AGI	- 200	
	$ 50	
Hospital, doctors	700	700
Medical insurance	600	600
	$1,350	$1,550
Less 5% of AGI	-1,000	-1,000
Medical expenses deduction	$ 350	$ 550

3. Capital expenditures for special equipment installed for medical reasons in a home or automobile are deductible as medical expenses to the extent the expenditures exceed the increase in value of the property

4. Deductible medical expenses include:

   1) Ambulance fees
   2) Artificial limbs
   3) Artificial teeth
   4) Chiropodists
   5) Chiropractors
   6) Christian Science practitioners
   7) Crutches
   8) Dental care
   9) Dentists
   10) Diagnostic services
   11) Doctors
   12) Eyeglasses
   13) Guide dogs (for the blind or deaf) and their maintenance
   14) Hearing aids and their component parts
   15) Hospital care
   16) Insurance premiums for hospitalization and medical care
   17) Laboratory services
   18) Meals and lodging furnished by a hospital or similar care facility
   19) Medicine, prescribed and nonprescribed in 1983; only prescribed medicine and insulin beginning in 1984
   20) Nurses (including nurses' board paid by you)
   21) Nursing services, including those rendered by a practical nurse
   22) Optometrists
   23) Osteopaths
   24) Physicians
   25) Podiatrists
   26) Psychologists
   27) Psychiatrists
   28) Special equipment, such as wheelchairs
   29) Special food or beverages prescribed solely for treatment of an illness
   30) Surgeons
   31) Transportation primarily for and essential to medical care (out-of-pocket expenses or 9¢ per mile if you use your own car)
   32) Therapy
   33) X-ray services

5. Items not deductible as medical expenses include:

1) Antiseptic diaper service
2) Bottled distilled water
3) Care of a normal and healthy baby by a nurse
4) Cosmetics
5) Domestic help
6) Funeral and burial expenses
7) Health club dues
8) Illegal operation or treatment
9) Maternity clothes
10) Meals and lodging not furnished by a hospital or similar institution as a necessary incident to medical care
11) Social activities, such as dancing lessons, etc., for the general improvement of your health, even though recommended by your doctor
12) Toiletries
13) Toothpaste
14) Trips for general improvement of health
15) Vitamins for general health
16) Program to stop smoking or lose weight
17) Premiums on life insurance policies, or on policies providing repayment for loss of earnings

6. Reimbursement for expenses deducted in an earlier year may be gross income in the period received under the tax benefit rule

7. Reimbursement in excess of expenses is includible in income to the extent the excess reimbursement was paid by policies provided by employer

B. Taxes

1. The following taxes are <u>deductible as a tax</u> in year paid if they are imposed on the taxpayer:

a. Income tax (state, local, or foreign)

1) The deduction for state and local taxes includes amounts withheld from salary, estimated payments made during the year, and payments made during the year on a tax for a prior year

2) A refund of a prior year's taxes is not offset against the current year's deduction, but is generally included in income

b. Real property tax (state, local, or foreign)

1) When real property is sold, the deduction is apportioned between buyer and seller on a daily basis within the real property tax year, even if the parties do not apportion the taxes at the closing

c. Personal property tax (state or local)
d. General sales tax (state or local)

1) An individual may deduct the amount of sales tax actually paid, or an amount determined from the "Optional State Sales Tax Tables"

a) Tables are based on:

1] Taxpayer's total available income (i.e., AGI plus nontaxable income), and
2] Total number of exemptions shown on return, not counting exemptions for being 65 or over or blind

        b)   The sales tax paid on the purchase of a car, motorcycle, motor home, truck, boat, plane, mobile home, or materials used to build a new home can be added to the table amount

2. The following taxes are <u>deductible only as an expense</u> incurred in a trade or business or in the production of income (above the line):

    a. Social security and other employment taxes paid by employer

    b. Federal excise taxes on automobiles, tires, telephone service and air transportation

    c. Customs duties

    d. State and local taxes not deductible as such (stamp or cigarette taxes) or charges of a primarily regulatory nature (licenses, etc.)

    e. Gasoline taxes

3. The following taxes are <u>not deductible</u>:

    a. Federal income taxes

    b. Federal, state, or local estate or gift taxes

    c. Social security and other Federal employment taxes paid by employee (including self-employment taxes)

    d. Social security and other employment taxes paid by an employer on the wages of an employee who only performed domestic services (maid, etc.)

C. Interest Expense

Interest expense is generally deductible if it results from an actual debtor-creditor relationship and a valid obligation to pay

1. Examples of <u>deductible</u> interest expense include:

    a. Mortgage interest
    b. Finance charges separately stated
    c. Bank credit card interest
    d. Mortgage prepayment penalty
    e. Late-payment charge by public utility
    f. Note discount interest
    g. Redeemable ground rents
    h. Amortization of bond premiums (straight-line)

2. <u>Prepaid interest</u> is not deductible when paid, it must be amortized over the period for which the loan applies

    a. Mortgage "points" as loan origination fees are a common example of prepaid interest

        1) However, they are deductible when paid if they are paid on a mortgage of the taxpayer's principal residence, are the normal charge in the area, and are not for specific services

    b. Another example of prepaid interest is when a percentage of a loan is retained by the creditor (i.e., note is discounted)

        EXAMPLE: You sign a one-year note for $1,200 on March 27, 1983, agreeing to pay it in 12 equal installments beginning on April 30, 1983. The interest ($1,200 x 6% = $72) was subtracted from the face value of the note and you received $1,128. Assuming payments are timely made, both cash and accrual method taxpayers would prorate the interest over the period of the loan. $54 (9/12 of $72) is deductible in 1983; the remainder in 1984.

3. Examples of items which are <u>not deductible</u> as interest:

   a. "Points" paid by a seller (treated as reduction of selling price)
   b. Service charges
   c. Credit investigation fees
   d. Loan fees
   e. Nonredeemable ground rents
   f. Interest relating to tax-exempt income, e.g., interest to purchase or carry municipal bonds
   g. Interest paid to carry "single-premium" life insurance
   h. Premium on a convertible bond
   i. Rental payments

4. Interest payments on installment or similar purchases are deductible if they are separately stated or can be definitely determined

5. <u>Investment interest</u> is interest paid or accrued on indebtedness incurred to purchase or carry property held for investment

   a. Limited to $10,000 plus net investment income per year

      1) Net investment income is the excess of investment income (e.g., interest, dividends, STCG) over investment expenses (e.g., expenses connected with the production of investment income including SL depreciation but excluding investment interest). Note: LTCG is not investment income.

   b. Special rule applies if taxpayer (including spouse and children) owns 50% or more of a corporation or partnership. The $10,000 limitation is increased by the lesser of (1) $15,000, or (2) the interest on the debt used to acquire the 50% or more ownership.
   c. Disallowed interest is carried over for unlimited period of time

D. <u>Charitable Contributions</u>

   Contributions to qualified domestic organizations are deductible in the year actually paid or donated (for both accrual and cash basis taxpayers) with some carryover allowed. A "pledge" is not a payment; charging the contribution on your bank card does constitute payment.

1. <u>Qualified organizations</u> include:

   a. A state, a U.S. possession, or political subdivision, or the District of Columbia if made exclusively for public purposes
   b. A community chest, corporation, foundation, etc., operated exclusively for charitable, religious, educational, scientific, or literary purposes, or for the prevention of cruelty to children or animals, or for fostering national or international amateur sports competition (unless they provide facilities or equipment)

      1) No part of the earnings may inure to any individual's benefit
      2) May not attempt to influence legislation or intervene in any political campaign

   c. Church, synagogue, or other religious organizations
   d. War veterans' organizations

   e. Civil defense organizations created under federal, state, or local law
   f. Domestic fraternal societies operating under the lodge system

      1) Only if the contribution is to be used exclusively for the charitable purposes listed in "b." above

   g. Nonprofit cemetery companies if the funds are irrevocably dedicated to the perpetual care of the cemetery as a whole, and not a particular lot or mausoleum crypt

2. Dues, fees, or assessments paid to qualified organizations are deductible to the extent that payments exceed benefits received. Not deductible to:

   a. Veterans' organizations
   b. Lodges
   c. Fraternal organizations
   d. Country clubs

3. Out of pocket expenses to maintain a <u>student</u> (domestic or foreign) in a taxpayer's home are deductible if:

   a. Student is in 12th or lower grade
   b. Not a dependent or relative
   c. Based on written agreement between taxpayer and qualified organization
   d. Deduction limited to $50/month for each month the individual is a full-time student

4. Payments to qualified organizations for goods or services are deductible to the extent the amount paid exceeds the fair market value of benefits received

5. Out of pocket expenses incurred while rendering services to a charitable organization without compensation are deductible

   a. E.g., actual auto expenses or standard rate of 9¢ per mile may be taken

6. <u>Nondeductible</u> contributions include contributions to/for:

   a. Civic leagues
   b. Social clubs
   c. International organizations
   d. Communist organizations
   e. Chambers of commerce
   f. Labor unions
   g. The value of your time or services
   h. The use of property
   i. Less than an entire interest
   j. Blood donated
   k. Tuition or amounts in place of tuition
   l. Payments to a hospital for care of particular patients
   m. "Sustainer's gift" to retirement home
   n. Raffles, bingo, etc. (but may qualify as gambling loss)
   o. Contributions made directly to a foreign organization
   p. Contributions to domestic fraternal societies are not deductible if they are used to defray sickness or burial expenses of members

7. Gifts of property to qualified organizations are <u>deductible</u>:

   a. At fair market value when FMV is below basis
   b. At basis when fair market value exceeds basis and if sold gain would be short-term capital gain or ordinary income, e.g.,

      1) Gain would be ordinary because of depreciation recapture or if property is inventory

  c. At fair market value if long-term capital gain property, but:

      1) Contribution must be reduced by 40% of any long-term capital gain that would have been realized if the property had been sold if:

        a) Contribution is tangible personal property and is unrelated to the purpose or the function of the charity, or

        b) Contributed to certain private nonoperating foundations

  d. The contribution must be reduced by interest prepaid or interest liability on a loan assumed by the donee

  e. Appraisal fees on donated property are a miscellaneous deduction

8. The overall limitation for contribution deductions is 50% of adjusted gross income (before any net operating loss carryback). A second limitation is that contributions of capital gain property (where gain is not reduced by 40%) are limited to 30% of AGI. A third limitation is that contributions to certain charities are limited to 20% of AGI or a lesser amount.

  a. Contributions to the following are taken first and may be taken up to 50% of AGI limitation

      1) Public charities

        a) Churches
        b) Educational organizations
        c) Tax exempt hospitals
        d) Medical research
        e) States or political subdivisions
        f) U.S. or District of Columbia

      2) All private operating foundations

        a) Operating foundations spend their income directly for the active conduct of their exempt activities, e.g., public museums

      3) Certain private nonoperating foundations that distribute proceeds to public and private operating charities

  b. Deductions for contributions of capital gain property (when the gain is not to be reduced by 40%) to organizations in "8.a." above are limited to 30% of adjusted gross income

      1) May elect to reduce all appreciated capital gain property by 40% of the gain and not be subject to this 30% limitation

  c. Deductions for contributions to charities that do not qualify in "8.a." above are limited to lesser of (1) 20% of AGI, or (2) (50% x AGI) - gifts to "8.a." charities

      1) These are usually private nonoperating foundations, e.g.:

        a) War veterans' organizations
        b) Domestic fraternal organizations
        c) Nonprofit cemeteries

2) Taken after deductions to organizations in "8.a." above without the 30% limitation on capital gain property in "8.b." above

EXAMPLE: AGI of $9,000. $1,000 of 50% limited contributions. $4,000 of 30% limited contributions. $2,000 of 20% limited contributions. None of the $2,000 is deducted because $1,000 and $4,000 (without 30% limit for this calculation) equals $5,000 which exceeds the $4,500 limit (50% of $9,000).

9. Contributions in excess of the 50% and 30% limitations can be carried forward for 5 years and remain subject to the 50% and 30% limitations in the carry-forward years

   a. Contributions subject to, but in excess of the 20% limitation cannot be carried forward

   EXAMPLE: Your adjusted gross income is $50,000. During the year you gave your church $2,000 cash and land (held for investment more than one year) having a fair market value of $30,000 and a basis to you of $10,000. You also gave $5,000 cash to a private foundation to which the 20% limitation applies.

   Since your allowable contributions to an organization to which the 50% limitation applies (disregarding the 30% limitation) exceed $25,000 (50% of $50,000), your contribution limited to 20% is not deductible.

   The $2,000 cash donated to the church is deducted first. The donation for the gift of land is not required to be reduced by 40% of the appreciation in value, but is limited to $15,000 (30% x $50,000). Thus, you may deduct only $17,000 ($2,000 + $15,000). The unused portion of the land contribution ($15,000) is carried over to the next year, still subject to the 30% limitation.

   Alternatively, you may elect to reduce the land by 40% of its appreciation (40% x $20,000 = $8,000) and not be subject to the 30% limitation. In such case your current deduction would be $25,000 ($2,000 cash + $22,000 land + $1,000 cash to private foundation), but there would be no carryovers. The benefit of an increased current deduction of $8,000 versus a $15,000 carryover would have to be considered.

10. The flowchart on the next page summarizes the rules for deducting charitable contributions as an itemized deduction for individuals

11. Deduction for nonitemizers. For 1983, an individual who does not itemize his personal deductions is allowed to deduct a direct charitable deduction from AGI for 25% of the first $100 ($50 if married filing separately) of charitable contributions. For 1984, the deduction is 25% of the first $300 ($150 if married filing separately) of charitable contributions.

E. Casualty and Theft Losses

Loss of property from a casualty or theft is deductible whether the property was used in business or for personal use. If the property were used in business, the loss is deductible as an "above the line" deduction and is deductible in full. If nonbusiness property, the loss is generally deductible as an itemized deduction, although the first $100 of each casualty or theft loss is not deductible. Beginning

A CHARITABLE CONTRIBUTION FLOWCHART FOR INDIVIDUALS

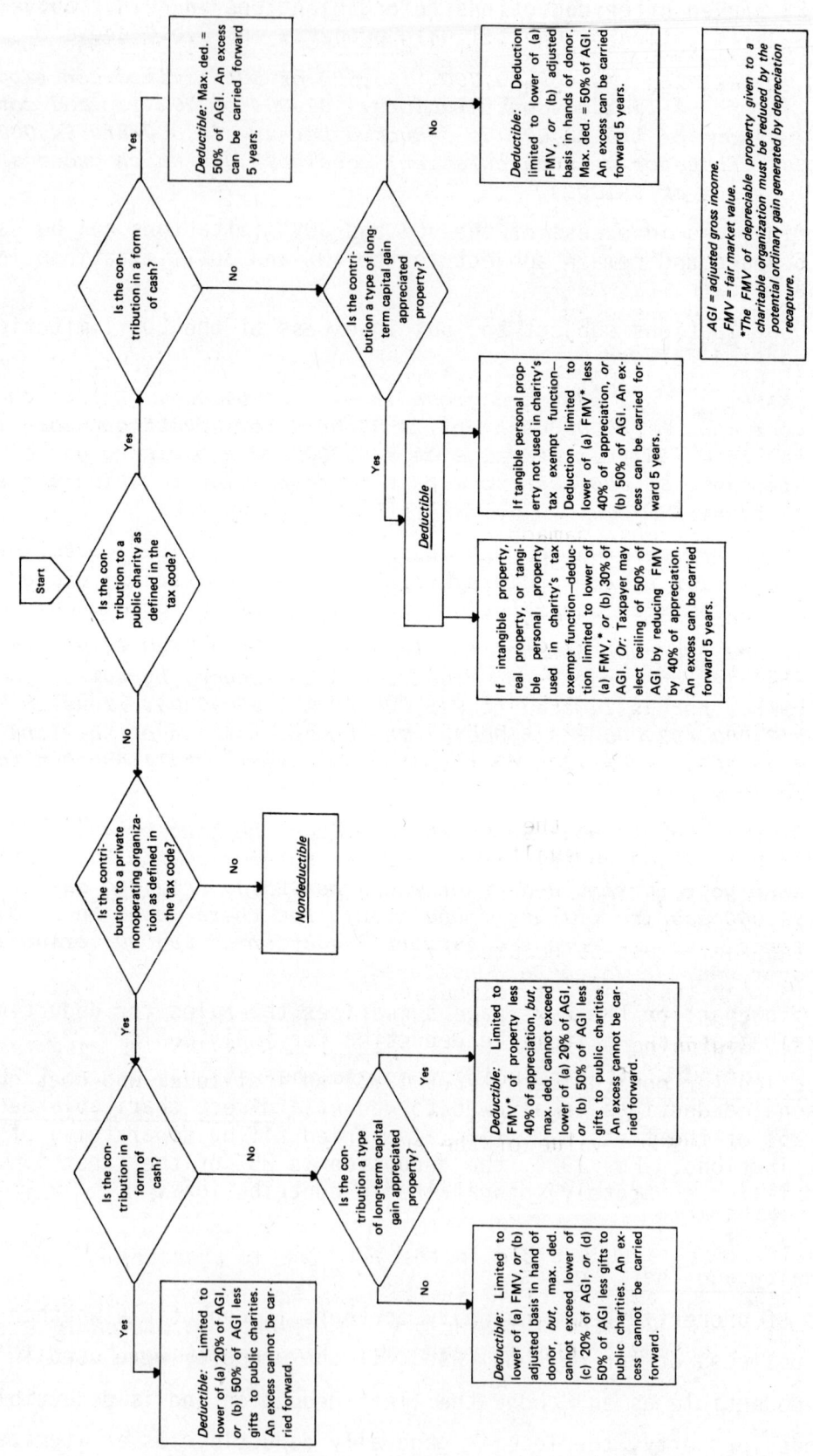

in 1983, nonbusiness casualty and theft losses are deductible only to the extent the total amount of such losses (after reduction for the $100 floor for each loss) exceeds 10% of the taxpayer's AGI.

1. A casualty loss must be identifiable, damaging to property, and sudden, unexpected, or unusual. Casualty losses include:

    a. Damage from a fire, storm, or accident
    b. Mine cave-in
    c. Sonic boom
    d. A loss from vandalism
    e. Damage to trees and shrubs if there is a decrease in the total value of the real estate

2. Losses not deductible as casualties include:

    a. Losses from the breakage of china or glassware through handling or by a family pet
    b. Disease
    c. Expenses incident to casualty (temporary quarters, etc.)
    d. Termite or moth damage
    e. Progressive deterioration through a steadily operating cause and damage from normal process. Thus, the steady weakening of a building caused by normal or usual wind and weather conditions is not a casualty loss.
    f. Losses from nearby disaster (property value reduced due to location near a disaster area)
    g. Loss of future profits from, for example, ice storm damage to standing timber that reduces the rate of growth or the quality of future timber is not deductible. To qualify as a casualty, the damage must actually result in existing timber being rendered unfit for use.

3. The amount of loss is the lesser of (1) the decrease in the FMV of the property resulting from the casualty, or (2) the adjusted basis of the property

    a. For business property completely destroyed, loss is the adjusted basis of the property
    b. The above must be reduced by:

        1) Any insurance or reimbursement
        2) $100 "floor" for each separate nonbusiness casualty
        3) Beginning in 1983, total nonbusiness casualties must be reduced by 10% of AGI (after reducing the unreimbursed loss by the $100 limitation)

4. The amount of a casualty loss on real property is determined by comparing the decrease in market value of the entire property with its adjusted basis

    a. If personal property is also destroyed, its loss must be determined separately

5. Casualty loss is deductible in the year the loss occurs

    a. Theft loss is deductible in the year the loss is discovered
    b. Loss in a declared disaster area is deductible either in the year loss occurs or the preceding year (by filing an amended return)

EXAMPLE: Frank Jones' lakeside cottage which cost him $13,600 (including $1,600 for the land) on April 30, 1975, was partially destroyed by fire on July 12, 1983. The value of the property immediately before the fire was $16,000 ($14,000 for the building and $2,000 for the land), and the value immediately after the fire was $12,000. He collected $1,050 from the insurance company. It was Jones' only casualty for 1983 and his AGI was $25,000. Jones' casualty loss deduction from the fire would be $350, computed as follows:

1.	Value of entire property before fire	$16,000
2.	Value of entire property after fire	12,000
3.	Decrease in fair market value of entire property	$ 4,000
4.	Adjusted basis (cost in this case)	$13,600
5.	Loss sustained (lesser of 3 or 4)	$ 4,000
6.	Less insurance recovery	1,050
7.	Casualty loss	$ 2,950
8.	Less $100 limitation	100
9.	Loss after $100 limitation	$ 2,850
10.	Less 10% of AGI	- 2,500
11.	Casualty loss deduction	$ 350

6. Sec. 1231 requires a separate netting of all casualty gains and losses on property held more than one year (See p. 1192)

F. Miscellaneous Deductions

1. Education expenses are deductible by an employee

   a. Only deductible if:

      1) To maintain or improve skills required in employee's present job, or
      2) To meet requirements to keep job

   b. Not deductible if:

      1) Required to meet minimum educational requirements in employee's job, or
      2) The education qualifies the employee for a new job, e.g., CPA review course, even if a new job is not sought

   c. Deductible expenses for tuition, books, supplies, etc., are itemized deductions
   d. Travel, transportation, and reimbursed expenses related to deductible education expenses are "above the line" deductions

2. Qualified adoption expenses connected with the adoption of a child with special needs are deductible up to $1,500

   a. Expenses include adoption fees, court costs, attorney fees, and other expenses connected with the adoption

   b. "Child with special needs" is one eligible to receive payments under the Social Security Act adoption assistance program because of ethnic background, age, physical or mental handicap, etc.

3. Union or professional dues

4. Tax counsel and assistance

5. Gambling losses (only to the extent of winnings included in gross income)
6. Expenses for the production of income other than those incurred in a trade or business or for production of rents or royalties (then an "above the line" deduction) e.g., investment counsel fees, clerical help, safe deposit box rental, etc.
7. Other "below the line" <u>deductible</u> employee expenses

    a. Uniforms not adaptable to general use
    b. Employment agency fees to secure employment in same occupation
    c. Subscription to professional journals
    d. Dues to professional societies
    e. Union dues
    f. Physical examinations required by employer
    g. A college professor's research, lecturing, and writing expenses
    h. Amounts a teacher pays his/her substitute
    i. Surety bond premiums
    j. Malpractice insurance premiums
    k. A research chemist's laboratory breakage fees
    l. Small tools and supplies

8. Example of <u>nondeductible</u> other expenses

    a. Fees and licenses, such as auto licenses and marriage licenses, and dog tags
    b. Home repairs, insurance, rent
    c. Personal legal expenses
    d. Life insurance
    e. Burial expenses
    f. Capital expenditures
    g. Illegal bribes and kickbacks
    h. Fines and tax penalties
    i. Collateral
    j. Commuting to and from work
    k. Professional accreditation fees
    l. Bar examination fees and incidental expenses in securing admission to the bar
    m. Accounting certificate fees paid for initial right to practice accounting
    n. Medical and dental license fees paid to obtain initial licensing
    o. Campaign expenses of a candidate for any office are not deductible, nor are registration fees for primary elections, even if taxpayer is the incumbent of the office to be contested
    p. Cost of midday meals or meals while working late (except while traveling away from home)
    q. Political contributions

IV. EXEMPTIONS

Exemptions are like excess itemized deductions in that they are deducted from adjusted gross income ("below the line" deductions). Exemptions of $1,000 each are allowed for the taxpayer, spouse, and dependents if taxpayer is a U.S. citizen or resident.

1. Each exemption results in a $1,000 deduction from adjusted gross income
2. Personal exemption for taxpayer

    a. Even if a dependent of another taxpayer
    b. Additional exemption if 65 or older at end of year (deemed 65 on day before 65th birthday)
    c. Additional exemption if blind at end of year
    d. Full exemptions even if birth or death occurred during the year

3. Exemption(s) for spouse

    a. Exemption on joint return
    b. Age and blindness exemptions as above
    c. Not allowed if divorced or legally separated at end of year
    d. If a separate return is filed, taxpayer may claim spouse exemption only if the spouse had no gross income and was not the dependent of another taxpayer

4. Exemptions for <u>dependents</u> (no age or blindness exemptions)

    a. Full exemption even if death or birth occurred during the year
    b. Each dependent must meet 5 tests:

        1) <u>Support.</u> Taxpayer must furnish over one-half of support.

            a) Support includes lodging, meals, clothing, medical, etc.
            b) Support excludes scholarships, life insurance, taxes, etc.

        2) <u>Gross income.</u> Dependent had less than $1,000 gross income.

            a) Does not apply to children of the taxpayer less than 19 at end of year
            b) Does not apply to taxpayer's child if a full-time student (at least 5 months out of the year) whatever child's age
            c) Gross income does not include tax-exempt income, e.g., social security

        3) <u>Household or relationship.</u> Dependent must either be of specified relationship (closer than cousin), or live with taxpayer the entire year.

            a) Temporary absences excepted
            b) Indefinite confinement in a nursing home excepted
            c) Death or birth during the year excepted

        4) <u>Citizenship.</u> Dependent must be a citizen, resident, or national of U.S., Canada, or Mexico.

        5) <u>Joint return.</u> Dependent cannot file a joint return, unless joint return is filed solely for refund of tax withheld.

    c. A <u>multiple support agreement</u> can be used if no single taxpayer furnishes more than 50% of the support of a dependent. Then any taxpayer (who meets the other requirements) contributing <u>more than 10%</u> can claim the dependent provided others furnishing more than <u>10%</u> agree not to claim the dependent as an exemption.

    d. <u>Child of divorced or separated parents</u> is treated as receiving over one-half of support from parent who has custody for the greater part of the year

        1) Parent who does not have custody will be treated as providing over one-half of support if:

a) Divorce decree or written agreement entitles that parent to the exemption and that parent provides $600 or more for the child's support, or

b) Noncustodial parent provides $1,200 or more for each child's support and other parent does not provide a larger contribution to the child's support

V. TAX COMPUTATION

A. Tax Tables

1. Tax tables contain precomputed tax liability based on taxable income

   a. AGI less excess itemized deductions and exemptions
   b. Filing status

      1) Single
      2) Head of household
      3) Married filing separately
      4) Married filing joint return
      5) Surviving spouse

2. The zero bracket amount is built into the tax tables

3. Tax tables must be used by taxpayers unless:

   a. Taxable income is $50,000 or more, or
   b. Income averaging is used

4. A special tax computation is required for a dependent child if the child's unearned income is $1,000 or more, and itemized deductions and earned income are each less than $2,300

   a. TI = AGI + [ZBA - (greater of earned income or itemized deductions)] - personal exemption

EXAMPLE: A dependent child has adjusted gross income of $4,000, composed of $1,400 of earned income from part-time employment and $2,600 of unearned income from interest. The child's itemized deductions total $400. The child's taxable income would be computed as follows:

Adjusted gross income		$4,000
Zero bracket amount	$2,300	
Earned income	−1,400	900
		$4,900
Personal exemption		−1,000
Taxable income		$3,900

B. Tax Rate Schedules

1. Tax schedules begin at the zero bracket amount and contain marginal tax rates that range from 11% to 50% in progressively higher income brackets

2. Married persons (married at year end or at death of spouse) file joint or separate returns

3. Surviving spouse can use joint return rates for two years after death of spouse if:

   a. Dependent child lives with surviving spouse, and
   b. Surviving spouse was eligible to file joint return in year of spouse's death, and

   c. Surviving spouse pays over one-half of costs of maintaining household, and
   d. Surviving spouse does not remarry before year end

      1) If remarried, no longer a surviving spouse, but may file joint return
          with new spouse

4. Head of household status applies to unmarried person not qualifying for surviving spouse status but who maintains a household for the entire year for:

   a. An unmarried child or other descendant (who need not be a dependent), or
   b. Relative (except a cousin) who is a dependent

      1) Includes a married child or married descendant

   c. Parents need not live with head of household, but parents' household must
       be maintained by taxpayer, e.g., nursing home
   d. Unmarried requirement is satisfied if spouses are living apart under a
       separate maintenance decree

C. Income Averaging (Schedule G)

1. Substantially increased income of a particular period may be averaged over a
   5-year period by individuals who:

   a. Are citizens or residents of U.S. and
   b. Have furnished at least one-half of their support during the previous four
       years (there are 3 exceptions to this rule)

2. Almost all income is subject to averaging

3. To calculate "averageable" income:

   a. Determine base period income for each of last 4 years
   b. Multiply the sum of the past 4 years' base period income by 30%

      1) This is 120% of the average income of the past 4 years

   c. If the difference between current adjusted taxable income and 120% of the
       average income of the past 4 years is more than $3,000, income averaging is
       permitted

      1) This difference is called averageable income
      2) 120% of the average income of the past 4 years is nonaverageable income

   d. The tax liability is the sum of:

      1) The tax liability on nonaverageable income, plus
      2) Five times:

         a) The tax liability on 1/5 of averageable income plus nonaverageable
             income, minus
         b) The tax liability on nonaverageable income

             *EXAMPLE: Jean Jones, who is an eligible individual, has never been
             married, and her tax year is the calendar year. Her only income for
             the computation year and her base years is her salary. Her taxable
             income for these years is:*

                               1983 $38,000
                               1982 $30,000
                               1981 $25,000
                               1980 $17,000
                               1979 $12,000

Jean's total base period income is $84,000. No adjustments are necessary to her 1983 taxable income.

Jean's averageable income for 1983 is $12,800, determined by subtracting $25,200 (30% of $84,000, her total base period income) from $38,000 (her taxable income for 1983). Since this is more than $3,000, Jean may use the income averaging method.

Jean then computes her tax as follows:

1.	30% of total base period income (30% x $84,000)	$25,200
2.	1/5 of averageable income (1/5 x $12,800)	2,560
3.	Sum of items (1) and (2)	$27,760
4.	Tax on amount on line (3) ($27,760)	$ 5,712
5.	Tax on 30% of total base period income (tax on $25,200)	4,893
6.	Tax on 1/5 of averageable income [item (4) - item (5)]	$ 819
7.	Tax on averageable income ($819 x 5)	$ 4,095
8.	Tax for 1983 [sum of items (5) and (7)]	$ 8,988

Under the regular tax computation method, her tax on $38,000 taxable income would be $10,913.

D. Alternative Minimum Tax (Form 6251)

1. The alternative minimum tax is computed by applying a 20% tax rate to alternative minimum taxable income (AMTI)

   a. Applies only if it exceeds the amount of regular tax
   b. Is reduced by only foreign tax credits
   c. Does not apply to corporations

2. The computation of AMTI begins with AGI, which is then:

   a. Increased by certain **tax preferences**:

   1) The capital gain deduction; but does not include gain from sale of personal residence
   2) Excluded dividends, and interest on All Savers certificates
   3) Accelerated cost recovery on real property and leased personal property--excess of recovery deductions over straight-line

   4) Excess deductions for mining exploration and development, pollution control facilities, magazine circulation, and research and experimental expenditures--generally in excess of ratable amortization over 10 years

   b. Decreased by certain itemized deductions:

   1) Medical expenses (to extent in excess of 10% of AGI), casualty, theft, and wagering losses, and charitable contributions
   2) Qualified housing interest
   3) Other interest (to extent of net investment income)

c. Decreased by exemption amount:

1) $40,000 for joint return
2) $30,000 for single taxpayer
3) $20,000 for married, filing separate return

> EXAMPLE: A married taxpayer filing a joint return has AGI of $175,000, and a regular tax liability of $43,075 for 1983. Included in his tax computation were a capital gain deduction of $200,000 and excess recovery deductions of $40,000. His itemized deductions included interest of $10,000 on his personal residence, and charitable contributions of $20,000. The AMT computation would be:

Adjusted gross income	$175,000
Add: Capital gain deduction	200,000
Excess recovery deductions	40,000
Less: Housing interest	(10,000)
Charitable contributions	(20,000)
Less AMT exemption	(40,000)
AMTI	$345,000
Tax @ 20%	$ 69,000
Tax payable--greater of	
AMT or regular tax	$ 69,000

E. Other Taxes

1. Social security (FICA) tax is imposed on both employers and employees (withheld from wages) at a rate of 6.7% of the first $35,700 of wages paid to each employee for 1983 (7.0% for employer and 6.7% for employee on first $37,800 of wages paid to each employee for 1984)

2. Federal unemployment (FUTA) tax is imposed only on employers at a rate of 3.5% of the first $7,000 of wages paid each employee in 1983 and 1984

3. Self-employment tax is imposed on individuals who work for themselves (e.g., sole proprietor, independent contractor, partner) at a rate of 9.35% of the first $35,700 of self-employment income for 1983 (11.3% of the first $37,800 of self-employment income for 1984)

a. Income from self-employment generally includes all items of business income less business deductions. Does not include personal interest, dividends, rents, capital gains and losses, gains and losses on the disposition of business property, and the self-employment tax.

b. Wages subject to FICA tax are deducted from $35,700 in determining the amount of income subject to self-employment tax

c. No tax if self-employment income is less than $400

VI. TAX CREDITS/ESTIMATED TAX PAYMENTS

Tax credits directly reduce tax liability. The tax liability less tax credits equals tax payable. Taxes which have already been withheld on wages, and estimated tax payments are credited against tax liability without limitation, even if the result is a refund due the taxpayer.

A. Investment Tax Credit (ITC)

1. A 10% tax credit for qualified investment in new or used property depreciable under ACRS, or other depreciable property having a useful life of at least 3 years

   a. Credit is available for year property is placed in service
   b. Qualified investment in new property is unlimited; used property is limited to $125,000 per year

2. Qualifying property (Sec. 38 property) is generally tangible personal business property (e.g., trucks, equipment, etc.), but also includes:

   a. Research and storage facilities used in manufacturing or production
   b. Livestock (except horses)
   c. Single purpose agricultural or horticultural structures (e.g., greenhouses, poultry houses)
   d. Elevators and escalators

3. Nonqualifying property includes:

   a. Buildings and structural components (e.g., heating or air conditioning systems, plumbing and lighting fixtures, sprinkler systems)
   b. Property used in lodging facilities (except hotels and motels) such as furniture and appliances
   c. Property amortized over 60 months (except 100% of cost of certified pollution control facility qualifies)
   d. Property predominantly used outside U.S., by tax-exempt organizations, or by government agencies

4. Amount of qualified investment is a percentage of the basis of new property or the cost of used property

ACRS Property		Other Property	
Class	Percent	Useful Life	Percent
5, 10, & 15 yr.	100%	7 or more yrs.	100%
3 yr.	60%	5 yrs. but less than 7	66 2/3%
		3 yrs. but less than 5	33 1/3%
		Less than 3 yrs.	-0-

EXAMPLE: Taxpayer purchased 5-year ACRS property for $20,000 and 3-year ACRS property for $10,000. The taxpayer's qualified investment and ITC would be:

Cost	Percent	Qualified Investment	ITC @10%
$20,000	100%	$20,000	$2,000
$10,000	60%	6,000	600
		$26,000	$2,600

5. Reduction in asset basis. For property placed in service after 1982, asset basis must generally be reduced by 50% of the regular ITC, by 50% of the business energy ITC, and by 50% of the credit for certified historic structures

EXAMPLE: Using the facts in the above example, the amounts recoverable through ACRS deductions would be:

    5-year property: $20,000 - (.50)($2,000) = $19,000
    3-year property: $10,000 - (.50)($600) = $9,700

6. Election to reduce credit. For property placed in service after 1982, instead of reducing an asset's basis by 50% of the regular ITC, a taxpayer may elect to reduce his regular ITC by 2 percentage points. This election is made on a property-by-property basis. For purposes of this computation, qualified investment is considered to be 100%, and the reduced percentages are:

   a. 8% for 5, 10, and 15-year property
   b. 4% for 3-year property

   EXAMPLE: If the election had been made for the property acquired in "4." above, the reduced ITC would be:

Cost	Percent	Qualified Investment	ITC %	ITC
$20,000	100%	$20,000	8%	$1,600
$10,000	100%	$10,000	4%	400
				$2,000

   Then the entire unadjusted basis of the property would be recovered through ACRS deductions; $20,000 over a 5-year recovery period, $10,000 over a 3-year recovery period.

7. Credit is limited to:

   a. Tax liability, if $25,000 or less
   b. $25,000 plus 85% of tax liability in excess of $25,000

   EXAMPLE. Taxpayer has a tax liability of $65,000. His investment tax credit cannot exceed $59,000 [$25,000 + (.85 x $40,000)].

   c. Excess ITC is carried back 3 years and forward 15 years
   d. Credits are applied in FIFO order each year

      1) First, carryovers (oldest first)
      2) Second, current credits
      3) Third, carrybacks (oldest first)

8. All or a part of the ITC may be recaptured if ACRS property is disposed of before the end of the recapture period, or other property is disposed of before the end of its estimated life

   a. Each full year that ACRS property is held before disposition earns 1/5 of the ITC for 5, 10, and 15-year property

   b. If 3-year ACRS property is held:

Years	Recapture %
Less than 1 year	100%
1, but less than 2	66%
2, but less than 3	33%
3 or more	0%

   c. Recapture for other property is the excess of the credit allowed over the credit that would have been allowed based on the time the property was actually held

EXAMPLE: If the property acquired in "4." were disposed of after being held one full year, the ITC recapture would be:

Original ITC	Portion Recaptured	ITC Recapture
$2,000	4/5	$1,600
600	66%	396
Additional tax liability for year of disposition		$1,996

B. Business Energy Credit

1. The business energy credit is 10%, 11%, or 15% of qualified investment in energy property, depending on the type of property (e.g., 10% for recycling equipment, 15% for solar or wind energy property)

    a. The property must be new property
    b. Energy property may qualify for the business energy credit and the regular ITC if it meets the qualifications for both

2. Amount of credit limited to 100% of tax liability. If taxpayer has both regular ITC and business energy credit, first compute regular ITC, then apply the business energy credit.

3. The recoverable basis of energy property must be reduced by 50% of the amount of business energy credit for property placed in service after 1982

C. Credit for Rehabilitation Expenditures

1. Special investment credit (in lieu of regular ITC and energy credits) for qualified expenditures incurred after 1981 to substantially rehabilitate old buildings

    a. Credit percentages are:

        1) 15%--for 30-39 year-old buildings
        2) 20%--for 40 or more year-old buildings
        3) 25%--for certified historic structures

    b. 15% and 20% credits are limited to nonresidential buildings; the 25% credit applies to both residential and nonresidential

2. To qualify for credit:

    a. 75% of external walls must remain in place

    b. Building must be substantially rehabilitated--rehabilitation expenditures during 24-month (or 60-month) period ending on last day of taxable year must exceed the greater of (1) the adjusted basis of the property at the beginning of such period, or (2) $5,000

    c. Rehabilitation costs must be recovered using the straight-line method and a recovery period of 15 years

        1) Costs eligible for recovery must be reduced by the full amount of the 15% or 20% credit; or, by half the amount of 25% credit
        2) Cost of acquiring or enlarging building does not qualify

D. Research Credit

1. Credit is <u>25%</u> of the excess of the qualified research expenses ("in-house" research expenses and 65% of contract research expenses) for the taxable year over the average of research expenses for the previous three-year base period

   a. Only research expenses incurred after 6/30/81 in carrying on a trade or business qualify for credit
   b. Base period research expenses are deemed to be not less than 50% of research expenses for current year
   c. Unused credits are carried back 3 years and forward 15 years

   EXAMPLE: Taxpayer incurred qualified research expense of $100,000 in 1983. He had never before incurred any research expenses. The research credit for 1983 would be [25% ($100,000 - $50,000 deemed average base period expenses)] $12,500.

2. Credit is available regardless of whether taxpayer elected to expense or amortize research expenditures

E. Credit for the Elderly

1. Available under different rules to:

   a. Taxpayers 65 and older
   b. Taxpayers under 65 on a public retirement pension

2. Marital status:

   a. Must file a joint return if married to get the credit unless taxpayers have not lived together at all during year
   b. If one spouse is 65 or over and the other is under 65 and on a public retirement pension,

      1) Both may claim the 65 or over credit, or
      2) Both may claim the under 65 credit

3. <u>65 or over credit</u> is 15% of:

   a. Initial amount of:

      1) $2,500 for single or joint return where only one spouse is eligible
      2) $3,750 for joint return where both spouses are eligible
      3) $1,875 for married filing separate return

   b. Reduced by amounts excluded from gross income, e.g.,

      1) Social security and railroad retirement
      2) Pensions and other retirement benefits not includable in gross income
      3) Except not reduced by annuities, life insurance, compensation for injuries or sickness, compensation under accident and health plans, receipts from employee's trusts

   c. Also reduced by 1/2 of adjusted gross income over:

      1) $7,500 if single
      2) $10,000 for joint return
      3) $5,000 for married filing separate return

4. <u>Under 65 credit</u> is 15% of the lesser of:

   a. Retirement income which is:

      1) Public retirement system pension if under 65, or
      2) Pensions and annuities, interest, rents, and dividends, if spouse is 65 or over

   b. Or $2,500 ($3,750 for marrieds filing joint return) less:

      1) Social security, railroad retirement, and other excluded income, and
      2) If under 62, any earned income in excess of $900, and
      3) If 62 through 72, (no reduction for those over 72):

         a) 1/2 of earned income in excess of $1,200 but not in excess of $1,700, and
         b) All of earned income in excess of $1,700

         EXAMPLE: Husband is over 65 and has wages of $2,600. Wife is under 65 and has a public retirement pension of $3,500 that is fully taxable. They file a joint return.

            1. Using the over 65 method, they would have a credit of 15% of $3,750 = $563. The $3,750 is not reduced, because AGI is not over $10,000 and nothing was excluded from gross income.

            2. Using the under 65 method, they would have a credit of 15% of $2,600 = $390. The $3,750 is reduced by 1/2 of income from $1,200 to $1,700 ($250) and all earned income over $1,700 ($900).

            3. Therefore they would use the over 65 method.

F. <u>Child Care Credit</u>

1. The credit may vary from <u>20% to 30%</u> of the amount paid for qualifying household and dependent care expenses incurred to enable taxpayer to be gainfully employed. Credit is 30% if AGI is $10,000 or less, but is reduced by 1 percentage point for each $2,000 (or portion thereof) of AGI in excess of $10,000 (but not reduced below 20%).

   EXAMPLE: For 1983, Able, Baker, and Charlie have AGIs of $10,000, $20,000, and $40,000 respectively, and each incurs child care expenses of $2,000. Able's child care credit is $600 (30% x $2,000); Baker's credit is $500 (25% x $2,000); and Charlie's credit is $400 (20% x $2,000).

2. <u>Eligibility</u> requirements include:

   a. Expenses must be incurred to enable taxpayer to be gainfully employed

   b. Married taxpayer must file joint return. If divorced or separated, credit available to parent having custody longer time during year

   c. Taxpayer must furnish more than half the cost of maintaining a household that is the principal residence of both taxpayer and <u>qualifying individual</u>, who is:

      1) Dependent under 15 years of age, or
      2) Dependent or spouse who is physically or mentally incapable of self-care

    d. <u>Qualifying expenses</u> are those incurred for care of qualifying individual, and for household services that were partly for care of qualifying individual

        1) Expenses incurred outside taxpayer's household qualify only if incurred for (1) a dependent under age 15, or (2) any other qualifying individual who regularly spends at least 8 hours each day in taxpayer's household

        2) Payments to taxpayer's child under age 19 do not qualify

        3) Payments to a relative do not qualify if taxpayer is entitled to a dependency exemption for that relative

3. <u>Maximum amount of expenses</u> that qualify for credit is lesser of:

    a. Actual expenses incurred, or

    b. $2,400 for one, $4,800 for two or more qualifying individuals, or

    c. Taxpayer's earned income (or spouse's earned income if smaller)

        1) If spouse is a student or incapable of self-care and thus has no earned income, spouse is treated as having earnings of $200 per month for one, $400 per month for two or more qualifying individuals

EXAMPLE: Husband and wife have earned income of $10,000 each, resulting in AGI of $20,000 for 1983. They have one child, age 3. They incurred qualifying household service expenses of $1,500 and child care expenses at a nursery school of $1,200 in 1983.

Household expenses	$1,500
Add child care outside home	1,200
Total employment-related expenses	$2,700
Maximum allowable expenses	$2,400
Credit = 25% x $2,400	$ 600

G. <u>Foreign Tax Credit</u>

1. Foreign income taxes on U.S. taxpayers are either an itemized deduction or used as a credit at the option of the taxpayer each year

    a. Usually used as a credit because credits reduce taxes more than deductions

2. The credit is limited to the overall limitation of:

    a. $\dfrac{\text{TI From All Foreign Countries}}{\text{Taxable Income - Exemptions - ZBA}}$ x (U.S. tax - credit for elderly)

3. Foreign taxes in excess of the overall limitation are subject to a 2-year carryback and a 5-year carryover

4. There is no limitation if foreign taxes are used as a deduction

H. <u>Political Contribution Credit</u>

1. Taxpayers may take a credit equal to 50% of political contributions limited to the lesser of:

    a. $50 ($100 on a joint return), or

    b. Tax liability reduced by:

        1) Credit for the elderly

        2) Investment credit

        3) Foreign tax credit

2. Qualifying political contributions are those to:

   a. A candidate for federal, state, or local elective political office

   b. A committee, association, or organization organized and operated exclusively for the purpose of furthering the nomination or candidacy of an individual described in "a."

   c. The national, state, or local committee of a national political party

I. Earned Income Credit

1. It is 10% of the first $5,000 of earned income reduced by 12.5% of earned income (or adjusted gross income if larger) that exceeds $6,000

2. To be eligible a taxpayer must:

   a. Maintain a household for himself and child in the U.S., and be:

      1) A married person entitled to a dependency exemption for the child, or
      2) A surviving spouse, or
      3) A head of household and child is either unmarried, or a married child for whom taxpayer may claim a dependency exemption

   b. File a joint return if married

3. Credit in excess of tax liability will be <u>refunded</u>

J. Residential Energy Credit

1. <u>15% of first $2,000</u> expended for energy-conserving items, e.g., insulation, storm windows, weather-stripping, (not aluminum siding)

   a. Energy-saving items must be new and installed in/on principal residence
   b. Principal residence must have been completed before 4/20/77

2. <u>40% of first $10,000</u> expended for renewable energy devices (e.g., solar, geothermal, or wind energy devices) installed on new or used principal residence

3. A new $2,000 (or $10,000) limit applies when taxpayer moves to another principal residence

4. Unused credits can be carried over through 1987

K. Targeted Jobs Credit

1. Through 1984, the targeted jobs credit is 50% of the first $6,000 of qualified first-year wages and 25% of the first $6,000 of qualified second-year wages paid to each qualified new employee

   a. Qualified new employees are those from economically disadvantaged families if age 18 to 24, Vietnam veterans under age 35, or ex-convicts; also those on welfare and those handicapped undergoing vocational rehabilitation
   b. Limited to 90% of employer's tax liability reduced by specified credits
   c. For employees of a trade or business only; wage deduction reduced by amount of credit
   d. It is elective
   e. Excess credit carried back 3 and forward 15 years

L. Estimated Tax Payments

1. Estimated tax payments must be made if:

   a. Estimated tax is $300 ($400 for 1984) or more, and
   b. Estimated gross income includes more than $500 of income not subject to withholding, or
   c. Estimated gross income exceeds:

      1) $20,000 for single individual, head of household, surviving spouse, or married individual and spouse has no income
      2) $10,000 for married individual and spouse has income
      3) $5,000 for married individual not eligible to file joint return

2. Estimated tax must be paid in installments by the 15th day of the 4th, 6th, and 9th month of the taxable year, and by the 15th day of the 1st month of the following year

VII. FILING REQUIREMENTS

A. Form 1040 must generally be filed if gross income exceeds the sum of the taxpayer's ZBA plus personal exemptions allowable (e.g., generally $2,300 + $1,000 = $3,300 for single taxpayer)

1. $1,000 filing requirement applies to

   a) Dependent with unearned income of $1,000 or more
   b) Married person filing separate return

2. Self-employed individual must file if net earnings from self-employment are $400 or more

B. Return must be filed by 15th day of 4th calendar month following close of taxable year

VIII. STATUTE OF LIMITATIONS

A. Claims for Refund

1. A taxpayer must file a claim for refund within 3 years from date return was filed, or 2 years from payment of tax, whichever is later

   a. A return filed before its due date is treated as filed on the due date
   b. The 3-year period is extended to 7 years for claims resulting from worthless securities or bad debts
   c. If the refund claim is the result of a carryback (e.g., NOL, ITC, corporate capital loss), the 3-year period begins with the return for the year in which the carryback arose

B. Assessments

1. The normal period for assessment of a tax deficiency is 3 years after the due date of the return, or 3 years after the return is filed, whichever is later

   a. The assessment period is extended to 6 years if gross income omissions exceed 25% of the gross income stated on the return
   b. There is no time limit for assessment if no return is filed, if the return is fraudulent, or if there is a willful attempt to evade tax

TRANSACTIONS IN PROPERTY

A. <u>Sales and Exchanges</u>

A sale or exchange is a transaction which generally gives rise to the recognition of income, in the form of a gain or loss. These gains or losses may be taxed as ordinary or capital gains/losses. If an exchange is nontaxable, the recognition of income is generally deferred until sale of the acquired asset. This is done by giving the asset received in a nontaxable exchange the basis of the old asset.

1. The <u>basis of property</u> to determine gain or loss is usually its cost or purchase price

   a. The cost of property is generally the amount paid for it in cash or the FMV of other property, plus expenses connected with the purchase

      1) If property is acquired subject to a debt, or the purchaser assumes a debt, this debt is also included in cost

   b. If acquired by <u>gift</u>, the basis for gain is the basis of the donor (substituted basis) increased by any gift tax paid attributable to the net appreciation in the value of the gift

      1) Basis for loss is lesser of gain basis (above), or FMV on date of gift

         a) Because of this rule, no gain or loss is recognized when use of the basis for computing loss results in a gain, and use of the basis for computing gain results in a loss

         EXAMPLE: A taxpayer received an airplane from his father as a gift. Father's adjusted basis was $10,000 and FMV was $8,000. If taxpayer sells the plane for $9,200, no gain or loss is recognized.

   c. If <u>acquired from decedent</u>, basis is property's FMV on date of decedent's death, or alternate valuation date (6 months after death)

      1) Use FMV on date of distribution if alternate valuation date is elected and property is distributed, sold, or otherwise disposed of during 6-month period following death
      2) FMV rule not applicable to appreciated property acquired by the decedent by gift within one year before death if such property then passes from the donee-decedent to the original donor or donor's spouse. The basis of such property to the original donor (or spouse) will be the adjusted basis of the property to the decedent immediately before death.

   d. The basis of <u>stock received as a dividend</u> depends upon whether it was included in income when received

      1) If included in income, basis is its FMV at date of distribution
      2) If nontaxable when received, the basis of shareholder's original stock is allocated between the dividend stock and the original stock in proportion to their relative FMVs. The holding period of the original stock "tacks on" to the holding period of the dividend stock.

         EXAMPLE: T owns 100 shares of X Corp. common stock that was acquired in 1980 for $12,000. In 1984, T receives a nontaxable distribution of 10 X Corp. preferred shares. At date of distribution the FMV of the 100 *common shares was $15,000, and the FMV of the 10 preferred shares was $5,000. The portion of the $12,000 basis allocated to the preferred and common shares would be:*

Preferred = $\dfrac{\$\ 5,000}{\$20,000}$ ($12,000) = $3,000

Common = $\dfrac{\$15,000}{\$20,000}$ ($12,000) = $9,000

e. The basis of <u>stock rights</u> depends upon whether they were included in income when received

1) If rights were nontaxable and allowed to expire, they have no basis
2) If rights were nontaxable and exercised or sold

a) Basis is zero if FMV of rights is less than 15% of FMV of stock
b) If FMV of rights is at least 15% of FMV of stock, or if taxpayer elects, basis is

$$\frac{\text{FMV of rights}}{\text{FMV of rights + FMV stock}} \quad \text{x} \quad \begin{array}{c}\text{basis in}\\\text{stock}\end{array}$$

1] Use FMV at date of acquisition

3) If included in income, basis is FMV at date of distribution

f. Detailed rules for basis are included in following discussions of exchanges and involuntary conversions

2. In a <u>sale</u>, the gain or loss is generally the difference between
a. The cash or cash value received, and
b. The adjusted basis of the property sold
c. If the property sold is mortgaged (or encumbered by any other debt) and the buyer assumes or takes the property subject to the debt

1) Include the amount of the debt in the amount realized because the seller is being relieved of the obligation

EXAMPLE: Property with $10,000 mortgage, basis of $15,000, is sold for $10,000 cash and buyer assumes mortgage. Amount realized is $20,000 and gain is $5,000.

2) If the amount of the mortgage exceeds basis, use the same rules

EXAMPLE: Property with $15,000 mortgage, basis of $10,000, is given away subject to the mortgage. Amount realized is $15,000 and gain is $5,000.

d. Casual sellers of property (other than dealers) reduce selling price by any selling expenses in computing amount realized

3. In a <u>taxable exchange</u>, the gain or loss is the difference between the adjusted basis of the property exchanged and the FMV of the property acquired

a. E.g., exchange of asset held for personal use such as a personal car traded for another car
b. Basis of property received in a taxable exchange is its FMV

4. <u>Nontaxable exchanges</u> generally are not taxed in the current period. Questions concerning nontaxable exchanges usually require a determination of the basis of property received, and the effect of "boot" on the recognition of gain.

a. Like-kind exchange--an exchange of business or investment property for
    property of a like-kind

    1) Does not apply to property held for personal use
    2) Does not apply to inventory, stocks, bonds, notes, or intangible
       evidences of ownership
    3) Property held for business use may be exchanged for investment property;
       or, vice versa
    4) Like-kind means "same class of property"

       a) Real estate must be exchanged for real estate; personal property
          exchanged for personal property, e.g.:

          1] Land held for investment exchanged for apartment building
          2] Real estate exchanged for a lease on real estate to run 30 years
             or more
          3] Truck exchanged for a truck

       b) Exchange of personal property for real property does not qualify

    5) The basis of like-kind property received is the basis of like-kind
       property given

       a) + Gain recognized
       b) + Basis of boot given (money or property not of a like-kind)
       c) - Loss recognized
       d) - FMV of boot received

          1] If un-like property is received, its basis will be its FMV on
             the date of the exchange

    6) If property is exchanged solely for other like-kind property, no gain
       or loss is recognized

       a) The basis of the property received is the same as the basis of the
          property transferred

    7) If "boot" (money or property not of a like-kind) is given, no gain or
       loss is generally recognized

       a) Gain or loss is recognized if the "boot" given consists of property
          with a FMV different from its basis

          *EXAMPLE: Real estate held for investment plus shares of stock are
          exchanged for investment real estate with a FMV of $13,000. The
          real estate transferred had an adjusted basis of $10,000 and FMV of
          $11,000; the stock had an adjusted basis of $5,000 and FMV of
          $2,000. A $3,000 loss is recognized on the transfer of stock. The
          basis of the acquired real estate is $12,000 ($10,000 + $5,000 -
          $3,000).*

    8) If "boot" is received

       a) Any realized gain is recognized to the extent of the lesser of (1)
          the realized gain, or (2) the FMV of "boot" received

       b) No loss is recognized

          *EXAMPLE: Investment real estate purchased for $10,000 was ex-
          changed for other investment real estate with a FMV of $9,000, an
          automobile with a FMV of $2,000, and $1,500 in cash. The realized*

gain is $2,500. Even though $3,500 of "boot" was received, the recognized gain is only $2,500 (limited to the realized gain). The basis of the automobile (un-like property) is its FMV $2,000; while the basis of the real estate acquired is $9,000 ($10,000 + $2,500 gain recognized - $3,500 boot received).

9) Liabilities assumed (or liabilities to which property exchanged is subject) on either or both sides of the exchange are treated as "boot"

   a) Boot received - if the liability was assumed by the other party
   b) Boot given - if the taxpayer assumed a liability on the property acquired

      1] If liabilities are assumed on both sides of the exchange, they are offset to determine the net amount of "boot" given or received

      EXAMPLE: A owns investment real estate with an adjusted basis of $50,000, FMV of $70,000, but which is subject to a mortgage of $15,000. B owns investment real estate with an adjusted basis of $60,000, FMV of $65,000, but which is subject to a mortgage of $10,000. A and B exchange real estate investments with A assuming B's $10,000 mortgage, and B assuming A's $15,000 mortgage. The computation of realized gain, recognized gain, and basis for the acquired real estate for both A and B is as follows:

	A	B
FMV of real estate received	$65,000	$70,000
+ Liability on old real estate assumed by other party (boot received)	15,000	(1) 10,000
Amount realized on the exchange	$80,000	$80,000
- Adjusted basis of old real estate transferred	-50,000	-60,000
- Liability assumed by taxpayer on new real estate (boot given)	-10,000	(2)-15,000
Gain realized	$20,000	$ 5,000
Gain recognized (1) minus (2)	$ 5,000	$ -0-
Basis of old real estate transferred	$50,000	$60,000
+ Liability assumed by taxpayer on new real estate (boot given)	10,000	15,000
+ Gain recognized	5,000	-0-
- Liability on old real estate assumed by other party (boot received)	-15,000	-10,000
Basis of new real estate acquired	$50,000	$65,000

   c) Boot given in the form of an assumption of a liability does not offset boot received in the form of cash or un-like property; however, boot given in the form of cash or un-like property does offset boot received in the form of a liability assumed by the other party

      EXAMPLE: Assume same facts as above except that the mortgage on B's old real estate was $6,000, and that A paid B cash of $4,000 to make up the difference. The tax effects to A remain unchanged.

However, since the $4,000 cash cannot be offset by the liability assumed by B, B must recognize a gain of $4,000, and will have a basis of $69,000 in his new real estate.

b. Involuntary Conversions

1) Occur when money or other property is received for property that has been destroyed, damaged, stolen, or condemned (even if property is transferred only under threat or imminence of condemnation)

2) If payment is received and gain is realized, taxpayer may <u>elect</u> not to recognize gain if converted property is replaced with property of similar or related use

   a) Gain is recognized only to the extent that the amount realized exceeds the cost of the replacement

   b) The replacement must be purchased within a period beginning with the earlier of the date of disposition or the date of threat of condemnation, and ending 2 years after the close of the taxable year in which gain is first <u>realized</u> (3 years for condemned real property).

   c) Basis of replacement property is the cost of the replacement decreased by any gain not recognized

   EXAMPLE: Taxpayer had unimproved real estate (with an adjusted basis of $20,000) which was condemned by the county. The county paid him $24,000 and he invested $21,000 in unimproved real estate. $1,000 of the $4,000 realized gain would not be recognized. His tax basis in the new land would be $20,000 ($21,000 - $1,000).

   EXAMPLE: Assume the same facts as above except the taxpayer reinvested $25,000 in unimproved real estate. None of the $4,000 realized gain would be recognized. His basis in the new land would be $21,000 ($25,000 - $4,000).

3) If property is converted directly into property similar or related in service or use, complete nonrecognition of gain is mandatory

   a) The basis of replacement property is the same as the property converted

4) The meaning of <u>property similar or related in service or use</u> is more restrictive than "like-kind"

   a) For an owner-user—property must be functionally the same and have same end use (business vehicle must be replaced by business vehicle that performs same function)

   b) For a lessor—property must perform same services for <u>lessor</u> (lessor could replace a rental manufacturing plant with a rental-wholesale grocery warehouse even though tenant's functional use differs)

   c) A purchase of at least 80% of the stock of a corporation whose property is similar or related in service or use also qualifies; cost of stock is treated as a direct purchase of the underlying "similar" assets

   d) More liberal "like-kind" test applies to real property held for business or investment that is converted by seizure, condemnation, or threat of condemnation (improved real estate could be replaced with unimproved real estate)

5) If property is not replaced within the time limit, an amended return is filed to recognize gain in the year realized

6) Losses on involuntary conversions are recognized whether the property is replaced or not

    a) Exception--a loss on condemnation of property held for personal use (e.g., personal residence) is not deductible

c. Sale or Exchange of Residence

1) Gain on the sale or exchange of a principal residence is not recognized to the extent an amount equal to the adjusted sales price is reinvested in another principal residence 2 years before or after date of sale

    a) If more than one residence is purchased within the time period, only the last residence purchased will qualify as a replacement unless the taxpayer has relocated for employment purposes, in which case any sale incident to such a move will qualify

2) The adjusted sales price is the sales price less

    a) Selling expenses, e.g., sales commissions, advertising

    b) Fixing-up expenses, i.e., the aggregate of the expenses for work performed on the old residence in order to assist its sale, made within 90 days before contract to sell is entered into and paid no later than 30 days after sale

        1] E.g., painting, cleaning, etc. (but not capital expenditures)

    c) Any gain excluded under "4)" below

3) Basis in the new house is cost less gain not recognized

EXAMPLE: Taxpayer's house cost $100,000 in 1978. In preparation for sale, he had it painted for $5,000 in May 1983. He sold the house on June 15, 1983, for $240,000 and paid a $10,000 sales commission. He bought another house for $110,000 on July 14, 1983. The following computations would be made:

Selling price	$240,000			
- Selling expenses	-10,000			
Amount realized	$230,000	Amount realized	$230,000
- Basis of old house	-100,000	- Fixing-up expenses	- 5,000
Gain realized	$130,000	Adjusted sales price	$225,000
Adjusted sales price	$225,000	Cost of new house	$110,000
Cost of new house	-110,000	- Gain not recognized	- 15,000
Gain recognized	$115,000	Basis of new house	$ 95,000

4) Taxpayer age 55 or older may elect to exclude up to $125,000 of the gain realized on the sale or involuntary conversion of a principal residence

    a) Election may only be made once in lifetime

    b) Taxpayer must have owned and occupied the residence for at least 3 of the 5 years ending on date of sale

    c) Exclusion reduces the gain realized and adjusted sales price, but does not reduce the basis of replacement property

        d) If taxpayer and spouse own residence in joint tenancy and file joint return for year of sale, exclusion may be elected even though only one of them satisfies the age and use tests

> *EXAMPLE: In example above, if taxpayer had made the once-in-lifetime election to exclude $125,000 of gain, the realized gain would be $5,000, the adjusted sales price would be $100,000, the recognized gain would be zero, and the basis of the new house would be ($110,000 - $5,000 of gain not recognized) = $105,000.*

    b) Loss on sale of personal residence is not deductible; does not affect basis of new home

  d. **Exchange of Insurance Policies**

    1) No gain or loss is recognized on an exchange of certain life, endowment, and annuity contracts to allow taxpayers to obtain better insurance

5. **Sales and Exchanges of Securities**

  a. Stocks and bonds are not included under like-kind exchanges

  b. Exchange of stock of <u>same</u> corporation

    1) Common for common, or preferred for preferred is nontaxable
    2) Common for preferred, or preferred for common is taxable, unless exchange qualifies as a recapitalization (see p. 1226)

  c. Exercise of conversion privilege in convertible stock or bond is nontaxable

  d. Wash Sales

    1) Wash sale occurs when stock is sold at a loss and within 30 days before or after the sale, substantially identical stock or securities in the same corporation are purchased
    2) Wash sale loss is not deductible, but is added to the basis of the new stock
    3) Wash sale rules do not apply to gains

> *EXAMPLE: X has 100 shares of "B" stock bought at $10/share. He sells it at $8/share and 20 days later buys 100 shares of "B" stock at $9/share.*
>
> *The $200 loss is not recognized, and the basis of the new stock is $1,100.*
> *The holding period in the new stock includes the time the old stock was held.*

    4) Does not apply to stock traders and dealers

  e. Worthless Securities

    1) Treated as a capital loss as if sold on the last day of the year the securities become worthless
    2) Treated as an ordinary loss if securities are those of an 80% or more owned corporate subsidiary that derived more than 90% of its gross receipts from nonpassive sources

  f. The first-in, first-out (FIFO) method is used to determine the basis of securities sold unless the taxpayer can specifically identify the securities sold

6. Losses, Expenses, and Interest Between Related Taxpayers

   a. No loss is allowed on sale or exchange of property to "related taxpayer"

      1) On a later resale, any gain recognized is reduced by the amount of the disallowed loss unless the loss initially sustained was a wash sale (then no reduction is allowed)

   b. Otherwise deductible expenses and interest are not allowed if accrued by accrual basis taxpayer and payable to related cash basis payee, but not actually (or constructively) received by payee within taxable year accrued or within 2 1/2 months thereafter

   c. Related taxpayers are:

      1) Members of a family, including only husband and wife, brothers, sisters, ancestors, and lineal descendants
      2) A corporation and a more than 50% stockholder
      3) Two corporations, more than 50% of each owned by the same stockholder (brother-sister corporations), if either corporation was a personal holding company during preceding year
      4) An individual and an exempt organization controlled by taxpayer or family
      5) Certain related individuals in a trust, including the grantor or beneficiary and the fiduciary

   d. In determining the stock ownership of an individual, the holdings of partners, family, corporations, etc., are considered constructively owned by the taxpayer

      EXAMPLE: X owns an interest-bearing note and 60% of the stock of Y Corporation. X is on cash basis; Y is on accrual basis. $500 interest on the note for 1983 is accrued by Y, but not actually (or constructively) received by X during 1983 or within 2 1/2 months thereafter. Result: The $500 interest deduction is disallowed to Y for 1983 and all subsequent years although still income to X when finally received.

7. Gain from the sale or exchange of property will be entirely ordinary gain (no capital gain) if the property is depreciable in hands of transferee and the sale or exchange is between:

   a. Husband and wife
   b. An individual and an 80% or more owned corporation or partnership
   c. Two corporations or partnerships at least 80% owned by the same individual

8. Installment sales (see Tax Accounting Methods)

B. Capital Gains and Losses

   Capital gains and losses result from the sale or exchange of capital assets. They are subject to special rules. LTCGs are beneficial because they are effectively taxed at a lower rate. Individuals are taxed at a maximum of 20% (40% x maximum rate of 50%) on net LTCG in excess of net STCL.

   Capital losses (LTCL and STCL) are not as useful as ordinary losses. For noncorporate taxpayers, only $3,000 of capital loss can be offset against ordinary income in any year. STCL are deducted dollar-for-dollar when they offset ordinary income. But it takes $2 of LTCL to offset each $1 of ordinary income. Corporations cannot deduct capital losses from ordinary income.

The mechanics of netting capital gains and losses may be summarized as follows. Take all of the capital asset transactions and divide them into four categories: long-term capital gain (LTCG), long-term capital loss (LTCL), short-term capital gain (STCG), short-term capital loss (STCL). Net any LTCG against any LTCL. Also, net any STCG against any STCL. Finally, offset a net LTCG against a net STCL, or a net LTCL against a net STCG.

1. The term capital assets includes investment property and property held for personal use. The term specifically excludes

   a. Stock in trade, inventory, or goods held primarily for sale to customers in the normal course of business
   b. Depreciable or real property used in a trade or business
   c. Copyrights or artistic, literary, etc., compositions created by the taxpayer

      1) Capital assets only if bought by taxpayer
      2) Patents are generally capital assets in the hands of the inventor

   d. Accounts or notes receivable arising from normal business activities
   e. An agreement (i.e., covenant) not to compete for a fixed number of years that is separable from goodwill

2. Whether short-term or long-term depends upon the holding period

   a. Long-term if held more than 1 year; short-term if held 1 year or less
   b. The day property was acquired is excluded and the day it is disposed is included
   c. Use calendar months, e.g., if held from January 4 to January 4 of the following year it is held exactly 12 months regardless of how many days in each month
   d. Securities sold through a broker by a cash-basis taxpayer are considered sold on the transaction date if sold at a loss; settlement date if sold at a gain. If the settlement date occurs in the taxable year following the year of sale, an installment sale has been made:

      1) The taxpayer may elect out of the installment method and recognize the gain in year of sale
      2) If no election is made, the gain is reported for the year in which the settlement date occurs

      EXAMPLE: A cash-basis taxpayer sells stock through a broker at a gain on December 30, 1983. The proceeds of sale are received by the taxpayer on the settlement date, January 5, 1984. The taxpayer may elect out of the installment method by including the full amount of gain in gross income for 1983. If no election is made, the gain is includible in gross income for 1984.

   e. The holding period of property received in a nontaxable exchange (e.g., like-kind exchange, involuntary conversion) includes the holding period of the property exchanged, if the property that was exchanged was a capital asset or Sec. 1231 asset

f. If the basis of property to a prior owner carries over to the present owner (e.g., gift), the holding period of the prior owner "tacks on" to the present owner's holding period

   1) If using FMV on date of gift to determine loss, then holding period begins on date of gift

   EXAMPLE: X purchased property on July 14, 1983, for $10,000. X made a gift of the property to Z on June 10, 1984, when its FMV was $8,000. Since Z's basis for gain is $10,000, his holding period for a disposition at a gain extends back to July 14, 1983. Since Z's $8,000 basis for loss is determined by reference to FMV at June 10, 1984, his holding period for a disposition at a loss begins on that date.

g. Property received from a decedent is always given long-term treatment, regardless of how long the property was held by the decedent or beneficiary

3. Computation of capital gains and losses for all taxpayers

   a. First net STCG with STCL and net LTCG with LTCL to determine

      1) Net short-term capital gain or loss (NSTCG or NSTCL)
      2) Net long-term capital gain or loss (NLTCG or NLTCL)

   b. Then net these two together to determine whether there is a NCG or NCL

4. The following rules apply to individuals

   a. If there is a net capital gain the following rules apply

      1) If NLTCG exceeds NSTCL, 60% of the excess is an above the line deduction

         a) The effect is to tax 40% of the gain at ordinary rates

      2) If NSTCG exceeds NLTCL, this excess is taxed as ordinary income

         a) There is no capital gain deduction

      3) If there are both NLTCG and NSTCG, then both are included in income and there is a deduction for 60% of the NLTCG only

      EXAMPLE: In 1983 taxpayer had a $5,200 long-term capital gain, $800 of short-term capital gain, and $1,000 of short-term capital loss. These capital gains and losses increased his adjusted gross income by $2,000, determined as follows:

NLTCG	$5,200
NSTCL	(200)
NCG (long-term)	$5,000
Less 60% deduction	(3,000)
Increase in AGI	$2,000

   b. If there is a net capital loss the following rules apply

      1) The loss is an above the line deduction, but limited to the lesser of:

         a) $3,000
         b) Taxable income reduced by zero bracket amount, or
         c) The sum of:

            1] NSTCL, plus
            2] 50% of NLTCL

2) STCLs reduce ordinary income dollar-for-dollar, but it takes $2 of LTCL to reduce ordinary income by $1

3) Apply STCLs first

> *EXAMPLE: In 1983 taxpayer had $2,000 of long-term capital gain, $6,000 of long-term capital loss, and $500 of short-term capital loss. These capital gains and losses decreased his adjusted gross income by $2,500, determined as follows:*

NSTCL (deducted first)		$ 500
NLTCL	$4,000	
Less 50%	(2,000)	
		2,000
Decrease in AGI (limit is $3,000)		$2,500

5. Capital loss carryovers for <u>individuals</u>

   a. The amount of the capital loss that exceeds the allowable deduction may be carried over for an unlimited period of time

   b. The carryover retains its character as a short-term and/or long-term loss

      1) Short-term loss carryovers offset short-term gains before offsetting long-term gains

      2) Long-term loss carryovers offset long-term gains before offsetting short-term gains

   c. Losses are applied in the order of occurrence, but all STCL are applied before LTCL when offsetting ordinary income

> *EXAMPLE: A taxpayer has taxable income of $9,000, a $200 short-term capital gain, a $900 short-term capital loss, a $1,000 long-term capital gain, and a $5,800 long-term capital loss. He will have a long-term capital loss carryover of $200, determined as follows:*

Capital loss deduction limit	$3,000
Less: Net STCL	700
Remaining capital loss deduction	$2,300
Net LTCL	$4,800
Less: Amount needed to reach	
$3,000 limit ($2,300 x 2)	4,600
LTCL carryover to next year	$ 200

6. <u>Corporations</u> have special capital gain and loss rules

   a. Taxed on net long-term capital gain at lower of

      1) Ordinary corporate tax rates, or

      2) 28%

   b. No capital gain deduction allowed (unlike individuals who are allowed a 60% deduction of long-term capital gain)

   c. Capital losses only offset capital gains, not ordinary income

   d. 3-year carryback and 5-year carryover for a net capital loss; all carrybacks and carryovers are treated as <u>short-term</u>

C. Gains and Losses on Business Property

Although property used in a business is excluded from the definition of "capital assets," Sec. 1231 extends capital gain and loss treatment to business assets if the gains from these assets exceed losses. However, before Sec. 1231 becomes operative, Sections 1245 and 1250 provide for recapture of depreciation (i.e., gain is taxed as ordinary income to the extent of certain depreciation previously deducted).

1. All gains and losses are <u>ordinary</u> on business property <u>held 1 year or less</u>
2. <u>Section 1231</u>
    a. All assets included must have been held for <u>over 1 year</u>
        1) Section 1231 gains and losses include those from:
            a) Sale or exchange of property used in trade or business (or held for production of rents or royalties) and which is not:
                1] Inventory
                2] A copyright or artistic composition
            b) Casualty, theft, or condemnation of:
                1] Property used in trade or business
                2] Capital assets
            c) Infrequently encountered items such as cut timber, coal and domestic iron ore, livestock, and unharvested crop
    b. The combining of Sec. 1231 gains and losses is accomplished in <u>two steps.</u> <u>First</u>, net all casualty and theft gains and losses on assets held for more than 1 year.
        1) If the losses exceed gains, treat them all as ordinary losses and gains and do not net them with other Sec. 1231 gains and losses
        2) If the gains exceed losses, the net gain is combined with other Section 1231 gains and losses
    c. <u>Second</u>, net all Section 1231 gains and losses (except casualty and theft net loss per above)
        1) Include casualty and theft net gain
        2) Include gains and losses from condemnations (other than nondeductible personal condemnation losses)
        3) Include gains and losses from the sale or exchange of property used in trade or business
    d. If losses exceed gains, treat all gains and losses as ordinary
    e. If gains exceed losses, treat the Sec. 1231 net gain as a long-term capital gain

    EXAMPLE: Taxpayer has a gain of $10,000 from the sale of land used in his business, a loss of $4,000 on the sale of depreciable property used in his business, and a $2,000 (noninsured) loss when a car used in his business was involved in a collision.

    The net gain or loss from casualty or theft is the $2,000 loss. The net casualty loss of $2,000 is treated as an ordinary loss and not netted with other Section 1231 gains and losses.

    The $10,000 gain is netted with the $4,000 loss resulting in a net Sec. 1231 gain of $6,000, which is then treated as a long-term capital gain.

3. Section 1245 Recapture

    a. Requires the recapture as <u>ordinary income</u> of all gain attributable to:

        1) <u>Post-1961 depreciation</u> on the disposition of Sec. 1245 property
        2) <u>Post-1980 recovery deductions</u> on the disposition of Sec. 1245 recovery property (including amount expensed under Sec. 179 expense election)

    b. <u>Sec. 1245 property</u> generally includes depreciable tangible and intangible personal property, e.g.

        1) Desks
        2) Machines and equipment
        3) Cars and trucks
        4) Special purpose structures, storage facilities, and other property (but not buildings and structural components) e.g., oil and gas storage tanks, grain storage bins and silos, and escalators and elevators

    c. <u>Sec. 1245 recovery property</u> means <u>all</u> ACRS recovery property other than:

        1) 15-year real residential rental property
        2) 15-year real property used outside the U.S.
        3) 15-year subsidized low-income housing
        4) 15-year real property for which a straight-line election was made

        Note: If the cost of 15-year nonresidential real property is recovered using the prescribed percentages of ACRS, all gain on disposition is ordinary income to extent of all ACRS deductions. Such recapture is no longer limited to the excess of accelerated depreciation over straight-line. However, if the straight-line method is elected for 15-year real property, there is no recapture and all gain is Sec. 1231 gain if property held over 12 months. If property held 12 months or less, gain is recaptured as ordinary income to the extent of all depreciation (including straight-line).

    d. Upon the disposition of property subject to Sec. 1245, any recognized gain will be ordinary income to the extent of post-1961 depreciation or post-1980 recovery deductions

        1) Any remaining gain after recapture will be Sec. 1231 gain if property held over 12 months
        2) If the disposition is not by sale, use FMV of property (instead of selling price) to determine gain
        3) Sec. 1245 overrides some nonrecognition provisions, e.g., a corporation generally recognizes no gain or loss on the distribution of property to shareholders as a dividend or in liquidation, yet it must recognize recapture

        EXAMPLE: Corporation distributes depreciable personal property to its shareholders as a dividend. The property cost $7,800, has a FMV of $5,200, and an adjusted basis of $3,000; depreciation deducted totaled $4,800. Corporation must recognize ordinary income of $2,200 (i.e., lower of (1) $2,200 excess of FMV over basis, or (2) $4,800 of depreciation deducted) because of Sec. 1245.

        a) When boot is received in a like-kind exchange, Sec. 1245 will apply to the recognized gain

EXAMPLE: Taxpayer exchanged his old machine (adjusted basis of $2,500) for a smaller new machine worth $5,000 and received $1,000 cash. Depreciation of $7,500 had been taken on the old machine. The realized gain of $3,500 ($6,000 - $2,500) will be recognized to the extent of the $1,000 "boot," and will be treated as ordinary income as the result of Sec. 1245.

b) In the case of an involuntary conversion, the recognized gain under Sec. 1245 shall not exceed:

1] The gain recognized without regard to Sec. 1245, plus
2] The FMV of property acquired which is not Sec. 1245 property, and which is not taken into account in "1]"

EXAMPLE: Taxpayer received $117,000 of insurance proceeds as a result of a fire that destroyed his machinery. After deducting depreciation of $15,000, the machinery had an adjusted basis of $100,000 when destroyed. Taxpayer spent $105,000 for replacement machinery and $9,000 for stock of a corporation that qualifies as replacement property. Ordinary income of $12,000 would be recognized (i.e., $3,000 without regard to Sec 1245 + $9,000 FMV non-Sec. 1245 property acquired).

If, instead of buying $9,000 in stock, taxpayer had bought $9,000 more of replacement machinery, only $3,000 of ordinary income would be recognized above.

c) Sec. 1245 recapture does not apply to transfers by gift (including charitable contributions) or transfers at death

4. Section 1250 Recapture

a. Applies to all real property (e.g., buildings and structural components) that is not Sec. 1245 recovery property

1) If Sec. 1250 property was held 12 months or less, gain on disposition is recaptured as ordinary income to extent of all depreciation (including straight-line)
2) If Sec. 1250 property was held more than 12 months, gain is recaptured as ordinary income to the extent of post-1969 excess depreciation (generally depreciation in excess of straight-line)

EXAMPLE: An office building with an adjusted basis of $200,000 was sold by individual X in 1983 for $350,000. The property had been purchased for $300,000 in 1976 and $100,000 of depreciation had been deducted. Straight-line depreciation would have totaled $70,000.

Total gain ($350,000 - $200,000)	$150,000
Post-1969 excess depreciation recaptured as ordinary income	(30,000)
Remainder is Sec. 1231 gain	$120,000

b. Beginning in 1983, the ordinary income element on the disposition of Sec. 1250 property by corporations is increased by 15% of the additional amount which would have been ordinary income if the property had been Sec. 1245 property or Sec. 1245 recovery property. (Not applicable to the disposition of a pollution control facility for which a 5-year amortization election was made.)

EXAMPLE: *Assuming the same facts as in the above example except that the building was sold by* <u>Corporation X</u> *in 1983, the computation of gain would be*

Total gain ($350,000 - $200,000)	$150,000
Post-1969 excess depreciation recaptured as ordinary income	(30,000)
Additional ordinary income-- 15% of $70,000 (the additional amount that would have been ordinary income if the property were Sec. 1245 property)	(10,500)
Remainder is Sec. 1231 gain	$109,500

5. <u>Summary of Gains and Losses</u>. The treatment of gains and losses on property held for <u>more than 1 year</u> is summarized in the following <u>4 steps</u> (also enumerated on flowchart at end of this section).

   a. Separate all recognized gains and losses into four categories

       1) Ordinary gain and loss
       2) Sec. 1231 casualty and theft gains and losses
       3) Sec. 1231 gains and losses other than by casualty or theft
       4) Gains and losses on capital assets (other than by casualty or theft)

           a) Note that "2)" and "3)" are only temporary classifications and that all gains and losses will ultimately receive ordinary or capital treatment

   b. Any gain (casualty or other) on Sec. 1231 property is treated as ordinary income to extent of Sec. 1245 and 1250 depreciation recapture

   c. After depreciation recapture, any remaining Sec. 1231 casualty and theft gains and losses are netted

       1) If losses exceed gains--the losses and gains receive ordinary treatment
       2) If gains exceed losses--the net gain is combined with other Sec. 1231 gains and losses in "d." below

   d. After recapture, any remaining Sec. 1231 gains and losses (other than by casualty or theft), are combined with any net casualty or theft gain from "c." above

       1) If losses exceed gains--the losses and gains receive ordinary treatment
       2) If gains exceed losses--the net gain receives LTCG treatment

EXAMPLE: Taxpayer incurred the following transactions during the current taxable year:

Loss on condemnation of land used in business held 15 months	($500)
Loss on sale of machinery used in business held 2 months	($1,000)
Bad debt loss on loan made 3 years ago to friend	($2,000)
Uninsured casualty loss on personal auto held 2 years (excess over $100 floor and 10% of AGI)	($3,000)
Loss on sale of business equipment held 3 years	($4,000)
Gain on sale of land held 4 years and used in business	$5,000
Gain from insurance reimbursement for tornado damage to residence held 10 years	$6,000

The gains and losses would be treated as follows. Note that the loss on machinery is ordinary because it was not held more than 1 year.

	Sec. 1231 Casualty	Sec. 1231 Other	Capital L-T	Capital S-T
Ordinary				
($1,000)	($3,000)	($ 500)		($2,000)
	6,000	(4,000)		
		5,000		
	⟶	3,000		
		⟶	$3,500	
($1,000)			$3,500	($2,000)

TAX TREATMENT OF GAINS AND LOSSES ON PROPERTY HELD MORE THAN 1 YEAR

Start

Ordinary gain and loss items (e.g., sale of inventory, stock-in-trade, etc.)

Sec. 1231 Casualty and Theft gains (losses) on business property and capital assets held more than 1 year

Gains to extent of Sec. 1245 & 1250 recapture

Remaining Sec. 1231 Casualty and Theft gains (losses) after Sec. 1245 & 1250 recapture

Gains > Losses

Losses > Gains

Other Sec. 1231 gains (losses) on property held more than 1 year and used in business, held for production of rent, or royalties, etc.

Gains to extent of Sec. 1245 & 1250 recapture

Net Sec. 1231 Casualty and Theft gain, plus remaining other Sec. 1231 gains (losses) after Sec. 1245 & 1250 recapture.

Losses > Gains

Gains (losses) on capital assets (other than by casualty or theft)

Ordinary Income (Loss) Treatment

Gains > Losses

Long-Term Capital Gain (Loss) Treatment

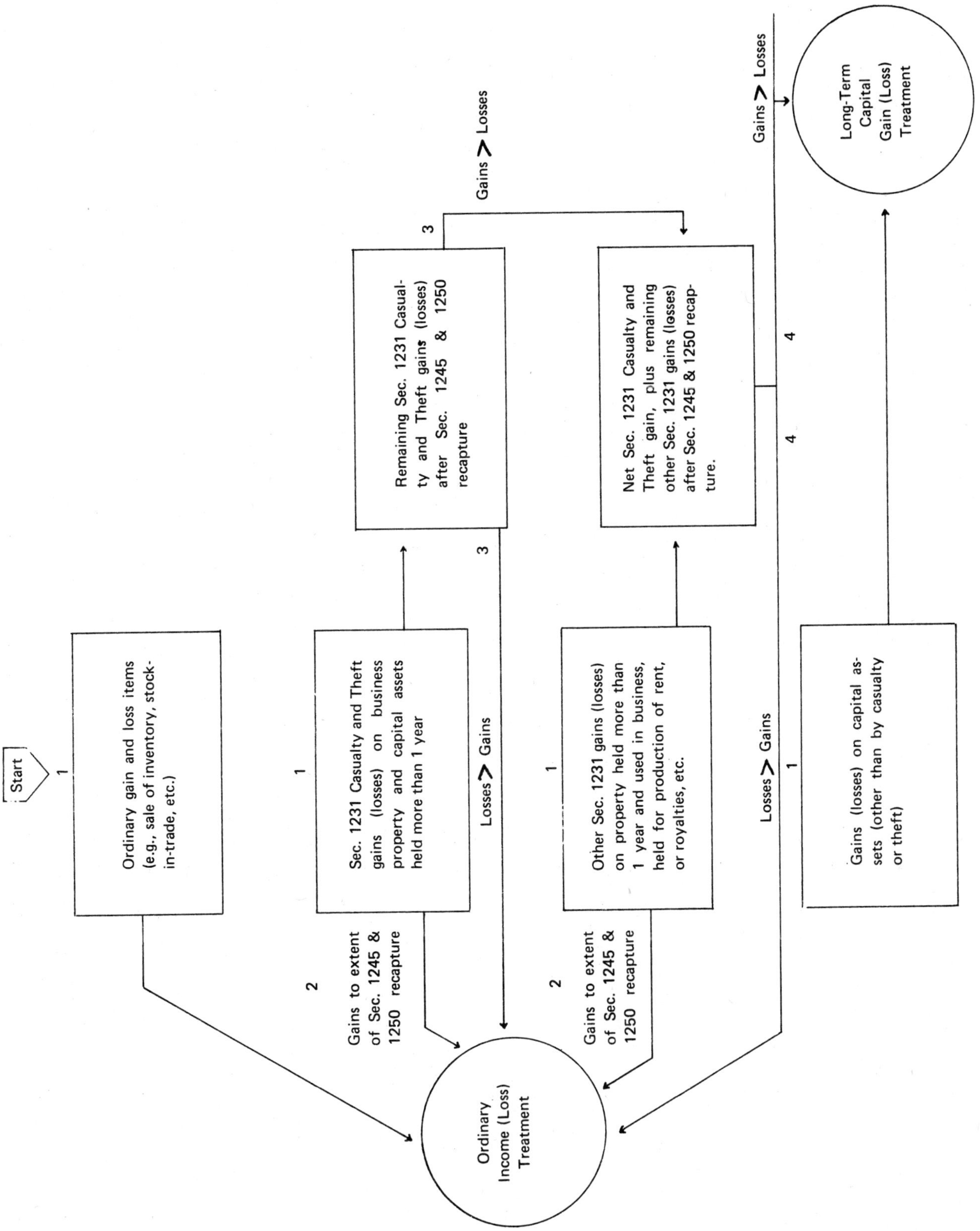

PARTNERSHIPS

Partnerships are organizations of two or more persons to carry on business activities. For tax purposes, partnerships also include a syndicate, joint venture or other unincorporated business through which any business or financial operation is conducted. If a partnership is found to be an association for tax purposes, it will be taxed as a corporation. A partnership will be treated as an association if it has more than two of the following corporate characteristics: continuous life, central management, unrestricted transferability of interests, no personal liability of owners.

Partnerships are not taxpayers; they are merely conduits to "flow-through" tax items to the partners. Partnerships file an informational return (Form 1065), and partners report their share of partnership taxable income or loss and other items on their individual returns. The nature or character (e.g., taxable, nontaxable) of income or deductions is not changed by the "flow-through" nature of the partnership.

A. Partnership Formation

1. As a general rule, no gain or loss is recognized by a partner when there is a contribution of property to the partnership in exchange for an interest in the partnership. There are three exceptions

    a. A partner must recognize income when property is contributed which is subject to a liability, and the resulting decrease in his individual liability exceeds his basis (see p. 1202 "2.d.1)")

        1) The excess of liability over adjusted basis is generally treated as a capital gain from the sale or exchange of a partnership interest

            a) The gain will be treated as ordinary income if the property transferred was subject to depreciation recapture under Sec. 1245 or 1250

EXAMPLE: A partner acquires a 20% interest in a partnership by contributing property worth $10,000 but with an adjusted basis of $4,000. There is a mortgage of $6,000 that is assumed by the partnership. The partner must recognize a gain of $800, and has a zero basis for his partnership interest, calculated as follows:

Adjusted basis of contributed property	$4,000
Less: portion of mortgage allocated to other partners (80% x $6,000)	(4,800)
	$ (800)
Plus recognized gain	800
Partner's basis	$ -0-

    b. Gain will be recognized on a contribution of property to a partnership in exchange for an interest therein if the partnership would be an investment company if incorporated

c. Partner must recognize compensation income when he receives an interest in partnership capital (as opposed to profits) in exchange for services rendered

   EXAMPLE: X received a 10% capital interest in the ABC Partnership in exchange for services rendered. On the date X was admitted to the partnership ABC's net assets had a basis of $30,000 and a FMV of $50,000. X must recognize ordinary income of $5,000.

2. Property contributed to the partnership has the same basis as it had in the contributing partner's hands (a carryover basis)

   a. The partner's basis for his partnership interest is increased by the adjusted basis of property contributed
   b. No gain or loss is generally recognized by the partnership upon the contribution

3. The partnership's holding period for contributed property includes the period of time the property was held by the partner

4. A partner's holding period for his partnership interest includes the holding period of property he contributed, if the contributed property was a capital asset or Sec. 1231 asset in his hands

B. Partnership Income and Loss

1. Since a partnership is not a separate taxable entity, but instead acts as a conduit to "flow-through" items of income and deduction to individual partners, the partnership's reporting of income and deductions requires a two-step approach

   a. First, all items having special tax characteristics (i.e., subject to partial or full exclusion, % or dollar limitation, etc.) must be segregated and taken into account separately by each partner so that any special tax characteristics are preserved

      1) These special items are listed separately on Schedule K of the partnership return and include

         a) Capital gains and losses
         b) Dividends qualifying for exclusion
         c) Charitable contributions
         d) Foreign taxes
         e) Sec. 179 expense election for depreciable property ($5,000 per partnership in 1983); $7,500 in 1984
         f) Etc. (see Form 1065 outline at the beginning of this chapter)

   b. Second, all remaining items (since they have no special tax characteristics) are ordinary in nature and are netted in the computation of partnership taxable income (referred to as "ordinary income or loss" on Form 1065)

      1) Frequently encountered ordinary income and deductions found in the computation of partnership taxable income include

         a) Sales less cost of goods sold, interest, rent, and royalty income
         b) Business expenses such as wages, rents, bad debts, and repairs
         c) Guaranteed payments to partners
         d) Depreciation

4
2

e) Amortization (over 60 months or more) of partnership organization expenses. Note that syndication fees (expenses of selling partnership interests) are neither deductible nor amortizable.

f) Sec. 1245, 1250, etc., recapture

g) See Form 1065 outline at beginning of chapter for more detail

2. A person sitting for the examination should be able to calculate book income of the partnership by adjusting partnership taxable income (or partnership taxable income by adjusting book income)

EXAMPLE: A partnership's accounting income statement for 1983 shows net income of $75,000 (i.e., book income). The three partners share profit and losses equally. Supplemental data indicate the following information has been included in net income:

	Dr.	Cr.
Net sales	$	$160,000
Cost of goods sold	88,000	
Tax-exempt income		1,500
Dividends received from domestic corporations		9,000
Section 1231 gain		6,000
Section 1250 gain		20,000
Long-term capital gain		7,500
Short-term capital loss	6,000	
Guaranteed payments ($8,000 per partner)	24,000	
Charitable contributions	9,000	
Advertising expenses	2,000	
	$129,000	$204,000

Partnership taxable income is $66,000, computed as follows:

Book income		$ 75,000
Add		
Charitable contributions	$ 9,000	
Short-term capital loss	6,000	15,000
		$ 90,000
Deduct		
Tax exempt income	$ 1,500	
Dividends received	9,000	
Section 1231 gain	6,000	
Long-term capital gain	7,500	24,000
		$ 66,000

Each partner's share of partnership taxable income is $22,000.

EXAMPLE: Using example above, assume one partner and his wife have $10,000 of personal dividends. Their taxable dividends on a joint return would be $12,800 ($3,000 + $10,000 - $200 exclusion = $12,800).

3. A partnership net operating loss (NOL) and capital losses from a partnership are deductible by the partner only to the extent of the partner's basis in the partnership

a. For this computation only, basis does not include liabilities for which the partner is not personally liable (e.g., nonrecourse debt)

1) This basis limitation does not apply to real estate ventures

2) This is effectively the "at risk" rule for partnerships. See Business Income in Individual Taxation for detail (p. 1147).

EXAMPLE: A partner's share of a net operating loss is $3,000, but his partnership basis is only $2,200 at the end of the taxable year. The partner can deduct only a $2,200 NOL on his individual tax return. The remaining $800 must be carried forward and deducted when the partner obtains additional basis in the partnership.

C. Partnership Agreements

1. A partner's distributive share of income or loss is generally determined by the partnership agreement. Such agreement

   a. Can have different ratios for income or loss
   b. May agree to allocate other items (e.g., credits and deductions) in varying ratios
   c. All allocations must have substantial economic effect, i.e., not just tax avoidance
   d. If no allocation is provided, or if the allocation of an item does not have substantial economic effect, the partners' distributive shares of that item shall be determined by the ratio in which the partners generally divide the income or loss of the partnership
   e. Gains and losses must be prorated according to the portion of the year a partner owns a partnership interest

2. Distributable shares of income and guaranteed payments are reported by partners for their taxable year during which the end of the partnership fiscal year occurs

   a. Guaranteed payments are payments to a partner determined without regard to income of the partnership, e.g., salary, interest

      1) Guaranteed payments are deductible by the partnership and reported as income by the partners
      2) A partner's partnership basis is not affected by guaranteed payments

   EXAMPLE: Z (on a calendar-year) has a 20% interest in a partnership that has a fiscal year ending May 31. Z received a guaranteed payment for services rendered of $1,000 a month from 6/1/83 to 12/31/83, and $1,500 a month from 1/1/84 to 5/31/84. After deducting the guaranteed payment, the partnership had ordinary income of $50,000 for its fiscal year ended 5/31/84. Z must include $24,500 in income on her calendar-year 1984 return ($50,000 x 20%) + ($1,000 x 7) + ($1,500 x 5).

   b. Partners are not considered to be employees for the purposes of fringe benefits

3. Family partnerships are subject to special rules because of their potential use for tax avoidance

   a. If the business is primarily service oriented (capital is not a material income-producing factor), the family member will be considered a partner only if he shares in the management or performs needed services, in addition to possibly contributing some capital
   b. A family member is generally considered a partner if he actually owns a capital interest in a business in which capital is a material income-producing factor
   c. Where a capital interest in a partnership in which capital is a material income-producing factor is created by gift, the distributive shares of partnership income of the donor and donee are determined by first making a

reasonable allowance for services rendered to the partnership, and then allocating the remainder according to the relative capital interests of the donor and donee

D. Partner's Basis in Partnership
1. A partner's original basis is generally the money plus adjusted basis of property contributed

   a. Plus gain recognized
   b. Adjusted for liabilities (See "2.d." below)

2. As the partnership operates, the partner's basis increases or decreases

   a. A partner's basis is increased by the adjusted basis of any subsequent capital contributions
   b. Also, a partner's basis is increased by his/her distributive share of

      1) Partnership taxable income
      2) Capital gains and other special income items
      3) Tax-exempt income of the partnership
      4) The excess of the deduction for depletion over the partnership's basis of the property subject to depletion

   c. A partner's basis is decreased (but not below zero) by

      1) Distributions received from the partnership
      2) Any distributive share of any losses of the partnership
      3) Distributive share of special expense items
      4) Amount of partner's deduction for depletion on oil and gas wells

      EXAMPLE: In the first example in "2." on page 1200, one partner's tax basis (who had a $15,000 tax basis at the beginning of 1983) would be $40,000 at the end of the year, calculated as shown below:

Beginning basis		$15,000
Add:		
Distributive share of partnership		
taxable income	$22,000	
Tax-exempt income	500	
Dividends	3,000	
Section 1231 gain	2,000	
Long-term capital gain	2,500	30,000
		$45,000
Less:		
Short-term capital loss	$ 2,000	
Charitable contributions	3,000	5,000
Ending basis		$40,000

   d. Changes in liabilities affect the partner's basis

      1) Any decrease in a partner's individual liability by reason of the assumption by the partnership of such individual liabilities is considered to be a distribution of money to the partner by the partnership (i.e., partner's basis is reduced)
      2) Any increase in a partner's individual liability by reason of the assumption by the partner of partnership liabilities is considered to be a contribution of money to the partnership by the partner. Thus, the partner's basis is increased.

3) An increase in the <u>partnership's</u> liabilities, (e.g., loan from the bank, increase in accounts payable) increases each partner's basis in his partnership interest by his share of the increase

4) Any decrease in the <u>partnership's</u> liabilities is considered to be a distribution of money to each partner and reduces his basis in the partnership by his share of the decrease

EXAMPLE: A partnership owns a warehouse with an adjusted basis of $120,000 subject to a mortgage of $90,000. Each of 3 partners owns a one-third interest in the partnership's profits, losses, and capital. Partner X has a basis for his partnership interest of $75,000. If the partnership transfers the warehouse and mortgage to Partner X as a current distribution, X's basis for his partnership interest immediately following the distribution would be $15,000, calculated as follows:

Beginning basis	$ 75,000
Individual assumption of mortgage	+ 90,000
	$165,000
Distribution of warehouse	-120,000
Partner's share of decrease in	
partnership's liabilities	- 30,000
Basis after distribution	$ 15,000

EXAMPLE: Assume in the example above that one of the other one-third partners had a basis of $75,000 immediately before the distribution. What would the partner's basis be immediately after the distribution to Partner X? $45,000 (i.e., $75,000 less 1/3 of the $90,000 decrease in partnership liabilities).

E. Transactions Between Partnership and Partners

1. Transactions between partnership and partners are treated as arm's-length transactions except

a. No losses are deductible on sales to or from a <u>more than</u> 50% partner or between partnerships which are <u>more than</u> 50% owned by the same persons

1) A later realized gain on sale by transferee will not be recognized to extent of disallowed loss

b. Gains recognized on sales to or from a more than 80% partner, or between partnerships which are more than 80% owned by the same persons, are treated as ordinary income if the property is not a capital asset in the hands of the buyer

c. Gains recognized on transactions between a partnership and an 80% or more partner, or between partnerships 80% or more owned by the same partner, are treated as ordinary income if the property is depreciable in the hands of the transferee

2. For purposes of losses and expenses under Sec. 267, a transaction between a partnership and a person related to a partner is treated as occurring between the person and individual partners

EXAMPLE: X owns 100% of X Corp. and also has a 1/4 interest in WXYZ Partnership. X Corp. sells property to WXYZ Partnership at a $1,200 loss. $300 of loss is disallowed.

F. Taxable Year of Partnership and Partners

1. A partnership may not change to or adopt a taxable year other than that used by
    its principal partners (a partner with a 5% or more interest in capital or
    profits)

    a. A new partnership must adopt a calendar year if its principal partners have
        different taxable years
    b. A principal partner may not change to a taxable year other than that used by
        the partnership

        1) Partnership and principal partners can all change to the same taxable
            year

    c. To deviate from above requires business purpose and IRS permission

        *EXAMPLE: In exchange for a 5% profits interest, W (on a calendar year)
        merges his accounting practice into the already existing XYZ Partnership
        which uses an August 31 fiscal year. W and the XYZ Partnership may keep
        their different taxable years, since neither is attempting to "adopt" or
        "change" a taxable year.*

2. The taxable year of a partnership ordinarily will not close as a result of
    the death or entry of a partner, or the liquidation or sale of a partner's
    interest

    a. But the partnership's taxable year closes as to the individual partner who
        sells or liquidates his entire interest

        *EXAMPLE: A partner sells his entire interest in a calendar-year partner-
        ship on March 31. His pro rata share of partnership income up to March 31
        is $15,000. Since the partnership year closes with respect to him at the
        time of sale, the $15,000 is includible in his income and increases the
        basis of his partnership interest for purposes of computing gain or loss on
        the sale.*

        *EXAMPLE: X (on a calendar year) is a partner in the XYZ Partnership which
        uses a June 30 fiscal year. X dies on October 31, 1983. Since the partner-
        ship year does not close with respect to X at his death, X's final return
        for the period January 1 thru October 31 will only include his share of
        partnership income for the partnership year ended June 30, 1983. His share
        of partnership income after June 30 will be reported by his estate or other
        successor in interest.*

G. Termination or Continuation of Partnership

1. A partnership will terminate when it no longer has at least two partners
2. A partnership and its taxable year will terminate for all partners if there is
    a sale of 50% or more of the total interest in partnership capital and profits
    within a 12-month period
3. In a merger of partnerships, the resulting partnership is a continuation of the
    merging partnership whose partners have a more than 50% interest in the result-
    ing partnership

    *EXAMPLE: Partnership AB has a June 30 fiscal year; Partnership CD and part-
    ners A, B, C, and D are on a calendar year. Partnerships AB and CD merge on
    April 1, forming the ABCD Partnership in which the partners' interests are as
    follows: Partner A, 30%; B, 30%; C, 20%; and D, 20%.*

*Partnership ABCD is a continuation of the AB Partnership and will file its
return on a June 30 fiscal year basis. The CD Partnership is considered terminated and its taxable year closed on April 1.*

4. In a division of a partnership, a resulting partnership is a continuation of
    the prior partnership if the resulting partnership's partners had a more
    than 50% interest in the prior partnership

    *EXAMPLE: Partnership ABCD (on a June 30 fiscal year) is owned as follows: A,
    40%; and B, C, and D each own a 20% interest. The partners agree to separate
    and form two partnerships--AC and BD. Partnership AC is a continuation of ABCD
    and will continue to use a June 30 fiscal year. BD is considered a new partner-
    ship and must adopt a taxable year, as well as make any other necessary tax
    accounting elections.*

H. Sale of a Partnership Interest

1. Since a partnership interest is usually a capital asset, sale of a partnership
    interest generally results in a capital gain or loss

    a. Gain is excess of amount realized over adjusted basis for partnership in-
        terest
    b. Include share of partnership liabilities in amount realized because selling
        partner is relieved of them

2. Gain is ordinary (instead of capital) to extent that gain is attributable to
    substantially appreciated inventory or unrealized receivables (Sec. 751 items)

    a. "Unrealized receivables" generally refer to the accounts receivable of a
        cash-basis taxpayer, but for this purpose also include any potential re-
        capture under Secs. 1245, 1250, 1251, and 1252
    b. "Inventory" is all assets except capital assets and Section 1231 assets.
        Thus unrealized receivables are included in this definition of "inventory."
    c. Inventory is substantially appreciated if its fair market value

        1) Exceeds 120% of its adjusted basis, and
        2) Exceeds 10% of the fair market value of all assets except money

    *40% interest to Z for $50,000. X's basis in his partnership is $22,000 and
    the cash-basis partnership had the following receivables and inventory:*

	Adjusted Basis	Fair Market Value
Accounts receivable	$ 0	$10,000
Inventory	4,000	10,000
Potential Sec. 1250 recapture	0	10,000
	$4,000	$30,000

    *X's total gain is $28,000 (i.e., $50,000 - $22,000). Since the Sec. 1250
    recapture is treated as "unrealized receivables" and the inventory is sub-
    stantially appreciated, X will recognize ordinary income to the extent that
    his selling price attributable to Sec. 751 items ($30,000 x 40% = $12,000)
    exceeds his basis in those items ($4,000 x 40% = $1,600), i.e., $10,400.
    The remainder of X's gain ($28,000 - $10,400 = $17,600) will be treated as
    capital gain.*

I. Pro Rata Distributions from Partnership

1. Partnership recognizes no gain or loss on a distribution

2. Partner recognizes gain only to the extent money received exceeds his partnership basis

   a. Remember relief from liabilities is deemed a distribution of money
   b. Gain is capital except for gain attributable to unrealized receivables and substantially appreciated inventory
   c. If property other than money is received, gain is not recognized until disposition of the property

3. Partner recognizes loss only upon complete liquidation of his partnership interest through receipt of only money, unrealized receivables, or inventory

   a. The amount of loss is the partner's basis for his partnership interest less the money and the partnership's basis in the unrealized receivables and inventory received. The loss is generally treated as a capital loss.

4. If property other than money, unrealized receivables, or inventory is distributed in complete liquidation of a partner's interest, no loss is recognized

   a. The partner's basis for any receivables or inventory received will generally be the same as the partnership's basis for those items

   b. The partner's basis for his partnership interest is reduced by the amount of money and the partnership's former basis for any unrealized receivables and inventory he receives, with any remaining basis allocated to other property received in proportion to their adjusted bases to the partnership

5. In nonliquidating distributions, a partner's basis in distributed property is the same as the partnership's former basis in the property; but limited to the partner's basis for his partnership interest less any money received

   EXAMPLE: S receives a nonliquidating distribution from her partnership at a time when the basis for her partnership interest is $10,000. The distribution consists of $7,000 cash and Sec. 1231 property with an adjusted basis of $5,000 and a FMV of $9,000. No gain is recognized by S since the cash received did not exceed her basis. After being reduced by the cash, her partnership basis of $3,000 is reduced by the basis of the property (but not below zero). Her basis for the property is limited to $3,000.

6. Payments to a retiring partner are allocated between amounts paid for the partner's interest in partnership property (resulting in capital gain or loss), and other payments (resulting in ordinary income)

   a. Amounts received for a partner's share of unrealized receivables and substantially appreciated inventory are treated as ordinary income

   b. Amounts treated as ordinary income by retiring partner are either

      1) Deductible by the partnership, or
      2) Reduce the income allocated to remaining partners

J. Non Pro Rata Distributions from Partnership

1. A non pro rata (disproportionate) distribution occurs when

   a. A distribution is disproportionate as to a partner's share of substantially appreciated inventory or unrealized receivables

      1) Partner may receive more than his share of these assets, or

2) Partner may receive more than his share of other assets, in effect giving up his share of unrealized receivables or substantially appreciated inventory

b. The partner may recognize gain or loss

1) The gain or loss is the difference between the FMV of what he received and the basis of what he gave up
2) The gain or loss is limited to the disproportionate amount of unrealized receivables or substantially appreciated inventory which is received or given up
3) The character of the gain or loss depends upon the character of the property given up

c. The partnership may likewise recognize gain or loss when there is a disproportionate distribution with respect to substantially appreciated inventory or unrealized receivables

EXAMPLE: A, B, and C each own a one-third interest in a partnership. The partnership has the following assets:

	Adjusted Basis	FMV
Cash	$ 6,000	$ 6,000
Inventory	6,000	12,000
Land	9,000	18,000
	$21,000	$36,000

Assume that A has a $7,000 basis for his partnership interest and that all inventory is distributed to A in liquidation of his partnership interest. He is treated as having exchanged his 1/3 interest in the cash and the land for a 2/3 increased interest in the substantially appreciated inventory. He has a gain of $3,000. He received $8,000 (2/3 x $12,000) of inventory for his basis of $2,000 (1/3 x $6,000) in cash and $3,000 (1/3 x $9,000) of land. The gain is capital if the land was a capital asset. The partnership is treated as having received $8,000 (FMV of A's 1/3 share of cash and land) in exchange for inventory with a basis of $4,000 (basis of inventory distributed in excess of A's 1/3 share). Thus, the partnership will recognize ordinary income of $4,000.

K. Optional Adjustment to Basis of Partnership Property

1. On a distribution of property to a partner, or on a sale by a partner of his partnership interest, the partnership may elect to adjust the basis of its assets to prevent any inequities that otherwise might occur

a. Once election is made, it applies to all similar transactions unless IRS approves revocation

2. Upon the distribution of partnership property, the basis of remaining partnership property will be adjusted for all partners

a. Increased by

1) The amount of gain recognized to a distributee partner, and
2) The excess of the partnership's basis in the property distributed over the basis of that property in the hands of distributee partner

> EXAMPLE: If election were made under facts in the example on page 1206 $2,000 of basis that otherwise would be lost will be allocated to remaining partnership Sec. 1231 property.

b. Decreased by:

1) The amount of loss recognized to a distributee partner, and
2) The excess of basis of property in hands of distributee over the prior basis of that property in the partnership

3. Upon the sale or exchange of a partnership interest, the basis of partnership property to the transferee (not other partners) will be

a. Increased by the excess of the transferee's basis for his partnership interest over his share of the adjusted basis of partnership property

b. Decreased by the excess of transferee's share of adjusted basis of partnership property over his basis for his partnership interest

> EXAMPLE: Assume X sells his 40% interest to Z for $80,000 when the partnership balance sheet reflects the following:

XY Partnership

Assets	Basis	FMV
Accounts Receivable	$ -0-	$100,000
Real Property	30,000	100,000

Capital		
X (40%)		$ 80,000
Y (60%)		120,000

> Z will have a basis for his partnership interest of $80,000, while his share of the adjusted basis of partnership property will only be $12,000. If the partnership elects to adjust the basis of partnership property, it will increase the basis of its assets by $68,000 ($80,000 - $12,000) solely for the benefit of Z. The basis of the receivables will increase from -0- to $40,000 with the full adjustment allocated to Z. When the receivables are collected, Y will have $60,000 of income and Z will have none. The basis of the real property will increase by $28,000 to $58,000, so that Z's share of the basis will be $40,000 (i.e., $12,000 + $28,000).

CORPORATIONS

Corporations are separate taxable entities, organized under state law. Although corporations may have many of the same income and deduction items as individuals, corporations are taxed at different rates and some tax rules are applied differently. There also are special provisions applicable to transfers of property to a corporation, and issuance of stock.

A. Transfers to a Controlled Corporation (Sec. 351)

1. No gain or loss is recognized if property is transferred to a corporation solely in exchange for stock or securities and immediately after the exchange those persons transferring property control the corporation (i.e., own at least 80% of stock)

a. "Property" includes everything but services
b. "Securities" are corporate debt obligations with at least a 5-year maturity
c. Receipt of boot (e.g., cash, short-term notes, etc.) will cause recognition of gain (but no loss)

1) Corporation's assumption of liabilities treated as boot only if there is a tax avoidance purpose, or no business purpose
2) Shareholder recognizes gain if liabilities assumed by corporation exceed the total basis of property transferred

2. Shareholder's basis for stock and securities = adjusted basis of property transferred:

a. + gain recognized
b. - boot received (assumption of liability always treated as boot for purposes of determining stock basis)

3. Corporation's basis in property = transferor's adjusted basis + gain recognized to transferor

EXAMPLE: Individuals A, B, & C form ABC Corp. and make the following transfer to their corporation:

Item transferred	A	B	C
Property - FMV	$10,000	$ 8,000	$ -0-
- Adjusted basis	1,500	3,000	-0-
Liability assumed by ABC Corp.	2,000	-0-	-0-
Services	-0-	-0-	1,000
Consideration received:			
Stock (FMV)	$ 8,000	$ 7,600	$ 1,000
2-year note (FMV)	-0-	400	-0-
Gain recognized to shareholder	$ 500	$ 400	$ 1,000
Basis of stock received	-0-	3,000	1,000
Basis of property to corp.	2,000	3,400	1,000*

*Expense or asset depending on nature of services rendered.

B. Section 1244 - Small Business Corporation (SBC) Stock

1. Sec. 1244 stock permits shareholders to deduct an ordinary loss on sale or worthlessness of stock, but

    a. Shareholder must be the original holder of stock, and an individual or partnership
    b. Stock must be common stock
    c. Ordinary loss limited to $50,000 ($100,000 on joint return); any excess is capital loss
    d. The corporation during the 5-year period before the year of loss, received less than 50% of its total gross receipts from royalties, rents, dividends, interest, annuities, and sales or exchanges of stock or securities

2. SBC is any domestic corporation whose aggregate amount of money and adjusted basis of other property received for stock, as a contribution to capital, and as paid-in surplus, does not exceed $1,000,000

C. Variations from Individual Taxation

1. Filing and payment of tax

    a. A corporation must file a return (Form 1120) every year even though it has no taxable income
    b. The return must be filed by the 15th day of the third month following the close of its taxable year (e.g., March 15 for calendar-year corporation)
    c. Estimated tax payments must be made by every corporation whose estimated tax is expected to be $40 or more

        1) Quarterly payments are due on the 15th day of the fourth, sixth, ninth, and twelfth months of its taxable year (April 15, June 15, September 15, and December 15 for a calendar-year corporation). Any balance due must be paid by the due date of the return.
        2) A corporation with $1 million or more of taxable income in any of its three preceding tax years must pay at least 90% of its current year's tax liability as estimated tax

2. Corporations are subject to

    a. Regular tax rates

Taxable Income	Rate
1) $0 - $25,000	15%
2) $25,001 - $50,000	18
3) $50,001 - $75,000	30
4) $75,001 - $100,000	40
5) $100,001+	46

    b. Alternative capital gains rate of 28% of the excess of NLTCG over NSTCL may be used in lieu of regular rates

        1) Use 28% when lower than regular corporate tax rate (e.g., taxable income above $50,000)

    c. 15% minimum tax on tax preference items reduced by the greater of

1) $10,000, or
2) 100% of regular tax liability
3) Tax preference items include

   a) ACRS deductions on 15-year real property to the extent more than straight-line depreciation using 15-year recovery period and no salvage value
   b) 18/46 of net capital gains
   c) Excess % depletion
   d) Excess amortization of pollution control and child care facilities
   e) Excess intangible drilling costs

   Note: Only 71.6% of the reduced amount of certain preferences is included in determining the minimum tax liability (i.e., of the remaining Sec. 1231 gain in the example on page 1195, only 71.6% x $109,500 = $78,402 would be a minimum tax preference item).

d. See subsequent discussion for penalty taxes on

   1) Accumulated earnings
   2) Personal holding companies

3. <u>Gross income</u> for a corporation is quite similar to the rules for an individual taxpayer. However, there are a few differences.

   a. A corporation does not recognize gain or loss on the issuance of its own stock, or the later sale of treasury shares

      1) It may recognize gain (but not loss) if it uses appreciated property to redeem its stock
      2) Assessments against shareholders are not income (they are capital contributions)
      3) Capital contributions by other than a shareholder are excluded from income, and the basis of the contributed property is zero

         a) If money is received, the basis of property purchased within 1 year afterwards is reduced by the money contributed
         b) Any money not used reduces the basis of depreciable property

   b. No gain or loss is recognized on the issuance of <u>debt</u>

      1) Premium or discount on bonds payable is amortized as income or expense over the life of bonds
      2) Principal payments are not deductible expenses
      3) Ordinary income/loss is recognized on the repurchase of a corporation's bonds determined by the relationship of the repurchase price to the net carrying value of the bonds (issue price plus or minus the discount or premium amortized)
      4) Interest earned or gains recognized in a bond sinking fund are income to the corporation

   c. Income from the discharge of an indebtedness of a corporation (including "b.3)" above) may be excluded from gross income if the corporation consents to reduce the basis of the asset associated with the indebtedness

   d. Property dividends received by a domestic corporation are included in income at the lesser of

      1) Fair market value at distribution, or

    2) Adjusted basis of the property to the distributing corporation plus gain recognized to the distributing corporation

  e. Gains are treated as ordinary income on sales to or from an 80% or more shareholder, or between corporations which are 80% or more owned by the same individual, if the property is subject to depreciation in the hands of the buyer

4. Deductions for a corporation are much the same as for individuals. However, there are some major differences.

  a. Adjusted gross income is not applicable to corporations since all deductible expenses are business expenses

  b. Organizational expenditures may be amortized over 60 months or longer if elected in the first tax return

    1) Otherwise deductible only in year of liquidation
    2) Election applies to expenditures incurred before the end of the corporation's first tax year (even if unpaid by cash basis corporation)
    3) Amortization period starts with the month that business operations begin
    4) Expenditures connected with issuing or selling shares of stock, or listing stock on an exchange are neither deductible nor amortizable

  c. The deduction for charitable contributions is limited to 10% of taxable income before the contributions deduction, the dividend received deduction, a net operating loss carryback (but after carryover), and a capital loss carryback

    1) Generally the same rules apply for valuation of property contributed as for individuals except

      a) Where an individual reduces FMV by 40% of appreciation, a corporation reduces it by 28/46
      b) Deduction for donations of inventory and other appreciated ordinary income-producing property is the donor's basis plus one-half of the unrealized appreciation but limited to twice the basis, provided:

        1] Donor is a corporation (but not an S corporation)
        2] Donee must use property for care of ill, needy, or infants
        3] No deduction allowed for unrealized appreciation that would be ordinary income under recapture rules

      c) Deduction for donation of scientific personal property to an educational organization is the donor's basis plus one-half the unrealized appreciation but limited to twice the basis, provided

        1] Donor is a corporation (but not an S corporation, PHC, or service organization)
        2] Property was constructed by donor and contributed within 2 years of substantial completion
        3] Donee must use property for research or experimentation
        4] No deduction allowed for unrealized appreciation that would be ordinary income under recapture rules

    2) Deductible in period paid unless corporation is an accrual basis taxpayer and then deductible when authorized by board of directors if payment is made within 2 1/2 months of tax year end, if corporation elects

    3) Excess contributions over the 10% limitation may be carried forward for up to five years

EXAMPLE: The books of a calendar year, accrual basis corporation for 1983 show a net income of $350,000 after deducting a charitable contribution of $50,000. The contribution was authorized by the Board of Directors on December 24, 1983, and was actually paid on January 31, 1984. The allowable charitable contribution deduction is $40,000, calculated as follows: ($350,000 + $50,000) x .10 = $40,000.

d. An 85% dividend received deduction (DRD) is allowed for qualified dividends from domestic taxable corporations

   1) DRD may be limited to 85% of taxable income before the dividend received deduction, the net operating loss deduction, and a capital loss carryback

   2) Exception: The 85% of taxable income limitation does not apply if the full 85% DRD creates or increases a net operating loss

EXAMPLE: A corporation has income from sales of $20,000 and dividend income of $10,000, along with business expenses of $21,500. Since taxable income before the DRD would be $8,500 (less than the dividend income), the DRD is limited to $7,225 (85% x $8,500). Thus, taxable income would be: $1,275 ($8,500 - $7,225).

EXAMPLE: In the example above, assume that all facts are the same except that business expenses are $21,501. Since the full DRD ($8,500) would create a $1 net operating loss ($8,499 - $8,500), the exception would apply and the full DRD ($8,500) would be allowed.

   3) A 100% DRD is permitted for dividends received from affiliated corporations

      a) There must be at least 80% ownership
      b) See page 1216 for discussion of affiliated corporations

e. Losses in the ordinary course of business are deductible

   1) Losses are disallowed if the sale or exchange of property is between

      a) Corporation and over 50% shareholder
      b) Two corporations each owned in excess of 50% by the same shareholder, if either corporation were a personal holding company in the prior year
      c) The transferee on subsequent disposition only recognizes gain to the extent it exceeds the disallowed loss

   2) Capital losses are deductible only to the extent of capital gains (i.e., may not offset ordinary income)

      a) Unused capital losses are carried back 3 years and then carried forward 5 years to offset capital gains
      b) Unlike individuals, for whom capital loss carryforwards retain their original short-term or long-term character, all corporate capital loss carrybacks and carryforwards are treated as short-term

   3) Bad debt losses are treated as ordinary deductions
   4) Casualty losses are treated the same as for an individual except

      a) There is no $100 floor
      b) An entire loss is measured by the property's adjusted basis
      c) A partial loss is measured the same as for an individual, i.e., the lesser of the decrease in FMV, or the adjusted basis

     5) A corporation's <u>net operating loss</u> is computed the same way as its taxable income

       a) The dividend received deduction is allowed without limitation

       b) No deduction is allowed for a NOL carryback or carryover from other years

       c) A NOL may be carried back 3 years and forward 15 years to offset taxable income in other years

       d) Carryback is first made to third preceding year, but corporation may elect to forgo carryback and only carryforward 15 years

f. Depreciation and depletion are similar to that for individuals

g. Research and development expenditures of a corporation may be treated under one of three alternatives

   1) Currently expensed in year paid or incurred

   2) Amortized over a period of 60 months or more if life not determinable

   3) Capitalized and depreciated over determinable life

h. Contributions to a pension or profit sharing plan

   1) Defined benefit plans

     a) Maximum deductible contribution is actuarially determined

     b) There also are minimum funding standards

   2) Defined contribution plans

     a) <u>Maximum deduction</u> for contributions to qualified profit-sharing or <u>stock bonus plans</u> is generally limited to 15% of the compensation paid or accrued during the year to covered employees

       1] If more than 15% is paid, the excess can be carried forward as part of the contributions of succeeding years to the extent needed to bring the deduction up to 15%

       2] If an employer pays less than 15% in one year, the deficiency may be carried forward and added to the maximum (15%) otherwise deductible. Then the aggregate limitation, including deficiency carryforwards, is 25% of compensation.

5. In working a corporate problem, certain calculations must be made in a specific order [e.g., charitable contributions (CC) must be computed before the dividends received deduction (DRD)]. The following memory device is quite helpful

   Gross income
       <u>less deductions (except CC and DRD)</u>
   = Taxable income before CC and DRD
       less charitable contributions (CC): limited to 10% of TI before CC,
       <u>DRD, capital loss carryback, and NOL carryback</u>
   = Taxable income before DRD
       less dividend received deduction (DRD): may be limited* to 85% of TI
       <u>before DRD, capital loss carryback, and NOL deduction</u>
   = Taxable income
       <u>times applicable rates</u>
   = Tax liability before tax credits
       <u>less tax credits</u>
   = Tax liability

     *Limitation not applicable if full 85% of dividends received creates or increases a NOL.

6. A person sitting for the CPA examination should be able to reconcile book and taxable income

    a. If you begin with book income to calculate taxable income, make the following adjustments:

        1) Increase book income by:

            a) Federal income tax expense

            b) Excess of capital losses over capital gains because a net capital loss is not deductible

            c) Income items in the tax return not included in book income (e.g., prepaid rents, royalties, interest)

            d) Charitable contributions in excess of the 10% limitation

            e) Expenses deducted on the books but not on the tax return (e.g., amount of business gifts in excess of $25, non-deductible life insurance premiums paid, provision for cash discounts)

        2) Deduct from book income:

            a) Income reported on the books but not on the tax return (e.g., tax exempt interest, insurance proceeds)

            b) Expenses deducted on the tax return but not on the books (e.g., ACRS depreciation above straight-line, charitable contribution carryover)

            c) The dividend received deduction

    b. When going from taxable income to book income, the above adjustments would be reversed

    c. Schedule M-1 of Form 1120 provides a reconciliation of income per books with taxable income before the NOL and DRD. There are two types of Schedule M-1 items:

        1) Permanent differences, e.g., tax-exempt interest

        2) Timing differences--items are reflected in different periods, e.g., accelerated depreciation on tax return and straight-line on books

        EXAMPLE: A corporation discloses that it had net income after taxes of $36,000 per books. Included in the computation were deductions for charitable contributions of $10,000, a net capital loss of $5,000, and federal income taxes paid of $9,000. What is the corporation's TI?

Net income per books after tax	$36,000
Nondeductible net capital loss	+ 5,000
Federal income taxes paid	+ 9,000
Charitable contributions	+10,000
Taxable income before CC	$60,000
CC (limited to 10% X 60,000)	− 6,000
Taxable income	$54,000

    d. Schedule M-2 of Form 1120 analyzes changes in the Unappropriated Retained Earnings per books between the beginning and end of the year:

Balance at beginning of year

Add: Net income per books
        Other increases (e.g.,
        refund of a prior
        year's tax)

Less: Dividends to shareholders
        Other decreases (e.g.,
        addition to reserve for
        contingencies)

Balance at end of year

D. Affiliated and Controlled Corporations

1. An affiliated group is a parent-subsidiary chain of corporations in which at
    least 80% of all classes of stock (except nonvoting preferred) are owned by in-
    cludible corporations

    a. They may elect to file a consolidated return. Election is binding on all
        future returns.
    b. Possible advantages of a consolidated return include the deferral of gain on
        intercompany transactions and offsetting operating/capital losses of one
        corporation against the profits/capital gains of another

        EXAMPLE: P Corp. owns 80% of the stock of A Corp., 40% of the stock of B
        Corp., and 45% of the stock of C Corp. A Corp. owns 40% of the stock of B
        Corp. A consolidated tax return could be filed by P, A, and B.

2. A controlled group of corporations is limited to one $25,000 amount in each
    taxable income bracket (the lower tax rates on the first $100,000 of TI), one
    $250,000 accumulated earnings credit, one $10,000 tax preference exclusion, etc.
    There are three basic types of controlled groups.

    a. Parent-subsidiary--basically same as P-S group eligible to file consoli-
        dated return. Affiliated corporations are controlled.

    b. Brother-sister--2 or more corporations at least 80% owned by 5 or fewer in-
        dividuals, estates, or trusts, who also own more than 50% of each corpora-
        tion when counting only identical ownership in each corporation. The 80%
        test is applied by including only the shares of those shareholders that hold
        stock in each corporation of the group being tested.

EXAMPLE: Individual Shareholder	Corporations W	X	Stock Considered for 50% Test
A	30%	20%	20%
B	5%	40%	5%
C	30%	35%	30%
D	15%	5%	5%
E	20%	–	–
	100%	100%	60%

        Corporations W and X are a controlled group since four individuals own at
        least 80% of each, and also own more than 50% when counting only identical
        ownership.

EXAMPLE:	Individual Shareholder	Corporations Y	Z	Stock Considered for 50% Test
	F	79%	100%	79%
	G	21%	--	___
		100%	100%	79%

Y and Z are not a controlled group because the 80% test is not met for Corporation Y. Since G owns no stock in Z, G's stock in Y can not be added to F's Y stock for purposes of applying the 80% test.

c. Combined--the parent in a P-S group is also a member of a brother-sister group of corporations

EXAMPLE: Individual H owns 100% of the stock of Corporations P and Q. Corporation P owns 100% of the stock of Corporation S. P, S, and Q are members of one controlled group.

E. Dividends and Distributions

1. Corporate distributions to shareholders on their stock are taxed as dividends to the extent of the corporation's current and/or accumulated earnings and profits

2. Most distributions fall into the dividend category

   a. But if distribution is in excess of the corporation's earnings and profits, it is a nontaxable return of capital

      1) If a return of capital, it reduces the shareholder's stock basis
      2) If return of capital exceeds stock basis, the excess is treated as capital gain

      EXAMPLE: Corporation X has earnings and profits of $6,000 and makes a $10,000 distribution to its sole shareholder, A, who has a basis of $3,000 for her X stock. The $10,000 distribution to A will be treated as a dividend of $6,000, a nontaxable return of stock basis of $3,000, and a capital gain of $1,000.

   b. Corporation recognizes gain on the distribution of property only if property is

      1) Subject to depreciation recapture
      2) Appreciated LIFO inventory (gain is excess of FIFO value over LIFO basis)
      3) Distributed with liability in excess of basis (gain is excess of liability over basis)
      4) An installment obligation (gain is excess of FMV over basis)
      5) Appreciated property used to redeem stock (gain is excess of FMV over basis)

   c. Corporate distributee includes in income cash received plus the lesser of (1) the fair market value, or (2) adjusted basis of property + gain recognized to distributing corporation; reduced by any liabilities assumed, or liabilities to which property is subject

   d. Noncorporate distributee (individuals, etc.) includes in income cash received plus the fair market value of other property; reduced by any liabilities assumed, or liabilities to which property is subject

e. A shareholder's tax basis in dividend property will be the same as in "c." and "d." above, except not reduced by liabilities

3. Earnings and Profits

a. Current earnings and profits (CEP) are essentially book income, but are computed by making adjustments to taxable income

1) Add--tax exempt income, dividend received deduction, excess of ACRS depreciation over straight-line, etc.
2) Deduct--federal income taxes, net capital loss, excess charitable contributions, expenses relating to tax exempt income, penalties, etc.

b. Accumulated earnings and profits (AEP) represent the sum of prior years' CEP, reduced by distributions and NOLs of prior years

c. Distributions reduce earnings and profits (but not below zero) by

1) The amount of money
2) The face amount of obligations of the distributing corporation, and
3) The adjusted basis of other property distributed

a) Above reductions must be offset by any liability assumed by the shareholder

EXAMPLE: Z Corp. has two 50% shareholders--B Corp. and Mr. C. Z Corp. distributes a parcel of land to each shareholder. Each parcel of land has a FMV of $12,000, basis of $8,000; and each shareholder assumes a liability of $3,000 on the property received.

	B Corp.	Mr. C
Dividend	$5,000	$ 9,000
Tax basis for property received	8,000	12,000
Effect on Z's earnings & profits	(5,000)	(5,000)

4. Stock Redemptions

a. If stock is redeemed, it is treated as a sale by the shareholder and not a dividend only if

1) The redemption is not essentially equivalent to a dividend (i.e., there is a meaningful reduction in shareholders' rights to vote, share in earnings, and share in assets upon liquidation), or

2) The redemption is substantially disproportionate (i.e., after redemption, shareholder's percentage ownership is less than 80% of his percentage ownership prior to redemption, and less than 50% of shares outstanding), or

3) All of the shareholder's stock is redeemed, or
4) The redemption is from a noncorporate shareholder in a partial liquidation, or
5) The distribution is a redemption of stock to pay death taxes under Sec. 303

5. Complete Liquidations

a. A corporation generally recognizes no gain or loss on the distribution of its property in liquidation. Gain will be recognized when it distributes

1) Installment obligations
2) Property subject to recapture

3) Appreciated LIFO inventory (gain to extent of excess of FIFO value over LIFO basis)

b. If a corporation distributes all of its assets within 12 months following the adoption of a plan of complete liquidation under Sec. 337, no gain or loss is recognized to the corporation on the <u>sale</u> or <u>exchange</u> of its property during the 12-month period

1) Nonrecognition does not apply to

a) Sale of inventory (unless bulk sale)
b) Sale of property subject to recapture

2) Not applicable if shareholders elect to defer gain under "d." below

c. Amounts received by shareholders in liquidation of a corporation are treated as received in exchange for stock, generally resulting in capital gain or loss

d. Shareholders (except excluded corporations) may elect under Sec. 333 to defer recognition of gain if the liquidation takes place within one calendar month

1) Shareholder's realized gain is recognized only to the extent of the greater of (1) the shareholder's ratable share of the corporation's earnings and profits, or (2) the amount of money and securities received

2) A noncorporate shareholder's recognized gain is treated as dividend income to the extent of his ratable share of earnings and profits

e. No gain or loss is recognized to a parent corporation under Sec. 332 on the receipt of property in complete liquidation of an 80% or more owned subsidiary

6. <u>Stock purchases treated as asset acquisitions</u>

a. An acquiring corporation that has purchased at least 80% of a target corporation's stock within a 12-month period may elect under Sec. 338 to have the purchase of stock treated as an acquisition of assets

b. Old target corporation is deemed to have sold all its assets on the acquisition date in a single transaction to which Sec. 337 applies (12-month liquidation), and is treated as a new corporation that has purchased those assets on the day after the acquisition date

1) Acquisition date is the date on which at least 80% of the target's stock has been acquired by purchase within a 12-month period

2) Generally no gain or loss is recognized to old target corporation on deemed sale of assets except for installment obligations, depreciation recapture, and ITC recapture

3) The deemed sales price and resulting bases for the target corporation's assets is generally the FMV of the target's assets as of the close of the acquisition date

F. <u>Collapsible Corporations</u>

1. Rules to prevent taxpayers from using corporations to convert ordinary income into long-term capital gain by

    a. Forming a corporation to construct or produce an item of property

    b. Before corporation realizes ordinary income from the property, taxpayers sell stock or liquidate corporation

    c. Thus taxpayers attempt to realize a LTCG on the sale or liquidation instead of recognizing ordinary income through continued operation of the corporation

2. May result in what would otherwise be reported by shareholder as LTCG, must instead be reported as ordinary income if corporation is collapsible

G. Personal Holding Company and Accumulated Earnings Taxes

1. Personal holding companies (PHC) are subject to a penalty tax on undistributed PHC income to discourage taxpayers from accumulating their investment income in a corporation taxed at lower than individual rates

    a. A <u>personal holding company</u> is any corporation

        1) During anytime in the last half of the tax year, 5 or fewer individuals own more than 50% of the corporation, directly or indirectly, and

        2) The corporation receives at least 60% of its adjusted ordinary gross income as "personal holding company income," e.g., dividends, interest, rents, royalties, and other passive income

    b. Taxed

        1) At ordinary corporate rates on taxable income, plus

        2) 50% of undistributed PHC income

    c. The PHC tax

        1) Is self-assessing (i.e., computed on Schedule PH and attached to Form 1120)

        2) May be avoided by dividend payments sufficient in amount to reduce undistributed PHC income to zero

2. Corporations may be subject to an <u>accumulated earnings tax</u> (AET), in addition to regular income tax, if they accumulate earnings beyond reasonable business needs in order to avoid shareholder tax on dividend distributions

    a. The tax is not self-assessing, but is based on a determination of the existence of tax avoidance intent

    b. AET is not applicable to PHCs

    c. Accumulated earnings credit allowed for greater of

        1) $250,000 ($150,000 for personal service corporations) minus the accumulated earnings and profits at end of prior year, or

        2) Reasonable needs of the business (e.g., expansion, working capital, to retire debt, etc.)

    d. Balance of accumulated taxable income is taxed

        1) At 27 1/2% on the first $100,000

        2) At 38 1/2% on the remainder

    e. The AET may be avoided by dividend payments sufficient in amount to reduce accumulated taxable income to zero

H. S Corporations

The Subchapter S Revision Act of 1982 made fundamental changes (generally effective after 1982) in the tax treatment of subchapter S corporations and their shareholders. The changes make their treatment similar to partnership taxation. Electing small business corporations are now designated as S corporations, all other corporations are referred to as C corporations.

1. Eligibility requirements for S corporation status

    a. Domestic corporation

    b. Not a member of an affiliated group (but inactive affiliated subsidiaries are allowed if they have not begun business and do not have any taxable income

    c. Only one class of stock issued and outstanding. A corporation will not be treated as having more than one class of stock solely because of differences in voting rights among the shares of common stock.

    d. Shareholders must be individuals, estates, trusts created by will (only for a 60-day period), voting trusts, or a trust all of which is treated as owned by an individual

        1) The latter trust may continue to be shareholder for 60 days beginning with date of death of the deemed owner, or

        2) For 2 years if entire corpus of trust is includible in the deemed owner's estate

    e. No nonresident alien shareholders

    f. Number of shareholders limited to 35

        1) Husband and wife (and their estates) are counted as one shareholder

        2) Each beneficiary of a voting trust is considered a shareholder

        3) If a trust is treated as owned by an individual, that individual (not the trust) is treated as the shareholder

2. An election must be filed anytime in the preceding taxable year or on or before the 15th day of the third month of the year for which effective

    a. All shareholders on date of election, plus any shareholders who held stock during the taxable year but before the date of election, must consent to the election

        1) If an election is made on or before the 15th day of the third month of taxable year, but either (1) a shareholder who held stock during the taxable year and before the date of election does not consent to the election, or (2) the corporation did not meet the eligibility requirements before the date of election, then the election is treated as made for the following taxable year

        2) An election made after the 15th day of the third month of the taxable year is treated as made for the following year

    b. A valid election is effective for all succeeding years until terminated

3. A corporation making a subchapter S election after 1982 must generally adopt a calendar taxable year

    a. A corporation must establish a business purpose and receive permission from the IRS to adopt any other taxable year

b. A corporation that was an S corporation prior to October 20, 1982 may retain its existing tax year so long as at least 50% of the stock in the corporation continues to be owned by those same persons who owned the stock on December 31, 1982. Stock acquired by reason of death or as a gift from a family member is generally not treated as owned by a different person.

4. Termination of S corporation status may be caused by

   a. Shareholders holding more than 50% of the shares of stock of the corporation consent to revocation of the election

      1) A revocation made on or before the 15th day of the third month of the taxable year is generally effective on the first day of such taxable year

      2) A revocation made after the 15th day of the third month of the taxable year is generally effective as of the first day of the following taxable year

      3) Instead of the dates mentioned above, a revocation may specify an effective date on or after the date on which the revocation is filed

      EXAMPLE: A revocation not specifying a revocation date that is made on or before 3/15/84, is effective as of 1/1/84. A revocation not specifying a revocation date that is made after 3/15/84 is effective as of 1/1/85. If a revocation is filed 3/11/84 and specifies a revocation date of 7/1/84, the corporation ceases to be an S corporation on 7/1/84.

   b. The corporation failing to satisfy any of the eligibility requirements listed in "1." Termination is effective on the date an eligibility requirement is failed.

   c. Passive investment income exceeding 25% of gross receipts for 3 consecutive taxable years if the corporation has Subchapter C earnings and profits

      1) Subchapter C earnings and profits means earnings and profits accumulated during a taxable year for which a Subchapter S election was not in effect

      2) Includes taxable years beginning after 12/31/81

      3) Termination is effective as of the first day of the taxable year beginning after the third consecutive year of passive investment income in excess of 25% of gross receipts

      EXAMPLE: T corporation had passive investment income in excess of 25% of its gross receipts for its calendar-years 1982, 1983, and 1984. Its S corporation status would terminate 1/1/85.

   d. Generally once terminated, S corporation status can only be reelected after 5 non-S corporation years

      1) The corporation can request IRS for an earlier reelection

      2) IRS may treat an inadvertent termination as if it never occurred

      3) The 5-year waiting period does not apply to terminations prior to 1983 (e.g., if a Subchapter S election were terminated for 1981, the corporation could reelect S corporation status for 1983)

5. An S corporation generally pays no federal income taxes, but may have to pay a tax on its net capital gain, or on its excess passive net income if certain conditions are met (see page 1225)

a. The S corporation is treated as a conduit--the character of any item of income, expense, gain, loss, or credit is determined at the corporate level, and passes through to shareholders retaining its identity

b. The taxable income of an S corporation is computed the same as for an individual except (1) certain items must be separately stated for each shareholder; (2) deductions are denied for personal exemptions, charitable contributions, net operating losses, itemized deductions, and deductions (or credits) for foreign taxes; and (3) a deduction is allowed for amortization of organizational expenses

c. An S corporation must recognize gain on the distribution of appreciated property (other than its own obligations) to its shareholders

   1) Gain is recognized in the same manner as if the property had been sold to the distributee at its FMV

   EXAMPLE: An S corporation distributes property with a FMV of $900 and an adjusted basis of $100 to its sole shareholder. Gain of $800 will be recognized by the corporation. The character of the gain will be determined at the corporate level, and passed through and reported by its shareholder.

   2) The above gain recognition rule does not apply to distributions in complete liquidation

d. An S corporation is treated as an individual for purposes of being a shareholder in a C corporation (i.e., property distributed to an S corporation will be included in gross income at FMV)

   EXAMPLE: An S corporation receives a distribution of property with a FMV of $500 and an adjusted basis of $200 to the distributing corporation. The S corporation will report dividend income of $500.

e. Expenses and interest owed to cash-basis shareholders owning 2% or more of the stock are deductible by the corporation only when paid. Note that deductions will no longer be lost if payment is made after 2 1/2 months after the end of the corporation's taxable year.

   EXAMPLE: A calendar-year S corporation accrues $10,000 of salary to an employee (a 60% shareholder) during 1983, but does not make payment until April, 1984. The $10,000 will be deductible by the corporation in 1984, and reported by the shareholder-employee as income in 1984.

f. An S corporation will not generate any earnings and profits for taxable years after 1982. All items are reflected in adjustments to the basis of shareholders' stock and/or debt.

6. A shareholder of an S corporation must separately take into account (for the shareholder's taxable year in which the taxable year of the S corporation ends) (1) his pro rata share of the corporation's items of income (including tax-exempt income), loss, deduction, or credit the separate treatment of which could affect the tax liability of any shareholder, plus (2) his pro rata share of all remaining items which are netted together into "nonseparately computed income or loss"

a. Some of the items which must be separately passed through to retain their identity include

   1) Net long-term capital gain (loss)
   2) Net short-term capital gain (loss)

       3) Net gain (loss) from Sec. 1231 casualty or theft
       4) Net gain (loss) from other Sec. 1231 transactions
       5) Tax-exempt interest
       6) Charitable contributions
       7) Dividends eligible for exclusion
       8) Foreign taxes
       9) Depletion
      10) Investment interest expense

   b. All separately stated items plus the nonseparately computed income or loss
       are allocated on a daily per share basis to anyone who was a shareholder
       during the year. Items are allocated to shareholders' stock (both voting
       and nonvoting); but not to debt.

7. A shareholder's allocation of the aggregate <u>losses and deductions</u> of an S cor-
    poration can be deducted by the shareholder to the extent of his basis for stock
    plus basis of any debt owed the shareholder by the corporation

   a. An excess of loss over combined basis for stock and debt can be carried for-
       ward indefinitely and deducted when there is basis to absorb it

   b. Once reduced, the basis of debt is later increased (but not above the
       original basis) by net income items before any increase is made to the stock
       basis

       *EXAMPLE: An S corporation incurred losses totaling $50,000. Its sole
       shareholder had a stock basis of $30,000 and debt with a basis of $15,000.
       The shareholder's loss deduction is limited to $45,000. The losses first
       reduce stock basis to zero, then debt basis is reduced to zero. The excess
       loss of $5,000 can be carried forward and deducted when there is basis to
       absorb it.*

8. A shareholder's S corporation <u>stock basis</u> is

   a. Increased by all income items (including tax-exempt income), plus depletion
       in excess of the basis of the property subject to depletion

   b. Decreased by distributions which were not includible in income, all loss
       and deduction items, nondeductible expenses not charged to capital, and
       percentage depletion on oil and gas wells

9. The treatment of <u>distributions</u> (cash + FMV or other property) to shareholders
    depends upon whether the corporation has accumulated earnings and profits

   a. Corporation <u>without</u> accumulated earnings and profits

       1) Distributions are nontaxable and are applied to reduce the shareholder's
           stock basis
       2) Distributions in excess of stock basis are treated as gain from the
           sale of stock

   b. Corporation <u>with</u> accumulated earnings and profits

       1) Distributions are nontaxable to the extent of the Accumulated Adjust-
           ments Account (AAA) and are applied to reduce the AAA and the share-
           holder's stock basis. [The AAA represents the cumulative sum of the
           S corporation's net income (i.e., gross income minus deductible ex-
           penses) which was not previously distributed to shareholders.]

       2) Distributions in excess of the AAA are treated as ordinary dividends
           to the extent of the corporation's accumulated earnings and profits

3) Distributions are next nontaxable and are applied to reduce the basis of stock
4) Distributions in excess of stock basis are treated as gain from the sale of stock

c. Before applying the above distribution rules, the basis of a shareholder's stock and the AAA are first adjusted for the corporate items passed through from the taxable year of the corporation during which the distribution is made

EXAMPLE: A calendar-year S corporation had accumulated earnings and profits of $10,000 at December 31, 1982. During calendar-year 1983, the corporation had net income of $20,000, and distributed $38,000 to its sole shareholder on June 20, 1983. Its shareholder had a stock basis of $15,000 at January 1, 1983.

The $20,000 of net income passes through and is includible in gross income by the shareholder for 1983. The shareholder's stock basis is increased by the $20,000 of income (to $35,000), as is the AAA which is increased to $20,000. Of the $38,000 distribution, the first $20,000 is nontaxable and (1) reduces stock basis to $15,000, and (2) the AAA to zero; the next $10,000 of distribution is reported as dividend income (no effect on stock basis); while the remaining $8,000 of distribution is nontaxable and reduces stock basis to $7,000.

EXAMPLE: Assume the same facts as above except that the corporation had no accumulated earnings and profits. The $20,000 of income increases stock basis to $35,000. Of the distribution of $38,000, the first $35,000 is nontaxable and reduces stock basis to zero; while the remaining $3,000 is treated as gain from the sale of stock.

10. An employee-shareholder owning more than 2% of an S corporation's stock is treated the same as a partner in a partnership for purposes of employee fringe benefits (i.e., an S corporation's payments for its fringe benefits are nondeductible). These benefits include the cost of up to $50,000 of group-term life insurance, the cost of meals and lodging furnished for the convenience of the employer, amounts paid to or for certain accident and health plans, and the the $5,000 death benefit exclusion.

11. An S corporation may have to pay a capital gains tax (and possibly minimum tax) if

a. NLTCG exceeds NSTCL by more than $25,000; exceeds 50% of TI; and, TI exceeds $25,000
b. Tax is lesser of (1) [(NLTCG - NSTCL) - ($25,000)] x 28%; or, (2) TI x regular corporate rates
c. It is computed the same as for a C corporation except that the NOL and dividends received deductions are not allowed

d. Tax won't apply if corporation had a subchapter S election for 3 preceding years or has had a subchapter S election for entire period of existence

e. The tax paid reduces the amount of LTCG passed through to shareholders

EXAMPLE: James Corporation, organized in 1970, is in its second year of subchapter S election. It had TI of $40,000 for 1983, of which $30,000 was NLTCG. Its capital gain tax is $1,400 (i.e., $5,000 x 28%). The amount of NLTCG passed through to shareholders would be $30,000 - $1,400 = $28,600.

12. Beginning in 1982, if an S corporation has C corporation accumulated earnings and profits, and its <u>passive investment income</u> exceeds 25% of gross receipts, a tax is imposed at a rate of 46% on the lesser of (1) excess net passive income (ENPI), or (2) taxable income

a. $\text{ENPI} = \begin{pmatrix} \text{Net Passive} \\ \text{Income} \end{pmatrix} \left[\dfrac{(\text{Passive Investment Income}) - (25\% \text{ of Gross Receipts})}{\text{Passive Investment Income}} \right]$

b. The tax paid reduces the amount of passive investment income passed through to shareholders

> *EXAMPLE: An S corporation has gross receipts of $80,000, of which $50,000 is interest income. Expenses incurred in the production of this passive income total $10,000. The ENPI if $24,000.*

$$\text{ENPI} = (\$50,000 - \$10,000) \left[\frac{(\$50,000) - (25\% \times \$80,000)}{\$50,000} \right]$$

I. Corporate Reorganizations

Certain exchanges, usually involving the exchange of one corporation's stock for the stock or property of another, result in deferral of gain.

1. There are seven types of reorganizations given nonrecognition treatment under the IRC

   a. Statutory mergers or consolidations (Type "A")

      1) Merger is where one corporation absorbs another
      2) Consolidation is where two corporations form a new corporation, the former ones dissolving

   b. The acquisition of at least 80% of the voting power and 80% of each non-voting class of stock of one corporation by another, in exchange <u>solely</u> for all or a part of its voting stock. No "boot" may be exchanged (Type "B").

   c. The acquisition of substantially all the properties of one corporation by another, in exchange solely for all or a part of its voting stock (Type "C")

      1) In determining whether the acquisition is made solely for stock, the assumption by the acquiring corporation of a liability of the other, or the fact that the property acquired is subject to a liability, shall be disregarded
      2) "Substantially all" means at least 90% of the FMV of the net assets and at least 70% of the FMV of the gross assets

   d. A transfer by a corporation of all or a part of its assets to another if immediately after the transfer the transferor, or one or more of its share-holders, or both, own at least 80% of the voting power and 80% of each non-voting class of stock (Type "D")

   e. A recapitalization (where the equity of a corporation is readjusted in amount, priority, etc.) (Type "E")

   f. A mere change in identity, form, or place of organization (Type "F")

   g. A bankruptcy reorganization (Type "G")

2. For the reorganization to be tax-free, it must meet one of the above definitions and the exchange must be made under a plan of reorganization involving the
   affected corporations as parties to the reorganization. It must satisfy the
   judicial doctrines of continuity of interest, business purpose, and continuity
   of business enterprise.

3. If "boot" is received in a reorganization, gain is recognized (but not loss)

   a. "Boot" includes the FMV of an excess of principal (i.e., face) amount of
      securities received over the principal amount of securities surrendered

   b. Recognized gain will generally be treated as a dividend to the extent of
      the shareholder's ratable share of earnings and profits of the acquired
      corporation

      *EXAMPLE: Pursuant to a merger of Corporation T into Corporation P, Smith
      exchanged 100 shares of T that he had purchased for $1,000, for 80 shares
      of P having a FMV of $1,500 and also received $200 cash, which was not in
      excess of Smith's ratable share of T's earnings and profits. Smith's
      realized gain of $700 is recognized to the extent of the cash received of
      $200, and is treated as a dividend. Smith's basis for his P stock is
      $1,000 ($1,000 + $200 recognized gain - $200 cash received).*

4. Carryover of tax attributed

   a. The tax attributes of the acquired corporation (e.g., NOL carryovers, earn-
      ings and profits, accounting methods, etc.) generally carry over to the
      acquiring corporation in an acquisitive reorganization

   b. The amount of an acquired corporation's NOL carryovers that can be utilized
      by the acquiring corporation for its first taxable year ending after the
      date of acquisition is limited to:

$$\begin{bmatrix} \text{Acquiring} \\ \text{corporation's} \\ \text{TI before} \\ \text{NOL deduction} \end{bmatrix} \left(\frac{\text{Days after acquisition date}}{\text{Total days in taxable year}} \right)$$

*EXAMPLE: Corporation P (on a calendar year) acquired Corporation T in a
statutory merger on October 19, 1983. If T had a NOL carryover of $50,000,
and P has taxable income (before an NOL deduction) of $90,000, the amount of
T's $50,000 NOL carryover that can be deducted by P for 1983 would be*

$$(\$90,000) \left(\frac{73}{365} \right) = \$18,000$$

GIFT AND ESTATE

The federal gift tax is an excise tax (imposed on donor) on the transfer of property by gift during a person's lifetime. The federal estate tax is an excise tax on the transfer of property upon death. The Tax Reform Act of 1976 combined these taxes into a <u>unified transfer tax</u> rate schedule that applies to both life and death transfers.

To remove relatively small gifts and estates from the imposition of tax, a unified transfer tax credit is allowed against gift and estate taxes as follows:

Year of gift or death	Unified transfer tax credit	Equivalent gift or estate transfer exempt from tax
1983	$79,300	$275,000
1984	$96,300	$325,000

A. The Gift Tax

1. Gift tax formula

Gross gifts (cash plus FMV of property at date of gift)		$XXX
Less:		
One-half of gifts treated as given by spouse	$ X	
Annual exclusion (up to $10,000 per donee)	X	
Charitable gifts (remainder of charitable gifts after annual exclusion)	X	
Marital deduction (remainder of gifts to spouse after annual exclusion)	X	XX
Taxable gifts for current year		$ XX
Add: Taxable gifts for prior years		X
Total taxable gifts		$ XX
Unified transfer tax on total taxable gifts		$ XX
Less: Unified transfer tax on taxable gifts made prior to current year		X
Unified transfer tax for current year		$ XX
Unified transfer tax credit	$XX	
Less: Unified transfer tax credit used in prior years	X	X
Net gift tax liability		$ XX

2. <u>Gross gifts</u> include any transfer for less than an adequate and full consideration

    a. The creation of joint ownership in property is treated as a gift to the extent the donor's contribution exceeds his/her retained interest

    b. The creation of a joint bank account is not a gift; but a gift results when the noncontributing tenant withdraws funds

3. Gross gifts less the following deductions equal taxable gifts

    a. <u>Gift-splitting</u>--a gift by either spouse to a third party may be treated as made one-half by each, if other spouse consents to election. Gift-splitting has the advantage of using the other spouse's annual exclusion and unified transfer tax credit

    b. <u>Annual exclusion</u>--of up to $10,000 per donee is allowed for gifts of present interests (not future interests)

        EXAMPLE: H is married and has three sons. H could give $20,000 per year to each of his sons without incurring any gift tax if H's spouse consents to gift-splitting.

	<u>H</u>	<u>W</u>
Gifts	$60,000	
Gift-splitting	(30,000)	$30,000
Annual exclusion		
(3 x $10,000)	(30,000)	(30,000)
Taxable gifts	$ -0-	$ -0-

    c. <u>Charitable gifts</u>--(net of annual exclusion) are deductible without limitation

    d. <u>Marital deduction</u>--is allowed without limitation for gifts to a donor's spouse

        1) The gift must not be a terminable interest (i.e., donee spouse's interest ends at death with no control over who receives remainder)

        2) If donor elects, a gift of <u>qualified terminable interest</u> property (i.e., property placed in trust with income to donee spouse for life and remainder to someone else at donee spouse's death) will qualify for the marital deduction if the income is paid at least annually to spouse and the property is not subject to transfer during the donee spouse's lifetime

4. The <u>tax computation</u> reflects the cumulative nature of the gift tax. A tax is first computed on lifetime taxable gifts, then is reduced by the tax on taxable gifts made in prior years in order to tax the current year's gifts at applicable marginal rates. Any available transfer tax credit is then subtracted to arrive at the gift tax liability.

5. For taxable gifts made after 1981, a gift tax return must be filed on a calendar-year basis, with the return due and tax paid on or before April 15th of the following year

6. The <u>basis</u> of property acquired by gift

    a. Basis for gain (and depreciation)--basis of donor plus gift tax attributable to appreciation

    b. Basis for loss--lesser of gain basis or FMV at date of gift

**4
4**

B. The Estate Tax

1. Estate Tax Formula

Gross estate (cash plus FMV of property at date of death, or alternate valuation date)		$XXX
Less:		
Funeral expenses	$X	
Administrative expenses	X	
Debts and mortgages	X	
Casualty losses	X	
Charitable bequests (unlimited)	X	
Marital deduction (unlimited)	X	XX
Taxable estate		$XXX
Add: Post-76 adjusted taxable gifts		XX
Total taxable life and death transfers		$XXX
Unified transfer tax on total transfers		$ XX
Less:		
Unified transfer tax on post-76 taxable gifts	$X	
Unified transfer tax credit	X	
State death, foreign death, and prior transfer tax credits	X	X
Net estate tax liability		$ XX

2. Gross estate includes the FMV of all property in which the decedent had an interest at time of death

    a. Jointly-held property

        1) If property was held by tenancy in common, only the FMV of the decedent's share is included

        2) Include one-half the FMV of community property, and one-half the FMV of property held by spouses in joint tenancy or tenancy by the entirety

        3) Include one-half of FMV if the property held in joint tenancy was acquired by gift, bequest, or inheritance

        4) If property held in joint tenancy was acquired by purchase by other than spouses, include the FMV of the property multiplied by the percentage of total cost furnished by the decedent

    b. For decedents dying after 1981, the old rule that gifts made within 3 years of death are automatically included in the decedent's gross estate no longer applies

    c. The FMV of transfers with retained life estates and revocable transfers are included in the gross estate

    d. Include the FMV of transfers intended to take effect at death (i.e., the donee can obtain enjoyment only by surviving the decedent, and the decedent prior to death had a reversionary interest of more than 5% of the value of the property)

    e. Include any property over which the decedent had a general power of appointment (i.e., decedent could appoint property in favor of herself/himself, her/his estate, or creditors of herself/himself or her/his estate)

    f. Include the value of life insurance proceeds from policies payable to the estate, and policies over which the decedent possessed an "incident of ownership" (e.g., right to change beneficiary)

g. Include annuities received by a beneficiary designated by decedent, except those payable under a qualified employee benefit plan, Keogh plan, or individual retirement plan

3. Property is included at FMV at date of decedent's death; or executor may elect to use FMV at alternate valuation date--a date six months subsequent to death

a. If alternate valuation date is elected, but property is disposed of within six months of death, then use FMV on date of disposition

b. Election applies to all property in estate, cannot be made on an individual property basis

4. Estate tax deductions include funeral expenses, administrative expenses, debts and mortgages, casualty losses during the estate administration, charitable bequests (no limit), and an unlimited marital deduction for the FMV of property passing to a surviving spouse

a. A terminable interest granted to surviving spouse will not generally qualify for marital deduction

b. If executor elects, the FMV of "qualified terminable interest property" is eligible for the marital deduction if the income from the property is paid at least annually to spouse and the property is not subject to transfer during the surviving spouse's lifetime

5. Post-76 taxable gifts are added back to the taxable estate at date of gift FMV. Any gift tax paid is not added back.

6. A unified transfer tax is computed on total life and death transfers, then is reduced by the tax already paid on post-76 gifts, the unified transfer tax credit, state death taxes (limited to table amount), foreign death taxes, and prior transfer taxes (i.e., percentage of estate tax paid on the transfer to the present decedent from a transferor who died within past 10 years)

7. For 1983, an estate tax return must be filed if the decedent's gross estate exceeds $275,000 ($325,000 in 1984). The return must be filed within 9 months of decedent's death, unless extension of time has been granted.

8. The basis of property received from a decedent is generally the FMV at date of decedent's death, or the alternate valuation date if elected for estate tax purposes

a. The above rule does not apply to appreciated property acquired by the decedent by gift within one year before death if such property then passes from the donee-decedent to the original donor or donor's spouse. The basis of such property to the original donor (or spouse) will be the adjusted basis of the property to the decedent immediately before death.

b. *EXAMPLE: Son gives property with FMV of $40,000 (basis of $5,000) to terminally ill father within one year before father's death. The property is included in father's estate at FMV of $40,000. If property passes to son or son's spouse, basis will remain at $5,000. If passed to someone else, the property's basis will be $40,000.*

ABBREVIATIONS

AAA	*Accumulated Adjustments Account*		DDB	*Double Declining Balance*
AAA	*American Accounting Association*		DL	*Direct Labor*
AC	*Absorption Costing*		DLH	*Direct Labor Hours*
ACRS	*Accelerated Cost Recovery System*		DM	*Direct Materials*
AcSEC	*Accounting Standards Executive Committee (AICPA)*		DRD	*Dividends Received Deduction*
			EDA	*Excess Deductions Account*
AEP	*Accumulated Earnings & Profits*		EDP	*Electronic Data Processing*
AET	*Accumulated Earnings Tax*		EFT	*Electronic Funds Transfer*
AGI	*Adjusted Gross Income*		EI	*Ending Inventory*
AH	*Actual Hours*		ENPI	*Excess Net Passive Income*
AICPA	*American Institute of CPAs*		EOQ	*Economic Order Quantity*
AJE	*Adjusting Journal Entry*		E&P	*Earnings and Profits*
AMTI	*Alternative Minimum Taxable Income*		EPS	*Earnings Per Share*
			ERISA	*Employee Retirement Income Security Act*
A/P	*Accounts Payable*			
AP	*Actual Price*		ESIC	*Enterprise Standard Industrial Classification*
APB	*Accounting Principles Board*			
AQ	*Actual Quantity*		ESOP	*Employee Stock Option Plan*
A/R	*Accounts Receivable*		EU	*Equivalent Units*
AR	*Actual Rate, Analytical Review, Accounting and Review Services (Citation for AICPA Professional Standards Volume)*		EUP	*Equivalent Units of Production*
			EWIP	*Ending Work in Process*
			F	*Favorable*
			FA	*Fixed Asset*
ARB	*Accounting Research Bulletin (AICPA)*		FAS	*Free Along Side*
			FASB	*Financial Accounting Standards Board*
ARR	*Accounting Rate of Return*			
ARS	*Accounting Research Study (AICPA)*		FC	*Fixed Cost*
			FCPA	*Foreign Corrupt Practices Act*
ASOBAT	*A Statement of Basic Accounting Theory*		FCU	*Foreign Currency Unit*
			FDEPS	*Fully Diluted Earnings Per Share*
ASR	*Accounting Series Release (SEC)*		FEI	*Financial Executives Institute*
AU	*Auditing (Citation for AICPA Professional Standards Volume)*		FG	*Finished Goods*
			FICA	*Federal Insurance Contribution Act*
AudSEC	*Auditing Standards Executive Committee (AICPA)*		FIFO	*First-In, First-Out*
			FMV	*Fair Market Value*
AVGP	*Analysis of Variation in Gross Profit*		FOB	*Free on Board*
BFP	*Bona Fide Purchaser*		FPC	*Finite Population Correction Factor*
BI	*Beginning Inventory*			
B of D	*Board of Directors*		FTC	*Federal Trade Commission*
BV	*Book Value*		FUTA	*Federal Unemployment Tax Act*
BWIP	*Beginning Work in Process*		FV	*Future Value*
CA	*Current Assets*		FY	*Fiscal Year*
CAP	*Committee on Accounting Procedures*		GAAFR	*Governmental Accounting Auditing & Financial Reporting*
CASB	*Cost Accounting Standards Board*		GAAP	*Generally Accepted Accounting Principles*
CC	*Charitable Contributions*			
CD	*Certificate of Deposit*		GAAS	*Generally Accepted Auditing Standards*
CEP	*Current Earnings and Profits*			
CGM	*Cost of Goods Manufactured*		GAO	*General Accounting Office*
CGS	*Cost of Goods Sold*		GCAP	*Generalized Computer Audit Programs*
CIF	*Cost, Insurance, and Freight*			
CIP	*Construction in Progress*		GFA	*General Fixed Asset Group of Accounts*
CL	*Current Liabilities*			
CLADR	*Class Life Asset Depreciation Range*		GI	*Gross Income*
CM	*Contribution Margin*		G/L	*General Ledger*
CNI	*Consolidated Net Income*		GLTD	*General Long-term Debt Group of Accounts*
COD	*Collect on Delivery*			
COM	*Computer Output to Microfilm*		GP	*Gross Profit*
CPA	*Certified Public Accountant*		GW	*Goodwill*
CPFF	*Cost Plus Fixed Fee (Contract)*		HDC	*Holder in Due Course*
CPI	*Consumer Price Index*		IC	*Internal Control*
CPU	*Central Processing Unit*		INV	*Inventory*
CRE	*Consolidated Retained Earnings*		IRA	*Individual Retirement Account*
CRT	*Cathode Ray Tube*		IRC	*Internal Revenue Code*
CSE	*Common Stock Equivalent*		IRR	*Internal Rate of Return*
CSV	*Cash Surrender Value*		IRS	*Internal Revenue Service*
CVP	*Cost-Volume-Profit*		ITC	*Investment Tax Credit*
DBA	*Data-Base Administrator*		ITF	*Integrated Test Facility*
DBMS	*Data-Base Management System*		LCM	*Lower of Cost or Market*
DB	*Declining Balance*			
DC	*Direct Costing*			

LIFO	Last-In, First-Out		SARs	Stock Appreciation Rights
LP	Linear Programming		SAS	Statements on Auditing Standards (AICPA)
LTCG	Long-Term Capital Gain		SBC	Small Business Corporation
LTCL	Long-Term Capital Loss		SCFP	Statement of Changes in Financial Position
MAS	Management Advisory Services		SDLC	Systems Development Life Cycle
MAT	Material		SE	Stockholders' Equity
MC	Marginal Cost		SEC	Securities and Exchange Commission
MI	Minority Interest		SFAC	Statement of Financial Accounting Concepts (FASB)
MOH	Manufacturing Overhead		SFAS	Statement of Financial Accounting Standards (FASB)
NAA	National Association of Accountants		SFR	Standard Fixed Rate
NBV	Net Book Value		SH	Standard Hours
NCA	Noncurrent Asset		SIC	Standard Industrial Classification
NCG	Net Capital Gain		S&L	Savings and Loan
NCGA	National Council on Governmental Accounting		SL	Straight-Line
NCL	Noncurrent Liability, Net Capital Loss		SOP	Statements of Position (AICPA)
NI	Net Income		SP	Standard Price
NLTCG	Net Long-Term Capital Gain		SQ	Standard Quantity
NLTCL	Net Long-Term Capital Loss		SQCS	Statements on Quality Control Standards (AICPA)
NOL	Net Operating Loss		SR	Standard Rate
NPV	Net Present Value		SS	Social Security
N/R	Note Receivable		SSARS	Statements on Standards for Accounting and Review Services (AICPA)
NRV	Net Realizable Value			
NSF	Nonsufficient Funds		STCG	Short-Term Capital Gain
NSTCG	Net Short-Term Capital Gain		STCL	Short-Term Capital Loss
NSTCL	Net Short-Term Capital Loss		STR	Standard Total Rate
O/H(OH)	Overhead		SVR	Standard Variable Rate
OLRT	Online Real-Time		SYD	Sum-of-the-Years-Digits
O/S	Outstanding		TC	Total Costs
PBGC	Pension Benefit Guarantee Corporation		TD	Test of Detail
PEPS	Primary Earnings Per Share		TE	Tolerable Error
PERT	Program (Problem) Evaluation and Review Technique		TI	Taxable Income
PHC	Personal Holding Company		TS	Treasury Stock
PIC	Paid-in Capital		TVMF	Time Value of Money Factor
P&L	Profit and Loss		TX	Tax Practice (Citation for AICPA Professional Standards Volume)
POC	Percentage-of-Completion		U	Unfavorable
PP&E	Property, Plant, and Equipment		UCC	Uniform Commercial Code
PPS	Probability Proportional to Size		ULPA	Uniform Limited Partnership Act
PTI	Previously Taxed Income		UPA	Uniform Partnership Act
PV	Present Value		UR	Ultimate Risk
R&D	Research and Development		UTI	Undistributed Taxable Income
RE	Retained Earnings		VAR	Variance
REITS	Real Estate Investment Trusts		VC	Variable Costs
REV	Revenue		WA	Weighted-Average
RM	Raw Materials		WC	Working Capital
ROI	Return on Investment		WIP	Work In Process
S	Sales		ZBA	Zero Bracket Amount

NOTE FOR INDEX USAGE: Where <u>uninterrupted</u> discussion of a topic covers two or more consecutive pages, only the first of these page numbers is listed in the index. For example, "Contracts, Acceptance," discussed from page 390 to page 392, is referenced simply as 390.

A

OTHER ACCOUNTING TEXTBOOKS FROM JOHN WILEY & SONS

BUSINESS LAW TEXTBOOKS FROM JOHN WILEY AND SONS

Cut Here

Fold here

NO POSTAGE
NECESSARY
IF MAILED
IN THE
UNITED STATES

BUSINESS REPLY MAIL

FIRST CLASS   PERMIT NO. 2277   NEW YORK, N.Y.

POSTAGE WILL BE PAID BY

JOHN WILEY & SONS, INC.

1 Wiley Drive
Somerset, N.J. 08873

Staple or tape closed

CPA PUBLICATIONS ORDER FORM

The **TWO VOLUME SET** consists of **Volume I** containing outlines and study guides for each section of the exam and **Volume II** with multiple choice questions, problems, and essay questions—with accompanying solutions.

☐	Quantity	Gleim/Delaney CPA EXAMINATION REVIEW Set, 11th Edition	1-80081-3	$63.90
☐	Quantity	Gleim/Delaney CPA EXAMINATION REVIEW, Vol I, 11th Edition	1-80083-X	$31.95
☐	Quantity	Gleim/Delaney CPA EXAMINATION REVIEW, Vol II, 11th Edition	1-80082-1	$31.95

The **THREE PART FORMAT** lets students purchase **THEORY and PRACTICE, AUDITING** or **BUSINESS LAW** separately. Each of these new volumes combines outlines and study guides with problems and solutions.

☐	Quantity	Delaney/Gleim: CPA EXAMINATION REVIEW: CPA Set 1984	1-88220-8	$75.85
☐	Quantity	Delaney/Gleim: CPA EXAMINATION REVIEW: Theory & Practice 1984	1-88221-6	$31.95
☐	Quantity	Delaney/Gleim: CPA EXAMINATION REVIEW: Business Law 1984	1-88219-4	$21.95
☐	Quantity	Delaney/Gleim: CPA EXAMINATION REVIEW: Auditing 1984	1-88222-4	$21.95

Delaney/Gleim CPA EXAMINATION SOLUTIONS features all the multiple choice questions from each exam with Delaney & Gleim's clear, concise explanations of the answers; solutions for each Accounting Practice problem along with detailed Solution Guides for applying the authors' solutions approach; and the answers for each Essay problem along with answer outlines.

☐	Quantity	Delaney/Gleim CPA Examination Solutions: Nov 1982*	1-89821-X	$15.95
☐	Quantity	Delaney/Gleim CPA Examination Solutions: May 1983*	1-89825-2	$15.95

*For complete most recent examination answers and explanations we recommend you investigate the National Association of State Boards of Accountancy (NASBA) CPA Examination Critque Program, 545 Fifth Avenue, Suite 506, New York, New York 10017.

For prompt service check with your local bookstore, or remove and complete this form and return it to John Wiley and Sons, Inc., One Wiley Drive, Somerset, NJ 08873, or call our hotline (815)756-8486.

Full credit is guaranteed, if not satisfied, when books are returned within 30 days in saleable condition. We normally ship within ten days. If payment accompanies order and shipment cannot be made within 90 days, full payment will be refunded. Complete the following information and mail it (**by envelope if sending check**) to the address above.

☐ Check Enclosed ☐ Bill Me ☐ Charge to my Credit Card

Charge Card Expiration Date

Credit Card No. (All Digits Please)

Mastercard ☐ Visa ☐ American Express ☐

_____
signature

Note:

1. If ordering by credit card, list complete card number, expiration date and sign order with full signature. Mastercard, Visa, and American Express honored.
2. If your order totals $126.00 or more, please attach a company purchase order or enclose 25% partial payment.
3. **Proprietary Schools Note:** To expedite orders at time of need, if you do not already have an account established at Wiley, contact in advance, **Marvin Willig, Credit Manager, John Wiley and Sons, Inc., One Wiley Drive, Somerset, NJ 08873.** Provide bank name and three credit references.

BILL TO _____ SHIP TO _____

ADDRESS _____ ADDRESS _____

CITY _____ CITY _____

STATE _____ ZIP _____ STATE _____ ZIP _____

For details regarding future issues and advance purchase plans write or call CPA Examination Review, P.O. Box 886, DeKalb, Illinois 60115, (815) 756-8486.

PRICES SUBJECT TO CHANGE WITHOUT NOTICE

ORDER INFORMATION FOR ACCOUNTING RELATED TITLES

☐ INTERMEDIATE ACCOUNTING, 4th edition by Donald E. Kieso and Jerry J. Weygandt
  (0 471 08871 4)   1983   1297 pp. $34.95

☐ ADVANCED ACCOUNTING, 2nd edition by Andrew A. Haried, Leroy F. Imdieke, and Ralph E. Smith
  (0 471 08717 3)   1982   912 pp. $32.50

☐ MODERN AUDITING, 2nd edition by Walter G. Kell and Richard E. Ziegler
  (0 471 87749 2)   1983   706 pp. $30.95

☐ AUDITING, 2nd edition by Donald H. Taylor and G. William Glezen
  (0 471 08166 3)   1982   931 pp. $32.95

☐ MONTGOMERY'S AUDITING, 10th edition, College Version, by Philip L. Defliese, Henry R. Jaenicke,
  Jerry D. Sullivan, and Richard A. Gnospelius
  (0 471 07756 9)   1984   1275 pp. $32.95

☐ AN INTRODUCTION TO STATISTICAL SAMPLING IN AUDITING by Dan M. Guy
  (0 471 04232 3)   1981   229 pp. $21.95

☐ INFORMATION SYSTEMS: THEORY AND PRACTICE, 3rd edition by John G. Burch, Felix Strater,
  and Gary Grudnitski
  (0 471 06211 1)   1983   656 pp. $31.95

☐ ACCOUNTING INFORMATION SYSTEMS: CONCEPTS AND PRACTICE FOR EFFECTIVE DECISION MAKING
  by Stephen A. Moscove and Mark G. Simkin
  (0 471 03369 3)   1984   800 pp. $30.95

☐ ACCOUNTING AND INFORMATION SYSTEMS by Joseph W. Wilkinson
  (0 471 04986 7)   1982   845 pp. $33.95

☐ EDP AUDITING: A PRIMER by Joseph Sardinas, John G. Burch, and Richard Asebrook
  (0 471 12305 6)   1981   224 pp. $18.95

☐ APPROACHING THE CPA EXAMINATION: A PERSONAL GUIDE TO EXAMINATION PREPARATION
  by Alvin Stenzel
  (0 471 08699 1)   1981   102 pp. $12.95

☐ BUSINESS LAW, 3rd edition by Michael P. Litka and Marianne Jennings
  (0 471 87390 X)   1983   1040 pp. $29.95

For prompt service check with your local bookstore, or remove and complete this form and return it to John Wiley and Sons, Inc., One Wiley Drive, Somerset, NJ 08873, or call our hotline (815)756-8486.

Full credit is guaranteed, if not satisfied, when books are returned within 30 days in saleable condition. We normally ship within ten days. If payment accompanies order and shipment cannot be made within 90 days, full payment will be refunded. Complete the following information and mail it (**by envelope if sending check**) to the address above.

☐ Check Enclosed   ☐ Bill Me   ☐ Charge to my Credit Card

☐☐   ☐☐☐☐☐☐☐☐☐☐☐☐☐☐☐☐☐☐
Charge Card   Credit Card No. (All Digits Please)
Expiration Date

Mastercard   Visa   American Express

☐   ☐   ☐   _____
                                                              signature

Note:

1. If ordering by credit card, list complete card number, expiration date and sign order with full signature. Mastercard, Visa, and American Express honored.
2. If your order totals $126.00 or more, please attach a company purchase order or enclose 25% partial payment.
3. **Proprietary Schools Note:** To expedite orders at time of need, if you do not already have an account established at Wiley, contact in advance, **Marvin Willig, Credit Manager, John Wiley and Sons, Inc., One Wiley Drive, Somerset, NJ 08873.** Provide bank name and three credit references.

BILL TO _____   SHIP TO _____
ADDRESS _____   ADDRESS _____
CITY _____   CITY _____
STATE _____ ZIP _____   STATE _____ ZIP _____

For details regarding future issues and advance purchase plans write or call CPA Examination Review,
P.O. Box 886, DeKalb, Illinois 60115, (815)756-8486.

PRICES SUBJECT TO CHANGE WITHOUT NOTICE

··· **Fold here** ···

||| |||

NO POSTAGE
NECESSARY
IF MAILED
IN THE
UNITED STATES

BUSINESS REPLY MAIL

FIRST CLASS   PERMIT NO. 2277   NEW YORK, N.Y.

POSTAGE WILL BE PAID BY

JOHN WILEY & SONS, INC.

1 Wiley Drive
Somerset, N.J. 08873

Staple or tape closed

Cut Here

COMING SOON . . .

DELANEY/GLEIM: CPA EXAMINATION REVIEW
AUDIO CASSETTES

- Three basic packages — Auditing, Business Law, and Theory and Practice

- Can be purchased separately by topical area or as a set of three

- Can be purchased and used in conjunction with the **Three Part Set**, Delaney/Gleim, *CPA Examination Review: Auditing, Business Law,* and/or *Theory and Practice* and can also be used with the **Two Volume Set**, Gleim/Delaney, *CPA Examination Review: Volume I* and *Volume II*

- For more information when available, tear out this sheet, staple, and mail postage free

- -

Please send me more information about the Delaney/Gleim New Audio Cassette Package when available.

Name _____

Address _____

City _____ State _____ Zip _____

081-5-1107

······················· Fold here ···

NO POSTAGE
NECESSARY
IF MAILED
IN THE
UNITED STATES

BUSINESS REPLY MAIL

FIRST CLASS   PERMIT NO. 2277   NEW YORK, N.Y.

POSTAGE WILL BE PAID BY

JOHN WILEY & SONS, INC.

1 Wiley Drive
Somerset, N.J. 08873

Staple or tape closed

Cut Here